THE LIGHT OF KABBALAH

Introduction to the Book of Zohar

VOLUME ONE

The Science of Kabbalah (Pticha)

THE SPIRITUAL SECRET OF KABBALAH

ORIGINAL TEXTS OF RAV YEHUDA ASHLAG

IN HEBREW AND ENGLISH

Commentary by Rav Michael Laitman PhD

THE LIGHT OF KABBALAH

Introduction to the Book of Zohar

VOLUME ONE

The Science of Kabbalah
(Pticha)

LAITMAN
KABBALAH PUBLISHERS

THE SPIRITUAL SECRET OF KABBALAH

ORIGINAL TEXTS OF RAV YEHUDA ASHLAG
IN HEBREW AND ENGLISH

Commentary by Rav Michael Laitman PhD

We wish to extend our gratitude
to the following people who made
a major contribution
to the creation of this book:

Executive Editor: Talib Din
Editor: Clive Borkum
Project Coordinator: Lenny Estrin
Translation: David Brushin
Drawings: Roman Ferber, Eugene Nemirovsky, Michael Gonopolsky
Production Manager: Tony Kosinec
Proofreading: Chaim Ratz
Type Setting: Baruch Khovov
Book Design: The George Partnership

Laitman Kabbalah Publishers Website:
www.kabbalah.info

Laitman Kabbalah Publishers Email:
info@kabbalah.info

INTRODUCTION TO THE BOOK OF ZOHAR

VOLUME ONE

The Science of Kabbalah
(Pticha)

Published by Laitman Kabbalah Publishers,
1057 Steeles Avenue West, Suite 532, Toronto, ON, M2R 3X1, Canada.

Printed in Canada.

ISBN: 0-9732315-6-4

FIRST EDITION: MARCH 2005

Introduction to the Book of Zohar

VOLUME ONE

The Science of Kabbalah (Pticha)

CONTENT

TO THE READER

For many centuries, the wisdom of Kabbalah was inaccessible to anyone who could not read Hebrew. Now, for the first time in the history of the Western World, readers of the English language and serious students of Kabbalah have the opportunity to learn the Wisdom of Kabbalah from the 20th Century's greatest Kabbalist, Baal HaSulam. In this text,* the student will find a systematic, graduated exposition of Kabbalah unlike any treatment found in other available texts. This text comes with a brilliant commentary by Michael Laitman, a scientist and Kabbalist who received the Tradition from that illustrious chain that includes the Ari, Baal HaSulam, and his teacher, Rabash.

"The Wisdom of Kabbalah" is an exhaustive text that the reader will certainly make a steady companion in his exploration of the Upper Worlds for many years to come. Enjoy!

Talib Din, Executive Editor
Bnei Baruch
May 16, 2004

* As Rav Laitman did not translate the Hebrew text word for word, the reader will find that the English translation does not strictly follow the Hebrew text.

- If you still ask yourself, "Where am I from?", "Where has everything around me come from?", you cannot manage without this book.
- If you are interested in the world where you live and want to know what it is like – you cannot manage without this book.
- If you want to study Kabbalah or at least take an interest in it – you cannot manage without this book.
- If you have been studying Kabbalah for a long time or even started teaching it, again you will not manage without this book.

"The Preamble to the Wisdom of Kabbalah" is the principal article that helps man enter the world of Kabbalah. One of the greatest Kabbalists of all times, Rabbi Yehuda Leib Alevi Ashlag, wrote it as one of the introductions to The Book of Zohar. Without the comprehension of this article, it is impossible to understand correctly a word in The Book of Zohar.

Without this book, one cannot succeed in Kabbalah. It is the key to all Kabbalistic literature: to "The Study of the Ten Sefirot", the principal modern Kabbalistic textbook, to the Book of Zohar, to the books of the great Ari. It is the key to the door that leads from our world to the spiritual world.

For a long time, I could not begin its translation and commentaries. My second book was an attempt to show the basic structure of the universe. It was published in 1983. In recent times, it has become very urgent to publish a textbook in English on the birth, basic structure, and correction of the worlds and souls.

It is hard and "clumsy" to describe Kabbalistic terms in translation, to relate Kabbalistic notions in another language. A Hebrew word contains endless information: its numeric meaning, transposition of letters, their inscription, and substitution of one kind of letter with another according to certain laws – all this makes it impossible to render in a different language.

To be honest, I had to receive my Teacher's permission. My Teacher is Rabbi Baruch Shalom Alevi Ashlag - Baal HaSulam's eldest son and the last Kabbalist of past generations. The period of the Descending Upper Wisdom stopped with him, and a new personal, group period of apprehending the creation has begun; it is the last stage of correction and its obvious manifestation.

I spent 12 years with my Teacher and he instructed me to continue the great mission of spreading Kabbalah in the world. I called my Kabbalistic School *Bnei Baruch*, in his honor. This school is open to anyone who really wants to study and devote himself to the ascent to the Upper worlds.

The material of the book was tape-recorded during my studies with beginners. It was typed, translated from Hebrew, proofread, edited, and prepared for publishing by dozens of my students. I am very glad that they participated in the publishing of this and other books, since those who circulate Kabbalah receive spiritual reward from above, i.e., advancement.

The book contains the original (Hebrew) text of the article "The Preamble to the Wisdom of Kabbalah" by Rabbi Y. Ashlag and its translation (*in italics*), supplemented by my commentaries (in regular print).

Drawings of every spiritual process were specially made for this book. It also contains 52 lectures, delivered by me on the article "The Preamble to the Wisdom of Kabbalah"; fourteen lessons on "The Introduction to the Commentaries of the Sulam"; four talks on the "Introduction to the Preamble to the Wisdom of Kabbalah", and other pertinent information.

A great spiritual wealth needed for self-knowledge and advancement to spirituality is found in this book. The rest depends on the reader!

My students and I are grateful to the Creator for the opportunity to publish this book, for the chance to reveal Kabbalah to the English reader, opening thereby the source of attaining Perfection, Happiness, and Eternity.

We invite you to travel to the unknown upper worlds, which are awaiting you and to reveal their secrets to all those, who really desire it.

M. Laitman

THE INTRODUCTION TO THE ARTICLE "THE PREAMBLE TO THE WISDOM OF KABBALAH"

All introductions composed by Rabbi Y. Ashlag (The Baal HaSulam) are written to allow a reader to enter the essential material, understand, and absorb it. As well, all introductions are separate Kabbalistic compositions, possessing their own spiritual power and depth.

א) איתא בזוהר ויקרא פרשת תזריע דף מ' תא חזי דכל מה די בעלמא לא הוי אלא בגיניה דאדם, וכלהו בגיניה מתקיימי וכו', הדא הוא דכתיב וייצר ה' אלקים את האדם, בשם מלא, כמה דאוקימנא, דאיהו שלימותא דכלא וכללא דכלא וכו', וכל מה דלעילא ותתא וכו' כלילן בהאי דיוקנא. עש"ה. הרי מפורש, שכל העולמות העליונים והתחתונים כלולים כולם בהאדם, וכן כל המציאות הנמצאת בעולמות ההם אינם רק בשביל האדם. ויש להבין הדברים, המעט לו לאדם העולם הזה וכל אשר בו בכדי לשמשו ולהועילו, אלא שהוא נצרך גם לכל העולמות העליונים וכל אשר בהם, כי לא נבראו אלא לצרכיו.

> *1) It is said in The Book of Zohar (weekly chapter Tazriya, p.40): "All worlds, the Upper and the lower, are inside man. All that is created in the world is for man's sake and everything lives and develops because of man."*
>
> *It is necessary to understand: Is man not content with this world and everything that is in it, existing to serve and develop him, that he desires the Upper worlds too?*

The Torah is a Kabbalistic book. It was written by the greatest Kabbalist Moses. The Book of Zohar is a Kabbalistic commentary for the

Torah. The Book of Zohar, as well as the Torah, is divided into 5 books and weekly chapters. One of the weekly chapters is entitled "*Tazriya*".

It is said: "The Creator created man with a full name. And everything that is created is absolutely perfect; everything is found in it." From the above statement, we see that all worlds, the Upper, and the lower, everything that fills and animates them, **all except the Creator, is inside man.**

ב) והנה בכדי להסביר הענין הזה על מילואו הייתי צריך להביא כאן לפנינו את כל חכמת הקבלה, אמנם בדרך כלל בשיעור המספיק להבין את פתיחת הדברים יתבאר לפניך בפנים הספר. והתמצית הוא, כי כוונת השי"ת בבריאה היתה כדי להנות לנבראיו כנודע. והנה ודאי הוא, שבעת שעלה במחשבה לברוא את הנשמות ולהנותם מכל טוב, הנה תיכף נמשכו ויצאו מלפניו בכל צביונם וקומתם ובכל גבהם של התענוגים שחשב להנותם, כי אצלו ית' המחשבה לבדה גומרת ואינו צריך לכלי מעשה כמונו. ולפי"ז יש לשאול למה ברא העולמות צמצום אחר צמצום עד לעוה"ז העכור והלביש הנשמות בהגופין העכורים של העוה"ז.

2) In order to explain the above, one would need to expound the entire wisdom of Kabbalah. Through further studying, the meaning of these statements will be revealed at a later stage.

The point is that the Creator's intention is to bestow delight. The moment the Creator thought to create souls and delight them, they instantly appeared before Him in their perfection and exaltedness. They were filled with infinite pleasure, which the Creator thought to bestow upon them. His thought alone completed the entire Creation and required no physical actions.

A question arises accordingly: Why did He create worlds, restriction upon restriction, down to our relatively tiny world, and then place the souls - the created beings - into the insignificant bodies of this world?

If the Creator is omnipotent, why did He not provide man with everything necessary? Why did He not allow each of us to do something of our own will? If desire alone were enough – each of us would have created a much better world than this. Why then did the Creator do it all this way?

If we are suffering now in whatever manner to reap the benefit in the future – it also points to imperfection.

ג) והתשובה על זה איתא בע"ח שהוא כדי להוציא לאור שלמות פעולותיו (ע"ח ענף א') ויש אמנם להבין איך אפשר זה שמהשלם יצאו פעולות בלתי שלמות עד שיהיו צריכים להשלימם ע"י פועל ומעשה שבעולם הזה. והענין הוא כי יש להבחין בהנשמות בחינת אור ובחינת כלי, כי עצם הנשמות שנבראו הוא הכלי שבהם, וכל השפע שחשב ית' להנותם ולענגם הוא האור שבהם. כי מאחר שחשב ית' להנותם הרי עשה אותם בהכרח בבחינת רצון לקבל הנאתו, שהרי לפי מידת הרצון לקבל את השפע כן יגדל ההנאה והתענוג. ותדע שהרצון לקבל ההוא הוא כל עצמותה של הנשמה מבחינה התחדשות ויציאת יש מאין, ונבחן לבחינת כלי של הנשמה. ובחי' ההנאה והשפע נבחן לבחינת אור של הנשמה הנמשך יש מיש מעצמותו.

3) The answer is in the Ari's book "The Tree of Life". "...It is created by Him so as to demonstrate the perfection of His actions". However, we need to understand: how could such imperfect action emanate from the perfect Creator? Moreover, the created beings must correct and spiritually elevate themselves through actions in this world.

Why did He create such a seemingly low world with imperfect bodies and put infinite souls in them? Was it done so that afterwards they might discover what perfection means? That is to say, the Creator created the most insignificant world and the most insignificant man, whereas man himself has to sweat in order to achieve perfection. Is this the aim and perfection of the Creator's actions?

The fact is that two parts should be distinguished in the souls: the light and the vessel. The essence of the soul is its vessel (Kli), and the abundance with which the Creator thought to delight the souls is the light (Ohr), which fills the vessel.

Since the Creator thought to bestow pleasure upon the souls, He was bound to fashion it in the form of a desire to receive delight. The size of the desire to receive pleasure determines the amount of pleasure received. You should know that the desire to receive pleasure is the essence of the soul. It is created from nothing, and is called "Kli"

– the soul's vessel. The abundance and delight that fill the vessel are defined as the light of the soul, emanating from the Creator.

This light spreads out from the Creator. Only the desire (*the Kli*), the vessel, was created. The light emanates from the Creator Himself as pleasure and fills the vessel. In other words, the primary goal was to bestow, the secondary – to create someone who would desire to receive pleasure. Overall, there are two components in the creation:

1. The vessel – the desire to receive pleasure, the soul, *Adam HaRishon*, creation.
2. The delight that emanated from the Creator.

ד) ביאור הדברים. כי בריאה פירושו התחדשות דבר מה שלא היה מקודם שהוא הנבחן ליש מאין, אמנם איך נצייר זה שיהיה דבר מה שאינו כלול בו ית'. הלא כל יכול וכוללם יחד, וכן אין לך נותן מה שאין בו. ובאמור אשר כלל כל הבריאה שברא ית' אינו אלא בחינת הכלים של הנשמות שהוא הרצון לקבל, מובן זה היטב, שהרי הכרח הוא שאינו כלול ח"ו מהרצון לקבל כי ממי יקבל. וא"כ הוא בריאה חדשה ממש שלא היה אף זכר ממנו מקודם לכן, וע"כ נבחן ליש מאין.

4) Creation is something that did not exist before, i.e., something born out of nothing. Yet, how can we imagine something non-existent in the Creator? He must include absolutely everything. It is said that the entire creation is no more than a vessel (a Kli) of the soul, a desire to receive pleasure. So it is quite clear that such a desire is absent in the Creator. Hence, the desire to receive is a totally new creation, non-existent before, and is defined as born out of nothing.

We cannot imagine what "nothing" is. Everything that exists in our world has its prehistory, its previous form; it is born out of something. For example, solid matter is formed out of gas. What does it mean to be formed out of nothing? We are unable to understand it. Afterwards, while apprehending spirituality, we will become participants in the comprehension of this process.

ה) ויש לדעת, שהחיבור ופירוד הנוהג ברוחניים אינו אלא בהשואת הצורה ובשינוי הצורה, כי אם ב' רוחניים הם בצורה אחת הרי הם מחוברים יחד והם אחד ולא שנים. שהרי אין מה שיבדילם זה מזה, ואי אפשר להבחינם לשנים זולת בהמצא שינוי צורה מזה לזה. וכן לפי מדת גודלה של השתנות הצורה ביניהם כן שיעור התרחקותם זה מזה, עד שאם הם נמצאים בהפכיות הצורה זה מזה אז נבחנים רחוקים כרחוק מזרח ממערב, דהיינו בתכלית המרחק המצוייר לנו בהמציאות.

5) One should know that, in spirituality, closeness and remoteness are determined by equivalence (similarity) or distinction of properties. If two spiritual objects have the same form, i.e. the same properties, they are bound together constituting a single whole. If there is no distinction between the two objects, they cannot be divided into two. The division is possible only if a difference between their properties is found.

The degree of distinction in their properties will determine the distance between them. If all the properties of two spiritual objects are opposite, then they are infinitely remote from each other, i.e., in a state of absolute remoteness.

In our world, when we say one object resembles another, it means they both exist, but are identical. In the spiritual world, this is impossible. Everything in it differs by the distinction of their properties. If there is no distinction, the two objects merge and form one. If there is a partial similarity of properties, then they merge in their common properties as two overlapping circles. A segment of one circle overlaps with a segment of the other, thus forming a common area.

In the spiritual world, there are two properties: (i) "to receive pleasure" and (ii) "to bestow pleasure". There is nothing except these two. If we juxtapose one with the other, we will see they are completely opposite and have no point of contact between them. However, if the property "to receive" is changed into the property "to bestow", i.e., the creation and the Creator will have some common desires, then they will move closer and bond with one another in these properties. The rest of their opposing desires will stay remote. Initially creation was created as absolutely opposite to the Creator.

ו) והנה בהבורא ית' לית מחשבה תפיסא ביה כלל וכלל, ואין לנו בו ח"ו שום הגה או מלה. אמנם מבחינת ממעשיך הכרנוך, יש לנו להבין בו ית', שהוא בבחי' רצון להשפיע, שהרי ברא הכל בכדי להנות לנבראיו, ולהשפיע לנו מטובו ית'. ולפי"ז נמצאים הנשמות בבחינת הפכיות הצורה אליו ית' שהרי הוא כולו רק להשפיע ואין בו ח"ו רצון לקבל משהו, והנשמות נטבעו ברצון לקבל לעצמם, כנ"ל, שאין הפכיות הצורה רחוקה מזו. ונמצא אם היו הנשמות נשארים בפועל בבחינת הרצון לקבל, היו נשארים נפרדים ממנו ית' ח"ו לעולמי עד.

> *6) Human thought is unable to grasp the infinite Creator's perfection. There is no way to express or describe Him. However, by feeling His influence, we can understand that He desires to bestow delight upon us, for his only goal is to give us pleasure, fill us with bliss.*
>
> *The souls' properties are absolutely opposite to those of the Creator. Whereas He is a giver with no trace of the desire to receive in Him, souls were created with only the desire to receive delight. Hence, there is no greater antithesis of properties and remoteness from each other than this. Therefore, had the souls remained in their egoistical desire to receive pleasure, they would have been forever separated from the Creator.*

No words of our language may describe Him, for we are separated from Him by our properties, and cannot feel Him.

It is worth pointing out here that this Introduction was written by a man, the Baal HaSulam, who had grasped it all in himself. He says he felt the Creator and His actions, saw His absolute kindness. At our level of understanding, we are yet unable to feel it.

Why is it not enough just to desire delight in order to receive it? Why do I have to approach near to the Creator, make my properties equal to His, merge with Him completely? Why could He not create such a state where the creation would, on the one hand, would receive pleasure, and on the other, bestow pleasure as does the Creator? In fact, then the Final Correction would come immediately, creation would merge with the Creator, being filled with His light, becoming equal to Him.

Why do we have to accomplish this entire evolutionary process in our senses, perceive each desire as egoistical and opposite to the Creator;

then correct it, make it altruistic, similar to Him? Why do we have to feel how we approach Him, merge with Him? What do we gain from it?

ז) עתה תבין מ"ש (בעץ חיים ענף א' הנ"ל) שסבת בריאת העולמות הוא לפי שהנה הוא ית' מוכרח שיהיה שלם בכל פעולותיו וכוחותיו וכו' ואם לא היה מוציא פעולותיו וכוחותיו לידי פועל ומעשה לא היה כביכול נקרא שלם וכו' עכ"ל. שלכאורה תמוהים הדברים, כי איך אפשר שמתחילה יצאו פעולות בלתי שלמות מפועל השלם עד שיהיו צריכים לתיקון. ובהמתבאר תבין זה כיון שעיקר כלל הבריאה אינו, רק הרצון לקבל, הנה הגם שמצד אחד הוא בלתי שלם מאוד להיותו בהפכיות הצורה מהמאציל, שהוא בחינת פירוד ממנו ית', הנה מצד הב' הרי זה כל החידוש והיש מאין שברא, כדי לקבל ממנו ית' מה שחשב להנותם ולהשפיע אליהם. אלא עכ"ז אם היו נשארים כך בפירודא מהמאציל לא היה כביכול נק' שלם, כי סוף סוף מהפועל השלם צריכים לצאת פעולות שלמות. ולפיכך צמצם אורו ית' וברא העולמות בצמצום אחר צמצום עד לעוה"ז, והלביש הנשמה בגוף מעוה"ז וע"י העסק בתורה ומצוות משגת הנשמה את השלימות שהיה חסר לה מטרם הבריאה, שהוא בחינת השואת הצורה אליו ית'. באופן, שתהיה ראויה לקבל כל הטוב והעונג הכלול במחשבת הבריאה, וגם תמצא עמו ית' בתכלית הדבקות, שפירושו השואת הצורה, כנ"ל.

7) Now we can understand what is written in the book "The Tree of Life". The creation of all the worlds is a consequence of the Creator's perfection in all His actions. However, if He had not revealed His powers in the actions He is performing on created beings, He would not have been called "perfect". Nonetheless, it is still not clear how imperfect deeds could come out of the perfect Creator?

Moreover, the Creator's actions are so imperfect that they need to be corrected by man. It is clear from the above statements that creation is a desire to receive pleasure. Although it is quite imperfect due to its being completely opposite to and infinitely remote from the Creator, it is nonetheless this specially created property of "reception" that is necessary for Creation to receive the Creator's delight.

Here arises a question: "What did the Creator create everything for?"

A Kabbalist who speaks only out of what he has attained asserts that He created us to bestow His delight upon us.

For example, say that I come to visit a person and see before me a magnificent palace. The host comes out to meet me saying: "I have waited for you all my life. Come and see what I have prepared for you." Then he begins to display all the delicacies and offer them to me. I ask him:

- Why are you doing all this?
- I am doing it to delight you.
- What is in it for you if I am delighted?
- I need nothing but to see you delighted.
- How can it be that you do not need anything?
- You have the desire to receive pleasure and I do not. Therefore, my delight is in giving pleasure to you.

On the finite human level, we cannot understand what it means to give without receiving anything in return. This property is absolutely opposite to our nature. Hence, it is said: "Only in my sensations can I know Him." Above it, I am unable to grasp. I have no way of knowing if the host has some secret idea or intention.

If the Creator has intentions as regards us, but does not reveal them, we are unable to know them. Each of us being created as a vessel can understand only what enters it. That is what fills our hearts and minds. When we develop our vessels to the maximum, we will receive in them everything that emanates from the Creator. Then we will feel that He is absolutely kind and has no thoughts other than to bestow delight upon man.

There are the so-called 7th, 8th, 9th and 10th millennia, after the 6th millennium – the 6 thousand levels of the Creation's attainment of the Creator. It reveals His thoughts, merges with Him so completely that no questions remain. It is not because the vessel is filled, but because the Creator allows the vessel inside of Himself.

This equivalence of form can be achieved in two ways. Either we improve our properties or the Creator will worsen His. The correction of souls occurs when the Creator descends to their level by worsening His properties and merging with them; He then starts to improve His properties, simultaneously improving those of the souls, as if pulling them out of their taint.

For example, a teacher joins a group of youngsters, pretending to be as frivolous as they are; he starts to liken his properties to theirs, and then, by improving himself, begins to make them a little better. In this way he corrects them, elevates them from their low level towards the light of the true intelligence.

Therefore, there needs to be an initial worsening of the Creator's properties in order to become equal with the creation, followed by the improvement and subsequent correction of the created souls.

This process depends on the Creator; it is carried out by Him and therefore is defined as "the Creator's work" (*Avodat Hashem*). However, man must be willing to go through this process if he wants the Creator to change him. Hence, he has to prepare himself and have the strength and understanding to justify the Creator's work. Such a person is called "a righteous man", for he is able to justify the Creator's actions.

The desires to receive and to bestow constitute two opposite moral and spiritual vectors, intentions. One is directed inwardly, the other is directed outwardly. However, the fact is that later, in the process of the evolution of creation, these desires take many different forms.

Each *Sefira* and *Partzuf* represents different kinds of desires. We study desires in their "pure" form, but in fact, a Kabbalist who grasps them, feels them as much more complex. However, the desire to receive pleasure is always at the heart of creation, whereas the desire to bestow is at the heart of the Creator's influence upon created beings.

Outwardly, the Creator may act as if He desires to receive, as is illustrated by the Baal HaSulam's example of the host and the guest. This example includes all elements of our relations. The host says, "I prepared it all for you; chose only the things you like. I will be delighted to watch you eat. Can you not give me that pleasure?" Thus, he can make the guest sit down and eat. After such persuasion, the guest feels he is obliged to eat and enjoy the meal. Otherwise, how would the guest reciprocate with the host for all his efforts?

However, the guest has a different problem; whatever he does, the desire to receive pleasure is constantly "burning" inside him. That is how he is created, and there is no getting away from it. He can only enjoy what he receives. How can he give? By receiving: to give for the sake of receiving. As a result, his act of giving is nothing more than a means to receive what he desires.

According to my nature, I can receive both in action and in intention. My action may be giving or receiving, but my goal is the same – to receive pleasure. Man unknowingly seeks delight; it is our natural desire. In other words, the essence of my action depends solely on my intentions.

With the help of intention, I can reverse the essence of my action. I can receive by giving as in the example of the host and the guest. In any case, I can only receive; I am unable to give anything. With the help of intention, I can only receive, either "for my own sake" or "for someone else's".

Therefore, the relations between the Creator and man may take innumerable forms. They change on each level of man's spiritual growth. The Creator changes with regard to us through a system of His concealments, demonstrating one of His properties at a time in accordance with our ability to be equal to Him.

If the Creator shows us His genuine, absolutely perfect properties, the way He is, we will not be able to become equal to Him. That is why he diminishes, coarsens, and rather adapts Himself to us. We only have to rise onto this tiny level, become similar to the Creator in one little property.

As soon as we do that, the Creator starts revealing Himself in this property on a slightly higher level, and in other properties too. Through a system of worlds, He conceals His perfection, allowing us to liken ourselves to Him and ascend spiritually.

"*Olam Hazeh*" ("our world") is man's **inner** sensation of being in a state of absolute egoism. It is in this state that man feels that there is a Creator Who is extremely remote and completely hidden from him.

In view of his created properties, man is totally opposite to the Creator and spiritually distant from Him. Such an inner sensation is called "*Olam Hazeh*." One may sit in his room and simultaneously be in "*Olam Hazeh*", or in the worlds of *Assiya, Yetzira, Beria*, and *Atzilut* – man's inner states that link him to the spiritual levels.

The Creator is in a constant state of absolute calm. What does this mean? The Host, havingfound out what you like most, prepared a special meal, and is waiting for you. When you come to Him, He persuades you to accept his treat. In spite of all these actions, we still say the Creator is in a state of absolute calm, since His intention "to bestow upon creation" is invariable.

By absolute calm, we mean a constant unchanging desire. It exists only in the Creator, in all His deeds. These deeds are countless, infinite and vast. Since all these variations of deeds remain unchanged and seek only after one goal, we define them as a state of absolute calm.

Here we see no movement, since there is no change. Yet how shall we give for the sake of receiving pleasure? In our world, we are constantly doing it. For example, somebody brought me a cup of tea. Why did he do that? Because he enjoyed doing it, otherwise he would not have done it. Our action of giving or receiving does not matter at all. Mechanical action does not determine anything.

Everything is determined only by the intention. There are four combinations of an intention and action:

- reception for the sake of reception;
- giving for the sake of reception;
- giving for the sake of giving;
- reception for the sake of giving.

The first two combinations, "action-intention", exist in our world. The third and the fourth exist in the spiritual world. If man can achieve such an intention, it means he is in the spiritual world. Spirituality begins when one gives in order to please. This is something we do not understand; giving for the sake of pleasing. Where am I here? I am "cut off" from my ego, from my desire to receive. I give something and please somebody without receiving anything in return... Can this be possible?

Then there is also "reception for the sake of giving". When we study it in the spiritual objects - *Galgalta, AB, SAG* – it seems quite simple. Actually, we are unable to imagine such a phenomenon in our life.

The fact is that to receive pleasure through giving is not forbidden. However, bestowal must be purely spiritual, without a trace of 'for one's own sake'. First, man makes a *Tzimtzum* (a restriction), "ascends" to such a spiritual level, and acquires a quality of complete disregard for his own needs. Only then can he bestow and be delighted, receive pleasure through giving, i.e., the delight he feels is not as a result of his bestowal, but a consequence of someone enjoying his act.

Tzimtzum Aleph (The First Restriction) is not just an action performed in the world of Infinity. If man is able to restrict himself and not think of his own benefit, he then starts to ascend, "to count" his spiritual levels.

Movement is defined as a change of desire, or more accurately, the desire to which he can add his intention "for the sake of the Creator" and not "for his own sake". If your desire is constant in size and direction, you are considered to be motionless. Suppose you wish me well only in 20% of your intention. If your desire is only such, then you are absolutely motionless. If it changes with regard to me, then you are in motion.

While climbing the spiritual levels, man is in constant motion with regard to the Creator. It also seems to man that, regarding himself, the Creator is constantly moving towards him. This is because as man rises to a higher level, the Creator's revelation of Himself to him increases, i.e., he sees that the Creator is more kind and wants to bestow upon him. In man's sensations, the rapprochement is mutual.

However, we say, "the Upper Light is absolutely motionless", the Upper Light, not the one that comes upon him, i.e., the Creator's intention, not His light. We cannot feel the Upper Light until it enters the vessel. Inside the *Kli* we can feel the different varieties of light, and the way it affects us. However, the Creator, the Upper Light, is absolutely motionless, for His only unchanging desire is to bestow delight upon us.

How do we know this? There are people who have ascended to such a high level, where they could fully grasp the Creator's desire with regard to creation. They reached the level of the largest *Kli* and entirely filled it with the Creator's light. They are unable to rise higher, but can see that everything that comes from the Creator to creation is absolute kindness.

"From Thy deeds I will know Thee" – I cannot know the Creator's thoughts; I can only verify that everything He does is meant for me, for my ultimate good, demonstrating His infinite kindness. Then I may say His attitude to me is absolutely kind.

What is it to be absolutely kind? We do not mean He Himself, but rather His properties regarding me. The Creator Himself is incomprehensible. If man in his *Kli*, be it the Baal HaSulam, the Ari or Rabbi Shimon, achieves The Final Correction (*Gmar Tikkun*) and receives from the Creator everything he can – he becomes the sole receiver! Perhaps he alone enjoys the Creator's attitude and others do not. We see that in our world the Creator treats one better and another worse. How can we assert that He is absolutely kind to all?

The fact is that, while climbing the spiritual levels, man absorbs all the vessels of all the souls, attaches all created souls to his. He absorbs their sufferings and performs their corrections. It is called "he who suffers with the whole world is rewarded by the whole world". Man receives the light descending to all souls. Therefore, in his ultimate state, each Kabbalist is afforded such sensations as if he alone was created and he is *Adam HaRishon*. Hence, he knows and feels what the Creator does with each soul.

We all exist in one perfect state, but do not feel so. Our sensations are unimproved and distorted; according to them, our state is imperfect. Our inner feelings are so unrefined that we nevertheless perceive our most blissful state as imperfect.

Even now, we are in an absolutely perfect state. However, we are sent such thoughts and feelings that it seems to us that we are in a different, bad state, as it is said, "When we return to the Creator, we will see it was a dream".

Then we will realize that our sensations were totally unimproved, that we saw reality quite differently from what it really was at the time. We could not perceive it correctly, for our senses were incorrectly tuned.

In fact, all souls are in a perfect state. No bad state was ever created by the Creator. He created a perfect soul that is in full confluence with Him. It is completely filled with the light and is delighted by His greatness and power.

Why then do other states exist? Because there is no way we can presently feel this perfection. Why are all worlds inside us? For unless we correct these concealments and distortions inside, we will not be able to sense where we really are.

Actually, we are in there and feel it, but not in our present state. A Kabbalist in this world is constantly performing corrections. He suffers and worries while making these corrections in himself. Further, there are special souls in our world that take upon themselves the general corrections of the entire world, thus "pulling" it towards the universal good.

Even in our most "lifeless" states, we go through tremendous changes. We cannot feel them. Oftentimes, a day flashes by like one moment, but at other times drags on for eternity...

Question: "What does it mean when the *Partzuf* receives the light and then expels it?"

In our world, it is impossible to return what was already received inside. Nevertheless, as we speak about spirituality, we mean sensations. Imagine feeling wonderful, then wretched, then wonderful again, and wretched again. This is in some way similar to receiving the light and expelling it. This example demonstrates the impossibility of juxtaposing spiritual actions with our material body. They are of a very different type.

The *Kli's* desire to acquire a screen and liken its properties to the Creator's after the First Restriction is just one of a number of "external" corrections, so-called "attires". The inner property, the desire to receive pleasure, remains unchanged in accordance with the spiritual law that holds: "desire remains unchanged". In other words, the size of the created desire never changes.

The Creator created the desire in absolute conformity to the light with which He wishes to fill creation. Neither the size of this desire, nor its quality, is subject to change. Only the creation's intention during reception alters. Reception can be either "for the Creator's sake" or "for one's own sake". There is a host, but I can neither see nor feel him; all that I see I use for my own sake. This state is called "our world".

Feeling the Creator and being able to push away what He offers me means that I have crossed the *Machsom* – a partition between the spiritual world and ours. I already have an intention not to use my egoism: desire remains and is by no means diminished, but its use was modified from "for one's own sake" to "for the Creator's sake".

First, I only restrain myself from receiving "for my own sake"; then I can correct my intention and make my screen so powerful that I will be able to use my egoism "for the Creator", i.e., begin to receive "for His sake".

My spiritual level, my place in the spiritual worlds, depends on how much I can receive for His sake. If I can thus receive one fifth of the light destined for me, then I am in the world of *Assiya*; if I can receive two fifths – I am in the world of *Yetzira*; if I receive three fifths – I am in the world of *Beria*; if I receive four fifths – I am in the world of *Atzilut*, and if I receive five fifths – I am in the world of *Adam Kadmon*. Once I am able to receive everything that emanates from the Creator, I return to *Olam Ein Sof* (the world of Infinity), i.e., the world of Unlimited Reception.

That was the world of Unlimited Reception without the screen, before *Tzimtzum Aleph* (*TA*). Now, I can also receive the light endlessly, but with the help of the screen. This state, which is so strikingly different from reception prior to *TA*, is called the Final Correction. There are no levels in the world of Infinity, although more and more new conditions for reception arise.

We do not study the state of creation once it achieves the world of Infinity, since everything related to the state after the Final Correction is called "*Sitrey Torah*" (secrets of the Torah). Everything related to the state before the Final Correction is called "*Ta'amey Torah*" (tastes of the Torah). *Ta'amey Torah* may and must be studied by all. Everyone is obliged to grasp them. They may be apprehended in two ways (more often in their combination): by "way of suffering" or by "way of the Torah"; in any event, the result will be the same, differing only in time and sensation. All people will have to apprehend *Ta'amey Torah*, i.e., master Kabbalah - the science of attaining the light of Torah.

Thus, as it was said above, the desire itself remains unchanged. It is only the screen that changes. In accordance with the screen's magnitude, I take only the part of my desire that I can use for the Creator's sake. In any case, whatever part of my desire I may use, I always receive a certain part of the light in all my five levels of soul.

Suppose there are five dishes on the table in front of me. I have to cut some layer off each dish, whereas "the thickness" of the layer would depend on the magnitude of my screen. I always have *NaRaNHaY* – five lights-pleasures (*Nefesh*, *Ruach*, *Neshama*, *Haya*, and *Yechida*) felt in five parts of my desire to receive delight (*Keter*, *Hochma*, *Bina*, *Zeir Anpin*, and *Malchut*).

If I received the light in one of my desires, it means that I received it in five parts of the desire (five *Sefirot*) being on the same level of *Aviut*. It means that this reception of the light (*Partzuf*) emerged (was born) because of one *Zivug de Haka'a* (the screen interacting with the light).

It is similar to ordering a set meal. There are various kinds worth $10, $20, $30, $100, and $1000, but each consists of five courses, since I always have a combination of five desires. This is how my desire to receive was originally designed. Similarly, I have five senses. Each dinner consists of my five desires, *Keter*, *Hochma*, *Bina*, *ZA*, and *Malchut*;inside them, I receive the lights, *Nefesh*, *Ruach*, *Neshama*, *Haya*, and *Yechida*.

The vessel and the light are common names, but the *Partzufim* have specific names. For example, *Partzufim* in the world of *Adam Kadmon* are called *Galgalta*, *AB*, *SAG*, *MA*, and *BON*, in the world of *Atzilut* – *Atik*, *Arich Anpin*, *Abba ve Ima*, *ZON*, etc.

After the 'Fall', creation, the common soul, *Adam HaRishon*, split into thousands of souls. In the process of their correction, the souls ascend and occupy certain places in the spiritual worlds. In order to give these levels brief and accurate names, they are called Abraham, Isaac, Jacob, *Beit HaMikdash* (the Temple), *Cohen HaGadol* (the High Priest), *Shemesh* (the Sun), *Yareach* (the Moon). In correspondence with these levels and states, names were given to the weekdays, Sabbaths, holidays, etc., depending on how the worlds and the souls in them ascend and descend.

Now we can understand what the Torah really speaks about: it describes only spiritual reality – worlds, *Partzufim*, *Sefirot* and souls. For describing the souls and what happens to them, "the language of branches" taken from our world is used. Hence, you will not find Kabbalistic names like *Keter*, *Hochma*, *Bina*, *Atik*, and *Arich Anpin* in the Torah. More precise, specific names, designating a definite level or a part of it in a certain state, are applied. In such a case, this level would for example be called a place of rest in a desert or some action, etc.

Regardless of ascents or descents of the world, the soul is always enveloped in some outer shell. At the moment, we call our shell "this world" or "our world". If man works on himself and crosses the *Machsom*, alongside this world he would feel another world, i.e., more outward forces, a greater manifestation of the Creator; man will distinctly see the light emanating from Him, establish a tangible contact with Him.

Man reaches this or that level in accordance with the magnitude of the acquired screen, because each world and each level represent a filter: from the world of Infinity to our world, there are 125 levels, i.e., 125 filters between the world of Infinity and our world.

I was completely filled with the light in the world of Infinity. In our world, I am totally deprived of the light, and can neither see nor feel it because all these filters conceal it from me. Supposedly, each filter conceals 125-th part of the light. Since there are five worlds, each containing five *Partzufim*, which in turn include five *Sefirot*, they total 5x5x5=125 levels. What is the meaning of these levels?

As with glass, each of them restrains the light. For example, take a piece of red glass. Why is it red? It is because it restrains the color red. How can I prevent this level from restraining the light coming to me? It is very simple. I have to match the properties of that level. In other words, it restrains the light for me because I am not allowed to receive it.

If it reaches me without being deferred by the filter, I will receive it "for myself", since I have no screen for it. Therefore, my screen must be equal to the properties of that level's filter, in which case I myself would be able to weaken the light. Thus, if I acquire a screen as powerful as this particular level, I match its properties and all its restrictions disappear for me; they cease to exist.

Therefore, gradually, level by level, I abolish all these levels-filters until they all vanish and only the light remains. Such a state signifies attainment of the world of Infinity. It is endless and has no limitations, since I neutralized them all.

When I reach a certain level, I begin to feel and grasp everything on it quite distinctly. I myself become the property of that level. Hence the Torah says, "Everyone has to be like Moses", i.e., must rise to the level reached by him, since in the spiritual worlds "Moses" is the name of a certain level, and anyone who reaches it is considered to be like Moses.

Each time, man increases the magnitude of his screen according to the properties of the level before him. Any level above me is defined as the Creator; I cannot see anything beyond it since it is His manifestation for me. Therefore, each time, I have to match my properties to the Creator in front of me. On each level, He is different, revealing Himself to me more and more.

To what extent? Suppose a person might steal $1000 lying before him, but if there is only $100, he would not do so. It means that he already has a screen for $100, so this sum may be placed before him; he will be able to reject it, altruistically work with it. Therefore he is not affected by the ban "Do not steal" with regard to $100.

If he is able to strengthen his screen and not to steal $1000, then this amount will not be a limitation for him, and it could be placed before him. Likewise, he must strengthen his screen before the infinite light that is destined to fill him "is placed" before him.

When man is able to receive all this light for the Creator's sake, he will experience a delight 625 greater than *Malchut* (creation) in the world of Infinity. Why will he receive more pleasure? Why was *Malchut's* (soul's) descent from the world of Infinity to our world necessary? For what purpose was the separation from the Creator and gradual return to Him?

It was done so that, with the help of the freedom of choice, by will and power, he might achieve an elevated state like the world of Infinity. Being in the world of Infinity was initially determined by the Creator, not by man. If he achieves this state by himself, he acquires his own new vessels, his own screen, his own sensations, earns his own eternity and perfection.

The fact is that because of man's independent efforts, he prepares himself for feeling what is really bestowed upon him in the world of Infinity. When *Malchut* of the world of Infinity was born by the Creator's thought, received the light and later restricted itself from further reception, it felt only a tiny part of it, for its vessel was not yet ready.

As creation begins to ascend from a point totally opposite to the Creator, from complete darkness, when hunger and the desire to enjoy this light are gradually accumulated, creation consequently begins to be delighted with the same light, but the delight is already 625 times greater than before the beginning of correction.

The light does not change; everything depends on hunger, on the desire to receive the light. If man is not hungry, he will not be able to enjoy even the best delicacies. If he is starving, even a crust of bread will become a source of tremendous pleasure. Thus everything depends on how strong the hunger is, not on the light. One can receive a scanty measure of the light, but the vessel will have a huge pleasure in that.

On the contrary, the light can fill everything around, but if the vessel feels no hunger, it will feel, out of all this light, only *Ohr Nefesh*, a very small light. The entire Universe and its control are designed exactly to prepare the *Kli* for receiving perfect delight; in other words, that it might really feel what the Creator bestows upon it. For that, it must move away, then gradually and independently draw nearer.

"The language of branches" exists only in Hebrew, but it could be made on the basis of any other language. In other languages, the relation between the spiritual root and its consequences in our world cannot be traced. It does not exist even in Modern Hebrew. Nevertheless, if we take basic Hebrew with all its roots, then there is a clear connection between the root and the consequence.

Such a connection exists in every language, but in other languages, no one has ever tried to find it. No Kabbalist is pointing out the connection between the spiritual and the material in Chinese hieroglyphs or in Latin letters, etc. In Hebrew, thanks to Kabbalists, we know these correspondences, for example, why the letter "*Aleph*" is written this way and not another.

What do we really express by it? We express human sensations. One can take the language of music, colors, or any other language. Everything that can be used to express human sensations, notions, comprehension, can be utilized as a language. It is possible to speak about spirituality in any language. Hebrew is unique in that it has a ready code. However, if there is a Kabbalist who knows the roots of any other language, he will be able to do the same with it.

The forces standing behind Hebrew letters form combinations expressed in a certain letterform. Hebrew is within the root of other languages. Inscription of the letters in other languages actually come from the same root as the Hebrew letters. However, they are modified, so the connection between letters in other languages and their spiritual roots are different.

When we comprehend a certain spiritual level or sensation, when we feel something in the spiritual world, we know what to call this sensation. So what can be done if we have not yet comprehended the spiritual, when the sensations cannot be expressed in words, when we do not have an appropriate language? What should be done to find this language?

In the spiritual world, there is no language, no worlds, and no letters; there is only the vessel's sensation of the light. The fact is that every spiritual vessel has its branch in this world; everything descends from the world of Infinity downwards to our world. Then all the sensations of our world rise to the world of Infinity. Therefore, if we take any point in the world of Infinity, it is possible to trace a straight line passing through all the worlds down to our world, to its branch.

Thus it is possible to say that the soul of *Adam HaRishon*, broken into 600 thousand parts, exists in each of the spiritual worlds. The arrangement of the spiritual worlds is absolutely identical. The difference is only in the material from which they are built. In any world, the soul feels its condition, the influence on it, and its interaction with a certain spiritual level.

If one takes the projection of this soul on our world, one will find in Hebrew the notions corresponding to spiritual conditions. Then we can take words from our world, assuming that with their help, we speak not about the objects of our world, but with the help of these words, we speak about the objects, forces, and actions in the spiritual world. Such complete correspondence is a result of our use of one and the same language. The difference is only in the plane of this or "that" world, where the intended notion exists.

Our language is a description of objects, actions, sensations, reactions, interactions.

Everything we have in our world exists in the spiritual one - the similar picture on all 5 levels. Hence, on each stage, on any of the 125 levels, regardless of where you are, you can always take our language and describe what is going on at that level. However, only someone who has already been on that level can really understand you. The one who has not yet been there will suppose that you are talking about our world, or the level he is on at the moment of reading or listening to your account.

The Torah is written in the language of branches at the level of the world of *Atzilut*. However, unprepared people understand what is written in the Torah literally, thinking that it is talking about our world. They take it as a collection of stories. Thus, the language of branches describes spiritual actions that take place simultaneously on all levels.

"The Preamble to the Wisdom of Kabbalah" studies the birth, development, and arrangement of the worlds. When the Upper worlds spread down to the level of our world, the souls begin to rise from our world to the world of Infinity.

The soul rises because it absorbs all the qualities, knowledge, and revelations from the previous levels. Therefore, it knows exactly what happens on all the lower levels. Kabbalists are in the world of *Atzilut*. So how do they call the actions taking place there by the names of our world? The fact is, they do not lose the connection with our world; they live in both worlds, feeling simultaneously what is going on in the world of *Atzilut* and in our world.

They know exactly the correspondence between one and the other; therefore, they call the objects in the world of *Atzilut* according to the properties of those that appear in our world as a projection coming from the spiritual worlds. In the world of *Atzilut*, there are no man-made objects (e.g. radio sets, computers etc), but all other objects and forces are present there. The Kabbalist sees that a certain object in our world is the consequence of the same object in the world of *Atzilut*. Therefore, he gives the object (root) in the world of *Atzilut* the same name born by the corresponding object (branch) in our world.

There is no connection between Kabbalistic comprehension and meditation or any other "mystical" notions. Everything that is studied by esoteric specialists, mystics, and pseudo-kabbalists, belongs to the human psyche, and is in no way connected with spirituality, attainment of the Creator or Kabbalah.

Most of these people do not have the slightest idea of what a screen is, and without the screen, spirituality cannot be grasped. Pseudo-Kabbalists who have heard about the screen, believe they already have it, imagining they are already in the world of Infinity. Kabbalah is a secret science; it cannot be "narrated" to anyone. Only the one who feels is able to understand.

Therefore, all methods, teachings, and religions belong to the comprehension of the latent qualities of the human psyche, to the product of human brain activity. These people can do a lot. They can cure, foretell the future, and relate the past - everything that refers to the body. Man has potential powers to do whatever he wants with the physical body.

However, to enter the spiritual world, one must have a screen. That is why the various kinds of predictions, tricks, miracles, including those that really exist, must not be confused with Kabbalah. One may foretell the future the way Wolf Messing and Nosrtadamus did; one can know the past by looking at a person, but none of this has anything to do with spirituality.

Whatever refers to the body, to our world, can be predicted and changed; there is nothing supernatural in that. Each of us, if he so desires, may move away from the disturbances of civilization, and start cultivating such powers, and abilities. We lost these capabilities because they were substituted by the products of civilization.

Every person has these natural inclinations. People with these kinds of abilities who are capable of looking at themselves critically, say that there is a Creator, but they know nothing about Him, or have nothing to do with Him. However, predicting man's future, seeing his past, or making something against his will, is not connected to the world of spirit. Since these abilities are unconnected with the soul, they die together with a person.

The soul is a vessel, created with the help of the screen. If there is no screen, there is no soul. While there is no screen, there is only "a point in the heart", the soul embryo. In the process of acquiring the screen, the first (still very small) ten *Sefirot* begin to emerge. The larger the screen gets, the larger the ten *Sefirot* under it become, but there are always 10 of them.

If man has no screen, then he will die as he was born, no matter what great abilities he had or what he did in this world.

Do you think that when a yogi does not breathe, it makes him spiritual? To enter the spiritual world, man must devote all of his strength, time, and desires to that end. Only the desires necessary for one's existence in this world need attending. For the spiritual world to open up, a real desire is necessary. Only the one who really desires it will enter the spiritual world. If you combine Kabbalah studies with something else, other than for taking care of your existence, it means that your desire is split.

Right now, man can judge only from the level on which he is. He cannot know what he will be like on the next one. Everything completely changes on another level, man's entire inner world. Thoughts, desires, reactions and outlook – everything changes. Everything is taken out of you, leaving only flesh, your outer shell; the rest is reinstalled anew.

Hence, we cannot understand how this desire can be the only one. We cannot understand it now, since we are not yet on that level. When we gradually ascend to a higher level, we will feel that this desire is really formed. This desire is the only requisite for entering the spiritual worlds; and when you meet this condition, the gates of spirituality will open up before you.

It should be pointed out that even a great Kabbalist cannot predict man's potential abilities. A fortuneteller might correctly predict his earthly, material future, but not man's spiritual future. Moreover, when coming across a Kabbalist, a genuine fortuneteller feels that a prediction of his future is beyond his abilities.

A Kabbalist is not interested in developing the abilities to predict his future. Forces of our world are necessary for this, and as a rule, they are totally undeveloped in a Kabbalist.

A fortuneteller can name all the ailments and bodily problems of a Kabbalist. However, he has nothing to say about his "self". He can only determine his physical condition at a given moment.

A Kabbalist is constantly looking for the connection with the Creator and does not try to guess how or what he has to do to earn a better future. It would never cross a Kabbalist's mind to know his future. Such a desire belongs to the impure forces and not to Kabbalah. By grasping the Upper world, a Kabbalist comprehends the ways of correction of all souls.

All information in the spiritual world consists of five parts (*Behinot*). One *Zivug de Haka'a* in the *Peh de Rosh*, although it involves only one kind of light, leads to formation of a *Partzuf* made of five parts. What does it mean - one light? One light is a general state. It consists of five parts that differ from each other quantitatively and qualitatively. However, they must always be together, as a whole set. It is similar to a sensation that is the product of five composite sub-sensations in our five senses: touch, smell, sight, hearing, and taste.

Since five lights come to me, there must be five desires inside me. The difference between them has to be both quantitative and qualitative. However, all of them ultimately act together. I cannot make one desire bigger and another smaller. They form a certain combination. The light entering the vessel passes four levels. In turn, the vessel consists of five levels of the desire to receive pleasure.

Now let us review paragraph 7:

7) And now understand what is written in the first part of the book "The Tree of Life": "The creation of all worlds is a consequence of the Creator's perfection in all His actions. However, if He had not revealed His powers in the actions that He is performing on the created beings, He would not have been called "perfect".

Thus, since the Creator is perfect, all of His actions must be perfect. That is why He created the worlds. On the contrary, the worlds are a concealment of the Creator, the remoteness from Him.

On the face of it, however, it is not clear how imperfect deeds could come out of the perfect Creator. Moreover, the Creator's actions are so imperfect that they need to be corrected by man.From the above statement, understand that, since the essence of creation is a desire to receive pleasure, it is quite imperfect due to its being absolutely opposite to the Creator (while He is perfect and giving, the creation only receives, is imperfect, and its properties are opposite to His). On the one hand, it is infinitely remote and detached from Him. On the

> *other hand, it is something new, born out of nothing. Creation was created to receive, and be filled with the Creator's delight.*

This means that the desire to receive pleasure, albeit quite contrary to the Creator and absolutely imperfect, is, nevertheless, exactly what the Creator had to create.

> *However, if the creations had been distanced from the Creator by their properties, He could not have been called the Perfect One, since imperfect actions cannot come from someone Perfect. Therefore, the Creator restricted His light, created the worlds, restriction after restriction down to our world, and put the soul into the body of our world.*

By "our world", we do not mean our physical world, but the set of egoistical desires corresponding to the lowest stage of development of the worlds.

> *"To study the Torah" means to learn for the sake of correction, not to read a book called "the Torah". "To observe precepts," means to perform spiritual actions with a screen, not to carry out mechanical actions. Through studying the Torah and observing its precepts, the soul achieves a perfection that it lacked in the beginning of creation. It signifies the equivalence of its properties with those of the Creator. The soul would deserve to receive all the pleasure that was in the Thought of Creation. Now it will completely merge with the Creator.*

It means that, apart from the delight, an additional reward is prepared for the soul, and this reward is called "merging with the Creator". Thus it is not just a reception of the entire light, but a merging with the Creator, a receiving of the light that appeared because of an equivalence of properties.

The equivalence of properties and merging with the Creator is much higher than just receiving the light, since because of the equivalence of properties, the soul rises to the level of the Creator. It not only receives the light from the Creator, but also ascends to His level. Thus, it rises from the level of creation to the Creator's level and also comprehends that which is above its nature.

ח) וענין הסגולה שבתורה ומצוות להביא את הנשמה לדבקה בו ית', הוא רק בבחינת העסק בהם שלא לקבל שום פרס רק בכדי להשפיע נחת רוח ליוצרו בלבד, כי אז לאט לאט הולכת הנשמה וקונית השואת הצורה ליוצרה, כמ"ש לפנינו במאמר ר' חנניא בן עקשיא בהתחלת הספר, עש"ה. כי יש בזה ה' מדרגות כוללות נפש רוח נשמה חיה יחידה המקובלים מה' העולמות הנקראים א"ק, אצילות, בריאה, יצירה, עשיה. וכן יש ה' מדרגות נרנח"י פרטיות המקובלים מפרטיות ה' פרצופין שיש בכל עולם מה' העולמות, וכן יש נרנח"י דפרטי פרטיות המקובלים מהעשר ספירות שבכל פרצוף, כמ"ש בפנים הספר. שע"י תורה ומצוות להשפיע נ"ר ליוצרו זוכים ומשיגים לאט לאט לכלים מבחי' הרצון להשפיע הבאים בהמדרגות האלו מדרגה אחר מדרגה עד שבאים בהשוואת הצורה לגמרי אליו ית'. ואז מקויימת בהם מחשבת הבריאה לקבל כל העונג והרוך והטוב שחשב ית' בעדם, ועוד נוסף להם ריוח הכי גדול, כי זוכים גם לדבקות אמיתי, מכח שהשיגו הרצון להשפיע כיוצרם.

8) Only through indulging in the Torah and the Commandments with an intention not to receive any reward for it, but for pleasing the Creator, generates a special power ("Segula") that enables the soul to reach the state of absolute unity with the Creator. Gradually, the soul advances by acquiring more and more new properties equal to the Creator's, as is said in the article "The Preamble to the Wisdom of Kabbalah".

This ascent, merging with the Creator, consists of five levels: Nefesh, Ruach, Neshama, Haya, and Yechida. These are received from five worlds: AK, Atzilut, Beria, Yetzira, and Assiya.

When the soul rises to the world of *Assiya*, it receives the light of *Nefesh*. When it rises to the world of *Yetzira*, it receives the light of *Ruach*. In the world of *Beria*, it receives the light of *Neshama*. In the world of *Atzilut*, it receives the light of *Haya*; and in the world of *Adam Kadmon*, it receives the light of *Yechida*.

Each of these five levels is in turn divided into its own five sub-levels also called Nefesh, Ruach, Neshama, Haya, and Yechida. It receives them from the five Partzufim that form each of the five worlds. Each sub-level has its own NaRaNHaY, which it receives from the ten Sefirot forming each Partzuf.

With the help of the Torah and the Commandments with an intention to please the Creator, created beings gradually acquire vessels-desires from the above-named levels until they completely merge with the Creator.

Thus, a greater desire to bestow is gradually formed in the soul. In accordance with this, the soul is filled with more and more light until it achieves a complete equivalence of properties with the Creator.

At this stage, the fulfillment of the Thought of Creation takes place in the souls: reception of all the delight the Creator prepared for them. Moreover, since the souls acquired the desire to bestow, they fully merge (Dvekut) with the Creator and experience a perfect, eternal and infinite pleasure, much greater than the reception of the light.

So the creation achieves:

1) The reception of pleasure prepared for it in the form of *NaRaNHaY*.
2) The equivalence of properties with the Creator, i.e. it rises to the Creator's level and gains a perfection equal to His.

We cannot yet imagine this level. We are used to operating with such notions as life, death, time, and pleasure. However, when it refers to the spiritual levels, we have neither words nor sensations to imagine or describe such states.

In the process of acquiring the screen, man begins to modify his properties, accordingly receiving the light and gradually ascending. Five major levels (worlds) are divided into five sub-levels (*Partzufim*), which in turn consist of their own levels (*Sefirot*) - and all of these are characterized by greater and greater likeness to the Creator.

While man is yet uncorrected, each of these levels is a concealment of the Creator from him. When man receives correction, the same level becomes a revelation of the Creator and a light for him. That is to say, on the one hand, each stage is the concealment of the Creator, and on the other – His revelation.

Each stage is a certain level of the Creator's properties. Let us assume that the world of Infinity corresponds to 100% of the Creator's properties, and is the highest level. Then our world corresponds to 0% of the Creator's properties. The remaining spiritual Universe is between them, and is divided into 125 levels, which correspond to 125 measures of the Creator's properties.

As it was said, we have to rid ourselves of egoism, because egoism is an inferior *Kli,* or vessel. The moment it starts feeling pleasure, the feeling eliminates the desire; as a result, the pleasure dies away. This means that the moment the desire is satisfied, the pleasure immediately disappears. Thus an egoistical *Kli* can never be satisfied. Therefore, egoism is given to us only for its correction, that we may be able to feel eternal and perfect delight in it.

Man feels that he has reached a certain level only when he is there. Then he knows what level he is on and what level he has already passed. He sees the next level before him, the one he has to reach. While seriously studying genuine Kabbalah from the authentic books, in the right group, he begins to understand the next level of his ascent.

At the beginning, he feels only the concealment of that level, i.e., the Creator is hidden from him in it. Then man begins to grasp what properties the Creator possesses and how he can acquire them. There are many stages along this path, but the first one is the most difficult. Compared to the first stage, comprehension of the rest of them is much easier.

It proceeds from the fact that on the first level, the largest *Kelim*-desires are being born; precisely those *Kelim* that appear on the first level, afterwards show up on the last one. This is because there is a so-called inverse relationship between the lights and the vessels.

Right now, we are in a condition wherein we do not know really which *Kelim* we are using. Although we are using very complex *Kelim* already, they have not yet manifested in our sensations. The biggest *Aviut* from *Shoresh, Aleph, Bet, Gimel,* and *Dalet* is in the world of *Assiya*. However, the biggest screen is in the world of *AK* - this is the screen of *Dalet*, in *Atzilut* - the screen of *Gimel*, in *Beria* - the screen of *Bet*, in *Yetzira* - the screen of *Aleph* and in *Assiya* – the screen of *Shoresh*.

One should always pay attention to what we refer to – whether it is the screen or the desire this screen is "dressed on". Therefore, this is the most difficult stage of our work. Entering the spiritual world is the major problem in man's entire spiritual quest.

Afterwards man confronts other problems and the work becomes completely different. He already knows clearly what to do; gets an idea of the 10 *Sefirot* he acquired, has some true comprehension of the entire Universe. The Universe is built according to one principle, so if man has acquired his own (even the smallest) 10 *Sefirot*, then he readily knows what the Torah talks about, albeit on the level of his 10 *Sefirot*.

If, for example, a man born in the jungle were brought to the civilized world, he would not know how to use certain technical devices. A person who grew up in a developed country, may not know the processes inside those devices, but he knows how to use them, because he lives among these objects. The same principle applies to a person who has reached the minimum level in the spiritual world. He has a slight idea about spirituality, already has *Kelim* (albeit the smallest). The innermost processes are perceived on the higher levels.

When a man acquires a screen, he makes a *Zivug de Haka'a* and receives the Inner Light inside, which gives him an idea about spirituality. We do not feel anything outside of us, we feel the world within, the spiritual world. This Inner Light, which fills the *Kli*, provides the measure, which we call "the level" or the light, the level of "*Nefesh*", "*Ruach*", "*Neshama*", "*Haya*", and "*Yechida*".

To go forward, man should constantly absorb, pass Kabbalistic texts through his mind and heart, be filled with it all the time. There is no other method apart from studying Kabbalah with the right books, guided by a Teacher, and working in a group. Collective efforts are very important. Even a group of beginners is already a spiritual force, despite the fact that its members hardly imagine what they study Kabbalah for and what goals they have. It will be able to attract very strong spiritual light by its own efforts in the future.

King David described all the spiritual states that a soul or a man goes through, from the lowest to the highest. King David (David *HaMelech*, *Malchut*) is called so, because he himself passed through all the spiritual states and described them. His book "*Tehilim*" ("Psalms") is the highest level in Kabbalah, which includes all possible states of the soul.

If man acquires all properties of the Creator, all His desires, habits, powers, such a state is called merging with the Creator.

It means that man becomes equal to Him. What does he create? By giving to the Creator, he creates himself, creates the screen, or rather becomes the Creator's equal partner in creating himself.

The Creator created egoism, man; and man makes altruism, the Creator out of egoism, out of himself. Naturally, he does not create it out of nothing ("*Yesh mi Ayn*") as the Creator has made our desire to receive pleasure, egoism, out of nothing. However, turning this desire into its opposite is man's goal. This process is called "correction" (*Tikkun*). Actually, it is a birth of a completely new quality. Indeed, the Creator created man's egoism and man creates the Creator.

What does it mean that the creation is made out of nothing? We know it from Kabbalists. They study all the Creator's properties and see that He is absolutely kind and complete. Hence, He made the Creation out of nothing. When man ascends, making his properties equal to the Creator's on the high levels called "the tenth millennium", where the Torah's secrets are revealed, he sees the creation itself and the way it was created by the Creator.

The only sources we study are the book of the "Zohar", the Ari's books, the books written by the Baal HaSulam and the Rabash. Nothing else can be read independently. One can read the books of the series "Kabbalah - the Secret Science", but nothing else. The Pentateuch can be read only when man can understand that it has an inner, Kabbalistic meaning, and is not merely an historical narrative.

A long time passes before man automatically begins to see the spiritual actions behind the words of the Torah. It is better to read the Book of Psalms; there at least human feelings are described. Although spiritual feelings are meant there, they are more or less equivalent in our world. One will not be misled as much as by reading the Torah.

It is necessary to study how to observe the precepts in our world. There is the "*Shulchan Aruch*" for that purpose. The commandments should be kept on a "simple" level. Josef Caro wrote the "*Shulchan Aruch*" especially for those who wish to study Kabbalah, and want to know how the precepts should be observed without having to study the Gemarra folios and having no time left for Kabbalah. One may not read The Zohar in Aramaic, only the Baal HaSulam's commentary.

ט) ומעתה לא יקשה לך להבין דברי הזוהר הנ"ל, אשר כל העולמות העליונים והתחתונים וכל אשר בתוכם לא נבראו אלא בשביל האדם. כי כל אלו המדרגות והעולמות לא באו אלא כדי להשלים הנשמות במדת הדבקות שהיה חסר להם מבחינת מחשבת הבריאה, כנ"ל. שמתחילה נצטמצמו ונשתלשלו מדרגה אחר מדרגה ועולם אחר עולם עד לעולם החומרי שלנו בכדי להביא את הנשמה בהגוף של עוה"ז, שהוא כולו לקבל ולא להשפיע, כמו בהמות וחית הארץ. כמ"ש עייר פרא אדם יולד, שהוא בחינת הרצון לקבל הגמור שאין בו מבחינת השפעה ולא כלום, שאז נבחן האדם להפכי גמור אליו ית', שאין התרחקות יותר מזה. ואח"ז בכח הנשמה המתלבשת בו הולך ועוסק בתורה ומצוות שאז משיג צורת ההשפעה כיוצרו לאט לאט בדרך המדרגות ממטה למעלה דרך כל אותם הבחינות שירדו בעת השתלשלותם מלמעלה למטה, שהם רק מדות ושיעורים בצורת הרצון להשפיע. שכל מדרגה עליונה פירושה שהיא יותר רחוקה מבחינת הרצון לקבל ויותר קרובה רק להשפיע, עד שזוכה להיות כולו להשפיע ולא לקבל כלום לעצמו, ואז נשלם האדם בדבקות אמיתי בו ית', כי רק בשביל זה נברא. הרי שכל העולמות ומלואם רק בשביל האדם נבראו.

9) It will not be difficult for you to understand now what is written in The Book of Zohar, that all the worlds – Upper and lower - and everything that exists in them were created only for man. All these levels were created only to fill up the souls, to direct them to perfection, to the degree of merging with the Creator, which is absent from the moment of the Thought of Creation.

In the beginning of creation, five worlds were formed from the Creator's level down to our world to place the soul into the material body of our world. The material body is the desire to receive without giving anything in return. This is the final form of the desire to receive pleasure for itself. That is why man's properties in our world are absolutely opposite to the Creator.

By studying Kabbalah, man gradually begins to comprehend the properties of giving. According to his comprehension, he gradually ascends, learning the properties of the descending levels that have the property of bestowal. Then he reaches the level of the desire only to give, receiving nothing in return. As a result, man completely merges with the Creator, i.e., reaches the state forwhich he was created. Therefore, all the worlds were created for man's sake.

Thus, all the worlds are created to help man ascend from point zero, upwards, opposite to the Creator, and finally to reach the last point - merging with the Creator, to cover the entire journey beginning from the complete concealment of the Creator, passing 125 levels, each representing a greater revelation of the Creator.

We have already spoken about the fact that the Creator deliberately concealed Himself behind five worlds, each consisting of five *Partzufim*, each *Partzuf* having five *Sefirot*, overall, 125 levels of concealment. All this was done for making man absolutely remote from the Creator.

Man cannot feel the Creator, he thinks he is independent, believes he has freedom of will – freedom to develop and utilize his egoism as he sees fit. Such conditions are called "our world"; in fact, they are the Creator's forces affecting us in a state of complete concealment.

Everything that surrounds us in this world is just the last level of the various forces that influence us on behalf of the Creator. Whatever man feels, inside and around himself, everything we call "our world", is the last level that can possibly exist in the Universe.

As soon as man, with the help of his inner work, is able to eliminate the nearest level of the Creator's concealment from him, to draw this curtain apart, he immediately starts feeling the Creator in this minimal 125th part.

It does not mean that 125 levels conceal the Creator from us proportionally. The lower the level, the more it conceals the Creator. As soon as man pulls away the lowest curtains separating him from the next level, the Creator's light immediately begins to shine upon him, and he begins to see the Creator behind all that exists around him in this world.

The still, vegetative, animal and human levels of nature - all that is around man and inside him, all his animal cravings and desires for power, honor, fame, aspiration for knowledge - for him, everything now becomes a manifestation of the Creator.

He feels how the Creator affects him, his "self", with the help of his surroundings and inner properties. The first level of revelation, though the most difficult, is the most important, because by overcoming it, man immediately establishes contact, albeit minimal, with the Creator, and never loses it. There is no way back. Thus, the correct beginning is paramount.

Sometimes, man seems to have lost all he had gained, and has fallen from his level. However, this sensation is deliberately sent to allow him to rise even higher. The spiritual levels are built in such a way that the concealment of the Creator on each of them depends on man's correction. The concealment is given to him on a level he is able to overcome.

Let us suppose that man has corrected 10% of his intention to receive. This means that he receives pleasure in these 10% not for himself, but for the sake of the Creator. Therefore, the measure of concealment and revelation of the Creator is the same level, its back and front parts. In other words, there is nothing outside man; all the levels are built for him and are inside him.

All the spiritual worlds are inside man's soul, forming a ladder between him and the Creator. That is, they are 125 levels of our properties. Around us, there is only one thing: the completely altruistic property to bestow and please us. We call this property the Creator. However, our inner property is absolutely egoistic.

The gradual correction of man's inner properties is the purpose of his existence in our world. Everyone must correct himself. The sensation of the Creator that man gains during his correction is called "spiritual ascent" from one level to another, or from one world to the next. All this takes place solely internally.

We have already said that the surrounding world is just a reaction of our inner properties to the Creator's influence, i.e., all worlds, *Partzufim*, *Sefirot*, everything that we ever talk about is inside the person; there is nothing outside. One may say that outside there are only the four properties of the Direct Light.

The descending light creates man and all his inner properties. All the spiritual worlds in us are just the measures of sensing the Creator. All the angels, devils, dark and light forces are no more than man's inner forces, specially created in him by the Creator to help him constantly correct and overcome his natural egoism.

Initially, they were systematically restricted, world-by-world, and descended to the level of this material world to insert the soul into the body, to dress man's "self" in absolutely egoistic properties, infinitely remote from the Creator, the most opposite to His properties.

They are called "the qualities of this world". What is meant here is not a number of material objects surrounding us - liquids, gases, solids. By material world, we mean absolutely egoistical qualities, from the least to the most developed, regardless of whether it is a baby or the greatest grown-up egoist in the world.

When the Kabbalists say "the body of this world", they mean the desire to receive. There is the body of our world – an egoistic desire to receive, and there is the spiritual body - the same desire to receive, but already with the screen, which means an egoistic desire transformed into an altruistic one.

As stated, in order to make man wish only to receive, the Creator put the soul into the body of our world. This is the so-called "animal" state, as the proverb says, "man is born like a wild donkey". Thus, when man descends to this world, he receives egoistic desires called "body" and with his properties becomes absolutely opposite to the Creator, infinitely remote from Him.

The Creator gives man only one little altruistic quality called the "soul". If man starts indulging into the Torah and the commandments with the right intention, he gradually acquires the Creator's desire "to bestow".

The highest level is the desire only to bestow without receiving anything for oneself. Achieving this state, man completes his way to the Creator and merges with Him. Closeness and remoteness of the spiritual objects take place because of an equivalence or difference of properties. Therefore, by achieving the state of absolute desire to bestow, i.e., the last 125-th level, man is rewarded with complete revelation of the Creator.

Thus, all the worlds with everything that fills them are created only for man's sake and for his correction. Observing the Torah and the commandments, with the intention to bestow pleasure upon the Creator without receiving anything in return, means adherence to the spiritual laws that man learns as he climbs these steps.

Each time, when he is in a certain spiritual state, there is always a choice before him, what to do, how to think, feel, choose his thoughts, intentions, inner decisions. Although the Creator has not yet revealed

Himself to us, we have to try to compare all our thoughts, decisions, and opinions with our intention to acquire His desire to bestow.

The way we analyze and choose each opinion and decision, is called "a commandment" (*Mitzvah*). When man fulfills this law correctly, he stimulates the candle, allowing a little more light to enter his spiritual desire.

On the higher levels, upon man's entering into the spiritual worlds, he corrects his absolutely egoistic desire, and with the help of a *Zivug de Haka'a* (Stroke Contact) receives a portion of the light. The light he receives is called variously "the Torah", "the Creator" or "the light of the soul".

There is a so-called Essence of the Creator (*Atzmuto HaBoreh*). We do not feel the Essence of the Creator, but only His influence. We are like a black box: whatever penetrates through our five senses - sight, hearing, touch, smell, and taste, or with the help of these devices, which only widen the range of our sensations - all this creates a picture of this world in us, seemingly existing outside of us.

However, this world is only a product of our inner sensations, something pressing us from outside. It is like making a body out of clay and giving it a kind of sensitivity. When I press on it, it will have an inner reaction. It feels this pressure in its sensations; somehow, it is reflected in it. The body calls this outside influence (or rather its reaction to it) a certain property.

Now, if someone pricks it, the body will call this outside stimulation (or its reaction to it) some other property. It has no idea what affects it from outside, but feels only its reactions to whatever presses on it. All the creation's reactions to the numerous outside influences create inside it a feeling of "the surrounding" world.

If aperson is deprived of one of his senses from birth, say the sight, he must build a picture of the surrounding world with the help of the remaining four. The resulting picture differs from ours.

If we are able to widen somehow the range of our senses (we cannot add any more senses), then the picture of the world will instantly change.

At any rate, we will perceive only what "enters" us (that is how we call our reactions to the external influences), and not what is outside.

Another additional stimulation, called the Creator's light, will enter us. He Himself will enter us, not just press us like a piece of clay from outside. He will enter and start filling us according to the extent of the equivalence of our properties to His. All our essence is "a piece of egoistic clay"; if this "piece" succeeds in acquiring the Creator's properties, i.e. learns to give, then there will be no difference between them. The outer boundary between Him and the "piece" will disappear. They will merge into one; the Creator will fill this "clay" from inside, and it will be in complete harmony, fully merged with whatever is outside.

This state is the most perfect, comfortable, eternal, and absolutely good. "The piece of clay" must achieve this level. Man must reach it, beginning with the lowest level, called "our world". The soul dressed into the body, forces it to work before it can ascend.

The soul at its zero stage is an egoistic property, but in its final state, it must be transformed into an altruistic one. In case man is reluctant to do it on his own free will, he will be assisted from above, and then, spurred by hard sufferings, "he" will be compelled to agree. Each of these "pieces of egoism" (souls) has to overcome all 125 levels. These "pieces" are divided only because each of them feels its own small desire.

In the process of likening their properties to the Creator's, they begin to feel the commonness and inseparable continuity of their mass, the absolute unity of all these egoistic splinters. They understand that they represent a single whole. The more man is corrected, the more he sees himself as an absolutely inseparable part of the whole, i.e., he depends on everybody and everybody depends on him.

If the creation is one whole organism, then it does not matter which part of it receives and which part gives. It is easier to be corrected as a small piece, and when all the pieces have corrected themselves, they merge in their sensations into a single whole – this is what they call: the merging of the souls.

There is much interference, all specially sent to us. Finally, only persistence wins. Man does not have to possess any special inclinations, intellect, particular qualities, or properties. He should only be persistent, or rather, show the ability and courage to endure; only this will lead to victory.

Each of us is the way the Creator made him; nothing can be done about it. All our inner changes in thoughts, desires, and ambitions - all of these are programmed in us from above, and they all must be corrected. It is that very material, that 'piece of clay' that we must work on.

A corrected egoistic property, which the Creator's light enters, is called a "*Kli*" (the vessel). A person who has just begun his study of Kabbalah can be told everything; everything enters him, nothing is forgotten, and nothing disappears. When necessary, he will recall it, but will do so only after his correction. When he has the minimal inner vessels and this information is necessary for his work, it will emerge, "surface" out of his subconscious.

Man himself will have to sort out this information and work with it. At this stage, he should not be given ready answers to his questions; now he has to search and find the answers.

Being on the high levels of the spiritual development, man suffers not because the souls on lower levels feel bad. He suffers from an inability to fulfill the Creator's desire as regards these souls, their present state; i.e., from the fact that not all souls feel the unity with the Creator the way he does. In addition, he naturally tries to accelerate this process by dissemination of Kabbalah, by spreading the knowledge about the necessity of correction, while others interfere with his mission.

Man needs the entire world in order to complete his spiritual work, because it consists not only in self-correction, but also on each level there is certain mutual work to be done with the rest of the souls.

A Kabbalist must feel the entire world, feel its sufferings, absorb them on his level, and correct them. Moreover, on each level, the inclusion of all the souls into his and his own into all other souls takes place.

י) ועתה אחר שזכית להבין ולדעת כל זה, כבר מותר לך ללמוד חכמה זו בלי שום פחד של הגשמה ח"ו. כי המעיינים מתבלבלים מאד, שמצד אחד נאמר שכל הע"ס והפרצופין מתחילת ע"ס האצילות עד סוף הע"ס דעשיה הוא אלקיות ואחדות גמור. (ע"ח שער מ"ד שער השמות פרק א') ומצד הב' נאמר שכל אלו העולמות מחודשים ובאים אחר הצמצום, ואיך יתכן אפילו להרהר זה באלקיות. וכן בחינת מספרים ומעלה ומטה וכדומה מהשנוים ועליות וירידות וזווגים, ומקרא כתוב אני הויה לא שניתי וכו'.

10) Now after having grasped this much, you may study Kabbalah without fear of materializing the spiritual. The beginners in Kabbalah are confused because it is said that all 10 Sefirot and Partzufim beginning from the world of Atzilut and down to the 10 Sefirot of the world of Assiya are absolutely divine and spiritual, i.e., in fact it is the Creator Himself.

On the other hand, it is said that all these worlds were created because of the Tzimtzum (restriction). Then how can one say the divine Sefirot, which refer to the Creator, appeared after the Tzimtzum? Besides, how should one take such notions as quantity, up, down, rise, fall, spiritual merging, separation etc.? How can all this be said about the divine and perfect?

It is said, "I change nothing; I am everywhere, the only One unchanging Creator". How can one say that transformations and restrictions exist in the perfect One, since any change speaks of imperfection?

The question is simple: what we call worlds - is it the Creator or the creation? Why are beginners confused by it?It is because, as a rule, they materialize it. They try to imagine these worlds in the form of material objects. It is a natural reaction for a man limited by his reality. Yet, how can he be given the correct perception; is it possible at all?

There are risks for people who study Kabbalah without a true guide, a person that would constantly direct them, prevent them from getting off the right track, and from materializing spirituality. For this reason, Kabbalah was kept away from the masses for centuries. If, at the beginning, man deviates one millionth of a degree from the right way, then in time, this deviation from the goal will gradually increase.

Consequently, the more he advances and, as it seems to him, draws nearer to the goal, the more he moves away from it. Therefore, the Kabbalists made certain demands and restrictions for those who wanted to study Kabbalah. It is better to remain on the mechanical level of observing the commandments (the common Surrounding Light shines upon man and purifies him slowly) than to study Kabbalah alone.

Unfortunately, we see self-taught Kabbalists and to what it has led them;they fabricate their own concepts about the spiritual world, populate it with all kinds of bodies, forces and their interactions, with winged angels, devils, witches, hell, and paradise, etc. They do this without understanding that the spiritual world is only inside of man's soul, while only the Creator is outside.

The Kabbalists were deeply concerned about all this. The principal commandment is not to make an idol out of your own egoism. Whether you want it or not, you worship it anyway - it is an idol made inside of you; from your birth, you worship only your own desires, thinking only about how to satisfy them.

Not to make an idol means not putting your own idol in place of the Creator. If you truly desire to enter spirituality, to have any contact with it, do not make a false picture of it in your imagination, for it leads astray. It is said, "To sit and do nothing is preferable to making a mistake".

A question arises: Can a man studying Kabbalah interfere with other people's matters? Can he explain anything to them? He can and should, but very carefully. A book can be given to read; one can talk a little about Kabbalah, but never argue the point.

It can be harmful to you. You will lose everything you have gained by your own efforts and studies. Kabbalah should be popularized unobtrusively, never try to convince a person. It will not help anyway. Man's egoism is stronger than any influence from outside. You will never make him change his mind. You can direct him only if he wants it. Man perceives something only when he feels he can fill his desire.

יא) ובהמתבאר לפנינו מובן היטב כי כל אלו העליות וירידות והצמצומים, והמספר, אינם נבחנים אלא בבחינת הכלים של המקבלים, שהם הנשמות. אלא שיש להבחין בהם בחינת כח ובחינת פועל, בדומה לאדם הבונה בית שסוף מעשה במחשבתו תחילה, אמנם תכונת הבית שיש לו במחשבה אין לו שום דמיון להבית הצריך לצאת בפועל, כי בעוד הבית במחשבה הוא רוחניות מבחינת חומר מחשבתי, ונחשבת לבחינת החומר של האדם החושב, כי אז נמצא הבית רק בבחינת "כח", משא"כ בעת שמלאכת הבית מתחילה לצאת בפועל כבר מקבלת חומר אחר לגמרי דהיינו חומר של עצים ואבנים. כן יש להבחין בבחינת הנשמות כח ופועל, אשר בחינת התחלת יציאתם מכלל מאציל לבחינת נשמות "בפועל" מתחיל רק בעולם הבריאה, וענין התכללותם בא"ס ב"ה מטרם הצמצום בבחינת מחשבת הבריאה, כנ"ל באות ב', הנה זה אמור רק בבחי' "הכח" בלי שום הכר ממשי כלל וכלל. ומבחינה זו נאמר שכל הנשמות היו כלולים במלכות דא"ס המכונה נקודה האמצעית, כי נקודה זו כלולה ב"כח" מכל הכלים של הנשמות העתידים לצאת ב"פועל" מעולם הבריאה ולמטה. וענין הצמצום א' לא נעשה רק בנקודה האמצעית הזו, והיינו רק בדיוק באותו הבחינה והשיעור שהיא נחשבת לבחינת "כח" לנשמות העתידים, ולא כלום בעצמותה. ותדע כי כל הכלים של הספירות והעולמות עד לעולם הבריאה המשתלשלים ויוצאים מנקודה זו או בסבת הזווג דהכאה שלה הנק' אור"ח המה ג"כ בבחינת כח לבד בלי שום מהות של הנשמות, אלא שהשינוים הללו עתידים לפעול אח"כ על הנשמות שמהותם מתחיל לצאת מעולם הבריאה ולמטה כי שם עדיין לא יצאו ממהות המאציל ית'.

11) From the above statement, we can conclude that all these worlds, Partzufim and the processes taking place in them (ascents, descents, restrictions etc.), are all man's inner vessels of reception, the properties of his soul.

That is to say, everything about which one reads in Kabbalah transpires inside of man's soul, and has two aspects: what happens in thought and what happens in action. It is similar to a situation in which a man builds a house: the end of his action is already integrated into his original plan.

The image of a house, the very notion "house" in man's thoughts, is different from the real house, because the structure existing only as a plan is made of the material of his ideas. As the process of build-

ing begins, the plan acquires other qualities, different properties that gradually materialize, and turn into a structure made of wood and stone, etc.

The thought materializes more and more until it comes to its final form, expressed in the materialized idea – a house. Also with regard to the souls, one should differentiate between the two parts: the plan and the action. The state of souls in the world of Infinity, i.e., when they were united with the Creator, before all restrictions, one with the Thought of Creation, is called "the souls in the Thought of Creation".

In the Thought of Creation, these souls are in the Creator without any distinction between them. This state is called Ein Sof – the world of Infinity. A similar state continues in the worlds of Adam Kadmon and Atzilut. The state, wherein souls receive, and are separated from the Creator, is called "the souls in the act of creation". This separation takes place on the level of the world of Beria.

The world of *Beria* (the word "*Beria*" derives from the same root as the word "bar" which means "out of", "except for") is the first one below the world of *Atzilut*, under the *Parsa*. Starting from the world of *Beria*, there is a transition of the souls into the state of "action".

The world of *Beria* is the first world, where the souls, as it were, fall out of the Creator's plan and become more materialized, "independently" existing. All the thoughts and desires in our world and in the spiritual ones descend to us from above. What one should do with these thoughts and desires in our world and in the spiritual ones is the subject of our studies.

Nothing that is inside or outside you is created by you. You react to any outside irritation according to your animal nature. Any reaction of this kind can be calculated in advance and your actions can be predicted in any given situation. So where is even the slightest freedom of choice or freedom of will here? Freedom of will is only in the effort to understand how the Creator would act in my place and react similarly.

Somehow or other, the entire world obeys the Creator's will; not even an atom can move against it. The difference lies in the fact that a Kabbalist consciously tries to correlate his actions with those of the Creator. With all his desires, he wants to follow the stream that the Creator set in motion for the entire Universe. Thus, he enters the most comfortable state of absolute "relaxation" (freedom and eternal peace).

Time stops, everything disappears except for the sensation of infinity, because there are no disturbances, no contradiction between you, the entire Universe and the Creator. It is said that every soul is included in *Malchut* of the world of Infinity, called "the central point", for this point is the Thought, and all the vessels come out of it, all the properties of the soul in action. This action begins in the world of *Beria* and continues into the worlds of *Yetzira* and *Assiya*.

Everything found in the worlds of Infinity, *Adam Kadmon* and *Atzilut*, still belongs to the Creator's Thought. We know it from the emanation of the four phases of Direct Light. The light coming out of the Creator is called "*Behina Shoresh*". Then the light completes the creation of the *Kli*, but it has no independent sensations. This phase is called "*Behina Aleph*".

In phase *Shoresh*, the light came out of the Creator; in the phase, *Aleph*, the *Kli* came out of the Creator. Both of these phases are still under the Creator's complete power, totally in His Thought; they are not yet separated from Him. The world of *Adam Kadmon* corresponds to phase *Shoresh*; the world of *Atzilut* corresponds to phase *Aleph* (*Galgalta* is *Shoresh le Ohrot*, *AB* is *Shoresh le Kelim*).

> *Tzimtzum Aleph (the First Restriction) was performed on that central point, i.e., on its property, to the extent that it is a Thought as regards the future souls. Regarding the Creator, there is no restriction in this point, only concerning the souls coming out of this central point.*

You must know that all these vessels, Sefirot, and worlds down to the world of Beria, which descend from this central point in consequence of the Zivug de Haka'a, are called "Ohr Hozer" (the Reflected Light). They are all considered as "The Thought of Creation", without being distinguished as independent souls. However, these transformations are already included in the plan, then realized in action, in the process of the souls' descent from the world of Beria. Before the world of Beria, they are still inseparably connected to the Creator's properties.

The introductions to the Kabbalistic books are very complicated; their purpose is to dispose the man who studies Kabbalah correctly, to channel his inner efforts in the right direction. If one deviates from this course, he is unable to understand a Kabbalistic book.

Man's task is to realize what happens to him, and how the Creator works with him from above, so that he will completely agree with the Creator's actions. The righteous person is the one who justifies the Creator's actions. When man gives completely and enjoys, he lets in the Upper Light through himself, which then returns to its Source; it is the Reflected Light (*Ohr Hozer*), which comes from above as Direct Light (*Ohr Yashar*) and is reflected, completely filling the entire vessel. *Ohr Yashar* dresses onto *Ohr Hozer* and man becomes a single whole with the Creator.

Man approaches the Universe in essentially two ways: (i) called "*Da'at Ba'alabaitim*" – petty owners' opinion, i.e., the opinion of egoistic masses. (ii) – "*Da'at Torah*". The word "Torah" derives from the word light (*Ohr*, *Ohra'a* - the way to the Creator). These two approaches are absolutely contrary to each other.

The problem is that while we are still in the bounds of our world and have not yet acquired the spiritual properties, we cannot understand that those two approaches to the Universe are opposite to each other. It happens because as man acquires the spiritual properties, time and space merge into one point for him and all movement stops.

This is when he begins to see everything as absolutely static, nothing happens around him, but everything takes place inside him. According to his inner spiritual state, his spiritual qualities, and properties, man begins to see a totally different world around him.

Every time these qualities are transformed in him, he sees a completely different picture. Then he discovers that the entire picture around him is in fact absolutely static, and it changes only inside him, according to the transformation of his properties, the organs of receiving "external" information (external – illusory, in fact only man is changing).

In fact, there is static, amorphous, homogeneous spiritual light around us, which is called "The Creator". Similarly, with our five senses, we also have five spiritual ones: spiritual eyes (sight), ears (hearing), nose (smell), mouth (taste), and hands (touch). Depending on their qualities, carrying capacity and sensitivity, we will constantly receive different impressions from this homogeneous spiritual light. The most primitive impression is the one we receive today.

The homogeneous spiritual light is perceived in our senses; it forms a cumulative picture of the Universe in our consciousness, which we call "our world", "this world". If our senses change a little bit, i.e., become less opposite to this light, come closer to it in their properties and receive altruistic properties, then they will begin to perceive it more correctly, more as it actually is.

Such complex sensations of oneself through one's own five senses will give him a picture, which is called the world of *Assiya*. The world of *Assiya* is no more than the measure of sensation of one's correction or difference from the light, from the Creator. Therefore, it is said that all worlds are inside man.

If we develop our senses even more, by changing our egoism into spiritual altruism, we will receive an even more correct picture of the light, called the world of *Yetzira* and so on. On the highest level, when we completely correct ourselves, we will perceive an undistorted picture of the Upper Light, i.e., the homogeneous light will fill us, enter through our five senses, and then we will feel the Creator Himself in all His true properties, thoughts, and desires as regards us.

Man must reach this state of complete merging with the Creator while still being in our world. Man's attitude to everything around him, as well as his reactions, are dictated by the level he is on, i.e., everything is determined by his present, partially corrected and uncorrected properties.

You cannot change your attitude about what is going on, nor react differently to it until you change yourself. Then your inner, improved, new properties will naturally earn you a different and better attitude.

When man begins to study Kabbalah, it seems to him that he will be able to progress with the help of his reasoning mind, analyzing, researching, and making conclusions. One writes a summary, another is tape-recording the lessons - it is natural, because the mind is our tool of perception and analysis of the world. However, this is true only in the bounds of our world.

In fact, spiritual comprehension occurs differently. When man makes an effort, although his intentions are absolutely egoistical, he attracts upon himself an increased emanation of the Surrounding Light (*Ohr Makif*). This surrounding emanation is already directed at a certain person, and not at the masses.

A person who studies according to the Kabbalistic method, attracts to himself a personal emanation of the Surrounding Light. This light begins to push man forward to spirituality; it "pulls" him up. This is a totally different way: not with the help of one's mind; it actually deprives man of his earthly mind: little by little he is sent circumstances with which he is bound to struggle. The light forces him to act; it "throws" him from side to side, from one circumstance into another, to arouse new sensations in him, to prepare him to feel spirituality.

The emanation of the Surrounding Light intensifies and we begin to feel worse. Why? We feel that, there is something on the outside, stronger, and better, that cannot enter us. Thus, we experience periods of depression. In fact, this means that the actual reason for our depressions is that we receive from above a more powerful emanation.

Man can in no way predict the next level in his spiritual development by his own mind. A possibility to somehow consciously control one's spiritual states (actually, they are not spiritual yet) disappears. Indeed, it is done to bring man to part with his earthly mind, to let him acquire a mind of a different sort: faith above reason. It is called "enter *Ibur*" (enter into the state of an embryo) inside a higher spiritual *Partzuf*.

It can only be done when man completely shuts off his intellectual, analytical properties belonging to this world. He totally surrenders to the higher force and wants to be completely included in it. The masses shun this approach. In Kabbalah, when man progresses by faith above reason, he first controls what is going on with him and then consciously switches off his mind.

The masses exist in faith below reason. The Zohar calls them "*Domem de Kedusha*". "*Domem*" means 'still', 'lifeless', "*Kedusha*" means 'holy', i.e., "the holy still level". What does this mean? There are five levels in the Universe:

-still

-vegetative

-animal

-human

-and one more, the highest level - **Divine**.

These are the five levels of nature. In the spiritual world, according to this division, there are also five levels of development of man's inner properties.

What is the meaning of the lowest "spiritually still" level? One is in the same static, "motionless" state, one similar to the 'still life' in nature, perhaps even a stone. This is because you were created so, and were told how everything should be done.

One makes everything on a "still" level, without an attitude of one's own, without a personal spiritual intention, one just carries out certain spiritual actions that correspond to the spiritual laws, but performs them "mechanically", without involving one's personal "self".

In the spiritual world, interaction between the human soul and the Creator takes place. The general interaction between man and the Creator is divided into 620 different actions, called commandments, 620 laws, spiritual actions that man carries out when he passes all levels, beginning from our world and up to the level of completely merging with the Creator.

There are 620 levels separating us from the Creator, each of which is overcome by the fulfillment of a certain spiritual action, which is called a commandment (a law or condition).

This spiritual action is fulfilled only by man's intention, or rather by changing his intention from "for himself" to "for the sake of the Creator". The size of the altruistic intention with which man performs the action is determined by the spiritual level he has reached.

If we carry out all 620 spiritual actions, in only mechanical way, without correcting the intention, as do the masses, we attract a Surrounding Light that maintains these masses in the way that it preserves 'still nature' in a certain form. This light inspires them to continue to do what they were taught, but does not move them forward, does not turn them from the spiritually 'still nature' into the 'vegetative' one.

To pass from the spiritually 'still nature' into the spiritually 'vegetative', one must have the special method that we study here. The moment man passes this threshold and becomes spiritually 'vegetative'; he has already entered the spiritual world. Then later, when he first develops his vegetative nature, that is, if he performs certain spiritual actions, constantly corrects his intentions, and thus carries out, perhaps, 100 precepts, this refers to the vegetative spiritual layer. Next, if he performs 100-

150 precepts, this refers to the animal spiritual layer. After performing 200-300 precepts, this refers to the human spiritual layer. The remaining precepts belong to the Divine layer, *Keter*. I offer this idea as an illustration, not as a specific example.

All spiritual levels, from zero to 620, are based on the principle that man changes himself internally, constantly improving, becoming more and more similar to the Creator, until there is no difference between them.

However, on our present lowest level, we can observe the commandments only mechanically. Mechanical action will never let us pass from the 'spiritually still' level to the 'vegetative' one. Only with the help of Kabbalah, one can break through it. This method attracts onto us the special Surrounding Light and pulls us out of this world, transforming "a stone" into "a plant".

Man is born as any other animal in this world, and there is nothing spiritual in him. The only thing you can say about man, with all the "intricacies" one can acquire from all kinds of oriental teachings, is that all this belongs to the inner "mental" (let us just put it this way) level of an animal called "man of our world". These various 'wisdoms' speak about forces that accompany our physical body.

Auras, Chakras etc. all exist, but they are biological, bio-energy structures of the human body. Animals possess them too; as a rule, they are even more sensitive to bio- and psycho- fields than man is. Anyone can develop these abilities.

All this refers to the physical body, but science has not pursued this research. Nowadays it has started developing more, and many things are not clear yet, but in principle, all this is subject to tests and research on an absolutely scientific basis, involving no spiritual corrections of man himself. Of course, man morally influences these fields, but still remains an egoist, or rather an egoistic altruist (gives for his own sake).

Thus, man is born with all these mental dispositions, which he can develop. There is only one more peculiarity: apart from egoistic desires, man can be given only one more desire, which is non-existent in our world. This is a desire to give, which is a spiritual desire. It is called "*Nekuda she baLev*" (a point in the heart).

Later we will examine how it is inserted into a human heart. In fact, it is inserted into man's egoistic "self", i.e., our entire organism is built on our egoistic "self". All of a sudden, a point, an embryo of the spiritual, altruistic "self", enters egoism. In principle, this point has nothing to do with man, because he is a totally egoistic creature.

Biologically, man is very similar to animals. He differs from them only by this "black point". Why is it called "black"? Is it not spiritual? It is because it is not yet filled with the light. With the help of Kabbalah, when the individual Surrounding Light begins to shine, it illuminates this "black point", and thus it begins to feel tension, disparity between itself and the light.

Continuing to study, man gradually begins to develop this point; it expands, until ten *Sefirot* are formed in it. As soon as there are the first ten *Sefirot* in the "black point", they are included in the structure of the higher spiritual *Partzuf*; this is then called "*Ibur*" (conception). This point is an embryo of the soul. The first 10 *Sefirot* acquired by man are called the soul, the vessel of the soul. The light that fills them is called "the light of the soul".

Man should develop this point up to a degree where it will enable him to turn all his egoistic properties into altruistic ones. A "black point" begins "to swell" as man adds egoism to it and turns it into altruism. This point is *Sefira Keter*. Out of it, with the help of additional egoism, 10 *Sefirot* begin to develop. The more egoism man adds to it, the bigger spiritual *Kli*, called "soul", he receives.

However, if this does not happen, then as man was born an animal, so he will die. On the other hand, if he has developed his spiritual

Kli even a little bit, albeit he has not reached the spiritual world, and if he has been influenced by the spiritual light, it remains in him forever. Because this newly formed quality does not refer to the body, does not die with it, it refers to the "black point", which is spiritual, i.e., eternal. Therefore this work, this effort is not lost.

How can one make at least 10 of the smallest *Sefirot* out of this point? Let us assume that we take one gram of our egoism and provide it with a screen. Egoism plus the screen combined with this point gives us the smallest spiritual *Kli*. There is no need for a screen as far as the "black point" is concerned, because man receives it from above.

Now let us come back to the question of free will. In the Baal HaSulam's book, "*Pri Hacham. Igrot*", it is written, "As I have already said on behalf of the Baal Shem Tov, before one performs any spiritual action (a commandment is meant), there is no need to think about the Creator's personal Providence, but on the contrary, man must say: 'If I don't help myself, then who will?'"

However, after he completes this action with the absolute confidence that everything depends only on him and the Creator does not exist at all, he has to collect his thoughts and believe that he has performed this spiritual action not by his own efforts, but only thanks to the Creator's presence, because such was His initial intention.

One should also act similarly in everyday, regular proceedings, because the spiritual and the earthly are alike. So before man leaves home to earn what he has to earn during the day, he must completely switch off the thought of the Creator's personal Providence saying: "If I don't help myself, then who will?", and do exactly what the rest of the people who earn their living do in the world.

But in the evening, when he comes back home with what he has earned, he should by no means think he has earned it by his own efforts, but believe that if he had not left home at all, he would have got the same. Since it was planned by the Creator in advance how much he had to earn during that day, in the evening he had to receive it anyway.

In spite of the fact that in our mind, these two approaches to the same action contradict each other, and neither our mind nor our heart perceives them, man must believe it anyway. It seems contradictory to us, because our properties are contrary to the Creator's, and have not entered the spiritual space yet, where all opposites unite in a single whole and all contradictions disappear, "drown" in the Unity.

There is the Divine Providence called *HaVaYaH* - which means that the Creator controls everything and man can in no way take part in this control, and that all his thoughts, desires, actions, etc., are given to him from outside. Then there is the Divine Providence called "*Elokim*" with *Gematria* (numerical value of Hebrew letters and words) equal to "*Teva*" (nature). This is Providence through nature, when man, regardless of the Creator's absolute control, acts according to his nature.

If man tries to combine these two kinds of Providence inside him (although they do not match in his mind, nor in his heart, he actually goes above his mind), these attempts finally lead to their union, and he sees there is no contradiction. However, until we reach such unity, we will ask the same question all the time: who has done this - the Creator or I? Moreover, there is no getting away from these questions until we come to the level where *HaVaYaH* – *Elokim* concur; then we may understand.

We speak here about man's attitude to action. Before acting, man consciously decides to be under the control of *Elokim*; it gives him an opportunity to analyze his actions and his attitude toward them. Thus, he juxtaposes these two systems and brings his "self" to the likeness with the Creator, constantly remembering their existence.

If man forgets or does not know about the existence of the two systems, he is influenced only by nature (*Elokim*), not by the Creator's personal Providence (*HaVaYaH*). Without juxtaposing these two systems, accepting only one of them (either He controls everything or I do), it turns out that either the Creator or man does not exist. Man's advancement to the Creator is only possible when he can forcefully combine these two providential systems in himself before each action.

יב) ואמשול לך מהויות דעולם הזה, למשל האדם המתכסה ומעלים את עצמו במיני כיסוים ולבושים שלא יראנו חברו ולא ירגישו, הכי יעלה על הדעת שהוא עצמו יש לו איזה התפעלות משהו של העלמה וכדומה מחמת ריבוי הכסוים שמתכסה, כן למשל הע״ס שאנו קוראים בשמות כתר חכמה בינה חסד גבורה ת״ת נצח הוד יסוד מלכות, הם רק עשר כסוים שא״ס מתכסה ומתעלם בהם, אשר הנשמות העתידים לקבל ממנו יהיו מחויבים לקבל באותם השיעורים והע״ס מודדים להם, ונמצאים המקבלים מתפעלים על ידי המספר הזה שבע״ס, ולא כלל אורו ית׳ שהוא אחד יחיד בלי שינוי, משא״כ המקבלים נחלקים לעשר מדרגות ממש לפי תכונת השמות הללו. ולא עוד אלא אפילו אלו בחינות הכיסוים שאמרנו אינם בערך האמור רק מעולם הבריאה ולמטה, כי רק שם כבר נמצאות הנשמות המקבלות מהעשר ספירות ההם, משא״כ בעולמות א״ק ואצילות עוד אין שום מציאות אפילו להנשמות כי שם הם רק בבחינת הכח. ולפיכך ענין העשר כיסוים האמורים בע״ס הם שולטים רק בג׳ עולמות התחתונים הנק׳ בריאה יצירה עשיה. אמנם גם בהעולמות בי״ע נבחנים העשר ספירות לאלקיות עד סוף עשיה, ממש כמו בא״ק ואבי״ע וכמו מטרם הצמצום, רק ההפרש הוא בהכלים של הע״ס, אשר בא״ק ואצילות אין להם עוד אפילו בחינת גילוי של שליטה, להיותם שם רק בבחי׳ ״כח״ כנ״ל, ורק בבי״ע מתחילים הכלים של הע״ס לגלות כח ההעלמה והכיסוי שבהם. אמנם באור שבע״ס אין שום שינוי של משהו מחמת הכסוים הללו כנ״ל במשל וז״ס אני הוי״ה לא שניתי וכו׳.

12) I will give you an example from our world. Let us assume that a man is hiding from strangers, so that no one can see or feel him, but he is not able to hide from himself. It is likewise with the 10 Sefirot that we call Keter, Hochma, Bina, Hesed, Gevura, Tifferet, Netzah, Hod, Yesod, and Malchut. They are just 10 curtains behind which the world of Infinity is concealed. The souls will have to receive whatever light the 10 Sefirot transfer to them from the Infinity in the future.

Note well, there are Infinity, the 10 hidden screens and the Souls.

If a soul is behind all 10 "covers", it does not feel the world of Infinity at all. As the soul "takes off" these "covers", it approaches the world of Infinity and begins to feel it more and more.

The measures of sensation of the world of Infinity are called the worlds: *Adam Kadmon, Atzilut, Beria, Yetzira, Assiya,* or levels of the spiritual ladder, 620 levels, 125 levels, 10 levels, *Sefirot*.It does not matter how one calls them; the path and the distance are the same.

Souls acquire the properties of the light depending on how much of it and from which level of the 10 *Sefirot* they receive, behind whatever "cover" they happen to be. The light inside the 10 *Sefirot* is absolutely homogeneous and static on all levels of all the worlds, whereas the receiving souls are divided into 10 levels, corresponding to the properties of the names of these levels.

This means that the Creator is indivisible and unchanging in Infinity. Being on one of the levels, the soul receives through the screens-concealments of the Creator and, naturally, it already receives the distorted light.

Each of these names - *Keter, Hochma, Bina, Hesed, Gevura, Tifferet, Netzah, Hod, Yesod* and *Malchut* - means a certain property, concealing and at the same time revealing. On the one hand, each name speaks of how much it conceals the Creator, on the other hand, it speaks of how much I reveal the Creator if I ascend to that level. These are two contrary directions - the measure of concealment and the measure of revelation.

All of these concealing screens about which we now speak act only in the world of Beria and below, for the souls receiving this light are only in these three worlds Beria, Yetzira and Assiya.

What does this mean? The souls can even be higher than the worlds of *Beria, Yetzira,* and *Assiya,* but only as they ascend with these worlds. In other words, the souls are always in these three worlds. The notion "ascent of the worlds" means that, if man leaves this world, he can be in the world of *Assiya*, then in the world of *Yetzira*, then in the world of *Beria*, but he cannot ascend above the world of *Beria*. If he ascends, he does it only inside these worlds. Through his efforts, he makes these worlds ascend with him. These worlds are his cover. With these worlds he ascends to *Atzilut*, and then to the world of Infinity.

In the worlds Adam Kadmon and Atzilut, the souls exist only in Thought, being inseparable from the Creator. Hence, these 10 "covers" act only in the 10 Sefirot in the worlds Beria, Yetzira, and Assiya. Nevertheless, even in these worlds the 10 "covers" are considered absolutely divine, down to the very end of the world of Assiya.

There is no distinction between the Sefirot and the Creator, exactly as before all restrictions. The difference is only in the Kelim that the 10 Sefirot consist of, since in the worlds Adam Kadmon and Atzilut, the power of the 10 Sefirot has not yet manifested sufficiently, for these 10 Sefirot are only in a Thought. Their Kelim begin to express their concealing power only in the worlds of Beria, Yetzira, and Assiya.

However, due to "the covers", the light in these 10 *Sefirot* remains unchanged, as stated: "I never change, - the Creator says about Himself, - I am omnipresent and "change" only in man's eyes, depending only on his ability to feel Me and the degree of correctionof his properties, his eyes".

יג) ואין לשאול, כיון שבא"ק ואצילות אין עוד שם שום גילוי למהות הנשמות המקבלים, א"כ מה משמשים הכלים ההם הנק' ע"ס ולמי המה מעלימים ומכסים בשיעוריהם הללו. ויש בזה ב' תשובות: הא', שכן דרך ההשתלשלות כמו שתמצא בפנים הספר. והב' הוא כי גם הנשמות עתידים לקבל מהע"ס ההם שבא"ק ואצילות, דהיינו בדרך עליות הג' העולמות בי"ע אליהם, כמ"ש להלן באות קסג, ולפיכך יש להבחין גם בא"ק ואצילות אלו השינוים שבע"ס, כפי מה שהם עתידים להאיר להנשמות בשעה שהם יעלו שמה עם העולמות בי"ע, כי אז יקבלו לפי המדרגה שבע"ס ההם.

13) Questions may arise: if there is no manifestation of the souls receiving the light in the worlds Adam Kadmon and Atzilut, then why are the 10 Sefirot there, the 10 Kelim? What arethe worlds Adam Kadmon and Atzilut for, if there are no souls there? If these worlds do not conceal or hamper anything, then what is their role? Also, if they hamper the light by various measures, then who is it for? There are two answers:

a) All the worlds and the Sefirot must develop this way. b) In the future, souls must receive from the 10 Sefirot in the worlds

Adam Kadmon and Atzilut, due to the ascent of the worlds Beria, Yetzira and Assiya to Atzilut, and then to Adam Kadmon. Hence, there must be steps, places prepared in advance in these worlds, so that the worlds Beria, Yetzira, and Assiya could ascend there, enter them, and receive a greater revelation of the Creator.

Otherwise, a soul cannot ascend; it can do so only with the worlds of *Beria, Yetzira,* and *Assiya,* because this is the way the souls will have to ascend there, and these worlds will shine upon the souls at the time. Then each of them will receive its level out of these 10 *Sefirot.*

יד) הרי נתבאר היטב, שענין העולמות ובחינת החידוש והשינוים ומספר מדרגות וכדומה, כל זה לא נאמר אלא בבחינת הכלים המשפיעים להנשמות ומעלימים ומודדים להם שיכלו לקבל מאור א"ס ב"ה שבהם בדרך המדרגה, והם אינם עושים שום התפעלות של משהו באור א"ס ב"ה עצמו, כי אין כיסוים פועלים על המתכסה רק על השני הרוצה להרגיש אותו ולקבל ממנו כנ"ל במשל.

14) Thus, we see that Kabbalah speaks about all the worlds and levels, about everything but the Creator. It refers to the Kelim, the vessels that measure off the states of concealments for the souls, so that afterwards they will be able to receive the light from the world of Infinity according to their levels. All these concealing curtains affect only those who are supposed to receive the light and not the One, who like the Source, hides behind them, i.e., they do not influence the Creator.

The worlds are levels like lifeless filters in our world; they hamper the light, but contrary to the live souls, they cannot consciously take part in the process of communication with the Creator. The *Sefira* (screen, world) by itself is a lifeless device for concealing the spiritual light from the souls. What kind of a device is that? We have already spoken about it - this device inside us is our egoism.

טו) ובדרך כלל, יש להבחין בהספירות ובפרצופין, בכל מקום שהם, את ג' בחינות הללו: עצמותו ית', כלים ואורות. אשר בעצמותו ית' לית מחשבה תפיסא בו כלל, ובכלים יש תמיד ב' הבחנות הפכים זה לזה, שהם העלמה וגילוי, כי ענין הכלי מתחילתו הוא מעלים על עצמותו ית', באופן שאלו העשרה כלים שבע"ס הם עשר מדרגות של העלמות. אמנם אחר שהנשמות מקבלים להכלים הללו בכל התנאים שבהם הנה אז נעשים אלו ההעלמות לבחי'

של גילויים להשגות הנשמות. הרי שהכלים כוללים ב' הבחנות הפכיות זו לזו שהם אחת, כי מדת הגילוי שבכלי הוא ממש כפי מדת ההעלמה שבהכלי וכל שהכלי יותר עב, דהיינו שהוא יותר מעלים על עצמותו ית' הוא מגלה קומה יותר גדולה הרי שב' הפכים הללו הם אחת. וענין האורות שבהספירות פירושן, אותו שיעור קומה הראוי להתגלות להשגת הנשמות. כי מתוך שהכל נמשך מעצמותו ית' ועם זה אין השגה בו רק בתכונתם של הכלים כנ"ל, ע"כ יש בהכרח עשרה אורות בעשרה כלים הללו, דהיינו עשר מדרגות של גילוים אל המקבלים בתכונת אותם הכלים. באופן שאין להבדיל בין אורו ית' לעצמותו ית' רק בזה, אשר בעצמותו ית' לית השגה תפיסא ביה כלל זולת המגיע אלינו ממנו ית' דרך התלבשותו בהכלים של הע"ס, ומבחינה זו כל הבא בהשגה אנו מכנים בשם אורות.

15) Hence, we may divide these Sefirot and Partzufim into three parts: the Creator's Essence, the vessels, and the light. We have no way of understanding or feeling the Creator Himself, neither in our sensations, nor in our mind.

There are always two opposite properties in the vessels, "concealment" and "revelation", because the vessel first conceals the Creator, so that these 10 vessels, called the 10 Sefirot, represent the levels of concealment. However, after the souls are corrected, according to the spiritual conditions dictated by the 10 Sefirot, these levels of concealment turn into the levels of revelation, attainment of the Creator.

Thus, it turns out that the vessels consist of two properties contrary to one another, and the degree of revelation inside the vessel (man, the soul) is the same as the degree of concealment. The rougher the vessel (the soul), i.e., the more it conceals the Creator and the more egoistic it becomes in the process of correction, the more powerful the light that is revealed in it at the end of correction . Thus, these two opposite properties are in fact just a single one.

The light inside the Sefirot is a measure of the Creator's light received by the souls according to their corrected properties. Everything comes out of the Creator: both the vessels and the light that fills them. Therefore, there are always 10 lights inside the 10 vessels, i.e., 10 levels of revelation according to the properties of the vessels.

We cannot distinguish between the Creator and His light. Outside of the vessel, He is imperceptible, impossible to grasp. We can attain only what enters our Kelim, our corrected properties. We comprehend only what comes from Him, what dresses onto our vessels, i.e., our properties consisting of the 10 Sefirot. Hence, whatever we perceive in the Creator we call the light, although it is a subjective sensation inside the corrected properties of our souls.

The vessel feels that it exists independently, but this is an illusion. What can we understand about the Creator? We reveal our own corrected properties. According to what we call them, kindness, mercy, etc., we attribute these properties to the Creator. The purpose of creation, the degree of our unity with the Creator, lies in an absolute likeness to Him, in revealing all His greatness, eternity and perfection.

“THE PREAMBLE TO THE WISDOM OF KABBALAH”

CONTENT

FOREWORD

The article **"The Preamble to the Wisdom of Kabbalah"** was written by the Baal HaSulam as one of the forewords to "The Book of Zohar". Overall, the Baal HaSulam wrote three forewords to the book of the Zohar: **"The Foreword to the Book of Zohar"**, **"Preface to the Book of Zohar"** and **"The Preamble to the Wisdom of Kabbalah".**

For an understanding of "The Book of Zohar", we should know the entire structure of creation; how all the worlds are built, the laws of their functioning, how they influence the souls, and vice versa, how the souls affect the worlds, how the Creator governs the entire Universe, and how created beings influence His Providence.

The purpose of studying Kabbalah is to feel the spiritual worlds and the scope of the Universe in their full measure; to experience sensations beyond the power of birth and death; to transcend time; to reach in one of the incarnations a state such that man can live in all the worlds at the same time, completely merged with the Supreme force; to fully comprehend the Creator, - i.e., to attain the purpose of man's existence in this world; and all while still living in this world.

Kabbalah studies provide man with the answers to all of his questions. He studies all cause-and-effect connections in this world; he studies the Upper world from which everything descends to ours. The revelation of the Upper worlds happens constantly, gradually, and inside of man. Man creates within himself additional senses, more sensitive than his regular ones, which allow him to feel the additional forces of the Universe, the part of it that is concealed from the common person.

Kabbalah is called a secret wisdom, because only he who comprehends, who feels the real picture of the Universe, it is only for him that this science becomes obvious. Because it educates man quite differently, Kabbalah has always been distinguished from common religion. It develops in him a sense of criticism, analysis, clear intuitive and conscious research of himself and of his surroundings. Without these qualities, man can research neither this world, nor the Upper one.

One can see how far apart Kabbalah stands from common religion by the fact that the greatest experts on religious laws and commandments in our world – many Rabbis and leaders of the religious masses, neither study nor know about Kabbalah. This ignorance in no way prevents them from physically observing the commandments or leading a religious life. It relates to the fact that Kabbalah speaks not about performing something in action, but about the way to create the right intention "for the sake of the Creator", which has nothing to do with common religion.

Kabbalistic education is entirely individual and completely contradicts the education of the masses. A Kabbalist must be given the freedom of self-knowledge, the tools, the means with the help of which he can constantly develop. In no way should his inner development be limited. If man is given all kinds of instructions, he ceases to be free, for someone else's model is imposed on his "self". The Torah says "The knowledge (opinion) of the Torah is contrary to the knowledge (opinion) of the egoistic masses". Hence, Kabbalists represent an entirely separate and autonomous group, though they were formally associated with the religious community.

During recent years, the general attitude toward Kabbalists has drastically changed. If during the previous centuries their books were burned and they were persecuted by the religious masses, today the situation is different, and the religious world treats genuine Kabbalists with much more tolerance. There are spiritual reasons for that, since all that happens in our world is a consequence of the spiritual phenomena in the Upper worlds.

We are at the end of the period of human development, on the eve of the whole of humanity's entering the spiritual world. There have never been so great a number of people taking an interest in Kabbalah. Today, Kabbalah studies are considered honorable and prestigious. All this shows that great changes have been sent from above.

Just 200 years ago, during the period of the so-called Enlightenment (*Haskala*), there was a retreat from traditional religion. It was sent from above so that the same souls might later return to the Torah by themselves; not only to its general open part, but also to Kabbalah.

Each generation consists of souls from previous generations dressed in new bodies. These souls descend into our world, accumulating experience with each reincarnation. In addition, with time external spiritual conditions also change.

400 years ago, a great Kabbalist known as the Ari founded the modern Kabbalah. His writings are destined for the souls that began to descend to this world from his time onward. Since that period, a qualitative change in the souls descending to our world began. There appears an obvious striving for spirituality among them. Hence, the ban on Kabbalah studies was rescinded. In the Ari's book "The Foreword to "The Gates of the Ascent", he says that, from his time on, Kabbalah may be studied by anyone who has that desire.

Today, a mass dissemination of Kabbalah should begin all over the world. The world has come to the moment when all spiritual roots have already descended from above; everything described in the Torah has already happened in our world. There have already been exiles, destructions. The only thing that has not yet happened is the attainment of spirituality by the souls, the elevation of this world to the level of the spiritual one and merging of these two worlds. This process began in the twenties of the 20th century, and now it is gathering momentum like a snow-ball.

By using the internet (**http://www.kabbalah.info**), we can see how the interest in Kabbalah is rapidly growing among those who until recently had nothing to do with it. People already understand that Kabbalah is not a teaching about some astrological-spiritual force. They begin clearly to realize that Kabbalah provides an understanding of the entire Universe. What are the forces governing the world? They realize that only this knowledge will save humankind from imminent disaster.

People who cannot find satisfaction on this world's level come to Kabbalah, hoping to receive answers to their most vital questions. In the future, millions of people will study Kabbalah. Those who are studying today will teach it to the succeeding generations.

In the process of man's life, his intentions go through constant changes.They move from the animal-like desires to settle comfortably in this world, to benefit from everything, to the aspiration for knowledge, and then to spiritual elevation.

We are built that way. Gradually, by studying Kabbalah, man changes his desires of this world to the higher, spiritual ones, to discover the spiritual world and enter it.

Subsequently, man's properties become altruistic. An egoistic vessel is very small and cannot include every pleasure prepared for us by the Creator. Therefore, by changing egoistic properties into altruistic ones, we infinitely expand the capacity of our vessel to receive all the spiritual information into it, to achieve a state of eternity and perfection.

There is a mistaken opinion that the person who has comprehended the spiritual, especially who has already reached a certain spiritual level, should appear as if he soars in the sky, and is "not of this world", as if there are no negative qualities in him.

Man ascends to the spiritual world internally to the extent of his "descent", to the degree that he senses and understands his own egoism. Man ascends as his natural egoism is progressively revealed to him . By correcting it to a certain extent, man rises to a higher spiritual level, which corresponds to the measure of his correction.

The higher a person becomes, he will possess increasingly greater egoistic properties. However, they receive correction. My Rabbi was a great Kabbalist. At the same time, he was able to be irritated or feel joy much more than any common human being.

Egoism is the stuff we are made of. It was the only thing created by the Creator, and the entire Universe is made only of this egoistic material. We cannot correct egoism itself; we can only modify the way we use it. By being corrected, man does not cut off his egoistic *Kli* from himself. He changes the intention for which he applies it.

A *Kli* with an altruistic intention is called spiritual. This *Kli* is a vessel of receiving pleasure and knowledge that changes, undergoes correction, and grows in size during the process of spiritual development.

A Kabbalist will not be recognized by his external appearances. All of them are energetic, purposeful people who neither give up this world, nor hide (except for special cases, when it is the Creator's direct command). Many temptations lie in wait for a Kabbalist as he advances spiritually; many unforeseen troubles suddenly come his way. It is only upon reaching a higher level that he sees why he had been given all of his hardships. Nothing is done in vain; everything is given only for further spiritual advancement; whatever is sent to man on a certain level must be accepted by faith above reason. Note this well.

A person who is ready to give up everything, who needs nothing, cannot move forward. While studying Kabbalah, man becomes more egoistic; all of his negative qualities become exposed. He seems rotten in his own eyes. This continues until he cannot bear his own properties anymore. Next, he is finally forced to cry out to the Creator for help. At this moment, he begs the Creator to rid him of his egoism and to replace it with altruism, for he clearly sees how much he loses because of his egoistic qualities.

On the other hand, the one who does not feel it cannot see these negative qualities in himself. He cannot even believe that man is even able to come to making such requests. Hence, there is no urging or coercion in Kabbalah, only the method leading a disciple to the realization of his negative egoistic qualities by way of feeling how contrary he is to eternity and perfection.

Only Kabbalah can lead man to transform his properties that they may come into agreement with the higher spiritual ones. There are two parts to the Torah: the obvious, open part and the secret concealed one. The open part speaks about mechanically observing the commandments. It is called open because it is quite obvious how man fulfils it. This part of the Torah is studied and carried out by the masses.

Therefore, a restriction is imposed on this part, "nothing to add and nothing to reduce".

For example, one must not add on more *Tzitzit* (frills on a ritual prayer shawl) to one's clothes, or put one more *Mezuzah* (a box containing an excerpt from the Holy Scriptures secured on the door-post of a Jewish home), or check the fitness of food with microscope, where one is instructed to check it with his naked eye and so on. Quite often, those who do not understand the essence of the Torah and its purpose in this world, concentrate more on mechanical performance.

The second part of the Torah, the secret one, speaks about man's intention (*Kavana*) in all his actions. Only this focused intention can change man's action into its opposite, without suppression, by using his natural egoism. Since man's intention is concealed from those around him, the part of the Torah that teaches the right intention is called the secret part, or Kabbalah. It instructs one how to receive everything prepared for him by the Creator.

This part of the Torah encourages a constant increase of intention, so that the bigger it is, the more man attains the spiritual world.

He feels the spiritual world to the extent of his intention, starting from the lowest level of the universe up to the complete intention on his entire true egoism – the highest level of the universe, a complete merging with the Creator.

During the past 6000 years, various types of souls have descended to our world, from the purest in the first generations of the world, to the most corrupt ones of our time. For the correction of the first souls, even the Torah was not necessary. The very fact of their existence, their animal suffering already meant their correction. The process of accumulating suffering during the soul's existence in a body of our world leads to the spiritual need (concealed from the soul) to enter the Upper world while still living in this one.

However, the first souls did not accumulate enough sufferings to feel the necessity to give up their own egoism. Their primitive, animal way of thinking (insufficient *Aviut*) could not generate in them the necessity of the spiritual elevation, did not push them towards the Creator.

All the private emotional experiences, sufferings and knowledge of the descending souls are accumulated in a common spiritual vessel, a general soul called "*Adam*". After two thousand years of accumulating this common experience, humankind felt the necessity for a mechanical, unconscious fulfillment of the commandments, while the rules of the spiritual world, which have no bearing on our world, are in no any way related to it.

Consequently, to those who do not know their true spiritual origin, they seem so odd. At this period, the Torah was given to humankind, although only to a small group of people. In the next and the last two thousand-year period, a conscious desire for the spiritual and the necessity for self-correction begins to manifest. It becomes especially strong at the time of the great Kabbalist Ari and continues right up to our generation.

The ultimate state of the entire universe is the Final Correction (*Gmar Tikkun*), where the lowest point of creation achieves the same state as the highest. The Creator at one stroke created this state. We are all in it already. Then why are we given the instruction for its attainment? It concerns the fact that we cannot feel our true state with our present egoistic desires.

According to Kabbalah, if we do not evolve or correct our senses according to the instruction ("the Torah" derives from the word *Ohra'a*, instruction), we will be urged, compelled by force and suffering. The instruction is given for shortening the suffering period by increasing the speed of this rite of passage, making suffering different in character and substituting suffering of hatred for suffering of love.

Why does the Creator need our suffering? He could have made the process of our spiritual growth painless. Of course, He could have. However, He wanted us to bear some kind of grievance against Him so that we might turn to Him for help, come into contact with Him, feel the necessity for Him. This connection with Him is the true purpose of the creation, while the correction is only a means to this end.

The arising of the need for the Creator's help, with regard to connection with Him, is possible only when we feel a real hunger for spiritual delight. The sensation of the lack of perfection must precede the feeling of perfection. Everything in the creation is comprehended only from its opposite state. First, a desire is created; only then can one sense pleasure from its fulfillment by the thing desired. We cannot feel our final, perfect condition at this time without preceding sufferings from the absence of this perfection.

We all feel our present condition as imperfect due to the absence of corresponding corrected *Kelim* (desires). If we begin to correct them, then by each corrected *Kli* we will begin feeling part of a true perfect state. Moreover, once we correct all of our *Kelim*, we will feel complete perfection. In order to complete our correction, we must create in ourselves the possibility of feeling every nuance of perfection.

This comprehensive process takes 6000 years, i.e., 6000 levels of correction which are called the period of the existence of this world, in other words, the period of feeling our imperfection. We all exist in biological bodies in which "a biological computer is installed. Ours is more sophisticated than that of animal organisms because ours serves a larger egoism. This computer is our mind. It is no more than a mechanical calculator thatallows us to choose the best, most comfortable state for any given moment.

This has nothing to do with spirituality. Spirituality begins when a "black point in the heart", which is planted into man from above, begins striving after the Upper world. It should be developed to the state of a full spiritual desire -"the *Partzuf*", in which later one receives spiritual information, spiritual sensations.

If there is no such point in a person, he may be a genius, but according to the spiritual criteria, he remains no more than a highly developed animal on the levels of the spiritual world.

We stated that Kabbalah deals with the most important question in man's life. We exist in an absolutely incomprehensible world, which we investigate with the help of our five senses. Whatever penetrates us from outside through these senses is processed in our mind, which synthesizes and presents us this information as a picture of the world. Therefore, what seems to us to be the surrounding reality is no more than our unimproved senses' interpretation of the outer light.

In fact, this is only a fragment of the universe. It means that what we perceive is a tiny part of what surrounds us. If we had different senses, we would perceive another fragment, i.e., we would sense this world differently. It would seem to us that the world around us has changed, while in fact all changes occur in us, in our perceptions, while the world wouldremain the same. This is because, outside of us, only the Creator's simple, Upper Light exists.

We sense how our organism reacts to outside influences. Everything depends on the sensitivity of our organs. If they were more sensitive, we would feel how atoms strike our bodies. We would comprehend, feel, perceive not the objects themselves, but their interaction; not their essence, but their outer form and material. Similarly, no device invented by us can register an action in itself; only the reaction to it.

Anything we might like to know about our world, in order to understand the meaning of our existence in it, depends on the framework of our comprehension, on the kind of questions we ask. Our nature, our innate qualities, dictates to us the level of our intellectual curiosity. The Creator, having programmed our properties, somehow dictates to us from inside what to take interest in, what to research, what to comprehend, what to discover. Ultimately though, the Creator leads us to revealing Himself.

The various sciences that deal with humans reveal only matters about man himself. All that is outside of man remains inaccessible. Therefore, the question about the meaning of our life cannot be solved with the help of science because the sciences do not discover anything outside of us, only what is in connection with us, with our senses, with our devices, with our reactions and those of our devices that communicate with the outer world.

The most global human questions, birth, the meaning of life and death, can be solved only by comprehending what is outside of us; not by discovering and researching our reactions to the outer world, but by objective knowledge concerning the outer world. This is exactly what is inaccessible to scientific research. Only when man enters the spiritual world, does he receive the gift of comprehending objective reality; how and what truly exists outside of him.

There is a method with whose help one can receive complete information about the entire universe; i.e., what exists beyond the bounds of human sensations and feelings, what is happening outside of oneself. This method is called Kabbalah. The one who masters it is called a Kabbalist.

This is a very special, ancient method. It was created by people who, while living in our world, managed to sense the spiritual worlds and pass their sensations on to us. The Kabbalistic method that they used throughout the centuries was described with more and more meticulousness, taking into consideration the properties of the generation for which it was meant. It went this way until its arrival in the form we are able to study today. This is the result of five thousand years of spiritual development.

Each succeeding generation of Kabbalists, guided by previous experience, worked on developing a method of mastering the spiritual, outer world, suitable for their generation. The textbooks they used for studying Kabbalah 2-3 thousand years ago, or even 400-500 years ago, are of no good use to us. We can use them only in a very limited capacity. The last great Kabbalist who adapted Kabbalah for the use of our generation was Rabbi Yehuda Leib Alevi Ashlag (1885-1955). He wrote the commentary to The Book of the Zohar and to the books of the Ari. His 6-volume textbook, "The Study of the Ten Sefirot", is the principal work on Kabbalah and is the only practical instruction for us to master spirituality.

To help the beginners studying this fundamental work, Rabbi Y. Ashlag wrote "The Preamble to the Wisdom of Kabbalah", which is a concise summary of what is written in "The Study of the Ten Sefirot". It provides an understanding of the structure of the universe,slightly lifting the veil for the attainment of this goal and explains the role of our world in grasping the entire universe.

THREE MAIN CONCEPTS IN KABBALAH
ג' יסודות של חכמה

א) "רבי חנניא בן עקשיא אומר: רצה הקב"ה לזכות את ישראל, לפיכך הרבה להם תורה ומצות, שנאמר ה' חפץ למען צדקו יגדיל תורה ויאדיר" (מכות כ"ג ע"ב). ונודע שזכות הוא מלשון הזדככות. והוא ע"ד שאמרו ז"ל "לא נתנו מצות אלא לצרף בהן את ישראל" (ב"ר רפמ"ד). ויש להבין ענין הזכות הזה, שאנו משיגים ע"י תורה ומצות. וכן מהי העביות שבנו, שאנו צריכים לזכותה ע"י התורה ומצות.

וכבר דברנו מזה בספרי "פנים מסבירות" ו"תלמוד עשר הספירות". ונחזור כאן בקיצור, כי מחשבת הבריאה היתה כדי להנות לנבראים, כפי מתנת ידו הרחבה ית' וית'. ומכאן הוטבע בהנשמות רצון וחשק גדול לקבל את שפעו ית'. כי הרצון לקבל הוא הכלי על מדת התענוג שבהשפע.

כי לפי מדת גדלו ותוקפו של הרצון לקבל את השפע, כן הוא מדת התענוג והחמדה שבשפע. לא פחות ולא יותר. והם מקושרים זה בזה, עד שאין לחלק ביניהם. זולת בהיחס, שהתענוג מיוחס להשפע, והרצון הגדול לקבל את השפע מיוחס לנברא המקבל. ובהכרח ב' אלה נמשכים מהבורא ית'. ובאו בהכרח במחשבת הבריאה. אלא שיש לחלק בהם על דרך הנזכר, אשר השפע הוא מעצמותו ית', כלומר שהוא נמשך יש מיש, והרצון לקבל הכלול שם, הוא השורש של הנבראים, כלומר הוא השורש של חידוש, שפירושו יציאת יש מאין. כי בעצמותו ית' ודאי שאין שם בחינת הרצון לקבל ח"ו. וע"כ נבחן שהרצון לקבל האמור, הוא כל חומר של הבריאה, מראשה עד סופה. עד שכל מיני הבריות המרובות ומקריהן, שאין להן שיעור, ודרכי הנהגתן, שכבר נתגלו והעתידים להתגלות, אינם רק שיעורים ושינוי ערכים של הרצון לקבל.

וכל מה שיש בהן באותן הבריות, דהיינו כל מה שמקובל ברצון לקבל המוטבע בהן, כל זה הוא נמשך מעצמותו ית' יש מיש, ואינו כלום מבחינת הבריאה המחודשת יש מאין, כי אינו מחודש כלל. והוא נמשך מנצחיותו ית' יש מיש.

1) Rabbi Hanania ben Akashia said, "The Creator wished to reward Israel, so He gave them the Torah and the Commandments..." In Hebrew "to award" ("Lizkot") is similar to the word "to purify" ("Lezakot"). Midrash "Bereshit Rabbah" says, "The Commandments are given only to purify Israel with their help". Here two questions arise:

-What is the privilege that the Creator awarded to Israel?
-What is this "impurity" and "coarseness" that is in us and from which we have to purify ourselves with the help of the Torah and the Commandments?

These matters have been discussed in my books "Panim Meirot uMasbirot" and "The Study of the Ten Sefirot". Let us review them briefly.

The Creator's intention was to give pleasure to created beings. For this, He prepared an enormous desire in the souls to receive this pleasure contained in the Shefa (the abundance which the Creator wants to bestow upon us). The "desire to receive" is a vessel for the reception of the delight contained in the Shefa.

The greater the "desire to receive", the more pleasure enters the vessel. These two notions interconnect in such a way that it is impossible to separate them.

It is only possible to point out that the pleasure refers to the Shefa (i.e., to the Creator) while the "desire to receive" refers to the Creation.

Both of these notions come directly from the Creator and are included in the Thought of Creation. While the abundance descends directly from the Creator, the "desire to receive" it, also included in the Shefa, is the root, the source of created beings.

The "desire to receive" is something essentially new, something that never existed before, because there is no trace of "desire to receive" in the Creator. It turns out that the "desire to receive" is the essence of the creation, from beginning to end, the only "material" the creation is made of. All of the various created beings are merely different "portions" of the "desire to receive". Moreover, all events that happen to them are the changes that happen to this "desire to receive".

Everything that fills the created beings and satisfies their "desire to receive" comes directly from the Creator. Therefore, everything that exists around us actually comes out of the Creator, either directly as abundance, or indirectly as, for example, the "desire to receive", that does not exist in the Creator Himself, but was created by Him for delighting His creatures.

Since the Creator's desire was to bestow upon the created beings, He had to create someone capable of receiving his abundance. Consequently, He integrated into the Creation the desire to receive pleasure. Why? There is a rule: the Creator created everything that exists in our nature. The question "Why did we receive such nature?" refers to the state of being prior to the beginning of the Creation and is beyond our grasp. We are able only to attain that which refers to the Creation, but not before or after it. Therefore, our nature allows us to receive only the pleasure that is in equilibrium with our desire for it.

For example, if a man is hungry he enjoys the meal; whereas, if he is offered food while not being hungry, he derives no pleasure. Everything is a combination of a deficiency and the filling of it. The stronger the desire, the greater is the pleasure from filling it.

ב) וכפי האמור, כלול הרצון לקבל בהכרח תכף במחשבת הבריאה, בכל ריבוי ערכים שבו, ביחד עם השפע הגדול שחשב להנותם ולהעניקם. ותדע שז"ס אור וכלי, שאנו מבחינים בעולמות עליונים. כי הם באים בהכרח כרוכים יחד, ומשתלשלים יחד ממדרגה למדרגה.

ובשיעור שהמדרגות יורדות מאת אור פניו ומתרחקות ממנו ית', כן הוא שיעור ההתגשמות של הרצון לקבל הכלול בשפע. וכן אפשר לומר להיפך, אשר כפי שיעור התגשמות של הרצון לקבל בשפע, כן הולך ויורד ממדרגה למדרגה. עד המקום הנמוך מכולם, דהיינו שהרצון לקבל מתגשם שם בכל שיעורו הראוי.

נבחן המקום ההוא בשם "עולם העשיה". והרצון לקבל נבחן לבחינת "גופו של אדם". והשפע שמקבל נבחן למדת תוכנו של "החיים שבגוף" ההוא. ועד"ז גם בשאר בריות שבעוה"ז. באופן, שכל ההבחן שבין העולמות העליונים לעוה"ז הוא, כי כל עוד שהרצון לקבל הכלול בשפעו ית' לא נתגשם בצורתו הסופית, נבחן שעודו נמצא בעולמות הרוחנים, העליונים מעוה"ז, ואחר שהרצון לקבל נתגשם בצורתו הסופית, הוא נבחן שכבר הוא מצוי בעוה"ז.

2) Therefore, the "desire to receive" in all its variety was included in the Thought of Creation from the very beginning. It was inseparably linked to the delight that the Creator prepared for us. The "desire to receive" is a vessel, while the Shefa is the light that fills the vessel. These lights and vessels are the only components of the spiritual worlds. They are inseparably connected to one another. Together they descend from above, level by level.

The farther away from the Creator these levels are, the greater and coarser the "desire to receive" becomes. On the other hand, the greater and coarser the "desire to receive" becomes, the more remote it is from the Creator. This happens until it comes to the lowest point where the "desire to receive" reaches its maximum size. This condition is desirable and necessary for the beginning of the ascension toward the correction.

This place is called "the world of Assiya". In this world the "desire to receive" is defined as "man's body", while the light is called "man's life". The difference between the Upper worlds and this world (Olam Hazeh) is that in the Upper worlds the "desire to receive" is not yet coarse enough, and is not yet separated completely from the light. In our world, the "desire to receive" reaches its final development and becomes completely separated from the light.

ג) וסדר השתלשלות האמור עד להביא את הרצון לקבל על צורתו הסופית שבעוה"ז, הוא על סדר ד' בחינות שיש בד' אותיות של השם בן ד'. כי ד' אותיות הוי"ה שבשמו ית' כוללות את כל המציאות כולה, מבלי יוצא ממנה אף משהו מן המשהו. ומבחינת הכלל הן מתבארות בהע"ס: חכמה, בינה, ת"ת, מלכות, ושרשם. והם עשר ספירות, כי ספירת התפארת כוללת בעצמה ששה ספירות, הנקראות חג"ת נה"י.

והשורש נקרא כתר. אמנם בעיקרם הם נקראים חו"ב תו"מ. והן ד' עולמות הנקראות: אצילות, בריאה, יצירה, עשיה. ועולם העשיה כולל בתוכו גם את עוה"ז. באופן, שאין לך בריה בעוה"ז, שלא תהיה מחודשת מא"ס ב"ה, דהיינו במחשבת הבריאה, שהיא בכדי להנות לנבראיו.

והיא בהכרח כלולה תיכף מאור וכלי. כלומר, מאיזה שיעור של שפע עם בחינת רצון לקבל את השפע ההוא. אשר שיעור השפע הוא נמשך מעצמותו ית' יש מיש, והרצון לקבל השפע הוא מחודש יש מאין. ובכדי שהרצון לקבל ההוא יבא על תכונתו הסופית, הוא מחויב להשתלשל עם השפע שבו דרך הד' עולמות אצילות, בריאה, יצירה, עשיה. ואז נגמרת הבריה באור וכלי, הנקרא "גוף" ו"אור החיים" שבו.

3) The above-mentioned descending order of the development of the "desire to receive" is divided into four levels (Behinot). This order is encoded in the mystery of the Creator's Name. The Universe submits to the order of these four letters, HaVaYaH (Yud-Hey-Vav-Hey). These letters correspond to the ten Sefirot: Hochma, Bina, Tifferet (or Zeir Anpin), Malchut and their root. Why are there ten? It is because the Sefira Tifferet includes 6 Sefirot: Hesed, Gevura, Tifferet, Netzah, Hod and Yesod.

The root of all these Sefirot is called Keter, but often it is not included in the Sefirot count; hence, one says HuB-TuM. These four Behinot correspond to the four worlds: Atzilut, Beria, Yetzira, and Assiya. The world of Assiya also includes this world ("Olam Hazeh"). There is no single created being in this world whose root is not in the world of Infinity, in the plan of the creation. The plan of the creation is the Creator's desire to please all the created beings.

It includes both the light and the vessel. The light comes directly from the Creator, while the desire to receive pleasure was created by the Creator anew out of nothing. For the "desire to receive" to reach its final development, it must pass together with the light through the four worlds of Atzilut, Beria, Yetzira, and Assiya (ABYA). Then the development of the creation is completed with the creation in it of the light and the vessel, called "the body" and "the light of Life".

The connection between the Creator and the creation is called "the world of Infinity" (the *Ein Sof*). Lower spiritual objects as they comprehend it give the names of the Upper Light. Since the Creator's desire was to bestow pleasure upon the created beings, He created someone who would be able to receive this pleasure from Him, and the creation of the desire to receive pleasure called "*Malchut*" or "the world of Infinity" was sufficient for that.

Since in this state *Malchut*, receives for its own sake, making no restriction on reception, *Malchut* later performs a restriction on the reception of the light-pleasure.

It is said that the "desire to receive" was finalized in the world of *Assiya*. So does it mean that the biggest "desire to receive" exists in this world of *Assiya*? Yet, while the world of *Assiya* is only *Behinat Shoresh* and has the weakest light, there is the light of *Keter* in the world of A"K.The notion the world of *Assiya* has two meanings:

a) The entire *Behina Dalet* is called the world of *Assiya.*
b) The world of *Assiya* by itself.

To understand the meaning of the first notion one needs to know that the finished vessel is called "*Behina Dalet*"; but, in fact the true vessel (the *Kli*) is already present in *Behina Aleph. Keter* is "the "desire to bestow" pleasure upon the creation"; *Hochma* is "the "desire to receive" this pleasure" and is completely filled with the light. Nevertheless, the *Kli* should pass four more levels to its final development.

We study everything from the point of view of our nature because all laws come out of the spiritual roots. In our world, the value of man's pleasure depends on the force of his striving for it. Unbearable passion brings great pleasure, while a tiny desire leads to small pleasure. For man to grasp a true desire, two conditions are necessary:

a) Man cannot strive for something that he has never heard of before. He has to know what he wants, i.e., once he has already had it.
b) But he cannot be striving for something he already has. Therefore four levels of development of the *Kli* are necessary for it to receive the final form.

Malchut had the entire light in the world of Infinity. However, the vessel is characterized by the difference of its properties from those of the Creator, which did not exist in the world of Infinity. With the following development of the vessel, we realize that the true vessel is the lack of the light.

In the world of *Assiya,* the *Kli* does not receive anything at all, because it wants only to receive; hence, it is defined as a genuine vessel. It is so far from the Creator that it knows nothing about its root. As a result, man has to believe that he is created by the Creator, although he is unable to feel it.

Conclusion: the vessel is not someone or something that has a lot; on the contrary, it is someone or something extremely remote. It is totally disconnected from the light. While receiving only for its own sake, the vessel has no "desire to give"; all it can do is to believe that such desire exists... Man just cannot understand why he has to strive for giving.

What is the point of existence for such a vessel that has no spark of the light and is extremely remote from the Creator? Such vessels have to begin working for the sake of bestowal with objects that are, so far, unreal.

The Baal HaSulam gives the following example. In the past, everything was very expensive, so children were taught to write first on the blackboard with a piece of chalk. Then they could erase what they had mistakenly written, and only those who had learned to write correctly were given real paper.

The same is true with us. First, we are given playthings, and then, if we learn to add the intention for the Creator's sake to our desire, we will be able to see the true light. The *Kli* is created in such a way as to get used to the real work.

Before the souls appear all actions are performed by the Creator. By this He shows the souls how they should act. For example, how does one learn to play chess? The moves are made for the pupil and in this way, he learns. That is why the worlds descend from above. The Creator carries out all the actions relating both to the higher levels and to the lower ones. Then at the second stage, the souls begin to ascend by themselves.

Meanwhile, we strive for playthings and not for spirituality; hence, the light of the Torah is concealed from us. Man would not be able to receive the enormous delights offered to him for the Creator's sake.

The Baal HaSulam gives us an example. A man puts all of his valuables on the table – gold, silver, diamonds. Suddenly, strangers come to his house.He fears they may steal his treasures. What can he do? He switches off the light so that no one can see that there are precious things in the house.

We do not lack the desire for spirituality because the "desire to receive" is absent in us; rather, because we cannot see anything. We cannot see the wood for the trees. The more man "purifies himself", the better he begins to see. Then his *Kli* (the "desire to receive") gradually grows, for he wants to feel greater pleasures.

For example, if one manages to receive 0.5 kg of pleasure for the sake of bestowal, he is given 1kg. Then, if that amount was also received with the intention for the Creator' sake, he is given 2 kg of pleasure, and so on.

The sages said about it: "He who has reached higher levels of Torah has bigger desires." Yet we cannot see anything until our desires acquire the intention to receive for the sake of bestowal. In this sense, the only distinction between a secular and religious person is that the former aspires to receive only the pleasures of this world, while the latter also desires the delight of the world to come.

The power of the desire to receive over all created beings is so great that the sages said about it, "The law ruling over people is this: Mine is mine, and yours is yours; and only fear stops man from saying, 'Yours is mine'."

ד) והצורך להשתלשלות הרצון לקבל על ד' בחינות האמורות שבאבי"ע, הוא מפני שיש כלל גדול בענין הכלים, אשר התפשטות האור והסתלקותו הוא עושה את הכלי רצוי לתפקידו.

פרוש, כי כל עוד שהכלי לא נפרד פעם מהאור שלו, הרי הוא נכלל עם האור "ובטל אליו כנר בפני האבוקה".

וענין הביטול הזה הוא, מפני שיש הפכיות ביניהם הרחוקה מקצה אל הקצה. כי האור הוא שפע הנמשך מעצמותו ית' יש מיש. ומבחינת מחשבת הבריאה שבא"ס ית' הוא כולו להשפיע, ואין בו מבחינת רצון לקבל אף משהו.

והפכי אליו הוא הכלי, שהוא הרצון הגדול לקבל את השפע ההוא, שהוא כל שורשו של הנברא המחודש. הנה אין בו ענין של השפעה כלום. ולפיכך בהיותם כרוכים זה בזה יחד, מתבטל הרצון לקבל באור שבו, ואינו יכול לקבוע את צורתו, אלא אחר הסתלקות האור ממנו פעם אחת. כי אחר הסתלקות האור ממנו, הוא מתחיל להשתוקק מאד אחריו. והשתוקקות הזאת

קובעת ומחליטה את צורת הרצון לקבל כראוי. ואח"ז, כשהאור חוזר ומתלבש בו, הוא נבחן מעתה לב' ענינים נבדלים: כלי ואור, או גוף וחיים. ושים כאן עיניך, כי הוא עמוק מכל עמוק.

4) The necessity to develop the "desire to receive" on four levels (Behinot) through the four worlds of ABYA is caused by the existing rule, according to which only the spreading of the light followed by its subsequent expulsion make the vessel fit for use.

An explanation: when the vessel is filled with the light, they are inseparably connected. The vessel is in fact non-existent; it abolishes itself as the flame of a candle disappears in the flame of a torch.

The desire is satisfied, so it ceases to exist. It can reappear only after the light exits from it, stops filling it. The reason for this self-annihilation of the vessel lies in its total contrast with the light. The light comes directly from the Creator's essence, from the Thought of Creation. This light is a "desire to bestow" and has nothing to do with a "desire to receive". The vessel is absolutely opposite to it; it is a huge "desire to receive" the light.

The vessel is a root, a source of something very new, non-existent before the creation. The vessel has no "desire to give". Since the light and the vessel are inseparably connected, the "desire to receive" is annulled by the light. The vessel acquires a certain form only after the expulsion of the light from it. Only then, the vessel starts craving for the light. This passionate desire determines the necessary form of 'his "desire to receive". When the light reenters the vessel, they become two separate objects – the vessel and the light, or body and life. Take a good note of it, because these are most profound notions.

When the *Kli* begins to receive, it must feel: "Now I receive pleasure". But the light carrying that pleasure does not let this "I" open and be felt by the *Kli*. Hence, the "I" annuls itself. It means that the *Kli* does not feel that it receives, although it does so.

Rabbi Baruch Ashlag gives this example. An old man won $100.000 in a lottery. His friends were afraid to tell him the news, thinking he might have a heart attack and die of over-excitement.

One of them said he could pass the information without causing any harm. He came to the old man and asked him, "Would you share $10 with me if you won in the lottery?" - "Of course I would!", answered the old man. "And if you won $100, would you still be willing to share the prize with me?" "Why not?" answered the old man. It went on and on until the sum reached $100.000, then the guest asked, "Are you ready to sign our agreement?" – "I certainly am!" – exclaimed the old man. At that very moment the guest collapsed on the floor and died.

We see that man can die of great joy, since too powerful a light annuls the "desire to receive". In such a case, the *Kli* disappears and the light is bound to exit to encourage the *Kli* to strive after it.

Why then does the light not annul the *Kli*, the *Behina Dalet*, upon returning to it? When the *Ohr* and *Kli* are together in the *Behina Aleph*, both the "desire to bestow" and the "desire to receive" must spread there. However, since they are opposite to one another, the "desire to bestow" annuls the "desire to receive", i.e., prevents it from spreading.

After the *Behina Dalet* was formed, the light cannot annul it, since they represent two existing forces. In the *Behina Aleph* the light does not let the "desire to receive" spread and grow; but once it has developed, it cannot interfere with it.

For example, two men are fighting. One of them prevents the other from entering his house. Does it matter if they are fighting outside or the intruder is already inside? If we say that, nothing exists but the Creator, who wishes to bestow pleasure and the creation that strives after this pleasure, it is sufficient to have *Keter* as a giver and *Hochma* as a receiver!

In the phase of *Hochma* the "desire to receive" is one with the light, the latter preventing it from feeling as it receives. This state is not perfect though, since the *Kli* must feel that it receives. For instance, man gives something to his friend, but he cannot feel it. In this case the giver violates the commandment, "do not destroy".

Hence, it is clear why we are not given important (precious) things. Since we are quite content with scanty pleasures, we are not worthy to be given valuable things. Therefore, the development of 4 phases is necessary for the birth of the *Kli*, which feels as it receives.

ה) ולפיכך צריכים לד' בחינות שבשם הוי"ה, הנקראות חכמה בינה ת"ת מלכות. כי בחי"א, הנקראת חכמה, היא באמת כל כללותו של הנאצל, אור וכלי. כי בו הרצון לקבל הגדול עם כל כללות האור שבו, הנקרא אור החכמה או אור החיה, כי הוא כל אור החיים שבהנאצל המלובש בהכלי שלו.

אמנם בחינה הא' הזו נבחנת לכלו אור, והכלי שבה כמעט שאינו ניכר, כי הוא מעורב עם האור ובטל בו כנר בפני האבוקה. ואחריה באה בחי"ב. והוא, כי כלי החכמה בסופו הוא מתגבר בהשואת הצורה לאור העליון שבו. דהיינו שמתעורר בו רצון להשפיע אל המאציל, כטבע האור שבתוכו, שהוא כולו להשפיע.

ואז ע"י הרצון הזה שנתעורר בו, נמשך אליו מהמאציל אור חדש, הנקרא "אור חסדים". ומשום זה כמעט שנפרש לגמרי מאור החכמה, שהשפיע בו המאציל. כי אין אור החכמה מקובל רק בהכלי שלו, שהוא הרצון לקבל הגדול בכל שיעורו. באופן, שהאור וכלי שבבחי"ב משונים לגמרי מבחי"א. כי הכלי שבה הוא הרצון להשפיע, והאור שבה נבחן לאור החסדים, שפירושו אור הנמשך מכח הדבקות של הנאצל בהמאציל. כי הרצון להשפיע גורם לו השואת הצורה למאציל. והשואת הצורה ברוחניות הוא דבקות.

ואחריה באה בחינה ג'. והוא כי אחר שנתמעט האור שבהנאצל לבחינת אור חסדים בלי חכמה כלל, ונודע שאור החכמה הוא עיקר חיותו של הנאצל, ע"כ הבחי"ב בסופה התעוררה והמשיכה בקרבה שיעור מאור החכמה, להאיר תוך אור החסדים שבה. והנה התעוררות הזו המשיכה מחדש שיעור מסוים מהרצון לקבל, שהוא צורת כלי חדש, הנקרא בחינה ג' או ת"ת. ובחינת האור שבה נקרא "אור חסדים בהארת חכמה". כי עיקר האור הזה הוא אור חסדים, ומיעוטו הוא אור חכמה.

ואחריה באה בחינה ד'. והוא כי גם הכלי דבחי"ג בסופו התעורר להמשיך אור חכמה במילואו, כמו שהיה בבחי"א. ונמצא התעוררות הזו היא בחינת השתוקקות, בשיעור הרצון לקבל שבבחי"א ונוסף עליו. כי עתה כבר נפרד מאור ההוא. כי עתה אין אור החכמה מלובש בו, אלא שמשתוקק אחריו. ע"כ נקבע צורת הרצון לקבל על כל שלימותו. כי אחר התפשטות האור והסתלקותו משם, נקבע הכלי. וכשיחזור אח"כ ויקבל בחזרה את האור, נמצא הכלי מוקדם להאור. וע"כ נבחנת בחינה ד' הזאת לגמר כלי. והיא נקראת "מלכות".

5) As stated above, the creation develops according to four phases, Behinot, encoded in the name HaVaYaH and called Hochma, Bina, Tifferet and Malchut. Behina Aleph (1) is called "Hochma", which contains both the light and the vessel made of the "desire to receive". This vessel contains the entire light called Ohr Hochma (the light of wisdom) Ohr Haya (the light of life), because it is the entire light of life inside the creation.

Nevertheless, Behina Aleph is still regarded as the light and the vessel in it has not manifested yet, existing potentially. It is still inseparably connected with the light in the state of self-abolishment. Afterwards, Behina Bet (2) comes into being, because by the end of its development Hochma wished to acquire the equivalence of properties with the light that is inside it. The "desire to bestow" upon the Creator has awakened in it.

The nature of the light is a pure "desire to give". As an answer to the awakening of that desire, the Creator sent a new and different light called "Ohr Hassadim" (the light of mercy). Hence, Behina Aleph almost completely got rid of Ohr Hochma, given by the Creator. Ohr Hochma may only be present in the proper vessel, i.e., the "desire to receive". Both the light and the vessel in Behina Bet are totally different from those in Behina Aleph, since the vessel in Behina Bet is the "desire to bestow" and the light is Ohr Hassadim. Ohr Hassadim is the pleasure of being like the Creator.

The "desire to bestow" leads to the equivalence of properties with the Creator that, in the spiritual worlds, leads to merging with him. Then Behina Gimel emerges. After the light inside the creation passes to the level of Ohr Hassadim in the almost complete absence of Ohr Hochma (as we know Ohr Hochma is the principal life force in the creation), Behina Bet felt its deficiency. At the end of its development, it attracted a portion of the Ohr Hochma so that it could start shining inside its Ohr Hassadim.

To this end, it reawakened a portion of its inner desire to receive and formed a new vessel called Behina Gimel, or Tifferet. The light inside it is Ohr Hassadim with the luminescence of Ohr Hochma because the main part of this light is Ohr Hassadim, Ohr Hochma being less significant. Behina Dalet follows it because the vessel of Behina Gimel also wished to attract Ohr Hochma at the end of its development, but this time it wanted all of it, as it had been in Behina Alef.

It turns out that this awakened desire leads to a situation where Behina Dalet feels the passionate desire that Behina Aleph had. Moreover, now, after expelling the light once, the creation knows how bad it feels, so it desires this light much more than at the earlier stage of Behina Aleph.

Therefore, the emanation of the light and its subsequent expulsion create a vessel. If the vessel now receives the light again, it will precede the light. Therefore, the Behina Dalet is a final phase in the creation of the vessel called Malchut.

Why did the light itself become a reason for the *Kli's* wish to give? We observe a law in our nature: each branch longs to be like its root. That is why, as soon as the light of *Hochma* came, the *Kli* received it. However, when it felt that the light had come from the Giver, it wished to be like the Source and not to receive. It means that two actions come out of *Keter*:

a) the desire to bestow pleasure upon the creation, which created the "desire to receive", and it is *Behina Aleph.*
b) the desire to bestow acts in the creation, because the latter feels that the light it receives comes from the desire of the superior giver, and thusalso wants to give.

We can see an example of this in the material world. One person gives another a present, and the latter receives it. Then he begins to think and understands: "He is a giver and I am a receiver! I should not take it!" That is why he returns the gift. At the beginning when he received the present, he was under the giver's influence and did not feel he was a receiver. However, after the reception he began to feel that he is a receiver, which made him decline the present.

It is necessary to point out that this person has a "desire to receive", because he did receive the present at the beginning. But he did not ask for it! Hence, it is not called a *Kli*. The *Kli* is a state in which one feels that there is pleasure, begs, and pleads to the giver to give it to him.

Why is *Bina's Aviut* bigger than that of *Hochma*, i.e., why does it have a bigger "desire to receive", but wishes only to give? *Hochma* is the vessel that does not yet feel that it receives; the giver controls it completely. Nevertheless, *Bina* already feels itself as a receiver; therefore, its *Aviut* is bigger.

There are two kinds of light:

a) The light of the Purpose of the creation called "*Ohr Hochma*" comes from the Creator (the "desire to bestow" upon the creation); it is *Behina Aleph*.
b) The light of the Correction of the creation called "*Ohr Hassadim*", which spreads thanks to the creation; it is termed *Behina Bet*.

How can one say that *Ohr Hassadim* spreads thanks to the creation? Is not the Creator the source of the light and pleasure? It is because the Creator's pleasure comes to the creation owing to its merging with the Source of pleasure.

The beginning of the Creation happens as follows:

The light comes out of the Creator, the *Ohr* - pleasure. This emanation of the light from the Creator is called the zero phase (0), or the root (*Shoresh*).

The light creates the *Kli*, which is able to feel, absorb all pleasure contained in the light. Let us assume that the Creator wanted to give the creation 1kg of pleasure. In that case, He should have created the "desire to receive" that pleasure (*Kli*) with the capacity of 1kg, which could absorb the entire delight.

Such a state of the *Kli's* being completely filled with the Creator's light is called phase *Aleph* (1). This phase is characterized by the desire to receive pleasure. The light, carrying the pleasure is called "*Ohr Hochma*". The *Kli* in this phase receives the *Ohr Hochma*; hence, the phase itself is called "*Hochma*".

The *Kli* receives the Creator's light, feels absolute pleasure and acquires its property - the "desire to give", to please. As a result, instead of receiving, the *Kli* now desires to give, and stops receiving the light. Since a new desire, contrary to the initial one appears in the *Kli*, it passes to a new state, which is called phase *Bet* (2), the "desire to give", or *Bina*.

The *Kli* has stopped receiving the light. The light continues to interact with the *Kli* and says to it, that by refusing to receive the light, it neither fulfils the Purpose of the creation, nor the Creator's desire. The *Kli* analyses this information and comes to a conclusion that it really does not fulfill the Creator's desire.

What is more, the *Kli* feels the light is a vital force, and that it cannot do without it. Hence, the *Kli*, still willing to give, decides to start receiving an essential portion of the light. It turns out that the *Kli* agrees to receive the light for two reasons: first, because it wants to fulfill the Creator's desire, this reason being the main one; and secondly, it feels that it really cannot exist without the light.

The appearance of a new, though, a tiny "desire to receive" the light in the *Kli*, creates a new phase that is called *Behina Gimel* (3), or *Zeir Anpin*.

While simultaneously giving and receiving a little in phase *Gimel*, the *Kli* begins to realize that the Creator's desire is to fill completely the *Kli* with the light so it might be able to enjoy it infinitely. Since the *Kli* has already acquired a little bit of the light of *Hochma* necessary for its existence, it now decides to receive the rest of the light. This is the Creator's desire, and the *Kli* resumes receiving the Creator's light the way it did in phase 1.

The new phase is called *Behina Dalet* (4). It differs from phase 1, in that it independently expressed its "desire to receive".

The first phase was unconsciously filled with the light by the Creator's desire. It had no desire of its own. The 4th phase is called "the kingdom of desires", or *Malchut*. This state, *Malchut*, is called "the world of Infinity' (the *Olam Ein Sof*) - infinite, unlimited desire to receive pleasure, to be filled with the light.

Behinat Shoresh (0) is the Creator's desire to create the creation and give it maximum pleasure. In this phase, as in a seed, or embryo, all subsequent creation is included from its beginning to the end, encompassing the Creator's attitude to the future creation.

Behinat Shoresh (0) is the Thought of the entire creation. All subsequent processes are only the realization of this Thought. Each subsequent phase is the logical consequence of the previous one. The development goes on from above and each preceding phase is "higher" than the following one, i.e., the preceding phase includes all the subsequent ones.

In the course of this development from the Creator down to our world, new levels come into being; everything evolving from perfect to imperfect. The Creator created the light, the pleasure, out of Himself, out of his Essence. Hence, it is said that the light is created "*Yesh mi Yesh*" (existent out of existent), i.e., that the light has existed forever. However, with the appearance of phase 1 of the desire to receive pleasure, the vessel, the *Kli*, is called "*Yesh mi Ayn*" (existent out of non-existent), i.e., the Creator made it out of nothing; because there cannot be even the slightest "desire to receive" in the Creator.

The creation's first independent desire occurs in phase two. In this phase, the "desire to bestow" appears for the first time. This desire appeared under the influence of the light, which was received from the Creator, and had already been included in the Thought of Creation. However, the *Kli* feels it as its own, independent desire. The same is true of our desires: all of them are sent from above, from the Creator; but we consider them to be our own.

By feeling the "desire to give" in phase two, contrary to the "desire to receive", the *Kli* ceases to feel pleasure from receiving, stops sensing the light as pleasure. The light filters out and leaves it remaining empty.

In phase one, the desire to receive pleasure was created. It is the only desire that is absent in the Creator. This very desire *is* the creation. Subsequently, there are only variations of this desire of phase 1 in the entire Universe; the desire to receive pleasure either from receiving or from giving, or from the combination of these two desires. Apart from the Creator there is only one thing – the desire to receive pleasure.

The vessel (the *Kli*) always wants to receive. The material it is made of does not change. Man can understand it only when he realizes the evil and comprehends his egoistic nature. All that is incorporated into our nature; in every cell of our body, there is no more than the desire to receive pleasure.

Phase two, now empty, stops feeling that it exists; it is created by the light and being without it, feels like dying. Hence, it desires to receive at least a little bit of the Creator's light. The pleasure from receiving the light is called "*Ohr Hochma*", while the pleasure from giving is called "*Ohr Hassadim*".

Phase two (*Bina*) wants to give, but it finds out it has nothing to give, that it "is dying" without *Ohr Hochma*. That is why it decides to receive a little bit of the *Ohr Hochma*.

This is what constitutes the third phase, *Behina Gimel* (3). In this phase, there are two different desires in the vessel: the "desire to receive" and the "desire to bestow". But the "desire to give" prevails. In spite of the fact that it has nothing to bestow upon the Creator, the "desire to give" still exists in it. This desire is filled with the light of *Hassadim*. It has in it also a little bit of the light of *Hochma*, which fills the "desire to receive".

The fourth phase, *Malchut*, is being gradually born from the third one. The "desire to receive" grows stronger, pushing out the "desire to give", and after awhile the "desire to receive" remains as the sole one. Therefore, this phase is called "*Malchut*", i.e., the kingdom of desire, the desire to absorb everything, the entire pleasure *(Ohr Hochma).*

This phase is a completion of the creation, and since it receives everything infinitely, endlessly, it is called "the world of Infinity".

These are the four phases of the Direct Light coming from the Creator. The rest of the creation, all the worlds, angels, *Sefirot*, souls - everything is only a part of *Malchut*. Since *Malchut* desires to be like the phases preceding it, the entire creation is a reflection of these 4 phases.

To understand it, to explain how these four phases are reflected in each of the worlds, how this affects our world; how we, by working actively with the help of feedback from above, can affect them and join in the general process of the Universe; this is the purpose of the science called Kabbalah. Our goal is to comprehend it all.

ו) ואלו ד' ההבחנות הנ"ל ה"ס עשר ספירות, הנבחנות בכל נאצל וכל נברא. הן בכלל כולו, שהן ד' העולמות, והן בפרט קטן ביותר שבמציאות. ובחי"א נקראת "חכמה" או "עולם האצילות". ובחי"ב נקרא "בינה" או "עולם הבריאה". ובחי"ג נקרא "תפארת" או "עולם היצירה". ובחי"ד נקרא "מלכות" או "עולם העשיה".

ונבאר את הד' בחינות הנוהגות בכל נשמה. כי כשהנשמה נמשכת מא"ס ב"ה ובאה לעולם האצילות, היא בחי"א של הנשמה. ושם עוד אינה נבחנת בשם הזה. כי השם "נשמה" יורה שיש בה איזה הפרש מהמאציל ב"ה, שע"י ההפרש הזה יצאה מבחינת א"ס ובאה לאיזה גילוי לרשות בפני עצמה. וכל עוד שאין בה צורת כלי, אין מה שיפריד אותה מעצמותו ית', עד שתהיה ראויה להקרא בשם בפני עצמה.

וכבר ידעת שבחי"א של הכלי אינה ניכרת כלל לכלי וכולה בטלה להאור. וז"ס הנאמר בעולם אצילות שכולו אלקיות גמור, בסוד "איהו וחיוהי וגרמוהי חד בהון". ואפילו נשמות שאר בעלי החיים, בהיותם עוברים את עולם אצילות, נחשבים כעודם דבוקים בעצמותו ית'.

6) The four above-mentioned phases correspond to the ten Sefirot of which every created being consists. These four phases correspond to the four worlds of ABYA, which include the entire Universe, and all the details existing in reality. Behina Aleph is called Hochma, or the world of Atzilut. Behina Bet is called Bina, or the world of Beria. Be-

hina Gimel is called Tifferet, or the world of Yetzira. Behina Dalet is called Malchut,or the world of Assiya.

Now let us understand the nature of these four Behinot existing in every soul. Each soul (Neshama) originates in the world of Infinity and descends to the world of Atzilut, acquiring the properties of Behina Aleph there. In the world of Atzilut, it is not yet called "Neshama", for this name points to a certain degree of separation from the Creator that leads to a fall from the level of Infinity, from a state of complete unity with the Creator, and acquires some "independence". However, it is not yet a completely formed vessel, so nothing separates it from the Creator's Essence thus far.

As we already know, while in Behina Aleph, the vessel is not yet such, for at this stage it annuls itself as regards the light. Hence, in the world of Atzilut, everything is said to be still absolutely Divine – "He is one and His Name is one". Even the souls of other creatures passing through this world merge with the Creator.

ז) ובעולם הבריאה כבר שולטת בחינה הב' הנ"ל, דהיינו בחינת הכלי של הרצון להשפיע. וע"כ כשהנשמה משתלשלת ובאה לעולם הבריאה, ומשגת בחינת הכלי ההוא אשר שם, אז נבחנת בשם "נשמה". דהיינו, שכבר יצאה ונתפרדה מבחינת עצמותו ית' והיא עולה בשם בפני עצמה, להקרא "נשמה". אמנם כלי זה זך מאוד, להיותו בהשואת הצורה להמאציל, וע"כ נחשבת לרוחניות גמורה.

7) Behina Bet rules in the world of Beria; i.e., its vessel is the "desire to bestow". Consequently, when the soul arrives in the world of Beria, it reaches this stage of the vessel's development and is already called "Neshama". This means it separated from the Creator's Essence and acquired a certain degree of independence. Nevertheless, this vessel is still very "pure", "transparent", i.e., very close in its properties to the Creator. Thus, it is regarded as being completely spiritual.

ח) ובעולם היצירה כבר שולטת בחינה הג' הנ"ל, שהיא כלולה מעט מצורת הרצון לקבל. וע"כ כשהנשמה משתלשלת ובאה לעולם היצירה, ומשגת הכלי ההוא, יצאה מבחינת הרוחניות של הנשמה, ונקראת בשם "רוח". כי כאן הכלי שלו כבר מעורב בעביות מועטת, דהיינו מעט

הרצון לקבל שיש בו. אמנם עדיין נבחנת לרוחני, כי אין שיעור עביות זאת מספיק להבדילו לגמרי מן עצמותו ית', להקרא בשם "גוף, עומד ברשות עצמו".

8) Behina Gimel rules in the world of Yetzira; it contains a certain amount of the "desire to receive". Therefore, when the soul comes to the world of Yetzira, reaches this stage of the vessel's development, it exits the state of "Neshama", and is now called "Ruach". This vessel already possesses certain Aviut, i.e., some portion of the "desire to receive". It is nevertheless still considered as spiritual, since this quantity and quality of the "desire to receive" is insufficient to be completely separated in its properties from the Creator's Essence. A complete separation from the Creator's Essence is a body, which is now fully and clearly "independent".

ט) ובעולם עשיה כבר שולטת בחינה הד', שהיא גמר הכלי של הרצון לקבל הגדול. וע"כ משגת בחינת גוף נפרד ונבדל לגמרי מעצמותו ית', העומד ברשות עצמו. והאור שבו נקרא "נפש", המורה על אור בלי תנועה מעצמו. ותדע, שאין לך פרט קטן בהמציאות, שלא יהיה כלול מכל האבי"ע.

9) Behina Dalet rules in the world of Assiya; it is the final stage of the vessel's development. At this level, the "desire to receive" reaches the peak of its evolution. The vessel turns into a body totally separated from the Creator's Essence. The light inside Behina Dalet is called "Nefesh". This name points to the lack of independent movement in this type of the light. In addition, remember that nothing exists in the Universe that does not consist of its own ABYA (four Behinot).

What is the difference between the "desire to receive" and the soul? The "desire to receive" is called *Behina Dalet*. It is the heart of everything; it feels and attains all levels. As a rule, "the light" is named "soul". The light without the one who comprehends it is called "light". The light together with the one who attains it is called "the soul".

For example, five people are watching an airplane through binoculars, and each one has better binoculars than another does. Now, the first one says that the size of the plane is 20 cm. The second claims it to be 1 m. Each of them speaks the truth because they base their speculations on what they see, but their opinions in no way affect the plane.

The reason for the difference of opinions consists in the difference of quality of the binoculars' lenses. The same occurs with us; there is no change in the light, all the changes are in those who attain it, and whatever we grasp is called "the soul". In our example the binoculars are the equivalence of properties, and in this sense there are differences between those who attain, and all the more so in that which is attained, the soul.

י) והנך מוצא, איך שהנפש הזאת, שהיא אור החיים המלובש בהגוף, נמשכת יש מיש מעצמותו ית' ממש. ובעברה דרך ד' עולמות אבי"ע, כן היא הולכת ומתרחקת מאור פניו ית'. עד שבאה בכלי המיוחד לה, הנקרא "גוף". ואז נבחן הכלי לגמר צורתו הרצוי. ואם אמנם גם האור שבה נתמעט מאד, עד שאין ניכר בו עוד שורש מוצאו.

עכ"ז ע"י העסק בתורה ומצות ע"מ להשפיע נחת רוח ליוצרו, הוא הולך ומזכך את הכלי שלו, הנקרא "גוף", עד שנעשה ראוי לקבל את השפע הגדול בכל השיעור, הכלול במחשבת הבריאה בעת שבראה. וזה שאמר ר' חנניא בן עקשיא: "רצה הקב"ה לזכות את ישראל, לפיכך הרבה להם תורה ומצוות".

10) The Nefesh, the light of life installed in the body, comes directly from the Creator's Essence. Passing through the four worlds of ABYA, it gradually moves away from the Creator until it acquires a vessel, a body assigned to it. Only then is the vessel considered as completely formed. At this stage of the vessel's development, the light inside it is so small that its source cannot be felt, i.e., the creation (the vessel) stops feeling the Creator.

However, with the help of the Torah and the Commandments with the intention to bestow delight upon the Creator, the creation can purify its vessel called the body, and receive all the light prepared for it by the Creator in the Thought of Creation. That is what Rabbi Hanania ben Akashia meant by saying, "The Creator wished to reward Israel, so He gave them the Torah and the Commandments..."

Here he explains the notion "*Aviut*", which we have to "*Lezakot*", purify. *Behina Dalet* is called *Aviut*, because it receives for the sake of self-enjoyment. The purpose is to achieve the equivalence of the properties, i.e., to receive for the sake of bestowal. That is what is defined as "*Zakut*" - purification. One can reach such a level by learning the Torah with the intention to acquire the "desire to give".

There cannot be two contrary desires simultaneously in the *Kli*; it is either the "desire to receive" or the "desire to give". If there are two desires in one *Kli*, it is divided into two parts, into two *Kelim*, proportionately.

"Time" in the spiritual world is the cause-and-effect connection between spiritual objects, the birth of the lower out of the higher. There are causes and effects in the spiritual worlds, but there are no time gaps between the two. In our world, as a rule, some time passes between a cause and an effect.

If we say "before", we mean the cause; but if we say "after", we mean the effect. We will gradually get used to such notions as "the absence of time and space". Rambam wrote that all our matter, the entire Universe, is below the speed of light. If anything exceeds the speed of light, time stops, and space contracts into a point. This is also known from Einstein's theory of relativity.

What is beyond it? Beyond it is the level of the spiritual world where space and time do not exist, i.e., they are taken by a person comprehending them as equal to zero. Spiritual space can be compared to our inner spiritual world where one feels either satisfied or drained.

There are only the Creator and the creation in the world. The creation is the "desire to receive" the light, pleasure from the Creator. In our world, this desire is unconscious; we cannot feel the source of life, of pleasure. In our world, the desire to receive pleasure is egoistic. If man can correct it and start using it altruistically, he begins to feel the light, the Creator, the spiritual world in the same *Kli*. The spiritual world and the Creator are the same.

Man's corrected desire is called "the soul". A soul is divided into different parts, private souls. Then they become diminished and move away from the Creator according to their properties and enter into man born in this world. A soul can enter a grown-up person at any time of his life. It happens according to a program given from above.

The souls supersede one another in one and the same person during his life. In fact, it is similar to the clothes that a man changes all the time. The same is true with the soul; it changes its material dress, its physiological body, leaving it, and being replaced by another soul. The body dies, but the soul changes its dress for another one.

Man's purpose is, while still living in this world, being in this body, in spite of all its egoistic desires, to strive to reach the spiritual level from which his soul descended. By achieving this goal, man reaches a spiritual level, which is 620 times higher than the present one. It corresponds to the 613 principal and seven additional commandments.

All the souls have the same task - to achieve their complete correction. That means to rise 620 times higher. Man can rise to that level with the help of the bodily encumbrances. That is the meaning of being in our world, in our body. The only difference between the souls is in their initial and final conditions, depending on the soul's character and on which part of the common soul it comes from. When all the souls combine into one, a completely new state of quantity and quality of the common desire and the volume of information emerges.

There are certain types of souls that have already completed their own correction and have descended to our world to correct others. Such is the soul of Rabbi Shimon bar Yochai, which later incarnated into the Ari, and then finally into the Baal HaSulam. Sometimes such a soul descends to influence the world as a whole, sometimes to bring up future Kabbalists.

After the final correction, there will be no difference between souls. The distinction between them exists only in their way to the Goal. It is said, that the people of Israel went into exile to disseminate the knowledge about spirituality and thus drew other peoples to the way of correction, those who were worthy of correction and elevation.

Note well, the material action similar to the spiritual one takes place in our world, in our bodies.

The connection between the spiritual and the material worlds is unilateral; it comes from above, from the spiritual to the material. Man is pushed ahead by the feeling of shame. Upon feeling shame, *Malchut* of the world of Infinity contracted and stopped receiving pleasure. The shame was so unbearable, that it was greater than the pleasure.

What is shame? It is absolutely different from the feeling we know. Spiritual shame arises exclusively when man feels the Creator. It is the feeling of spiritual variance between the Creator and man. Although receiving everything from the Creator, man cannot give him the same in return. Shame is characteristic only of the higher souls that have already entered the spiritual world and ascended to the levels where the Creator can be felt.

The sensations cannot be conveyed. If man knows this or that feeling, it can be aroused in him from outside, but not be made afresh. Spiritual sensations are particularly indescribable because only the one who attains them feels them. Both in our world and in the spiritual one, the man who feels something can neither convey nor prove his sensations to anyone else. It is an intensely personal experience.

We feel only that which enters us. We do not know what is outside of us, what does not pass through our senses. Science constantly discovers something new, but we do not know what has not been uncovered yet, and there is no way we can know it in advance. It is still beyond us, around us; it has not yet entered our mind and sensations.

By its "discoveries", science only ascertains the existence of certain facts in nature. The undiscovered realm continues to exist around us and outside of our sensations. Kabbalah is also a science; however, it researches not our world, but the spiritual one, providing man with an additional sense. By entering the spiritual world, we can better understand ours. All events that take place in the spiritual world descend to us, while all the effects of our world ascend to the spiritual world according to the law of constant circulation and interaction of all information.

Our world is the last, lowest level of all the existing worlds. Hence, the Kabbalist, who enters the spiritual world, can see the descending and ascending souls, the causes and effects of all spiritual and material processes.

Is the science of Kabbalah verifiable? Looking at our world from above, one can see that all the teachings and religions end where man's inner world, his inner psychology comes to the limit. As long as it is impossible to demonstrate anything spiritual on the level of our world, it will be impossible to prove anything. Only the one who ascends will see it. Hence, Kabbalah is called a secret science. If man is born blind in our world, it is impossible to explain to him the meaning of "seeing".

In Kabbalah, there is a method of strictly scientific, reasonable, critical self-attainment. When an additional sense emerges, man begins to talk with the Creator, to feel Him. The Creator begins to open his own inner world - the only thing man can feel and understand. As any other created being, man can feel only what descends to him from the Creator.

Perhaps the Creator has something else He does not speak about? Of course, He does. We also receive more and more new information, new sensations, which He has not introduced into us before. However, one cannot pass judgment about something he has not yet received from the Creator.

Man attains everything in Kabbalah by going through the 6000 levels, or so-called "six thousand years". Having completed his spiritual ascent, consisting of 6000 levels, man rises to the higher level of attainment - the 7th millennium or "*Shabbat*".

Then three more ascents come– the 8th, 9th and 10th millennia, where man attains the highest *Sefirot: Bina, Hochma and Keter*. These levels are above the creation. They completely belong to the Creator who gives the corrected souls such attainments, such merging with Him.

Nothing is written about this anywhere; there is no language capable of describing it. It refers to the Torah secrets. Hence, when one asks about the Creator Himself, we cannot answer anything. We speak only about the light that emanates from Him. We attain the light and thus attain the Creator. Whatever we attain, we call "The Creator", something that created us. It turns out that we actually attain ourselves, our inner world, and not Him.

Being completely filled with the light, *Malchut* felt that, although it had pleased the Creator by receiving His light, it was totally opposite to Him in its properties. It only wants to receive pleasure, while the Creator's only desire is to give pleasure.

At this stage of development, *Malchut*, for the first time, felt a burning shame because it had seen the Giver and His properties, and all the vast difference between Him and itself.

As a result of this sensation, *Malchut* decides to completely free itself from the light, as in phase 2 (*Bina*), with the only difference being that here the creation passionately desires to receive pleasure and feels how much this desire is contrary to the Creator's.

The expulsion of the light out of *Malchut* is called "*Tzimtzum Aleph*" (*TA*). Because of *TA*, *Malchut* remains completely empty. The Creator acted up to phase four. Beginning with the feeling of shame, the creation starts acting as if "independently", the feeling of shame being its driving force.

After the restriction, *Malchut* does not want to receive any more light. *It* feels its contrast to the Creator Who gives it this pleasure. Being filled with the light, and thus fulfilling the Creator's desire, *Malchut* now has finally become contrary to the Creator. What should it do so as not to feel shame and be similar to the Creator, i.e., to receive, because He wants it to, and to give the way He does?

Malchut can achieve such a state if it receives not for its own sake, not for satisfying its own desire to receive pleasure, but for the sake of the Creator. This means that it will now receive the light only because, by doing so, it gives pleasure to the Creator. It is similar to the guest who, even though very hungry, refuses to receive the treat for his own sake, but receives to please the host.

For this purpose, *Malchut* creates a screen - a force resisting the egoistic desire to receive pleasure for its own sake, which pays no attention to the Giver. This force pushes away all the light coming to it. Then, with the help of the same screen, *Malchut* calculates what amount of the light it can receive for the sake of the Creator.

Malchut opens up only to the portion of the light measured by the screen that it can receive for the Creator's sake. The remaining part of *Malchut*, i.e., the rest of its desires, remains empty. If it could fill itself completely with the light and receive for the sake of bestowal, it would have become similar to the Creator by its properties. It would finish the correction of its egoism and begin using it only to give pleasure to the Creator.

Such a state of absolute correction of *Malchut* is "the purpose of the creation" and is called "The End of the Correction" (of egoistic desire to receive pleasure). But it is impossible to reach such a state in one moment, one action, because it is completely contrary to *Malchut's* egoistic nature. *Malchut* receives its correction in parts, in portions over a period of time.

The light that enters the *Kli* is called "*Ohr Yashar*" (the Direct Light). The *Kli's* intention to receive the light only for the Creator's sake is called "*Ohr Hozer*" (the Reflected Light). With the help of this intention, the *Kli* reflects the light. The part of the *Kli* that receives the light is called

"*Toch*" (inner part). The remaining empty part of the *Kli* is called "*Sof*" (end). Together, *Toch* and *Sof* form the "*Guf*" (body) - the desire to receive pleasure. One should take into consideration that, when Kabbalistic books speak about "the body", a "desire to receive" is always meant.

With the exception of our world, the entire spiritual Universe is built on this single principle - to receive for the sake of the Creator. It appears that the Universe is only variations of *Malchut* emptied in *TA*, which now fills itself with the help of the screen. The outer, less significant part of this *Malchut* is called the worlds of *Adam Kadmon, Atzilut, Beria, Yetzira* and *Assiya*. However, the remaining inner part of *Malchut* is called "the soul", *Adam*.

The process of filling *Malchut* with the light is qualitative and quantitative. This is the very process we are going to study. It consists in the fact that each tiny part of *Malchut that*descended into our world must correct itself by merging with the Creator. And each such particle is inside man. It is his real "self".

The part of *Malchut that* does not yet receive the light, but just makes a preliminary analysis, calculating how much light it can receive for the Creator's sake, is called "the *Rosh*" (head). As much light as *Malchut* can receive, so much pleasure can it give to the Creator. *Malchut* has a complete freedom of will; it can choose either not to receive at all, or to receive as much as it wants. It controls its egoism and chooses just this state to be similar to the Creator. It works with its egoism, i.e., not only it chooses not to receive for its own sake, but receives for the sake of the Creator.

Malchut has to feel pleasure, because this is the Creator's desire; but the intention must be altruistic. That is why it cannot receive for the Creator's sake all the light coming from Him. There arises a contradiction between the intention and the pleasure itself. If *Malchut*does not enjoy, neither would the Creator. All His pleasure is in pleasing *Malchut*.

The light that entered the *Toch* of *Malchut* is called "*Ohr Pnimi*" (the Inner Light). The place where the screen sits is called "the *Peh*" (mouth). The screen in Hebrew is "*Masach*". The boundary where the *Kli* stops receiving the light is called "the *Tabur*" (navel). The line signifying the end of the *Kli* is called "the *Sium*" (completion) *or* "*Etzbaot Raglin*" (toes).

The part of the light that *Malchut* cannot receive, because of a weak screen remains outside and is called "*Ohr Makif*" (the Surrounding Light). The light that *Malchut* receives inside should correspond to its intention to receive this light for the Creator's sake. This intention, as is known, is called "the Reflected Light". Therefore, the light from the head enters the body and mixes with the Reflected Light.

The *Toch*, filled with the light, is absolutely similar to the Creator and is in a state of constant exchange of pleasure with Him. The Creator emanates pleasure, which is felt by the souls according to their measure of "hunger", the desire to receive it. The problem here is to desire to feel the Creator and to receive pleasure from Him. This is what Kabbalah teaches us.

One can feel the Creator only to the degree of similarity of his own properties. The sense that perceives, that feels the Creator, is called "the *Masach*" (screen). The entrance into the spiritual world starts with a minimal screen emerging in man, when he begins to feel the outer world and understands that it is the Creator.

Then, by studying Kabbalah, man increases the magnitude of his screen and begins to feel the Creator more and more. The screen is the force of resistance to one's egoism and the measure of one's similarity to the Creator. It allows him to harmonize his intention according to the intention of the Creator. To the extent that man's desires are equal in their measure of likeness to those of the Creator's, he begins to feel the Creator.

Nothing exists in the Universe except the Creator's desire "to bestow" and the creation's initial desire "to receive". Every subsequent process is the correction of this desire "to receive" with the help of the desire "to bestow". Yet, how can man change something that was created by the Creator - the desire "to receive", if it is his very essence?

The answer is that it occurs only with the help of the intention "to receive for the sake of bestowal". The creation becomes equal to the Creator in its properties, its spiritual level. Every created being should achieve such a state either during one or several lifetimes. This process takes place throughout every generation. We are the consequence, the product of the previous generations; our souls have been here more than once, and have descended yet again and again. They accumulate the experience of suffering and the readiness to approach nearer to the spiritual...

Man's nature is one of laziness, and it is a very good feeling. Unless he had it, he would have scattered himself all over the different kinds of pursuits, without giving preference to anything. One should not be afraid of laziness; it protects us from unnecessary activities.

The Creator's actions become apparent in the first two phases:

The Zero phase, called "the root", is the light emanating from the Creator.

The First phase, called *"Hochma"* is the "desire to receive" the light, the vessel (the *Kli*), created by the light itself, that it may receive the pleasure contained in this light. Furthermore, until the end of the entire creation, everything happens only as the *Kli*'s reaction to the light inside it. Everything occurs only due to the interconnection between these two components - the light and the vessel, the "desire to give" pleasure and the "desire to receive" that pleasure.

The Second phase, called *"Bina"*, is the first reaction of the *Kli* to the light that fills it; the *Kli* borrows the property of "bestowal" from the light and wants to be equal to it. That is why it expels the light.

The Third phase, called *"Tifferet"*, or *"Zeir Anpin"*, is the first action performed by the *Kli*. It understands that the Creator wants it to receive and enjoy the light. Therefore, it begins receiving a little bit of the light. This "desire to receive" is the third phase.

The Fourth phase is called "*Malchut*". In the third phase the *Kli*'s "desire to receive" the entire light of *Hochma* emanating from the Creator develops, and this desire is then called *Malchut.*

This fourth phase is the complete desire, the only creation. We can see that the creation has only one desire - to receive and enjoy the light of *Hochma*. Initially, the only possibility for bestowal is by not receiving for its own sake, but for the sake of the Creator.

However, to become a giver it is necessary to feel the Creator and to receive only for the sake of bestowing pleasure upon Him.You become partners.

He gives to you and you give to Him. You become equal in your properties and aspirations; you suffer if He does not receive pleasure, but He also suffers if you do not enjoy what he has prepared for you. He and you become one whole.

The fourth phase, *Malchut,* is then subdivided into five parts. This happens, because it cannot correct all of its egoism at once, i.e., it is unable to receive the entire light prepared for it for the Creator's sake. The "desire to receive" for someone else's sake is unnatural; hence, the creation should gradually "get used" to this desire.

Malchut wants to be similar to the preceding phases. Hence, it divides itself into five parts:

(a) **The root part** of *Malchut* is similar to the root phase of the Direct Light;
(b) **The first part** of *Malchut* is similar to the first phase of the Direct Light;
(c) **The second part** of *Malchut* is similar to the second phase of the Direct Light;
(d) **The third part** of *Malchut* is similar to the third phase of the Direct Light;

(e) **The fourth part** of *Malchut* is *Malchut* itself, which is not similar to any of the previous properties. Therefore, it is absolutely egoistic.

These phases are correspondingly called:

1. Still
2. Vegetative
3. Animal
4. Human and
5. Spiritual

The souls are created out of the last part of *Malchut*. The rest of the Universe, the worlds and everything that fills and inhabits them, is created out of the preceding parts of *Malchut*. The difference between the levels of the creation is in the degree of the desire to receive pleasure: from the least in the still nature to the biggest in man and to the highest in the souls.

Through reincarnations, man feels all kinds of desires. The one who has even an unconscious desire to become closer to the Creator has also the rest of rougher desires. The question becomes, in what proportion are these desires represented in him, and which desire should he choose for his actions?

With the help of the group and the Rabbi (Teacher), one can replace all of his desires with the single one of attaining the Creator. While moving towards that Goal, the rest of the desires grow and interfere with this advancement. There come all kinds of desires, including sex, money, power, fame, knowledge, and the various idols of the material world.

Man is given all kinds of temptations from above; he is lured by the possibility of growing rich, of being promoted to a high post etc. It happens so that man can get to know himself, to realize his aspirations and weaknesses, his insignificance in withstanding tempting pleasures. All of this is only that he may learn what this desire to receive pleasure is that the Creator has fashioned in him.

Kabbalah is a science of self-knowledge, of revealing the Creator in oneself. Man realizes what is most important to him. It matters what man does with his free time, what he thinks about the rest of the time. A Kabbalist should work. Free time can be used in the right way only if it is planned beforehand. If you think about the question "What am I living for?" during your free time, then it will allow you to think correctly the rest of the time.

To ascend spiritually, one should have an objective to correct, i.e., it is necessary to have the "desire to receive", egoism. Only this, the "desire to receive", corrected with the help of the intention to receive for the sake of the Creator, becomes the vessel into which the light intended by the Creator enters. It turns out that the more egoistic man becomes the better. For man's egoism steadily grows during his approach to the Creator. It is necessary to make a bigger egoist out of man. In this way, he might come to feel that something in him requires correction.

Egoism makes man negatively perceive the positive manifestation of the Creator. Nevertheless, this very negative sense of the Creator brings us to Him. During the spiritual ascent, drawing nearer to the Creator, all negative emotions turn into positive ones.

Man's inner "self" is the Creator. We feel separated from Him only because our egoism is not yet corrected.

The entire creation consists of five *Behinot*: *Keter*, *Hochma*, *Bina*, *Tifferet* or *Zeir Anpin* and *Malchut*, to which correspond 10 *Sefirot*. Why are there 10? The matter is that *Tifferet* consists of 6 *Sefirot*: *Hesed*, *Gevura*, *Tifferet*, *Netzah*, *Hod*, *Yesod*. Let us point out that the name "*Tifferet*" means both one of the 5 *Behinot*, and one of its private *Sefirot*.

This private *Sefira*, one of the 6, determines the character of the common *Tifferet*. However, it is more usual to use the name *Zeir Anpin* (ZA) instead of *Tifferet*. This name (the tetragrammaton) is more accepted, especially in the school of the Ari. These 10 *Sefirot* include the entire Universe.

These five *Behinot: Keter, Hochma, Bina, ZA, Malchut,*are also the five worlds that we otherwise call by the name of the Creator (*Yud-Hey-Vav-Hey*). This name is usually pronounced as HaVaYaH. It has an infinite multitude of meanings, because it provides the framework, the basis of all the names of all the creations:

Sefira	World	Letter
Keter	Adam Kadmon	The point of the letter *Yud (Kutzo shel Yud)*
Hochma	Atzilut	*Yud*
Bina	Beria	*Hey*
ZA	Yetzira	*Vav*
Malchut	Assiya	*Hey*

Our world is a part of the world of *Assiya*. Although our world is formally under its lowest spiritual level, as there is no place for such an egoistic property as the one ruling over our world in the spiritual realm, this is considered to be the final level of the world of *Assiya*.

The reason for the creation of the worlds consists in the fact that, in order to give pleasure to the creation, the Creator has to create in it several conditions:

-The creation must want to receive pleasure.
-This desire must come from the creation itself.
-It must be independent, which is not the same as in the previous condition.
-The creation must be able to rule over this desire, so that the desire may neitherhave power over the creation, nor dictate its behavior.
-The creation must be independent to choose whether it will receive pleasure by being a creation, or by being similar to the Creator.

The creation must be able to act freely between the two contrary forces: its own egoism and the Creator; it must independently choose its path and set out upon that path.

In order to provide the creation (man) with these conditions, the Creator should:

- Distance the creation from the light;
- Create the condition for freedom of will;
- Create an opportunity to attain the Universe and evolve;
- Create an opportunity (what is the difference between a condition and an opportunity?) for freedom of action.

The Creator gradually creates such conditions for the creation. By creation, we mean man in our world, in the state where he already begins to realize himself in relation to the Universe or starts climbing the spiritual levels. Such a state is desirable for the beginning of man's spiritual work and is called "this world".

Why did the Creator, Who is at the highest spiritual level, have to form the creation out of an egoistic property that is contrary to Him? Why did He initially completely fill creation with the light, which then empties itself of the light, and by doing so lower creation to the state of "this world" (*Olam Hazeh*)?

The matter is that creation is not independent; even though it is filled with the light, for it is completely suppressed by the light. The light dictates its conditions to the creation, and the desire to receive pleasure, the *Kli*, transfers its properties to it.

For the creation of an independent *Kli*, absolutely free from the light's assistance, the light should completely move away from it. There is a simple rule: the spreading of the light inside the *Kli*, with the subsequent expulsion of it, makes the *Kli* suitable for its function of independently realizing and choosing the way of filling. Such a genuine, independent *Kli* can emerge only in our world.

The descent of the light from above through all the worlds to man in this world presents the preparatory phase of formation of the genuine the *Kli*. At each phase, only the light determines all the forms, stages, and character of the *Kli*. As soon as the *Kli* completely expels the light, it becomes absolutely independent and is able to take on different decisions.

Any soul (one more name for the *Kli*) that descends from a certain spiritual level is considered as part of the Creator and is filled with His light, until it dresses into man's body-desire and until he starts working with it.

Only after a soul descends to our world and learns Kabbalah does it comprehend its real state. Then man, in whom a desire for spiritual advancement emerged, may ask the Creator to fill him with the spiritual light that will elevate him. However, man does not rise spiritually to the level from which his soul descended, but 620 times higher.

How does man advance? If he were given from above an incentive for the attainment of the spiritual, he must not lose it. Man can be pushed several times from above, by providing him with the interest for spirituality. However, if he does not use this desire correctly, he will eventually be left in peace until his next incarnation.

The *Kli* is forced to rise spiritually by the Surrounding Light, *Ohr Makif*. It shines from outside, because it cannot enter the egoistic *Kli* yet. But this light affects man's desire for spirituality and makes it grow so considerably, that all he wants is the spiritual ascent. Then he receives help from above. To increase the influence of the Surrounding Light and thus to start feeling the spiritual sensations, to break into the spiritual space one can only do this:

a) under the guidance of a true Kabbalist;
b) with the help of studyinggenuine books;
c) through communication with the members of his group (collective studies, work, meals).

Olam Hazeh **("this world")** is the state where man already feels that the Creator conceals Himself from him. At this time, we do not feel it yet. We are told that the Creator exists, we hear about it, but in any case, we cannot feel it. When man starts feeling that there is something outside of our world, something that hides from him, it is called the double concealment of the Creator.

Egoism is man's property that automatically makes him derive benefit from everything he does. Only in this does he see the purpose of his actions. Altruism is a property we are totally unable to comprehend; it is when person does something without any benefit to himself. Nature endowed us only with the egoistic properties. Altruism is beyond the limits of our understanding.

Only someone who feels the Creator can acquire this property. Using the language of Kabbalah, when the light enters the *Kli*, it will pass its altruistic properties to it. Man cannot be corrected all by himself, and he is not required to. Under his Teacher's guidance, during the group lessons, he has to arouse such spiritual desires that would cause the light to enter him.

To obtain that one should work hard on his thoughts and desires to know what is exactly necessary, although he cannot yet desire it. If man performs an action in our world that seems outwardly altruistic, it actually means that he calculated its future reward in advance.

Any movement, even the slightest one, is made only based on a calculation. As a result, it seems to man that he would be better off than he is now. If man did not make such calculations, he would not be able to move, for a certain amount of energy is needed for movement even at the molecular level of nature, and this energy is our egoism, i.e., the desire to receive pleasure. This law then "dresses" into general physical-chemical laws. In our world, man can only receive or give for the sake of receiving.

It is worth noting here that the desires that make all humankind happy are also egoistic, for man, seeing himself as a part of humankind, desires to please this very part of him...

Kabbalah permits the description of both the inner actions performed by man, and those the Creator performs on him, i.e., their interactions. Kabbalah is a physical-mathematical description of the spiritual objects and their actions, expressed in formulas, graphs and tables.

All of them describe a Kabbalist's inner spiritual actions, and only the one who can reproduce these actions in himself, and thus understand what these formulas mean, can know what stands behind them.

A Kabbalist can pass this information on to his disciple only when the latter reaches at least the first spiritual level. Such information is passed "by word of mouth" (*mi Peh le Peh*), because the screen is at the level of "*Peh*" of the spiritual *Partzuf*. If a student has not yet acquired the screen, he cannot really understand anything; he cannot yet receive anything from his teacher.

When a Kabbalist reads a Kabbalistic book, he should feel each word, each letter internally, just as blind people feel each letter of the alphabet using the Braille system.

We have studied four phases of the formation of the *Kli* (0-*Shoresh* or *Keter*, 1-*Hochma*, 2-*Bina*, and 3-*Tifferet*). Why are there four and not five? It is because the fifth one is the *Kli* itself, and not the phase of its formation. Starting from *Malchut*, there are no more phases; the *Kli* is completely created, born, formed in its egoistic desire to receive pleasure from the light of *Hochma*. The *Kli* is independent not only in its desire, but in the implementation of its desire to act.

However, if the light, the pleasure, fills the *Kli*, it dictates to the *Kli* the way it should act, because it suppresses it by filling it with delight. That is why the *Kli* is truly free in its intention only when it is not filled with the light. Still that is not enough yet; the light should not be felt even from afar; i.e., the Creator should conceal Himself completely from the *Kli, Malchut.* Only then can *Malchut* be independent, free in its decisions and actions.

When the *Kli* can realize its desires independently, when it is completely free from the influence of the light and pleasure, and the light cannot dictate to the *Kli* its conditions, such a state, is called "our world", or "this world". This state can be achieved if the light is removed not only from the inner part of the *Kli*, but gradually distances itself from outside of the *Kli.* In our world, man feels the Creator neither on the inside northe outside; i.e., hedoes not believe in His existence.

The expulsion of the light from the *Kli* is called the restriction of the desire to receive pleasure, or simply the restriction, *Tzimtzum Aleph.* Moving the light away from outside of the *Kli* is attained with the help of a system of darkening screens that are called worlds. There are only five such screens; i.e., there are five worlds. Each of these worlds consists of five parts called "*Partzufim*" (plural of *Partzuf*). Each *Partzuf* includes five parts called "*Sefirot*" (plural of *Sefira*). As a result, *Malchut* is so remote from the light that it does not feel it at all. This is man in our world.

In Kabbalah, we study the properties of the worlds, *Partzufim* and *Sefirot*; i.e., the properties of screens that conceal the spiritual world, the Creator from us. Thepurpose of this study is to know what properties man should acquire so as to neutralize the concealing actions of all these worlds, *Partzufim* and *Sefirot*; to rise to the level of this or that spiritual level of *Sefira, Partzuf* or world.

By acquiring the properties of a certain *Partzuf* in a certain world, man immediately neutralizes the concealing action of this level and attains it.

At this time, only the higher levels hide from him the Creator, the light. Gradually he should attain all the properties of all the levels, starting from the lowest one immediately above our world, and up to the highest level, his final correction.

Let us return to *Malchut*, the 5th phase of the development of the *Kli*. When *Malchut* feels that it receives whilst the Creator gives, it perceives the contrast of its state to the Creator's to be so disgusting that it decides to stop receiving pleasure. Since there is no compulsion in the spiritual world, and pleasure cannot be felt, if there is no desire for it, the light disappears, stops being felt in the *Kli*.

Malchut performs *Tzimtzum Aleph* (*TA*). In the previous phases, the *Kli* had not felt itself receiving, and only in the 5th phase, when it independently decides to receive, the *Kli* feels its opposition to the Creator. Only *Malchut* can make *TA*, for to make the *Tzimtzum*, one should first feel its complete opposition to the Creator.

Another name for *Malchut* is soul, but the name "soul" may refer both to the *Kli*, and to the light in it. While reading a text, one should always remember whether it speaks about the creation or about what it is filled with. In the first case, it is a part of the creation itself, a desire. In the second case, it is the Creator's part, the light.

When a soul descends to the world of *Atzilut* from the world of Infinity, it becomes the soul of phase *Aleph*, but not the real soul. The distinction between it and the Creator is not yet felt. It is as a baby in its mother's womb; it cannot be called independent yet, although it already exists. It is still in the interim phase.

The world of *Atzilut* is absolutely spiritual, because the *Kli* is not felt in it; it is completely suppressed by the light and is a single whole with the light. The souls of the rest of the created beings, for example, animals, descending from above through the world of *Atzilut*, are also considered one with the Creator. However, in our world, the created beings are completely empty of the light and infinitely remote from the Creator.

The worlds are levels of closeness to the Creator in man's ascent and the measures of remoteness from Him in the descent of the souls. It does not matter about what kind of souls we speak. Although all nature presents a single whole, some types of created beings, differing in the degree of their freedom of choice, can be singled out as more or less free in the choice of the Goal.

Of all created beings, only man has a true freedom of will; the rest of nature ascends or descends with him, because everything in our Universe is related to man. It is impossible to speak about a certain number of souls that pass this way, for it is difficult to give a quantitative estimate.

Particles of other stronger and higher souls may appear in each of us. They begin to speak in us and push us forward. In fact, the soul is not something predetermined, permanent, something that accompanies our physiological body during its entire biological life. For example, the Ari, in his book *"Shaar HaGilgulim"* ("The Gates of Reincarnation") describes the kind of souls and in what succession they took root in him.

A soul is not something indivisible. It constantly merges and separates, creates new parts according to the demands of the correction of the common soul. Even during man's life, some of the souls' parts take root or leave him; souls constantly "flow" one into another.

The world of *Beria* corresponds to the phase *Bet-Bina*, the "desire to bestow", to please. The *Kli* in the world of *Beria* is called *"Neshama"*; for the first time it has its own desire, albeit the "desire to bestow"; hence, it is very "clear", non-egoistic in its desires and considered to be absolutely spiritual.

The world of *Yetzira* corresponds to the phase *Gimel-Tifferet*, or ZA, in which both the "desire to bestow" (approximately 90%) and the "desire to receive" (approximately 10%) emerge. There is a little bit of the light of *Hochma* on the bright background of *Ohr Hassadim*. The *Kli* in this phase passes from the state of *Neshama* to *Ruach*. Although the desires of the *Kli* are already egoistic to some degree, all the same the "desire to bestow" prevails; therefore, the *Kli* in the world of *Yetzira* is still quite spiritual.

The completely egoistic fourth phase, *Malchut*, rules in **the world of** *Assiya*. Here the "desire to receive" is itself the *Guf* (body), which is absolutely remote from the Creator. The light that fills the *Kli* in the world of *Assiya* is called "*Nefesh*"; this name suggests that the *Kli* and the light are spiritually motionless similarly to the still nature of our world.

The *Kli* becomes coarser as it gradually descends through the levels of the worlds, and moves away from the light until it is completely empty, i.e., it does not feel the light at all. Therefore, it becomes completely free from the light and the Creator in its thoughts and actions.

Now, if the *Kli* itself prefers the path of spiritual development to "petty" egoistic pleasures, it will gradually be able to ascend through the levels of the worlds of *Assiya, Yetzira, Beria, Atzilut, Adam Kadmon*, and reach the world of Infinity, i.e., infinitely merge with the Creator, become equal with Him.

Each man has a so-called black point in his heart, an embryo of the future spiritual state. In different people, this point is in a different state of readiness for the spiritual perception. There are people who cannot grasp spiritual notions at all; they have no interest in them. However, there are people who suddenly wake up, and are puzzled by the fact that they suddenly become interested in such "abstract" matters.

As with all other animals, man lives under the influence of his parents, the environment, traits of his character. Having no freedom of will, he only processes the available information according to outer and inner factors. Then he performs the actions that seem best to him.

Yet, everything changes when the Creator starts awaking man. A person wakes up under the influence of a small portion of the light that the Creator sends to him in advance. Upon receiving this portion, his inner point begins to demand further filling, forcing him to look for the light. Therefore, he starts to search for it in different occupations, ideas, philosophies, doctrines, study groups, until he comes to Kabbalah. Each soul on the Earth has to go along the same path!

Until, with the help of the screen, his black point, reaches the size of a small *Partzuf*, man is considered to have no soul, no *Kli*, and naturally, no light in him. The presence of even the smallest spiritual *Partzuf*, having the lights of *Nefesh, Ruach, Neshama, Haya, Yechida (NaRaNHaY)*, indicates man's birth and his leaving of the animal state (which we are used to consider human, by the way).

Man refers to such a spiritual state where one has already passed the spiritual barrier (*Machsom*) separating this world from the spiritual one, the world of *Assiya*; i.e., one who has acquired the spiritual *Kli* called the soul.

The experience accumulated by the soul in each of its incarnations in this world remains with it, and passes from generation to generation, only changing its physiological bodies as one would change a shirt. All bodily physical sufferings also register in the soul, and at a certain moment, bring man to a desire to attain spirituality.

The dressing of a soul into a woman's body signifies that it does not have to go through any personal spiritual correction in this incarnation. A woman does not advance spiritually by herself, except by helping to circulate the wisdom of Kabbalah and receiving spiritual elevation through her husband.

The Torah says that the hearts of those who rule the world are in the hands of the Creator. This refers to all politicians, heads of states, dictators - all those on whom humankind depends. All of them are nothing but marionettes in the hands of the Creator, through whom He controls everything.

There is only one law in the spiritual realm - the law of the equivalence of the spiritual properties. If the properties of two people are equal, similar, they are spiritually close. If people differ in their thoughts, viewpoints, they feel separated and distant from one another, even if they are physically close.

Spiritual proximity or distance depends on the similarity of the objects' properties. If the objects completely coincide in their properties, desires, they merge. If two desires are contrary to one another, they are said to be remote one from the other. The more similar two desires are, the closer they are in the spiritual world.

If only one out of the numerous desires of the objects coincides, these two objects have contact only in one point. If there is not even one desire in us that is similar to the Creator's, it means that we are absolutely remote from Him and have nothing with which to feel Him. If there appears just one desire in me that is similar to the Creator, then with it I will be able to feel the Creator.

Man's task is gradually to make all his desires similar to those of the Creator. Then man will completely merge into one spiritual object with Him, and there will be no distinction between them. Man will achieve everything the Creator has: eternity, absolute knowledge, and perfection. This is the ultimate purpose of the correction of all man's natural desires.

Malchut, upon expelling all the light in *TA*, decided to receive it with the help of a screen. The Direct Light comes to it, presses on the screen, wanting to get inside. *Malchut refuses* to receive the light, remembering the burning shame it felt when it was filled with it. Refusal to receive the light means reflecting it with the help of the screen. Such light is called "*Ohr Hozer*" (the Reflected Light). The reflection itself is called "*Haka'a*" (a stroke) of the light into the screen.

The reflection of pleasure (the light) takes place inside of man with the help of the intention to receive this pleasure only for the Creator's sake. Man calculates how much he can receive to please the Creator. He, as it were, dresses the pleasure he wants to receive onto the intention to bestow upon the Creator; to receive, to enjoy for the sake of the Creator.

The dressing of the Direct Light onto the Reflected Light allows *Malchut*, after *TA*, to expand and receive a portion of the light. It means that, at this point it becomes similar to the Creator by merging with Him. The Purpose of the creation is to fill *Malchut* completely with the

Creator's light. Then all reception of the light will be equal to bestowal and will mean total merging of the entire creation with the Creator.

By dressing the coming pleasure into its intention (the Reflected Light), *Malchut* announces that it wants to feel this pleasure only because, by doing so, it delights the Creator. In this case, reception is equal to bestowal, since the meaning of an action is determined by the *Kli's* intention, not by the mechanical direction of the action, inward or outward. Pleasure felt in this case will be twofold: from receiving it and from bestowing it upon the Creator.

Rabbi Ashlag wonderfully illustrates the situation with the example of a relationship between a guest and his host, the guest, receiving pleasure from the host, turns it as it were into giving. He pays a visit to the host, who knows exactly what he likes most. The guest sits down in front of the host, and the host puts his five most favorite dishes before him, the exact amount to match his appetite.

If the guest had not seen the giver, the host, he would have shamelessly pounced on the food and gulped down all the delicacies without leaving a bit, since they are exactly what he desires.However, the host, sitting in front of him, embarrasses him, so the guest refuses to eat. The host insists, explaining how much he wishes to please him, to give him delight.

Finally, by trying to talk the guest into eating, the host says that the guest's refusal makes Him suffer. Upon realizing that by eating the dinner he will give pleasure to the host, turning himself into a giver instead of a receiver, i.e., becoming equal with the host in his intentions and properties, only then does the guest agree to eat.

If a situation arises where the host wants to please the guest by putting the treat before him, and the guest, in return, eats it with the intention to return the pleasure to the host, enjoying it at that, this condition is called interaction by stroke *(Zivug de Haka'a)*. However, it can take place only after the guest's prior complete refusal to receive pleasure.

The guest only accepts the treat when he is sure that he pleases the host by receiving it, as if doing him a favor.He receives it only to the extent of his ability to think not about his own pleasure, but about pleasing the host, in other words, the Creator.

So, why do we need all these pleasures in our world if they are all based on suffering? When a desire is fulfilled, the pleasure "is extinguished" and disappears.

Pleasure is felt only when there is a burning "desire to receive" it. With the help of the correction of our desires, by adding to them the intention "for the sake of the Creator", we can enjoy infinitely, without feeling "hunger" before receiving pleasure. We can receive enormous delight by granting pleasure to the Creator, with the help of constantly increasing in ourselves the feeling of His greatness.

Since the Creator is eternal and infinite,we, by feeling His greatness, create in ourselves the eternal and infinite *Kli* - hunger for Him. Thus, we can enjoy eternally and infinitely. In the spiritual world any reception of pleasure promotes an even larger "desire to receive" it, and it goes on forever.

Filling becomes equal to giving: man gives, sees how much the Creator enjoys it, and acquires an even bigger "desire to give". However, the pleasure from giving should also be altruistic, i.e., for the sake of bestowal, and not for the sake of receiving pleasure from it. Otherwise, it will be giving for self-enjoyment, as when we give while pursuing our own ends.

Kabbalah teaches man to receive pleasure from the light with the intention for the sake of the Creator. If man can screen all the pleasures of this world, he will be able instantly to feel the spiritual world. Then man falls under the influence of the spiritually impure forces. They gradually provide him with additional spiritual egoism. He builds a new screen on it with the help of the pure forces, and then he can receive a new portion of the light, which corresponds to the quantity of egoism corrected by him. Thus, man always has the freedom of will.

The notion of "screen" contains the difference between the spiritual and material. Receiving pleasure without the screen is a common egoistic pleasure of our world. The point is to prefer spiritual pleasures to the material ones and by developing the screen, to receive eternal pleasure, which is intended for us according to the Thought of Creation.

However, the screen can appear only under the influence of the light of the Creator, on the egoistic desire of the *Kli*. The moment the Creator reveals Himself to man, his question of who needs his efforts, instantly disappears. So all our work boils down to just one thing: to feel the Creator.

To overcome any level of concealment, man must acquire the properties of this level. By doing so, he "neutralizes" the restriction, takes upon himself the influence of the concealing level, so that the concealment turns into revelation and attainment.

For example, let us take a person whose every property belongs to our world. His properties are so unimproved that he is under the influence of the concealment of all five worlds. If, because of the correction, his properties become similar to those of the world of *Assiya*, then this world stops concealing the Creator's light from him, which means that man has spiritually ascended to the level of *Assiya*.

A person , whose properties and sensations are already in *Assiya*, feels the concealment of the Creator on the level of the world of *Yetzira*. By correcting his properties according to those of *Yetzira*, he neutralizes the concealment of the Creator's light on this level and begins to feel Him on the level of *Yetzira*. It turns out that the worlds are the screens that conceal the Creator from us. However, when man puts the screen on his egoism similar to those levels, he by doing so, reveals the part of the Creator's light that this screen, this world was concealing.

The one who is in a certain spiritual world will feel the concealment on that level and the one above it, but not on the one below. So, if man is on the level of *Sefira Hesed* of the *Partzuf* ZA of the world of *Beria*, then from this level downwards, all the worlds, all the *Partzufim* and all the *Sefirot* are already in him in their corrected state. These passed levels are the levels of revelation for him; he absorbed their egoism, corrected it with the help of the screen, and thus revealed the Creator on this level.

However, the Creator is still concealed from him on all the higher levels. Overall, there are 125 levels from our world to the Creator: five worlds with five *Partzufim* in each world, with five *Sefirot* in each *Partzuf*.

The main thing is to take the first step into the spiritual world; afterwards it becomes much simpler. All the levels are similar to one another, and the difference between them is only in the material, not in the design. The world of *Adam Kadmon* consists of five *Partzufim*: *Keter (Galgalta), Hochma (AB), Bina (SAG* or *Abba ve Ima,* or *AVI* in short), *ZA* (sometimes it is called *Kadosh Baruch Hu, Israel), Malchut (Shechina, Leah, Rachel).*

On each spiritual level, man as it were, changes his name, and according to where he is now, is called either Pharaoh, Moshe (Moses), or Israel. All of these are the Creator's names, man's levels of attaining Him. As a rule, the Kabbalistic books are written by Kabbalists who have passed all these levels of the correction.

The levels that follow are not the levels of correction, but an individual's attainment and personal contact with the Creator. They are not studied. They belong to the so-called "secrets of the Torah" (*Sodot Torah*) that are given as a gift to the one who has completely corrected himself. Unlike these, the levels of correction belong to the tastes of the Torah (*Ta'amey Torah*); they must be studied to be attained.

The conveying of Kabbalistic information is the conveying light. The transferring of properties from the higher spiritual level to the lower one is called "descent" or "influence", and from the lower to the higher one - "request", "prayer", MAN. The connection exists only between two adjacent *Partzufim*, one above the other. No communication is possible between two discontinuous levels. Each higher level is called the Creator with regard to the lower one; its relationship to the lower level can be likened to a ratio of the Universe to a grain of sand.

יא) ועם זה תבין גדר האמיתי להבחין בין רוחניות לגשמיות: כי כל שיש בו רצון לקבל מושלם בכל בחינותיו, שהוא בחי"ד, הוא נקרא "גשמי". והוא נמצא בפרטי כל המציאות הערוכה לעינינו בעוה"ז. וכל שהוא למעלה משיעור הגדול הזה של הרצון לקבל, נבחן בשם "רוחניות". שהם העולמות אבי"ע, הגבוהים מעוה"ז, וכל המציאות שבהם.

ובזה תבין, שכל ענין עליות וירידות האמורות בעולמות העליונים, אינן בבחינת מקום מדומה ח"ו, רק בענין ד' הבחינות שברצון לקבל. כי כל הרחוק ביותר מבחי"ד, נבחן למקום יותר גבוה. וכל המתקרב אל בחינה ד', נבחן למקום יותר תחתון.

11) Now we can understand the difference between the spiritual and the material. If the "desire to receive" has reached its final development, i.e., achieved the stage of Behina Dalet, it is called "material" and belongs to our world (Olam Hazeh). If the "desire to receive" has not yet reached its final development, then such a desire is considered spiritual and corresponds to the four worlds of ABYA, which are above the level of our world.

You should understand that all ascents and descents in the Upper worlds are not by any means movements in some imaginary space, but are merely changes in the magnitude of the "desire to receive". The object most remote from Behina Dalet is in the highest point. The closer an object is to Behina Dalet, the lower is its level.

Here the name "*Olam Hazeh*" means the world of *Assiya*.

The "desire to receive" in *Behina Dalet* is absolutely complete; this is the desire just to receive without giving anything in return. All ascents and descents in the spiritual world in no way refer to the notion of place they speak solely about the increase or decrease of the similarity of man's inner properties to those of the Creator.

If one likens it to our world, then the ascent can be imagined as a burst of joy and high spirits, while the descent would be a dismal mood. We speak about the similarity of properties though, when the mood only accompanies the realization of the spiritual ascent. In Kabbalah, all actions refer to man's inner feelings.

It depends on man himself what property he should use. What really matters is the measure of egoism that man works with right now and "for whose sake", i.e., for the sake of the Creator, which will be an ascent, or for his own, which corresponds to a fall. It is important how he uses his egoism and in what direction.

יב) אמנם יש להבין: כיון שכל עיקרו של הנברא ושל כל הבריאה בכללה, הוא רק הרצון לקבל בלבד, ומה שיותר מזה אינו לגמרי בכלל בריאה, אלא נמשך יש מיש מעצמותו ית', א"כ למה אנו מבחינים את הרצון לקבל הזה לעוביות ועכירות, ואנו מצווים לזכות אותו על ידי תורה ומצות, עד שזולת זה לא נגיע אל המטרה הנעלה של מחשבת הבריאה?

> *12) One should understand that the essence of each vessel and the entire Creation is only the "desire to receive". Nothing outside the framework of this desire has anything to do with the creation, but refers to the Creator. Then why do we regard the "desire to receive" as something coarse, disgusting and requiring correction? We are instructed to "purify" it with the help of the Torah and the Commandments; otherwise, we will not be able to achieve the ultimate purpose of the Creation.*

The desire to receive pleasure was formed by the Creator and therefore not subject to change. Man can only choose what size of a desire he can use now and "for whose sake". If each of his desires he uses only for his own benefit, then it is egoism or "spiritual impurity". If man wants to use his desires to receive pleasure while simultaneously delighting the Creator, then he has to choose only those of his desires with which he can really do so.

Therefore, wishing to act altruistically, man should first check what kind of desires he can use to receive pleasure so that it returns to the Creator. Only then can he start filling them with pleasure. All of man's desires are the desires of *Malchut*. They are divided into 125 parts called levels. Gradually, using larger and larger egoistic desires for the sake of the Creator, man ascends spiritually. The use of all of *Malchut's* 125 private desires is called 'the complete correction of egoism'.

Sometimes it is more convenient to divide *Malchut's* desires into 620 instead of 125 parts. Such parts of the desire or rather their use for the sake of the Creator are called "commandments", actions for His sake. By fulfilling these 620 actions, commandments, man ascends to the same 125-th level.

יג) והענין הוא, כי כמו שהגשמיים נפרדים זה מזה ע"י ריחוק מקום, כן נפרדים הרוחנים זה מזה ע"י שינוי הצורה שבהם. ותמצא זה גם בעוה"ז. למשל שני בני אדם, הקרובים בדעתם זה לזה, הם אוהבים זה את זה. ואין ריחוק מקום פועל עליהם, שיתרחקו זה מזה. ובהפך, כשהם רחוקים זה מזה בדעותיהם, הרי הם שונאים זה את זה, וקרבת המקום לא תקרב אותם במאומה.

הרי ששינוי הצורה שבדעתם, מרחקם זה מזה, וקרבת הצורה שבדעתם, מקרבם זה אל זה. ואם למשל, טבעו של האחד הוא הפוך בכל בחינותיו כנגד טבעו של השני, הרי הם רחוקים זה מזה כרחוק המזרח ממערב. ועד"ז תשכיל ברוחניות, שכל הענינים של התרחקות והתקרבות וזווג ויחוד, הנבחנים בהם, הם משקלים של שינוי צורה בלבד. שלפי מדת שינוי הצורה, הם מתפרדים זה מי זה, ולפי מדת השואת הצורה, הם מתדבקים זה בזה.

ועם זה תבין, שהגם שהרצון לקבל הוא חוק מחויב בהנברא, כי הוא כל בחינת נברא שבו, והוא הכלי הראוי לקבל המטרה שבמחשבת הבריאה, עכ"ז הוא נעשה ע"ז נפרד לגמרי מהמאציל, כי יש שינוי צורה עד למדת הפכיות בינו לבין המאציל. כי המאציל הוא כולו להשפיע, ואין בו מנצוצי קבלה אפילו משהו ח"ו. והוא כולו לקבל, ואין בו מנצוצי השפעה אף משהו. הרי אין לך הפכיות הצורה רחוקה יותר מזה. ונמצא ע"כ בהכרח כי הפכיות הצורה הזו מפרידה אותו מהמאציל.

13) As all material objects are separated from one another by distance in space, spiritual objects are also separated from one another due to the difference in their inner properties. Something like this can be seen in our world. For example, two men have similar views, sympathize with one another, and no distance can influence the empathy between them. On the contrary, when their views are very different, they hate one another and no proximity can unite them.

Therefore, the similarity of views draws people together, while the differences separate them. If one person's nature is absolutely opposite to the nature of the other, these people are as remote from one another as East is from West. The same occurs in the spiritual worlds: moving away, rapprochement, merging – all these processes happen only according to the difference or resemblance between the inner properties of the spiritual objects. The difference in properties separates them, while their similarity brings them closer.

The "desire to receive" is the principal element of the creation; this is the vessel necessary for the realization of the Purpose included in the Thought of the Creation. This is the desire that separates the creation from the Creator. The Creator is the absolute "desire to bestow"; He does not have a trace of the "desire to receive". It is impossible to imagine a greater contrast than this: between the Creator and the creation, between the "desire to bestow" and the "desire to receive".

The spiritual place means being with one's properties on one of the 125 levels of the spiritual ladder. From this, it follows that the notion of "place" means quality, property, measure of correction. Even in our world, closeness in physical space does not bring two different characters close to one another; it is only the similarity of their properties, thoughts and desires that can bridge the gap between them. On the contrary, the difference in properties, thoughts, and desires moves the objects away from one another.

יד) ובכדי להציל את הנבראים מגודל הפירוד הרחוק הזה, נעשה סוד הצמצום הא', שענינו הוא, שהפריד הבחי"ד מן כל פרצופי הקדושה. באופן, שמדת גדלות הקבלה ההיא נשארה בבחינת חלל פנוי וריקן מכל אור. כי כל פרצופי הקדושה יצאו בבחינת מסך מתוקן בכלי מלכות שלהם, שלא יקבלו אור בבחי"ד הזו.

ואז, בעת שהאור העליון נמשך ונתפשט אל הנאצל, והמסך הזה דוחה אותו לאחוריו, הנה זה נבחן כמו הכאה בין אור העליון ובין המסך, המעלה אור חוזר ממטה למעלה, ומלביש הע"ס דאור העליון. כי אותו חלק האור הנדחה לאחוריו, נקרא "אור חוזר". ובהלבשתו לאור העליון, נעשה אח"כ כלי קבלה על האור העליון במקום הבחי"ד.

כי אח"ז התרחבה כלי המלכות, באותו שיעור האו"ח, שהוא אור הנדחה, שעלה והלביש לאור העליון ממטה למעלה, והתפשטה גם ממעלה למטה, שבזה נתלבשו האורות בהכלים, דהיינו בתוך אור חוזר ההוא. וה"ס ראש וגוף שבכל מדרגה. כי הזווג דהכאה מאור העליון במסך, מעלה אור חוזר ממטה למעלה, ומלביש הע"ס דאור העליון בבחינת ע"ס דראש, שפירושו שרשי כלים.

כי שם עוד לא יכולה להיות הלבשה ממש. ואח"ז כשהמלכות מתפשטת עם האו"ח ההוא ממעלה למטה, אז נגמר האור חוזר, ונעשה לבחינת כלים על אור העליון. ואז נעשית התלבשות האורות בכלים. ונקראת "גוף של מדרגה" ההיא, שפירושו כלים גמורים.

14) In order to save the creation from such remoteness from the Creator, the Tzimtzum Aleph (TA, the First Restriction) took place and separated Behina Dalet from the spiritual objects. This happened in such a way that the "desire to receive" turned into a space void of the light. After the Tzimtzum Aleph, all the spiritual objects have a screen on their vessel-Malchut in order to avoid receiving the light inside Behina Dalet.

The moment the Upper Light tries to enter the creation, the screen pushes it away. Thisprocess is called a Stroke (Haka'a) between the Upper Light and the screen. Because of this blow, the Reflected Light rises and dresses the 10 Sefirot of the Upper Light. The Reflected Light, dressed on the Upper Light, is becoming a vessel instead of Behina Dalet.

After this, Malchut expands in accordance with the height of the Reflected Light, then spreads downwards, thus letting the light get inside. One says that the Upper Light dresses onto the Reflected Light. This is called the "Rosh" (head) and the "Guf" (body) of each level. The Stroke Contact of the Upper Light with the screen causes the lifting of the Reflected Light. The Reflected Light dresses onto the 10 Sefirot of the Upper Light, thus forming the 10 Sefirot de Rosh.

The 10 Sefirot de Rosh are not the real vessels yet; they only pass for their roots. It is only after Malchut, with the Reflected Light, spreads downwards, that the Reflected Light turns into the vessels for the reception of the Upper Light. Then the lights dress into the vessels, called "the body" of this particular level. The real, complete vessels are called "the body".

The creation is formed as absolutely egoistic. Moreover, according to this property it is as remote as can be from the Creator. To help the creation out of such a state, the Creator fashioned in *Malchut* a desire to make *TA*, i.e., to separate *Behina Dalet* from all pure *Behinot*, leaving it absolutely empty in the space filled with nothing.

On its way to the creation, the Upper Light (*Ohr Elion*) collides with the screen, which is in front of *Behina Dalet's* desire to receive pleasure, and which completely pushes it back. This phenomenon is defined as an interaction by the stroke between the Upper Light and the screen and is called "*Haka'a*" (stroke). Divided by the screen into 10 parts, *Sefirot*, the Reflected Light, dresses onto the Upper Light, thus dividing it into 10 *Sefirot*. The combination of 10 *Sefirot* of the Reflected Light and the 10 *Sefirot* of the Upper Light forms the *Rosh* (head) of the *Partzuf* (spiritual object).

Thus the Reflected Light, i.e., the desire to return to the Creator the pleasure that one receives from Him, becomes the condition of receiving this pleasure, i.e., the vessel of reception (*Kli Kabbalah*) instead of *Behina Dalet. Behina Dalet* is unable to receive pleasure without the screen because of its egoistic desires. We see that the screen can change its intention from egoistic into altruistic, turn it into the "desire to receive" for the Creator's sake. Only after the creation builds such an intention can the higher light spread into the vessel and dress it into the desires-*Kelim*, formed by the Reflected Light.

טו) הרי שנעשו בחינת כלים חדשים בפרצופי דקדושה במקום בחי"ד אחר הצמצום א', שהם נעשו מאור חוזר של זווג דהכאה בהמסך. ויש אמנם להבין את אור חוזר הזה: איך הוא נעשה לבחינת כלי קבלה, אחר שהוא מתחילתו רק אור נדחה מקבלה, ונמצא שמשמש תפקיד הפוך מענינו עצמו?

ואסביר לך במשל מהויות דחיי העולם. כי מטבע האדם לחבב ולהוקיר מדת ההשפעה. ומאוס ושפל בעיניו מדת הקבלה מחברו. ולפיכך, הבא לבית חברו, והוא מבקשו שיאכל אצלו, הרי אפילו בעת שהוא רעב ביותר, יסרב לאכול. כי נבזה ושפל בעיניו להיות מקבל מתנה מחברו.

אכן בעת שחברו מרבה להפציר בו בשיעור מספיק, דהיינו עד שיהיה גלוי לו לעינים, שיעשה לחברו טובה גדולה עם אכילתו זו, הנה אז מתרצה ואוכל אצלו. כי כבר אינו מרגיש את עצמו למקבל מתנה, ואת חברו להמשפיע. אלא להיפך, כי הוא המשפיע ועושה טובה לחברו, ע"י קבלתו ממנו את הטובה הזאת. והנך מוצא, שהגם שהרעב והתאבון הוא כלי קבלה המיוחד

לאכילה, והאדם ההוא היה לו רעבון ותאבון במדה מספקת לקבל סעודת חברו, עכ"ז לא היה יכול לטעום אצלו אף משהו, מחמת הבושה.

אלא כשחברו מתחיל להפציר בו, והוא הולך ודוחה אותו, הרי אז התחיל להתרקם בו כלי קבלה חדשים על האכילה. כי כחות ההפצרה של חברו וכחות הדחיה שלו, בעת שהולכים ומתרבים, סופם להצטרף לשיעור מספיק, המהפכים לו מדת הקבלה למדת השפעה. עד שיוכל לצייר בעיניו, שיעשה טובה ונחת רוח גדולה לחברו עם אכילתו. אשר אז נולדו לו כלי קבלה על סעודת חבירו. ונבחן עתה, שכח הדחיה שלו נעשה לעיקר כלי קבלה על הסעודה, ולא הרעב והתאבון, אע"פ שהם באמת כלי קבלה הרגילים.

15) After the First Restriction, new vessels of reception appear in place of Behina Dalet. They are formed because of a Stroke Contact between the light and the screen. However, we still need to understand how this light turned into a vessel of reception after being the light reflected from such a vessel. It turns out that the light becomes a vessel, i.e., starts playing an opposite role.

To explain the above, let us take an example from this world. Man naturally respects a "desire to give", at the same time, he resents receiving without giving something in return. Let us suppose that a person comes to his friend's house, and is offered a meal. Naturally, he would refuse to eat no matter how hungry he may be, because he hates to be a receiver who gives nothing in return.

His host, however, starts persuading him, making it clear that by the guest's eating his food, he would please his host immensely. When the guest feels that what the host says is true, he will consent to accept the meal, since he would not feel as a receiver anymore. Moreover, now the guest feels he is giving to the host, delighting him with his readiness to eat. It turns out that in spite of his hunger - a genuine vessel of receiving food - the guest could not even touch the delicacies until his shame was placated by the host's persuasions.

Now we see how a new vessel for receiving the food comes to life. The gradually growing power of the host's persuasion and the guest's resistance finally turn reception into bestowal. The act of receiving remained unchanged; only the intention was transformed. Just the force of resistance and not hunger (the true vessel of reception) turned into the reason for accepting the treat.

Wherever *Behina Dalet* is mentioned, *Malchut* is meant, i.e., reception for the sake of reception. There is an action and the reason of this action. What is the reason for reception before the Restriction? It is the desire to receive pleasure. It means that receiving is an action for the sake of receiving. After the Restriction, the *Partzufim* do not use *Behina Dalet*; the only light received by it is that coming from the screen and the Reflected Light.

The reason for receiving that existed before the Restriction remained afterwards too, because without a desire and striving for something, it is impossible to receive. Nevertheless, this reason is not enough for reception; it should be accompanied by an additional reason i.e., the intention for the sake of bestowal.

Malchut is ready to renounce animal pleasures; it performs the Restriction on them. It receives only because it is the Creator's desire. According to that, reception for the sake of bestowal looks different. The act of receiving does not arise from the first reason, but from the second - receiving for the sake of giving; however, the first reason must accompany the second, for if there is no desire to receive pleasure, how will it be able to enjoy?

For example, there is a commandment to enjoy the Sabbath meal; but if there is no hunger, how can one receive pleasure from eating? Hence the first reason - the "desire to receive" should remain (albeit because of the shame it is unable to receive), but only in the presence of the additional reason - the "desire to give".

טז) ומדמיון הנ"ל בין אדם לחברו אפשר להבין ענין הזווג דהכאה ואת האו"ח העולה על ידו, שהוא נעשה כלי קבלה חדשים על אור העליון במקום בחי"ד. כי ענין ההכאה של אור העליון, המכה בהמסך ורוצה להתפשט אל בחי"ד, יש לדמותו לענין ההפצרה לאכול אצלו. כי כמו שהוא רוצה מאד שחברו יקבל את סעודתו, כן אור העליון רוצה להתפשט למקבל. וענין המסך, המכה באור ומחזירו לאחוריו, יש לדמותו לדבר הדחיה והסירוב של חברו לקבל את

סעודתו. כי דוחה את טובתו לאחור. וכמו שתמצא כאן, אשר דוקא הסירוב והדחיה נתהפכו ונעשו לכלי קבלה נכונים לקבל את סעודת חברו, כן תוכל לדמות לך, כי האו"ח, העולה ע"י הכאת המסך ודחיתו את אור העליון, הוא שנעשה לכלי קבלה חדשים על אור העליון, במקום הבחי"ד ששמשה לכלי קבלה מטרם הצמצום א'.

אמנם זה נתקן רק בפרצופי הקדושה דאבי"ע. אבל לא בפרצופי הקליפות ובעוה"ז, שבהם משמשת הבחי"ד עצמה לכלי קבלה. וע"כ הם נפרדים מאור העליון, כי שינוי הצורה של הבחי"ד מפריד אותם. וע"כ נבחנים הקליפות וכן הרשעים למתים, כי הם נפרדים מחיי החיים ע"י הרצון לקבל שבהם.

16) With the help of the example of the host and the guest we can now understand what a Zivug de Haka'a (Stroke Contact) is, which results in the birth of new vessels of receiving the Upper Light instead of the Behina Dalet. The interaction takes place because the light hits the screen wishing to enter the Behina Dalet. It resembles a host who tries to convince his guest to eat. The force of the guest's resistance is similar to the screen. As the refusal to eat turns into a new vessel, so does the Reflected Light become a vessel of receiving instead of the Behina Dalet, which played that role before the First Restriction.

However, we should keep in mind that it happens only in the spiritual objects of the worlds of ABYA, whereas in the objects related to the impure forces and to our world, the Behina Dalet continues to be a receiving vessel. Hence neither in the impure forces nor in our world is there any light, because of the difference between the properties of the Behina Dalet and those of the Creator. Therefore, the Klipot (impure forces, a "desire to receive" the light without the screen) and sinners are called dead, since the desire to receive the light without the screen separates them from the Life of Lives, the Creator's light.

FIVE LEVELS OF MASACH
ה' בחינות שבמסך

יז) והנה נתבאר עד הנה ג' יסודות הראשונים שבחכמה; הא' ענין אור וכלי, שהאור הוא המשכה ישרה מעצמותו ית', והכלי הוא בחינת הרצון לקבל הכלול בהכרח באור ההוא, שבשיעור הרצון הזה יצא מכלל מאציל לנאצל. והרצון לקבל הזה היא בחינת המלכות הנבחנת באור העליון, וע"כ נק' מלכות, שמו, בסוד הוא ושמו אחד, כי שמו בגימטריא רצון. ענין הב', הוא ביאור הע"ס וד' עולמות אבי"ע, שהם ד' מדרגות זו למטה מזו. שהרצון לקבל מחויב להשתלשל על ידיהן עד לקביעות כלי על תוכנו. ענין הג', הוא ענין הצמצום ומסך שנעשה על כלי הקבלה הזה שהוא בחי"ד, ותמורתו נתהוו כלי קבלה חדשים בע"ס הנק' אור חוזר. והבן ושנן היטב אלו הג' יסודות הם ונימוקיהם כפי שנתבארו לפניך, כי זולתם אין הבנה אף במלה אחת בחכמה הזו.

17) The three basic definitions are now clear to us:

1) The Ohr is a direct emanation of the Creator's light, while the Kli is a "desire to receive" created by the light. The light initially contains an unexpressed "desire to receive", but as this desire develops, the vessel (Malchut) is separated from it. Malchut is called "His Name" (Shemo) ("He and His Name are one"). The numerical value of the word "Shemo" is identical to the word "Ratzon" (desire).

2) The 10 Sefirot or the 4 worlds of ABYA correspond to the 4 Behinot (phases). They must be present in any created being. The "desire to receive", or the Kli, "descends" from the Creator's level through these 4 worlds and achieves its full development in our world.

3) The First Restriction and the Masach of Behina Dalet bring forth a new vessel instead of Behina Dalet. The vessel is an intention to bestow to the Creator, and is called "Ohr Hozer". The quantity of the received light depends on the intensity of the desire.

יח) ועתה נבאר ה' בחינות שיש בהמסך, שעל פיהם משתנים שיעורי הקומה בעת הזווג דהכאה שעושה עם אור העליון.

ויש להבין תחלה היטב, כי אע"פ שלאחר הצמצום נפסלה הבחי"ד מלהיות כלי קבלה על הע"ס, והאו"ח העולה מהמסך ע"י זווג דהכאה, נעשה לכלי קבלה בתמורתה, עכ"ז היא

מוכרחת להתלוות עם כח הקבלה שבה אל האו"ח. וזולת זה לא היה האו"ח מוכשר כלל להיות כלי קבלה.

ותבין זה ג"כ מהמשל הנ"ל באות ט"ו. כי הוכחנו שם, אשר כח הדחיה והסירוב לקבל הסעודה, נעשה לכלי קבלה במקום הרעב והתאבון. כי הרעב והתאבון, שהם כלי קבלה הרגילים, נפסלו כאן מלהיות כלי קבלה, מחמת הבושה והבזיון להיות מקבל מתנה מחברו. ורק כחות הדחיה והסירוב נעשו במקומם לכלי קבלה. כי מתוך הדחיה והסירוב נתהפכה הקבלה להיות השפעה. והשיג על ידם כלי קבלה מוכשרים לקבל סעודת חברו. ועכ"ז אי אפשר לומר, שעתה כבר אינו צריך לכלי הקבלה הרגילים, שהם הרעב והתאבון. כי זה ברור, שבלי תאבון לאכילה לא יוכל למלאות רצון חברו ולעשות לו נחת רוח עם אכילתו אצלו.

אלא הענין הוא, כי הרעב והתאבון, שנפסלו בצורתם הרגילה, נתגלגלו עתה, מחמת כח הדחיה והסירוב, וקבלו צורה חדשה, שהוא קבלה ע"מ להשפיע. ועי"ז נהפך הבזיון להיות כבוד. הרי, אשר הכלי קבלה הרגילים עדיין פועלים עתה כמו תמיד, אלא שקבלו צורה חדשה. וכן תקיש בענינינו כאן: כי אמת הוא שבחי"ד נפסלה מלהיות כלי קבלה על הע"ס, שהוא מחמת העוביות שבה. שפירושו שינוי הצורה כלפי המשפיע, המפריד מהמשפיע.

אמנם ע"י תיקון המסך בהבחי"ד, המכה על אור העליון ומחזירו לאחוריו, הנה נתגלגלה צורתה הקודמת הפסולה, וקבלה צורה חדשה, הנקראת "או"ח", בדומה לגלגול צורת הקבלה בצורת השפעה. אשר התוכן של צורה הראשונה לא נשתנה שם, כי גם עתה אינו אוכל בלי תאבון. כן גם כאן, כל העוביות, שהיא כח הקבלה שהיה בבחי"ד, נתגלגל ובא תוך האו"ח. וע"כ נעשה האו"ח מוכשר להיות כלי קבלה.

ולפיכך יש להבחין תמיד בהמסך ב' כחות: א. קשיות, שהוא כח הדחיה שבו כלפי האור העליון, ב. עוביות, שהוא שיעור הרצון לקבל מבחי"ד הנכלל בהמסך, אשר ע"י זווג דהכאה מכח הקושיות שבו, נתהפכה העוביות שבו להיות זכות, דהיינו התהפכות הקבלה להשפעה. ואלו ב' הכחות שבהמסך פועלים בה' בחינות, שהם ד' הבחינות חו"ב תו"מ, ושורשם הנקרא "כתר".

18) We will now clarify the five Behinot of the screen according to which the size of the Kli is changed during the Stroke Contact with the Upper Light.

After the First Restriction, Behina Dalet ceases to be a receiving vessel. The Reflected Light (Ohr Hozer), which rises above the screen because of the Stroke Contact, now plays that role instead. However, Behina Dalet with its powerful "desire to receive" has to accompany the Ohr Hozer. Without it, the Ohr Hozer is absolutely unable to be a vessel of reception.

Remember the situation between the host and his guest. The guest's force of refusal to eat has become a receiving vessel taking on the role of hunger, which lost that function because of shame. During that refusal, receiving actually turns into an act of giving. However, we cannot say that the guest has no need for the usual vessels of receiving. Without them, he will not be able to please the host by eating his delicacies.

By way of refusal, hunger (the "desire to receive") acquires a new form – a "desire to receive" for the sake of bestowing to the host, the Creator. Shame has now become a merit. It turns out that the usual vessels of reception keep functioning as before, but acquire a new intention, i.e., to receive for the Creator's sake. The coarseness of Behina Dalet, the state of being opposite to the Creator, prevents it now from being a receiving vessel.

However, thanks to the screen set in Behina Dalet, which hits and reflects the light, it takes a new form called the Ohr Hozer – the Reflected Light – while receiving turns into giving, as in the example with the host and the guest. Nevertheless, the essence of the form remains the same, because the guest would not eat without an appetite. Yet all the power of Behina Dalet's desire to receive pleasure is included in the Ohr Hozer, making it a proper vessel.

There are two forces always present in the screen. The first is Kashiut, the force of resistance to receiving light; the second is Aviut, the force of Behina Dalet's "desire to receive". Because of a Stroke Contact of Kashiut with the light, Aviut totally changes its properties, turning reception into bestowal. The two forces function in all five parts of the screen: Keter, Hochma, Bina, Tifferet, and Malchut.

Five parts are in the screen through which it receives the light (five *Zivugey de Haka'a*). The *Ohr Hozer* is not a genuine vessel; it can only assist in the receiving of light. The desire to receive pleasure, *Behina Dalet*, which was a vessel before the First Restriction, still retains that role; only its intention changes.

The larger man's egoism, the more light he is able to receive, provided there is a screen matching his egoism. Instead of resenting his unworthy desires, man should only ask the Creator for a screen that will correct those desires by making them altruistic.

Oftentimes we know neither what motivates our actions nor what our real desires are. Sometimes we feel a need for something but have no idea what it is. Man is in a constant dream-like state until Kabbalah wakes him up and opens his eyes. Initially we do not even possess a genuine desire to receive pleasure. Kabbalah works with the spiritual desires, which are much more powerful than those of our world are.

Thanks to the *Kli*'s new intention, the "desire to receive" obtains a new form: a "desire to bestow", or more precisely, a "desire to receive" for the sake of the Creator. Man now starts receiving in order to please the Creator. Upon discovering the difference between its own properties and the Creator's, *Behina Dalet* feels shame. The screen set up by *Malchut* reflects the light and thus changes the intention. The essence of the "desire to receive" remains, but now it is receiving for the Creator's sake.

Kabbalah is a logical science. Every phenomenon leads to a certain consequence, which in turn becomes a reason for the next, thus forming a chain of cause and effect connections. Our problem, however, consists in that we are not yet really connected to what we study. While reading about the spiritual worlds, the *Partzufim* and the *Sefirot*, we cannot yet feel them.

There are two levels in Kabbalah studies. The first is for beginners, when there is no sensation of the material studied. After further study though, a Kabbalist receives a feeling of the phenomena and terms described in the book.

One should point out that the light is actually motionless; it neither enters anything nor exits from anywhere. However, depending on its inner properties, the vessel feels the light differently, distinguishing in it different "tastes" or pleasures. If the vessel enjoys direct reception of the light, then such pleasure is called *Ohr Hochma*. If the creation receives pleasure from the likeness of its properties to those of the Creator, then this kind of delight is called *Ohr Hassadim.* The alternate reception of either *Ohr Hochma* or *Ohr Hassadim* creates "movement".

When man starts on his spiritual path, he initially realizes how evil his nature is. This thought leads him to the beginning of correction. As a result, he ascends, starts feeling more and more subtle influences of the supreme forces.

The light descending from the Creator after the First Restriction represents a narrow ray of light coming from Infinity to the central point of the universe. All spiritual worlds *(AK* and *ABYA)* are dressed onto this ray. From the point of the Creator's influence, we are at the very center of all the worlds.

The Creator's personal providence is implemented with the help of the light ray. This ray descends to a certain soul, dressing it in all the worlds, starting from *Adam Kadmon (AK),* then continuing to *Atzilut, Beria, Yetzira* and the outermost, *Assiya.*

A common person differs from a Kabbalist by the fact that he has no screen, hence he cannot feel, reflect the light, or create his own spiritual vessel. Such a vessel is *Toch,* the inner part of the *Partzuf* where the creation receives the Creator's light. Strictly speaking, what we call the Creator is His light, since we are unable to attain the Creator's Essence.

The Creator influences all people as though they had never left the world of Infinity (*Ein Sof*), i.e., they are in an unconscious state. Such an influence is called "*Derech Igulim*", with the help of circles and spheres, i.e., through the general light surrounding the entire creation. The spreading of the light in the form of a circle signifies the absence of a limiting force, the screen.

Man's task is to take into his own hands a partial control over his destiny, thereby becoming the Creator's partner. Then the Creator will no longer treat him as He does all other creatures, but individually, with the help of the light ray (*Derech Kav*). In this case, man himself takes control instead of the Creator.

יט) כי הגם שביארנו שג' בחינות הראשונות אינן נחשבות עוד לבחינת כלי, אלא רק הבחי"ד לבדה נחשבת לכלי, עכ"ז מתוך שג' בחינות הראשונות הן סבות וגורמות להשלמת הבחי"ד, באופן שהבחי"ד אחר שנשלמה, נתרשמו בה ד' שעורים במדת הקבלה שבה: החל מבחי"א, שהוא שיעור היותר קלוש שבה ממדת הקבלה, ואח"כ בחי"ב, שהיא משהו עב ביותר מבחי"א במדת הקבלה שבה.

ואח"כ בחי"ג, העבה יותר מבחי"ב במדת הקבלה שבה, ולבסוף בחי"ד, שהיא בחינתה עצמה העבה יותר מכולם, שמדת הקבלה שלה מושלמת בכל תוכנה. גם יש להבחין בה עוד, אשר גם השורש של הד' בחינות כלול בה, שהוא הזך מכולם. ואלו הן ה' בחינות הקבלה הכלולות בבחי"ד. ונקראות ג"כ בשמות הע"ס כח"ב תו"מ, הכלולות בבחי"ד. כי הד' בחינות הם חו"ב תו"מ והשורש נקרא "כתר".

19) As stated, the three first Behinot are not considered vessels yet. Only Behina Dalet is a true vessel. Since these three first Behinot are the reasons, phases preceding the creation of Behina Dalet, it adopted their properties upon completion of its development. They were somewhat imprinted in it, creating inside of Behina Dalet its own four levels of the "desire to receive". Everything begins with the Behina Aleph, the "purest", "weakest" "desire to receive". Then follows the Behina Bet, which is a bit "coarser" and has a bigger Aviut than the Behina Aleph, i.e., it is a higher level of the "desire to receive".

Behina Gimel has an Aviut even greater than that of the Behina Bet. Finally comes the turn of the Behina Dalet, which has the largest Aviut, i.e., the greatest "desire to receive". Its desire reached the highest, most perfect and ultimate level. It should be pointed out that the root (Shoresh) of these four Behinot is Keter (known as the highest of all and the closest to the Creator), which also left its imprint in Behina Dalet. Thus we mentioned all five levels of the "desire to receive" included in Behina Dalet, which are otherwise called Keter, Hochma, Bina, Tifferet and Malchut.

The three *Behinot* preceding *Malchut* are called "the light"; only *Malchut* is the *Kli*, for it wants to receive for its own sake.As a result, it becomes a separate independent part. The previous *Behinot* are not separated from the Creator; hence, they are defined as the light.

When the last phase or *Malchut* is completely filled with the light, it begins to feel the properties of all the preceding *Behinot:* first the adjacent *Tifferet,* then *Hochma,* which created *Bina,* then the source (*Shoresh*) and finally the overall Thought – *Keter.*

This means that all the previous properties of all the *Behinot* are included in *Malchut* and influence it. It is then *Dalet de Dalet* (i.e., the last part – *Dalet* of the entire *Dalet*) and all the previous properties it acquired from the light. Apprehending the light that fills it, *Behina Dalet* attains the Creator's greatness. It discovers in itself the striving to become similar to the "desire to bestow"; to the way the Creator does it.

What is "to bestow"? The Creator is the source of the light. The *Kli* cannot bestow anything; it can only intend to do so. The Creator created the "desire to receive", the rest being just different degrees of it. Only an intention can change from "for one's own sake" to "for the sake of the Creator".

What is the difference between *Aviut Keter* and *Aviut Bina?* Are they not both called "the "desire to bestow""? *Keter* is the "desire to give", *Hochma* receives, and *Bina,* upon receiving the light, returns it to the Creator. This can be understood from the example taken from the *Mishna.* "Man studies the Torah for the sake of the Creator" means that he refuses to receive anything that corresponds to *Aviut Keter.* "The Torah secrets are revealed to him" means that he did not ask for this, but received them from above – from *Behinat Hochma.*

Upon receiving, man has to overcome himself and say, "I refuse it, because all I want is to bestow". Now look what a difference it makes: man wishes to give after receiving the light or before receiving it!

כ) ומה שה' בחינות הקבלה שבבחי"ד נקראות בשם הספירות כח"ב תו"מ הוא, כי הבחי"ד מטרם הצמצום, דהיינו בעוד שהבחי"ד היתה כלי הקבלה על הע"ס הכלולות באור העליון בסוד "הוא אחד ושמו אחד", כי כל העולמות נכללים שם, נבחן שם הלבשתה להע"ס ע"פ אותן ה' הבחינות.

שכל בחינה מה' הבחינות שבה הלבישה הבחינה שכנגדה בהע"ס שבאור העליון: כי בחינת השורש שבבחינה ד' הלבישה לאור הכתר שבע"ס, ובחי"א שבבחי"ד הלבישה לאור החכמה

שבעשר ספירות, ובחי"ב שבה הלבישה לאור הבינה, ובחי"ג שבה הלבישה לאור הת"ת, ובחינתה עצמה הלבישה לאור המלכות. ולפיכך גם עתה אחר הצמצום א', אחר שהבחי"ד נפסלה מלהיות עוד כלי קבלה, נקראות ג"כ ה' בחינות העוביות שבה על שם ה' הספירות כח"ב תו"מ.

20) The five levels of the "desire to receive" included in Behina Dalet are called by the names of the 10 Sefirot of the Upper Light because Behina Dalet was a vessel receiving this light before TA ("He and His Name are One"). All the worlds, the entire Universe, was included in Behina Dalet of the Direct Light (Malchut of the world of Infinity).

Each Behina contained in Malchut adopted the properties of the corresponding Behina in the 10 Sefirot of the Upper Light. Behina Shoresh of the Behina Dalet adopted the properties of Keter, "dressed in it", one of the 10 Sefirot of the Upper Light. Behina Aleph of the Behina Dalet "dressed" into the light of Hochma of the 10 Sefirot, and so on. Even after TA, when Behina Dalet ceased to be a vessel of reception, its five levels of the "desire to receive" still bear the names of the five Sefirot: Keter, Hochma, Bina, Tifferet, and Malchut.

We are *Behina Dalet de Dalet*, whereas all the preceding four *Sefirot* are the worlds. By interacting with the worlds, we can receive their properties in order to correct the *Behina Dalet*. All the worlds are inside of us, as well as all spiritual work. Our task is to feel the Creator's light as *Malchut* did in the world of Infinity and thus get corrected.

What does it mean that *Behina Dalet* attains the properties of the preceding *Behinot*? It means that it begins to feel that, with the exception of the "desire to receive", there is also the "desire to bestow", which was absent in it. *Malchut* still wants to receive pleasure; however, it is now imbued with the "desire to give"; i.e., it now strives to receive delight from giving.

The properties and desires inside the *Kli* gradually change from a yearning for simple reception of the light to a "desire to give" everything.

These changes are caused by the light; the *Kli*'s behavior depends solely on this influence.

We study the 10 *Sefirot*, the 10 aspects of the relationship between the Creator and the creation. First, *Malchut* completely reflects the light, and then it calculates how much it can receive inside. If it worked with all its five desires, it could receive the light in all its five parts. If *Malchut* does not have enough anti-egoistic force to receive all the light for the Creator's sake, it receives only that portion out of five parts of the light for which it has a screen.

The ability to withstand the desires to receive pleasure is termed willpower. The force of resistance in the screen is called rigidity *(Kashiut)*. The intensity of the desire to receive pleasure, the passion for fulfillment, is called thickness *(Aviut)*. Inside the screen, two of *Malchut*'s properties collide: these are "reception" and the screen's anti-egoistic force of "bestowal". If my egoistic "desire to receive", has an *Aviut* that equals 100%, and a force of resistance or rigidity, that equals only 20%, then I can receive for the Creator's sake no more than 20%. Only *Kashiut* determines what amount of egoism I may use.

After *TA*, *Malchut* wants to change only the method of applying its desire. *Malchut* understands its "egoism", it realizes that the "desire to receive" is its nature. However, this property is not negative; everything depends solely on the method of its use. The sensation of the Creator's properties, of the "desire to bestow" and of the previous *Behinot* arises inside the egoistic desire *(Behina Dalet)*. Now *Malchut* only has to become like them, i.e., it must makeits desire to receive pleasure similar to theirs.

For that purpose, it pushes the entire light away from its egoism by performing *Tzimtzum* (Restriction) on itself. It then calculates to what extent it can assimilate the Creator's properties – *Behinot* 0, 1, 2, and 3.

The screen knows exactly how much light it may let in according to its egoism. The screen's *Kashiut*, its will power, the force of resisting temptation to receive pleasure, must match precisely its *Aviut*, the "desire to receive".

The memories left from the previous state of being filled with the light, which help *Malchut* calculate her future actions, are called "a record" or "a memory" (the *Reshimot*). Spiritual attainment is called investing.

כא) וכבר ידעת, שחומר המסך בכללו מתבאר בהשם "קשיות", שפירושו כמו דבר קשה מאד, שאינו מניח למי שהוא לדחוק במשהו תוך גבולו. כן המסך אינו מניח משהו מאור העליון לעבור דרכו אל המלכות, שהיא בחי"ד. שעם זה נבחן, שכל שיעור האור הראוי להתלבש בכלי המלכות, מעכב עליו המסך ומחזירו לאחוריו. גם נתבאר, שאותן ה' בחינות העביות שבבחי"ד, נכללות ובאות בהמסך ומתחברות במדת הקשיות שבו. ולפיכך נבחנים בהמסך ה' מינים של זווגים דהכאה ע"פ ה' שיעורי עביות שבו.

שזווג דהכאה על מסך שלם מכל ה' בחינות העביות, מעלה או"ח המספיק להלביש הע"ס כולן, דהיינו עד קומת כתר, וזווג דהכאה על מסך החסר מעביות דבחי"ד, שאין בו רק עביות דבחי"ג, הנה האו"ח שהוא מעלה, מספיק להלביש הע"ס רק עד קומת חכמה, וחסר מכתר.

ואם אין בו אלא עביות דבחי"ב, הנה או"ח שלו קטן יותר ואינו מספיק להלביש הע"ס רק עד קומת בינה, וחסר מכתר חכמה, ואם אין בו אלא עביות דבחי"א, הנה האו"ח שלו מוקטן יותר, ומספיק להלביש רק עד לקומת ת"ת, וחסר מכח"ב, ואם הוא חסר גם מעביות דבחי"א, ולא נשאר בו אלא עביות דבחינת שורש, הנה ההכאה שלו קלושה מאוד, ומספיק להלביש רק לקומת מלכות בלבדה, וחסר מט"ס הראשונות, שהם כח"ב ות"ת.

21) We have already learned that the screen's material is called Kashiut. It is similar to a solid body that does not allow anything to enter it. Likewise, the screen prevents the Upper Light from entering Malchut, i.e., Behina Dalet. The screen stops and reflects all the light that was destined to fill Malchut. The five Behinot of Aviut in Behina Dalet are included in the screen according to its kashiut. Hence, the screen performs five Stroke Contacts (Zivugey de Haka'a) with the light according to its five Behinot of Aviut.

The light reflected by the screen, consisting of all the five Behinot of Aviut, rises back, envelops the coming light and reaches its source, the Behina Shoresh. However, if only 4 out of 5 parts of the Aviut are present in the screen, then its Reflected Light will "see" only four portions of pleasure.

In the absence of Behinot Dalet and Gimel, the 5-th and the 4-th parts of rigidity in the screen, it can reflect the Ohr Hozer only up to the level of Bina. If there is only the Behina Aleph in the screen, then its Ohr Hozer is very small and can envelop the Direct Light only up to the level of Tifferet in the absence of Keter, Hochma, and Bina. If there is only the Behina Shoresh of Kashiut in the screen, then its resisting power is quite weak and the Ohr Hozer can envelop Malchut's coming light, while the nine first Sefirot are absent.

The screen is characterized by two properties. One of them is *Kashiut* (strength); it does not let the light enter *Malchut*. Any measure of the light that comes to the screen is pushed back and reflected.

The second property of *Masach* is its coarseness, egoism, *Aviut* (thickness). This is what can be added to the strength of the screen of *Behina Dalet* and be used for reception for the Creator's sake.

Since there are five desires for five kinds of pleasure in *Malchut*, it reflects all of them, thus avoiding the egoistic reception of pleasure.

The screen is like a curtain that I can draw when the sunlight disturbs me. In the material world, we know of what material a curtain is made. In the spiritual world, the material of the screen is called "*Kashiut*", which is its strength, hardness, or rigidity. One describes as"very hard, tough" a person who does not accept other people's opinions but sticks vehemently to his own.

The conclusion: The Creator (the "desire to bestow" delight upon created beings) prepared the "desire to receive" and wishes to fill it. However, the creation is adamant in its decision to receive nothing for its own sake. This is the purpose of the screen.

Here we need to make an important note: there is no restriction of the desire! If man sees pleasure before him, he instantly wants to receive it in full. However, he can only receive by applying the intention for the sake of bestowal; but this does not mean that the "desire to receive" the entire pleasure is absent in him. Now we can formulate a law: man makes a restriction on the pleasure he cannot refuse and receives the pleasure he can give up.

For example, man says to his body on Yom Kippur; "Know that today you must not receive food, so don't feel the hunger!" Nevertheless, his body does not listen... Why is it designed in such a way? The Creator created the "desire to receive"; therefore, it is invariable. If this desire disappears, then man is no longer alive.

Some people speak about the elimination of desires. Here is what Rabbi Israel from Ruzhin said in this connection: "He, who eliminated one desire, will receive two instead". It is impossible and unnecessary to eliminate the "desire to receive"; one should pray for an opportunity to use it with the intention for the Creator's sake.

The difference between created beings depends on the size of the "desire to receive". Someone with big aspirations is called big; someone with a small "desire to receive" is called small.

My spiritual level is determined by how completely my Reflected Light can envelop the entire Direct Light coming to me, all the pleasures anticipated by me, so that I would be able to receive them for the Creator's sake. I can be on the level of *Malchut*, *ZA*, *Bina*, or maybe even *Hochma* or *Keter*.

Malchut of the world of Infinity divides into many parts, but they all differ from one another only by the screen's properties. In the world of *Assiya*, *Malchut* is similar to the Creator in perhaps 20%, 40% in the world of *Yetzira*, 60% in the world of *Beria*, 80% in the world of *Atzilut*, and in the world of *Adam Kadmon (AK) Malchut* is 100% equal to the Creator.

The levels differ only by the strength of their screen. There is no screen in our world. Hence, we cannot feel the Creator and exist in an absolutely empty space. As soon as man acquires the screen, he already starts feeling the spiritual world on the lowest level of the world of *Assiya*. We ascend with the help of increasing the strength of the screen.

What is the transition from one spiritual level to another? It means to acquire the properties of a new, higher level. If at a certain level, man can increase his screen's magnitude; this can elevate him to the next level. The higher the level is, the more different is the sensation, the attainment of the universe.

We have said that when there are five *Behinot* of *Aviut* in the screen, the *Ohr Hozer* reaches the highest level (the light of *Keter*, *Ohr Yechida*). Then the *Kli* receives all the lights: *Keter, Hochma, Bina, Tifferet,* and *Malchut* from all the preceding *Behinot*.

In the absence of the coarsest *Behina* (*Dalet*) in the screen, i.e., the intention for the Creator's sake on the most intense desires, the highest light (*Keter, Yechida*) is also absent in the *Kli*, while the screen reaches the level of the light of *Hochma (Ohr Haya)*. In the absence of *Aviut Dalet* and *Gimel* in the screen, the lights of *Keter* and *Hochma (Ohr Yechida* and *Haya)* are absent in the *Kli*; it works with *Aviut Bet* and the light of *Bina (Ohr Neshama)*.

If the *Aviut* of the screen is *Aleph*, then the lights of *Tifferet* and *Malchut (Ohr Ruach* and *Nefesh)* are present. Finally, the screen with the *Aviut Shoresh* raises the *Ohr Hozer* only up to the level of the light of *Malchut (Ohr Nefesh)*, and only this light is present in the *Kli*. To make it easier, we usually say that the *Masach* is set before *Malchut*, although we have to understand that the *Masach* spreads over the entire *Malchut*, over all the desires of the *Kli*.

Why is the highest light missing in the absence of *Aviut Dalet*? It happens because there is an inverse relationship between the *Ohr* and the *Kli*, the light and the vessel. If the screen has a maximum *Aviut*, it raises the *Ohr Hozer* to the highest level, i.e., to the light of *Keter*. It means that with the "strongest" screen, the *Ohr Hozer* can envelop all pleasures standing before the screen and let them inside the *Partzuf*.

כב) והנך רואה איך ה' שיעורי קומות של ע"ס יוצאים ע"י ה' מיני זווג דהכאה של המסך, המשוערים על ה' בחינות עוביות שבו. ועתה אודיעך טעם הדברים, כי נודע שאין אור מושג בלי כלי.

גם ידעת שה' בחינות עוביות הללו, באות מה' בחינות העוביות שבבחי"ד, שמטרם הצמצום היו ה' כלים בהבחי"ד, שהלבישו להע"ס כח"ב תו"מ (אות י"ח), ואחר הצמצום א' נכללו בה' בחינות של המסך, אשר עם האו"ח שהוא מעלה, הם חוזרים להיות ה' כלים מבחינת או"ח על הע"ס כח"ב תו"מ, במקום הה' כלים שבבחי"ד עצמה שמטרם הצמצום.

ועל פי זה מובן מאליו, שאם יש במסך כל ה' בחינות עביות הללו, אז יש בו ה' כלים להלבשת הע"ס. אבל בעת שאין בו כל הה' בחינות, כי חסר לו העביות דבחי"ד, הרי אין בו אלא ד' כלים. וע"כ אינו יכול להלביש רק ד' אורות חו"ב תו"מ. והוא חסר מאור אחד, שהוא אור הכתר, כמו שחסר לו כלי אחד, שהוא העביות דבחי"ד.

וכמו כן בעת שחסר בו גם בחי"ג, שאין בהמסך רק ג' בחינות עביות, דהיינו רק עד בחי"ב, הרי אז אין בו רק ג' כלים. וע"כ אינו יכול להלביש רק ג' אורות, שהם בינה ת"ת ומלכות. והקומה חסרה אז מב' האורות כתר וחכמה, כמו שחסרה מב' הכלים בחי"ג ובחי"ד.

ובעת שאין בהמסך רק ב' בחינות עוביות, דהיינו מבחינת שורש ומבחי"א, הרי אין בו אלא ב' כלים. וע"כ אינו מלביש רק ב' אורות, שהם אור ת"ת ואור מלכות. ונמצאת הקומה חסרה מג' אורות כח"ב, כמו שחסרה ג' הכלים, שהם בחי"ב ובחי"ג ובחי"ד.

ובעת שאין בהמסך רק בחינה אחת דעביות, שהיא בחינת שורש העביות לבד, הרי אין לו אלא כלי אחד. לכן אינו יכול להלביש רק אור אחד, שהוא אור המלכות. וקומה זו חסרה מד' אורות כח"ב ות"ת, כמו שחסרה מד' הכלים, שהם עוביות דבחי"ד ודבחי"ג ודבחי"ב ודבחי"א.

הרי ששיעור הקומה של כל פרצוף תלוי בדיוק נמרץ בשיעור העביות שיש במסך: שהמסך דבחי"ד מוציא קומת כתר, ודבחי"ג מוציא קומת חכמה, ודבחי"ב מוציא קומת בינה, ודבחי"א מוציא קומת ת"ת, ודבחינת שורש מוציא קומת מלכות.

22) The five levels (Behinot) of the 10 Sefirot of the Reflected Light emerge because of five kinds of Zivugey de Haka'a (Stroke Contact) of the Upper Light with the five levels of the screen's Aviut. This light is not perceived or attained by anyone if there is no vessel to receive it.

These five phases emerge from five Behinot of Aviut of Behina Dalet, which were five receiving vessels of Behina Dalet before TA; they enveloped the 10 Sefirot: Keter, Hochma, Bina, Tifferet, and Malchut. After TA, these same five Behinot merge with the five Behinot of the screen, and with the help of the Reflected Light again become receiv-

ing vessels instead of the five Behinot of Behina Dalet, which played that role before TA.

Now we can understand that if the screen has all these five Behinot of Aviut, then it possesses five vessels for enveloping the 10 Sefirot, i.e., for receiving the Upper Light. If the Aviut of the Behina Dalet is absent in the screen, it has only four vessels and can receive only the four lights corresponding to Hochma, Bina, Tifferet and Malchut but cannot receive the light of Keter.

If the Aviut of Behina Gimel is absent in the screen, it has only three vessels and can receive only the three lights corresponding to Bina, Tifferet and Malchut. The lights corresponding to Keter and Hochma as well as the vessels corresponding to Behinot Gimel and Dalet are absent in it.

If the screen has only two levels of Aviut, Shoresh, and Behina Aleph, it possesses only the two vessels corresponding to the lights of Tifferet and Malchut. It turns out that such a Partzuf lacks the three lights of Keter, Hochma and Bina, as well as the three vessels corresponding to Behinot Bet, Gimel, and Dalet. If the screen has only Aviut Shoresh, then it has only one vessel with only the light of Malchut (Nefesh).

The remaining lights, Keter, Hochma, Tifferet and Malchut, are absent in it. Therefore, the size of each Partzuf depends only on the screen's Aviut (thickness). The screen with the Aviut of Behina Dalet creates a Partzuf consisting of five levels including Keter. The screen with Aviut of Behina Gimel creates a Partzuf consisting of four levels up to Hochma, and so on.

There are five levels of the desire to receive pleasure in the screen, i.e., 5 levels of anti-egoistic force of resistance to pleasure. Two of its forces, thickness (*Aviut*) and strength (*Kashiut*), must be balanced.Then *Malchut* has the freedom of will and can make its own decisions, since it is independent of its own desires and pleasures.

The *Ohr Yashar* is equal to the *Ohr Hozer*, which means that the creation wishes to bestow upon the Creator the very pleasure He prepared for it. The *Ohr Hozer* (intention) dresses, as it were, on the Creator's delight; this demonstrates that the *Kli* does not want it for itself, but returns the delight to Him.

In the absence of one more desire (the absence of the "desire to bestow" is meant and not an egoistic "desire to receive", since the latter never disappears), *Gimel*, the screen can envelop only three lights in its Reflected Light. Therefore, it will not be able "to see" the lights of *Yechida* and *Haya*. That is why we cannot feel the Creator's light in our world. Initially we do not possess the screen and the light reflected by it without which it is impossible to see or feel the Creator's light.

The amount of the Reflected Light depends on the screen's strength: the stronger the screen, the higher the level of the Reflected Light, the farther the *Kli* sees and the more it can receive for the Creator's sake. As the screen grows weaker, the *Kli* sees less and accordingly can receive less for the Creator's sake.

There are no changes in the screen. All changes are only in *Aviut*. The screen is the force of resistance to egoism; it is present in each property. The difference is in the *Aviut*, in the number of egoistic desires provided with the screen. We study only four levels of *Aviut*, since *Keter* has no *Aviut* (the "desire to receive"); it only wants to bestow.

The desire to give pleasure to the created beings – *Keter* – called forth the "desire to receive" in the lower *Sefirot*; therefore, *Keter* is a root of *Aviut*. When the lower spiritual object is unable to receive with the intention for the sake of the Creator, it uses the *Aviut* Shoresh, i.e., it can perform only acts of giving with the intention for the Creator's sake.

There are the light – pleasure, the *Kli* – the "desire to receive" and the screen – the force of resisting pleasure. The *Kli* creates the screen to become like the Creator. There is nothing else in the entire universe!

One should constantly remember this and try to interpret Kabbalah with the help of these three components.

We cannot feel any spiritual pleasures because we lack even a minimal screen. The screen's will power determines with what pleasure the Kabbalist works. After *TA* the *Kli* includes not just the "desire to receive" but also the "desire to receive" with the screen, i.e., not for self-satisfaction, but for the Creator.

When there is no screen for a certain desire, it means a Kabbalist cannot work with it, i.e., it is unfit to be filled with the light; hence we say it is absent. It does not disappear; it is just not worked with. The spiritual level (*Koma*) of a *Partzuf* depends on the intensity of desire fitted to the screen.

The opposition to the most intense desire – *Dalet*, gives birth to the *Partzuf* of the highest level – *Keter*. The opposition to the desire of the level *Gimel* gives birth to the *Partzuf* of *Hochma*, which is one step below *Keter*. The force of opposition to the desire *Bet* creates the *Partzuf* of the level of *Bina*, a step lower than the preceding one, i.e., it can liken itself to the Creator even less than with the screen *Gimel*.

If the screen can resist the desire - *Aleph*, it means that the Kabbalist's spiritual level is *Tifferet*. If it can resist the smallest desire - *Shoresh*, then it gives birth to the tiniest *Partzuf, Malchut*.

Egoistic desires should be used only to the extent of the will power to resist them. One cannot work with uncorrected desires without the screen; they should be neutralized and restricted. Desires neither appear nor disappear; they are created by the Creator. Only their use depends on man.

Everything depends on the screen's force of resistance, the intention, which turns a receiver into a giver. That is what the "game" between the Creator and the creation is all about: transforming an egoistic desire into an altruistic one, i.e., directing it towards the Creator.

All desires are in *Malchut* of the world of Infinity; it uses them in accordance with the screen, which emerges in it in each case. There are screens with the help of which *Malchut* builds worlds and those that form various *Partzufim*. Certain types of screens promote the appearance of souls. These are all parts of *Malchut* of the world of Infinity.

Giving up a certain pleasure is easier than receiving it from someone who gives it to you. One can always receive less light for the sake of the Creator than one can give up. Or one can choose not to "work" with it at all.

If a *Kli* decides to receive egoistically, i.e., has a desire without a screen, the light first approaches the *Kli* (the *Kli* attracts the light), but as soon as the light wishes to get inside it, the law of *TA* snaps into action and the light retreats.

When *Malchut* or the world of Infinity performed *TA*, the Creator accepted this law. Hence, we cannot openly use our egoism. We are under the influence of this law; therefore, we cannot feel any spiritual pleasures until we succeed in creating a screen for them.

In addition, what are the pleasures of this world? They constitute the micro-dose of the light (the *Ner Dakik*) of the entire *Malchut* of the world of Infinity, which was allowed to be felt by us and can exist outside *TA*. Transcending this world is possible only through acquiring the screen.

If there is the screen for a greater pleasure, then it is also available for a smaller one. In order to stop receiving delight for oneself, one should add an intention to that pleasure (the *Ohr Hozer*) and receive it for the sake of the Giver.

Movement in the spiritual world occurs only because of a strengthening or weakening of the screen. The entire creation, *Malchut* of the world of Infinity, gradually acquires the screen for all of its desires. When all of *Malchut's* desires are fitted with the screen, it will achieve the state of "the Final Correction" (the *Gmar Tikkun*). This is the meaning of all of creation's actions.

The creation of the screen, its interaction with the light, the *Ohr Hozer* enveloping the light, is called "a commandment", a *Mitzvah*. The received light is called "the Torah". Overall there are 620 levels, steps, measures of the screen's interaction with the light so as to receive all the light particles in all *Malchut's* desires. When *Malchut* is completely filled with the Creator's light, it means it has received the entire Torah and has achieved perfection.

כג) אמנם עוד נשאר לבאר: למה בחוסר כלי מלכות בהמסך, שהוא בחי"ד, הוא נחסר מאור הכתר? ובחוסר גם כלי הת"ת, נחסר מאור חכמה וכו'? ולכאורה היה צריך להיות בהיפך: שבחוסר כלי מלכות במסך, שהיא בחי"ד, יחסר בקומה רק אור מלכות, ויהיו בה ד' אורות לכח"ב ות"ת? וכן בחוסר ב' כלים בחי"ג ובחי"ד, יחסרו האורות מת"ת ומלכות, ויהיה בקומה ג' אורות לכח"ב? וכו' עד"ז.

> *23) We need to understand why, in the absence of the vessel of Malchut, the light of Keter is missing, and why the light of Hochma is missing when the vessel of Tifferet is also absent.On the face of it, everything should be the other way around.If the Aviut of the Behina Dalet is absent in the screen, then the light of Malchut (Nefesh) should be missing. If two vessels are absent –Behina Gimel and Behina Dalet - the lights of Tifferet and Malchut should also be missing.*

Supposedly, if there is no force of resistance for the greatest desire *(Malchut)*, then the light of *Malchut* should presumably be missing, i.e., the light that fills this desire. Then why do we claim that the greatest light *(Keter)* is missing in this case? Is this not the light, which fills *Behina Keter?*

This can be explained by the inverse relationship between the light and the vessel, i.e., first the smallest desire *(Keter)* is filled with the smallest light of *Malchut (Nefesh)*, so far unrelated to the formed *Kli* and temporarily taking its place. However, as the desire gradually grows, or rather by acquiring the screen for more desires, greater lights fill the *Kli Keter.* Meanwhile *Hochma, Bina, Tifferet,* and *Malchut are* filled with the various lights until *Malchut* is finally filled with the light of *Nefesh* and *Keter* - with the light of *Yechida.*

כד) והתשובה היא, כי יש תמיד ערך הפכי בין אורות לכלים. כי מדרך הכלים הוא, שהכלים העליונים נגדלים תחילה בפרצוף. שמתחלה נגדל הכתר, ואחריו הכלי דחכמה וכו', עד שכלי המלכות נגדל באחרונה.

וע"כ אנו מכנים לכלים בסדר כח"ב תו"מ מלמעלה למטה, כי כן טבע גידולם. והפכי אליהם האורות, כי באורות, האורות התחתונים נכנסים תחלה בפרצוף. כי מתחילה נכנס הנפש, שהוא אור המלכות, ואח"כ הרוח, שהוא אור הז"א וכו', עד שאור היחידה נכנס באחרונה.

וע"כ אנו מכנים לאורות בסדר נרנח"י ממטה למעלה, כי כן סדר כניסתם מתתא לעילא. באופן, בעת שעוד לא נגדל בפרצוף רק כלי אחד, שהוא בהכרח כלי העליון כתר, הנה אז לא נכנס בפרצוף אור היחידה, המיוחס לכלי ההוא, אלא רק אור התחתון מכולם, שהוא אור הנפש, ואור הנפש מתלבש בכלי דכתר.

וכשנגדלו ב' כלים בפרצוף, שהם ב' העליונים כתר וחכמה, הנה אז נכנס בו גם אור הרוח, ויורד אז אור הנפש מכלי דכתר אל כלי דחכמה, ואור הרוח מתלבש בכלי דכתר. וכן כשנגדל כלי ג' בפרצוף, שהוא כלי הבינה, אז נכנס בו אור נשמה. ואז יורד אור הנפש מכלי דחכמה לכלי דבינה, ואור הרוח לכלי דחכמה, ואור הנשמה מתלבש בכלי דכתר.

וכשנגדל בפרצוף כלי ד', שהוא כלי דת"ת, הנה נכנס בפרצוף אור החיה. ואז יורד אור הנפש מכלי דבינה לכלי דת"ת, ואור הרוח לכלי דבינה, ואור הנשמה לכלי דחכמה, ואור החיה בכלי דכתר.

וכשנגדל כלי חמישי בפרצוף, שהוא כלי מלכות, נכנס בו אור היחידה. ואז באים כל האורות בכלים המיוחסים להם. כי אור הנפש יורד מהכלי דת"ת לכלי דמלכות, ואור הרוח לכלי דת"ת, ואור הנשמה לכלי דבינה, ואור החיה לכלי דחכמה, ואור היחידה לכלי דכתר.

24) The fact is that there is an inverse relationship between the lights and the vessels. First, the higher vessels emerge and start growing in the Partzuf, from Keter and down to Hochma and so on until Malchut.

Hence we call the vessels according to the order of their growth: Keter, Hochma, Bina, Tifferet and Malchut (KaHaB-TuM), from up downwards. The lights enter the Partzuf in an opposite order, first the lower ones: the lowest light – Nefesh (its place is inside Malchut), then Ruach (Zeir Anpin's light) and so on until Yechida.

Hence, we name the lights in the following order: Nefesh, Ruach, Neshama, Haya and Yechida (NaRaNHaY), from down upwards, according to the order of their entering into the Partzuf. When the Partzuf has only one vessel (this can be only Keter), the first light to enter it is not Yechida, which must be inside it, but Nefesh, the lowest light.

When two higher vessels, Keter and Hochma, emerge in the Partzuf, then the light Ruach also enters it. The light Nefesh exits the vessel Keter and descends to the vessel Hochma, whereas the light Ruach enters the vessel Keter. When the third vessel Bina emerges in the Partzuf, the light Nefesh exits the vessel Hochma and descends to the vessel Bina, while the light Ruach descends to the vessel Hochma and the light Neshama enters the vessel Keter.

When the fourth vessel Tifferet emerges in the Partzuf, the light Haya enters it; the light Nefesh exits the vessel Bina and descends to the vessel Tifferet. While the light Ruach descends to the vessel Bina, the light Neshama enters the vessel Hochma and the light Haya enters the vessel Keter.

When the fifth vessel Malchut emerges in the Partzuf, the light Yechida enters it. All the lights are now in their places, since the light Nefesh exits the vessel Tifferet, and descends to the vessel Malchut, while the light Ruach descends to the vessel Tifferet, the light Neshama enters the vessel Bina, the light Haya enters the vessel Hochma, and the light Yechida enters the vessel Keter.

When the Partzuf consisting of five parts of the "desire to receive" (the Kelim Keter, Hochma, Bina, Tifferet and Malchut) is filled with the light, Nefesh is in Malchut, Ruach is in Tifferet, Neshama is in Bina, Haya is in Hochma and Yechida is in Keter. This is what a completely filled Partzuf looks like.

However, the formation, i.e., correction of the *Kelim*, their acquiring the screen, occurs from the most unselfish (*Keter*) to the most egoistic (*Malchut*) from up downwards. Their filling with the lights starts from the weakest one (*Nefesh*) to the most intense pleasure (*Yechida*).

Gradually, all the lights first enter *Keter*, one after the other. The filling of the *Partzuf* always occurs in the following order: *Keter – Hochma – Bina – Tifferet – Malchut*.The lights enter in the following order: *Nefesh – Ruach – Neshama – Haya – Yechida*. The rule states: the *Kli* starts growing from the uppermost *Sefira*, while the lights enter from the lowest one. It is similar to two cylinders entering one another.

According to the order of their entering the *Partzuf* from *Nefesh* to *Yechida*, the lights are abbreviated *NaRaNHaY*, from the smallest to the largest; while the *Kelim* are abbreviated according to their descending order *KaHaB-TuM*.

We see the same occurrence in our life: if I want to resist some pleasure while remaining somehow connected to it, I always start from the smallest one, gradually passing to more and more intense delights, until I am quite sure that even the biggest pleasures I can receive are not for my own sake.

When we say that a new *Kli* is born, it means that there is a screen for the corresponding pleasure, the force of resisting this delight, the intention to receive for the Creator's sake. Consequently, the *Partzuf* is being filled with the light that matches the opposing force.

The screen appears as a result of focused studies and work in a group with the proper intention. When a Kabbalist acquires a screen for the smallest desire, he only works with it. The rest of his desires are simply put aside and restricted. Because of man's efforts, the screen grows stronger, i.e., an additional force of resisting a bigger desire emerges and man starts working with two desires and receives two lights.

This continues until there is a screen for all five desires, when all the lights can be received for the sake of the Creator. Every time a man can work with new desires, the preceding ones come nearer to perfection, for along with the light that was in it, a new more powerful light enters bringing greater pleasure.

If a person, who consistently studies in a group of like-minded people and listens to the Teacher's explanations, can afterwards concentrate on the same spiritual matters, while being in various states and circumstances of our world, then the next time he comes to study he will feel more than the previous time. He will receive a higher light, for he now works with purer *Kelim* and does not think about animal pleasures. This is what the inverse relationship between the *Ohrot* and the *Kelim* (the lights and the vessels) means.

The land of Israel differs from all other places by its highest level of egoism. It is the most difficult place for the spiritual work. However, at the same time, it is unique and most favorable.

This land has a special spiritual potential. The Baal HaSulam wrote that Jerusalem is a place of the destruction of the Temple. The most powerful force is present there, but so are the mightiest impure forces, the *Klipot.*

Is the *Kli Keter*, the *Aviut de Shoresh*, designed for the smallest or the biggest pleasure? – It is meant for the biggest delight – the *Ohr Yechida*, which enters *Keter* last, when the *Masach* gets strong enough to oppose the most intense desire of *Malchut. In other words,* by working with the lowest desires, creating for them the intention to receive pleasure for the Creator's sake, the Kabbalist receives the greatest delight – the *Ohr Yechida*, which enters the purest *Kli Keter.*

If, by filling his coarsest animal desires, man can think about the Creator and the Purpose of Creation, then while learning, studying Kabbalistic texts and also by praying, he will surely establish better contact with the Creator.

There are five desires to receive pleasure in the *Kli.* Its "size" or "volume" depends only on the screen. The level of desire it can resist determines the light that will enter the *Kli*, i.e., the *Kli*'s level. First, one works with the *Kli* of *Aviut de Shoresh* and gradually creates the screen for *Aviut Aleph.*

When this process is over, you will be able to receive the same screen for *Aviut Aleph* and work with it. Next, little by little, you create a screen for *Aviut Bet, Gimel,* and *Dalet.* The *Kli* with the initial *Aviut Shoresh* must have rudiments of the screen for all the five *Behinot*, to build the screen for all these kinds of *Aviut.*

The *Kli* gradually builds itself going from the tiniest desires to the biggest. It happens in this order to avoid the egoistic reception of pleasure. The desires are measured according to the intensity of the pleasure felt. That is how humankind progresses from small desires to bigger ones.

Beginning to work with the smallest desire (*Keter*), man transforms it into an altruistic one with the help of the screen. Then he receives the light *Nefesh*, feeling great pleasure, because the Creator is partially revealed in it, i.e., according to the size of the *Kli's* correction, he becomes equal to the Creator.

The *Ohr Nefesh* is a delight of being united with the Creator in the smallest, fifth part, where one is able to feel eternity, wisdom, absolute knowledge, exquisite delight and perfection.

Such a state of the *Kli* means transcending the bounds of our world, our nature. So far, the *Kli* is unable to see beyond that state. Nevertheless, as it develops further, it starts feeling more and more perfect states, receiving greater and greater pleasures.

Man's reception of *Ohr Nefesh* means reception of all five parts of that light: *Nefesh de Nefesh, Ruach de Nefesh, Neshama de Nefesh, Haya de Nefesh, and Yechida de Nefesh* ("*de*" means "of"). Any *Kli*, any reception, also consists of five parts. It is similar to the way we receive information in this world through our five senses: sight, hearing, smell, taste and touch.

All these five lights must manifest in the *Kli Keter*, where the light *Nefesh* enters first. The same happens with the rest of the lights. All external religious trappings just hint at spiritual actions. Great Kabbalists in each generation introduced certain rules into the life of the religious masses to bind them to the Torah and thus educate them.

For example, there is the tradition of putting on two robes, which symbolizes the two types of "*Levushim*" (clothes) that dress the soul in the world of *Atzilut*. All these religious rituals have a Kabbalistic meaning.

The principal spiritual law is the equivalence of man's properties, his desires, with those of the Creator.

The Creator's light is homogeneous by nature. A certain *Kli*, depending on its inner parameters, distinguishes in the homogeneous light various "tastes", i.e., different kinds of pleasure: the *Ohr Yashar,* the *Ohr Hozer,* the *Ohr Elion,* the *Ohr Pnimi,* the *Ohr Makif,* etc. This is the same light; everything depends on how the *Kli* perceives it. Prior to entering the *Kli,* it is called the simple Upper Light (the *Ohr Elion Mufshat*), since no diversity of properties can be distinguished in it.

This resembles the Baal HaSulam's example about the heavenly manna, which has no taste, whereas everyone senses the taste that corresponds to his properties. If the simple Upper Light shines in the head of the *Partzuf,* it is called "the *Ohr Yashar*" (the Direct Light). The light reflected by the screen (the *Ohr Hozer)* envelops *the Ohr Yashar,* and when they both enter the *Kli,* this light receives another name – the *Ohr Pnimi* (the Inner Light) or *Ta'amim* (tastes).

Since the *Partzuf* receives only a certain portion of the coming light, the uncollected part of it is left outside of the *Kli.* This part of the light is called "the *Ohr Makif*" (the Surrounding Light). The *Partzuf* will gradually receive this light in small portions. The state in which the entire Surrounding Light will be able to enter the *Partzuf* is called *Gmar Tikkun* (the Final Correction).

The light exiting the *Kli* is called "*Nekudot*" – points, because *Malchut* is called a point, a black point, due to its egoistic properties, which are unable to receive the light after *TA.* Upon filling the *Partzuf* with the Inner Light, the Surrounding Light presses on the screen in the *Tabur,* so that the *Kli* might receive the light left outside.

However, the *Partzuf* does not have the proper *Masach* for this light. Hence, if it receives it (it already lacks the intention for the Creator's sake), such a reception will be egoistic. Since the restriction on receiving the light is a consequence of *Malchut's* egoistic desire (the black point), the light exiting *Malchut* is called *"Nekudot"*.

When the Inner Light exits the *Partzuf* and shines on it from afar, it provokes a special sensation, an impression inside the *Kli*, called recollections (*Reshimot*). These recollections constitute the vital information without which the *Partzuf* cannot know what to do next.

כה) הרי שכל עוד שלא נגדלו כל ה' הכלים כח"ב תו"מ בפרצוף, נמצאים האורות שלא במקומם המיוחס להם. ולא עוד, אלא שהם בערך ההפכי, שבחוסר כלי מלכות חסר שם אור היחידה, ובחוסר ב' הכלים תו"מ חסרים שם יחידה חיה, וכו'. שהוא מטעם שבכלים נגדלים העליונים תחילה, ובהאורות נכנסים האחרונים תחילה.

גם תמצא, שכל אור הבא מחדש, הוא מתלבש רק בכלי דכתר. והוא מטעם, שכל המקבל מחויב לקבל בהכלי היותר זך שבו, שהוא הכלי דכתר. ומטעם זה מחויבים האורות, שכבר מלובשים בפרצוף, לרדת מדרגה אחת ממקומם, בעת ביאת כל אור חדש. למשל בביאת אור הרוח, מחויב אור הנפש לירד מהכלי דכתר לכלי דחכמה, כדי לפנות מקום הכלי דכתר, שיוכל לקבל את האור החדש, שהוא הרוח.

וכן אם האור החדש הוא נשמה, מחויב גם הרוח לרדת מהכלי דכתר לכלי דחכמה, לפנות מקומו דכתר לאור החדש שהוא נשמה. ומשום זה מחויב הנפש, שהיה בכלי דחכמה, לרדת לכלי דבינה. וכו' עד"ז. וכל זה הוא כדי לפנות הכלי דכתר בשביל אור החדש.

ושמור הכלל הזה בידך. ותוכל להבחין תמיד בכל ענין, אם מדברים בערך כלים ואם בערך אורות. ואז לא תתבלבל, כי יש תמיד ערך הפכי ביניהם. והנה נתבאר היטב ענין ה' בחינות שבמסך, איך שעל ידיהן משתנים שיעורי הקומה זה למטה מזה.

25) Until the formation of all the five Kelim in the Partzuf has been completed, their five lights are not in their places; moreover, they are arranged in an inverse order. In the absence of the Kli Malchut, the light Yechida is missing in the Partzuf. In the absence of the two vessels Malchut and Tifferet, there are no lights Yechida and Haya. On the one hand, the pure vessels are born, from Keter to Malchut; on the other hand, the weaker lights (starting from Nefesh) are the first to enter them.

Since any reception of the light occurs in the purest vessels, each new light must enter the Kli Keter. As the new light enters the Kli Keter, the light that was there descends to the Kli Hochma. When there is a Masach for the vessel Hochma, Ohr Ruach enters the Kli Keter and the Ohr Nefesh descends to Hochma.

As the screen grows stronger, the following vessels are formed: Bina, Tifferet and Malchut, and the lights Neshama, Haya, and Yechida are able, one by one, to pass through Keter and fill all the vessels. All the lights enter their rightful places: Nefesh in Malchut, Ruach in Tifferet, Neshama in Bina, Haya in Hochma and Yechida in Keter.

Remember this rule about the inverse relationship between the lights and vessels, and you will always be able to distinguish whether the lights or the vessels are meant in a certain context without getting confused. We have learned about the five Behinot (levels) of the screen and how the levels of the Kli emerge one under the other in correspondence with them.

Each new light is billions of times more intense than the preceding one. Hence, each subsequent level is perceived as a totally different world. In our world, where we have no screen at all, we cannot see the light that is before us. One can only see with the help of the Reflected Light (the *Ohr Hozer)* and only to the extent of *Malchut's* reflecting it.

However, by studying Kabbalah we stimulate the *Ohr Makif* until it creates in us the primary *Kli Keter,* where we will instantly receive the *Ohr Nefesh.* This state signifies our spiritual birth, crossing the barrier (the *Machsom*) between our world and the spiritual one. It means we are on the lowest level of the world of *Assiya.*

By continuing to work on our correction, we acquire the next screen of the *Aviut Aleph* and receive the light *Ruach.* Next, we acquire the screens for the *Kelim Bet, Gimel,* and *Dalet* and accordingly receive the lights *Neshama, Haya,* and *Yechida.* Now all the lights are in their correct places.

How can we set up a screen? If I could know and feel my egoistic properties today, I would run away from the corrections! There is nothing my egoism hates more than the screen. Nevertheless, I cannot escape the spiritual for the reason that I am unaware of my own egoism or do not understand my properties. Such an "unconscious" initial state is deliberately created that we may not resent spirituality, but that we may aspire to it out of a curiosity and desire to improve our future.

Therefore, the principle consists in crossing the barrier in spite of our own nature. It happens unconsciously; man does not know what he is heading for or when it might happen. After crossing the *Machsom*, man begins to see that, until that moment, he was in a dream-like state.

Two processes precede the crossing of the Machsom, the first being a comprehension of one's own evil. Man begins to understand how harmful his egoism is for him. The second process consists in the realization that spirituality is very attractive, and there is nothing more worthwhile, magnificent, or eternal than that.

These two opposite points (realization of the evil and attraction of the spiritual) come together in the common person to create a zero level. As they advance spiritually, they begin to move away from one another. At the same time, spirituality gets elevated in man's eyes, while his egoism is perceived as evil.

This difference between them, one's own appraisal of the spiritual and criticism of egoism, increase so tremendously that it evokes one's inner outcry, a request about a solution to the problem. If this outcry reaches the required intensity, the screen is given to one from above.

The study of egoism, its correction and proper use, constitutes man's entire journey from the initial state to the ultimate end (the *Gmar Tikkun*). In the spiritual worlds, man continues to study his egoism on each level. The higher we ascend, the more egoism is added to us, so that by working with it, we are able to turn it into altruism.

Everything we say is seen from the point of view of the creation. We cannot say anything about the Creator, since we do not really know who He is. On a personal level, I just know how He is perceived in my sensations. Only philosophers have the time to speculate about something that can never be attained. Hence, this science has completely degenerated.

Kabbalah operates only with what the Kabbalists sensed and quite distinctly drew upon themselves and related to us in a special Kabbalistic language. Everyone can reproduce that process internally as in a strict scientific experiment.

The instrument of such an experiment is the screen that man must create in the central point of his own egoism; this "I" develops with the help of the method called Kabbalah.

There are two kinds of screen. The first is positioned in front of the *Kli* in the *Peh de Partzuf*, i.e., in *Malchut de Rosh*. It reflects the entire light, as if standing guard over the implementation of *TA*. The second screen receives the light; it works with the *Aviut* that is positioned in *Malchut de Guf*. It absorbs all the egoism that can be transformed into reception for the sake of the Creator.

Generally, the screen is always in *Malchut*, the lowest point of the *Partzuf*. Reflection and reception are two of its actions. The first forms *Rosh* while the second forms the *Guf* of the *Partzuf*. For further details, see Part 3 ("*Histaklut Pnimit*"), chapter 14, p. 5 of "The Study of the Ten Sefirot".

THE FIVE PARTZUFIM OF THE WORLD ADAM KADMON

ה' פרצופי א"ק

כו) אחר שנתבאר היטב ענין המסך שנתקן בכלי המלכות, שהיא הבחי"ד אחר שנצטמצמה, וענין ה' מיני זווג דהכאה אשר בו, המוציאים ה' קומות של ע"ס זו למטה מזו, נבאר עתה ה' פרצופי א"ק, הקודמים לד' עולמות אבי"ע.

וזאת כבר ידעת, שהאו"ח הזה, שעולה ע"י זווג דהכאה ממטה למעלה ומלביש הע"ס דאור העליון, הוא מספיק רק לשרשי כלים, המכונים "ע"ס דראש הפרצוף". ובכדי לגמור את הכלים, מתרחבת המלכות דראש מאותם הע"ס דאו"ח שהלבישו לע"ס דראש.

והיא מתפשטת מינה ובה ממעלה למטה, באותו שיעור קומה שבעשר ספירות דראש. ובהתפשטות הזה נגמרו הכלים, שהם נקראים "גוף הפרצוף". באופן שב' בחינות של ע"ס יש להבחין תמיד בכל פרצוף: ראש וגוף.

26) We clearly understand the notion of the Masach (screen), placed over the Kli Malchut (Behina Dalet) after TA, and also the five kinds of Zivugeyde Haka'athat occur on this screen to create five levels of 10 Sefirot, one beneath the other. Now we shall learn about the five Partzufim of the world of Adam Kadmon (AK) that precedes the four worlds of ABYA.

We know that the Ohr Hozer that rises as a result of the Zivug de Haka'a dresses the 10 Sefirot of the Upper Light; this is sufficient only to create "the roots" of the future Kelim defined as the 10 Sefirot de Rosh .

Malchut spreads from up downwards, according to the height of the level of the 10 Sefirot de Rosh. It results in the creation of the Kelim called "Guf"(body) of the Partzuf (see §14). Therefore, there are always two kinds of the 10 Sefirot in the Partzuf: the Rosh and the Guf.

In each *Partzuf*, two kinds of the 10 *Sefirot* should be determined: the *Rosh* and the *Guf*. Those who do not know Hebrew find it much easier to study Kabbalah, because they do not take literally such Kabbalistic terms as *Peh*-mouth, *Rosh*-head, *Guf*-body, *Tabur*-navel etc. They can understand them abstractedly, and such people do not make a materialistic picture out of these terms.

These students easily perceive all the above-mentioned terms as forces, desires, intentions, not as body parts. There are no bodies in the spiritual world, only the desire to receive pleasure, the intention for the sake of what or whom one can receive this pleasure, and the pleasure itself.

The place where the reflecting *Masach* resides is called the *Peh*. At first, the *Masach* pushes away all the *Ohr Yashar* that is before it, as if to say it does not want to receive anything for its own sake. Then a calculation is made in the *Rosh* to determine how much can be received anyway, not for its own sake, but for the sake of the Creator. Then, the *Ohr Hozer* dresses the 10 *Sefirot* of the Upper Light *(de Ohr Elion)* from down upwards.

It is sufficient only for making a clear decision; the vessel roots *(Shorshey Kelim)*. The 10 *Sefirot* of the Reflected Light that dress the 10 *Sefirot* of the Direct Light together form the 10 *Sefirot* of the *Rosh* of the *Partzuf*.

To complete the formation of the *Kelim* and truly receive the light, the 10 *Sefirot de Ohr Yashar* dress into the 10 *Sefirot de Ohr Hozer*. They "pass" through the *Masach*, spread from up downwards, thus widening the tenth *Sefira* of the *Rosh* - *Malchut de Rosh* for its own 10 *Sefirot* - from *Keter* to *Hochma* and forming the *Kelim de Guf* .

Before *Malchut* could receive for the sake of the Creator, it was compressed, restricted to the size of a point. Nevertheless, by receiving the screen, it acquired a new intention to receive for the sake of the Creator, and then it "expanded" from a point to the 10 *Sefirot*, receiving the light into the *Guf*.

כז) והנה תחילה יצא הפרצוף הראשון דא"ק. כי תיכף אחר צמצום א', אשר הבחי"ד נצטמצמה מלהיות כלי קבלה על אור העליון, והיא נתקנה במסך, הנה אז נמשך אור העליון להתלבש בכלי מלכות כדרכו. והמסך שבכלי מלכות עיכב עליו והחזיר את האור לאחוריו. וע"י הכאה זו שהיתה ממסך דבחי"ד, העלה או"ח עד קומת כתר שבאור העליון. ואותו או"ח נעשה ללבוש ובחינת שורשי כלים לע"ס שבאור העליון, הנקרא "ע"ס דראש" של הפרצוף הראשון דא"ק.

ואח"ז התרחבה והתפשטה המלכות ההיא עם האו"ח, מכח ע"ס דראש, מינה ובה, לע"ס חדשות ממעלה למטה. ואז נגמרו הכלים בבחינת הגוף. וכל שיעור הקומה, שיצא בע"ס דראש, נתלבש ג"כ בהע"ס דגוף. ובזה נגמר הפרצוף הא' דא"ק ראש וגוף.

27) As soon as the first Partzuf of the world of Adam Kadmon is born, after TA, Behina Dalet immediately stopped being a Kli for receiving the Upper Light, being thus corrected by way of the screen. The Upper Light descended to be dressed in the Kli Malchut according to its nature.

However, the screen, which positioned itself before Malchut, reflected and returned it to the Source. Because of this Stroke Contact, the Ohr Hozer ascended to the level of Keter de Ohr Elion. This Ohr Hozer has become the embryo of the vessels ("the Shorshey Kelim") for the 10 Sefirot de Rosh of the first Partzuf of Adam Kadmon.

Afterwards, by using the power of the 10 Sefirot de Rosh, Malchut de Rosh together with Ohr Hozer expanded and spread from up downwards, thus creating inside itself 10 new Sefirot, which are true and complete Kelim. All that potentially existed in the Rosh has finally manifested and taken form in the Guf. Thus, the creation of the Rosh and the Guf of the first Partzuf of the world Adam Kadmon was completed.

After TA, when *Malchut* made a restriction on reception of the light, it decided to receive a portion of it with the help of the screen for the sake of the Creator. The first reception formed the first *Partzuf* of the world of *Adam Kadmon* (*Keter* or *Galgalta*). Overall, there are five *Partzufim* in the world of *Adam Kadmon*.

The *Masach* in the *Kli Malchut* pushed away the entire Upper Light. With the help of a stroke (*Haka'a*) into the *Masach*, whose force was equal to all five *Behinot*, the Reflected Light (the *Ohr Hozer*) rose to the level of *Keter* of the Direct Light (the *Ohr Yashar*) and dressed the 10 *Sefirot de Rosh* of the first *Partzuf* of AK. Then *Malchut* expanded, and the light spread inside it, forming the 10 *Sefirot de Guf.*

The part of the *Kli* (*Guf*), which was filled with the light, is called the *Toch* (the inner part), and the light in it is called "the *Ohr Pnimi*" – the Inner Light. The part of the *Guf* that remained empty is called the *Sof* (end), and the light in it is called the *Ohr Hassadim.*

This part refuses to receive any pleasure, because it does not have a proper screen; so if it receives the light, this will lead to the reception of pleasure for its own sake. The boundary separating the *Toch* and the *Sof* is called the *Tabur* (navel). The light that has not entered the *Kli* is called the *Ohr Makif* (the Surrounding Light).

Each *Partzuf* sees what light is in front of it only with the help of the Reflected Light. If the power of the Reflected Light equals the power of the screen on all five *Behinot,* it can see the light of *Keter.* It divides this light into five parts, fills the *Toch* with them, leaving the *Sof* empty. Light of any intensity can shine in the *Rosh* of *Partzuf,* but *Malchut de Peh de Rosh* will see only as much as the *Ohr Hozer* allows it to.

Our senses are based on the same principle. Make them more sensitive and they will see micron-sized objects, feel microbes etc. In other words, everything depends not on what really surrounds us, but on whatever we are able to detect, on the perceptibility of our sensors.

Each subsequent *Partzuf* has a screen of a smaller quantity and quality of desires (*Behinot*) than the preceding one; therefore, its *Ohr Hozer* is smaller and it sees the light of a lower level. It resembles a person whose eyesight has deteriorated and who can see objects only at a short distance.

If the screen has the strength of the *Behina Gimel,* it can see the light of the level of *Hochma* as regards the preceding *Partzuf.* Regarding itself, it receives the same five parts of the light of *NaRaNHaY,* but of the general level of *Hochma,* not *Keter.* Let us take the example of this world: a tall person and a short one naturally consist of the same "parts". However, we say that one of them is a whole head taller than the other, i.e., the latter is, as it were, short by a head.

We study the descending worlds. When the Universe came into being, the *Partzuf Adam HaRishon* (the First Man) was created. Then this *Partzuf* split into 600,000 fragments called souls. Each of these fragments has to receive its part of the Upper Light.

When the soul, i.e., a fragment of the *Partzuf Adam HaRishon,* reaches a certain level in the spiritual world, it receives a little of its part of the light. Although it has not yet received the entire light assigned to it, the soul perceives this state as absolutely perfect. Then a little more egoism is added to it (the soul) and again it begins to wish for more. By correcting this portion of egoism, it receives a new portion of the light in the newly corrected vessels, and only then realizes that there is a greater perfection to be attained.

If a man lacks this inner desire, the need or point in his heart, he is unable to understand how one can be interested in spirituality. By the way, fortune telling, amulets, alternative medicine and blessings have nothing to do with spirituality. Kabbalah interprets the spiritual as the aspiration for the Creator, His properties. In fact, we always discover that whatever seemed supernatural to us turns out to be the work of more or less talented frauds who use the forces of our world unknown to most people, as well as psychology and the inner powers of the human body.

כח) ואח"ז חזר ונשנה אותו הזווג דהכאה על מסך המתוקן שבכלי מלכות, שאין בו רק עביות דבחי"ג. ואז יצא עליו רק קומת חכמה. ראש וגוף. כי מתוך שחסר במסך העביות דבחי"ד, אין בו רק ד' כלים כח"ב ת"ת. וע"כ אין מקום באו"ח להלביש רק ד' אורות לבד, שהם חנר"נ, וחסר בו אור היחידה. ונקרא "ע"ב דא"ק".

ואח"כ חזר אותו הזווג דהכאה הנ"ל על מסך שבכלי מלכות, שאין בו רק עביות דבחי"ב. ואז יצאו עליו ע"ס ראש וגוף בקומת בינה. והוא נקרא פרצוף "ס"ג דא"ק", שחסרים בו ב' הכלים דז"א ומלכות וב' האורות דחיה יחידה.

ואח"כ יצא הזווג דהכאה על מסך שאין בו רק עביות דבחי"א. ואז יצאו ע"ס ראש וגוף בקומת ת"ת. וחסרים בו ג' כלים בינה ז"א ומלכות, וג' אורות נשמה חיה יחידה, ואין בו אלא רוח ונפש מהאורות, המלובשים בכתר חכמה דכלים. והוא הנקרא פרצוף מ"ה וב"ן דא"ק. וזכור כאן את ערך ההפכי שבין כלים לאורות (כנ"ל באות כ"ד).

28) After the above, there was one more Stroke Contact with the screen of the Kli Malchut. However, this time the Behina Dalet was absent in it. The screen now has only four vessels: Keter, Hochma, Bina, and Tifferet. Therefore, the next Partzuf of the world of Adam Kadmon, which emerged one level below the Partzuf Galgalta, on the level of Hochma, is called AB. In this case, the Ohr Hozer dresses onto the four lights of the NaRaNH while the fifth part, the Ohr Yechida, is absent.

The Behinot Dalet and Gimel are absent in the screen of the third Partzuf. Hence, it emerged one level lower than the Partzuf AB, i.e., on the level of Bina, and the lights Yechida and Haya are absent in it. It is two steps lower than the first Partzuf and only one step lower than the second. It is called Bina or SAG.

Then a *Zivug de Haka'a* occurred on the *Masach* with the *Aviut Aleph*; thus, the *Rosh* and the *Guf* emerged on the level of *Tifferet* with the lights *Nefesh* and *Ruach*, whereas the lights *Neshama, Haya,* and *Yechida* are absent. There are no *Kelim Dalet, Gimel,* and *Bet*; therefore, the corresponding lights are also missing. This Partzuf is called *Tifferet* or MA.

The final fifth *Partzuf* emerged on the *Aviut Shoresh* with the light *Nefesh*. It is called *Malchut* or *BON*.

כט) והנה נתבארו אופן יציאתם של ה"פ א"ק, הנקראים גלגלתא ע"ב ס"ג מ"ה וב"ן, זה למטה מזה, שכל תחתון חסר בחינה עליונה של העליון שלו. כי לפרצוף ע"ב חסר אור יחידה. ובפרצוף ס"ג חסר גם אור החיה, שיש להעליון שלו, שהוא ע"ב. ובפרצוף מ"ה וב"ן חסר גם אור הנשמה, שיש בהעליון שלו, שהוא ס"ג. והוא מטעם שזה תלוי בשיעור העוביות שבהמסך, שעליו נעשה הזווג דהכאה. (אות י"ח). אמנם צריכים להבין: מי ומה גרם שהמסך ילך ויתמעט, בחינה אחר בחינה משיעור עוביותו, עד שיתחלק לה' שיעורי קומה שבה' מיני זווגים הללו?

29) So we have investigated the formation of the five Partzufim of the world of Adam Kadmon called Galgalta, AB, SAG, MA and BON, where each subsequent Partzuf is one step lower than the preceding one. For example, there is no light of Yechida in the Partzuf AB, and no light of Haya in SAG (it was in AB). The light of Neshama is absent in the Partzuf MA. The level of each Partzuf depends on the thickness of the screen on which a Zivug de Haka'a is made (see §18). However, we have not yet clarified the reason for the lessening of the screen's thickness at the formation of a new Partzuf.

After *TA Malchut* acquires a screen with five degrees of hardness, hence it can work with all five levels of its desires. Using the screen's force, it reflects the entire light and in the Reflected Light reaches the level of *Keter*. It "sees" all five parts of the coming light: the lights in the *Sefirot Keter, Hochma, Bina, Tifferet, and Malchut,* which are in the *Rosh*. Approximately 20% of each light can be received in the *Toch*.

The general level of this light is determined according to the highest light – *Yechida,* which corresponds to the level of *Keter (Komat Keter)*. In the second *Partzuf, Malchut* can receive less light, since it loses one higher level of desire – the *Aviut Dalet* and the light *Yechida*.

The amount of light in the third, fourth and fifth *Partzufim* is even smaller.Their level gets lower and lower because of the decreasing *Aviut* that occurs from *Gimel* to *Bet* in the third *Partzuf*, from *Bet* to *Aleph* in the fourth and from *Aleph* to *Shoresh* in the fifth. According to the degree of *Aviut*, there are no lights *Yechida* and *Haya* in the third *Partzuf* SAG, *Yechida, Haya and Neshama* – in the fourth and *Yechida, Haya, Neshama* and *Ruach* – in the fifth.

The *Partzufim* look this way only as regards one another, where each *Partzuf* that follows is "one head" lower than the preceding one by the level of the light, strength, and quality. However, each of them has its own 5 (or 10, for *Sefira Tifferet* consists of 6 *Sefirot*) *Sefirot KaHaB-TuM* and 5 lights *NaRaNHaY*, respectively.

Each *Partzuf* must have a set of all those 10 parts of which the creation consists. The *Partzufim* differ only by the strength of their screen. Therefore, when the screen grows weaker, a new *Partzuf* is born one-step lower than the preceding one.

After *TA*, the *Kli* consists of the "desire to receive" and the *Masach*. The filling of the *Kli* happens in accordance with the strength and size of this *Masach*. The screen can push away the pleasures corresponding to its five, four, three, two, or one desires. Every *Partzuf* consists of five parts, defined as:

Keter	The point of beginning the letter *Yud*
Hochma	*Yud*
Bina	*Hey*
Tifferet	*Vav*
Malchut	*Hey*

These letters are the shell of the *Partzuf*, the five permanent parts that constitute its *Kli*. According to the strength of the screen, the *Partzuf* fills these parts with more or less intensive light – the *Ohr Hochma* or the *Ohr Hassadim*. *Ohr Hochma* is denoted by the letter *Yud* and the *Ohr Hassadim* – by the letter *Hey*. Therefore, we can designate each *Partzuf* by a letter code or a number.

As it was explained in the article "The Letters of Amnon-Saba" (p.104): "Each *Partzuf* consists of five parts = 5 *Sefirot:* a point and 4 letters: *Keter*-point+*Hochma-Yud*+*Bina-Hey*+*ZA-Vav*+*Malchut-Hey*=*HaVaYaH*". The difference between all 125 *Partzufim* is in the light that fills them, while the shell *HaVaYaH* remains the same. This is because the desire cannot be formed unless the Creator's light goes through five preliminary stages, where only the fifth stage constitutes the birth of the new creation – a new desire.

The entire Universe and all the worlds are only the 10 *Sefirot*, or the Creator's name *HaVaYaH:*

Sefira	Letter	Partzuf	World	Light
Keter	Point	Galgalta	AK	Yechida
Hochma	*Yud*	AB	Atzilut	Haya
Bina	*Hey*	SAG	Beria	Neshama
ZA	*Vav*	MA	Yetzira	Ruach
Malchut	*Hey*	BON	Assiya	Nefesh

The filling of *HaVaYaH* with the light is called its revelation, for it is to that degree that the Creator reveals Himself in this desire. By this action, the letters emerge out of the state of concealment and emptiness.

Overall, there are five *Partzufim: Keter (Galgalta), AB, SAG, MA, BON. Keter* is the principal *Partzuf*, the source of the rest of them. Within *Keter's* 10 *Sefirot* is a simple or inner *HaVaYaH.* Moreover, each of the four letters of its *HaVaYaH* gets outside and creates a new *Partzuf* that dresses onto the *Partzuf Galgalta.*

So, the following Partzufim emerge from Keter-Galgalta:

Yud	Partzuf Hochma, AB
Hey	Partzuf Bina, SAG
Vav	Partzuf ZA, MA
Hey	Partzuf Malchut, BON

Thus, the *Partzuf* Keter is denoted by a simple *HaVaYaH*, while the *Partzufim* that dress onto it are denoted by a *HaVaYaH* with fillings. The registration of *HaVaYaH* with the light that fills it is called "*Milluy*" (filling). For a short designation of the *Partzuf, the* notion *Gematria* (numerical value of the fillings) was introduced.

The letters of the alphabet:

Name	Pronunciation	Gematria
Aleph	[a], [e]	1
Bet	b, v	2
Gimel	g (gate)	3
Dalet	d	4
Hey	[a], [e]	5
Vav	v, [u], [o]	6
Zayn	z	7
Het	h (how)	8
Tet	t	9
Yud	y, i (in)	10
Chaf	h, k	20
Lamed	l	30
Mem	m	40
Nun	n	50
Samech	s	60
Ayn	[a], [e]	70
Pey	p	80
Tzady	tz	90
Kuf	k	100
Reish	r	200
Shin	sh, s	300
Tav	t	400

The *Gematria* of the *Partzuf* that is not filled with the light, i.e., the *Gematria* of the empty *HaVaYaH* is equal to *Yud+Hey+Vav+Hey*=10+5+6+5=26.

The *filling of each letter forms the Gematria of the filled HaVaYaH*: each Hebrew letter has a full name: A – *Aleph,* B – *Bet* and so on, according to the table.

Hence, there are 4 kinds of fillings of *HaVaYaH*: a) *AB*; b) *SAG*; c) *MA*; d) *BON*.

a) **HaVaYaH with the filling of AB**:

- **Yud**: *Yud+Vav+Dalet*=10+6+4=20
- **Hey**: *Hey+Yud*=5+10=15
- **Vav**: *Vav+Yud+Vav*=6+10+6=22
- **Hey**: *Hey+Yud*=5+10=15

Total: 72=20+15+22+15=*AB*, where the letter A stands not for *Aleph*=1, but for *Ayn*=70 (they are just pronounced the same way, therefore in English they are marked by the same letter).

HaVaYaH, filled with such light, is called the *Partzuf AB*, the *Partzuf Hochma, because the letter Yud* in its filling means the *Ohr Hochma*. Such filling of *HaVaYaH* is called *HaVaYaH* with the filling of *Yud*.

b) **HaVaYaH with the filling of SAG**. The *Partzuf*, filled with the light of *Hassadim*, is called SAG, because such is its *Gematria*: SAG=*Samech* (60) +*Gimel* (3) = 63:

- **Yud**: *Yud+Vav+Dalet*=10+6+4=20
- **Hey**: *Hey+Yud*=5+10=15
- **Vav**: *Vav+Aleph+Vav*=6+1+6=13
- **Hey**: *Hey+Yud*=5+10=15

Total: 63= 60+3= *Samech* + *Gimel* = SAG. If the *Kelim* and their filling originate in the *Tzimtzum Aleph (TA)*, then there is **Yud** in the filling of the *HaVaYaH*. We will learn that later there was another restriction *Tzimtzum Bet (TB)*. Therefore, if the *Kelim* are filled with the light from the Second Restriction, then in their filling of *HaVaYaH* **the letter Aleph** is present instead of *Yud*.

The difference between *AB* and SAG is in the filling of the letter *Vav*: in *AB* the *Gematria* of *Vav*=22 from the filling with the light of *Hochma*, and in SAG the *Gematria* of the letter *Vav* =13, from filling with the light of *Hassadim*. From the above statement, it is clear that *AB* originates in *TA* and in the *Partzuf* SAG its letter *Vav*, or *ZA*, derives from *TB*.

c) **HaVaYaH with the filling of MA**:

- **Yud**: *Yud+Vav+Dalet* = 20
- **Hey**: *Hey+Aleph* = 6
- **Vav**: *Vav-Aleph-Vav* = 13
- **Hey**: *Hey+Aleph* = 6

Such a filling of *HaVaYaH* is called: 20+6+13+6=45=40+5=*Mem+Hey*=MA. The letter *Hey* is pronounced as [a].

d) **HaVaYaH with the filling of BON**:

- **Yud**: *Yud+Vav+Dalet* = 20
- **Hey**: *Hey+ Hey* = 10
- **Vav**: *Vav+ Vav* = 12
- **Hey**: *Hey+ Hey* = 10

Such a filling of *HaVaYaH* is called 20+10+12+10 = 52 = 50+2 = *Nun+Bet*, and is pronounced in the reversed order: *BON*.

Malchut of the World of Infinity is a simple "desire to receive". The screen, by way of dividing *Malchut* into different parts, calls forth the variety of its forms:

- The division of *Malchut* into five general parts is called "worlds".
- The division of each world into five more parts is called "*Partzufim*".
- The division of each *Partzuf* into five more parts is called "*Sefirot*".

Each *Sefira* in turn consists of five more sub-*Sefirot*, which in turn consists of its own 10 *Sefirot*, and so on ad infinitum.

Our world is a reflection of the lowest spiritual world, and it has the same types and kinds of objects as in the spiritual world, except they are, as it were, made of a different substance. They consist of a material desire to receive pleasure without the screen, from the portion of light, completely detached from the Creator. We feel it as pleasure, but we do not feel its source. Therefore, by studying the spiritual world, one can completely attain the entire nature of our world, all its laws.

THE WEAKENING OF THE MASACH FOR THE CREATION OF THE PARTZUF
הזדככות המסך לאצילות פרצוף

ל) בכדי להבין ענין השתלשלות המדרגות בה' שיעורי קומה זה למטה מזה, שנתבאר בה' פרצופין דא"ק לעיל, וכן בכל המדרגות המתבארים בה"פ של כל עולם ועולם מד' העולמות אבי"ע עד המלכות דעשיה, צריכים להבין היטב ענין הזדככות המסך דגוף, הנוהג בכל פרצוף מפרצופי א"ק ועולם הנקודים ובעולם התיקון.

30) In order to understand the development of the spiritual levels, expressed by the five degressive Partzufim of the world AK, and all levels of the five Partzufim of each of the four worlds of ABYA, down to Malchut of the world of Assiya, we have to learn properly what the thinning of Masach de Guf is. This occurs in all the Partzufim of the worlds AK, Nikudim and Atzilut (the world of Correction).

All the levels, beginning with the World of Infinity (the *Olam Ein Sof*) and down to our world, are created according to one and the same scheme. The more removed a level is from the World of Infinity, the thinner and weaker the screen becomes. Because of this, *Malchut* receives less and less light each time its levels descend lower and lower, until gradually *Malchut* descends from its highest state – the *Olam Ein Sof* and reaches its lowest state - our world.

לא) והענין הוא, שאין לך פרצוף או איזה מדרגה שהיא, שלא יהיה לה ב' אורות, הנקראים אור מקיף ואור פנימי. ונבארם בא"ק. כי האור מקיף של פרצוף הא' דא"ק ה"ס אור א"ס ב"ה, הממלא את כל המציאות. אשר לאחר הצמצום א' והמסך שנתקן במלכות, נעשה זווג דהכאה מאור הא"ס על המסך הזה.

וע"י האו"ח שהעלה המסך, חזר והמשיך אור העליון לעולם הצמצום, בבחינת ע"ס דראש וע"ס דגוף (אות כ"ה).

אמנם המשכה זו שבפרצוף א"ק מא"ס ב"ה אינה ממלאת את כל המציאות כמטרם הצמצום, אלא שנבחן בראש וסוף: הן מבחינת מלמעלה למטה, כי אורו נפסק על הנקודה דעוה"ז, שה"ס מלכות המסיימת בסו"ה "ועמדו רגליו על הר הזיתים".

הן מבחינת מבפנים לחוץ. כי כמו שיש ע"ס ממעלה למטה כח"ב תו"מ והמלכות מסיימה את הא"ק מלמטה, כן יש ע"ס כח"ב תו"מ מפנים לחוץ, המכונים מוחא עצמות גידין בשר ועור, אשר העור, שהוא סוד המלכות, מסיימת את הפרצוף מבחוץ.

אשר בערך הזה נבחן פרצוף א"ק, כלפי א"ס ב"ה הממלא את כל המציאות, רק כמו קו דק בלבד. כי פרצוף העור מסיימת אותו ומגבילה אותו סביב סביב מבחוץ, ואינו יכול להתרחב למלא את כל החלל שנצטמצם. ונשאר רק קו דק עומד באמצעו של החלל.

והנה שיעור האור שנתקבל בא"ק, דהיינו קו הדק, נקרא "אור פנימי". וכל ההפרש הגדול הזה, שבין האו"פ שבא"ק ובין אור א"ס ב"ה שמטרם הצמצום, נקרא "אור מקיף". כי הוא נשאר בבחינת או"מ מסביב פרצוף א"ק, כי לא יכול להתלבש בפנימיות הפרצוף.

31) The fact is that any Partzuf, or even any spiritual level, has two kinds of the light: the Ohr Makif (the Surrounding Light) and the Ohr Pnimi (the Inner Light). As was made clear, in the first Partzuf of the world AK Galgalta the Surrounding Light is the light of the World of Infinity, which fills the entire Universe. After TA and emerging of Masach, the Stroke Contact (the Zivug de Haka'a) between the entire light of the World of Infinity with this Masach takes place.

The Ohr Hozer that emerged as a result of this Zivug allowed a part of the Upper Light to enter the world of Restriction (the Olam HaTzimtzum) and thus created the ten Sefirot de Rosh and the ten Sefirot de Guf, as was said in § 25.

However, the entire light did not enter the Partzuf Galgalta. Now the light of the World of Infinity does not fill the entire Universe, as was the case before TA. Now there are Rosh and Sof, i.e., while the ten Sefirot spread downwards, the light stops at the point of "this world", in "limiting" Malchut (Malchut Masayemet), as said: "his feet are standing on the Mount of Olives"...

Furthermore, now there is a notion "from inside out". Similarly to the downward spreading of the ten Sefirot Keter, Hochma, Bina, Tifferet, Malchut (KaHaB-TuM) and limiting Malchut, there also exists the spreading of the ten Sefirot KaHaB-TuM from inside out.

Here the Sefirot are called: Mocha-brain (Keter), Atzamot-bones (Hochma), Gidin-tendons (Bina), Basar-flesh (Tifferet), and Or-skin (Malchut; "Or" with the letter "Ayn", not with "Aleph", i.e., "the light"). Concerning the World of Infinity, where the entire Universe was filled with the light of the Partzuf Galgalta, there is just a thin ray of light. Or-skin (Malchut) limits the Partzuf on the outside, preventing the light from "widening" further and filling the empty space.

The amount of light (its thin ray) received in Galgalta is called "the Ohr Pnimi" (the Inner Light). The enormous amount of light of the World of Infinity, which did not enter Galgalta, remained outside. Now this light is called the Ohr Makif (the Surrounding Light). It cannot enter the Partzuf but rather surrounds it on all sides.

Any part of *Malchut* is called a level, if it has filled each of its desires with the light by using a screen. Each level received by *Malchut* divides the coming light into two parts: the *Ohr Pnimi*, which enters the *Partzuf*, and the *Ohr Makif*.

The screen sees the entire light coming to it with the help of the *Ohr Hozer*, and then determines how much it can receive with the help of the screen for the sake of the Creator, and how much it must leave outside. The screen always divides the light into two parts.

The *Ohr Pnimi* (the received part) is only a thin ray of light, which entered *Malchut*, i.e., the empty space, departed after *TA* (before *TA Malchut* was completely filled). We see the strength of egoism, which allowed just a thin ray of light to enter *Malchut* with the help of the screen. Moreover, it only refers to the first *Partzuf* of *AK* - *Galgalta*. The remaining *Partzufim* are filled with even less light.

Then, with the help of this ray of light, additional *Partzufim* are created. In the very center of this dark sphere – *Malchut*, after *TA*, there is our world. In the world of *Atzilut* a very special *Partzuf*, *Adam HaRishon*, is born. It consists of two components: the qualities of *Bina* and *Malchut*. Then this *Partzuf* splits into numerous separate *Partzufim*, called "souls".

By acquiring the screen, the formed souls can gradually fill the entire sphere with the light. Such a state is called "The Final Correction" of the souls with the help of the screen-"the *Gmar Tikkun*". After that, the further widening of *Malchut* consists in the attainment of the Creator, not inside itself, but above its properties.

This already refers to that part of Kabbalah called "the secrets of the Torah". The rest of Kabbalah, everything that is below this level and refers to "*Ta'amey Torah*", can and must be studied by all. Kabbalists must open "*Ta'amey Torah*" to everyone but conceal "the secrets of the Torah".

There are many kinds of the *Ohr Makif* as well as the *Ohr Pnimi*. One of them shines upon man when he has no screen yet, no corrected feeling - and man starts longing for the spiritual. It happens owing to the *Ohr Makif* that shines upon him. Here the light is primary and the desire is secondary.

The *Ohr Makif* starts shining when man does not yet understand where this luminescence comes from, but spirituality begins to attract him. As he starts learning, he arouses upon himself the luminescence of another kind, which gradually corrects him; with its help, man begins to see his shortcomings, more and more opening the surrounding world. Gradually the light creates the spiritual picture before him, which gets clearer and clearer, as if emerging out of a fog.

We are surrounded by the Creator, Who is behind all objects around us, and wishes to bring us nearer to Him. For this purpose, He uses the objects of nature. In our world, He does it with the help of people - family, boss, acquaintances. He deliberately sends us complicated situations and sufferings, so that by trying to escape from them, we would come closer to Him.

However, man is inclined to see the reason of all his misfortunes in his shrewish wife, angry boss or the people who surround him. However, that is the way it should be, because the Creator is concealed from him. Man has not yet reached the level where he can only see the Creator behind all that happens to him. Moreover, he should react according to his own feelings, not as if it is only the Creator Who exists in the world.

While on the material level, it is impossible to see the spiritual forces in the surrounding objects.

We depict the *Partzufim* very relatively. Though it is said that *Galgalta* looks like a thin ray of light, we imagine it in the form of a rectangle to show the correlation between the parts of the *Partzuf*. The *Partzuf* with its parts is gradually created in man's sensations. We study how from a point, a *Sefira* is created in man, then an embryo-*Partzuf*; next, it grows as man starts receiving the Upper Light into it.

It is said, "his feet will ascend onto the Mount of Olives and will stand on it'. Olive oil symbolizes the *Ohr Hochma*. The entire process of reception and the grading of the *Ohr Hochma* are extremely complicated. In Hebrew *Har* (mountain) also means "*Hirhurim*" - doubts, sufferings and efforts while climbing a mountain. From below, on our part, this ascent continues until the *Machsom*, where the spiritual world begins. In the *Gmar Tikkun*, the *Ohr Hochma* will fill not only the *Toch*, but also the *Sof* of *Galgalta*.

לב) ונתבאר היטב סוד האו"מ דא"ק, שלגדלו אין קץ ותכלית. אמנם אין הכונה שא"ס ב"ה, הממלא את כל המציאות, הוא עצמו הוא בבחינת או"מ לא"ק. אלא הכונה היא, שבעת שנעשה הזווג דהכאה על המלכות דראש א"ק, אשר א"ס הכה במסך אשר שם, שפירושו שרצה להתלבש בבחי"ד דא"ק כמו מטרם הצמצום, אלא המסך שבמלכות דראש א"ק הכה בו, שפירושו שעיכב עליו מלהתפשט בבחי"ד, והחזירו לאחוריו (אות י"ד).

שבאמת האו"ח הזה שיצא ע"י החזרת האור לאחוריו, נעשה ג"כ בחינת כלים להלבשת אור העליון. אמנם יש הפרש גדול מאוד בין קבלת הבחי"ד שמטרם הצמצום, ובין קבלת האור חוזר שלאחר הצמצום. שהרי לא הלביש אלא בחינת קו דק בראש וסוף. אשר כל זה פעל המסך בסבת הכאתו על אור העליון.

הנה זה השיעור, שנדחה מא"ק בסבת המסך, כלומר כל אותו השיעור, שאור העליון מא"ס ב"ה רצה להתלבש בבחי"ד, לולא המסך שעיכב עליו, הוא הנעשה לאו"מ מסביב הא"ק. והטעם הוא, כי אין שינוי והעדר ברוחני. וכיון שאור א"ס נמשך להא"ק להתלבש בבחי"ד, הרי זה צריך להתקיים כן. לכן אע"פ שעתה עיכב עליו המסך והחזירו לאחוריו, עכ"ז אין זה סותר להמשכת א"ס ח"ו. אלא אדרבא, הוא מקיים אותו! רק באופן אחר.

והיינו ע"י ריבוי הזווגים בה' העולמות א"ק ואבי"ע, עד לגמר התיקון, שתהיה הבחי"ד מתוקנת על ידיהם בכל שלימותה. ואז א"ס יתלבש בה כבתחילה. הרי שלא נעשה שום שינוי והעדר

ע"י הכאת המסך באור העליון. וזה סוד מ"ש בזוהר: "א"ס לא נחית יחודיה עליה עד דיהבינן ליה בת זוגיה".

ובינתים, כלומר עד הזמן ההוא, נבחן שאור א"ס הזה נעשה לאו"מ, שפירשו שעומד להתלבש בו לאחר מכן. ועתה הוא מסבב ומאיר עליו רק מבחוץ בהארה מסוימת, שהארה זו מסגלתו להתפשט באותם החוקים הראוים להביאהו לקבל האו"מ הזה בהשיעור שא"ס ב"ה נמשך אליו בתחילה.

32) Now let us clear up what is the Ohr Makif of the world AK (or rather Galgalta), which is infinitely great and inexhaustible. It is not a question of the light of the World of Infinity being the Ohr Makif. It means that, when the Stroke Contact took place, the enormous light of the World of Infinity hit the screen of the Malchut de Rosh Galgalta. Although it wished to enter Behina Dalet, as if no TA had ever happened, the screen stopped and reflected it, preventing it from getting inside Behina Dalet (see § 14).

This Ohr Hozer has virtually become the vessel of reception of the Upper Light. However, there is a tremendous difference between the reception by Behina Dalet before TA and the reception with the help of the Masach and the Ohr Hozer after it. As we have already said, the light that entered Galgalta is just a thin ray compared to what it was before TA.

The part of the Upper Light that could not enter the Partzuf has turned into the Ohr Makif of Galgalta. There is a rule: nothing ever disappears in the spiritual world, hence the light of the World of Infinity that was meant for Behina Dalet has not vanished; it is bound to fulfill its predestination and enter Malchut, so now it starts filling the worlds AK and ABYA, albeit according to a totally different principle. Now the creation gets only that part of the light that it can receive, not for its own sake, but for the sake of the Creator.

It happens due to a large number of Stroke Contacts between the light and the Masachim of the worlds and the Partzufim, until Behina Dalet corrects itself with their help and reaches the state of absolute perfection, conceived by the Creator at the beginning of the creation.

Then the entire light of the World of Infinity will enter it; but now the creation will be the Creator's partner in creating itself, "earning" the reception of the light. Therefore, the Stroke Contact between the light and the Masach does not lead to a disappearance or a transformation of the light.

But for the time being, before the Final Correction (the Gmar Tikkun) the light of Infinity turns into the Ohr Makif (the Surrounding Light), which means that it will have to enter this Partzuf in the future. However, for the present moment it surrounds the Partzuf and shines upon it as if from "outside".

This outside luminescence spreads through all the worlds in the form of corrections, capable of leading Malchut to being completely filled with the light of the World of Infinity.

As we have already said, the light reflected by the screen dresses onto the Direct Light (the *Ohr Yashar*) and serves as the *Kli*for receivingthe *Ohr Pnimi* into the *Guf*. The *Ohr Hozer* is *Kavanah* (intention), thanks to which the light can enter the *Guf* for the sake of the Creator. The screen has enough strength only to dress and receive just a small portion of the light into the *Toch* as compared to the light that *Malchut* was filled with in *Behina Dalet* in the world of *Ein Sof*. The empty desires form the *Sof* of the *Partzuf*; whereas the light that was unable to enter them and was left around the *Partzuf*, is called "the *Ohr Makif*".

In the spiritual world, all processes take place according to the cause-and-effect relation. There is no time, nothing changes or disappears there. All that was continues to be, and everything new merely dresses onto it. The previous continues to exist and is the cause, while all the new becomes its effect.

The screen that pushed away the *Ohr Yashar* did not prevent it from spreading in *Malchut*, but just gave the process a new form. Now it happens in the way of a partial receiving with the help of numerous "*Zivugey de Haka'a*" in the five worlds of *AK*, *Atzilut*, *Beria*, *Yetzira* and *Assiya*.

This process goes on until the Final Correction, when the *Behina Dalet* will be corrected in all its perfection. Then the light of Infinity will spread into it as it had done before *TA*. In this process, the *Masach* has not introduced anything that would interfere with achieving perfection.

The light of the World of Infinity will not rest until it fills the entire *Malchut*. So far it surrounds it from outside as the *Ohr Makif*, ready to enter it the instant the screen appears. The luminescence of the *Ohr Makif* is able to correct *Malchut* and allow it to receive the light inside.

The light hits the screen, because such is its nature; as it wanted to fill the *Behina Aleph*, so later it constantly wishes to fill the vessel of reception - the "desire to receive". For example, sometimes man has some kind of a hidden desire; the outside pleasure strikes it and awakens this desire, arouses it. Then man begins to feel that this pleasure wants to enter him.

In the spiritual world, each action is new because the creation makes a *Zivug de Haka'a* on every new portion of the "desire to receive" that has not yet been involved in the correction. Each new action is the effect of the preceding one and the cause of the subsequent one. The light emanating from the Creator is one and the same, simple light; but with each new desire, the *Kli* singles out the various kinds of pleasure in it that correspond to this new desire.

Everything depends on the *Kli*. According to its inner properties, desires (whether it wants to receive for its own sake or for the sake of the Creator, whether it wants to receive at all) it distinguishes certain kinds of pleasure in the light. The vessel (the *Kli*) must be created so that it will be able to pick out all those numerous pleasures in the light that were incorporated in it from the beginning.

On the one hand, the light emanating from the Creator creates the *Masachim*, screens, which assist the gradual filling of different parts of *Malchut* with the light, and it continues in this way until the *Gmar Tikkun*. On the other hand, we must say that the light is the cause that arouses the desire of the *Kli*, whereupon it should work hard to create its own screen.

לג) ועתה נבאר ענין הביטוש דאו"פ ואו"מ זה בזה, המביא להזדככות המסך ולאבידת בחינה אחרונה דעביות. כי בהיות ב' האורות הללו הפוכים זה מזה וקשורים יחד שניהם במסך שבמלכות דראש א"ק, ע"כ מבטשים ומכים זה בזה.

פירוש: כי אותו זווג דהכאה הנעשה בפה דראש א"ק, דהיינו במסך שבהמלכות דראש, הנקראת "פה", שהיה הסבה להלבשת אור פנימי דא"ק ע"י האו"ח שהעלה, הנה הוא ג"כ הסבה ליציאת האו"מ דא"ק. כי מחמת שעיכב על אור א"ס מלהתלבש בבחי"ד, יצא האור לחוץ בבחינת או"מ. דהיינו כל אותו חלק האור שהאו"ח אינו יכול להלבישו כמו הבחי"ד עצמה, הוא יצא ונעשה לאו"מ. הרי שהמסך שבפה הוא סבה שוה לאור מקיף כמו לאו"פ.

33) Now, the time has come to learn about the impact between the Ohr Makif and the Ohr Pnimi, which leads to a thinning of the screen and the subsequent loss of its highest level of Aviut. These two kinds of light have quite opposite properties, although the screen, positioned in Malchut's Peh de Rosh of the Partzuf, inseparably connects them.

They are in constant contradiction, leading to concussion between them. The same Zivug de Haka'a that happened on this screen, on the one hand, called forth a filling of the Partzuf with the Inner Light (the Ohr Pnimi); on the other hand, the same Zivug de Haka'a produced the Surrounding Light (the Ohr Makif). In this way, it prevented the light of Infinity from entering Behina Dalet.

The screen, positioned at the *Peh de Rosh* divides the simple light descending from above into two contrary, albeit, connected kinds: the *Ohr Pnimi*, partially received inside by the *Partzuf*with the help of the *Ohr Hozer* and the *Ohr Makif*, which the screen prevents from entering the *Guf (Behina Dalet)* and leaves it outside.

Thanks to the same intention of man (to receive for the Creator's sake), one part of the light is received, while the other is left outside. The *Partzuf* (man) receives exactly as much light as he can receive with the intention for the sake of the Creator.

לד) ונתבאר שהאו"פ והאו"מ שניהם קשורים במסך, אלא בפעולות הפוכות זה לזה. ובה במדה שהמסך ממשיך חלק מאור העליון לפנימיות הפרצוף ע"י האו"ח המלבישו, כן הוא מרחיק את או"מ מלהתלבש בהפרצוף. ומתוך שחלק האור הנשאר מבחוץ לאו"מ גדול הוא מאוד, מפאת המסך המעכב עליו מלהתלבש בא"ק, ע"כ נבחן שהוא מכה במסך המרחיק אותו, במה שהוא רוצה להתלבש בפנימיות הפרצוף.

ולעומתו נבחן ג"כ, אשר כח העביות וקשיות שבמסך מכה באו"מ, הרוצה להתלבש בפנימיותו ומעכב עליו, ע"ד שהוא מכה באור העליון בעת הזווג. ואלו ההכאות שהאו"מ והעביות שבמסך מכים זה בזה, מכונים "ביטוש האו"מ באו"פ". אמנם ביטוש זה נעשה ביניהם רק בגוף הפרצוף, כי שם ניכר ענין התלבשות האור בכלים, המשאיר את האו"מ מחוץ לכלי. משא"כ בע"ס דראש, שם אינו נוהג ענין הביטוש הזה, כי שם אין האו"ח נחשב לכלים כלל, אלא לשרשים דקים לבד.

ומשום זה אין האור שבהם נחשב לאו"פ מוגבל, עד להבחין באור הנשאר מבחוץ לבחינת או"מ. וכיון שאין הבחן הזה ביניהם, לא שייך הכאה דאו"פ ואו"מ בע"ס דראש. אלא רק אחר שהאורות מתפשטים מפה ולמטה לע"ס דגוף, ששם מתלבשים האורות בכלים, שהם הע"ס דאו"ח שמפה ולמטה, ע"כ נעשה שם הכאה בין האו"פ שבתוך הכלים ובין האור מקיף שנשאר מבחוץ.

34) The Ohr Pnimi and the Ohr Makif are concerned with the Masach, even though their actions are contrary to one another. According to the ability of the Masach to let a part of the Ohr Yashar that has dressed on the Ohr Hozer inside the Partzuf, it prevents the Ohr Makif from entering it. The amount of the Surrounding Light left outside the Partzuf exceeds by far the Ohr Pnimi.

The screen, with its Aviut and Kashiut, does not allow the Ohr Makif to enter the Partzuf as much as it resists the Ohr Yashar. The concussion between the Ohr Makif and the screen's Aviut is called Bitush – the impact between the Ohr Makif and the Ohr Pnimi. This impact happens only in the Guf of the Partzuf, since that is where the reception of the light in the vessels took place; however, a considerable part of the light was left outside. In the 10 Sefirot de Rosh, this impact does not occur, for the Ohr Hozer is not yet regarded as a true vessel of reception. It only forms the Shorshey Kelim (roots, sources of the vessels).

Therefore, the light that is in them is not yet genuine *Ohr Pnimi*. Due to the same reason, the *Ohr Makif* cannot be distinguished there either. Since there is still no difference between them, there cannot be any impact in the *Rosh* of the *Partzuf*. Only after the light spreads downwards from the *Peh* by way of the 10 *Sefirot de Guf* (where the lights dress into the vessels, i.e., the 10 *Sefirot* of the Reflected Light), then the impact between the *Ohr Pnimi* and the *Ohr Makif* takes place.

The amount of *Ohr Makif* surrounding the *Partzuf* is incomparably greater than the *Ohr Pnimi* inside it. In an attempt to enter the *Partzuf*, the *Ohr Makif* strikes the *Masach* that gave birth to it. What does it mean that the *Ohr Makif* strikes the screen? *Malchut* has a passionate desire to receive pleasure. It feels that the light contains just the pleasure it would so much like to receive. Hence, it begins to attract the light.

This demonstrates that, in order to feel and then receive pleasure, one should have an appropriate vessel, a vessel that has passed through an intricate inner development. Why do we perceive the *Ohr Makif* as being outside us? Because, in the *Sof* of each *Partzuf*, there are unfilled desires that feel the light as pleasures that are so far out of their reach. Or rather, these empty desires feel as though the outer light strikes them, "demanding" to be enjoyed.

Mutual strokes of the Surrounding Light (pleasure), with the desire of *Malchut* to receive pleasure and the strength of the screen resisting these desires, are called the *Bitush Pnim u Makif*, the impact between the Inner and the Surrounding Lights. Strictly speaking, the *Ohr Makif* nor the *Ohr Pnimi* do not collide. Rather, both of them strike into the screen between them. It happens in the *Masach* positioned in the *Tabur* of the *Partzuf*, where the reception of the light clearly ends.

It becomes clear only in the *Tabur* how much light (pleasure) entered the *Partzuf*, and how much remained outside of it. In the 10 *Sefirot de Rosh*, there is no such impact, because the *Ohr Hozer* is not yet the vessel for receiving the *Ohr Yashar*, but serves only as an embryo of the *Kli*. The impact begins only after the *Ohr Yashar*, dressed in the intention (the *Ohr Hozer*), spreads into the *Toch* down to the *Tabur*.

Spirituality cannot be attained through the mind; the spiritual *Kli* is a sense that does not understand the Creator, but feels Him. If man can feel the Creator, the spiritual realm, then understanding gradually comes to him.

לה) והנה הביטוש הזה נמשך, עד שהאו״מ מזכך את המסך מכל עוביותו, ומעלה אותו לשרשו העליון שבפה דראש. כלומר, שמזכך ממנו כל העביות שממעלה למטה, המכונה ״מסך ועביות דגוף״. ולא נשאר בו רק השורש דגוף, שהוא בחינת המסך דמלכות דראש, הנקרא ״פה״. דהיינו שנזדכך מכל העביות שממעלה למטה, שהוא החוצץ בין או״פ לאו״מ. ולא נשאר רק העביות שממטה למעלה, ששם עוד לא נעשה ההבדל מאו״פ לאו״מ. ונודע שהשואת הצורה מדביק הרוחניים להיות אחד. ע״כ אחר שנזדכך המסך דגוף מכל עביות של הגוף, ולא נשאר בו רק עביות השוה למסך דפה דראש, ונעשה צורתו שוה אל המסך דראש, הנה נכלל עמו להיות אחד ממש, כי אין ביניהם מה שיחלק אותם לשנים. וזה מכונה, שהמסך דגוף עלה לפה דראש. וכיון שנכלל המסך דגוף בהמסך דראש, נמצא נכלל שוב בזווג דהכאה שבמסך דפה דראש, ונעשה עליו זווג דהכאה מחדש. ויוצאות בו ע״ס בקומה חדשה, הנקרא ״ע״ב דא״ק״ או ״פרצוף חכמה דא״ק״. והוא נחשב לבן ותולדה של הפרצוף הא׳ דא״ק.

> *35) This impact continues until the Ohr Makif liquidates the Aviut of Masach de Guf in the Tabur. As a result of this, the Masach de Guf starts ascending towards the screen, positioned at the Peh de Rosh, which is the root, the cause of the screen de Guf. After merging with the screen in the Peh de Rosh, the Masach of Tabur also gets involved in the Zivug de Haka'a, which is constantly taking place between the Masach in Peh de Rosh and the light. This Zivug results in the formation of a new Partzuf and the emergence of 10 new Sefirot called AB de AK or the Partzuf Hochma of the world of Adam Kadmon. In relation to the first Partzuf Galgalta-Keter, this new Partzuf is considered its result, its "son".*

The Surrounding light puts great pressure upon the screen in an attempt to enter the *Kli* that ispositioned at the *Tabur*. However, the

Masach cannot bear it. On the one hand, it is unable to receive more light with the intention for the sake of the Creator; on the other hand, it cannot remain under such pressure.

Therefore, the best solution is to return to its previous state in the *Peh de Rosh*, altogether refusing to receive the light. The *Masach* begins to rise from the *Tabur* to the *Peh*. On its way, it banishes all the light from the *Kli* and merges with the *Masach* in *Peh de Rosh*, i.e., it returns to the previous state where the light was only in the *Rosh* of the *Partzuf*, but absent from the *Guf* of the *Partzuf*.

The small pleasure that the *Kli* enjoyed by receiving the light in the *Toch* has given it an idea of the great pleasure that is waiting outside. Reception of this pleasure only weakened the screen. It is much easier to refuse altogether a certain pleasure than to receive it in small portions, for the pleasure that was received inside weakens the will power, i.e., the intention to receive pleasure for the sake of the Creator.

As *Ohr Pnimi* and *Ohr Makif* both press upon the screen with their pleasure, the screen weakens under this double pressure, and is forced completely to stop receiving the light. It gets free from all the *Aviut*, rises to the *Peh de Rosh* and fully merges with the *Masach*, which receives nothing at all, but just pushes the light away.

Further on, the material studied may become more technical, but one should not despair. Studying Kabbalah is a complicated inner process. Sometimes Kabbalah is perceived in sensations (and it is the best way), but sometimes it is not perceived at all. That is natural.

One should continue with persistent learning. At a certain moment, you will feel the material penetrating inside. Meanwhile, even if it is impossible to understand, one should continue to study so as not to lose touch with the general scheme, and at each time add another new element to it.

The general scheme looks like this: the light, gradually growing thicker and thicker, creates the *Kli* out of itself and for itself. The *Kli* passes through four phases of its development, turning into *Malchut,* i.e., the only creation.

Then the aim becomes complete separation of it from the Creator; the creation should feel neither the *Ohr Pnimi* nor the *Ohr Makif*, i.e., neither inner, nor outer pleasures, which could dictate their conditions to it.

It needs to acquire absolute freedom of will and the possibility of its own desires and actions, directed at the correction of its egoistic desires and spiritual advancement towards the Creator.

The first independent desire of *Malchut* was to become like the Creator in its properties. That is why it makes the First Restriction on its "desire to receive", on *Behina Dalet*, and leaves it without the light. Then it creates the system of descending worlds. The spiritual worlds are nothing but the phases of restriction; they are curtains, screens. In all, there are five of them: the worlds of *AK* and *ABYA (Adam Kadmon, Atzilut, Beria, Yetzira and Assiya).*

Upon creating the worlds from above down to the lowest point, the creation finds itself in absolute emptiness and darkness; it does not feel the Creator at all. Humankind is in such state.

When, as a result of studying, man begins to vaguely feel that the *Ohr Makif* shines on him, that the omnipotent Creator is hiding somewhere behind it all, that each phenomenon has its own cause and effect, it means that he is already on a certain spiritual level called the *Olam Hazeh.*

Now we are studying the descending structure of all the screens and the worlds that conceal the Creator from *Malchut*. Then, if *Malchut,* by the power of its own desire, creates the screen, protecting it from the light-pleasure, it becomes, as it were, equal to this screen, this level, and the screen serves as revelation of the Creator.

If man independently desires to observe all 620 laws of the Creator's revelation, they stop being restrictive for him, and then the corresponding screen is neutralized on each level. Man acquires the properties of the screen, and there is no sense in concealing the Creator on this phase, since there is no danger that he will receive the light for his own sake.

While spiritually ascending, Kabbalists internally perceive all these processes, having previously studied the descent of the worlds. On the one hand, it is necessary to study Kabbalah to acquire knowledge; on the other hand, man should feel everything he studies.

לו) ואחר שפרצוף ע״ב דא״ק יצא ונשלם בראש וגוף, חזר גם עליו ענין הביטוש דאו״מ באו״פ, ע״ד שנתבאר לעיל בפרצוף הא׳ דא״ק. והמסך דגוף שלו נזדכך ג״כ מכל עביות דגוף, עד שהשוה צורתו לבחינת מסך דראש שלו.

ונמצא אז שנכלל בזווג שבפה דראש שלו. ונעשה עליו זווג דהכאה מחדש, שהוציא קומה חדשה של ע״ס, בשיעור קומת בינה, הנקרא ״ס״ג דא״ק״. והוא נחשב לבן ותולדה של פרצוף הע״ב דא״ק, כי יצא מהזווג דפה דראש שלו. ועד״ז יצאו ג״כ הפרצופים שמס״ג דא״ק ולמטה.

36) After the Partzuf AB de AK was born and completed its development by forming the Rosh and the Guf, the process of the Bitush Ohr Pnimi be Ohr Makif resumed in it, as in the first Partzuf of AK. Its Masach de Guf (the screen of its spiritual body) gradually lost all its Aviut and merged its properties with the Masach de Rosh.

Now this Masach happens to be involved in a Zivug between the Upper Light and the screen that is positioned in the Peh de Rosh. In it the Zivug de Haka'a was renewed and gave birth to a new Partzuf at the level of Bina, which is called SAG de AK. It is considered to be the consequence of the Partzuf AB de AK, since it emerges because of a Zivug on the Masach positioned at the Peh de Rosh. The Partzufim, starting from SAG and further down, emerge according to the same principle.

As it was stated, the second Partzuf AB of the world AK was formed after Galgalta; it felt Bitush Pnim u Makif, expelled the light, then brought the screen de Guf and the screen at Peh de Rosh together.

Then *AB* felt the pressure of those two lights and behaved exactly as *Galgalta* did, i.e., it began to get rid of its *Aviut Gimel*. It raised the

Masach de Guf to the *Peh de Rosh*, where *Zivugim* constantly take place, and became equal to it in its properties.

This means that it stops receiving pleasure for the sake of the Creator. Then a new *Zivug de Haka'a* takes place on this screen, but on a new portion of egoism, one that corresponds to the level of *Bina*. This is how the third *Partzuf* SAG *de* AK was formed.

When *Malchut* of the World of Infinity performed *TA* and established the screen, four *Behinot* lay between it and the Creator. The light cannot reach it through these four *Behinot*, and *Malchut* understands that it is absolutely remote from the Creator. This is a most terrible state, where it is ready completely to rid itself of the infinite delight, whoseabsence turns into suffering, pain and bitterness.

Now, thanks to the screen, it begins to see the light of the four *Behinot* and understands that the Creator wants it to receive pleasure. It makes a calculation and receives a small part of the light, from the *Peh* down to the *Tabur*. As soon as *Malchut* receives this small portion of the light, it starts feeling the pressure from the *Ohr Makif* in the *Tabur*, which wants to enter it, paying no attention to *TA*.

Malchut finds itself at an impasse, for it cannot receive the light just yet; so it should somehow get out of this situation. The way out consists in returning to the initial state. However, by making the first screen, it has already placed a curtain between itself and the Creator, thus creating the first *Partzuf* and receiving 20 per cent of the light. What is it supposed to do when the remaining 80 per cent of the light comes to it? The way out is to try working with a smaller amount of egoism for the sake of the Creator and make the screen for it.

For example, Ruben asks Simon to wake him up at 2 a.m. that he might be able to come to the lesson on time. On the next day, he turns to Simon: "It is so hard for me to get up at 2 a.m., please wake me up at 3 a.m.". The next day, regretting it all, he asks to wake him up at four in the morning, then at five. Seeing that even this is difficult for him, he altogether stops coming to the lessons...

If earlier Malchut could liken itself to the Creator in 20 per cent, it tries now to do it to a lesser degree; by making the screen for 15 per cent of the light, (the numbers serve strictly as an example). Thus, *Malchut* is separated from the Creator by two screens. It then becomes even more remote from Him.

By creating these *Partzufim*, *Malchut* tries to liken itself to *Behina Shoresh, Aleph, Bet, and Gimel* of the Direct Light, to the Creator's properties. However, the egoistic core made the *Tzimtzum*. Becoming like the Creator in these *Behinot*, it isolated itself from Him, as it were, by these *Partzufim* creating an empty space. Now being spiritually empty, it can independently look for the way to become like the Creator.

Although we endow these *Partzufim* with the properties of living beings, we should nevertheless understand that they are not actually alive. They are the weakening screens that shield the spiritual delight from the egoistic desire to receive pleasure.

Only man's soul, which we will discuss later, feels the Creator; therefore, only the soul is a living being. All the rest of the objects are no more than robots, programmed by the Creator to fulfill this or that function, which is somehow connected with man's correction.

All newly created *Partzufim*, levels and their previous states, exist at the same time. An example can be given by analogy with a movie. The scrolled film disappears from our field of sight, but it exists as if in a still state. Similarly, each previous *Partzuf* is like a sequence in this film.

The entire picture, from the first moment and until the last one, is very diverse. A great number of actions take place in it, but all together, because of merging of the present, past and future states, form one sphere, a closed system. The lower *Partzufim* can influence the higher ones, because through them they receive the light from the World of Infinity.

For example the *Partzuf AB*, which receives the light from *Galgalta*, forces it to change too, for the light passing through it is already similar to the properties of *AB*, which alsotransforms *Galgalta*. From this follows the diversity, interconnection, and interdependency of all the spiritual processes.

The very last desire of *Malchut*, which realized that it is absolutely contrary to the Creator in its properties, that wants to receive only for the sake of itself without giving anything in return, is called the true "creation", or "the soul". Although we are not there yet, this very part of *Malchut* is the "material" of which a human soul will be created later on.

The rest is not the creation, but only an auxiliary tool for the merging of the creation with the Creator. These forces assist the Creator in governing creation. There are only two existing entities: the Creator and the creation. Everything else is the system of their communication, with whose help they find one another.

The *Partzufim* do not make the actions. Being on a certain level and performing actions corresponding to this or that *Partzuf*, Kabbalists see the light that they can push away and consequently receive it inside. All Kabbalistic books appeared in the following way: a Kabbalist, ascending the spiritual levels, describes his spiritual sensations on paper...

The entire world of *AK* is similar to *Malchut* of *Ein Sof,* on the level of *Shoresh*; *Atzilut* is similar to *Malchut* on the level of *Behina Aleph*; *Beria* corresponds to *Behina Bet* of *Malchut*; *Yetzira* - to *Behina Gimel*, and the world of *Assiya* is similar to *Behina Dalet* of *Malchut*. The light in *Galgalta* is the *Ohr Nefesh*.

לז) והנה נתבאר יציאת הפרצופים זה למטה מזה, הנעשה מכח הביטוש דאו״מ באו״פ, המזכך המסך דגוף עד שמחזירו לבחינת מסך דפה דראש. ואז נכלל שם בזווג דהכאה, הנוהג בפה דראש.

ומוציא ע״י זווגו קומה חדשה של ע״ס. שקומה חדשה זו נבחן לבן אל פרצוף הקודם. ובדרך הזה יצא הע״ב מפרצוף הכתר, והס״ג מפרצוף ע״ב, והמ״ה מפרצוף ס״ג. וכן יתר המדרגות בנקודים ואבי״ע. אלא עוד צריכים להבין: למה יצאו הע״ס דע״ב רק על בחי״ג ולא על בחי״ד. וכן הס״ג רק על בחי״ב וכו׳? דהיינו, שכל תחתון נמוך במדרגה אחת כלפי עליונו? ולמה לא יצאו כולם זה מזה בקומה שוה?

37) Thus, we have made clear the consecutive emerging of the Partzufim (one under another), which happened due to the impact between the Inner and the Surrounding Lights (Bitush Ohr Pnimi u Makif). This impact weakens the Masach so that it loses its strength and returns to the Peh de Rosh (coincides with it in its qualities), thus getting involved in the Zivug de Haka'a constantly occurring at the Masach de Rosh.

Owing to this Zivug, a new Partzuf emerges as an offspring of the previous one. So AB is a result of the Partzuf Keter, SAG is an offshoot of AB, MA – of SAG and so on in all subsequent levels of the worlds of Nikudim and ABYA. However, we also have to understand why the Partzuf AB can only reach the level of Behina Gimel and not Dalet. SAG reaches only Behina Bet. I.e., each following Partzuf is one level lower than the previous. Why are they not all equal?

לח) ותחילה יש להבין, למה נחשב הע"ס דע"ב לתולדה של פרצוף הא' דא"ק. כי מאחר שיצא מהזווג דפה דראש דפרצוף הא', כמו הע"ס דגוף הפרצוף עצמו. וא"כ במה יצא מבחינת פרצוף הא', להיות נחשב כפרצוף שני ותולדה אליו?

וצריך שתבין כאן ההפרש הגדול ממסך דראש למסך דגוף. כי יש ב' מיני מלכיות בפרצוף: א. הוא מלכות המזדווגת, בכח המסך המתוקן בה, עם אור העליון, ב. היא מלכות המסיימת, בכח המסך המתוקן בה, את אור העליון שבע"ס דגוף.

וההפרש ביניהם כרחוק מאציל מנאצל. כי המלכות דראש המזדווגת בזווג דהכאה עם אור העליון, נחשבת לבחינת מאציל אל הגוף. כי המסך המתוקן בה לא הרחיק אור העליון עם הכאתו בו, אלא אדרבא, שע"י אור חוזר שהעלה, הלביש והמשיך את האור העליון בבחינת ע"ס דראש. ונמצא מתפשט ממעלה למטה עד שנתלבשו הע"ס דאור העליון בהכלי דאו"ח, הנקרא "גוף".

וע"כ נבחן המסך והמלכות דראש בבחינת מאציל להע"ס דגוף, ולא ניכר עדיין שום בחינת מגביל ומדחה במסך ומלכות הזאת. משא"כ המסך והמלכות דגוף, שפירושו, שאחר שהע"ס נתפשטו מפה דראש ממעלה למטה, אינם מתפשטים רק עד המלכות שבע"ס ההם. כי אור העליון אינו יכול להתפשט תוך המלכות דגוף, מפני המסך המתוקן שם המעכבו מלהתפשט אל המלכות. וע"כ נפסק הפרצוף שם ונעשה סוף וסיום על הפרצוף.

הרי שכל כח הצמצום והגבול מתגלה רק בהמסך והמלכות הזאת של הגוף. ולפיכך כל הביטוש דאו"מ באו"פ אינו נעשה רק במסך דגוף בלבד, כי הוא המגביל ומרחיק את האו"מ מלהאיר

בפנימיות הפרצוף. ולא במסך דראש, כי המסך של הראש הוא רק הממשיך ומלביש האורות, ואין עדיין כח הגבול מתגלה בו אף משהו.

38) First, we have to understand why the Partzuf AB is regarded as the offspring of the Partzuf Keter. After its birth because of the Zivug at Peh de Rosh of the Partzuf Galgalta, its height corresponds precisely to the 10 Sefirot de Guf of the Partzuf. So why is it unable to continue as part of the Partzuf Galgalta and not as an individual Partzuf, the result of the first one?

Here you should realize what an enormous difference there is between the Masach de Guf and the Masach de Rosh. There are two kinds of Malchut in the Partzuf. The first is Malchut Mizdaveget, i.e., Malchut that interacts with the Upper Light owing to its corrected intentions (Masach); the second is Malchut Mesayemet, which with the help of its screen prevents the spreading of the Upper Light into the 10 Sefirot de Guf of the Partzuf.

The distinction between them is as great as between the Creator and the creation. It is because Malchut de Rosh ,in the Stroke Contact with the Upper Light, is considered to be the Creator as regards the Guf of Partzuf. Its screen does not push away the light when it strikes. Rather, following the dressing of the Ohr Hozer onto the Ohr Yashar, the 10 Sefirot de Rosh emerge, allowing the light to spread downwards, until the 10 Sefirot of the Upper Light dress in the Kli de Ohr Hozer, called the Guf (body of the Partzuf).

Hence, the Masach and Malchut de Rosh are regarded as the Creator for the 10 Sefirot de Guf. However, so far there is absolutely no resisting power in this Malchut and in its Masach. It will happen thanks to Malchut and the Masach of the Guf de Partzuf. Let us explain: after the 10 Sefirot spread from the Peh de Rosh downwards, they could only reach the Malchut of these 10 Sefirot, for the Upper Light cannot spread into Malchut de Guf. The Masach positioned there prevents the light from filling it; therefore, the Partzuf ends and the Behina Sof (End of Partzuf) appears there.

Since all the power of the Restriction manifests in this Masach of Malchut de Guf, the impact between the Inner and the Surrounding Lights occurs only in the Masach de Guf (the screen of the body) of the Partzuf. It restrains and repels the Ohr Makif, preventing it from shining inside the Partzuf. The Masach de Rosh does not do it, since it only attracts and dresses the light, but the resisting power is not yet apparent in it.

As we have already said, there are two screens in each *Partzuf*. The first is at *Peh de Rosh*, which says that it will not receive pleasure for its own sake; hence, it pushes away all the light. The second is the *Masach de Guf*, which appears together with the intention to receive the light for the sake of the Creator, i.e., to dress it into the *Ohr Hozer*.

This *Masach* descends with the light and ascends when the light exits the *Guf*. The first screen is always in action and is in the spiritual world. The second one determines the position of the *Kli* on the straight line from zero level until the *Gmar Tikkun*. These two screens do not contradict one another.

לט) ונתבאר, שמכח הביטוש דאו"מ באו"פ, חזר המסך דמלכות המסיימת להיות לבחינת מסך ומלכות המזדווגת (אות ל"ה). כי הביטוש דאור מקיף טיהר את המסך המסיים מכל העביות דגוף שהיה בו, ולא נשאר בו רק רשימות דקות מהעביות ההיא, השוות לעביות דמסך דראש. ונודע שהשתוות הצורה מדביק ומיחד הרוחניים זה בזה. לפיכך, אחר שהמסך דגוף השווה צורת עביותו למסך דראש, הנה תיכף נכלל בו ונעשה עמו כאלו היו מסך אחד. ואז קבל כח לזווג דהכאה, כמו מסך דראש.

ויצאו עליו הע"ס דקומה החדשה. אמנם יחד עם זווגו זה, נתחדשו בו במסך דגוף הרשימות דעביות דגוף, שהיו בו מתחילה. ואז חזר וניכר בו שוב שינוי הצורה באיזה שיעור בינו למסך דראש הנכלל עמו. והכר של השינוי הזה מבדילהו ומוציאהו מהפה דראש דעליון.

כי אחר שחזר וניכר מקורו הראשון, שהוא מפה ולמטה דעליון, הנה אז אינו יכול לעמוד עוד למעלה מפה דעליון. כי שינוי הצורה מפריד הרוחניים זה מזה. ונמצא שהוכרח לירד משם למקום שמפה ולמטה דעליון. ולפיכך נבחן בהכרח לגוף שני כלפי העליון. כי אפילו הראש של הקומה החדשה נבחן כלפי העליון כגופו בלבד, להיותו נמשך ממסך דגוף שלו.

ולפיכך שינוי הצורה הזו מבדיל אותם לב' גופים נבדלים. וכיון שהקומה החדשה היא כולה תולדה של המסך דגוף של פרצוף הקודם, ע"כ נחשב כבן אליו, וכמו ענף הנמשך ממנו.

39) As stated above, the impacts between the Ohr Pnimi and the Ohr Makif have turned the Masach of Malchut Mesayemet into the Masach of Malchut, which makes a Zivug at Peh de Rosh. The Bitush of the Ohr Makif so weakened the restraining power of the Masach that, out of all the Aviut de Guf of Masach de Rosh, only the thin Reshimot (equal to Aviut of Masach de Rosh) remained, which led to the merging of the Masach de Guf with the Masach de Rosh. As a result, it enabled the Masach de Guf to make the same Zivug de Haka'a as the Masach de Rosh.

Out of this Zivug emerged a new Partzuf that has its own 10 Sefirot, whose level is one-step lower than the preceding one. At the same time, the Reshimot de Aviut that had originally been in the Masach de Guf were renewed there; therefore, the difference between the properties of both screens reappears. This difference separates the Masach de Guf from the Masach de Rosh.

When its true nature manifests, it cannot remain in the Peh of the higher Partzuf, since in the spiritual world the changing of properties separates one object from another. Therefore, it is forced to descend and become an individual Partzuf. Even the Rosh of the new Partzuf is at the level of the Guf of the higher one, because it was born out of its Masach de Guf.

This distinction between them divides them into two different Partzufim, and since the new Partzuf emerged out of the Masach de Guf of the previous one, it relates to its superior as a branch relates to its root.

The *Reshimot* are the *Ohr Makif*, which was inside the *Partzuf* and exited it. That is why it retains a special connection with the *Kli*.

The screen has already made a *Zivug de Haka'a* on its previous desires, received the light and made sure that it has reached only the

Tabur. It knows that this way is wrong and cannot lead to the *Gmar Tikkun*. Now, when its desires to receive the light for the sake of the Creator reactivate, they emerge one level lower. This means that the new *Partzuf* will receive the light on a lesser level.

The first and second portions of the light are added together to equal the total quantity of the light that entered *Malchut* of the World of Infinity. Now *Malchut* has to receive all the light that was inside it before *TA*, with the new intention to receive, not for its own sake, but to please the Creator, i.e., with the help of the *Masach* and the *Ohr Hozer*.

The second *Partzuf* differs in its properties from the first; hence, it emerges not from the *Peh*, as the previous one did, but lower than the *Peh*, i.e., it is as if it is a head shorter than the previous *Partzuf*. Even its head is considered the *Guf* of the previous *Partzuf*, because it emerges from the *Masach de Guf* of the previous *Partzuf*. The second *Partzuf* is a complete outcome of the first one and branches off it as a frond out of the trunk.

When the first *Masach* at the *Peh de Rosh* pushes away the light, it puts itself into an independent position as regards the giver. The second *Masach* in the *Guf* says that it can receive even for the sake of the host. It has five desires; the *Partzuf* fills each of them by 20 per cent. The rest of the desires remain unfilled, because the *Masach* is not strong enough.

By receiving the light inside, the second screen descends. The *Ohr Makif* continues to interact with the *Partzuf*; it presses and tries to fill the remaining desires. The *Masach de Guf* cannot withstand it, and ascends to the level of the *Masach de Rosh*, and the light leaves the *Partzuf*. The united *Masach* makes a new *Zivug*, and as a result, a new *Partzuf* appears one level below the previous one and it differs in the quality of the light.

The peculiarity is that the *Partzuf AB* is not born from the *Masach de Rosh* of *Galgalta*, but from the *Masach de Guf*. It is strange, because a *Zivug* on the *Behina Gimel* took place in the *Rosh* of *Galgalta*. It is explained in "The Study of the Ten Sefirot", part three, answer 310. While the *Masach de Guf*, i.e., the *Masach de Behina Dalet*, ascends to the *Peh de Rosh*, it unites with the *Aviut de Rosh*, which is "an ascending *Aviut*". However, it is an *Aviut* of *Behina Gimel*, and not *Dalet*, because the *Aviut* of *Behina Dalet* is the *Masach de Guf*, which has never used the *Aviut Gimel*.

Here we can determine two major notions:

1) **The Essence**. This is the *Masach de Guf* and it rises to the *Rosh*, demanding to be filled. That is why the *Masach de Rosh* of *Galgalta* makes a *Zivug* on the *Behina Gimel*. When the essence of the elevated *Masach* becomes clear, it descends into the *Guf* again, not to the *Tabur (Behina Dalet)*, but to the *Chazeh (Behina Gimel)*. This *Behina* is not called "the son or offspring", but the "*Partzuf AB Pnimi*", i.e., the *Partzuf AB*, which spreads into the empty inner *Kelim* of *Galgalta* and is considered the *Guf de Galgalta*, because it emerged from a *Zivug* in the *Rosh* of *Galgalta*.

2) **The Inclusion**. After the *Masach de Guf* descends to the *Chazeh*, the *Reshimot* of the "descending" *Aviut* are activated during their presence in the *Malchut de Rosh*.

It turns out that, as regards the *AB Pnimi*, this is the *Masach HaMesayem* (limiting the spreading of the light), born from a *Zivug* on the *Aviut Gimel* at the *Peh de Rosh* of *Galgalta*. However, regarding the property of "the inclusion", it is *Masach HaMizdaveg* (interacting with the light).

Then it attracts the light again, making a *Zivug de Haka'a* on the *Behina Gimel*, so that the *Rosh AB* emerges from the *Chazeh* up to the *Peh de Galgalta*. The *Peh de AB* is at the level of the *Chazeh de Galgalta*, while the *Guf de AB* spreads downward to the *Tabur* of *Galgalta*. It turns out that the *AB Pnimi* spreads into the *Kelim de Galgalta* and the *AB Hitzon* (outside) dresses onto it so that even its *Rosh* is in the place of the *Guf* of *Galgalta*.

The *AB Pnimi* spreads from the *Rosh* of *Galgalta (Behina Dalet)* into the empty *Kelim* of the *Behina Dalet*, but the *AB Hitzon* has absolutely no connection with the *Behina Dalet*.

Two united objects are completely similar in their desires. As much as the *Masach* can withstand egoism, the *Kli* becomes similar to the Creator in its properties, receiving the light inside with the intention for the Creator's sake. A comparison of the properties is a comparison of the intentions, but it does not mean that both of them become one and the same object. They remain two objects, but their properties are so close that, at this moment, from our point of view, there is no difference.

The more the *Partzuf* receives, the more it becomes similar to the Creator in its intention, and the less in its action. To become equal with the Creator, one should develop one's egoism, to receive more for His sake, but that will lead to an even bigger difference between the creation and the Creator in action. When the *Masach* at the *Peh de Rosh* pushes away all the light, it becomes, as it were, similar in action to the Creator (it does not receive either), but it is isolated from Him in its intention.

The method of self-restraint is wrong. There is no need to fast and give up pleasures; on the contrary, the Creator increases man's egoism to the extent that he can apply the screen and work with it. So out of the two above-mentioned screens, the screen of the *Guf* can lead out into the spiritual.

However, if the screen is only at the *Peh de Rosh*, then man is as if a stone that does not need anything, has no inner movement. It has always been unclear how egoism can lead to the spiritual, when the purpose of the Creation implies reception of delight.

The *Kli* does not see what is outside it. All our names: the "*Ohr Makif*", "presses from outside", "hasn't entered yet" – are notions belonging to the language of our world that we need to imagine somehow a spiritual action. Nevertheless, there is in fact no light pressing from outside, and there is no delight in it. Man's internal *Kli* will feel pleasure, if this light is inside it.

Hence, in order to have an appetite sufficient for the pleasure, I must somehow imagine and sense this pleasure. The light is an inner reaction of the *Kli* for some kind of influence emanated by the Creator, i.e., the light corresponds to our "resistance". Everything depends on how the *Kli* will react to this influence. Only the *Ohr Pnimi* that enters the *Kli* is the measure of similarity to the Creator.

All of the *Partzufim*, from the World of Infinity down to our world, were born according to the same principle: the lower *Partzuf* was born from the higher one.

Man should never think about what will happen to him at the next moment. One should always use the present moment, constantly trying to penetrate into its depth. The next moment will be born out of this one; but one should neither wait for it to come nor think about what it will be like. The entrance into the spiritual world depends on inner penetration into the present.

מ) ויש עוד דבר נוסף בהבדל מהתחתון לעליון. והוא, כי כל תחתון יוצא מבחינת שיעור קומה אחרת שבה׳ בחינות שבמסך (אות כ״ב).

וכל תחתון חסר הבחינה העליונה של האורות דעליון, והבחינה התחתונה של הכלים דעליון.

והטעם הוא, כי מטבע הביטוש דאו״מ במסך, להאביד מהמסך את בחינה אחרונה דעביות שלו. ולמשל, בפרצוף הא׳ דא״ק, שהמסך יש לו כל ה׳ בחינות עביות שלו, דהיינו עד לבחי״ד, הנה ע״י הביטוש דאו״מ בהמסך דגוף, מזכך את העביות דבחי״ד לגמרי, ואינו מניח ממנו אפילו רשימו של העביות ההיא.

ורק הרשימות מהעביות דבחי״ג ולמעלה נשארים במסך. ולפיכך, כשהמסך ההוא נכלל בראש ומקבל שם זווג דהכאה על העביות שנשאר בהרשימות שלו מהגוף, נמצא הזווג יוצא רק על בחי״ג דעביות שבמסך בלבד, כי הרשימו דעביות דבחי״ד נאבדה ואינה שם. וע״כ הקומה שיוצאת על המסך הזה, הוא בשיעור קומת חכמה לבד, הנקרא "הוי״ה דע״ב דא״ק" או "פרצוף ע״ב דא״ק". ונתבאר באות כ״ב, אשר קומת חכמה, היוצאת על המסך דבחי״ג, חסרה המלכות דכלים ובחינת אור יחידה מהאורות, שהוא אור הכתר. הרי שפרצוף הע״ב חסר הבחינה אחרונה דכלים דעליון, והבחינה עליונה דאורות דעליון. ומשום שינוי הצורה הרחוקה הזו, נבחן התחתון לפרצוף נבדל מהעליון.

40) The difference between the lower and the higher Partzufim consists in the fact that each lower Partzuf appears at a different level, lower than the preceding one. As was mentioned, this level is determined by the Aviut of Masach, consisting of the five Behinot.

The highest level of the light and the lowest Behina of the Kelim of the previous Partzuf are absent in each subsequent one. The smaller the desire I use with the screen, the lower the quality of the light I receive in my Partzuf.

The Impact between the Ohr Makif, and the Ohr Pnimi in the screen that separates them, contributes to the loss of the last Behina of the Aviut of this Masach. Therefore, Behina Dalet disappears in the Partzuf Galgalta, so that no Reshimot are left from it.

After the *Masach de Guf* rises and merges with the *Masach de Peh* making a *Zivug de Haka'a* on the *Aviut* left in the *Reshimot* of *Masach*, the *Partzuf* of one level lower emerges, i.e., the *Partzuf Hochma*. The *Behina Dalet* of the vessels is absent in it as well as the light of *Yechida*. Because of the transformation of properties, a new *Partzuf AB* separates from the *Partzuf Galgalta* and becomes independent, but is considered its offspring.

If I can accept 20 per cent of five portions, it means that I receive the *Ohr Yechida* and the *Behina Dalet*. The next time a *Partzuf* is born with the smaller light of *Haya* and the *Kli Gimel*, then the *OhrNeshama* and the *KliBet*, then with the *Ohr Ruach* and the *KliAleph*, and the last one with the *Ohr Nefesh* and the *Kli Shoresh*. Then the desires recommence, and for 20 per cent of the remaining desires, the five *Partzufim* of the world of *Atzilut* are born, and so on, until all the desires of *Malchut* of the World of Infinity are used.

All the *Partzufim* of the five worlds have received as much light as there was in *Malchut* of the World of Infinity, only gradually and with the help of the screen. No matter what portion we take as an example, it will always consist of five parts, albeit very small. The *Kli* is created out of the five desires, and it is necessary to make a *Zivug de Haka'a* on each of them.

If man has not yet corrected his *Kelim*, then the less egoism he has, the closer he is to the Creator. When he acquires the screen, then the bigger his egoism is, the better, for the closer he is to the Creator. Everything depends on the presence of the screen.

To make a *Kli* suitable for use, the light needs to enter it first, and then disappear, so that the *Kli* becomes completely remote from the Creator. With further correction, it will be able to make a choice and merge with the Creator again.

The exit into the spiritual world is possible only if there is a screen for all of your desires. However, if there are no desires, a *Masach* is not necessary either. Hence, without having desires, man cannot enter the spiritual world, since he has nothing to correct.

The ascent to the spiritual levels goes in three lines: left, right and middle. By receiving new portions of egoism, man applies a stronger screen to them. A *Zivug de Haka'a* takes place between the screen and the light; as a result, man receives a new portion of the light and ascends to the next level.

If man has big desires, while the strength of his resistance to them (the screen) is small, then he receives the light according to his screen and generates a small *Partzuf*. Then, when he is able to withstand a new portion of egoism, his *Partzuf* will expand on and on, until he receives a screen for absolutely all of his desires.

This is called "*Gmar Tikkun*". The "bigger" man is, the more desires he has, the stronger the screen he acquires; such a man has great attainments because he is able to rule over his coarsest desires. The desires are given to man from Above when he can ask for their correction.

The scanty desires of our world, the *Ner Dakik*, turn our heads, occupy our thoughts and have such command overus, that we do not know what to do with them, how to get rid of them. All our life is concerned with looking for an opportunity to fill these animal desires. Egoism itself must not be destroyed; one should only put two kinds of screen on it: first – to stop receiving for one's own sake, then to start receiving for the sake of the Creator.

A *Zivug de Haka'a* takes place in the *Rosh*, i.e., I calculate how much I can receive with the intention for the sake of the Creator. The calculation is followed by the reception of the light into the *Guf*, from the *Peh* down to the *Tabur*. The *Tabur* is the borderline of the reception with the intention for the Creator's sake. The light that the *Kli* was unable to receive, the *Ohr Makif*, offers it to receive more; otherwise it does not fulfill the Purpose of creation. But the *Kli* knows that it cannot receive more for the sake of the Creator; provided it receives even a little bit more, this will already be for its own sake.

There is no way out except to overcome this deadlocked state, i.e., expel all the received light. The *Kli* understands that, even if it can receive in the future, it will not be the same amount as it has now, but smaller and with a weaker *Masach*.

The *Masach* loses strength, rises to the *Peh de Rosh* together with the *Reshimot* it received from the four lights in the four *Kelim*. The *Aviut Dalet* was lost in the *Tabur* after the *Bitush* of the *Ohr Makif* in the *Masach*; therefore, the *Kli* will not be able to receive the *Ohr Yechida* henceforth. However, it has not yet made the restriction on the remaining levels of the *Aviut*; hence, it just does not know what it will or will not be able to receive.

Now, when the *Masach* is at the *Peh de Rosh*, the *Kli* feels it can receive some more light. Then all its *Reshimot* awake, and it tries to receive on the *Behina Gimel*. The *Masach* descends to the *Chazeh*, makes a *Zivug de Haka'a* there, and then a new *Partzuf AB* is born. However, all the *Reshimot* of *AB* come from the *Guf* of *Galgalta*.

What is the difference between the two notions: the screen and the Restriction, the *Masach* and the *Tzimtzum*? A restriction means complete refusal to receive. The screen means reception of one part and pushing away the rest. Rabbi Baruch Ashlag gives the following example: each time a drunkard attended a wedding, he would drink himself to oblivion, fall down, and lay on the ground; even his wife would not let him into the house. Ashamed of his disgrace, the man decided to stop attending weddings altogether, because he could not control himself. And so he commenced.

After awhile, he decided he could be present at the festivities and allow himself to drink half a glass of wine, an amount that would not harm him. So he did. Conclusion: a restriction means to abstain from attending celebrations, while the screen means that one attends, but decides to receive a small amount.

There are two kinds of *Reshimot*. The first is the *Reshimo de Itlabshut*, i.e., the memories of the pleasures I was filled with. The second kind is the *Reshimo de Aviut*. It is a recollection of the desires with the help of which I did that, and how strong and hard the screen I used was.

The "desire to receive" in the *Kli* is created by the Creator. The *Kli* received the "desire to give" from Him. How can it use these absolutely opposite desires right now? First, the *Kli* measures the size of its "desire to give", i.e., opposes its genuine, natural "desire to receive".

Let us assume that I have 20 per cent of the "desire to give". It is called the hardness of the screen. I can resist my desire to receive pleasure by 20 per cent. It means that in these 20 per cent I can receive the light, for in them I receive not for my own sake, but for the sake of the Creator. It is similar to a mother who receives pleasure when her baby is delighted. The Creator enjoys when I receive pleasure. The remaining desires, not included in these 20 per cent, remain empty; I do not work with them.

What is Kabbalah? First, we take our inner desires, break them into small cells or vectors and build various graphs. This is the inner psychology of man; not as a creature of this world, but of some entity brought forth by the Creator with all the forces that the Creator gave to him.

Then we study how, with the help of those forces, man attains the Creator. This is a brief explanation of what Kabbalah is. One should not see it as some mystical teaching about secret, supernatural forces that exist outside the Universe. The main idea of Kabbalah suggests that, in the process of accumulating anti-egoistic forces, one can take a certain portion of egoism and work with it in a different direction.

First, the screen that was at the *Peh de Rosh* did not want to receive anything, then it calculated how much it could receive for the sake of the Creator. It is a bigger effort than not receiving anything at all for one's sake. As a result, the screen that is at the *Peh de Rosh* is divided into two screens. The first says that I do not want to receive anything for myself. It is a complete reflection of the light, its rejection, its observance of *TA*. The second screen, which is inactive so far, also stays there. After meeting the conditions of *TA*, I begin to try to receive a little bit of light for the sake of the Creator.

מא) ועד"ז אחר שנתפשט פרצוף ע"ב לראש וגוף, ונעשה הביטוש דאו"מ על המסך דגוף דע"ב, שהוא מסך דבחי"ג, הנה הביטוש הזה מעלים ומאביד ממנו את הרשימו דעביות של הבחינה האחרונה שבמסך, שהוא בחי"ג. ונמצא בעת עלית המסך אל הפה דראש, ונכלל בו בהזווג דהכאה, נעשה ההכאה רק על עביות דבחי"ב, שנשארה במסך הזה. כי הבחי"ג נאבדה ממנו ואינה. וע"כ הוא מוציא רק ע"ס בקומת בינה, הנקרא "הוי"ה דס"ג דא"ק" או "פרצוף ס"ג". ויחסר ז"א ומלכות דכלים וחיה יחידה דאורות. ועד"ז כשנתפשט הפרצוף ס"ג הזה לראש וגוף. ונעשה הביטוש דאו"מ·בהמסך דגוף שלו, שהוא מסך דבחי"ב. הנה הביטוש הזה מעלים ומאביד ממנו הבחינה אחרונה דעביות שבהמסך, שהוא בחי"ב, ולא נשארו במסך אלא הרשימות דעביות שמבחי"א ולמעלה. וע"כ, בעת עלית המסך לפה דראש, ונכלל בזווג דהכאה אשר שם, נעשה ההכאה רק על מסך דבחי"א, שנשאר במסך. כי הבחי"ב כבר נאבדה ממנו. וע"כ הוא מוציא רק ע"ס בקומת ת"ת, הנקרא "קומת ז"א". והוא חסר בינה ז"א ומלכות דכלים, ונשמה חיה יחידה דאורות. וכו' עד"ז.

41) After the formation of the Partzuf AB, the impact between the Ohr Makif and the Ohr Pnimi on the Masach de Guf of AB (with Aviut Gimel) takes place. This impact makes for the loss of the last Behina of the Reshimo de Masach. The Masach rises to the Peh de Rosh and makes a Zivug de Haka'a there only on the Aviut de Behina Bet. This Zivug forms the 10 Sefirot on the level of Bina, i.e., the Partzuf SAG of the world of Adam Kadmon, which has neither the Kelim of ZA and Malchut, nor the lights of Yechida and Haya.

When the Partzuf SAG spreads into the Rosh and the Guf, it leads to a Bitush Ohr Makif on its Masach de Guf and the loss of the last Behina de Aviut of the Masach, the Behina Bet takes place. The Masach with the Reshimot de Aviut from the Behina Aleph and higher rises to the Peh de Rosh and makes a Zivug on the Behina Aleph there, which forms the 10 Sefirot on the level of Tifferet (or ZA). The Kelim Bina, ZA and Malchut and the lights Yechida, Haya and Neshama are absent in this Partzuf.

Does the *Behina Dalet* in SAG have desires, or does it restrict them and the desires of the *Behina Gimel*? Are there any desires in *Behina Dalet* in *AB*, or does it restrict them too?

Everyone has these desires; we speak only about the "desire to receive", without which there is no creation. However, there was a danger that the souls might "steal", receive for their own sake; hence, the correction took place, making them unable to see anything.

Now let us understand the saying, "All the earth is full of His Glory", i.e., everyone has to feel His existence. Yet why can we not actually feel it? It is because, from the direction of the Creator, "All the earth is full of His Glory"; but to prevent the creation from receiving for its own sake, the Restriction took place. Seeing no delight in it, man does not aspire after spirituality.

The Introduction to "The Study of the Ten Sefirot" says that if punishment and reward were revealed so that the one who eats something forbidden would instantly choke with it, who would dare to eat the forbidden food? On the contrary, if man felt great pleasure while putting on the *Tzitzit* (a ritual prayer shawl), he would never take it off. Therefore, if we felt the spiritual delight, we would immediately wish it for our own sake.

There is only one law inherent in egoism: "To work less and to receive more", it knows nothing else. So what can one do if one can neither see nor receive anything? The Creator tells us: "I give everything freely and you should give freely".

We must reach the same level where we can give without expecting any reward. Hence, there was the *Tikkun* (correction) - we can neither see nor "steal". It is written in the *Gemara* (Treatise "Sanhedrin"): "*Adam HaRishon* was a thief" (he stole from the Creator).

In the beginning there was the Creator's domain, i.e., all that *Adam HaRishon* did was for the sake of bestowal; nothing for his own benefit. However, upon seeing the enormous light, he could not receive it with the intention for the sake of giving and got it for himself. This is called, that he takes the light from the Creator's domain to his own; hence, he is called "a thief".

To prevent this from ever happening again, the correction took place in the souls; that is why they cannot see anything. Man should not ask for attainment and spiritual heights, only for the *Kelim* to be able to see.

To give a name to the *Partzuf* there is no need to say that a *Zivug* on some *Behina* takes place; it is enough to give its numeric value, the *Gematria*, to know what it is like qualitatively. *Yud-Hey-Vav-Hey* is the basis of any *Kli*. *Malchut* of the world of Infinity and the entire Universe consist of this one and only structure.

The amount of matter on this structure, i.e., the use of a desire with the right intention is equal to the light received by the *Partzuf*. The numerical value speaks about the quantity and the quality of this light in the *Partzuf*.

The *Partzuf Galgalta* corresponds to the entire *Malchut* of the World of Infinity and has the biggest screen in the Universe. If it received the maximum of what it could for the sake of the Creator, how can there be a place for another *Partzuf*? What can *AB* add to what *Galgalta* has not yet received?

It turns out that *AB* also corresponds to *Malchut* of the World of Infinity, and it can receive the light that *Galgalta* could not. The screen in the next *Partzuf* is weaker; it interacts with the light of a different quality, much less powerful than that of *Galgalta*; hence, *AB* can receive an additional portion of the light.

Each subsequent *Partzuf* receives the light of lower quality. Each new *Partzuf* is an absolutely new state. *AB* draws its desires from the *Sof* of *Galgalta*, i.e., it works with the desires that the previous *Partzuf* could not deal with. *Galgalta* wanted to receive the *Ohr Yechida*, whereas *AB* – only the *Ohr Haya*.

When *Malchut* in the World of Infinity pushes away all the light, it is called *Dalet de Aviut* and *Dalet de Hitlabshut*. It shows that the *Reshimot* of the entire World of Infinity are in it. *Galgalta* starts working with these *Reshimot*, makes a *Zivug de Haka'a* on *Dalet /Dalet* and receives the corresponding light. When the *Bitush Pnim u Makif* takes place, the *Dalet de Hitlabshut* and the *Gimel de Aviut* remain. *Dalet de Aviut* disappears because the *Partzuf* decides not to work with it anymore, and annuls it.

There is an inverse relation between the *Kli* and the light. The smaller the *Kli*, the closer it is in its properties to the light. Let us assume that I have five egoistic desires, from the purest to the coarsest. My purest desire is the nearest to the Creator, the coarsest one is the most remote. *Malchut* has five desires: *Shoresh*, *Aleph*, *Bet*, *Gimel* and *Dalet*.

To put it more precisely, these are the five phases of development of one and the same "desire to receive". The *Shoresh* is the purest, most elevated desire; therefore, it is the closest to the Creator.

When *Malchut* puts the screen over its egoistic desire, the law that states that the purest desire is the closest to the Creator remains unchanged. Besides, the intention for the sake of the Creator is put on it, and exactly this intention allows it to receive more light than such a small desire was supposed to. *Malchut* with the *Masach* "attracts" the light, but Keter (the purest, loftiest part of the *Kli*) receives it and not *Malchut*.

The main elements of the Universe are:
-the light emanating directly from the Creator;
-the egoistic "desire to receive" delight that was created by Him;
-the screen that emerged as a reaction to the received light.

Kabbalah studies these elements in their various states. Harmonious correspondence between the screen, the light, and the desire constitutes the soul, which dictates its laws to the angels, the *Levushim* and material objects.

Each *Partzuf* fills *Malchut* of the World of Infinity; thus the *Partzufim* cover its innermost point from the light. We are the central point. Therefore, as regards us, all the worlds, all the *Partzufim* are the restraining screens.

On the one hand, we say that all the worlds were created in descending order, i.e., before the existence of man. The Worlds are the measures of concealment of the Creator. *Galgalta* conceals the Creator from the lower *Partzuf* by 20 per cent. *AB* only sees 80% of the Creator. Nevertheless, these 80 % are the Creator for it, so they are in fact 100 % for *AB*.

Thus, it goes until the five worlds that consist of the five *Partzufim*, where each *Partzuf* in turn consists of five *Sefirot*, completely conceal the Creator's light from us behind 125 screens. The light does not reach our world at all. We are behind the screen and can neither see nor feel the Creator.

On the other hand, as man ascends and reaches the level of some *Partzuf*, he puts up the screen equal to this *Partzuf* and by doing so eliminates the concealment of the Creator on this level. Rising to the next level, man neutralizes its concealment with the help of his screen, attains the Creator on this level et cetera. When he annuls all the filters, he will completely grasp all the levels that separate him from the Creator.

The worlds are created to teach us how to act in each situation. Therefore, the Creator's concealment is descending, while the revelation happens in the opposite direction. The steps, which the soul climbs, as it were, disappear thereupon.

The lower *Partzuf* knows the previous one and understands that it cannot receive as much light as the one before it does. However, to provide the lower *Partzuf* with the light, each higher one should send its request for the light (called MAN) to the *Partzuf* above it.

Since each new *Partzuf* is an absolutely new desire, which after *TA* has never been filled with the light, each new *Partzuf* leads to a new attainment, exceeding the previous one both qualitatively and quantitatively.

The light received by each subsequent *Partzuf* arrives to it via the previous one. All the *Partzufim* it passes through, receive their part of the light, and this portion is immeasurably bigger than the amount of the light that will be received by the last one in this chain. Only *Galgalta* receives the light directly from the World of Infinity.

All our actions are based on our desires. The mind plays only an auxiliary role at that. The mind consciously perceives only what enters the senses; it calculates and analyses them. The wider and deeper the sensations are, the bigger the mind necessary for their processing.

If we take a person who studies Kabbalah and indulges in some kind of inner work, then the more subtle this work is, the more flexible and precise his mind should be to differentiate and analyze his senses and make adequate conclusions. However, the mind always remains only an auxiliary tool of the desire. The mind is needed only for gaining the desired object. All of us want pleasure, and the mind assists us in achieving it. If man wants to enjoy scientific research, his mind helps him there. Man thinks that he lives only by his mind; therefore, he stands above all other creatures.

מב) ונתבאר היטב הטעם של ירידות הקומות זו למטה מזו בעת השתלשלות הפרצופים זה מזה, שהוא משום שהביטוש דאו"מ באו"פ, הנוהג בכל פרצוף, מאביד תמיד שם את הבחינה אחרונה דרשימו דעביות אשר שם.

ויש לדעת, אמנם שבאלו הרשימות, הנשארות במסך לאחר הזדככותו, יש בהם ב' בחינות: א. נקרא רשימו דעביות, ב. נקרא רשימו דהתלבשות. למשל, אחר שנזדכך המסך דגוף דפרצוף הא' דא"ק, אמרנו שהבחינה האחרונה דרשימות דעביות, שהיא הרשימו דבחי"ד, נאבדה ממנו. ולא נשאר בהמסך, אלא הרשימו דעביות דבחי"ג. אמנם הרשימו דבחי"ד כוללת ב' בחינות כנ"ל: דהתלבשות ודעביות. ולא נאבד מהמסך בסבת ההזדככות ההיא רק הרשימו דעביות דבחי"ד. אבל הרשימו דהתלבשות דבחי"ד נשארה בהמסך ההוא ולא נאבד ממנו. ופירושו של הרשימו דהתלבשות, הוא בחינה זכה מאד מהרשימו דבחי"ד, שאין בה עביות מספיק לזווג דהכאה עם אור העליון. ורשימו זו נשארה מהבחינה אחרונה שבכל פרצוף בעת הזדככותו. ומה שאמרנו, שהבחינה אחרונה נאבדה מכל פרצוף בעת הזדככותו, הוא רק הרשימו דעביות שבה בלבד.

42) Now we will understand the meaning of the consecutive descent of the levels during the development of the Partzufim one after another because of the Bitush Ohr Makif and Ohr Pnimi, which governs in each Partzuf and contributes to the loss of its last Behina of the Reshimo de Aviut.

The Reshimot left after the thinning of the screen are of two kinds: the Reshimo de Aviut and the Reshimo de Hitlabshut. Therefore, after the weakening of the Masach of the Partzuf Galgalta, the Reshimo de Aviut of the Behina Gimel remained, while the Reshimo de Hitlabshut of the Behina Dalet did not change.

The *Reshimo de Hitlabshut* is a very thin part of the *Reshimo* that does not have sufficient *Aviut* for a *Zivug de Haka'a* with the light. Like *Galgalta*, any *Partzuf* with the weakening of its *Masach* loses only the last *Reshimo de Aviut*, but not the *Reshimo de Hitlabshut*.

We have studied that there is an inverse relation between the light and the vessel, and there are two rules here:

1) "*Lefum Tza'ara – Agra*", i.e., the reward is given according to the merit (suffering); in other words, the amount of the light revealed to man depends on the amount of efforts he made.

2) The light wants to enter the clearest *Kli*. The *Kli* is considered clear if it refuses to receive anything the coarse *Kli* wants to receive.

For example, it is easier to work with the intention for the sake of bestowal during prayer, when man is covered with a *Tallit*, and crowned with a *Tefillin*; he does not want to receive anything, only to fulfill the commandment. But while studying, it is more difficult to have the intention for the sake of bestowal, much more difficult to have it during the family meal, and still more difficult to apply during one's work.

However, according to the first rule, the bigger hindrances one can overcome, the more powerful light one can receive. That is why if man can do business with the intention for the sake of the Creator, without doubt he is worthy of a high level. We say about such person that "His knowledge is deep and his prayer is strong!"

The second rule springs from the first one: the highest level corresponds to the lightest *Kelim*, although there it is easier to intend for the sake of the Creator. On the other hand, the height of the level is determined by its most corrected property, and the light goes through it and descends to the lower level.

Therefore, the *Reshimo de Aviut* is a deficiency, the "desire to receive". But one should not forget that, in spirituality, the "desire to receive" always means the desire with a *Masach*. Therefore the *Reshimo de Aviut* means that there is a memory in it of how much it can receive for the sake of giving, i.e., the previous strength of resistance disappeared in it. Its lightest *Kli*, the *Kli de Keter*, cannot disappear under the influence of the surrounding light, because it has no *Aviut*. Hence, *Reshimo* of the light that was there once is left in it, which is called the *Reshimo de Hitlabshut*.

There is always some *Reshimo* left from the presence of the light. Two notions should be cleared up:

1) The light comes from the giver's direction.
2) The *Aviut* and the *Masach* come from the receiver's direction.

Whatever comes from the giver leaves a memory, and whatever comes from the receiver – meets with resistance and disappears.

Rabbi Baruch Ashlag gives the following example: "Once I found myself in a place where old people were resting. I looked around and saw that all of them were dozing, paying no attention to anything. It is said about it: "the day is devoid of passion". I came up to one of them and began talking to him. First I asked him where he was from, then how he made his living, so I got him talking, and he began telling me about his past businesses.

Little by little, he was getting more and more excited and enthusiastic, recalling his achievements and the various events he went through, i.e., in the language of Kabbalah the *Reshimot* of the past delights awoke in him. At the end, I asked him, "Would you like to relive it all over again, traveling from town to town making deals and striking bargains the way you did before? That very instant his eyes grew dim, for he recalled the present and the bygone strength, which he had no more".

Thus, we see that the *Reshimo* of a man's delight remains in him, while the strength is all gone. We may conclude that he has no more *Aviut* in him, i.e., he cannot receive for the sake of giving. The *Reshimo de Hitlabshut* – the reminiscence of the pleasure dressed in the *Kli*-desire remained, but, having no screen, he is unable to return to the bygone delights.

מג) וההשארה של הרשימו דהתלבשות מהבחינה אחרונה, שנשארה בכל מסך, גרם ליציאת ב' קומות זכר ונקבה בראשים דכל הפרצופים. החל מע"ב דא"ק, וכן בס"ג דא"ק, וכן במ"ה וב"ן דא"ק, ובכל פרצופי אצילות.

כי בפרצוף ע"ב דא"ק, שאין שם במסך אלא רשימו דעביות דבחי"ג, המוציא ע"ס בקומת חכמה, הנה הרשימו דהתלבשות מבחי"ד, הנשארת שם במסך, שאינה ראויה כלל לזווג עם אור העליון משום זכותה, הנה היא נכללת עם העביות דבחי"ג ונעשת לרשימו אחת. ואז קנתה הרשימו דהתלבשות כח להזדווגות עם אור העליון.

וע"כ יצא עליה זווג דהכאה עם אור העליון, המוציא ע"ס בקירוב לקומת כתר. והוא מטעם, היות בה בחינת התלבשות דבחי"ד. והתכללות זה נקרא התכללות הנקבה בזכר. כי הרשימו דעוביות מבחי"ג נקרא נקבה, להיותה הנושא לבחינת העביות. והרשימו דהתלבשות דבחי"ד נקרא זכר, משום שבא מקומה גבוה ממנה, ומשום שהוא זך מעביות.

ולפיכך, הגם שהרשימו דזכר בלבד אינו מספיק לזווג דהכאה, אמנם ע"י התכללות הנקבה בו, נעשה גם הוא ראוי לזווג דהכאה.

43) The disappearance of the Reshimo de Hitlabshut in each last level left in the Masach leads to the formation of two stages: Zachar and Nekeva ("male" and "female" essence) in the Rosh of each Partzuf, starting from AB de AK, but also in SAG, MA, BON and in all the Partzufim of the world of Atzilut.

There is the Reshimo de Aviut of the Behina Gimel in the screen of the Partzuf AB. It elevates the 10 Sefirot of the Reflected Light only up to the level of Hochma, but the Reshimo de Hitlabshut of the Behina Dalet that is left there is unfit for Zivug with the Upper Light, due to its Zakut (the absence of the "desire to receive", but wishing to be like the Creator). By absorbing the Reshimo de Aviut and forming one common Reshimo with it, it now receives enough strength for a Zivug de Haka'a with the Upper Light.

Then a Zivug de Haka'a with the Ohr Elion takes place, and as a result, the Partzuf of the level close to that of Keter emerges, as the Reshimo de Hitlabshut of the Behina Dalet is present in it. This merging is called the inclusion of Nekeva in Zachar; since the Reshimo de Aviut of the Behina Gimel is called "Nekeva". This is because it is determined by the property of Aviut (the sensation of the "desire to receive"). However, the Reshimo de Hitlabshut of the Behina Dalet is called Zachar, because it corresponds to a higher state and does not have Aviut.

The Reshimo de Zachar cannot make a Zivug by itself. A Zivug de Nekeva determines the level of the emerging Partzuf, the quality and the quantity of the light that will really enter the Partzuf.

Owing to the memory of its previous state, i.e., the previous *Partzuf*, *Zivug de Zachar* gives to the emerging *Partzuf* a kind of additional, auxiliary luminescence.

Such interaction of *Zachar* and *Nekeva* starts from the *Partzuf* AB. Therefore beginning with it, all the *Partzufim* have two heads (*Rashim*) and two *Zivugim*.

There is a rule: regarding the lower level, the upper one is called perfection (*Shlemut*). *Zachar* is called perfection because it is the *Reshimo* of the light and there is no deficiency in it.

מד) ואחר זה יש גם התכללות הזכר בנקבה. דהיינו שהרשימו דהתלבשות נכלל בהרשימו דעביות. ואז יוצא זווג דהכאה על קומת הנקבה בלבד, שהוא רק קומת בחי"ג, שהיא קומת חכמה, הנקרא "הוי"ה דע"ב".

והנה הזווג העליון, שהנקבה נכללה בהזכר, נבחן לקומת הזכר, שהיא קומת כתר בקירוב. וזווג התחתון, שהזכר נכלל בהנקבה, נבחן לקומת הנקבה, שהיא קומת חכמה בלבדה. אמנם קומת הזכר, מתוך שהעביות שבו אינו מעצמו, אלא ע"י התכללות עם הנקבה, הנה הגם שמספיק ליציאת קומת ע"ס ממטה למעלה, הנקרא "ראש", עכ"ז אין קומה זו יכולה להתפשט ממעלה למטה לבחינת גוף, שפירושו התלבשות האורות בכלים.

כי זווג דהכאה על עביות הבא מבחינת התכללות, אינו מספיק להתפשט לבחינת כלים. ולפיכך אין בקומת הזכר רק בחינת ראש בלי גוף. וגוף הפרצוף נמשך רק מקומת הנקבה, שיש לה עביות מבחינת עצמותו. ומשום זה אנו מכנים את הפרצוף רק על קומת הנקבה בלבד, דהיינו בשם פרצוף ע"ב. כי עיקרו של הפרצוף הוא הבחינת גוף שלו, שהוא התלבשות האורות בכלים. והוא יוצא רק מקומת הנקבה כמבואר. ע"כ נקרא הפרצוף על שמה.

44) There is also the inclusion of Zachar in Nekeva. This means that the Reshimo de Hitlabshut unites with the Reshimo de Aviut. In this case a Zivug occurs only on the level of Nekeva, i.e., on Behina Gimel (Hochma), which is called HaVaYaH (Yud-Hey-Vav-Hey, the unutterable Name of the Creator) de AB.

There are the so-called "upper" and "lower" Zivugim. The upper Zivug corresponds to the inclusion of Nekeva in Zachar. Because of this Zivug, the Partzuf whose level is close to Keter emerges. The lower Zivug corresponds to the inclusion of Zachar in Nekeva. This Zivug leads to the creation of a Partzuf whose level is only Hochma. Aviut, which corresponds to the level of Zachar, does not belong to it, as was mentioned above; it was acquired because of the "inclusion", the interaction with Nekeva.

Therefore this Aviut is sufficient only for creating the 10 Sefirot bottom-up (called Rosh), but not for spreading top-down, which forms the Guf – the true vessels. The Guf of the Partzuf is formed with the help of the level of Nekeva, which has its own Aviut. Hence, we call the Partzuf according to the level of Nekeva, in this particular case AB. The main part of the Partzuf is the Guf; it is where the reception of the light in the vessels takes place.

מה) ועי"ד שנתבארו ב' הקומות זכר ונקבה בראש דפרצוף ע"ב, ממש על אותו דרך יוצאים ב' הללו גם בראש הס"ג. אלא שם קומת הזכר הוא בקירוב לבחינת חכמה, משום שהוא מהרשימו דהתלבשות דבחי"ג בהתכללות העביות דבחי"ב. וקומת הנקבה היא בקומת בינה, דהיינו מהעביות דבחי"ב.

וגם כאן נקרא הפרצוף רק על שם קומת הנקבה, משום שהזכר הוא ראש בלי גוף. ועד"ז בפרצוף מ"ה דא"ק. ושם קומת הזכר הוא בקירוב לקומת בינה, המכונה "קומת ישסו"ת", להיותו מרשימו דבחי"ב דהתלבשות בהתכללות עביות מבחי"א. וקומת הנקבה היא קומת ז"א לבד. כי היא רק בחי"א דעביות. וגם כאן אין הפרצוף נקרא אלא על שם הנקבה, דהיינו פרצוף מ"ה או פרצוף ו"ק, משום שהזכר הוא ראש בלי גוף. ועד"ז תשכיל בכל הפרצופים.

45) Similar to the formation of the two levels of Zachar and Nekeva in the Rosh of the Partzuf AB, the same levels emerge in the Partzuf SAG. The only difference is that, in the former case, the level of Zachar is approximately Hochma, since it emerges as a result of a Zivug on the inclusion of Aviut Bet (Bina) in the Reshimo Gimel de Hitlabshut (Hochma). The level of Nekeva in SAG is a pure Bina with Aviut Bet.

In the case of SAG, the Partzuf is also called according to the level of Nekeva (Bina), since the level of Zachar has only the Rosh without the Guf. Zachar of the Partzuf MA of the world AK is at the level close to Bina and is called YESHSUT, since it results from the interaction between the Reshimo Bet de Hitlabshut and the Reshimo Aleph de Aviut. Nekeva of this Partzuf is at the level of ZA, since it has only Aleph de Aviut. The rest of the Partzufim of the world AK are constructed similarly.

VAK de Bina is called YESHSUT, and Gar de Bina is called the upper Abba ve Ima.

TA'AMIM, NEKUDOT, TAGIN, AND OTIOT
טעמים נקודות תגין ואותיות

מו) אחר שנתבאר הביטוש דאו"מ באו"פ, הנוהג אחר התפשטות הפרצוף לבחינת גוף, שבסבתו מזדכך המסך דגוף, וכל האורות דגוף מסתלקים, והמסך עם הרשימות הנשארים בו עולים לפה דראש, ומתחדשים שם בזווג דהכאה מחדש, ומוציאים קומה חדשה בשיעור העביות שברשימות, נבאר עתה ד' מיני אורות טנת"א, הנעשים עם הביטוש דאו"מ ועליות המסך לפה דראש.

46) We said above that because of the Bitush Ohr Makif in the Masach de Guf, the Masach weakens, rises until it joins the Masach de Rosh, and becomes a single whole with it. Then both screens perform a Zivug de Haka'a, which leads to the emergence of a new Partzuf in concordance with the Aviut in its Reshimot. Now let us study the four kinds of the light TANTA (Ta'amim, Nekudot, Tagin and Otiot – in Hebrew the word begins with the letter Aleph), which stem out of the Bitush de Ohr Makif and the rise of the Masach to the Peh de Rosh.

מז) כי נתבאר, שע"י הביטוש דאו"מ במסך דגוף, הוא מזכך למסך מכל עביות דגוף, עד שנזדכך ונשתוה למסך דפה דראש. שהשתוות הצורה עם הפה דראש, נמצא מיחדהו כבחינה אחת עמו, ונכלל בזווג דהכאה שבו. אמנם נבחן, שאין המסך מזדכך בבת אחת, אלא על פי סדר המדרגה. דהיינו, מתחילה מבחי"ד לבחי"ג, ואח"כ מבחי"ג לבחי"ב, ואח"כ מבחי"ב לבחי"א, ואחר כך מבחי"א לבחינת שורש, עד שנזדכך מכל בחינת עביותו ונעשה זך כמו המסך דפה דראש. והנה אור העליון אינו פוסק מלהאיר אף רגע, והוא מזדווג עם המסך בכל מצב ומצב של הזדככותו.

47) However, the Masach does not lose its strength at one go; it happens in a certain order. First, the Masach loses Behina Dalet, then Behina Gimel, then Bet, then Shoresh and Aleph, until the Masach is totally free from all the Aviut and merges with the Masach de Rosh. The Upper Light never stops shining; it continues to interact with the Masach in whatever state it may be during the process of its weakening.

The egoistic desire that made *TA* now wants to work only in an altruistic mode and enjoy receiving for the sake of the Creator. However, at the beginning it receives only 20 per cent, then gradually gets free from the light, because it cannot receive any more as the result of the *Bitush* of the *Ohr Makif* and the *Ohr Pnimi*.

In fact, the light neither enters nor exits anything. The light is constantly inside the vessel (the *Kli*). Everything depends on whether the particular vessel is able to feel the light inside it or not. Similarly, we are filled with the Creator's light, but do not feel it due to the lack of correction, the screen. If we begin to correct ourselves and acquire the screen against our egoism, we will feel the Creator and His light.

Now that the decision to expel the light is made, *Malchut*, wishing to feel and reveal the Creator, starts modifying its inner sensations. The Upper Light never stops shining, but constantly makes *Zivugim* with the *Masach* in each state as it ascends.

> *When the Masach de Guf ascended one level above the Tabur, i.e., from the Malchut de Guf to the Zeir Anpin de Guf, there was an intermediate Zivug in the Masach de Rosh. Because of this Zivug, the intermediate Partzuf of the level of Hochma emerged.*
>
> *Then the Masach de Guf continues to rise. From ZA de Guf it rises to Bina de Guf. At this time, there is another intermediate Zivug de Haka'a on the Masach de Rosh, which leads to the formation of the Partzuf of the level of Bina and so on.*
>
> *There are four such interim Zivugim during the transition from Galgalta to AB. These Zivugim lead to the formation of four intermediate Partzufim called Hochma de Galgalta, Bina de Galgalta, ZA de Galgalta, and Malchut de Galgalta.*
>
> *Thus, we learned that the second Partzuf AB is born with the help of four Zivugim, which gradually emerge during the weakening of the Masach de Guf on its way to complete merging with the Masach de*

Rosh. A similar process takes place during the transition from AB to SAG or any other Partzuf.

There is a general rule: the Masach cannot get free from its Aviut at one go; it is a gradual process. The Ohr Elion, which is constantly shining, makes a Zivug on each level.

כי אחר שנזדכך מבחי"ד, ונסתלק כל הקומת כתר הזו, והמסך בא לעביות דבחי"ג, הרי אור העליון מזדווג עם המסך על פי העביות דבחי"ג הנשארת בו, ומוציא ע"ס בקומת חכמה.

ואחר כך, כשנזדכך המסך גם מבחי"ג, ונסתלק גם קומת חכמה, ולא נשאר במסך רק בחינה ב', נמצא אור העליון מזדווג עמו על בחי"ב, ומוציא ע"ס בקומת בינה. ואחר כך כשמזדכך גם מבחי"ב, ונסתלקה הקומה הזו, ולא נשאר בו רק עביות דבחי"א, הנה אור העליון מזדווג עם המסך על עוביות דבחי"א הנשארת בו, ומוציא קומת ע"ס בקומת הז"א. וכשנזדכך גם מעביות דבחי"א, וקומת הז"א מסתלקת, ולא נשאר בו אלא שורש העביות, מזדווג אור העליון גם על העביות דשורש הנשארת בהמסך, ומוציא ע"ס בקומת המלכות. וכשנזדכך המסך גם מעביות דשורש, וגם קומת המלכות נסתלקה משם, כי לא נשאר במסך עוד שום עביות דגוף, הנה אז נבחן שהמסך ורשימותיו עלו ונתחברו עם המסך דראש, ונכלל שם בזווג דהכאה, ויוצאים עליו הע"ס החדשות, הנקראות בן ותולדה לפרצוף הראשון.

והנה נתבאר, שענין הביטוש דאו"מ באו"פ, המזכך להמסך דגוף של הפרצוף הא' דא"ק, ומעלהו לפה דראש שלו, שעי"ז נולד ויוצא פרצוף שני ע"ב דא"ק, אין זה נעשה בבת אחת, אלא על סדר המדרגה, אשר אור עליון מזדווג עמו בכל מצב ומצב מהד' מדרגות, שהולך ובא עליהם במשך זמן הזדככותו, עד שנשתווה לפה דראש. ועד"ז שנתבאר יציאת ד' קומות במשך זמן הזדככות הגוף דפרצוף א' לצורך ע"ב, כן יוצאות ג' קומות במשך זמן הזדככות המסך דגוף דפרצוף ע"ב, בעת אצילותו לפרצוף ס"ג. וכן בכל המדרגות.

כי זה הכלל: אין המסך מזדכך בבת אחת אלא בסדר המדרגה. ואור העליון, שאינו פוסק להתפשט לתחתון, נמצא מזדווג עמו בכל מדרגה ומדרגה שבדרך זיכוכו.

מח) אמנם אלו הקומות שיוצאות על המסך במשך זמן הזדככותו ע"פ סדר המדרגה, אינן נחשבות להתפשטות מדרגות אמיתיות, כמו הקומה הראשונה שיצאה מטרם התחלת הזדככות, אלא שהן נחשבות לבחינות נקודות. ומכונות בשם "אור"ח ודין". כי כח הדין של הסתלקות האורות כבר מעורב בהם.

כי בפרצוף הא', הנה תיכף כשהביטוש התחיל לפעול וזיכך את המסך דגוף מבחי"ד, הנה נחשב כאלו כבר נזדכך כולו. כי אין מקצת ברוחני. וכיון שהתחיל להזדכך, כבר מוכרח להזדכך כולו. אלא מתוך שמדרך המסך להזדכך על סדר המדרגה, יש שהות לאור העליון להזדווג עמו בכל מדרגה של עביות שהמסך מקבל במשך זמן הזדככותו, עד שמזדכך כולו. וע"כ אלו הקומות היוצאות במשך זמן הסתלקותו, כח ההסתלקות מעורב בהן, ונחשבות רק לבחינות נקודות ואור"ח ודין.

48) These interim, inner Partzufim are called "Nekudot". Nekudot are the Ohr Hozer, per se. Besides, the Nekudot are inseparably connected with the category of "Din" (judgment), because the force of this judgment-restriction is already included in them.

There are no half-decisions in spirituality. Therefore, when the Partzuf, affected by a Bitush Pnim u Makif, decides to expel the light, this process cannot be stopped. However, as was said above, during the expulsion of the light, i.e., during the ascent of the Masach from the Tabur (Malchut de Guf), intermediate Zivugim de Haka'a take place and create intermediate Partzufim called Nekudot.

Any reception of the light inside the *Partzuf* (including what occurred because of such a *Zivug*) is a reception of pleasure. It means that, even while passing from one level to another lower one (e.g. from *Galgalta* to *AB*, from *AB* to *SAG* and so on), the *Partzuf* continues to receive the light (pleasure).

ולפיכך אנו מבחינים בכל פרצוף ב' מיני קומות, בשם: טעמים, ונקודות. כי הע"ס דגוף שיצאו בראשונה בכל פרצוף נקראות בשם "טעמים". ואותם הקומות היוצאות בפרצוף בדרך זיכוכו, דהיינו אחר שכבר התחיל המסך להזדכך עד שמגיע לפה דראש, הן נקראות בשם "נקודות".

Thus, we can distinguish two levels in each Partzuf: the Ta'amim and the Nekudot. The Nekudot were defined above. The Ta'amim are the first 10 Sefirot de Guf of the Partzuf, emerging because of the first regular Zivug de Haka'a, which leads to the formation of this particular Partzuf.

The first spreading of the light – the *Ta'amim* - came to shine on this level; but the *Nekudot*, although they have the Direct Light and also spread in the form of *Rosh*, *Toch* and *Sof*, do not emerge to shine on this level because the *Ohr Makif* annuls the screen and the entire level disappears.

However, since the screen consists of the four *Behinot*, the light cannot leave the level at one go. It resembles a situation in which a person sitting in the fourth room is asked to leave. He cannot leave the house from the fourth room without passing through the other three. When he enters the third room, he does not intend to remain there, for he wishes only to pass through it.

A person falling down from the fifth floor cannot stop during the fall, can he? He must fall down to the fourth floor, then to the third and so on, until he reaches the ground. A clever person falling down from the fifth level considers the fourth level the lowest; in this case, he can stop immediately and must not continue falling. Someone less smart, falling from the fifth level to the fourth one, thinks: "There are people worse than I am". This person must fall to the bottom.

There is another example. Two workers received their salary. The first one got $800 and is very pleased; the second got $900 and is very sad. The first one used to receive $600 before; hence, he was pleased to receive $800. The second one used to receive $1000, so he was sad when his salary was cut. The reduced salary brings no pleasure, only judgment and restriction.

It is defined as "the power of judgment", the power of outcome, which arises from the disappearance of the screen and according to the law that imposes a ban on the egoistic reception. These phases of the light's withdrawal are called "the Returned Light". Yet in fact, they are the Direct Light since they shine at the time of departure, during "the return of the light to its root".

Since there are no half-decisions in the spiritual world, we may conclude that, if we wish to attain spirituality, we should prefer it to everything else and go on until the end.

מט) ואלו הרשימות הנשארות למטה בגוף אחר הסתלקות האורות דטעמים, נקראות בשם "תגין". ואלו הרשימות הנשארות מקומות הנקודות נקראות בשם "אותיות", שהם "כלים". והתגין, שהם הרשימות מהאורות דטעמים, הם חופפים על האותיות והכלים, ומקיימים אותם.

ונתבאר ד' מיני אורות, הנקראים "טעמים", "נקודות", "תגין", "אותיות". אשר הקומה הראשונה היוצאת בכל פרצוף מה"פ, הנקראים "גלגלתא", "ע"ב", "ס"ג", "מ"ה" "ב"ן", נקראת בשם "טעמים". וקומות היוצאות בכל פרצוף אחר שכבר התחיל להזדכך, עד שמזדכך

כולו, נקראות בשם "נקודות". והרשימות הנשארות מהאורות דטעמים שבכל קומה אחר הסתלקותם, נקראות בשם "תגין". והרשימות הנשארות מהאורות של קומות הנקודות אחר הסתלקותם, נקראות בשם "אותיות" או "כלים". ותזכור זה בכל ה"פ הנקראים "גלגלתא", "ע"ב", "ס"ג", "מ"ה", "ב"ן", כי בכולם יש הזדככות ובכולם יש אלו ד' מיני אורות.

49) The Reshimot (memories) that remain from the Ta'amim in the Guf of the Partzuf are called "Tagin". The Reshimot that remain from the interim stages of Nekudot are called "Otiot" or "Kelim". The Tagin (Reshimot from the lights of Ta'amim) are placed above the letters (Otiot - the genuine Kelim), and enliven them.

Therefore, the ten Sefirot that emerged from the first Zivug de Haka'a and the subsequent descent of the light are called the "Ta'amim". The ten Sefirot or, rather, ten interim Partzufim (or five, if we consider ZA one Sefira), which emerged from the nine (or four) intermediate Zivugim during the rise of the screen from the Tabur to the Peh, are called "Nekudot". The Reshimot of Ta'amim are called "Tagin" and the Reshimot of Nekudot – "Otiot".

Nothing ever appears or disappears; everything depends on the attitude of the *Partzuf* to the light. It either perceives the light as pleasure or as darkness. *Malchut* of the World of Infinity sensed the light as egoistic pleasure, and then saw emptiness in it. Therefore, it disappeared (in the language of Kabbalah, *Malchut* "expelled" the light).

Now it does not derive pleasure from egoistic reception, but from receiving for the sake of bestowal. The filling of it from the *Peh* to the *Tabur* is the sensation of pleasure from giving to the Creator. Being too weak to keep this pleasure, *Malchut* loses the desire for it, and it leaves. However, the reminiscence of this pleasure stays behind; it is called the *Reshimo*, i.e., the outside light, as it were, shines from afar upon this *Partzuf*.

In fact, all sensations are inside; so the meaning of "outside" is purely relative. There are dozens of kinds of *Reshimot* (memories) and of course, all of them are felt inside. The *Ohr Makif* (the Surrounding, Outer

Light) is inside me, but the attitude to it is different now. We must learn to think internally, turning all our attention and thoughts "inside".

Being empty of pleasure creates the *Kelim*. Man had already experienced the previous state, passed it, and sensed all its transformations. Now, he can proceed to the next. Without the state of being filled and the following emptiness, it is impossible to acquire a genuine *Kli*.

Longing for spirituality or being indifferent to it, striving after animal pleasures – only this determines man's advancement. It does not depend on us how many levels we will go through. We can only determine the speed. This means that man can shorten the duration of the correction ("Israel shortens the time"). This is the main task of Kabbalah.

It turns out that the *Ta'amim*, i.e., the spreading of the light from above, only marks the contours of the future *Partzuf*. It is only *Keter*, the sketch of the future ten *Sefirot*. The *Nekudot* are the ten *Sefirot* that already appear according to the contours outlined by the *Ta'amim*. The *Nekudot* are the next stage of the creation of the *Partzuf*, the *Kli*. The *Tagin* are the ten *Sefirot* that were also placed on the borders created earlier by the *Ta'amim* and the *Nekudot*. The *Otiot* are the ten *Sefirot* that appeared after the expulsion of the light.

Otiot, i.e., the state where there is no light, but there is a very strong "desire to receive" it, are the very final phase in the development of the *Kli*. One must remember that well, because the weakening of the screen, the expulsion of the light and the emergence of four kinds of the light, *Ta'amim*, *Nekudot*, *Tagin* and *Otiot*, take place in all the *Partzufim*.

The light enters or exits the *Kli*, but the *Reshimot* are also the light that shines with small intensity, as it cannot be retained anymore.

When man ascends the spiritual levels, all these *Reshimot* are already inside him. He knows in advance that there will be difficulties; hence, foreseeing a fall, he can use it as a springboard for a future ascent. By working, putting his efforts into something, man is rewarded with knowledge and pleasant sensations. The moment he starts enjoying them, there comes a fall.

Nevertheless, while man is descending, he cannot feel the fall yet; it still pleases him. When he feels it, it means that he is already down. Therefore, to avoid the sensation of a fall, to sweeten its bitterness, man, when he achieves something good, should consider it a fall. Then he can continue ascending. This refers to the practical studies of Kabbalah.

The answers to the questions that come to one's mind during the study of the material should be attained internally. If man starts feeling the Creator just a little bit, then the questions he used to ask others are revealed to him. Only by receiving a personal answer to his question, by attracting a spark of the light, does he discover the essence of phenomena, and it is never forgotten; it remains inside him, in his sensations.

Such answers depend on the amount of effort man puts forth and have nothing to do with the bulk of his accumulated knowledge. Nor does it depend on his educational level or intellect. This is the main difference between Kabbalah and all other sciences. Kabbalah is called a science because it is based on the reception of the spiritual light – the *Ohr Hochma*, which enters the spiritual *Kli* with the help of the screen, but not through knowledge or intellect.

Spiritual knowledge is the light that enters the *Kli*, the desire to receive pleasure for the sake of the Creator. All other kinds of knowledge enter our 'desire to acquire'; the knowledge itself constitutes egoistic information.

The discovery of spirituality means that one should not seek knowledge; rather one must be eager to acquire the intention to receive for the sake of the Creator. Spiritual information must enter the spiritual vessel. While studying, I should connect with the material; find something that speaks about me. I have to understand where my past, present and future are, and how they are related to the material I study. If man has not yet entered the spiritual world, it means that the quality and the quantity of his efforts were not sufficient.

Or, perhaps man has made considerable effort; but their quality was not adequate enough, i.e., during his studies he did not concentrate on how the Upper Light would purify and elevate him above our world. Instead, he tried to understand the material and fill his mind with it.

ROSH, TOCH, SOF, AND DRESSING OF THE PARTZUFIM ON ONE ANOTHER

ענין רת"ס שבכל פרצוף וסדר התלבשות הפרצופים זב"ז

נ) הנה כבר ידעת את ההבחן שיש ב' מיני מלכיות בכל פרצוף, שהם מלכות המזדווגת ומלכות המסיימת. והנה מהמסך שבמלכות המזדווגת יוצאות ע"ס דאו"ח ממנה ולמעלה, המלבישות לע"ס דאור העליון, שהם נקראות "ע"ס דראש", כלומר שרשים לבד.

ומשם ולמטה מתפשטות הע"ס דגוף הפרצוף, דהיינו בבחינות התלבשות האורות בכלים גמורים.

ואלו הע"ס דגוף מתחלקות לב' בחינות של ע"ס, הנקראות "ע"ס דתוך" ו"ע"ס דסוף". שהע"ס דתוך מקומן מפה עד הטבור, ששם מקום התלבשות של האורות בכלים. והע"ס דסיום וסוף הפרצוף, מקומן מטבורו ולמטה עד סיום רגליו, שפירושן, אשר המלכות מסיימת לכל ספירה וספירה עד שמגיעה לבחינתה עצמה, שאינה ראויה לקבל שום אור, וע"כ נפסק שם הפרצוף.

ובחינת הפסק זה מכונה "סיום אצבעות רגלין של הפרצוף", שמשם ולמטה חלל פנוי וריקן בלי אור. ותדע, שב' מיני ע"ס הללו נמשכים מהע"ס דשרשים, הנקראים "ראש". כי שניהם נכללים במלכות המזדווגת. כי יש שם כח הלבשה, שהוא האו"ח, העולה ומלביש לאור העליון.

גם יש שם כח העיכוב של המסך על המלכות, שלא תקבל האור, שעי"ז נעשה הזווג דהכאה המעלה אור חוזר. וב' כחות הללו המה בהראש רק שורשים בעלמא. אלא כשמתפשטים מלמעלה למטה, הנה כח הא', שהוא כח ההלבשה, יוצא לפועל בע"ס דתוך, שמפה ולמטה עד הטבור. וכח הב', שהוא כח העיכוב על המלכות מלקבל אור, יוצא לפועל בע"ס דסוף וסיום, שמטבור ולמטה עד סיום אצבעות רגלין.

וב' מיני ע"ס הללו נקראים תמיד חג"ת נהי"מ. שהע"ס דתוך, שמפה עד הטבור, נקראות כולן בשם "חג"ת". והע"ס דסוף שמטבור ולמטה, נקראות כולן בשם "נהי"מ".

50) As was stated above, there are two kinds of Malchut in each Partzuf: Malchut that makes a Zivug and Malchut that prevents the light from entering. Because of the Zivug de Haka'a that occurs on the Masach of the first Malchut, the 10 Sefirot of the Reflected Light emerge. They rise and dress onto the Upper Light, dividing it into ten Sefirot de Rosh, i.e., purely the roots of the Kelim.

Then this Malchut expands downwards from the Masach via the ten Sefirot, spreading by the ten Sefirot de Guf, which means dressing of the light in the finished Kelim.

The ten Sefirot de Guf are divided into two parts: the Toch and the Sof. The position of the ten Sefirot de Toch is from the Peh to the Tabur, where the lights dress in the Kelim. From the Tabur down to the "Sium Reglav" is the place of the ten Sefirot de Sof and Sium. It means that here Malchut restricts the reception of the light in each Sefira, having reached the maximum corresponding to the particular size of the Masach, until it reaches Malchut de Malchut, which is totally unfit to receive the light.

This stage is called "the toe-tips of the Partzuf". From that point and below there is an empty space devoid of the light ("Halal Panuy"). Both kinds of ten Sefirot de Toch and Sof descend from the ten Sefirot de Rosh and are included in Malchut Mizdaveget, since it has power to dress the Ohr Hozer on the Ohr Elion.

There is also the force of the Masach that prevents the light from entering Malchut and raises the Ohr Hozer. These two forces are merely the roots, the germs of the Kelim. Then the first force of dressing the light from the Peh to the Tabur in the Toch of the Partzuf is activated, while the second restricting force starts acting in the ten Sefirot de Sof and Sium, from the Tabur down to the Sium Reglav.

If we examine the entire Partzuf, i.e., the Rosh, Toch and Sof as a single whole like the common ten Sefirot, it turns out that the Rosh corresponds to the Sefirot Keter, Hochma and Bina – KaHaB, Gimel Rishonot, Gar (the three first Sefirot). Toch, i.e., the area from the Peh to the Tabur corresponds to the Sefirot Hesed, Gevura, and Tifferet (HaGaT). Sof, i.e., the area from the Tabur and below corresponds to the Sefirot Netzah, Hod, Yesod and Malchut (NHYM).

As it was said, the science of Kabbalah operates with its own special language of formulas, definitions, symbols, and graphs. The light is the sensation of the most exquisite pleasure. Then this sensation is graded into different parts according to its quantity and the quality. This is the source of the five lights of *NaRaNHaY*; each of them in turn consists of its own five lights.

They depend on the sensation, the desire, the quality, and property of this desire, its intention and its selective abilities. Then the text describes the connection between the receiver's properties (the *Kli*, sensor) and the perceptible information that it feels. In other words, all the perceptible information becomes strictly scientific, which allows one to describe these feelings.

Neither psychology nor psychiatry can graduate it all, for they lack this mathematical data. Each person reacts in his own way in a certain situation; there is no common approach. In Kabbalah, the desire created by the Creator reveals itself completely. Everything is most accurately defined and described. Kabbalah provides the general method of attainment of the entire Universe.

When man is on a certain spiritual level, he can qualitatively and quantitatively measure his own actions, vis-à-vis someone else who has already mastered and described this level.

Each fragment of the Universe includes some other fragment in one of its *Sefirot*. So each person in one of his private sensations can feel someone else, i.e., include that person in himself or be included in the other. Thus, through self-knowledge and learning about his source with the help of Kabbalah, man gets to know other people and the entire Universe.

The desire, *Behina Dalet*, is positioned in the area from the *Peh* to the *Sium*, i.e., these are the *Toch* and the *Sof* of the body of the spiritual *Partzuf*. Depending on its screen, it divides itself into two parts. First, it pushes away the light and refuses to receive it in any of its desires. At this time, the *Ohr Hassadim* spreads inside *Malchut*. Then the desire to receive a portion of the light for the sake of the Creator spreads through it.

What does this reception for the sake of the Creator mean? Let us take an example from our world. Suppose you would like to do something really nice for a certain person. If he finds out that you did something for him, you will definitely derive some benefit from it; say respect etc. In the spiritual world, neither I, nor someone I want to please, must know about it. Otherwise it will not be true giving.

Let us assume that man wishes to absorb everything. Later he refused to receive anything for himself, and afterwards feels the "desire to give" everything to someone else to please him. This last stage is called *Bina*. When man is in this state, the *Ohr Hassadim* (pleasure from giving) enters him.

However, the one he wished to please says, "If you really want to please me, start receiving." Now you, as it were, should act in defiance of your previous "desire to give" and start receiving for his sake. This is extremely difficult to do. You cannot use all your "desire to give" on receiving for someone's sake.

It is very difficult to receive for someone else's sake. You have to act in accordance with your innate egoism, i.e., to receive, but with an intention opposite to egoism – receive for the sake of the giver. Hence, it can only be done gradually.

We see it in the example of *Galgalta*, which accepted the light only in the *Toch*, leaving the *Sof* empty; then the light of the *Hassadim* filled it.

"Halal Panuy" constitutes those egoistic desires that have no screen. However, they will manifest only after the Breaking of the *Kelim*.

Galgalta acts according to the law of *TA*. Later on, we will study the structure of the *Partzufim* in compliance with the law of *TB (Tzimtzum Bet)*. All elements created there will be reflected in the structure of man's soul.

נא) עוד יש לדעת, כי ענין הצמצום לא היה אלא על אור החכמה, שהכלי שלה הוא הרצון לקבל הנגמר בבחי"ד, שבה נעשה הצמצום והמסך. אבל על אור דחסדים לא היה שום צמצום כלל, כי הכלי שלו הוא הרצון להשפיע, שאין בו שום עביות ושינוי הצורה מהמאציל, ואינו צריך לשום תיקונים.

ועכ"ז לפי שבע"ס דאור העליון נמצאים אלו ב' האורות חכמה וחסדים, מקושרים יחדיו בלי שום הפרש ביניהם, להיותם אור אחד המתפשט לפי תכונתו, לפיכך כשבאים בהתלבשות בכלים אחר הצמצום, הנה גם אור דחסדים נפסק על המלכות, אעפ"י שעליו לא נעשה צמצום.

כי אם היה אור דחסדים מתפשט במקום, שאין אור החכמה יכול להתפשט שם אף משהו, דהיינו במלכות המסיימת, היתה נעשת שבירה באור העליון. כי האור דחסדים היה מוכרח להפרד לגמרי מאור החכמה. ולפיכך נעשה מלכות המסיימת לבחינת חלל פנוי וריקן לגמרי ואפילו מאור דחסדים.

51) One also has to know that TA was referred exclusively to the Ohr Hochma, which was in the Kli, the "desire to receive", which ended in the Behina Dalet. A Tzimtzum was made and the Masach was created on this specific Behina. The Ohr Hassadim, however, was not restricted at all, since its Kli is the "desire to bestow", which has no Aviut, and whose properties do not differ from those of the Creator, hence require no correction.

As was already stated, the Creator's light is one and indivisible; the Ohr Hochma and the Ohr Hassadim are inseparably connected and spreading together, filling the vessels. According to its inner properties, the Kli distinguishes various kinds of pleasure in the light – the Ohr Hochma (pleasure from the direct reception of the light) and the Ohr Hassadim (pleasure from the equivalence of the vessel's inner properties with those of the Creator).

Therefore when, after TA, the light exits from the Kelim, the Ohr Hassadim stops spreading in Malchut as well as the Ohr Hochma, while there was no Restriction on the Ohr Hassadim. If the Ohr Hassadim had been able to enter Malchut, which resisted the light of Hochma, the light would have been shattered in it, for the Ohr Hassadim would have had to completely separate from the Ohr Hochma. Nevertheless, since that is impossible, Malchut Mesayemet is left quite empty of even the light of the Hassadim.

One can give infinitely; there is no ban on it. Everything that was ever created in *Malchut* of the World of Infinity is based on the restriction imposed on the "desire to receive". If man feels a powerful desire and it is genuine, he will hear the Creator say "If you really wish to give, start receiving".

This will be the measure of giving. In fact, there is nothing man can possibly give, since he does not generate the light; but only consumes it. We can "give" only our intention; in action, we can at most either receive or not receive.

Man's true natural desire is to receive. Look at a small child; it is pure egoism in action. We are born with it. In our world, I can refrain from using this desire. I want to receive or do something, but I will restrict myself, will not take advantage of my desire. To that end, I must imagine a gain that, by my abstinence, may be more considerable than by fulfilling my desire.

The process of purchase and sale takes place here. If I think of some nice profit from the restriction, I will be able to work with my egoistic desire. Let us suppose that I want to steal some money lying on the table. In this case, I need clearly to imagine how the theft will lead me to jail and how I will only lose from it. Then it is not worth it.

Everything is precisely evaluated in our world. Both giving and receiving are in any case egoistic here. You just do what seems to be the most favorable thing in the given situation. In the spiritual world, one can only be exposed to the Upper Light, which transforms your true natural property of reception. It provides you with the screen. We cannot understand what it means. However, with its help we stop thinking about filling our egoism. The first correction consists in gaining strength to stop filling yourself.

If you can meet this condition, it is called the *Tzimtzum Aleph*. You see that reception for the sake of reception is detrimental for you. Then you are given a stronger desire – to receive through giving to the Creator. Where does it come from? You begin to see that there is something called the Creator, that He is so enormous and great, that He includes you in Himself. This feeling grips you so that you wish to give to Him; you acquire the screen for the egoistic desires.

When the screen for the *Behinot Shoresh*, *Aleph*, and *Bet* appears, the desire is still not very strong. When there is a screen for *Behinot Gimel* and *Dalet*, you become one great "desire to give". However, what can you actually give? Here the Creator tells you that only by receiving His light and enjoying it can you give to Him. Having transformed the intention from egoistic to altruistic, for the Creator's sake, you start receiving. The end of correction comes when you acquire the intention for the sake of the Creator on all your egoistic desires and receive all His light.

The "desire to receive" for the sake of the Creator is not egoistic, since it went through several phases of correction. The "desire to receive" for one's own sake turns first into the desire to receive nothing at all. Then the "desire to give" everything to the Creator appears; and finally, the desire to receive everything from the Creator with the intention to bestow upon Him.

נב) ועם זה תבין תוכנם של הע"ס דסוף הפרצוף שמטבור ולמטה. כי אי אפשר כלל לומר שהן רק בחינת אור החסדים בלי חכמה כלל, כי אין האור דחסדים נפרד לעולם לגמרי מאור החכמה. אלא שיש בהן בהכרח הארה מועטת גם מאור החכמה. ותדע שהארה מועטת הזו אנו מכנים תמיד בשם "ו"ק בלי ראש". והנה נתבארו ג' בחינות הע"ס שבפרצוף, הנקראות "ראש", "תוך", "סוף".

52) Now, we can understand what the 10 Sefirot from the Tabur and below are. It would be wrong to say there is only the Ohr Hassadim without any Ohr Hochma. There has to be some faint luminescence of the Ohr Hochma called VAK bli Rosh (6 ends without a head). There are 10 Sefirot in any Partzuf: the Gar is Keter, Hochma, and Bina: the Ohr Hochma is present there in all its greatness. Hesed, Gevura, Tifferet, Netzah, Hod and Yesod form VAK, where there is the Ohr Hassadim and a little Ohr Hochma. The tenth Sefira Malchut remains empty.

נג) ועתה נבאר ענין סדר הלבשת הפרצופים גלגלתא ע"ב וס"ג דא"ק זה לזה. וזה ידעת, כי כל תחתון יוצא ממסך דגוף דעליון, אחר שנזדכך ונעשה בהשואת הצורה אל המלכות והמסך שבראש. כי אז נכלל במסך שבראש בזווג דהכאה שבו.

ואחר שנעשה עליו הזווג דהכאה בב' הרשימות עביות והתלבשות הנשאר במסך דגוף, הנה הוכרה העביות שבו, שהיא מבחינת עביות דגוף. וע"י הכר ההוא נבחן לנו, שהקומה יוצאת מבחינת ראש דפרצוף הא' דא"ק, ויורדת ומלבשת לבחינת הגוף שלו, דהיינו במקום שורשה, כי ממסך דגוף היא.

ובאמת היה צריך לירד המסך עם המלכות המזדווגת של הפרצוף החדש למקום הטבור דפרצוף הא', כי שם מתחיל המסך דגוף עם מלכות המסיימת של פרצוף הא', שמשם שורש הפרצוף החדש ואחיזתו. אלא מתוך שהבחינה האחרונה דעביות נאבדה מהמסך, בסבת הביטוש דאו"מ באו"פ (אות מ) ולא נשאר במסך זולת בחי"ג דעביות. אשר בחי"ג הזאת דעביות נקרא חזה. ולפיכך אין למסך ומלכות המזדווגת דפרצוף החדש שום אחיזה ושורש בטבור דעליון, אלא רק בחזה שלו. והוא דבוק שם כענף בשורשו.

53) And now let us examine the order in which the Partzufim Galgalta, AB and SAG dress on one another. It is known that each subsequent Partzuf emerges from the Masach de Guf of the previous one after losing its Aviut, ascending, and merging with the Masach de Rosh.

A Zivug de Haka'a with this screen is made on two kinds of the Reshimot left in the Masach de Guf of the previous Partzuf: Aviut and Hitlabshut. The Partzuf that emerges from the Rosh of the previous one descends to its Guf and dresses onto it, i.e., on its root, the Masach de Guf.

In fact, the Masach of the new Partzuf and Malchut Mizdaveget are supposed to descend to the Tabur of the previous Partzuf, since that is the place of the root and the attachment of the new Partzuf. However, owing to the Ohr Makif and Pnimi, the Masach of the previous Partzuf lost the last Behina de Aviut. Thus, only Behina Gimel de Aviut (Chazeh) remained; hence, the Masach and Malchut of the new Partzuf have no connection with the Tabur of the previous one, but only in its Chazeh, where it is attached as a branch to its root.

We learn how the entire Universe consisting of five worlds was created. We learn what preceded the creation of our universe, man. We have also learned how the Upper forces gradually transformed, weakened, divided, deteriorated in quality and size, in order to recreate everything to allow the Creation to achieve the most perfect state, become equal to the Creator. It was necessary to create such an interaction between all forces that would gradually and following a certain order, influence the entire Creation, and raise all its elements to the highest spiritual level.

In fact, the Universe is a shell that, on the one hand, separates the Creator from the Creation, and, on the other hand, unites them. The creation of this shell required a huge number of levels on which the future Creation, corresponding to the properties of each level, was modeled. To that end, each of these levels had to be fully adapted to the Creation. Now we are beginning to study how the supreme power (the Creator) adjusts itself to the inferior system.

נד) ולפיכך נמצא, שהמסך דפרצוף החדש יורד למקום החזה דפרצוף הא'. ומוציא שם ע"י זווג דהכאה עם אור העליון ע"ס דראש ממנו ולמעלה, עד הפה דעליון, שהוא המלכות דראש דפרצוף הא'. אבל את הע"ס דראש של פרצוף העליון אין התחתון יכול להלביש אף משהו, להיותו רק מבחינת מסך דגוף של העליון.

ואח"כ מוציא ע"ס ממעלה למטה, הנקראות "ע"ס דגוף", בתוך וסוף של התחתון. ומקומם מחזה דפרצוף העליון ולמטה עד הטבור שלו בלבד. כי מטבור ולמטה הוא מקום הע"ס דסיום של העליון, שהיא בחי"ד, ואין להתחתון אחיזה בבחינה אחרונה של העליון, כי נאבדה ממנו בעת הזדככותו (אות מ).

וע"כ פרצוף התחתון ההוא, הנקרא "פרצוף החכמה דא"ק" או "פרצוף ע"ב דא"ק", מוכרח להסתיים למעלה מטבור של פרצוף הא' דא"ק. ונתבאר היטב, שכל רת"ס דפרצוף ע"ב דא"ק, שהוא התחתון דפרצוף הא' דא"ק, המה עומדים ממקום שמתחת הפה דפרצוף הא' עד מקום הטבור שלו. באופן, שהחזה דפרצוף הא' הוא מקום פה דראש של פרצוף ע"ב, דהיינו מלכות המזדווגת. והטבור דפרצוף הא' הוא מקום סיום רגלין דפרצוף ע"ב, דהיינו מלכות המסיימת.

54) Therefore, the Masach of the new Partzuf (AB) descends to the Chazeh of the previous one (Galgalta). With the help of a Zivug de Haka'a with the Upper Light it creates the ten Sefirot de Rosh from the Chazeh and above – up to the Peh of the previous Partzuf, where its Malchut de Rosh is. The lower Partzuf is unable to dress the ten Sefirot de Rosh of the higher one, because it is born from the Masach de Guf of the higher Partzuf and not from its head.

Each subsequent Partzuf can attain only the Guf of the preceding one, its root, and not the Rosh – the calculations, the thoughts and the mind of the previous Partzuf. Next, the screen creates ten Sefirot de Guf of the new Partzuf from the Chazeh down to the Tabur of the previous one, while from the Tabur and below, there are ten Sefirot de Sium of the previous Partzuf. In other words, there is Behina Dalet, with which the new Partzuf cannot work due to the loss of the last Behina de Aviut during the weakening of the screen.

Therefore, the position of the Rosh, Toch, and Sof of the Partzuf AB is from the Peh de Galgalta to the Tabur. At that, the Chazeh de Galgalta is the Peh de AB, i.e., Malchut Mizdaveget, and the Tabur de Galgalta is the Sium de AB (Malchut Mesayemet).

נה) וכמו שנתבאר בסדר יציאת פרצוף ע"ב מפרצוף הא' דא"ק, כן הוא בכל הפרצופים עד סוף עולם העשיה, שכל תחתון יוצא ממסך דגוף דעליון שלו, אחר שנזדכך ונכלל במסך דמלכות דראש דעליון בזווג דהכאה אשר שם, ואח"ז יורד משם למקום אחיזתו בגוף דעליון, ומוציא גם במקומו ע"י זווג דהכאה עם אור העליון את הע"ס דראש ממטה למעלה, וגם מתפשט ממעלה למטה לע"ס דגוף בתוך וסוף, ע"ד שנתבאר בפרצוף ע"ב דא"ק. אלא בענין סיום הפרצוף יש חילוקים, כמ"ש במקומו.

55) The order of the creation of the Partzuf AB from Galgalta applies to the formation of on the rest of the Partzufim, down to the lowest Sefira of the world of Assiya. It consists in the fact that each subsequent Partzuf emerges from the Masach de Guf of the previous one. After the Masach loses its strength, it ascends and merges with the Masach of Malchut de Rosh of the preceding Partzuf, making a Zivug de Haka'a with it. Then it descends to the Chazeh of the previous Partzuf and there, after a Zivug with the Upper Light, the ten Sefirot de Rosh arise as well as ten Sefirot Toch and Sof de Guf, thus forming the Partzuf AB of the world of Adam Kadmon.

THE TZIMTZUM BET: CALLED THE TZIMTZUM NHY DE AK
צמצום ב׳ הנקרא צמצום נה״י דא״ק

נו) והנה נתבאר היטב ענין הצמצום א׳, שנעשה על כלי המלכות, שהיא הבחי״ד, שלא תקבל לתוכה אור העליון. וכן ענין המסך, והזווג דהכאה שלו עם האור העליון, המעלה אור״ח, שהאו״ח הזה נעשה לכלי קבלה חדשים במקום הבחי״ד. וכן ענין ההזדככות של המסך דגוף, הנעשה בגופים דכל פרצוף, מפאת הביטוש דאו״מ באו״פ, המוציאה ד׳ הבחינות טנת״א דגוף דכל פרצוף, והמעלה את המסך דגוף לבחינת מסך של ראש, ומכשרתו לזווג דהכאה עם אור העליון, שעליו נולד פרצוף שני, הנמוך במדרגה אחת מהפרצוף הקודם. וכן יציאת ג׳ פרצופים הראשונים דא״ק, הנקראים "גלגלתא", "ע״ב", "ס״ג", וסדר הלבשתם זה את זה.

56) Thus, we have cleared up the meaning of TA, which was made on Behina Dalet – the Kli Malchut, as it stopped receiving the light. We have also spoken of the Masach and its Zivug de Haka'a with the Upper Light. It raises the Ohr Hozer, which plays the role of the new vessel of reception instead of Behina Dalet.

Then we discussed the weakening of the *Masach de Guf* that happened because of the impact between the *Ohr Makif* and the *Ohr Pnimi*. These processes led to the formation of the *Ta'amim, Nekudot, Tagin* and *Otiot de Guf* in each *Partzuf*, and the ascent of the *Masach* to the *Peh de Rosh* and its *Zivug de Haka'a* with the Upper Light. As a result, the second *Partzuf* is born one level below the first and then the third. These *Partzufim* of the world of *Adam Kadmon* are called *Galgalta, AB* and *SAG*. Each subsequent *Partzuf* dresses onto the preceding one from the *Peh de Rosh* and below.

נז) ותדע, שבאלו הג׳ הפרצופים גלגלתא ע״ב וס״ג דא״ק, אין עוד אפילו שורש לד׳ העולמות אבי״ע. כי אפילו בחינת מקום לג׳ עולמות בי״ע עוד לא היה כאן. שהרי פרצוף הפנימי דא״ק היה נמשך עד הנקודה דעוה״ז. וכן לא נגלה עוד שורש לענין תיקון הנרצה, שבסבתו נעשה הצמצום. כי כל הנרצה בדבר הצמצום, שנעשה בבחי״ד, היה בכדי לתקנה, שלא תהיה בה שום שינוי צורה עם קבלתה את אור העליון (אות יר״ד). והיינו, כדי לברוא גוף האדם מבחינה ד׳ ההיא, ועם העסק שלו בתורה ומצוות על מנת להשפיע נ״ר ליוצרו, יהפך את כח הקבלה שבבחי״ד, שיהיה ע״מ להשפיע, שבזה משווה צורת הקבלה להשפעה גמורה, ואז יהיה גמר התיקון.

כי בזה תחזור הבחי"ד להיות לכלי קבלה על אור העליון, וגם תהיה בדביקות גמורה עם האור, בלי שום שינוי צורה כלל. אמנם עד עתה לא נגלה עוד שורש לתיקון הזה. כי לענין זה צריך האדם להיות כלול גם מבחינות העליונות שלמעלה מבחי"ד, כדי שיהיה בו ההכשר לעשות מעשים טובים של השפעה.

ואם היה האדם יוצא מהמצב של פרצופי א"ק, היה כולו מבחינת חלל פנוי. כי הבחי"ד, הצריכה להיות לשורש גופו של האדם, היתה כולה מלמטה מרגלי א"ק, בבחינת חלל פנוי וריקן בלי אור, להיותה נמצאת בהפכיות הצורה מאור העליון, שנבחנת משום זה לבחינת פרודא ומיתה.

ואם היה נברא האדם ממנה, לא היה יכול לתקן מעשיו כלל. כי לא היה בו שום ניצוצים של השפעה. והיה נמשל כבהמות, שאין בהם מבחינת השפעה ולא כלום, שכל חייהם הוא אך לעצמם. וכדוגמת הרשעים, השקועים בתאות הקבלה לעצמם, "ואפילו החסד דעבדין, לגרמייהו עבדין". שעליהם נאמר: "רשעים בחייהם נקראים מתים", להיותם בהפכיות הצורה מחי החיים.

57) You must know that there is not even a hint of the creation in the four worlds of ABYA in these three Partzufim; there was not even a place for them, for the Galgalta of the world of Adam Kadmon reaches the point of our world. The root of the desired correction has not yet been revealed, that being the reason for the Tzimtzum Aleph. It was made to provide Behina Dalet with an opportunity to receive the Upper Light, and then create man from it, who, with the help of the Torah and the Commandments for the sake of the Creator, could transform reception into giving.

Then Behina Dalet would become the vessel of reception of the Upper Light, merging with it by its properties. However, the root of such correction has not yet even been revealed in the world of Adam Kadmon. For that, man should consist not only of the Behina Dalet – the "desire to receive" – but also possess the properties that refer to the first nine Sefirot, i.e., the "desire to bestow", allowing him "to perform good deeds" (to give).

If man had appeared at the state in which the Partzufim de Adam Kadmon had been, he would have had no light at all, because the Behina Dalet, being the root of man's spiritual body, would have been below the Sium of the world of Adam Kadmon in total darkness and absolutely opposite to the light by its properties.

Had man been created of such "material", he would never have corrected himself due to the lack of even the slightest "desire to give". He would have been considered an animal, living only for itself. Similarly, sinners bogged down in their "desire to receive" only for themselves, even while doing good deeds, are called dead during their life.

The Creator created a single creation –*Behina Dalet* – the "desire to receive", egoism, man, *Malchut*. Having received the light inside, *Behina Dalet* felt emptiness. In the spiritual world, such straightforward reception leads to death.

Upon realizing this, it wished to be like the Creator and stopped receiving the light by making a *Tzimtzum*. By doing this, it did not become like the Creator, but rather stopped being opposite to Him in its properties. The Creator allotted His own properties to the four phases of *Malchut's* development. However, since *Malchut* itself is no longer His property, it is called the "creation", the "desire to receive".

How can *Malchut* be made equal to the Creator? To this end, it must receive, but only for His sake. If *Malchut* sees that by receiving it pleases the Creator, it must begin to do so.

Where can *Malchut* get such altruistic properties?It must come from *Bina*, for *Bina* is the "desire to bestow". To accomplish this, we need to combine *Bina's* desire not to receive anything with *Malchut's* "desire to receive" for its own sake. If that can be done, it will be possible to give *Malchut* the intention to receive for the Creator's sake. A desire cannot be transformed. It is our nature and is not subject to change.

If it is possible to give *Malchut* such an intention, it can receive the Creator's entire light and reach the *Gmar Tikkun*. How can we bring together and mix these two opposing properties? We must have something common between them. For this, we must break *Bina* and *Malchut* – the "desire to receive" and the "desire to give" – and mix the fragments very thoroughly so that each spiritual object that emerged after this breaking may possess these two desires.

For this purpose, one of *Bina's* properties must be "spoiled", in order for it somehow to become similar to *Malchut*. In other words, *Bina's* intention to bestow for the sake of the Creator must be "spoiled", converted, as it were, into the "desire to give" for the sake of reception. Its intentions would become similar to those of *Malchut*, even though *Bina* receives nothing, while *Malchut* wants to get everything. In this way, *Bina* "spoils" its intention and becomes selfish like *Malchut*. Now it is necessary to inculcate *Bina's* property into *Malchut*.

This is done with the help of the stroke penetration, an explosion that will mix their properties so thoroughly that it will be practically impossible to divide them. If this can be done, we will be able to irradiate this common mass with the Upper Light until *Bina* retrieves its previous intention for the sake of the Creator. Then *Malchut*, in this mass, will also acquire the intention to receive for the sake of the Creator.

In the world of *Adam Kadmon*, the *Partzuf Galgalta* is *Keter*; *AB* is *Hochma*; *SAG* is *Bina*. It should be noted that everything that is in the *Sof* of *Galgalta*, or below its *Tabur*, is *Malchut*.That is why, in order to mix *Bina* with *Malchut*, it should be placed under the *Tabur* of *Galgalta*. *Malchut* passes three states:

1. When it received everything prior to the *Tzimtzum Aleph*
2. The state of correction
3. The state of reception for the sake of the Creator.

Throughout this time, *Malchut* never changed its action – neither before the *Tzimtzum Aleph*, nor after it. The correction consisted merely in transforming the intention to receive for itself into receiving for the sake of the Creator. This is what the Universe was created for. This intention is received from *Bina*.

Malchut of the World of Infinity that is mixed with *Bina* is called *Adam*, man. The entire system of the worlds, the Universe, is aimed only at changing *Malchut's* intention. The reception for the sake of the Creator is called Kabbalah.

נח) וז"ס מ"ש חז"ל (ב"ר ספי"ב): "בתחלה עלה במחשבה לברא את העולם במדת הדין. וראה שאין העולם מתקיים, והקדים מדת הרחמים ושתפה למדת הדין". פירוש: כי כל "תחילה ואח"כ", הנאמר ברוחניות, פירושו "סבה ומסובב". וז"ש, שהסבה הראשונה של העולמות, דהיינו פרצופי א"ק, שנאצלו תחילת כל העולמות, נאצלו במדת הדין, דהיינו בבחינת מלכות לבד, הנקראת "מדת הדין", דהיינו הבחי"ד, שנצטמצמה ויצאה בבחינת חלל פנוי וסיום לרגלי א"ק. שה"ס הנקודה דעוה"ז, הנמצאת למטה מסיום רגלי א"ק בבחינת חלל פנוי וריקן מכל אור.

"וראה שאין העולם מתקיים". דהיינו כנ"ל, שבאופן זה לא היה שום אפשרות לאדם, הצריך להברא מבחי"ד הזו, שיוכל לסגל מעשים של השפעה, שעל ידו יתקיים העולם במדת התיקון הנרצה, לכן "הקדים מדת הרחמים ושתפה למדת הדין".

58) In the beginning, the Creator's conception was to create the world with the properties of "Din" (judgment). This means that, if something were created from the "material" taken from the first nine Sefirot, it would possess only the "desire to give". On the other hand, something created from the "material" taken from under the Tabur would have only the "desire to receive".

Then the Creator "saw" that the world could not exist this way. So He mixed the desire to receive with the desire to give. What does this mean? Did He not know in advance that the world would not be able to exist this way? Everything that was, is and will be – the entire Universe, was built according to the principle of "cause and effect". There is neither beginning nor end; only cause and effect.

Moreover, the first cause of the worlds, (the Partzufim of the world of Adam Kadmon, created before all other worlds) was the property of judgment, i.e., Malchut's decision not to receive the light for its own pleasure. As was already said, if man had been created from Behina Dalet (Malchut) at this stage (Malchut de Malchut, Dalet de Dalet, i.e., the complete "desire to receive", the only Creation, and the rest being the transition from the Creator to the creation), he would never have been able to correct the egoistic "desire to receive".

When it is said that, in the beginning the Creator created the world with the properties of judgment, this means that He initially created the world *Adam Kadmon* as distinctly divided into two kinds of vessels: "giving" and "receiving" – *Malchut.* However, inside this *Malchut* there was not even a single spark of the "desire to give", i.e., it could not receive at all, thus failing to fulfill the Purpose of the Creation (to please the Creator). The Creator mixed the "desire to give" *(Bina)* with the "desire to receive" *(Malchut)* so that *Malchut* could receive with the altruistic intention.

פרוש: ספירת בינה נקראת "מדת הרחמים". וספירת המלכות נקראת "מדת הדין", משום שעליה נעשה הצמצום. והמאציל העלה מדת הדין, שהוא כח הסיום הנעשה בספירת המלכות, והעלה אותה אל הבינה, שהיא מדת הרחמים. ושיתף אותם יחד זה בזה, שע"י השתתפות הזה נעשית גם הבחי"ד, שהיא מדת הדין, כלולה מניצוצי השפעה, שבהכלי דבינה. ובזה נעשה הכשר לגוף האדם, היוצא מבחי"ד, שיהיה כלול גם ממדת ההשפעה, אשר יוכל לעשות מעשים טובים ע"מ להשפיע נ"ר ליוצרו, עד שיהפך מדת הקבלה שבו שתהיה כולה ע"מ להשפיע, שעי"ז יתקיים העולם לתיקון הנרצה מבריאת העולם.

To this end He raised the property of judgment, i.e., the force of restriction that is in Malchut to Bina, and mixed them until Behina Dalet included the sparks of the "desire to give" that are present in Bina. This allowed man, who was later created from Behina Dalet, to acquire the sparks of giving, so that afterwards, by doing good deeds, he would completely change his properties (the "desire to receive") and thus ensure the existence of the world.

It should be noted that the mixing of *Bina* and *Malchut* is an extremely complex process that passed several phases, which we are about to examine. Ultimately, the Creator broke both *Bina* and *Malchut* into many tiny fragments and thoroughly mixed them. It turned out that each fragment had properties of both *Bina* and *Malchut.* This fragment is man's soul.

"Our world" is a spiritual category, a spiritual property of absolute egoism, which remains empty and unable to receive anything.

Before the souls were created, and fell to the lowest possible level, everything is thought to have been made by the Creator. In fact, only man, totally detached from the Creator, can be called the creation.

When the creation is filled with the light, it does not understand anything; it is blind. It has no freedom of choice; everything is predetermined inside and outside of it. It is only to the extent of acquiring the *Masach* that *Malchut* begins to ascend to the Creator's level.

All the *Partzufim* of the world *AK (Galgalta, AB, SAG, MA* and *BON)*, end above the *Tabur* of *Galgalta*. So how can these *Partzufim* suddenly descend below that level? We can understand the descent of the *Partzuf Nekudot de SAG* below the *Tabur*, since this *Partzuf* is pure *Bina*, which desires nothing for itself.

There is no *Tzimtzum* on the light of *Bina* (the *Ohr Hassadim)*; hence, it can descend under the *Tabur*. The *Partzuf Nekudot de SAG* feels perfectly well in any situation, in any place in the spiritual space. Bina is characterized by a freedom of choice and behavior that are above all restrictions.

As the soul acquires the properties of *Bina*, it becomes more and more free. The *Partzuf Nekudot de SAG* is reluctant to receive anything, ignoring even the most intense desire – the *Aviut Dalet*; hence, it could descend under the *Tabur de Galgalta* unrestricted.

Both the *Ohr SAG (Bina)* and the *Ohr AB (Hochma)* descend to the world of *Nikudim*. How is it possible? *AB* can descend under the *Tabur* in order to correct the lower *Partzufim*; it becomes similar to them in its properties, although its mission is quite different.

All the worlds are not the created beings, but constitute the Creator's attire, made in the power and quality of their restriction in such a way that each soul receives only a certain portion of the light. The souls strive after the Creator while retaining their freedom of will, some sort of illusionary choice.

All the worlds and the *Partzufim* are still objects, "robots". They have no independence, no freedom of choice. Only man – the combination of Malchut de Malchut, the essence of the "desire to receive", with *Bina*, the "desire to bestow" – can be considered the creation.

As in all other worlds, *AK* consists of five *Partzufim*. These *Partzufim* emerge because of the same process – the weakening and rising of the *Masach*. *Keter*, *Hochma*, and *Bina* (the higher *Partzufim*) control the lower ones. They are direct representatives of the Creator, of His desire to fulfill the Thought of the Creation.

Keter *(Behina Shoresh)* is the Creator's thought to create and bestow delight upon the created beings.

Hochma *(Behina Aleph)* is the delight the Creator wishes to bestow upon the created beings. It is both the vessel and the light of *Hochma* inside it.

Bina (*Behina Bet*) is the Creator's own property, the desire not to receive anything. All three upper Sefirot represent the Creator's properties. With these, He created the creation and instilled into it two opposing desires. On the one hand, there is the desire to receive pleasure; conversely, there is the desire to bestow. This duality is completely realized in *Behina Dalet*.

ZA (*Behina Gimel*) and **Malchut** *(Behina Dalet)* are not the Creator's properties. They are rather by now their consequences, their realization.

The Creator's properties are defined differently in each world. In the world of the *Nikudim* they are *Keter* and *Abba ve Ima*. In the world of *Atzilut*, they are called *Atik*, *Arich Anpin*, and *Abba ve Ima*. The names differ, but the meaning is the same.

At all stages of the creation, there are five essential levels. The end result is important: how does *Behina Dalet* achieve perfection? How can each of the five properties, which in turn consist of their own five, be elevated to the level of perfection? Each property of the soul corresponds to the specific force that pulls it up, corrects it, and leads it to absolute perfection.

Soon we will begin to study the world of the *Nikudim*. This world emerged and broke in order that each "broken" fragment of the light would adapt itself to a fragment of the soul, and find points of contact with it for future correction..

נט) והנה השיתוף הזה של המלכות בבינה נעשה בפרצוף ס"ג דא"ק, וגרם לצמצום ב' בעולמות שממנו ולמטה. כי נעשה בו סיום חדש על אור העליון, דהיינו במקום הבינה. ונמצא, שהמלכות המסיימת, שהיתה עומדת בסיום רגלי הס"ג דא"ק, ממעל הנקודה דעוה"ז, עלתה וסיימה את אור העליון במקום חצי בינה דגוף הס"ג דא"ק, הנקרא ת"ת.

כי כח"ב דגוף נקרא חג"ת. ונמצא הת"ת היא בינה דגוף. וכן מלכות המזדווגת, שהיתה עומדת במקום הפה דראש הס"ג דא"ק, עלתה למקום נקבי עינים דא"ק, שהוא חצי בינה של ראש. ונעשה שם הזווג לצורך המ"ה דא"ק, הנקרא "עולם הנקודים", במקום נקבי עינים.

59) The interaction between the properties of Malchut and Bina in the Partzuf SAG brought about the Tzimtzum Bet in the worlds below. This led to the emergence of a new Sium of the Upper Light in the place where Bina is. Malchut, which prevented the light from spreading into the Sof of Galgalta at the level of the Sium Reglav (positioned a little above the point of this world), rose to Bina de Guf of the Partzuf Nekudot de SAG. It then restricted the light of the upper half of Bina de Guf, called Tifferet.

Indeed, Hesed, Gevura, and Tifferet correspond to Keter, Hochma and Bina de Guf; so it turns out that Bina de Guf is Tifferet. Malchut, which was in the Peh de Rosh, rose to the Nikvey Einaim (pupils of the eyes), i.e., to the line separating the vessels of bestowal (Galgalta) from the vessels of reception (AHP) of Bina de Rosh. From there, it made a necessary Zivug for the creation of the Partzuf MA de AK, called the world of Nikudim (or the lower MA).

The *Partzuf* SAG has the *Reshimot Gimel* (3) *de Hitlabshut* and *Bet* (2) *de Aviut*. This means that, in principle, SAG is the *Partzuf Bina* with the *Ohr Hassadim* inside, which is determined by the main *Reshimo Bet de Aviut*. However, SAG has also the *Hitlabshut Gimel* – the memory of the previous state (the *Partzuf AB*, the *Partzuf Hochma*). Hence, there is a slight luminescence of the *Ohr Hochma* inside the *Partzuf* SAG. As long as this luminescence is inside SAG, it cannot descend below the *Tabur*.

Before the rise of its *Masach*, the *Partzuf* SAG still has some properties of the *Partzuf Hochma* – "*Hochma be Kiruv*". Because of the rise of the *Masach* and expulsion of the light caused by the impact between the *Ohr Pnimi* and the *Ohr Makif*, some radical changes take place in SAG. As was stated, each rise of the screen from one level to another is accompanied by a series of intermediate *Zivugim de Haka'a* that lead to the formation of interim *Partzufim* called "the *Nekudot*" (in this case the *Nekudot de* SAG).

The very first rise of the screen (from *Malchut de* SAG to ZA *de* SAG), which leads to expulsion of the light *Yechida de Bina*, naturally calls forth the expulsion of luminescence of the *Ohr Hochma*,stimulated by the presence of the *Reshimo de Hitlabshut Gimel* in SAG. Because of this, "*Hochma be Kiruv*" disappears, and SAG turns into the *Partzuf* of pure *Bina*, which has the *Reshimot Bet de Aviut* and *Bet de Hitlabshut*.

The *Reshimot Bet de Aviut* and *Bet de Hitlabshut* - pure *Bina* – can descend below the *Tabur*. Therefore, the *Nekudot de* SAG freely descended under the *Tabur* of the world of AK, since even the *Masach de Galgalta* was too weak to fill these desires below the *Tabur* with the *Ohr Hochma*. Generally, the process of transition takes place from the *Partzuf* SAG (*Gimel/Bet*) to the *Partzuf* MA (*Bet/Aleph*). Hence, the *Nekudot de* SAG, which has the *Reshimot Bet/Bet*, constitutes an intermediate *Partzuf*.

Like all the other *Sefirot*, *Bina* in turn consists of its own five: *Keter, Hochma, Bina*, ZA and *Malchut*. ZA represents an interim stage between the three upper *Sefirot* and the vessel of reception – *Malchut*. This is a common property of the Creator and *Malchut*. In a sense, it links them together and consequently consists of six *Sefirot*: *Hesed* is similar to *Keter*; *Gevura* to *Hochma*; *Tifferet* to *Bina*. While *Netzah* is the property of ZA itself, *Hod* is similar to *Malchut* and *Yesod* is the sum of all the properties.

Therefore, *Tifferet* in ZA is *Bina*. If we also divide it crosswise, it will similarly consist of *Keter, Hochma, Bina (KaHaB), Hesed, Gevura, Tifferet (HaGaT)* and *Netzah, Hod, Yesod* and *Malchut (NHYM)*. If we divide Tifferet into one third and two thirds, it will turn out that the light descends only to its upper third, spreading no further. The point where the vessels of bestowal get separated from the vessels of reception, *Bina* from *Malchut*, is called "the *Parsa*".

The desires *KaHaB-HaGaT* are called GE (*Galgalta ve Eynaim*) – the altruistic desires. The desires NHYM, the egoistic *Kelim*, are called *Awzen*. The lower part of *Tifferet – Netzah* and *Hod* are *Hotem*, while *Yesod* and *Peh* are *Malchut*. This combination is called *AHP (Awzen, Hotem, and Peh)*. Now the creation can work only with GE, whereas the *Kelim* with a touch of egoism *(AHP)* are not used.

The *Tzimtzum Bet* is a source of all our souls. The Torah (the chapter *Bereshit*) begins at this very moment. From this point, we start speaking about man's soul; until then there was no root of the creation. First it was necessary to make *Tzimtzum Aleph*, then descend to the *Nekudot de SAG* to make *Tzimtzum Bet*, break all the good and bad properties in order to mix them, and finally to start building a totally new system. This system is a combination of Good and Evil, the right and the left line, the systems of pure and impure forces.

Bina (the Creator's properties) has to descend to such a level where it can become equal to the properties of *Malchut*, i.e., spoil itself to the extent of becoming similar to the property of reception for its own sake. How can this happen?

Malchut divides *Bina* into GE and *AHP*, stands between them, and influences the lower part of *Bina* (*Zat* – the seven lower *Sefirot de Bina*) so that its properties become equal to those of *Malchut*. The upper part of *Bina (Gar)* remains altruistic as before. This is called *Tzimtzum Bet* (*TB*).

The Creator deliberately "spoils" *Bina*, i.e., His own property, so that it would become similar to the property of reception and merge with it. Next, He gradually shows it how much better His properties are, encouraging it to adopt them and slowly move up toward Him.

Above *Malchut*, there is a choice to apply the intention for the sake of bestowal; below *Malchut*'s domain, there is no such option. So, if *Malchut* ascends to Bina, from that point and downwards there is no choice. All of the *Behinot*, the properties below *Bina*, fell under the power of the egoistic desires.

Let us review in a general way the ascent of *Malchut* to *Bina*. Is it possible that the "desire to receive" appeared in *Bina*? First, let us clear up the notion "the *Tet Rishonot*", the nine upper *Sefirot*, and *Malchut* in general.

Rabbi Baruch Ashlag gives the following example: Man has the *Kelim* called eyes, ears, nose, and mouth that dress the sight, hearing, smell and speech. Of course, these *Kelim* are very important. If man's eyes are damaged, he cannot see; if his ears are damaged, he cannot hear. Nevertheless, sometimes man does not use his senses. When does this happen? When he goes to sleep.

It turns out that when man wants to receive pleasure through his senses, he uses them; but when he wants to enjoy rest, he ignores them. Hence, we see that the true *Kli* is a desire to receive pleasure. Our senses are not the *Kelim*; they only serve that desire.

In accordance with our example, the nine upper *Sefirot* are sight, hearing, smell and speech, i.e., the light and the vessel. Each type of light dresses into its corresponding *Kli*, but the *Kelim* of the first nine *Sefirot* are not genuine. This is because the *Kli* is a desire to receive pleasure and is present only in *Malchut*. These *Kelim* are necessary only for the dressing of the light, as in the example with sight, hearing etc. So who receives pleasure from the first nine *Sefirot*? It is the "desire to receive", called "*Malchut*".

Now let us return to the question of *Malchut* rising to *Bina*. Is it possible for an ear to have a "desire to receive"? Everything we discuss here refers to whatever *Malchut* receives from the first nine *Sefirot*. After the Second Restriction, *Malchut* attains only a half of *Bina* and above.

ס) וזה מכונה ג"כ "צמצום נה"י דא"ק". כי הס"ג דא"ק, שהיה מסתיים בשוה עם פרצוף גלגלתא דא"ק, ממעל הנקודה דעוה"ז, הנה ע"י השיתוף ועלית המלכות במקום בינה, נמצא מסתיים ממעל לטבור דא"ק הפנימי, דהיינו במקום חצי ת"ת, שהוא חצי בינה דגוף דא"ק הפנימי. כי שם עלתה מלכות המסיימת, ועכבה אור העליון, שלא יתפשט ממנה ולמטה.

וע"כ נעשה שם חלל פנוי וריקן בלי אור. ונמצאו התנה"י דס"ג, שנצטמצמו ונתרוקנו מאור העליון. ולפיכך נקרא הצמצום ב' בשם "צמצום נה"י דא"ק". כי ע"י סיום החדש, שנעשה במקום הטבור, נתרוקנו הנה"י דס"ג דא"ק מאורותיהם. וכן נבחן, שאח"פ דראש הס"ג, יצאו ממדרגת ראש הס"ג, ונעשו לבחינת גוף שלו. כי המלכות המזדווגת עלתה לנקבי עינים, ויצאו הע"ס דראש מהמסך שבנקבי העינים ולמעלה. ומנקבי העינים ולמטה כבר נקרא "גוף הפרצוף", כי אינו יכול לקבל רק הארה שמנקבי עינים ולמטה, שזו היא בחינת גוף.

והנה קומת הע"ס הללו, שיצאה בנקבי עינים דס"ג דא"ק, הן הע"ס הנקראות "עולם הנקודים". שירדו מנקבי עינים דס"ג, ובאו למקומן, שהוא למטה מטבור דא"ק הפנימי. ונתפשטו שם ראש וגוף. ותדע, כי הסיום החדש הנ"ל, הנעשה במקום הבינה דגוף, מכונה בשם "פרסה". ויש כאן פנימיות וחיצוניות. ורק הע"ס החיצוניות נקראים "עולם הנקודים". והעשר ספירות הפנימיות נקראים "מ"ה וב"ן דא"ק" עצמו.

60) Tzimtzum Bet is also called Tzimtzum NHYM de AK (if we divide the Partzuf Galgalta into the ten Sefirot, then the Rosh will be KaHaB, Toch – HaGaT and Sof - NHYM). This is because the Nekudot de SAG, which ended above the point of our world during Malchut's rising to Bina and interacting with it, end below the Tabur of Galgalta in Tifferet de Guf of Galgalta, where Malchut Mesayemet rose.

An empty space absolutely devoid of the light was formed under Malchut in the place of the egoistic desires NHYM de SAG, which restricted reception of the light and were left empty. The AHP de Rosh de SAG were separated from GE and began to play the role of the Guf. The ten Sefirot de Rosh rose from the Nikvey Eynaim (the boundary between Gar de Bina and Zat de Bina) and higher, while the Guf was formed underneath. This can receive only a slight luminescence emanating from the Rosh.

The ten Sefirot that emerged because of a Zivug de Haka'a in the Nikvey Eynaim de SAG are called the ten Sefirot of the world of Nikudim. They descended from the Nikvey Eynaim and took their place under the Tabur de AK. There they split into the Rosh and the Guf. The place, below which the Ohr Hochma cannot spread, is called "the Parsa". The world of the Nikudim is called "the outer part". The inner Sefirot are called the Partzufim MA and BON of the world of AK.

So why did *Tzimtzum Bet* take place? The fact is that when the *Nekudot de* SAG, which are actually the *Zat de Bina* (*Zat* means "*Zain Tachtonot*" – seven lower *Sefirot*), i.e., the vessels, which ZA and *Malchut* turn to for the light and which are ready to transfer that light downwards, descended under *Tabur*. They also encountered the *NHYM of Galgalta* – the enormous desires of *Dalet/Gimel* that, with regard to their properties,are close to *Dalet de Dalet*, i.e., to the Essence of the Creation.

The *Nekudot de* SAG adopted the desires of the *NHYM de Galgalta*. However, they did not have the appropriate screen; hence, *Nekudot de* SAG ran the danger of receiving the light for their own pleasure. To avert this, *Malchut*, which had made TA, rose to *Tifferet* (i.e., *Bina de Guf*), thus cutting the vessels of reception off from the vessels of bestowal. Now the *Nekudot de* SAG will not be able to receive delight for their own sake. This is the *Tzimtzum Bet*.

There are the ten *Sefirot KaHaB, HaGaT,* and *NHYM* in *Malchut* of the world of Infinity. After TA, it is possible to use the first nine Sefirot in order to receive as much light for the Creator's sake as the strength of the screen allows. Only *Malchut* cannot receive the Direct Light.It has just the *Ohr Hozer* (the Surrounding Light).

The *Tzimtzum Bet* puts forward additional conditions. Now it is impossible to receive the *Ohr Hochma*, even for the sake of the Creator. *Malchut* can only give, receiving the *Ohr Hassadim*, the pleasure from the equivalence of its properties with those of the Creator. If a ban is imposed on two or three desires, a *Zivug de Aka'a* is not made on them. They are not taken into account but remain unused.

Let us review the interaction between the qualities of judgment and mercy. During the rise of *Malchut* to *Bina*, the latter was restricted. How do we know that *Malchut* received so-called sweetening (the quality of mercy)? Is not the purpose of this action to provide *Malchut* (*Din*) with the qualities of mercy, and not vice versa, to give *Bina* (mercy) the property of judgment?

To answer this question, let us give an example that demonstrates how *Malchut* received the sweetening by way of *TB*.

The sages said: "In the beginning, the Creator thought to create the world by the quality of judgment, but saw that it cannot exist, and added the property of mercy". That world is *Malchut*, which restricted itself (the expression of the quality of judgment). Nevertheless, there are always *Sefirot* in each *Partzuf*, although *Malchut* made the Restriction on itself. *Malchut* does not yet have a complete *Partzuf*. However, the Creator's desire is to make it a full *Partzuf* so that it will receive the direct Light into its *Kelim* as before the Restriction.

We have learned that the place for such correction is *Malchut de* ZA of the world of *Atzilut*. Then it separates from ZA and becomes an independent *Partzuf* - *Malchut* of the world of *Atzilut*. As in all the other *Partzufim*, *Malchut* ascended to *Bina* in ZA, i.e., its *Malchut* rose to its ZA called "*Chazeh*". *NHY* fell into the power of *Malchut* from the *Chazeh* and downwards. It turns out that, owing to the rise of *Malchut* to *Bina*, ZA restricted itself; i.e., it does not use all of its ten *Sefirot*, but only down to the *Chazeh (Bina de Guf)*.

Then, thanks to a *Zivug* AB-SAG, *TB* was cancelled and *Malchut* returned to its place. The *Kelim NHY* were purified, so ZA can use them again. Here we see something quite new! Since nothing disappears in the spiritual world, we find that *Malchut* is still up with *NHY* under its power. However, by canceling the *TB*, the *Zivug* AB-SAG does not lower *Malchut*.

Therefore, *Malchut* acquired the *Kelim de NHY*, thanks to the *Gadlut de* ZA, and included them in itself. These *Kelim* refer to the Direct Light, called "sparks of the "desire to bestow"". Although they have no connection with *Malchut*, these vessels fell into it (the "desire to receive" for itself), so now it is able to bestow.

These *NHY* split into nine parts, joined *Malchut* in its upper position and formed the *Partzuf Malchut*. Now we see that, if it were not for *TB*, *Malchut* would have been totally unable to build its own *Partzuf*.

A calculation is made in the *Rosh* that only the first three *Sefirot* are the vessels of reception and can therefore be used. The lower, receiving vessels, i.e., *Sefirot* from *Malchut* up to the middle of *Tifferet*, cannot be used. A *Zivug de Haka'a* occurs only from mid-*Tifferet* and above. A similar action takes place in the *Guf*: I can use only *Sefirot* from *Keter* to mid-*Tifferet*. The rest of the desires remain empty. This is *TB*. It indicates that it is only possible to give for the Creator's sake, but not to receive.

The *Masach de Rosh* rose from the *Peh* to the *Nikvey Eynaim*; now only the vessels of bestowal above the screen can be used. There is no screen on the receiving desires, but it is possible to prevent these desires from receiving selfishly. They are just neutralized, ignored; only the desires of bestowal are worked with. The state of the *Partzuf* working only with the desires of bestowal is called "*Katnut*" (small state), since it uses only the giving vessels.

The state, when the *Partzuf*, having acquired anti-egoistic powers, will be able to receive the light in its vessels of reception and work with all ten desires, is called "*Gadlut*" (big state). Here a question arises: how can the tenth desire – *Malchut*, receive? Was it not impossible even before

TB? It can be done with the help of the *AHP de Aliyah* and "the three lines". But we will discuss this later.

Only the giving vessels (*GE*) are above the screen; below it are the vessels of reception (*AHP*), with which it does not work while in the state of *Katnut*. The GE *de Rosh* fills the GE *de Toch*, while no part of the *AHP* goes into the *AHP de Toch*.

Our body is designed in the image and likeness of the spiritual *Partzuf*. There is a dividing line - the diaphragm - which separates the respiratory system from the digestive. The respiratory system corresponds to the giving vessels, the digestive - to the vessels of reception.

Therefore, the letter *Aleph*, the first one in the Hebrew alphabet, consists of a slanting line - diaphragm - above which the upper letter *Yud* represents GE, and the lower - *AHP*. In fact, it is only after the *TB* the creation takes a definite form. Hence the letter *Aleph* embodies the beginning of this process.

When desires appear in man, he decides which of them he can or cannot use. This means that the screen is being created in him, and he starts working with it. What does it mean to wish to bestow without receiving anything in return. This is *Bina*, the *Behina Bet*.

It says it does not want to receive anything, since it understands that pleasure distances it from the Creator. It prefers not to receive at all in order to be closer to Him. It enjoys giving. We can receive pleasure either from reception or from giving, which is in fact also a kind of reception. It enjoys being close to the Creator.

The *Partzuf* SAG does not receive anything either. Then why does it have a *Rosh*, *Toch*, and a *Sof*? Why does it make a *Zivug de Haka'a*? On the face of it, only the *Ohr Hassadim* has to spread inside it. Yet it is not so. The *Ohr Hassadim* is an enormous pleasure of being similar to the Creator, from closeness to Him, from sharing the information that is in Him.

One gets to know His thoughts, feelings, attain whatever is in Him; one reaches the same level. It brings tremendous delight, which must also be provided with the screen, so that it would be felt in an altruistic way.

SAG cannot receive all the pleasures, hence it makes a *Zivug* in the *Rosh* and has the *Toch*; the *Sof*, however, cannot be filled.

Actually, the creation cannot have the vessels of bestowal. The creation is *Malchut* after the *TA*, i.e., the vessel of reception. This *Malchut* places the screen of this or that power and acts accordingly as *Keter, Hochma, Bina, ZA*, or *Malchut*. So, a part of these vessels of reception, that is *Keter, Hochma*, and *Gar de Bina*, which are equipped with the appropriate screen, can be used as the vessels of bestowal.

If the pure bestowal (this is only the Creator) existed, the creation would not be able to feel it at all, since it can only feel something that enters it. The upper *Partzuf* always gives birth to the lower one because it retains the *Reshimot*. The light filled *Malchut* of the World of Infinity and transferred all its powers and properties to it. Because of this, *Malchut* passionately desires to be like it and is ready to sacrifice everything to expel the light and to remain empty.

The strength of this desire drives the entire creation from the beginning to the very end – the *Gmar Tikkun*. All that happens to the creation (*Malchut's* desire to correct itself and become similar to the Creator) finds its reflection after the *TA*. In addition, *Malchut* has strength for that, since it was filled with the light that passed it its properties.

The higher state fully determines and gives rise to the lower, which is itself on a lower level. For instance, what is the difference between *Galgalta* and *AB*? It consists in the fact that *AB* works for the Creator with less power. Nevertheless, both of them use the egoistic *Kelim* for His sake.

The SAG is already unable to do that, for its screen is weaker than that of *AB*; like *Bina*, it can only refuse to receive anything. By receiving nothing, ignoring its receiving vessels, it can fill with the *Ohr Hassadim* those desires that no other *Partzufim* could. As was stated, there was no *Tzimtzum* on the *Ohr Hassadim*; hence, the *Partzuf* SAG can descend under the *Tabur*.

Then it creates the world of *Nikudim* and afterwards – the world of *Atzilut*. *Bina* (SAG), is the first and only desire of the creation that sets everything in motion. The *Behinat Shoresh* is the Creator's "desire to bestow" delight upon the created beings. The *Behina Aleph* is the creation created by the Creator. Only the *Behina Bet, Bina,* is the creation's reaction, its desire to be like Him. Henceforth, this property of *Bina* determines the direction of the entire creation's evolution, right up to the Final Correction.

SAG spread as the *Nekudot* both above the *Tabur de Galgalta* and below it. The *Partzufim* MA *Elion* and BON *Elion* emerged from the *Reshimot de* SAG above the *Tabur*. The SAG makes a *Zivug* on the *Reshimot* that rose from under the *Tabur de Galgalta* and creates a *Partzuf* called the world of *Nikudim*. The SAG was imbued with the desires *Dalet/Gimel* under the *Tabur* and wished to fill them.

Imagine that you have both the desire to give and to receive. Generally speaking, the creation does not have the altruistic desires to give; it was created out of pure egoism, the desire to receive pleasure. However, it is possible to enjoy the reception of the *Ohr Hochma*, i.e., directly receiving delight (the Creator's light), and the reception of the light of *Hassadim*, i.e., enjoying the similarity of one's properties to those of the Creator. We therefore define two desires of the creation: to receive and to give. Actually, the Creator created only one desire – to receive.

When man works only with his "desire to give", he restricts all his egoistic desires and is in the state of *Katnut*. How can this state be called forth? If all man's egoistic desires are bigger than his screen, there is nothing else for him to do but to refrain from using them as the vessels of reception. All of us are in such a state. The only thing we can do is not activate all our egoistic desires, ignore them. This state is called *"Ubar"* (embryo).

Malchut is the "desire to receive" for the sake of reception, a purely egoistic desire. If all man's desires are imbued only with this intention, it means that *Malchut* rose to *Bina*, i.e., it rules over all of its desires from *Bina* and below it. This is the *Tzimtzum Bet*.

We cannot correct independently such desires in ourselves. The only thing we can do is to work in a group under the guidance of a Teacher and study authentic, reliable sources of Kabbalistic knowledge. By introducing necessary efforts into such studies, we can attract the Creator's light, His influence, His sensation, all of which will help us to acquire anti-egoistic power, i.e., the screen.

As much as we can withstand our egoism, we will be able to feel the Creator; we will acquire the intention to work for His sake. The law states that when the smaller *Partzuf* begins to feel the higher one, it acquires the desire, the intention, to do everything for it.

If we still lack such desire, it is only because we cannot feel the higher *Partzuf*. The Creator conceals Himself from us, since egoism rules over us, suppresses altruism, and makes us feel our independence. However, when He is revealed, we will instantly become His slaves. To transform some of my qualities, I primarily need to realize they are harmful to me, and then ask the Creator to make them altruistic. This process is called "the realization of evil". All our studies are based on it.

We are either slaves of our own egoism or the Creator's slaves. The main thing is to understand what is preferable. Freedom consists in the ability independently to choose one or the other. The sensations of suffering determine man's behavior. The Creator provided a mother with the desire to nurture her child and to do everything for it. To some people, He gives the ability to feel the sufferings of others. Nevertheless, overall, everyone suffers from being unable to satisfy his egoistic desires.

סא) אמנם יש להבין, כיון שהע"ס דנקודים והמ"ה דא"ק נאצלו ויצאו מנקבי עינים דראש הס"ג, הנה היו צריכים להלביש להס"ג מפה דראשו ולמטה, כמ"ש בפרצופים הקודמים, שכל תחתון מלביש לעליונו מפה דראש ולמטה.

ולמה לא היה כן, אלא שירדו להלביש במקום שלמטה מטבור דא"ק? ובכדי להבין את זה, צריכים לידע היטב, איך נתהווה השיתוף הנ"ל, שהבינה והמלכות נתחברו לאחת?

61) It is necessary to understand that, since the 10 Sefirot of the world of the Nikudim and MA of the world of AK emerged from Nikvey Eynaim de SAG (the boundary between the "giving" and "receiving" vessels – Gar and Zat de Bina), they had to dress SAG from Peh de Rosh and below. This is similar to the way all previous Partzufim emerged – each lower Partzuf dresses onto the upper one from the Peh de Rosh and downwards.

סב) והענין הוא, כי בעת יציאת פרצוף ס"ג, הוא נסתיים כולו למעלה מטבור דא"ק הפנימי, כמו שנתבאר בפרצוף ע"ב דא"ק, כי לא יכלו להתפשט מטבור ולמטה. כי שם מתחלת שליטת הבחי"ד דא"ק הפנימי בבחינת ע"ס דסיום שלה, ובפרצופי ע"ב ס"ג אין בהם מבחי"ד ולא כלום (אות נ"ד).

אמנם כשהתחילו לצאת הנקודות דס"ג דא"ק, דהיינו אחר שנזדכך המסך דס"ג, שהוא בחי"ב דעביות, ע"י הביטוש דאו"מ בו, ובא לבחי"ב דהתלבשות ובחי"א דעביות, הנה אז נסתלקו הטעמים דס"ג, ויצאה קומת הנקודות על העביות הנשארת במסך, בו"ק בלי ראש. כי הע"ס היוצאות על בחי"א דעביות הן קומת ז"א בחסר ג"ר. וגם בקומת הזכר, שהוא בחי"ב דהתלבשות, אין שם בחינת בינה אלא בקירוב, שהוא נבחן לו"ק דבינה.

ולפיכך קומה זו דנקודות דס"ג, נשתוה צורתה עם הע"ס דסיום שלמטה מטבור דא"ק, שגם הן בבחינת ו"ק בלי ראש (אות נ"ב). ונודע שהשתוות הצורה מקרבת הרוחניים לאחד. וע"כ ירדה קומה זו למטה מטבור דא"ק, ונתערבה שם עם הזו"ן דא"ק, ושמשו כאחד יחד, להיותם שוים בשיעור קומה.

62) The fact is that when the Partzuf SAG emerged, as did AB, it ended above the Tabur de Galgalta, because it could not descend below the Tabur, where Behina Dalet de Galgalta rules as the ten Sefirot de Sium. The Partzufim AB and SAG have nothing to do with the Behina Dalet.

But when, after the weakening of the Masach, the Nekudot de SAG began to emerge from the Bet de Aviut and the Gimel de Hitlabshut

> *to the Aleph de Aviut and the Bet de Hitlabshut and the Ta'amim de SAG disappeared, then the level of the Nekudot de VAK (six Sefirot) appeared, i.e., ZA without the first three Sefirot. There is no Ohr Hochma there, only the Ohr Hassadim.*
>
> *This state completely corresponds to the property of the ten Sefirot de Sium below the Tabur, which are also in the state of VAK. We know that the equivalence of properties in the spiritual world unites them into one. Therefore, the Nekudot de SAG descended under the Tabur and merged with ZON (ZA and Malchut) of the world of AK.*

We should remember, that the "*Nekudot de SAG*" do not refer to *Bina*, which does not wish to receive the *Ohr Hochma*. All we speak about is no more than *Malchut*! *Malchut* is called "*Bina*", since it knows that it will not be able to withstand the pleasure of the *Ohr Hochma*; hence it does not want to subject itself to temptation; it is not interested in the light of *Hochma*, only in the light of *Hassadim*.

Let us examine the notion "raising MAN". MAN stands for "*Mey Nukvin*", the plural of the words *Maim* (water) and *Nukvin* (female). Before merging, *Bina* and *Behina Dalet* existed separately. When *Bina* descended under the *Tabur*, it was mixed with *Malchut*; now there are two kinds of *Bina*: *Bina de Bina* and *Bina* included in *Malchut*. There are also two kinds of *Malchut*: *Malchut de Malchut* and *Malchut* included in *Bina*.

Bina is known as *Maim* (water) and the plural of two *Malchut* – *Nukvin* – together form "*Mey Nukvin*". This hints to the fact that, beginning from this moment on, with each raising of MAN, *Malchut* must be sweetened by *Bina*. Pure *Malchut* is not called MAN, but the *Masach* or "the property of judgment".

Many things in this paragraph raise questions, but the Baal HaSulam did not provide all the answers. That was never his goal; he always gave his disciples an opportunity to make an effort to find the required answer.

Our work is in the field of the application of necessary efforts; not in the means to understand the spiritual worlds. Understanding comes only in the measure of our ability **to feel** the Creator. When man's property is similar to the property of the Creator, it turns into the spiritual vessel of reception, with the help of which man can sense spiritual information.

The Creator reveals Himself only after man applies a sufficient quantity and quality of efforts. If you simply memorize the text, and remember that *Nekudot de SAG* descends under the *Tabur* and mixes with *NHYM de Galgalta*, it will be enough for your further advancement. The facts must be rooted well in your head. This information does not vanish with biological death.

סג) ואין להקשות: הרי עדיין יש ביניהם מרחק רב מצד העביות שבהם, כי הנקודות דס"ג באו מעביות דבחי"ב, ואין בהם מבחי"ד ולא כלום? והגם שהם קומת ז"א, אין זה עוד דומה לקומת ז"א של הלמטה מטבור דא"ק, שהוא ז"א דבחי"ד, הרי שיש בהם הפרש גדול?

התשובה היא, כי אין העביות ניכרת בפרצוף בעת התלבשות האור, רק אחר הסתלקות האור. וע"כ בעת שהופיע פרצוף הנקודות דס"ג בקומת ז"א, ירד ונתלבש בקומת זו"ן שמטבור ולמטה דא"ק, ואז נתערבו הבחי"ב בהבחי"ד זה בזה, וגרם לצמצום הב', שנעשה סיום חדש במקום בינה דגוף של פרצוף ההוא. וכן גרם להשתנות מקום הזווג, ונעשה הפה דראש במקום נקבי העינים.

63) However, we must understand that there is a significant distinction between the Nekudot de SAG and the NHYM de Galgalta. The Nekudot de SAG have the Behina Bet de Aviut and are totally unconnected with the Behina Dalet, which is below the Tabur, although both of them are on the level of ZA, but with a different degree of the Aviut.

The fact is that the Aviut does not show in the Partzuf when it is filled with the light that overwhelms the vessel (the desire). However, after the light exits the Partzuf, the necessary Aviut becomes obvious in it.This allows the Nekudot de SAG to descend under the Tabur and be mixed with the NHYM de Galgalta. This led to TB and the formation of a new Sium in the position of Bina de Guf of the

Partzuf. The place of the Zivug also changed; Malchut moved from the Peh de Rosh to the Nikvey Eynaim.

It is written that there is a similarity of properties between the *Nekudot de* SAG and the ZON *de* AK, since both of them make up the *Partzuf* VAK *(Katnut)*. The level of the *Partzuf* SAG is *Bet-Aleph*, which is defined as *VAK*. However, the ZON *de AK* are *VAK* due to a different reason. It is not according to their height, which is *Dalet-Gimel*, but because they are under the *Tabur* – the ten *Sefirot* of *Sium de Partzuf*. So what is the similarity between these *Partzufim*?

The *Partzuf Galgalta* is called "inner *AK*"; it has the inner *HaVaYaH* (the unutterable four-letter name of the Creator – *Yud, Hey, Vav, Hey* – the base of any *Kli*). This means that it is divided according to a certain order, regardless of the height of the *Partzuf*.

The head is called *Keter* and is *Kotzo* (the beginning) of the letter *Yud*. From the *Peh* to the *Chazeh* is *Hochma*,the *Yud* of the name *HaVaYaH*; from the *Chazeh* to the *Tabur* is *Bina*, the first *Hey* of *HaVaYaH*; from the *Tabur* downwards are MA and *BON*, the letters *Vav* and *Hey* of the name *HaVaYaH*; they are *VAK*. According to this order, it turns out that their height is the same, i.e., both of them are *VAK* and have the light of *Hassadim* with the luminescence of *Hochma*; not, however, because they are *Vav* and *Hey*, but because these are the ten *Sefirot* of *Sium de Partzuf*.

סד) והנך מוצא, שמקור השיתוף של המלכות בבינה, הנקרא "צמצום ב"', נעשה רק למטה מטבור דא"ק, ע"י התפשטות פרצוף נקודות דס"ג שמה. ולפיכך לא יכלה קומת ע"ס זו דנקודים, הבאה מצמצום ב', להתפשט למעלה מטבור דא"ק, כי אין שום כח ושליטה יכול להתגלות למעלה ממקור יציאתו. ומתוך שמקום התהוות הצמצום ב' התחיל מהטבור ולמטה, ע"כ הוכרחה גם קומת הנקודים להתפשט שם.

64) It turns out that the source of the interaction between Malchut and Bina (TB) became apparent only below the Tabur of the world of AK, when the Partzuf Nekudot de SAG spread there. Hence, the ten Sefirot of the world of Nikudim that emerged according to the laws of TB could not spread above the Tabur de AK, because nothing can manifest above its source, its root. Since TB rules from the Tabur and below it, the world of Nikudim was bound to spread there as well.

As in all the other *Partzufim* affected by the impact between the Inner and the Surrounding Lights, the screen of the *Partzuf* SAG began losing strength and rising to the *Peh de Rosh*. Because of this intermediate state, the *Partzuf Nekudot de* SAG began to take form. It has the *Reshimot Bet/Bet*, i.e., constitutes pure *Bina*. Hence, it can spread anywhere, including under the *Tabur* of *Galgalta*, and fill the desires that the previous *Partzufim* could not.

The *Nekudot de* SAG can use their desires in a way that neither the *Galgalta* (it used only 20% for the Creator's sake above the *Tabur*, restricting the remaining desires, *NHYM*, under the *Tabur de Galgalta*), nor SAG could.

The SAG could not receive for the Creator's sake at all. It can only bestow without receiving anything. If it starts receiving, the reception will be egoistic. It has no screen on its egoistic desires.

Why does the SAG not immediately descend under the *Tabur*? It is because the SAG has *Gimel de Hitlabshut*, a slight luminescence of the *Ohr Hochma*, which does not allow it to descend under the *Tabur*. When the *Masach* rises to the *Peh de Rosh* and the *Gimel de Hitlabshut* disappears, leaving only the *Bet de Hitlabshut* (pure *Bina* without *Ohr Hochma*), the *Nekudot de* SAG can descend under the *Tabur*, refuse to receive anything in their *Kelim* and wish to enjoy giving, i.e., receive the *Ohr Hassadim*. This is the work of pure Bina.

When it descends under the *Tabur*, the SAG encounters desires that it cannot resist. The *Galgalta* and *AB* also refuse to receive anything under the *Tabur*, but in addition to the *Ohr Hassadim* there was some luminescence of the *Ohr Hochma*, which they received in their *Kelim* above the *Tabur* for the Creator's sake.

The *Nekudot de SAG*, which by nature do not want to receive anything and by their structure are similar to the *NHYM de Galgalta*, begin to mix with them. However, seeing the luminescence of the *Ohr Hochma*, which brings enormous pleasure, they suddenly "desire to receive" that delight, although they have no screen for it; hence, they are totally unfit to receive.

The law of *TA* instantly snaps into action, preventing the light from entering the egoistic vessels. As a result, the light disappears from them, and *Malchut* of the World of Infinity rises to *Bina* and restricts the reception of the light in the receiving vessels. This is how the *Tzimtzum Bet* (the Second Restriction, *TB*) takes place.

Even the *SAG* could not use its egoistic vessels for the Creator's sake. More, the subsequent *Partzufim*, *MA* and *BON*, which do not have the appropriate screen, will not be able to receive anything for the sake of the Creator.

The *Tzimtzum Bet* makes the use of the egoistic *Kelim* impossible. They are forbidden to be used and must be isolated. Only the altruistic *Kelim* are worked with. When such information rises to the *Rosh de SAG*, the structure of the future *Partzuf* is planned there in advance, taking into consideration the *Tzimtzum Bet*. Then a *Zivug* is made, not in the *Peh de Rosh*, but in the *Nikvey Eynaim*. From this point and above there are only the desires of bestowal.

The same calculation must be made in the *Guf* of the *Partzuf*, where the light can enter only the vessels of *KaHaB HaGaT*, i.e., up to the middle of *Tifferet*. In fact, in the *Rosh* and in the *Guf*, the same 10 *Sefirot* remain; only the level on which they are used changes. This means that each *Sefira* – *Keter, Hochma, Bina* etc. – is used not up to 100%, but only up to 60%. Now, we say that a *Zivug* is made only in GE, *KaHaB HaGaT*. However, these are mere terms.

It is possible to use the *AHP*, i.e., the vessels of reception, only if they are referred to as the vessels of bestowal, "raising" them above the boundary between the receiving and the giving vessels, i.e. the *Parsa*. However, despite the fact that the *AHP* are now considered as vessels of bestowal and fit to receive only the *Ohr Hassadim*, the ascended *AHP* naturally and automatically attract a slight luminescence of the *Ohr Hochma*. This process is called the "*AHP de Aliyah*" – the ascent of egoistic desires; in other words, they achieve their correction by merging with the upper *Partzuf*.

The *Masach* that stands at the *Peh de Rosh* of the *Galgalta* had the *Aviut Dalet* and made a *Zivug* on all the desires. However, only 20 % of each of them is used for the Creator, while 80 % do not take part in the reception for the Creator's sake. The anti-egoistic force in the screen is not sufficient for them. Only altruistic vessels placed above the *Nikvey Eynaim* are used in the *Nekudot de SAG* after the *Tzimtzum Bet*, because they have the "desire to give" for the sake of bestowal.

The entire universe represents one cause-and-effect chain that began from the first state when *Malchut* of the World of Infinity was completely filled with the light and up to its final correction when it will be filled with the light again. This process is controlled with the help of the *Reshimot*. Starting from the World of Infinity, *Malchut* gradually sorts out all its delights and builds a screen on them. It then leaves *Reshimot* from each of the previous states, up to its final correction.

The *Reshimot* alone determine the birth of the next *Partzuf* from the previous one. It is just this information about the past that provides the possibility to work with the screen. Only the light that filled the previous *Partzuf* can give to the next *Partzuf* the information about the pleasure and desires that were in it, and then pass them on to the next. Otherwise, there would be no idea about the light or the pleasure. The *Reshimot* in the *Partzuf* make it desire, seek, and move towards something new. We merely follow the instructions of our *Reshimot*.

There are no concepts such as 'was', 'is', or 'will be' existing separately in the spiritual world. These three concepts are already included in each new spiritual state. The *Reshimo* is a state in which I exist, but it shines from afar, attracting me from the future, arousing the desire to reach it. This light, which was inside the vessel, left and is now shining upon it from outside.

There are many kinds of *Reshimot*; they are reminders of what was inside each *Partzuf*. Unlike *Reshimot*, the *Ohr Makif* is the light that has not yet entered the vessel, but is shining upon it from outside. After the expulsion of the light from each *Partzuf*, lots of spiritual information remains around it. Meanwhile, we need only a tiny picture of the creation, some clear idea of the spiritual worlds. Everything around is in the state of absolute peace.

Although one must try to read what is written with understanding, a person should not take it as an assessment of his state: where he is now, where he is going, what he should do. Only the quantity and quality of efforts can be the criterion, for only they promote spiritual growth. Only your efforts can reveal the Creator, not your knowledge. Nevertheless, knowledge is also necessary, though minimal.

If you understand that your work, family, children and, of course, the studies are needed for achieving only one Goal – revealing the Creator – all these are counted as your efforts. Whatever you do in life, whatever you study, everything must remind you about the Purpose of the creation. This leads accordingly to the accumulation of efforts that reach the necessary result.

THE PLACE OF THE FOUR WORLDS ABYA AND THE PARSA BETWEEN ATZILUT AND BYA

המקום לדי העולמות אבי״ע ועניין הפרסא שבין אצילות לבי״ע

סה) והנה נתבאר, שכל עיקרו של צמצום הב׳ נעשה רק בפרצוף נקודות דס״ג, שמקומו מטבור ולמטה דא״ק עד סיום רגליו, דהיינו עד ממעל לנקודה דעוה״ז. ותדע שכל אלו השינויים, שנעשו בעקבות צמצום הב׳ הזה, באו רק בפרצוף נקודות דס״ג ההוא, ולא למעלה ממנו. ומה שאמרנו למעלה, שע״י עלית המלכות לחצי ת״ת דא״ק וסיימה שם הפרצוף, יצאו חצי ת״ת התחתון ונהי״מ דא״ק לבחינת חלל פנוי, לא נעשה זה בתנה״י דא״ק עצמו, אלא רק בתנה״י דפרצוף נקודות דס״ג דא״ק. אבל בא״ק עצמו נבחנים השנוים הללו רק לבחינת עליית מ״ן לבד, שפירושו, שהוא נתלבש בשינוים הללו, כדי להאציל לע״ס דנקודים בבחינתן. אבל בא״ק עצמו לא נעשה שום שינוי.

65) Thus it turns out that the essence of the TB was revealed exclusively in the Partzuf Nekudot de SAG from the Tabur down to the Sium Reglav above the point of this world (HaOlam Hazeh). Know that all changes called forth by TB happened only in the Partzuf Nekudot de SAG and not above it.

As was already said above, because of the ascent of Malchut to mid-Tifferet of the Sefirot de Sof of the world AK, which cut off its vessels of reception at this point, the lower part of Tifferet and the NHYM de Sof de AK turned into an empty space. It happened not in AK, but in the Partzuf Nekudot de SAG de AK. The changes that took place in AK are considered the raising of MAN, which means that AK only performs these changes for creating the ten Sefirot of the world of the Nikudim. There were no changes in AK itself.

After *TA*, *Malchut* of the World of Infinity, which decided not to receive anything, makes a new decision. It chooses to receive the *Ohr Hochma* for the Creator's sake by building the anti-egoistic screen, i.e., by acquiring the intention to receive for the sake of the Creator. The first *Zivug de Haka'a* and reception of the light are called *Galgalta*, the second – *AB* and the third – *SAG*. All the above-mentioned *Partzufim* could receive the light only above the *Tabur de Galgalta*. This is because the desires beneath the *Tabur* are so egoistic that they can only be ignored.

When the screen of *Partzuf* SAG weakens and *Nekudot de* SAG (the *Partzuf* of pure *Bina*) emerge, they can fill those desires under the *Tabur de Galgalta* with *Ohr Hassadim*, which neither *Galgalta*, *AB*, nor SAG could fill.

The *Nekudot de* SAG want nothing for themselves; they receive pleasure only from giving, i.e., from *Ohr Hassadim*. Hence, the *Nekudot de* SAG can refuse to work with its vessels of reception, and fill the desires with *Ohr Hassadim* instead.

But as soon as the desires under the *Tabur* are filled with the *Ohr Hassadim*, it turns out that there are *Zat de Bina* in *Nekudot de* SAG, i.e., the lower part that connects *Bina* with ZA, and obliges it to fulfill ZA's request for the *Ohr Hochma*. For that, *Bina* needs to receive this light, although by nature it desires not to receive at all. This quality of *Zat de Bina* became apparent already during the formation of the four *Behinot de Ohr Yashar*, where *Bina*, at the end of its development, decides to receive a little of the *Ohr Hochma* in order to create ZA.

For that purpose, Bina had to restrict slightly its desire not to receive and create in itself the "desire to receive", but only for the sake of giving, that it may be somewhat similar to the Creator. Now, having met with the enormous desires to receive, *Bina* (the *Nekudot de* SAG) had to submit to them and pass them some *Ohr Hochma*, which it has to request from above.

Such tremendous, newly acquired desires *(Dalet/Gimel)* are incomparably greater than the strength of the screen of the *Nekudot de* SAG; hence, there is a hazard that the *Nekudot de* SAG would receive the light for their own sake. To avert this, *Malchut* of the World of Infinity, which earlier decided to make *TA*, ascends from the *Sium de Galgalta*, where it was so far, to mid-*Tifferet* of the *Partzuf Nekudot de* SAG, thus cutting off the vessels of reception – the lower part of *Tifferet, Netzah, Hod, Yesod* and

Malchut, thereby restricting their use. Why are these particular *Sefirot* separated?

The upper *Sefirot Keter, Hochma, Bina, Hesed, Gevura*, and the upper part of *Tifferet*, are by nature vessels of bestowal; therefore, they did not take on the desires of the *NHYM de Galgalta (Dalet/Gimel)*. Only the *TNHYM* of *Nekudot de* SAG, albeit similar vessels with smaller *Aviut*, reacted to them. Recall that the *NHYM de Galgalta* have the *Reshimot Dalet/Gimel*, while *Nekudot de* SAG is a transition from *Reshimot Bet/Bet to Bet/Aleph*.

The upper light can pass through *Galgalta, AB*, SAG, descend under the *Tabur*, pass through *Keter, Hochma, Bina, Hesed, Gevura* and the upper half of *Tifferet*, i.e., the light can reach *Malchut*, which is now at mid-*Tifferet*. The light cannot descend under *Malchut*, because of the egoistic desires that remain in absolute emptiness and darkness.

In this manner, *Malchut* divided *Nekudot de SAG* into the vessels of bestowal that are above it and the vessels of reception that are below it. The line that separates them is called "*Parsa*". Any kind of light, including *Ohr Hochma*, can be above that line, for that is where the giving vessels or *GE* are. This is the place where the world of *Atzilut* will later emerge.

This world of *Atzilut* is completely altruistic; it will rule over the entire creation, create the worlds *BYA*, the *Partzuf* of *Adam HaRishon*, and facilitate its "sin" and consequent breaking into six hundred thousand souls. Afterwards, it will begin correcting all the broken vessels; it will lift them up to their Final Correction (the *Gmar Tikkun*) during 6000 years-levels.

The second half of *Tifferet*, i.e., *Zat de Bina* that lies under the *Parsa*, has the properties of Bina; therefore, the future world of *Beria (Bina)* will be formed in its place. Below it, in the place of *Netzah, Hod* and *Yesod*, the world of *Yetzira* will emerge, and the world of *Yetzira* - in the place of *Malchut*.

This is the general scheme of the creation of the worlds. Meanwhile, we have learned that the notion of "place" has nothing to do with our everyday physical definition. By "place", we mean the *Nekudot de SAG* from the *Tabur* to the *Sium de Galgalta* that are divided by the *Parsa* into the places of *Atzilut* and *BYA*.

We should also note such properties of the future worlds as ascent and descent. Indeed, their place may ascend and descend with them or remain where it is. The worlds always go up or down together with the souls.

סו) והנה תיכף בעת הצמצום, דהיינו בעת עלית המלכות לבינה, עוד מטרם העלית מ"ן והזווג שנעשה בנקבי עינים דא"ק, גרם זה שיתחלק פרצוף הנקודות דס"ג דא"ק לד' חלוקות: א. כח"ב חג"ת עד החזה שלו, הנבחנים למקום אצילות, ב. ב"ש ת"ת שמחזה ולמטה עד סיום הת"ת, שנעשה למקום בריאה, ג. ג' הספירות נה"י שלו, שנעשה למקום עולם היצירה, ד. המלכות שבו, שנעשה למקום עולם העשיה.

66) The division of the Partzuf Nekudot de SAG happened already during the TB (ascent of Malchut to Bina), i.e., before the raising of MAN and the Zivug made in the Nikvey Eynaim of the Rosh de SAG. This division occurred in the following way: Keter, Hochma, Bina, Hesed, Gevura, and the upper third of Tifferet, down to its Chazeh, is the place of Atzilut; two thirds of Tifferet, from the Chazeh to the end of Tifferet, is the place of Beria; Netzah, Hod and Yesod is the place of Yetzira; and Malchut is the place of Assiya.

סז) וטעם הדברים הוא, כי מקום עולם אצילות, פירושו המקום הראוי להתפשטות אור העליון. ומתוך עלית המלכות המסיימת למקום בינה דגוף, הנקרא ת"ת, נמצא מסתיים שם הפרצוף. ואין האור יכול לעבור משם ולמטה. הרי שמקום האצילות נסתיים שם בחצי ת"ת על החזה. וכבר ידעת, שסיום החדש הזה שנעשה כאן, נקרא בשם "פרסא", שמתחת עולם האצילות.

ובאלו הספירות, שהן למטה מהפרסא, יש בהם ג' חלוקות. והוא מטעם, כי באמת לא היו צריכים לצאת למטה מהאצילות רק ב' הספירות זו"ן דגופא, הנקרא נהי"מ. כי מאחר שהסיום נעשה בהבינה דגופא, שהוא ת"ת, נמצאים רק הזו"ן שלמטה מת"ת, שהם למטה מהסיום, ולא הת"ת. אמנם גם חצי ת"ת התחתון יצא ג"כ למטה מסיום. והטעם הוא, כי הבינה דגוף נכללת ג"כ מע"ס כח"ב זו"ן. ומתוך שהזו"ן הללו דבינה הם שרשים של הזו"ן דגוף הכוללים, שנכללו בהבינה, הם נחשבים כמוהם.

67) The place of the world of Atzilut is assigned to the spreading of the Upper Light down to Tifferet, where the Partzuf ends, i.e., the place of the ascent of Malchut Mesayemet to Bina, below which the light cannot enter. Thus, the place of the world of Atzilut ends in the Chazeh, i.e., at the boundary between the upper third of Tifferet and the lower two thirds of it. The new frontier, called the Parsa, is below the world of Atzilut.

Below the Parsa, the place was divided into three parts, although it was to be divided only into two: the ZON de Guf (ZA and Nukva) of NHY. Nevertheless, after a new Sium emerged in Bina de Guf (or Tifferet), only the ZON is below it. However, two thirds of Tifferet also descended under the Parsa. The fact is that Bina de Guf (Tifferet) in turn consists of its ten Sefirot KaHaB and ZON; and since ZON de Bina is the root of the ZON de Guf, ZON de Bina already possesses properties similar to those of ZON.

It means that they already have the "desire to receive", not for themselves, but for passing the light down to the ZON.

וע"כ יצאו גם הזו"ן דבינה למטה מהפרסא דאצילות ביחד עם הזו"ן הכוללים. ומטעם זה נסדקה ספירת הת"ת לרחבה במקום החזה. כי המלכות שעלתה לבינה עומדת שם, ומוציאה גם את הזו"ן דבינה לחוץ, שהם ב"ש הת"ת שמחזה ולמטה עד סיומו.

ועכ"ז יש הפרש בין ב"ש ת"ת לבין נהי"מ. כי הב"ש ת"ת שייכים באמת להבינה דגוף, ולא יצאו למטה מסיום האצילות מחמת עצמם, רק מפני שהם שורשי הזו"ן. לכן אין הפגם גדול בהם, כי אין יציאתם מחמת עצמם. וע"כ נבדלו מהנהי"מ ונעשו לעולם בפני עצמו, והוא הנקרא "עולם הבריאה".

Hence, together with the ZON de Guf, the ZON de Bina is also under the Parsa. For this reason, Sefira Tifferet split in all its width in Chazeh de Partzuf, since Malchut, which rose to Bina, stands there, leaving the ZON de Bina (two thirds of Sefira Tifferet below the Chazeh) outside (under the Parsa).

That explains the distinction between the upper part of Tifferet above the Parsa, which refers exclusively to Bina, and the lower part of Tifferet (ZON), which is under the Parsa against its will. It is the root of the real ZON and in the future will have to provide them with the light. There is not much evil in it, since it emerged not by its free choice. It separated from the NHYM (actual ZON), positioned below it, and formed the world of Beria.

סח) גם הזו"ן דגוף, הנקרא נהי"ם, נתחלקו ג"כ לב' בחינות. כי המלכות להיותה בחינת נוקבא, נמצאת פגמה יותר קשה, והיא נעשית למקום עולם העשיה. והז"א, שהוא נה"י, נעשה לעולם היצירה, למעלה מעולם עשיה.

והנה נתבאר, איך נחלק פרצוף הנקודות דס"ג בסבת הצמצום ב', ונעשה מקום לד' עולמות: אצילות, בריאה, יצירה, עשיה. אשר הכח"ב חג"ת עד החזה שבו - נעשה מקום לעולם אצילות. וחצי ת"ת התחתון שמחזה עד סיום הת"ת - נעשה מקום לעולם הבריאה. והנה"י שבו - לעולם היצירה. והמלכות שלו - לעולם העשיה.

ומקומם מתחיל מנקודת הטבור דא"ק ומסתיים ממעל לנקודת עוה"ז, דהיינו עד סיום רגליו דא"ק, שהוא סוף שיעור הלבשת פרצוף נקודות דס"ג לפרצוף גלגלתא דא"ק.

68) The ZON de Guf also split into two parts: ZA (NHY – Netzah, Hod and Yesod) became the world of Yetzira, while Malchut (or Nukva) formed the world of Assiya under Yetzira.

Here we have learned how, because of TB, the Partzuf Nekudot de SAG was divided and the place for the four worlds, Atzilut, Beria, Yetzira and Assiya, was formed. Keter, Hochma, Bina, Hesed, Gevura and Tifferet down to the Chazeh formed the place for the world of Atzilut. The lower two thirds of Tifferet, from the Chazeh down to the end of Tifferet, formed the place for the world of Beria. Netzah, Hod and Yesod prepared the place for the world of Yetzira and Malchut created the place for the world of Assiya.

The common place for all the worlds begins at the point of the Tabur of the world AK and ends above our world, i.e., reaches Sium Reglav de AK where the dressing of the Nekudot de SAG on the Partzuf Galgalta comes to an end.

Desires are created by the Creator and cannot be changed. All desires are created as *Malchut* of the World of Infinity. One can only decide how and when to apply them. Each desire can be used, worked with, or left aside until better times.

If you can do it, you are called "man" in the spiritual sense of the word and means that you already have the screen. You are the master of your actions and desires. If, with the help of the screen, you can use some of your desires, then depending on the strength of your screen, you may fill them with the Creator's light.

The desires are called the vessel of your soul; the light is called the light of the soul. The soul constitutes those desires you work with for the sake of the Creator. The filled vessel is like the soul.

TA was aimed neither at restricting the use of desires nor at neutralizing them. We have no power over that. We always want something. The restriction was made only on receiving for one's sake, whereas one can receive for the Creator's sake at any time. *Malchut*, from the *Peh* to the *Tabur*, began receiving the *Ohr Hochma* for the sake of the Creator in the desires that were there.

The ten *Sefirot* of *Nekudot de SAG* are under the *Tabur*. The *Parsa* divided the *Nekudot de SAG* into two parts – altruistic and egoistic. The altruistic vessels end in *Tifferet de Tifferet*.

As was stated, we need to understand the material in order to grasp the general picture, the meaning of Kabbalah, to see where it leads us and with what it provides us. How can we start working with a set of our desires? Which of them do I have to begin with? Can I use them? If so, under what conditions may they be used?

THE STATES OF KATNUT AND GADLUT IN THE WORLD OF NIKUDIM

ענין הקטנות והגדלות, שנתחדש בעולם הנקודים

סט) והנה אחר שידעת בדרך כלל ענין הצמצום ב', שנעשה בפרצוף הנקודות דס"ג לצורך אצילות הע"ס דעולם הנקודים, שהוא פרצוף הרביעי דא"ק, נחזור ונבאר ענין יציאת הע"ס דנקודים בפרטיות. וכבר נתבאר ענין יציאת פרצוף מפרצוף, שכל פרצוף תחתון נולד ויוצא ממסך דגוף דעליון, אחר הזדככותו ועליתו להתחדשות הזווג להפה דעליון, והגורם להזדככות הזה הוא הביטוש דאו"מ במסך דפרצוף העליון, המזכך למסך מעביות דגוף שבו, ומשווה אותו לבחינת עביות דראש (אות ל"ה).

שבדרך זה יצא פרצוף ע"ב דא"ק מפרצוף הכתר דא"ק, וכן פרצוף ס"ג דא"ק מפרצוף ע"ב דא"ק. והנה גם פרצוף הד' דא"ק, הנקרא ע"ס דעולם הנקודים, נולד ויצא מהעליון שלו, שהוא ס"ג דא"ק, ג"כ באותו הדרך.

69) Having acquired some general idea of the TB in the Partzuf Nekudot de SAG, we now proceed to a more detailed analysis of the creation of the ten Sefirot of the world of Nikudim, the fourth Partzuf of the world AK. We already know how one Partzuf takes form out of another. It happens when each lower Partzuf emerges from the Masach de Guf of the upper one, after it loses its strength and rises to the Peh to resume a Zivug de Haka'a. Bitush of the Ohr Makif in the Masach facilitates a loss of the Aviut of Masach de Guf down to Aviut de Rosh.

This allows the creation of a new Partzuf from the previous one. In this way, the Partzuf AB (Hochma) emerged from the Partzuf Galgalta (Keter); similarly, the fourth Partzuf of the world of AK, called the ten Sefirot of the world of Nikudim, emerged from the Partzuf SAG (Bina).

This means that, unless the *Nekudot de SAG* had descended under the *Tabur de Galgalta*, followed by the *TB*, the world, or rather, the *Partzuf Nikudim*, would simply have been the *Partzuf ZA* of the world of *AK*. However, the above-mentioned events have resulted in a considerable difference between the *Partzuf Nikudim* and the previous *Partzufim*.

The rising of the *Masach de Guf* to the *Peh de Rosh* means that, by its properties, it becomes equal to the screen at *Peh de Rosh*. As was already said, there are actually no rises or descents in the spiritual world. Kabbalists simply use the notions "ascent", "descent" and so on, to explain to us the processes that happen there. For example, if I am on a certain level, then provided I have the properties of the higher level, it means that I ascend to it.

ע) אמנם יש כאן ענין נוסף, כי בפרצופים הקודמים, בעת הזדככות המסך והעליה לפה דראש דעליון, לא היה המסך כלול רק מהרשימות דעביות דגוף העליון בלבד. משא"כ כאן בהזדככות המסך דס"ג דא"ק לצורך הנקודים, היה המסך הזה כלול מב' מיני רשימות.

כי מלבד שהוא כלול מרשימות העביות של עצמו, דהיינו מבחינת הספירות דגוף דס"ג דא"ק, הנה הוא כלול עוד מרשימות העביות דזו"ן דא"ק שלמטה מטבור. והוא מטעם התערבותם יחד למטה מטבור דא"ק, כמ"ש (אות ס"א) שהנקודות דס"ג ירדו למטה מטבור דא"ק ונתערבו יחד עם הזו"ן דא"ק אשר שם.

70) Now, what is the fundamental difference between the Partzuf (the world) Nikudim and the previous Partzufim? The fact is that, during the creation of the previous Partzufim, a Zivug de Haka'a was always made on one pair of Reshimot – de Hitlabshut and de Aviut. In this case, however, two pairs of Reshimot rose to Rosh de SAG.

This is because it consists not merely of Reshimot of its own Aviut, i.e., reflects the properties of the Sefirot of Guf de SAG, but it also includes the Reshimot of Aviut de ZON of Partzuf AK below the Tabur. This happened because they were mixed under the Tabur of Partzuf AK; as said in § 61, the Nekudot de SAG descended under the Tabur de AK and merged there with ZON de AK.

The first pair is the usual *Bet/Aleph*, i.e., the *Reshimot* that emerge one after the other, following the weakening of the screen of *Partzuf* SAG *(Gimel/Bet)*. A *Zivug de Haka'a* is made on these *Reshimot*, which leads to the creation of the *Partzuf* MA *Elion*. This *Partzuf*, as well as the following *BON Elion*, have nothing to do with us, i.e., the actual creation.

These *Partzufim* exist only for the completion of the world *AK*. As is well known, each spiritual object is supposed to consist of five *Behinot*. Similarly, the world *AK* must have its own five parts.

The second pair is also *Bet/Aleph*, but these *Reshimot* are completely different. First, they contain the information about *TB* that occurred in the *Nekudot de* SAG, and the ban on direct use of any desires of reception, i.e., it is forbidden to receive *Ohr Hochma* directly, even with the intention for the Creator's sake.

It means that, now, only the vessels down to *Gar de Bina* (included) can be used. Secondly, these *Reshimot* contain information about the presence of *Nekudot de* SAG under *Tabur. Zivug de Haka'a* is made on these *Reshimot*, which leads to the creation of *Katnut* (the small state) of the world of *Nikudim*.

The third pair is *Dalet/Gimel*, i.e., the enormous desires, which are close to the Essence of the Creation by their properties, that were taken on by the *Nekudot de* SAG from the *NHYM de Galgalta*. A *Zivug de Haka'a* is made on these *Reshimot*, which leads to the creation of *Gadlut* (the big state) of the world of *Nikudim*. In fact, a *Katnut de Nikudim* is the *Partzuf*, while a *Gadlut* de *Nikudim* is already the world.

Just the availability of these enormous desires, this additional *Aviut*, allows for the creation of the world, which consists of several *Partzufim*. Thus, the awakening of the *Reshimot Dalet/Gimel* leads to the emergence of the world.

The study of Kabbalah is a cumulative process. The Creator knows exactly how much time you spend sitting at the lessons, listening to texts and struggling with sleep. He considers everything and then turns on the tap. Everyone has his own way. There are no bright or stupid people here. What is important are the efforts made to withstand the egoistic desires.

However, there is no need to do anything artificially. One must persistently advance without fear of being thrown back. To avoid it, one must do something for the group, translate articles, and spread Kabbalah wherever possible. Man does not know until the last moment when he is going to reach the next level. It is now advisable to learn to think in spiritual categories.

עא) ומכח זה נתחדש כאן בפרצוף הנקודים ענין קטנות וגדלות. אשר מבחינת הרשימות דעביות שבמסך, יצאו עליהם ע"ס דקטנות נקודים. ומבחינות הרשימות דזו"ן דא"ק שלמטה מטבור, שנתחברו ונתערבו עם הרשימות של המסך, יצאו עליהם הע"ס דגדלות נקודים.

71) Owing to the merging of the Sefirot under the Tabur of the Partzuf AK, new states of Gadlut and Katnut (big and small states) emerged in the Partzuf Nikudim. The ten Sefirot de Katnut of Nikudim emerged on the Reshimot de Aviut in the Masach of Partzuf SAG. The ten Sefirot de Gadlut of Nikudim emerged on the Reshimot ZON de AK under the Tabur that were mixed with the Reshimot of the Masach.

עב) גם תדע, אשר הע"ס דקטנות נקודים שיצאו על המסך, נחשבים לעיקר הפרצוף נקודים, משום שיצאו על סדר המדרגה, דהיינו מעצם המסך דגוף דעליון, ע"ד שיצאו ג' פרצופים הקודמים דא"ק. אבל הע"ס דגדלות נקודים נבחנות רק לתוספת בלבד על פרצוף הנקודים, משום שיצאו רק מזווג על הרשימות דזו"ן דא"ק שלמטה מטבור, שלא באו על סדר המדרגה, אלא שנתחברו ונתוספו על המסך מסבת ירידתו דפרצוף נקודות דס"ג למטה מטבור דא"ק (אות ע).

72) Know that the ten Sefirot of Katnut of the world of Nikudim are considered the principal Partzuf, since it emerged similarly to the three previous Partzufim of the world AK. It was born because of a Zivug de Aka'a on the Reshimot Bet/Aleph in the Masach de Guf of the upper Partzuf. The ten Sefirot de Gadlut are only an addition to the Partzuf Nikudim, because they appeared, not in the order of the emergence of levels, but from a Zivug on the Reshimot of ZON de Galgalta, which were added to the screen as a result of the descent of Nekudot de SAG under the Tabur.

At first, man wants to "understand" Kabbalah, but comprehension comes through applying efforts, not by absorbing information. The study merely allows us "to contact" the spiritual world. The information provides just the general outline; the way things are designed. But how can we touch it, find out where it is, in what virtual space we can get hold of it, feel it, what the connection is between certain phenomena? It is similar to a musician who feels each note. Any specialist in his field instantly understands the meaning, internally feels it in his mind, his senses, then passes it through himself and builds an inner picture.

Man always perceives with his senses. For many years, I used to work with fighter planes. New digital computing equipment was introduced at that time. A pilot, however, saw only arrows on his control panels. However, while a man cannot concentrate on digits during the flight, he can instantly evaluate the situation by casting a glance at the arrows, This is because images play the most important role in our perception.

What we learn here technically only provides a formal basis, but the principal purpose is to create inner images in ourselves, upon which all technical information can be gradually dressed. This depends on the efforts we put into it.

Spiritual sensation is born in man as an addition to his five senses. It is in no way connected to the mind or any other senses. Hence, it is irrelevant in what language man reads Kabbalistic books. It is important to attract the Surrounding Light.

There are methods of promoting a more powerful influence. Man's mind plays no role in it. Only persistence and desire will allow us to enter the Creator's domain. My Rabbi did not permit me to move to the city of Bnei Brak for a long time, so I had to come from Rechovot twice a day. At 10 p.m., I used to return home, only to be back to the lesson by 2 a.m.

I was tired, slept at the lessons, but the Rabbi used to say that I would learn everything I needed to. The efforts have played their part. If man thinks there is no sense in attending a class, because he overslept and would not comprehend anything, it demonstrates his failure to understand that spiritual efforts are not measured by time or physical strength, but by an inner resistance to egoism, even if it is instantaneous...

There was a man in our group who finished working late, so he came in a taxi to catch the final ten minutes of the evening class. These ten minutes gave him more than someone else who spent two hours studying.

I do not have a grudge against those who spend their time sitting in a bar or in front of the TV set. They have not been given the desire for Kabbalah. This life will pass, and then a couple more lives, until their souls finally mature. We went through the same process in the previous incarnations; I can clearly see it on the people sitting here...

עג) והנה תחילה נבאר הע"ס דקטנות נקודים. וכבר ידעת, כי אחר התפשטות הס"ג דא"ק, נעשה בו הביטוש דאו"מ באו"פ, דהיינו על המסך שלו, וזיכך אותו על דרך המדרגה. אשר הקומות היוצאות בדרך הזדככותו, נקראות "נקודות דס"ג". והן שירדו למטה מטבור דא"ק ונתערבו עם הבחי"ד אשר שם (אות ס"ב). והנה אחר שנגמר להזדכך מכל העביות דגוף שבמסך, ולא נשאר בו רק בחינת עביות דראש, נבחן שעלה לראש הס"ג, וקבל שם זווג מחדש, על שיעור העביות שנשארו ברשימות שבמסך (אות ל"ה).

73) First, let us examine the process of the birth of the Partzuf Katnut de Nikudim. As we know, after the spreading of Partzuf SAG, the Bitush Ohr Pnimi and Makif takes place in its Masach. It weakens the Masach and forces it to return to the Peh de Rosh. With that, the intermediate Partzufim, called Nekudot de SAG, emerge and descend under the Tabur of the Partzuf AK. There they are mixed with Behina Dalet. After the Masach lost all of its Aviut and only the Masach de Rosh is left in the Partzuf, the Masach de Guf supposedly rises to the Peh de Rosh and leads to a new Zivug on the Aviut de Reshimot that remained in the Masach.

עד) וגם כאן נבחן, שבחינה אחרונה דעביות, שהיא העביות דבחי"ב שהיתה במסך, נאבדה לגמרי, ורק רשימו דהתלבשות נשאר ממנה. ומהעביות לא נשאר כי אם בחי"א בלבד.

ולפיכך (אות מ"ג) קבל המסך שם בראש הס"ג ב' מיני זווגים: א. מהתכללות בחי"א דעביות תוך בחי"ב דהתלבשות, הנקרא "התכללות הרשימו דנקבה בהרשימו דזכר, יצאה עליהן קומת בינה בקירוב, שהוא בערך ו"ק דבינה. וקומה זו נקרא "ספירת הכתר דנקודים".

ב. מהתכללות הזכר בהרשימו דנקבה, דהיינו התכללות הרשימו דבחי"ב דהתלבשות בבחי"א דעביות, יצאה קומת ז"א, שהוא בחינת ו"ק בלי ראש, הנקרא "אבא ואמא דנקודים אב"א".

וב' קומות הללו נקראות "ג"ר דנקודים", כלומר בחינת ע"ס דראש נקודים. כי כל ראש מכונה בשם ג"ר או כח"ב. ויש חילוק ביניהם, כי הכתר דנקודים, שהוא קומת הזכר, אינו מתפשט לגוף ורק בראש הוא מאיר, ואו"א דנקודים, שהם קומת הנקבה, היא לבדה מתפשטת לגוף, הנקרא "ז"ס תחתונות דנקודים" או "חג"ת נה"י דנקודים".

74) As always, the last level (in this case the Aviut of the Behina Bet) completely disappeared after the return of the Masach to the Rosh. Only the Reshimo de Hitlabshut and the Behina Aleph de Aviut remained.

As in all the previous Partzufim, two Zivugim occur in the Rosh de SAG after the Reshimot that were left from the intermediate Partzuf Nekudot de SAG rose there. One of them happens because of the inclusion of the Reshimo de Aviut (Nekeva) in the Reshimo de Hitlabshut (Zachar).

In this case, the matter concerns the emergence of the world of Nikudim; hence, this is the Reshimo Aleph de Aviut and Bet de Hitlabshut. Because of this Zivug, the Sefira of the level called "Bina be Kiruv" or "VAK de Bina" emerges, i.e., the interim state between Bina and ZA. This Sefira is called Keter of the world of Nikudim.

A second Zivug happened because of the inclusion of the Reshimo de Hitlabshut (Zachar) in the Reshimo de Aviut (Nekeva), from which the Sefira of the level of ZA or "VAK bli Rosh" emerged. This Sefira is called Abba ve Ima of the world of Nikudim, and they are in a back-to-back position (Achor be Achor).

These two levels are called two heads of the world of Nikudim. However, there is a difference between them. It consists in the fact that Keter de Nikudim, i.e., the level of Zachar, does not spread into the Guf, but shines only in the Rosh, whereas Abba ve Ima de Nikudim, i.e., the level of Nekeva, spreads into the Guf and is called HaGaT NHYM de Nikudim.

The *Nikudim* is the first world that is built according to *TB*; hence, there are certain elements in it that are related to our world.

The distance between the Creator and us can be divided as follows: the *Rosh de Galgalta* is, roughly speaking, the *Dalet Behinot de Ohr Yashar* (four phases of emergence and development of the Direct Light). Then, *Malchut* of the World of Infinity is positioned from the *Peh de Galgalta* downwards. It decides to accept some part of the light *(Ta'amim)* into the *Toch* after the *TA*.

Further pressure of the *Ohr Makif* on the *Masach* leads to its weakening and to the gradual emergence of the *Partzufim de Galgalta, AB, SAG, MA* and *BON*. Then the *Nekudot de SAG* descend under the *Tabur* and form the 10 *Sefirot*, which consist of *GE* (the vessels of bestowal) and *AHP* (the vessels of reception). An enormous "desire to receive" the light for themselves manifests in the vessels of reception. Thus, observing the conditions of *TA*, *Malchut* of the World of Infinity rises to *Bina* and prevents the reception of the light by those vessels. This is how *Tzimtzum Bet* took place.

The screen of *Nekudot de SAG* commenced rising with the *Reshimot Bet de Hitlabshut/Aleph de Aviut*, the *Reshimot* of *TB* and of the *NHYM de Galgalta (Dalet/Gimel)*. A *Zivug* is then made on the first pair or *Reshimot* (usual *Bet/Aleph*), which leads to the formation of the *Partzufim MA Elion* and *BON Elion*. One more *Zivug* is made on the *Reshimot Bet/Aleph*, plus the information of *TB*, and the light spreads only in *GE*. The *Partzuf* that emerged on this pair of *Reshimot* is called *Katnut* of the world of *Nikudim* (see above).

When people who study "The Preamble to the Science of Kabbalah" reach this point, they feel a sudden change, and have to start learning from the beginning. This turning point is not random, since beginning from *TB* and on, we begin to study the origins of our soul. *TA* and its consequences are not directly connected with our soul. Starting from the first *Partzuf* based on *TB* – the world of *Nikudim* and further, we begin to see the development of our soul, properties and aspirations that originate from the fragments of the common soul of *Adam HaRishon*. There is no doubt that the laws of *TA*, although having no direct influence on us, generally affect the entire Universe.

After their descent under the *Tabur*, the *Nekudot de SAG* acquired additional desires *(Dalet/Gimel)*, for which they did not have a proper screen, i.e., the force of resistance. A surplus of the egoistic desires was formed, and because of this *Malchut* rose to *Bina* up to the upper third of *Tifferet*. Now the light cannot spread below the *Parsa*.

For the light to spread from the *Tabur* to the *Parsa*, SAG has to make a prior calculation in the *Rosh*. To that end, it raises the screen from the *Peh* to the *Nikvey Eynaim*. This is the boundary between *Gar de Bina* and *Zat de Bina de Rosh*, i.e., between the vessels of bestowal and reception. This happens in the the *Rosh de SAG* under the *Tabur de AK*, taking into account that the light would spread only down to the *Parsa* in the *Guf de Nikudim* under the *Tabur de AK*. Here the *Partzuf Katnut de Nikudim* emerges. It has two heads *(Keter and Abba ve Ima)* and *Guf (ZON)*. Both heads are in a back-to-back position *("Achor be Achor")*. There is a notion "combination of the *Partzufim*" in the spiritual world. As the light gradually spreads from one *Sefira* to another in ten *Sefirot* of each *Partzuf*, the upper part of the *Sefira* is the receiving one, the middle part is the *Sefira* proper, and the lower part gives the light to the next *Sefira*.

Abba ve Ima de Nikudim are in a back-to-back position. It means that none has the *Ohr Hochma*. Another explanation suggests that they received the correction called *"Achor be Achor"* or *"Ki Hafetz Hesed"*, i.e., they have only the *Ohr Hassadim*.

Normally the word *"Achoraim"* (back part) means the part used either for reception or for bestowal. "*Panim*" (face) has the opposite meaning; it is the property being used. The correction, *"Achor be Achor"*, is also called "the correction of *Achoraim de Ima*", which is *Bina de Ohr Yashar*. It is unwilling to receive the *Ohr Hochma*, just the *Ohr Hassadim*.

Abba ve Ima is ZA, the *Behinat VAK* (the lack of *Ohr Hochma*), but thanks to the received correction, they only want the *Hassadim*. Hence, it is considered as the *Rosh* and *Gar*. They received this correction through *Zachar*, which has the *Bet de Hitlabshut. Abba ve Ima - Behina Aleph de Aviut* - was included in the *Bet de Hitlabshut*. Consequently, when a *Zivug* was made on their *Behinot*, they were also involved in a *Zivug* with their property *"Kli Hafetz Hesed"*.

The same happens in the world of the *Nikudim*. Two objects may be in four states: *Achor be Achor, Achor be Panim, Panim be Achor* and *Panim be Panim*. When *Abba ve Ima* are in the state of *Achor be Achor, Abba* is unable to give *Ima* anything, while *Ima* does not want to receive anything from *Aba*. Only in the state of the *Panim be Panim* can *Abba* transfer the light to *Ima*. There are two kinds of *Zivugim*: the spiritual, when no *Partzuf* is born, and "corporeal", which leads to the birth of a new *Partzuf*.

עה) באופן שיש כאן ג' מדרגות זה תחת זה: א. הוא הכתר דנקודים, שיש לו קומת ו"ק דבינה. ב. הוא קומת או"א דנקודים, שיש להם קומת ז"א. והם שניהם בחינת ראש. ג. הוא ז"ת דנקודים חג"ת נהי"מ, שהם בחינת הגוף דנקודים.

> *75) Here, we speak about the three levels, one under the other, in the world of Nikudim:*
>
> *a) Keter de Nikudim on the level of VAK de Bina;*
> *b) Abba ve Ima on the level of ZA – the two heads;*
> *c) Zat or HaGaT NHYM – the Guf de Nikudim.*

Recall that *Galgalta (Keter)* has the *Reshimo Dalet/Dalet* (4/4), *AB (Hochma)* has the *Reshimo Dalet/Gimel* (4/3), and SAG *(Bina)* has the *Reshimo Gimel/Bet* (3/2). The next *Partzuf* is the world of *Nikudim*. It is *Partzuf* ZA or MA (shortened due to *TB*). Therefore, *Abba ve Ima* and *ZON de Nikudim* constitute just this common ZA of the world *AK*.

Note that the world of *Nikudim in Katnut* is no more than the fourth *Partzuf (ZA)* of the world AK. Keter of the world of the *Nikudim* represents *VAK de Bina*, the interim level between the *Partzuf Bina (SAG)* and the *Partzuf* ZA (the world of *Nikudim*).

Previously we paid no attention to the fact that the *Partzuf* has two heads, although this was present in each *Partzuf*. Since there are two kinds of *Reshimot* – *Hitlabshut* and *Aviut*, there are also two types of *Zivugim*, and consequently two heads. However, they did not play a major role before, so we never mentioned them. Here, in the state of *Katnut de Nikudim*, they play a very special part and are very important.

Let us learn to "adapt" ourselves to the laws of the spiritual worlds. There is a soul, man. Previously he had the screen on all his desires, with the help of which he could receive a certain amount of the light for the Creator's sake. Now he cannot knowingly use all his desires for the Creator, since there are those among them that wish to receive for their own sake. Hence, he chooses not to use them, but puts them aside and works only with the altruistic desires: *Keter, Hochma, Bina, Hesed, Gevura,* and a part of *Tifferet*.

Now, there appears a basis for the emergence of the observed desires-commandments, which refer to *Sefirot* above the *Parsa*, and the forbidden desires, which refer to *Sefirot* below the *Parsa*. When, at the Final Correction, the *Partzuf* acquires the screen for the forbidden desires and they turn into the ones to be observed, he will be able to completely fill himself with the light.

The light is pleasure. If I enjoy the reception, it is called egoism. If I enjoy the act of giving, it is still egoism, but of a totally "different kind". There is no *Ohr Hochma* or *Hassadim* under the *Parsa* after *TB*, only absolute darkness. When the worlds *Beria, Yetzira,* and *Assiya* are formed under the *Parsa*, some light appears in them, the so-called *Ohr Tolada*, i.e., a small luminescence destined for the spiritual birth and correction, but not for the reception of pleasure.

In our rise to the *Parsa*, we climb 6000 steps or levels to reach and cross this barrier that separates us from the spiritual worlds. Then the *Mashiah* (the Upper Light) comes, resurrects the dead, egoistic desires, and corrects them. Then they can be used for the reception of the light-pleasure. This process is called "the resurrection of the dead".

We should stress that there is a fundamental difference between the creation of the worlds (the process we are studying) and creation of souls. Strictly speaking, the worlds are not the creation; they are the levels of the Creator's concealment, still objects, robots.

Only man, who climbs these steps, turning them into the levels of the Creator's revelation, animates them. We have spoken about this. Nevertheless, it is so important that it merits repeated mentioning.

Now, as we study the structure of the worlds, we learn about the creation of the spiritual environment for the future souls. The worlds promoted the creation of the soul of Adam HaRishon. Then this soul broke into many fragments. Each of them represents a human soul, which, upon its correction, will be able to receive the light, tearing off the spheres and filters during its ascent.

The *Parsa* is called "the point of the world to come". The *Sium* of *Galgalta* is "the point of this world". The difference between the two points is the place of the worlds *BYA*. The world of *Atzilut* is called *Gan Eden* (Paradise).

In our world, we have the task of acquiring the vessels of bestowal *(GE)*. This is achieved by crossing the barrier (the *Machsom)* and advancing to the *Parsa*. Only in the world of *Atzilut* do we begin to correct the vessels of reception *(AHP)*. This means that, during 6000 years or levels, we only acquire the altruistic desires.

Upon entering the seventh millennium, the world of *Atzilut*, we will be able to start correcting the egoistic desires. This is called the resurrection of the dead egoistic desires, which were forbidden to be used. This process takes 4000 more years. The tenth millennium already refers to the secrets of the Torah, of which we may not speak. There is no time, as we understand it, in spirituality. The so-called millennium can be passed in one day, provided the necessary corrections are made. The spiritual level is called "a year", since while passing a certain level, the soul's desires go through a full cycle of changes.

We study the most necessary science in our life, through which all others are attained. Imagine an empty space in which your "I" emerges.

This "I" is endowed with senses, with the ability to feel. Whatever you feel inside your senses is called your world. Who provides you with these sensations? The Creator does. He emerges from nowhere, existing outside, but you can feel Him only inside of you.

People differ by their sets of desires to receive pleasure. One strives after power, while another is drawn to money; one longs for animal pleasures, yet another is attracted to science. Similar phenomena exist in the spiritual world. It is impossible "to enter" the spiritual essence of another human being.

Therefore, we should never compare our sensations with those of others, since everyone runs them through his own set of desires. We cannot compare two different people's sensations of the same food, even though in both cases it will be, say, sweet. Only the Creator's light is common for all.

Whatever is necessary for man's existence is not considered egoism, although people's needs are quite diverse. Had I been satisfied with receiving nothing for my existence, I would have been free from all and totally independent. However, I still have to devote some time to satisfying the needs of my body. The Creator made me this way, and, although I would be happy not to do it, this does not depend on me.

Egoism means following one's own desire. Here man must determine what is necessary for the existence of his body, and what is superfluous and serves the satisfaction of his egoistic desires. However, the goal is to feel the Creator. Gradually increasing the sensation of the Creator will give us strength, confidence and the opportunity to move forward, correctly evaluating the current situation.

Kabbalah does not turn man into a fanatic nor oblige him to give something up. On the contrary, it wishes to lead him to absolute perfection and delight. Only the thoughts that cross your mind during the reading of a genuine text, combined with the explanations of a true

Teacher, can lead to a good result. If you are away from the book and your thoughts divert you from Kabbalah, consider yourself outside of it.

Kabbalah leads us to a state in which we can already feel the point in the heart. In this state we can evaluate ourselves, not from the angle of the egoistic desires, but according to the apprehension of the Universe and our own place in it, i.e., from the altruistic standpoint. Then a contradiction, between egoism and altruism arises, which forces man to cry out to the Creator for help, for deliverance from his egoism.

There are two kinds of *Rosh* in each *Partzuf*: the *Rosh de Hitlabshut* and the *Rosh de Aviut*. The *Rosh de Hitlabshut* contains information about the light that was present in the previous *Partzuf*. The *Rosh de Aviut* says which *Masach* is available at this moment. These two kinds of information are all there is in the entire Universe: the power of the light and the strength of the vessel. They provide us with two notions: the power of delight in the Creator's light and the strength of the screen in the *Kli*. Then, after making such a calculation in the *Rosh*, the vessel receives some part of the light in the *Guf* for the Creator's sake.

As was stated, the *Rosh de Hitlabshut* in the world of *Nikudim* is called *Keter*, and the *Rosh de Aviut - Abba ve Ima*. Yet there is the third head in the world of *Nikudim* – the *YESHSUT*. However, we usually disregard it, since it refers to *TA*, is under the *Tabur* and is considered a part of the *Partzuf SAG*. *Keter* and *Abba ve Ima* already refer to *TB*.

Each *Reshimo* should give birth to a thought that can emerge in action. The thought that was born because of the previous pleasure, the *Reshimo de Hitlabshut*, the *Rosh de Keter*, cannot come to realization for the lack of proper screen. It can emerge only by a *Zivug* on the *Reshimo de Aviut*, the body of the *Partzuf*.

The world of *Nikudim* consists of the *Rosh de Keter*, the *Rosh de Abba ve Ima* and the *Guf* – *ZON*, which itself includes seven *Sefirot*. The *AHP de ZON* is under the *Parsa* and joins the *Partzuf* only in the state of *Gadlut*. In this way, the *AHP* passes its egoistic desires on to the altruistic vessels, i.e., *GE*, which in accordance with *TA*, leads to the loss of the screen, the breaking of the vessels and the disappearance of the light. Only the empty egoistic desires remain.

Now we are studying the state of *Katnut* of the world of *Nikudim* that emerged as a result of a *Zivug* made on *Reshimot Bet/Aleph*. We come across some entirely new notions that need to be very thoroughly examined, since our *Kli*, our soul, is based on them. We are created because of the laws of *TB*. By overcoming the 6000 years or levels, we cover the distance from our world to the *Parsa*, and then enter the world of *Atzilut*.

The descending structure of the Universe described by Kabbalists, and man's attainment of the spiritual worlds, pass through the same levels. In fact, the Creator created all the spiritual worlds so that they would serve as steps-levels in man's attainment. The Kabbalists left us a detailed description of the descent; the ascent is attained by each man individually and is impossible to describe. We study the laws of the spiritual Universe and must know them if we wish to exist in the spiritual world.

The laws of *TB* apply to this world, but we see them in their material form: physical, chemical, biological and social. All these laws are expressed in their outward appearance, but if we look closely enough, we will see that they are also based on the spreading of the light, the formation of the screen etc. We study the basic laws of the Universe, reaching into the very depths of it.

עו) ותדע, שמכח עלית המלכות לבינה, נבחנות אלו המדרגות דנקודים, שבעת יציאתן נתבקעו לב' חצאים, הנקראים "פנים" ו"אחורים". כי מאחר שהזווג נעשה בנקבי עינים, אין בראש אלא ב' ספירות וחצי, שהם גלגלתא ועינים ונקבי עינים, דהיינו כתר חכמה וחצי העליון דבינה. והם מכונים "כלים דפנים". והכלים דאח"פ, שהם חצי בינה התחתון וז"א ונוקבא, יצאו מהע"ס דראש ונעשים לבחינתה של המדרגה שלמטה מהראש, ועל כן אלו הכלים דראש, שיצאו לחוץ מהראש, נבחנים לכלים דאחורים. ועד"ז נבקעה כל מדרגה ומדרגה.

76) Know that all the levels of the Nikudim are determined by the rising of Malchut to Bina. Moreover, they divide into two parts: "Panim ve Achoraim" (front and back of the Partzuf). After making a Zivug in the Nikvey Eynaim, there are only two and a half Sefirot in the Rosh: GE and Nikvey Eynaim, i.e., Keter, Hochma, and the upper third of Bina, which are actually the Kelim de Panim. AHP, which consists of the lower two thirds of Bina, ZA and Nukva (Malchut) got outside the ten Sefirot de Rosh and is now called the Kelim de Achoraim, which are not taken into account during a Zivug. Each subsequent level is divided similarly.

So, a *Zivug de Haka'a* cannot be made on *AHP*. No calculations and no reception of the light are possible. These Sefirot may not be used, since they are under the screen. Only the vessels of bestowal above the screen are taken into account. Accordingly, only the two and a half upper *Sefirot* are filled with the light in the *Guf of Partzuf – Keter, Hochma,* and the *Gar de Bina*. Such a state, when the receiving vessels are not used, is called *Katnut*. Only the vessels of bestowal are worked with.

It is similar to the situation where a host puts 10 different dishes before his guest. The guest, however, tells him that he can only enjoy watching this culinary abundance without touching anything. By not receiving, the guest likens himself to the giver. According to the force, which resists his egoism, he can receive only two salads for the sake of the host.

The *Partzuf* SAG, which refuses to receive anything, has the *Rosh*, the *Toch*, and the *Sof*. By not receiving, it enjoys tremendously its connection with the Creator, His revelation. Since the SAG is similar to the Creator by its properties, the *Ohr Hassadim* spreads in it. A question arises: should a *Zivug de Haka'a* be made on the *Ohr Hassadim*? Previously we only dealt with a *Zivug de Haka'a* on the *Ohr Hochma*.

It turns out that a *Zivug* must also be made on the *Ohr Hassadim*. As we have already said, the Creator's light is indivisible, and only the vessel distinguishes the various kinds of pleasure in it, according to its properties. Since there is a screen and a *Zivug de Haka'a*, there are also the *Rosh*, the *Toch*, and the *Sof* of the *Kelim*, in which the *Ohr Hassadim* spreads. They are called GE – *Keter, Hochma* and *Gar de Bina* (the vessels of bestowal), whereas the light does not enter *AHP*.

The Creator created the ten *Sefirot*. They are always present. Everything depends only on the strength of our screen and the ability to work with it. Now the screen is weak and can work only with the *Kelim de Panim* (the vessels of bestowal). There are the *Kelim de Panim* in the *Rosh*, the *Toch* and the *Sof*. However, we cannot work with the *Kelim de Achoraim* (the vessels of reception) that are also present there. Hence, the screen rises from the *Peh* to *Nikvey Eynaim*.

The entire *Partzuf* takes a different form: the *Peh* is in *Nikvey Eynaim*, the *Tabur* is where the *Peh* was, and the *Sof* is where the *Chazeh* was. Thus, after *TB*, the *Partzufim* use only the uppermost, giving, parts of their desires. According to the law of the inverse relation between the vessels and the lights, the light that fills them is correspondingly smaller than that which fills the *Partzufim* in *TA* (the lower, coarser *Kelim* the *Partzuf* uses, the higher light fills it). Due to the rise of the screen, which leads to using only the giving vessels, the *Partzuf* can entirely descend under the *Tabur* of *Galgalta* and work with the coarse desires, using only the giving part of each of them. The *Partzufim* of the world of *AK* are unable to use these coarse desires, because they make a calculation on both the giving and the receiving parts. *Partzufim* of the world of *AK* can descend under the *Tabur* only for passing the light to the lower *Partzufim* that function in *TB*, for at that stage, they do not make any calculation with regard to themselves, but with regard to those they bestow upon.

The notions "*Panim*" and "*Achoraim*" are self-explanatory: *Panim* is a more significant stage, *Achoraim* – less significant. *Panim* is used for both giving and receiving; *Achoraim* is a stage that is used for neither giving nor reception.

עז) ונמצא לפי"ז, שאין לך מדרגה, שאין בה פנים ואחורים. כי האח"פ דקומת זכר, שהם הכתר דנקודים, יצאו ממדרגת הכתר וירדו למדרגת או"א דנקודים, שהם קומת הנקבה. ואח"פ דקומת הנקבה, שהם או"א דנקודים, ירדו ונפלו למדרגת הגוף שלהם, דהיינו למדרגות ז"ס חג"ת נה"י דנקודים. ונמצא, שאו"א כלולים מב' בחינות פנים ואחורים, כי בפנימיותם נמצאים אחורים של מדרגת הכתר, דהיינו האח"פ דכתר, ועליהם מלביש הכלים דפנים דאו"א עצמם, דהיינו גלגלתא ועינים ונקבי עינים שלהם עצמם. וכן הז"ת דנקודים כלולים מפנים

ומאחורים. כי הכלים דאחורים דאו"א, שהם אח"פ שלהם, נמצאים בפנימיות הז"ת. והכלים דפנים דז"ת נמצאים מלבישים עליהם מבחוץ.

77) There is no level in the world of the Nikudim that would not divide into Panim and Achoraim. Therefore, the AHP de Keter, i.e., the Zachar de Nikudim, descended to the level of the Panim de Rosh, Abba ve Ima; in other words, to the level of Nekeva. AHP, i.e., Achoraim de Nekeva of Abba ve Ima, descended to the Guf, i.e., to HaGaT NHYM de Nikudim. Thus, both Keter and Abba ve Ima consist of two parts: Panim and Achoraim. In other words, Panim de Abba ve Ima dress onto the Achoraim de Keter that descended from above. Achoraim de Abba ve Ima, which descended to the Guf, constitutes the inner part on which Panim de Guf dress.

For example, there were five thoughts in the *Rosh* and correspondingly five desires in the *Guf* to receive pleasure from the light that is in the *Rosh*. Now, there are only two and a half thoughts in the *Rosh* and two and a half desires to receive pleasure. The rest of the desires are inside the lower level and are not used.

עח) וענין זה דהתחלקות המדרגות לב' חצאים גרם ג"כ, שאי אפשר להיות בכל אלו המדרגות דנקודים יותר מבחינת נפש רוח, דהיינו ו"ק בחסר ג"ר. כי מתוך שחסר בכל מדרגה ג' הכלים בינה וזו"ן, הרי חסר שם ג"ר דאורות, שהם נשמה חיה יחידה (אות כ"ד). והנה נתבארו היטב הע"ס דקטנות נקודים, שהן ג' מדרגות הנקראות: כתר, או"א, ז"ת. ואין בכל מדרגה זולת כתר חכמה דכלים ונפש רוח דאורות, כי הבינה וזו"ן דכל מדרגה נפלה למדרגה שמתחתיה.

78) The division of each level into two parts led to the presence of only the lights of Nefesh and Ruach in each upper part of the level, i.e., VAK, and the vessels Keter, Hochma and a part of Bina. Therefore, there are three levels in Katnut de Nikudim: Keter, Abba ve Ima and Zat, i.e., the vessels Keter, Hochma and a part of Bina, and the lights Nefesh and Ruach, since Zat de Bina and ZON descended from their level to the lower one.

RAISING OF MAN AND GADLUT OF THE WORLD OF NIKUDIM
עלית מ"ן ויציאת הגדלות דנקודים

עט) ועתה נבאר הע"ס דגדלות הנקודים, שיצאו על המ"ן דרשימות של הזו"ן דא"ק שלמטה מטבורו (אות ע"א). ויש לידע מקודם ענין עלית מ"ן. כי עד עתה לא דברנו כי אם מעלית המסך דגוף לפה דראש דעליון, אחר שנזדכך. שעל הרשימות הנכללות בו, נעשה שם הזווג דהכאה, המוציאות קומת ע"ס לצורך התחתון. אמנם עתה נתחדש ענין עלית מיין נוקבין, כי אלו האורות שעלו מלמטה מטבור דא"ק לראש הס"ג, שהם הרשימות דזו"ן דגופא דא"ק, מכונים בשם "עלית מ"ן".

79) Now we will learn about the ten Sefirot de Gadlut de Nikudim that emerged on MAN from the Reshimot of ZON de AK below the Tabur. Until now, we have not spoken about the raising of MAN. We discussed the rise of the Masach de Guf from the Tabur to the Peh de Rosh of the upper Partzuf, and a Zivug de Haka'a in the Rosh that was made on the Reshimot included in Masach, which led to the formation of the ten Sefirot of the lower Partzuf. Now let us talk about the light that rose from under the Tabur de AK to the Rosh de SAG, i.e., about the Reshimot of the ZON de Guf of the world of AK that are called "Mey Nukvin" (rising of female waters) or "Aliyat MAN".

"*Aliyat* MAN" is the rise of the desire, a request from the lower spiritual object to the upper one about making a *Zivug de Haka'a*. *Malchut* asks *Bina* (the soul turns to the Creator) to fill its emptiness, to correct its property of reception, to make *Malchut* similar to Him, the Creator, the "desire to give". It is called female waters because this is a request for the light of *Hassadim*, the altruistic desire.

Malchut had the 10 *Sefirot* completely filled with the light in the World of Infinity. Wishing to be like the Creator, it expelled the 10 *Sefirot*, i.e., it did not want to feel them. Nevertheless, they did not cease to exist because of it. *Malchut* chooses either to feel pleasure from them or not, but its nature remains unchanged.

After *TA* the *Rosh*, *Toch* and *Sof* are created in *Malchut*; it begins to calculate how much light it can receive for the Creator's sake. The *Partzuf* formed consists of three parts; each part contains ten *Sefirot*. The *Sof* emerged because *Malchut* began calculating its possibilities and understood that not all of them coincide with its desires, that it can fill with the light only 20% of its desires to receive for the Creator. 80% of the desires cannot be filled, so *Malchut* restricts them - makes the *Sof* and leaves it empty.

It will continue to be so until the *Gmar Tikkun*, when all 100% of the desires for the Creator's sake will be filled with His light. Then there will not be any need for the *Rosh* or any calculations. *Malchut* will be able to receive the Creator's entire light without any preliminary testing of its own powers. There will not be any uncorrected desires left. The angel of death will turn into the angel of holiness. Only the *Toch* will remain.

However, in the process of correction, calculations are essential. Restrictions may be quantitative (the *Galgalta*, *AB*, and *SAG*) when the light is received (although only a certain amount, in accordance with *TA* laws) in each of the ten *Sefirot*, and qualitative when not all ten *Sefirot* are filled with the light, but only some of them, depending on their properties.

Such qualitative division took place after *TB*, the state wherein only the small desires (of bestowal) are filled. On the other hand, *Katnut* is the state in which the big desires are not worked with. The lights that fill only the small desires are called *Nefesh* and *Ruach*. In this state, the creation feels only two and a half *Sefirot* out of its ten and does not work with the rest. If the creation gains additional powers and can activate the remaining *Sefirot* for receiving for the Creator's sake, it enters the state of *Gadlut*.

Now we are examining, according to the laws of *TB*, the transition from *Katnut* to *Gadlut*. In the course of our advancement from one level to another, the two states will alternately supersede one another. As soon as we enter the spiritual reality, climb its first level, we will gradually pass from *Katnut* to *Gadlut*. Then the *AHP* of the upper level will instantly lower us into the state of *Katnut*, but already of its own higher level on which we will have to achieve again *Gadlut* in order to descend into *Katnut* of the new level, and so on.

All the 6000 descending levels are built so that the *AHP* of the upper level is inside the *GE* of the lower one, and is dressed onto it. Hence, all the levels string one onto the other forming one ladder *(Sulam)* from the lowest point of the creation to its perfection – the Creator. Thanks to this close connection between the *AHP* and *GE*, each soul can ascend by climbing one level after another until the Final Correction. Such advancement can be roughly compared to the peristalsis of intestines while pushing the digested food forward by way of contracting muscles.

Any upper level is considered inner as regards the lower one, since it is closer to the Creator; it has a more powerful screen and bigger desires under the screen. Therefore, the levels become wider as they descend, which resembles a pyramid.

פ) ודע שמקורו של עלית מ"ן הוא מהז"א ובינה של הע"ס דאו"י (אות ה). ונתבאר שם, אשר הבינה, שהיא בחינת אור דחסדים, בעת שהאצילה את ספירות הת"ת, הנקרא בחי"ג, חזרה להתחבר עם החכמה, והמשיכה ממנו הארת חכמה בשביל הת"ת שהוא ז"א. ויצא הז"א בעיקרו מבחינת אור חסדים של הבינה ומיעוטו בהארת חכמה.

ומכאן נעשה קשר בין הז"א והבינה: שכל אימת שהרשימות דז"א עולות אל הבינה, מתחברת הבינה עם החכמה, וממשיכה ממנו הארת חכמה, בשביל הז"א. והעליה הזו של הז"א אל הבינה, המחברת אותה עם החכמה, מכונה תמיד בשם "עלית מ"ן". כי בלי עלית הז"א להבינה, אין הבינה נחשבת לנוקבא אל החכמה, בהיותה בעצמותה רק אור דחסדים ואינה צריכה לאור החכמה. ונבחנת שהיא תמיד אחור באחור עם החכמה, שפירושו, שאינה רוצה לקבל מהחכמה.

ורק בעת עלית הז"א אליה, חוזרת להעשות נוקבא לחכמה, כדי לקבל ממנו הארת חכמה, בשביל הז"א. הרי שעלית הז"א עושה אותה לנוקבא. לפיכך מכונה עליתו בשם "מיין נוקבין". כי עליתו דז"א מחזירה פנים בפנים עם החכמה, שפירושו שמקבלת ממנו כבחינת נוקבא מהדכר. והנה נתבאר היטב סוד עלית המ"ן.

80) You should know that ZA and Bina of the 10 Sefirot de Ohr Yashar (i.e., before Malchut de Ein Sof) are the source of raising MAN. This is what happened with them there: Bina, which is the Ohr Hassadim and the Behina Bet, gave birth to Tifferet (or ZA, the Behina Gimel) and reunited with Behinat Hochma to ask for the Ohr Hochma to pass on to ZA, which consists of the Ohr Hassadim and some luminescence of the Ohr Hochma.

In this way, contact was established between ZA and Bina. Each time the Reshimot of ZA rise to Bina, the latter merges with Hochma and draws a small amount of the Ohr Hochma for ZA. Such a rise of ZA to Bina, and Bina's connection with Hochma, is called the raising of MAN. Without this action, Bina itself has no need for the Ohr Hochma. Its essence is the Ohr Hassadim and it is always in the Achor be Achor (back-to-back) position with Hochma.

Only the request of ZA prompts Bina to receive the Ohr Hochma for it and turns it to Nukva; hence, this rise is called "female waters" (i.e., the receiving Sefira) as regards Hochma and changes their position from back-to-back to face-to-face (Panim be Panim).

All our corrections, prayers, during the 6000 years are made with the help of raising MAN. We (the souls) are parts of a general *Malchut*. Our request for correction arouses *Malchut*, which rises to *Bina*, forces it to receive the *Ohr Hochma* and pass it through ZA back to *Malchut*, which in turn transfers it to the souls. This chain rises like a call for help (raising MAN) from the direction of *Nukva* and then descends as the *Ohr Hochma* (male waters). Here lie all our opportunities for spiritual enlightenment, exaltedness, and revelation of the Creator. Gradually, we have to clear up these two principles.

We are now coming closer to the material that relates directly to us, our souls. First, it will seem difficult, muddled, but it needs to be mastered; with time it will enter into our sensations.

פא) וכבר ידעת שפרצוף ע"ב דא"ק הוא פרצוף החכמה. ופרצוף הס"ג דא"ק הוא פרצוף הבינה. דהיינו, שהם נבחנים לפי בחינה העליונה של הקומה שלהם. כי הע"ב שבחינה העליונה שלו הוא חכמה, נחשב לכולו חכמה. והס"ג, שבחינה העליונה שלו היא בינה, נחשב לכולו בינה. ולפיכך, בעת שהרשימות דזו"ן דגוף שלמטה מטבורו דא"ק, עלו לראש הס"ג, נעשו שמה למ"ן אל הס"ג, שבסבתם נזדווג הס"ג, שהוא בינה, עם פרצוף ע"ב, שהוא חכמה. והשפיע הע"ב להס"ג אור חדש לצורך הזו"ן, שלמטה מטבור שעלה שמה.

ואחר שקבלו הזו"ן דא"ק אור חדש הזה, חזרו וירדו למקומם, למטה מטבור דא"ק. ששם נמצאים הע"ס דנקודים. והאירו את אור החדש תוך הע"ס דנקודים. והוא המוחין דגדלות של הע"ס דנקודים. והנה נתבאר הע"ס דגדלות, שיצאו על המין הב' דרשימות, שהם הרשימות דזו"ן שלמטה מטבור דא"ק (אות ע"א). אמנם המוחין דגדלות האלו גרמו לשבירת הכלים, כמ"ש להלן.

81) We already know that AB is the Partzuf Hochma and SAG is the Partzuf Bina. They are defined according to their highest property. AB has the Aviut Gimel; hence, it is called Hochma. SAG has Aviut Bet, called Bina. When the Reshimot ZON de Guf (ZA and Malchut) rise from under the Tabur up to the Rosh de SAG (Bina), this process is called raising MAN to SAG. There, a Zivug between the SAG and the AB (between Bina and Hochma) is made, which results in the transfer of the Ohr Hochma from AB to SAG.

After ZON (Zeir Anpin and Nukva) receive the "new light", they descend under the Tabur again to shine upon the 10 Sefirot of the world of Nikudim, which leads to the emergence of the 10 Sefirot of Gadlut de Nikudim. However, we will find out later that just these 10 Sefirot contributed to the breaking of the vessels.

The Creator created only the "desire to receive" delight. The amount of light filling each of these desires determines the essence of the *Partzuf*. All the *Sefirot* of each *Partzuf* possess the qualities that correspond to its essence. For example, the 10 *Sefirot* of the *Partzuf AB* are ruled by its highest property of *Hochma*. *Keter* in *AB* has the property of *Hochma*, so does *Hochma de AB*, etc. In the *Partzuf SAG (Bina)*, the highest *Sefira Keter* already has the property of *Bina*, and not *Hochma* as in *AB*.

The *Reshimot* that the *Nekudot de SAG* received from the *NHYM de Galgalta (ZA)* demand *Ohr Hochma*, which *SAG (Bina)* does not have.

Therefore, *SAG* turns to *AB*, receives *Ohr Hochma*, and makes a *Zivug* on it. According to the demand of the *Reshimot Dalet/Gimel* of *NHYM de Galgalta*, the light from this *Zivug* must spread from the *Tabur* to the lowest point (the law of *TA*). From here, the world of *Nikudim* receives *Gadlut* by adding the *AHP* to itself, i.e., now it consists of 10 full *Sefirot* and uses all its desires.

Tzimtzum Bet represents the state where one may just passively observe, refusing to receive anything. If you can hold out in such a state without using your vessels of reception, then you are in *Katnut*. It means that you work only with the vessels of bestowal. In this state, you are somehow connected with the Creator, since He does not receive anything either. Hence, these ten *Sefirot* of yours are filled with the *Ohr Hassadim*.

Galgalta and *AB* received by bestowing upon the Creator. *SAG* already could not receive, just gave, or, rather, could passively exist in the spiritual space. *Nekudot de* SAG, being a part of SAG, also passively exist and do not want to receive anything. However, when a pleasure that is bigger than their screen (with the *Reshimot Bet/Bet*) can cope with (the *Reshimot Gimel/Bet*) comes their way, they catch this desire, being unable to resist it.

Any *Partzuf* is egoistic, but the screen that withstands egoism protects the *Partzuf* from receiving for its own sake, by the power it has. As the *Partzuf* meets with delight *Dalet/Gimel*, the screen instantly loses its strength and has no other option but to become a slave of its own desires and submit to them.

The difference between *Katnut* and *Gadlut* lies in the fact that, in the state of *Katnut*, the *Partzuf* activates only a half of its *Kelim* (GE), and correspondingly, if the *Kelim Netzah-Hod-Yesod* (the *AHP*) are missing, then the *Gar* of the lights are absent too. Even if there had been no *TB* and a *Zivug* on the middle line, there would not have been the *Aleph de Aviut* and the *Bet de Hitlabshut* on the level defined as the *Ohr Hassadim*. This state is called "*Katnut*".

The *Aviut Gimel* is used in *Gadlut*, which is defined as the *Kli* for the *Ohr Hochma*. In this case, *TB* is cancelled, since it allows only the use of the *Kelim* of bestowal. In other words, *Gadlut* means being filled with the *Ohr Hochma*.

The pure (clear) parts of the *Kli* are called the *Panim*, i.e., the *Kelim de Ashpa'a*, the desires of bestowal. The state wherein only such *Kelim* are present (where the screen for using the more egoistic desires *(Achoraim)* is unavailable) is called "*Katnut*". However, when there is a screen for the *Kelim de Achoraim*, the desire to receive the *Ohr Hochma*, i.e., the Inner Light called the light of *Gadlut*, enters the *Kli*.

פב) ונתבאר לעיל באות ע"ד, שיש ב' מדרגות בראש דנקודים, הנקראות כתר ואו"א. ולפיכך, כשהאירו הזו"ן דא"ק את אור החדש דע"ב ס"ג אל הע"ס דנקודים, האיר תחילה אל הכתר דנקודים דרך טבורו דא"ק, ששם מלביש הכתר, והשלימו בג"ר דאורות ובינה וזו"ן דכלים. ואח"כ האיר אל או"א דנקודים דרך היסוד דא"ק, ששם מלבישים או"א, והשלימם בג"ר דאורות ובינה וזו"ן דכלים.

> *82) We already know that there are two heads in the world of Nikudim: Keter and Abba ve Ima. When the new light of Hochma (AB-SAG) from the Rosh de SAG (requested by the ZON de Galgalta) begins to shine upon the ten Sefirot de Nikudim, it first enters the Rosh de Keter via the Tabur de AK. The world of Nikudim fills the Rosh de Keter with the light of Gar and elevates Sefirot Bina and ZON (i.e., AHP) de Keter, which have so far been in the Rosh de Abba ve Ima. Then the light AB-SAG enters the Rosh de Abba ve Ima of the world of Nikudim via Yesod de AK, fills them with the light of Gar and elevates Sefirot Bina and ZON de Abba ve Ima, which have been in the Gar de Guf. Thus, both heads, Keter and Abba ve Ima, enter the state of Gadlut.*

We see that the request rising from *ZON*, the creation's appeal to the Creator about getting strength for receiving the light for His sake, for the first time appears after *TB*. Ahead, we will observe the constant requests of the lower *Partzuf* to the upper one; we will see this connection that allows them to be incorporated into the entire system of the Universe, become similar to it, and become permanent partners with it.

In spirituality, a desire is considered existing if it can be used for the Creator's sake, i.e., for giving. If such an intention is absent, one may say the desire is non-existent, since it is suppressed by the *Partzuf*. Any *Partzuf* consists of 10 *Sefirot*, 10 desires, but if it works only with one of them, then, in fact, only this particular desire exists. The rest do not, because they take no part in reception.

In *Gadlut* the desires *Netzah, Hod, Yesod* and *Malchut* join the desires *Keter, Hochma, Bina, Hesed, Gevura,* and *Tifferet (Katnut)*. These desires become active because they acquired the anti-egoistic screen.

When the lower part of *Tifferet, Netzah, Hod, Yesod* and *Malchut* (*AHP* of each *Partzuf*) are inactive, there is no schematic description of them. Each *Partzuf* of the world of *Nikudim* has only GE, while its *AHP* (*Awzen, Hotem, Peh*) descend to the lower *Partzuf* and are, as it were, concealed inside its GE, which are dressed on them. This means that, as the light *AB-SAG* fills the GE of the upper *Partzuf* and then descends to the GE of the lower one, the light enters the *AHP* at the same time, which means the equivalence of the properties of GE of the upper *Partzuf* with the *AHP* of the lower one.

This temporary fall of the *AHP* is necessary for pulling the GE of the lower *Partzuf* up together with the rise of the *AHP* of the upper *Partzuf* to its place in *Gadlut*. The GE of the lower *Partzuf* joins the *AHP* of the upper *Partzuf* on the level of the lower one, i.e., in *Katnut*. It happens owing to the presence in both of them of the intention to give to the same upper *Partzuf*. The commonness of the intention also remains when they both rise to the level of the upper *Partzuf*, where they form the 10 full *Sefirot*. The *Partzuf* that is formed from the GE of the lower one and the *AHP* of the upper one is new in the creation. Its formation depends on man's spiritual prayer, while both the upper and the lower *Partzufim* are the Creator's work.

Thus, the lower *Partzuf* can rise to a higher level with the help of the upper one, which temporarily likened itself (its properties) to the lower one. The same laws apply to the souls. The main thing is to feel the upper *Partzuf* inside, do everything in your power for establishing contact and merging with it, so that, when it starts lifting its *AHP* attached to your *GE*, it will elevate you as well.

When the *AHP* of the upper *Partzuf* descends to the *GE* of the lower and merges with it, this combination takes place only from the point of view of the upper *Partzuf*. Now the lower *Partzuf* has to put effort into merging with it, preferring contact with the Creator, despite the emptiness it feels in the *AHP* of the upper *Partzuf*. Furthermore, when the upper *Partzuf* begins to fill its *AHP* with the light, elevating it, the lower one must hold on to this *AHP*, not for the delight it now feels in it, but out of longing to merge with it, become like it.

We can see it in the example of the granting of the Torah. The desires *GE* in the *Partzuf* (in man) are those that strive for the Creator. They are called Israel (from the Hebrew words "*Yashar El*" – "straight to the Creator"). The entire process of their emergence, correction and filling is described in the Torah. This book is a manual for the spiritual work. All that is written in it happens inside man's desires, in his heart, in the point that represents his true "I" and longs only for merging with the Creator.

It is a major delusion to perceive this book as a collection of stories, although the historical facts also took place, since everything in our world is a reflection of the spiritual worlds in man's heart. At the foot of Mount Sinai, only the Torah (the light of correction), emanating from the *AHP* of the upper *Partzuf* was granted. Israel (*GE* of the lower *Partzuf*) is yet unable to accept it. The Torah was given, but not yet received. The only desire in man's heart, called *Moshe* (Moses), can climb Mount Sinai, i.e., rise above its doubts and receive the Torah there.

Afterwards, this desire pulls ("*Moshech*") Israel after it. How many wars, births, and inner transformations must happen before the Temple (the vessel for receiving the light of the Torah) is rebuilt. This example demonstrates the fundamental difference between the descent of the *AHP* of the upper *Partzuf* into the *GE* of the lower and the state, where thanks to their own efforts, *GE* merge with this *AHP*, so that the upper *Partzuf* will be able to fill all of them with the light of the Purpose of Creation.

פג) ונבאר תחילה ענין הגדלות, שגרם אור חדש הזה אל הע"ס דנקודים. והענין הוא, כי יש להקשות על מ"ש באות ע"ד, שקומת הכתר ואו"א דנקודים היו בבחינת ו"ק, משום שיצאו על עביות דבחי"א. והלא אמרנו, שע"י ירידת הנקודות דס"ג למטה מטבור דא"ק, נתחברה הבחי"ד במסך דנקודות דס"ג שהוא בינה. הרי יש במסך הזה גם רשימו של בחי"ד דעביות. וא"כ היה צריך לצאת על המסך, בעת התכללותו בראש הס"ג, ע"ס בקומת כתר ואור היחידה, ולא קומת ו"ק דבינה בספירת הכתר, וקומת ו"ק בלי ראש באו"א?

והתשובה היא: כי המקום גורם! כי מתוך שהבחי"ד נכללה בבינה, שהיא נקבי עינים, נעלמה שם העביות דבחי"ד בפנימיות הבינה, ודומה כמו שאיננה שם. וע"כ לא נעשה הזווג, רק על הרשימות דבחי"ב דהתלבשות ובחי"א דעביות, שהם מעצם המסך דבינה לבד (אות ע"ד) ולא יצאו שם אלא אלו ב' הקומות: ו"ק דבינה וו"ק גמורים.

83) First, let us find out what Gadlut is, the transition that was caused by the spreading of the new light (AB-SAG) into the ten Sefirot of the world of Nikudim. We should point out that the levels Keter and Abba ve Ima de Nikudim were on the level of the VAK, since their Aviut was Aleph. However, we previously said that, during the descent of Nekudot de SAG under the Tabur, they were mixed with Dalet/Gimel of the NHYM de Galgalta, which means that the Masach that rose to the Peh de Rosh has the Reshimo Dalet. Therefore, after such a Zivug in the Rosh de SAG, ten Sefirot de Nikudim of the level of Keter with the light of Yechida were supposed to emerge there, and not the VAK de Bina.

The fact is that, due to the inclusion of the Behina Dalet into Bina de Nikvey Eynaim, Behina Dalet takes no part in a Zivug; it, as it were, disappears as regards Bina. Moreover, a Zivug took place not in the Peh de SAG, but rose higher, to the Nikvey Eynaim. Here, TB occurred on Bet de Hitlabshut and Aleph de Aviut, which is the essence of the Masach de Bina. Two levels emerged from this Zivug:

the VAK de Bina (Bet de Hitlabshut) and the complete VAK (Aleph de Aviut, the level of ZA).

פד) ולפיכך עתה, אחר שהזו"ן דא"ק שלמטה מטבור המשיכו את האור החדש ע"י המ"ן שלהם מע"ב ס"ג דא"ק, והאירו אותו לראש דנקודים (אות פ"א), הנה מתוך שפרצוף ע"ב דא"ק אין לו שום נגיעה בצמצום ב' הזה, שהעלה את הבחי"ד למקום נקבי עינים, ע"כ כשהאור שלו נמשך לראש דנקודים, חזר וביטל בו את הצמצום ב', שהעלה מקום הזווג לנקבי עינים. והוריד בחזרה את הבחי"ד למקומה לפה, כמו שהיתה בעת הצמצום הא', דהיינו במקום הפה דראש.

ונמצאו ג' הכלים אוזן חוטם ופה, שמסבת צמצום הב' נפלו מהמדרגה (אות ע"ו), הנה עתה חזרו ועלו למקומם למדרגתם כבתחילה. ואז ירד שוב מקום הזווג מנקבי עינים אל הבחי"ד במקום הפה דראש. ומאחר שהבחי"ד כבר היא במקומה, יצאו שם ע"ס בקומת כתר. והנה נתבאר, שע"י אור החדש, שהמשיך הזו"ן דא"ק אל הראש דנקודים, הרויח ג' האורות נשמה חיה יחידה, וג' הכלים אח"פ, שהם בינה וזו"ן, שהיו חסרים לו בעת יציאתו מתחילה.

84) Now, after the ZON de AK, which positioned under the Tabur, attracted the new light from the AB-SAG by raising MAN, this light shone on the Rosh de Nikudim and cancelled TB for the lack of any connection between the Partzuf AB and the TB (it originated in TA). Behina Dalet de AK under the Tabur, which rose to the Nikvey Eynaim after TB, now returned to the Peh de Rosh, as in TA.

Hence, the vessels AHP in the Rosh de SAG, which descended from under the screen due to TB, now rose again and took their previous position under the vessels of GE, while the place of Zivug descended from Nikvey Eynaim to Peh de Rosh, Behina Dalet. The return of Behina Dalet to its place led to the emergence of the Partzuf of the level of Keter with the light of Yechida. Thus, with the help of the new light, the Partzuf gained three more kinds of the Ohr Hochma: Neshama, Haya and Yechida, and the vessels Bina and ZON that were absent in it in the state of Katnut.

The principal task is to fill *Malchut* of the World of Infinity completely with the light. *Malchut* represents the *Galgalta*. If it were filled with the light from the *Peh* to the *Tabur* and from the *Tabur* down to the *Sium*, the Final Correction would come. However, according to the law of TA, only a part of *Malchut* from the *Peh* to the *Tabur* can be filled with the light so far. Filling *Malchut* with the light from the *Tabur* to the *Sium*, with the help of *TA*, a usual *Zivug de Aka'a* is simply impossible. Neither *Galgalta*, nor *AB* nor any of the subsequent *Partzufim*, whose screen was even weaker than that of the *Galgalta*, could do that.

The only way is to somehow liken the properties of *Malchut* to those of Bina, mix the egoistic vessels of *NHYM de Galgalta* with the altruistic vessels of the SAG *(Bina)*, receive their altruistic properties, and gradually start filling the corrected vessels with the light.

Being the intermediate *Partzuf* between *Bina* (the SAG) and ZA (the MA, the world of *Nikudim*), the *Nekudot de* SAG, on the one hand, have the properties of *Bina*; on the other hand, the *Aviut Aleph*. Hence, it has also the properties of ZA or, rather, *VAK*, so it is somewhat similar to the *NHYM de Galgalta (ZA)*. That is why just the *Partzuf Nekudot de SAG* proves useful to achieve that goal – filling *Malchut* of the World of Infinity with the light under the *Tabur*. It descended under the *Tabur* and filled the *NHYM de Galgalta* with the *Ohr Hassadim*.

Then, as we already know, since the "desire to receive" for one's sake was activated in the lower part of *Nekudot de SAG*, *Tzimtzum Aleph* snapped into action. *Malchut* instantly rose to *Tifferet (Bina de Guf)* and restricted reception of the light in the lower two thirds of it and in the *NHY*. The new restriction received the name *Tzimtzum Bet* and divided each level into *Gar* and *Zat*, GE and *AHP*.

The result of *TB* is that all the properties are mixed. SAG acquires egoistic properties and *Malchut* – altruistic vessels. This general mix of properties constitutes the world of *Nikudim* in *Katnut*, which says that now only the altruistic desires (GE) may be used. In fact, the world of *Nikudim* also consists of ten *Sefirot*, but of all these ten desires, it may use only the altruistic ones; hence, they say it has only GE.

After the emergence of the world of *Nikudim* in the state of *Katnut* (the screen is in the *Nikvey Eynaim*, the *Reshimot Bet/Aleph*), its ZON raise MAN on *Reshimot Dalet/Gimel* asking for the filling of their desires.

To receive the *Ohr Hochma* and pass it on to the *ZON*, *SAG* turns to *AB*, since *AB* has a sufficiently strong screen to work with the *Reshimot Dalet/Gimel.*

Light *AB-SAG* passes through the *Tabur* to the *Rosh de Keter* and *Rosh de Abba ve Ima* of the world of *Nikudim*, dictating its properties. It annuls *TB*, elevates *AHP* to *GE* in the *Rosh de Keter* and *Abba ve Ima*, and then makes them enter the state of *Gadlut*. The light corrects and fills the vessels. The correction of our souls will take place in a similar fashion, with the help of the raising of *MAN*. There are just three components in this process: the egoistic "desire to receive" created by the Creator, the screen and the light.

Malchut of the World of Infinity slowly moves through the entire process of transition from the first state (of being completely filled with the light) to the third state (the *Gmar Tikkun*) during 6000 years or levels. This process represents the second stage of gradual correction of the vessels and fills them with portions of the light. Kabbalah is a practical science that deals with the filling of desires with the light. Like other sciences, it possesses its special instrument called the screen and the methods for building it, the so-called "*Birur*" (analysis) and the "*Tikkun*" (correction). The screen is not just an instrument, or the vessel to be filled; it also contains the *Reshimot* – the information about the previous state.

We have never heard of the additional light that comes and allows the vessel to transform itself. The *Partzuf* in the state of *Katnut*, filled with the *Ohr Hassadim* is unable to change anything by itself, give birth to a new state. Only the *Partzuf* filled with the *Ohr Hochma* can do this.

Galgalta above the *Tabur* has exhausted all its *Reshimot* because of *Zivugim*, on which the five *Partzufim* of the world of *AK* emerged. Now the world of *Nikudim* in *Katnut* is under the *Tabur*, together with the *Reshimot Dalet/Gimel* on four unused desires after *TB*. These vessels want to receive the light, since they feel that their desires are not filled. They demand the *Ohr Hochma* from the upper *Partzuf*. However, the vessel must acquire a screen with sufficient power to resist its egoistic desires, i.e., the intention to receive for the Creator's sake.

To correct the vessels of the world of *Nikudim*, *SAG* turns to *AB*, receives the *Ohr Hochma* from it, then passes the combined light *Hochma-Hassadim (AB-SAG)* to *Nikudim*. This light is not pleasure; it is the light of correction, which means that it allows even the egoistic vessels to receive for the sake of the Creator.

How can such a light enter the egoistic vessels when the law of *TA*, which forbids the light from entering the *Kli* without the *Masach*, is effective? The Light *AB-SAG* acts in the following way: it allows the vessel to see the Creator's greatness from afar. This sensation of significance of spirituality lets the vessel act in an altruistic way.

The *Ohr AB-SAG* is a very specific kind of light that we will discuss later. Having no *Ohr Hochma*, the *SAG* turns to *AB*. The *Ohr AB-SAG* is the light that corrects the creation. In order to be corrected, one needs to know what correction is, what it means to be filled with wisdom and knowledge. The Light *AB-SAG* contains all this information. Both the light of *AB* and *SAG* are necessary to show the lower *Partzuf* the entire diversity of the spiritual attainment.

From the state of complete emptiness, performing each new action for the sake of the Creator, *Malchut* of the World of Infinity accumulates more and more altruistic properties. These are the *Partzufim Galgalta*, *AB* and *SAG*. Seemingly, it should get closer and closer to the Creator. The birth of each new *Partzuf* is like a manifestation of a new altruistic property of *Malchut*. Yet in reality, each new action moves *Malchut* away from the Creator.

Perhaps it is drawing nearer and not moving away? On the one hand, the more distant the *Partzuf* is from the Creator, the more independent it becomes. On the other hand, there lies its weakness; it loses contact with the Creator, and feels less of the power of His light.

Every action in the spiritual world is either perfect or must approximate perfection. Now *Malchut* realizes the Creator's goal: to be completely filled with His light.Hence, each new action is supposed to draw it nearer to this goal and must be better than the previous. The vessels' properties become more and more revealed. *Malchut* moves farther away from the Creator, but from the point of its self-knowledge, it is a very positive process. However, one can come to know oneself only with the help of the powerful light, whereas each subsequent *Partzuf* contains less and less of it.

A phenomenon can be properly examined only by summarizing all actions. Everything should be looked upon from the viewpoint of the creation, i.e., *Malchut* of the World of Infinity. First, turning into new worlds and *Partzufim*, it moves farther and farther away from the Creator. Then, reaching the point of our world and turning into the human soul, it starts ascending, being the initiator of all actions. The actions performed from above refer exclusively to the Creator.

פה) ונתבאר היטב הקטנות והגדלות דנקודים. אשר צמצום הב', שהעלה את ה"ת, שהיא בחי"ד, למקום נקבי עינים, ונגנזה שם, גרם לקומת הקטנות דנקודים, שהוא קומת ו"ק או ז"א באורות דנפש רוח, והיו חסרים שם בינה וזו"ן דכלים ונשמה חיה יחידה דאורות. וע"י ביאת אור חדש דע"ב ס"ג דא"ק אל הנקודים, חזר הצמצום א' למקומו. וחזרו הבינה וזו"ן דכלים לראש, כי ה"ת ירדה מנקבי עינים וחזרה למקומה למלכות, הנקראת "פה".

ואז נעשה הזווג על בחי"ד, שחזרה למקומה. ויצאו הע"ס בקומת כתר ויחידה. ונשלמו הנרנח"י דאורות והכח"ב זו"ן דכלים. ולשם הקיצור מכאן ואילך: נכנה להצמצום ב' והקטנות בשם "עלית ה"ת לנקבי עינים וירידת אח"פ למטה", ואת הגדלות נכנה בשם ביאת אור דע"ב ס"ג, המוריד ה"ת מנקבי עינים ומחזיר האח"פ למקומם.

גם תזכור תמיד שגו"ע ואח"פ הם שמות דע"ס כח"ב זו"ן דראש, והע"ס דגוף מכונים בשם חג"ת נהי"מ. וגם הם נחלקים לפי גו"ע ואח"פ, כי החסד וגבורה ושליש עליון דת"ת עד החזה - הם גלגלתא ועינים ונקבי עינים, וב"ש ת"ת ונהי"ם הם אח"פ.

גם תזכור, שגלגלתא ועינים ונ"ע או חג"ת עד החזה הם מכונים כלים דפנים, ואח"פ או ב"ש ת"ת ונהי"מ שמחזה ולמטה מכונים כלים דאחורים, וכן תזכור ענין בקיעת המדרגה, שנעשה עם צמצום ב', אשר לא נשאר בכל מדרגה רק הכלים דפנים לבד. וכל תחתון, יש בפנימיותו הכלים דאחורים של העליון (אות ע"ז).

85) We have cleared up the meaning of Katnut and Gadlut of the world of Nikudim, where TB lifted Malchut to Nikvey Eynaim and concealed it there. This caused the emergence of the world of Nikudim in Katnut. This is the state in which the vessels Keter, Hochma and Gar de Bina are filled with the lights Nefesh and Ruach, while the vessels the Zat de Bina and ZON, and the lights Neshama, Haya, and Yechida are absent. Then, as the new light AB-SAG descends from the world AK to the world of Nikudim, TA returns; as a result, the vessels Zat de Bina and ZON in the Rosh joined the upper vessels and the screen descended from Nikvey Eynaim to Peh.

Then a Zivug is made on Behina Dalet, which returned to its position in Peh de Rosh. This leads to the formation of ten Sefirot of the level of Keter. From this moment, TB and Katnut are defined as the ascent of Malchut to Nikvey Eynaim and the downfall of AHP. The state of Gadlut is characterized by the appearance of the light AB-SAG, the descent of Malchut to its previous position (as in TA) and the rise of AHP.

As was stated above, GE and AHP are names of the 10 Sefirot KaHaB ZON de Rosh. The 10 Sefirot de Guf are correspondingly called the HaGaT NHYM, which in turn consist of their GE (Hesed, Gevura and the upper third of Tifferet down to the Chazeh) and the AHP (two lower thirds of Tifferet and NHYM).

You should also remember that GE (HaGaT down to the Chazeh) is also called the **Panim** *(face, front part), and the AHP (two thirds of Tifferet and the NHYM) is called the* **Achoraim** *(back part). You should not forget about the division of the levels after TB, when only GE remained on each level, while the AHP fell into the GE of the lower level, whose AHP in turn fell to the GE of the level below, etc.*

THE NEKUDOT: HOLAM, SHURUK, HIRIK
ביאור ג' הנקודות חולם שורק חירק

פו) דע, שהנקודות נחלקות לג' בחינות ראש תוך סוף, שהם: נקודות עליונות, שממעל לאותיות, הנכללות בשם "חולם", ונקודות אמצעיות, שבתוך האותיות, הנכללות בשם "שורק" או "מלאפום", דהיינו ו' ובתוכה נקודה, ונקודות תחתונות, שמתחת האותיות, הנכללות בשם "חירק".

86) You must know that there are three kinds of Nekudot (dots, points): the Rosh, the Toch and the Sof. The upper Nekudot, positioned above the Hebrew letter as dots, are called Rosh, or **Holam**. *The middle Nekudot inside the letters, as in Vav with a dot, is called Toch, or* **Shuruk**. *The lower Nekudot, placed under the letters, are called Sof, or* **Hirik**.

What does this mean in the spiritual world? The letters are the vessels, while the dots are the lights. If the dot is above the letter, it symbolizes the light that has not yet entered the vessel, but is destined to do so in the future. This kind of a dot is called *Holam*. If the dot is inside the vessel, in its Toch, it is called *Shuruk*. If the dot left the vessel and is under it, it is called *Hirik*.

פז) וזה ביאורם. כי אותיות פירושם כלים, דהיינו הספירות דגוף. כי הע"ס דראש הם רק שרשים לכלים ולא כלים ממש. ונקודות פירושם אורות, המחיים את הכלים ומנענעים אותם. והיינו אור החכמה, הנקרא "אור חיה". והוא בחינת אור חדש, שהזו"ן דא"ק קבלו מע"ב ס"ג והאירו להכלים דנקודים, והורידו את ה"ת בחזרה לפה דכל מדרגה, והשיבו להמדרגה את האח"פ דכלים וג"ר דאורות.הרי שאור הזה מנענע הכלים דאח"פ ומעלה אותם מהמדרגה שלמטה, ומחבר אותם לעליונה כבתחילה, שז"ס "נקודות המנענעות להאותיות". וזה האור להיותו נמשך מע"ב דא"ק, שהוא אור חיה, ע"כ הוא מחיה לאותם הכלים דאח"פ ע"י התלבשותו בתוכם.

87) The letters constitute the vessels, i.e., the Sefirot de Guf. The ten Sefirot de Rosh are called the roots of the vessels. The Nekudot are the lights that animate these vessels. Hence, the Ohr Hochma is called the light of life (Ohr Haya). This new light AB-SAG passes through the ZON of the world of AK. It then shines upon the vessels of the world of Nikudim, causes Malchut to descend from Nikvey

Eynaim to Peh on each level, and thus brings the AHP back. As a result, all the lights return to their places. This light moves the Kelim from the state of TB to the state of TA, from Katnut to Gadlut. Accordingly, the light AB-SAG animates and arouses the vessels by dressing into them.

In the *Katnut de Nikudim, Abba ve Ima* dressed on the *AHP de Keter*, the ZON dressed on the *AHP de Abba ve Ima*, and the *AHP de ZON* were under the *Parsa*. This state appeared after a *Zivug* in *Nikvey Eynaim* of the *Rosh de* SAG. Now, under the influence of the new light *AB-SAG*, the screen in *Rosh de SAG* descended from *Nikvey Eynaim* to the *Peh de Rosh* and made a *Zivug* with the *Ohr Hochma* of *AB*. First, the light descended to the *Rosh de Keter* and attached the *AHP* and the light of *Gar* to *Keter*. This light let the vessel understand what the Creator means. The vessel is totally imbued with altruism and is now able to work with all of its ten desires, making a *Zivug de Haka'a* on them. Thus, the vessel passes from *Katnut* to *Gadlut*.

פח) וכבר ידעת, שהזו"ן דא"ק האירו את אור החדש הזה להע"ס דנקודים דרך ב' מקומות: דרך הטבור האיר להכתר דנקודים, ודרך היסוד האיר לאו"א דנקודים. ותדע, שהארה דרך הטבור מכונה בשם "חולם", המאיר לאותיות מלמעלה מהם.

והוא מטעם, שהארת הטבור אינו מגיע אלא לכתר דנקודים, שהוא קומת הזכר דראש הנקודים (אות ע"ד). וקומת הזכר אינו מתפשט לז"ת של הנקודים, שהם הכלים דגוף שנקראים "אותיות". לפיכך נבחן שהוא מאיר אליהם רק ממקומו למעלה ואינו מתפשט באותיות עצמם. וההארה דרך היסוד מכונה בשם "שורק". דהיינו ו' עם נקודה שהיא עומדת תוך שורת האותיות. והטעם, כי הארה זו מגיע לאו"א דנקודים, שהם קומת הנקבה דראש הנקודים, שאורותיה מתפשטים גם לגוף, שהם הז"ת דנקודים, הנקראים "אותיות". וע"כ נמצא נקודת השורק תוך שורת האותיות.

88) We already know that ZON of the world of AK affected the ten Sefirot de Nikudim with the new light in two ways: through the Tabur, it shone upon Keter de Nikudim, and through Yesod – upon Abba ve Ima de Nikudim. You should know that the light passing through the Tabur is called Holam. It shines above the letters only in

Keter, representing the level of Zachar (active male essence), or Hitlabshut, and cannot spread to the vessels of the Guf, called letters.

That is why it is considered to be shining only above the letters without spreading inside them. The light passing through Yesod is called Shuruk, Vav with a dot, which means it is inside the letters and enters Abba ve Ima, the female essence of the Rosh de Nikudim. This light also spreads in the Guf, i.e., the Zat de Nikudim, called letters. Thus, the Nekudat Shuruk is inside the letters.

When we look at the Hebrew alphabet of the *Torah*, we will see that there are many dots inside of letters (not just *Vav* with a dot): for example, *Pey* and *Fey*, *Bet* and *Vet*. *Mem* and *Tav* can also have dots. All these laws derive from the rules of the spiritual world. Later we will study the Hebrew alphabet, which actually originates in *Bina*, ZA and *Malchut* of the world of *Atzilut*, and fully correspond to the ZON and the *AHP de Abba ve Ima* of the world of *Nikudim*. The first letters from *Aleph* to *Tet* are in *Bina*, the letters from *Chav* to *Tzadik* are in ZA, the last four letters: *Kuf*, *Reish*, *Shin*, and *Tav* are in *Malchut*.

Every dot, whether over the letters (crowns), inside the letters, or under them, speaks only about the spiritual state of the *Partzuf*. Every word in Hebrew says something about the Universe and signifies the reception of some spiritual light in the vessel. The combination of the vessel and the light is expressed in a code called "word". This code contains all relations between the light and the vessel, the screen, *Aviut* etc.

Each letter of the alphabet carries a tremendous amount of information in its shape, the relation to the previous letter. This information points exclusively at spiritual actions. When man pronounces a word, he expresses his feelings in each letter; they register in the screen and speak about the spiritual level of the *Partzuf*.

In our world, we do not feel the spiritual conformity between the vessel and the light. While using a language, we do not understand the inner spiritual meaning of the words that come from the Torah, which carry clear spiritual information. It is impossible to call something by a different name. For example, the word *Maim*, which consists of two letters, *Mem* (one of which is terminal – *Sofit*) and certain dots, precisely expresses the essence of water; so does each word.

Kabbalists are known to perform some actions with the letters. This does not at all mean they write something on parchment or paper. When they say that Kabbalists operate with letters, it means that they perform strictly spiritual actions, i.e., they fill their vessels with the help of the screen and the Reflected Light. No eye can see these actions.

פט) והנה נתבארו היטב החולם והשורק. אשר הארת אור חדש דרך הטבור, המוריד ה"ת מנקבי עינים דכתר לפה, ומעלה בחזרה האח"פ דכתר, הוא סוד נקודת החולם, שממעל לאותיות. והארת אור חדש דרך היסוד, המוריד ה"ת מנקבי עינים דאו"א להפה שלהם, ומשיב להם את האח"פ, ה"ס נקודת השורק, שבתוך האותיות. מטעם שמוחין אלו באים גם בז"ת דנקודים, הנקראים "אותיות".

89), We have learned the meaning of the dots Holam and Shuruk. The luminescence of the new light passing through the Tabur, which lowers the screen from Nikvey Eynaim de Rosh of Keter to its Peh and returns the AHP de Keter to its level, is called Nekudat Holam. The luminescence of the new light passing through Yesod lowers the screen from Nikvey Eynaim de Abba ve Ima to the Peh and returns their AHP de Keter to its place. This light shines inside the letters and is called Shuruk. These Mochin (the light of Gar) also spread to the Zat de Nikudim, called letters, i.e., the vessels receiving this light.

However, from the *Rosh de Abba ve Ima* (called the *Rosh de Aviut* as distinct from the *Rosh de Keter* called the *Rosh de Hitlabshut*), the light spreads to the *Guf de ZON*.

צ) וסוד החירק, הוא בחינת האור חדש, שהז"ת עצמם מקבלים מאו"א, להוריד בחינת ה"ת המסיימת, העומדת בחזה שלהם, אל מקום סיום רגלי א"ק. שעי"ז חוזרים אליהם האח"פ שלהם, שהם הכלים שמחזה ולמטה, שנעשו למקום בי"ע. אשר אז יוחזרו הבי"ע להיות כמו אצילות.

אמנם הז"ת דנקודים לא יכלו להוריד הה"ת מהחזה, ולבטל לגמרי את הצמצום ב', והפרסא, והמקום בי"ע. אלא בעת שהמשיכו האור לבי"ע, נשברו תיכף כל הכלים דז"ת. כי כח ה"ת המסיימת, העומדת בפרסא, היה מעורב בכלים האלו. והיה האור מוכרח תיכף להסתלק משם. והכלים נשברו ומתו ונפלו לבי"ע. ונשברו גם הכלים דפנים שלהם, העומדים למעלה מפרסא, דהיינו הכלים שמחזה ולמעלה. כי גם מהם נסתלק כל האור. ונשברו ומתו ונפלו לבי"ע. וזה היה מחמת חיבורם עם הכלים דאחורים לגוף אחד.

90) Hirik is the new light received by Zat directly from Abba ve Ima, which lowers Malchut from the Chazeh to the Sium de AK; as a result, the AHP de ZON returns to its place from under the Parsa. These AHP de ZON formed the worlds BYA under the Parsa. So now, under the influence of the light of Hirik, these worlds are supposed to become similar to the world of Atzilut.

However, the ZON de Nikudim could not lower Malchut from the Chazeh and completely cancel TB and the Parsa, thus changing the place of the worlds BYA. The moment the light spread to BYA, all the vessels of the Zat broke, for the law of Malchut Mesayemet (in the Chazeh) was still effective. The lights instantly left the vessels, which broke, died and fell to BYA. The Kelim de Panim also broke. Even though these vessels were under the Parsa, they wanted to unite with the AHP in one Partzuf.

They also died and fell to *BYA*, because the light had disappeared from them. In fact, the worlds *Atzilut* and *BYA* have not been there yet, but the vessels from which they would later be created, already existed.

All was well until the light disappeared from *Keter* and *Abba ve Ima*. After the light descended under the *Parsa,* to the *AHP de ZON*, there occurred the breaking of the vessels. *GE* had the screen above the *Parsa*, which could bestow everything upon the Creator, while under the *Parsa* (the receiving vessels) the law restricting any reception ruled entirely, even though the "desire to receive" was concentrated there. When the light *AB-SAG* came, it gave the strength to the common vessel to receive this entire light for the sake of the Creator, and fill the *NHY de Galgalta* with it.

However, *Rosh de Keter* and *Abba ve Ima* failed to take into account the fact that the light *AB-SAG*, which spread under the *Parsa*, would arouse the egoistic desire in the vessels present there. The fact is that not just two heads, *Keter* and the *Abba ve Ima*, maintain the *Parsa*, but also by the third, the *YESHSUT* that is under the *Tabur*. This very head restrains the light *AB-SAG*, preventing it from spreading under the *Parsa*.

This is deliberately done to break all the vessels, deprive them of the screen, and move them as far from the Creator as possible. However, because of this, the altruistic and egoistic vessels completely mixed with one another. Now each fragment contains both the "desire to bestow" and the "desire to receive". This was exactly what breaking of the vessels aimed at.

The *ZON* of the world of *Nikudim* embodies the entire *Malchut* of the World of Infinity. The purpose is to fill its part under the *Parsa* with the Creator's light. How can that be done? Only by the above-mentioned explosive method, when *Abba ve Ima* and *ZON* get the wrong impression that they can receive the light for the Creator's sake under Parsa. The *ZON* really seem to start receiving the light for the sake of the Creator, but then realize they receive it in an egoistic way.

The light disappears; the vessel finds itself in a desperate situation, where not only its own properties, but also those of *GE* become egoistic. They fall under the *Parsa* and mix with the egoistic vessels. Now these fragments of the egoistic vessels have sparks of altruism. When the light shines upon them, it will arouse their altruistic sparks and correct them.

צא) והנך רואה, שנקודת החירק לא יכלה לצאת לשליטתה בעולם הנקודים, כי אדרבה היא גרמה לשבירת הכלים. והיינו משום שרצתה להתלבש בתוך האותיות, דהיינו בתנהי"מ שלמטה מפרסא דאצילות, שנעשו לבי"ע. אמנם אח"כ, בעולם התיקון, קבלה נקודת החירק את תיקונה. כי שם נתקנה להאיר מתחת האותיות.

דהיינו שבעת שהז"ת דאצילות מקבלים את אור הגדלות מאו"א, הצריך להוריד את ה"ת המסיימת ממקום החזה לסיום רגלין דא"ק, ולחבר את הכלים דתנהי"מ לאצילות, והאורות יתפשטו למטה עד סיום רגלין דא"ק - אינם עושים כן, אלא שהם מעלים התנה"י הללו ממקום בי"ע אל מקום האצילות שלמעלה מפרסא. ומקבלים האורות בהיותם למעלה מפרסא

דאצילות, כדי שלא יארע בהם שוב שביה"כ כבעולם הנקודים. וזה נבחן, שנקודת החירק, המעלה את הכלים דתנה"י דז"ת דאצילות, עומדת מתחת אלו הכלים תנהי"מ שהעלתה, דהיינו שעומדת במקום הפרסא דאצילות. הרי שנקודת החירק משמשת מתחת האותיות. והנה נתבאר סוד ג' נקודות חולם שורק חירק בדרך כלל.

91) We see that the world of Nikudim was not ready to receive the light that corresponded to the point of Hirik; hence it made for the breaking of the vessels. It happened because it wanted to get inside the letters, i.e., the vessels Tifferet, Netzah, Hod, Yesod and Malchut under the Parsa in the worlds of BYA. Afterwards, in the world of Correction (Atzilut), the point of Hirik is corrected and shines below the letters.

When Zat of the world of Nikudim received the light of Gadlut from Abba ve Ima, which had to lower Malchut from the Chazeh to the Sium de AK and unite the vessels of the AHP with the GE de Nikudim, the light began spreading under the Parsa. This led to the breaking of the vessels. To prevent this from happening again, the corrected point of Hirik in the world of Atzilut elevates Tifferet, Netzah, Hod, Yesod and Malchut from under the Parsa (the worlds BYA) to the world of Atzilut above the Parsa, and stays below them, i.e., on the level of the Parsa. Thus, we have learned the meaning of the three dots: Holam, Shuruk, and Hirik.

How can the desire be elevated above the *Parsa*? This becomes possible only after the breaking of the vessels, when each desire of *Malchut* is mixed with *Bina* and has a chance to be corrected. This material is difficult to understand without certain inner sensations. Kabbalah is impossible to grasp by the mind alone. If man persistently tries to do that, he commits a most serious violation. Yet, there is so far no other way out, for we have no alternative connection with spirituality.

Let us review the material we have studied. We know that *Nekudot de SAG* descended under the *Tabur de Galgalta* and mixed with the *NHYM de Galgalta*. Then they rose to *Rosh de SAG* with the *Reshimot Bet/Aleph* and the information about the *TB*, which produced the *Katnut de*

Nikudim with *Keter, Abba ve Ima* and ZON reaching the *Parsa*. *Keter* is the *Rosh de Hitlabshut*, *Abba ve Ima* is the *Rosh de Aviut* and ZON is the *Guf*.

In fact, *Nikudim* in *Katnut* is not a world; it is still only a small *Partzuf*. Nevertheless, it is called the world because later it will in fact appear there. This will happen as a result of a *Zivug* on the *Reshimot Dalet/Gimel*, which were received from the *NHYM de Galgalta* and were also present in the screen ascending to the *Rosh de SAG*.

When the world of *Nikudim* emerge in the state of *Katnut*, the *Reshimot Dalet/Gimel* awaken in the *Rosh de SAG*. They now wish to receive the entire *Ohr Hochma* destined for the vessels of *Galgalta* under the *Tabur*. Light AB-SAG descends in response to this request. The SAG demonstrates what the "desire to bestow" is; *AB* shows how it is possible to receive for the Creator's sake. Both of them enable the vessel in *Katnut* to pass to the state of *Gadlut*.

In order to receive the light AB-SAG, a *Zivug* is made not in *Nikvey Eynaim*, but again in the *Peh de Rosh*, where the screen descends. First, this new light descends through the *Tabur* to *Keter de Nikudim*, and by filling it, provides it with strength to attach its own *AHP* and pass to *Gadlut*. The light cannot spread beyond *Keter* (the *Rosh de Hitlabshut)*. It spreads to *Yesod de Galgalta*, where the *Rosh de Abba ve Ima* is dressed. Thus, the second head (the *Abba ve Ima)* can receive light AB-SAG and, with its help, achieve the state of *Gadlut*.

The light in *Keter* is called *Holam* (dot above letter). This means that the light does not spread farther than the *Rosh*. The light in *Abba ve Ima* is called *Shuruk* (dot inside letter). Then the light enters GE *de* ZON and tries to descend to *AHP de* ZON under the *Parsa*, to the egoistic vessels. If it could get under the *Parsa*, it would unite GE *de* ZON with their *AHP*. However, it cannot get there to give the *AHP* the altruistic properties.

Therefore the *AHP* does not join GE *de* ZON; *AHP* retain their "desire to receive" for their own sake, which leads to breaking of the vessels. The light disappears, since according to *TA* it cannot be inside egoistic vessels. The *Kelim de GE* and the *AHP de ZON* become absolutely egoistic; having no screen, they fall under the *Parsa*, which means their properties are totally opposite to the Creator's. The light that tries to get under the *Parsa* is called the point of *Hirik*.

Later on, the correction takes place in the world of *Atzilut*. This world has the following structure. It also has *Keter, Abba ve Ima* and *ZON*. The principle of correction is quite simple. The *Parsa* cannot be eliminated. The only way is to raise the *AHP* (the vessels of reception) above the *Parsa* and attach them to the *GE de ZON*, thus creating the ten *Sefirot* above the *Parsa* and filling them with the light. This process is called "*AHP de Aliyah*" – the ascending vessels of reception. This state is called the Final Correction.

Afterwards, the light from above will come to eliminate the *Parsa*. When it is out of the way, it will lower the *AHP* to its place under the now non-existent *Parsa*. This is called the *AHP Amiti'im* (real *AHP*) or the *AHP de Yeridah* (descending *AHP*). Thus, the light completely fills *Galgalta* down to the *Sium Reglav*. This light is called the *Ohr HaMashiach*. It corrects and fills all vessels.

This correction is going on in the Universe. So where is man in this scheme? All we discuss happens for the sake of the souls that will be created later on, and which will have to go through all the levels prepared for them. Right now, the worlds seem to be the goal; man seems to have no place in them. This is not so. The worlds represent the system that controls the souls, whereas the souls can in turn control the worlds. We will talk about it later.

The state where the *AHP* rises above the *Parsa* is called "the ascent of the worlds on *Shabbat* and on holidays". When the *AHP* is under the *Parsa*, it is called "weekdays". That is the origin of time.

Why were there not any letters before the world of *Atzilut*? It is because there were no real vessels, just their roots. The formation of the vessel is gradual. A clear-cut vessel-desire requires information about the *Reshimo* (the desire of the *Kli*) and a total absence of the desired pleasure. First, the light must enter the vessel, whose desires are opposite to this light.

It happens that, in the preliminary vessels, the light is primary while the vessel's reaction to it is secondary. However, in the case where the true vessel is primary, the light is secondary. The real vessel emanates its own desire, aspiration to something, which is beyond its absolute darkness and remoteness from the Creator.

When man studies Kabbalah, he knows that some previously unknown information is delivered to him: information about the light, the *Sefirot*, the *Partzufim*, the worlds etc. In order to feel it, he needs to have the screen, and then all the information turns into light, which previously surrounded him. This information is all around, but there are no vessels able to perceive it so far.

We should not imagine anything, for all our images will be wrong until we have the screen. If you were reading a book about delicious and healthy food recipes, you would instantly imagine the tastes and the smells of the described delicacies. Any images in Kabbalah are totally groundless if no adequate vessels are available.

The plan, the Thought of Creation, all further actions, their initial and final states, are concealed in *Behina Aleph* of the Direct Light, its first point called *Keter de Ohr Yashar.* Then it develops as the four *Behinot, Malchut* of the World of Infinity, the world *AK*, the world of *Nikudim*, the worlds of *BYA*, the breaking of the vessels, *Adam HaRishon* etc.

The properties of both the light and the vessel were determined in the Thought of Creation, so the way from the initial state to the final is known in advance. There are no unforeseen obstacles or unnecessary actions on this way, which might lead to unexpected results. Everything evolves according to a precisely planned program. Either you feel the tough influence of nature, mercilessly pushing you towards the Purpose of Creation, or you take control into your own hands and move quickly to leave the blows behind. Thus, you accelerate the entire process. This quick movement will not be a burden to you; on the contrary, it will seem delightful.

As regards the Creator, the initial point of the creation merges with the final; they continue to exist as one. As regards us, the first point gradually unfolds as a series of consecutive actions, until this way ends in its final point. No horoscopes, fortune telling, or corrections of destiny will help us to avoid blows.

The light is amorphous. The vessel surrounded by the light feels more or less in accordance with its spiritual properties - the screen. There are 12 kinds of *Ohr Hozer*, 12 kinds of *Reshimot*, 10 kinds of the *Kelim*, seven kinds of *Masachim*, and six kinds of *Ohr Yashar*. In order to feel it all, one must have the appropriate vessels. For instance, when we hear the word "*Lechem*" (bread), we can sense its smell, its taste. What do we sense when words such as "*Ohr*", "*Reshimo*" or "*Kli*" are pronounced? ...

The *Gadlut* of the world of *Nikudim* symbolizes the *Gmar Tikkun*, when the light fills the *AHP de ZON*, but it will happen in the sensations of the souls. The state wherein each soul can correct itself is called its birth.

RAISING OF MAN OF ZAT DE NIKUDIM TO ABBA VE IMA

ענין עלית מ"ן דז"ת דנקודים לאו"א וביאור ספירת הדעת

צב) כבר נתבאר, שבסבת עלית ה"ת לנקבי עינים, שנעשה בצמצום ב', דהיינו לעת יציאת הקטנות דע"ס דנקודים, נחלקה כל מדרגה לב' חצאים: גלגלתא ועינים - נשארים במדרגה ונקראים משום זה "כלים דפנים", ואזן חוטם פה - הנפולים מהמדרגה להמדרגה שמתחתיה, נקראים משום זה "כלים דאחורים". באופן, שכל מדרגה ומדרגה נעשית כפולה מפנימיות וחיצוניות, באשר הכלים דאחורים דעליונה נפלו בפנימיות הכלים דפנים של עצמה. ונמצאים אח"פ הנפולים דכתר נקודים מלובשים תוך גלגלתא ועינים דאו"א, ואח"פ הנפולים דאו"א מלובשים תוך גלגלתא ועינים דז"ת דנקודים (אות ע"ו).

92) We have already explained that, because of Malchut rising to Nikvey Eynaim (caused by TB) and the emergence of the world of Nikudim in Katnut, each level divided into two parts. GE, remain on their level and are therefore called Kelim de Panim, and AHP, which fall from their level to the lower one and are called Kelim de Achoraim. Thus, each level now consists of inner and outer parts. The AHP de Keter of the world of Nikudim is inside the GE de Abba ve Ima. The AHP de Abba ve Ima fell into the GE de ZON of the world of Nikudim.

So, starting from *TB*, each level consisting of 10 *Sefirot* is divided into GE, which include *Keter, Hochma, Bina, Hesed, Gevura* and the upper third of *Tifferet*, and the *AHP* that include the lower third of *Tifferet, Netzah, Hod, Yesod* and *Malchut*.

The light can enter the upper part (the *GE*), which may be used. The *AHP* cannot receive the light and these desires may not be used. The upper *Sefirot* are called the altruistic desires, the lower *Sefirot* – egoistic. The former bestow, the latter receive. Each level may actively work only with its upper part, i.e., the *GE*.

If before *TB* all levels were one under the other, after *TB* all *AHP's* of the upper levels are inside the *GE* of the lower ones, which allowed an exchange of information in both directions. This entire structure is called a "*Sulam*" (ladder); the souls descend and ascend it.

There are two entities: the Creator and the Creation. The Creator is an entirely altruistic desire, whereas the Creation is an absolutely egoistic desire.

The Creator's goal is to make the Creation similar to Himself, so that by the end of its correction, it will achieve absolute perfection. This can be done only by way of passing the Creator's properties to *Malchut*, i.e., by mixing the nine upper altruistic *Sefirot* with the egoistic *Malchut*. However, they are completely opposite to one another. To bring them closer, a special force is created in the system of the worlds. With its help, the egoistic properties of *Malchut* can mix with the sparks of altruistic properties by a stroke contact between them.

Now we begin to study the formation of these forces (external as regards the souls) in the worlds, so that with their help the souls could be elevated to the Creator's level.

We have learned that there are four phases of development of the light: *Hochma, Bina, ZA* and *Malchut*. Being completely filled with the light, *Malchut* expels it and makes *TA*, which leaves it absolutely empty. Then *Malchut* invents a system that allows it to begin receiving a little light, but for the sake of the Creator. *Bina* is an interim stage between *Malchut* and *Keter*. It consists of two parts: *Gar (Gimel Rishonot)* and *Zat (Zain Tachtonot)*. *Bina* does not want to receive anything in the first three parts, but agrees to receive in the seven lower parts on condition that the reception be for someone else's sake. This someone is ZA, which agrees to receive only 10 % for *Malchut*. Such is the property of *Zat de Bina*: receiving for the sake of giving to someone else.

However, if a light more powerful than *Bina's* screen comes, then *Behina Bet* starts desiring it for itself. However, *TA* forbids egoistic reception; hence, the *Zat de Bina* begins to contract and assume the egoistic properties of *Malchut*. The further goal is to reverse this process: elimination of the egoistic properties in *Zat de Bina* and passing the true altruistic properties to *Malchut*. This can be achieved by breaking of the vessels, which we will study later. With this, the entire system turns into such a combination of both egoistic and altruistic vessels that, as in our world, there will be no distinction between them.

To change this situation, an additional portion of the Creator's light is necessary. With its help, it will be possible to distinguish between the two kinds of desires. The entire process of correction is based on this principle.

In fact, *Zat de Bina* is the central part of the creation. Much depends on it, so we will discuss it at length. During the descent of *Nekudot de SAG* under the *Tabur*, i.e., when *Zat de Bina* meets the more powerful desires of *NHYM de Galgalta*, *Zat de Bina* contract and assume *Malchut's* properties. *TA* was made by *Malchut* to restrict itself; *TB* is the restriction of *Bina*. In other words, the Creator, as it were, takes on the egoistic properties of the creation.

This is done in order that the Creator gradually passes His altruistic properties to the creation, corrects it, and fills it with the light. To correct someone, one has to possess the same properties that will later be corrected. The spiritual ladder is built so that its last spiritual level, the *AHP*, enters us, partially acquiring our egoistic properties. In this way, it establishes contact with us to elevate us later on to the spiritual world.

In fact, the worlds do not turn egoistic (they are still completely altruistic), but they are covered with an external curtain of coarseness, which enables them to be in contact with the souls of our world. Alternatively, rather, the worlds are the curtains that the Creator puts on, which weakens His light to the extent of becoming similar to the "spoiled" created beings, for the purpose of keeping contact with them.

Therefore, on all levels in the spiritual worlds, there is the same measure of imperfection that is present in the created beings. The *TB* is a restriction in the worlds.

Then the soul of *Adam HaRishon* emerges and goes through the process of splitting and descending to the point of this world. The descending levels of the worlds and the ascending steps of the soul are identical. So, when the soul finds itself in our world, the whole ladder of worlds is prepared for its consecutive ascent.

The properties of the entire creation are installed in four phases of the development of the Direct Light. Later on, they will affect *Malchut* in the worlds. The worlds represent *Malchut*, which affects the first nine *Sefirot*. The soul is *Malchut*, the tenth *Sefira* that acquired the properties of the first nine. They gradually contract, coarsen, "get spoiled" and turn into the egoistic desire of *Malchut*. This state is called the worlds.

The worlds are the Creator's properties that gradually descend, coarsen, and contract in order to become similar to the properties of *Malchut*. Each world includes the properties of the others. The first nine *Sefirot* gradually acquire the properties of *Malchut* to affect later on its egoistic desires, correcting and elevating them to the highest level.

צג) ומכאן נמשך, שגם בביאת האור חדש דע"ב ס"ג דא"ק להמדרגה, המוריד בחזרה את הה"ת למקומה לפה, דהיינו לעת הגדלות דנקודים, אשר אז מחזרת המדרגה אליה את האח"פ שלה, ונשלמים לה הע"ס דכלים והע"ס דאורות, נבחן אז, אשר גם המדרגה התחתונה, שהיתה דבוקה על אח"פ דעליונה, עולה גם היא עמהם ביחד לעליונה. כי זה הכלל: "אין העדר ברוחני". וכמו שהתחתונה היתה דבוקה באח"פ דעליון בעת הקטנות, כן אינם נפרדים זה מזה בעת הגדלות, דהיינו בעת שהאח"פ דעליונה שבים למדרגתם. ונמצא, שמדרגה התחתונה נעשתה עתה לבחינת מדרגה עליונה ממש. כי התחתון העולה לעליון נעשה כמוהו.

93) From this, it follows that, when the new light AB-SAG comes to a certain level, it lowers Malchut to its previous place in the Peh de Rosh and leads the world of Nikudim to the state of Gadlut. With this, the AHP return to its level, complementing it to ten Sefirot-vessels and Sefirot-lights. The GE, of the lower level, rises together with the ascending AHP. This is because nothing disappears in the spiritual world. If the lower level were connected with the AHP of the upper level in Katnut, it would also remain attached to it during

Gadlut. In other words, during the rise of the AHP, the lower level acquires the properties of the upper.

When the light *AB-SAG* enters the vessel, it imparts its altruistic qualities to it, so the vessel can use its *AHP*. Furthermore, the *GE* of the lower level (*Abba ve Ima* with *AHP de Keter* inside) is corrected. Now there are the *GE de Keter*, the *AHP de Keter*, and the *GE de Abba ve Ima* on the level of *Keter*.

We are in our world now. There is a special spiritual point inside us ("*Nekuda she ba Lev*"), which has no screen so far; hence, it is totally egoistic. Inside our egoistic vessel, there is the *AHP* of the lowest spiritual level (the world of *Assiya*). If the *Ohr AB-SAG* comes, the world of *Assiya* will elevate its *AHP* and together with it our spiritual vessel.

This means that man will cross the barrier and enter the spiritual world, i.e., he will not just rise from one spiritual level to another, but will make a quantum leap from the material world to the spiritual. This opportunity - to pass from one level to a higher one up to the highest with the help of the *Ohr AB-SAG* - was created by a *TB* that divided each level into two parts, and lowered the AHP of the upper level into the GE of the lower.

We see that now in *Keter* there are the *GE de Keter*, the *AHP de Keter*, and the *GE de Abba ve Ima* of the lower level. Yet that is not all. The *GE de Abba ve Ima* can receive its *AHP* (necessary to form its own 10 *Sefirot*) from the *AHP de Keter*, since its power is much greater than the GE de Abba ve Ima need.

Thus, *Abba ve Ima* start using the egoistic desires and enter *Gadlut*. However, these are not their own desires; hence, such a state is called the 1st *Gadlut*, as distinct from the 2nd *Gadlut*, where *Abba ve Ima* begin using their own *AHP*. As the lower Partzuf enters the 1st *Gadlut*, it somewhat learns to use the desires from the upper one, imitates it. This is a transition between the state of *Katnut* and the real *Gadlut*. (For details see § 134)

צד) ונמצא, בעת שאו"א קבלו האור חדש דע"ב ס"ג, והורידו הה"ת מנקבי עינים בחזרה אל הפה שלהם, והעלו אליהם את האח"פ שלהם, הנה גם הז"ת, המלבישים האח"פ אלו בעת קטנות, עלו עתה גם הם עמהם ביחד לאו"א. ונעשו הז"ת למדרגה אחת עם או"א. והנה עליה הזו של הז"ת לאו"א נקרא בשם "עלית מ"ן". ובהיותם מדרגה אחת עם או"א, נמצאים מקבלים גם אורותיהם דאו"א.

94) When Abba ve Ima receive the light AB-SAG, their Malchut naturally descends to the Peh de Rosh and their AHP rise from the lower level of the ZON, taking with it the GE de ZON to the level of Abba ve Ima, constituting a single whole with it and allowing it to receive the light of this level. The ascent of the ZON to Abba ve Ima is called raising MAN.

Generally speaking, the *GE* of the lower *Partzuf* is called *MAN*, and the *AHP* of the upper *Partzuf* is called in this case "the *Kli* raising *MAN*".

צה) ומה שנקרא בשם מ"ן, הוא מטעם שעלית הז"א אל הבינה מחזיר אותה פנים בפנים עם החכמה (אות פ). ונודע שכל ז"ת הם זו"ן. וע"כ בעת שהז"ת נתעלו עם האח"פ דאו"א למדרגת או"א, נעשו מ"ן אל הבינה דע"ס דאו"א. והיא חוזרת עם החכמה דאו"א פב"פ, ומשפעת הארת חכמה אל הזו"ן, שהם הז"ת דנקודים שעלו אליהם.

95) The ascent of ZON to Bina, i.e., the raising MAN, places Bina face-to-face with Hochma. As we know, each Zat (seven lower Sefirot) is a ZON; therefore, when Zat rose together with the AHP de Abba ve Ima to the level of Abba ve Ima, they turned to MAN as regards the 10 Sefirot de AVI. Then Bina returns to a face-to-face state with Hochma de AVI and passes the luminescence of the Ohr Hochma to ZON (Zat de Nikudim).

The *NHYM de Galgalta* is a criterion according to which we can see how much is corrected and how much is left to correct until the *Gmar Tikkun*. As with any other *Partzuf*, the light passing to the lower *Partzuf* fills the *NHYM de Galgalta*. All the upper *Partzufim* transfer the light to the lower. There is no other way for the light to get through. It descends from the World of Infinity and has to go through the *Partzufim AB, SAG* and so on, until it reaches the lowest one. The upper worlds are filled with the light that passes through them to the lower worlds.

How does the light pass from one *Partzuf* to the next, from *Malchut* of the upper to *Keter* of the lower? *Malchut* receives all; *Keter* bestows all. How is it possible? This subject is studied in Part 3 of "The Study of Ten *Sefirot*". We deal with the inverse transition of *Malchut* into *Keter* and vice versa. There is a notion *"Nitzutz Boreh and Nitzutz Nivrah"* (spark of the Creator and spark of the creation). The creation is something made of nothing. The Creator's "absence" in any place is the root of the creation.

There are five vessels: *Keter, Hochma, Bina, ZA* and *Malchut*; and five lights: *Nefesh, Ruach, Neshama, Haya* and *Yechida*. Actually, there is no such thing as "a variety of the lights". The light depends on the sensation of the vessel, which, while receiving the amorphous light, distinguishes whatever it feels now and gives this light an appropriate name. There is no variety of the lights outside of the vessel; only one amorphous light called 'the Creator'.

The lights generally divide into *Ohr Hochma* and *Ohr Hassadim*. If the vessel can only bestow and is yet unable to receive for the Creator's sake due to the lack of the screen, the lights *Nefesh, Ruach* and *Neshama* spread in it. The lights *Haya* and *Yechida* are absent. If the vessel acquires the screen and starts receiving the light for the sake of the Creator, the lights *Haya* and *Yechida* fill it.

The *ZON*, which rise together with the *AHP* to *Abba ve Ima (AVI)* become *MAN*, the request to *Abba ve Ima* to make a *Zivug de Haka'a* and pass the light of *Hochma* down to *GE de ZON*. This resembles a child's request directed to its mother, in whom the child's source is rooted. It turns for help to this very source.

צו) אמנם עלית הז"ת לאו"א שאמרנו, אין הפירוש שנעדרו ממקומם לגמרי ועלו לאו"א, כי "אין העדר ברוחני". וכל "שינוי מקום" הנאמר ברוחניות, אין הפירוש שנעדרה ממקומה הקודם ובאה למקום החדש, כדרך העתקת מקום בגשמיות, אלא רק תוספת יש כאן, כי באו למקום החדש וגם נשארו במקומם הקודם. באופן, שהגם שהז"ת עלו לאו"א למ"ן, מכל מקום נשארו ג"כ במקומם במדרגתם למטה כמקודם לכן.

96) However, the rise of ZON to Abba ve Ima does not mean they disappeared from their place. Nothing ever disappears in the spiritual world and a change of place does not lead to disappearance of any particular object from its place as it happens in our world. Only a minor addition to the previous state is meant in spirituality: an object moves to another place while remaining where it was. The same refers to ZON, which rose to Abba ve Ima and retained their original position.

צז) וכן עד"ז תבין, אע"פ שאנו אומרים, שאחר שעלו הזו"ן למ"ן לאו"א וקבלו שם אורותיהם, יוצאים משם וחוזרים למקומם למטה, הנה גם כאן אין הפירוש שנעדרו ממקומם למעלה ובאו להמקום שלמטה. כי אם היו הזו"ן נעדרים ממקומם למעלה באו"א, היה נפסק הזווג פב"פ דאו"א תיכף, והיו חוזרים אב"א כמקודם לכן. ואז היה נפסק השפע שלהם. וגם הזו"ן שלמטה היו אובדים את המוחין שלהם. כי כבר נתבאר למעלה, שהבינה מטבעה חושקת רק באור דחסדים, בסו"ה "כי חפץ חסד הוא", ואין לה ענין כלל לקבל אור חכמה. וע"כ נמצאת עם החכמה אב"א. ורק בעת עלית הזו"ן להם למ"ן, חוזרת הבינה בזווג פב"פ עם החכמה, בכדי להשפיע הארת חכמה אל הז"א (אות פ). ולפיכך הכרח הוא, שהזו"ן ישארו שם תמיד, כדי ליתן קיום והעמדה אל הזווג דאו"א פב"פ. וע"כ אי אפשר לומר שהזו"ן נעדרו ממקום או"א בעת שבאים למקומם למטה. אלא כמו שאמרנו, שכל "שינוי מקום" אינו אלא תוספת בלבד. באופן, שהגם שהזו"ן ירדו למקומם למטה, מכל מקום נשארו ג"כ למעלה.

97) We should also understand that the ZON rising to Abba ve Ima, together with their AHP (raising MAN), receive the Ohr Hochma from a Zivug between Abba ve Ima, and then descend to their place. They do not disappear from the level of Abba ve Ima, since such disappearance would lead to stopping a Zivug between Abba ve Ima and a consecutive change of their position to Achor be Achor. This will prevent the spreading of the Ohr Hochma in the ZON below, because Bina by nature does not need the Ohr Hochma, only the Ohr Hassadim.

It needs the light of Hochma only for passing it on to ZA in answer to its request. If the request stops, the light of Hochma ceases to descend. Only the raising of MAN de ZON to Abba ve Ima returns them to a face-to-face Zivug and resumes the passage of the Ohr Hochma to ZA. Hence, the ZON must always be above, constantly renewing their request for the Ohr Hochma.

As we have already stated, any change of place in the spiritual worlds is just an addition to the previous state. Consequently, the ZON are above and below, simultaneously. The GE de ZON that is above passes the light to GE de ZON below.

From this example, we see that an exchange of properties takes place. The same property can be located in a number of different places. If I write a letter to my boss asking for something, it does not mean that, upon sending the letter, I will stop having the desire for what I asked in my letter. This desire will simultaneously be in me and will pass to my boss.

We are studying the transition of the world of *Nikudim* to the state of *Gadlut*. It happens that *Keter*, *Abba ve Ima* and the ZON in *Katnut* consisted only of GE. Now *Keter*, which uses all of its ten *Sefirot* again, lifted the GE *de Abba ve Ima* up to its own level. Having received its ten *Sefirot*, *Abba ve Ima* lifted the GE *de* ZON. Later on, we will study how the light AB-SAG reached the *Parsa* and wished to get inside; but there met with enormous desires that led to breaking of the vessels.

Now we encounter the notion "*Sefira Da'at*" for the first time. Until now, we said that there are only five *Behinot* in the *Partzufim* of AK: *Keter, Hochma, Bina,* ZA and *Malchut*. Beginning with the world of *Nikudim* and further on, we come across one more *Sefira* called *Da'at*, which we include in the general number of *Sefirot* called *HaBaD: Keter, Hochma, Bina* and *Da'at* (*Keter* is usually omitted). There was no notion of "Raising MAN" in the world of AK.

The Creator created the first four *Behinot de Ohr Yashar: Hochma, Bina,* ZA and *Malchut*, which emerged from *Keter* (the four phases of the vessel development). The rest is the consequence of these four phases called *Yud-Hey-Vav-Hey* (the Creator's Name). Any vessel or desire, any development, takes place within these four phases. They contain all the information about the vessel and the light.

Afterwards, the light fills the fourth phase, *Malchut*, and gives it its properties. It makes a *Tzimtzum* and then starts analyzing its relations with the light; it wishes to receive the light on different conditions, according to the properties installed both in *Malchut* and in the light. Nothing new happens, only the relations between the light and the vessel continue to develop. If later on you find something that is difficult to understand, you should each time go back to these four phases.

The Creator's light can enter *Malchut* only when *Bina* fills its *Zat* with the *Ohr Hochma* and passes it to ZA and on to *Malchut*. How does *Bina* receive the *Ohr Hochma?* It turns to *Hochma*, makes a *Zivug de Haka'a* on this light, and then passes it to ZA. If for some reason, ZA and *Malchut* cannot or do not want to receive the light, *Bina* understands and refrains from passing it to them. At this moment, its seven lower *Sefirot* are filled only with the *Ohr Hassadim*. The property of *Bina*, to receive the *Ohr Hochma*, manifests only when it can pass this light on to someone else. *Bina* does not need this light.

We may see this picture in the world of *Nikudim* where the seven lower *Sefirot* of *Bina* (i.e., of the *Partzuf Abba ve Ima*) are in the state of *Achor be Achor*; *Bina* does not want to receive anything. It waits until the ZON start receiving the *Ohr Hochma*, which may happen only when they (the ZON) decide to pass from *Katnut* to *Gadlut*. The *Ohr AB-SAG* provides them with such an opportunity.

For that, the ZON must turn to *Abba ve Ima*, which turn face to face, make a *Zivug* on the *Ohr Hochma*, and pass it to ZON. The request ZON sends to *Ima* is called Raising MAN. When *Ima* starts giving *Ohr Hochma*, the ZON descend with this request and become the receiver of the *Ohr Hochma*. However, being below and receiving the light, the ZON must be constantly close to Ima with their request to ask it to continue making a *Zivug* on the *Ohr Hochma* with *Abba* for passing it down.

The request of the ZON must be genuine; otherwise it cannot be called Raising MAN and will not be answered. The request of ZON, which remained above while the ZON descended, is called *Sefira Da'at*. This is not an additional *Behina* or the eleventh *Sefira*; it simply points to the state of the *Partzuf*.

Abba ve Ima may be in three states: *Achor be Achor* (back to back), where the ZON do not need the *Ohr Hochma*, so it is also absent in *Abba ve Ima*. Such a state is called *Holam* and *Katnut*. The second state comes when there is *Ohr Hochma* in *Keter* and in *Sefirat Abba* of the world of *Nikudim* and *Sefirat Abba* faces *Ima's* back. This state is called *Shuruk* and *Yenika*. In the third state, ZON raises MAN to *Sefirat Ima*, which turns its face to *Aba*. This state is called *Hirik* and *Gadlut*.

The Light AB-SAG allows the ZON to receive the *Ohr Hochma* like AB, and to acquire the "desire to bestow" inherent in SAG.

There are two kinds of *Reshimot*: of *Katnut* – *Bet/Aleph* and of *Gadlut* – *Dalet/Gimel*. The first allows the world of *Nikudim* to enter the state of *Katnut*. When the second kind of *Reshimo* awakens, the vessel begins to ask the AB-SAG for strength to receive the *Ohr Hochma*. There is no pressure from above unless there is a request from below. Although the *Reshimot* provoke such a request, the vessel ascribes it to itself.

> *The Light AB-SAG is the light of correction. It provides strength and desire to feel the Creator and do something for Him. The Ohr Hochma, which the vessel receives for the sake of the Creator, is a result of the correction made by the Ohr AB-SAG, and is called the light of the Purpose of Creation. For this reason, we speak about two different kinds of the light.*

צח-צט) ומכאן תבין סוד ספירת הדעת, שנתחדש בעולם הנקודים. כי בכל פרצופי א"ק עד הנקודים אין שם כי אם ע"ס כח"ב זו"ן. ומעולם הנקודים ואילך כבר יש גם ספירת הדעת, ואנו חושבים כחב"ד זו"ן. והענין הוא שגם ענין עלית מ"ן לא היה בפרצופי א"ק אלא רק ענין עלית המסך לפה דראש (אות ע"ט). ותדע, שספירת הדעת נמשך מעלית מ"ן דזו"ן אל או"א. כי נתבאר, שזו"ן, שעלו שם למ"ן לחו"ב, המה נשארים שם גם אחר יציאתם משם למקומם למטה, בכדי ליתן קיום והעמדה להזווג דאו"א פב"פ. והזו"ן האלו, הנשארים באו"א, נקראים "ספירת הדעת". וע"כ יש עתה לחו"ב ספירת הדעת, המקיים ומעמיד אותם בזווג פב"פ. שהם הזו"ן שעלו שמה למ"ן, ונשארו שמה גם אחר יציאת הזו"ן למקומם. וע"כ אנו חושבים מכאן ואילך את הע"ס בהשמות כחב"ד זו"ן. אבל בפרצופי א"ק, שמקודם עולם הנקודים, שעוד לא היה שם ענין עלית מ"ן, ע"כ לא היה שם ספירת הדעת. גם תדע, שספירת הדעת מכונה תמיד בשם "ה' חסדים וה' גבורות". כי הז"א הנשאר שם הוא בחינת ה"ח, והנוקבא שנשארה שם היא בחינת ה"ג.

98-99) We can now understand what the Sefira Da'at, which appeared in the world of Nikudim, is. As was stated above, such a notion was absent in the Partzufim of the world of AK. There were just the 10 Sefirot of KaHaB ZON, and the rise of the screen to Peh de Rosh; the notion "Raising MAN" still did not exist. The Sefira Da'at emerges because of the MAN de ZON rising to Abba ve Ima and its permanent staying there. From the world of Nikudim and further, we already speak about the Sefira Da'at and the Sefirot are now called the HaBaD ZON. The Sefira Da'at is also called Hey (5) Hassadim, Hey (5) Gvurot, since ZA, which remained there, is Hey (5) Hassadim, and Nukva is Hey (5) Gvurot.

ק) ואין להקשות על מה שכתוב בספר יצירה, שהע"ס הן עשר ולא תשע, עשר ולא אחד עשר". ולפי האמור שבעולם הנקודים נתחדש ספירת הדעת, הרי יש אחד עשר ספירות כחב"ד זו"ן?

והתשובה היא, שאין זה הוספה של כלום על הע"ס. כי נתבאר, שספירת הדעת היא הזו"ן, שעלו למ"ן ונשארו שם. וא"כ אין כאן הוספה, אלא שיש ב' בחינות זו"ן: א. הם הזו"ן שבמקומם למטה, שהם בחינת גוף, ב. הם הזו"ן שנשארו בראש באו"א, מטעם שכבר היו שם בעת עלית מ"ן. ואין העדר ברוחני. הרי שאין כאן שום הוספה על הע"ס, כי סוף סוף אין כאן אלא ע"ס כח"ב זו"ן בלבד. ואם נשארו גם בחינת הזו"ן בראש באו"א, אין זה מוסיף כלום על בחינת הע"ס.

100) We should not think that there are 9 or 11 Sefirot. Since the Sefira Da'at emerged in the world of Nikudim, it seems to complement the 10 Sefirot with the 11th. It is not so, because in reality it is the ZON, which raised MAN to Abba ve Ima and stayed there. There are two kinds of the ZON: the first are in their place below and receive the light of Hochma; the second are in Abba ve Ima above, with a constant request for this light. Therefore, they cannot be considered an addition to the 10 Sefirot.

Malchut reaches the state of perfection when it receives the entire light of Hassadim from Bina and the entire light of Hochma from Hochma. First, Bina must gain strength for using its AHP for the Creator's sake and then receive information about the ZON's "desire to receive" the Ohr Hochma, i.e., the ZON must raise their MAN, and then Bina will pass the light of Hochma down to them.

BREAKING OF THE VESSELS AND THEIR FALL TO THE WORLDS OF THE BYA

ענין שבירת הכלים ונפילתם לבי״ע

קא) ונתבאר היטב סוד עלית מ״ן וספירת הדעת, שהם בחינת הכלים דפנים דז״ת דנקודים, שנמשכו ועלו לאו״א. כי או״א קבלו אור החדש דע״ב ס״ג דא״ק מן הזו״ן דא״ק בסוד נקודת השורק, והורידו הה״ת מנקבי עינים שלהם אל הפה, והעלו את הכלים דאחורים שלהם, שהיו נפולים בהז״ת דנקודים. שמתוך כך עלו גם הכלים דפנים דז״ת הדבוקים בהכלים דאחורים דאו״א (אות פ״ט-צ״ד). ונעשו הז״ת דנקודים שם בבחינת מ״ן. והחזירו או״א בבחינת פב״פ. ומתוך שה״ת, שהיא בחי״ד, כבר חזרה למקומה במקום הפה, ע״כ הזווג דהכאה, שנעשה על המסך הזה דבחי״ד, הוציא ע״ס שלמות בקומת כתר באור היחידה (אות פ״ד). ונמצאים הז״ת, הנכללות שם בסוד מ״ן, שגם הן קבלו אורות הגדולים ההם דאו״א. וכל זה הוא רק בבחינת ממטה למעלה. כי או״א הם בחינת הראש דנקודים, ששם נעשה הזווג, המוציא ע״ס ממטה למעלה. ואח״ז מתפשטים ג״כ לבחינת גוף, דהיינו ממעלה למטה (אות נ). ואז נמשכו הז״ת עם כל האורות שקבלו באו״א אל מקומם למטה. ונגמר הראש והגוף של פרצוף הגדלות דנקודים. והתפשטות זו נבחן לבחינת הטעמים דפרצוף גדלות הנקודים (אות כ״ו).

101) The Sefira Da'at is the GE de ZON of the world of Nikudim that rose to Abba ve Ima, for Abba ve Ima had received the light AB-SAG from the ZON de AK, which is called Shuruk. Then Malchut descends from Nikvey Eynaim to Peh, thus lifting the AHP de Abba ve Ima that fell to GE de ZON of the world of Nikudim. The vessels GE de Zat of the world of Nikudim rise together with them and form the Behinat MAN, which turns the Sefirot Abba ve Ima face to face (Panim be Panim).

A Zivug de Haka'a on the screen in Behina Dalet led to the formation of 10 complete Sefirot on the level of Keter with the light of Yechida. The Zat de Nikudim in Abba ve Ima (MAN, Sefirat Da'at) receive powerful light from the Rosh de Abba ve Ima, since Abba ve Ima constitute the Rosh de Nikudim, where a Zivug that lifted ten Sefirot took place. This light then spreads downwards into the Guf de ZON, and consequently into the Rosh and Guf of the world of Nikudim in the state of Gadlut. Such spreading of the light is called Ta'amim.

As was mentioned, the rise of the desire from *ZON* to Bina is called Raising *MAN*. Previously, *Abba ve Ima* did not interact, and such a state is called *Panim be Achor*. There is the light of *Hochma* in the *Partzuf Abba*, but *Ima* does not want to receive it. *MAN* stimulates *Ima*'s need to receive *Ohr Hochma* from *Abba*; hence, it turns its face to it.

The world of the *Nikudim* consists of three parts: *Keter* and *Abba*, where the lights is, the second part is *Ima*, which does not want to receive the light, and the third is the *ZON*. If the *ZON* ask *Ima* for the light, it will make *Ima* meet *Abba*, receive the light and pass it on to *ZA*.

The desires that manifest in us, besides those of the animal level, are a consequence of breaking of the vessels, which caused tiny sparks of the light to enter us.

A special *Partzuf* emerges after *TB – Katnut de Nikudim*. As we already said, it consists of three parts: *Keter*, *Abba ve Ima* and the *ZON*. TB restricts the vessels of reception and allows working only with the vessels of bestowal. Hence, there is only the *Galgalta* in *Rosh de Keter*, while the *AHP* is inside the *GE de Abba ve Ima*. The *AHP de Abba ve Ima* is in the *GE de ZON*. *AHP de ZON* is under the *Parsa*, having desires to receive for itself, and cannot be worked with. None of the *AHP*'s has either light or screen. All of them (except the *AHP de ZON*, which do not receive the light at all) receive just a small luminescence from *GE*.

Then the aroused *Reshimot Dalet/Gimel* ask to do something for the *AHP*. Why does this desire appear? A *TB* was made on the *Aviut Bet*. The *Partzuf Nikudim* emerged because of a *Zivug* on *Aviut Aleph*. Now this *Partzuf* decides to try to work with the *AHP*. Afterwards, the *Partzufim AB* and SAG make a *Zivug*, pass the light down to *Keter*, enabling it to enter the state of Gadlut, i.e., to lift its *AHP* from the *GE de Abba ve Ima*. For this purpose, *Malchut* in the *Rosh de Keter* descends from *Nikvey Eynaim* to the *Peh* and makes a *Zivug* on ten complete *Sefirot*.

Being dressed on the *AHP de Keter*, *Abba* rises (achieves *Gadlut*) together with it. Now there is *Ohr Hochma* both in the ten *Sefirot de Keter* and in *Abba*, so it turns its face to Ima. However, *Ima* wants only *Hassadim* and not *Hochma*, so it is still with its back to *Abba*. How can it be compelled to receive the *Ohr Hochma*? It can be done only if the *ZON* ask for it. To this end, the "desire to receive" the *Ohr Hochma* must be aroused in the *ZON*.

The *ZON de Nikudim* dress onto *NHYM de Galgalta* of the world of *AK*, then pass the *Ohr Hochma* to the *ZON*. The *ZON* turn with their request to *Ima, Ima* then turns face to face with *Abba*. Thus, the light descends; but when it reaches the *Parsa* and wishes to get under it, the light encounters the enormous egoistic "desire to receive", which, in defiance of *TB*, received a portion of the light. The light instantly disappears, and the vessels of *GE de ZON* and the *AHP de ZON* break and mix with one another. This isso that each fragment might have a little of the *Ohr Hochma*.

All of them fall to the lowest level under the *Parsa*, moving as far from the Creator as possible. This led to the presence of tiny sparks of the light in all the egoistic desires of *Malchut*. On the other hand, their egoism is sufficiently formed, since it has already received the *Ohr Hochma*.

The "desire to receive" the *Ohr Hochma* and egoism were not yet developed in the World of Infinity. The egoistic vessels of the *AHP* were first created in *Nekudot de SAG*. From the world of *Nikudim*, such vessels are called *Klipot, Tuma*. The light's properties are absolutely opposite to these vessels, but the "desire to receive" is so huge that it craves even for a spark of the light, which it retains, but is unable to enjoy. Hence, during all our life, we chase after any expression of the light that dresses in the various attires of this world. It seems sometimes that we are about to touch this spark of the light, but it instantly disappears.

Then we rush after another expression of that spark. Thus, the sparks of light are a moving force of our egoism; they pull man forward, give him an aspiration to conquer the entire world. However, there are sparks that, when taking root in our hearts, endow us with the aspiration to spirituality.

The *Gadlut* of the world of *Nikudim* depends only on the *Reshimot Dalet/Gimel.* They start up this entire system, which ultimately leads to breaking of the vessels. After this breaking, *Malchut* on its lowest level is called *Adam,* and we are its parts.

The place of the creation (i.e., this or that part of *Malchut* of the World of Infinity) is determined only by the strength of the screen. There is no screen under the *Parsa*, so all egoistic desires are concentrated there. Depending on their closeness to the Creator (i.e., on the measure of their egoism), they have their places in the worlds of *BYA*. Everything interacts to the extent of the similarity between the vessel and the light. It is determined by the screen, which serves as a link between the light and the vessel, when the creation crosses the barrier between the material world and the spiritual.

קב) כי גם בפרצוף נקודים נבחנים ד' הבחינות: טעמים נקודות תגין אותיות (אות מ"ז). כי כל הכחות שישנם בעליונים, הכרח הוא שיהיו גם בתחתונים. אלא בתחתון נתוספים ענינים על העליון. ונתבאר שם, שעיקר התפשטות כל פרצוף נקראת בשם "טעמים".

ואחר התפשטותו נעשה בו הביטוש דאו"מ באו"פ, שע"י הביטוש הזה מזדכך המסך בדרך המדרגה, עד שמשתוה לפה דראש. ומתוך שאור העליון אינו פוסק, נמצא אור העליון מזדווג במסך בכל מצב של עביות שבדרך זיכוכו. דהיינו, כשמזדכך מבחי"ד לבחי"ג, יוצא עליו קומת חכמה. וכשבא לבחי"ב, יוצא עליו קומת בינה. וכשבא לבחינה א', יוצא עליו קומת ז"א. וכשבא לבחינת שורש, יוצא עליו קומת מלכות. וכל אלו הקומות, שיוצאים על המסך בעת הזדככותו, נקראים בשם "נקודות".

והרשימות, הנשארים מהאורות אחר הסתלקותם נקראים בשם "תגין". והכלים, הנשארים אחר הסתלקות האורות מהם נקראים בשם "אותיות". ואחר שהמסך מזדכך כולו מהעביות דגוף, נמצא נכלל במסך דפה דראש בזווג אשר שם. ויוצא עליו שם פרצוף שני.

102) The four stages, Ta'amim, Nekudot, Tagin and Otiot, are also present in the world of Nikudim, since the forces that act on the higher levels must have their reflections below, but with the additional information about the higher forces. The spreading of each Partzuf downwards is called Ta'amim.

Then, because of Bitush of the Ohr Makif and the Ohr Pnimi, the screen loses its Aviut and gradually rises to the Peh de Rosh, where it finally merges with the screen positioned there. However, since the Upper Light never stops spreading, a Zivug between the light and the screen occurs at each stage of its weakening.

The level of Hochma emerges when the Aviut Dalet passes to Gimel; the transition to Aviut Bet gives birth to Bina, ZA emerges on the Aviut Aleph and Malchut – on Aviut Shoresh. All the levels emerging during Zivugim, together with the weakening screen, are called Nekudot.

The Reshimot remaining after the light exits are called Tagin. The vessels left without the light are called Otiot. In other words, Otiot are the Reshimot that remain on the level of the Nekudot. When the Masach de Guf finally rids itself of all its Aviut and joins the Masach de Rosh in the Peh with the help of a Zivug, the Partzuf emerges.

Moving away from the light is considered a positive factor in the development of the vessels. When man feels disappointed, spiritually depressed, he should understand that the genuine vessels are being developed in him, the desire to receive the spiritual light. It is first decided how much light man can accept for the Creator's sake; only then can he actually receive. The decision is made in the *Rosh*, where the quality and quantity of the light is calculated in advance. It may then be received in the *Toch*. The part of the vessel devoid of the light is called the *Sof*. *Malchut* of the World of Infinity did not have the *Rosh*; it calculated nothing, receiving everything into the *Toch*.

The *Galgalta*, *AB*, and *SAG* could not fill the *Sof* with the light. Only *Nekudot de SAG* could get there and fill *Malchut*, although not with the *Ohr Hochma*, but with the *Ohr Hassadim*. Of course, *Malchut* wants the *Ohr Hochma* for its own delight, but the *Ohr Hassadim* also gives it enormous pleasure from giving.

Spiritual advancement is possible only under the light's influence. If the vessel is filled with the light, it has enough strength to act against its own nature; the light is more powerful than the vessel. At that, the vessel makes a *Tzimtzum* on the reception of pleasure and acquires some opportunity to receive for the sake of the Creator.

The *Galgalta*, *AB*, and *SAG* are the first three actions that *Malchut* performs for the Creator's sake. The fourth action prevents it from receiving the light for the Creator's sake, due to the small *Aviut Bet*. Now it can only bestow, so, when it still tries to receive something, the enormous egoistic desires emerge, and since *Malchut* is unable to work with them, *TB* is made. The next reception of the light is *Katnut* of the world of *Nikudim*; in this state, the vessel can only give for the sake of bestowal. Because of this, the *Ohr Hassadim* enters it.

Then the great reinforcement comes to this *Partzuf* in the form of the light *AB-SAG*. The *Partzuf AB* can receive an enormous amount of the *Ohr Hochma*; the *Partzuf SAG* can receive only the *Ohr Hassadim*. These two *Partzufim* seem to be opposite to one another, but they are opposite only in their actions, while their intentions are the same – to bestow. That is why they can give the *Partzuf* maximum power. In this particular case, both lights descend upon the small *Partzuf* that works only with its altruistic desires. The *Katnut de Nikudim* does not use any pleasure for its own sake.

The light *AB-SAG* reveals the Creator's greatness in the *Nikudim*. It shows the importance of merging with Him, without tempting it with pleasures. Because of this, the *Partzuf* has powers to receive for the sake of the Creator, to acquire the screen and pass on to *Gadlut* in the *Partzufim Keter* and *Abba ve Ima*. The *AHP de ZON* also try to enter *Gadlut*, but they cannot receive the light; therefore, the vessels break. They tasted the pleasures of *Gadlut*, and after breaking of the vessels, they retain the *Reshimot*, which speak only about the egoistic pleasures. Thus, the fragments of the broken vessels fall into the *Klipot*. The place where the *Klipot* are found is called the *Mador* (area) *Klipot*.

We have learned that *Malchut* rose to the level of *Bina* in *TB* and restricted the reception of the light in the *Kelim* of *GE*. Together with the acquired *Kelim de AHP*, *Malchut* is not yet a *Klipah* at this stage, since it restricts its egoistic reception of the light. Now, during the breaking of the vessels, the egoistic desire of *Malchut* feels delight without having the appropriate screen, begins to want it for itself, and thus turns into a *Klipah*. However, the *Klipah* does not have the real light. All it has is the *Reshimot* (fragments of the broken screen).

If the creation were not to go through the stage called *Klipot*, it would not have its own true desire. All previous desires, created by the Creator, constitute a single whole with Him. The genuinely created beings have no connection with the Creator; hence, they feel independent. Now, in order to allow the creation to achieve complete merging with the Creator, a spark of altruistic desire must be installed in it. It is accomplished with the help of the breaking of the vessels and mixing all fragments together.

The *Reshimot* of the Inner Light that departed after leaving the vessel are *called "Tagin"*. The *Kelim*-desires that remain after the light disappears from them are called *Otiot*.

It is said about the world of AK that the *Tagin* are the *Reshimot* of *Ta'amim* and *Otiot* are the *Reshimot* of *Nekudot*.

Thus, we find an additional explanation:

- *Ta'amim – Keter;*
- *Nekudot – Hochma;*
- *Tagin – Bina;*
- *Otiot – ZON*

קג) והנה ממש על דרך זה נעשה גם כאן בפרצוף נקודים. כי גם כאן יוצאים ב' פרצופין: ע"ב, ס"ג. זה תחת זה. ובכל אחד מהם: טעמים, נקודות, תגין, אותיות. וכל ההפרש הוא, כי ענין הזדככות המסך לא נעשה כאן מחמת הביטוש דאו"מ באו"פ, אלא מחמת כח הדין דמלכות המסיימת, שהיה כלול בכלים ההם (אות צ). ומטעם זה לא נשארו הכלים הריקים בפרצוף אחר הסתלקות האורות, כמו בג' הפרצופין גלגלתא ע"ב ס"ג דא"ק, אלא נשברו ומתו ונפלו לבי"ע.

103) As in the world of AK, two Partzufim also emerge in the world of Nikudim: AB and SAG, one under the other, each having its own Ta'amim, Nekudot, Tagin and Otiot. The difference lies in the weakening of the Masach that happened, not as a result of the Bitush Ohr Makif with the screen, as in the world of AK, but because Malchut Mesayemet (Din) emerged, and, standing in the Parsa, sees to it that TB is observed. Therefore, when the light disappears, the vessels are not left empty as they were in Galgalta, AB and SAG. Instead, they break, die and fall into the worlds of BYA.

קד) והנה פרצוף הטעמים, שיצא בעולם הנקודים, שהוא פרצוף א' דנקודים, שיצא בקומת כתר, יצא בראש וגוף, שהראש יצא באו"א, והגוף הוא התפשטות הז"ת מפה דאו"א ולמטה (אות ק"א). והנה התפשטות הזאת שמפה דאו"א ולמטה נקרא "מלך הדעת". והוא באמת כללות כל הז"ת דנקודים, שחזרו ונתפשטו למקומם אחר העלית מ"ן. אלא מתוך ששרשם נשאר באו"א לקיום והעמדה לפב"פ דאו"א (אות צ"ח), שנקרא שם בשם "מוח הדעת", המזווג לאו"א, לפיכך גם התפשטותם ממעלה למטה לבחינת גוף נקרא ג"כ בשם הזה, דהיינו "מלך הדעת". והוא מלך הא' דנקודים.

104) The first Partzuf, Ta'amim of the world of Nikudim, emerged on the level of Keter, its root being in Abba ve Ima, while the Guf spreads downwards. Such a Partzuf is called Melech HaDa'at; it contains everything found in Zat de Nikudim, i.e., it includes all their vessels.

Unlike the upper *Partzufim AB* and *SAG*, the lower *Partzufim* are called the *Melachim*. *Abba ve Ima* makes a *Zivug de Haka'a* on the *Reshimot Dalet/Gimel* and send powerful light downwards. The state of *Abba ve Ima* interacting is called *Da'at*, since a *Zivug* is made on the *Ohr Hochma*. The *Partzuf* that descends from them is called *Melech HaDa'at*. These *Partzufim* are called the *Melachim* because they originate in *Malchut*. Then this *Partzuf* breaks and leaves fractured vessels that merge with the *AHP* and fall down.

The actions that take place in the world of *Nikudim* are similar to those happening in AK. First, a *Zivug* on the *Reshimo Dalet/Gimel* is made, where the *Partzuf Melech HaDa'at* emerges in correspondence to

AB. Then the *Partzuf* loses the *Aviut Gimel*, and *Zivugim* on the *Reshimot Gimel/Bet* (as in SAG), *Bet/Aleph*, and *Aleph/Shoresh* take place.

The desire created by the Creator cannot be changed; we can just try to change our intention. Everything boils down to the screen and the intention (for the sake of bestowal or for the sake of reception). We can either increase or decrease them depending on the conditions.

If I have desires for all five dishes placed before me, and there are no restrictions to hold me back, I will naturally gobble them down; my desires match the available delight. Such was the situation in *Malchut* of the world of Infinity, where it wanted to enjoy everything the Creator had given it. This is not defined as the *Klipah*, since there was no restriction from the Creator's direction. However, having filled *Malchut*, the light gave it such power that now it can resist the pressure of delight. It does not want to receive it for its own sake, although the desire remains. Furthermore, *Malchut* not only refuses to receive for itself, but also acquires additional powers to receive a part of the light for the sake of the Creator.

The *Tzimtzum Bet* states that there is no more strength to receive for the Creator's sake. Now it is only possible to sit at the table without touching anything. Having the properties similar to those of the Creator secures a right to be in the spiritual world. However, such a state is undesirable to both the Creator and the creation. Hence, *Abba ve Ima* make a *Zivug* on the *Ohr Hochma* to pass it down, failing to take into account the fact that the light *AB-SAG* cannot descend under the *Parsa* and correct the vessels there. The intentions in the *Rosh* were good, but impossible to implement.

The same happens to us: we suddenly embark on doing something with good intentions, but then forget about them and fall into egoistic desires, turning into their slaves. This occurs because the very first sensation of pleasure completely seizes our desires and there is no power to resist them. As a result, all the vessel's desires under the *Parsa* break, lose their screen, and pass to the *Mador Klipot*. Man is sitting at the table, sees all the dishes, and is craving to swallow them in one gulp. He is driven by his egoistic desires and pays no attention to the host.

There is a fundamental difference between the desires of *Malchut* after *TA*, when it restricted its egoistic desires and refused to receive anything (although it saw all pleasures before it). In addition, *Malchut*, after the breaking of the vessels, just wishes to receive pleasure in any way possible, using the giver, but fails. Later, we will study how the *Klipot* influence man in such a way that, during all his life, he chases them, but is never able to receive ultimate pleasure.

No egoistic desires are the true created beings, since the Creator made them. The only genuine creation is that in which its **own** desire for spirituality arises. It is the aspiration for the Creator, longing to receive for His sake. Such a desire is absent in Him; it derives from the lowest black point of the creation as a result of the light's constant influence upon the vessel, like the constant dropping of water wears away the stone. This desire is called a soul; it marks man's birth out of an animal. Then, as the creation receives larger and larger portions of the light, the soul gradually reveals the Creator and finally merges with Him.

We have said that the two *Partzufim, AB* and *SAG*, emerged under the *Tabur* in the world of *Nikudim*. As we know, the world of *Nikudim* under the *Tabur* is in the state of *Katnut* on the *Reshimot Bet/Aleph*. Then it enters the state of *Gadlut* on the *Reshimot Dalet/Gimel*. This is the first *Partzuf* of the world of *Nikudim* that is similar to *AB de AK*, which also emerged above the *Tabur* on the *Reshimot Dalet/Gimel*.

Next, the screen loses strength, not because of the *Bitush Pnim u Makif* as in *AK*, but because of the breaking. Then another *Partzuf* (similar to *SAG de AK*) emerges under the *Tabur* on this *Reshimo*. However, both of these *Partzufim* are called *Melachim*, since the *Malchut* that rose to *Bina* rules over them. Both *AB* and *SAG* of the world of *Nikudim* include four inner *Partzufim*: one from *Ta'amim* and three from *Nekudot*, i.e., 8 *Melachim*, all in all. The intermediate *Partzufim* that emerge on *Aviut Shoresh* are not taken into account, since they do not spread into the *Guf*.

The first *Partzuf* is called *Melech HaDa'at*. As its screen weakens, it begins to include three more: *Melech Hesed*, *Melech Gevura*, and *Melech Shlish Elion de Tifferet*. The second *Partzuf* is called the *Shnei Shlish Tachton de Tifferet*, *Melech Netzah ve Hod*, *Melech Yesod*, and *Melech Malchut*. The *Partzufim* of the world of *Nikudim* are called by the names of the *Sefirot de Guf*, because they emerge in the *Guf* of *Partzuf Nikudim*. All of these eight *Melachim* are various measures of the light received under the *Parsa* for the Creator's sake. However, the screens with anti-egoistic power disappeared; the light left them, so they are considered fallen below all spiritual desires.

Why is the number of *Aviut* levels in the *Partzuf* determined differently in various places? The language of the ten *Sefirot* is very laconic. Using it for the explanation of certain phenomena in a certain aspect, Kabbalists often apply the same terms and definitions for the description of different interrelations. Thus, examining the *Partzuf AB*, we say that it consists of five inner *Partzufim*. In general, five levels of *Aviut* may be distinguished in any spiritual object, since it is a part of *Malchut* of the World of Infinity. However, when we look upon *AB* in relation to *Galgalta*, we say that it has only four levels of *Aviut*, because the *Aviut Dalet* is absent in it.

Thus, the description of spiritual objects depends on the aspect in which they are examined. Similarly, when describing a person, we may say he is a whole head shorter than another man, but it does not at all mean he has no head.

All that is described in this book happens in man's soul. Therefore, in order to understand the material, one does not have to possess abstract thinking or the ability to look at an object from different angles. This requires finding all the described phenomena and processes in one's relations with the Creator. Then comprehension will come and everything will take its place. However, if man imagines the spiritual worlds as something existing outside him, as some abstract system beyond his own feelings, then eventually he will reach a deadlock. In such a case, he will find it a lot more difficult to study Kabbalah, since he will have to give up his abstract ideas. If this material seems tangled to you, try to combine it with reading other books of this series, e.g. Book 4 ("Attaining the Worlds Beyond"). Make an effort to feel that they speak about the same subjects.

What is the *Midat haDin* (category of judgment)? *Din* is the only restriction, ban or the only "desire to receive" for its own sake. *Malchut* assumed this restriction already during *TA*, when it refused to receive for its own sake and remained empty. Prior to that, it could easily receive pleasure for itself. After *TA*, anyone who violates this law is considered a sinner, a *Klipah*, an impure force etc.

The "desire to receive" in its four phases is the only creation. If someone decides to change his nature and acquire altruistic desires, it will be his personal affair. However, since man is unable to accomplish such transformation on his own, he will have to ask the Creator for help. Still, the desire for pleasure remains; only the intention for the use of this desire changes.

Malchut is called the *Midat haDin*. It demands filling. If this desire has no anti-egoistic screen, it remains egoistic. However, if *Malchut* receives power from above and acquires the screen, its intentions become altruistic. The *Midat haDin* disappears and the *Midat haRachamim* (the light of the *Hassadim*, the Reflected Light, the screen) takes its place.

קה) ונודע, שכל הכמות והאיכות שבע"ס דראש, מתגלה ג"כ בהתפשטות ממעלה למטה לגוף. ולפיכך, כמו שבאורות דראש חזרה וירדה מלכות המזדווגת ממקום נקבי עינים למקום הפה, וגו"ע ונ"ע, שהם הכלים דפנים, חזרו וחיברו להם את הכלים דאחורים, שהם האח"פ, והאורות נתפשטו בהם, כן בהתפשטותם ממעלה למטה לגוף, נמשכו האורות גם לכלים דאחורים שלהם, שהם התנהי"מ שבבי"ע למטה מפרסא דאצילות.

אמנם לפי שכח מלכות המסיימת שבפרסא דאצילות מעורב בכלים ההם, ע"כ תיכף בפגישת האורות דמלך הדעת בכח הזה, נסתלקו לגמרי מהכלים ועלו לשורשם. וכל הכלים דמלך הדעת נשברו פנים ואחור, ומתו, ונפלו לבי"ע. כי הסתלקות האורות מהכלים הוא כמו הסתלקות החיות מגוף הגשמי, הנקרא "מיתה". ואז נזדכך המסך מהעביות דבחי"ד, מאחר שהכלים האלו כבר נשברו ומתו. ונשאר בו רק עביות דבחי"ג.

105) You should know that whatever is present in the ten Sefirot de Rosh is also found in the Guf in the same quantity and quality. Thus, as in the Rosh, Malchut descended from Nikvey Eynaim to the Peh, its GE joined their AHP and the light spread there. The light reached the Kelim de Achoraim, i.e., Tifferet, Netzah, Hod, Yesod and Malchut under the Parsa.

However, since the power of Malchut in the Parsa affects these vessels, the light Melech haDa'at disappears from them and rises to its root, while all the vessels of both the Panim and the Achoraim of Melech haDa'at break, die and fall into the BYA. This is because the disappearance of the light from the vessel is similar to life leaving a biological body and is therefore called death. Upon the downfall and death of the vessels, the screen loses the Aviut Dalet, so the Aviut Gimel remains.

When we speak about *Aviut Gimel*, we should bear in mind that the matter concerns the first *Partzuf* of the world of *Nikudim* that reached *Hitlabshut Dalet* and *Aviut Gimel*. Nevertheless, there are inner *Partzufim* with *Aviut Dalet, Gimel, Bet, Aleph,* and *Shoresh* inside the *Partzuf* with *Aviut Gimel*. Now only the first inner *Partzuf* with *Aviut Dalet* disappeared, leaving *Aviut Gimel*. The light cannot spread in desires that have no intention to be filled, so they remain empty and do not break.

קו) וכמו שנתבטלה העביות דבחי"ד מהמסך דגוף מחמת השבירה, כן נתבטלה העביות ההיא גם בהמלכות המזדווגת של ראש באו"א. כי העביות דראש ועביות דגוף דבר אחד הוא. אלא שזה כח וזה פועל (אות נ).

ולכן נפסק הזווג דקומת כתר גם בראש באו"א. והכלים דאחורים, שהם האח"פ, שהשלימו לקומת כתר, חזרו ונפלו למדרגה שמתחתיה, דהיינו להז"ת. וזה מכונה "ביטול האחורים דקומת כתר מאו"א". ונמצא, שכל קומת הטעמים דנקודים, ראש וגוף, נסתלקה.

106) As Aviut Dalet disappeared (as a result of the breaking of the vessels) from the Masach de Guf, so does Aviut Dalet in Malchut. Malchut makes a Zivug in the Rosh de Abba ve Ima, since Aviut de Rosh and Aviut de Guf are identical, although the first Zivug (in the Rosh) is only potential, while the second one (in the Guf) really happens.

For this reason, a Zivug on the level of Keter disappears also in the Rosh. The AHP, which complemented Keter, returned to the previous lower level, that is to say, to the seven lower Sefirot. This is called the elimination of the AHP de Keter in the Partzuf Abba ve Ima. Thus, the entire level of the Ta'amim de Nikudim (both the Rosh and the Guf) disappears.

Abba ve Ima makes a *Zivug* only to fill ZON with their light. The moment ZON become unable to receive the light and their request to *Ima* stops, *Ima* instantly terminates its *Zivug* with *Abba*. In this case, we see that the *Guf* sends a command to the *Rosh*, which immediately stops a *Zivug*.

First, the world of *Nikudim* was in *Katnut*, then, upon raising MAN, the *AHP* rose to their GE, but the breaking of the vessels followed. These vessels will continue to split into more and more desires until all the desires of ZON *de Nikudim* are totally broken. These are *Dalet, Gimel, Bet, Aleph* and *Shoresh* of level *Gimel.* Then the same happens with level *Bet, Aleph* and *Shoresh,* down to the very last desire. All this was necessary for the mixing of altruistic and egoistic properties. The breaking of the vessels has far-reaching and positive consequences.

Only the very first level – the *Shoresh* – is called the Creator's intention as regards the future creation. The other levels constitute development, realization of the intention and its transformation into the Creation. The first Creation is called *Dalet de Dalet (Malchut de Malchut)* of the World of Infinity. Everything could have stopped at this point, but, under the influence of the light, the first Creation wished to become similar to the Creator in its intentions, although its actions remained unchanged.

To change the intention, one must first completely refuse to receive the light, and then create an anti-egoistic force (the screen). It is necessary for the reception of the light for the Creator's sake. This development begins with a reception of a small portion and proceeds up to complete merging with the Creator. Such a process of the screen's development begins after *TA*. This is achieved by breaking the desire *Dalet de Dalet* into certain parts and creating the screen on all desires, from the smallest to the biggest.

The screen is prepared during the descent of the worlds. To create the minimal screen, both the Creator's and the creation's intentions and desires must mix. Only then will sparks of altruistic desire appear in the creation, i.e., in *Dalet de Dalet*. This is achieved with the help of the breaking of the vessels.

Nevertheless, none of these processes disappears; they constantly exist and the future connection with the Creator is conceived in them. The light does not enter the *Guf* during breaking of the vessels; it is in the *Rosh* and enters only the *GE* of each *Sefira*, although it also wants to enter the *AHP* (the egoistic vessels). However, in accordance with *TA*, it cannot do that. Still, a very brief contact takes place, so the vessel starts wishing to receive the light for its own sake, realizing what such reception could mean.

Previously, the creation did not understand it. The matter concerns the development of egoism from a stage where the reception of the light is restricted, to that of a passionate "desire to receive" it no matter what. During the emergence of the worlds and *Partzufim*, we are dealing with the gradual formation of a more advanced, albeit coarser egoism, an egoism that understands what it means to enjoy the light, and desires it more and more. When the vessel reaches the last stage of its development (our world), it becomes most suitable for its role.

When the vessel breaks, the egoistic desire (the *Reshimo* of the screen) is left in it, while the light that was to enter the vessel ascends. However, the connection between the *Reshimo* of the screen and the vanished light still exists, giving the vessel some luminescence, some memory of the screen it once had.

What is the difference between the weakening of the screen due to the *Bitush Pnim u Makif* and that owing to the breaking of the vessels? In the first case, the vessel, pressed by the *Ohr Makif* that wants to get inside, understands that it cannot receive the light in an altruistic way. Egoistic reception is forbidden, so the vessel decides to expel the light rather than violate the ban. In the second case, the vessel's initial intentions seem to be good, but it suddenly discovers that it wants to receive in a purely egoistic way; therefore, *TA* instantly snaps into action, and the weakening of the screen is expressed here as the breaking of the vessel, as its death.

Previously, we explained how the breaking of the vessels took place. The light *AB-SAG* came and began spreading in the *Rosh de Keter,* the *Rosh de Abba ve Ima,* the *GE de ZON,* and upon reaching the *Parsa,* the vessels began to break and to lose their screen.This is because the light met with the egoistic desires without the screen. Here the *TA* prohibition worked; the light rose to the *Rosh de Nikudim* and then to the *Rosh de SAG,* while the vessels that wanted to receive pleasure for themselves broke and fell into the *Klipot.*

There is the light of the Thought of Creation and the light of Correction of Creation. The light that created *Malchut* and its desire to enjoy it is called the *Ohr Hochma* or the light of the Thought of Creation. The light that corrects *Malchut,* reveals the higher properties in it, and enables it to feel pleasure from giving is called the *Ohr Hassadim.* One can feel the Creator either by enjoying the contact with Him (delight from reception of the *Ohr Hochma*), or by feeling His properties and enjoying similarity to Him (delight from the *Ohr Hassadim*).

Unless egoism begins to feel the Creator's properties, it will neither make *Tzimtzum Aleph,* nor ever wish to be like the Creator. The Creator created an egoism that would be able to develop and feel both the delight as well as the One who provides it. Indeed, the future ability to be like the Creator was already included in the initial phase of the development of egoism.

The information that stimulates the sensation of the Giver comes to the vessels together with the light *AB-SAG*. This is the light of correction, the light of a very different nature. It arouses in man very subtle feelings of the Giver's significance and the desire to be like Him. The *TA* is an extremely cruel act of the creation that rather pushed the Creator aside, saying that it wanted nothing from Him, depriving Him of an opportunity to be the Giver. It rendered His desires uncalled for, until it begins to understand that the Thought of Creation suggests, not refusing to receive the light, but reception of it for the sake of the Creator.

The primary role in the creation of the *Partzufim* after *TA* belongs to the screen; action is secondary and the entire process develops from big to small. After *TB*, when the *Partzuf* restricted itself, the desire to pass from *Katnut* to *Gadlut* appeared for the first time. This required strength; the strength came from the light *AB-SAG*. All the vessels above the *Parsa*: *Keter, Abba ve Ima, GE de ZON*, can feel an opportunity to pass to *Gadlut*. However, this light cannot get under the *Parsa*. The *AHP de ZON* cannot feel it; hence, they remain in the same state. The *Nekudot de SAG* under the *Parsa* are empty after the *TB*. They form a place for the worlds *Atzilut, Beria, Yetzira,* and *Assiya*.

When we say that there is no light, it actually means that the *Kli* simply cannot feel it. The light itself is amorphous; there are no distinctions in it; in other words, the vessel is unable to detect any shades, any variations of pleasure in the light. Such was the state of *Malchut* in the World of Infinity. When it felt the light's properties, it made *TA*. *Malchut* began to distinguish nine previous *Sefirot* in the light, starting from the closest. As it discovered the last one *(Keter)* and felt the contrast between their properties (*Keter* only bestows and *Malchut* only receives), it instantly made a *Tzimtzum*.

ZA consists of *Hochma* and *Bina*. It is called "a small face", which refers to the amount of light in it, as compared to *Malchut*, which wishes to be big and receive all the light of *Hochma*. *Keter* gives all, *Malchut* receives all, and *Bina* does not receive anything. These are the characteristics of the four phases of the Direct Light and their root called *Keter*.

While studying Kabbalah, one should constantly remember that there are no such notions as place, time or space (as we understand them) in spirituality. The notion of place first appeared only after *TB*. The *Nekudot de* SAG under the *Parsa* remain empty after *TB* and form a place for the worlds of *ABYA*. Thus, by "place", we usually mean the *Nekudot de* SAG; to be precise, the vessels working in compliance with the law of *TA* as regards the vessels working according to *TB*, which form the worlds beginning from *Atzilut*. Now we can understand the fundamental difference between these two modes of working with desires.

The vessels of *TB* are not exactly the vessels of *TA*, which use only half of their desires. It is a cardinally different principle of work. We will be studying the so-called ascents of the worlds wherein the "place" may or may not ascend together with the worlds.

In spirituality, we understand time as a number of necessary actions aimed at achieving a certain spiritual level. These actions form a cause-and-effect chain. The less corrected man is, the more the Creator conceals Himself from him; the more man's way to the Creator turns from a sequence of spiritual actions into an unconscious flow of time.

In the spiritual world everything is connected to the intention for the sake of the Creator, hence nothing ever disappears there. Only the *Klipot*, the desires for one's self can disappear. Our world is below the *Klipot*, therefore we observe in it such a phenomenon as disappearance.

We have spoken about the breaking of the vessels. The light AB-SAG came and began to spread in the *Rosh de Keter*, the *Rosh de Abba ve Ima*, the *GE de* ZON, and as soon as it reached the *Parsa*, the vessels began to split, lose the screen, for the light came across desires to receive for one's own sake without a screen. The *TA* snapped into action, the light rose to *Rosh de Nikudim*, and then to *Rosh de* SAG; the egoistic vessels broke and fell into the *Klipot*.

קז) ומתוך שאור העליון אינו פוסק מלהאיר, נמצא שחזר ונזדווג על העביות דבחי"ג, הנשאר במסך של ראש באו"א. ויצאו ע"ס בקומת חכמה. והגוף שממעלה למטה, נתפשט לספירת החסד. והוא מלך הב' דנקודים. וגם הוא נמשך לבי"ע ונשבר ומת. ואז נתבטלה גם העביות דבחי"ג מהמסך דגוף ודראש. וגם הכלים דאחורים, האח"פ, שהשלימו לקומת חכמה זו דאו"א, חזרו ונתבטלו ונפלו למדרגה שמתחתיה, לז"ת, כנ"ל בקומת כתר.

ואח"כ נעשה הזווג על העביות דבחי"ב, שנשאר במסך. ויצאו ע"ס בקומת בינה. והגוף שממעלה למטה נתפשט בספירת הגבורה. והוא מלך הג' דנקודים. וגם הוא נמשך לבי"ע ונשבר ומת. ונתבטלה גם העביות דבחי"ב בראש וגוף. ונפסק הזווג דקומת בינה גם בראש. והאחורים של קומת בינה דראש נפלו למדרגה שמתחתיה בהז"ת.

ואח"כ נעשה הזווג על העוביות דבחי"א, שנשאר בהמסך. ויצאו עליה ע"ס בקומת ז"א. והגוף שלו ממעלה למטה נתפשט בשליש עליון דת"ת. וגם הוא לא נתקיים ונסתלק האור ממנו. ונזדככה גם העוביות דבחי"א בגוף וראש. והאחורים דקומת ז"א נפל למדרגה שמתחתיה, לז"ת.

107) The Upper Light never stops shining; it makes a new Zivug on the Aviut Gimel, which remained in the Masach de Rosh of Abba ve Ima. Because of this Zivug, a Partzuf consisting of 10 Sefirot emerges with the level of Hochma, while the Guf, with the level of Hesed, spreads down, and is called the second Melech of the world of Nikudim. As with the first, the Melech haDa'at, it spreads in the BYA, breaks and dies. The Aviut Gimel disappears from the Masachim de Guf and de Rosh. The AHP, which completed the Partzuf at the level of Hochma, broke and fell to the lower level.

Then a Zivug on Aviut Bet produces 10 Sefirot of the level of Bina, while the Guf spreads down to Gevura, and is called the third Melech of the world of Nikudim. It spreads down to BYA, breaks and dies. Aviut Bet disappears from the Guf and the Rosh and a Zivug on the level of Bina also stops in the Rosh. The AHP of Bina de Rosh fall to the lower level, into the seven lower Sefirot.

The next Zivug is made on Aviut Aleph; the 10 Sefirot with the level of ZA appear, while the Guf spreads to the upper third of Tifferet. It also ceases to exist, the light leaves it, and Behina Aleph disappears from the Guf and the Rosh. The AHP de ZA falls to the lower level of Zat.

Why are the *Partzufim* in the world of *Nikudim* called *Melachim*? It is because they are in *Gadlut* (big state), which emerges from *Katnut* (small state) with the *Ohr Nefesh*, also called the *Ohr Malchut*. Regardless of the eight levels, only seven *Melachim* exist, since there are only seven lower parts, levels. Similarly, there are just seven *Shorashim* (roots) in the *Rosh* for their spreading.

קח) וכאן נגמרו כל האחורים דאו"א לירד, שהם האח"פ. כי בשבירת מלך הדעת, נתבטלו באו"א רק אח"פ השייכים לקומת כתר. ובשבירת מלך החסד, נתבטלו באו"א רק אח"פ השייכים לקומת חכמה. ובשבירת מלך הגבורה, נתבטלו האח"פ השייכים לקומת בינה. ובהסתלקות שליש עליון דת"ת, נתבטלו האח"פ דקומת ז"א.

ונמצא שנתבטלה כל בחינת הגדלות דאו"א, ולא נשאר בהם רק הגו"ע דקטנות. ונשאר במסך רק עביות דשורש. ואח"כ נזדכך המסך דגוף מכל עביותו, ונשתוה למסך דראש. אשר אז נמצא נכלל בזווג דהכאה של ראש. ומתחדשים שמה הרשימות שבו חוץ מהבחינה האחרונה (אות מ"א). ובכח התחדשות הזה יצא עליו קומה חדשה, הנקראת ישסו"ת.

108) After the last Zivug on Aviut Aleph was terminated, all the AHP de Abba ve Ima stopped descending; therefore, when the Melech haDa'at de Abba ve Ima broke, the AHP de Keter disappeared. When the vessels of the Melech haHesed in Abba ve Ima broke, the AHP de Hochma disappeared. When the vessels of the Melech haGevura in Abba ve Ima broke, the AHP de Bina disappeared. When the Melech Shlish Elion de Tifferet broke, the AHP de ZA disappeared.

Thus, the entire level of Gadlut in Abba ve Ima ceased to exist. Only the vessels of the GE de Katnut with Aviut Shoresh in the Masach remained. Afterwards the Masach de Guf loses all its Aviut, merges with the Masach de Rosh, and joins a Zivug de Haka'a in the Rosh. All the Reshimot except for the last Behinot are renewed in it. From this renewal (Zivug), a new level arises called the YESHSUT.

Let us review the whole process briefly. The world of *Nikudim* was in *Katnut* where there were only the vessels of GE in *Keter*, *Abba ve Ima* and ZON. Then *Keter* and *Abba ve Ima* made a *Zivug* on *Dalet de Hitlabshut* and *Gimel de Aviut*, and the light spread to the *Guf*. The *Guf* broke and only *Aviut Gimel-Bet* remained. *Keter* and *Abba ve Ima* want to make a *Zivug* on that *Aviut* and hope that the *Guf* will be able to receive this light for the Creator's sake, since it is one level lower. Because of this *Zivug*, a *Partzuf* of a different spiritual level emerges; hence, it is already called the *YESHSUT* and not *Abba ve Ima*.

קט) ומתוך שהבחינה אחרונה נאבדה, לא נשאר בו כי אם בחי"ג. ויוצאים עליו ע"ס בקומת חכמה. וכשהוכרה עביות דגוף שבו, יצא מהראש מאו"א, וירד והלביש במקום החזה דגוף דנקודים (אות נ"ה). ומוציא מחזה ולמעלה הע"ס דראש. והראש הזה מכונה "ישסו"ת". והגוף שלו הוא מוציא מהחזה ולמטה בב"ש ת"ת עד סיום הת"ת. והוא מלך הד' דנקודים.

וגם הוא נמשך לבי"ע ונשבר ומת. ונזדככה העביות דבחי"ג ראש וגוף. והכלים דאחורים של ראש נפלו למדרגה שמתחתיה במקום גוף שלהם. ואח"כ נעשה הזווג על עביות דבחי"ב, הנשאר בו. ויצא עליו קומת בינה. והגוף שלו שממעלה למטה נתפשט בב' הכלים נצח והוד. והם שניהם מלך אחד, דהיינו מלך ה' דנקודים.

וגם הם נמשכו לבי"ע ונשברו ומתו. ונזדככה גם העביות דבחי"ב בראש וגוף. והכלים דאחורים של הקומה נפלו להמדרגה שמתחתיה, לגוף. ואח"כ נעשה הזווג על עביות דבחי"א, שנשארה בו. ויצא עליו קומת ז"א. והגוף שלו שממעלה למטה נתפשט בכלי דיסוד. והוא מלך הו' דנקודים. וגם הוא נמשך לבי"ע ונשבר ומת. ונזדככה גם העביות דבחי"א בראש וגוף. והכלים דאחורים שבראש נפלו למדרגה שמתחתיהם, לגוף. ואח"כ נעשה הזווג על העביות דבחינת שורש, הנשאר במסך. ויצא עליו קומת מלכות. והממעלה למטה שלו נמשך לכלי דמלכות. והוא מלך הז' דנקודים. וגם הוא נמשך לבי"ע ונשבר ומת. ונזדככה גם העביות דשורש בראש וגוף. והאחורים דראש נפלו למדרגה שמתחתיה, בגוף. ועתה נגמרו להתבטל כל הכלים דאחורים דישסו"ת, וכן שביה"כ דכל ז"ת דנקודים, הנקראים ז' מלכים.

109) After the disappearance of the last degree of Aviut (Dalet), the Behina Gimel brought forth 10 Sefirot of the level of Hochma. The Partzuf begins from the Chazeh de Abba ve Ima so that the Sefirot of its Rosh rise above the Chazeh and are called the YESHSUT; whereas below the Chazeh, including the lower two thirds of Tifferet, the 10 Sefirot de Guf are formed. This is the fourth Partzuf called the Melech of the world of Nikudim.

It also spreads to BYA, breaks and dies. The Aviut de Behina Gimel disappears both in the Rosh and in the Guf. The AHP de Rosh falls to the lower level (Guf). Then a Zivug on Aviut de Behina Bet brings forth the level of Bina. The Guf of the new Partzuf spreads to the vessels Netzah and Hod. This fifth Partzuf is called the Melech of the world of Nikudim.

It also spreads to BYA, breaks and dies. The Behina Bet disappears both in the Rosh and in the Guf, while the AHP de Rosh falls to the lower level (Guf). The next Zivug on Aviut Aleph produces the level of ZA, while its Guf spreads down to the vessel of Yesod. This is the sixth Melech of the world of Nikudim, which reaches the BYA, breaks, and dies. The Aviut Aleph disappears both in the Rosh and in the Guf, while the AHP de Rosh falls to the lower level (Guf).

After that, the last *Zivug* is made on the *Aviut Shoresh* that is left in the *Masach*. It brings forth the level of *Malchut*, which spreads to the vessel of *Malchut*. This is the seventh *Melech* of the world of *Nikudim*. As with all the preceding *Melachim*, it breaks and dies. The last *Aviut de Shoresh* disappears in both the *Rosh* and in the *Guf*, and the *AHP de Rosh* fall to the lower level (to its *Guf*). Thus, all the *AHP de YESHSUT* disappeared and all the seven lower *Sefirot de Nikudim* (i.e., all the seven *Melachim*) broke.

Tifferet constitutes the entire *Guf* of the *Partzuf*. Because of *TB*, *Tifferet* divides into three parts: the upper third of *Tifferet* is called the *Chazeh*, the middle third of *Tifferet* is called the *Tabur*, and the lower third of *Tifferet* is called *Yesod*.

קי) והנה נתבארו הטעמים ונקודות שיצאו בב' הפרצופים או"א וישסו"ת דנקודים, הנקראים ע"ב ס"ג.

שבאו"א יצאו ד' קומות זה למטה מזה, שהם קומת כתר, הנקראת הסתכלות עיינין דאו"א, קומת חכמה, הנקראת "גופא דאבא", קומת בינה, הנקראת "גופא דאמא", קומת ז"א, הנקראת יסודות דאו"א. שמהם נתפשטו ד' גופים, שהם: מלך הדעת, מלך החסד, מלך הגבורה, מלך ש"ע דת"ת עד החזה. וד' הגופים אלו נשברו פנים ואחורים יחד.

אבל מבחינת הראשים, דהיינו בד' הקומות שבאו"א, נשארו בהקומות כל הכלים דפנים שבהם, דהיינו בחינת הגו"ע ונ"ע דכל קומה, שהיה בהם מעת הקטנות דנקודים. ורק הכלים דאחורים, שבכל קומה שנתחברו בהם בעת הגדלות, הם בלבדם חזרו ונתבטלו בסבת השבירה, ונפלו למדרגה שמתחתיהם, ונשארו, כמו שהיו לפני יציאת הגדלות דנקודים (אות ע"ו-ע"ז).

110) We have learned about the Ta'amim and the Nekudot that emerged in two Partzufim: Abba ve Ima and YESHSUT of the world of Nikudim, and are called the AB and the SAG.

Four levels, one under the other, appear in Abba ve Ima: Keter is called "Histaklut Eynaim Abba ve Ima" (looking into one another's eyes); Hochma is called "Gufa de Aba"; Bina is called "Gufa de Ima"; and ZA is called "Yesodot de Abba ve Ima". Four bodies emerge from the above-mentioned levels: the Melech haDa'at, the Melech haYesod, the Melech Gevura and Melech of the upper third of Tifferet down to the Chazeh. The Gufim of all of these four levels broke, both Panim and Achoraim, i.e., both GE and AHP.

However, in the Rashim (heads) of these four levels of Abba ve Ima, all the Kelim de Panim of each level that were during Katnut de Nikudim, that is to say, the GE and Nikvey Eynaim (Keter, Hochma and Gar de Bina), remained in their places. Only the Kelim de Achoraim (i.e., the AHP de Rosh, the Zat de Bina, ZA, and Malchut) of each level, which joined the GE during Gadlut, disappeared because of the breaking of the vessels. They fell to the lower level, i.e., to where they had been during Katnut.

קיא) ועד"ז ממש היה בפרצוף ישסו"ת יציאת ד' קומות זה למטה מזה: שקומה הא' היא קומת חכמה ונקראת הסתכלות עיינין דישסו"ת זה בזה, וקומת בינה, וקומת ז"א, וקומת מלכות. שמהם נתפשטו ד' גופים, שהם: מלך ב"ש תתאין דת"ת, מלך נו"ה, מלך היסוד, המלכות. וד' הגופים שלהם נשברו פנים ואחור יחד. אבל בהראשים, דהיינו בד' הקומות דישסו"ת, נשארו הכלים דפנים שבהם, ורק האחורים בלבד נתבטלו בסבת השבירה. ונפלו למדרגה שמתחתיהם. והנה אחר ביטול אלו ב' הפרצופים או"א וישסו"ת, יצא עוד קומת מ"ה בנקודים. ולפי שלא נתפשט ממנה לבחינת גוף אלא רק תיקוני כלים בלבד, לא אאריך בו.

111) Similarly, four levels, one under the other, emerged in the Partzuf YESHSUT. The first level (Hochma) is called the Histaklut Eynaim de YESHSUT, the second level (Bina), followed by ZA and Malchut, brings forth 4 bodies: the Melech of two lower thirds of Tifferet, the Melech Netzah-Hod, the Melech Yesod and the Melech

Malchut. These four Gufim broke (both Panim and Achoraim), but the Kelim de Panim remained in the Rashim de YESHSUT. Their Achoraim disappeared because of the breaking of the vessels, and fell to the lower level. After the two Partzufim Abba ve Ima and the YESHSUT broke, one more Partzuf emerged – MA of the world of Nikudim. However, since no Guf spreads from it (only "Tikuney Kelim"), we will not characterize it here.

Thus, because of a *Zivug* on the *Reshimot Dalet/Gimel*, four *Melachim* emerged in the *Rosh de Abba ve Ima (Gadlut de Nikudim).* Then there was a *Zivug* in the *Rosh de YESHSUT* on the *Aviut Gimel/Bet*, which led to the emergence of four more *Melachim*. All of them received the *Ohr Hochma*, but not for the Creator's sake; hence, they lost the screen, broke and fell from their spiritual level. Each of them retained the *Reshimo* of the light and the *Ohr Hozer* – a tiny portion of the screen's light, which they wanted to work with, but could not.

This tiny portion of the light is called a "*Nitzutz*" (spark). The fact that it resides inside the egoistic desire makes it possible to start correcting the broken vessels. Had the vessels never been broken, this altruistic spark would have never gone under the *Parsa*, and the vessels of the *AHP* found there would have had no possibility for correction. This will be the task of the MA *Hadash* (new MA) or the World of Correction, *Atzilut*, which emerged from the *Rosh de AK* because of a *Zivug* on the *Aviut de Shoresh*. This level is called the *Metzah* (forehead).

The screen in *Galgalta* lost its strength, the light disappeared, and the *Masach de Guf* rose to join the *Masach de Rosh*. The *Reshimot Dalet/Gimel* was left from the light of *Hochma* in the *Toch* and *Dalet/Gimel* from the light of the *Hassadim* in the *Sof*. *Reshimot Dalet/Gimel* of the light of *Hassadim* means that, although the *Ohr Hochma* is felt and desired owing to the *Aviut Gimel*, nevertheless, the creation just wants to merge with the Creator. That is to say, it wants to be filled with *Ohr Hassadim* and not with *Ohr Hochma* (the light of Purpose of the Creation), for it is unable to receive *Ohr Hochma* for the Creator's sake. The *Partzuf AB* emerges on the *Reshimot de Toch* and the *Gadlut de Nikudim* emerges on the *Reshimot de Sof*. After the light leaves the *Partzuf AB*, the *Partzuf SAG* emerges above the *Tabur* in the world of AK.

As a result of a *Zivug* on the *Reshimo Dalet/Gimel* under the *Tabur*, *Gadlut* of the world of *Nikudim* called the lower *AB* or *Abba ve Ima* emerges. When it disappears, a *Zivug* on the *Reshimo Gimel/Bet* takes place under the *Tabur*. As a result, the second *Partzuf* called the lower SAG or the *YESHSUT* springs up. The properties of the *Partzufim* both above and under the *Tabur* are similar in the sense that the light of *Hochma* spreads in the lower *AB*, while the light of *Hassadim* with luminescence of *Hochma* spreads in the lower SAG. The correction of the *ZON* and *Malchut* under the *Tabur* will consist in lifting them to the level of the *Partzufim AB* and SAG.

After the disappearance of the light in the *Partzufim*, pure egoism remains, which remembers what it means to receive the light. All the previous *Reshimot* were based on the reception of the light for the sake of the Creator. Now, when the vessels of *Malchut* were broken, the "desire to receive" the light at any cost appears for the first time. However, this is not the final point of development of egoism; a very long way lies ahead of it.

Malchut senses the light long before it enters it. The same happens in our world. We feel pleasure before we actually receive it. Once we get it, it instantly disappears. It only seems to us that we feel delight. Each time we have to perform certain actions that would help us feel pleasure, but the moment we come in contact with it, the vessel ceases to exist and the pleasure vanishes.

However, we all live only for the sake of achieving such contact. If we were filled with constant imperishable pleasure, we would not make a single move in the direction of new delight, since we would be overfilled with the previous one. Like drug addicts, we would enjoy an injected dose, doing nothing until the need for a new dose is felt. Only egoism (if corrected) that has reached a state of absolute opposition to the Creator may become equal to Him. Then the received pleasure will not vanish; the desire for it will remain, whereas we, not for a moment stopping to enjoy, will rush towards new reception for the sake of the Creator.

The light wanted to enter the vessel under the *Tabur* and the vessel was eager to receive it for the Creator's sake according to the strength of its screen. The vessel discovered too late that there was no screen. All pleasures were already inside and imposed their will on it. However, *TB* expelled the light and the vessel remained empty of the desires it could not satisfy. This terrible state accompanies the breaking of the vessels, death and a downfall. All desires become isolated and undirected at one goal.

When man is firm of purpose, all his desires (both altruistic and egoistic) pursue the same goal. If he is not, he has many different desires that do not aim at one target. Such a person cannot succeed.

When the *Melachim* fall, the highest of them, having lost the screen, falls lower than the rest. All the eight *Melachim* were of different levels. The vessel of *Keter* fell down to *Malchut*. The vessel of *Bina* (the vessel of bestowal) did not fall as low.

The Sefirot de Rosh have the following names:

Gar de Keter	*Metzah*
Hochma	*Eynaim*
Gar de Bina	*Nikvey Eynaim*
Zat de Bina	*Awzen*
ZA	*Hotem*
Malchut	*Peh*

THE WORLD OF CORRECTION BORN FROM METZAH OF THE WORLD OF AK
עולם התיקון ומ"ה החדש, שיצא מהמצח דא"ק

קיב) והנה נתבאר היטב מתחילת הפתיחה עד כאן ד' פרצופים הראשונים דא"ק:

פרצוף הא' דא"ק, הנקרא "פרצוף גלגלתא", שהזווג דהכאה נעשה בו על בחי"ד, והע"ס שבו הן בקומת כתר.

112) Now, let us examine all the spiritual worlds, the entire spiritual Universe as a single whole. We will see that in the Galgalta (Partzuf Keter of the entire Universe) a Zivug was made on all the five Reshimot – Dalet/Dalet.

In fact, the screen stood in *Malchut (Peh)* of the common *Rosh* of the entire Universe (this *Rosh* is actually "*Rosh*" of *Malchut* of the World of Infinity).

פרצוף הב' דא"ק, נקרא ע"ב דא"ק, אשר הזווג דהכאה נעשה בו על עביות דבחי"ג, והע"ס שלו הן בקומת חכמה. והוא מלביש מפה ולמטה דפרצוף הגלגלתא, פרצוף הג' דא"ק נקרא ס"ג דא"ק, שהזווג דהכאה נעשה בו על עביות דבחי"ב. והע"ס שלו הן בקומת בינה. והוא מלביש מפה ולמטה דפרצוף ע"ב דא"ק.

Then the screen rises from Malchut to ZA (Hotem) of this Rosh. A Zivug on Reshimot Dalet/Gimel in this screen creates AB (Partzuf Hochma of the entire Universe). So now, the screen stands in ZA of the common Rosh. Then the screen continues rising. This time it ascends from ZA to Bina of the common Rosh and there a Zivug on the Reshimot Gimel/Bet creates the Partzuf SAG (Bina of the entire Universe).

Afterwards, as we know, *TB* takes place and renders the *AHP* (the vessels of *Zat de Bina, ZA* and *Malchut*) of each *Sefira* unfit for use. Because of *TB*, *Bina* of the common *Rosh* happens to divide into two parts: the *Gar* (**Nikvey Eynaim**) and the *Zat* (**Awzen**). Now the screen stands on the borderline between these *Gar* and *Zat*, i.e., between the **Nikvey Eynaim** and the **Awzen**. With some reserve, it may be said that the *Partzuf*

Nekudot de SAG, which is an intermediate stage between *Bina* and ZA of the entire Universe (essentially it is *Zat de Bina*, *YESHSUT*), emerged because of a *Zivug* made on the screen positioned there.

Then the screen continues "rising" to *Hochma* of the common *Rosh*, i.e., the **Eynaim**, but it should be stressed that now, after the *TB*, the screen stands not at the bottom of each level as before, but in the **Nikvey Eynaim**, that is to say, on the border between *Gar de Bina* and *Zat de Bina*. Hence, the world of the *Nikudim* (ZA of the entire Universe and *Partzuf* MA) emerges from a *Zivug* in **Nikvey Eynaim** *de* **Eynaim**, i.e., the screen stands on the border between *Gar* and *Zat de Hochma* of the common *Rosh*.

This *Zivug* was made on the *Reshimot Bet/Aleph* with the additional information of *TB* (ban on using the vessels of reception). So now the *Partzufim*, as it were, consist only of two and a half *Sefirot*. Then, upon breaking of the vessels, the screen moves to the **Nikvey Eynaim** *de Keter* of the common *Rosh (Metzah)*. There a *Zivug* on the *Reshimot Aleph/Shoresh* creates the world of *Atzilut*, also called the world of *Vrudim* or MA *Hadash* (new MA).

We will explain later on why *Atzilut* is called MA *Hadash*. The world of *Atzilut* corrects the broken vessels, gives birth to the soul of *Adam haRishon*, the soul that descends to the lowest point and only then becomes the true Creation, for now it is infinitely remote from the Creator and can start correcting itself and ascend back to Him.

We should have a general idea of the world of *Atzilut*, which controls everything. The creation is constantly connected with this system. As the result of a gradually achieved correction, we ascend 6000 levels and reach the world of *Atzilut*. Then the 7th, 8th, 9th, and 10th millennia come, accessible only to those who rise to the level of the Final Correction (the *Gmar Tikkun*).

פרצוף הד' דא"ק נקרא מ"ה דא"ק, שהזווג דהכאה נעשה בו על עביות דבחי"א, והע"ס שבו הן בקומת ז"א. ופרצוף זה מלביש מטבור ולמטה דס"ג דא"ק. והוא נחלק לפנימיות וחיצוניות,

שהפנימיות נקרא מ"ה וב"ן דא"ק, והחיצוניות נקרא "עולם הנקודים". וכאן נעשה ענין השיתוף של המלכות בבינה, הנקרא צמצום ב', והקטנות, והגדלות, ועלית מ"ן, וענין הדעת, המכריע והמזווג החו"ב פב"פ, וענין שבירת הכלים. כי כל אלו נתחדשו בפרצוף הד' דא"ק, הנקרא מ"ה או "עולם הנקודים".

The fourth Partzuf of the world of AK is called MA. It emerges from a Zivug de Behina Aleph, and its 10 Sefirot have the level of ZA. It dresses onto Galgalta from the Tabur and below, where the Nekudot de SAG spread. The Partzuf MA has an inner part called MA and BON of the world of AK, and an outer – Nikudim, which dresses onto the inner part. In this place, Malchut joins Bina, i.e., TB, Katnut, Gadlut, the raising of MAN, the emergence of Sefira Da'at. This in turn promotes a Zivug between Hochma and Bina Panim be Panim, the breaking of the vessels – all of which occurred in the fourth Partzuf MA or the world of Nikudim.

The *Partzuf* MA, born from the SAG on the *Aviut Bet/Aleph*, refers to *TA* and is considered an inner *Partzuf* as regards the MA that was born from the *Nekudot de SAG*, and under the *Tabur*, refers to the *TB*. We see this entire process as a cause-and-effect chain, but in fact, this is not a process; it is a constantly existing static picture.

There are *Ta'amim*, *Nekudot*, *Tagin* and *Otiot* in each *Partzuf*. The processes that occur in *Nekudot de SAG* – the descent under *Tabur*, the mixing with *NHYM de Galgalta*, *TB*, whose *Reshimo* brings forth the world of *Nikudim* in *Katnut* and *Gadlut*, the breaking of the vessels – all this may be referred to the *Nekudot de SAG* and to one of the parts of the *Partzuf* SAG.

The *Gematria* (numeric value) of SAG consists of *Yud-Key-Vav-Key*, but the filling, the light that is in the *Kelim* of *Hochma*, *Bina*, ZA and *Malchut*, amounts to 63. The filling of the letter *Vav (Vav-Aleph-Vav)* includes the letter *Aleph*, which points to *TB* and the *Partzuf Nikudim*. The following letter, *Key*, again includes *Yud* and not *Aleph*, which refers to *Gadlut de Nikudim*. Therefore we do not view *Nikudim* (when taken separately) as the world. So why do we not say that the SAG got broken? These changes do not affect the SAG since it is under the *Tabur*, and all that happened refers to its outer *Partzufim* (so-called *Partzufey Searot*), which dress onto it. The *Partzufey Searot* (hair) are examined in detail in Part 13 of "The Study of the Ten Sefirot" on the example of the *Partzuf Arich Anpin* of the world of *Atzilut*.

The first spreading of the light down from *Peh de Rosh* to the *Tabur* on *Aviut Dalet* is called *Ta'amim*. Then next *Partzufim-Nekudot* emerge *on Gimel de Dalet, Bet de Dalet, Aleph de Dalet* and *Shoresh de Dalet*, although we do not give them names under the *Tabur de AK*. Under the *Tabur* in the world of *Nikudim*, we call them *Sefira Da'at, Melech Da'at, Melech Hesed, Melech Gevura* and *Melech* of the upper third of *Tifferet*. At that, the *Partzuf* emerging on *Aviut Shoresh* does not spread into the *Guf*; hence, it is not taken into account and is not called a *Melech*.

When can we see that the *Guf* influences the *Rosh*? Raising MAN makes *Abba ve Ima* turn *Panim be Panim* to make a *Zivug* on the *Ohr Hochma* for passing it on to the lower *Partzufim*. Such a request of ZA to *Abba ve Ima* leads them to a state called the *Sefira Da'at*. As the vessels break, this desire in *Abba ve Ima* disappears and they terminate their *Zivug*. As the lower *Partzuf* turns to the upper with a request, it changes the way it is controlled. When we long to change our state from below, we must raise MAN to the upper *Partzuf* and receive correction.

קיג) ואלו ה' בחינות עביות שבמסך נקראים על שם הספירות שבראש, דהיינו גלגלתא עינים ואח"פ: שהעביות דבחי"ד נקרא "פה", שעליה יצא פרצוף הא' דא"ק, ועביות דבחי"ג נקרא "חוטם", שעליה יצא פרצוף ע"ב דא"ק, ועביות דבחי"ב נקרא "אזן", שעליה יצא פרצוף ס"ג דא"ק, ועביות דבחי"א נקרא "נקבי עינים", שעליה יצא פרצוף מ"ה דא"ק ועולם הנקודים, ועביות דבחינת שורש נקרא "גלגלתא" או "מצח", שעליה יצא עולם התיקון. והוא נקרא מ"ה החדש. כי פרצוף הד' דא"ק הוא עיקר פרצוף מ"ה דא"ק, כי יצא מנקבי עינים בקומת ז"א, המכונה בשם הוי"ה דמ"ה. אבל פרצוף החמישי דא"ק, שיצא מן המצח, דהיינו בחינת הגלגלתא, שהיא בחינת עביות דשורש, אין בו באמת אלא קומת מלכות הנקרא ב"ן. אמנם מטעם שנשארה שם גם בחי"א דהתלבשות, שהוא בחינת ז"א, ע"כ נקרא גם הוא בשם מ"ה. אלא בשם מ"ה שיצא מהמצח דא"ק, שפירושו, מהתכללות עביות דשורש, הנקרא "מצח". וכן הוא נקרא בשם מ"ה החדש, בכדי להבדילו מהמ"ה שיצא מנקבי עינים דא"ק. ופרצוף מ"ה החדש הזה נקרא בשם "עולם התיקון" או "עולם אצילות".

113) The five levels of Aviut in the screen are called by the names of the Sefirot in the Rosh: the Galgalta ve Eynaim and the AHP. The first Partzuf of the world of AK emerged on Aviut de Behina Dalet, called the Peh, and the Partzuf AB of the world of AK emerged on Aviut de Behina Gimel, called the Hotem. The Partzuf SAG de AK emerged on Aviut de Behina Bet, called the Awzen. The Partzuf MA and the world of Nikudim emerged on Aviut de Behina Aleph, called Nikvey Eynaim. The Partzuf MA Hadash, or the world of correction (Atzilut), emerged on Aviut de Behina Shoresh, called the Metzah. Unlike all the other Partzufim, the name of Atzilut is determined not by the Aviut, but by the Hitlabshut Aleph, which plays a most significant role in the world of Atzilut. Therefore, it is not called BON, but MA Hadash.

Does not the appearance of MA *Hadash* signify that up to now the entire way of *Malchut* of the World of Infinity was faulty? There is no such notion as "a mistake" in spirituality. The entire way is just phases of the rise of the genuine desire.

Any level, even the lowest, corresponds to the entire Universe, reality. However, on the lowest levels, everything happens in the coarsest way, whereas on the highest levels it takes the most open, sophisticated and perfectly analyzed form. This difference provides all the strength, all the taste that is in the sensation of the Creator. There is *NaRaNHaY* on all levels. All see the same picture, but everyone perceives it differently on various levels. Alternatively, rather, each level bears in itself a deeper attainment, which provides information that is more extensive. These sensations cannot possibly be expressed with words from our world. The lower level is unable to comprehend the upper one.

קיד) אמנם יש להבין: למה ג' הקומות הראשונות דא"ק, הנקראות "גלגלתא", ע"ב, ס"ג אינן נבחנות לג' עולמות, אלא לג' פרצופים? ולמה נשתנה פרצוף הד' דא"ק להקרא בשם "עולם"? וכן פרצוף החמישי דא"ק, כי פרצוף הד' נקרא בשם "עולם הנקודים" ופרצוף הה' נקרא בשם "עולם האצילות" או בשם "עולם התיקון".

114) We should understand why the three first levels of the world of AK are called Partzufim and not worlds. Why is the fourth level of AK called the world of Nikudim and the fifth – the world of Atzilut.

The first three levels of *AK*, called *Galgalta*, *AB* and *SAG*, are *Keter, Hochma*, and *Bina*. Why is the fourth *Partzuf* (if it is just ZA with the *Aviut Aleph*) called "the world of *Nikudim*" and the fifth (having only *Aviut Shoresh*) – "the world of *Atzilut*"?

The dot is the light of *Malchut* in the *Kli de Keter*. The creation's task is to expand this dot to the size of a complete, fully corrected *Partzuf* of *Adam haRishon*. The preparation stages are:

1. The outer body is similar to our material *(Homer)*, "the dust of the earth", i.e., the egoistic desire to receive pleasure.
2. Reaching the level of *"Nefesh-Ruach"* in the worlds *Yetzira* and *Assiya* and then *"Neshama"* in the world *Beria*.
3. Reaching the levels *"Nefesh-Ruach-Neshama"* in the world of *Atzilut*.
4. As a result of the "Sin", *Malchut* falls from the world of *Atzilut* to the worlds of *BYA* and acquires the properties "the dust of the earth", loses all its achievements in the world of *Atzilut*, and retains only the point of *Keter*.
5. The broken soul split into 600,000 fragments, from which our souls were formed.
6. Thus, the *Behina Dalet*, i.e., *Adam HaRishon*, emerged to begin correcting the intention.

קטן) וצריכים לידע ההפרש מפרצוף לעולם. והוא, כי בשם פרצוף נקרא כל קומת ע"ס, היוצאת על המסך דגוף דעליון, אחר שנזדכך ונכלל בפה דראש דעליון (אות נ). שאחר יציאתו מהראש דעליון, הוא מתפשט בעצמו לרת"ס. גם יש בו ה' קומות זה למטה מזה, הנקראות "טעמים" ו"נקודות" (אות מ"ז). אמנם נקרא רק על שם קומת הטעמים שבו.

ועד"ז יצאו ג' פרצופים הראשונים דא"ק: גלגלתא, ע"ב, ס"ג (אות מ"ז). אבל "עולם" פירושו, שהוא כולל כל מה שנמצא בעולם העליון ממנו, כעין חותם ונחתם, שכל מה שיש בחותם עובר כולו על הנחתם ממנו.

115) We should know the difference between a Partzuf and a world. A Partzuf is any level consisting of ten Sefirot, which emerge as a result of Zivug with the Masach de Guf of the upper Partzuf upon the weakening of the Masach, and its merging with the Masach in the Peh de Rosh of the upper Partzuf. When it emerges from the Rosh of the upper Partzuf, it spreads to the Rosh, the Toch and the Sof and has 5 levels, one under the other, called the Ta'amim and the Nekudot. However, it receives its name only from the Ta'amim.

Similarly, the three first Partzufim, Galgalta, AB and SAG of the world of AK, emerged and received names from their Ta'amim, Keter, Hochma and Bina. As far as the worlds are concerned, each consecutive world contains all that was in the preceding one, the way an imprint is the copy of a seal.

The entire Torah is constructed from the Creator's names. Each time man rises to a certain spiritual level and is filled with a certain kind of light, he feels this level and gives it a corresponding name, which he himself receives too. The *Masach* and the *Ohr Hozer* are called *"Milluy"* (filling), since the light filling the vessel depends on it.

קטז) ולפי זה תבין, שג' פרצופים הראשונים גלגלתא ע"ב ס"ג דא"ק, נבחנים רק לעולם אחד, דהיינו עולם הא"ק, שיצא בצמצום הראשון. אבל פרצוף הד' דא"ק, שבו נעשה ענין הצמצום ב', נעשה לעולם בפני עצמו, מטעם הכפילות שנעשה במסך דנקודות דס"ג בירידתו למטה מטבור דא"ק. כי נכפל עליו גם העביות דבחי"ד, בסוד ה"ת בעינים (אות ס"ג).

אשר בעת גדלות חזרה הבחי"ד למקומה לפה, והוציאה קומת כתר (אות פ"ד). ונמצאת קומה זו נשתוה לפרצוף הא' דא"ק. ואחר שנתפשט לרת"ס בטעמים ובנקודות, יצא עליו פרצוף ב' בקומת חכמה, הנקרא ישסו"ת. והוא דומה לפרצוף ב' דא"ק, הנקרא ע"ב דא"ק. ואחר התפשטותו לטעמים ונקודות, יצא פרצוף ג', הנקרא מ"ה דנקודים (אות קי"א). והוא דומה לפרצוף ג' דא"ק.

הרי שיצא כאן בעולם הנקודים כל מה שהיה בעולם א"ק, דהיינו ג' פרצופים. זה תחת זה. שבכל אחד מהם טעמים ונקודות וכל מקריהם, בדומה לג' פרצופים גלגלתא ע"ב ס"ג דא"ק שבעולם הא"ק. וע"כ נבחן עולם הנקודים, שהוא נחתם מעולם הא"ק. ונקרא משום זה עולם שלם בפני עצמו. (ומה שג' פרצופי נקודים אינם נקראים גלגלתא-ע"ב-ס"ג אלא ע"ב-ס"ג-מ"ה, הוא מטעם שהבחי"ד שנתחברה במסך דס"ג אין עביותה שלמה, מפאת מקרה ההזדככות שהיה מכבר בפרצוף הא' דא"ק. וע"כ ירדו לבחינת ע"ב ס"ג מ"ה).

116) As was already stated, the Partzufim of the world of AK, Galgalta, AB and SAG, are called by one common name, AK. They emerged in accordance with TA. However, the fourth Partzuf (in which TB occurred) is called the world, because when Nekudot de SAG descended under the Tabur, they acquired the additional Reshimot Dalet/Gimel.

During Gadlut, Behina Dalet returned to its place in the Peh de Rosh; the level of Keter emerged there, very similar to the first Partzuf of the world of AK. Then it spread to the Rosh, the Toch and the Sof, the Ta'amim and the Nekudot. The Partzuf Bet with the level of Hochma, called YESHSUT, follows. It is similar to the Partzuf AB de AK. Then the third Partzuf of the world of Nikudim arises. All three Partzufim stand one above the other; each has the Ta'amim and the Nekudot and all that is found in the three Partzufim of AK.

Hence, Olam HaNikudim is considered an imprint, a mould of the world of AK and is called the world. The three Partzufim of the world of Nikudim should rather be called not Galgalta, AB and SAG, but AB, SAG and MA, since the Nekudot de SAG received only Dalet/Gimel (not Dalet/Dalet, which was in the Galgalta before the light was expelled) from the NHYM de Galgalta. That is why the first Partzuf of the world of Nikudim (it adopted these Reshimot from the Nekudot de SAG and would later pass them on to the world of Atzilut) corresponds to AB (the Reshimot Dalet/Gimel and not Dalet/Dalet).

קיז) והנה נתבאר איך עולם הנקודים נחתם מעולם הא"ק. ועד"ז נחתם פרצוף הה' דא"ק, דהיינו המ"ה החדש, שנחתם כולו מעולם הנקודים. באופן שכל הבחינות ששמשו בנקודים, אע"פ שנשברו ונתבטלו שם, מכל מקום חזרו כולם ונתחדשו במ"ה החדש.

וע"כ הוא נקרא עולם בפני עצמו. ונקרא "עולם האצילות", מטעם שנסתיים כולו למעלה מפרסא, שנתקנה בצמצום ב'. ונקרא ג"כ "עולם התיקון", מטעם שעולם הנקודים לא נתקיים, כי היה בו ביטול ושבירה. אלא אחר כך במ"ה החדש, שחזרו כל הבחינות ההם, שהיו בעולם הנקודים, ובאו במ"ה החדש, הנה נתקנו שם ונתקיימו. וע"כ נקרא "עולם התיקון". כי באמת הוא עולם הנקודים עצמו, אלא שמקבל כאן במ"ה החדש את תיקונו משלם. כי ע"י מ"ה

החדש חוזרים ומתחברים לג"ר כל אלו האחורים שנפלו לגוף מן או"א וישסו"ת, וכן הפנים ואחורים דכל הז"ת, שנפלו לבי"ע ומתו, חוזרים ועולים על ידו לאצילות.

117) We know that the world of Nikudim is an imprint of the world of AK. Similarly, the fifth Partzuf de AK (MA Hadash) was formed. It is considered an exact copy of the world of Nikudim in the sense that all the Behinot used in Nikudim that broke and disappeared there were renewed and reconstructed in MA Hadash.

This world is also considered independent and is called Atzilut. Its position is between the Parsa (formed after TB) and the Tabur. It is also called the world of Correction. After the world of Nikudim broke and disappeared, the world of Atzilut was formed from the same broken Behinot. Thus, the world of Nikudim gets corrected with the help of MA Hadash, where all the AHP's that fell into the Guf de Abba ve Ima and the YESHSUT gather and return to Gar. All the Panim and Achoraim of all the Zat, which fell into the BYA and died, now return and ascend to Atzilut with the help of MA Hadash.

The *Tabur* is an imaginary line above which the light of *Hochma* may be received. Under the *Tabur*, there is no screen so far, so reception is forbidden. The *Parsa* is also an imaginary line; the vessels of bestowal (*GE*) that require no light of *Hochma* are above it, while the vessels of reception are below it and may not receive the light of *Hochma*.

The world of *Atzilut* is between the *Tabur de Galgalta* and the *Parsa*. It is the world of Correction and has in it the *Ohr Hochma*. How can that be? This world elevates the fallen vessels of reception, attaches them to the vessels of bestowal, and fills them with the light of *Hochma*. This action takes place gradually. As soon as the *AHP* of all levels ascend to *Atzilut*, the state called *Gmar Tikkun* or the 7th millennium will be achieved.

Then there are also the 8th, 9th and 10th millennia, when the *AHP* start to be filled with light under the *Parsa* as well. When the world of *Atzilut* lowers the *AHP* to the place of the world of *Beria*, the 8th millennium will come. The *AHP de Atzilut* in *Yetzira* will mark the 9th millennium and the *AHP de Atzilut* in *Assiya* will mark the 10th millennium.

Then absolutely every vessel will be filled with light in accordance with the Purpose of Creation. However, the *Gmar Tikkun* is 6000 levels, all that we can correct by ourselves, whereas further correction will come with the help of the light of *Mashiach*.

קיח) וטעם הדברים, כי כל פרצוף תחתון חוזר וממלא הכלים דעליון, אחר הסתלקות אורותיהם בעת הזדככות המסך. כי אחר הסתלקות האורות דגוף דפרצוף הא' דא"ק, מפאת הזדככות המסך, קבל המסך זווג חדש בקומת ע"ב, אשר חזר ומילא הכלים הריקים דגוף דעליון, דהיינו דפרצוף הא'.

וכן אחר הסתלקות האורות דגוף דע"ב, מפאת הזדככות המסך, קבל המסך זווג חדש בקומת ס"ג, שחזר ומילא הכלים הריקים דעליון, שהוא ע"ב. וכן אחר הסתלקות האורות דס"ג, מפאת הזדככות המסך, קבל המסך זווג חדש בקומת מ"ה, שיצא מנקבי עינים, שהם הנקודים, שחזר ומילא את הכלים הריקים דעליון, שהוא הנקודות דס"ג.

וממש עד"ז, אחר הסתלקות האורות דנקודים, מחמת ביטול האחורים ושבירת הכלים, קבל המסך זווג חדש בקומת מ"ה, שיצא מהמצח דפרצוף ס"ג דא"ק, וממלא את הכלים הריקים דגוף דעליון, שהם הכלים דנקודים שנתבטלו ונשברו.

118) Each lower Partzuf returns and fills the vessels of the upper one after the expulsion of the light from it. When the light disappeared from the body of the first Partzuf de AK, due to the weakening of its screen, a new Zivug was made in the screen on the level of AB.Then it returned and filled the empty vessels of the upper Partzuf.

After the expulsion of the light from the body of Partzuf AB, because of the screen weakening, a new Zivug was made in the screen on the level of SAG, which returned and filled the empty vessels of Partzuf AB. After the expulsion of the light from the body of Partzuf SAG, due to the weakening of the screen, a new Zivug was made in the screen on the level of MA, which emerged from Nikvey Eynaim and filled the empty vessels of SAG.

Similarly, after the expulsion of the light from the world of Nikudim, due to the disappearance of the Achoraim and the breaking of the vessels, a new Zivug made in the screen on the level of MA, emerged from the Metzah of Partzuf SAG de AK and filled the empty vessels of the world of Nikudim, which broke and disappeared.

We have always studied the development of creation "from above". The Creator created the only creation – *Malchut* of the World of Infinity. It constitutes the unity of all desires (vessels) and pleasures (the light). Whatever happens afterwards is just a sequence of various intentions *Malchut* uses in order to fill itself. We learn that *Malchut* gradually begins to move away from the Creator to become fully independent of Him.

Malchut stops feeling the Creator, coarsens, transforms its properties into egoistic ones and becomes opposite to the Creator, infinitely remote from Him. When the process of evolution reaches its lowest point, the creation is ready to begin the reverse process – gradual advancement towards the Creator.

Each higher *Partzuf* is nearer to perfection that the previous one, has a stronger screen, and is closer to the Creator. How can it be that each consecutive *Partzuf* fills the preceding one with light, although it is weaker? Does it not originate from it? It fills the preceding *Partzuf* by demanding to be filled.

When the *Partzuf Galgalta* completely expels the light, its *Masach de Guf* merges with the *Masach de Rosh* and the lower level of *Aviut* disappears. A new *Partzuf* is born and demands strength from the previous in order to fill itself with the light. To receive such light, the preceding *Partzuf* has to make a *Zivug de Haka'a* with the light of Infinity, decrease the intensity of this light by one degree to pass it to the lower level, which feels it in the *Rosh* and perceives it as the light of the World of Infinity.

For instance, *Malchut* of the world of *Assiya* sees the light diminished 125 times in its *Rosh*, but perceives it as the light of the World of Infinity, although it passed through all 125 degrees of weakening. *Malchut* perceives it as absolute Infinity. The filling of the preceding *Partzuf* happens through the consecutive *Partzuf's* desire to be filled with the light of the preceding one.

When *SAG* asks *AB* to fill it with the light, *AB*, having nothing, turns to *Galgalta*, which has nothing else to do but to ask *Malchut* of The

World of Infinity for the light. Why is it so? We say that the entire light is in the *Rosh de Galgalta*. It is really so, but it must now give SAG the appropriate light of *Bina*. Therefore, *Galgalta* turns to *Malchut* of The World of Infinity, or, rather, to its *Behina Bet*, which corresponds to the light of *Bina*. It passes this light first through *Bina de Galgalta*, then through *Bina de AB* and only then to the *Rosh de SAG*.

Overall, there are five *Partzufim* and five lights. The *Partzuf* receives each light from *Malchut* of the World of Infinity, or, rather, from one of its *Sefirot*. Any *Bina* of any *Partzuf* or world can receive the light of *Bina* only through all *Binot* of all the *Partzufim* and worlds preceding it. The other *Sefirot* – *Keter*, *Hochma*, ZA and *Malchut* – receive the light by including themselves in the desires of the requesting vessel. The consecutive *Partzuf* complements the preceding one with the desires (the vessels), while the preceding *Partzuf* fills these desires with the light.

The lower *Partzuf* always turns to the upper, from which it originated. The *Partzuf AB* emerges from *Hochma de Galgalta* and is connected with *Galgalta* only through Hochma. *Galgalta* turns to the *Sefirat Hochma* of *Malchut* of the World of Infinity, receives *Ohr Hochma*, but cannot pass it to *AB*. It must transform it into *Ohr Hochma* that would suit *AB*, and only then pass it on to it.

The smallest, but true request of the tiniest *Partzuf* fills all the worlds up to *Galgalta* with the light. At that, the higher the *Partzuf* is, the more light it receives. Therefore, being filled with the light, the Tree of Life is revived by the raised *MAN*.

קיט) אמנם יש הפרש גדול כאן במ"ה החדש. כי הוא נעשה לבחינת דכר ובחינת עליון להכלים דנקודים, שהוא מתקן אותם. משא"כ בפרצופים הקודמים, אין התחתון נעשה לדכר ולעליון אל הכלים דגוף דעליון, אע"פ שהוא ממלא אותם ע"י קומתו.

והשינוי הזה הוא, כי בפרצופים הקודמים לא היה שום פגם בהסתלקות האורות, כי רק הזדככות המסך גרם להסתלקותם.

אבל כאן בעולם הנקודים, היה פגם בהכלים. כי כח מלכות המסיימת היה מעורב בהכלים דאחורים דז"ת. ואינם ראוים לקבל האורות. שמסבה זו נשברו ומתו ונפלו לבי"ע. לפיכך הם תלויים לגמרי במ"ה החדש: להחיותם, לבררם, ולהעלותם לאצילות. ומתוך זה נחשב המ"ה

החדש לבחינת זכר ומשפיע. ואלו הכלים דנקודים הנבררים על ידו נעשו בחינת נוקבא אל המ"ה. ולכן נשתנה שמם לשם ב"ן. כלומר שנעשו בחינת תחתון אל המ"ה. ואע"פ שהם עליון למ"ה החדש, כי הם כלים מעולם הנקודים ובחינת מ"ה ונקבי עינים, שבחינה עליונה שבו הוא ר"ק דס"ג דא"ק (אות ע"ד), מ"מ נעשו עתה לתחתון אל המ"ה החדש. ונקרא ב"ן מטעם האמור.

119) However, there is a fundamental distinction in MA Hadash, called the world of Atzilut. It consists in the fact that, being the Partzuf that follows the world of Nikudim, it affects and corrects all of its vessels. However, in the previous Partzufim, each lower one could not influence the Kelim de Guf of the upper one, even though it filled them with the light of its level.

This change in MA happened because the power of Malchut restricting the light in the world of Nikudim intervened with the AHP de Zat. This led to the loss of the screen, expulsion of the light, breaking of the vessels, their death and fall into BYA. In the previous Partzufim, there was no "spoiling" of the vessels during the light expulsion, which was connected exclusively with the weakening of the screen and its rising to the Rosh of the Partzuf.

However, here in the world of Nikudim, the vessels become spoiled and their existence now depends on the world of Atzilut, which has power to correct and lift them up. Hence, the world of Atzilut is considered new and bestowing (Zachar) as regards the vessels of the world of Nikudim (Nekeva in regards to it); hence, they change their name from Nikudim (the Aviut of MA) to BON, i.e., they descend below MA Hadash.

The world of *Nikudim* emerged on the *Masach* in *Nikvey Eynaim (Bina de Hochma)*; the world of *Atzilut* emerged on the *Masach* in *Nikvey Eynaim de Metzah (Bina de Keter)* of the *Rosh de* SAG. The world of *Nikudim* was supposed to be MA and *Atzilut* – *BON*, but owing to the breaking of the vessels, they switch places: *Atzilut* becomes MA, while the broken vessels of *Nikudim*, which it attaches to itself, become the *BON*.

FIVE PARTZUFIM OF THE WORLD OF ATZILUT, MA AND BON IN EACH PARTZUF
ה״פ אצילות וענין מ״ה וב״ן שבכל פרצוף

קכ) ונתבאר, שקומת מ"ה החדש נתפשטה ג"כ לעולם שלם בפני עצמו כמו עולם הנקודים.

120) Now, the MA Hadash turned into an independent world like the Nikudim.

Each *Partzuf* in the world of *AK* emerged on one pair of *Reshimot* (e.g. *Dalet/Dalet* etc.). As was already stated, the *Nekudot de SAG* under the *Tabur* also received *Reshimot Dalet/Gimel* from the *NHYM de Galgalta* in addition to those upon which this *Partzuf* emerged.

Thus, there are two kinds of *Reshimot* under the *Tabur*: the *Bet de Hitlabshut – Aleph de Aviut*, and *Dalet de Hitlabshut – Gimel de Aviut*. The first brought forth the world of *Nikudim* in *Katnut*, whereas the second gave rise to a series of *Partzufim* similar to *AB-SAG*. The world of *Atzilut* emerged on *Aleph de Hitlabshut and Shoresh de Aviut*, although the *Reshimo Dalet-Gimel* remains.

Therefore, a second desire emerges in the *Masach*, which also rises to the *Rosh de SAG*: to receive light from *Dalet-Gimel*. Therefore, as with the world *Nikudim*, *Atzilut* also initially emerges in *Katnut*, and then wants to pass to *Gadlut*.

וטעם הדבר הוא, כמו שנתבאר בקומת הנקודים, שהוא מכח כפילות המסך גם מבחי"ד (אות קט"ז). כי הגם שהארת הזו"ן דא"ק שהאיר דרך הטבור והיסוד לג"ר דנקודים החזירה הצמצום א' למקומו, וה"ת ירדה מנקבי עינים לפה, שעי"ז יצאו כל אלו הקומות דגדלות נקודים (אות ק"א), אמנם כל אלו הקומות חזרו ונתבטלו ונשברו, וכל האורות נסתלקו. וע"כ חזר הצמצום ב' למקומו. והבחי"ד חזרה ונתחברה במסך.

The luminescence of ZON de AK through the Tabur and Yesod in the Gar de Nikudim returned Malchut from Bina to its place, i.e., from the Nikvey Eynaim to the Peh. Thus, all levels of the world of Nikudim emerged in Gadlut, but later, as we know, they disap-

peared, broke, and the light exited them. TB returned to its place; Behina Dalet joined the Masach.

The state of *Gadlut*, which happened in the world of *Nikudim*, also took place in *Atzilut*, although according to the laws that prevented the vessels from breaking.

קכא) ולפיכך גם במ"ה החדש, שיצא מהמצח, נוהג ג"כ ב' בחינות קטנות וגדלות, כמו בעולם הנקודים. אשר תחילה יוצאת הקטנות, דהיינו לפי העביות המגולה במסך, שהוא: קומת ז"א דהתלבשות, המכונה חג"ת, וקומת מלכות דעביות, הנקרא נה"י. מטעם ג' הקוין, שנעשה בקומת מלכות: שקו ימין נקרא "נצח", וקו שמאל נקרא "הוד", וקו אמצעי "יסוד". אמנם כיון שאין מבחי"א רק בחינת התלבשות, בלי עביות, ע"כ אין בה כלים. ונמצאה קומת חג"ת בלי כלים. והיא מתלבשת בכלים דנה"י. וקומה זו נקראת "עובר". שפירושו, שאין שם אלא שיעור עביות דשורש, שנשאר במסך אחר הזדככותו, בעת עליתו לזווג במצח דעליון. שקומה, היוצאת שם, היא רק קומת מלכות. אמנם בפנימיותה יש בחינת ה"ת בגניזו. והוא בחינת ה"ת במצח. ואחר שהעובר מקבל הזווג בעליון, יורד משם למקומו (אות נ"ד). ואז מקבל מוחין דיניקה מהעליון, שהם עביות דבחי"א, בבחינת ה"ת בנקבי עינים. ועי"ז קונה כלים גם לחג"ת, מתפשטים החג"ת מתוך הנה"י. ויש לו קומת ז"א.

121) Therefore, as in the world of Nikudim, the two forces also rule in MA Hadash, which emerged from Metzah: Katnut and Gadlut, i.e., first Katnut on Hitlabshut Aleph (ZA,) called the HaGaT, and Malchut (Shoresh) de Aviut, called NHY, due to the appearance of "three lines" in it. The three lines are the right line (Netzah), the left line (Hod) and the middle line (Yesod). However, since there is only the Behinat Hitlabshut without the Aviut in the Behina Aleph, it has no Kelim, so the level of the HaGaT, for the lack of its own vessels, uses the Kelim de NHY. Such a Partzuf is called Ubar (embryo). Then it grows to the Aviut Aleph and receives the name of Katan (small). Upon reaching the Aviut Gimel, it enters Gadlut.

There were only two states in the world of *Nikudim: Katnut* and *Gadlut*; and three – in *Atzilut*. *Gadlut* was instantly born in *AK*. The world of *Nikudim* is called ZA or the *HaGaT*; the world of *Atzilut* is first called *Ubar* or *NHY*, then *Katan* (ZA), or *HaGaT-NHY*. In *Gadlut*, it is called *HaBaD-HaGaT-NHY*, the *Aviut Bet-Gimel-Dalet*. When the *Partzuf* is born in the state of *Ubar*, it has *Aviut de Shoresh*, the vessel of *Keter* and the lights *Nefesh* and *Ruach*.

So where is *Ohr Ruach*? It turns out to be together with *Ohr Nefesh*. However, it is true that *Malchut* hides inside the *Ubar*, for *Reshimo Dalet-Gimel*, on which a *Zivug* was not made, is still there. Later on, in the state of *Aviut de Shoresh*, the *Ubar* receives light from the previous *Partzuf* and grows to *Aviut Aleph*, while the screen descends from the *Metzah* to *Nikvey Eynaim (de Eynaim)*. The *Partzuf* in this state is called *Katan*. If the screen descends lower, the *Partzuf* will be in *Gadlut*, gradually passing from *Aviut Bet* to *Gimel* and then to *Dalet*.

When a *Partzuf* is born, it means that a screen is born, no more. Desires are created by the Creator, while the light preceded the desires. Now only the intention to receive for the sake of the Creator is brought forth. The screen is an inversion of what I may do with the pleasure I can feel. The entire ladder, from us to the Creator, is graduated in accordance with the screens – from 0%, the lowest level, up to 100%, the highest level. The *Partzuf* is a measure of the screen's reaction to the Upper Light. After its birth, the *Partzuf* instantly descends to its place according to its screen. In *TB*, only *GE* (the vessels of bestowal) are used in all the states of the *Partzuf* from *Shoresh* to *Dalet*.

קכב) והנה אח"ז עולה פעם ב' למ"ן להעליון. ונקרא "עיבור ב"". ומקבל שם מוחין מע"ב ס"ג דא"ק. ואז יורדת הבחי"ד מנקבי עינים למקומה לפה (אות ק"א). ואז נעשה הזווג על בחי"ד במקומה. ויוצאות ע"ס בקומת כתר. והכלים דאח"פ מתעלים וחוזרים למקומם בראש. ונשלם הפרצוף בע"ס דאורות וכלים. ואלו המוחין נקראים "מוחין דגדלות" של הפרצוף. וזהו קומת פרצוף הא' דאצילות, הנקרא "פרצוף הכתר" או "פרצוף עתיק" דאצילות.

122) After its birth in Katnut, the Partzuf raises MAN for the second time in the Rosh de SAG, and is called the Ibur Bet (the 2nd conception). There it receives Mochin, i.e., the light AB-SAG of the world of AK. Then Behina Dalet descends from Nikvey Eynaim to its place in Peh de Rosh. A Zivug on Behina Dalet gives birth to 10 Sefirot de Keter. The vessels of AHP return to its place in the Rosh. Thus, the Partzuf is extended to 10 Sefirot (both the vessels and the lights). This light is called the Mochin de Gadlut of the Partzuf. This is how the first Partzuf of the world of Atzilut, called Keter or Atik de Atzilut, emerged.

The name *Atik* derives from the word "*Ne'etak*", i.e., isolated from the rest of the lower *Partzufim*. It is a kind of intermediary between the worlds of *AK* and *Atzilut*. *Atik* works according to the laws of *TA*, but dresses in "*Searot*" (the outer *Partzufim*), which is already in *Rosh de SAG* and is perceived by other *Partzufim* as the *Partzuf* that exists according to the laws of *TB*. Concerning *Galgalta*, the *Atik* is on the level of *Hochma*, since it emerges on *Reshimo Dalet-Gimel*. This corresponds to the *Partzuf AB (Hochma de Galgalta)*. As regards the world of *Atzilut*, it is the first *Partzuf* of the level of *Keter*, which initiates the entire network of *Partzufim* of the world of *Atzilut*, to which it will bestow.

In fact, *Keter de Atzilut* is not *Atik*, which is so isolated and concealed that it is practically unable to contact any other *Partzuf*. It passes its functions to the second *Partzuf* of the world of *Atzilut* –*Arich Anpin*, which is in fact *Keter* and carries out all corrections of the vessels.

Four out of 6 volumes of "The Study of the Ten Sefirot" speak about the world of *Atzilut*. The general control of the entire Universe, the connection between the souls and the Creator, originates there. Almost nothing is said about *Atik*, since it, as it were, has nothing to do with the world of *Atzilut*. Actually, *Atzilut* begins with *Arich Anpin*, which, as regards all the other *Partzufim*, plays the role of *Galgalta* of the world of *AK*. All the *Partzufim* of the world of *Atzilut* are also dressed on it.

קכג) וכבר ידעת, שאחר שביה"כ חזרו ונפלו כלהו אח"פ מהמדרגות, כל אחד למדרגה שמתחתיו (אות ע"ז, ק"ו). ונמצאים אח"פ דקומת כתר דנקודים בגו"ע דקומה חכמה. ואח"פ דקומת חכמה בגו"ע דקומת בינה, וכו'. ולפיכך בעת העיבור ב' דגדלות דפרצוף הא' דאצילות, הנקרא "עתיק", שחזרו ונתעלו האח"פ שלו, הנה עלו עמהם יחד גם הגו"ע דקומת חכמה. ונתקנו יחד עם האח"פ דקומת עתיק. וקבלו שם עיבור הא'.

123) You already know that, after the breaking of the vessels, all the AHP fell again from their level to the one below. The AHP of Keter de Nikudim is now on the level of the GE de Hochma. The AHP of Hochma is on the level of GE de Bina, and so on. Now, during Ibur Bet, i.e., in Gadlut of the Partzuf Atik, its AHP rose, with GE de Hochma, and was corrected together. The GE de Hochma reached Behinat Ibur Aleph.

When a *Partzuf* is born in *Katnut*, its *AHP* do not receive the light and are inside GE of the lower level. As the upper *Partzuf* starts lifting its *AHP* and filling them with the light, the *Reshimot* GE of the lower still unborn *Partzuf* rise together with them. The *AHP* of the upper *Partzuf* prepare a place for the birth of this *Partzuf*. The upper *Partzuf* passes through *Ibur Bet*, while GE of the lower *Partzuf* pass through *Ibur Aleph*.

Thus, the fall of each *AHP* by one level created an opportunity, with their return to the original level, to elevate and correct GE of the lower level, in other words, their fall allowed GE of the lower *Partzuf* to enter *Ibur Aleph*, while the upper *Partzuf* entered *Ibur Bet*.

After the breaking of the vessels in the world of *Nikudim*, the egoistic desires without a screen (*Reshimot*) remained. They cannot come out of that state by themselves. Because there are *Reshimot* of the GE of the following *Partzuf* in all the fallen *AHP*, it becomes possible to correct the GE of the lower *Partzuf* during the rise and correction of the *AHP*. The miracle of *TB* and the breaking of the vessels lie in this process.

קכד) ואחר שהגו"ע דחכמה קבלו קומת העיבור והיניקה שלהם (אות קכ"א), חזרו ועלו לראש דעתיק. וקבלו שם עיבור ב' שלהם למוחין דגדלות. וירדה הבחי"ג למקומה לפה. ויצאו עליה ע"ס בקומת חכמה. והכלים דאח"פ שלהם חזרו ועלו למקומם בראש. ונשלם פרצוף החכמה בע"ס דאורות וכלים. ופרצוף זה נקרא פרצוף "אריך אנפין" דאצילות.

124) After the GE de Hochma pass through the Ibur and the Yenika (Ibur Aleph, Katnut), Hochma passes to Ibur Bet, so as to receive Mochin de Gadlut. Then Behina Gimel descends to the Peh de Rosh, and a Zivug on it forms all the 10 Sefirot de Hochma; its AHP rises and accomplishes this level. In this way, the Gadlut of the second Partzuf de Atzilut, called the Arich Anpin, emerged.

The transition to *Gadlut* happens with the help of the light *AB-SAG*, which allows the acquisition of a screen and begins to work with the vessels of reception (the *AHP). Arich Anpin* means a long face. *Hochma* symbolizes a face. "Long" suggests that there is a lot of *Ohr Hochma* in *Arich Anpin*, unlike in *ZA* (small face), where there is just a little *Ohr Hochma*. When the creation begins to understand the Creator's greatness with the help of the light *AB-SAG*, it starts working with the previously unused vessels of reception.

קכה) ועם אח"פ הללו דא"א עלו ביחד גם גו"ע דקומת בינה. וקבלו שם עיבור הא' ויניקה שלהם. ואח"ז עלו לראש דא"א לעיבור ב'. והעלו האח"פ שלהם וקבלו המוחין דגדלות. ונשלם פרצוף הבינה בע"ס דאורות וכלים. ופרצוף זה נקרא או"א וישסו"ת. כי הג"ר נקראות או"א, והז"ת נקראות ישסו"ת.

125) The vessels of GE de Bina rose together with the AHP de Arich Anpin and received Ibur Aleph and Yenika there. Then they rose to the Rosh de Arich Anpin for Ibur Bet, lifted their AHP and received Mochin de Gadlut. Next, the Partzuf of Bina began using all of its 10 Sefirot, both the vessels and the lights. This third Partzuf of the world of Atzilut is called Abba ve Ima and YESHSUT, where Abba ve Ima are Gar de Bina and YESHSUT is Zat de Bina.

GE has *Aviut Shoresh* and *Aleph*. When the *Partzuf* passes all the stages of the screen's formation, *Shoresh, Aleph, Bet, Gimel* and *Dalet* of the *Aviut de Shoresh*, it constitutes conception. Then the screen emerges on *Shoresh, Aleph, Bet, Gimel*, and *Dalet* of *Aviut de Aleph*. This is the *Yenika* and the birth of the *Partzuf* in *Katnut*, i.e., the use of only the *GE* (the *Aviut Shoresh* and *Aleph*). Then this *Partzuf* rises again to the *Rosh* of the previous one. This is a stage of *Ibur Bet* (the second conception). Then, it lifts its *AHP* and receives *Mochin de Gadlut*, i.e., the full 10 *Sefirot*.

קכו) ועם אח"פ הללו דאו"א עלו ביחד גם גו"ע דזו"ן. וקבלו שם העיבור א' שלהם והיניקה. ובזה נשלמים הזו"ן בבחינת ו"ק לז"א ונקודה להנוקבא. והנה נתבארו ה"פ מ"ה החדש, שיצאו בעולם האצילות בבחינת קביעות, הנקראים עתיק א"א או"א וזו"ן.

שעתיק יצא בקומת כתר, וא"א בקומת חכמה, ואו"א בקומת בינה, וזו"ן בו"ק ונקודה, שהוא קומת ז"א. ובאלו ה' הקומות לא יארע שום מיעוט לעולם. כי בג"ר אין מעשי התחתונים מגיעים אליהם, שיוכלו לפוגמם. וז"א ונוקבא, שאליהם מגיעים מעשי התחתונים, היינו דוקא בכלים דאחורים שלהם, שמשיגים בעת הגדלות. אבל בכלים דפנים, שהם גו"ע באורות דו"ק ונקודה, הנה גם בהם לא יגיעו מעשי התחתונים. ולפיכך נבחנים ה' הקומות הנ"ל לבחינת מוחין הקבועים באצילות.

126) GE de ZON rose together with AHP de Abba ve Ima and YESHSUT and received Ibur Aleph and Yenika there. Thus, the Partzuf ZON was completed and reached the level of Vak de ZA and Nekudah de Nukvah. So all five Partzufim of the world of MA Hadash or Atzilut are in its minimal state: Atik, Arich Anpin, Abba ve Ima and ZON.

The Partzuf Atik emerged on the level of Keter, Arich Anpin – on the level of Hochma; Abba ve Ima is on the level of Bina and the ZON is on the level of Vak and Nekudah, i.e., ZA and Malchut. There cannot be any descent of these five levels. No actions of the lower Partzufim can reach Atik, Arich Anpin and Abba ve Ima, so they are unable to spoil them. As far as ZA and Nukvah are concerned, as they achieve Gadlut, the actions of the lower spiritual objects (the souls) can reach only their AHP, but not their GE.

The lower objects are the souls in the *AHP de ZON* of the world of *Atzilut*. They cannot correct themselves, but can raise MAN to *ZON de Atzilut*, which raise their *AHP*. As MAN makes a *Zivug* on them, it simultaneously gives birth to *Katnut* of the particular soul.

The task consists in providing the broken vessels with a new screen and gradually filling them with light. This work is carried out from down up. It starts with the less egoistic vessels and ends with the coarsest and most egoistic, i.e., proceeds from the easy-to-correct vessels to the most difficult. The work begins with the birth of the world of *Atzilut*.

After the vessels break, the screen ascends to *Rosh de* SAG and makes a *Zivug de Haka'a* on the purest *Reshimot*, which results in the emergence of the first *Partzuf Atik*. Then *Atik* makes a *Zivug* on the purest *Reshimot*, which leads to the emergence of *Arich Anpin*. *Arich Anpin* takes the purest of the remaining *Reshimot* and makes a *Zivug* on them, which creates the *Partzuf Abba ve Ima*. From the remaining *Reshimot*, *Abba ve Ima* create the ZON.

After that, a *Zivug* could be made on no more pure *Reshimot*. Only the *Reshimot* that can lead to *Katnut* of the world of *Atzilut* are activated. Similarly, *Katnut* of the world of *Nikudim* was created in its own time. These worlds resemble one another; the difference being that *Atzilut* is constructed so that the vessels in it cannot break.

Actually, there are 12 *Partzufim* in the world of *Atzilut*. Each of them is divided into two parts: up and down, left and right, etc. All these intermediate states are created for using the *AHP* to the maximum, correcting them without breaking the vessels.

How can the *AHP* be used after the breaking of the vessels, when they are forbidden to use? *TA* and *TB* must not be violated. However, *TA* is in effect forever, while *TB* - only during 6000 levels. The entire process of correction is controlled by *TB*. What is the meaning of *Tzimtzum Bet*? Out of five desires, only *Keter* and *Hochma*, which are almost unselfish, may be used. The three remaining desires, *Bina*, ZA, and *Malchut*, i.e., the *AHP*, are not to be used for their egoistic nature; they require great willpower, a very strong screen.

After *TB*, the *Kelim* that have no strength to work with the egoistic vessels emerge. Nevertheless, the desires do not disappear. It is only possible to forbid their use. The desires of *GE* may be used only within certain limits. When you are in *Katnut*, you do not receive anything and enjoy only the equivalence of properties with the Creator. You are similar to the Creator – that is a lot, but insufficient for fulfilling the Purpose of Creation, which is being filled with the light of *Hochma*. To achieve that, you need to have the vessels of reception. Such an opportunity is yet unavailable to you.

The only solution is to use the egoistic vessels of the *AHP*, including them in the altruistic *GE*. The vessels of *AHP* want to receive *Ohr Hochma* exclusively, which is forbidden. Only the light of *Hassadim* may be received. However, when the light of *Hochma* is pushed away, a small amount of it enters the vessels. The *AHP* may be used only if they are lifted above the *Parsa*. If all the *AHP* in the world of *Nikudim* were lifted above the *Parsa*, and the light of *Hochma* received in 10 Sefirot formed in this manner, the vessels would not have broken. The *AHP* can be lifted and filled with light only if this light will be passed on to the lower *Partzuf*. That is one of corrections made by the world of *Atzilut*.

Raising *MAN*, filling the lower *Partzufim* with light, in answer to a request for correction, corrects the broken vessels, from which they receive portions of the light. Thus, the system of spreading and receiving (Kabbalah) light emerges in the spiritual world. Similarly, one can come to reveal the Creator only in a group of those who wish to be corrected by joining the system of circulation of Kabbalah.

Desires are constant; they are our very essence created by the Creator. We cannot change ourselves, but we can modify our intentions. There is no need to work on actions, only on the intentions that accompany them. The purpose of your actions is either your own good feeling, the health of your family, money, or the reward to be received from the Creator in the world to come – all this remains within the limits of your egoism.

It is a very different matter if the Creator endows you with an opportunity to realize His greatness to such an extent that, whatever you do, is only for His sake. This requires the Creator's revelation. Only constant, persistent, work with books and in a group under the guidance of a true Teacher can attract the Surrounding Light and lead to the Creator's revelation. The spiritual path does not begin with an action, but with inner reflection.

Nothing disappears in the spiritual realm. This rule applies to the souls. Today I am on a certain level, tomorrow I will pass to another. All my previous states are included in this new one. Today I can still remember what happened 20 years ago. The past states are rather lit up by today's condition. The light that shines in the present also fills the past.

In the *Gmar Tikkun*, all the previous states are condensed into one big *Partzuf* filled completely with light. All the successive vessels give additional desires to those preceding them so that each time they receive a more powerful light.

All the screens broke together with the vessels. During the correction, they start growing from zero to 100%. New desires for which you do not have a screen are added to provide for passage to the next level, whereas the previous one has exhausted itself. Such a state is called a fall. A moment ago, you were in a wonderful state, you had a screen, but now you "have fallen". You were given more egoistic desires; hence, you do not want anything spiritual.

In this state, some serious inner work must be done in order to acquire a new screen, which will allow you to receive an even more powerful light. The work on the screen consists only in active studies.

At the first encounter with "The Preamble to the Wisdom of Kabbalah", the human brain cannot comprehend all the information; it creates confusion, especially while studying the world of the *Nikudim*, then *Atzilut* and so on. One should stop for a while, contemplate about the things heard and perhaps review the previous chapters. Listening to audio cassettes is highly recommended. Gradually the material settles down and is absorbed, because building the spiritual vessels (and that is exactly what happens to you), requires time and efforts.

קכז) וסדר הלבשתם זא"ז ולפרצוף א"ק הוא, כי פרצוף עתיק דאצילות אע"פ שיצא מראש הס"ג דא"ק (אות קי"ח), מכל מקום לא יכול להלביש מפה ולמטה דס"ג דא"ק רק למטה מטבור. כי למעלה מטבור דא"ק הוא בחינת צמצום א', ונקרא "עקודים".

והן אמת, שפרצוף עתיק, להיותו בחינת ראש הא' דאצילות, עדיין אין הצמצום ב' שולט בו. וא"כ היה ראוי שילביש למעלה מטבור דא"ק. אמנם כיון שהצמצום ב' כבר נתקן בפה דראשו, בשביל שאר פרצופי אצילות, שממנו ולמטה, ע"כ אינו יכול להלביש רק למטה מטבור דא"ק.

ונמצא קומת עתיק מתחלת מטבור דא"ק. והיא מסתיימת בשוה עם רגלי א"ק, דהיינו למעלה מנקודה דעוה"ז. וזהו מפאת פרצופו עצמו. אמנם מפאת התקשרותו עם שאר פרצופי אצילות, שמבחינתם נבחן שהוא כלול ג"כ מצמצום ב', הנה מבחינה זו הוא נבחן שרגליו מסתיימים למעלה מפרסא דאצילות. כי הפרסא הוא הסיום החדש של הצמצום ב' (אות ס"ח).

127) The Partzufim "dress" one onto the other in the following way: although Atik de Atzilut emerged from the Rosh de SAG of the world of AK, it cannot dress onto SAG from the Peh to the Tabur, but only under the Tabur, since above it, the power of the TA rules entirely.

It is also known that the Partzuf Atik (its alternative name is Akudim) is essentially the first Rosh of the world of Atzilut, where the TB does not rule yet; so, in principle, it can dress onto the AK above the Tabur. However, TB comes into effect in the Rosh de Atik with regard to the subsequent Partzufim of Atzilut; hence, Atik dresses onto AK only under the Tabur.

The level of Atik stretches from the Tabur to the Sium de AK, i.e., above the point of our world. This refers to Atik itself. As far as its connection with the rest of the Partzufim of the world of Atzilut is concerned, it is considered to be ruled by TB; from this point of view its feet end above the Parsa de Atzilut (new Sium of TB).

Therefore, there are two kinds of *Atik*: one abides by the laws of *TA*, while the other obeys *TB*. All the other *Partzufim* of the world of *Atzilut* born after *Atik* submit to the laws of *TB*. *Atik* contains all information about all the *Partzufim* that follow it, down to our world.

All the *Partzufim* of the world of *Atzilut* emerged in the state of *Katnut*. They do not require the light of *Hochma*, although they can pass to *Gadlut* at any time, receive this light through a request of the lower *Partzufim*, and transfer it to them.

Out of all the *Reshimot* left from the breaking of the vessels, *Partzuf Atik* selects the purest, the best, and makes a *Zivug* on the level of *Keter*. As *Atik* reaches its ultimate state, it transfers only the *Ohr Hochma* and gives birth to the *Partzuf Arich Anpin*. Similarly, *Arich Anpin* chooses the purest *Reshimot* related to *Bina* and creates the *Partzuf Abba ve Ima*.

קכח) ופרצוף הב' דמ"ה החדש, הנקרא א"א, שהוא נאצל ויצא מפה דראש עתיק, הנה קומתו מתחיל ממקום יציאתו, דהיינו מפה דראש עתיק. ומלביש את הז"ת דעתיק, המסתיימים למעלה מפרסא דאצילות. ופרצוף הג', הנקרא או"א, שנאצלו מפה דראש א"א, הם מתחילים מפה דראש א"א ומסתיימים למעלה מטבור דא"א. והזו"ן מתחילים מטבור דא"א ומסתיימים בשוה עם סיום א"א, דהיינו למעלה מפרסא דאצילות.

128) The second Partzuf of the world of Atzilut is called Arich Anpin. It emerges from the Peh de Rosh of the Partzuf Atik and dresses onto its seven lower Sefirot, which end above the Parsa de Atzilut. The third Partzuf of the world of Atzilut, called Abba ve Ima, emerges from the Peh de Rosh of Arich Anpin and ends above the Tabur de Arich Anpin. The fourth and fifth Partzufim of the world of Atzilut, called ZON, stretch from the Tabur de Arich Anpin to the Sium de Arich Anpin, i.e., above the Parsa de Atzilut.

Atik emerges from the *Metzah* of *Rosh de SAG* and under the influence of *TA* spreads from the *Tabur de Galgalta* down to its *Sium*. *TA* can no longer affect the *Partzufim* of the world of *Atzilut*. *Atik* is created according to the laws of *TA*, since it receives light from the *Partzufim* of the world of *AK* (created according to the laws of *TA*), but it then transforms the light for the lower *Partzufim*, ruled by *TB*.

Arich Anpin, born from *Atik*, spreads from the *Peh de Rosh de Atik* down to the *Parsa*. The third *Partzuf* of the world of *Atzilut*, called *Abba ve Ima*, emerges from the *Peh de Rosh* of *Arich Anpin* and ends at the level of the *Tabur de Arich Anpin*. *Abba ve Ima*, i.e., *Bina de Atzilut*, gives birth to two *Partzufim* that can be viewed as one: *ZA* and *Malchut* or *ZON*. This *Partzuf* dresses onto *ZON de Arich Anpin* and reaches the *Parsa*.

Later on we will study how the world of *Atzilut* changes, affected by the upper and the lower spiritual objects. Stimulation from above is expressed in holidays, Sabbaths, the beginnings of months, which appear regardless of what happens below in the worlds of the *BYA*. Stimulation from below comes from the souls in the worlds of *BYA*, which demand from *Atzilut* to be elevated, corrected, and filled with light. In this case, *Atzilut* is obliged to react to the request from below. This reaction includes the reception of light from above and passing it on down.

As in the world of *Nikudim*, there are six upper *Sefirot* of ZA called *HaBaD-HaGaT* in *Atzilut be Katnut*. Only one *Sefira*, *Keter de Malchut*, is above the *Parsa*, while the three lower *Sefirot (NHY)* of ZA and nine lower *Sefirot* of *Malchut* (from *Hochma* to *Malchut de Malchut*) are under the *Parsa*.

As was already stated, *Malchut* did not have its own *Sefirot* before *TB*; it was just a point. Because of *TB*, *Malchut* rose and received all the *Sefirot* that are now below it (the lower third of *Tifferet*, *Netzah*, *Hod* and *Yesod*), turning into an independent *Partzuf*. Then, these four *Sefirot* are restructured into ten according to special laws.

A *Sefira* is a certain property of the Creator that *Malchut* takes as firm and unchanging. The *Sefira Da'at* is a request that ZA and *Malchut* raise to *Bina* in order to receive the *Ohr Hochma*. The *Sefira Da'at* has no constant place of its own; it constitutes the "desire to receive" *Ohr Hochma*, which *Bina* feels owing to the request of the *ZON*. As soon as ZA starts breaking up, its request to *Bina* gradually begins to subside: first, *Sefira Keter* is lost, then *Hochma* etc., until the last one finally disappears.

קכט) ותדע, שכל קומה וקומה מה"פ אלו דמ"ה החדש, בעת שיצאה, ביררה וחיברה לעצמה חלק מהכלים דנקודים, שנעשה לה לבחינת נוקבא: כי הנה בעת שיצא פרצוף עתיק, לקח וחיבר אליו כל הג"ר דנקודים, שנשארו שלמים בעת שביה"כ. דהיינו, בחינת הגו"ע שבהם, שיצאו בעת קטנותם, הנקראים "כלים דפנים" (אות ע"ו).

שבקטנות הנקודים לא באו עמהם רק מחציתה העליונה דכל מדרגה, שהם גו"ע ונקבי עינים. ומחציתה התחתונה דכל אחת, הנקראים אח"פ, ירדו למדרגה התחתונה. ולפיכך נבחן, שפרצוף עתיק דמ"ה החדש לקח לו מהכלים דנקודים את מחציתה העליונה דכתר, ומחציתה העליונה דחו"ב, וז' השרשים דז"ת הכלולים בג"ר דנקודים. והם נעשו לבחינת פרצוף נוקבא אל העתיק דמ"ה החדש. ונתחברו יחד זה בזה. והם המכונים "מ"ה וב"ן דעתיק דאצילות". כי הזכר דעתיק נקרא מ"ה, והכלים דנקודים שנתחברו אליו נקראים ב"ן (אות קי"ט). וסדר עמידתם הוא פו"א: העתיק דמ"ה בפנים והעתיק דב"ן באחוריו.

> *129) You should know that as each level of the five Partzufim of MA Hadash emerged, it sorted out and added a certain part of the Kelim de Nikudim, which became like a Nukvah (that, which asks to be filled with the light) as regards this particular level. Therefore, Atik attached all the Gar de Nikudim that remained intact upon breaking of the vessels, i.e., the GE, the upper halves of each level.*

Thus, the Partzuf Atik added to itself only the upper halves of Keter, Hochma and Bina (Abba ve Ima), and the seven Ketarim of the seven lower Sefirot. All the parts added to Atik received the names MA and BON de Atik de Atzilut. MA is the giving part in Atik called Zachar (male essence). BON is the receiving part in Atik called Nekeva (female essence). With regard to one another, they are Panim (Atik de MA – Ma de Atik) and Achoraim (Atik de BON and BON de Atik).

In general, all the *Partzufim* of the world of *Atzilut* are built similarly. All the vessels of *Atzilut* that emerged from a *Zivug* on *Reshimot Aleph/Shoresh*, i.e., its own *Sefirot Keter*, *Hochma* etc., form the right line of *Atzilut*, have light in them, and are called MA and *Zachar*.

Each of these *Sefirot (Partzufim)* takes the broken, empty and eliminated vessels from the world of *Nikudim* and builds the left line out of them, which requires correction and filling with light. These vessels are called *BON* or *Nukvah*.

Thus, the world of *Atzilut* contains five pairs of *Partzufim* (actually, there are six of them; we will study that in detail in "The Study of the Ten Sefirot").These are *Atik* and its *Nukvah (Keter)*, *Arich Anpin* and its *Nukvah (Hochma)*, *Abba(Zachar) ve Ima (Nukvah)* – the *Partzuf Gar de Bina*, *Israel Saba (Zachar) ve Tvunah (Nukvah) (YESHSUT)* – the *Partzuf Zat de Bina*, ZA and its *Nukvah* and also *Malchut*, for which the souls that require correction play the role of *Nukvah*.

Tvunah is a part of *Bina*, in which a root of the future *Sefira* (or *Partzuf*) ZA emerges. In other words, this part of *Bina* can be called a womb. In Hebrew, it is called exactly so: "*Rechem*". This is a place of a *Zivug*, conception, and birth.

Atik, which has nothing to do with the breaking of the vessels, selects and attaches to itself the entire vessels of *GE de Keter* and *Abba ve Ima* (left empty after the breaking) and commits itself to filling them with its light. The world of *Atzilut* is in fact *Nikudim*; only it has a special system of protection against the breaking of the vessels. This system is based on the reception of small portions of light by large vessels. The *Sefira*, which was in the world of *Nikudim*, now turns into a whole *Partzuf* in *Atzilut*. The force of resistance to egoism will be a lot more powerful than this egoism.

Any giving part of the *Partzuf* is called MA and the receiving – *BON*. However, in the world of *AK*, the *Ohr Hochma* shines in MA and *BON*, while in *Atzilut* – the *Ohr Hassadim*. The world of *Atzilut* is called giving, *Zachar*, the correcting and male part. Concerning *Atzilut*, the world of *Nikudim* is called *Nekeva*. It receives from and is corrected with the help of *Atzilut*.

It is not the case that every upper vessel will be called giving, and the subsequent one receiving. For instance, *Bina* does not want to receive anything, so is it MA or *BON*? Only ZA and *Malchut (Nukvah)* may be called MA and *BON*. If the giver and the receiver face one another, they are both ready: the one to bestow, the other to receive the light.

If we speak of transferring the light of *Hassadim*, the notions "right" and "left" arise, since *Ohr Hassadim* provides the breadth of spiritual attainment, not the height. Where there is an abundance of *Ohr Hassadim*, it is defined as "right"; where there is only a little of it, it is called "left".

קל) ופרצוף א"א דמ"ה החדש, שיצא בקומת חכמה, בירר וחיבר אליו את חציו התחתון דכתר הנקודים, שהם האח"פ דכתר, שבעת הקטנות היו בהמדרגה שמתחת הכתר, דהיינו בחכמה ובינה דנקודים (אות ע"ז). ונעשה לבחינת נוקבא אל הא"א דמ"ה החדש. ונתחברו יחד זה בזה. וסדר עמידתם הוא ימין ושמאל: א"א דמ"ה, שהוא הזכר, עומד בימין, וא"א דב"ן, שהיא הנוקבא, עומדת בשמאל.

ומה שפרצוף עתיק דמ"ה לא לקח גם את חציו התחתון דכתר נקודים, הוא, כי עתיק מתוך שהוא ראש הא' דאצילות, שמעלתו גבוהה מאד, לכן לא חיבר אליו רק הכלים דפנים דג"ר דנקודים, שבהם לא אירע שום פגם בעת השבירה. מה שאין כן בחצי הכתר התחתון, שהם

אח"פ, שהיו נפולים בעת הקטנות בחו"ב, ואח"כ בעת הגדלות עלו מחו"ב ונתחברו בכתר דנקודים (אות פ"ד), אשר אח"כ בעת שבירת הכלים חזרו ונפלו מהכתר דנקודים ונתבטלו, הרי המה כבר נפגמו עם נפילתם וביטולם, ואינם ראוים משום זה לעתיק. ולכן לקח אותם א"א דמ"ה.

130) The Partzuf Arich Anpin (the level of Hochma) sorted and attached to itself the lower half of the Keter de Nikudim, i.e., the AHP de Keter, which were on the lowest level (Hochma and Bina, Abba ve Ima) of the world of Nikudim. Arich Anpin turned these AHP into its Nukvah. MA (Zachar) de Arich Anpin is on the right, while its Nukvah (BON) is on the left.

The Partzuf Atik did not attach the lower part (AHP) of the Keter de Nikudim to itself, since it corresponds to the first Rosh of the world of Nikudim, and its level is very high. Hence, only Gar de Keter and Gar de Abba ve Ima were attached to it, i.e., the vessels unspoiled during the breaking. This cannot be said about the AHP de Keter that fell to a lower level during Katnut and then returned to its place during Gadlut by merging with Keter. When the vessels broke, the AHP fell again and disappeared. Therefore, only Arich Anpin, but not Atik, can attach the AHP de Keter to itself.

Only the light and the vessel exist; but there are countless varieties of their combinations and interactions. Only man who reached this level can clearly confirm or deny it. We know too little. It is just a figment of our imagination. No Kabbalist ever made a point of describing everything. They wrote their books so that we could ascend and feel it for ourselves, and not just spend time reading thick bulky volumes. We can exist in our world, and then start researching nature, whereas in the spiritual world, we must first attain it and only then start living in it. Spirituality is attained through perception.

קלא) ופרצוף או"א דמ"ה החדש, שהם בקומת בינה, בררו וחיברו להם את חצים התחתון דחו"ב דנקודים, שהם האח"פ דחו"ב, שבעת הקטנות היו נפולים בהז"ת דנקודים. אלא אח"כ בעת הגדלות נקודים, עלו ונתחברו לחו"ב דנקודים (אות צ"ד).

ואשר בעת שביה"כ חזרו ונפלו להז"ת דנקודים ונתבטלו (אות ק"ז). ואותם בררו להם או"א דמ"ה לבחינת נוקבא אליהם. והם מכונים ז"ת דחכמה ו"ת דבינה דב"ן.

כי בחינת החסד דבינה נשארה עם הג"ר דחו"ב דב"ן בפרצוף עתיק. ולא נשאר בחציה התחתון דבינה כי אם ו"ת מגבורה ולמטה. ונמצא הזכר דאו"א הוא קומת בינה דמ"ה, והנוקבא דאו"א היא ז"ת דחו"ב דב"ן. ועמידתם הם בימין ושמאל: או"א דמ"ה בימין, ואו"א דב"ן בשמאל. והישסו"ת דמ"ה, שהם הז"ת דאו"א, לקחו המלכיות דחו"ב דב"ן.

131) The Partzuf Abba ve Ima de MA Hadash on the level of Bina sorted out and attached to itself the lower part of Partzuf Hochma-Bina of the world of Nikudim, i.e., their AHP, which were on the level of the Zat de Nikudim. Then, during the Gadlut de Nikudim, they rose to join GE de Abba ve Ima.

However, as the vessels broke, these AHP fell to the Zat de Nikudim and disappeared. These broken vessels were sorted out by Abba ve Ima de MA Hadash (as Nukvah) and are now called Zat de Hochma and the six lower Sefirot (Vav Tachtonot) de Bina, as regards BON. Why are there six Sefirot in BON de Bina and not seven?

It is because Hesed de Bina remained in Partzuf Atik together with Gar de Hochma and Bina de BON. Only the six lower Sefirot from Gevura to Malchut were left in the lower half of Bina. Thus, Bina de MA Hadash is considered Zachar de Abba ve Ima, while Zat of Hochma-Bina de BON is Nukvah de Abba ve Ima. The YESHSUT de MA, i.e., the Zat de Abba ve Ima, attached to itself Malchut of Hochma-Bina de BON.

Here we learn how the *Rashim de Nikudim* were attached to the *Rashim de Atzilut*. The world of *Nikudim* was first in *Katnut*, then in *Gadlut*, where its heads, *Keter* and *Abba ve Ima*, attached their *AHP* and received the light of *Gadlut*. They passed it to *GE de ZON*, but some sparks of the light went under the *Parsa*. This led to a breaking of the vessels, their downfall and death. The *Rashim de Nikudim* lost the light of *Gadlut* and returned to *Katnut*, whereupon *Atzilut* emerged instead of *Nikudim*.

The purpose of the world of *Atzilut* is to correct the broken vessels, lift them up, absorb, and fill them with the light, while at the same time avoiding another breaking. The world of *Atzilut* is in fact similar to the world of *Nikudim*, but its mode of operation is correct. There can be no errors in *Atzilut*, because it has the *Reshimot* of the broken vessels and knows how to act to avoid repeating that state.

The *Partzuf Atik de Atzilut* attached to itself the purest vessels: the upper part of *Keter de Nikudim*, the upper part of *Abba ve Ima de Nikudim* and *Zat de Nikudim*, i.e., the 7 roots *(Ketarim)* with the information of the future *Guf de Nikudim*. *Arich Anpin* takes upon itself to correct, attach and fill the *AHP de Keter* of the world of *Nikudim* with light.

The *Partzuf Abba ve Ima* is responsible for the correction and filling of the *AHP de Abba ve Ima de Nikudim* with light. *Abba ve Ima* forms a combination of two *Partzufim*: *Hochma* and *Bina*. The *Partzuf Hochma*, i.e., *Abba de Atzilut*, attached the *AHP de Abba de Nikudim*, but *Ima de Atzilut* did not attach all the *AHP de Ima de Nikudim* (excluding *Hesed*), since *Hesed* is a giving part of *Bina* and refers to the *Rosh*.

While studying the interconnections between the corrected and uncorrected properties (vessels) in the world of *Atzilut*, we better understand what we will possess in the future. We learn what spiritual properties we will be connected with and how, for our souls are actually the broken vessels.

The attachment of the *Kelim de Nikudim*, which are to the left of the *Kelim de Atzilut*, speaks of the *Ohr Hassadim* that always spreads from right to left. The light of *Hochma* spreads downwards. From this, it becomes clear that the height of the *Partzuf* depends on the amount of the *Ohr Hochma*, while its capacity depends on the *Ohr Hassadim* (correction). These parameters complement one another. The light of *Hochma* spreads only together with the light of *Hassadim*.

קלב) ופרצוף זו"ן דמ"ה החדש, שהם בקומת ו"ק ונקודה, בירור וחיברו אליהם את הכלים דפנים דז"ת דנקודים, מתוך שבירתם בבי"ע. דהיינו בחינת הגו"ע של הז"ת דנקודים (אות

ע"ח). והם נעשו לנוקבא אל הזו"ן דמ"ה. ועמידתם הוא בימין ושמאל: הזו"ן דמ"ה בימין, והזו"ן דב"ן בשמאל.

132) The Partzuf ZON de MA Hadash, which has only the Sefirot ZA and Keter in Malchut, sorted out and attached to itself (as Nukvah) the GE de Zat de Nikudim, positioning them on the left, being itself on their right. The YESHSUT de MA (seven lower Sefirot de AVI) attached the Sefirot of Malchut (Behinot Hochma and Bina of Partzuf BON).

The GE *de Zat de Nikudim* did not just disappear; they were broken with the vessels under *Parsa*. Consequently, they cannot be attached to the ZON *de Atzilut* the way the other *Partzufim* of MA *Hadash* attaches *Nukvot* from the world of *Nikudim*. The *Kli* of *Zat de Nikudim* must be corrected first by raising MAN and other consecutive actions.

There is only one vessel – the desire to receive pleasure, which later acquires the Creator's properties, i.e., the 9 upper *Sefirot*, by using them to work with its egoism. As the egoism is gradually corrected, *Malchut* begins to approach differently the properties received from the Creator in its nine *Sefirot*. On each level, the combinations of the nine properties and *Malchut* are completely different from those of the previous level.

The same is true about people. One differs from another by his character traits. We cannot even catch all the nuances of the differences in these traits, be that external appearance or inner content. It seems to us that the spiritual forces and objects are rather simple.

There are ten parts, which in turn, consist of their own ten. That is all. However, we should understand why there is such a remarkable subdivision in the spiritual world, and what is in it for us. Above all, this multitude of desires must be united by one intention, imparting completeness and perfection to them: the intention for the sake of the Creator.

Perfection in itself is very simple, impossible to divide. If it can be divided, it suggests some differences; and it cannot be called perfection. In spirituality, common intention leads to perfection. Until that happens, we are overwhelmed with a swarm of desires with all their connections, an awesome system of control and unpredictability. Ideally, it is only *Malchut* of the World of Infinity, completely filled with the light, that exists outside of us.

In his manuscripts (which, by the way, are still unpublished, because people are not yet ready for what they say), Baal HaSulam writes about extremely complicated interactions; he gives them special names and describes such levels of attainment that are not even mentioned in "The Study of the Ten Sefirot". He can speak about these processes because he himself was in a state of simple perfection.

The higher your head (which sees the simplicity and wholeness of the entire system) is, the more minute the details you can distinguish, seeing the same perfection and simplicity in the general confusion. It resembles a scientist who sees the interconnections between all elements of the general picture as he penetrates deeper into his science.

קלג) והנה נתבאר המ"ה וב"ן שבה"פ אצילות. אשר ה' הקומות דמ"ה החדש, שיצאו בעולם האצילות, בירו להם מהכלים הישנים ששימשו בזמן הנקודים, ונתקנו להם לבחינת נוקבא, הנקראת בשם ב"ן.

שהב"ן דעתיק נעשה ונתקן ממחציתן העליונה דג"ר דנקודים, והב"ן דא"א ואו"א נבררו ונתקנו ממחציתן התחתונה דג"ר דנקודים, ששמשו להם בעת גדלות דנקודים וחזרו ונתבטלו, והב"ן דזו"ן נברר ונתקן מהכלים דפנים, שיצאו בעת קטנות דנקודים, שבעת הגדלות נשברו ונפלו ביחד עם הכלים דאחורים שלהם.

133) So, we know what MA and BON are in the 5 Partzufim of the world of Atzilut, where 5 levels of MA Hadash (Kelim de Atzilut) sorted out the old vessels of the world of Nikudim, selected the suitable ones, and corrected them (using them as Nukvah called BON).

Thus, MA de Atik corrected the upper part of Gar de Nikudim, and MA de Arich Anpin and Abba ve Ima sorted out and corrected the vessels of the lower half of Gar de Nikudim, which had been used during Gadlut de Nikudim and later broke, fell and disappeared.

MA de ZON sorted out and corrected the vessels of GE de Zat of the world of Nikudim, which had also broken during Gadlut and disappeared together with their AHP.

Overall, 320 parts have been broken. The count is as follows: eight *Melachim*, each containing *HaVaYaH – Yud-Key-Vav-Key* with the 10 *Sefirot* inside. In all, there are 8x4x10=320. Out of these 320 parts, 32 *Malchuyot* are called *"Lev haEven"* (stone heart). The remaining 288 parts, called *Rapach*, refer to the first nine *Sefirot*.

Each fragment of a broken vessel is a spark that remained from the screen of the *Partzuf* in its previous unspoiled state.

There are GE *de Keter* and GE *de Abba ve Ima* above the *Parsa*. The *AHP de Abba ve Ima* fell to the place of GE *de ZON de Nikudim*, while the broken vessels fell under the *Parsa*. In place of the world of *Nikudim*, there emerged the world of *Atzilut* with its five *Partzufim*. The entire *Gar de Atzilut* takes the *Gar de Nikudim*, corrects them and fills with the light of *Gadlut*. *ZON de Atzilut* correct GE *de ZON* of the world of *Nikudim*. Both the GE and the *AHP de ZON* break and fall under the *Parsa*.

When the vessels break, all their fragments mix and penetrate one another. Why do the GE and the *AHP* interpenetrate during the breaking of the vessels? Does the intention "to receive" unite them more than the intention "to bestow"? Prior to the breaking, the GE and the *AHP* possessed a common intention to bestow. Afterwards, in their uncorrected state, the intention is again the same– to receive. Hence, the connection between them is also preserved after the breaking, despite the fact that each fragment feels separated from the others. However, the GE and the *AHP* do not make up a single whole anymore; therefore, the connection between them (if it exists) is characterized only as inclusion. Thus, there are the four following kinds of broken vessels (left):

1. The GE (the vessels of bestowal);
2. The GE inside the *AHP*;
3. The *AHP* inside the GE;
4. The *AHP* (the vessels of reception).

The ZON *de Atzilut* take the vessels that refer to the GE. The *AHP* are the egoistic vessels that cannot be corrected yet and are called *Lev haEven*. There are two more kinds of vessels: the GE inside the *AHP* and the *AHP* inside the GE. These vessels can somehow be corrected. The GE inside the *AHP* are the vessels of bestowal inside the vessels of reception. This combination can be used for the formation of the worlds of BYA under the *Parsa*: *Beria* – GE in the *Awzen (Bina)*, *Yetzira* – GE in the *Hotem (ZA)* and *Assiya* – GE *in* the *Peh (Malchut)*. These vessels are sorted out and born by *Malchut* of the world of *Atzilut*.

With the help of the *AHP* inside the GE, we can pass to *Gadlut* of the world of *Atzilut*. If *Atzilut* remains only in *Katnut*, it will not be able to correct anything under the *Parsa*, i.e., the vessels referring to the *AHP de* ZON of the world of *Nikudim*. It is precisely because the *AHP* are inside the GE of the broken vessels that they can be lifted above the *Parsa* and subjected to correction, by their use as vessels of bestowal.

That is what man's work is all about. A special *Partzuf* (common soul) *Adam* is created. The correction of this part depends on *Adam's* correction. However, this is not the topic of our research for the time being. The vessels of reception cannot be corrected when they exist separately. This can be done only when they are united with the vessels of bestowal.

By way of an explosion, the Creator mixes these vessels, i.e., He actually mixes His own "desire to bestow" with the creation's "desire to receive". Now a part of the broken vessels will possess both the "desire to receive" and the "desire to bestow", although each in its own proportion. That is what the breaking of the vessels, "the sin" of *Adam* and other fragmentations, were needed for.

THE UNCHANGING STATE AND THE ASCENTS OF THE WORLDS OF BYA

כלל גדול בעניני המוחין שבקביעות ובעליות הפרצופים והעולמות, הנוהגין בשתא אלפי שני

קלד) כבר נתבאר, שיציאת הגדלות של הג"ר וז"ת דנקודים באו בג' סדרים, בסוד ג' הנקודות חולם שורק חירק (אות פ"ו). ומשם תבין שיש ב' מינים של השלמת הע"ס לקבלת המוחין דגדלות:

א. הוא מצד עליתו והתכללותו בעליון. דהיינו בעת שהזו"ן דא"ק האירו את האור חדש דרך הטבור אל הכתר דנקודים, והורידו הה"ת מנקבי עינים דכתר להפה שלו, שבזה נתעלו האח"פ הנפולים דכתר שהיו באו"א, וחזרו למדרגתם לכתר והשלימו הע"ס שלו.

הנה נבחן אז שעלו עמהם גם גו"ע דאו"א, שהיו דבוקים על האח"פ דכתר. ונמצאים גם או"א נכללים בהע"ס השלמות של הכתר, כי התחתון העולה לעליון נעשה כמוהו (אות צ"ג). ונבחן משום זה, שגם או"א השיגו האח"פ החסרים להם להשלמת ע"ס שלהם, מכח התכללותם בהכתר. וזהו מין הא' של מוחין דגדלות.

Having failed to receive all the light at one go, the world of *Nikudim* could not exist, so the light was left above the *Parsa* in the world of *Atzilut*, while correction of the broken vessels continues above the *Parsa*. The total amount of light above the *Parsa* divides into 6000 parts; each of them must go through 6000 levels or corrections. It resembles a huge column consisting of 6000 people (called one generation). Each generation must climb all 6000 steps.

The world of *Atzilut* corrects the vessels only up to the *Ateret haYesod*, i.e., the vessels of *Malchut*, while the *Zat de Yesod* receives no light. Hence, due to the inverse relation between the lights and the vessels, only the following lights can enter the *Partzufim* of the world of *Atzilut*: *Nefesh*, *Ruach*, *Neshama*, and *Vak de Haya*. The lights *Yechida* and *Gar de Haya* do not enter the *Partzuf*. This means that we use only the vessels of *GE* (with lights *Nefesh* and *Ruach* inside), while of *AHP*, only their inclusion in the *GE* (with the lights *Neshama* and *Gar de Haya*) is used. *Atzilut* conditions the correction in this way, so that the law of *TB* would never be violated. Real *AHP* cannot be worked with; it is impossible to fill them with light. The only opportunity is to lift them to GE, i.e., work only with those *AHP* that are able to become similar to GE.

Each fragment that feels the desire to be corrected consists of 10 *Sefirot* or four *Behinot*. *Keter*, *Hochma* and *Gar de Bina* can be corrected and filled with light, but *Zat de Bina*, ZA and *Malchut* cannot. Only a very small part of the desires that receives an insignificant amount of light is corrected. This continues until the *Mashiach* comes; then the entire *AHP* rise to the world of *Atzilut* and are filled with the light, which means the *Gmar Tikkun*.

> *134) We already know that the transition to Gadlut took place in three stages: 1) Holam (a point above the letter), 2) Shuruk (a point inside the letter) and 3) Hirik (a point under the letter). According to this, now let us examine two kinds of supplementations of the 10 Sefirot with the subsequent reception of the Mochin de Gadlut.*
>
> *The first kind of supplementation occurs because of the rise of the Partzuf by way of its inclusion into the upper one. For example, when ZON de AK pass the new light to Keter de Nikudim through the Tabur and lower Malchut from Nikvey Eynaim de Keter to its Peh, this leads to the rise of AHP de Keter from the Rosh de Abba ve Ima, which create 10 complete Sefirot in Keter.*
>
> *The GE de Abba ve Ima rose together with AHP de Keter and joined the 10 complete Sefirot de Keter, since the lower object rising to the level of the upper becomes equal to it. Hence, it is assumed that when the AHP de Keter rose, Abba ve Ima also received the AHP for the completion of 10 Sefirot by including them in Keter.*

Keter acquires its own *AHP*, completes its *Partzuf* to 10 *Sefirot*, and receives the light of *Mochin de Gadlut*. So what *AHP* is received by GE *de Abba ve Ima*? It is definitely not their own *AHP*. The rise of one's own *AHP* requires a lot more power, since each lower object is worse off than the one above it. *Keter* received the light according to its anti-egoistic force. The rise of the *AHP de Abba ve Ima* requires a more powerful light than that which lifted the *AHP de Keter*; therefore, the GE *de Abba ve Ima* take the *AHP de Keter*.

There is no quantitative division in the spiritual world; one can receive as much as one wants. The division is qualitative. *Keter* and *Abba ve Ima* passed to the state of *Gadlut* with the help of the same *AHP de Keter*.Supplementing Abba ve Ima to 10 *Sefirot* is called the First Supplementation.

When man reaches the next level, it means that he equals its measure of correction, but not by his personal properties, "chromosomes". In other words, two people on the same level merge into one new vessel according to the measure of their altruistic intention. Only the extent of correction unites people on the same level and makes them equal to it.

The light that descends from above for correcting a certain *Partzuf* does not have enough power to correct the one below it, because it is more egoistic; hence, its correction requires more power. The light *AB-SAG* allows the vessel to feel the Creator's greatness and become like Him, i.e., to start doing altruistic actions.

Keter of the world of *Nikudim* gains this power, but GE *de Abba ve Ima* receive light from *AHP de Keter*, along with the opportunity to rise to *Keter*, together with them. However, this is the level of *AHP de Keter*, whereas *AHP de Abba ve Ima* remains in its place so far. Meanwhile, GE *de Abba ve Ima* also rise, at the same time staying in their place, since nothing disappears in the spiritual worlds. Hence, *GE de Abba ve Ima*, which rose similarly as *GE de Keter*, also receive a new state with the help of *AHP de Keter*.

If something changes in *Atzilut*, this world and the worlds *BYA* simultaneously move up one or more levels. Similarly, they can also descend, but not lower than their constant state of *Katnut*. There are three states in *Gadlut*: the use of *Bet de Aviut (Awzen)*, *Gimel de Aviut (Hotem)*, and *Dalet de Aviut (Peh)*. The three ascents of the worlds *ABYA* take place in compliance with these three states of *Gadlut*.

In the state of *Katnut*, the vessels work only with *GE*, but not with *AHP*; hence, the latter are hidden inside of the *GE* located below. The light *AB-SAG* comes from above and gives the *Partzuf Keter* power to lift and attach its own *AHP*, which fell into the *GE de Abba ve Ima*. This process is called *AHP de Aliyah* (*AHP* of Elevation). The *GE de Abba ve Ima* is partially filled at the expense of *AHP de Keter*; to be completely filled, they must use their own *AHP*.

קלה) ומין הב' הוא, שהמדרגה נשלמת בע"ס בכחה עצמה. דהיינו בעת שהזו"ן דא"ק האירו את האור חדש דרך היסוד דא"ק, הנקרא "נקודת השורק", לאו"א, והוריד הה"ת מנקבי עינים דאו"א עצמם להפה שלהם, שבזה העלה את הכלים דאח"פ דאו"א ממקום נפילתם בז"ת אל הראש דאו"א, והשלימו להם הע"ס, שעתה נשלמים או"א ע"י עצמם.

כי עתה השיגו הכלים דאח"פ ממש החסרים להם. משא"כ במין הא', בעת שקבלו שלמותם מהכתר ע"י הדבקות באח"פ שלו, הרי באמת היו עוד חסרים אח"פ. אלא ע"י התכללותם בכתר, קבלו על ידו הארה מאח"פ שלהם, שהספיק רק להשלימם בע"ס בעודם במקום הכתר, ולא כלל בעת יציאתם משם למקומם עצמם.

135) The Second Supplement of the Partzuf to 10 Sefirot consists in the fact that a certain level acquires its 10 Sefirot by its own strength. This happens when the new light shines through Yesod of the world of AK (called Nekuda de Shuruk – a point inside the letter).

This luminescence was destined for Abba ve Ima de Nikudim. Assisted by it, Malchut descended from the Nikvey Eynaim to the Peh de Abba ve Ima and elevated its AHP from GE de ZON to Rosh de Abba ve Ima, which completed the vessels of Abba ve Ima to 10 Sefirot by their own strength, i.e., with the help of their own AHP. In the first case, the completion to the 10 Sefirot were at the expense of the connection between GE de Abba ve Ima and the AHP de Keter that waspreserved during their ascent and attachment to Keter. In the second case, it happened with their own AHP in their own place.

קלו) ועד"ז נמצא ב' מיני השלמות גם בז"ת: א. בעת הארת השורק ועלית אח"פ דאו"א. שאז גם הגר"ע דז"ת הדבוקים בהם נתעלו יחד עמהם ועלו לאו"א. וקבלו שם בחינת אח"פ

להשלמת הע״ס שלהם. שאח״פ אלו אינם עוד אח״פ הממשיים שלהם, אלא רק הארת אח״פ, המספיק להשלמת ע״ס בעודם באו״א, ולא כלל בירידתם למקומם עצמם.

ב. השלמת הע״ס, שהשיגו הז״ת בעת התפשטות המוחין מאו״א אל הז״ת. שעי״ז הורידו גם הם בחינת ה״ת המסיימת מהחזה שלהם אל מקום סיום רגלי א״ק, והעלו את התנה״י שלהם מבי״ע, וחיברו אותם למדרגתם לאצילות. שאז, לולא נשברו ומתו, היו נשלמים בע״ס שלמות ע״י עצמם. כי עתה השיגו את האח״פ הממשיים החסרים להם.

136) Similarly, there are two methods of supplementing the Zat de Nikudim to 10 Sefirot. The first is with the help of luminescence through Shuruk and elevation of AHP de Abba ve Ima to GE de Abba ve Ima. This is accompanied by the rise of GE de Zat, with their subsequent reception of AHP de Abba ve Ima for supplementing their Sefirot to 10. These AHP de Abba ve Ima are not real AHP de Zat de Nikudim, and their insignificant luminescence is sufficient only for supplementing the Sefirot de Zat to 10 in the place of Abba ve Ima (i.e., one level higher), and not in their own location.

The second method consists in the fact that the light from Abba ve Ima reaches the Zat, which start lowering their screen from the Chazeh to the Sium de AK, and elevate their Tifferet-Netzah-Hod-Yesod from the BYA in order to attach them to their GE. Had there been no breaking of the vessels, they would have had to supplement the GE de Zat to 10 Sefirot by their own strength, i.e., with the help of their actual AHP, whereupon the entire process of filling Malchut de Ein Sof with the light would have been done.

As soon as *ZON* wished to supplement itself to 10 *Sefirot*, the vessels broke. Later on, we will study how the *AHP* will attach to their *GE* in the world of *Atzilut* in order to avoid a new breaking. In *Atzilut*, this method will prevent independent attachment of the *AHP*, i.e., the second method of supplementation that led to the breaking must be abolished.

Keter is just the 10 *Sefirot*. *Abba ve Ima* consist of two parts: *Abba* (the upper part, *Panim*, able to receive the light) and *Ima*, which is *Achoraim* as regards *Abba* and receives light only on a request from *ZON*. Then it turns its face to *Abba*, accepts the light from it and passes it to

ZON. Both *Abba* and *Ima* have *GE* and *AHP*, but *Abba* is above *Ima*, so its *GE* and *AHP* are filled and supplemented by *Keter*. The GE and *AHP de Ima* may receive only because of the *MAN* raised by ZON. The light that *Gadlut* gives to *Keter* also elevates *Abba*, leaving *Ima* below. Thus, we may say that *Abba* is the *GE* of their common *Partzuf*, and *Ima* is their common *AHP*. Distinctions and definitions are applied according to what we wish to emphasize.

Therefore, we have learned about two kinds of supplementation to 10 *Sefirot*. For example, *Abba ve Ima* can receive *Gadlut* with the help of the *AHP de Keter*, i.e., through the rise of *GE de Ima* to *Keter*, or while remaining in its place, be supplemented with the help of their own *AHP*. The same would have been the case with *ZON de Nikudim* had their vessels not been broken.

קלז) וגם בד' פרצופים, שיצאו מאו"א לכלים דחג"ת, וכן בד' הפרצופים, שיצאו מהישסו"ת לכלים דתנהי"מ (אות ק"ז-ק"ט), הנה גם בהם נמצאים אלו ב' מיני השלמות הע"ס. כי מבחינה אחת היה נשלם כל אחד מהם ע"י התדבקותם באח"פ דאו"א וישסו"ת בעודם בראש, שהיא השלמת ע"ס דמין הא'. ואח"כ שנתפשטו לבי"ע, היו רוצים להשתלם בהשלמת הע"ס דמין הב'. וענין זה נוהג גם בפרטי פרטיות.

> *137) As with the Rashim, there are two kinds of supplementation to 10 Sefirot in the 4 Partzufim (Melachim) that emerge from Rosh de Abba ve Ima (Reshimot Dalet/Gimel). They are called Da'at, Hesed, Gevura, and Tifferet.The same is true for the four Partzufim that emerge from the Rosh de YESHSUT (Reshimot Gimel/Bet) that replaced Abba ve Ima. They are Tifferet, Netzah-Hod, Yesod and Malchut.*
>
> *On the one hand, the 10 Sefirot de Guf are supplemented at the expense of the AHP of their Rashim, rising to where the Rashim are. On the other hand, they spread in the BYA wishing to be increased to 10 Sefirot by way of attaching their own AHP, i.e., using the second method. This rule is also effective in each individual case.*

The division of the *Partzuf* into *GE* and *AHP* is purely qualitative and means that only the vessels of bestowal may be worked with, while the vessels of reception stay inactive. Now the *AHP* of the upper object are not in *GE* of the lower as before. They are located exactly under their own *GE*, but remain idle. They can transfer the light downward. Creation, designed in this way, cannot change its structure or location. It can change only the intention, the way it will work with its parts.

קלח) ותדע, כי אלו ה"פ אצילות, עתיק וא"א ואו"א וזו"ן, שנתקנו בקביעות ואין שום מיעוט נוהג בהם (אות קכ"ו), שעתיק יצא בקומת כתר, וא"א בקומת חכמה, ואו"א בקומת בינה, וזו"ן בקומת ז"א, ו"ק בלי ראש.

הנה הכלים דאח"פ, שנתבררו להם מעת הגדלות, היו מבחינת השלמת ע"ס דמין הא'. והיינו על דרך נקודת החולם, שהאיר בכתר דנקודים. שאז נשלמו גם או"א על ידי הכתר והשיגו הארת כלים דאח"פ (אות קל"ד). ולפיכך אע"פ שהיה לכל אחד מעתיק וא"א ואו"א ע"ס שלמות בראש, מ"מ לא הגיע מזה בחינת ג"ר לגופים שלהם. ואפילו פרצוף עתיק לא היה לו בגוף אלא בחינת ו"ק בלי ראש. וכן א"א ואו"א.

והטעם הוא, כי כל הזך נברר תחילה. וע"כ לא נברר בהם רק השלמת ע"ס דמין הא', שהוא מצד עליתו בעליון. דהיינו בחינת הארת כלים דאח"פ, המספיק להשלים הע"ס בראש. אבל אין עוד התפשטות מהראש לגוף. כי בעת שאו"א נכללו בכתר דנקודים, היה מספיק להם הארת אח"פ מכח הכתר, ולא כלל בהתפשטותם למקומם עצמם, מפה דכתר דנקודים ולמטה (אות קל"ה). וכיון שהגופים דעתיק וא"א ואו"א היו בו"ק בלי ראש, מכ"ש הזו"ן עצמם, שהם בחינת גוף הכולל דאצילות, שיצאו בו"ק בלי ראש.

138) You must know that the 5 Partzufim of the world Atzilut: Atik, Arich Anpin, Abba ve Ima and ZON, have their minimal state below which they cannot descend. Atik has the level of Keter, Arich Anpin – of Hochma, Abba ve Ima – of Bina and ZON – of ZA.

The AHP that joined them during Gadlut supplemented their Sefirot to 10 through the point of Holam, which shone upon Keter de Nikudim. The GE de Abba ve Ima rose together with the AHP de Keter and received the same luminescence. Despite the fact that the Rashim of Atik, Arich Anpin, and Abba ve Ima have the full 10 Sefirot, they did not receive the lights that correspond to the Gar in their Gufim. Even the Guf de Atik had the level of the Vak like Gufim de Arich Anpin and Abba ve Ima.

It is known that the purer Partzufim are corrected first; consequently, they were corrected only according to the first method when the AHP rose to their GE and supplemented them to 10 Sefirot in the Rosh. However, the light has not yet spread from the Rosh into the Guf. Therefore, Abba ve Ima rose to Keter and received the light of AHP de Keter. This light, though, was insufficient for shining upon their own AHP, which remain below. Since the bodies of Atik, Arich Anpin, and Abba ve Ima have only the level of Vak, the ZON de Atzilut (its body) also has the same level.

No *Guf* of the *Partzuf* in the world of *Atzilut* receives *Gadlut*. They stay in *Katnut*, while only the *Rosh* of each *Partzuf* receives *Gadlut*.

In the world of *Atzilut*, *Gadlut* can be received only when the lower *Partzuf* rises to the upper. All ascents of the worlds on holidays, Sabbaths and the new moons are based on this principle, which prevents the breaking of the vessels.

קלט) אמנם בא"ק לא היה כן. אלא כל הכמות שיצא בהראשים דפרצופי א"ק, נתפשט ג"כ לגופים שלהם. ולפיכך נבחנים כל ה"פ אצילות, שהם רק בחינת ו"ק דפרצופי א"ק. וע"כ הם מכונים מ"ה החדש או מ"ה דה"פ א"ק. דהיינו קומת ז"א, שהוא מ"ה. בחוסר ג"ר, שג"ר הן גלגלתא ע"ב ס"ג. כי עיקר המדרגה נבחנת ע"פ התפשטותה אל הגוף מפה ולמטה, וכיון שגם לג' פרצופים הראשונים אין מהם התפשטות לגוף רק ו"ק בלי ראש, ע"כ הם נבחנים לבחינת מ"ה, שהוא קומת ו"ק בלי ראש אל ה"פ א"ק.

139) In the world of AK, the picture was different. The amount of the light in the Rosh spread to the Guf. In the world of Atzilut, the light that spread in the Rosh, even in the state of Gadlut, does not spread to the Guf. Hence, the world of Atzilut, as regards the world of AK, is defined as Vak (ZA) and is called MA Hadash or MA of the 5 Partzufim de AK, i.e., the level of ZA, which constitutes MA without Gar.

It is similar to the state of the *Partzufim* of the world of AK, provided each of them will have only the *Vak* without the *Gar*. Let us examine it in more detail. Each *Partzuf de AK*, i.e., *Galgalta*, *AB*, *SAG*, *MA* and *BON* (*Keter*, *Hochma*, *Bina*, ZA and *Malchut*) in turn, consists of *Gar* (*Galgalta* – *Keter*, *AB* – *Hochma* and *SAG* - *Bina*) and *Vak* – MA and *BON*. So, all the *Partzufim* of the world of *Atzilut* correspond only to MA *de* AK. *Atik de Atzilut* equals MA *de Galgalta*, *Arich Anpin* – the MA *de* AB, *Abba ve Ima* – the MA *de* SAG and the ZON – MA and *BON de* AK. There is no spreading of light in the *Guf*, i.e., all of these *Partzufim* are in the state of *Vak*.

קמ) באופן, שעתיק דאצילות, שיש לו בראש קומת כתר, נבחן לבחינת ו"ק לפרצוף הכתר דא"ק. וחסר נשמה חיה יחידה דכתר א"ק. וא"א דאצילות, שיש לו בראש קומת חכמה, נבחן לבחינת ו"ק לפרצוף ע"ב דא"ק שהיא חכמה. וחסר נשמה חיה יחידה דע"ב דא"ק.

ואו"א דאצילות, שיש להם בראש קומה בינה, נבחנים לבחינת ו"ק של פרצוף ס"ג דא"ק. וחסר לו נשמה חיה יחידה דס"ג דא"ק. והזו"ן דאצילות נבחנים לבחינת ו"ק דפרצוף מ"ה וב"ן דא"ק. וחסר להם נשמה חיה יחידה דמ"ה וב"ן דא"ק. וישסו"ת וזו"ן הם תמיד במדרגה א': זה ראש וזה גוף.

140) Rosh de Atik of the world of Atzilut has the level of Keter, which is defined as Vak (MA) with regard to Partzuf Galgalta de AK. It has only the lights Ruach and Nefesh, while Neshama, Haya, and Yechida de Galgalta are absent. The Rosh de Arich Anpin, with the light of Hochma, corresponds to Vak (MA) de AB and has the lights Nefesh and Ruach, while Neshama, Haya and Yechida de Hochma de AB are absent.

Abba ve Ima de Atzilut, whose Rosh has the light of Bina, is defined as Vak de SAG without the lights of Neshama, Haya and Yechida de Bina de SAG. The Partzuf ZON de Atzilut, which has the level of ZA and Malchut in its Rosh, is defined as the Vak of the Partzufim MA and BON de AK, without the lights of Neshama, Haya and Yechida de MA and BON de AK.

קמא) וע"י העלאת מ"ן ממעשים טובים של התחתונים, נבררים השלמת האח"פ דע"ס דמין הב'. דהיינו השלמתם דאו"א מבחינת עצמם, על דרך בחינת נקודת השורק. שאז או"א עצמם

מורידים הה"ת מנקבי עינים שלהם, ומעלים אליהם האח"פ שלהם. שאז יש להם כח גם להשפיע אל הז"ת, שהם זו"ן. דהיינו אל הגופים ממעלה למטה. כי הגו"ע דזו"ן, הדבוקים באח"פ ואו"א, נמשכים עמהם לאו"א ומקבלים מהם השלמת ע"ס (אות צ"ד).

ואז נמצא כל כמות המוחין שישנם באו"א מושפעים ג"כ לזו"ן, שעלו אליהם ביחד עם האח"פ שלהם. ולפיכך, בעת שה"פ אצילות מקבלים השלמה זו דמין הב', אז יש ג"ר גם להגופים דג' פרצופים הראשונים, שהם עתיק וא"א ואו"א דאצילות. וכן להזו"ן דאצילות, שהם גוף הכולל דאצילות.

ואז עולים ה' פרצופי אצילות ומלבישים לה"פ א"ק. כי בעת התפשטות הג"ר גם אל הגופים דה"פ אצילות, הרי הם משתוים עם ה"פ א"ק. ועתיק דאצילות עולה ומלביש לפרצוף כתר דא"ק, וא"א לע"ב דא"ק, ואו"א לס"ג דא"ק, וזו"ן למ"ה וב"ן דא"ק.

ואז מקבל כל אחד מהם נשמה חיה יחידה מהבחינה שכנגדו בא"ק.

141) The souls in the worlds BYA raise MAN, thus causing the descent of additional light This leads to a supplementing of the Partzufim to 10 Sefirot according to the second method wherein the light comes through NHY de Galgalta to the ZON de Nikudim (and Atzilut), via the point of Shuruk. Abba ve Ima lowers its Malchut from Nikvey Eynaim to Peh and elevates their AHP. GE de ZON (merged with the AHP de Abba ve Ima) rise to Abba ve Ima together with the AHP, and increase to 10 Sefirot.

Then the entire amount of Mochin (the light) in Abba ve Ima affects the ZON, which rise together with the AHP de Abba ve Ima. Since the five Partzufim de Atzilut are supplemented according to the second method, the three first Partzufim have the lights of Gar in their Gufim as well as in the ZON, which makes up the common Guf of the world of Atzilut.

Then the five Partzufim of the world of Atzilut rise and dress upon the five Partzufim de AK, since the spreading of Gar in the Gufim de Atzilut equates them with the five Partzufim de AK.This is so that Atik might rise and dress upon the Partzuf Keter de AK (Galgalta), the Arich Anpin – on AB de AK, Abba ve Ima – on SAG de AK, and ZON – on MA and BON de AK.

Such a dressing of the *Partzufim* of the world of *Atzilut* onto the corresponding *Partzufim* of the world of *AK* means that each of them receives the lights *Neshama, Haya* and *Yechida* on the level of the world of *AK*.

After the vessels break, all the *Partzufim* of the world of *Atzilut* emerge in *Katnut*, both in the *Rosh* and in the *Guf*. The first *Partzuf, Atik*, is born. The *Reshimot* of *Arich Anpin* begin to appear in it; it later emerges from *Atik*. Thus, *Atik* does not fully enter *Gadlut*, but only to the extent of being able to give birth to *Arich Anpin*. In this way, all the *Partzufim* of *Atzilut* and the worlds *BYA* emerge. Then the light of *Holam* on the *Reshimot Dalet/Gimel* descends from above. As in the world of *Nikudim*, this light enters *Keter*, which attaches its *AHP* and *Abba ve Ima* to itself, etc. This is the first case when all the *Rashim* receive *Gadlut*, while all the *Gufim* remain in *Katnut*.

The second way of receiving *Gadlut* requires awakening from below, desire. In the world of *Nikudim*, the desire was received from *NHY de Galgalta*. The light shone upon them, and the *ZON de Nikudim* began asking for light from *Abba ve Ima*. True requests to *Abba ve Ima* in the world of *Atzilut* cause all the *Partzufim* to pass to *Gadlut*, according to the second method.

If the *Rashim de Atzilut* receive *Gadlut* through the first method, why does this light not pass to the *Gufim*? The reason lies in the fact that *Gadlut* of the *Rashim* does not happen at their own expense; rather, they are elevated by the higher *Partzufim* and lifted with their light. The *Rosh* did not rise to a higher level by its own strength. Neither was it filled by its own effort. Hence, upon receiving *Gadlut*, it also remained in *Katnut*, in its place below. It can in no way pass the light to its *Guf* below. All the *Rashim de Atzilut* received this kind of *Gadlut*.

The second state of *Gadlut* in the *Gufim* occurs when the lower *Partzufim* ask the upper for strength to make a *Zivug* and pass to *Gadlut* in their own places, without rising; consequently, they can spread the light to their bodies.

Spiritual states do not disappear. Everything depends on what you wish to see at a particular moment and upon one's point of view. We are now interested in the specific states, first according to the initial method (*Gadlut Rashim*), then – to the second (*Gadlut Gufim*).

Before the vessels were broken, we spoke about the *Bitush Pnim u Makif*. After the breaking, we do not speak about it anymore, since the vessels start to be corrected, acquire a screen. Next, they are filled with light from below. From our various desires, we take the smallest, the least egoistic, the one we can correct most easily, and fill it with light in accordance with its correction.

Now, the light that comes to the vessel is no more than it can receive. In the world of *AK*, a *Zivug* on the entire *TA* was made, and it was possible to withstand the light of Infinity pressing the vessel to receive the light. After the break, it is no longer possible to withstand even a gram of light. It is only upon acquiring the tiniest screen that we can receive the light according to its strength.

קמב) אמנם כלפי הזו"ן דאצילות נבחנים המוחין הללו רק לבחינת מין הא' דהשלמת הע"ס. כי אלו האח"פ אינם אח"פ גמורים, רק הארת האח"פ, שהם מקבלים ע"י או"א, הוא בעת שהם במקום או"א. אבל בהתפשטותם למקומם עצמם, הרי הם עוד חסרים האח"פ שלהם (אות קל"ו). ומטעם זה נבחנים כל המוחין שהזו"ן משיג בשתא אלפי שני בשם "מוחין דעליה". כי אי אפשר להם להשיג מוחין דג"ר, רק בעת עלותם למקום ג"ר. כי אז נשלמים על ידם. אמנם אם אינם עולים למעלה למקום הג"ר, אי אפשר להיות להם מוחין. כי עדיין לא נבררו לזו"ן בחינת המוחין דמין הב', שזה לא יהיה זולת בגמר התיקון.

> *142) The ZON de Atzilut receives light according to the first principle, that is to say, through "AHP de Aliyah". These AHP are not yet final. The light they receive is just the luminescence coming through Abba ve Ima, when ZON is on their level. However, on their own level, they do not have the AHP, so the light received by the ZON during 6000 years is called Mochin de Aliyah, for the light of Gar can be attained only while being on the level of the Gar, which increase them to 10 Sefirot. Until they reach the level of Gar, the ZON are unable to receive the entire light. However, the ZON have not yet*

received their correction of the second kind. This will happen only in the Gmar Tikkun.

When the *ZON* rise to *Abba ve Ima*, they compel them to make a *Zivug* and to receive light. The request of *ZON* is made for the comprehensively selected desires that are now unfit. It is necessary to find out whether they can be corrected. To that end, there is a special mechanism in the *Rosh de Arich Anpin*, through which it rules over *Abba ve Ima*, which in turn control *ZON*.

The light that *Arich Anpin* sends down allows seeing fallaciousness only in nine *Sefirot*, but not in the 10-th, *Malchut*. Hence, the light of *Arich Anpin* is less powerful than it is supposed to be, but it provides an opportunity to correct the vessels of reception, which rise and join the vessels of bestowal.

קמג) והנה נתבאר, שהמוחין דה"פ הקבועים באצילות, הם מבחינת בירורי כלים דמין הא' דאו"א, שבעולם הנקודים מכונה הארה זו בשם "הארת הטבור", או "נקודת החולם". שאפילו או"א אין להם השלמה, אלא מבחינת מין הא'. וע"כ אין מגיע מהראשים דעתיק וא"א ואו"א להגופים שלהם עצמם וכן להזו"ן שום הארת ג"ר. כי גם הז"ת דנקודים לא קבלו כלום מהארה זו דבחינת החולם (אות פ"ח).

והמוחין דשתא אלפי שני עד גמר התיקון הבאים ע"י העלאת מ"ן של התחתונים, הם מבחינת בירורי כלים להשלמת ע"ס דמין הב' דאו"א, שבעולם הנקודים מכונה הארה זו בשם "הארת היסוד" או "נקודת השורק".

כי אז מעלה או"א את האח"פ של עצמם, שעליהם דבוקים גם הגו"ע דז"ת. וע"כ גם הז"ת מקבלים במקום או"א בחינת מוחין דג"ר. ולפיכך מגיע המוחין הללו גם להגופים דה"פ אצילות ולזו"ן הכוללים. אלא בלבד שהם צריכים להיות למעלה במקום הג"ר ולהלביש אותם.

ולעתיד לבא בגמר התיקון יקבלו אז הזו"ן את בחינת השלמת ע"ס דמין הב'. ויורידו ה"ת המסיימת מבחינת החזה שלהם, שהוא הפרסא דאצילות, אל מקום סיום רגלי א"ק (אות קל"ו). ואז יתחברו התנה"י דזו"ן שבבי"ע אל מדרגת הזו"ן דאצילות. וישתוה סיום רגלין דאצילות לסיום רגלים דא"ק. ואז יתגלה מלכא משיחא. בסו"ה "ועמדו רגליו על הר הזיתים". ונתבאר היטב, שבשתא אלפי שני אין תיקון לעולמות רק בדרך עליה.

143) The light received by the five permanent Partzufim of the world of Atzilut is called the correction of the Kelim de Abba ve Ima. They supplement their Sefirot to ten by using the first method. In the world of Nikudim, this light is called "luminescence through the Tabur" or

"Nekudat Holam". Thus, no light de Gar spreads from the heads of Atik, Arich Anpin and Abba ve Ima, to their bodies and to ZON, for in the past, the Zat de Nikudim did not receive anything from this luminescence.

The Mochin (the light) received during 6000 years until the Final Correction comes as an answer to the request – MAN – raised by the lower Partzufim, including the souls in the worlds BYA, i.e., by the second method. In the world of Nikudim, it is called "luminescence through Yesod" or "Nekudat Shuruk".

According to this method, Abba ve Ima elevate their own AHP,and merge with GE de Zat, which receive the light Mochin de Gar on the level of Abba ve Ima. In this way, Mochin spread to the Gufim of the five Partzufim de Atzilut, including ZON, but on the condition that they will be above, in the place of Gar.

In the future, after the Gmar Tikkun, ZON will be increased to 10 Sefirot according to the second method, and Malchut will descend from the Parsa to the Sium Raglin de AK. Then Netzah, Hod and Yesod de ZON in the BYA will join ZON de Atzilut, while the Sium de Atzilut will have the same properties as Sium de AK. At that period, the Melech-haMashiach will come and "His feet will stand on the Mount of Olives". Then it will be clear that the complete correction of the worlds during 6000 years can happen only through their ascent.

THE WORLDS OF BERIA, YETZIRA AND ASSIYA
ביאור ג' העולמות בריאה יצירה ועשיה

קמד) ז' עיקרים כוללים יש להבחין בג' העולמות בי"ע:

א. מהיכן נעשה המקום לג' העולמות הללו.

ב. שיעורי קומת פרצופי בי"ע ועמידת העולמות בראשונה, בעת שנאצלו ויצאו מהנוקבא דאצילות.

ג. כל אלו שיעורי קומה מהמוחין דתוספת ומצב עמידתם, שהשיגו מטרם חטאו של אדה"ר.

ד. המוחין שנשתיירו בפרצופי בי"ע, ומקום נפילת העולמות לאחר שנפגמו בחטאו של אדה"ר.

ה. המוחין דאמא, שקבלו פרצופי בי"ע אחר נפילתם למטה מפרסא דאצילות.

ו. בחינת פרצופי האחור דה"פ אצילות, שירדו ונתלבשו בפרצופי בי"ע ונעשו להם לבחינת נשמה לנשמה.

ז. בחינת המלכות דאצילות, שירדה ונעשית בחינת עתיק לפרצופי בי"ע.

144) We must learn seven interrelated fundamentals about the worlds of BYA:

1. Where the place for the three worlds come from.

2. The level of the Partzufim of BYA and the initial position of the worlds at the time of their formation and separation from Nukvah de Atzilut.

3. The ascents of the worlds and their positions before the sin of Adam haRishon.

4. The Mochin that the worlds of BYA received, and the place of their fall after they were broken due to the sin of Adam haRishon.

5. The Mochin, the light of Gadlut from Ima de Atzilut received by the worlds of BYA after they fell under the Parsa de Atzilut.

6. The meaning of the back parts of the five Partzufim de Atzilut that fell under the Parsa into the worlds of BYA and became as Neshama de Neshama for them.

7. The level of Malchut de Atzilut that fell into the worlds of BYA and plays the role of Atik for the Partzufim de BYA.

We have learned that the source of all, the Creator, cannot be attained by us. He thought to bestow delight upon the future creations. The light (the thought of creation and bestowal) emanates from Him and builds a vessel that will "desire to receive" His delight.

All of creation's desires correspond to the thought (the light) that emanates from the Creator. If that vessel were filled with the light, it would achieve the state of perfection. However, there is only one perfection – the Creator; thus creation has to reach His level independently.

For that purpose, the creation must be put into the Creator's position; it should start creating something out of nothing. It must make the Creator out of itself. This is achieved by ascending the levels. Such work includes several requirements:

1. The advancement of creation by means of the descending ladder of the worlds and the *Partzufim*.
2. The arrangement of necessary conditions for the creation, which is thoroughly detached from the Creator, so that it might ascend the "steps-levels" prepared in advance.

We have learned about the formation of the steps from above: the structure of the world of AK, *Nikudim*, and then *Atzilut*. Had the world of *Nikudim* received the entire light, it would have meant the *Gmar Tikkun*. *Malchut* of the World of Infinity would have been completely filled with the light (fulfillment of the Thought of Creation). However, as we know, this did not happen; the vessels broke and fell under the *Parsa*. Now the world of *Atzilut* must correct the broken vessels and elevate them above the *Parsa*.

Atzilut consists of the five *Partzufim*, *Atik*, *Arich Anpin*, *Abba ve Ima* and ZON (ZA and *Malchut*). *Malchut* rises to *Bina* to pass from *Katnut* to *Gadlut* and to receive an opportunity to create its next state – the world of *Beria*. Prior to that, *Malchut* was a point; for the creation of the next state, it needs to acquire *Aviut Bet*. Hence, it rises to *Bina* and sorts its vessels.

Before the vessels were broken, they consisted of only two kinds: the giving and the receiving. Afterwards, these two kinds are supplemented with two more: the vessels of reception that mixed with the vessels of bestowal, and the vessels of bestowal that mixed with the vessels of reception.

The ZON *de Atzilut* are created from the *Kelim de* GE, sorted out from all the broken and mixed vessels that fell under the *Parsa*. All vessels that have only the "desire to receive" are put aside; they cannot be corrected yet. This is the so-called *Lev haEven* that will be corrected only after the *Gmar Tikkun*.

After that, only the vessels of reception that mixed with the vessels of bestowal, and the vessels of bestowal that mixed with the vessels of reception, remain. Thus, the Creator's and the creation's properties were mixed together.

How can they be corrected? The worlds of *BYA* are created from the vessels of bestowal that are inside the vessels of reception (the GE inside the *AHP*). The vessels of reception that are inside the vessels of bestowal (the *AHP* inside the GE) may be used by way of elevating them to the world of *Atzilut*.

Nothing can exist under the *Parsa*; it is the place of very distinct egoistic vessels. However, as the fragments of the altruistic vessels break and fall into them, some form of spiritual light, called the *Ohr Tolada* (the secondary light), can already shine there.

This is necessary for the souls below the worlds of *BYA* (under the *Sium*, beneath the barrier, in the point of our world) to mature enough to enter the spiritual world, and receive that property without which they cannot exist. They then cross the barrier and proceed to creating a screen for turning the egoistic properties into altruistic ones.

Entering the place where the vessels of bestowal are inside the vessels of reception, the souls can communicate with them. They receive the light from the fragments of the vessels of bestowal (the right line), simultaneously receiving additional desires from the fragments of the vessels of reception (the left line) in the worlds of *BYA*, rising systematically from one level to another.

Generally, all the worlds are built according to one scheme. The difference is in the fact that the lower the world is, the more it conceals the Creator's light. Egoism lies at the heart of nature. If it receives a screen it is corrected, and acquires altruistic properties. There are broken vessels that can be corrected during the 6000 years (the levels of the worlds of *BYA*, 2000 in each).

The vessels uncorrected during 6000 years are called *Klipot*. These can be corrected only after the coming of the *Mashiach*. The ascending soul contains all kinds of vessels: those that can be corrected, and the *Klipot*. While ascending, it is important to sort out the vessels correctly in order to separate and ignore the *Klipot*, using only the remaining vessels. This is called the work in three lines.

The entire way of ascent is covered with darkness. Each consecutive level can be felt only when the light of *Hochma* enters the corrected vessels. One can advance only by alternately moving between the right and left lines, Creation was not made just for receiving, as was the case with *Malchut* of the World of Infinity.

Hence, man's state is suspended between the earth (egoism) and the sky (altruism). On each level, we have to go through all the states from *Katnut* to *Gadlut*. Having climbed a certain level, man believes he has achieved everything. Then he receives additional desires and resumes his ascent, not knowing what awaits him ahead.

קמה) הנה הבחן הא' כבר נתבאר (אות ס"ו), שמפאת עלית המלכות המסיימת, שמתחת סיום רגלי א"ק, למקום החזה דז"ת דנקודות דס"ג, הנעשה בזמן צמצום ב', יצאו ונפלו ב"ש תתאין דת"ת ונהי"ם למטה מנקודת הסיום החדשה שבחזה דנקודות. ואינם ראויים עוד לקבל אור העליון. ונעשו מהם המקום לג' העולמות בי"ע: שמב"ש תתאין דת"ת נעשה מקום עולם הבריאה, ומג' ספירות נה"י נעשה מקום עולם היצירה, ומהמלכות נעשה מקום עולם העשיה.

> *145) The first definition: as was stated above, as a result of Malchut rising to Bina (Tifferet) of the Nekudot de SAG, the lower two thirds of Tifferet, Netzah, Hod, Yesod and Malchut of this Partzuf fell under the Parsa, and formed the place for the worlds of BYA there. The lower two thirds of Tifferet have become the place of the world of Beria, three Sefirot, Netzah, Hod and Yesod, have become the place of the world of Yetzira, and Malchut has become the place of the world of Assiya.*

Therefore, the place of the worlds of *BYA* are the vessels of *Nekudot de SAG*, specifically, they are in fact the *Kelim de AK* that submit to the laws of *TA*.

Each consecutive *Partzuf* dresses upon the previous one, which afterwards turns out to be inside it. Place means desire. The larger the desire is, the larger the place. This is how it was before *TA*. After *TA*, place is determined not by the size of the desire, but by the strength of the screen. The vessel can receive light only in accordance with the size of the screen and not the desire, since there are usually desires in the *Partzuf* that the screen cannot affect.

We should note that the worlds of *BYA* were created by *Malchut de Atzilut*, so they actually constitute the *AHP de Malchut* of the world of *Atzilut* or *Atzilut* as a whole. The worlds of *BYA* descended to the existing "place of *BYA*", which, as we said before, was formed by the vessels of the *Nekudot de SAG*. As the vessels got broken, the *Kelim* of bestowal (the *GE*) *de ZON* also fell to "the place of *BYA*".

After the creation of the worlds of *BYA*, one more *Partzuf* was created inside them. Its name is *Adam haRishon*. As the worlds began ascending, *Adam haRishon* rose together with them. These ascents continued until it "committed a sin". The places of the worlds of *BYA*, i.e., the *Nekudot de SAG*, ascended together with the worlds. After *Adam's* sin and downfall, the worlds of *BYA* and their place descended. So now, their place (the *Nekudot de SAG* forming a kind of a frame of the worlds of *BYA*) does not ascend, but constantly remains under the *Parsa*. The worlds of *BYA* rise together with the souls living in them.

קמו) והבחן הב' הוא שיעורי קומת פרצופי בי"ע ומקום עמידתם בעת יציאתם ולידתם מבטן הנוקבא דאצילות. דע, שבעת הזאת כבר השיג הז"א בחינת חיה מאבא, והנוקבא כבר השיגה בחינת נשמה מאמא. וכבר ידעת, שאין הזו"ן מקבלים המוחין מאו"א אלא בדרך עליה והלבשה (אות קמ"ב). וע"כ נמצא: הז"א מלביש את אבא דאצילות, הנקרא או"א עילאין, והנוקבא מלבשת לאמא דאצילות, הנקרא ישסו"ת. ואז הנוקבא דאצילות בירה והאצילה את עולם הבריאה בכללות ה"פ שבו.

> *146) The second definition: the level of attainment of the Partzufim de BYA and their position at the time of emergence and birth from the Beten de Nukvah of the world of Atzilut. Malchut de Atzilut creates the worlds of BYA. Then, ZA de Atzilut reached the level of Haya (Hochma) of Abba, and Nukvah reached the level of Neshama of Ima. As you already know, the ZON receive Mochin from Abba ve Ima only by way of their elevation and dressing upon the upper Partzuf. ZA dresses onto the Partzuf Abba de Atzilut, called the upper Abba ve Ima, and Malchut dresses onto Ima de Atzilut, called YESHSUT. Being in this state, Malchut de Atzilut chooses suitable, yet uncorrected, vessels and creates of them the world Beria with the five Partzufim.*

We know that a *Partzuf* emerges from the screen of the previous one, which rose to the *Peh de Rosh* and made a *Zivug* there. So it was in the world of AK. However, in the worlds of *BYA*, the *Partzufim* are born from the *Beten*, "abdomen" of the previous *Partzuf*.

In the four *Behinot de Ohr Yashar*, we see that *Shoresh* creates *Behina Aleph*, which wants to receive the light. Then *Behina Bet* emerges from *Behina Aleph* and refuses to receive the light. After that, a partial "desire to receive" the light is born in it; this *Behina* is called ZA. However, such a desire is born in the lower part of *Bina*, the *Zat de Bina*, which wants to receive for the Creator's sake. Only the lower part of *Bina* is related to the creations; its upper part does not want to receive anything.

Malchut rises to *Zat de Bina*. Only this part of *Bina* gives birth to the next *Partzuf* from its *Peh* (if we view the *Zat de Bina* as an independent *Partzuf*, it will be positioned from the *Tabur de Bina*, and below; another independent *Partzuf* of common *Bina* – the *Gar de Bina* will be above the *Tabur*). Thus, the *Peh de Zat* is on the level of the *Beten* of the common *Partzuf Bina*.

קמז) וכיון שהנוקבא עומדת במקום אמא, הרי היא נחשבת למדרגת אמא, כי התחתון העולה לעליון נעשה כמוהו. ולפיכך עולם הבריאה, שנבררה על ידה, נבחנת למדרגת ז"א, להיותה מדרגה תחתונה להנוקבא, שהיא בחינת אמא. והתחתון מאמא הוא ז"א. ונמצא אז עולם הבריאה, שעומדת במקום ז"א דאצילות, מתחת להנוקבא דאצילות, שהיתה אז בחינת אמא דאצילות.

147) Since Malchut is in the place of Ima (Bina), it reaches the level of Ima. Hence, the world of Beria, created from the Beten de Malchut (Nukvah) is one level below Ima, and therefore one level below Nukvah, which rose to Ima and reached its level. Thus, at the moment of its birth, the world of Beria is on the level of ZA de Atzilut.

קמח) ועל פי זה נבחן עולם היצירה, שנברר ונאצל ע"י עולם הבריאה, שהוא אז במדרגת הנוקבא דאצילות, להיותה מדרגה תחתונה לעולם הבריאה, שהיה אז בחינת הז"א דאצילות. והתחתון מהז"א היא בחינת נוקבא. אמנם לא כל הע"ס דעולם היצירה הם בחינת הנוקבא דאצילות, אלא רק הד' ראשונות דיצירה בלבד. והטעם הוא, כי יש ב' מצבים בנוקבא, שהם פב"פ ואב"א: שבהיותה פב"פ עם הז"א, קומתה שוה אל הז"א.

ובהיותה אב"א, היא תופשת רק ד' ספירות תנה"י דז"א. ומשום שאז היה מצב כל העולמות רק אב"א, לא היה בבחינת הנוקבא אלא ד"ס לבד. וע"כ גם עולם היצירה אין לו במקום הנוקבא דאצילות רק ד"ס ראשונות שלו. ושאר ששה תחתונות דיצירה היו בששה ספירות ראשונות דעולם הבריאה של עתה. דהיינו ע"פ תכונות מקום בי"ע שבהבחן הא' (אות קמ"ה), ששם נפלו העולמות בי"ע אחר חטאו של אדה"ר, ושם היא מקום קביעותם עתה.

148) The world of Yetzira was created in a similar way. It was birthed after the world of Beria, on the level of Nukvah (Malchut) de Atzilut, which follows ZA. However, only four out of the ten Sefirot of the world of Yetzira are in the place of Nukvah de Atzilut. Concerning

ZA de Atzilut, Nukvah has two states. If it is at Panim be Panim with ZA, then it is on one level with it and dresses upon it. Both of them have 10 Sefirot in this state.

When Nukvah is at Achor be Achor with ZA, it has only its four first Sefirot dressed on the 4 lower Sefirot of ZA. The six upper Sefirot of Nukvah descend one level, i.e., under the Parsa, and take the place of the first 6 Sefirot of the world of Beria. Therefore, when Nukvah is at Panim be Panim with ZA, the world of Yetzira is entirely in the place of Nukvah, i.e., in the world of Atzilut, above the Parsa.

In Achor be Achor, when Nukvah (Malchut) de Atzilut has only four Sefirot above the Parsa, the world of Yetzira also has only 4 upper Sefirot above the Parsa. The remaining six Sefirot of the world of Yetzira are on the level of the first six Sefirot of the world of Beria.

The place by itself constitutes the vessels of *TA*. *Malchut* of the World of Infinity, *Galgalta* with all the *Partzufim* dressed on it; the world of *Atzilut* and the worlds of the *BYA*, as it were, fill the place, which never changes. All ascents and descents are measured according to place. If places were not constant, we would not be able to determine the movement, defined by change of one object with regard to another.

As we said, one should differentiate between the worlds of *BYA* and their places. The place of *BYA* was formed by the vessels of *Nekudot de SAG* and is under the *Parsa*. Two thirds of *Tifferet* is the place of the world of *Beria*. *Netzah*, *Hod* and *Yesod* make up the place of the world of *Yetzira*. *Malchut* is the place of *Assiya*. As far as the worlds are concerned, *Beria* is in the place of *ZA de Atzilut* at the time of its birth, i.e., on one level with it. The world of *Yetzira* is either on the level of *Nukvah de Atzilut* (in *Panim be Panim*) or has only 4 *Sefirot* on this level, while 6 lower *Sefirot* are under the *Parsa* in the place of the 6 upper *Sefirot* of *Beria*.

The lowest 10th part of any *Partzuf* is called *Malchut*. After *TB* and up to the Final Correction, its use is forbidden. Therefore, a circumcision takes place; this *Sefira* is removed and a *Zivug* is made on the *Ateret haYesod*.

Each member of our group donates the tenth part of his income that cannot be used until the *Gmar Tikkun*. Only the corrected nine parts may be worked with. This is done in correspondence with the spiritual worlds.

קמט) ועולם העשיה, שנברר ע"י עולם היצירה, נבחן למדרגת בריאה של עתה. כי מתוך שעולם היצירה היה אז במדרגת הנוקבא דאצילות, נמצא המדרגה שמתחתיה עולם העשיה, שהוא בבחינת עולם הבריאה של עתה. אלא מתוך שרק הד"ר דיצירה היה בבחינת הנוקבא דאצילות, והשש תחתונות שלה היו בעולם הבריאה, לכן גם עולם העשיה שמתחתיה, נמצאים רק הד"ר שלו בבחינת ד"ס תחתונות דעולם הבריאה, והשש התחתונות דעולם העשיה היו במקום שש ראשונות דעולם היצירה של עתה.

ונמצאו אז י"ד הספירות, שהם נהי"ם דיצירה של עתה, וכל הע"ס דעולם עשיה של עתה, היו ריקנות מכל קדושה. ונעשו למדור הקליפות. כי רק הקליפות היו נמצאות במקום י"ד ספירות הללו. כי העולמות דקדושה נסתיימו במקום החזה דעולם היצירה של עתה. והנה נתבאר מדרגות שיעורי הקומה של פרצופי בי"ע ומקום עמידתם בעת שנאצלו בראשונה.

149) The world of Assiya corrected with the help of the world of Yetzira is defined as the level, taken by the world of Beria today. This is because previously the world of Yetzira was on the level of Nukvah de Atzilut. That is why the level below it refers to the world of Assiya – today's Beria. However, only the 4 first Sefirot de Yetzira were on the level of the Nukvah de Atzilut, while its 6 lower Sefirot were on the level of Beria. Hence, the 4 first Sefirot de Assiya are on the level of the 4 lower Sefirot de Beria, and the 6 first Sefirot de Assiya are in the place of the 6 upper Sefirot of the actual location of Yetzira.

Thus, the four Sefirot de Netzah, Hod, Yesod and Malchut of today's Yetzira and all the 10 Sefirot of the actual world of Assiya stopped being related to Kedusha (holiness) and passed to the Klipot (the uncorrected desires). The level from the Chazeh de Yetzira to the Sium de Assiya cannot be taken by anything but the Klipot; the pure worlds are located above the Chazeh of today's Yetzira. Now we know the levels taken by the worlds of BYA and their place, created before the actual formation of those worlds.

So, before the sin of *Adam haRishon*, at the moment of creation of the worlds of *BYA*, the worlds and the *Partzufim* were positioned in the following way:

1. *ZA de Atzilut* was on today's level of *Arich Anpin (Abba, Hochma).*

2. *Malchut (Nukvah) de Atzilut* was on the level of *Abba ve Ima (Bina).*

3. The world of *Beria* was on the level of today's *ZA de Atzilut.*

4. The four upper *Sefirot* of the world of *Yetzira* were on the level of *Malchut de Atzilut* and the six lower *Sefirot* – on the level of the six upper *Sefirot* of today's world of *Beria*. We may say that the places of *Malchut* and *ZA de Atzilut* in *Gadlut* (10 *Sefirot* in each) are not one under the other, but on the same level. When *Malchut* is in *Katnut*, its four upper *Sefirot* are on the level of the four lower *Sefirot* of *ZA*, and its six lower *Sefirot* are under the *Parsa*.

5. The four upper *Sefirot* of the world of *Assiya* were on the level of the four lower *Sefirot* of today's world of *Beria*; its six lower *Sefirot* were on the level of today's world of *Yetzira*. Thus, previously all the worlds were 14 *Sefirot* higher than they are now.

After the breaking of the vessels, the screen rose to the *Rosh de* SAG with all the *Reshimot* left from the breaking above the *Parsa* and with all the fragments that fell down. The screen is in *Nikvey Eynaim de Keter* of the *Rosh de* SAG. It begins to make *Zivugim* on the *Reshimot* left in it after the breaking. Since the breaking of the vessels included the entire *Malchut* of the World of Infinity, there were *Reshimot* left on all kinds of broken vessels that fell under the *Parsa*.

First, the *Masach* selects the best *Reshimot* and makes a *Zivug* on them. Further *Zivugim* are performed on the remaining *Reshimot* according to their deterioration. These *Zivugim* lead to the birth of the *Partzufim* one after another, from the best to the worst. First, Atik is born, then

Arich Anpin, Abba ve Ima, YESHSUT, ZA and *Nukvah de Atzilut*. All the *Reshimot* of *GE* (the vessels of bestowal) end here.

In addition to the vessels that have only one desire – either to bestow or to receive, vessels emerge that have both of these desires mixed. Now they can be sorted out and create additional *Partzufim*. *Malchut* of the World of Infinity undertakes this mission.

Initially, it is just a point with a single *Sefira, Keter*. Then it rises to ZA and receives the state of *Katnut* there. After that, it rises to *Bina* and grows to match its size. Now it can give birth like the higher Partzufim. Being on the level of *Bina*, it makes a *Zivug* on *Bet de Aviut* and gives birth to the world of *Beria*, which has to descend one level below its mother, i.e., to the level of ZA *de Atzilut*.

The world of *Yetzira* is born from a *Zivug de Haka'a* on *Gimel de Aviut* and descends below ZA, i.e., to *Nukvah de Atzilut*. *Nukvah* is not completely under ZA, but dresses its four upper *Sefirot* on it, its six lower *Sefirot* being under the *Parsa*. Hence, the world of *Yetzira* takes the place of *Nukvah* and its four upper *Sefirot* cover the four lower *Sefirot* of ZA, while its six lower *Sefirot* dress onto six lower *Sefirot de Nukvah*, under the *Parsa*, i.e., overlap with the six first *Sefirot* of the place of *Beria* in its actual location.

If some *Partzuf* ascends to or descends from a certain level, it means that it assumes the properties of the level on which it currently rests.

Even in our world, if a person feels the desire to do something good, he is thought to be improving his properties and spiritually rising. "I ascend," means that my properties do not correspond to the level I was on previously, but reach a higher level that I dress upon, so to speak.

Now, we begin to study how all the *Partzufim* of the world of *Atzilut* dress, one after the other, onto their corresponding *Partzufim* of the world of *Adam Kadmon*. The spiritual world's ladder is permanent; it can move up and down as a whole with regard to something. Nothing disappears in the spiritual realm. Hence, even while moving, the spiritual ladder stays in its place.

קנ) ועתה נבאר הבחן הג', שהוא שיעורי קומה דפרצופי בי"ע ומצב עמידתם, שהיה להם מהמוחין דתוספת, מטרם חטאו של אדה"ר. והוא, כי ע"י הארת תוספת שבת, היה להם אז ב' עליות: א. בשעה חמשית בערב שבת, שבו נולד אדה"ר. שאז מתחיל להאיר תוספת שבת, בסוד הה' דיום הששי.

ואז השיג הז"א בחינת יחידה ועלה והלביש לא"א דאצילות, והנוקבא בחינת חיה, ועלתה והלבישה לאו"א דאצילות, והבריאה עלתה לישסו"ת, והיצירה עלתה כולה לז"א, והד"ס ראשונות דעשיה עלו למקום הנוקבא דאצילות, והשש תחתונות דעשיה עלו במקום שש ראשונות דבריאה.

ב. היתה בערב שבת בין הערבים. שע"י תוספת שבת, עלו גם הו' תחתונות דעשיה למקום הנוקבא דאצילות, והיו עומדים עולם היצירה ועולם העשיה בעולם האצילות במקום זו"ן דאצילות בבחינת פב"פ.

150) Now we clear up the third definition: the height of the Partzufim of BYA during the reception of the additional light of the Mochin after the sin of Adam haRishon. There were two ascents of the worlds with the help of the additional light on Shabbat. The first ascent took place on the fifth hour of Erev (eve) Shabbat, when Adam haRishon was born. Then the additional light of Shabbat called "Hey de Yom haShishi" began to shine.

At that time, ZA reached the level of Yechida, rose, and dressed upon Arich Anpin de Atzilut. The Nukvah reached the level of Haya, then rose and dressed upon Abba ve Ima de Atzilut. Beria rose to YESHSUT, Yetzira – to ZA; the four first Sefirot de Assiya rose to the place of Nukvah de Atzilut. The six lower Sefirot de Assiya rose to the six upper Sefirot de Beria.

The second ascent of the worlds took place on Erev of Shabbat when, with the help of the additional light on Shabbat, the six lower Sefirot de Assiya rose to the place of Nukvah de Atzilut. Thus, both worlds, Yetzira and Assiya, rose above the Parsa and found their place in ZON de Atzilut in the state of Panim de Panim.

The worlds of *BYA* were born before *Adam haRishon*. Then *Partzuf Adam haRishon* emerged. It was born from *Malchut de Atzilut* that had risen to *Bina*. What is the difference between the births of *Adam haRishon* and the worlds of *BYA*?

The worlds of *BYA* are created from *GE*, which fell to *AHP* of *ZON de Nikudim*. *Adam haRishon* is a totally new construction that derives from the inner thought of creation. When the 4 phases of Direct Light were completed and *Malchut* of the World of Infinity emerged, it began to receive the light that gradually revealed its previous parts, *Gimel, Bet, Aleph,* and *Shoresh*, which had given birth to it.

Malchut cannot overstep its own limits, but it discovers the previous phases due to the deeper attainment of light that fills it. *Malchut* gradually starts building up nine more *Sefirot* (the light properties) out of the initial point and attains them little by little. The tenth part is *Malchut* itself.

It makes a *Tzimtzum* on this tenth part (on itself) and wishes to become similar to the nine *Sefirot-Partzufim*. Not all worlds and *Partzufim* are *Malchut* itself. They are just its attempts to copy the light, mere lifeless objects. The central point of the creation – *Malchut* of the World of Infinity, starts working after the completion of all the worlds and the breaking of the vessels.

A special combination between *Malchut de Malchut* (the Essence of the Creation) and the nine first *Sefirot* is called *Adam haRishon*. It is destined to become equal to the Creator.

During *TB*, *Malchut* of the World of Infinity rose to *Tifferet* of *Nekudot de SAG*, separating the vessels of reception from the vessels of bestowal. It remained there ever since.

Malchut de Atzilut, which is also on the level of the *Parsa*, is its direct representative. Then *Malchut de Atzilut* rises to *Bina* and makes a *Zivug de Haka'a* only on the *GE*; it does not work with the *AHP*.

The created *Partzuf*, which has so far only the vessels of *GE*, is called *Adam haRishon*. The direct participation of *Malchut* of the World of Infinity in the creation of *Adam haRishon* turns it into the most important *Partzuf*. In fact, it is the true Creation. The difference between *Adam haRishon* and all other spiritual objects is enormous.

Since it was also born from *Malchut de Atzilut*, which gave birth to the worlds of the *BYA*, *Adam haRishon* is inside these worlds. Its head begins below *Malchut* located in *Bina*, in the place of *ZA de Atzilut*. Its throat corresponds with the four upper *Sefirot* of *Malchut de Atzilut* above the *Parsa*. The body from the shoulders to the *Tabur*, is below the *Parsa*, in the place of the first six *Sefirot* of the world *Beria*, or in the place of the six lower *Sefirot* of the world *Yetzira* or in the place of the six lower *Sefirot* of the *Malchut de Atzilut*.

Then the *Partzuf Adam haRishon* spreads from the *Chazeh* of the world of *Beria* to its end; its feet end on the level of *Chazeh de Yetzira*, where the world of *Assiya* ends in this particular state. The height of *Partzuf Adam haRishon* is equal to that of the worlds of *BYA*. Such was the state of the *Partzuf Adam haRishon* at the moment of its birth.

A totally new structure was born. If previously only the environment for correction of the creation (called the central point or the *Malchut* of the World of Infinity) was being created, now it can be completely corrected. The common soul of *Adam* must be broken into fragments that altruistic desires will later enter. The breaking of the *Partzuf Adam haRishon* was similar to the breaking of the *Kelim de Nikudim*. The vessels of bestowal will enter the central point. This could not be achieved before.

Now let us see how the breaking of the *Partzuf Adam haRishon*, which is inside the worlds of *BYA* and can ascend and descend only together with them, took place.

Adam HaRishon, with its vessels of bestowal, performed all kinds of different actions, but then it realized that the most significant action for the Creator's sake can be done only through receiving the light of *Hochma*. It must have the vessels of reception, which are absent in it, or, rather, not yet corrected. Its intentions were quite clear.

Hence, it starts attaching to itself the vessels of reception, whereupon they break (as they previously did in the world of *Nikudim*) inside its *Guf*, both the *GE* and the *AHP*. After the breaking, altruistic sparks penetrate the vessels of reception. From this point on, the work of each fragment of *Adam's* soul (feeling separate from one another) begins.

All this corresponds to what must be done by everyone in this world. When *Adam's* soul was broken, in addition to the downfall of the vessels from the level of *Atzilut*, a whole system of impure worlds was formed: *Atzilut*, *Beria*, *Yetzira*, and *Assiya de Tuma*, which correspond to the four pure worlds. Human souls exist between these two systems.

Our present state is a consequence of the breaking of *Adam haRishon's* soul. We are a construction consisting of a biological body saturated with egoistic desires. As we mentioned, altruistic sparks, called the *"Ner Dakik"* (a tiny candle), fell inside these desires. If the *Ner Dakik* manifests in an altruistic desire, man starts longing for something uncertain, trying to satisfy that wish.

But there is nothing in our world that can fill this desire – all pleasures of this world are egoistic. Man would run around searching, until he finds a source that can (or so it will seem to him) somehow fill the void or will do so in the future. If this is a group of students headed by a Teacher-Kabbalist, then such a man will gradually begin to transform his egoistic vessels into altruistic ones, attaining the Creator in them.

How does this correction take place? There are 320 sparks inside each human being. Man must do exactly what happened in the world of *Atzilut*, i.e., sort out the 288 sparks and separate them from the *Lev haEven* (32 egoistic sparks), from its central point, (the egoistic essence, nature), and say that he stops working with them in order to become similar to the altruistic desires.

Man should do it consciously, by sparing no effort, overcoming the formidable resistance of his own egoism. This work forms the vessels that man did not have before. As a result, it allows him to work with the nine altruistic *Sefirot*, the *Lev haEven* remaining inactive. Upon sorting out all altruistic desires and restricting 32 egoistic desires, man achieves the *Gmar Tikkun*. By struggling against his egoism, he preferred to become equal to the Creator.

After that, the upper light descends from above and corrects the *Lev haEven* in such a way that it may now be used for receiving the *Ohr Hochma* for the sake of the Creator. Somehow, the light *AB-SAG* affects this point and corrects it. Such correction is called the arrival of the *Mashiach*; the *Malchut* of the World of Infinity completely merges with the Creator, i.e., reaches its third and final state. It is worth mentioning that the first state is the *Malchut* of the World of Infinity prior to *Tzimtzum Aleph*. The second state is the descending formation of the worlds and the creation's correction through gradual ascent.

The additional light for the ascent of *Adam haRishon* is called the "*Hey de Yom haShishi*", i.e., the 5th hour of the 6th day. *Adam haRishon* reaches this level together with the worlds of *BYA*. This is the first ascent (the 10 *Sefirot* of one world) on the eve of *Shabbat*. If before this ascent the feet of *Adam haRishon* and the world of *Assiya* were on the level of the *Chazeh de Yetzira*, then afterwards they ascend to the *Chazeh de Beria*.

The world of *Atzilut* has many states. We must be very attentive while studying the world of *Atzilut* – in accordance with the changes in man's sensations in the process of his correction. All the names of the Torah have definite roots in the world of *Atzilut* – one source of all that exists.

This includes the general and individual control, the soul's reincarnations, the ascents and descents, etc. If man studies the material correctly, he steps back each time he starts learning about *Atzilut*, realizing that it is over his head. This happens several times for a few years, until man begins to establish contact with this enormous system, when some form of connection with the world of *Atzilut* manifests inside him.

The purest desires rise during the first ascent, while the darkest, most egoistic sink, forming a division between the corrected and the uncorrected desires in both man and the worlds. The emptiness that formed between them, is called "*Tehum Shabbat*". In our world, it is symbolized by the distance a man may move away from a city wall without violating the laws of *Shabbat*.

Man is not allowed to leave "the domain of the One" for "the domain of the many". "The domain of the One" (the "*Reshut haYachid*") is a state, when all of man's thoughts, desires and prayers are directed to the Creator, when man always justifies Him and perceives all His deeds as those of "the Kind One Creating Goodness" ("*Tov ve Meitiv*"). Such desires are completely corrected and are in the world of *Atzilut*.

As well, man also has the desires that have not been corrected yet. He is still in doubt: does the Creator rule over everything or not, and if He does, is His rule good or bad? Perhaps the society, the boss, the wife, or the children are to blame in all his troubles. These diverse aspirations and thoughts in man are called "the domain of the many" ("*Reshut haRabim*"). These desires are below the *Chazeh de Yetzira* and down to the *Sium*. In all, they constitute 14 *Sefirot* and are called the *Mador* (section) *haKlipot*.

After the *Shabbat* ascents, the section from the *Parsa de Atzilut* to the *Mador haKlipot* is an empty space consisting of 16 *Sefirot*. These are in turn divided into two parts: the first part is made up of the six upper *Sefirot* of the world of *Beria*, the second part – the ten *Sefirot* from the *Chazeh de Beria* to the *Chazeh de Yetzira*. The first six *Sefirot* of the world of *Beria* are called "*Iburo shel Yir*" ("conception of a city"). This can be compared to a pregnant woman whose belly belongs to her, but which at the same time protrudes because there is a foreign body inside it. On the one hand, it is so far related to her, but, on the other – may be considered as a separate entity.

Such a state is called *Ibur*: still related to the upper one, but also to a new creation.

The world of *Atzilut*, the Creator's domain, is called "a city". In his thoughts, man can step out of the city's bounds (albeit no farther than the *Chazeh de Beria*) without committing a transgression. This additional section ("*Iburo shel Yir*") is the 70 *Amah* (an *Amah* is the distance from wrist to elbow, i.e., seven *Sefirot*: *HaBaD HaGaT*) from the *Chazeh*. This still refers to the city, although outside its walls.

At the end of the 70 *Amah* from the *Chazeh de Yetzira* to the *Chazeh de Beria*, an additional area of 2000 *Amah* stretches on. These are 10 *Sefirot* called "*Tehum Shabbat*". Man can step into these 2000 *Amah* without transgressing his unity with the Creator, called *Shabbat*, because there are no impure desires in this area. Such is the power of the *Shabbat* luminescence; it allows man, who is in the world of *Atzilut*, to descend to that level without losing his connection with the Creator. Thus, the 16 upper *Sefirot* of the worlds of *BYA* are still the vessels of bestowal; therefore, man can be in them without leaving the bounds of *Atzilut*.

We have examined the two ascents of the worlds of *BYA* and *Adam haRishon* to *Atzilut* (first, 6 *Sefirot*, then 10 more) that took place on the eve of *Shabbat*. Sixteen empty *Sefirot* are in this state below the world of *Atzilut* down to the *Chazeh de Yetzira*. They are still regarded as the vessels of bestowal; hence, their properties are very close to those of *Atzilut*.

As was stated above, the worlds of *BYA* were created from the broken vessels of the world of *Nikudim* that fell under the *Parsa* and intermixed. This created the following four kinds: vessels of bestowal, vessels of reception, vessels of reception mixed with vessels of bestowal and vessels of bestowal mixed with vessels of reception. First, the *Partzuf SAG* selects the vessels of bestowal out of all the broken fragments. These form the world of *Atzilut* that consists exclusively of *GE*, which even before the breaking were in the world of *Nikudim* as *GE de ZON*. *ZON de Atzilut* correspond to *ZON de Nikudim*.

Three kinds of vessels remain unused:

1. The egoistic vessels of reception. The *SAG* sorts them out, puts them aside, and does not work with them. This is the *Lev haEven*; no altruistic intentions can correct it until the *Gmar Tikkun*.

2. The vessels of bestowal that fell into the vessels of reception and cannot be separated from them. These are the worlds of *BYA*, which resemble a narrow lucid altruistic stripe within a mass of egoistic desires.

3. The vessels of reception are included in the vessels of bestowal. They are called "*AHP de Aliyah*" of the world of *Atzilut*. With their help, *Ohr Hochma* can be received in addition to *Ohr Hassadim* in *Atzilut*, thus allowing it to receive *Gadlut*. Thus, we have learned what can be received out of all four kinds of broken vessels of the *ZON de Nikudim*.

As *Adam's* soul breaks, four more kinds of broken vessels are formed. They are not in the worlds of *BYA* anymore, but fall to our world under the *Sium de Galgalta*. All these breakings lead to the fact that there are roots of the altruistic desires (the *AHP de Elion*) inside *GE de Tachton* (the lower *Partzuf*). Thus, it becomes possible to correct the vessels.

Now, if man begins to study in a proper group, guided by a true Teacher, he attracts the influence of the Surrounding Light (the *Ohr Makif*), which gradually purifies the fragments of *GE* inside his egoistic vessels. Inside himself, man builds his own world of *Atzilut* with the help of the corrected vessels of *GE*. On each level, the *Lev haEven* is not worked with.

Therefore, it turns out that man reflects all that seemingly happens outside of him, i.e., the worlds of *AK* and of *BYA*. As he corrects his vessels, man receives the light of *AK ABYA*. Upon completing his correction, he becomes equal to the distance between the central point of our world and the World of Infinity, i.e., he matches the size of *Galgalta*, and all the corrected fragments (all human souls) completely fill the entire *Malchut* of the World of Infinity with the light.

קנא) ועתה נבאר הבחן הד', שהוא קומת המוחין שנשתיירו בבי"ע. ומקום נפילתם לאחר החטא. והוא, כי מחמת פגם חטאו של עצה"ד, נסתלקו מהעולמות כל המוחין דתוספת, שהשיגו ע"י ב' העליות. והזו"ן חזר לו"ק ונקודה.

151) Now let us clear up the fourth definition – the level of the Mochin in the worlds of BYA and the place of these worlds' downfall after the sin of Adam haRishon. It is known that, due to the damage caused by Adam's sin, the Mochin completely disappeared from these worlds, i.e., all the additional light that the worlds received during the two ascents on Shabbat eve.

Furthermore, ZON *de Atzilut* returned to the state of *Vak* and *Nekuda*.

This means that now, as regards the vessels, ZA again has only the six upper *Sefirot, HaBaD HaGaT*, filled with the six "lower" lights, the *HaGaT NHY* (inverse relation between the lights and the vessels). Now *Malchut de Atzilut* has only one *Sefira* – *Keter* with the *Ohr Nefesh* under the *Parsa*.

וג' העולמות בי"ע, נשתיירו בהם רק המוחין שיצאו בהם בראשונה בעת אצילותם, שעולם הבריאה היה במדרגת הז"א שפירושו ו"ק, וכן היצירה ועשיה בשיעור הנ"ל (אות קמ"ח). ונוסף ע"ז, כי נסתלק מהם כל בחינת אצילות ונפלו למתחת הפרסא דאצילות בתכונת מקום בי"ע, שהוכן ע"י צמצום ב' (אות קמ"ה). ונמצאו ד"ת דיצירה וע"ס דעולם העשיה, שנפלו ועמדו במקום הי"ד ספירות של הקליפות (אות קמ"ט), הנקרא "מדור הקליפות".

The worlds of BYA are now filled only with the light that they had during their birth. They are in the state of Vak (ZA). Moreover, they fell under the Parsa to the place of the worlds of BYA, prepared for them after TB. Now the 4 last Sefirot of the world of Yetzira and all 10 Sefirot of the world of Assiya are in the place of the 14 Sefirot of the Mador haKlipot.

קנב) הבחן הה' הוא המוחין דאמא, שקבלו בי"ע במקום נפילתם. כי אחר שיצאו הבי"ע מאצילות ונפלו למתחת הפרסא דאצילות, לא היה בהם אלא בחינת ו"ק (אות קנ"א). ואז נתלבשו הישסו"ת בהזו"ן דאצילות. ונזדווגו הישסו"ת מבחינת התלבשות בזו"ן. והשפיעו מוחין דנשמה לפרצופי בי"ע במקומם: שעולם הבריאה קבל מהם ע"ס שלמות בקומת בינה, ועולם היצירה קבל מהם ו"ק, ועולם העשיה רק בחינת אב"א.

152) The fifth peculiarity of the worlds of BYA consists in the fact that, during the fall, they received the Mochin de Ima. When the worlds of BYA left Atzilut and fell under the Parsa, they were on the level of Vak. Then YESHSUT de Atzilut dressed upon ZON de Atzilut, made a Zivug on the Reshimo de Hitlabshut in ZON, and passed the light of Neshama to the worlds of BYA. Thus, the world of Beria received from it 10 full Sefirot on the level of Bina, the world of Yetzira –Vak de Bina, and the world of Assiya – only Behina Achor be Achor, i.e., one point of the Malchut de Bina.

קנג) הבחן הו' הוא בחינת נשמה לנשמה, שהשיגו פרצופי בי"ע מפרצופי האחור דה"פ אצילות. כי בעת מיעוט הירח נפל פרצוף האחור דנוקבא דאצילות ונתלבש בפרצופי בי"ע. והוא כולל ג' פרצופים, המכונים: עבור, יניקה, מוחין. ובחינת המוחין נפלה לבריאה, ובחינת היניקה נפלה ליצירה, ובחינת העיבור נפלה לעשיה. ונעשו בחינת נשמה לנשמה לכל פרצופי בי"ע, שהיא בחינת חיה אליהם.

153) The sixth peculiarity is the level of Neshama de Neshama (Haya) reached by the worlds of BYA from the five Partzufim de Achoraim of the world of Atzilut. It happened because during the lunar diminution (Miut haYareach), i.e., Malchut de Atzilut, nine of its lower Sefirot forming the "Partzuf de Achor de Nukvah" fell under the Parsa and dressed on the Partzufim BYA, which included three stages: Ibur, Yenika and Mochin. The Behinat Mochin (adult state) fell to the world of Beria, Behina Yenika fell to Yetzira, and Behina Ibur fell to Assiya. Thus, all three worlds of BYA received Behina Neshama le Neshama.

ZA builds *Malchut*, and gives it all the power. The final, ultimate state comes when ZA and *Malchut* become equal and establish full contact with one another. Then *Malchut* receives from ZA without restraint, at the same time being pleased to bestow delight upon it.

This final state is called a *Zivug de ZON Panim de Panim*. *Malchut* wished to achieve it already on the fourth day of creation. Eager to receive the light from *Bina*, *Malchut* rose to ZA, but discovered that its (of *Malchut*) vessels are defective; hence, instead of the light, it received total darkness.

Darkness is *Ohr Hochma* not dressed in *Ohr Hassadim*. Therefore, *Malchut* starts complaining that the two *Partzufim* cannot possibly receive the light from the same source. ZA has both *Ohr Hassadim* and *Ohr Hochma*. *Malchut*, however, has no *Ohr Hassadim*; it must correct its vessels, its intentions.

The only way out of this state is to contract into a point (one *Sefira*), assume its natural size and start gradually correcting its vessels, i.e., acquire a screen. The diminution of *Malchut* is called a *Kitrug haYareach*, i.e., the Moon's (*Malchut's*) complaint about being unable to shine like the Sun (ZA). It has to turn itself into a point and then start growing systematically, until it reaches the ultimate state. Still it will not be able to shine like the Sun, i.e., in any case *Malchut* will receive the light from ZA.

קנד) הבחן הז' הוא הנוקבא דאצילות, שנעשתה לרדל"א ולהארת יחידה בבי"ע. כי נתבאר, שבעת מיעוט הירח, נפלו ג' הבחינות עי"מ (עיבור, יניקה, מוחין) דפרצוף האחור דנוקבא דאצילות ונתלבשו בבי"ע. והם בחינת אחורים דט"ת דנוקבא, שהם עי"מ: שנה"י נקרא "עיבור", וחג"ת נקרא "יניקה", וחב"ד נקרא "מוחין".

אמנם בחינת האחור דבחינת הכתר דנוקבא, נעשתה לבחינת עתיק לפרצופי בי"ע. באופו שבחינת עיקר אורותיהם דפרצופי בי"ע של עתה, הם מהשירים שנשארו בהם אחר חטאו של אדה"ר, שהוא בחינת הו"ק דכל פרט מהם (אות קנ"א). ובחינת נשמה קבלו ממוחין דאמא (אות קנ"ב), ובחינת נשמה לנשמה, שהוא בחינת חיה, קבלו מט"ת דפרצוף האחור דנוקבא, ובחינת יחידה קבלו מבחינת האחור דכתר דנוקבא דאצילות.

154) The seventh peculiarity is the Sefira Keter of Nukvah de Atzilut, absolutely unattainable by the worlds of BYA, but which emanates faint luminescence of Ohr Yechida onto them. As it turned out, during the lunar diminution, Behinot Ibur, Yenika and Mochin of the back part of Nukva de Atzilut fell under the Parsa and dressed upon the worlds of the BYA. The NHY are called Ibur, HaGaT – Yenika and HaBaD –Mochin.

However, Achoraim of Keter de Nukva turn into Atik as regards the Partzufim de BYA, and are unattainable. The light shining in BYA is just a faint luminescence, compared to what it was prior to the "Fall" (sin). The worlds receive Ohr Nefesh from Ibur, Ohr

Ruach – from Yenika and Ohr Neshama – from Mochin de Ima. The Neshama de Neshama (the Ohr Haya) is received from the nine lower Sefirot de Nukva and Behinat Yechida – from the Achoraim de Keter of Nukva de Atzilut (the point of Malchut de Atzilut).

We have already mentioned that, on the fourth day of creation, a so-called lunar diminution took place. *Malchut de Atzilut* wishes to be like *ZA de Atzilut*, so it rises to *Bina*, but cannot receive the same light as ZA gets, for it neither has the intention to receive for the Creator's sake, nor the screen to resist the egoistic desires.

Only upon receiving the *Ohr Hassadim*, which would dress onto the *Ohr Hochma* and take it in, will it be able to acquire the properties of ZA. Hence, *Bina* refuses to receive the *Ohr Hochma*. Instead of *Ohr Hochma*, *Malchut* felt darkness. This happens when there are desires without the proper intentions.

Existing in our world, we feel neither darkness, nor light. We cannot feel the preliminary state of darkness for the lack of the necessary desire to receive pleasure, even for our own sake. When the enormous desire acquired for spiritual delight becomes as all-consuming as a great love, we will discover within ourselves the intention to receive the light for the sake of the Creator.

How can this be done? *Bina* advises *Malchut* to diminish itself. *Malchut* contracts into a point and begins gradually to acquire a screen in the three stages *Ibur*, *Yenika*, and *Mochin*.

THE ASCENTS OF THE WORLDS
ביאור ענין עליות העולמות

קנה) עיקר ההפרש מפרצופי א"ק לפרצופי עולם האצילות הוא, כי פרצופי א"ק הם מבחינת צמצום א'. שבכל מדרגה שבו יש בה ע"ס שלמות. ואין בע"ס רק בחינת כלי אחד, שהוא כלי מלכות. אבל הט"ס ראשונות הן רק בחינת אורות לבד.

משא"כ פרצופי אצילות הם מבחינת צמצום הב', בסו"ה "ביום עשות הוי"ה אלהים ארץ ושמים", ששיתף רחמים בדין (אות נ"ט). שמדת הדין, שהיא מלכות, עלתה ונתחברה בהבינה, שהיא מדת הרחמים. ונשתתפו יחד.

שעי"ז נעשה סיום חדש על אור העליון במקום הבינה. שהמלכות המסיימת את הגוף עלתה לבינה דגוף, שהיא ת"ת, במקום החזה. והמלכות המזדווגת שבפה דראש עלתה לבינה דראש, הנקרא "נקבי עינים", שעי"ז נתמעטו שיעור קומת הפרצופים לגו"ע, שהם כתר חכמה דכלים, בקומת ו"ק בלי ראש, שהוא נפש רוח דאורות (אות ע"ד). ונמצאו חסרים מאח"פ דכלים, שהם בינה וזו"ן, ומנשמה חיה יחידה דאורות.

155) The principal distinction between the worlds of AK and Atzilut consists in the fact that the Partzufim of the world of Adam Kadmon emerged as a consequence of Tzimtzum Aleph. Each of their levels includes 10 full Sefirot with one single vessel – Malchut. The nine first Sefirot constitute exclusively the light, the Creator.

The Partzufim de Atzilut is the result of Tzimtzum Bet. When we say that on that day the Creator created the Heaven and the Earth, we mean the Rachamim (mercy) were included in the Din (judgment) during the ascent of Malchut (the level of Din) to Bina (the level of Rachamim) and their merging.

As a result, a new Sium of the Upper Light appeared in Bina on the level of Chazeh (as Malchut Mesayemet rises to Bina). The Malchut Mizdaveget, which was in the Peh de Rosh, rose to Bina de Rosh called the Nikvey Eynaim, so that only the vessels Keter and Hochma remained on the level of Vak without the Rosh, i.e., the lights Nefesh and Ruach. Out of the five vessels, Bina, ZA and Malchut are absent as well as the lights Neshama, Haya and Yechida.

The worlds have two parts: the inner and the outer. The place of *ABYA* is called the outer worlds. Inside this place, there must be an inner part where the world of *Nikudim* is located. The root of the outer part of the worlds is the *Partzuf Nekudot de SAG* that merged with *Behina Dalet* during its descent under *Tabur de Galgalta*. From the merging of the *Behinot Bet* and *Dalet*, the place between the *Tabur* and the *Sium* split into two parts: the place of *Atzilut* and the place of *BYA*.

There are 10 vessels in each *Partzuf* of the worlds of *ABYA* and *Nikudim*. This was caused by the rise of *Malchut* to *Bina* of each *Sefira*. In *TA*, there is only one *Kli*, since below there is only one *Malchut*, that receives the light from the nine first *Sefirot*.

Ten *Kelim* are formed in *TB*. Due to the Second Restriction, *Malchut* ascends to the nine first *Sefirot* (*Tet Rishonot*). Are these *Sefirot* considered the lights? Does *Malchut* rise to the lights?

There is a rule: *Behina Dalet* is called the *Kli*, and the nine first *Sefirot* are called the lights. The "desire to receive" is *Behina Dalet*; hence, it is separated from the light. In the spiritual world, *Behina Dalet* is reception for its own sake without a hint of bestowal.

The first nine *Sefirot* are the lights and *Malchut* receives all that these nine *Sefirot* have to offer. Now this *Behina* pushes the light away, as if to say, if I can work with the altruistic intention like the light, then I should receive for the sake of bestowal. This transformation of the intention is the essential difference between work for the Creator's sake and reception for one's own.

קנו) והגם שנתבאר (אות קכ"ד), שע"י עלית מ"ן לעיבור ב' השיגו פרצופי אצילות הארת המוחין מע"ב ס"ג דא"ק, המוריד הה"ת מנקבי עינים בחזרה למקומה לפה, כבצמצום א', ומשיגים שוב האח"פ דכלים והנשמה חיה יחידה דאורות.

אמנם זה הועיל רק לבחינת הע"ס דראש של הפרצופים, ולא להגופים שלהם, כי המוחין הללו לא נמשכו מפה ולמטה אל הגופים שלהם (אות קל"ח). וע"כ גם לאחר המוחין דגדלות, נשארו הגופים בצמצום ב', כמו בזמן הקטנות.

ומשום זה נחשבו כל ה"פ אצילות, שאין להם רק קומת ע"ס היוצאת על עביות דבחי"א, שהוא קומת ז"א, ו"ק בלי ראש, הנקרא קומת מ"ה. והם מלבישים על קומת מ"ה דה"פ א"ק, דהיינו מטבור ולמטה דה"פ א"ק.

156) As was stated above, with the help of raising of MAN during the second Ibur, the Partzufim of the world of Atzilut received the light of Hochma from the Partzufim AB-SAG de AK. This light again lowered Malchut from Nikvey Eynaim de Rosh to Peh, as was the case before TB. Hence, the Partzufim again acquire the hitherto missing Kelim de Bina, ZA and Malchut and, correspondingly, the lights of Neshama, Haya, and Yechida.

This refers only to the 10 Sefirot de Rosh, but not to the Guf, since the light of Hochma has not yet spread from the Peh de Rosh to the Guf, so, even upon receiving the Mochin de Gadlut de Rosh, the Gufim still remained in the state of TB, as in Katnut.

Thus, the Partzufim de Atzilut are regarded as the level of the 10 Sefirot that emerged on Aviut de Behina Aleph. This corresponds to the level of ZA (Vak without Rosh), and is called the world of MA. They dress upon the Partzufim de MA (ZA) of the five Partzufim de AK, located below the Tabur.

A certain ban exists in the world of *Atzilut*: the light of the *Rosh* does not spread to the *Guf*. Once, *Gadlut* spread from the *Rosh* to the *Guf* in the world of *Nikudim*, which led to the breaking of the vessels. In the world of AK, we see that whatever is in the *Rosh* later spreads to the *Guf*.

After the breaking of the vessels in the world of *Nikudim*, the *Reshimot* remained. They clearly state that *Gadlut*, which occurred in the *Rosh* after the raising of MAN, will not pass to the *Guf* – it is forbidden. Hence, the light of *Gadlut* will never pass from the *Rosh to* the *Guf* in the world of *Atzilut*. Does it mean that the vessels of reception cannot be used? Then how will the correction take place?

The entire following process is a correction of egoism with the help of a very special method defined as the *AHP de Aliyah*, or the middle line.

However, in the world of *Atzilut* the light of *Gadlut* will never spread to the *Guf*, even provided an accurate calculation is made stating that it is quite safe to receive the light for the Creator's sake. It will never happen again in the spiritual world because of the remaining *Reshimot*.

All the *Partzufim* of the world of *Adam Kadmon* are divided in the following way: the *Rosh* is called *Keter*, the place from the *Peh* to the *Chazeh* is called *Hochma*, from the *Chazeh* to the *Tabur* – *Bina*, from the *Tabur* to *Yesod* – ZA, and the place from *Yesod* down to the *Sium* is called *Malchut*. If we take *Galgalta*, its *Rosh* is called *Keter*; from the *Peh* to the *Chazeh* is AB, from the *Chazeh* to the *Tabur* – SAG, from the *Tabur* to *Yesod* – MA and from *Yesod* to the *Sium* – *BON*.

Each *Partzuf* of the world of *Atzilut* dresses onto the corresponding part of the *Guf de AK*. For example, the *Partzuf Atik de Atzilut* refers to the *Partzuf Galgalta* as MA, i.e., the way ZA refers to *Keter*.

The *Rosh* of any *Partzuf* is a consequence of the previous state, which already passed and left the *Reshimot*. A new state appears based on these *Reshimot* with all the contiguous details. Hence, the *Rosh* contains all the information of the past.

As in our world, there is nothing unusual or unknown. Knowing the qualities of parents, we can more or less imagine and describe their future baby. As each new *Partzuf* emerges, one can very accurately foresee what it will be like.

However, what happened in the world of *Nikudim* does not seem to have been preprogrammed. There is one more *Rosh* – *YESHSUT*, which is under the *Tabur de Galgalta* and refers to *TA*. The lower *Rashim* are unaware of what happens in *TA*; they can find their bearings only within their own framework (*TB*).

The *YESHSUT* contains all information. As regards *TA*, it is interested in the further breaking. Had the *Kelim* de *Guf* of the world of *Nekudim* possessed the full information of *TB*, they would not have been able to receive the light for the Creator's sake, since their screen would not have withstood it.

After the breaking of the vessels, a special *Reshimo* in the *Rosh de Atzilut* prevents the light from spreading to the *Guf*. The *Guf* can be only in the state of *Vak*.

קנז) באופן: שפרצוף עתיק דאצילות מלביש על פרצוף הכתר דא"ק מטבורו ולמטה, ומקבל שפעו מקומת מ"ה דפרצוף הכתר דא"ק אשר שם, ופרצוף א"א דאצילות מלביש מטבור ולמטה דפרצוף ע"ב דא"ק, ומקבל שפעו מקומת מ"ה דע"ב דא"ק אשר שם. ואו"א דאצילות מלבישים מטבור ולמטה דפרצוף ס"ג דא"ק, ומקבלים שפעם מקומת מ"ה דס"ג אשר שם.

זו"ן דאצילות מלבישים מטבור ולמטה דפרצוף מ"ה וב"ן דא"ק, ומקבלים שפעם מקומת מ"ה דפרצוף מ"ה וב"ן דא"ק. הרי שכל פרצוף מה"פ אצילות אינו מקבל מפרצוף שכנגדו בא"ק, רק בחינת ו"ק בלי ראש, הנקרא קומת מ"ה.

ואע"פ שיש בראשים דה"פ אצילות בחינת ג"ר, מכל מקום אנו מתחשבים רק בהמוחין המתפשטים מפה ולמטה לגופים שלהם, שהוא רק ו"ק בלי ראש (אות קל"ט).

157) Atik de Atzilut receives the light from MA de Galgalta, i.e., dresses upon it from the Tabur to Yesod. The Partzuf Arich Anpin (AA) de Atzilut dresses onto the Partzuf AB from the Tabur and below and receives the light from MA de AB. The Partzuf Abba ve Ima de Atzilut dresses onto SAG de AK from the Tabur and below and receives the light from MA.

ZON de Atzilut dresses onto the Partzufim MA and BON of the world of AK and receive the light on this level. Thus, each Partzuf of the world of Atzilut receives light from the corresponding Partzuf de AK on the level of its Vak bli Rosh from the Tabur to Yesod, i.e., on the level of the MA de AK. However, it does not completely dress onto the corresponding Partzuf of the world of Adam Kadmon.

Despite the fact that the level of Ohr Hochma in the Rashim de Atzilut reaches the Gar, we take into account only that level of Hochma, which spreads from the Peh de Rosh to the Guf, i.e., the Vak bli Rosh or ZA.

The Universe consists of five worlds, that in turn include five *Partzufim*; each of them is divided into five parts in accordance with the degree of its *Aviut*. Starting with *TB*, each *Partzuf* has three states: *Ibur*, *Yenika*, and *Mochin*, one inside the other. The *AHP* of the upper *Partzuf* is inside the *GE* of the lower one. *Keter* of the lower *Partzuf* can receive the light only from *Malchut* of the upper.

Each *Partzuf* dresses onto the previous one from its *Peh* downwards as in *TB*. However, the *Partzufim* built according to *TB* have laws of their own. Everything depends on what function needs to be expressed. Besides, all the *Ketarim* are interconnected and so are *Hochmot*, etc. *Hochma* of the lower *Partzuf* cannot receive the light from *ZA* or *Bina* of the upper. *Hochma* receives from *Hochma* throughout the entire chain. Both overall and in particular, everything submits to the law of the similarity of properties.

Man starts attaining this entire intricate system only when he acquires the vessels corresponding to it. He becomes its integral part, can influence it, and is affected by it constantly.

קנח) ואין הכונה שה"פ אצילות מלבישים כל אחד על הבחינה שכנגדו בא"ק. כי זה אי אפשר, שהרי ה"פ א"ק מלבישים זה על זה. וכן ה"פ אצילות. אלא הכונה היא, שקומת כל פרצוף מפרצופי אצילות מכוונת לעומת הבחינה שכנגדו שבה"פ א"ק, שמשם מקבל שפעו (אילן, ציור ג').

158) This does not mean that each of the five Partzufim de Atzilut dresses onto the corresponding Behina in the world of AK. This is impossible, because the five Partzufim de AK dress one onto the other. The same happens to the five Partzufim de Atzilut. It means that the level of each Partzuf de Atzilut correlates with the level corresponding to it in the five Partzufim de AK and receives its light from there.

Now let us look at Diagram 3 in "*Sefer haIlan*" (The Book of the Tree) and the brief comment to it. It shows the permanent state of the five *Partzufim de AK*, from which the five *Partzufim de MA Hadash* (or *Atzi-*

lut) emerged in their permanency. Since they are the vessels of bestowal, no diminution ever happens in them, only *Gadlut*.

The book also examines the division of each *Partzuf* into *Keter* and *ABYA*, which are alternatively called *Keter*, *AB*, *SAG*, *MA* and *BON* or *Yechida*, *Haya*, *Neshama*, *Ruach* and *Nefesh*. Each *Rosh* down to its *Peh* is called *Keter* or *Yechida*. The distance from the *Peh* to the *Chazeh* in each of them is called *Atzilut*, *AB* or *Haya*; from the *Chazeh* to the *Tabur* – *Beria*, *SAG* or *Neshama*; below the *Tabur* – *Yetzira* and *Assiya*, *MA* and *BON*, or *Ruach* and *Nefesh*.

Now let us look at the order in which the *Partzufim* dress one onto the other. Each lower *Partzuf* dresses onto the upper from the *Peh* and below according to the following law: the *Rosh* of each lower *Partzuf* dresses onto the *AB* – *Atzilut* of the upper, *AB* – *Atzilut* of the lower – on the *SAG* – *Beria* of the upper; *SAG* - *Beria* of the lower – on the *MA* and the *BON* (*Yetzira* and *Assiya*) of the upper.

Thus, the *Peh* of the upper *Partzuf* is the level of *Galgalta* of the lower; the *Chazeh* of the upper serves the *Peh* of the lower; the *Tabur* of the upper is the *Chazeh* of the lower. The emergence of *MA Hadash* becomes clear in each of the five *Partzufim de Atzilut* and in the corresponding *Partzuf de AK*.

קנט) ובכדי שיושפעו המוחין מפה ולמטה אל הגופים דה"פ אצילות, נתבאר (אות קמ"א) שצריכים לעלית מ"ן מהתחתונים, שאז מושפעים להם השלמת הע"ס דמין הב' המספיק גם להגופים. והנה באלו המ"ן שהתחתונים מעלים, יש ג' בחינות.

כי כשמעלים מ"ן מבחינת עביות דבחי"ב, יוצאות עליהם ע"ס בקומת בינה, הנקראת קומת ס"ג, שהן מוחין דאור הנשמה. וכשמעלים מ"ן מעביות דבחי"ג, יוצאות עליהם ע"ס בקומת חכמה, הנקראת קומת ע"ב, שהן מוחין דאור החיה, וכשמעלים מ"ן מעביות דבחי"ד, יוצאות עליהם ע"ס בקומת כתר, הנקרא קומת גלגלתא, שהן מוחין דאור היחידה (אות כ"ט).

159) For the upper Partzufim to be able to spread the Mochin from the Peh down to the Gufim of the five Partzufim de Atzilut, the lower Partzufim must raise MAN. Only then can they receive an increase to the 10 Sefirot of the second kind sufficient for the Gufim. MAN is raised in three stages.

First, MAN, on Aviut Bet, gives birth to the 10 Sefirot de Bina, i.e., the SAG in Gadlut with the light of Neshama. Then MAN on Aviut Gimel creates the 10 Sefirot de Hochma, i.e., AB with the Mochin de Haya. When MAN is raised for the third time on Aviut Dalet, 10 Sefirot emerge on the level of Keter or Galgalta with Mochin de Yechida.

The light coming from above as a result of raised *MAN* increases the lower *Partzufim* to 10 *Sefirot* and provides them with enough strength to create a screen on their uncorrected properties and pass from the state of *Katnut* to *Gadlut* by using the second method, i.e., by adding *AHP* to *GE* in order to form the 10 *Sefirot*.

The light that enters a *Partzuf* depends on the *Aviut de Masach*, on the desire the *Partzuf* may use. Indeed, the amount of light that a *Partzuf* can absorb is equal to the degree to which it is willing to use the light for the Creator's sake.

As soon as something changes in one of the *Partzufim*, all the others are instantly transformed, for all of them are interrelated and interconnected. If man makes even a tiny correction, he immediately generates a tremendous light in all the *Partzufim* and the worlds. This is how important man's role is in changing the state of the world. Each element of the creation feels exactly what all others feel.

After the disappearance of the light, the *Reshimot* remain in the screen, which then rises to the *Rosh* and asks for strength in accordance with those *Reshimot*. After the breaking of the vessels in the world of *Nikudim*, the screen with all the *Reshimot* ascends, eager to be filled again, and wills to acquire the new power of intention.

Each consecutive level may be born only after the complete emergence of the previous one, i.e., the *Partzuf Arich Anpin* may not be born before *Atik* is fully formed. The *Rosh de SAG* analyses the *Reshimot Dalet-Gimel* and gives birth to *Atik*. *Behinat Hochma* cannot emerge before it is born.

After the *Rosh de SAG* fills *Atik* and brings it to the state of *Gadlut*, it passes to *Atik* all the *Reshimot* it had in order for *Atik* to select the smallest of them. Therefore, *Atik* chooses MAN (a screen) and the *Reshimot de Behinat Hochma*.

Then, after the formation of *Katnut* and *Gadlut* in AA, it receives all the *Reshimot* and selects the smallest for *Behinat Bina*. Now that AA has *Gadlut de Neshama*, it can give birth to *Katnut de Abba ve Ima (AVI)* in the place of *Bina de Atzilut (Bina de MA)*. In order to give the *AHP de AVI* strength to receive the light "for the sake of the Creator", a *Zivug AB-SAG* must be made. This light descends from SAG under the *Tabur* through all the *Partzufim de Atzilut* to the relevant place.

קס) ודע שהתחתונים הראוים להעלות מ"ן, הם רק בחינת נר"ן דצדיקים, שכבר כלולים מבי"ע, ויכולים להעלות מ"ן לזו"ן דאצילות, הנחשבים לבחינת העליון שלהם. ואז הזו"ן מעלים מ"ן אל העליון שלהם, שהם או"א. ואו"א יותר למעלה, עד שמגיעים לפרצופי א"ק.

ואז יורד אור העליון מא"ס ב"ה לפרצופי א"ק על המ"ן שנתעלו שמה. ויוצאות קומת ע"ס ע"פ מדת העביות של המ"ן שהעלו: אם הוא מבחי"ב הוא קומת נשמה, אם מבחי"ג הוא קומת חיה וכו'.

ומשם יורדים המוחין ממדרגה למדרגה דרך פרצופי א"ק, עד שבאים לפרצופי אצילות. וכן עוברים ממדרגה למדרגה דרך כל פרצופי אצילות, עד שבאים להזו"ן דאצילות, שהם משפיעים המוחין האלו אל הנר"ן דצדיקים, שהעלו את המ"ן הללו מבי"ע. וזה הכלל, שכל חידוש מוחין אינו בא אלא רק מא"ס ב"ה לבדו. ואין מדרגה יכולה להעלות מ"ן או לקבל שפע, רק מהעליון הסמוך לו.

160) The lower Partzufim that must raise MAN are the human souls (the "NaRaN de Tzadikim"), already included in the worlds of BYA and capable of raising MAN to the ZON de Atzilut, which in turn raise MAN to their own upper Partzufim: Arich Anpin, Abba ve Ima and above, until they reach the Partzufim de AK.

Then, in response to MAN, the upper light descends from the World of Infinity to AK. The 10 Sefirot emerge according to the Aviut de MAN present there. If it is Behina Bet, it corresponds to the level of Neshama, Behina Gimel equals the level of Haya, and Behina Dalet attracts the light of Yechida.

Gradually, the Mochin descends from the same level through Partzufim de AK to the Partzufim de Atzilut, until it reaches ZON de Atzilut. With the help of the Mochin, ZON de Atzilut compel the NaRaN de Tzadikim to raise MAN from BYA. The general rule states that each new Mochin comes directly from the World of Infinity. No level can raise MAN or receive the light of Hochma without the upper Partzuf closest to it.

The place of *Atzilut* is between the *Tabur de AK* to the *Parsa*. The worlds of *BYA* with the uncorrected souls are under the *Parsa*. If by certain actions these souls can receive strength for the correction of *ZON de Atzilut*, they elevate their request higher, to *Rosh de Galgalta* of the world of *AK*, which is in contact with the World of Infinity and draws the upper light in order to pass it on to *BYA*.

The light spreading from above is many times more powerful than was requested by the worlds of *BYA*, but while descending and passing through all the *Partzufim* and the worlds, it diminishes to the size of the request, so as not to harm the requestor.

Wherever the *Partzuf* might be, it feels only the one standing right above it. Its request is turned only to the upper *Partzuf* and not to the one several levels higher. In accordance with the accomplished correction and the acquired screen, its level will change, but the *Partzuf* will always address the one at its immediate, upper level.

The soul's correction begins in our world. Man of this world, a two-legged, albuminous creature, receives a signal from above and starts looking for something he cannot yet understand. Nevertheless, if he finds a Teacher, a group and books, then by persistent studies, together with other members of the group, and guided by the Teacher, a student can achieve the state of *Ibur* in the lowest spiritual *Partzuf*.

Then his vessels of bestowal (the *GE*) will be gradually born. Such a state is called *Katnut*. The emergence of *GE* marks the appearance of man's inner world of *Atzilut* with *Aviut Shoresh* and *Aleph*.

The continuation of studies generates in him a desire to turn to the upper level with a request for the vessels of reception, i.e., for *Gadlut*, in order to receive by way of bestowal. However, as we know, the vessels of reception were restricted by *TB*. The world of *Nikudim* wanted to receive them and was broken. So was *Adam haRishon* when it wished to work with them.

So how can they possibly be received? It can be done only with the help of the *AHP de Aliyah*. Man asks for strength to work with the vessels of reception without the risk of breaking them. If man asks for the measure of correction his vessels are ready for, and if he knows exactly what he needs, a spiritual force comes to him and answers his request.

If he previously had the *GE* with *Aviut Shoresh/Aleph*, now man starts working with the *AHP*, perhaps, of *Aviut Bet*. He passes the level of *Katnut* and receives the first level of *Gadlut* (the *Behina Bet*), and ascends for the first time. By further efforts, he gains more strength to work with *Aviut Gimel* and rises again. At last, he acquires the vessels of reception of the level *Dalet* and ascends for a third time to full *Gadlut*.

When man has *GE*, he is on the level of *ZON de Atzilut*. The first time in *Gadlut*, he rises to the level of *YESHSUT*, the second time – to *Abba ve Ima de Atzilut*, the third time – to *AA de Atzilut*, i.e., completely dresses onto *ZON de Nekudim* (broken) and corrects them. So, by his own efforts, man returns to his spiritual root, receives the entire spiritual light.

The *Tzadikim* are souls in a certain spiritual state in the worlds of *BYA* that are willing to justify the Creator's actions. Our only task is to achieve the level of the *Tzadik Gamur* (absolutely righteous), when all the Creator's actions are revealed to man. Seeing that all His actions are right and just, man calls Him the Righteous One. Hence, he himself is called a righteous man. If the Creator's actions are partially or completely concealed from man, he is called a partially righteous man, a partial or complete sinner.

Our state and name depend only on the extent of the Creator's revelation. Our desires and properties will change accordingly. Why is a soul called *Neshama*? The reason is that it is the most powerful light our soul can receive. The world of *Adam Kadmon* consists of five *Partzufim*, since the Creator affects all the five parts of *Malchut*.

ZON de Atzilut is the uppermost *Partzuf* for all worlds of *BYA*, the inclusion of all that is found under the *Parsa* and below. Any *MAN* first rises to the *Gar* of *ZON de Atzilut*. However, *ZON* cannot answer the request of the worlds of *BYA*. The light of correction or the light filling the vessel with delight can come from above only.

The light that the *Partzufim* enjoyed before the breaking is different from that which corrects and fills them. This speaks about how delighted I am while delighting the Creator. Hence, such light descends from the World of Infinity; it cannot be in *ZON de Atzilut*.

Any spiritual movement is altruistic. The upper *Partzuf* cannot possibly give the lower something that may harm it. The next *Partzuf* is always a natural continuation of the development (desires, thoughts) of the previous one. *Galgalta* completely exhausted all its resources. It can do no more for the Creator. Therefore, a new opportunity springs up: to accept some more light on a smaller *Aviut*, i.e., on the level of *AB*, which continues what *Galgalta* began doing.

After (below) the world of *Atzilut*, the first seven *Sefirot* from the *Parsa* to the *Chazeh de Beria* (70 *Amah*) are still somehow connected with *Atzilut*. Then the full 10 *Sefirot* from the *Chazeh de Beria* to the *Chazeh de Yetzira* (2000 *Amah*) may still be used on *Shabbat*, when the *Partzufim* rise to *Atzilut*. We see that the passage from *Chazeh de Yetzira* to *Chazeh de Beria* is much more difficult than from the *Parsa* to the *Chazeh de Beria*. Naturally, these estimates are relative.

קסא) ומכאן תדע, שאי אפשר שהתחתונים יקבלו משהו מהזו"ן דאצילות, מטרם שיתגדלו על ידיהם כל הפרצופים העליונים דעולם האצילות ועולם הא"ק. כי נתבאר, שאין חידוש מוחין אלא מא"ס ב"ה. אמנם אין הנר"ן דצדיקים יכולים לקבלם אלא מהעליון הסמוך להם, שהם זו"ן דאצילות.

ולפיכך צריכים המוחין להשתלשל דרך העולמות והפרצופים העליונים, עד שמגיעים אל הזו"ן, שהם המשפיעים לנר"ן דצדיקים. וכבר ידעת, שאין העדר ברוחני. וענין העברה ממקום למקום, אין הפירוש שנעדרים ממקום הא' ובאים למקום הב', כנוהג בגשמיים, אלא שנשארים במקום הא', גם אחר שעברו ובאו למקום הב', כמו מדליק נר מנר ואין חברו חסר.

ולא עוד, אלא זה הכלל, שעיקר ושורש האור נשאר במקום הא', ובמקום הב' נמשך רק בחינת ענף ממנו. ועם זה תבין, שאותו השפע העובר דרך העליונים עד שמגיע לנר"ן דצדיקים, נשאר בכל מדרגה ומדרגה שעבר דרכה. ונמצאות כל המדרגות מתגדלות בסבת השפע, שהם מעבירים לצורך נר"ן דצדיקים.

161) You should know that the lower Partzufim cannot receive the light from ZON de Atzilut before all the upper Partzufim de Atzilut and AK acquire Gadlut. The new Mochin descends only from the World of Infinity. However, the NaRaN de Tzadikim can receive the Mochin only from the previous Partzuf, i.e., from ZON de Atzilut.

Hence, the Mochin must descend and spread through all the Partzufim located above ZON de Atzilut, until it reaches it. Only after that, will the Mochin pass on to NaRaN de Tzadikim in the worlds of BYA. We already know that nothing ever disappears in the spiritual realm. Contrary to what happens in our world, a spiritual object passing from one place to another continues to remain in its initial position.

This can be compared to lighting one candle from another. As the first candle passes the fire to the next, it continues to remain alight. The rule holds that the primary light (the root) stays in place while the branch changes its position. Now you will understand that the same light that descends via all the upper worlds and reaches NaRaN de Tzadikim remains on each level it passes through. All the levels receive more light owing to the fact that they have to pass it to NaRaN de Tzadikim.

Tiny man's diminutive work below generates a tremendous light in all the worlds. Man's merit consists in the fact that the reception of the light is his personal achievement.

קסב) ובהאמור תבין, איך התחתונים במעשיהם גורמים עליות וירידות להפרצופין והעולמות העליונים. כי בעת שמטיבים מעשיהם ומעלים מ"ן וממשיכים שפע, הרי כל העולמות והמדרגות, שדרכם עברה השפע, מתגדלים ועולים למעלה בסבת השפע שמעבירים, כנ"ל, ובעת שחוזרים ומקלקלים מעשיהם, הנה מתקלקל המ"ן, והמוחין מסתלקים גם ממדרגות העליונות, כי נפסק ענין העברת השפע מהן לצורך התחתונים, ונמצאות חוזרות ויורדות למצבן הקבוע כבתחילה.

162) From the above, you should understand how, by their actions, the lower spiritual objects cause the rise of the worlds and the Partzufim. If their actions are correct, they raise MAN and attract the light. Then all the levels it passes through grow and rise. When their actions deteriorate, so does MAN; Mochin disappears from the levels, the upper worlds stop passing light to the lower; so, they descend to their initial permanent (minimal) state.

Nothing disappears; whatever was before continues to exist. Ascents and descents of the worlds are determined only as regards the souls, which by aggravating their actions, lower the worlds; however, by doing good deeds, they contribute to the ascent of the worlds.

All that happens in the worlds makes for correction and the approach of the *Gmar Tikkun*. Every thought, every event, and every action is just one more step towards correction. What does it mean that a soul is spoiled? It worked on itself, to make a spiritual action, to rise and merge with the Creator on some level. It raised *MAN*, received the light and strength to ascend. Once the new level is achieved, the soul cannot remain motionless.

To make it move, more egoism, for which it does not yet have a screen, is added to the soul. Affected by this load, it falls and deteriorates. Each fall is necessary for regaining powers, rising higher and, consequently, receiving another portion of egoism. Thus, all initially egoistic desires are gradually transformed into altruistic ones.

The Baal HaSulam gives the following example. A king, who wanted to move from one capital to another, did not know how to transfer all his treasures without being robbed. Hence, he dispensed a gold coin to each of his subjects. The king could trust them with that amount. Thus, by small portions, he was able to transfer his entire wealth. This example hints at the correction of the general egoism by way of dividing it into small parts that are then transferred to the world of *Atzilut*. There, they will again merge into one common vessel, one single soul.

קסג) ועתה נבאר סדר עליות ה"פ אצילות לה"פ א"ק, וג' העולמות בי"ע לישסו"ת וזו"ן דאצילות. החל ממצבם הקבוע, עד להגובה שאפשר להיות בהשתא אלפי שני מטרם גמר התיקון. שבדרך כלל הן רק ג' עליות. אמנם הן מתחלקות לפרטים מרובים.

והנה מצב העולמות א"ק ואבי"ע בקביעות כבר נתבאר לעיל, כי פרצוף הראשון הנאצל לאחר צמצום א', הוא פרצוף גלגלתא דא"ק, שעליו מלבישים ד' פרצופי א"ק: ע"ב ס"ג מ"ה וב"ן. וסיום רגלי א"ק הוא למעלה מנקודת העוה"ז (אות כ"ז, ל"א). ועליו מסבבים המקיפים דא"ק מא"ס ב"ה, שלגדלם אין קץ ושיעור (אות ל"ב). וכמו שא"ס ב"ה מקיף מסביב לו, כן הוא מתלבש בפנימיותו. והוא המכונה קו א"ס ב"ה.

163) Now we will clear up the way the five Partzufim de Atzilut rise to the five Partzufim de AK. We will also clarify the ascent of the three worlds of BYA to YESHSUT and ZON de Atzilut, starting with their minimal state (Katnut), up to the ultimate state that will be achieved by the end of a 6000-year period, in the Gmar Tikkun. Usually we speak about three main ascents that are divided into many special ones.

We know that the first Partzuf in the world of AK after TA was Galgalta. The four following Partzufim de AK dressed on it: AB, SAG, MA and BON. Sium Ragley de AK is above the point of our world. Galgalta is surrounded with the light of Infinity on all sides. This light is limitless and its magnificence is indescribable. The part of this light that enters Galgalta is called a line, or the Inner Light.

קסד) ובפנימיות מ"ה וב"ן דא"ק יש פרצוף תנהי"מ דא"ק, המכונה נקודות דס"ג דא"ק (אות ס"ג, ס"ו). שבעת צמצום הב' עלתה מלכות המסיימת, שעמדה ממעל לנקודה דעוה"ז, וקבעה

מקומה בהחזה דפרצוף הזה, מתחת שליש עליון דת"ת שלו. ונעשה שם סיום חדש על אור העליון, שלא יתפשט משם ולמטה. וסיום חדש הזה נקרא בשם "פרסא שמתחת האצילות" (אות ס"ח).

ואלו הספירות שמחזה ולמטה דפרצוף נקודות דס"ג דא"ק, שנשארו מתחת הפרסא, נעשו מקום לג' העולמות בי"ע: ב"ש ת"ת עד החזה, נעשה מקום לעולם הבריאה, ונה"י נעשו מקום לעולם היצירה והמלכות נעשה מקום לעולם העשיה (אות ס"ז). ונמצא שמקום ג' העולמות בי"ע מתחיל מתחת הפרסא ומסתיים ממעל לנקודה דעוה"ז.

164) There is a Partzuf called TNHYM de AK inside Partzufim MA and BON de AK. It is also defined as Nekudot de SAG de AK. During TB, Malchut Mesayemet, which was above the point of our world, rose to Tifferet and set a place in the Chazeh of this Partzuf below the upper third of Tifferet. A new Sium on the upper light (unable to spread lower) was formed there. This Sium was named Parsa under the world of Atzilut.

The Sefirot of the Partzuf Nekudot de SAG, which remained under the Parsa, formed a place for the the worlds of BYA in the following order: the lower two thirds of Tifferet down to Chazeh prepared a place for the world of Beria. Netzah, Hod, and Yesod prepared a place for the world of Yetzira. Malchut formed a place for the world of Assiya. Thus, the location of the three worlds of BYA begins from the Parsa and ends with the point of our world.

The *Parsa*, *Tifferet*, is called "*Bina de Gufa*". Affected by the *Tzimtzum* (restriction), it finds itself under the *Gar (Gimel Rishonot) de Bina*. One should remember that the *Guf* of the *Partzuf (Tifferet)* is divided into three parts: the upper third of *Tifferet* – the *HaBaD*, the middle third of *Tifferet* – the *HaGaT* and the lower third of *Tifferet* – the *NHY*. *Malchut* rises to the level under the *Gar de Bina* to a place called "the *Chazeh*". The law of *TB* rules from here downwards and the *Parsa* is formed under the world of *Atzilut*.

קסה) ונמצאים ד' העולמות אצילות, בריאה, יצירה ועשיה. שמתחילים ממקום למטה מטבור דא"ק ומסתיימים ממעל לנקודת העוה"ז. כי ה"פ עולם האצילות מתחילים ממקום שלמטה

מטבור דא"ק ומסתיימים ממעל להפרסא. מהפרסא ולמטה עד לעוה"ז עומדים ג' העולמות בי"ע. וזהו מצב הקבוע של העולמות א"ק ואבי"ע, שלעולם לא יארע בהם שום מיעוט.

וכבר נתבאר (אות קל"ח), שבמצב הזה אין בכל הפרצופים והעולמות אלא רק בחינת ו"ק בלי ראש. כי אפילו בג' הפרצופים הראשונים דאצילות, שיש ג"ר בראשים שלהם, מכל מקום אינן מושפעות מפה ולמטה שלהם. וכל הגופים הם ו"ק בלי ראש. וכ"ש בפרצופי בי"ע. ואפילו פרצופי א"ק, בערך המקיפים שלו, נבחנים ג"כ שהם חסרי ג"ר (אות ל"ב).

165) The four worlds, Atzilut, Beria, Yetzira and Assiya, are located between the Tabur and the point of our world. The world of Atzilut is between the Tabur de AK and Parsa. The place for the worlds of BYA was formed between the Parsa and the point of our world. The state of the worlds of AK and ABYA is now permanent, and there will never be any diminution in them.

All the Partzufim and the worlds in this state have only the level of Vak bli Rosh. In addition, even if Gar is in the Rashim of the first three Partzufim de Atzilut, the light cannot spread below the Peh, and all their Gufim are in the state of Vak bli Rosh. The same state is present in the worlds of BYA. Even in the Partzufim de AK, Gar is considered to be absent as regards the Surrounding Light (the Ohr Makif).

The *Gar* represents the *Rosh* and the genuine light of *Hochma*, while *Vak* represents *Ohr Hassadim* with a spark of *Ohr Hochma*.

So what happens in the world of *Atzilut*? Let us begin our explanation with *Galgalta*. *Galgalta* receives light from the World of Infinity. We know there is an inverse relation between the lights and the vessels. The coarser the vessel, the larger screen it may use, the more powerful light it can receive. Vice versa: the smaller the vessel, the weaker the screen it has and the less light it will receive.

Everything depends on how the lowest spiritual objects, the souls, will demand powers for the correction of their egoism. Until they are completely corrected, *Galgalta*, *AB* and *SAG* are filled with only the smallest light.

First, the light of *Nefesh* enters the *Kli Keter*. As the *Kli Hochma* appears, *Ohr Nefesh* passes to it, and *Ohr Ruach* enters *Keter* and so on, until *Malchut*, the largest vessel, is activated.Then the most powerful light of *Yechida* fills *Keter*. We see that for the reception of the uppermost light, the most egoistic vessel – *Malchut* – must start acting to build a screen.

Malchut de Malchut of the world of Infinity is forbidden (unable) to work with until *Gmar Tikkun*. Man is unable to correct or fill it with the true light of *Hochma* before the *Mashiach* comes. Hence, the *Gar* (the true light of *Hochma*) is absent in the *Partzufim Galgalta*, *AB* and *SAG*. It appears only when *Malchut* is used.

The breaking of the vessels demonstrated that it is impossible to work with the vessels of reception; they may be gradually included into the altruistic vessels – the *AHP de Aliyah*. It means that the light of *Hochma* in its entirety and perfection cannot enter the vessel until its final correction – the *Gmar Tikkun*.

As was mentioned numerously, after *TB* only the *Kelim de GE* (filled with the light of *Hassadim*) and the *Kelim de AHP* (receiving no light at all) included in the *GE* may be worked with. However, since they are still egoistic, by virtue of their nature, the *AHP* automatically attract the luminescence of *Hochma*, i.e., they have *Vak de Hochma* or *Vak bli Rosh*, but not the *Gar*.

All the laws of the world of *Atzilut* are created to allow no spreading of the powerful light below. There is *Ohr Hochma* in the *Rashim de Partzufim* of the world of *Atzilut*, but only a small part of it spreads below. If the *Rosh* has the *Gar*, only the *Vak* of this light spreads to the *Gufim*.

AB-SAG is not the light of pleasure. It descends to correct the vessels, to impart an altruistic intention to its desires. We have no control over our desires; they are given by the Creator. They may only be given an altruistic intention. Suppose, I would like a cup of coffee. I cannot change this desire. However, I can drink it, because either I want to receive pleasure, or I can do it for the sake of pleasing the Creator. This happens only when I feel Him and understand that He gives me, so I wish to return the delight to Him. For this, I must feel the Giver.

The light *AB-SAG* descends in order to correct a desire or, rather, impart an altruistic intention to it. Man starts revealing the Creator, whose greatness and magnificence he begins to feel. Then man is ready to do everything for His sake. The importance and greatness of spirituality are far above the level of our pleasures; hence, they give us strength to do everything for the Creator. In our world, upon seeing someone outstanding and important, we agree, with pleasure, to do everything for that person.

קסו) ולפיכך נוהגות ג' עליות כוללות, בכדי להשלים העולמות בג' הקומות נשמה חיה יחידה, החסרות להם. ועליות האלו תלויות בהעלאת מ"ן של התחתונים. העליה הא' היא, בעת שהתחתונים מעלים מ"ן מבחינת העביות דבחי"ב. שאז נבררים האח"פ דקומת בינה ונשמה מבחינת השלמת הע"ס דמין הב'. דהיינו מהארת נקודת השורק (אות קל"ה). אשר המוחין האלו מאירים גם לבחינת הז"ת והגופים. כמו בפרצופי א"ק, שכל הכמות שיש בע"ס דראשי פרצופי א"ק, עוברת ומתפשטת גם לגופים.

> *166) There are three general ascents for supplementing the worlds with three levels: Neshama, Haya and Yechida. These ascents depend on the MAN raised by the lower objects. The first ascent is when MAN rises on the level of Aviut de Behina Bet. Then the AHP de Bina (Ohr Neshama) is corrected by its supplementation to 10 Sefirot of the second type, i.e., with the help of the luminescence of Shuruk. At that, the Mochin also shines onto the Zat and the Gufim, as in the Partzufim de AK, where all levels of the 10 Sefirot of the Rashim also spread in their Gufim.*

The worlds of *ABYA* do not use their genuine *AHP*. Nevertheless, each of these worlds receives light in its *AHP* and gradually fills with the entire light necessary for the end of correction, its ultimate state. How does it happen?

First, all the *Partzufim* in addition to the *GE* (*Aviut Shoresh* and *Aleph*) also acquire the *Awzen* (*Aviut Bet*). Then a force comes and helps to receive *Bet de Aviut* and the light of *Neshama*. However, since the *AHP de Aliyah* (not their own *AHP*) is used, hence the worlds ascend one level (the 10 *Sefirot*).

At last, the light that corrects *Behina Dalet* (the *Peh*) comes, which leads to a third ascent of the worlds one level (the 10 *Sefirot*). In all, three ascents are necessary for the reception of all missing lights: *Neshama*, *Haya*, and *Yechida*.

Accordingly, the entire five *Partzufim de Atzilut* dress onto the five *Partzufim de AK*: each *Partzuf de Atzilut* dresses from the *Tabur* downwards onto the corresponding upper *Partzuf de AK*. The part of the *Partzuf* from the *Tabur* to the *Sium* is called *Vak*.

In its first ascent, the *Partzuf* in *Katnut* (*Nefesh-Ruach*, *GE*) is supplemented with the level of *Neshama*, *SAG*. Then it dresses onto the corresponding part of the world of *AK*, from the *Chazeh* to *Tabur*, because *Bina de Gufa* (*SAG* of each *Partzuf*) is located there.

In its second ascent, each *Partzuf* dresses onto the corresponding *Partzuf* of the world of *AK*, from the *Peh* to its *Chazeh*, i.e., on the level of *Hochma*, *Haya*, *AB*.

In its third ascent, each *Partzuf de Atzilut* dresses onto the *Rosh* of the corresponding *Partzuf de AK* and receives *Mochin* (the light) *de Yechida*.

Each *Partzuf* must dress onto the place where the *Reshimot* of the previous level of the *Gufa de Galgalta* shine. The *Rosh de AB* must dress, not on the *Rosh de Galgalta*, but from its *Peh* to the *Chazeh*, since the light must spread to where it disappeared, i.e., in the *Chazeh de Galgalta*, and not in its *Rosh*.

The *Rosh de Nekudim (YESHSUT)* dresses onto the *Rosh de Galgalta*. Keter dresses onto the *AB de AK*, *Abba ve Ima* – onto SAG *de* AK. Each has to fill the *Partzufim* in AK. Since in the *Gufim de Partzufim* of the *Gar de Atzilut* in "*Matzav haKavuah*" (its initial state) there is just the light of *Vak*, only three ascents of the worlds of *BYA* are possible.

When the lower *Partzufim* raise MAN, as if to request the strength to withstand our desires, to give us the properties of *Bina* that are in the world of *Beria*, then the power may be received from the light of *Shuruk*, i.e., the light descending from *Abba ve Ima Panim be Panim*; then one can start ascending spiritually.

קסז) ונמצא, בעת שהמוחין אלו עוברים דרך פרצופי האצילות, מקבל כל אחד מה"פ אצילות בחינת מוחין דבינה ונשמה, הנקרא מוחין דס"ג, המאירים ג"ר גם לפרצופים שלהם, כמו בא"ק. וע"כ נבחן אז, שהם מתגדלים ועולים ומלבישים על פרצופי א"ק, כפי מדת המוחין שהשיגו.

167) As the light passes through the world of Atzilut, each of this world's five Partzufim receives the light of Bina, called Neshama, or Mochin de SAG, which shines upon the Partzufim de Atzilut in the manner they had in AK. They receive the light of Gadlut and dress onto the Partzufim de AK according to the level of the Mochin they possess.

קסח) באופן, שבעת שפרצוף עתיק דאצילות השיג המוחין האלו דבינה, נמצא עולה ומלביש לפרצוף בינה דא"ק, המכוון נגד קומת ס"ג דפרצוף גלגלתא דא"ק. והוא מקבל משם בחינת נשמה דיחידה דא"ק, המאירה גם להז"ת שלו.

וכשהמוחין באים לפרצוף א"א דאצילות, הוא עולה ומלביש על ראש דעתיק דקביעות, המכוון נגד קומת הס"ג דפרצוף ע"ב דא"ק. והוא מקבל משם בחינת נשמה דחיה דא"ק, המאירה לז"ת שלו. וכשהמוחין באים לפרצוף או"א דאצילות, הם עולים ומלבישים לג"ר דא"א דקביעות, המכוון נגד קומת בינה דס"ג דא"ק. והם מקבלים משם בחינת נשמה דנשמה דא"ק, המאירה גם להז"ת שלהם.

וכשהמוחין האלו באים לישסו"ת וזו"ן דאצילות, הם עולים ומלבישים על או"א דקביעות, המכוון נגד קומת בינה דפרצוף מ"ה וב"ן דא"ק. ומקבלים משם בחינת נשמה דנפש רוח דא"ק. ואז מקבלים הנר"ן דצדיקים את המוחין דנשמה דאצילות. וכשהמוחין באים לפרצופי עולם הבריאה, עולה עולם הבריאה ומלביש את הנוקבא דאצילות. ומקבל ממנה בחינת נפש דאצילות.

וכשבאים המוחין לעולם היצירה, הוא עולה ומלביש לעולם הבריאה דקביעות. ומקבל ממנו בחינת נשמה וג"ר דבריאה. וכשהמוחין באים לעולם העשיה, הוא עולה ומלביש על עולם היצירה, ומקבל משם בחינת מוחין דו"ק שביצירה. והנה נתבאר העליה הא', שהשיג כל פרצוף מאבי"ע, בסבת המ"ן דבחי"ב, שהעלו התחתונים. (האילן, ציור ז').

168) As soon as Atik receives Mochin de Bina, it rises and dresses onto the Partzuf Bina of the world of AK, corresponding to the level of SAG (Bina) de Galgalta of AK. There it receives Behinat Neshama de Yechida of the world of AK, which shines in its Guf.

When the Mochin reaches Partzuf Arich Anpin de Atzilut, it rises and dresses onto the Rosh de Atik, corresponding to the level of the SAG of Partzuf AB de AK and receives Behinat Neshama de Haya de AK, which also shines in its Guf. When the Mochin reaches Partzuf Abba ve Ima, it rises by one level and dresses onto the *Gar de Arich Anpin, corresponding to the level of Bina de SAG de AK. From there it receives the light of the Neshama de Neshama de AK that shines in its Zat.*

When the Mochin reaches YESHSUT and ZON de Atzilut, they rise and dress onto Abba ve Ima de Atzilut, corresponding to Behinat Bina of the Partzufim MA and BON de AK. From there they receive the light of Neshama de Nefesh-Ruach de AK.Then the NaRaN de Tzadikim receive the Mochin de Neshama of the world of Atzilut. When the Mochin reaches the Partzufim de Beria, this world rises and dresses onto Nukvah de Atzilut, receiving from it Behinat Nefesh de Atzilut.

When the Mochin reaches the world of Yetzira, it rises and dresses onto the world of Beria, receiving Behinat Neshama and the Gar de Beria from it. Finally, as the Mochin reaches the world of Assiya, it rises and dresses onto the world of Yetzira, receiving from it Behinat Mochin de Vak de Yetzira. Thus, we have learned what each Partzuf received during the first ascent caused by MAN of the second type, raised by the souls in the worlds of BYA.

We see how, influenced by the requests and prayers raised by the souls from the worlds of *BYA*, they ascend through all worlds to the *Rosh de Galgalta*. It makes a *Zivug* with the light of the World of Infinity and receives it. Then the light passes through all the *Partzufim* of the worlds of *AK* and *ABYA*, and reaches the soul that attracted this light, filling it. The soul and all worlds are in a state of ascent. The thread that ties this soul with the World of Infinity links it to the Creator.

Nefesh and *Ruach* are two constant lights shining in the worlds. During the ascent, *Neshama* is added to them. Each *Partzuf* goes up one level. The *Rosh* of the lower *Partzuf* reaches the *Rosh* of the upper, attaining all of its thoughts and calculations.

Let us look at diagram 7 in the book *"Sefer haIlan"*. On diagram 3, we saw a minimal permanent state of the worlds of *BYA*. Diagram 7 shows the states of the worlds of *BYA* after the first ascent, when they received the light of *Neshama*. Let us note that the *Rosh* of each *Partzuf* dressed on the MA of the corresponding *Partzuf de* AK.

The *Rosh* of each *Partzuf de Atzilut* dresses onto the *SAG* of the corresponding *Partzuf de* AK. Thus, the worlds of *ABYA* shifted one level up as compared to the previous state and the world of *AK*. Receiving light from the World of Infinity, *AK* also rises. Here our goal is to see the additional light received by the worlds of *ABYA*. We may say that, thanks to the souls' request, all worlds received the light of *Neshama* and all vessels from the World of Infinity down to our world were filled with it.

קסט) העליה הב' היא בעת שהתחתונים מעלין מ"ן מבחינת העביות דבחי"ג, שאז נבררים האח"פ דקומת חכמה וחיה, מבחינת השלמת הע"ס דמין הב'. שמוחין אלו מאירים גם לבחינת הז"ת והגופים, כמו בפרצופי א"ק. וכשהמוחין עוברים דרך הפרצופים דאבי"ע, נמצא כל פרצוף עולה ומתגדל על ידיהם כפי המוחין שהשיג.

169) The second ascent took place as a result of the raising of MAN on Aviut de Behina Gimel, when the AHP de Hochma (Haya) is corrected. Gadlut and supplementation to 10 Sefirot of the second type take place as the Mochin shines in the Zat and the Gufin, as well as in the Partzufim AK. When the Mochin passes down through the worlds of BYA, each Partzuf affected by this light grows and ascends one more level.

The additional filling with light is called an ascent. In fact, nothing ascends or descends in the spiritual world. It is necessary to have an additional vessel that can be created through a request sent from below.

What other methods of correction and filling the vessels are available? The light can come from above and temporarily arouse a craving for spirituality. It corrects and sustains all the *Partzufim* and the souls in the worlds of *BYA*, filling them with scanty light. This happens on *Rosh Hodesh*, *Shabbat* and holidays.

Depending on the light descending from above, we can know what these days and holidays are. The diversity is determined by the light, its kind. Hence, we have the time calendar, introduced by the Creator. The light comes from above, arouses the vessels, fills, and empties them. This light is not connected with the souls' request.

In accordance with the kind and intensity of the request, raised by the soul, it can ascend one, two, or three levels. The soul's ascent through all three levels means it achieved the *Gmar Tikkun*. It corrected everything it could with the help of the *AHP de Aliyah*, i.e., included its own vessels into the vessels of bestowal and does not work with the *Lev haEven* that is corrected only with the arrival of the *Mashiach*.

Thus, there are two kinds of the souls' ascents. The first is stimulation from above; this is the work of the Creator, Who activates this most intricate mechanism called nature. The process is totally beyond our powers. The second kind includes a most thorough preparation for stimulation from below, surpassing the light's influence from above, paying no attention to it and rising independently.

By this, the *Klipot* descend and cease to be parallel to the pure worlds. This prevents them from exerting a negative influence. That is why, having completed the three ascents to the world of *Atzilut*, the souls completely break away from the *Klipot*. Up to that time, there is an opposition between the pure and the impure worlds. Man needs to analyze his thoughts, intentions, and feelings carefully and try to separate the altruistic from the egoistic.

קע) באופן, כשבאו המוחין לפרצוף עתיק דאצילות, עולה ומלביש לג״ר דפרצוף חכמה דא״ק, הנקרא ע״ב דא״ק, המכוון נגד קומת ע״ב דגלגלתא דא״ק. ומקבל משם בחינת אור החיה דיחידה. וכשהמוחין מגיעים לפרצוף א״א דאצילות, הוא עולה ומלביש לג״ר דס״ג דא״ק, המכוונים נגד קומת ע״ב דפרצוף ע״ב דא״ק. ומקבל משם בחינת אור החיה דחיה דא״ק.

וכשהמוחין מגיעים לפרצופי או"א דאצילות, הם עולים ומלבישים לג"ר דעתיק דקביעות, המכוונות נגד קומת ע"ב דפרצוף ס"ג דא"ק. ומקבל משם בחינת אור החיה דנשמה דא"ק, המאירה גם להז"ת והגופים. וכשהמוחין באים לישסו"ת דאצילות, הם עולים ומלבישים לג"ר דא"א דקביעות, המכוונות נגד קומת ע"ב דמ"ה דא"ק. ומקבלות משם אור החיה דמ"ה דא"ק.

וכשהמוחין באים לזו"ן דאצילות, הם עולים לג"ר דאו"א, המכוונים נגד קומת ע"ב דב"ן דא"ק. ומקבלים משם בחינת אור החיה דב"ן דא"ק. ומהזו"ן מקבלים נשמת הצדיקים. וכשמגיעים המוחין לעולם הבריאה, הוא עולה ומלביש על הז"א דאצילות. ומקבל ממנו בחינת רוח דאצילות.

וכשהמוחין באים לעולם היצירה, עולה היצירה ומלביש על הנוקבא דאצילות. ומקבל ממנה אור הנפש דאצילות. וכשבאים המוחין לעולם העשיה עולה ומלביש לעולם הבריאה ומקבל ממנו בחינת ג"ר ונשמה דבריאה. ואז נשלם עולם העשיה בכל הנר"ן דבי"ע. והנה נתבאר העליה הב' של כל פרצוף מפרצופי אבי"ע, שעלו ונתגדלו בסבת המ"ן דבחי"ג, שהעלו הנר"ן דצדיקים. (האילן, ציור ח').

170) When the Mochin reaches Partzuf Atik de Atzilut, Atik rises and dresses onto Partzuf Hochma de AK, called AB. This corresponds to the level of AB de Galgalta de AK and receives the light of Haya de Yechida. When the Mochin reaches Partzuf Arich Anpin de Atzilut, AA rises and dresses onto the Gar de SAG de AK, corresponding to the level of AB de AK, and receives the light of Haya de Haya de AK.

When the Mochin reaches Partzuf Abba ve Ima de Atzilut, it rises and dresses onto the Gar de Atik in Katnut. It corresponds to the AB de SAG de AK and receives the light of Haya de Neshama de AK, which also shines for the Zat and the Gufim. When the Mochin reaches the YESHSUT de Atzilut, it rises and dresses onto the Gar de Arich Anpin in Katnut. It corresponds to the AB de MA de AK and receives the light of Haya de MA de AK.

When the Mochin reaches Partzuf ZON de Atzilut, it rises and dresses onto Gar de Abba ve Ima. This corresponds to AB de BON de AK and receives the light of Haya de BON de AK. The souls of the Tzadikim receive light from ZON. If the Mochin reaches the world of Beria, it rises and dresses onto ZA de Atzilut and receives the light of Ruach de Atzilut.

When the world of Yetzira receives the Mochin, it rises and dresses onto Nukva de Atzilut, receiving the light Nefesh de Atzilut. If the Mochin reaches the world of Assiya, it rises and dresses onto the world of Beria and receives Behinat Gar and Neshama de Beria. Then the world of Assiya is filled with all lights of NaRaN de BYA. Thus, we have learned about the second ascent of each Partzuf de ABYA that rose and grew because NaRaN de Tzadikim had raised MAN de Behina Gimel.

The second ascent is identical to the first. As regards the world of *AK*, which remains in its place, the worlds of *ABYA* ascend. From diagram 8 at the end of the book, we see how the *Rosh* of each *Partzuf* dresses onto the corresponding place of *Partzuf AB* de *AK* (not *SAG*, as during the first ascent). *Atik* dresses onto *AB de Galgalta, Arich Anpin* – on *AB de AB, Abba ve Ima* – on *AB de SAG*, i.e., all of them receive the light of *Hochma* from *AB*.

קעא) העליה הג' היא בעת שהתחתונים מעלים מ"ן מעביות דבחי"ד. שאז נבררים האח"פ דקומת כתר ויחידה, מבחינת השלמת הע"ס דמין הב'. אשר המוחין אלו מאירים גם להז"ת והגופים שלהם, כמו בפרצופי א"ק. וכשהמוחין אלו עוברים דרך פרצופי אבי"ע, הרי כל פרצוף עולה ומתגדל ומלביש לעליונו כפי מדת המוחין ההם.

171) The third ascent of the worlds happens in response to MAN raised by the souls on Aviut Dalet. The AHP de Keter is corrected and the Partzuf receives the light Yechida by way of being supplemented to 10 Sefirot (second type). The Mochin also shines in its Zat and Gufim as it did in the Partzufim de AK. While passing through the Partzufim of the worlds of ABYA, each of them grows, rises, and dresses onto the corresponding upper one, depending on the kind of light in it.

The next paragraph describes the third ascent. From diagram 9, we may see how all the *Partzufim* of the worlds of *ABYA* ascend one more level and receive the light *Yechida*. By this, all of the *Partzufim de Atzilut* dress onto the corresponding *Partzufim de AK*. Thus, all the worlds of *ABYA* that were on the level of *GE (Keter-Hochma)*, with the help of the three ascents, now acquired the vessels *Bina*, *ZA* and *Malchut*, and were thus completely filled with light.

During the first ascent, the world of *Beria* ascended above the *Parsa* up to the world of *Atzilut*. During the second ascent, *Yetzira* reached *Atzilut*, and during the third ascent, *Assiya* rose above the *Parsa* up to *Atzilut*. During the first ascent, the world of *Assiya* rose to the level of *Yetzira*; during the second – to the level of *Beria*; and during the third - to the level of *Atzilut*.

All the *Reshimot* that remained from the breaking of the vessels form a certain chain from the weakest to the mightiest, coarsest, from an easy correction to a more difficult one. Each cycle of correction of certain souls is called a generation; they receive the light that corresponds to them from above. As the coarser souls descend, they require a more powerful light that leads to the considerable correction, both in the spiritual worlds and in ours. All of this continues until the Final Correction (*Gmar Tikkun*) comes.

קעב) באופן, שבעת ביאת המוחין לפרצוף עתיק דאצילות, עולה ומלביש לג"ר דפרצוף גלגלתא דא"ק. ומקבל משם בחינת אור היחידה דיחידה. וכשהמוחין מגיעים לפרצוף א"א דאצילות, עולה ומלביש להג"ר דפרצוף ע"ב דא"ק. ומקבל משם אור היחידה דחיה דא"ק.

וכשהמוחין מגיעים לפרצוף או"א דאצילות, הם עולים ומלבישים לג"ר דס"ג דא"ק. ומקבלים משם אור היחידה דנשמה דא"ק. וכשהמוחין מגיעים לפרצוף ישסו"ת, הם עולים ומלבישים לג"ר דמ"ה דא"ק. ומקבלים משם אור היחידה דמ"ה דא"ק. וכשהמוחין מגיעים לזו"ן דאצילות, הם עולים ומלבישים לג"ר דב"ן דא"ק. ומקבלים משם אור היחידה דב"ן דא"ק. ואז מקבלים הנר"ן דצדיקים את אור היחידה מהזו"ן דאצילות.

ובעת שהמוחין מגיעים לעולם הבריאה, עולה ומלביש לפרצוף ישסו"ת דאצילות. ומקבל משם נשמה דאצילות. וכשהמוחין מגיעים לעולם היצירה, עולה ומלביש לפרצוף ז"א דאצילות. ומקבל ממנו בחינת רוח דאצילות. וכשהמוחין מגיעים לעולם העשיה, עולה ומלביש לנוקבא דאצילות, ומקבל ממנה בחינת אור הנפש דאצילות. (האילן, ציור ט').

172) When the Mochin comes to the Partzuf Atik de Atzilut, Atik rises and dresses onto the Gar de Galgalta de AK and receives the light of Yechida de Yechida. When the Mochin reaches Arich Anpin de Atzilut, the latter rises to the level of the Gar de AB de AK and receives the light of Yechida de Haya de AK.

When the Mochin reaches AVI, this Partzuf ascends to the Gar de SAG de AK and receives the light of Yechida de Neshama de AK. When the Partzuf YESHSUT receives the Mochin, it rises to the Gar de MA de AK and receives the light of Yechida de MA de AK. When the Mochin reaches ZON, the latter rise to the Gar de BON de AK and receive the light of Yechida de BON de AK. Then NaRaN de Tzadikim receive the light of Yechida from ZON de Atzilut.

When the Mochin reaches Beria, this world rises to YESHSUT de Atzilut and receives the light of Neshama de Atzilut. The Mochin elevates the world of Yetzira to Partzuf ZA de Atzilut, receiving the light of Ruach de Atzilut. As the Mochin reaches Assiya, the world rises to Partzuf Nukva de Atzilut, receiving the light of Nefesh de Atzilut (see diagram 9 from "Sefer haIlan").

קעג) ונמצא עתה בעת עליה הג', אשר ה"פ אצילות, נשלמו כל אחד בג' הקומות נשמה חיה יחידה מא"ק, שהיו חסרים להם מבחינת הקביעות. ונבחן, שה"פ אצילות עלו והלבישו את ה"פ א"ק, כל אחד להבחינה שכנגדו בפרצופי א"ק. וגם הנר"ן דצדיקים קבלו בחינת הג"ר, שהיה חסר להם. וגם ג' העולמות בי"ע, שהיו נמצאים מתחת הפרסא דאצילות, שמבחינת הקביעות לא היה בהם אלא בחינת נר"ן דאור חסדים, הנפרשים מחכמה מכח הפרסא שעליהם. ועתה עלו למעלה מפרסא, והלבישו לישסו"ת וזו"ן דאצילות, ויש להם נר"ן דאצילות, שאור החכמה מאיר בחסדים שלהם.

173) It turns out that during the third ascent, each of the five Partzufim de Atzilut expanded at the expense of Neshama, Yechida and Haya de AK, by dressing onto the 5 corresponding Partzufim de AK. The NaRaN de Tzadikim and the worlds of BYA received the Gar as well and rose above the Parsa. Now the light of Hochma shines in their Hassadim.

קעד) ויש לדעת, שהנר"ן דצדיקים מלבישים בקביעות רק לפרצופי בי"ע שמתחת הפרסא:

הנפש מלביש לע"ס דעשיה, והרוח לע"ס דיצירה, והנשמה לע"ס דבריאה. ונמצא, שהגם שהם מקבלים מזו"ן דאצילות, עכ"ז הוא מגיע אליהם רק דרך פרצופי בי"ע, שמלבישים עליהם.

באופן, שגם הנר"ן דצדיקים עולים בשוה עם עליות הג' עולמות בי"ע. ונמצא שגם עולמות בי"ע אינם מתגדלים, אלא לפי מדת קבלת השפע של הנר"ן דצדיקים, דהיינו ע"פ המ"ן הנבררים על ידיהם.

174) One should know that the NaRaN de Tzadikim, (human souls living in the worlds of BYA) constantly dress only on the Partzufim of BYA, under the Parsa. Nefesh dresses onto the 10 Sefirot de Assiya, Ruach – on the 10 Sefirot de Yetzira, and Neshama – on the 10 Sefirot de Beria. Although the souls receive light from ZON de Atzilut, it comes to them through the worlds of BYA, onto which they dress. The NaRaN de Tzadikim rise together with the ascents of the three worlds of BYA. The worlds of BYA ascend in accordance with the reception of light by the NaRaN de Tzadikim, i.e., depending on the power of MAN raised by them.

We mentioned the *Partzuf Adam haRishon* that was broken and whose vessels were mixed and are now in the worlds of *BYA*. According to the request raised by each of these fragments, the worlds of *BYA* become agitated and in turn arouse *ZON de Atzilut*. Then, it passes on to the *Gar de Atzilut*, and then to *AK*, which receives light from the World of Infinity, moving gradually, through all worlds, lowering it to the soul that raised its *MAN*. The soul rises to its individual correction in accordance with the light received by it.

קעה) והנה נתבאר, שמבחינת הקביעות, אין בכל העולמות והפרצופים שבהם רק בחינת ו"ק בלי ראש. כל אחד כפי בחינתו. כי אפילו הנר"ן דצדיקים אינם אלא בחינת ו"ק. כי הגם שיש להם ג"ר דנשמה מעולם הבריאה, עכ"ז ג"ר אלו נחשבים רק בבחינת ו"ק בערך עולם האצילות. מטעם שהם בחינת אור חסדים, הנפרשים מחכמה.

וכן פרצופי אצילות, אע"פ שיש ג"ר בראשים שלהם, מכל מקום כיון שאינם מאירים לגופים, הם נחשבים רק לבחינת ו"ק. וכל המוחין המגיעים לעולמות, שהם יותר מבחינת ו"ק, אינם אלא ע"י המ"ן שמעלים הצדיקים.

אמנם המוחין האלו לא יוכלו להתקבל בפרצופים, זולת דרך עלית התחתון למקום העליון. והוא מטעם, כי אע"פ שהם נחשבים לבחינת השלמת הע"ס דמין הב', מכל מקום כלפי הגופים והז"ת עצמם עוד הם נחשבים לבירורי אח"פ דמין הא', דהיינו שאינם נשלמים במקומם עצמם, אלא רק כשהם נמצאים במקום העליון (אות קמ"ב).

ולפיכך לא יוכלו ה"פ אצילות לקבל נשמה חיה יחידה דא"ק, זולת בעת שהם עולים ומלבישים אותם.

וכן הנר"ן וג' עולמות בי"ע לא יוכלו לקבל נר"ן דאצילות, זולת רק בעת שהם עולים ומלבישים לישסו"ת וזו"ן דאצילות. כי אלו האח"פ דמין הב', השייכים להז"ת, שיש להם התפשטות ממעלה למטה, למקום הז"ת, לא יתבררו רק בגמר התיקון. ולפיכך בעת שהג' עולמות בי"ע עולים ומלבישים לישסו"ת וזו"ן דאצילות, נמצא אז, שמקומם הקבוע מפרסא ולמטה, נשאר ריקן לגמרי מכל אור קדושה. ויש שם הפרש בין מחזה ולמעלה דעולם היצירה, לבין מחזה ולמטה שלו.

כי נתבאר לעיל, שמחזה ולמטה דעולם היצירה, הוא מקום הקבוע רק לקליפות (אות קמ"ט). אלא מסבת פגם חטאו של אדה"ר, ירדו ד"ת דיצירה דקדושה וע"ס דעשיה דקדושה ונתלבשו שם (אות קנ"ו). ולפיכך בעת, עליות בי"ע לאצילות, נמצא שמחזה דיצירה ולמעלה, אין שם לא קדושה ולא קליפות. אבל מחזה דיצירה ולמטה, יש שם קליפות. כי שם המדור שלהם.

175) All the worlds and Partzufim that are in their usual permanent state have only the Vak bli Rosh. This means that each level uses only six of its upper Sefirot, filled with the 6 lower lights. Even the NaRaN de Tzadikim are no more than the Vak, in spite of the fact that they have the Gar de Neshama from the world of Beria. In comparison with the world of Atzilut, these Gar are the Vak.

The same may be said about Partzufim de Atzilut. Although there is the light of the Gar in their Rashim (heads), this light, nevertheless, does not spread to the Gufim; hence, these Partzufim are also considered Vak. The use of the additional vessels (Sefirot), which leads to the reception of more light, takes place only as a result of MAN raised by the Tzadikim (i.e., human souls in the worlds of BYA).

However, the reception of this light (the Mochin) is possible only through the rise of the lower Partzuf to the level of the upper. The upper Partzufim de Atzilut (AA, AVI and YESHSUT) are supplemented to 10 Sefirot according to the second type (with their own AHP). However, the ZON are supplemented to 10 Sefirot according to the first type, i.e., by ascending to the level of the upper Partzuf with its AHP, and not theirs.

This happens because the AHP de ZON de Atzilut are enormous desires to receive, similar to the Essence of Creation (Malchut de Malchut). These desires cannot be corrected before the Gmar Tikkun. Hence, the five Partzufim of the world of Atzilut can receive the lights Neshama, Haya and Yechida only during their ascent to the corresponding Partzufim de AK.

The worlds of BYA can also receive the lights Neshama, Haya, and Yechida during their ascent to YESHSUT and ZON de Atzilut. Beria dresses onto YESHSUT, Yetzira – on ZA and Assiya – on Malchut (Nukva) de Atzilut. It turns out that during this ascent, the space from the Parsa and below (the place of BYA) becomes empty of any light. However, on the one hand, there is a difference between the 10 Sefirot of Beria and the 6 upper Sefirot of Yetzira, and on the other, all of the other Sefirot.

Thus, 14 (out of 30) lower Sefirot of the place of BYA constitute a permanent location only for the Klipot (i.e."desire to receive" the light for their own pleasure without a screen). Just because of Adam's "sin", the 14 lower Sefirot de BYA descended to this place. Previously, as we know, these worlds stood at least 14 Sefirot higher. Therefore, after the ascent of the worlds of BYA to Atzilut, there is absolutely "nothing" in the space between the Parsa to the Chazeh (chest) de Yetzira, neither the worlds of BYA, nor the Klipot; while the space from the Chazeh de Yetzira and below is taken by the Klipot.

קעו) ולפי שהמוחין היתירים מקומת ר"ק אינם באים רק ע"י מ"ן של התחתונים, אינם נמצאים משום זה בקביעות בפרצופים, כי תלוים במעשי התחתונים. ובעת שהם מקלקלים מעשיהם, נמצאים המוחין מסתלקים (אות קס"ב). אמנם המוחין דקביעות שבפרצופים, שנתקנו מכח המאציל עצמו, לא יארע בהם שום שינוי לעולם, שהרי אינם מתגדלים ע"י התחתונים. ולכן אינם נפגמים על ידיהם.

176) Thus, the reception of the additional lights, Neshama, Haya, and Yechida, depends on MAN being raised by the lower Partzufim and, finally, on MAN being raised by the human souls (NaRaN de

Tzadikim). If something happens to the NaRaN de Tzadikim and, for some reason, they cannot raise MAN, the "additional" lights depart from all the Partzufim de ABYA. However, the permanent lights – Nefesh and Ruach, which fill the vessels Keter and Hochma in such states, never leave them.

קעז) ולא יקשה לך, הרי א"א דב"ן הוא נבחן לכתר דאצילות, ואו"א לע"ב (אות ק"ל).

כי א"א הוא מחצית הכתר התחתונה דב"ן, ואו"א הם מחצית התחתונה דחו"ב דנקודים. וא"כ הבחינה שכנגדו דא"א בא"ק היה צריך להיות פרצוף הכתר דא"ק, והבחינה שכנגדם דאו"א בא"ק היה צריך להיות ע"ב דא"ק. והתשובה היא, כי פרצופי הב"ן הן נוקבין, שאין להם שום קבלה מעצמם, אלא רק מה שהזכרים, שהם פרצופי המ"ה, משפיעים להם.

ולפיכך, כל אלו ההבחנות שבהעליות, שפירושם, השגת מוחין מהעליון, נבחנים רק בהזכרים, שהם פרצופי המ"ה. וכיון שא"א דמ"ה אין לו מבחינת כתר כלום, אלא רק קומת חכמה בלבד, ואו"א דמ"ה אין להם מבחינת חכמה כלום, אלא קומת בינה בלבד (אות קכ"ו). ע"כ נבחן הבחינה שכנגדם בא"ק: ע"ב דא"ק לא"א, וס"ג דא"ק לאו"א. ופרצוף הכתר דא"ק מתיחס רק לעתיק בלבד, שלקח כל הקומת כתר דמ"ה.

177) As was already stated, there is MA on the right side of the world of Atzilut, i.e., its own vessels, and BON on the left side, i.e., the broken vessels of the world of Nikudim, which are corrected with the help of the vessels of MA de Atzilut. Do not think it strange that Arich Anpin de BON is considered Keter de Atzilut and Abba ve Ima – AB de Atzilut.

Arich Anpin is the lower half of Keter de BON and Abba ve Ima is a lower half of Hochma and Bina de Nikudim. So, the Partzuf Keter de AK (Galgalta) must presumably correspond to AA de Atzilut. The fact is that all the Partzufim de BON are Nekevot, i.e., they have no opportunity of their own to receive; they can acquire only what the corresponding Partzufim de MA (Zeharim) give them.

Hence, all the ascents happen only with the Zeharim (Partzufim de MA). Since no vessels of AA de MA correspond to Keter, but only to Hochma, and AVI de MA have only the vessels corresponding to Bina, the Partzuf AB de AK corresponds to AA and the Partzuf SAG de AK corresponds to AVI. The Partzuf Keter de AK corresponds only to the Partzuf Atik, which took the entire level of Keter de MA.

During *Gadlut de Nikudim*, the *Rosh de YESHSUT* rose to the *Rosh de Galgalta*; the *Rosh de Keter* rose to *AB de AK*; while *AVI* rose to *Rosh de SAG*. During *Gadlut de Nikudim, Abba ve Ima* had the level of *Keter*. Then why is it said they had the level of *Hochma* and *Bina*?

The level of the 10 *Sefirot* of the Direct Light differs from that of *Gadlut*, since the phase of the Direct Light is the first point, called *Keter*. In the state of *Katnut, GE de Keter* was on its level, while its *AHP* were in *GE de Abba ve Ima*.

Keter in *Gadlut* had the level of *Keter*. *Abba ve Ima*, called *Hochma* and *Bina*, as the *Behinot de Ohr Yashar*, received the level (*Komah*) of *Keter* in *Gadlut* (they had the *Aviut Aleph* in *Katnut*).

קעח) גם צריך שתבחין בהאמור, כי סולם המדרגות, כפי שהם בהמוחין דקביעות, אינו משתנה לעולם, בסבת כל העליות הנ"ל. שהרי נתבאר לעיל, שסבת כל אלו העליות, הם מפאת שהנר"ן דצדיקים, העומדים בבי"ע, אי אפשר להם לקבל משהו, מטרם שכל הפרצופים העליונים מעבירים אותה להם מא"ס ב"ה. שבשיעור הזה נמצאים העליונים עצמם, עד א"ס ב"ה, מתגדלים ועולים גם הם. כל אחד להעליון שלהם (אות קס"א).

ונמצא, שבשיעור התעלות מדרגה אחת, כן מחויבים להתעלות כל המדרגות כולם, עד א"ס ב"ה. כי למשל, בהתעלות הזו"ן ממצבם הקבוע, שהוא למטה מטבור דא"א, ומלביש מחזה ולמטה דא"א, הרי גם א"א נתעלה באותה העת במדרגה אחת ממצבו הקבוע, שהיה מפה דעתיק ולמטה. ומלביש לג"ר דעתיק. שאחריו מתעלים גם מדרגות הפרטיות שלו. כי החג"ת שלו עלו למקום ג"ר הקבועות. והמחזה עד הטבור שלו עלו למקום חג"ת הקבועים, והמטבור ולמטה שלו עלו למקום המחזה עד הטבור.

אשר לפי זה נמצא הזו"ן, שעלה למקום מחזה עד הטבור דא"א הקבוע, שהוא עדיין למטה מטבור דא"א. שהרי בעת הזאת כבר עלה גם הלמטה מטבור דא"א למקום המחזה עד הטבור. (האילן, ציור ד' - עליות הזו"ן בערך הקבוע דה"פ דאצילות, שעולה ומלביש בעת השגת נשמה, לג"ר דישסו"ת, שעל גבי מפה ולמטה דאו"א, שעל גבי מחזה ולמטה דא"א).

אמנם גם כל פרצופי אצילות עולים בעת הזאת (האילן, ציור ז'). לכן תמצא שם את הזו"ן עדיין מלביש מפה ולמטה דישסו"ת, שעל גבי מחזה ולמטה דאו"א, שעל גבי מטבור ולמטה דא"א. הרי שסולם המדרגות לא נשתנה כלום מחמת העליה. ועד"ז בכל מיני העליות (האילן, מציור הג' עד סופו).

178) The order of Partzufim in all the worlds does not change as a result of these ascents. As we know, MAN raised by the NaRaN de Tzadikim caused an additional reception of light in all the higher Partzufim, which pass them the light from the World of Infinity, leaving a part of it for themselves, each according to its position, growing in size, ascending higher and higher.

Each Partzuf rises to the level of the higher one, i.e., all the Partzufim ascend without changing the order of their positions. For example, when ZON move from their permanent position under the Tabur de AA, they rise one level higher, i.e., to the Chazeh de AA. However, AA simultaneously goes up one level, i.e., from the Peh de Atik to the Gar de Atik.

Naturally, all of its Sefirot rise too. Its HaGaT reach the previous level of the Gar, while the Sefirot that were between the Chazeh and the Tabur rose to their place, etc. Thus, ZON are now on the level of the Tabur and below the Partzuf AA, i.e., their position remained unchanged (see diagram 4 in "Sefer haIlan", where during the reception of the light of Neshama, ZON rose to the Gar de YESHSUT, located below the Peh de Abba ve Ima, positioned below the Chazeh de AA).

However, all the Partzufim de Atzilut also ascended one level (see diagram 7 in "Sefer haIlan") during the reception of the light of Neshama. Hence, ZON still happen to be dressed on the space below the Peh de YESHSUT, located below the Chazeh de AVI, positioned below the Tabur de AA. Without exception, the ascents of all the Partzufim occur in a similar fashion (see diagrams 3 to 12 in "Sefer haIlan").

קעט) גם יש לדעת, שגם אחר עליות הפרצופים, הם משאירים כל מדרגתם במקום הקבוע או במקום שהיו שם מתחילה. כי אין העדר ברוחני (אות צ"ו). באופן, שבעת שהג"ר דאו"א עולים להג"ר דא"א, עוד נשארו הג"ר דאו"א במקום הקבוע מפה ולמטה דא"א. ונמצאים הישסו"ת, שעלו אז על גבי החג"ת דאו"א דעליה, שהם מקבלים מהג"ר דאו"א ממש, אשר היו שם מטרם העליה.

ולא עוד, אלא שנבחן שיש שם ג' מדרגות ביחד. כי הג"ר דאו"א דעליה, העומדות במקום ג"ר דא"א דקביעות, נמצאות משפיעות למקומם הקבוע שמפה ולמטה דא"א, ששם נמצאים עתה ישסו"ת. הרי הג"ר דא"א ואו"א וישסו"ת מאירים בבת אחת במקום אחד. ועד"ז נבחנים כל הפרצופים דא"ק ואבי"ע בעת העליות.

ומטעם זה יש להבחין תמיד בעלית הפרצוף, את ערך העליה כלפי העליונים במצבם הקבוע, ואת ערך שלו כלפי העליונים, שגם הם עלו מדרגה אחת כמותו. (ועיין כל זה באילן. כי בציור ג' תמצא מצב הפרצופים במצבם הקבוע. וג' עליות הז"א לפי ערכם של ה"פ אצילות הקבועים תמצא בציור ד', ה', ו'. וג' עליות של כל ה"פ אצילות, לפי ערכם של ה"פ א"ק הקבועים, תמצא בציורים ז', ח', ט'. וג' עליות של כל ה"פ א"ק, בערך קו א"ס ב"ה הקבוע, תמצא בהציורים י, י"א, וי"ב).

179) It should also be noted that, while ascending, all the Partzufim leave "traces" on all the previous levels. In other words, they both rise and stay in their places, for nothing disappears in the spiritual world. For example, although the Gar de AVI ascend to the level of the Gar de AA, they, at the same time, remain in their previous place – below the Peh de AA, where the YESHSUT now rose (to the HaGaT de AVI), received the same light that was received by HaGaT de AVI when they were in this place before the ascent.

Thus, there are now three Partzufim on that level at the same time; the Gar de AVI (after the ascent) now take the permanent place of the Gar de AA, pass the light to their previous position – from the Peh de AA and below. Now that level is taken by YESHSUT, since the Gar de AA, AVI and YESHSUT simultaneously shine upon one place. So, all the Partzufim de AK and ABYA line up during the ascents.

That is why, when the Partzuf rises, one must pay attention to the level of its ascent with regard to the permanent position of the higher Partzufim, their new places (see diagram 3 in "Sefer haIlan", where the permanent positions of the Partzufim are shown. On diagrams 4, 5 and 6 we can see 3 ascents of ZA as regards the permanent location of the Partzufim de Atzilut. On diagrams 7, 8 and 9 we can see three ascents of the five Partzufim de Atzilut as regards the five Partzufim de AK. On diagrams 10, 11, and 12 we can see three ascents of the five Partzufim de Atzilut as regards the permanent position of the Line of Infinity).

THE DIVISION OF EACH PARTZUF INTO KETER AND THE ABYA
ענין התחלקות כל פרצוף לכתר ואבי"ע

קפ) יש לדעת, שהכלל ופרט שוים זה לזה. וכל, הנבחן בכלל כולו יחד, נמצא גם בפרטי פרטיות שבו, ובפרט האחרון, שאך אפשר להפרט. ולפיכך, כיון שהמציאות בדרך כלל נבחן לה' עולמות א"ק ואבי"ע, שעולם הא"ק נבחן להכתר של העולמות, וד' עולמות אבי"ע נבחנים לחו"ב וזו"ן (אות ג).

כמו כן אין לך פרט קטן בכל ד' העולמות אבי"ע, שאינו כלול מכל ה' האלו, כי הראש של כל פרצוף נבחן להכתר שבו, שהוא כנגד עולם הא"ק. והגוף מפה עד החזה נבחן לאצילות שבו. וממקום החזה עד הטבור נבחן לבריאה שבו ומטבור ולמטה עד סיום רגליו נבחן ליצירה ועשיה שלו.

180) In the spiritual worlds, everything is built according to the same principle, i.e., one can judge the common by the particular, and vice versa, the particular by the common. The entire Universe is usually divided into the five worlds of AK and ABYA. The world of AK is regarded as Keter of all the worlds, while the four worlds of ABYA are correspondingly Hochma, Bina, ZA, and Malchut.

Therefore, any world, Partzuf or Sefira – in general, any spiritual object, can also be divided into the five worlds of AK and ABYA. The Rosh of any Partzuf is considered its Keter and the world AK. The Guf, from the Peh to the Chazeh, is considered the world of Atzilut (Hochma). The space from the Chazeh to the Tabur is considered the world of Beria, from the Tabur, and below – the worlds Yetzira and Assiya (the ZON).

קפא) וצריך שתדע, שיש כינויים מרובים לעשר ספירות כח"ב חג"ת נהי"מ. כי פעמים נקרא גר"ע ואח"פ, או כח"ב זו"ן, או נרנח"י, או קוצו של יוד וד' אותיות י"ה ו"ה, או הוי"ה פשוטה וע"ב ס"ג מ"ה וב"ן, שהם ד' מיני מילואים שבהוי"ה:

א) מילוי ע"ב הוא יוד הי ויו הי,
ב) מילוי ס"ג הוא יוד הי ואו הי,
ג) מילוי מ"ה הוא יוד הא ואו הא,
ד) מילוי ב"ן הוא יוד הה וו הה.

וכן הם הנקראים א"א ואו"א וזו"ן. שא"א הוא כתר, ואבא הוא חכמה, ואמא היא בינה, וז"א הוא חג"ת נה"י, והנוקבא דז"א היא מלכות. וכן נקראים א"ק ואבי"ע או כתר ואבי"ע. והמלכות דכתר נקרא פה, והמלכות דאצילות נקרא חזה, והמלכות דבריאה נקרא טבור, והמלכות דיצירה נקרא עטרת יסוד, והמלכות דכללות נקרא סיום רגלין.

181) Now, the Sefirot KaHaB HaGaT NHYM have many different names. Depending on what we wish to express, they may be called: 1) GE and AHP, 2) KaHaB ZON, 3) NaRaNHaY, 4) The dot of the letter "Yud" and the 4 letters "Yud", "Hey", "Vav" and "Hey".

5) A simple HaVaYaH (Galgalta) and AB, SAG, MA and BON, which constitute four kinds of the light filling (Milluyim):

a) Filling of the AB – יוד הי ויו הי
b) Filling of the SAG – יוד הי ואו הי
c) Filling of the MA – יוד הא ואו הא
d) Filling of the BON – יוד הה וו הה

6) The AA, AVI, and ZON:

a) The AA is Keter,
b) The Abbais Hochma,
c) The Ima is Bina,
d) The ZA is HaGaT NHY,
e) The Nukvah is Malchut.

7) AK and ABYA or Keter and ABYA.

Malchut de Keter is called "the Peh", Malchut de Atzilut – "the Chazeh", Malchut de Beria – "the Tabur", Malchut de Yetzira – "the Ateret Yesod", and the common Malchut – "the Sium Raglin".

קפב) ותדע שיש תמיד להבחין באלו שינוי השמות של הע"ס ב' הוראות: א. הוא ענין השואתו להספירה, שעל שמה הוא מתיחס, ב. הוא ענין השינוי שבו מאותו הספירה שמתיחס אחריה. שמסבה זו נשתנה שמו בהכינוי המיוחד. למשל, הכתר דע"ס דאו"י ה"ס א"ס ב"ה. וכל ראש של פרצוף נקרא ג"כ כתר. וכן כל ה"פ א"ק נקראים ג"כ כתר. וכן פרצוף עתיק נקרא כתר. וכן א"א נקרא כתר.

וע"כ יש להתבונן: אם הם כולם כתר, למה נשתנה שמם להקרא בהכינוים הללו? וכן אם הם מתיחסים כולם לכתר, הרי צריכים להשתוות להכתר?

אמנם האמת הוא, שמבחינה אחת הם כולם שוים לכתר, שהם בחינת א"ס. כי זה הכלל: שכל עוד שאור העליון לא נתלבש בכלי, הוא בחינת א"ס.

ולכן כל ה"פ א"ק נחשבים כלפי עולם התיקון שהם אור בלי כלי. כי אין לנו שום תפיסא בהכלים דצמצום א'. ולכן נחשב אצלנו אורותיו לבחינת א"ס ב"ה.

וכן עתיק וא"א דאצילות, הם שניהם מבחינת הכתר דנקודים. אמנם מבחינה אחרת הם רחוקים זה מזה. כי הכתר דאו"י הוא ספירה אחת, אבל בא"ק יש בו ה"פ שלמים, שבכל אחד מהם רת"ס (אות קמ"ב). וכן פרצוף עתיק הוא רק ממחצית הכתר העליון דנקודים, ופרצוף א"א הוא ממחצית הכתר התחתון דנקודים (אות קכ"ט). ועל דרך זה צריכים להבחין בכל מיני הכינוים של הספירות אותם ב' ההוראות.

182) There are two reasons why the 10 Sefirot are called differently. The first is the similarity of properties to the Sefira to which it refers. The second is the difference of properties with this Sefira, which leads to the emergence of a new and special name. For example, Keter of the 10 Sefirot de Ohr Yashar, on the one hand, is the light of Ein Sof (of Infinity); on the other hand, the Rosh of any Partzuf is also called "Keter". All five Partzufim de AK are also "Ketarim"; the Partzuf Atik is Keter and so is AA.

If all of them are "Ketarim", then why does each of them have its own name? Furthermore, we know that spiritual objects that have completely identical properties merge into a single whole. Then why do these spiritual objects (the Ketarim) not merge?

It happens because, although they have properties similar to those of Keter (they refer to Ein Sof), there is a rule saying that unless the upper light enters the vessel (spreads to the Guf), it is regarded as Ein Sof (unattainable Infinity).

Therefore, as regards the worlds of ABYA, all five Partzufim de AK are considered the light, which has not yet entered the vessel, since the AK, built according to the laws of TA, is utterly unattainable by the Partzufim de Atzilut, based on the laws of TB.

The Partzufim Atik and AA de Atzilut both correspond to Keter de Nikudim. It should be noted that during Katnut de Atzilut, AA is not Keter, its level in this state being Hochma. Meanwhile, the only Keter is Atik.

However, during Gadlut, all the Partzufim of Atzilut rise, Atik "leaves" for AK and AA takes advantage of its AHP de Aliyah and becomes the Partzuf Keter de Atzilut. Further, as with the entire Partzufim de AK, Atik is built in accordance with the laws of TA; hence, it is unattainable by the lower Partzufim and worlds ("Atik" derives from the word "Ne'etak" – "separated").

קפג) ותדע שההוראה המיוחדת לעצמה שבאלו הכינוים דע״ס בשם כתר ואבי״ע, הוא להורות, שהכונה היא על בחינת התחלקות הע״ס לכלים דפנים ולכלים דאחורים, שנעשו בסבת הצמצום ב׳ (אות ס׳), שאז עלתה מלכות המסיימת למקום בינה דגוף, הנקרא ת״ת במקום החזה, וסיימה שם את המדרגה, ונעשה שם סיום חדש, הנקרא ״פרסא שמתחת האצילות״ (אות ס״ח).

והכלים שמחזה ולמטה יצאה לבר מאצילות ונקראים בי״ע. שב״ש ת״ת שמחזה עד הסיום נקראים ״בריאה״, ונה״י נקראים ״יצירה״, והמלכות נקראת ״עשיה״. גם נתבאר, שמטעם זה נחלקה כל מדרגה לכלים דפנים וכלים דאחורים, שמחזה ולמעלה נקרא ״כלים דפנים״, ומחזה ולמטה נקרא ״כלים דאחורים״.

183) The ten Sefirot are called Keter and ABYA, because Kabbalists want to point to their division into Kelim de Panim (the "front" vessels) and Kelim de Achoraim (the "back" vessels), which took place during TB. As was stated above, Malchut Mesayemet rose from the level of Bina de Guf (called Tifferet) to the Chazeh, thus creating a new Sium de Partzuf called "the Parsa" and located below Atzilut.

The vessels that are below the Parsa "left" Atzilut and are called BYA. The lower two thirds of Tifferet are called Beria, the NHY are called Yetzira, and Malchut is called Assiya. It is worth mentioning that each Sefira was divided into the vessels of "Panim" and "Acho-

raim", so that those vessels above the Chazeh are Panim, while those beneath the Chazeh are Achoraim.

קפד) ולפיכך, הבחן זה של הפרסא במקום החזה, מחלק המדרגה לד' בחינות מיוחדות, הנקראות אבי"ע: האצילות עד החזה, והבי"ע מחזה ולמטה. וראשית ההבחן הוא בא"ק עצמו. אלא בו ירדה הפרסא עד הטבור שלו (אות ס"ח).

ונמצא בחינת אצילות שלו הוא הע"ב ס"ג המסתיימים למעלה מטבורו. ומטבורו ולמטה הוא בי"ע שלו, ששם ב' הפרצופים מ"ה וב"ן שבו. הרי איך ה"פ א"ק נחלקים על אבי"ע, מכח הסיום דצמצום ב', שנקרא "פרסא": שהגלגלתא הוא הראש, והע"ב ס"ג עד טבורו הוא אצילות, והמ"ה וב"ן שמטבורו ולמטה הוא בי"ע.

184) Since the Parsa is on the level of the Chazeh, each Sefira and each Partzuf splits into four levels called ABYA. Atzilut is the space above the Chazeh, BYA – under the Chazeh. In fact, this division was also present in the world of AK, the difference being that in AK the Parsa descended to the Tabur, whereas in Atzilut, it is on the level of the Chazeh.

It turns out that its own Atzilut is the Partzufim AB and SAG, which end above the Tabur, while its BYA, i.e., the Partzufim MA and BON, are under the Tabur. Therefore, Galgalta is Rosh; AB and SAG above the Tabur are Atzilut; MA and BON under the Tabur are BYA.

קפה) ועד"ז נחלקים ה"פ עולם האצילות בפני עצמם לכתר ואבי"ע: כי א"א הוא הראש דכללות אצילות, ואו"א עלאין, שהם ע"ב, המלבישים מפה ולמטה דא"א עד החזה, הם אצילות. ושם, בנקודת החזה, עומדת הפרסא, המסיימת בחינת האצילות של עולם האצילות.

וישסו"ת, שהם ס"ג, המלבישים מחזה דא"א עד טבורו, הם בריאה דאצילות. והזו"ן, שהם מ"ה וב"ן, המלבישים מטבור דא"א עד סיום האצילות, הם יצירה ועשיה דאצילות. הרי שגם עולם האצילות, בכללות ה"פ שבו, מתחלק לראש ואבי"ע, כמו ה"פ א"ק. אלא כאן עומדת הפרסא על מקומה, שהוא בחזה דא"א, ששם מקומה האמיתי (אות קכ"ז).

185) All five Partzufim de Atzilut are divided similarly. AA is the Rosh of the entire world of Atzilut; AVI Ilayin, which correspond to AB and dress onto the Partzuf AA from its Peh to Chazeh, are Atzilut de Atzilut (not to be confused with the common Parsa of the worlds of ABYA).

The YESHSUT that correspond to SAG and dress onto AA from its Chazeh to the Tabur are the Beria de Atzilut. The ZON, which correspond to MA and BON and dress onto AA from its Tabur to the Sium de Atzilut, are Yetzira and Assiya de Atzilut. Thus, we see that the world of Atzilut is also divided into its own Rosh and ABYA. As in the world of AK, the Parsa is in its place, i.e., at the level of the Chazeh de AA.

The principal *Partzuf de Atzilut*, *Arich Anpin*, has four kinds of dress: 1. *Abba*, 2. *Ima*, 3. *Israel Saba*, 4. *Tvunah*. All of them are the *Yud-Hey* of the name *HaVaYaH* and dress onto AA from the *Peh* to the *Tabur*. ZA and *Malchut de Atzilut* dress onto AA from the *Tabur* down to the *Parsa*; they are the *Vav-Hey* of the name *HaVaYaH*. There are only *Keter* and *Hochma* in the *Rosh de Arich Anpin*; its *Bina* exited the *Rosh* and split into the *Gar* and the *Zat*.

Abba ve Ima dress the light on the *Gar de Bina* and remain in the state of perfection felt in the *Rosh*, because they have properties of *Bina*, which desires nothing, hence stays unaffected. The *YESHSUT* takes the *Zat de Bina* of *Partzuf* AA (located under the *Chazeh de AA*), where the absence of *Ohr Hochma* is felt. This level is called "*Beria de Atzilut*".

קפו) אמנם בכללות כל העולמות, נבחנים כל ג' הפרצופים גלגלתא ע"ב ס"ג דא"ק לבחינת הראש דכללות. וה"פ עולם האצילות, המלבישים מטבור דא"ק ולמטה עד הפרסא דכללות, שהיא הפרסא שנעשתה בחזה דנקודות דס"ג (אות ס"ו), הנה שם הוא אצילות דכללות, מפרסא ולמטה, עומדים ג' העולמות בי"ע דכללות (אות ס"ז-ס"ח).

186) If we view the entire Universe as a single whole, we will see that the three Partzufim, Galgalta, AB and SAG of the world of Adam Kadmon, constitute its common Rosh; the five Partzufim de Atzilut, which dress onto the space from the Tabur de AK to the Parsa, are Atzilut of the Universe. The three worlds of BYA under the Parsa are the BYA of the Universe.

קפז) וממש על דרך הנ"ל מתחלקת כל מדרגה דפרטי פרטיות שבכל עולם מאבי"ע לראש ואבי"ע. ואפילו בחינת מלכות דמלכות שבעשיה. כי נבחן בו ראש וגוף. והגוף נחלק לחזה,

וטבור, וסיום רגלין. והפרסא, שמתחת האצילות של אותו המדרגה, עומדת בהחזה שלו ומסיימת האצילות. ומחזה עד הטבור הוא בחינת בריאה של המדרגה, שנקודת הטבור מסיימתה. ומטבור ולמטה עד סיום רגליו הוא בחינת יצירה ועשיה של המדרגה. ומבחינת הספירות נבחנים החג"ת עד החזה לאצילות. וב"ש תתאין דת"ת שמחזה עד הטבור לבריאה. ונה"י ליצירה. והמלכות לעשיה.

187) All individual Sefirot de Sefirot are divided in a similar way. Even Malchut de Malchut de Assiya has its own Rosh and Guf. The Guf is divided by its Chazeh, Tabur, and Sium Raglin. The Parsa, which is located under Atzilut of this level, stands in the Chazeh and limits it.

Beria of this level takes the space between the Chazeh and the Tabur. Yetzira and Assiya of this level are located between the Tabur and Sium Raglin. The Sefirot HaGaT of each level correspond to Atzilut. The lower two thirds of Tifferet from Chazeh to the Tabur are Beria, NHY – Yetzira and Malchut – Assiya.

קפח) ולכן הראש דכל מדרגה מיוחס לבחינת כתר, או יחידה, או לפרצוף גלגלתא. והאצילות שבו, שמפה עד החזה, מיוחס לחכמה, או לאור החיה, או לפרצוף ע"ב. והבריאה שבו, שמחזה עד הטבור, מיוחס לבינה, או לאור הנשמה, או לפרצוף ס"ג. והיצירה ועשיה שבו, שמטבור ולמטה, מיוחס לזו"ן, או לאורות דרוח נפש, או לפרצוף מ"ה וב"ן. (ותראה בהאילן, מציור ג' ואילך, איך כל פרצוף מתחלק לפי הבחינות הנ"ל).

188) Thus, the Rosh of each level refers to Keter or Yechida, or Partzuf Galgalta. Atzilut (from the Peh to the Chazeh) refers to Hochma or the light of Haya, or AB. Beria (from the Chazeh to the Tabur) refers to Bina or the light of Neshama, or SAG. Yetzira and Assiya (below the Tabur) refer to ZON or the lights Ruach and Nefesh, or Partzufim MA and BON (see diagrams 3 to 12 in "Sefer haIlan").

QUIZ TO THE ARTICLE "THE PREAMBLE TO THE WISDOM OF KABBALAH"

1. What is the substance ("*Homer*") of which the Creation is made? (§ 1)
2. What is the meaning of the light and the vessel described as the ten *Sefirot*?(§ 2)
3. Why are the ten *Sefirot* called only the four *Behinot HuB TuM*; where does the number 10 come from? (§ 3)
4. What is the reason for dividing each creation into ten *Sefirot*? (§ 5)
5. What is the difference between the worlds of *ABYA*? (§§ 6, 7, 8 and 9)
6. Why is the world of *Atzilut* considered as referring only to the Creator? (§ 6)
7. How was the soul (*Neshama*) separated from the Creator? (§ 7)
8. What is a "*Zivug de Haka'a*" of the Upper Light with a screen? (§ 14)
9. How did new vessels referring to the "desire to bestow" emerge? (§ 15)
10. Why is the *Aviut* inherent in the "desire to bestow" also present in the new vessels? (§ 18)
11. Why are the *Partzufim* positioned one under the other after their emergence?(§ 22)

12. Why are the vessels *KaHaB TuM* positioned in a descending order? (§ 24)
13. Why are the lights called *NaRaNHaY* in a descending order? (§ 24)
14. Why is there an inverse relation between the lights and the vessels? (§ 25)
15. What is the difference between the *Rosh* and the *Guf* of the *Partzuf*? (§ 26)
16. How did the five *Partzufim* of the world of *AK* (the *Rosh* and the *Guf*) emerge one under the other? (§ 27, 28)
17. Why did the world of *AK* turn into a thin line and fail to fill the entire Universe? (§ 31)
18. Why did the luminescence of *AK* stop above the point of our world? (§ 31)
19. What is the quantitative correlation between the Surrounding Light and the Inner Light in the world *AK*? (§ 32)
20. How and where is the Surrounding Light of *AK* manifested? (§ 32)
21. Why are the Surrounding and the Inner Lights connected with one another in one vessel? (§ 33)
22. What is the Impact between the Surrounding Light and the Inner Light? (§ 34)
23. How does the screen with the *Reshimot de Guf* rise to the *Peh de Rosh*? (§ 38)
24. What is the reason for the formation of the lower *Partzuf* out of *Peh* of the upper? (§ 39)
25. Why is each lower *Partzuf* smaller by one level (*Behina*) than the upper? (§ 40)
26. Why is the lower *Partzuf* separated from the upper and considered its "consequence", "son"? (§ 40)
27. What are the *Reshimo de Hitlabshut* and the *Reshimo de Aviut*? (§§ 42, 43)

28. Why are there two levels in the *Rosh* of all the *Partzufim* – *Zachar* and *Nekeva*? (§ 43)
29. Why is the level of the *Partzuf* determined by the level of *Nekeva* and not *Zachar*? (§ 44)
30. What are *Ta'amim, Nekudot, Tagin* and *Otiot*? (§§ 48, 49)
31. Why are the level of *Ta'amim* mercy (*Rachamim*) and the level of *Nekudot* – judgment (*Din*)? (§ 48)
32. Why is every *Partzuf* divided into *Rosh, Toch* and *Sof* and each of these parts – into ten *Sefirot*? (§ 50)
33. Why does each lower *Partzuf* dress onto the upper from the *Chazeh* and below? (§ 53)
34. What is the difference between *TA* and *TB*? (§ 58)
35. Why could not the worlds exist according to the laws of *TA*? (§ 57)
36. What is the principle benefit of *TB*? (§§ 57, 58)
37. What is Tzimtzum *NHY de AK* and what was the reason for it? (§ 60)
38. Why did the world of the *Nikudim* not dress onto the *Partzuf* SAG above the *Tabur*? (§ 62)
39. What is the essence of the *Parsa* located under the world of *Atzilut*? (§ 67)
40. How did three places for the worlds of the *BYA* emerge? (§ 67)
41. Why are there *Katnut* and *Gadlut* in each *Partzuf*? (§ 71)
42. Why did the Partzufim de *AK* not have the statesof *Katnut* and *Gadlut*? (§§70, 71)
43. Why did *Zachar* and *Nekeva* (*Dechar ve Nukva*) appear in the *Gar de Nikudim*, i.e., in *Keter* and the *AVI*? (§ 74)
44. Why does *Keter de Nikudim* not spread to the *Zat*? (§ 74)
45. Why did each level in the world of *Nikudim* split into two parts? (§76)

46. What led to the emergence of "the *Panim*" and "the *Achoraim*" in the world of Nikudim? (§ 76)
47. Why are the *Achoraim* of the upper *Partzuf* inside the *Panim* of the lower? (§ 77)
48. What is the reason for the raising of MAN? (§ 80)
49. Why did the *Mochin de Gadlut* emerge? (§ 84)
50. What is the light raised by the *AHP* of the vessels and the *Gar* of the lights? (§ 84)
51. What are the ascent of *Malchut* to the *Nikvey Eynaim* and the descent of the *AHP*? (§ 85)
52. What is the difference between the names of the *Sefirot* GE, *AHP* and *KaHaB TuM*? (§ 85)
53. Why do *Hesed, Gevura* and the upper third of *Tifferet* refer to the *Kelim de Panim*?(§ 85)
54. Why do the lower two thirds of *Tifferet* and the *NHYM* refer to the *Kelim de Achoraim*? (§85)
55. What are the lights *Holam, Shuruk* and *Hirik*? (§ 89)
56. Why does the point of the *Hirik* get broken as it emerges in the world of *Nikudim*?(§ 90)
57. Why is the *Hirik* under the letters (*Otiot*)? (§ 91)
58. How did the *Zat* raise MAN to the *Gar de Nikudim*? (§§ 93, 94, 95)
59. What is the *Sefira Da'at*, which first appears in the world of *Nikudim*? (§ 98)
60. Why does the *Sefira Da'at* not become the 11th *Sefira*? (§ 100)
61. What is the level of the *Partzuf Ta'amim de Rosh* and the *Guf* in the world of *Nikudim*? (§ 104)
62. What is the level of the *Partzufim Nekudot de Rosh* and the *Guf* in the world of *Nikudim*? (§ 104)

63. What is *Melech haDa'at* in the world of *Nikudim* and what is its level? (§ 107)

64. What is the reason for the breaking of the vessels? (§ 105)

65. Why is *Gadlut* in the world of *Nikudim* only an addition? (§ 72)

66. What are the names of the levels *AVI* and *YESHSUT* in the world of *Nikudim*? (§§ 110, 111)

67. What is the difference between MA *de Nikudim* from MA *Hadash (in Atzilut)*? (§ 113)

68. What is the difference between the *Partzuf* and the world? (§§ 115, 116)

69. What are the first and second *Ibur*? (§§ 121, 122)

70. What are *Ibur, Yenika,* and *Gadlut*? (§§ 121, 122)

71. How did five levels of the world of *Atzilut* emerge one under the other? (§§ 122-129)

72. What is the order of superposition ("dressing") of the five *Partzufim de Atzilut* one on the other? (§ 122-129)

73. What are MA and *BON* in each *Partzuf de Atzilut*? (§ 129, 133)

74. What are the two kinds of *Gadlut* that can exist in the world of *Atzilut*? (§ 134, 135)

75. What is the difference between supplementation to 10 *Sefirot* of the lower *Partzuf* at the expense of *AHP* of the upper and the use of its own *AHP* for that purpose? (§ 135-138)

76. What kind of supplementation to 10 *Sefirot* do the 5 permanent *Partzufim de Atzilut* use for reaching *Gadlut*? (§ 138)

77. What is the size of the *Gufim de AK* and thc *Gufim de Atzilut*? (§ 139)

78. Why do the worlds supplement their 10 *Sefirot* with the help of *AHP de Aliyah* (§§ 142, 143)

79. What are the seven basic peculiarities of the worlds of *BYA*? (§§ 144, 154)
80. Why do the worlds ascend when the souls of the *Tzadikim* receive the *Mochin*? (§§ 161, 162)
81. What is the order of the three ascents at that time? (§§ 163-176)
82. How do the five *Partzufim de Atzilut* dress onto the 5 *Partzufim de AK* during each of these ascents? (§§ 163-176)
83. What are the four fillings of the Name *HaVaYaH*: *AB*, *SAG*, *MA* and *BON*? (§ 181)
84. What are the four parts of the *Partzuf*? (§ 180)
85. What is the meaning of terms: "*Peh*", "*Chazeh*", "Tabur" and "*Sium Raglin*" (§ 181)
86. What is the reason for the division of the *Partzuf* into *Keter* and *ABYA*? (§ 180-185)

RECAPITULATION BY RABBI BARUCH ASHLAG

First, let us examine the issue: "The connection between the Creator and the Creation", having pointed out that the Creator's Essence is unattainable. We can only grasp His actions. This connection may also be called "The Thought of Creation", where the Creator's desire is to bestow delight upon created beings.

Therefore, from the moment of The Thought of Creation, the Universe begins its descending evolution: creation of worlds, nature, and then, out of its root called "the soul of Adam haRishon", human souls are born. All that was created before the birth of Adam's soul (or simply soul) was prepared as an environment in which this soul can exist, develop and improve until it reaches its ultimate spiritual level.

Let us speak about the top-down evolution of the worlds. Wishing to delight the created beings, the Creator intended to give them, perhaps, 100 kg of pleasure. Hence, He had to create such beings that would be willing to receive that pleasure. The entire essence of creation consists in this will to receive the Creator's delight. Hence, the name "*Yesh mi Ayn*", i.e., the essence created from something that was previously non-existent, prior to the Creator's Thought. This 'will to receive pleasure' was created for the single purpose of bestowing delight upon created beings.

The creation of a will to receive for delight must go through four phases of development, since man cannot enjoy anything without having a passionate desire for that pleasure. Therefore, a vessel is a passionate desire for delight. The size of the vessel is measured according to volume of its desire.

Two conditions are essential for a desire to appear:

1. You must know what you want to enjoy. Man cannot wish for something that he never saw or heard of. In other words, a pleasure has to be something previously felt and evaluated as such.

2. The vessel must not have this pleasure at this particular moment, since, if pleasure fills the desire, it extinguishes the aspiration to it.

To achieve these two conditions, i.e., to develop a genuine desire, the initial will to receive pleasure (that derives from nothingness, from the Creator's Thought) must pass four phases of its development:

Phase Shoresh, 0, *Keter* is "the Creator's "desire to bestow" delight upon the createdbeings".

Phase Aleph, 1, *Hochma* is "the Creator's "desire to bestow" delight upon the createdbeings" created "*Yesh mi Ayn*", out of nothing – a will to receive delight. Since the desire was created of the light – the pleasure prepared by the Creator, it emerged already filled with delight. Hence, there is no genuine striving after it.

Phase Bet, 2, *Bina*. Since the light emanates from the Creator and His property to bestow, the vessel gradually acquires that property of giving, i.e., the vessel wishes to be like the light. The emergence of a new desire in phase one turns it into a separate phase two.

Question: "If the desire of *Bina* is to give, why is it considered coarser and more remote from the Creator? Does it not have to be purer than *Hochma*?"

I would like to explain it with the following example. A person gives his friend a gift and he accepts it. Then, after thinking it over, decides not to, and returns it. First, he was under the giver's influence; hence, he took the gift. Yet, having received it, he felt himself a receiver, and this feeling of shame forced him to return the gift.

From this, we may conclude that *Behina Aleph* received under the influence of the giver and did not feel that it was receiving. However, when, affected by the light, it felt it was receiving, and then it stopped. Therefore, the sensation of desire to receive pleasure in *Bina* is greater than that in *Hochma* – the desire feels more egoistic, because it compares itself with the light, i.e., with the giver. Hence, it considers itself more remote from the Creator.

The light that enters the vessel, which wants to merge with the Creator by its properties, is called *Ohr Hassadim*. This light shines in *Bina*. However, *Bina* feels only the "desire to give", and it can only give to the light, to the Creator. *Bina* realizes that its goal is to receive, to enjoy. It can give the Creator only by receiving His pleasure.

Hence, phase two makes a compromise: now it will accept the light of *Hassadim* and a little light of *Hochma*. Since *Bina* had to generate the desire to enjoy the *Ohr Hochma* in order to receive it, the new desire for both *Hassadim* and *Hochma* is coarser than the previous. That is why **phase three** is farther away from the Creator and is called *Behina Gimel de Aviut*. This phase bears the name "*Zeir Anpin*" – a small face, because *Hochma* is called "*Panim*" ("*Anpin*" in Aramaic), i.e., a miniature spiritual object.

When phase three is completely filled with the light of *Hassadim* (and the luminescence of *Hochma*), it feels the "desire to receive" the entire light of *Hochma* and not just its part. This happens because the light lets ZA know that the Thought of Creation consists in receiving the entire light of *Hochma* prepared by the Creator. This awakening leads to an enormous desire for the *Ohr Hochma* rising up in the vessel. It wants to receive as much light as was in *Behina Aleph*. The difference lies in the fact that *Behina Aleph* did not have this passionate desire for the light that *Behina Dalet* (*Malchut*) has, so *Behina Aleph* did not feel delighted, since the light gave birth to desire, whereas here the desire attracts pleasure!

Therefore, **phase four** is defined as a genuine vessel, and all previous phases are called preparatory. *Malchut* is filled with limitless, infinite pleasure; hence, it is called the "World of Infinity" – 100 kg of delight filled 100 kg of desire.

However, when the light fills phase four, *Malchut*, it starts passing it its properties, as it was in phase one: phase one received the light, but with the delight it acquired the light's property of bestowal; hence, its "desire to receive" turned into a "desire to bestow", phase two.

Since this desire is absolutely opposite to its original, the natural will to receive pleasure, *Malchut* feels "shame" – a tremendous inner tension between its original desire and the one it acquired. Because of this, it decides to completely stop receiving the light, similar to phase one as it passed into phase two. Why did phase one not feel shame? It is because phase four already has a desire to receive pleasure that derives from the creation itself, and not the one created by the Creator.

The expulsion of pleasure from the desire (phase four, *Malchut*) is carried out by the creation; hence, it is called "the First Restriction" ("*Tzimtzum Aleph*").

The light passed its properties to *Malchut*, so that it would become like the light; but *Malchut* only stopped receiving pleasure. So how can the creation carry out the Creator's will – to receive the entire light of *Hochma* without being a receiver?

After the restriction, *Malchut* makes a decision: to receive the entire delight according to the Creator's wish, but only because He, and not *Malchut* itself, wants it.

Question: "The *Tzimtzum* was made only on *Behina Dalet*; only the desire "*Lekabel al menat Lekabel*" ("to receive pleasure for one's own sake", "reception for the sake of reception") was restricted (in contrast to "receiving for the sake of bestowal", which appears later). So why did the light disappear from all the previous *Behinot*?

Answer: The three first *Behinot* are not yet called "vessel", for they merely contribute to the formation of the genuine vessel in *Behina Dalet* – "reception for the sake of reception". The only true vessel is *Malchut*;

if it does not want to receive, it stops feeling the light, as if being non-existent in phases zero through three.

Malchut, having accepted the entire light, was filled with it. Such an absolute state is called whole or round, because a circle (or, rather, a sphere, since *Malchut* of the World of Infinity filled with the light is meant) is identical in all its parts; there are no "up – down", "better – worse" in it. If every desire is filled, it does not matter what size it is, big or small; they all receive infinite delight.

Only after the *Tzimtzum*, when the light disappears, the empty desires begin to differ in their properties, sizes, and closeness to the Creator. They divide into up and down according to their significance, become more or less spiritual, closer, or farther away from the Creator. The desires that are more distant from egoism are considered more important, those that are closer to it – less important.

After the *Tzimtzum*, "traces" were left in the empty desires – the *Reshimot* of the light that was inside them. These five phases, or the 10 *Sefirot* (because phase three, ZA, consists of six parts) are called the "ten round *Sefirot*" ("*Eser Sefirot de Igulim*") after the restriction. They are called round because there is no notion of "up – down" in them.

Since everything develops from the Creator to the creation, from perfection to imperfection, the upper object's desire always becomes a law for the lower. Hence, after deciding not to receive the light for its own sake, *Malchut* makes a restriction, which applies to all future parts of the creation.

Egoistic reception of pleasure would be impossible, and if some part of *Malchut*, e.g. man, has such desire, he will not be able to enjoy it, constantly chasing after pleasure. *Malchut* is the only creation. All that exists are its parts.

Although the decision to restrict itself was voluntary, it became law the moment *Malchut* made it. Now reception for its own sake is forbidden. Now that a ban is imposed, notions like "up – down" as regards this ban, come into being. Hence, reception for the Creator's sake is called "a *Kav*" ("line"), which spreads from the World of Infinity down to our world.

After the restriction, the empty round, *Sefirot* fill with the light by way of the line.

Thus, there are three states of the creation (desire, *Malchut*):

1. The will to receive created in the world of *Ein Sof*, which received the entire light. It is called *Malchut de Ein Sof* (*Malchut* of the World of Infinity).

2. The restricted desire called "*Olam haTzimtzum*" - the World of Restriction, *Malchut Metzumtzemet* (restricted, empty *Malchut*).

3. *Malchut de Kav* – *Malchut*, which decided to receive the light after the restriction, but only as much as it can accept for the Creator's sake.

After the restriction, *Malchut* decides to receive pleasure for the Creator's sake. It attracts the entire light that it expelled previously and calculates what part it can receive; not for itself, but to please the Creator. First, *Malchut* makes this decision in its mind (*be Koach*), then in action (*be Foahl*).

Such an interaction of *Malchut* with the light, antagonizing its desire to receive pleasure for itself and accepting the light in its "desire to bestow" upon the Creator, is called "a *Zivug de Haka'a Ohr be Masach*" (interaction between the light and the screen by stroke). *Malchut* puts a barrier before the coming light.

This screen reflects the entire light, and then *Malchut* calculates that it can accept, perhaps, 20% of it for the Creator's sake and receives it inside its desire, but this pleasure is dressed in the intention "for the Creator". *Malchut* feels such enormous delight in the remaining 80% of the light that, if it accepts it, it will not be for the Creator, so it decides not to receive more than 20%.

What is the difference between the *Tzimtzum* and the *Masach*? The *Tzimtzum* took place because of *Malchut's* independent decision to stop enjoying the infinite light, i.e., the entire pleasure emanating from the Creator that is inside it. The *Masach* is a law imposed by the superior spiritual object as regards the lower: even if the lower wants to receive, the superior will not allow it.

What is a *Zivug de Haka'a*? Wishing to bestow upon the created beings, the superior spiritual object creates a "desire to receive" the light in the lower. The lower wants to be like the superior, so it decides not to accept the light. Hence, they contradict one another, which results in their impact (*Haka'a*).

The superior and the lower objects are always the Creator and the creation, since each higher level, *Sefira*, *Partzuf*, world or soul represents a parent, a source from which the lower one originates and receives the light. Furthermore, the lower can attain only the level above it. So the superior is always perceived by the lower as the Creator.

Because of this conflict, when each one wants to bestow and not to receive, an impact (*Haka'a*) takes place. Both come to an agreement by way of a *Zivug* (merging): the lower receives the light since the superior wants it to, but only as much as it can accept with an intention to bestow. A *Zivug* is possible only if an impact (*Haka'a*), a contradiction, preceded it.

The whole process of a *Zivug de Haka'a* takes place in the part of the creation that precedes the action. Such comprehension and decision making (*be Koach*) is called the *Rosh* (head) or the *Shoresh* (root). Then the action (*be Foahl*) follows; it is called the *Guf* (body).

The *Rosh*, the preliminary estimate of the action, is necessary because there are desires that are not equipped with an altruistic intention; hence, *Malchut* is obliged to make a calculation (called the *Rosh*) before it actually receives the light in the *Guf*.

Therefore, it is said, "There were neither the *Rosh* nor the *Sof* before the creation came into being". Reception was not banned in the world of *Ein Sof*, so *Malchut* received without limit or preliminary evaluation. However, as soon as *Malchut* made its decision to receive only for the Creator's sake, the need to oppose its own decision arose; the *Sof* was defined and the *Rosh* (*be Koach*) and the *Guf* (*be Foahl*) were separated.

The 20% of the light *Malchut* received are called the *Toch*, i.e., the place where the light spreads inside the desire. A desire consists of the *Rosh*, the *Toch*, and the *Sof*. The *Rosh* ends in the *Peh* (mouth). The light is received in a space from the *Peh* to the *Tabur*. This part of a desire is called the *Toch*. *Malchut de Toch*, which received 20% of the light, stands in the *Tabur*. It also restricts the reception of 80% of the light in 80% of the empty desires. The light that is supposed to fill these desires of the *Sof* remains outside and is called "the *Ohr Makif*" ("the Surrounding Light").

When the vessel is filled with 20% of the light from the *Peh* to the *Tabur*, the remaining 80% of the light (the *Ohr Makif*) strikes into the screen, positioned at the *Tabur*. This tells *Malchut* that it is wrong, since it cannot fulfill the purpose of creation in this way. If it remains on the same level, it will never be able to receive more than 20% of the light. Since *Malchut* can neither accept more than these 20%, nor remain filled only with 20% (seeing now that this state is far from perfect), it decides to stop receiving the light altogether.

The collision of opinions of *Malchut*, which decided to receive only 20% of the light, and the Surrounding Light, is called the *Bitush Ohr Makif be Ohr Pnimi* or the *Bitush Ohr Makif be Masach de Tabur*.

Each spreading of the light consists in filling all the five parts of *Malchut*. Even if *Malchut* is filled by 20%, it means that each of its five parts receives 20%. Therefore, when *Malchut* decides to expel the received light, it does so systematically.

After the restriction, *Malchut* decides to receive 20% of the light, which it had in the state of being completely filled. That state left the *Reshimot* in *Malchut*, and it makes a *Zivug* on them.

The *Masach* gradually loses its *Aviut*: first, *Behina Dalet de Dalet*, then *Gimel de Dalet* and so on, until it reaches the *Peh de Rosh*, where the *Masach de Guf* originated. As it rises, the *Masach* uses smaller and smaller *Aviut* and consequently receives weaker light for the sake of bestowal. Being on the level of *Behina Dalet*, the *Masach* can receive the light of *Yechida*, on the level of *Behina Gimel* – *Haya*, on the level of *Behina Bet* – *Neshama*, on the level of *Behina Aleph* – *Ruach*. *Behina Shoresh* provides it with the light of *Nefesh* for the sake of bestowal, until it becomes completely unable to receive the light for the sake of bestowal.

A question arises: "What did the *Ohr Makif* gain by forcing the creation to fulfill the purpose of creation and receive more and more light? On the face of it, what happens is opposite to what the *Ohr Makif* wants: the *Masach* completely stops receiving the light and the vessel loses the little light it had".

Answer: There was no chance to receive any more light before the *Bitush*. Now that *Behina Dalet* disappeared, the vessel may receive more, i.e., in *Behina Gimel*. When *Behina Gimel* is lost, it receives light in *Behina Bet* and so on. New vessels were created with the help of the *Bitush*. So what is the gain, if each time the creation receives less and less? There is a rule: nothing ever disappears in the spiritual world. In other words, whatever was revealed remains; but it cannot be enjoyed. Only when the entire work is completed will all lights be revealed simultaneously. This will be the final gain.

There is a story about two men who were friends when they were young. Then their ways parted. One became a king, the other a beggar. Many years passed, when one day the beggar found out that his friend had become a king. He decided to travel to the country where his friend was ruling and ask him for help. When they met, he told the king about his distress. The story touched the king's heart and he gave the beggar a letter to his treasurer. The letter allowed the beggar to spend two hours inside the treasury and take as much money as he could within that time.

Upon receiving the treasurer's permission, the beggar began filling the cup he had used for collecting his alms with gold coins. When the cup was full, he moved to get out of the building, beaming with happiness. However, as he approached the door, a guard took the cup from his hands and emptied the contents onto the floor. The beggar burst out crying, but the guard told him: "Take your cup, go back, and refill it". The beggar did as he was told, but as he came to the door, the guard once again emptied his cup.

And so it went on until the two hours expired. As the beggar came to the door for the last time with the full cup in his hands, he began to implore the guard to let him have this last cupful, since his time was up. The guard told him that he could have not just the last cupful of money, but also all the coins that were scattered on the floor.

From the story, we may conclude that every time we receive light for the Creator's sake, it remains. However, if it does, there is no desire to accept more, since it is impossible to increase the intention for the Creator's sake and receive a larger portion than before. Hence, the previous level has to disappear, so that each consecutive level will allow the correcting of the vessels, until they are all completely corrected and all the lights simultaneously shine in them.

Let us explain the notion of the *Masach* again. The first spreading of the light from the *Peh* down is called the *Ta'amim*. As the *Masach* gets weaker, new levels emerge in the process. All these levels are called *Nekudot*. My Rabbi said that new vessels were formed with the help of the *Bitush*. This allowed the reception of new portions of the light. As long as the light shines inside the vessel, it has no need or "desire to receive" the light. Therefore, both the light and the vessel are identical. However, after the expulsion of the light, they (the light and the vessel) can be separately defined.

The levels that emerge during the weakening of the *Masach* are called *Nekudot* (*Nekudat Tzimtzum* is meant). What is this? *Malchut* without the light is called a black point. When the ban on egoistic reception is in force, darkness sets in. The point of the *Tzimtzum* starts acting in the place where the "desire to receive" for oneself arises. In our example, when the *Masach* loses *Behina Dalet*, the ban on egoistic reception applies to it and the point of the *Tzimtzum* snaps into action. Then this process spreads to *Behina Gimel* and so on.

Now let us clear up the difference between the *Rosh*, the *Toch*, and the *Sof*. The *Rosh* is *Behina be Koach*; there is no actual reception in it. Two parts spread from the *Rosh*: one can accept the light of *Hochma*, the *Ohr Pnimi*, the light of the Thought of Creation. Another part is a will to receive for one's own sake, which may not be used by the vessel, so the *Sof* (end of reception) is formed there. It is called the 10 *Sefirot de Sof*. The main distinction between the *Toch* and the *Sof* consists in the fact that the *Toch* is filled with the light of *Hochma*, while the *Sof* contains the light of *Hassadim* with luminescence of *Hochma*.

The light of *Hochma* shines upon the vessels of reception and depends on their level of *Aviut*. The light of *Hochma* spreads top-down, so the notions "*Aroch*" (long) and "*Katzar*" (short) are inherent in it.

The light of *Hassadim* neither spreads because of the *Aviut* nor depends on it; hence, the notions expressing width ("right" and "left") are applied to it. This hints at the luminescence on the same level regardless of the amount of *Aviut*.

We have so far discussed only the first *Partzuf de AK* called the *Galgalta* or the *Partzuf Pnimi de AK*. Each world has a so-called *Partzuf Pnimi*, which is dressed in four "garments". Let us make it clear in the case of AK. The *Partzuf Galgalta* consists of a complete *HaVaYaH* (the Creator's Name – "*Yud-Hey-Vav-Hey*").

An independent level emerges from each letter of *HaVaYaH*. The *Rosh* is unattainable; it is called *Keter* or *Kotzo shel Yud* (*point* of *Yud*). The part from the *Peh* to the *Chazeh* is called *Yud*. The second *Partzuf de AK* called *AB* emerges on this level and dresses onto it. The part from the *Chazeh* and below is called the first *Hey*. This is the third *Partzuf de AK*.

It is called SAG or *Bina*. Both *AB* and SAG are dressed above the *Tabur* and constitute the letters *Yud-Hey*.

The letters *Vav-Hey* of *HaVaYaH* are located below the *Tabur*. The *Vav* takes the upper third of *Netzah-Hod-Yesod*, called MA, from which the world of *Nikudim* later emerges. The last *Hey* takes the lower two thirds of *Netzah-Hod-Yesod*. The *Partzuf BON* or *Malchut* emerges from it. Later on, the world of *Atzilut*, using *Aviut Shoresh*, comes into being there.

When the light disappeared from *Galgalta*, *Reshimot* remained in the empty vessels. *Reshimo* is a passionate desire for something that was available in the past. *Reshimo* consists of two parts: pure transparent light and coarser light. The *Reshimo* of the transparent light is left by the *Ohr Yashar* (Direct Light), whereas the *Ohr Hozer* (Reflected Light) leaves the *Reshimo* of the coarser light. Both of them merge and dress in the common *Ohr Hozer*, which plays the role of a vessel.

When the light shines upon the vessel, it is impossible to separate one from the other, both perform the same duty. It may be compared to food and appetite. Both take part in one process. If there is an appetite without food, eating becomes impossible. The same is true when there is food without an appetite.

As soon as the light disappears from the *Partzuf*, the notion "vessel" arises. *Ohr Hozer* plays that role. This notion also refers to the *Reshimot*. When both the transparent and the coarse lights are combined together, they are called "light". When *Ohr Yashar* disappears from the *Reshimo*, the coarse light receives the name *Nitzutzin*. The light that vanished shines from afar.

Now we are going to discover the meanings of *Shoresh* of the vessels and *Shoresh* of the lights. There is a rule that states: all worlds emerge as "a seal and its imprint". The worlds develop in a descending order that corresponds unerringly to all the peculiarities that initially emerged.

The vessels first manifested in the *Partzuf Galgalta*; hence, it is called the *Shoresh* of the vessels. As long as the light shines inside the vessels, there is no opportunity to differentiate between the vessels and the lights. The vessels first manifest after the expulsion of the light and retain the *Reshimot* of it. Therefore, the *Kli Keter* retains the *Reshimo* of the light of *Keter*. The *Kli Hochma* holds the *Reshimo de Ohr Hochma*. Each light enters the purest vessel, i.e., *Keter*, which is called the *Shoresh* of the vessels.

Now what are *Tagin* and *Otiot*? The *Reshimo* of *Ta'amim* is called *Tagin*. The *Reshimo* of *Nekudot* is called *Otiot* (letters).

When the light exits the *Partzuf Galgalta*, two kinds of *Reshimot* remain. The *Reshimo* of the light *Keter*, which was inside the vessels, is called *Dalet de Hitlabshut*. The last degree of the *Masach's* power (*Dalet*) is lost and now only *Behina Gimel de Aviut* is left. The *Hitlabshut* is the *Reshimo* of *Ta'amim*; the *Aviut* is the *Reshimo* of *Nekudot*.

As the *Masach* in the *Partzuf Galgalta* grows weak and rises to the *Masach de Rosh*, two *Zivugim* took place in the *Rosh* of that level: one on *Dalet de Hitlabshut*, the other – on *Gimel de Aviut de Ohr Hochma*. Thus the *Partzuf AB* was born. The *Dalet de Hitlabshut* shines only in the *Rosh* of the level, preventing the light from spreading into the *Guf*. The *Gimel de Aviut* causes the light to spread in the *Guf de Partzuf*, i.e., in the vessels and the *Otiot*.

As the *Masach de Partzuf AB* loses the last degree of *Aviut Gimel*, only *Aviut Bet* and *Hitlabshut Gimel* remain. After two *Zivugim* on these *Behinot*, the *Partzuf* SAG emerges. The *Nekudot de SAG* is *Behina Hassadim*; therefore, they can spread under the *Tabur de Galgalta*. Regardless of the *Aviut Dalet* under the *Tabur* (the vessels of reception), the *Nekudot de* SAG still wish to bestow, and are not interested in receiving the light.

Having no *Masach* on *Behina Dalet* and being aware of the "desire to receive" present there, the *Nekudot de* SAG wished the light for themselves. However, the *Tzimtzum* is imposed on the "desire to receive", so the light instantly disappears. How is it that *Nekudot de* SAG (the vessels of bestowal) suddenly wanted to receive the light for themselves? The *Gar de Bina* did not want to receive. Only the *Zat de Bina* was supposed to get the *Ohr Hochma* to pass it on to ZA. Hence, the restriction took place only in the *Zat de Bina*, i.e., in the *AHP* that exceeded the bounds of the level. This is *Tzimtzum Bet* (*TB*). The *Gar de Bina*, i.e., the *Galgalta ve Eynaim* (GE) did not merge with *Behina Dalet*. Meanwhile this place is called *Atzilut*.

When the *Masach* of the *Partzuf* SAG began rising to the *Peh de Rosh*, the following *Zivugim* took place in the *Rosh*: a *Zivug on Reshimot de Ta'amim de* SAG, which did not descend under the *Tabur*, and on which the *Partzuf* MA *Elion*, emerged. A *Zivug on Reshimot de* SAG, which made *Tzimtzum* and merged with *Behina Dalet* under the *Tabur*. The *Partzuf* MA, called the world of *Nikudim*, emerged on them. This *Zivug* was made on one half of *Aleph de Aviut* and *Bet de Hitlabshut* with the information on *TB*.

There are two *Rashim* in the world of *Nikudim*: one is *Keter* –*Bet de Hitlabshut*; the other is *Abba ve Ima* –*Aleph de Aviut*. Since *Bet de Hitlabshut* cannot draw the light for the lack of desire, it needs to work together with the *Aviut*. We have learned that "the *VAK de Bina*" is *Behina* "*Hafetz Hesed*"; with its help, this level feels no need for the light of *Hochma*. This light is also called "the *Tikkun Kavim*" (correction of lines).

We know that in the world of *Nikudim* "the *Tikkun Kavim*" shines only in the *Rosh*, because the *Hitlabshut* cannot spread the light into the *Guf*. There was just some luminescence in the *Guf*, so the state of *Katnut* brought no satisfaction to the vessels. However, as the light of *Gadlut* came, even the vessels of bestowal break.

Only after the vessels break does an independent desire called "the creation" come into being and begins looking for the way to its source. Hence, there is no action in the Universe, from the beginning to the very end, which would not bring the creation closer to its goal – eternal, perfect, and infinite filling with the Supreme Light.

THE PREFACE TO THE COMMENTARY OF "THE SULAM" BY RABBI Y. ASHLAG

THE TEN SEFIROT

1. First of all, one should know the names of the ten *Sefirot*: *KaHaB HaGaT NHYM* (*Keter, Hochma, Bina, Hesed, Gevura, Tifferet, Netzah, Hod, Yesod and Malchut*). These ten *Sefirot* constitute the ten concealments of the Supreme Light, which exist in order to let the created beings receive that Light. It is impossible to look at the Sun without the help of some darkened glass that weakens sunlight and makes it suitable for visual perception.

With certain reserve, this may be compared to the reception of the light by the spiritual objects (created beings), for which the Creator's Light is too powerful; hence, it can be received only through these ten concealments. It should be noted that the lower the concealment is located, the more it weakens the Creator's Light.

2. These ten *Sefirot* correspond to the Creator's ten Sacred Names, mentioned in the Torah (*Zohar, Vayikra* §§ 156-177):

The Name אהיה (*Ekeh*) corresponds to *Sefira Keter*.
The Name יה (*Yah*, pronounced as "*Koh*") corresponds to *Hochma*
The Name יהו"ה (*HaVaYaH*, with the vowels of "*Elohim*") corresponds to *Bina*.
The Name אל (*El*) corresponds to *Hesed*.

The Name אלהים (*Elohim*) corresponds to *Gevura*.
The Name יהו"ה (*HaVaYaH*, with the vowels of *Shvah-Holam-Kamatz*) stands for *Tifferet*.
The Name צבאות (*Tzevaot*) corresponds to two *Sefirot Netzah* and *Hod*.
The Name שדי (*Shaddai*) is *Yesod*.
The Name אדני (*Adonai*) is *Malchut*.

3. Ten *Sefirot* correspond to the five *Behinot* (phases). The fourth *Behina Zeir Anpin* (ZA) or *Tifferet* contains six *Sefirot*: *Hesed, Gevura, Tifferet, Netzah, Hod, Yesod*. The reasons for it are explained in great detail in "The Book of Zohar" (See "*Hakdamat Sefer HaZohar*", "*Marot HaSulam*", p. 5). Thus, the 5 *Behinot* are called: *Keter, Hochma, Bina, Tifferet (or ZA) and Malchut* (See also "The Preamble to the Wisdom of Kabbalah", §§ 1-7).

WHY DOES TIFFERET CONSIST OF HAGAT NHY?

4. Each of the five *Behinot KaHaB TuM* in turn consists of its own five *Behinot KaHaB TuM*. However, the *Sefirot de Tifferet* are not called *KaHaB TuM*, but *HaGaT NH* (*Hesed, Gevura, Tifferet, Netzah, Hod*), since their level is lower than the *Gar*. *Sefira Yesod* unites all of them. The fact that *Behina Tifferet* includes six *Sefirot* does not at all mean it is higher and better than *Keter, Hochma* and *Bina*.

On the contrary, since the *Behina Tifferet* does not have the light of the *Gar*, its five *Sefirot KaHaB TuM* received new names - *HaGaT NH*. *Sefira Hesed* corresponds to *Keter*, *Gevura* – to *Hochma*, *Tifferet* – to *Bina*, *Netzah* – to *Tifferet* and *Hod* – to *Malchut*. *Sefira Yesod* is added to them. It is not a new level; it is rather a mixture of all the previous *Behinot*. *Tifferet* is otherwise called *VAK* - "*Vav Ktzavot*" (six edges), which means six *Sefirot*.

THE LIGHT AND THE VESSEL

5. We cannot speak about the light in the absence of the vessel. "The Preamble to the Wisdom of Kabbalah" in §§ 3-4 explains what the spiritual vessel is. First, there was just one vessel – *Malchut*. When we say, there are five *Behinot KaHaB TuM*, we actually mean that they constitute parts of *Malchut* called *Behina Dalet*. In fact, these *Behinot* are stages of the vessel's development, whereas *Malchut* is a final stage (See "The Preamble to the Wisdom of Kabbalah", § 5).

After the First Restriction (*Tzimtzum Aleph, TA*) the *Kli Malchut* puts up a screen (*Masach*), which prevents the light from getting inside it. As the Supreme Light tries to enter *Malchut*, it impacts the screen, and is reflected by it. This process is called "a *Zivug de Haka'a*" (a stroke interaction) between the light and the screen of *Malchut*. The light that bounces back is called "the ten *Sefirot* of the Reflected Light".

ROSH, TOCH, SOF, PEH, TABUR, SIUM RAGLIN

6. Because of the emergence of new vessels of the Reflected Light, three parts are formed in each *Partzuf*: the *Rosh*, the *Toch*, and the *Sof*. As was already stated, the screen blocked the reception of the light inside *Malchut*, which led to the Stroke Interaction (a *Zivug de Haka'a*) between the light and the screen. The ten *Sefirot* of the Reflected Light created by this *Zivug* "dressed" on the ten *Sefirot* of the Direct Light. The ten *Sefirot* of the Reflected Light combined with the ten *Sefirot* of the Direct Light form the ten *Sefirot de Rosh*. However, the ten *Sefirot* of the Reflected Light and the ten *Sefirot* of the Direct Light are not yet genuine vessels.

The word "vessel" points to a certain "*Aviut*" – the size of a "desire to receive". This means that the power of the category of Judgment, the ban inherent in the screen, prevents the light from entering *Malchut*. There is a rule: the power ofthe ban is effective only below the point of the restriction, but never above it. Since the ten *Sefirot* of the Reflected

Light rise above the screen, the restriction does not apply to it; therefore, it cannot be a genuine vessel.

The ten *Sefirot* of the Reflected Light are called "the *Rosh*". These ten *Sefirot* are not considered the real vessels. *Malchut* with a screen that makes a *Zivug de Haka'a* is called "the *Peh*" (mouth). Similar to a material mouth, which utters sounds designated by letters, the spiritual *Peh* forms the ten *Sefirot* of the Reflected Light called the five *Behinot KaHaB TuM* resulting from a *Zivug de Haka'a*. These *Sefirot* are the vessels for the Direct Light; these vessels are called "letters" ("*Otiot*"). Thus, now we know what the ten *Sefirot de Rosh* are.

7. When the ten *Sefirot* of the Direct Light, and the ten *Sefirot* of the Reflected Light spread under the screen, the ten *Sefirot* of the Reflected Light turn into the real vessels for the reception of the light. These in turn dress onto the ten *Sefirot* of the Direct Light. This happens because the screen that created the Reflected Light already rules over it with the help of its *Aviut*. These ten *Sefirot* (now genuine vessels) are called "the *Toch*" and "the *Guf*", i.e., they constitute the inner part of the *Partzuf*.

Malchut de Toch is called "*Tabur*". The *Tabur* is a center. It means that *Malchut de Toch* is a central, principal *Malchut*. The genuine vessels of the *Guf* were formed out of its Reflected Light. We may also add that the word *Tabur* (**טבור**) consists of the same combination of letters as the word **טוב אור** ("*Tov-Ohr*", good light). This suggests that the light is good when it is inside the vessels fit to receive it. Thus, now we understand the meaning of the ten *Sefirot de Toch* down to the *Tabur*.

8. There are two *Behinot* in *Malchut de Rosh*: 1. *Malchut Mesayemet* (limiting), i.e., the *Masach* in this place prevents the light from entering the vessels of *Malchut*; 2. *Malchut Mizdaveget*, which makes a *Zivug*. There would have been no vessels of reception, unless the light impacted on the screen (a *Zivug de Haka'a*) and elevated the Reflected Light. There would have been no light, because without the vessel the light does not exist.

These *Behinot* exist in *Malchut de Rosh* only as "*Shorashim*" – roots, sources. *Malchut Mesayemet de Rosh* is a root of the *Malchut Mesayemet*, which completes this level. *Malchut Mizdaveget de Rosh* causes the light to get inside the vessels. Both of these actions really happen only in the *Guf* of the *Partzuf*, i.e., in the space between the *Peh* and the *Tabur*, where the *Malchut Mizdaveget* rules, and so the Supreme Light enters the vessels.

Malchut Mesayemet rules in the space between the *Tabur* and the *Sium*, creating the ten *Sefirot de Sium* (end of the *Partzuf*). Each of these *Sefirot* has only luminescence of the Reflected Light; the Supreme light cannot enter them. The *Partzuf* ends at the point of *Malchut de Sium*, since this is exactly the *Malchut Mesayemet* that does not receive any light; it limits the spreading of the *Kli de Partzuf*. We also call it *Malchut* de "*Sium Raglin*" ("end of the legs"), which cuts the light off and limits the *Partzuf*.

These ten *Sefirot de Sium*, which spread from the *Tabur* down to the *Sium Raglin*, are called the ten *Sefirot de Sof*; they are all parts of *Malchut de Sof* and *de Sium*. By saying that there is only the Reflected Light inside these *Sefirot*, we do not mean they have no Direct Light at all. There is some luminescence of the Direct Light in them, but it is considered the *VAK bli Rosh* (See "The Preamble to the Wisdom of Kabbalah", § 50-53).

CHAZEH (CHEST)

9. Up to this point, we have spoken about the *Partzufim* of the world of *Adam Kadmon* (*AK*). However, a new *Sium* is added in the *Partzufim de Atzilut*, in the ten *Sefirot de Toch*. It happens because *Malchut de Toch*, called the *Tabur*, rose to *Bina* of the ten *Sefirot de Toch*, and restricted them. This new *Sium* (end) is called "*Chazeh*". This is where the *Parsa* is.

The Torah calls this boundary "the firmament" ("*Rakia*"); it separates "the upper waters" (i.e., *Keter* and *Hochma de Toch*) from "the lower waters" (the vessels of *Bina*, ZA and *Malchut*), which descended from the level of the *Toch* to the *Sof*. Because of this, the ten *Sefirot de Toch* split into two levels: a space from the *Peh* to the *Chazeh*, still considered the *Toch*, *Atzilut* and the *Gar de Guf*; and a space below the *Chazeh* and the *Tabur*, regarded as the ten *Sefirot de Sof*, *Beria* and also the *VAK bli Rosh* like the ten *Sefirot de Sof*.

THE INVERSE RELATION BETWEEN THE LIGHTS AND THE VESSELS

10. The lights and vessels are always inversely related. This happens because the upper vessels are the first to grow in the *Partzuf*: *Keter* emerges followed by *Hochma*, *Bina*, *Tifferet* (ZA) and *Malchut*. Hence, we call the vessels *KaHaB TuM*, i.e., top-down, according to the order of their emergence in the *Partzuf*.

The lights, however, enter the *Partzuf* in the opposite order, starting with the lowest: first, *Nefesh*, then *Ruach*, *Neshama*, *Haya* and *Yechida*. Thus, *Nefesh* (the smallest light), which corresponds to the *Sefira Malchut* is first to enter the *Partzuf*, whereas *Yechida* (the most powerful light), which corresponds to the *Sefira Keter*, is last to enter the *Partzuf*. Hence, we always call the lights *NaRaNHaY*, i.e., according to the sequence of their emergence inside the *Partzuf*.

11. It turns out that when there is only one upper vessel, *Keter*, which appears first, it is not filled by the light of *Yechida* that corresponds to it, but with the weakest light of *Nefesh*. When the second vessel *Hochma* appears in the *Partzuf*, the second light of *Ruach* enters it. By this, the light of *Nefesh* descends from *Keter* to *Hochma*, while *Ruach* fills *Keter*.

After the emergence of the third vessel, *Bina*, the light of *Nefesh* descends from *Hochma* to *Bina*, *Ruach* passes from *Keter* to *Hochma*, and the light of *Neshama* enters *Keter*. As the fourth vessel ZA appears, the light of *Nefesh* descends from *Bina* to ZA, *Ruach* passes from *Hochma* to *Bina*, *Neshama* – from *Keter* to *Hochma*, and *Haya* enters *Keter*. With the emergence of the fifth, last vessel, all lights take their rightful places: *Nefesh* enters *Malchut*, *Ruach* – ZA, *Neshama* – *Bina*, *Haya* – *Hochma* and *Yechida* fills *Keter*.

12. It turns out that before all the five vessels of the *KaHaB TuM* emerge, the lights are not in their places. Furthermore, the lights and vessels are inversely related, for unless *Malchut*, the smallest vessel, appears, the light of *Yechida* will remain outside the *Partzuf*. If two lower vessels,

ZA and *Malchut*, are absent in the *Partzuf*, the two upper lights, *Yechida* and *Haya*, will not be able to enter it.

13. By saying that because of the rise of *Malchut* to *Bina*, each level (*Partzuf*) ends after *Hochma* and only two *Sefirot* – *Keter* and *Hochma* remain in the *Partzuf*, while *Bina*, ZA and *Malchut* descended one level (See § 17), we mean only the vessels. Contrary to that, the lights *Nefesh* and *Ruach* remained on their level, and *Neshama*, *Haya*, and *Yechida* exited the *Partzuf*.

14. Certain places in "The Book of *Zohar*" say that since *Malchut* rose to *Bina*, only two letters מ"י of the five letters that make up the Name *Elokim* (אלהים) remained on the same level, while three letters אל"ה descended to the lower level (See The Introduction to the *Zohar*, p. 20). Other places inthe "*Zohar*" state the contrary, that because of this ascent, two letters א"ל remained on their level, while three letters הי"מ descended to the lower level (See "The *Zohar*", "*Bereshit* (Genesis) 1", § 59).

The fact is that the five letters of the Name אלהים constitute the five *Sefirot KaHaB TuM* or the five lights *NaRaNHaY*. When *Malchut* rises to *Bina*, two upper vessels remain on this level – *Keter* and *Hochma*, designated by letters א"ל, and three letters, הי"מ descended to the lower level. The opposite happens to the lights: the two last letters, מ"י, correspond to the two lower lights – *Nefesh* and *Ruach*. They retain their level while the first three letters, אל"ה, corresponding to the lights *Yechida*, *Haya*, and *Neshama* descended to the lower level. If one keeps that in mind and determines whether the lights or the vessels are meant in each particular case, many seeming contradictions will no longer be relevant.

THE RISE OF MALCHUT TO BINA

15.One should pay close attention to the correction of *Malchut* in *Bina*. This notion is the root, the source of all *Kabbalah*, since *Malchut* represents the category of judgment (restriction). The world, the spiritual Universe, cannot be based only on restriction. Hence, the Creator elevated *Malchut* (judgment, restriction) to *Sefirat Bina*, which is the category of mercy.

The sages say that the world was first created with the help of the category of judgment (restriction), i.e., *Malchut*, but seeing that such a world cannot exist, the Creator mixed the category of judgment (*Midat HaDin*) with the category of mercy (*Midat HaRachamim*), i.e., *Malchut* with *Bina*. Because of the rise to *Bina*, *Malchut* acquired its properties, i.e., the category of mercy. After that, *Malchut* starts ruling the world using its new properties. The process takes place on all levels, in all the *Sefirot* from the *Rosh de Atzilut* and down to the *Sof de Malchut* of the world of *Assiya*, because absolutely all levels, all worlds and the *Partzufim* consist of the ten *Sefirot* – *KaHaB HaGaT NHYM*.

THE DIVISION OF EACH LEVEL INTO TWO HALVES

16. All *Sefirot*, all levels, are known to end with the *Sefira Malchut*. This means that *Malchut* of each level does not let the light enter it. The reason for this lies in *TA* (restriction), which forbids *Malchut* from receiving the Supreme Light. Hence, the light spreads only down to *Malchut* without entering it; it stops, blocked by the screen.

A *Zivug de Haka'a* (stroke interaction) is made on this screen. Therefore, as *Malchut* of each level rises to *Bina*, it begins to restrict the light in its new place in the middle of *Bina*. The lower part of *Bina*, ZA, and *Malchut* are now below *Malchut Mesayemet*. They happen to be outside this particular level and by this form its second half.

Therefore, owing to the rise of *Malchut* to *Bina*, each level was divided into two levels. *Keter*, *Hochma* and the upper half of *Bina* remained on their level, while the lower half of *Bina*, ZA (which includes *HaGaT NHY*), and *Malchut* turned into the lower level. The new end created by *Malchut* in the middle of *Bina* is called "the *Parsa*".

17. As we know, there must be five lights on each level: *Yechida*, *Haya*, *Neshama*, *Ruach* and *Nefesh*, which are inside five vessels: *Keter*, *Hochma*, *Bina*, ZA and *Malchut*. After *Malchut* rose to *Bina*, only two

full vessels – *Keter* and *Hochma* – remained in each level; *Bina*, *ZA*, and *Malchut* are absent there.

Hence, only two lights – *Nefesh* and *Ruach* – were left in each level. They are inside the vessels *Keter* and *Hochma*. Three lights – *Neshama*, *Haya* and *Yechida* are absent for the lack of appropriate vessels. In the language of Kabbalah, this process is described in the following way: letter י (*Yud*) enters the word "אור" ("*Ohr*", "light"). As a result, the word "אור" turns into "אויר" ("*Avir*", "air"). It means that the rise of *Malchut* to *Bina* causes the loss of the three first lights called "*Ohr*", the light by each level.

It retains only the lights *Nefesh* and *Ruach*, called "*Avir*", air. Alternatively, this process can be described with the help of five letters of the Name "אלהים", which was divided in two parts – אל"ה מ"י, so that the two letters מ"י correspond to the two lights *Nefesh* and *Ruach* in two vessels *Keter* and *Hochma* that remained on their level. The remaining three letters אל"ה correspond to the three vessels *Bina*, *ZA*, and *Malchut*, which descended to the lower level.

DESCENT OF MALCHUT FROM BINA TO ITS OWN PLACE

18. Because of raising *MAN* (request, prayer) by the lower *Partzufim*, the upper luminescence descends from the *Partzufim AB* and *SAG* (*Hochma* and *Bina*). This forces *Malchut* to leave *Bina* and return to its own place. Now letter י' exits the word "אויר" ("*Avir*", "air"), turning it into "אור" ("*Ohr*", "light").

The vessels of *Bina*, *ZA*, and *Malchut* return to their level. Now each level again has the five vessels *KaHaB TuM* filled with the five lights *NaRaNHaY*. "*Avir*" turns to "*Ohr*", because the three upper lights of the *Gar*, called "*Ohr*", returned.

THE TIME OF KATNUT AND THE TIME OF GADLUT

19. Owing to the rise of *Malchut* to *Bina*, each level began to have two states, two periods: *Katnut* and *Gadlut*. After *Malchut* rose to *Bina*, the level ends under the *Sefirat Hochma*; *Bina*, *ZA*, and *Malchut* descend to the lower level. Only the vessels *Keter* and *Hochma* with the lights *Ruach* and *Nefesh* remain there.

This state is called *Katnut*. When because of raising *MAN* by the lower *Partzufim*, the luminescence of *Hochma* and *Bina* (light *AB* and *SAG*) descends from the world of *AK*; *Malchut* descends from *Bina* and returns to its position. The vessels of *Bina*, *ZA*, and *Malchut* rise to their level.

Thus, five vessels, *Keter*, *Hochma*, *Bina*, *ZA* and *Malchut* and five corresponding lights, *Nefesh*, *Ruach*, *Neshama*, *Haya*, and *Yechida* again make up each level. Such a state is called *Gadlut*. Therefore, the state without the *Gar*, without the three upper lights, is called *Katnut*. The state wherein the three vessels *Bina*, *ZA*, and *Malchut* return and the lights of the *Gar* reappear is called *Gadlut*.

THE RISE OF THE LOWER PARTZUF TO THE UPPER

20. The rise of *Malchut* to *Bina* creates an opportunity for each lower object to rise to the level of the upper. The rule states that the upper *Partzuf*, which descended to the lower, acquires its properties; and vice versa, the lower *Partzuf*, which ascended to the upper, becomes similar to it.

Thus, during *Katnut*, i.e., when *Malchut* rises to *Bina*, moving *Bina*, *ZA*, and *Malchut* to the lower level, these *Bina*, *ZA*, and *Malchut* become similar to that new level. During *Gadlut*, i.e., when *Malchut* returns to its place, *Bina*, *ZA* and *Malchut* rise to their level.

By this, they elevate the lower level, inside which they were before, to their own. Consequently, the lower level receives all the lights that were in the upper level. Thus, we have discovered how the connection between the levels is formed due to the rise of *Malchut* to *Bina*, which allows even the lowest level to reach the highest.

KATNUT AND GADLUT OF THE YESHSUT AND THE ZON

21. Now that we know what the rise of *Malchut* to *Bina* generally means in all phases of the worlds of *ABYA*, let us look at the details. For example, let us take to phases in the world of *Atzilut* called the *YESHSUT* and the *ZON*. Because of the rise of *Malchut de YESHSUT* to *Bina de YESHSUT* during *Katnut*, three *Sefirot* – *Bina*, *ZA*, and *Malchut* descended to the *ZON*. While being in the *ZON*, these three *Sefirot* acquired their properties.

During *Gadlut*, when *Malchut* descended to its place, *Bina*, *ZA*, and *Malchut* returned to theirs – in the *YESHSUT*. At the same time, they elevated the *ZON* (or, rather, *Keter* and *Hochma de ZON*), with which they actually constitute a single whole. As a result, the *ZON* also became the *YESHSUT*, i.e., acquired their properties and received the corresponding lights.

UNLESS MALCHUT RISES TO BINA, THE ZON CANNOT RECEIVE GADLUT

22. It should be stressed that the *ZON* cannot receive the light of *Gadlut* by themselves, since they refer to the space under the *Tabur de AK*. *Malchut* rules there, controlled by the power of *Tzimtzum* (Restriction), which prevents it from receiving the light. However, during *Gadlut*, when *Bina*, *ZA*, and *Malchut de YESHSUT* elevated the *ZON* with them, the *ZON*, in fact, turn into the *YESHSUT*; now they (like the *YESHSUT*) can receive the light of *Gadlut*.

23. Now we can understand what our sages meant by saying, "First, the Creator created the world in the category of judgment". The *ZON de Atzilut* is called "world". This word refers to our world, which receives the light from *ZON de Atzilut*. Whatever was received in *ZON de Atzilut* can be received by people in our world.

Conversely, whatever was absent in ZON *de Atzilut*, cannot descend to our world. As we said, the root (*Shoresh*), the source of ZON *de Atzilut*, is the space under the *Tabur de AK*, where *Malchut* rules in the state of restriction. Therefore, the ZON cannot receive the light and exist. All the more our world, located much lower and receiving from ZON *de Atzilut*, would be unable to exist.

That is exactly what the following words refer to: "Then the Creator saw that such world cannot exist, so He mixed mercy with judgment". It means that the Creator elevated the *Malchut* (judgment) of each level to *Bina* (mercy). In particular, the *Malchut de YESHSUT* rose to *Bina de YESHSUT*; as a result, *Bina*, ZA and the *Malchut de YESHSUT* descended one level, i.e., to the ZON. By this, they acquire that level's properties. In fact, the *Sefirot* and the ZON become a single whole after their descent.

Hence, during the *Gadlut de YESHSUT*, when *Malchut* descends to its own place from *Bina*, the three vessels – *Bina*, ZA, and *Malchut* also return to their position on the level of the *YESHSUT*. With that, they also elevate the ZON, with which they form a single whole. As a result, the ZON rise to the level of the *YESHSUT*. This means they can now receive the same lights that the *YESHSUT* gets. At the same time, they pass the light to our world allowing it to exist.

However, unless the categories of judgment and mercy were mixed i.e., unless *Malchut de YESHSUT* rose to *Bina de YESHSUT*, forcing *Bina* ZA and *Malchut* to descend one level to the ZON, the ZON would never be able to rise to the *YESHSUT*, or receive the Supreme Light for our world and allow its existence. Thus, we understand what the rise of *Malchut* to *Bina* means.

ALBUM OF DRAWINGS

How to associate diagrams and charts with the text:

The annotation P. on the diagrams indicates the associated paragraph number as found in the body of the text of Baal Ha Sulam e.g.

Figure 8. Olam HaTzimtzum
(The Preamble to the Wisdom of Kabbalah. P.14)

14) In order to save the creation from such remoteness from the Creator, the Tzimtzum Aleph (TA, the First Restriction) took place and separated Behina Dalet from the spiritual objects. This happened in such a way that the "desire to receive" turned into a space void of the light. After the Tzimtzum Aleph, all the spiritual objects have a screen on their vessel-Malchut in order to avoid receiving the light inside Behina Dalet.

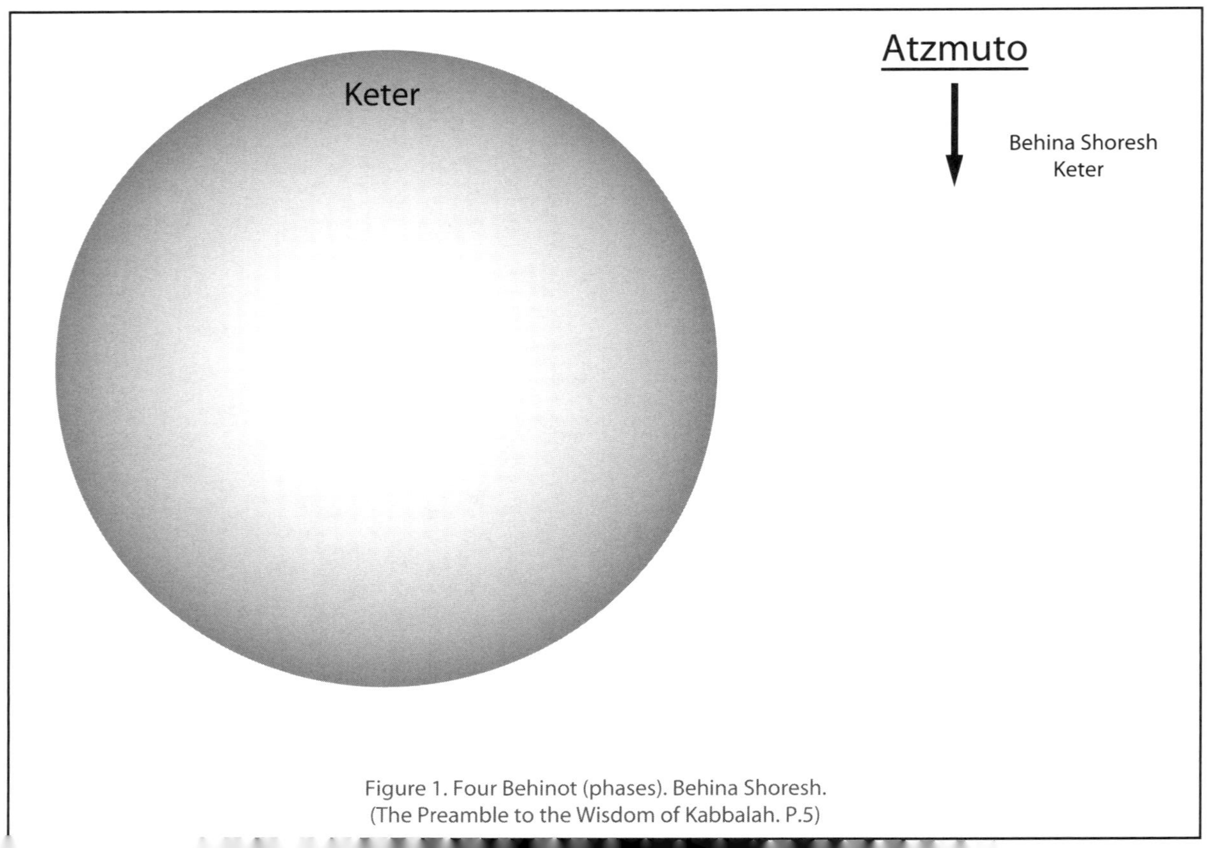

Figure 1. Four Behinot (phases). Behina Shoresh.
(The Preamble to the Wisdom of Kabbalah. P.5)

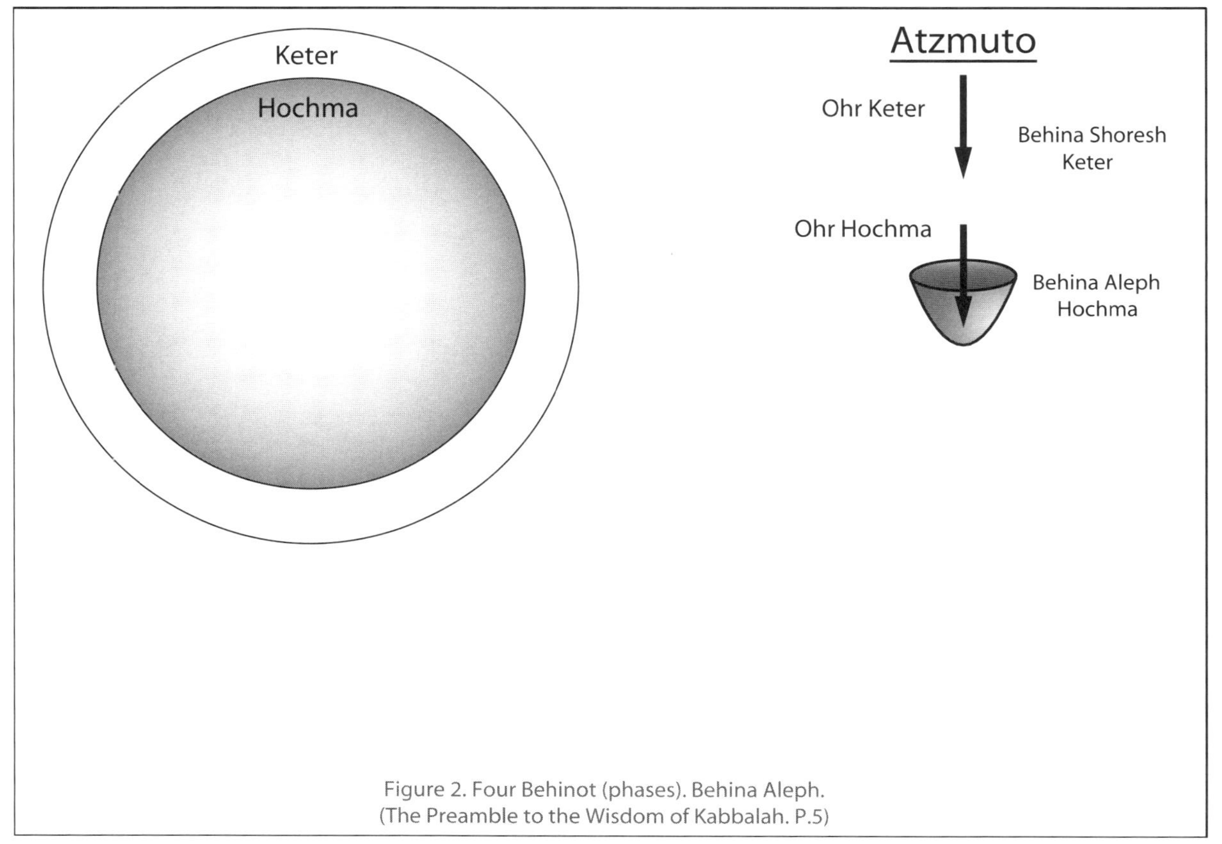

Figure 2. Four Behinot (phases). Behina Aleph.
(The Preamble to the Wisdom of Kabbalah. P.5)

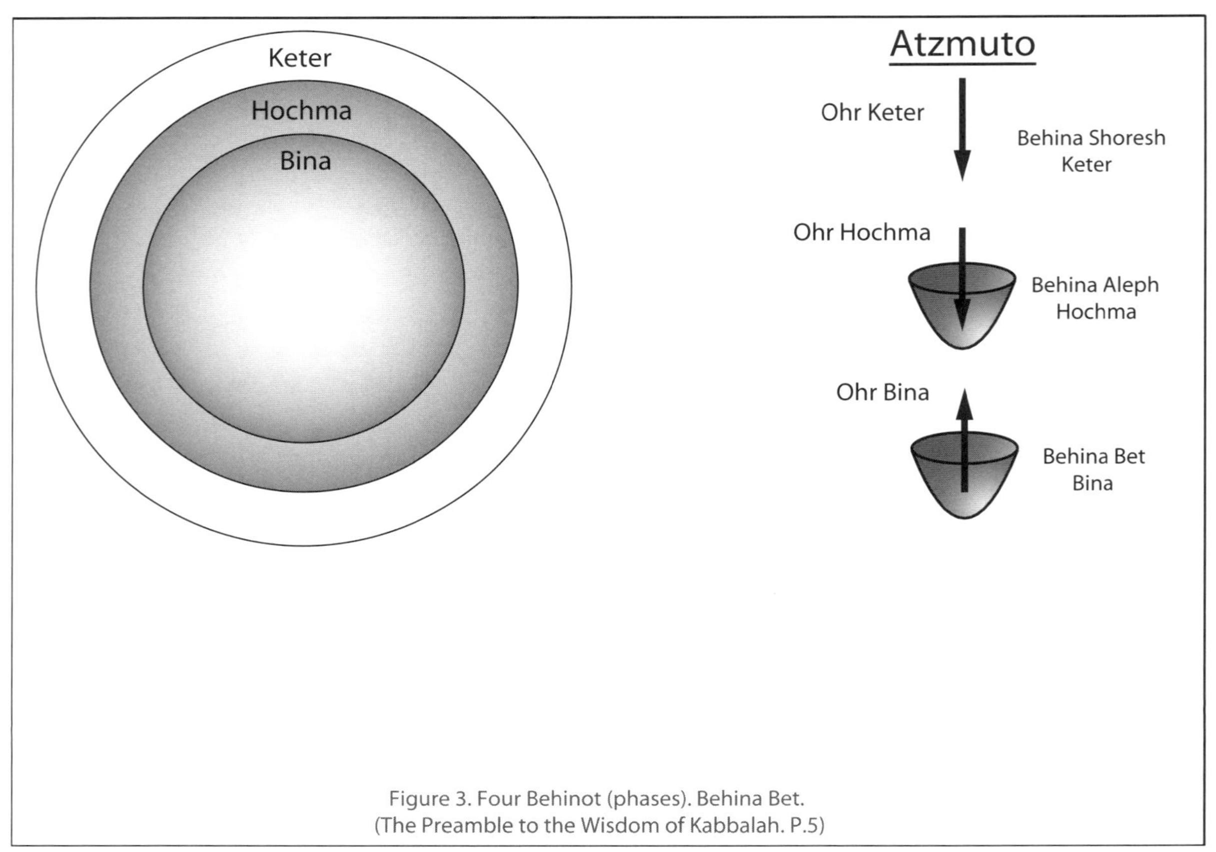

Figure 3. Four Behinot (phases). Behina Bet.
(The Preamble to the Wisdom of Kabbalah. P.5)

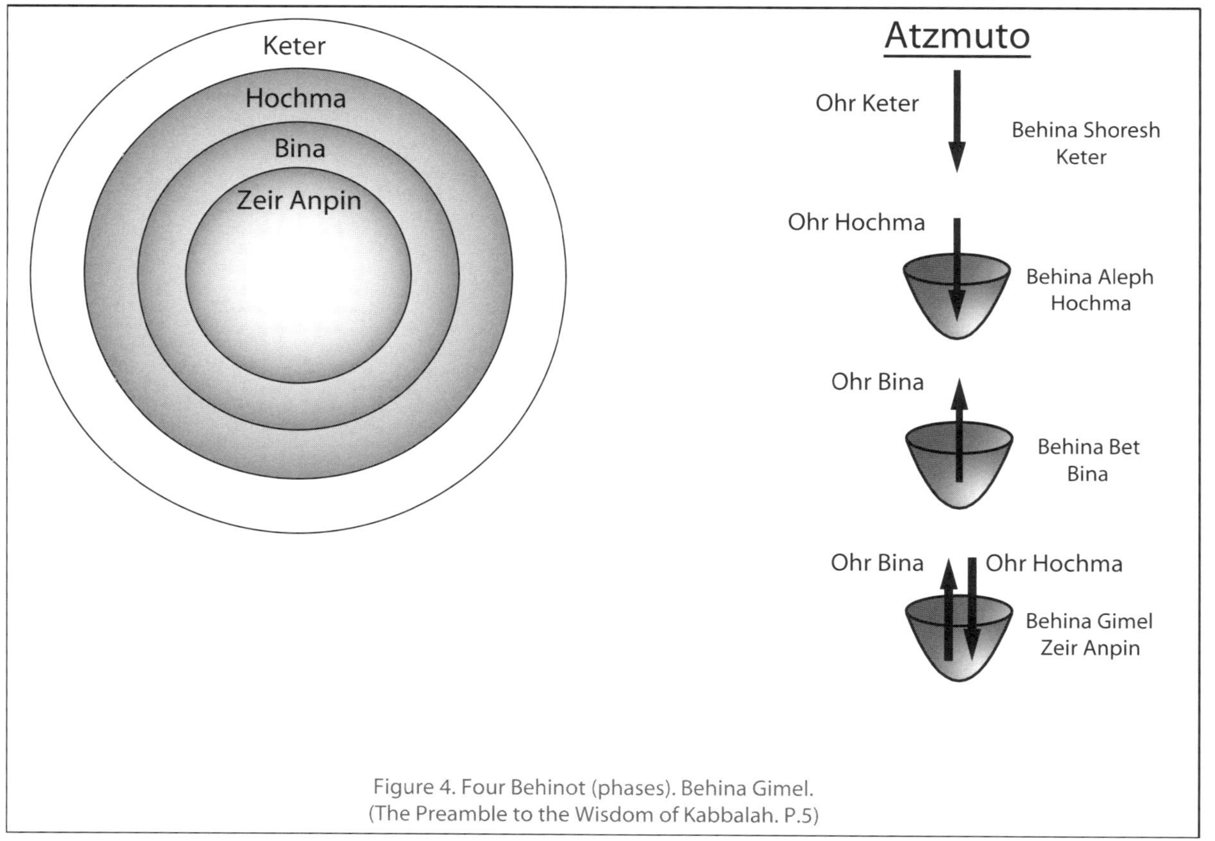

Figure 4. Four Behinot (phases). Behina Gimel.
(The Preamble to the Wisdom of Kabbalah. P.5)

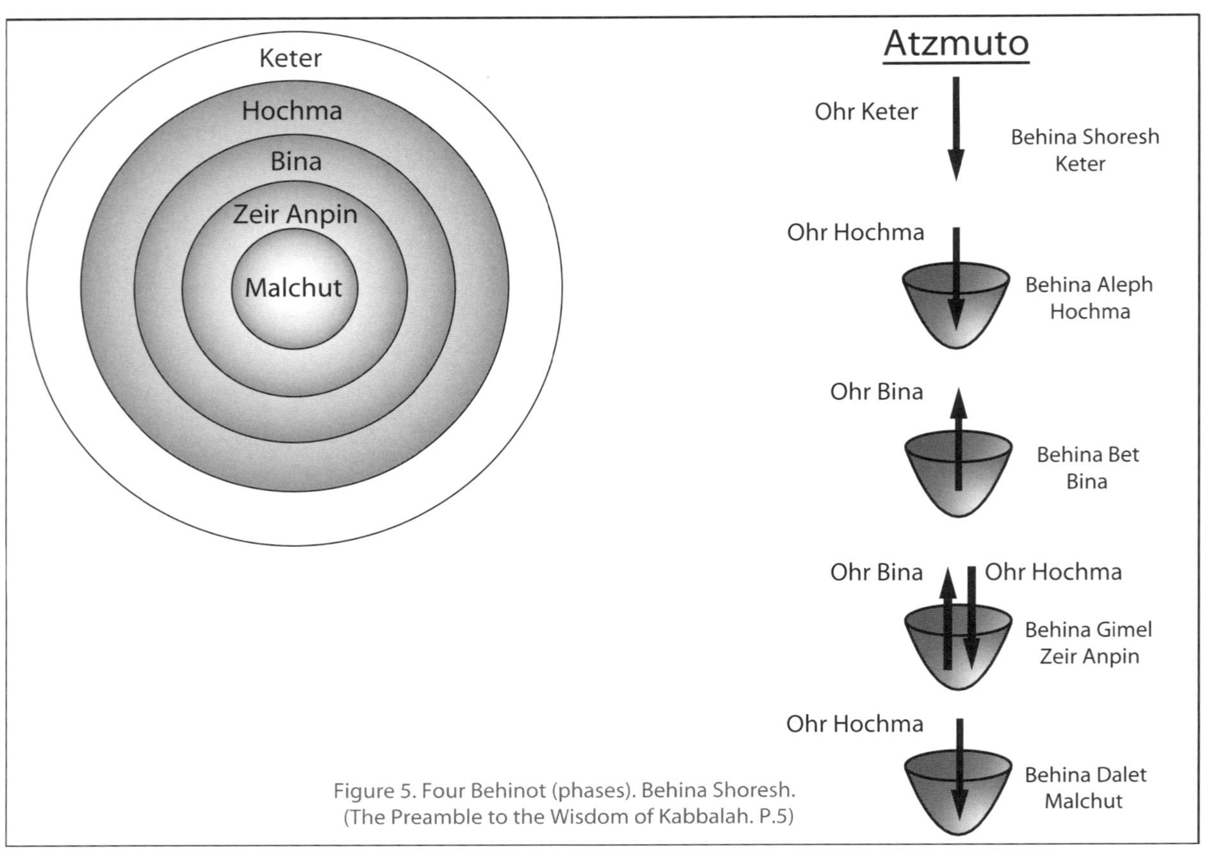

Figure 5. Four Behinot (phases). Behina Shoresh.
(The Preamble to the Wisdom of Kabbalah. P.5)

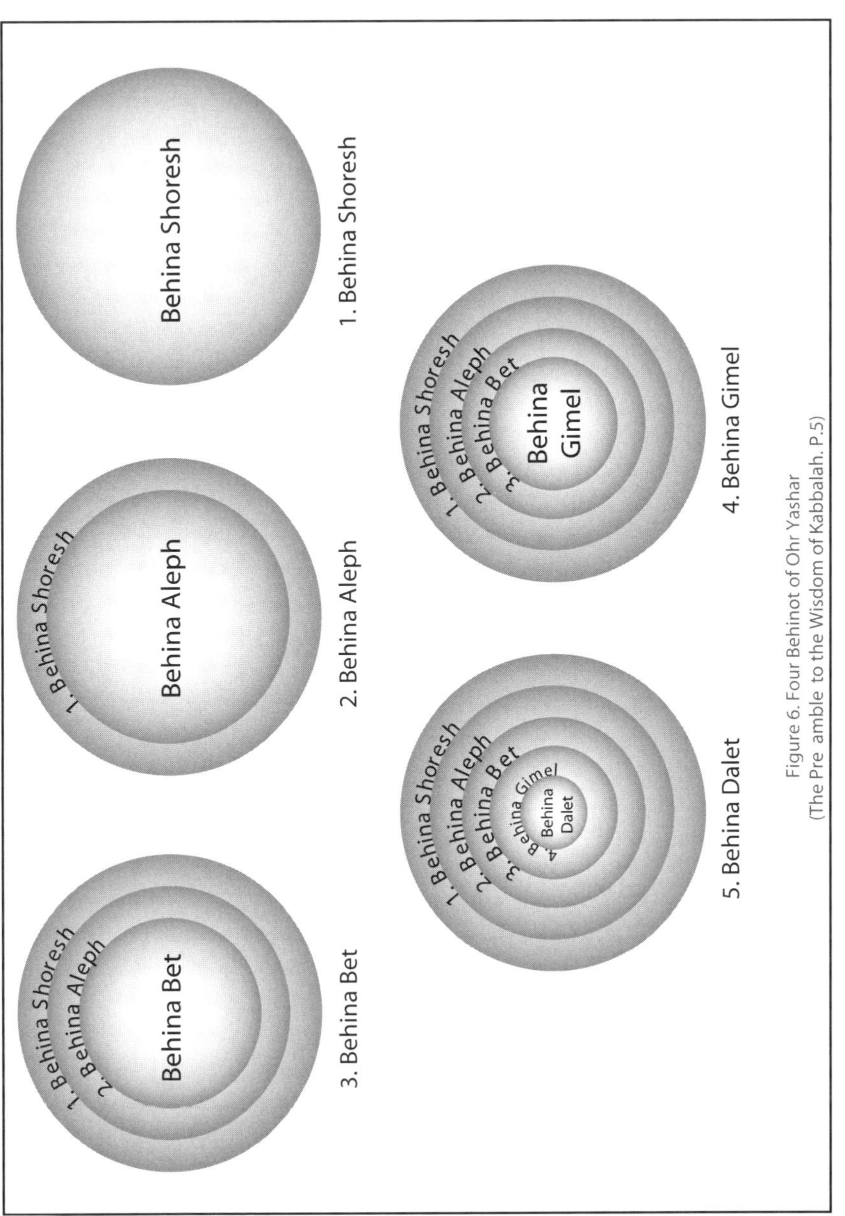

Figure 6. Four Behinot of Ohr Yashar
(The Pre amble to the Wisdom of Kabbalah. P.5)

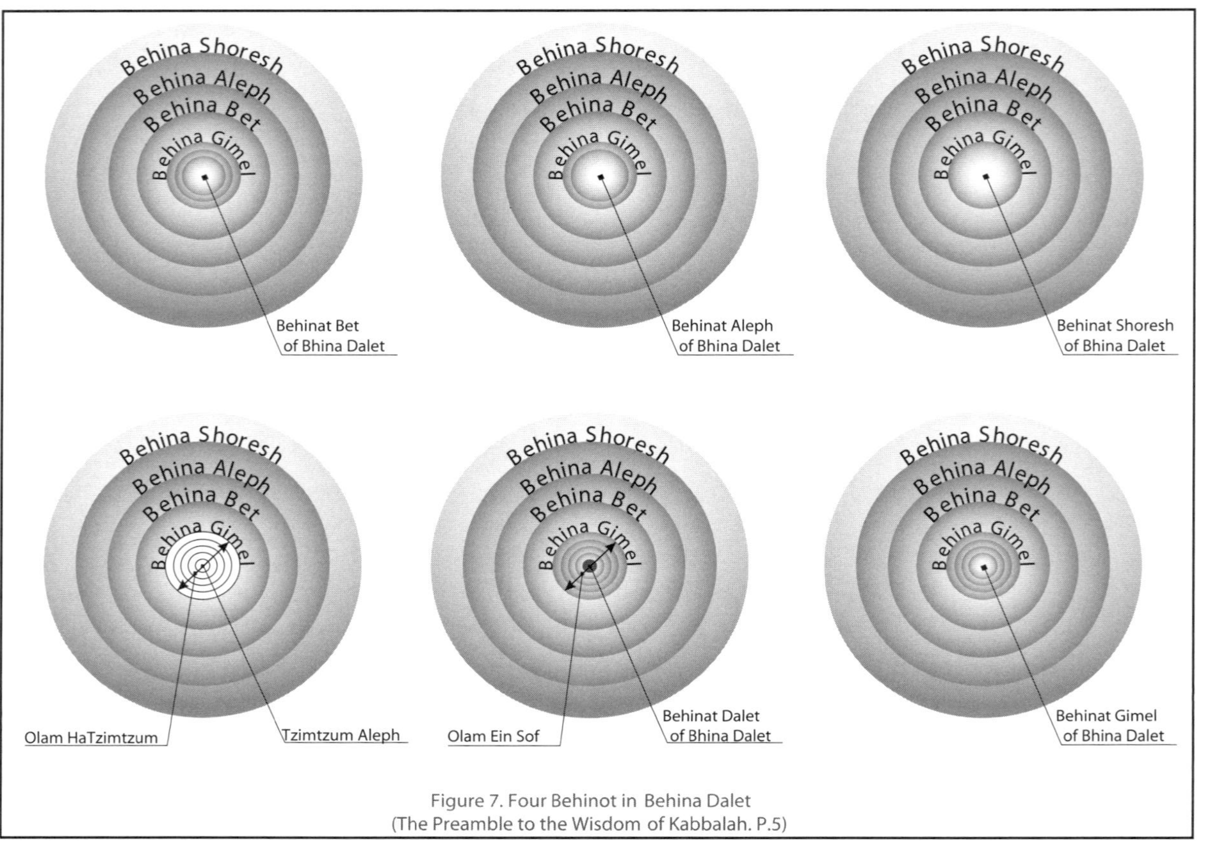

Figure 7. Four Behinot in Behina Dalet
(The Preamble to the Wisdom of Kabbalah. P.5)

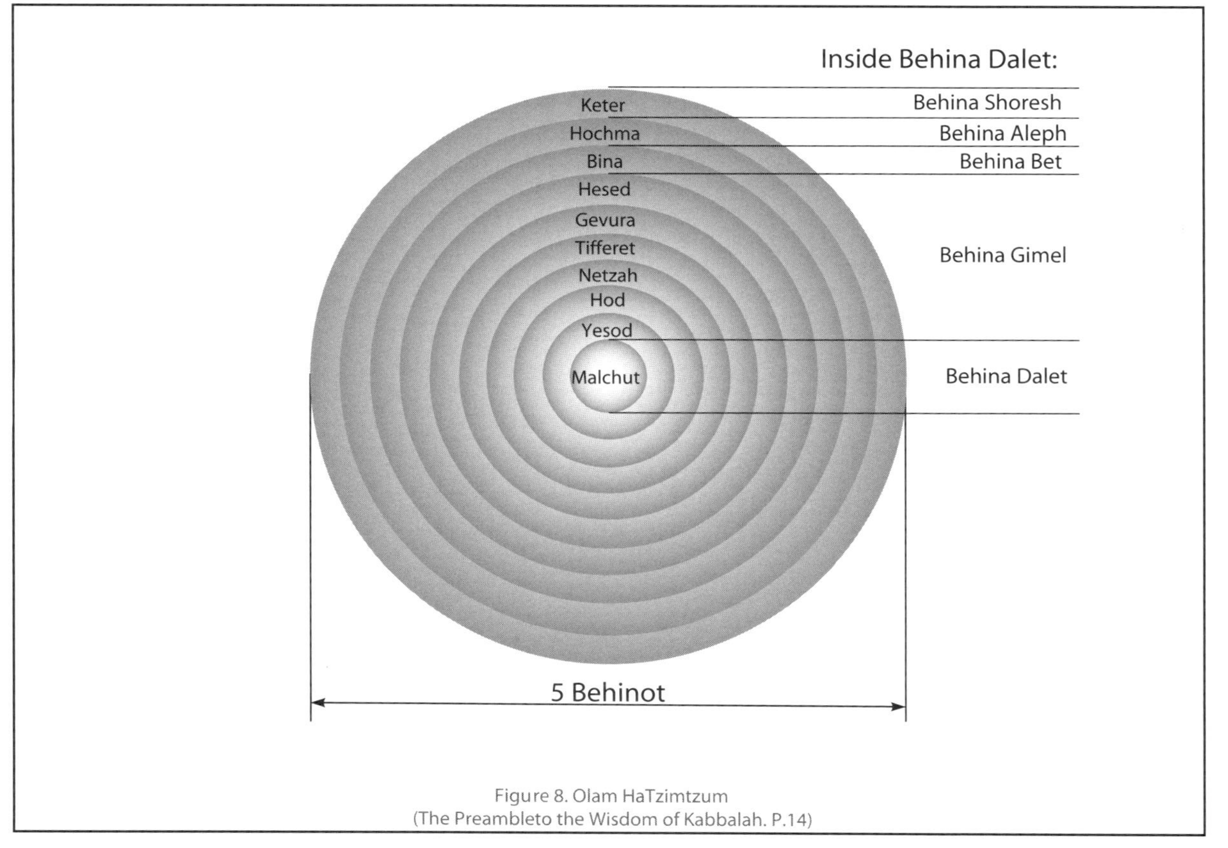

Figure 8. Olam HaTzimtzum
(The Preambleto the Wisdom of Kabbalah. P.14)

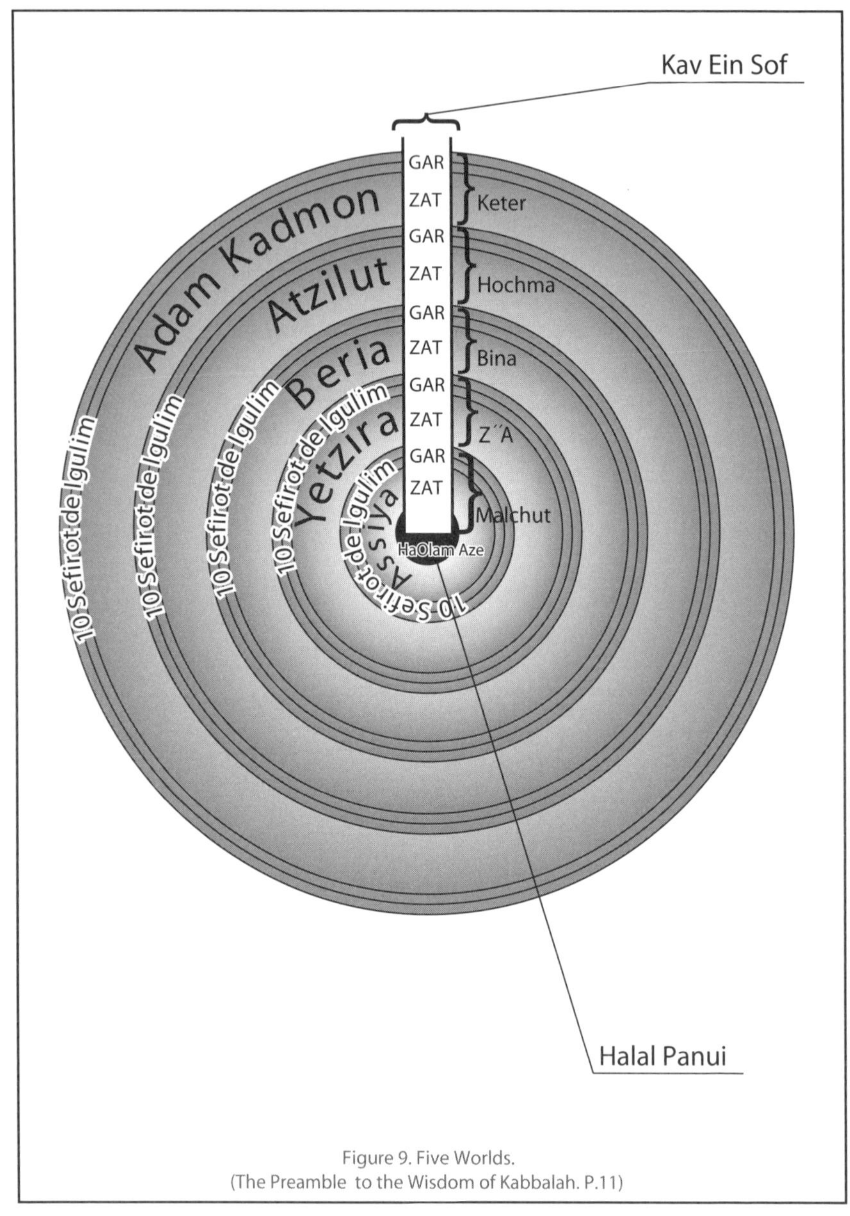

Figure 9. Five Worlds.
(The Preamble to the Wisdom of Kabbalah. P.11)

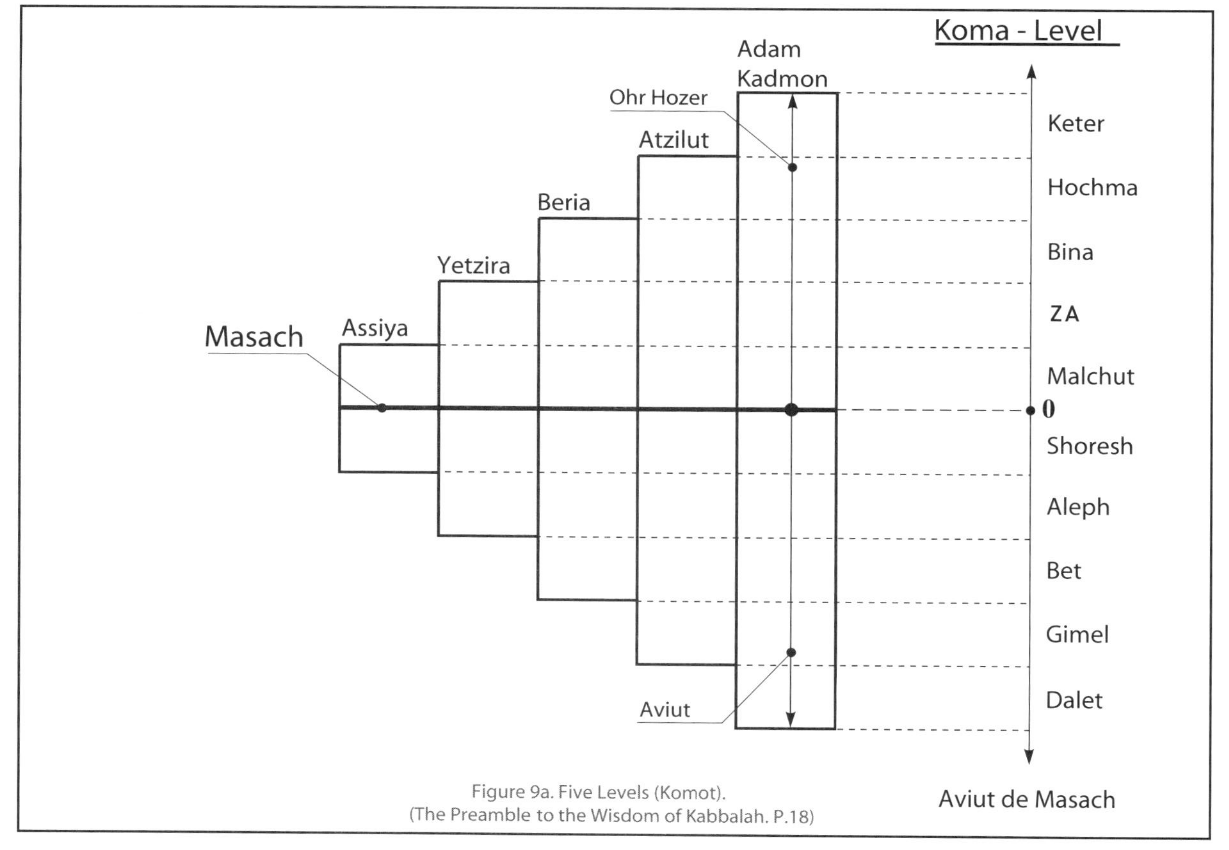

Figure 9a. Five Levels (Komot).
(The Preamble to the Wisdom of Kabbalah. P.18)

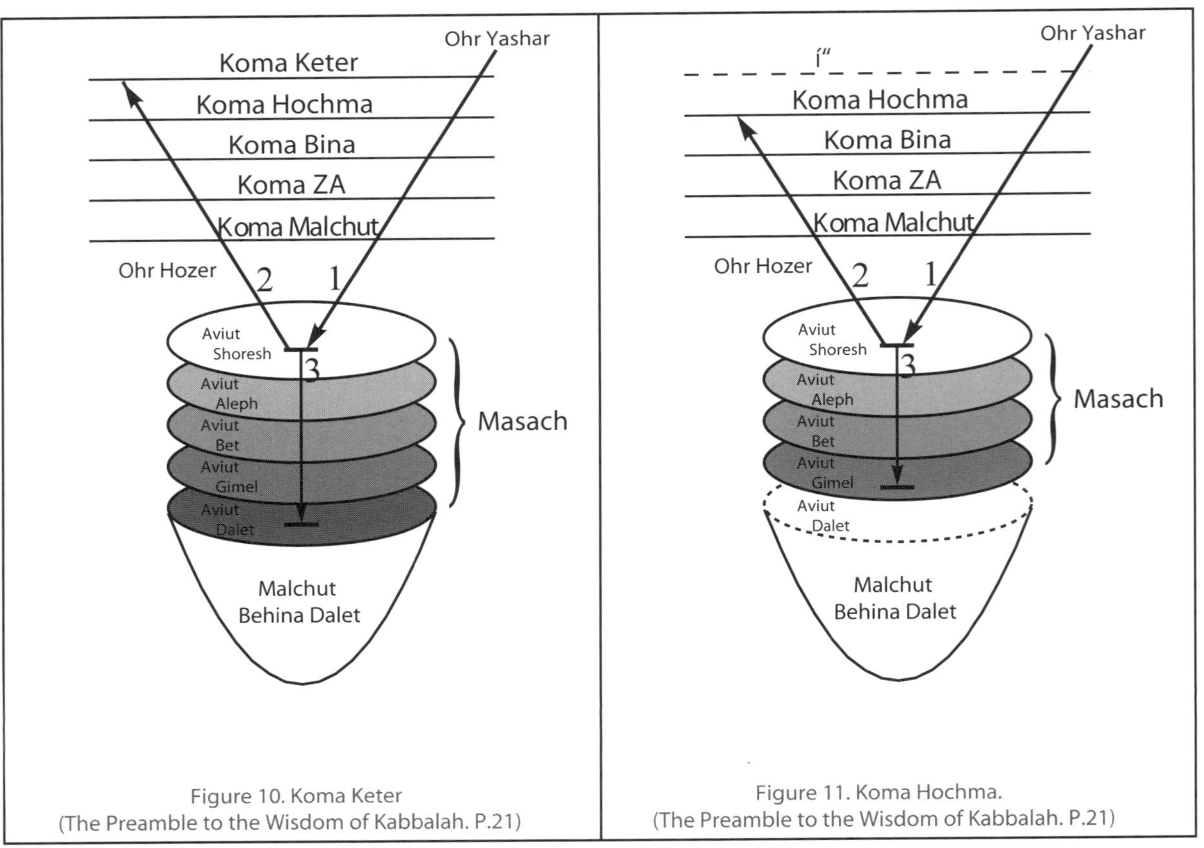

Figure 10. Koma Keter
(The Preamble to the Wisdom of Kabbalah. P.21)

Figure 11. Koma Hochma.
(The Preamble to the Wisdom of Kabbalah. P.21)

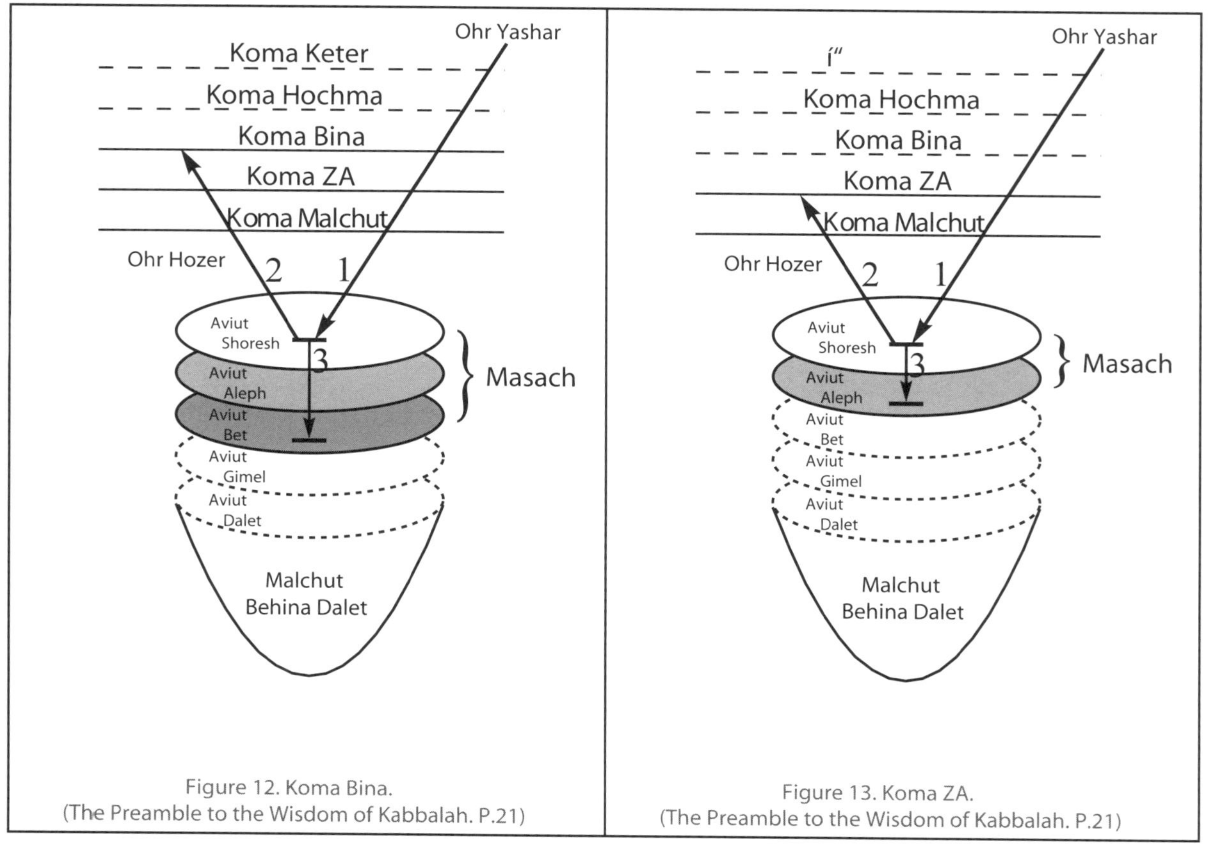

Figure 12. Koma Bina.
(The Preamble to the Wisdom of Kabbalah. P.21)

Figure 13. Koma ZA.
(The Preamble to the Wisdom of Kabbalah. P.21)

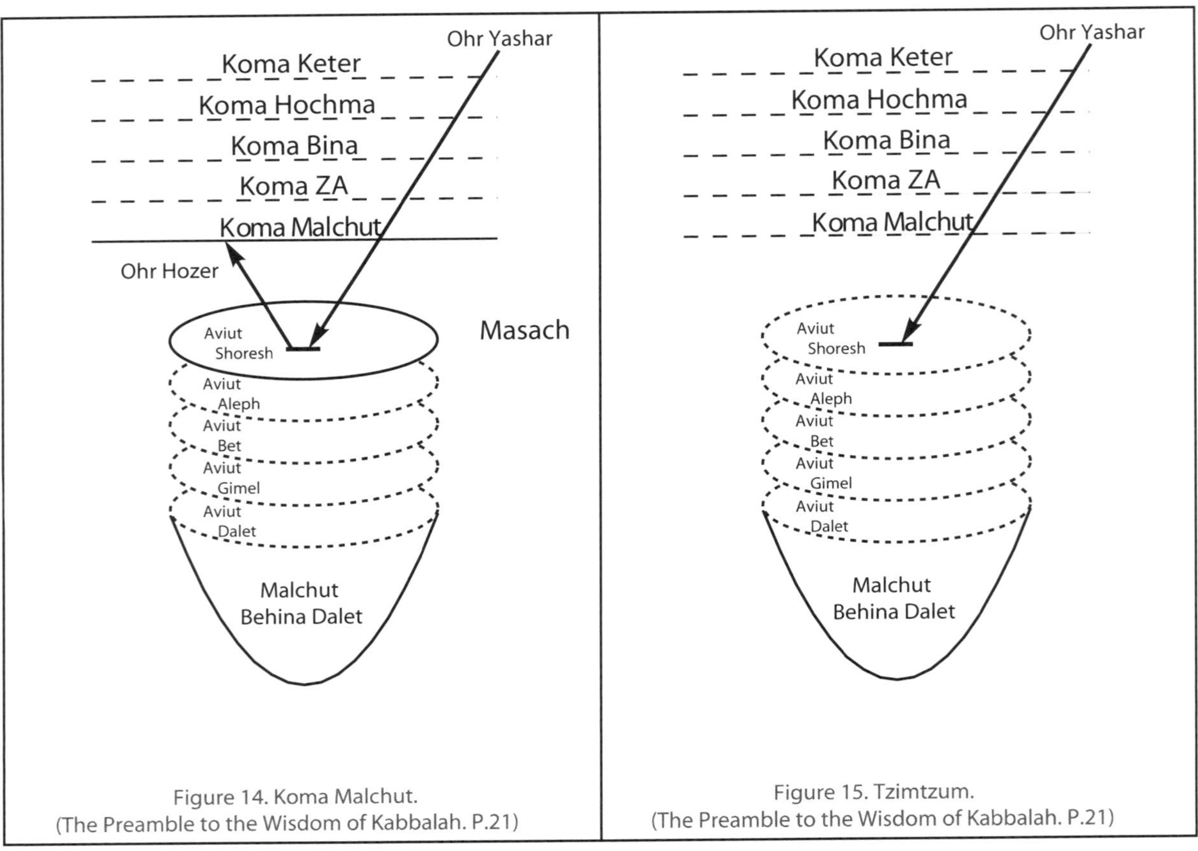

Figure 14. Koma Malchut.
(The Preamble to the Wisdom of Kabbalah. P.21)

Figure 15. Tzimtzum.
(The Preamble to the Wisdom of Kabbalah. P.21)

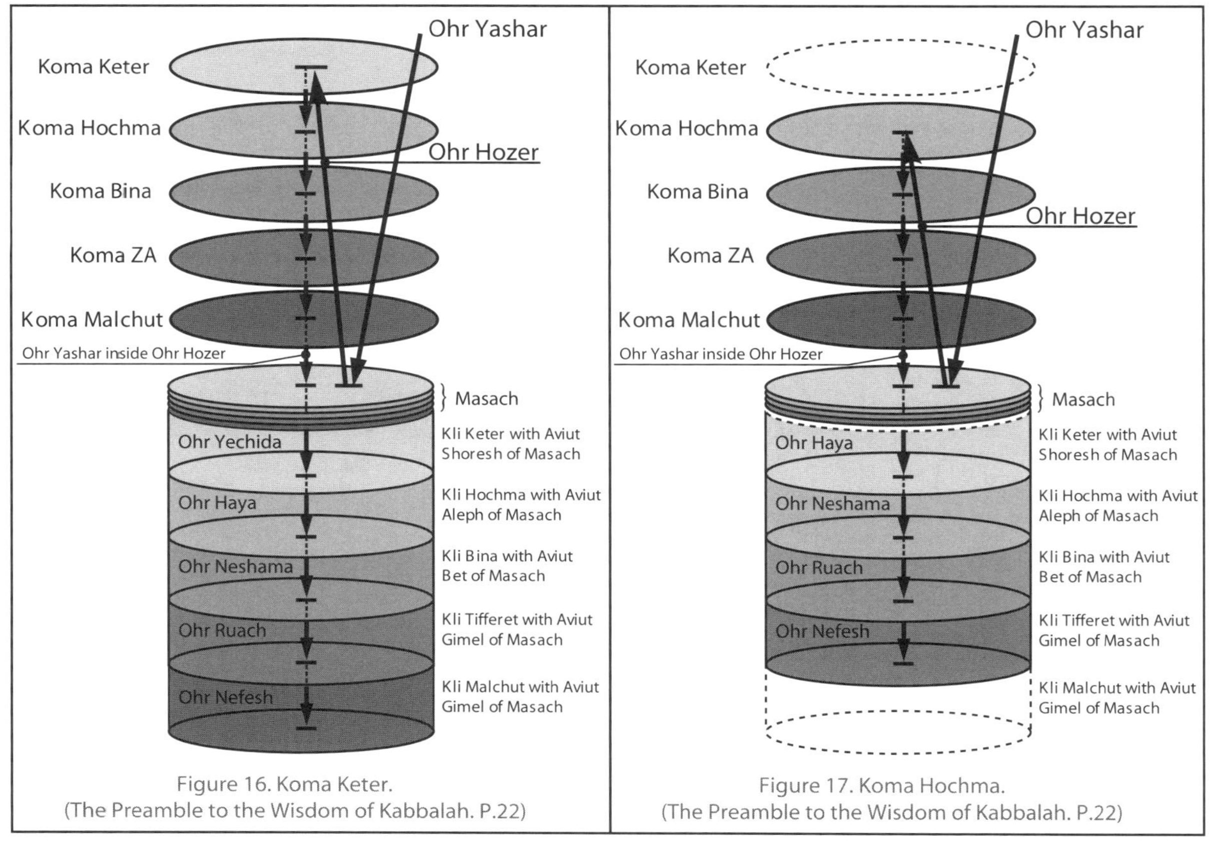

Figure 16. Koma Keter.
(The Preamble to the Wisdom of Kabbalah. P.22)

Figure 17. Koma Hochma.
(The Preamble to the Wisdom of Kabbalah. P.22)

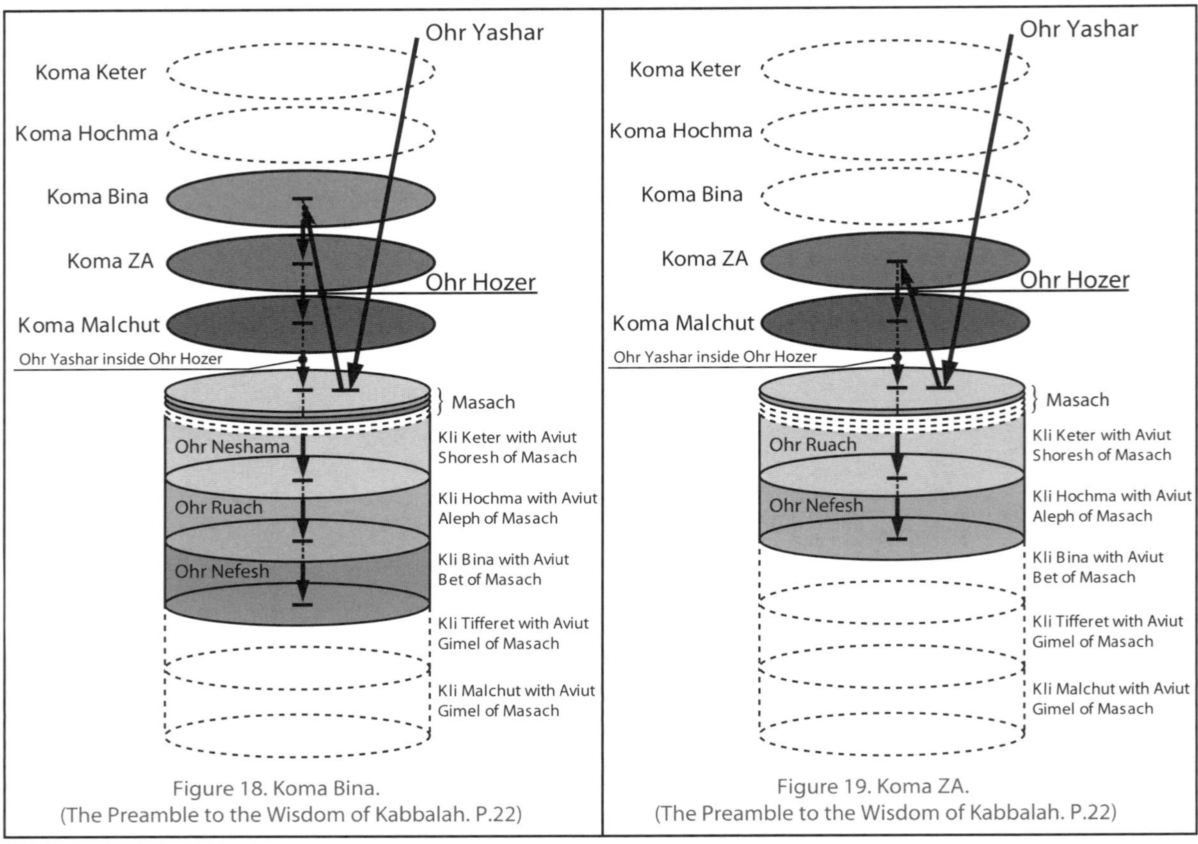

Figure 18. Koma Bina.
(The Preamble to the Wisdom of Kabbalah. P.22)

Figure 19. Koma ZA.
(The Preamble to the Wisdom of Kabbalah. P.22)

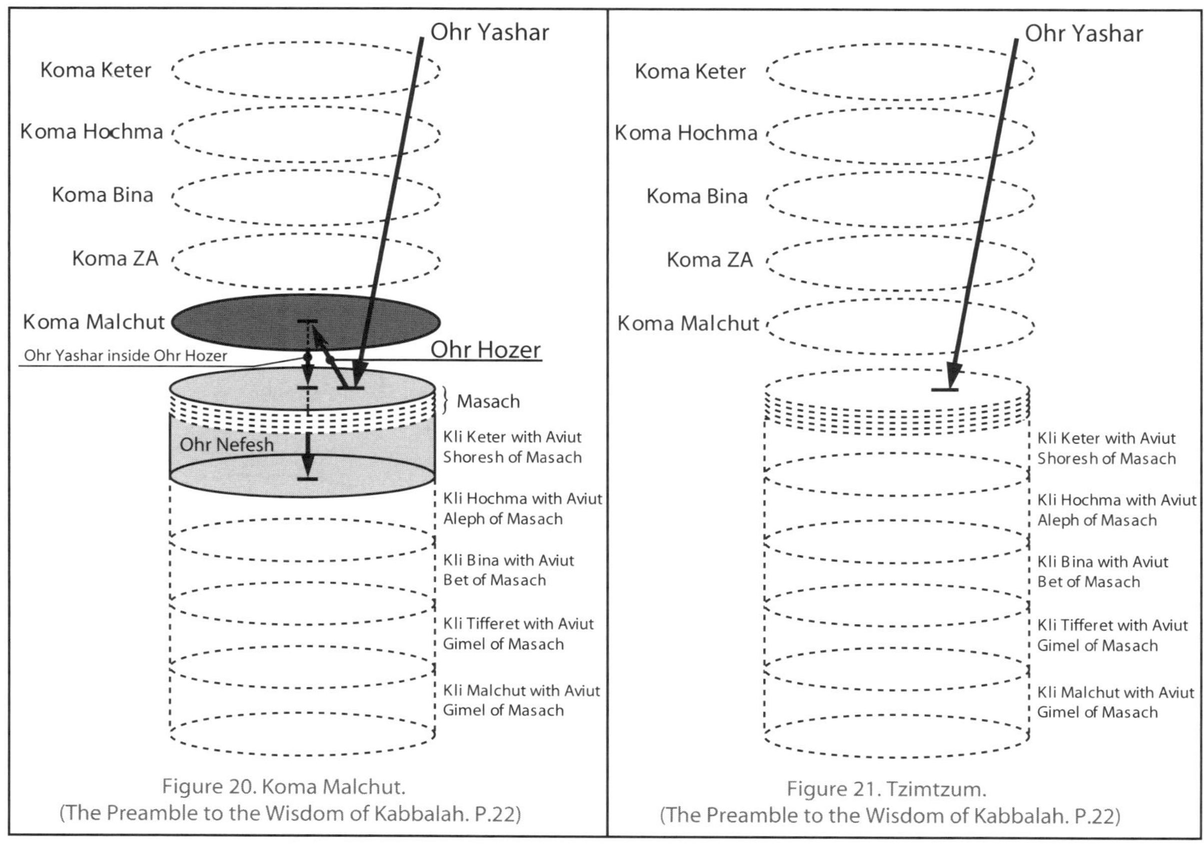

Figure 20. Koma Malchut.
(The Preamble to the Wisdom of Kabbalah. P.22)

Figure 21. Tzimtzum.
(The Preamble to the Wisdom of Kabbalah. P.22)

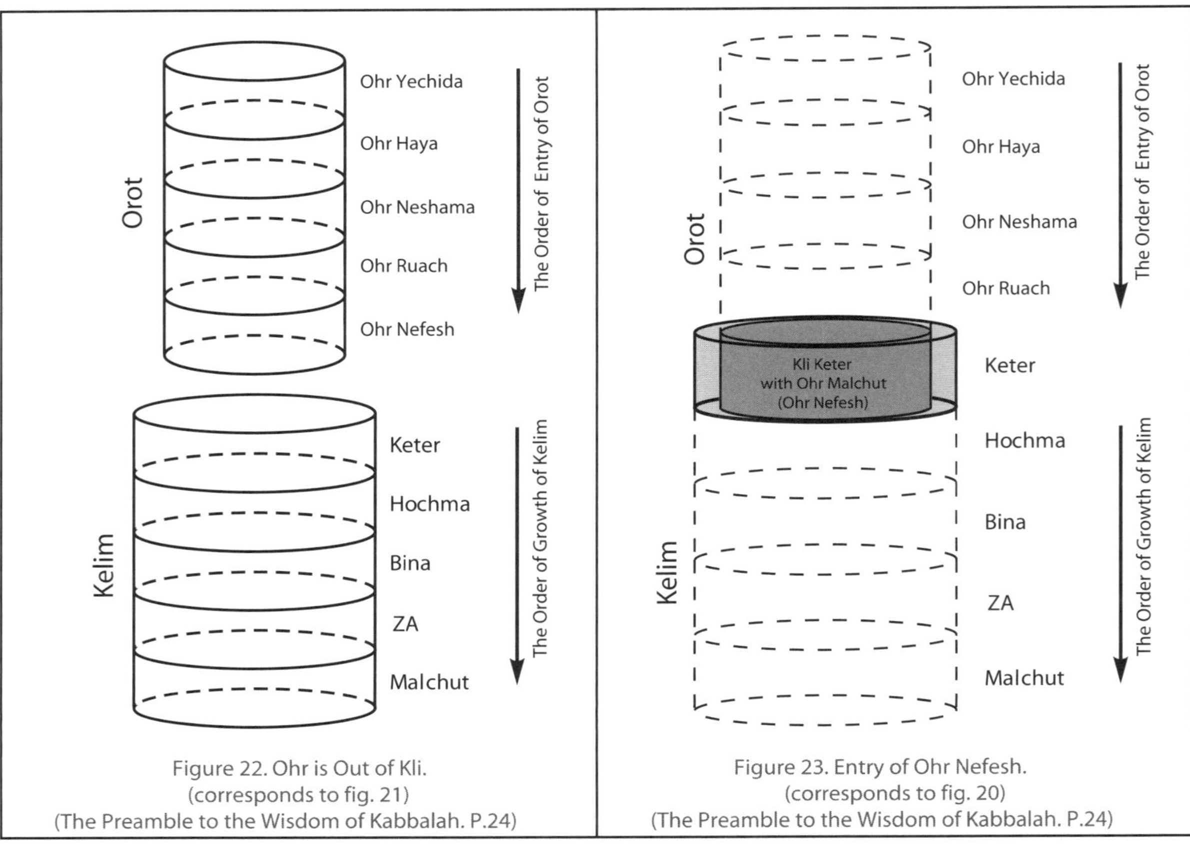

Figure 22. Ohr is Out of Kli.
(corresponds to fig. 21)
(The Preamble to the Wisdom of Kabbalah. P.24)

Figure 23. Entry of Ohr Nefesh.
(corresponds to fig. 20)
(The Preamble to the Wisdom of Kabbalah. P.24)

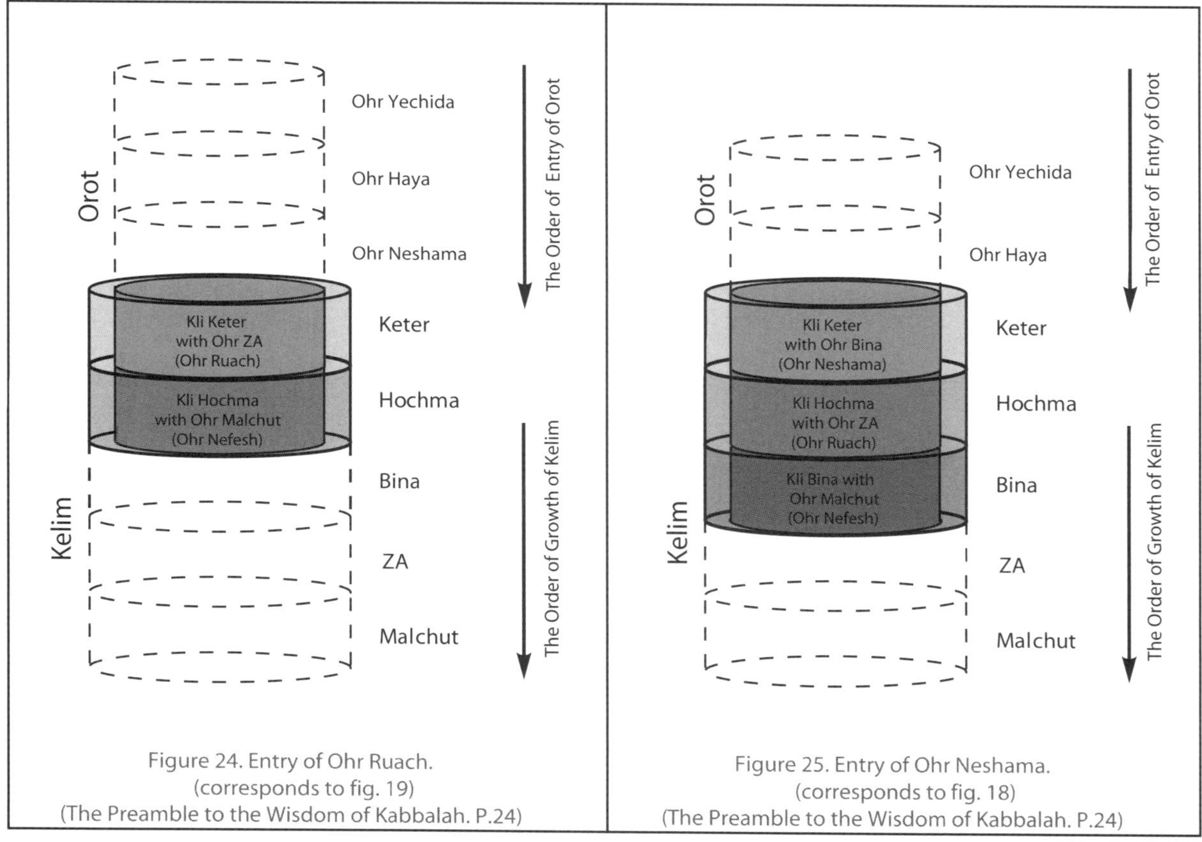

Figure 24. Entry of Ohr Ruach.
(corresponds to fig. 19)
(The Preamble to the Wisdom of Kabbalah. P.24)

Figure 25. Entry of Ohr Neshama.
(corresponds to fig. 18)
(The Preamble to the Wisdom of Kabbalah. P.24)

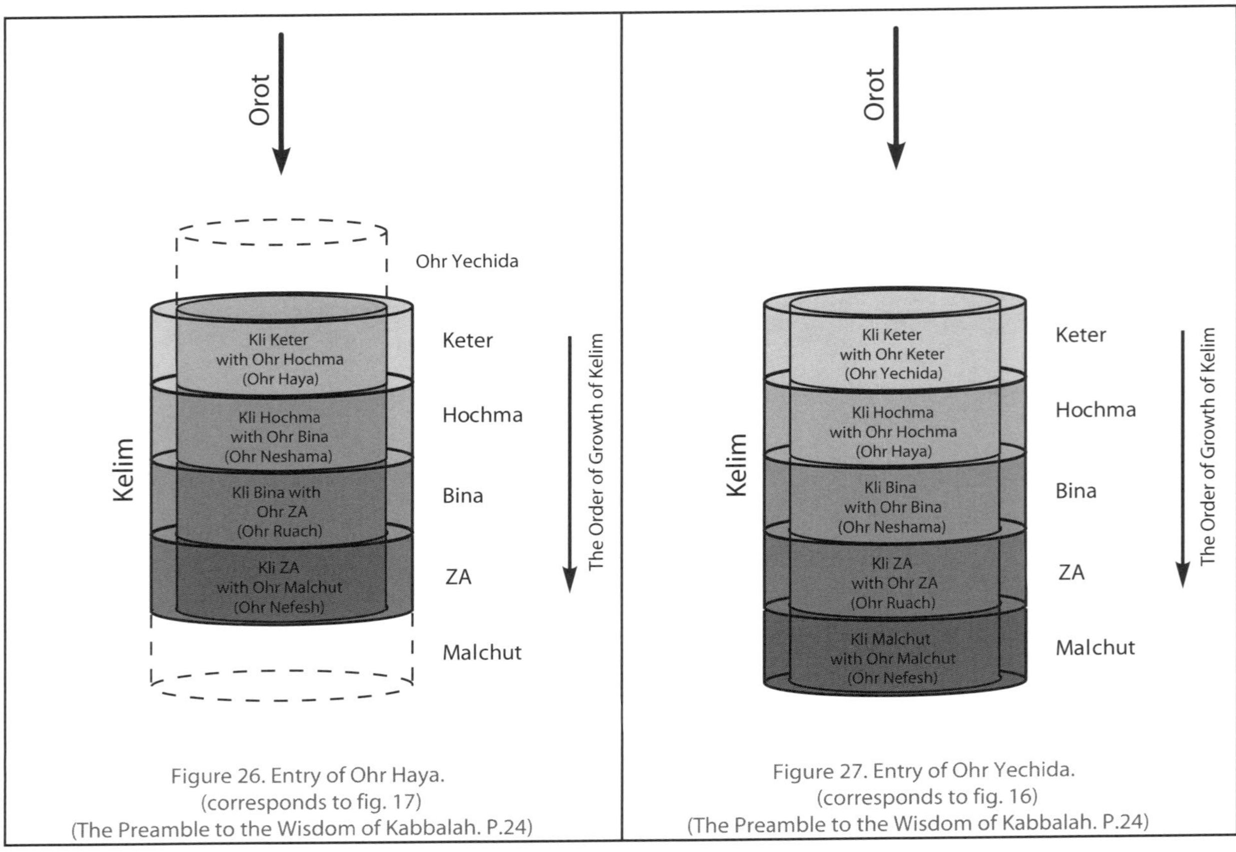

Figure 26. Entry of Ohr Haya.
(corresponds to fig. 17)
(The Preamble to the Wisdom of Kabbalah. P.24)

Figure 27. Entry of Ohr Yechida.
(corresponds to fig. 16)
(The Preamble to the Wisdom of Kabbalah. P.24)

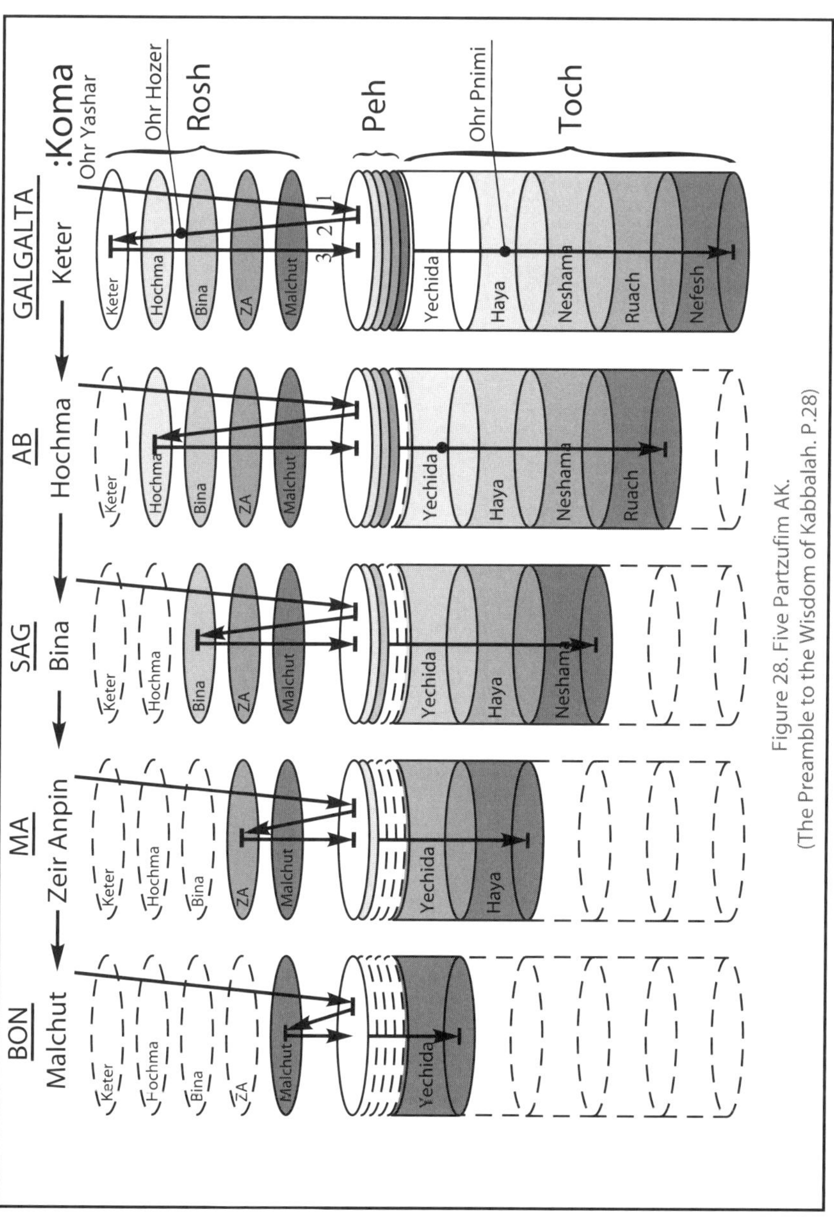

Figure 28. Five Partzufim AK.
(The Preamble to the Wisdom of Kabbalah. P.28)

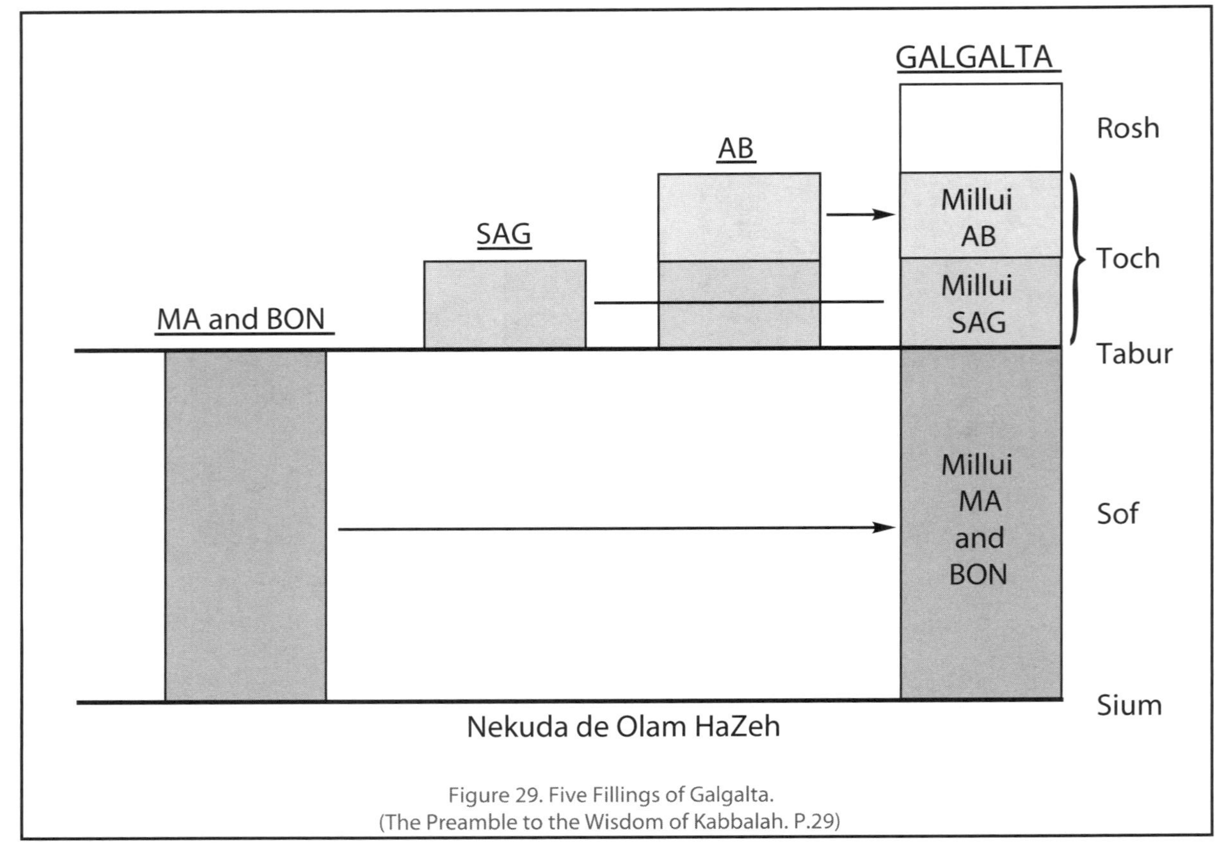

Figure 29. Five Fillings of Galgalta.
(The Preamble to the Wisdom of Kabbalah. P.29)

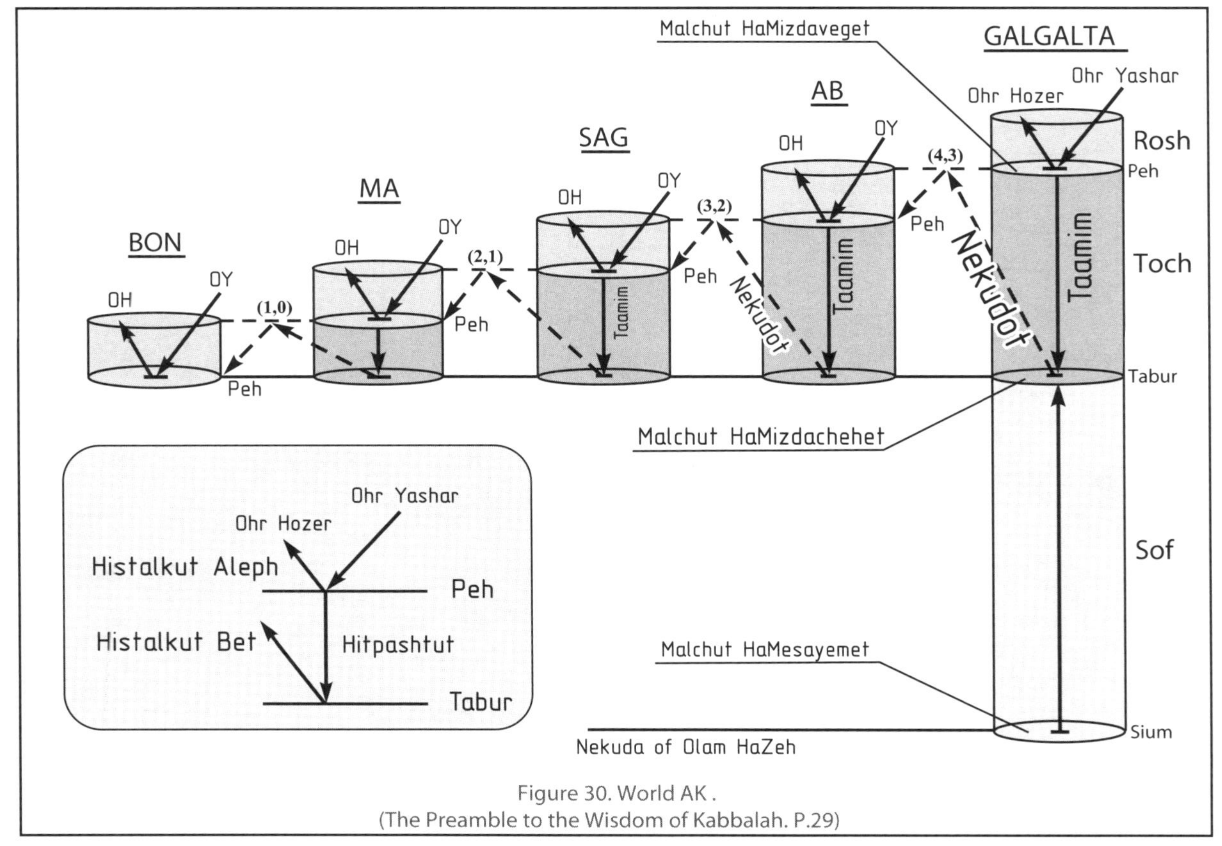

Figure 30. World AK.
(The Preamble to the Wisdom of Kabbalah. P.29)

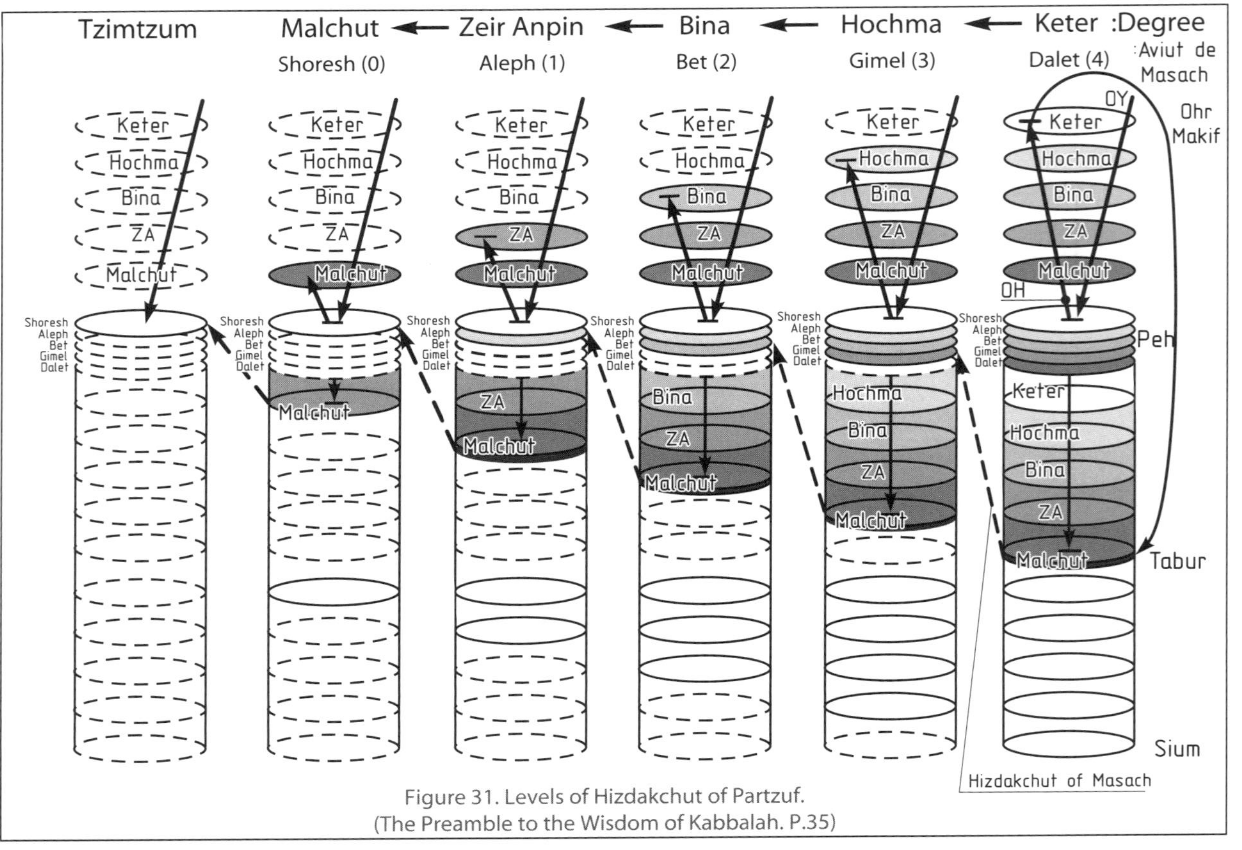

Figure 31. Levels of Hizdakchut of Partzuf.
(The Preamble to the Wisdom of Kabbalah. P.35)

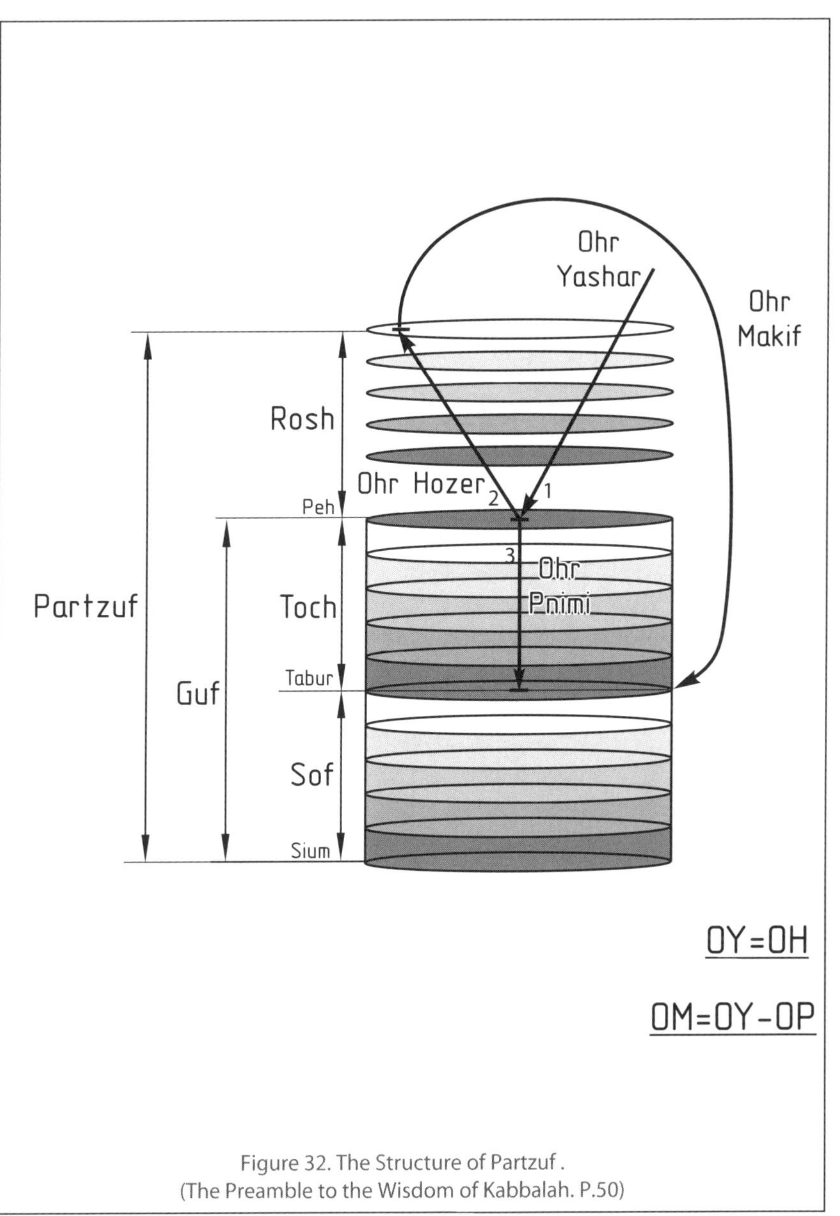

Figure 32. The Structure of Partzuf .
(The Preamble to the Wisdom of Kabbalah. P.50)

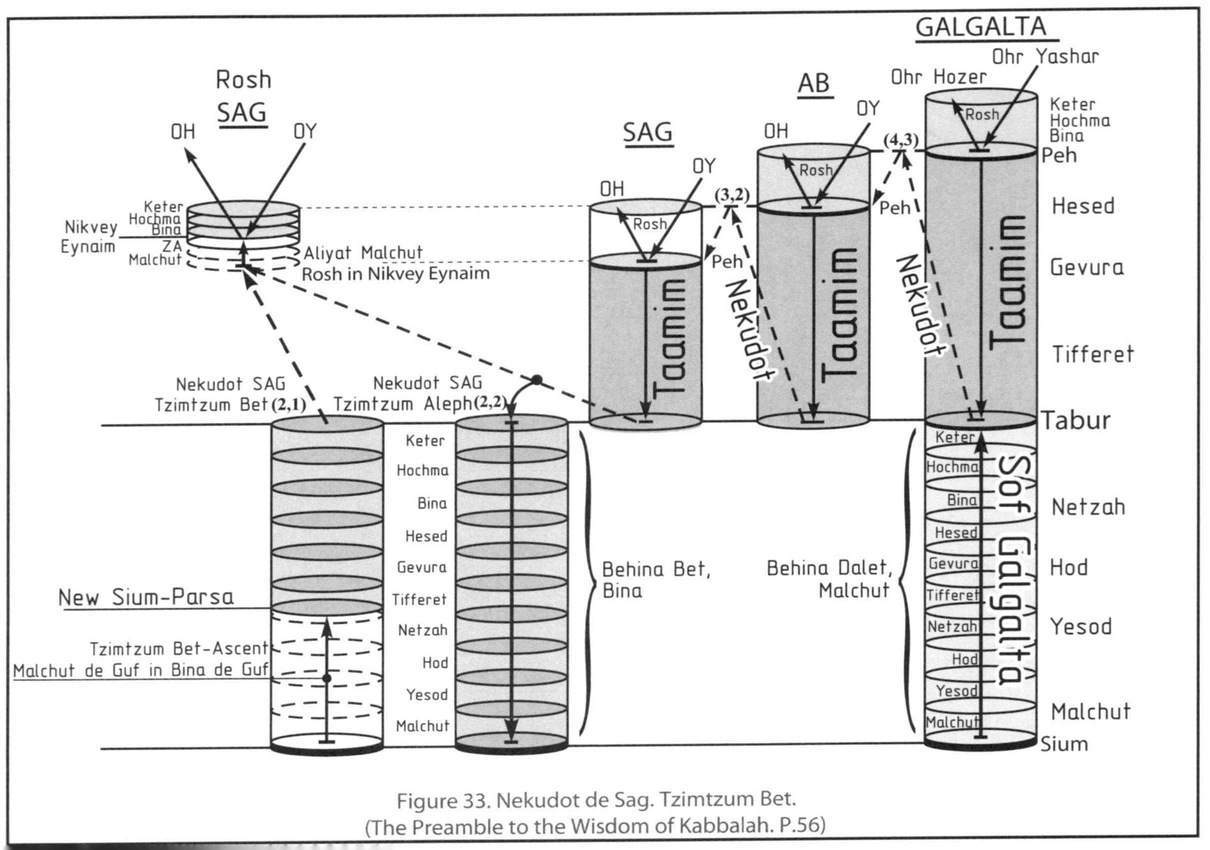

Figure 33. Nekudot de Sag. Tzimtzum Bet.
(The Preamble to the Wisdom of Kabbalah. P.56)

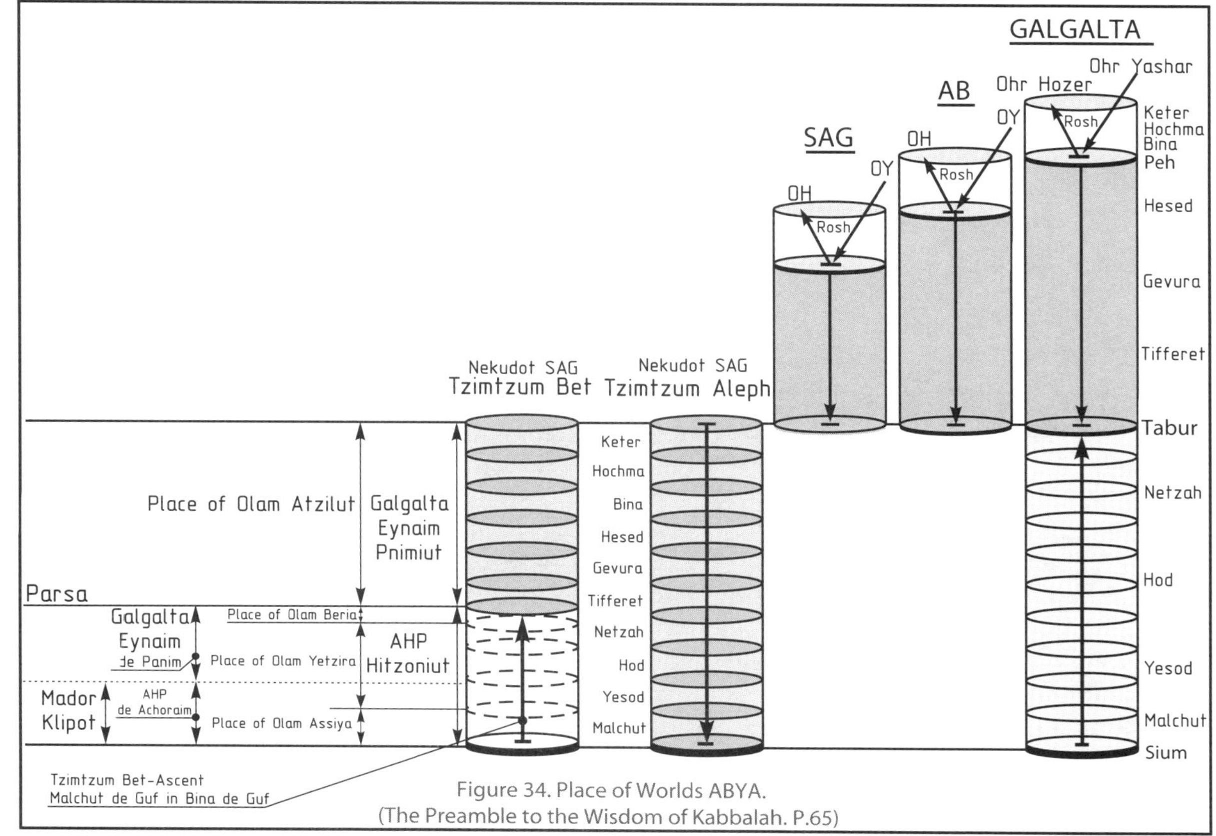

Figure 34. Place of Worlds ABYA.
(The Preamble to the Wisdom of Kabbalah. P.65)

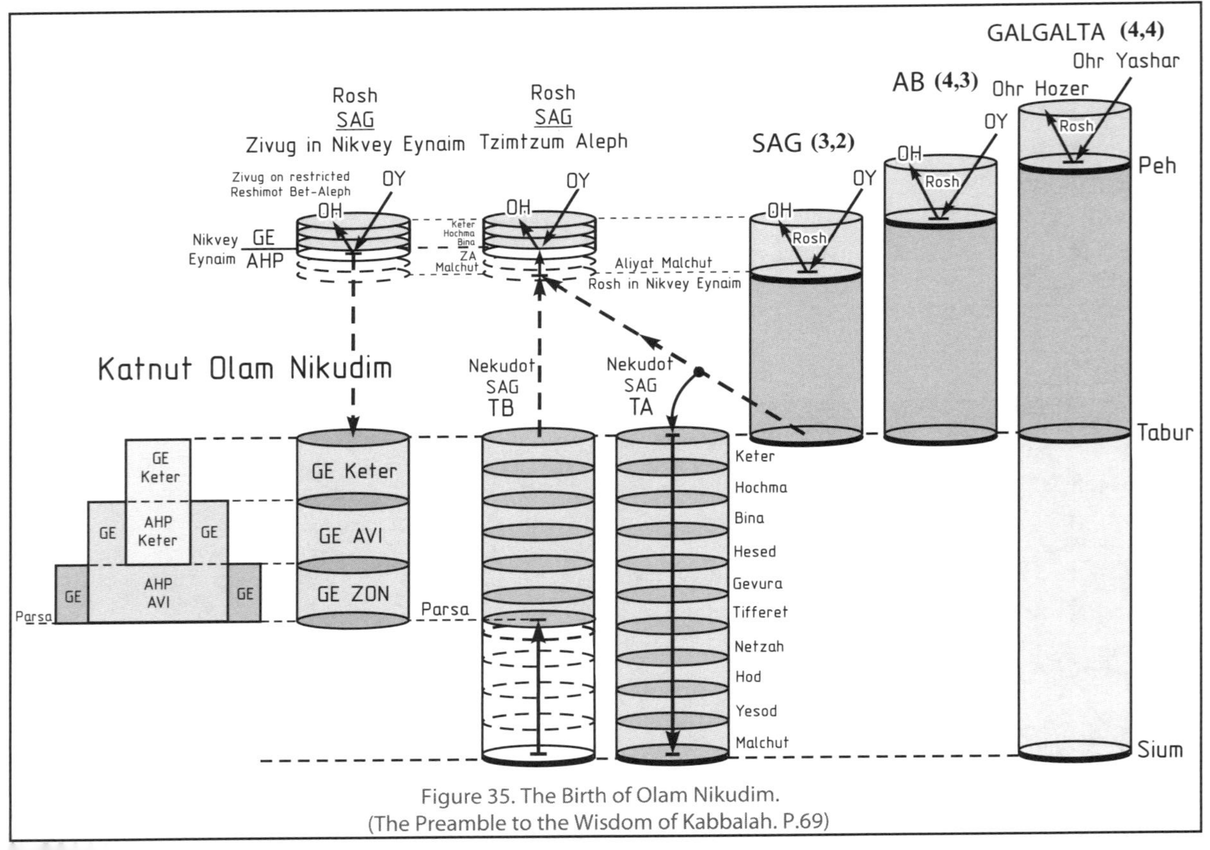

Figure 35. The Birth of Olam Nikudim.
(The Preamble to the Wisdom of Kabbalah. P.69)

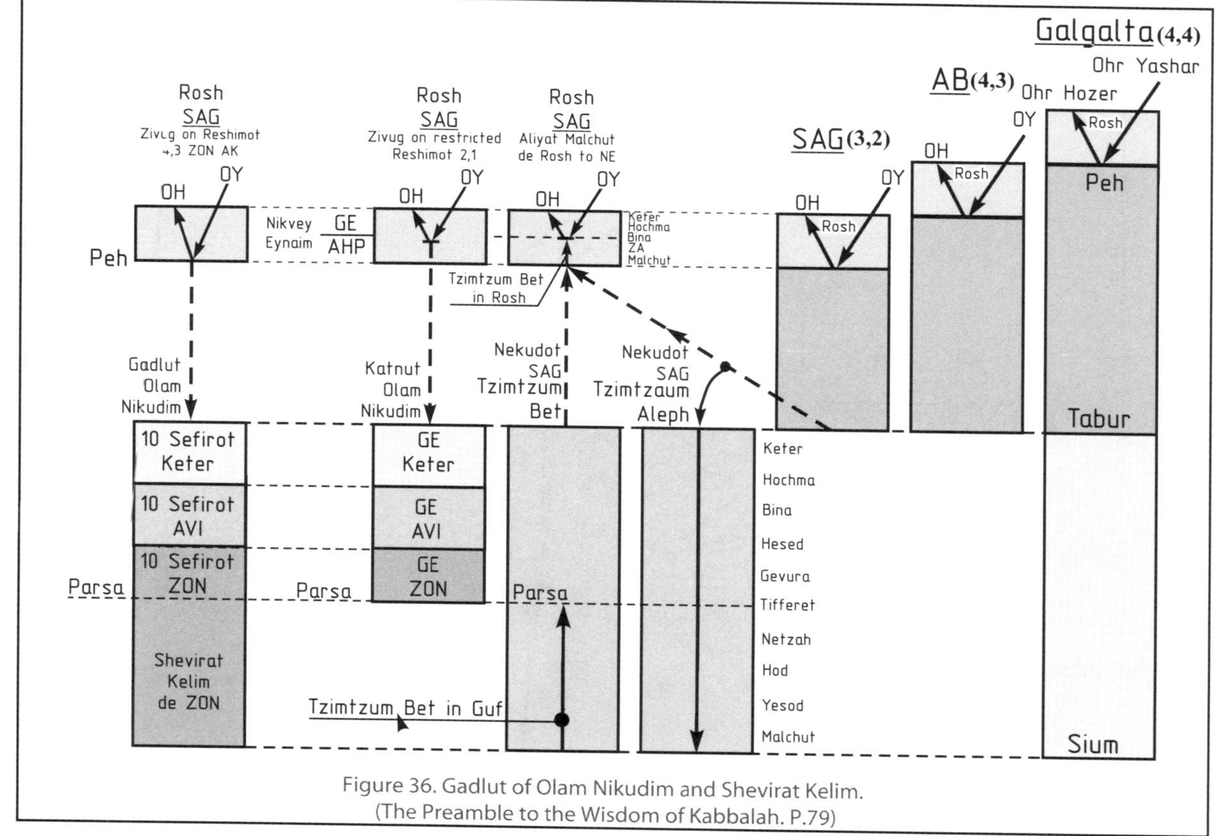

Figure 36. Gadlut of Olam Nikudim and Shevirat Kelim.
(The Preamble to the Wisdom of Kabbalah. P.79)

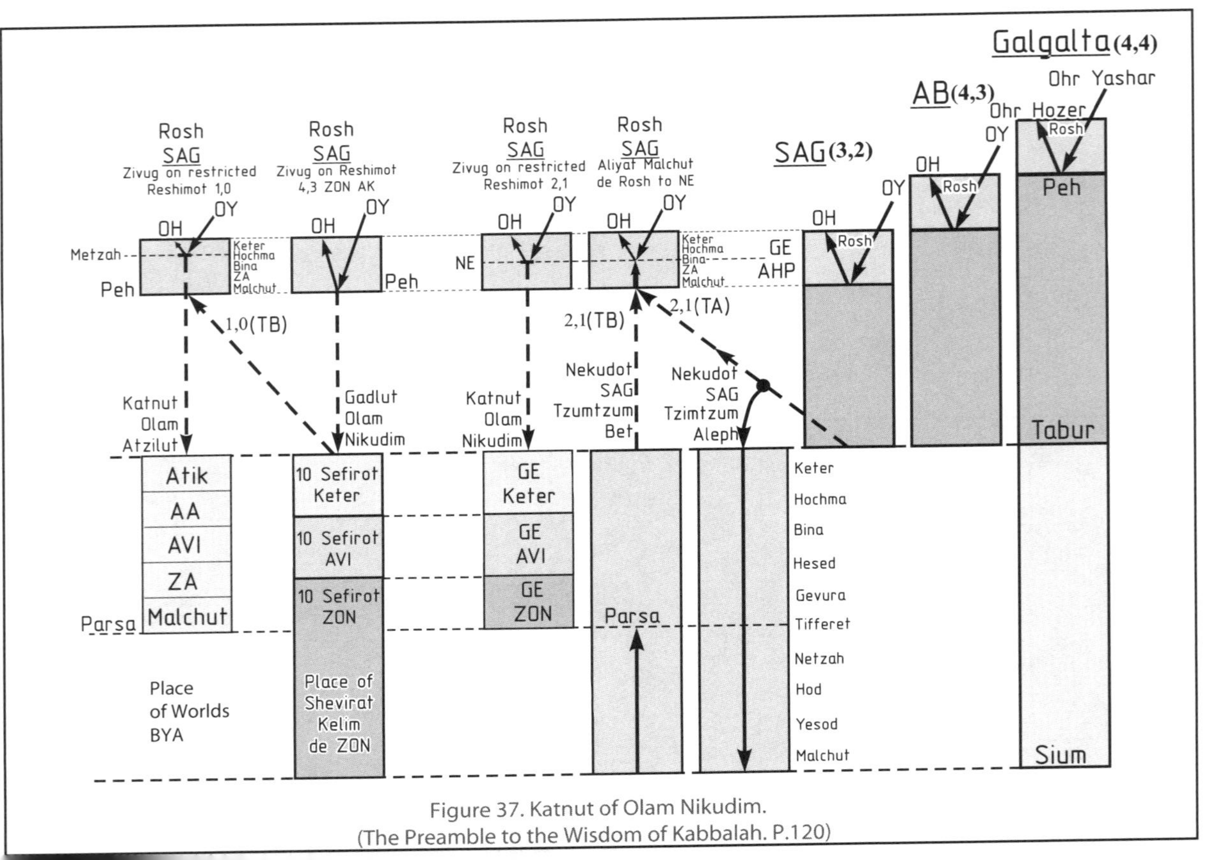

Figure 37. Katnut of Olam Nikudim.
(The Preamble to the Wisdom of Kabbalah. P.120)

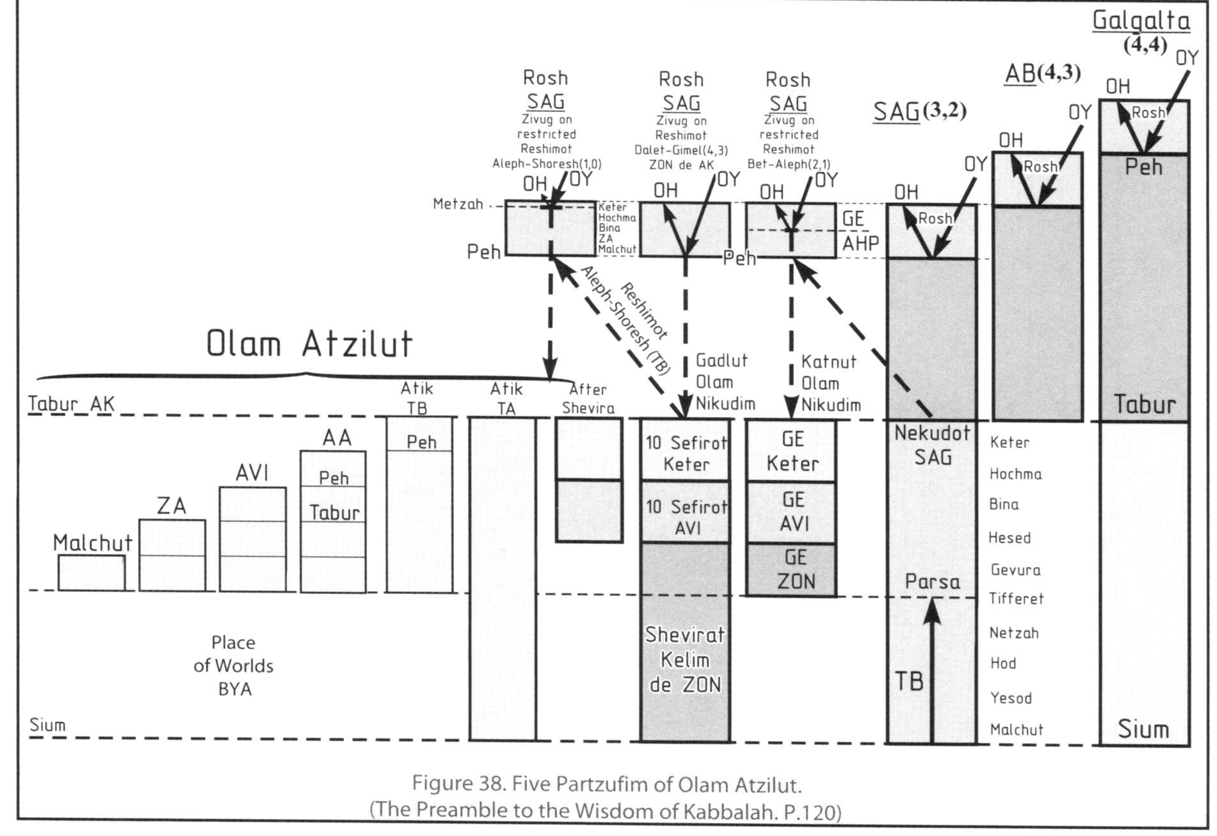

Figure 38. Five Partzufim of Olam Atzilut.
(The Preamble to the Wisdom of Kabbalah. P.120)

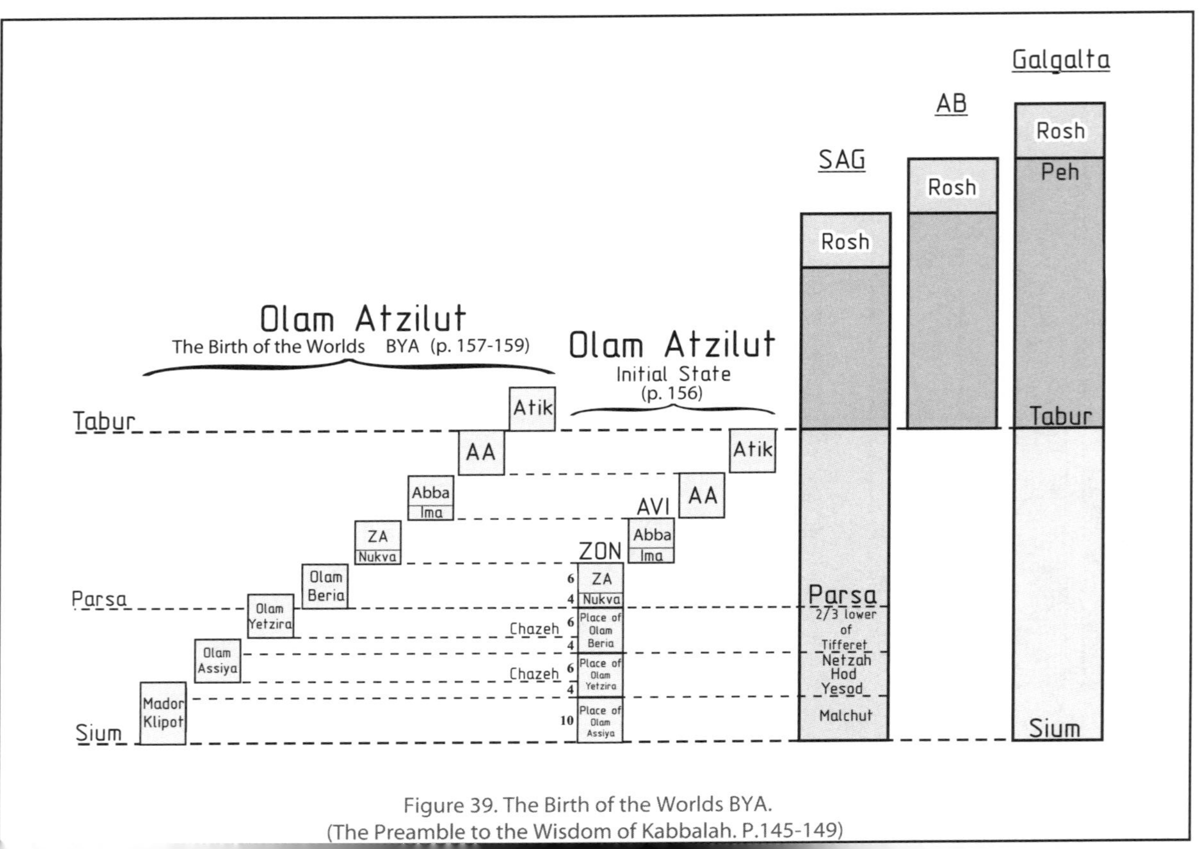

Figure 39. The Birth of the Worlds BYA.
(The Preamble to the Wisdom of Kabbalah. P.145-149)

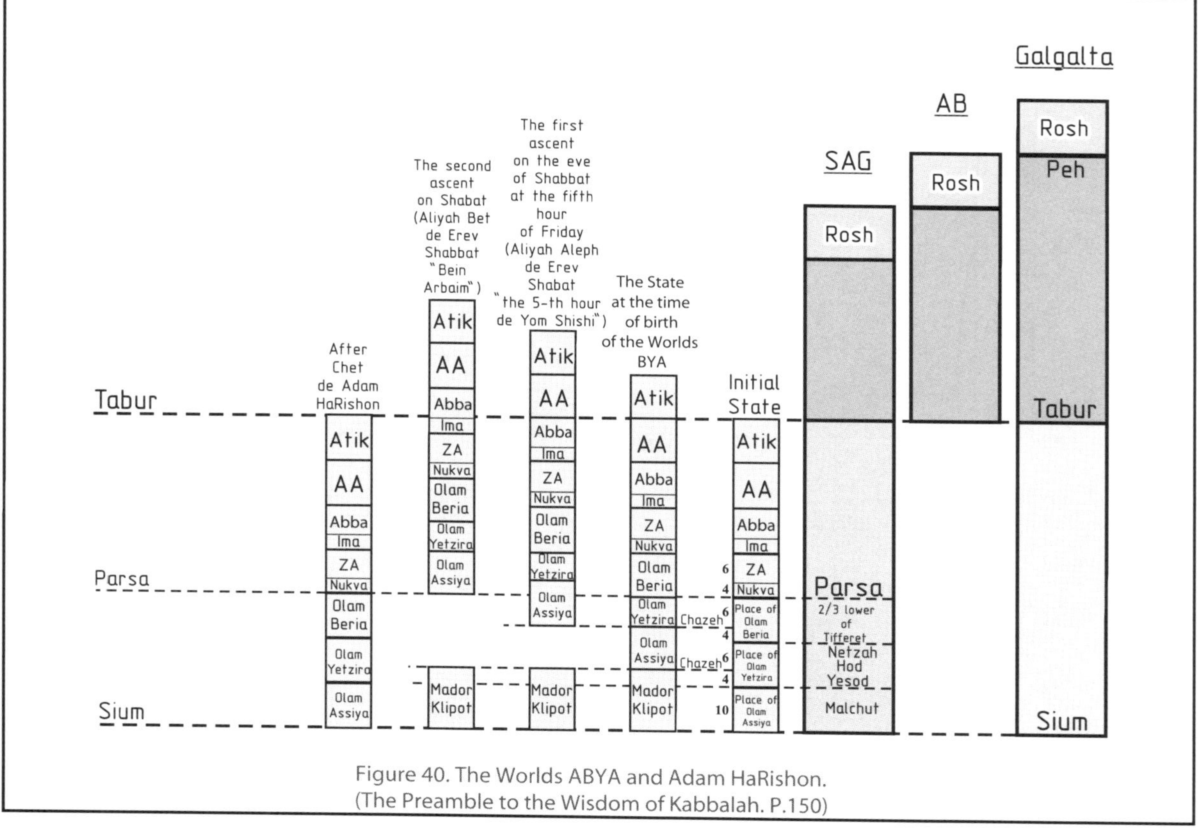

Figure 40. The Worlds ABYA and Adam HaRishon.
(The Preamble to the Wisdom of Kabbalah. P.150)

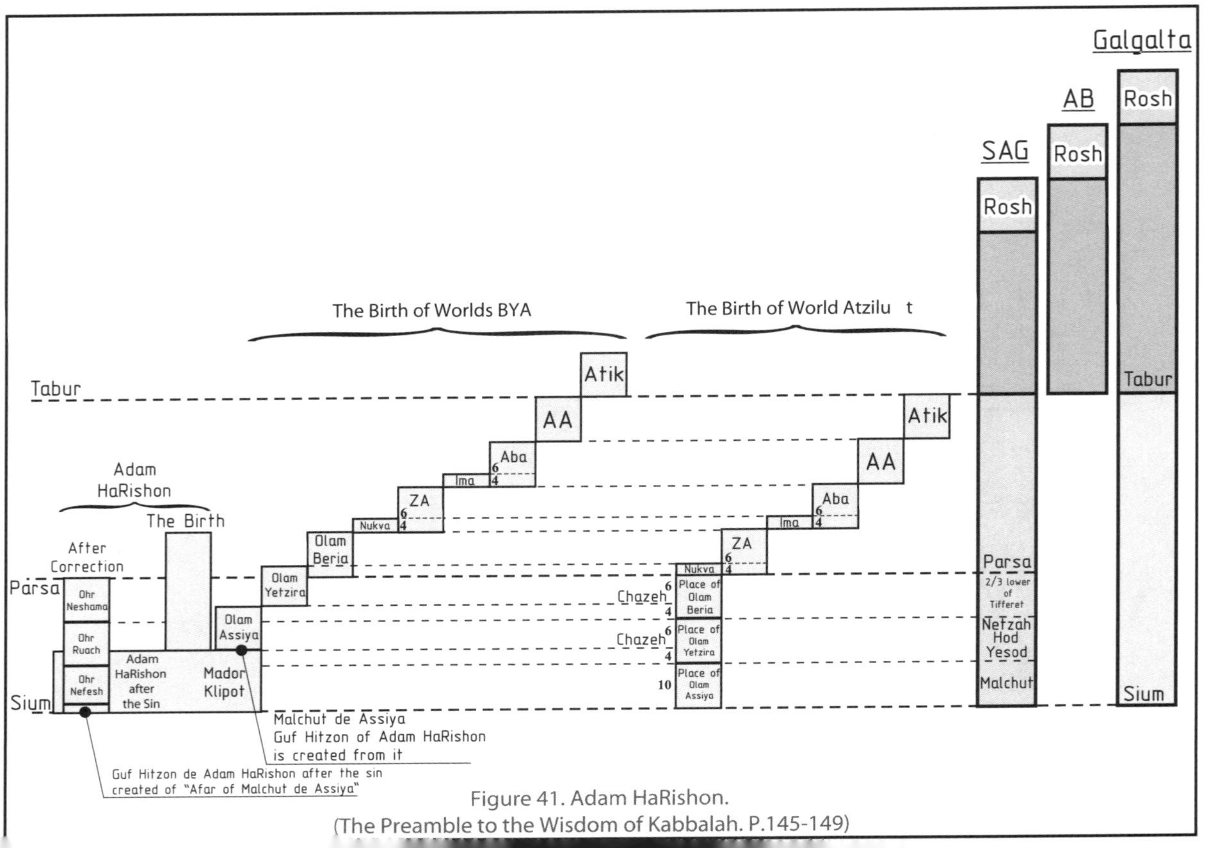

Figure 41. Adam HaRishon.
(The Preamble to the Wisdom of Kabbalah. P.145-149)

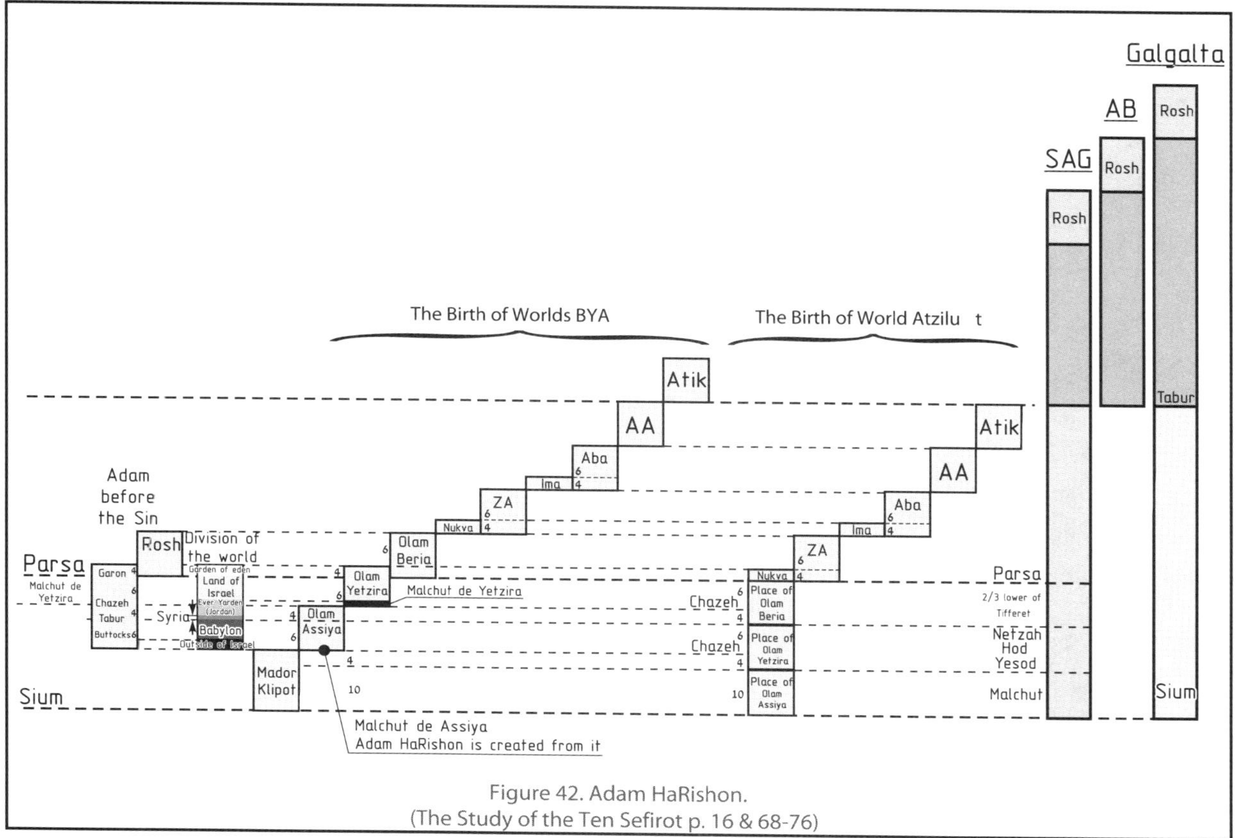

Figure 42. Adam HaRishon.
(The Study of the Ten Sefirot p. 16 & 68-76)

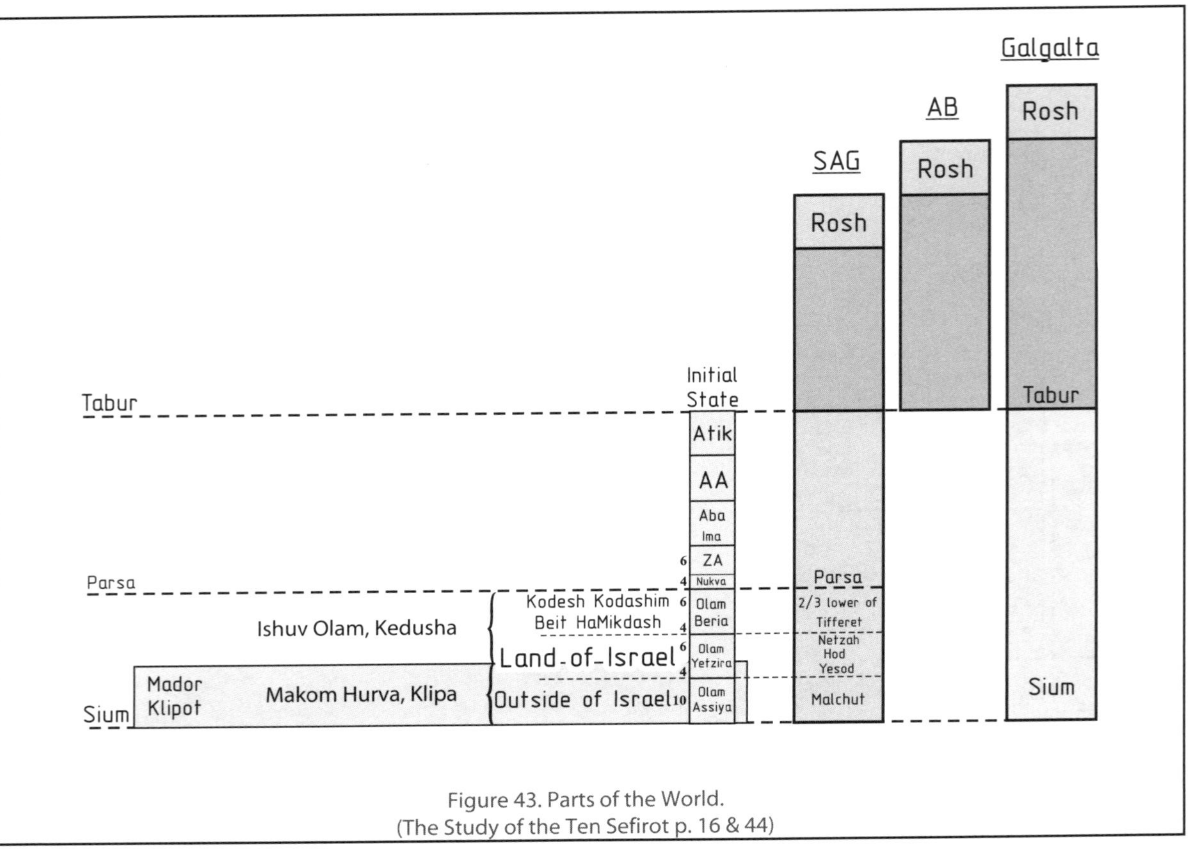

Figure 43. Parts of the World.
(The Study of the Ten Sefirot p. 16 & 44)

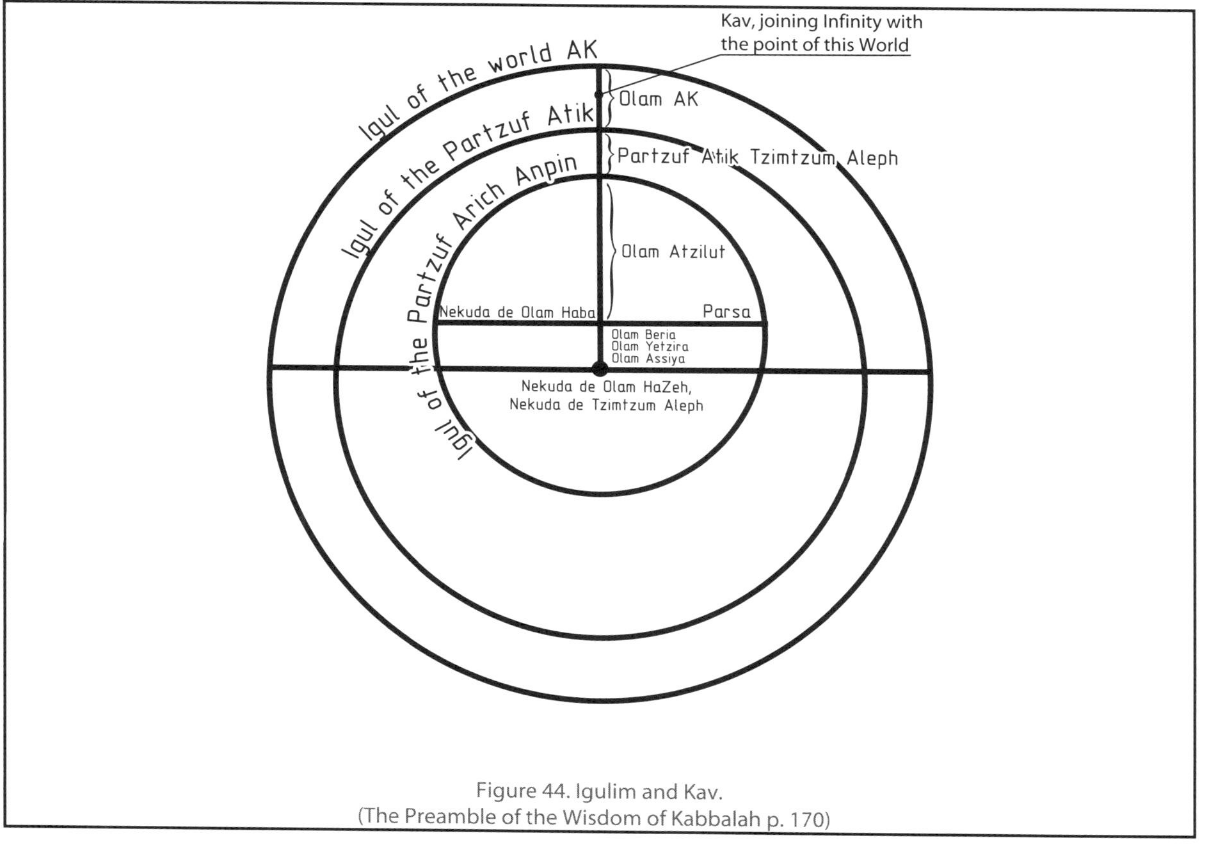

Figure 44. Igulim and Kav.
(The Preamble of the Wisdom of Kabbalah p. 170)

SEFER HA-ILAN

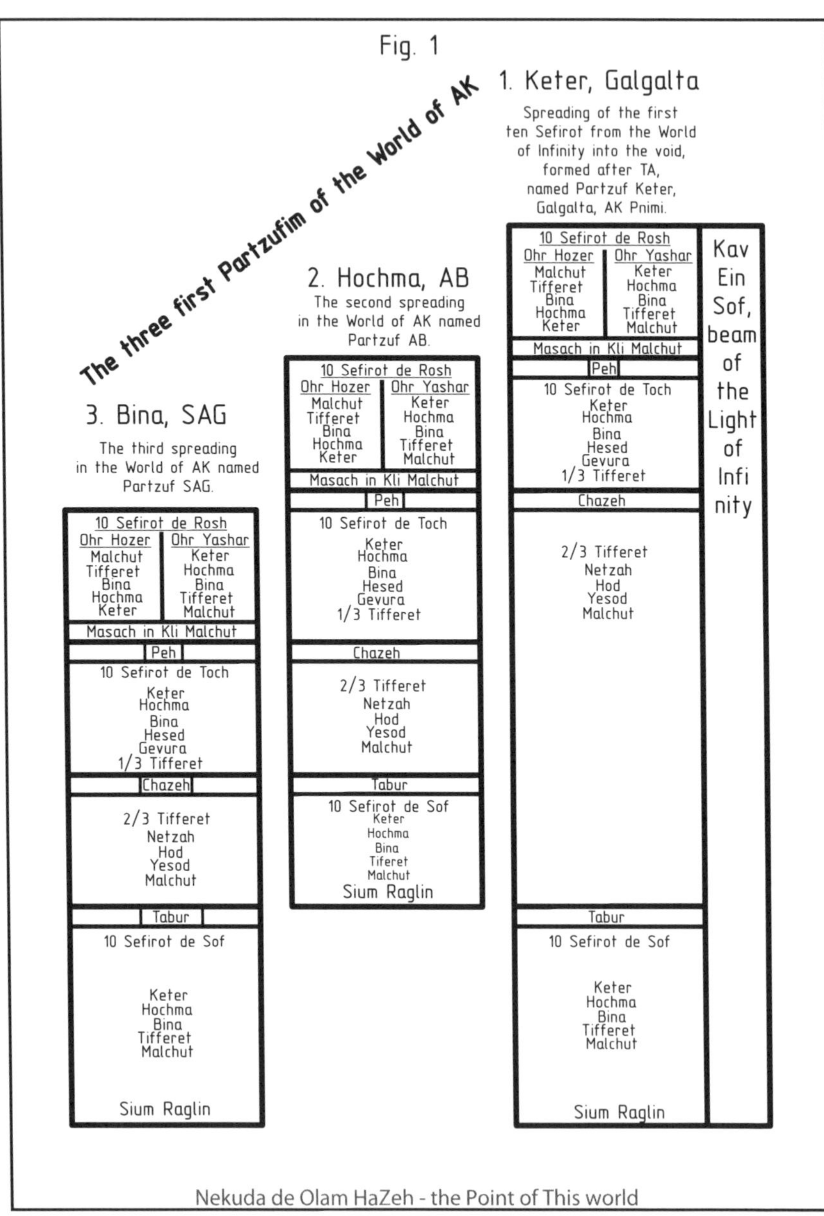
Fig. 1
The three first Partzufim of the World of AK
1. Keter, Galgalta
Spreading of the first ten Sefirot from the World of Infinity into the void, formed after TA, named Partzuf Keter, Galgalta, AK Pnimi.
10 Sefirot de Rosh
Ohr Hozer
Malchut
Tifferet
Bina
Hochma
Keter
Ohr Yashar
Keter
Hochma
Bina
Tifferet
Malchut
Masach in Kli Malchut
Peh
10 Sefirot de Toch
Keter
Hochma
Bina
Hesed
Gevura
1/3 Tifferet
Chazeh
2/3 Tifferet
Netzah
Hod
Yesod
Malchut
Tabur
10 Sefirot de Sof
Keter
Hochma
Bina
Tifferet
Malchut
Sium Raglin
Kav Ein Sof, beam of the Light of Infi nity
2. Hochma, AB
The second spreading in the World of AK named Partzuf AB.
10 Sefirot de Rosh
Ohr Hozer
Malchut
Tifferet
Bina
Hochma
Keter
Ohr Yashar
Keter
Hochma
Bina
Tifferet
Malchut
Masach in Kli Malchut
Peh
10 Sefirot de Toch
Keter
Hochma
Bina
Hesed
Gevura
1/3 Tifferet
Chazeh
2/3 Tifferet
Netzah
Hod
Yesod
Malchut
Tabur
10 Sefirot de Sof
Keter
Hochma
Bina
Tiferet
Malchut
Sium Raglin
3. Bina, SAG
The third spreading in the World of AK named Partzuf SAG.
10 Sefirot de Rosh
Ohr Hozer
Malchut
Tifferet
Bina
Hochma
Keter
Ohr Yashar
Keter
Hochma
Bina
Tifferet
Malchut
Masach in Kli Malchut
Peh
10 Sefirot de Toch
Keter
Hochma
Bina
Hesed
Gevura
1/3 Tifferet
Chazeh
2/3 Tifferet
Netzah
Hod
Yesod
Malchut
Tabur
10 Sefirot de Sof
Keter
Hochma
Bina
Tifferet
Malchut
Sium Raglin
Nekuda de Olam HaZeh - the Point of This world

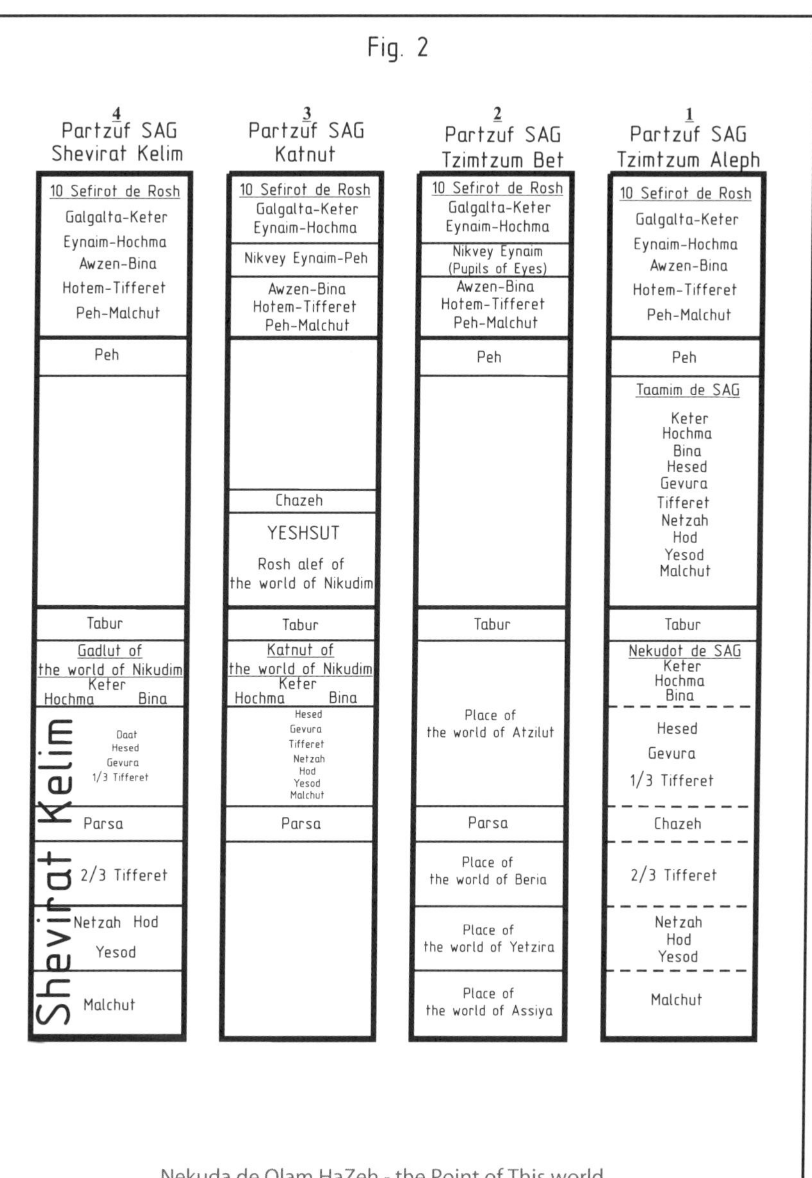
Fig. 2
4
Partzuf SAG
Shevirat Kelim
10 Sefirot de Rosh
Galgalta-Keter
Eynaim-Hochma
Awzen-Bina
Hotem-Tifferet
Peh-Malchut
Peh
Tabur
Gadlut of
the world of Nikudim
Keter
Hochma
Bina
Daat
Hesed
Gevura
1/3 Tifferet
Parsa
2/3 Tifferet
Netzah Hod
Yesod
Malchut
Shevirat Kelim
3
Partzuf SAG
Katnut
10 Sefirot de Rosh
Galgalta-Keter
Eynaim-Hochma
Nikvey Eynaim-Peh
Awzen-Bina
Hotem-Tifferet
Peh-Malchut
Chazeh
YESHSUT
Rosh alef of
the world of Nikudim
Tabur
Katnut of
the world of Nikudim
Keter
Hochma
Bina
Hesed
Gevura
Tifferet
Netzah
Hod
Yesod
Malchut
Parsa
2
Partzuf SAG
Tzimtzum Bet
10 Sefirot de Rosh
Galgalta-Keter
Eynaim-Hochma
Nikvey Eynaim
(Pupils of Eyes)
Awzen-Bina
Hotem-Tifferet
Peh-Malchut
Peh
Tabur
Place of
the world of Atzilut
Parsa
Place of
the world of Beria
Place of
the world of Yetzira
Place of
the world of Assiya
1
Partzuf SAG
Tzimtzum Aleph
10 Sefirot de Rosh
Galgalta-Keter
Eynaim-Hochma
Awzen-Bina
Hotem-Tifferet
Peh-Malchut
Peh
Taamim de SAG
Keter
Hochma
Bina
Hesed
Gevura
Tifferet
Netzah
Hod
Yesod
Malchut
Tabur
Nekudot de SAG
Keter
Hochma
Bina
Hesed
Gevura
1/3 Tifferet
Chazeh
2/3 Tifferet
Netzah
Hod
Yesod
Malchut
Nekuda de Olam HaZeh - the Point of This world

Fig. 3

The lowest initial state of the Worlds of AK and Atzilut

The dotted lines show connection and reception in Rosh of each Partzuf of the World of Atzilut and the corresponding Partzuf of AK

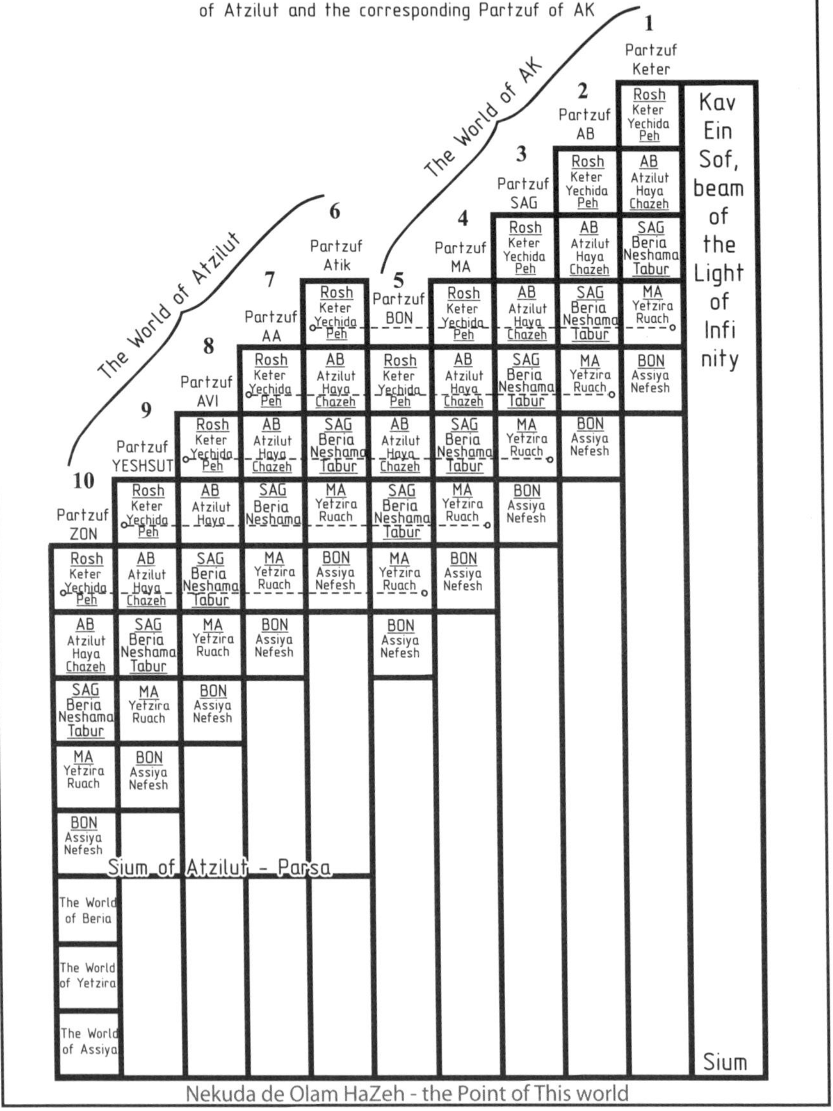

The World of AK

The World of Atzilut

1 Partzuf Keter
- Rosh — Keter, Yechida, Peh
- AB — Atzilut, Haya, Chazeh
- SAG — Beria, Neshama, Tabur
- MA — Yetzira, Ruach
- BON — Assiya, Nefesh

2 Partzuf AB
- Rosh — Keter, Yechida, Peh
- AB — Atzilut, Haya, Chazeh
- SAG — Beria, Neshama, Tabur
- MA — Yetzira, Ruach
- BON — Assiya, Nefesh

3 Partzuf SAG
- Rosh — Keter, Yechida, Peh
- AB — Atzilut, Haya, Chazeh
- SAG — Beria, Neshama, Tabur
- MA — Yetzira, Ruach
- BON — Assiya, Nefesh

4 Partzuf MA
- Rosh — Keter, Yechida, Peh
- AB — Atzilut, Haya, Chazeh
- SAG — Beria, Neshama, Tabur
- MA — Yetzira, Ruach
- BON — Assiya, Nefesh

5 Partzuf BON
- Rosh — Keter, Yechida, Peh
- AB — Atzilut, Haya, Chazeh
- SAG — Beria, Neshama, Tabur
- MA — Yetzira, Ruach
- BON — Assiya, Nefesh

6 Partzuf Atik
- Rosh — Keter, Yechida, Peh
- AB — Atzilut, Haya, Chazeh
- SAG — Beria, Neshama, Tabur
- MA — Yetzira, Ruach
- BON — Assiya, Nefesh

7 Partzuf AA
- Rosh — Keter, Yechida, Peh
- AB — Atzilut, Haya, Chazeh
- SAG — Beria, Neshama
- MA — Yetzira, Ruach
- BON — Assiya, Nefesh

8 Partzuf AVI
- Rosh — Keter, Yechida, Peh
- AB — Atzilut, Haya
- SAG — Beria, Neshama, Tabur
- MA — Yetzira, Ruach
- BON — Assiya, Nefesh

9 Partzuf YESHSUT
- Rosh — Keter, Yechida, Peh
- AB — Atzilut, Haya, Chazeh
- SAG — Beria, Neshama, Tabur
- MA — Yetzira, Ruach
- BON — Assiya, Nefesh

10 Partzuf ZON
- Rosh — Keter, Yechida, Peh
- AB — Atzilut, Haya, Chazeh
- SAG — Beria, Neshama, Tabur
- MA — Yetzira, Ruach
- BON — Assiya, Nefesh

Sium of Atzilut - Parsa

The World of Beria

The World of Yetzira

The World of Assiya

Kav Ein Sof, beam of the Light of Infinity

Sium

Nekuda de Olam HaZeh - the Point of This world

Fig. 4
The ascent of the World of Atzilut to the level of Neshama with regard to the initial state of the World AK.

The World of AK

The World of Atzilut

10 Partzuf ZON	9 Partzuf YESHSUT	8 Partzuf AVI	7 Partzuf AA	6 Partzuf Atik	5 Partzuf BON	4 Partzuf MA	3 Partzuf SAG	2 Partzuf AB	1 Partzuf Keter	
									Rosh Keter Yechida Peh	Kav Ein Sof, beam of the Light of Infinity
								Rosh Keter Yechida Peh	AB Atzilut Haya Chazeh	
							Rosh Keter Yechida Peh	AB Atzilut Haya Chazeh	SAG Beria Neshama Tabur	
				Rosh Keter Yechida Peh		Rosh Keter Yechida Peh	AB Atzilut Haya Chazeh	SAG Beria Neshama Tabur	MA Yetzira Ruach	
			Rosh Keter Yechida Peh	AB Atzilut Haya Chazeh	Rosh Keter Yechida Peh	AB Atzilut Haya Chazeh	SAG Beria Neshama Tabur	MA Yetzira Ruach	BON Assiya Nefesh	
		Rosh Keter Yechida Peh	AB Atzilut Haya Chazeh	SAG Beria Neshama Tabur	AB Atzilut Haya Chazeh	SAG Beria Neshama Tabur	MA Yetzira Ruach	BON Assiya Nefesh		
Rosh Keter Yechida Peh	Rosh Keter Yechida Peh	AB Atzilut Haya	SAG Beria Neshama	MA Yetzira Ruach	SAG Beria Neshama Tabur	MA Yetzira Ruach	BON Assiya Nefesh			
AB Atzilut Haya Chazeh	AB Atzilut Haya Chazeh	SAG Beria Neshama Tabur	MA Yetzira Ruach	BON Assiya Nefesh	MA Yetzira Ruach	BON Assiya Nefesh				
SAG Beria Neshama Tabur	SAG Beria Neshama Tabur	MA Yetzira Ruach	BON Assiya Nefesh		BON Assiya Nefesh					
MA Yetzira Ruach	MA Yetzira Ruach	BON Assiya Nefesh								
BON Assiya Nefesh	BON Assiya Nefesh									
The World of Beria										
The World of Yetzira										
The World of Assiya										
Place of the World of Assiya										Sium

Sium of Atzilut - Parsa

Nekuda de Olam HaZeh - the Point of This world

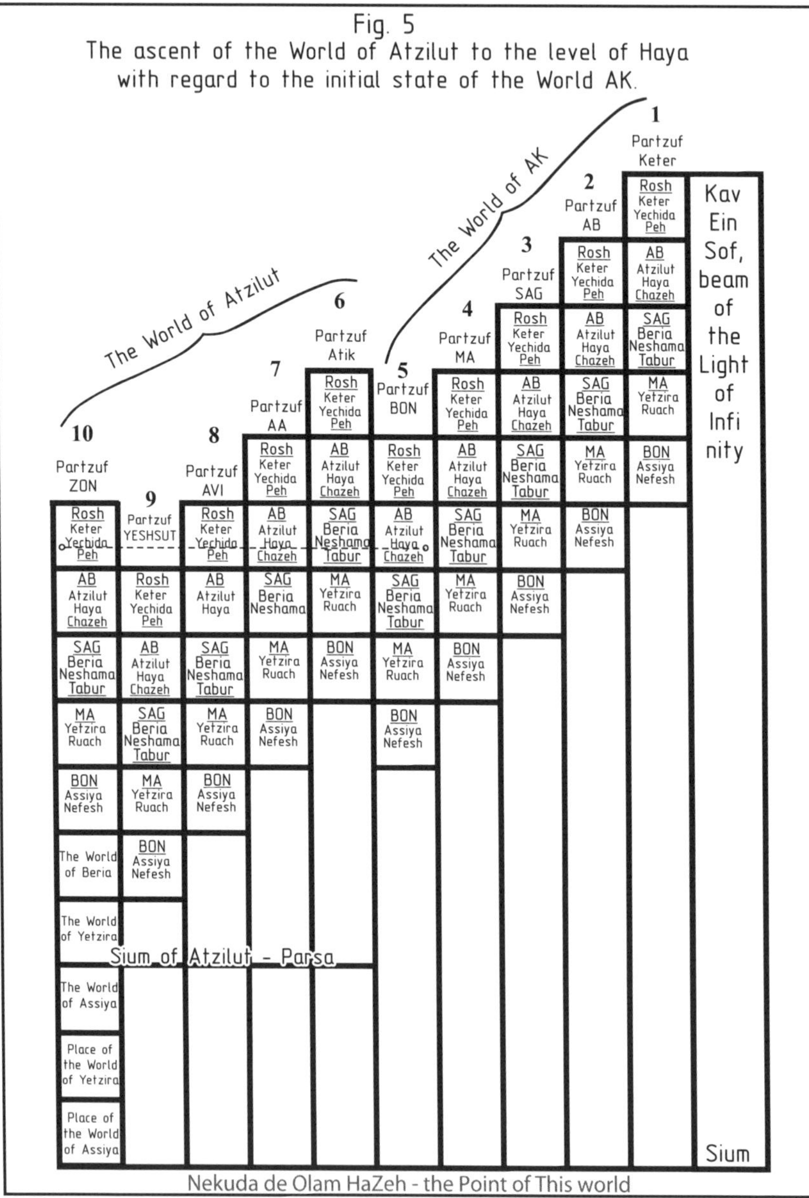

Fig. 5
The ascent of the World of Atzilut to the level of Haya with regard to the initial state of the World AK.

Fig. 6

The ascent of the World of Atzilut to the level of Yechida with regard to the initial state of the World AK.

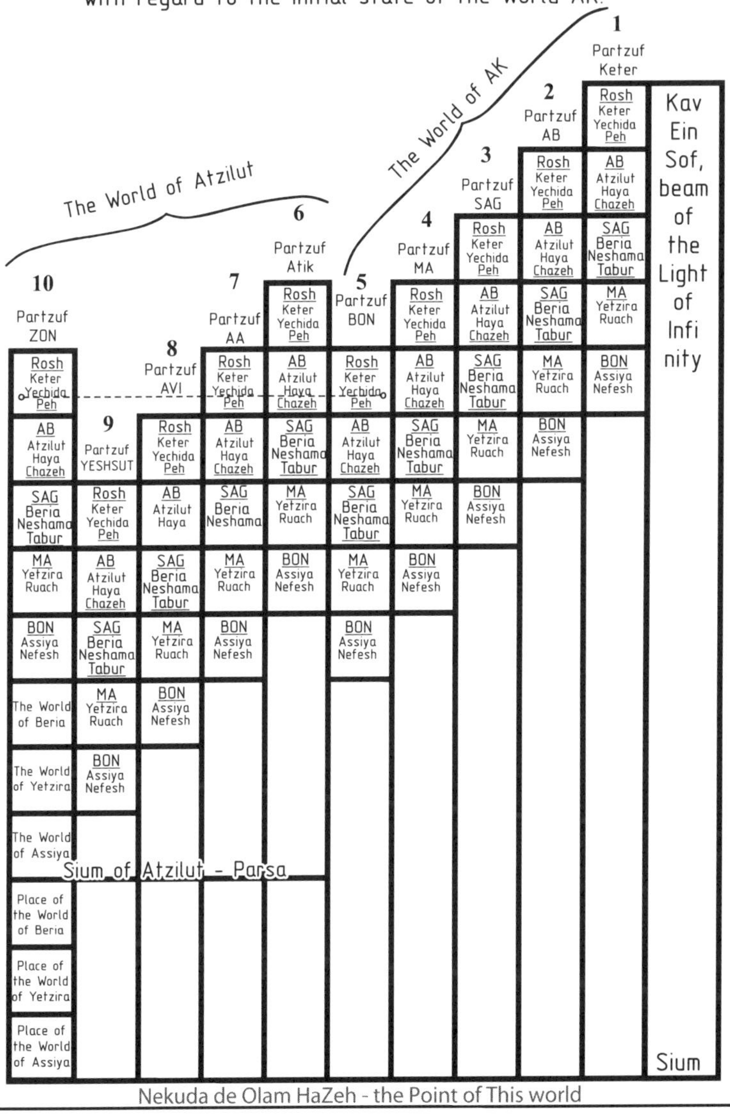

The World of AK

The World of Atzilut

1 Partzuf Keter
Rosh Keter Yechida Peh
AB Atzilut Haya Chazeh
SAG Beria Neshama Tabur
MA Yetzira Ruach
BON Assiya Nefesh

2 Partzuf AB
Rosh Keter Yechida Peh
AB Atzilut Haya Chazeh
SAG Beria Neshama Tabur
MA Yetzira Ruach
BON Assiya Nefesh

3 Partzuf SAG
Rosh Keter Yechida Peh
AB Atzilut Haya Chazeh
SAG Beria Neshama Tabur
MA Yetzira Ruach
BON Assiya Nefesh

4 Partzuf MA
Rosh Keter Yechida Peh
AB Atzilut Haya Chazeh
SAG Beria Neshama Tabur
MA Yetzira Ruach
BON Assiya Nefesh

5 Partzuf BON
Rosh Keter Yechida Peh
AB Atzilut Haya Chazeh
SAG Beria Neshama Tabur
MA Yetzira Ruach
BON Assiya Nefesh

6 Partzuf Atik
Rosh Keter Yechida Peh
AB Atzilut Haya Chazeh
SAG Beria Neshama Tabur
MA Yetzira Ruach
BON Assiya Nefesh

7 Partzuf AA
Rosh Keter Yechida Peh
AB Atzilut Haya Chazeh
SAG Beria Neshama
MA Yetzira Ruach
BON Assiya Nefesh

8 Partzuf AVI
Rosh Keter Yechida Peh
AB Atzilut Haya
SAG Beria Neshama Tabur
MA Yetzira Ruach
BON Assiya Nefesh

9 Partzuf YESHSUT
Rosh Keter Yechida Peh
AB Atzilut Haya Chazeh
SAG Beria Neshama Tabur
MA Yetzira Ruach
BON Assiya Nefesh

10 Partzuf ZON
Rosh Keter Yechida Peh
AB Atzilut Haya Chazeh
SAG Beria Neshama Tabur
MA Yetzira Ruach
BON Assiya Nefesh
The World of Beria
The World of Yetzira
The World of Assiya
Place of the World of Beria
Place of the World of Yetzira
Place of the World of Assiya

Kav Ein Sof, beam of the Light of Infinity

Sium

Sium of Atzilut - Parsa

Nekuda de Olam HaZeh - the Point of This world

Fig. 7
The ascent of the Worlds of ABYA to the level of Neshama with regard to the initial state of the World AK.
The dotted lines show connection and reception in Rosh of each Partzuf of the World of Atzilut and the corresponding Partzuf of AK

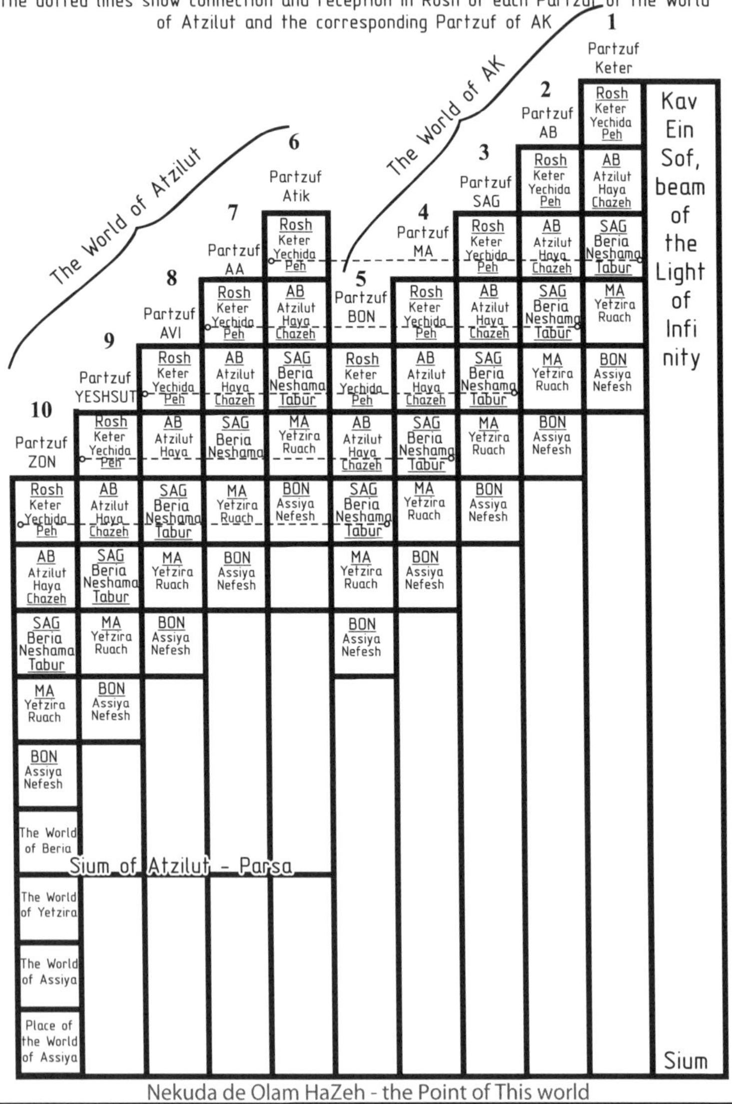

The World of AK
The World of Atzilut

1 Partzuf Keter
2 Partzuf AB
3 Partzuf SAG
4 Partzuf MA
5 Partzuf BON
6 Partzuf Atik
7 Partzuf AA
8 Partzuf AVI
9 Partzuf YESHSUT
10 Partzuf ZON

Rosh Keter Yechida Peh
AB Atzilut Haya Chazeh
SAG Beria Neshama Tabur
MA Yetzira Ruach
BON Assiya Nefesh

Kav Ein Sof, beam of the Light of Infinity

The World of Beria
Sium of Atzilut - Parsa
The World of Yetzira
The World of Assiya
Place of the World of Assiya
Sium

Nekuda de Olam HaZeh - the Point of This world

Fig. 8

The ascent of the Worlds of ABYA to the level of Haya with regard to the initial state of the World AK.

The dotted lines show connection and reception in Rosh of each Partzuf of the World of Atzilut and the corresponding Partzuf of AK

The World of AK

1 Partzuf Keter
- Rosh – Keter – Yechida – Peh
- AB – Atzilut – Haya – Chazeh
- SAG – Beria – Neshama – Tabur
- MA – Yetzira – Ruach
- BON – Assiya – Nefesh

2 Partzuf AB
- Rosh – Keter – Yechida – Peh
- AB – Atzilut – Haya – Chazeh
- SAG – Beria – Neshama – Tabur
- MA – Yetzira – Ruach
- BON – Assiya – Nefesh

3 Partzuf SAG
- Rosh – Keter – Yechida – Peh
- AB – Atzilut – Haya – Chazeh
- SAG – Beria – Neshama – Tabur
- MA – Yetzira – Ruach
- BON – Assiya – Nefesh

4 Partzuf MA
- Rosh – Keter – Yechida – Peh
- AB – Atzilut – Haya – Chazeh
- SAG – Beria – Neshama – Tabur
- MA – Yetzira – Ruach
- BON – Assiya – Nefesh

5 Partzuf BON
- Rosh – Keter – Yechida – Peh
- AB – Atzilut – Haya – Chazeh
- SAG – Beria – Neshama – Tabur
- MA – Yetzira – Ruach
- BON – Assiya – Nefesh

The World of Atzilut

6 Partzuf Atik
- Rosh – Keter – Yechida – Peh
- AB – Atzilut – Haya – Chazeh
- SAG – Beria – Neshama – Tabur
- MA – Yetzira – Ruach
- BON – Assiya – Nefesh

7 Partzuf AA
- Rosh – Keter – Yechida – Peh
- AB – Atzilut – Haya – Chazeh
- SAG – Beria – Neshama
- MA – Yetzira – Ruach
- BON – Assiya – Nefesh

8 Partzuf AVI
- Rosh – Keter – Yechida – Peh
- AB – Atzilut – Haya
- SAG – Beria – Neshama – Tabur
- MA – Yetzira – Ruach
- BON – Assiya – Nefesh

9 Partzuf YESHSUT
- Rosh – Keter – Yechida – Peh
- AB – Atzilut – Haya – Chazeh
- SAG – Beria – Neshama – Tabur
- MA – Yetzira – Ruach
- BON – Assiya – Nefesh

10 Partzuf ZON
- Rosh – Keter – Yechida – Peh
- AB – Atzilut – Haya – Chazeh
- SAG – Beria – Neshama – Tabur
- MA – Yetzira – Ruach
- BON – Assiya – Nefesh
- The World of Beria
- The World of Yetzira
- Sium of Atzilut – Parsa
- The World of Assiya
- Place of the World of Yetzira
- Place of the World of Assiya

Kav Ein Sof, beam of the Light of Infinity

Sium

Nekuda de Olam HaZeh - the Point of This world

Fig. 9
The ascent of the Worlds of ABYA to the level of Yechida with regard to the initial state of the World AK.

The dotted lines show connection and reception in Rosh of each Partzuf of the World of Atzilut and the corresponding Partzuf of AK

The World of Atzilut

10 Partzuf ZON
- Rosh – Keter – Yechida – Peh
- AB – Atzilut – Haya – Chazeh
- SAG – Beria – Neshama – Tabur
- MA – Yetzira – Ruach
- BON – Assiya – Nefesh
- The World of Beria
- The World of Yetzira
- The World of Assiya
- Place of the World of Beria
- Place of the World of Yetzira
- Place of the World of Assiya

9 Partzuf YESHSUT
- Rosh – Keter – Yechida – Peh
- AB – Atzilut – Haya – Chazeh
- SAG – Beria – Neshama – Tabur
- MA – Yetzira – Ruach
- BON – Assiya – Nefesh

8 Partzuf AVI
- Rosh – Keter – Yechida – Peh
- AB – Atzilut – Haya – Chazeh
- SAG – Beria – Neshama – Tabur
- MA – Yetzira – Ruach
- BON – Assiya – Nefesh

7 Partzuf AA
- Rosh – Keter – Yechida – Peh
- AB – Atzilut – Haya – Chazeh
- SAG – Beria – Neshama – Tabur
- MA – Yetzira – Ruach
- BON – Assiya – Nefesh

6 Partzuf Atik
- Rosh – Keter – Yechida – Peh
- AB – Atzilut – Haya – Chazeh
- SAG – Beria – Neshama – Tabur
- MA – Yetzira – Ruach
- BON – Assiya – Nefesh

Sium of Atzilut – Parsa

The World of AK

5 Partzuf BON
- Rosh – Keter – Yechida – Peh
- AB – Atzilut – Haya – Chazeh
- SAG – Beria – Neshama – Tabur
- MA – Yetzira – Ruach
- BON – Assiya – Nefesh

4 Partzuf MA
- Rosh – Keter – Yechida – Peh
- AB – Atzilut – Haya – Chazeh
- SAG – Beria – Neshama – Tabur
- MA – Yetzira – Ruach
- BON – Assiya – Nefesh

3 Partzuf SAG
- Rosh – Keter – Yechida – Peh
- AB – Atzilut – Haya – Chazeh
- SAG – Beria – Neshama – Tabur
- MA – Yetzira – Ruach
- BON – Assiya – Nefesh

2 Partzuf AB
- Rosh – Keter – Yechida – Peh
- AB – Atzilut – Haya – Chazeh
- SAG – Beria – Neshama – Tabur
- MA – Yetzira – Ruach
- BON – Assiya – Nefesh

1 Partzuf Keter
- Rosh – Keter – Yechida – Peh
- AB – Atzilut – Haya – Chazeh
- SAG – Beria – Neshama – Tabur
- MA – Yetzira – Ruach
- BON – Assiya – Nefesh

Kav Ein Sof, beam of the Light of Infinity

Sium

Nekuda de Olam HaZeh - the Point of This world

Fig. 10

The ascent of the Worlds of AK and ABYA to the level of Neshama with regard to the line of Infinity.

The dotted lines show connection and reception in Rosh of each Partzuf of the World of Atzilut and the corresponding Partzuf of AK.

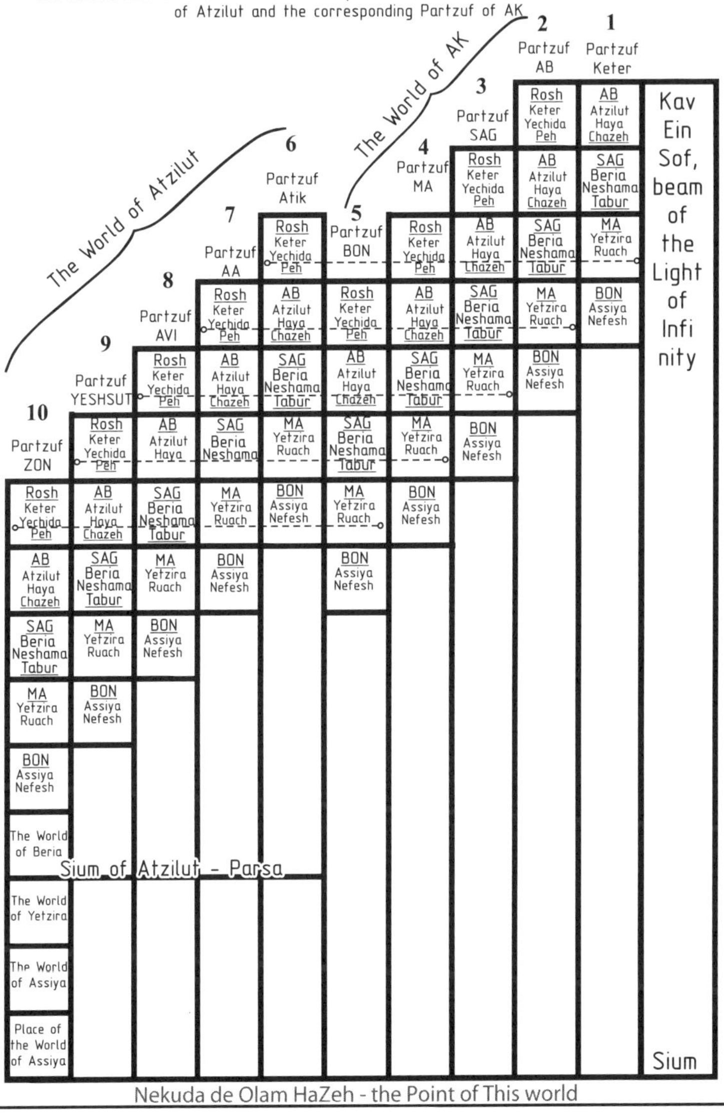

The World of AK

The World of Atzilut

1 Partzuf Keter
AB Atzilut Haya Chazeh
SAG Beria Neshama Tabur
MA Yetzira Ruach
BON Assiya Nefesh

2 Partzuf AB
Rosh Keter Yechida Peh
AB Atzilut Haya Chazeh
SAG Beria Neshama Tabur
MA Yetzira Ruach
BON Assiya Nefesh

3 Partzuf SAG
Rosh Keter Yechida Peh
AB Atzilut Haya Chazeh
SAG Beria Neshama Tabur
MA Yetzira Ruach
BON Assiya Nefesh

4 Partzuf MA
Rosh Keter Yechida Peh
AB Atzilut Haya Chazeh
SAG Beria Neshama Tabur
MA Yetzira Ruach
BON Assiya Nefesh

5 Partzuf BON
Rosh Keter Yechida Peh
AB Atzilut Haya Chazeh
SAG Beria Neshama Tabur
MA Yetzira Ruach
BON Assiya Nefesh

6 Partzuf Atik
Rosh Keter Yechida Peh
AB Atzilut Haya Chazeh
SAG Beria Neshama Tabur
MA Yetzira Ruach
BON Assiya Nefesh

7 Partzuf AA
Rosh Keter Yechida Peh
AB Atzilut Haya Chazeh
SAG Beria Neshama
MA Yetzira Ruach
BON Assiya Nefesh

8 Partzuf AVI
Rosh Keter Yechida Peh
AB Atzilut Haya
SAG Beria Neshama Tabur
MA Yetzira Ruach
BON Assiya Nefesh

9 Partzuf YESHSUT
Rosh Keter Yechida Peh
AB Atzilut Haya Chazeh
SAG Beria Neshama Tabur
MA Yetzira Ruach
BON Assiya Nefesh

10 Partzuf ZON
Rosh Keter Yechida Peh
AB Atzilut Haya Chazeh
SAG Beria Neshama Tabur
MA Yetzira Ruach
BON Assiya Nefesh
The World of Beria
The World of Yetzira
The World of Assiya
Place of the World of Assiya

Sium of Atzilut - Parsa

Kav Ein Sof, beam of the Light of Infinity

Sium

Nekuda de Olam HaZeh - the Point of This world

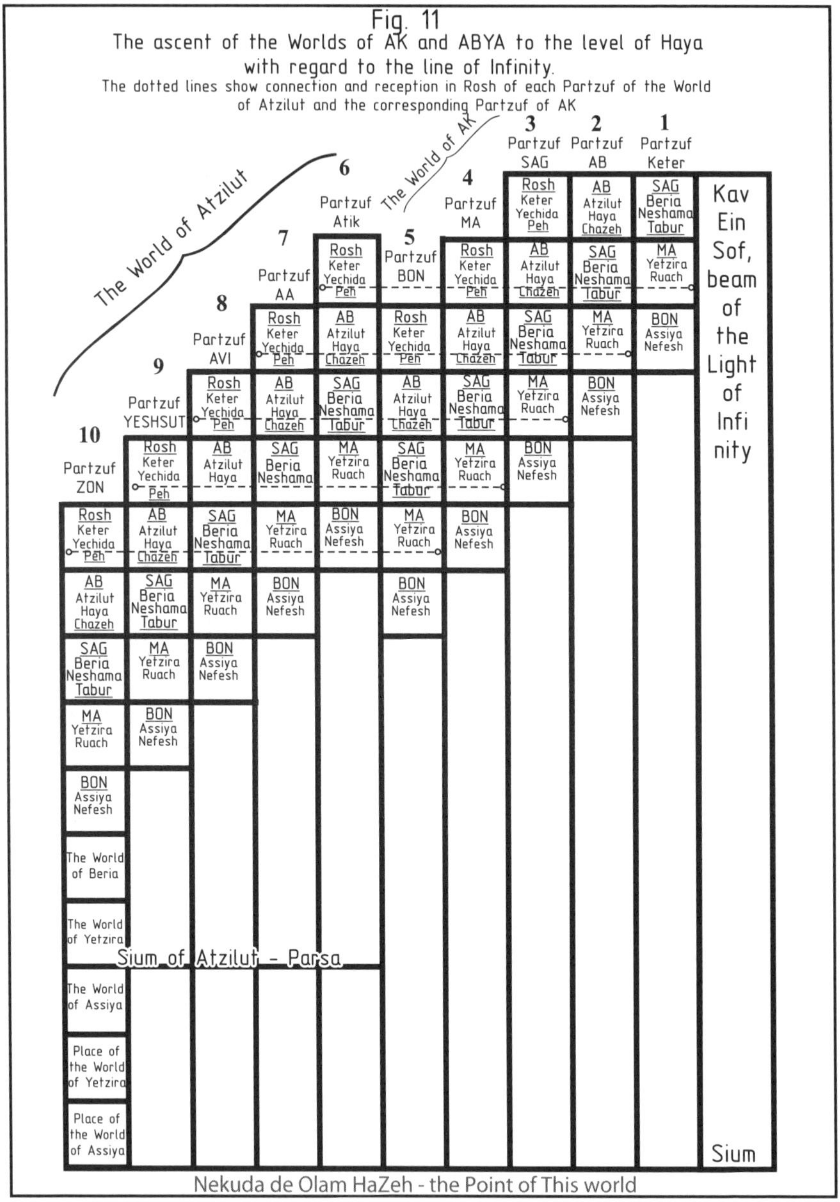

Fig. 11
The ascent of the Worlds of AK and ABYA to the level of Haya with regard to the line of Infinity.
The dotted lines show connection and reception in Rosh of each Partzuf of the World of Atzilut and the corresponding Partzuf of AK

The World of Atzilut
The World of AK

10 Partzuf ZON
Rosh Keter Yechida Peh
AB Atzilut Haya Chazeh
SAG Beria Neshama Tabur
MA Yetzira Ruach
BON Assiya Nefesh
The World of Beria
The World of Yetzira
The World of Assiya
Place of the World of Yetzira
Place of the World of Assiya

9 Partzuf YESHSUT
Rosh Keter Yechida Peh
AB Atzilut Haya Chazeh
SAG Beria Neshama Tabur
MA Yetzira Ruach
BON Assiya Nefesh

8 Partzuf AVI
Rosh Keter Yechida Peh
AB Atzilut Haya
SAG Beria Neshama Tabur
MA Yetzira Ruach
BON Assiya Nefesh

7 Partzuf AA
Rosh Keter Yechida Peh
AB Atzilut Haya Chazeh
SAG Beria Neshama
MA Yetzira Ruach
BON Assiya Nefesh

6 Partzuf Atik
Rosh Keter Yechida Peh
AB Atzilut Haya Chazeh
SAG Beria Neshama Tabur
MA Yetzira Ruach
BON Assiya Nefesh

5 Partzuf BON
Rosh Keter Yechida Peh
AB Atzilut Haya Chazeh
SAG Beria Neshama Tabur
MA Yetzira Ruach
BON Assiya Nefesh

4 Partzuf MA
Rosh Keter Yechida Peh
AB Atzilut Haya Chazeh
SAG Beria Neshama Tabur
MA Yetzira Ruach
BON Assiya Nefesh

3 Partzuf SAG
Rosh Keter Yechida Peh
AB Atzilut Haya Chazeh
SAG Beria Neshama Tabur
MA Yetzira Ruach
BON Assiya Nefesh

2 Partzuf AB
AB Atzilut Haya Chazeh
SAG Beria Neshama Tabur
MA Yetzira Ruach
BON Assiya Nefesh

1 Partzuf Keter
SAG Beria Neshama Tabur
MA Yetzira Ruach
BON Assiya Nefesh

Kav Ein Sof, beam of the Light of Infinity
Sium

Sium of Atzilut - Parsa

Nekuda de Olam HaZeh - the Point of This world

Fig. 12

The ascent of the Worlds of AK and ABYA to the level of Yechida with regard to the line of Infinity.

The dotted lines show connection and reception in Rosh of each Partzuf of the World of Atzilut and the corresponding Partzuf of AK

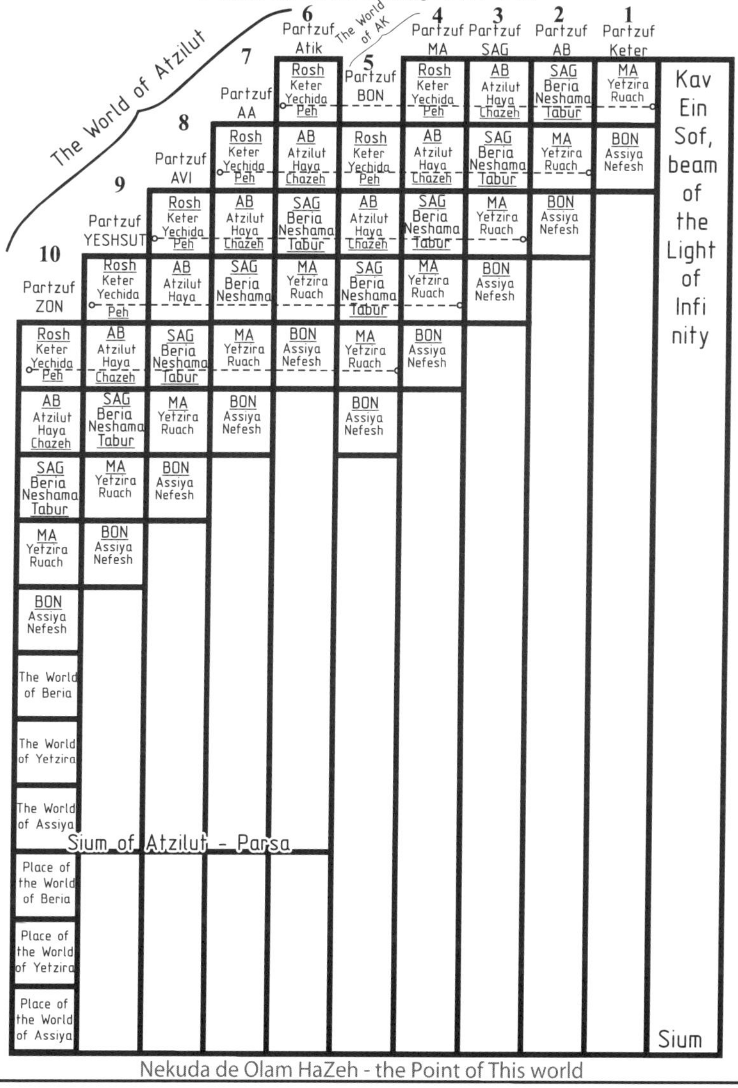

The World of Atzilut

The World of AK

1 Partzuf Keter: MA Yetzira Ruach; BON Assiya Nefesh

2 Partzuf AB: SAG Beria Neshama Tabur; MA Yetzira Ruach; BON Assiya Nefesh

3 Partzuf SAG: AB Atzilut Haya Chazeh; SAG Beria Neshama Tabur; MA Yetzira Ruach; BON Assiya Nefesh

4 Partzuf MA: Rosh Keter Yechida Peh; AB Atzilut Haya Chazeh; SAG Beria Neshama Tabur; MA Yetzira Ruach; BON Assiya Nefesh

5 Partzuf BON: Rosh Keter Yechida Peh; AB Atzilut Haya Chazeh; SAG Beria Neshama Tabur; MA Yetzira Ruach; BON Assiya Nefesh

6 Partzuf Atik: Rosh Keter Yechida Peh; AB Atzilut Haya Chazeh; SAG Beria Neshama Tabur; MA Yetzira Ruach; BON Assiya Nefesh

7 Partzuf AA: Rosh Keter Yechida Peh; AB Atzilut Haya Chazeh; SAG Beria Neshama; MA Yetzira Ruach; BON Assiya Nefesh

8 Partzuf AVI: Rosh Keter Yechida Peh; AB Atzilut Haya; SAG Beria Neshama Tabur; MA Yetzira Ruach; BON Assiya Nefesh

9 Partzuf YESHSUT: Rosh Keter Yechida Peh; AB Atzilut Haya Chazeh; SAG Beria Neshama Tabur; MA Yetzira Ruach; BON Assiya Nefesh

10 Partzuf ZON: Rosh Keter Yechida Peh; AB Atzilut Haya Chazeh; SAG Beria Neshama Tabur; MA Yetzira Ruach; BON Assiya Nefesh; The World of Beria; The World of Yetzira; The World of Assiya; Place of the World of Beria; Place of the World of Yetzira; Place of the World of Assiya

Kav Ein Sof, beam of the Light of Infinity

Sium of Atzilut - Parsa

Sium

Nekuda de Olam HaZeh - the Point of This world

KABBALISTIC TERMS GLOSSARY

A

ABYA, the impure worlds (אבי"ע של קליפות) - oppose the pure (holy) worlds of the *ABYA*, but take the space from the *ZON de Atzilut* and below. The *Klipot* are beneath the holy, pure forces in the place of absolute emptiness, below the line of *Sium* (end), under *Malchut*, which ends all pure desires (*Kedusha*). After the *Tzimtzum Aleph* their place was under the *Partzuf AK* (below the legs of *Adam Kadmon*). However, after the *Tzimtzum Bet*, when the *Malchut Mesayemet* rose to *Bina* in the *Guf de Partzuf Nekudot de SAG*, the "*Parsa*" (limit of holiness) was formed there. "The place" for the worlds of the *BYA* emerged under it. Since this place was free from holiness, it was completely occupied by the impure forces.

Achar Kach (אח"כ) after that - an effect of a certain cause.

Achiza (אחיזה) a grip - like a branch that sucks water from the root, the *Klipot* gather in the place of deficiency in holiness. The extent of the lack of holiness makes up "a pipe", through which they suck (receive) power and life energy.

Achor be Achor (אב"א) back to back - the correction with the help of the light of *Bina*. i.e., "*Hafetz Hesed*". In the absence of the *Ohr Hochma*, the *Kli* is corrected by means of the *Ohr Bina*, which provides it with the sensation of perfection.

Achor be Panim (אב"פ) back to face - the *Panim* (face) *de Malchut* is a reception of only the light of *Hochma*, which is possible only by dressing it in the light of *Hassadim*. Hence, *ZA* corrects *Malchut* by way of a *Zivug de Achor be Panim*, passing the *Ohr Hassadim de Achoraim* to the *Panim de Malchut*.

Achor, Achoraim (אחור, אחוריים) opposite side – 1) The *Kli* without the light of *Hochma*; 2) The *Kli* or its part, which does not work for the sake of reception or bestowal; 3) the part of the *Kli* below the *Chazeh* (chest) *de Partzuf*.

Achoraim shel Nukva (אחוריים של נוקבא) the opposite side of the *Nukva* – the *Sefirot NHY* (*Netzah, Hod* and *Yesod*) of the *Nukva Mesayemet* of the world of *Atzilut*; it borders on the *Klipot*, which stick to the *Achoraim* (the place where there's a lack of the *Ohr Hochma*).

Achsadrin (אכסדראין) "outer rooms" – the *NHY de Zeir Anpin*. Revelation, sensation of the light of Hochma.

Adam Kadmon (אדם קדמון) – The first world that emerged after the *TA*. It receives the light from the World of Infinity and spreads down to "our" world. It is called "*Adam*", because its *Sefirot de Yosher* with the light of bestowal is a root of man in our world. The name "*Kadmon*" (first, original) derives from the influence of the *TA* on it.

Adrin (אדרין) "inner rooms" – the *HaGaT de Zeir Anpin* filled with the light of *Hassadim* without the luminescence of *Hochma*; hence they are called "inner".

Agol (עגול) circular – when there's no difference between up and down in the four phases of the "desire to receive". Hence, the four *Behinot* are called four spheres, one inside another.

Aleph (א) – the first letter of the Hebrew alphabet; the numerical value is 1.

Aliyah (עליה) ascent, rise – purification, since there is a similarity of properties with the World of Infinity. The rule states: the purer object is higher, the coarser object is lower.

Alpaim Amah Tehum Shabbat (אלפיים אמה תחום שבת) two-thousand-*Amah* domain of the *Shabbat* – the real position of the worlds, their second state before the Fall, when ZA stands in the place of *Arich Anpin*, *Malchut* – in the place of *Abba ve Ima*, *Beria* – in the place of the *YESHSUT*, *Yetzira* –in the place of ZA, the four first *Sefirot* of the world of *Assiya* stand in the place of the *Nukva* and dress onto the world of *Yetzira*. The six last *Sefirot de Assiya* stand in the place of the six first *Sefirot de Beria*. The six first *Sefirot* of the place of *Beria* from the *Parsa* to the *Chazeh* are called "*Iburo shel haYir*" (conception of a city). They refer to the world of *Atzilut*, because the six lower *Sefirot de Assiya* remained there.

Ani (**אני**) I – *Malchut*, when it is revealed, is called "*Ani*". When *Malchut* is concealed, it is called "*Hu*" (He).

Arich Anpin (**א"א**) – The *Partzuf* filled with the light of *Hochma*. Small luminescence of *Hochma* is called *Zeir Anpin*.

Aroch (**ארוך**) long – reception (for the sake of bestowal) of the *Ohr Hochma*.

Assiya (**עשייה**) – the 10 *Sefirot* of *Malchut*, which receives the light from ZA.

Atzmut (**עצמות**) essence – the light of *Hochma*, since it is the essence of life of the creation.

Avir (**אויר**) air – The *Ohr Ruach*, the light of *Hassadim*.

Avir Reykani (**אויר ריקני**) – The light of *Hassadim* before being dressed on the light of *Hochma*.

Aviut (**עביות**) – a great "desire to receive", which attracts the light, hence it is called "the inner part of the *Kli*".

Avot (**אבות**) fathers – *Sefirot HaGaT* as regards *Sefirot NHY* (their "sons").

Awzen (**אוזן**) – the level of *Bina* of the 10 *Sefirot de Rosh*.

Ayn (**ע**) – the sixteenth letter of the Hebrew alphabet; the numerical value: 70.

The 24 *Sefirot* ("the space empty of the light") were left from the *Chazeh de Beria* to *Sium*. The 16 *Sefirot* from the *Parsa* to the *Chazeh de*

Yetzira are called "*Tehum Shabbat*". *Tehum Shabbat* constitutes of the 10 *Sefirot* from the *Chazeh de Beria* to the *Chazeh de Yetzira*, also called the 2000 *Amah*. The 14 *Sefirot* from the *Chazeh de Yetzira* to the *Sium* are called "*Mador haKlipot*" (the impure forces section). *Yir* (city) is the world of *Atzilut*. The *Parsa* is the *Sium* (end, limit) of a city.

The vessels got broken, because the light of *Hochma* descended from the *Rosh* (head) *de* SAG wishing to spread under the *Parsa* in all the ten *Sefirot* down to the *Sium de Galgalta*, as before the *TB*. This happened because the GE joined the *AHP* both in the *Rosh* and the *Guf* (head and body) of the *Partzuf Nekudim*. But before the light could pass through the empty space (*Halal Panui*), the vessels got broken and died, for the *Parsa* continued to exist. The light rose back, while the vessels fell under the *Parsa* and got mixed with the *Klipot* in the worlds of the *BYA*. The vessels of the *AHP de Guf* (but not the *Rosh*) *de Nekudim* fell under the *Parsa*. Hence, the *Klipot* are found only in the space from the *ZON de Atzilut* and below.

B

Bait, or Heichal (בית, היכל) house or palace – the part of *Malchut* detached from the inner *Kelim*, which turned into the *Kli* for reception of the Surrounding Light (*Ohr Makif*).

Bassar (בשר) flesh – the *Behina Gimel* called *Zeir Anpin*. In the ten *Sefirot* that spread outwardly we distinguish: *Mocha* (brain), *Atzamot* (bones), *Gidin* (tendons), *Basar* (flesh) and *Or* (skin).

Beer (באר) a well – the *Yesod de Nukva*, from which (like from a well) the Reflected Light rises.

Beit HaMikdash (בית המקדש) Temple – *Beria* of this world.

Ben (בן) son – the lower spiritual object as regards the upper.

Beria (בריאה) creation – the creation of "*Yesh mi Ayn*" (existence from absence). It manifests under the *Parsa* as the *Aviut*, "desire to receive".

Bet (ב) – the second letter of the Hebrew alphabet; the numerical value: 2.

Beten (בטן) abdomen – the lower third of the *Sefira Tifferet* in every *Partzuf*. This is where pregnancy and delivery take place.

Bina (בינה) – research by means of a "cause-and-effect" method.

Binyamin (בנימין) – a screen lifting the Reflected Light from the *Yud de Zeir Anpin*.

Birur (בירור) test, selection – separation, isolation of the *Behina Dalet*, which impedes reception the Supreme light.

Birur and Tikkun (בירור ותיקון) selection and correction – selection is a separation of 32 (*Lamed Bet*) sparks, *Malchuyot* as waste (*Psolet*). 288 (*Rapach*) sparks remain inside the system of holiness, which is corrected by the light of the the *Partzuf Aba*. A level, the *Partzuf* cannot exist without *Malchut*. So, thanks to the screen of *Partzuf Ima* the properties of *Bina-Ima* and *Malchut* get mixed. This is called "inclusion of judgment in mercy". As a result of this, 32 new *Malchuyot* from *Bina-Ima* are added to 288 pure sparks, which brings the number of the lights to 320 (*Shach*). Selection (*Birur*) of adequate properties "for the sake of bestowing upon the Creator" is possible only if the light of *Abba*is available: it does not shine in the *Behina Dalet*, thus it gets separated from all the other adequate *Behinot*, properties. Then correction is carried out by the light of *Ima*.

Bohu (בוהו) – *Arich Anpin*, in which the Creator is revealed.

Bolet (בולט) protruding – luminescence of the *Ohr Hochma*.

Boreh (בורא) the Creator – the name refers only to the creation of previously non-existent "desire to receive".

Brit (ברית) union – the place of the *Aviut* and a screen, where the interaction with the Supreme Light takes place.

BYA of This world (בי"ע שבעולם הזה): the place of the Temple – the world of *Beria*, the Land of Israel – the world of *Yetzira*, outside of Israel – the world of *Assiya*, desert – the place of the impure forces.

C

Chaf, Kaf (כ, ך) – the eleventh letter of the Hebrew alphabet; the numerical value: 20.

Chama BeNartika (חמה בנרתיקה) – the *Sefirot NHY de Zeir Anpin*, dressed in the *Toch de Nukva*.

Chazeh (חזה) chest – the end of the *Tzimtzum Bet*. Hence, there are the *Kelim de Panim*, the *GE*, face above the *Chazeh*. The *TB* has no power over them.

Chet (ח) – the eighth letter of the Hebrew alphabet; the numerical value: 8.

D

Dadei Behema (דדי בהמה) nipples of a beast – luminescence of *Malchut* without mitigation by the light of *Hassadim*, the lower third of the *Sefirot Netzah* and *Hod* of the *Partzuf Atik*, positioned in the world of *Beria*.

Dadim (דדים) nipples – mediator between the upper and the lower levels, when the upper affects the lower even before the lower can rise to it.

Dalet (ד) the fourth letter of the Hebrew alphabet; the numerical value: 4.

Dalet Tzurot (ד' צורות) four forms – the *Aviut* or desire in the created being is called its material. The four levels of the *Aviut* are called "the *Dalet Tzurot*".

Dalet Yesodot (ד' יסודות) four foundations – four properties of the *Aviut* in the *Kli de Malchut*.

Dam (דם) blood – the *Aviut de Malchut*, governed by the *TA*, which prevents the reception of the light. This makes *Malchut* "bleed"; it wishes to receive the light, hence it is called “blood”. When this *Aviut* refers to the *NHY*, it is called “*Dam BeMakor*” (blood in the source). Its reception is forbidden. However, when this *Aviut* rises to *HaGaT*, which is not its place, it is mitigated (sweetened) there and turns to “milk”.

Dam Lida (דם לידה) birth blood – when *MAN de Zeir Anpin* in the *AVI* rises, *MAN de Zeir Anpin* and all the *Partzufim* that would emerge from ZA in the future down to the last *Partzuf de Assiya*, simultaneously rise with it. During the months of pregnancy (*Ibur*) only *MAN de ZA* is purified. Its *Partzufey de Ibur* are born on this *MAN*. During birth each *MAN* unrelated to ZA gets outside as *Dam Lida*. Birth blood is also called “impure blood”.

Dam Mitapech LeHalav (דם מתהפך לחלב) – See **Dam**.

Dam Tameh (דם טמא) impure blood – birth blood.

Derech Tzar (דרך צר) narrow road – a limited reception the light in *Hassadim*.

Dibur (דיבור) speech – the 10 *Sefirot* of the light passing through the *Malchut de Rosh* called the *Peh* (mouth) to the *Toch* (body). The inner *Partzuf* of the *Nukva* is called “*Dibur*” (speech). If it disappears and the *Nukva* is left only with the outer *Partzuf*, it is called “*Ilem*” (mute), since the inner *Partzuf* is the *Gar* and the outer is the *Vak*.

Dmut (דמות) image – Letters *Yud*, *Hey* and *Vav* of the Name *HaVaYaH* constitute “*Tzelem*”, while the last letter *Hey* of *HaVaYaH* is *Dmut*.

Dofen (דופן) side – the *Aviut* of a screen is a vessel for reception of the light. It is called “*Dofen Kli*”, because each *Kli* is made up of its sides (*Dfanot*). Four degrces of the *Aviut* are four the *Klipot* (sides) in thickness of the *Dofen* dressed one on another inwardly and outwardly. The coarser property in *Dofen Kli* attracts more light and is regarded the inner part of the *Kli*, i.e., The *Behina Dalet* is more interior than the *Behina Gimel*, while the *Behina Gimel* is more interior than the *Behina Bet* etc.

Dormita (**דורמיטא**) sleep – when the lower *Partzuf* rises to the upper as MAN, all lights disappear from it; the *Partzuf* is considered to be below and has just enough light to sustain life, which is regarded as a state of "slumber".

Dvekut (**דבקות**) merging – similarity of properties in two spiritual objects.

E

Echad (**אחד**) One – The Supreme Light that emanates from the Creator and spreads down without any change.

Eden Elyon (**עדן עליון**) – *Yesod* of the world of *Beria*.

Eden Tachton (**עדן תחתון**) – *Yesod* of the world of *Assiya*.

Eichut Makom (**איכות מקום**) place quality. Place quantity is a number of levels in this place. Place quality is the importance of the level.

Ein (**אין**) non-existent – concealment of the *Ohr Hochma*. Presence of the *Ohr Hochma* is called "*Yesh*" (existent).

Elohim Acherim (**אלוהים אחרים**) "other gods" – the *Klipot* attached to the opposite side of the *Nukva*, since there is no perfection in its selection and correction up to the *Gmar Tikkun* (the End of Correction).

Elyon (**עליון**) supreme, upper one – more important.

Emtzai (**אמצעי**) a means, which unites two remote ends, properties.

Eretz Edom (**ארץ אדום**) – when *Malchut* is included in *Bina*, bina is called "*Eretz Edom*".

Eretz Elyona (**ארץ עליונה**) the Upper Land – *Bina*.

Eretz Israel (**ארץ ישראל**) – *Yetzira* of This world.

Eretz Tachtona (**ארץ תחתונה**) the Lower Land – *Malchut*.

Et (**את**) *Malchut* is called "*Et*", because it includes all letters from *Aleph* to *Tav*.

Et Ratzon (עת רצון) time of desire – time of a *Zivug* in *Gadlut*, when owing to the light *AB-SAG* "hair" disappears and the light of *Hochma* shines.

Etz (עץ) – *Yesod de ZA*, middle line, the place of a *Zivug*.

Etz HaChaim (עץ החיים) tree of life – a place from the *Chazeh* and above, where the light of *Hassadim* is concealed – the light of the opposite side of *Bina*; there are no *Klipot* there.

Etz HaDa'at (עץ הדעת) tree of knowledge - a place from *Chazeh* and below called "*Assiya*". *Yesod*, i.e., the middle line called "tree" is most important.

Etz HaDa'at Tov VeRa (עץ הדעת טוב ורע) the tree of knowledge of good and evil – stretches from the *Chazeh* down to *ZA*. There is some luminescence of *Hochma* there, hence the *Klipot* called "the evil" stick to that place.

Evel (הבל) – the Reflected Light that rises from a screen.

Eyvarim (איברים) organs – the *Sefirot de Guf* of *Partzuf*, parts of body of the *Partzuf*.

G

Gadlut (גדלות) big state – A level's *Ohr Hochma*.

Gadol (גדול) big – revelation of the light of *Hochma*. Lack of the light of *Hochma* makes the small *Partzuf* (*Katan*).

Gag (גג) roof – *Keter* of each level.

Galgalim (גלגלים) wheels – the *Sefirot de Igulim* (circles), since, having neither the *Aviut* nor the *Hizdakchut*, the lights that fill them take a circular form.

Galgalta (גלגלתא) the *Partzuf Keter*. The *Ohr Hochma* fills its *Kli*.

Gan Eden (גן עדן) Garden of Eden – *Malchut* of the world of *Atzilut*. *Eden* means *Hochma*, *Gan* is *Malchut*. Since the entire world of *Atzilut* is *Hochma*, the *Malchut de Atzilut* is called "*Gan Eden*".

Gan Eden Elyon (גן עדן עליון) – in the world of *Beria* (*Bina*).

Gan Eden Tachton (גן עדן תחתון) – the *Yesod de Malchut* in the world of *Assiya*.

Gar (ג"ר) the first three – the lights of the *Rosh* (head), which precede the vessels. The *Sefirot Keter*, *Hochma* and *Bina* called "the *Rosh de Partzuf*".

Gar of Guf (ג"ר של גוף) the first three *Sefirot de Guf* – *Hesed*, *Gevura* and *Tifferet*.

Gashmiut (גשמיות) corporeality – all that is perceived and felt by five senses, or whatever is determined by place and time.

Gidin (גידין) tendons – the *Kli de Bina* in the 10 *Sefirot* of one level.

Gimel (ג) the third letter of the Hebrew alphabet; the numerical value: 3.

Guf (גוף) body – the place, where the light is received in a level. Owing to the dressing of the Reflected Light (*OH*) on the Direct Light (*OY*) in the *Rosh*, both lights spread in the desire. This reception forms the *Guf* of the *Partzuf*.

Gvul (גבול) boundary – a screen of a particular level.

Gzar (גזר) verdict – separation of *Malchut* from the *Kelim* that fell into the worlds of the *BYA*. The entire correction is dependent on it.

H

Habatat Panim (הבטת פנים) manifestation of face – spreading of the *Ohr Hochma*.

Hachana Lekabel (הכנה לקבל) readiness to receive – a condition, when the *Partzuf* has a screen with the *Aviut* sufficient to attract the light and interact with it.

Hafradat HaSigim (הפרדת הסיגים) separation of admixture. *Sigim* is *Malchut* mixed with seven *Malachim*, which led to breaking of the world of the *Nikudim*. Hence, the correction consists in separating *Malchut* from all broken vessels. This happens owing to the light of *Hochma*, the *Ohr Aba*. This correction is called "*Hafradat HaSigim*".

Hagdala (הגדלה) enlargement – a transition from *Katnut* (small state) to *Gadlut* (big state).

Haka'a (הכאה) stroke – a contact between the light and the screen, similar to an interaction between two solid objects, when one wants to penetrate the other, which resists the penetration.

Halal (חלל) space, emptiness – the *Behina Dalet* without the light. Due to the *TA* it is still within the Creator, but as an empty space without the light.

Halal Panui (חלל פנוי) empty space – by the power of the *TA Malchut* restricts the reception of the Supreme Light. The boundary is above the point of This world. Owing to the *TB*, the limit of the spreading of the light rises from the *Sium de Galgalta* to the *Chazeh de Nikudim*. From there and below an empty space was formed, the place where the future impure forces would emerge. But with the fall of the bestowing vessels (the *GE*) under the *Chazeh*, only the 14 *Sefirot* remained to accommodate the impure forces in the place of the worlds of the *BYA*.

After the First Adam's Fall, the boundary of holiness descended to *Bina de Malchut* of *Assiya* called "the Land of the lower Garden of Eden" and an empty space was formed there. It turns out that by way of breaking the vessels and through First Adam's Fall the empty space shrank, since it descended from the *Parsa* to *Bina* of the *Malchut de Assiya*, but then the *Klipot* found powers to build four worlds down to the *ZON de Atzilut*.

Halav (חלב) milk – the lights of *Hassadim*, which *Bina* gives to ZA after its birth (Zman *HaYenika*, a biennial period feeding). In ZA the lights of *Hassadim* turn into *Hochma*. This is called "milk turns to blood".

Halon (חלון) window – the power of the Reflected Light that allows receiving the light in the *Kli*.

Hamtaka (המתקה) sweetening – as a result of the *Shevira* (breaking of the vessels), the *Kelim* are in need of the light that would correct them, sweeten their bitterness (power of judgment-restriction), so that the outer forces wouldn't seize them.

Harchaka (הרחקה) – the correction of the *Kli* by way of refusing to receive the *Ohr Hochma*, preferring the reception of the *Ohr Hassadim*.

Hash'ala (השאלה) borrowing – the *Kelim NHY de Ima*, which it (*Ima*) passes to *Zeir Anpin*, whereupon ZA receives the light in these *Kelim*.

Hashva'a Achat (השוואה אחת) equivalence of properties – when there is no distinction in the four phases of the "desire to receive".

HaVaYaH-ADNY (הויה"ה-אדני) – A *Zivug Panim be Panim* between ZA and the *Nukva* of the world of *Atzilut*, designated by a combination of their letters, where the first *Yud* means the *Hochma de* ZA and the last – the *Hochma de Malchut*.

Hay (חי) life, the numerical value: 18 – *Yesod*, since it elevates the 9 *Sefirot* of the Reflected Light and receives the 9 *Sefirot* of the Direct Light in them.

Haya (חיה) – the light of *Hochma*.

Hazara LeMa'atzil (חזרה למאציל) back to the Creator – spreading of the light during the weakening of a screen.

Heilot HaMalchut (חילות המלכות) see also **Tzvaot HaMalchut** – the *Partzufim* that emerge from *Malchut* of the worlds of the *BYA*.

Hevdel (הבדל) difference – a screen's action, which divides the *Partzuf*, so that no impure desires would stick to the light.

Hey (ה) – the fifth letter of the Hebrew alphabet; the numerical value: 5.

Hibuk Smol (חיבוק שמאל) embrace from left – spreading of the light from ZA to *Malchut* so that it would elevate the *AHP*.

Histaklut (הסתכלות) scrutinizing – spreading of the light from the World of Infinity to the screen. The light of the World of Infinity is always the *Ohr Hochma*, the light for the eyes, for the sight.

Histaklut Aleph (הסתכלות א') scrutinizing – See **Histaklut.**

Histaklut Bet (הסתכלות ב') - spreading of the light from the World of Infinity to the screen, which rises from the *Tabur* to the *Peh*. On its way up the screen makes *Zivugim* that lead to the emergence of the *Partzufey Nekudot*.

Hitchadshut HaNeshamot (התחדשות הנשמות) renewal of the souls – spreading of the light of *Hochma* in the souls, as was during the *Gadlut de Nikudim*, but disappeared after the breaking of the vessels. The souls also were in this state before the sin of *Adam HaRishon*, but again lost it after the breaking of the souls into many fragments.

Hitdabkut Klipot (התדבקות קליפות) adhesion of the *Klipot* – the *Klipot* stick to the opposite side of *Malchut*, because it limits the reception of the Supreme Light; below it is complete darkness. Therefore, the *Klipot* touch the bottom point of *Malchut*, which is called "*Hitdabkut Klipot*".

Hitkashrut (התקשות) connection – the 10 *Sefirot* of the Reflected Light, which rise from the *Masach de Rosh* of *Partzuf*, dress onto the 10 *Sefirot* of the Direct Light and connect with them, since the lights precede the vessels in the *Rosh de Partzuf*.

Hitpashtut (התפשטות) spreading – the light spreading from the Creator to the created being in accordance with its "desire to receive" the light.

Hitpashtut Aleph (**התפשטות א'**) – the light of the *Ta'amim*.

Hitpashtut Bet (**התפשטות ב'**) – the secondary entry of the light after purification (*Hizdakchut*) of the screen, because now there are vessels fit to receive the light.

Hitrachkut MiOhr Elyon (**התרחקות מאור עליון**) distancing from the Supreme Light – the closer an object is to spiritual emptiness, the farther it is from the Supreme Light.

Hitzoniut HaMalchut (**חיצוניות המלכות**) the outer part of *Malchut* – the purest part of the *Kli*, which is a vessel for the Surrounding Light.

Hochma (**חכמה**) wisdom – the knowledge of the final result of any existing phenomenon.

Hochma (**חכמה**) wisdom – the light of the essence of the creation.

Hochma Ila'a (**חכמה עלאה**) the supreme wisdom – the light of *Hochma* in ZA.

Hochma Keduma (**חכמה קדומה**) preceding wisdom – the light of *Hochma* in the *Partzuf Arich Anpin*, which does not shine in the world of *Atzilut*. Only the light of *Hochma shel Lamed-Bet Netivot* shines there.

Hochma shel Lamed-Bet Netivot (**חכמה של ל"ב נתיבות**) wisdom of 32 ways – the light of *Hochma* received by *Bina* for ZA, which constitutes 22 letters of *Bina* + the 10 *Sefirot* of the *ZON* in *Bina*.

Hochma Tata'a (**חכמה תתאה**) the lower wisdom – the light of *Hochma* in *Nukva*.

Holam (**חולם**) – the light above letters.

Homer (**חומר**) material – thickness of the *Partzuf* in the *Behina Dalet* ("desire to receive"). It possesses length, width, depth and 6 ends: up, down, east, west, north and south.

Hoshech (**חושך**) darkness – the *Behina Dalet* ("desire to receive") without the light because of *TA*.

Hotem (**חוטם**) nose – the *Sefira* of the ZA *de Rosh*.

Hotam (חותם) stamp – the Reflected Light, rising up from a screen and dressing the 10 *Sefirot de Rosh* of the *Partzuf*. "*Nihtam*" (imprint) is the same 10 *Sefirot* passing from the *Rosh* to the *Guf* of the *Partzuf*.

Hurva (חורבא) ruins, desert – the place of the *Klipot* of This world, a lifeless place.

Hutz LaAretz (חוץ לארץ) abroad – *Assiya* of This world. *Beria* is the place of the Temple. *Yetzira* is the Land of Israel.

I

Ibur (עיבור) conception – A *Zivug de Katnut*.

Ibur Aleph (עיבור א') – A *Zivug* on the conception of *Partzuf*.

Ibur Bet (עיבור ב') – A *Zivug* for reception of the additional light of *Hochma* in *Partzuf*.

Iburo Shel Yir (עיבורו של עיר) conception of a city – the first six *Sefirot* of *Beria* that protrude from the world of *Atzilut* like a pregnant woman's belly.

Ihud (יחוד) unity – two different properties that became similar in their corrected intentions.

Ilem-Dibur (אלם-דיבור) mute-speaking – the 10 *Sefirot* of the light, which pass through the *Malchut de Rosh* into the *Toch de Partzuf* called the "*Peh*" (mouth). The inner *Partzuf de Nukva* is called "*Dibur*" (speech). If it disappears, leaving the *Nukva* only with the outer *Partzuf*, then the *Nukva* is called "*Ilem*" (mute), because the inner *Partzuf* is the *Gar* and the outer – the *Vak*.

Ima Tata'a (אמא תתאה) the lower Mother – *Malchut* of the world of *Atzilut*.

Israel (ישראל) or Moshe and Israel – the *Gar de Zeir Anpin* or inner *Partzuf*.

K

Kaf, Chaf (כ, ך) – the eleventh letter of the Hebrew alphabet; the numerical value: 20.

Kaf-Bet (22 – כ"ב) letters of the Hebrew alphabet. The letters are the *Kelim*, which the light dresses in. There are 22 basic letters (beside 5 ending letters called *Mantzepach*), which define all the *Partzufim*.

Kaf-Zayin (27 – כ"ז) letters of the Hebrew alphabet. 22 basic letters and 5 ending letters (*Mantzepach*). Owing to the 5 ending (limiting) properties in a screen, the lights spread from the *Rosh* of the *Partzuf* to its *Guf* giving birth to the *Kelim*, i.e., the other 22 letters.

Kamatz (קמץ) – accumulation of the light, pointing at the 10 *Sefirot de Rosh* before they dress in the *Guf* of the *Partzuf*. Spreading of the light in the *Guf* is called "aperture", letting the light in.

Kamut Makom (כמות מקום) place quantity – a number of levels in a particular place. Place quality of is the importance of the level.

Karka (קרקע) ground – *Malchut* of any level or world.

Katnut (קטנות) small state – the *Partzufim de Ibur* (conception) and *Yenika* (feeding), hence they have neither the *Rosh* nor the light of the *Mochin* (brain).

Katzar (קצר) short – a decreased amount of the *Ohr Hochma*. "*Rahav*" (broad) suggests spreading of the *Ohr Hassadim*. "*Tzar*" (narrow) means the restriction of the *Ohr Hassadim*. Spreading of the *Ohr Hochma* I called "length".

Kav (קו) line – the name points to the presence of up and down, and also at the scanty amount of the *Ohr Hochma* as compared to the previous light. The 10 *Sefirot* of the *Direct Light*, *Kelim* are also called "a pipe"; filled with the light, they are called "a line".

Kaved (כבד) liver – the inner *Kli* with the light *Nefesh*.

Kelim Hitzoniim (כלים חיצוניים) the outer *Kelim* – the *Kelim* of the opposite side (כלים של אחוריים) – the *Kelim* below the *Chazeh de Partzuf*.

Kelim shel Achoraim - See **Kelim Hitzoniim**

Kelim shel Panim (כלים של פנים) - the *Kelim* above the *Chazeh de Partzuf*.

Kesher (קשר) connection – the name of the correction of the *Kelim*, because the *Sefirot* are connected to such an extent that there's no opposition between them.

Kesher Sefirot (קשר ספירות) – connection between the *Sefirot* – the rise of *Malchut* to the *Eynaim* (eyes) connects the *Sefirot*.

Keter (כתר) crown – the root (*Shoresh*) of any level. Being the purest part, it surrounds the *Partzuf* from above.

Kisseh (כסא) throne – the world of *Beria*. The word derives from "*Kissui*" (cover) and "*Alama*" (concealment), because the light of *Hochma* is concealed there. It is also called "*Kisse*", since the light of *Hassadim* passing through the *Parsa* is considered the light of the *Vak*. It means a sitting position as regards the *Ohr Hochma* – the light of the *Gar* (standing position).

Kisseh Din (כסא דין) throne of judgment – *Malchut* filled with the light of the *Partzuf Ima* dressed in the *Malchut de Beria*.

Kisseh HaKavod (כסא הכבוד) throne of honor – the 10 *Sefirot* of the light *de Partzuf Ima*, which spread in the world of *Beria*: the *Gar* is called "*Kisse*"; the *Vak* is called "six ascents (steps) to the throne". *Malchut* that dresses in the *Malchut de Beria* is called "*Din*" (judgment), *Tchelet* or *Sandalfon*.

Kisseh Rachamim (כסא רחמים) throne of mercy – the first nine *Sefirot* of the *Partzuf Ima*.

Kista DeHayuta (קיסטא דחיותא) a pocketful of life-force – a micro dose of the light left in the *Partzuf*, which rises with *MAN* to the upper *Partzuf*. The light of the *Mochin* disappears from it at this time.

Kli (pl. Kelim) (כלי) vessel – a will to receive in the creation.

Kli HaMa'ale MAN (כלי המעלה מ"ן) the *Kli* raising *MAN* – the *AHP* of the upper *Partzuf* during *Gadlut*.

Kli LeOhr Makif (כלי לאור מקיף) the vessel for the Surrounding Light – the outer *Dofen* (side) of the *Kli*, i.e., its purer part.

Kli LeOhr Pnimi (כלי לאור פנימי) the vessel for the Inner Light – the inner part of *Dofen* (side) of the *Kli*, i.e., its coarser part. The vessel for the Surrounding Light is a half of the outer *Dofen* (side) of the *Kli*, i.e., its purer part.

Klipat Noga (קליפת נוגה) – the property of the light sparks, in which good and evil are mixed. When *Noga* receives the light in its good part, it also shines in the bad part.

Klipot (קליפות) impure forces – the egoistic desires opposite to the Supreme Light, which wishes only to bestow. Hence, they are detached from life and are called "dead".

Knafaim (כנפיים) wings – *Malchut* of the *Partzuf Ima* is always in *Katnut* (the small state), separating and protecting the ZON from the outer *Kelim*, since only a small luminescence of *Hochma* passes through it. The *Parsa* below the world of *Atzilut* is also *Malchut* of the *Partzuf Ima* and is called "*Na'al*" (shoe), protecting "legs" of the ZON. However, no light of *Hochma* passes through it.

Knesset Israel (כנסת ישראל) assembly of *Israel* – the *Partzuf Gar de Malchut*, receiving (*Knesset*) the lights from the *Gar de Zeir Anpin* called *Israel*.

Koach (כוח) strength – a potential quality similar to that of a seed growing into a tree.

Koach HaKlipa (הקליפה כוח) power of dark forces – the dressing of the lights that exit their vessels, due to the admixture of evil in them, fall into the impure forces and strengthen them.

Kol ve Dibur (קול ודיבור) voice and speech – a *Zivug* of the two inner *Partzufim* – ZA and the *Nukva*; also called *Neshika* ("kiss").

Kotel (כותל) The Wailing Wall – the screen of the opposite side of the *Partzuf Ima*, which repels the *Ohr Hochma* by the power of its state "*Hafetz Hesed*", preventing it from entering the *ZON*, because they are in *Katnut* (small state).

Kuf (ק) - the nineteenth letter of the Hebrew alphabet; the numerical value: 100.

L

Lamed (ל) – the twelfth letter of the Hebrew alphabet; the numerical value: 30.

Lamed Madregot BeGuf shel Nukva (למד מדרגות בגוף של נוקבא) thirty levels: conception, feeding and adulthood of the opposite side of the *AHP de Nukva*, where every period consists of the 10 *Sefirot*.

Lamed-Bet Elokim DeMa'ase BeReshit (ל"ב אלוקים דמעשה בראשית) thirty two channels, through which the light of *Hochma* comes to *Bina* ("*Elokim*"). It selects 288 sparks (the nine upper *Sefirot*) out of 320, leaving *Malchut* (32 sparks) below as waste.

Le'at (לאט) slowly, gradually – spreading of the light in a level according to cause and effect.

LeAtid Lavo (לעתיד לבוא) in the distant future – the light of *Tvunah* may be in ZA, and so be called "the world to come". The light of Ima, which ZA receives on a still higher level, is called "*LeAtid Lavo*".

Lemala (למעלה) – the comparison of properties of the upper and the lower spiritual objects.

Lev (לב) heart – the *Kli* of the light *Ruach* in the *Sefirot HaGaT*.

Levush (לבוש) clothes – the properties of ZA (free of the Inner Light), which turns into the *Kli* for the Surrounding Light. Moreover, each upper *Partzuf* is dressed on the lower.

Lida (**לידה**) birth – the emergence of the *Aviut* in the *Guf de ZA*, which differs from the *Aviut de Ima*. It is considered the birth and separation from *Ima* due to the difference of properties and is similar to changing place in the material world.

Loven Elyon (**לובן עליון**) – the light prior to entering the *Kli*, since all hues are distinguished only by the *Kli*.

M

MA (**מ"ה**) *HaVaYaH* filled with the light of "*Alephim*" **יוד-הא-ואו-הא**.

Ma'atzil (**מאציל**) the Creator – each cause with regard to its effect. The *Malchut de Rosh* is considered the Creator as regards the *Guf de Partzuf*. The same applies to any upper level with regard to the lower.

Machtzevet HaNeshama (**מחצבת הנשמה**) – will to receive in the souls, which separates them from the Supreme Light. It is a transition from the world of *Beria* to the world of *Atzilut*.

Makom (**מקום**) place – the will to receive (filling, delight) in the created being. Place, time and movement constitute one notion.

Makom Ahizat HaKlipot (**מקום אחיזת הקליפות**) a place of attachment of the impure forces – lack of holiness and correction.

Makom BYA (**מקום בי"ע**) – a place under the *Parsa*. Emerges during the *TB*.

Makom HaHerayon (**מקום ההריון**) a place of pregnancy – the lower third of the *Sefira Tifferet* of the *Partzuf Abba ve Ima*, when it joins the *YESHSUT*.

Makom Hosheh (**מקום החושך**) a dark place – the *Sefira Malchut*, which limits the *Partzuf* by the power of the *Tzimtzum*, creating a dark place outside.

Makom Panui ve Halal (**מקום פנוי וחלל**) empty space – when ZA rises to the AA, which is its real place, since the AA dresses onto the ZA *de Nikudim*, the place of the worlds of the *BYA* remains empty of the light of *Atzilut*. During the *Gmar Tikkun Atzilut* descends under the *Parsa*.

Makom Yishuv (מקום ישוב) a place of settlement – the place of the worlds of the *BYA* is divided into the *GE* (holiness) and the 14 *Sefirot* of the *Mador HaKlipot*. Similarly, This world is divided into "a place of settlement" including the worlds of the *BYA*: the Temple, the Land of Israel, abroad and the deserts unpopulated by man.

Makor HaOrot (מקור האורות) – the *Malchut de Rosh*, since it produces the Reflected Light (the *Ohr Hozer*) dressed on the Direct Light (the *Ohr Yashar*) and filling the *Toch* of the *Partzuf* with the Inner Light (the *Ohr Pnimi*).

Malchut (מלכות) – the last phase called so, because it emanates absolute rule and power.

Malchut Ein La Ohr (מלכות אין לה אור) *Malchut* without the light – as a result of the weakening of the screen, it retains only the smallest *Aviut* (*Shoresh*), insufficient for a *Zivug*, hence it can receive the light only from a *Zivug* made in *ZA*.

Malchut Mesayemet (מלכות המסיימת) limiting *Malchut* – *Malchut de Guf*.

Malchut Mizdaveget (מלכות המזדווגת) Malchut that makes a *Zivug* – *Malchut de Rosh*.

Maleh (מלא) full – there is no deficiency in it and nothing can be added to its perfection.

MAN (מ"ן) – the cause of a *Zivug*.

MAN (מ"ן) – the *GE* (altruistic vessels) of the lower *Partzuf* that merged with the *AHP* of the upper during *Katnut*. Being one with the upper *Partzuf* in *Katnut*, the *GE* of the lower rises together with the *AHP* in *Gadlut*, which turns into the new *NHY*. The *Partzufim* of the *TB* are born similar to the way the *AB* is born from the interaction of the screen and the *Reshimot* of the future the *Partzuf AB* in the *Rosh de Galgalta*. The difference lies in the fact that a *Zivug* is made on *Yesod*.

MANTZEPA"CH (מנצפ"ך) - properties of a screen and the *Aviut* of the *Partzuf*, left in it from *Katnut*. *MAN* of the souls is merged with the *AHP* of the *Partzuf Nukva*, from which the lower one will be conceived. Hence, *MAN* of conception is included in *MANTZRPA"CH* of *Nukva*, which elevates it to ZA. A conception of the new *Partzuf* of the soul is made on this *MAN*.

Masach (מסך) screen - the force of Restriction, which emerges in the created being with regard to the Supreme Light, preventing it from entering the *Behina Dalet*. This means that the instant the light touches the *Behina Dalet* this power snaps into action, strikes the light and hurls it back. This force is called "a screen".

Mata (מטה) below - a qualitative diminution with regard to the upper one.

Mayin Nukvin (מיין נוקבין) female waters - during the spreading of the *Partzuf Nekudot de* SAG under the *Tabur* two kinds of the *Reshimot* joined: *Hey Rishona* (the first letter "*Hey*") of the Name *HaVaYaH*, *Bina* of the *Partzuf* SAG and the last *Hey* of the Name *HaVaYaH*, *Malchut* of the *Partzuf Galgalta*. Hence, the screen that included two *Nukvot* (*Bina* and *Malchut*) is called "*Mayin Nukvin*". Now each *Zivug* it makes includes two *Nukvot*.

Mazal (מזל) luck - *Yesod*, because it dispenses the *Ohr Hochma* in drops, intermittently. *Mazal* derives from the word "*Nozel*" (dripping).

Mazla (מזלא) beard hair, since its light drips until it is accumulated in the most powerful light available in the worlds.

Mechaber (מחבר) unite - *Malchut* of the upper one turns to *Keter* of the lower uniting the two levels, making them equal. Thus, all levels become equal.

Mechitzot (מחיצות) partitions - body of the *Partzuf*.

Mem (מ) – the thirteenth letter of the Hebrew alphabet; the numerical value: 40.

Meshulash (משולש) triangle – the level possessing only the three first properties (desires).

Metaltelin (מטלטלין) flipping – the *Vak*. Until the *Partzuf* reaches *Gadlut*, it is between judgment and mercy, being intermittently in one of the states, which is called "flipping".

Metzah (מצח) forehead – *Bina* of the *Sefira Keter*.

Metzah HaRatzon (מצח הרצון) – during a *Zivug* in *Gadlut*, when owing to the light *AB-SAG Ohr Hochma* shines, the *Partzufey Searot* disappear and the "*Et Ratzon*" (time of desire) manifests.

Mezonot (מזונות) sustenance – provides power for rising to a higher level.

Mi (מי) who – *Bina*.

Midbar (מדבר) desert – the place of the impure forces of This world.

Milemala Lemata (מלמעלה למטה) top-down – from the *Behina Aleph* to the *Behina Dalet*. Since the *Behina Dalet* remained empty, it is considered the lowest, while the *Behina Aleph* is the highest, since its desire is the purest.

Milemala Lemata (מלמעלה למטה) top-down – the light spreading from a pure property to a coarse one is called "the Direct Light".

Milemata Lemala (מלמטה למעלה) bottom-up – the light spreading from a coarse property to a pure one is called "the Reflected Light".

Milluy (מילוי) filling – a degree of the *Aviut de Masach*, since the *Kli* is filled according to it.

Milluy shel HaVaYaH (מילוי של הוי"ה) – the Name *HaVaYaH* constitutes ten *Sefirot*: *Yud-Hochma*, the first *Hey-Bina*, *Vav-Zeir Anpin* and the second *Hey-Malchut*. This, however, does not point to their height, which may be *Nefesh*, *Ruach*, *Neshama*, *Haya* or *Yechida*. It is determined by their filling. The level of *Nefesh* is filled with *HaVaYaH* (with infill of "*Hey*"), *Gematria* of the *BON*; *Ruach* – with infill of "*Aleph*", *Gematria* MA; *Neshama* – with infill of "*Yud*" and *Vav* with infill of *Aleph*, *Gematria of* the SAG; *Haya* – with infill of "*Yud*" in all letters, *Gematria* of the *AB*.

Milluy Shemot (מילוי שמות) filling of names – points to the height of the level. Dots above and under the letters designate the root of each particular level and determines whether it is included in the upper, in the lower or just exists by itself.

Milluyim (מילויים) an infill – the *Partzuf* consists of 10 empty *Sefirot: Keter, Hochma, Bina,* ZA and *Malchut*. They are denoted by the letters *HaVaYaH: Yud-Hochma, Hey-Bina, Vav-Zeir Anpin* and *Hey-Malchut*. The *Gematria* of *Yud-Hey-Vav-Hey* equals 10+5+6+5=26. But it does not reflect their height: *Nefesh, Ruach, Neshama, Haya* and *Yechida*. The height is determined by the filling of the ten *Sefirot* with the light.

Mita (מיתה) death – a place below the spreading of the Supreme Light, i.e., below the point of the Restriction (*Tzimtzum*), under the *Parsa*. Hence, the *Kelim* that fell under the *Parsa* are called "dead", since they are detached from the light of life.

Mita (מיתה) death – the light of *Atzilut* exiting the *Kli* in any place is considered death. That is why the light of Hochma is called "the light of life", because it provides the *Kelim* with life force.

Mitat Malachim (מיתת המלכים) death of the angels – unable to receive the *Ohr Hochma*, they get isolated from the Supreme Light, fall to the worlds of the *BYA* and die, since the light stops spreading in the world of *Atzilut*.

Mitbatel (מתבטל) self-elimination – when the properties of two spiritual objects completely coincide, so that there's not a slightest distinction between them, they turn into one, and the smaller object eliminates itself before the bigger one.

Miuchad (מיוחד) Uniting – ultimately turns into the One. The One is the Supreme Light that brings numerous levels to unity, equality.

Miut Yareach (מיעוט ירח) lunar diminution – the state of Malchut of the world of Atzilut, when it is unable to receive the light, due to the lack of correction.

Moach (מוח) brain – the *Sefira Keter* of 10 *Sefirot* of the same degree. The vessel of the *Ohr Neshama* in the *Gar*.

Mochin (מוחין) brain – the light of the *Gar* or the light of the *Rosh*.

Mochin shel Gadlut (מוחין של גדלות) – the light received by ZA during raising *MAN* after 9 years-levels. This is called "*Ibur Gimel*" (the third conception), or the "*Mochin shel Tolada*", since the *ZON* make a *Zivug* "face to face" and give birth to the souls.

Moshe and Israel (משה וישראל) – the *Gar de* ZA.

Motrei Mocha (מותרי מוחא) excessive light in the brain – the lights that the brain cannot bear due to the lack of correction, hence they get outside the *Partzuf Galgalta*. They are also called "hair".

a) The level of *Haya* is completely filled with "*Yud*" – the *Gematria* *AB*:

b) The level of *Nefesh* is determined by *HaVaYaH* filled with "*Hey*" – the *Gematria BON*:

c) The level of *Neshama* is filled with "*Yud*", except for the letter *Vav* filled with "*Aleph*" – the *Gematria SAG*:

d) The level of *Ruach* is filled with "*Aleph*" – the *Gematria* MA:

מ"ה = 45 = (1+5) + (6+1+6) + (1+5) + (4+6+10) =יוד-הא-ואו-הא

ב"ן = 52 = (5+5) + (6+6) + (5+5) + (4+6+10) =יוד-הה-וו-הה

ס"ג = 63 = (10+5) + (6+1+6) + (10+5) + (4+6+10) =יוד-הי-ואו-הי

ע"ב = 72 = (10+5) + (6+10+6) + (10+5) + (4+6+10) =יוד-הי-ויו-הי

N

NaRaNHaY (נרנח"י) – the *Kelim* of the 10 *Sefirot* called the *KaHaB ZON*. The lights of the 10 *Sefirot* are called: *Nefesh, Ruach, Neshama, Haya* and *Yechida*. The *Kelim* are called top-down and the lights – bottom-up in accordance with the order of their growth.

Nefesh (נפש) – the light received by the *Partzuf* from the one above and not from the World of Infinity. It is also called "the light of the *Nekeva*".

Nefila (נפילה) fall – descent of a level due to acquiring the properties of the lower level.

Nehtam (נחתם) imprint – the same 10 *Sefirot* that pass from the *Rosh* to the *Guf*. *Hotem* (stamp) is the Reflected Light, which rises from a screen and dressing the 10 *Sefirot de Rosh*.

Neiro Dakik (נהירו דקיק) minute light – tiny, weak luminescence, which enlivens and sustains the *Klipot*.

Nekeva, Nukva (נקבה, נוקבא) – *Malchut* of the world of *Atzilut*. It is called so, because it receives the light from ZA through *Nekev*, an opening in its *Chazeh*, which diminishes the light.

Nekuda (נקודה) point – *Malchut*, on which no *Zivug* is made. Black and empty, it does not raise the Reflected Light because of the *TA* that took place in the central point.

Nekuda Emtzait (נקודה אמצעית) central point – the *Behina Dalet* of the World of Infinity merged with the light of Infinity.

Nekudot (נקודות) points, dots – four levels emerging during a *Zivug* between the Supreme Light and a screen (as it loses strength). The lights of the *Tabur* – dots above the letters – the *Holam*; the lights of the *Sefira Yesod* – dots inside the letters – *Melaphon*; the light of the *Sium Reglaim* – dots under the letters.

Neshama (נשמה) soul – the light dressed in the *Kli de Bina*. It is called "breath" ("Linshom", "to breathe"), because ZA receives the light of "life spirit" from *Bina* by way of ascending and descending, as if breathing.

Neshamot Adam HaRishon (נשמות של אדם הראשון) the First Man's Souls – these are the lights of the *NaRaN de BYA*, which rose to the world of *Atzilut* before the Fall.

Neshamot Bnei Adam (נשמות בני אדם) human souls – the inner *Kelim KaHaB de Atzilut* called *Mocha*, *Atzamot* and *Gidin* with the lights of *NaRaN*. The lights *Haya* and *Yechida* dress in the light of *Neshama*. The *Kelim* ZA and *Malchut* got separated from the *Partzuf*, hence they are called "*Bassar*" and "*Or*", i.e., they are not the real (corrected) *Kelim*, but only dress onto the *Guf* from outside. The lights *Ruach* and *Nefesh*, which fill them, are received from the inner *Kelim*. Therefore, there are *Ruach* and *Nefesh* in both the inner and the outer *Kelim*. Human souls are born as a result of the interaction between the inner *Kelim*. The interaction between the outer *Kelim* gives birth to the souls of angels. The souls are considered the inner part of the worlds, since they are born out of the inner *Kelim* of the *Partzuf*. Angels are considered the outer part of the worlds, since they are brought forth by the outer *Kelim* of the *Partzuf*.

Neshamot Hadashot (נשמות חדשות) new souls – 1) really new souls – the light of *Hochma de Ohr Yashar*. These souls don't enter the world of Correction. 2) Renewed souls that emerged from *Hochma* of 32 ways, from *Bina* included in *Hochma*. With regard to the *ZON*, they are new, since they come from the *Partzuf MA Hadash* (only the old souls of the *BON*). There are also two distinctions in them:

a) New souls refer to the state "*Panim be Panim*" (at the time), when ZA was constantly on the level of the *AB*; *Beria* that determines the souls' properties was in *Atzilut*, therefore the souls were also in *Atzilut* and were considered to be in the state of "face to face".

b) After destruction of the Temple *Beria* descended under the *Parsa* and lost the light of *Atzilut*. It is in the state of "back to back", so the souls are considered to be in the same state.

Neshamot Malachim (נשמות מלאכים) the souls of angels – See **Neshamot Bnei Adam**.

Neshikin (נשיקין) kiss – A *Zivug* between the two inner *Partzufim* – ZA and the *Nukva*; also called "sound and speech".

Neshirat Evarim (נשירת איברים) – the downfall of the souls to the impure forces. With regard to the *Kelim* such a fall is called breaking.

Neshirat Evarim Adam HaRishon (האדם הראשון נשירת איברים) fall-off of the First Man's organs – before the Fall of *Adam HaRishon* had the lights of the *NaRaN de Atzilut*; after the Fall all parts of its soul fell off – only the light of *Nefesh* was left in the *Kelim* of the 100 *Ketarim*.

Nesira (נסירה) – separation of the *Nukva* from the ZA.

Netinat Orot (נתינת אורות) - passing the light from one *Sefira* to another as the screen loses its strength. All lights emanating from *Partzuf* come to *Keter*: as the screen rises from the *Tabur* to the *Peh*, all lights gradually rise to *Keter*.

Nikud Otiot (ניקוד האותיות) – points to the source of each particular *Sefira*: whether it emerged as an inclusion in the upper or the lower one, or by itself. The infill of a name (*Gematria*, *Milluy*) designates a level's height.

Nikuy Psolet (ניקוי פסולת) purifying the waste – the *Aviut* in MAN of the lower *Partzuf* rises and gets involved in a *Zivug* of the upper. The screen of the upper *Partzuf* analyses and corrects it there. The lower one can now make its own *Zivug*. Everything depends on a *Zivug* of the upper the *Partzuf*: if it is made on the *Aviut Aleph* of the screen, only the *Behina Aleph* gets purified, while the remaining *Behinot* are rejected as waste, since the screen was unable to correct them. Hence, this *Zivug* is called "a purification of the waste". Only the amount of waste included in the screen gets corrected and can make a *Zivug*.

Nikvey Awzen, Hotem, Eynaim (נקבי אוזן, חוטם, עיניים) – during the *TB Malchut* of each of the 5 *Sefirot de Rosh* of *Hochma* rose and made an opening in them: in the *Hotem* (nose), the *Awzen* (ear) and the *Eynaim* (eyes). Before the rise of *Malchut* there was only one opening in the *Rosh* of each *Sefira* – the *Peh* (mouth).

Nikvey Eynaim (נקבי עיניים) pupils of eyes – *Behina Aleph de Rosh. Hochma* is called "eyes". Owing to the rise of *Malchut* to the *Eynaim*, *Hochma* appeared in the *Nukva* as well.

Nimshach (נמשך) attraction – descent of the light through the power of the *Aviut*, i.e., desire in the creation is called "spreading" or "attraction".

Nitzutz (נצוץ) a spark (pl. *Nitzutzim*) – the Reflected Light. *Nitzutzin* (נצוצין) – sparks-reminiscences left from the lights of the *Partzuf Nikudim* after they disappeared from the broken vessels. There are two kinds of light in them: 1) the Direct Light (pure) called "the lights" left in the world of *Atzilut*; 2) the Reflected Light (coarse) called "sparks", which descended to the worlds of the *BYA*.

Noflim (נופלים) fall – when ZA is worthy of receiving the light, *Tvunah* rises to *Ima*, makes a *Zivug* on the *Aviut Bet* and passes the light to ZA. This is called "to support the falling ZON", since they receive the light from the *Gar*.

Nogeah (נוגע) touch – transformations that take place between the levels, although insufficient for the separation from the root.

Nukva (נוקבא) – the *Nukva* grows so as to be face to face with ZA in full height in one *Keter*. The smallest state of the *Nukva* is a point below the *Yesod de ZA*.

Nun (נ) – the fourteenth letter of the Hebrew alphabet; the numerical value: 50.

O

Ohr (pl. Orot) (אור) light – all that is inside the *Behina Dalet*, beside the desire to receive pleasure.

Ohr Atzilut (אור אצילות) – the light of *Hochma* (wisdom).

Ohr Beria (אור בריאה) – the light of *Hassadim* (mercy) without the light of *Hochma*.

Ohr Eynaim (אור עיניים) the light of the eyes – the light emerging as a result of interaction between the Direct light and the screen standing in the *Nikvey Eynaim, NE* (*Aviut Aleph*). The *Ohr Eynaim* spreads from the World of Infinity to the screen. Such light is always the *Ohr Hochma* or the *Ohr Eynaim*.

Ohr Hadash (אור חדש) new light – any light that emanates as a result of correction of the vessels in the world of *Atzilut* (the light felt in the corrected vessels in *Atzilut*).

Ohr Hochma (אור חכמה) the light of *Hochma*, the light of wisdom – the light emanating from the Creator to the creation, the essence and life of all that exists.

Ohr Hozer (אור חוזר) *OH*, the Reflected Light – the light rising from a coarser vessel to a purer one called the top-down emanation of the light. The Reflected Light is rejected by the *Behina Dalet* with the help of a screen.

Ohr Makif (אור מקיף) the OM, the Surrounding Light – any light rejected by a screen due to its weakness and inability to receive the light in the *Sof* of the *Partzuf*. The OM surrounds the *Partzuf* and presses on the screen intending to be received in the future.

Ohr Malchut (אור מלכות) See **Ohr Nefesh.**

Ohr Mit'agel (אור מתעגל) rounded light – the Direct Light descends to the *Kli* in accordance with its desire, the *Behina Dalet*, which resembles a heavy object falling to the ground. The *Kelim* without the

Aviut (i.e., a strong desire) don't have power to attract the light, so it becomes rounded.

Ohr Mugbal BeKli (אור מוגבל בכלי) the light limited by the vessel – when the light can spread in the vessel according to the degree of the *Aviut de Kli*.

Ohr Nefesh (אור נפש) the light of *Nefesh* – the light received by the *Partzuf* from the upper level and not from the World of Infinity. It is also called the "*Ohr Nekeva*" or the "*Ohr Malchut*".

Ohr Nekeva (אור נקבה) See **Ohr Nefesh.**

Ohr Panim (אור פנים) light of face – the light of *Hochma*.

Ohr Pnimi (אור פנימי) the *OP*, the Inner Light – the light dressed in the *Kli*.

Ohr Reshimo (אור רשימו) the light of reminiscence – that, which is left in the *Kli* after the light exits it.

Ohr Yashan (אור ישן) – the light that remained in the world of the *Nikudim* after breaking of the vessels.

Ohr Yashar (אור ישר) the Direct Light – the light descending from the World of Infinity to the spiritual objects, worlds and the *Partzufim*, not felt by the *Kelim de Igulim* (the circular vessels without an anti-egoistic screen), only by the *Kelim de Yosher* (*Kelim* with a screen, the corrected desires). The *Ohr Yashar* (OY) is the light received by a coarser vessel from a purer one. This is called the top-down emanation of the light.

Olam (עולם) world – the name "world" starts from the *Partzuf BON* of the world of *Adam Kadmon*, because ZA and *Malchut* of the inner vessels of the *Behina Dalet* disappeared, turning into the *Kelim* for the *Ohr Makif*. In this case they are called the *Heichalot* (palaces). **Olam** means "concealed" ("*Alama*" - concealment).

Olam HaBah (עולם הבא) the future world – the lights of *Tvunah* that constantly spread in the *ZON*. "*Le Atid Lavo*" (in the future) means the lights of the upper *Bina*, since they are to enter ZA in the future.

Olamot VeNeshamot (עולמות ונשמות) the worlds and the souls – the *AVI* make two *Zivugim*: 1) "back to back" to enliven the worlds with the light of *Hassadim*; 2) "face to face" to give birth to the souls. The first, outer *Zivug* produces "garments", the second, inner *Zivug* spreads the *Ohr Hochma* and gives birth to the souls. Hence there are three *Partzufim*: the outer and intermediate of the first *Zivug* and the inner of the second.

Orech (אורך) length – distance between the two opposite ends of the level, from the purest (the uppermost) property to the coarsest (the lowest).

Otiot (אותיות) – the *Kelim* (the vessels).

P

Panim (פנים) face – a place for reception or bestowal in the *Kli*.

Panim be Panim (פנים בפנים) face to face – when the *Nukva* receives the Supreme Light from the face of the *Zachar* to its own face.

Panim Lemala (פנים למעלה) face up – the weakening of the screen; directed to the smaller *Aviut*.

Panim Lemata (פנים למטה) face down – when the light spreads according to the *Aviut*.

Panui (פנוי) vacant – a place ready to be corrected.

Parsa (פרסא) boundary – a partition dividing the *Partzuf* into the vessels of reception and the vessels of bestowal.

Partzuf (פרצוף) – the 10 *Sefirot* one under another, which emerged due to the rise of *Malchut* to the Creator.

Pashut (פשוט) simply – no difference in levels and sides.

Pe'ah (פאה) *Malchut* – because it is the last *Sefira*.

Peh (פה) - *Malchut de Rosh*.

Perud (פרוד) – two levels having no common properties.

Petah (**פתח**) opening – spreading of the light in the *Guf*, which lets it in.

Pey (**פ**) – the seventeenth letter of the Hebrew alphabet; the numerical value: 80.

Pnei Nekeva (**פני נקבא**) woman's face – *Kelim* for the reception of the *Ohr Hochma*.

Pnei Zachar (**פני זכר**) man's face – spreading of the light of *Hochma*.

Pnimi (**פנימי**) inner – the *Partzufim* of conception, feeding and maturity dress ontoe into another so that the biggest of them is the innermost.

Pnimiut (**פנימיות**) – the *Aviut* of the screen, since it is a place where the light spreads.

Psolet (**פסולת**) waste – the *Kelim* left after their selection.

Ptihat Eynaim (**פתיחת עיניים**) open eyes – the light of the eyes, the light of *Hochma*.

R

Rachel (**רחל**) – *Nukva* of ZA located from its *Chazeh* and below.

Rachok (**רחוק**) far – the maximal transformation of properties. Small luminescence of the *Ohr Hochma*. "Near" means a great amount of the *Ohr Hochma*.

RADLA (**רדל"א**) – the 10 *Sefirot* of the *Partzuf Atik* called "unattainable head", because they use *Malchut* of the *TA*.

Rahav (**רחב**) broad – spreading of the light of *Hassadim*.

Rakia (**רקיע**) firmament – the *Yesod de ZA*, since it is its end, the upper waters, and the beginning of the *Nukva*, the lower waters.

Reiach (**ריח**) smell – the light in ZA *de Rosh* called "*Hotem*" (nose).

Resh (**ר**) - the twentieth letter of the Hebrew alphabet; the numerical value: 200.

Reshimo (רשימו) reminiscence - that, which the light leaves behind after its disappearance, which is the root of a new *Partzuf*.

Reshit (ראשית) in the beginning - *Hochma de Zeir Anpin*.

Ribuah (ריבוע) a square - the *Zivugim* made by *Malchut* as it rises from the *Behina Dalet* to the *Behina Gimel* to the *Behina Bet* etc., until it reaches the *Peh*. The name also derives from the four kinds of weakening of the screen.

Ribui Ohr (ריבוי אור) a large amount of the light - a large number of the *Reshimot*, which were not renewed during a *Zivug*, hence they require correction and raise *MAN* to a new *Zivug*.

Riyah (ראיה) sight - spreading of the light from the World of Infinity to a screen. The light descending from the World of Infinity is always the *Ohr Hochma* or the *Ohr Eynaim*, or the sight, or the *Ohr Hochma de Rosh*.

Rosh (ראש) head - the part of the creation most similar to the root. The 10 *Sefirot* of the Supreme Light spreading to the screen of *Malchut* so as to raise the Reflected Light are also called so, because they precede the screen and the *Ohr Hozer*. The 10 *Sefirot* of the Direct Light dressed in the 10 *Sefirot* of the Reflected light have the same name.

Rosh Shualim (ראש לשועלים) "head of a fox" - the *Rosh* of the lower level. It is simultaneously considered "a lion's tail" - the end of the upper level.

Ruach (רוח) spirit - the light of *Hassadim*, which fills the *Kli* of ZA. Its nature consists in rising to *Bina*, receiving the light and descending to *Malchut* so as to pass the light to it.

Ruchaniut (רוחניות) spirituality - abstract from all material notions, i.e., from categories of time, place, imagination, movement.

S

Said to the world: "Stop spreading" (אמר לעולמו די ולא תתפשטו יותר) – *Malchut* blocks the light from spreading in the *Chazeh* of the world of *Yetzira* and makes the boundary there.

Salik Beruta (סליק ברעותא) – a *Zivug* on the *Masach de Aviut Shoresh.*

Samech (ס) – the fifteenth letter of the Hebrew alphabet; the numerical value: 60.

Samuch (סמוך) near – similarity of the properties.

Sandalphon (סנדלפון) – *Malchut* of the light of the *Partzuf Ima* dressed in *Malchut* of the world of *Beria*.

Searot (שערות) hair – the light, which brain is unable to endure for the lack of correction, absence of a screen. Hence, it gets outside of the *Partzuf Galgalta*. It is also called "excessive brain" ("*Motrei Mocha*").

Sefira (ספירה) – the 10 *Sefirot* of the Direct Light dressed in the 10 *Sefirot* of the Reflected Light born in one *Zivug* are called "one *Sefira*" after the uppermost *Sefira*, despite the fact that it includes the 10 *Sefirot* in height and width.

Segol (סגול) violet – a hint at three points of *HaBaD*, where *Hochma* and Bina are positioned face to face.

Shadayim (שדיים) breasts – nipples are the source of the *Ohr Hassadim*; now the *Ohr Hochma* shines there as well.

Shana (6000 years - ששת אלפים שנה) – the world of *Assiya* is called "2000 years of *Tohu*", since *Tohu* means the *Klipot*; the entire world of *Assiya* is in the *Klipot*. The world of *Yetzira* is called "2000 years of the *Torah*", because *Yetzira* is the property of ZA (the written *Torah*). The world of *Beria* is called "2000 years of *Mashiach's* coming". Beria is the property of *Bina* (*Ima*), the source of deliverance called "*Leah, Mashiach* Ben-David's mother".

Shem (שם) name – a formula, which explains how the light designated by it gets revealed on this particular level, because each level is characterized by its own way (name) of attainment.

Shemiya (שמיעה) hearing – the light in the *Sefirat Bina de Rosh* (in head of the *Partzuf*).

Shena (שינה) sleep – when the *Partzuf* ascends with MAN, it is considered to be sleeping in its permanent place, i.e., instead of the *Ohr Hochma* (which is gone now) it retains just a sustaining luminescence.

Shevira (שבירה) breaking – disappearance of a screen's boundary.

Shevira (שבירה) breaking – the downfall of the *Kelim* into the impure forces. The process is also called the "*Neshirat Evarim*" (the "fall-off of organs").

Shin (ש) – the twenty-first letter of the Hebrew alphabet, the numerical value: 300.

Shoresh (שורש) root – all properties of *Keter*, the 10 *Sefirot de Rosh.*

Shvirat Kli (שבירת כלי) breaking of a vessel – when the *Kli* is unable to receive the light.

Sigim (סיגים) – *Malchut*, mixed with seven *Malachim*, which caused the breaking of the world of the *Nikudim*.

Sium Kelim shel Panim (סיום כלים של פנים) end of the vessels of "face" – the level of *Chazeh*.

Sium Ragley Adam Kadmon (סיום רגלי אדם קדמון) end of legs of the world of *Adam Kadmon* – the point of This world, where the line of the Supreme Light ends; the position of the Central point of all worlds.

Sium Ragley Atzilut (סיום רגלי אצילות) end of legs of the world of *Atzilut* – the *Bina de Gufa* of the *Partzuf Nekudot de* SAG (the middle of *Tifferet* in its *Guf*).

Sium shel Tzimtzum Aleph (סיום של צימצום א') End of the First Restriction – located above the point of This world.

Sium shel Tzimtzum Bet (סיום של צימצום ב') End of the Second Restriction – the *Parsa* below the world of *Atzilut*.

Sof, or Sium (סוף או סיום) – end, ending – the refusal of the *Behina Dalet* to receive the light. The *Behina Dalet* is called "end", because it blocks the reception of the light, thus ending the level.

Sovel (סובל) suffer – when the *Kli* is free to receive the light, but chooses not to.

Sovev (סובב) – a cause of a *Zivug*.

T

Ta'amim (טעמים) tastes – top-down spreading of the light from the *Peh* to the *Tabur*.

Tabur (טבור) navel – the *Malchut de Guf*, from which the actual rejection of the light starts.

Tabur Lev (טבור לב) – the place of the *Chazeh*.

Tachlit Kulam (תכלית כולם) the ultimate purpose – being the coarsest of all, the *Behina Dalet* is called the "*Sof*" (end). All the *Madregot* (levels, worlds etc.) were created only in order to correct and fill it.

Tardema (תרדמה) slumber – The state of ZA while raising MAN. It is also called "*Dormita*".

Tav (ת) the twenty-second letter of the Hebrew alphabet; the numerical value: 400.

Tchelet (תכלת) light blue – *Malchut* of the light of the *Partzuf Ima* dressed in *Malchut* of the world of *Beria*.

Techiyat Metim (תחיית מתים) resurrection of the dead – return from the *BYA* to *Atzilut*, since exiting *Atzilut* is called "death".

Tefillin (תפילין) – *Tzitzit* is hair of ZA that shines in the *Rosh de Nukva* and creates the *Tefillin* on its *Metzah* (forehead).

Tehum Shabbat (תחום שבת) – the boundary set by the power of *Malchut* for the spreading of the Supreme Light in the *Chazeh de Yetzira*.

Tenuah (תנועה) movement – any renewal of spiritual form (properties) with regard to the previous form (properties).

Terem ve Achar Kach (טרם ואחר כך) – when the relation between cause and effect is discussed, cause is called "*Terem*" and effect – "*Achar Kach*".

Tet (ט) – the ninth letter of the Hebrew alphabet; the numerical value: 9.

Tipa (טיפה) a drop – intermittent reception of the light, on and off.

Tipat HaHolada (טיפת ההולדה) – the light of *Hesed* of the *Partzuf Abba*lowering the screen from the eyes.

Tohu (תוהו) – the *Partzuf Atik* unattainable by the lower *Partzufim*. *Bohu* (**בוהו**) is the *Partzuf Arich Anpin* (AA), which can be attained.

Tohu (תוהו) – the unattainable *Atik*.

Torah (תורה) – the light of ZA.

Tosefet Shabbat (תוספת שבת) – the descent of the Supreme Light causing the ascent of the worlds at the fifth hour of the sixth day (*Erev Shabbat*).

Tzadi (צ) – the eighteenth letter of the Hebrew alphabet; the numerical value: 90.

Tzar (צר) narrow – the abatement of the *Ohr Hassadim*. *Rahav* (wide) means spreading of the *Ohr Hassadim*. Restriction of the *Ohr Hochma* is called "short". Spreading of the *Ohr Hochma* is called "long".

Tzela (צלע) – the name of the *Nukva*, when it is attached "back to back" to the opposite side of the *Chazeh de* ZA. Since it is attached to the *Guf de* ZA, both of them use the same *Keter*.

Tzelem (צל"ם) – dressing of the light of the *Mochin de* ZA.

Tzelem (צל"ם) – the Reflected Light that rises owing to the inclusion of the lower one's *MAN* into the upper one's screen and the *Aviut*. The 10 *Sefirot* of the Direct Light are dressed on it. This light refers to the upper one, but since it makes a *Zivug* for the lower one's sake (on its *Aviut*); the Reflected Light descends with the light that refers to the lower one. However, in order to receive it, the lower one has to consecutively diminish the light by three levels called "*M-L-Tz*", or, if read bottom-up by the lower one – "*Tze-Le-M*".

Tzere (צירה) – the name of *Hochma* and *Bina*, when *Bina* constitutes the opposite side of *Hochma* and has no point of *Da'at*, which leads to a *Zivug* with *Hochma*. *Bina* is also called "*Tzere*", since all parts of ZA take their form thanks to its *Aviut*.

Tzimtzum (צימצום) a restriction – overcoming one's desire. One restricts reception despite the passionate "desire to receive".

Tzimtzum Aleph (צימצום א') – a restriction imposed on *Malchut* (the *Behina Dalet*), hence the line of the World of Infinity ends in *Malchut* of the *NHY*.

Tzimtzum Bet (צימצום ב') – a restriction of the *NHY* of the world of *AK* (*Behina Bet*), hence the line of the World of Infinity ends in *Bina de NHY* of the world of *AK*, where the place of the *BYA* starts. The Second Restriction is a merging of two properties: mercy (of *Bina*) and judgment (of *Malchut*).

Tzinor (צינור) pipe – the *Kelim de Ohr Yashar* (the Direct Light), since they confine the light within their limits.

Tzion (ציון) – inner *Yesod* of the *Nukva*. "*Tzion*" derives from "*Yetzia*" (exit).

Tziporney Raglaim (ציפורני רגליים) toe-nails – end of any *Partzuf*.

Tzitzit (ציצית) – the hair of ZA that shines in the *Rosh de Nukva* and creates the *Tefillin* on its *Metzah* (forehead).

Tzura (צורה) form – four degrees of the *Aviut* in the *Masach* of *Malchut* called "*Hochma*", "*Bina*", "*ZA*" and "*Malchut*" (four forms).

Tzvaot Malchut ((צבאות מלכות (גם חילות) – the *Partzufim*, which emerge from *Malchut* in the worlds of the *BYA*.

Y

Ya'akov (יעקב) – the *Vak* of *Zeir Anpin* or the outer *Partzuf*.

Yamey Kedem (ימי קדם) past days – the *Sefirot* of the *Partzuf Atik*, since *Malchut* of the *TA* is concealed from all the other *Partzufim* of *Atzilut*.

Yarchey Ibur (ירחי עיבור) months of conception or months of pregnancy – time and place constitute a renewal of form, quality. The *Partzuf* perfects itself by way of numerous *Zivugim* and the lights in the process of 7, 9 or 12 months of pregnancy in accordance with the number of the lights necessary to completely feel the *Partzuf*.

Yashar (ישר) straight – the descent of the Supreme Light into the *Kelim* in precise correspondence with their desire, which resembles a heavy object falling to the ground. the *Kelim* without the *Aviut* (i.e., a strong desire) don't have power to attract the light, so it becomes rounded.

Yechid (יחיד) One – the Supreme Light leading to the unity of all properties. *Miuchad* means that in the *Gmar Tikkun* everything becomes one.

Yechida (יחידה) – the light in the *Sefirat Keter*.

Yenikat Klipot (יניקת קליפות) attachment of the impure forces – the substance of the *Klipot* is absolute evil; hence they cannot receive any light. However, when the vessels got broken, the *Kelim* of bestowal (the *GE*) fell into the impure forces of the *AHP* and became their soul and life.

Yerida (ירידה) descent (from a level) – it occurs during the second spreading of the light, when the *Ohr Hochma* comes and dresses in the *Kli Keter*. The level of *Keter* turns out to have descended to the level of *Hochma*, *Hochma* – to *Bina*, etc.

Yerida le Klipot (ירידה לקליפות) descent to the impure forces – as a result of *MAN* raised by the souls to the *ZON*, the *ZON* rise to the *AVI* to receive the new light. If the souls' actions (properties) deteriorate, the *ZON* lose the *Ohr Hochma*, because the light comes to *ZON* only as a result of *MAN* raised by the souls, when the *Kelim* rise from the worlds of the *BYA*, go through selection and dress in the *ZON*. If *MAN* disappears, the light exits and the *ZON* return to their place. The *Kelim NHY* of *ZA* and the 9 lower *Sefirot* of the *Nukva*, which rose to the *BYA* and dressed in the *ZON*, descend (fall) into the *Klipot*.

Yesh (יש) existing – the presence of the *Ohr Hochma* is called "*Yesh*". The disappearance of the *Ohr Hochma* is called "*Ain*" (absence).

Yetzia le Hutz (יציאה לחוץ) getting outside – transformation of properties in a certain part of the *Partzuf* leads to its coming out of that *Partzuf* and becoming independent. At that, no changes take place in the first *Partzuf*.

Yetziat Ohr Derech Eynaim (יציאת אור דרך עיניים) the light emanating from the eyes – when *Malchut* rises to the *Nikvey Eynaim* (*NE*) and makes a *Zivug*, the light of this *Zivug* shines through the pupils of the eyes and not through the mouth.

Yir (עיר) city – the state of the world of *Atzilut*, when the worlds ascend to it.

Yirushalayim (ירושלים) Jerusalem – the outer *Yesod de Malchut*.

Yosef (יוסף) – *Yesod* of *Zeir Anpin*.

Yotzer (יוצר) – spreading of the light in the worlds, which includes everything, but the will to receive.

Yud (י) – the tenth letter of the Hebrew alphabet; the numerical value: 10.

Yud-Aleph Simaney Ketoret (י"א סימני קטורת) eleven parts of incense burning – sparks of the light left for the resurrection of the *Lev HaEven* (stony heart).

Z

Zachar (זכר) male essence – the upper *Partzuf* gives the same light it has to the lower one.

Zanav LeArayot (זנב לאריות) lion's tail – end of the upper level, which turns into the *Rosh* of the lower level called "fox's head".

Zayin (ז) – the seventh letter of the Hebrew alphabet; the numerical value: 7.

Zeir Anpin (זעיר אנפין) – the literal meaning is "small face", since the essence of ZA is the light of *Hassadim* and a little light of *Hochma*. The *Ohr Hochma* is called "face", therefore *Keter* is called the "*Arich Anpin*" (big face), because it is filled with the light of *Hochma*.

Zivug Gufani (זיווג גופני) bodily *Zivug* – coition of *Abba*and *Ima* for passing the light to the souls (ZON).

Zivug Haka'a (זיווג הכאה) – an impact coition – a screen's action directed at pushing the light away from the *Behina Dalet* and returning it to the root, the source. There are two opposite actions present in this phenomenon: rejection of the light and consecutive interaction with it, which leads to reception of the light in the *Kli*, because the rejected light turns into the Reflected Light, i.e., into the *Kli* that reveals the light in the *Partzuf*.

Zivug Pnimi Shel Atzilut (זיווג פנימי של אצילות) the inner *Zivug* in the world of *Atzilut* – the inner *Kelim de Atzilut* are the *KaHaB* called "*Mocha*" (brain), "*Atzamot*" (bones) and "*Gidin*" (tendons), filled with the lights: *Nefesh*, *Ruach* and *Neshama*. Having no *Kelim* of their own, the lights *Haya* and *Yechida* dress in the light of *Neshama*. This is because the *Kelim* of ZA and *Malchut* that must be filled with the lights *Haya* and *Yechida* got separated from the *Partzuf*. Other ZA and *Malchut* called "*Bassar*" (flesh) and "*Or*" (skin) are used instead of them. These are not real complete vessels, but only dress the *Guf* from outside. They receive the lights *Ruach* and *Nefesh* that fill them from the inner *Kelim*. That is why *Ruach* and *Nefesh* fill both the inner and outer *Kelim*. A *Zivug* on the inner *Kelim* creates human souls and a *Zivug* on the outer *Kelim* creates the souls of angels. Hence, born from the inner *Kelim* of the *Partzuf*, the human souls are considered inner, while the souls of angels born from the outer *Kelim* of the *Partzuf* are regarded outer.

Zivug Ruchani (זיווג רוחני) – A *Zivug* that comes from the *Rosh de SAG* to the *Rosh de Nikudim* and corrects the *Gar de Nikudim*, but does not spread to the *Guf de Nikudim*. It is also called "coition by a kiss".

Zivug Shel Neshikin (זיווג של נשיקין) coition by a kiss – *Zivug* that comes from *Rosh de SAG* to *Rosh de Nikudim* and corrects *Gar de Nikudim*, but does not spread to *Guf de Nikudim*. It is also called "the spiritual coition".

Zivug Shel Yesodot (זיווג של יסודות) coition of bodies – corrects the *Zat* of the seven lower *Sefirot* of the *Partzuf*. It is also called "the lower *Zivug*" and "bodily *Zivug*".

Zivug Tadir (זיווג תדיר) permanent *Zivug* – coition of *Abba*and *Ima* in their places.

Zman (זמן) time – a certain number of properties, which develop one out of another as cause and effect.

ZON Shel Klipah (זו"ן של קליפה) - only the *Kelim* of the seven lower *Sefirot* got broken.

OUR OTHER BOOKS

Guide to the Hidden Wisdom of Kabbalah with Ten Complete Kabbalah Lesson: provides the reader with a solid foundation for understanding the role of Kabbalah in our world. The content was designed to allow individuals all over the world to begin traversing the initial stages of spiritual ascent toward the apprehension of the upper realms.

Attaining the Worlds Beyond: is a first step toward discovering the ultimate fulfillment of spiritual ascent in our lifetime. This book reaches out to all those who are searching for answers, who are seeking a logical and reliable way to understand the world's phenomena. This magnificent introduction to the wisdom of Kabbalah provides a new kind of awareness that enlightens the mind, invigorates the heart, and moves the reader to the depths of their soul.

Introduction to the Zohar: is the second in a series written by Kabbalist and scientist Rav Michael Laitman, which will prepare readers to understand the hidden message of "The Zohar". Among the many helpful topics dealt with in this companion text to The Science of Kabbalah, readers are introduced to the "language of roots and branches", without which the stories in the Zohar are mere fable and legend. Introduction to the Zohar will certainly furnish readers with the necessary tools to understand authentic Kabbalah as it was originally meant to be, as a means to attain the Upper Worlds.

Kabbalah for Beginners: By reading this book you will be able to take your first step in understanding the roots of human behaviour and the laws of nature. The contents present the essential principals of the Kabbalistic approach and describe the wisdom of Kabbalah and the way it works. Kabbalah for beginners is intended for those searching for a sensible and reliable method of studying the phenomenon of this world for those seeking to understand the reason for suffering and pleasure, for those seeking answers to the major questions in life. Kabbalah is an accurate method to investigate and define man's position in the universe. The wisdom of Kabbalah tells us why man exists, why he is born, why he lives, what the purpose of his life is, where he comes from, and where he is going after he completes his life in this world.

Root of All Science: The process of examining our world with the help of the human mind and manmade tools is called science. All fields of science deal with what is perceived through our natural five senses, yet the Wisdom of Kabbalah deals with acquiring knowledge that exceeds their limitations.

In Root of All Science, Rav Michael Laitman presents the differences between Kabbalistic scientific method and the current method used by scientists. The distinction is in the ability of Kabbalah to incorporate human awareness in a verifiable analysis of reality. The enormous significance of this additional focus, to both the scientific researcher and the seeker of spirituality, is that it provides the leap in dimensions enabling the observer to penetrate the causal level of all aspects of existence and all events that occur in this world.

Wondrous Wisdom: Today interest in Kabbalah has exploded world-wide. Millions of people are seeking answers as to what this ancient wisdom really is, and where they can find authentic instruction. With so many conflicting ideas about Kabbalah on the internet, in books, and in the mass media; the time has finally arrived to answer humanity's need, and reveal the wisdom to all who truly desire to know. In Wondrous Wisdom you will receive the first steps, an initial course on Kabbalah, based solely on authentic teachings passed down from Kabbalist teacher to student over thousands of years. Offered within is a sequence of lessons revealing the nature of the wisdom and explaining the method of attaining it.

But if you listen with your heart to one famous question, I am sure that all your doubts as to whether you should study the Kabbalah will vanish without a trace. This question is a bitter and fair one, asked by all born on earth: "What is the meaning of my life?"

Rav Yehuda Ashlag,
from "Introduction to
Talmud Eser Sefirot"

ABOUT BNEI BARUCH

Bnei Baruch is a non-profit group centered in Israel that is spreading the wisdom of Kabbalah to accelerate the spirituality of mankind. Kabbalist Michael Laitman PhD, who was the disciple and personal assistant to Kabbalist, Rabbi Baruch Ashlag, the son of Kabbalist Rabbi Yehuda Ashlag (author of the Sulam Commentary on the Zohar), follows in the footsteps of his mentor in guiding the group.

Rav Laitman's scientific method provides individuals of all faiths, religions and cultures the precise tools necessary for embarking on a highly efficient path of self-discovery and spiritual ascent. The focus is primarily on inner processes that individuals undergo at their own pace. Bnei Baruch welcomes people of all ages and lifestyles to engage in this rewarding process.

In recent years, an awakening of a massive worldwide quest for the answers to life's questions has been underway. Society has lost its ability to see reality for what it is and in its place easily formed viewpoints and opinions have appeared.

Bnei Baruch reaches out to all those who seek awareness beyond the standard view. It offers practical guidance and a reliable method for understanding the world's phenomena. The group's unique method not only helps overcome the trials and tribulations of everyday life, but initiates a process in which individuals extend themselves beyond the standard boundaries and limitations of today's world.

Kabbalist Rabbi Yehuda Ashlag left a study method for this generation, which essentially 'trains' individuals to behave as if they have already achieved the perfection of the Upper Worlds, here in our world.

In the words of Rabbi Yehuda Ashlag, "*This method is a practical way to apprehend the Upper World and the source of our existence while still living in this world. A Kabbalist is a researcher who studies his nature using this proven, time-tested and accurate method. Through this method, one attains perfection, and takes control over one's life. In this way, one realizes one's true purpose in life. Just as a person cannot function properly in this world having no knowledge of it, so also one's soul cannot function properly in the Upper World having no knowledge of it. The wisdom of Kabbalah provides this knowledge."*

The goal-orientated nature of these studies enables a person to apply this knowledge on both an individual and collective basis in order to enhance and promote the spirituality of humankind, and indeed the entire world.

HOW TO CONTACT BNEI BARUCH

Bnei Baruch
1057 Steeles Avenue West, Suite 532
Toronto, ON, M2R 3X1
Canada

E-mail address: info@kabbalah.info

Web site: www.kabbalah.info

Toll free in Canada and USA:
1-866-LAITMAN
Fax: 1-905 886 9697

PRISON WRITINGS

The Roots of Civilisation

Abdullah Ocalan

Translated by Klaus Happel

First published 2007 by Pluto Press, reprinted 2015
345 Archway Road, London N6 5AA

www.plutobooks.com

British Library Cataloguing in Publication Data
A catalogue record for this book is available from the British Library

Hardback
ISBN-13 978 0 7453 2616 0
ISBN-10 0 7453 2616 1

Library of Congress Cataloging in Publication Data applied for

10 9 8 7 6 5 4 3 2

Designed and produced for Pluto Press by
Chase Publishing Services Ltd, Fortescue, Sidmouth, EX10 9QG, England
Typeset from disk by Newgen Imaging Systems (P) Ltd, Chennai, India
Printed by CPI Antony Rowe, Chippenham, UK

Contents

PART 2 THE AGE OF FEUDALISM

PART 3 THE CIVILISATION OF THE AGE OF CAPITALISM

PART 4 IDEOLOGICAL IDENTITY AND TIME–SPACE CONDITIONS OF THE NEW DEVELOPMENT IN CIVILISATION

PART 5 CAN THE CULTURAL TRADITION OF THE MIDDLE EAST SERVE AS A SOURCE FOR A NEW SYNTHESIS OF CIVILISATIONS?

Preface

The analyses and theses in this book were originally part of my appeal to the European Court of Human Rights. Thus they had an additional purpose that went beyond a mere analysis of the state of civilisation in the Middle East.

I came to Europe in 1997 in the hope of reaching a settlement with our imperialist oppressors. I hoped that a reasonable solution according to democratic European criteria would end the necessity for the guerrilla campaign in the mountains – a campaign that had already started to take more lives than ever and which I did not want in the first place. Once, the mountains had been the ornaments of my dreams and it was only after waiting in vain for 40 years that I eventually and reluctantly set out into the mountains.

This time, because I knew it would be incompatible with my view of responsibility and ethics, I personally was not ready to embark on a guerrilla campaign again – a campaign which I knew would cause yet more sorrow to my comrades and my entire people.

I certainly did not foresee that my journey to Europe would end in tragedy. I have to admit that I underestimated the power of certain interests and the possibility of treason. They measured me, they weighed me, and then threw me to the real animals, in Africa, in a contemptible way. They boasted to the world about having taken me, tied me up expertly, and stowed away in Imrali, as in a coffin. In this way they had restored their interests, which they felt had been endangered.

These events were a violation of European law – if there is such a thing. To my mind, the attitude of the court is a measure of the state of a civilisation and, furthermore, I was under the impression that someone who turns to Europe for help in a state of surrender is always received warmly. With me, this was, and will not be, the case. Therefore, my relationship with Europe is based on my finding an antithesis. This in turn depends upon the Middle East's ability to formulate, from its own historical foundations, a distinct antithesis to European civilisation. This is the message that I want to convey and I feel that I am to some extent successful.

This book is also meant as a general answer to the opinions and criticism of many of my friends and comrades, voiced in letters that were successfully smuggled to me – and to the many that did not reach me. It is a necessary answer.

The considerations and the criticism I put forward in this book are meant as a defence, as an *apologia* in the original Greek sense of the word. They were written under the effects of the extraordinary plot that had brought me into this solitary cell that I now inhabit.

I am about to begin the second volume of my writings. It will in particular address methodically questions in Kurdish historiography; Kurdish–Turkish relations; the perspective of a democratic solution of the Kurdish question; the development of the plot that brought me here and its real meaning; European law and the significance of the European Court of Human Rights. I have paid attention to everything from which we may learn and I have tried to formulate a methodical approach, for what we need, more than anything else, is people who can think independently. Issues that I felt were important have been treated more extensively. I hope this will be helpful. The criticism that has already reached me gives me confidence.

There is always the danger that some of my remarks about God and religion could be distorted. I believe that the strongest points of my discourse lie exactly in the treatment of these issues and I am determined to push for the mental revolution I advocate here. Let me also emphasise my deep conviction that such a mental revolution will be followed by the development of a free and sensitive conscience. Without such a thorough mental revolution we will never become people with an ethical sensitivity, let alone revolutionaries. In this sense, I am convinced I have responded on different levels to all people who may have an interest in reading these contemplations.

There are, of course, many deficiencies in my discourse for which I alone should take responsibility.

I dedicate these writings to those fallen in the course of the prison revolt in Turkey and to all victims of similar cruelties.

Additionally, I hope to have answered at least some of the questions important to those close to me personally. I am theirs more than ever and while there is not much left of me which I can call my own, I would like to send them my deepest love and my sincere hopes for their well-being.

May humanity prevail!
Abdullah Ocalan
Imrali, 2 July 2001

Translator's Introduction

On 15 February 1999, Abdullah Ocalan, the leader of a Kurdish rebellion in Turkey that had lasted for more than a decade, was kidnapped on his way from the Greek embassy in Nairobi, Kenya, to the airport. He was tied up and taken to Turkey aboard the aircraft of a Turkish businessman. This act ended a week-long odyssey between Damascus, Moscow, Amsterdam, Rome and Athens. It was immediately speculated that his kidnapping in Kenya had been engineered by the CIA and Mossad in cooperation with the Turkish authorities.

Ocalan, born in Sanliurfa, south-eastern Turkey, in 1949, was the founder and chairman of the Kurdistan Workers Party (PKK), which had begun its armed struggle against the Turkish army in the Kurdish areas of Turkey in 1984. This struggle lasted for more than 15 years and took the lives of more than 30,000 people, many of them civilians. Numerous villages were destroyed and their populations driven away.

In 1998, Ocalan had to leave Syria, where he had had his headquarters for many years, after Turkey had threatened Syria with war. All his attempts to apply for political asylum in Europe and elsewhere failed, as did his attempts to find support among European politicians for his ideas for a political solution to the Kurdish question.

In 1999, the State Security Court in Ankara found Ocalan guilty of high treason and sentenced him to death. Because of increasing international pressure the sentence was not carried out. In 2002, following the abolition of the death penalty in Turkey during times of peace, the death sentence was commuted into one of life imprisonment.

Ocalan lodged an appeal against his verdict before the European Court of Human Rights in Strasbourg. From the beginning, this appeal was to serve two purposes: it was a statement of his defence for the court and at the same time a discussion of the Kurdish issue, including a political solution, which he called "unity in freedom", advocating a democratic approach and a call for peace. Ocalan knew that his only chance of getting his ideas to the outside world was by writing them as submissions to the court. These prison writings, which from the outset were intended for publication, also addressed the Kurds and the military and political leaders of the PKK, as well as public opinion in Turkey and the West.

In 2005 the European Court closed the Ocalan file with its final decision: Ocalan had not received a fair trial in Turkey, the verdict declared, ruling that Turkey had to reopen his case, if Ocalan submitted an appeal.

Since 16 February 1999, Abdullah Ocalan has been kept in solitary confinement on the Turkish prison island of Imrali, in the Sea of Marmara.

Today, the whole island of Imrali is kept under camera surveillance. The airspace above the island as well as the waters surrounding it are rigorously controlled by the military. Everyone going through the checkpoints or entering the high-security wing for the first time is subjected to an iris scan and a hand scan, the data of which are saved.

About 1,000 soldiers are deployed on the island for surveillance of the restricted area. These soldiers also serve as guards in the high-security wing.

* * *

Ocalan inhabits a cell of 13 square metres equipped with a single frosted-glass window, which can only be opened a finger's breadth. Fresh air is provided by air-conditioning. The cell is located in a two-storey building with special safeguards. There is a toilet and washing facility in the room. The cell is subject to 24-hour surveillance by camera and peephole by a team of carefully selected Turkish military officers, who are regularly rotated.

The cell is illuminated 24 hours a day, causing the prisoner severe sleep problems. In general, Ocalan is permitted to see his lawyers for one hour once a week in a room adjacent to his cell. These visits are often arbitrarily postponed or cancelled, resulting in complete week-long isolation.

Ocalan's closest relatives are permitted to see him once a month for one hour. They may only see him through a glass partition and speak to him by means of a telephone. Twice a day he is allowed to leave his cell for a one-hour walk in the yard. This yard is about 40 square metres in size; it is surfaced with gravel and surrounded by high walls surmounted with barbed wire.

Contact with the outside world, including access to information, has been reduced to an absolute minimum. Ocalan has no television, and the books and papers supplied by his lawyers are often handed over to him only in part and sometimes not at all. His mail is censored, and he is not allowed to answer any letters. He is allowed no more than three books at a time. His single source of up-to-date information is a radio, which only receives the state-run Turkish channel TRT.

As a result, the anti-torture committee of the Council of Europe (CPT), which has repeatedly sent delegations to Imrali, has requested an end to his solitary confinement and has called for a noticeable improvement in the prison conditions. Neither Turkey nor the Council of Europe have followed these recommendations as yet.

* * *

Ocalan's submissions to the European Court of Human Rights originally constituted a single book in nine parts. This was then split into two volumes, of which the present volume is the first. It contains the first six of the nine parts, and consists primarily of historical and theoretical considerations. The subsequent volume, containing the last three parts, discusses Kurdish and Middle Eastern history and in particular the struggles of the PKK in the light of the theoretical foundations laid in the present volume.

The first part of this volume analyses ancient slave-holding societies, from Sumer to Rome. The analysis yields results of general importance. Ocalan establishes (a) the dialectical relationship between the development of state-based, hierarchical civilisations and the communities putting up resistance to them as a major motive force in human history; (b) the realm of mythology, religion and philosophical thought as a site of this conflict; and (c) a growing tension between, on the one hand, permanent historical change on the ideological, economic, social, cultural and political plane, and, on the other hand, the preservation of the basic institutions of the state apparatus. He argues that the base and superstructure of state societies, from Sumer to the modern United States, take on forms of appearance that are merely modifications, but have not essentially changed. Sumerian hieratic rule becomes a metaphor for state-based, patriarchal, class societies in the wider historical sense.

In the second part, Ocalan deals with the medieval, feudal orders of Europe and the Middle East. He argues that Christianity was essentially an emancipatory ideology that emerged from the Middle Eastern struggle against the Roman Empire. Under the ideological guidance of Christianity, late Roman state structures and European pre-state tribal communities amalgamated into the Western medieval social order. On the other side of the world, the ideology of Islam allowed the Arab desert tribes to amalgamate with the existing Byzantine and Sassanian state structures into an Eastern feudal order.

Islam was originally a progressive ideology that advocated humanism and endowed all sections of society with rights that they had not possessed under previous Middle Eastern orders. However, it was soon hijacked by the Umayyad Dynasty, a group of people who stood at the intersection of parochial tribal zeal and the aggrandising powers afforded by the administrative structures they seized. Ocalan holds this "counter-revolution within Islam" chiefly responsible for the eventual degeneration of Islamic culture, which was to become the last grand form of Middle Eastern civilisation.

Ocalan argues that the first period of Islamic culture, from the eighth to the twelfth century CE, was an era of tremendous blossoming. Many of its achievements exerted a progressive influence on medieval Europe. However, a reactionary, oppressive aspect came to the fore from the late Abbasid period onwards and stifled all further development. The deeply entrenched Eastern culture of hieratic – or theocratic and autocratic – governance crushed the individual. Thus the lack of autochthonous development in the modern Middle East cannot be explained by reference to the supposedly innate backwardness of Islam; rather it must be discussed against the backdrop of the withering of an age-old cultural tradition, exhausted and ossified through its own contradictions. The Ottoman empire was merely the custodian of a graveyard, namely that of Middle Eastern civilisation.

Dogmatic, fatalist thought is one of the most destructive residues of this inveterate, defunct system, since it paralyses social agencies and impedes change. In contrast, Ocalan draws attention to heterodox Middle Eastern currents, e.g. Islamic mysticism, renegade sects, secular popular traditions in the arts and literature, and so on, as the backbone of a positive heritage.

In the face of a similarly conservative trend in late medieval Western civilisation, there emerged the European Renaissance, the starting point for an antagonistic development in world history. This is the subject of the third part of the present volume. European capitalist modernity introduced (a) the paramount social position of the individual vis-à-vis society; (b) non-religious thought; (c) a new mode of production based on the production of surplus value rather than the mere exaction of surplus product; (d) enormous scientific and technological progress; (e) new forms of political organisation: nation states, democracy, etc. However, European modernity, too, preserved the main traits of state-based, patriarchal class society, fused with an unfettered, ever-expanding, individual insatiability. Through unprecedented imperialist expansion, this form of civilisation is grafting itself onto most societies across the globe. It has evolved its own countertrend, the socialist movement, which however has failed to develop a viable alternative to capitalism, and thus to 5,000 years of state-based hierarchic civilisation.

Actually existing socialism, in its preoccupation with state power and the state sector of the economy, relapsed into the old tradition of state-centred, quasi-hieratic, administrative authority. It failed to promote individual freedom as opposed to social imperatives. Engulfed by capitalism, socialism finally collapsed into its arms, because it had to resort to a more backward form of coercion than post-industrialist capitalism.

After the collapse of both fascism and actually existing socialism, democracy became the paramount form of governance. Democracy enables oppressed groups to defend their interests to a certain extent and is apt to become the site of non-violent, democratic, political struggles for basic rights, freedoms and equality.

In the fourth part, Ocalan deals with the present world situation and the immediate future from a Middle Eastern perspective. The modern Middle East ought to adopt the advancements of European modernity: individual rights, non-religious thought, secular political structures, pluralism, etc. However, it is obvious that the Middle East is the principal world region to stubbornly resist the assimilation of Western civilisation. This historical inflexibility constitutes a chance to develop an alternative. At the beginning of the twenty-first century, the Middle East is ripe for a renaissance of its own historical traditions, a reformation of religion and a process of social enlightenment that draws on its native cultural and intellectual resources.

Democratisation is the key that can unlock the age-old chest. Women's liberation and the empowerment of minorities can help establish pluralist federative structures, which can provide the framework for the resolution of social, ethnic and religious conflicts. The existing centralist nation states must grow into decentralised federations, which can merge in a Democratic Middle Eastern Union. The main arena of the struggles to bring about these changes is civil society: neither the state sector nor traditional society can produce solutions. Both must be reformed. Eco-democratic, communal local governments can empower diverse populations to run their polities.

This objective provides an alternative to the fundamentalist religious and secular–nationalistic currents which at present confront Western powers but fail to provide any progressive perspective for society. The armed struggle for national liberation or dictatorship of the proletariat is an equally inadequate perspective, since the available historical examples have all resulted in backward, weak and autocratic regimes. Change must come through a thorough democratisation of society. However, organised armed defence against the onslaughts of reactionary powers is legitimate.

The Kurdish struggle links the populations of four central Middle Eastern states: Turkey, Syria, Iraq and Iran. Its concrete role in promoting the objective outlined above is discussed at length in the second volume of Ocalan's prison writings.

The wider perspective of the present book revives the initial idea of the PKK that the liberation of Kurdistan would be the starting point for the establishment of a socialist union of the Middle East. What has changed is Ocalan's outlook on state power as a tool to achieve that objective. He recently remarked that his approach is not anti-state but "a-state": drawing on new ideas developed by the libertarian social ecologist Murray Bookchin, feminist political theorists, leftist Foucauldians and critical Marxists, but mainly through sifting and critically reappraising his lifelong experience as a revolutionary leader, Ocalan advocates organised civil struggle at a point in the historical and geopolitical matrix of our world where every shock has immediate global repercussions.

* * *

This book was clearly written under extraordinary circumstances. Its handwritten pages were handed over to Ocalan's lawyers or relatives during their short and infrequent visits. Sometimes they were not even written down, but dictated to the lawyers, or the lawyers had to take notes while listening to what their client explained. This procedure could not fail to have had an influence on the resulting book. Ocalan also was unable to make his thoughts available for a broad and intense discussion. He could not provide annotations and a bibliography. The entire work, as it left his cell, was raw and unfinished in many aspects, and translating and editing it has been a complex process, which involved the help and participation of a number of people with the necessary sociological, political or historical expertise. We also had to maintain constant communications with lawyers, Kurdish politicians and other experts.

I wish to thank the team that has made this book possible: Hendrika Harm, Arjen Harm, Sonja Dekker, Leendert Dekker, and in particular John Tobisch-Haupt and his friends of the International Initiative "Freedom for Abdullah Ocalan". I could not have completed it without their support and help.

Klaus Happel
September 2006

Introduction

The Kurdish question is at the heart of my domestic trial, and of my application to the European Court of Human Rights. It is intimately linked with developments, correlations and contradictions pertaining to a certain social reality that once had its ample share in the birth and growth of civilisation, but is now facing a very peculiar kind of decay. Appraisals based on textbook structural analysis of Kurdish society along the lines of categories such as class and nation have failed to provide an understanding of the Kurdish question. Where these have been undertaken, they have been restricted to the realm of the abstract, and this, almost inevitably, has led to political conclusions that have proved to be fatally erroneous. The fact that the question has had repercussions surpassing the boundaries of the Middle East and has occupied the prominent global players of the twentieth century requires any analysis of it to have reference to the wider context of the history of civilisation. Without a correct definition of the basis on which this question rests, no sound legal findings can be made in a case resulting from it.

The European Convention on the Protection of Human Rights and Fundamental Freedoms and the European Court of Human Rights are among the latest democratic institutions of law designed by European civilisation. There can be no question that this most authoritative and well-established representation of contemporary civilisation is informed by European judgements of value. It seems somewhat ironic, though, that the Kurds, who are today seeking solutions to their own problems at the gates of Europe, are actually part of the source that informed European civilisation in the first place. An aged mother seeks justice with her children, whom she raised and nurtured over thousands of years, and who hardly recognise her any more. Will her rights be acknowledged? This, I think, is what the Kurdish question boils down to. The *power of socialisation* and the *power of individuation* (two terms I shall elaborate on) are standing face to face. East and West, Asia and Europe, Anatolia and Greece – these geographical terms form the background scenery to the drama of my capture, trial and imprisonment on Imrali island, each of them an episode of truly theatrical quality.

Any unbiased spectator will have to concede that there is a need to find satisfactory answers to the questions as to who drafted the script for this jurisdictional theatre, how the various parts were assigned, who played the leading roles and who the bit parts, and what message was supposed to be given to the audience. I fear that the framework in which the European Court has indicated that it would consider my application is construed in rather a narrow fashion, so as to reduce it to a matter of an individual petition. That makes it likely that the court will ignore a number of important issues related to my case and will inadvertently provide the stage for the final act in the said drama. I therefore respectfully invite the court to consider my submissions, the main part of which is dedicated to the task of shedding light on the dirty, bloody and truly unfortunate history that constitutes the background to my case. I am confident that the court, being, as it is, a legal institution itself established in reaction to historical events involving much bloodshed and suffering, will arrive at an unbiased judgement at the end of fair proceedings, or, failing that, will at least grant an opportunity for the unrestricted presentation of my case.

This presentation is structured in several main sections progressing from the general to the specific. I am acutely aware of the fact that it has a number of shortcomings, partly owing to the fact that I had to link a massive argument to the purpose of drafting a defence, and partly to the circumstances of spending years of solitary confinement in a prison cell, including the loss of mental faculty that this entails.

But historic trials call for historical arguments. In order for my application, which refers to events involving deep pain and tragic losses for all the parties to it, to become an opportunity for learning, and for progress, all those who played their part are called upon to give full accounts of it. I do hope that the following submissions qualify as such an account.

Part 1

Slave-owning Society and the Development of Civilisation

1

The Birth of Civilisation on the Banks of the Tigris and the Euphrates

According to research in archaeology, ethnology, religious studies and other branches of the social sciences, the earliest state-based society and the oldest written sources of human history can be found in the lands around the rivers Euphrates and Tigris in Lower Mesopotamia, and can be accredited to the *Sumerians*. Theirs is referred to as the first civilisation and hailed as the most consequential event in history. The initial development of the structures and establishments that make up a complex *body politic* doubtless amounts to a significant turning point in the history of humankind, for all its negative and positive consequences. After all, any contemporary state shares its functional outlines as a device for social organisation and as an overarching political institution with its Sumerian prototype. To learn about the Sumerians and their state, therefore, amounts to learning about ourselves and the times we live in. Had not some of the remnants of Sumerian culture been unearthed, this oldest and perhaps most influential source of civilisation would have been completely effaced from our cultural memory and, without any real knowledge of how history began, we would have remained oblivious to what we are ourselves. In fact, the Sumerians are our yesterdays, and they're as close to us as our immediate past.

Some of the earliest proofs of an economy based on agriculture and the domestication of cattle and of sedentary life have been found in Upper Mesopotamia. The term *neolithic revolution*[1] indicates that the transition to a subsistence based on food production and the concomitant establishment of fairly permanent settlements must have had far-reaching effects on human life. Sites at Cayonu in Diyarbakir, Hallan Cemi near Batman, and Nevali Cori in Urfa,[2] show traces of sedentary village life, sustained mainly through agriculture and animal husbandry, dating back 10,000 years. Many more of these early neolithic settlements must be buried under the countless mounds that one passes on an ordinary drive through the terrains that have been called Kurdistan since the times of the Iranian Seljuks. Despite the regrettably limited scope of the actual excavations undertaken here, there can be no doubt that this region – the Fertile Crescent – constituted one of the main centres of this intriguing era of prehistoric cultural developments. It was most likely the centre from where cultural innovations were transmitted to far-away regions.

In terms of their social ramifications, the cultures found in settlements dating back to the era from 6000 to 3000 BCE[3] prepared the material basis on which Mesopotamian civilisation emerged. These cultures, nurtured by the rivers Tigris and Euphrates, invented most of the facilities that featured in the making of civilisation – the earliest that one can speak of as far as our present knowledge of complex societies goes. The neolithic communities in Mesopotamia had command of advanced techniques of manufacturing painted pottery (by employing the wheel), of spinning and weaving flax and wool, and of grinding grains. The axe, the plough, and other tools made from copper ore, hearth and kiln, and elaborate communal buildings (including shrines) can be found in their settlements. Their religious beliefs, though varied, apparently involved some forms of astral symbolism and the veneration of female deities. The outstanding human products associated with this Mesopotamian "dawn of history" are of importance to the long-term development of human culture that only the European inventions of the sixteenth to twentieth centuries CE can be compared with.

Communities of the Late Ubaid and Uruk periods (mid-fifth to late fourth millennium BCE) achieved a remarkably high yield on the crops they cultivated in the alluvial marshlands near the Persian Gulf. The use of irrigation canals and a complex interplay of environmental factors rendered possible a population of settlements exceeding by far the size of the village communities found further north. A small upper layer of this population started using early forms of cuneiform script by 3100 BCE – an invention that has caused historians to exclaim that "History began at Sumer".[4]

There are innumerable ways of defining civilisation.[5] However, the most determining trait seems to be that human labour, once it yields significantly more produce than is required for immediate consumption, becomes subservient to a social elite that administers and appropriates such surpluses.

Thus the dimension of servitude is introduced into human relations, and with it the notion of property. The way this actually happened in Sumerian society was through the establishment of units that served as cultic locations, sites for the coordination of collective labour, and centres of social governance. These temples, or *ziggurats*, were apparently conceived as *earthly representations of the celestial order*, i.e. as representing social identity. They are now often regarded as the prototype of all later temples, parliaments, trade centres, military headquarters and centres of learning and the arts. We may thus say that the Mesopotamian ziggurat was the womb of state institutions. This human invention was sacrosanct even in its embryonic form, where its extraordinary fecundity was already appreciated by the ideologues of early Mesopotamian society, the priests.

In their hands, the state established a firm hegemony over the minds of the people and became the main source of political authority. On the one hand, this entailed that servile labour could henceforth be employed as an outstandingly efficient productive tool, while a certain section of the population could be exempted from immediate food production and be occupied with specialised handicrafts, or indeed religious and administrative tasks. On the other hand, through propagating the divine order envisioned by Sumerian theology, the moral and spiritual guidance emanating from this central institution could exercise a strong influence on the thoughts and sentiments of the community. Material and ideational developments supported one another. The sanctioning of private property and the institutionalisation of religion exercised a remarkable impact on the restructuring of family relations in a society that gradually transformed from one based on kinship bonds into one structured through social stratification and ideologically represented by new institutions.

The priests, who took the lead in the invention of the state at Sumer, displayed stunning capacities as ideologues, just as they stand out as skilled organisers of the process of production. Their *priesthood* formed the cell unit of political hierarchy[6] and prepared the grounds for the transition to dynastic kingship. On reading the extant Sumerian documents, one easily gets an idea why their authors should have referred to everything they did as being part and parcel of a divine order. For their contemporaries, however, it was by no means conceivable that here was a human order in the making. They would have believed that the sacred earthly order was fashioned in the image of the astral system established and mediated to them by the priests.

Perhaps no other ideology since has had as profound an impact on human thought as has Sumerian mythology. Not only was it systematised in the form of theology and installed as an official ideology that informed and legitimised a coercive political regime. It was also instituted as the point of departure and frame of reference for much of the religious and philosophical reasoning of subsequent cultures and, by extension, of science – as I shall set out further on in this book. Sumerian mythology found its original expression in various forms of naive but enchanting works of epic prose and fine arts. They account for a number of sources without the knowledge of which all written histories are doomed to be flawed. Unfortunately, the systematic examination of Sumerian culture has only begun and its seminal importance is still far from being widely acknowledged.

The basic contributions of early Mesopotamian civilisation to historical development include the invention of a highly influential system of writing (cuneiform),[7] mathematics and the calendar, and the earliest elaborate mythology and theology. The institution of the state and of *the politic*, fuelled by the formation of classes, saw the establishment of written legal norms regulating various forms of private, state-owned and collective property. At the core of social organisation was the holy household and, at its apex, dynastic rule. Early

Mesopotamia was the scene of a vibrant urban life grouped around temples, crafts and centralised trade. Apart from mythological poetry, epic prose and music, the Sumerians can be accredited with the first colonial settlements and imperial expansion. What was added later amounts to little more than the quantitative extension and elaboration of what we already find at Sumer. In other words, growing complexity basically means the functional differentiation and branching out of the initial institutions of archaic class society as found in early Mesopotamia. One concept highly cherished by the Sumerians themselves was that of *mè*, or basic law,[8] which served to delineate the traits of the civilisation they engendered. Roughly a hundred of them have been found in Sumerian texts, and to a modern Middle Eastern reader, these chime with the 99 attributes of God in Islam.

Another essential aspect of studying the Sumerians is the mythological expression of gender conflict in what seems to be the transition from a predominantly matrifocal social organisation to a patriarchal order. The goddess of birth, Nin-Hursag (Lady of the Foothills),[9] and Inanna, the goddess of fertility, love and war, were powerful deities in early Sumerian myth. Of their many fierce confrontations with the cunning male god Enki, one particularly worth mentioning is Inanna's coercion of Enki to return to her the *mè* for which she claimed creatorship. The story can be read as an account of Inanna's efforts to regain the cultural achievements of non-patriarchal Neolithic societies, usurped and locked away by Enki, and her struggle to make them again immanent in the world. Having got hold of the *mè*, Inanna returns from Eridu, the city under Enki's patronage, to Uruk, the city where she was at home and had an early and splendid temple.

In general, women command higher respect in Sumerian texts than they do in the documents of most subsequent cultures. But Mesopotamian texts also bear witness to the disenfranchisement of women in a patriarchal state system where the enslavement of human beings by others reinforced gender hierarchies and vice versa. Any conflicts among deities would usually have correlates in the class struggles and the conflicts among dynasties or city states. Mesopotamian sources that can be ascribed to different historical eras can help to reconstruct the social processes associated with the changes occurring in a society organised under a central authority. According to the position allocated to them in the Mesopotamian system of belief, human beings could clearly not appear as agents in such narratives. Only the gods possessed will-power; it was only they who acted. Their human subjects were mere shadows of divine glory. I think that this astonishing ideological hegemony was at the core of the concept and the institutional practices of the early centralised state. Later centralised states represented fully-fledged religious, legal and political orders, to which the individual was and still remains totally subjected. This ideological hegemony continues to exist in modern state societies, albeit in somewhat transmuted ways.

2
The Historical Role of Sumerian Civilisation

Although it constitutes the remarkable starting point of the process of civilisation, Sumerian culture has not been given sufficient prominence in the intellectual history of modernity. This is partly due to the fact that the memory of it was obliterated and its material remains only discovered at a comparatively late stage,[1] and partly due to the Eurocentric thinking so characteristic of modernity. The self-centeredness of Greco-Roman civilisation had played a huge role in the obliteration of Sumerian civilisation. It seems that each form of cultural complexity tends to regard cultural development as limited to itself and invents narratives of how it itself constituted the beginnings of civilisation. The Sumerians themselves certainly displayed this cultural egotism in laying claim to the entirety of the achievements of the neolithic and chalcolithic ages and ascribing the creation of all given cultural values to the gods who they said had created the Sumerian cities as their primal abodes.

The impact Sumerian culture has had on subsequent cultures can be discussed under a number of different headings.

THE EMERGENCE OF CLASS SOCIETY

The process of *socialisation*, of establishing cultural practices that both require and foster more or less conscious forms of cohesion in communities, is the most basic, but also the most far-reaching achievement of the human species. While all living species undergo a natural process of evolution, human societies are at the same time agents in this process by virtue of the faculty of comprehension and will-power. The ability to grasp things that happened in the material world fuelled the development of speech in *Homo sapiens*, which in turn allowed for the regulation of communal life through purposeful activities. The development of certain areas of the brain, along with the increasingly efficient use of tools and techniques, mediated through speech-based interaction, gave rise to a qualitative leap that distinguishes this species from other animals.

The main characteristic of this initial social revolution was the realisation of the advantages of living in communities. As in the formation of the elements in matter, durable units developed towards increasing complexity. This social history, measured in hundreds of thousands of years, precedes the history of civilisation.[2] Long before there evolved the perception of *individuality*, which forms one of the pillars of European civilisation and underlies the notion of individual human rights (discussed in my pending Court application), countless generations of hominids had to devote enormous effort towards creating *sociality*. Primitive fetishism, animism, totemism, matrilineal kinship systems and patriarchy, polytheist and monotheist religious structures, shamanism and prophethood, all served the purpose of committing the human species to a definite social order that entailed emancipation from biological instincts and compliance with cultural rules.

The methods employed may seem odd to us – but rituals and oblations, including human sacrifice, must be understood as an integral part of a basic process of education aiming at the realisation of the potential social power of the species. It was through these efforts that human beings developed forms of behaviour so distinct from that of animals, and that nature was rendered serviceable to human communities.[3] These methods form our cultural heritage in a more acute sense than we may envision, and civilisation is founded on them.

The *agrarian revolution* of the Neolithic age constitutes the second stage in the emergence of class society. Its effects on the material and intellectual culture of humankind persist even through our post-industrial age. The main elements sustaining complex cultures over millennia originate from sedentary agricultural society. Firstly, the products derived from agriculture and animal husbandry, which still form the basis of subsistence all over the world, and the exploitation of mineral ores. Secondly, many of our concepts, and their linguistic manifestations, derived from these activities. Without the cultural devices developed in the piedmonts of the Zagros and plains of the Fertile Crescent, and the social structures arising from them, there would have been neither Sumerian class society, nor state and superstructure institutions, nor, indeed, the subsequent line of development in civilisation that we today construe. Hypothetically speaking, if these developments had not occurred in the Fertile Crescent in the way outlined, present day world civilisation might well have evolved in some other way, from other sources, and might have brought about different cultural constellations from the ones we are presently discussing. But since we are concerned with actually existing history, in which we are real agents, any awareness of its intricacies entails a discussion of ancient south-west Asia.

Non-European societies in general and Middle Eastern societies in particular will gain self-confidence, and perhaps some corrective guidelines for their present political life, from a more thorough understanding of their own part in world history. One particularly dangerous dimension of the imperialist aspect of European civilisation is its ideological hegemony. Without challenging it, we shall never be able to enter an independent path of political and economic development and share in a sustainable and just world order.

The story of how human beings became human beings in the first place should never be forgotten when discussing how the ancient mythologies and religions, irrational though they may appear to us, were invented. The process of socialisation as generating an outburst of collective cultural energy can be compared to the fusion of hydrogen atoms into helium, which accounts for the energy radiated by the sun. Ancestry, magic, priesthood and prophecy were agents in this process. (Now, one of the prominent features of Western civilisation is that it has initiated a counterpoising process. Historical agents in modernity attempted to dismantle those social structures they found detrimental to their personal short-term interests, and lionised the *individual* in the name of freedom. Capitalist personalities and institutions, more authoritarian and richer than any of the coercive elites history had hitherto known, emerged from these attempts. They are now destroying the social resources built up through hundreds of thousands of years of human labour along with the natural resources that labour drew upon, ravaging all the material and moral aspects of world cultures that they find unprofitable, while ruthlessly appropriating those on which they can capitalise. Whether this will lead towards higher forms of civilisation or towards its fatal derailment and imminent catastrophe has been vividly discussed by some of the most eminent modern philosophers.[4] This question and the related one of whether socialism, which has arisen as a reaction to this very tendency, can constitute an alternative, are discussed in the relevant chapters of this volume.)

Initial class differentiation and stratified state society in early Mesopotamia can only be understood on the basis of what we know about the communities preceding it. Abstract models of the "slaveholding mode of production" are of limited explanatory value, especially where they are not informed by an analytical understanding of the concrete way in which Sumerian society was organised. Most theories of slavery draw their general outlook from looking at the slave system in Athens and Rome.[5] Whilst these provide important examples of mature and disintegrating slave-owning societies respectively, the formative process of class societies as the pivot of the history of civilisation needs to be studied from its oldest and perhaps most significant sources in early Mesopotamia. The distinctive details that differentiate Sumer from, say, the Greek world deserve to be taken into account. The outlines of the almost 3,000 years of early Mesopotamian state societies need to be determined as precisely as possible in order to establish the main lines of historical development in the ancient world. Failing that, our consciousness of history will remain seriously flawed. I believe that a certain line of historical development begins at Sumer. This often escapes the attention of historians and social scientists and leaves them entangled with misconceptions of later processes. One purpose of my drafting these submissions was to call for an approach to international historical and social issues that does them justice.

The transition from a society organised in kinship units to a political one hinged on the institution of slavery.[6] It provided the material basis for profound change. Servile labour in the collective economy was a decisive factor in the production of surplus far above what was needed for consumption. It allowed a layer of merchants and specialised craftspeople to arise as a distinct and novel social group, as well as an administrative elite that no longer relied on the kinship bonds of tribal federations.[7] Thus, a three-level social stratification came into being that continues to exist in most societies to the present day.

This class differentiation was probably much more complex and certainly less clear-cut than this schematic description suggests, and kinship ties may, to some extent, have remained the connective tissue of Sumerian civilisation. We do not have any articulate, direct account of this process. But its description through sophisticated myth was one of the main occupations of Sumerian scribes and poets. Enslavement is described in striking terms as an integral part of the divine order that people had better not complain about.[8] The ideological hegemony established through Sumerian myth must have been quite sweeping, considering that probably all layers of this early society would have interpreted reality in terms of this matrix. Enslaved subjects in Mesopotamia were mere shadows, subordinate creatures, throughout several thousand years. The social system coordinated from the temples required everyone, from the god–king to the agricultural labourers, to act according to the predestined position they were allocated. Everything on earth followed the well-laid-out plans of the various gods, as did the stars and planets in the sky. Even to thoughts, dreams and emotions would be attached a meaning determined by the will of the gods. The world continued without end and with little change, as was decreed by the divine masters. This is the first recorded ideological opus of a coercive ruling class relying on servile labour and it is truly awe-inspiring.[9] Indeed, several Mesopotamian god–kings seem to have been entombed along with their life retinue. One grave adorned with royal insignia at Ur contained the remains of 74 elaborately dressed bodies, mostly females, thought to be human sacrifices, perhaps servants, interred upon the god–king's death.[10]

Most slaves and dependent labourers in Sumer were not employed in the royal, or any other private household, but were in the service of the temple collectives. (Private ownership of slaves was the predominant form of property in Athens and Rome, but not in Mesopotamia.) The idea of sacrificing human life for some higher purpose associated with divine authority pervades early Mesopotamian society. It is part of the ideological power sanctioning slavery and confiscatory behaviour. This ideological hegemony has been renewed and revised by exploitative ruling classes throughout the history of civilisation vis-à-vis the awakening human will-power and reason. The chain remains unbroken. The Sumerian state apparatus was the most naive, and perhaps most credible, tool of coercion – later forms of state rule have increasingly perfected their hierarchical order by means of innumerable forms of ideological hegemony. Although humankind has waged heroic struggles for freedom, we are still a far cry from doing away with the hegemony of this particular form of slavery. On the contrary, it has been consolidated through educational institutions, and its circumference expanded through elaborate techniques. Some of its protagonists have even suggested they could soon control and manipulate the genetic structure of human beings by means of modern technologies.

GENDER INEQUALITY

The specific quality that gender differences assumed in Sumerian society is another of the important "firsts" they realised. Women formed a prominent part of the productive force of the Neolithic cultures that preceded and surrounded Sumerian society. Both agriculture and the domestication of animals would certainly not have evolved without the active contributions of women. Sedentary modes of living are often said to have been adopted in response to females' requirements pertaining to the rearing of children.[11] Pottery, weaving and the pounding and grinding of cereal grains were central activities, and they were principally performed by women. Kinship relations crystallised around females in what is often described as matrilineal or matrifocal modes of social organisation. These found their ideological expression in religious symbolism, in which many aspects of nature were conceived as female goddesses. Gendered hierarchies developed in Sumerian society in conjunction with class hierarchies. These hierarchies are colourfully reflected in mythical texts of different periods, where increasing differences in status lead to reconceptions of earlier themes. In the early narratives, the goddesses occupy a pre-eminent position that progressively fades as time passes, until they receive a mortal blow as signified in the slaughter of the Babylonian mother goddess Tiamat by Enki's offspring Marduk.[12] Marduk, the city god of Babylon, does not appear in earlier texts, but in the Babylonian culture of the second millennium BCE he assumes the position of a predominant god. His rise in status, which has sometimes been interpreted as a proto-form of monotheism,[13] signifies the ancient Near Eastern culture of male dominance that has its repercussions in the tradition of the monotheist religions referring to Abraham as their founder.[14] Women initially held positions in the Sumerian temples that were equal to those of male priests, but females soon assumed subordinate roles in the households, which constituted the core units of the early stratified society. The institutionalisation of marriage, and that of prostitution, is also an invention of the Sumerians. Nevertheless, the status of women in early Mesopotamian society is not quite as debased as it is in the second wave of civilisations, i.e. in the Israelite, Phoenician, Greek and Roman societies. Judging from the textual evidence, compromise appears to be the principal form in which tensions between the genders are played out in Sumerian culture.

THE URBAN REVOLUTION[15]

While the neolithic age was based on an agrarian, sedentary revolution, civilised society is chiefly defined by reference to urbanisation and the creation of a state, the latter being based on the former. The reorganisation of human communities on an unprecedented scale[16] was made possible by the rise of formalised and hierarchical institutions in the economic basis of society and in its conceptual superstructure – the centralised state. Life in large and complex social contexts must have precipitated a new mentality and the search for new institutions. The practice of writing, both in administrative and in sacral–literary contexts; the calculation of quantities of goods, tides, seasons and other natural cycles; the practice of medicine and education were established as distinct professions. These were probably social markers in a changing context in which status would increasingly be measured in terms of occupation instead of, or complementary to, kinship affiliation. The social institutions and modes of inter-human relations established in Sumerian society are fundamentally those that prevail in modern societies, where their dimensions and the specificity of their subsections have grown to varying degrees. It would therefore be erroneous to analyse subsequent societies, or indeed the condition of our age, without having recourse to this primal link in a chain of complex, hierarchical civilisations.

THE ECONOMIC INSTITUTIONS OF SUMER

There is evidence of both collective and private ownership of land in Sumer. Tenure, lease and property rights were highly codified. The urban elite of the Sumerian cities exacted tributes in the form of products or labour payments (*corvée*).[17] Large institutional estates undoubtedly constituted a major component of the economy.[18] The crafts were separated from the process of food production and became independent professions that accounted for an important dimension of Sumerian economic and social life. Merchants, potters, silversmiths, metallurgists, leather-workers, fishermen, bricklayers, smiths, weavers and scribes were organised into separate guilds, which apparently had a cultic function. The superiority of Sumerian urban civilisation over its agrarian hinterland is to some extent a product of these specialised professions. Social phenomena like the institution of sages and prophethood, that permeate the history of the Middle East, have these guilds as sources of influence.

THE SUPERSTRUCTURE INSTITUTIONS

The seminal formation of state institutions in Sumer involves types of hierarchic organisation that can be found in most subsequent states, namely institutions such as kingship, the military, vizierate, administrative bureaucracy, and a representative city assembly (*ukkin*).[19] Early Mesopotamian society created a set of values and *institutions* that have been handed down to present-day cities and have undergone a process of continuous modification and refinement without their basic content being altered. The mythological fabrications of the Sumerians, their rituals and practices of worship, constituted the oil that fuelled and kept the machinery of social institutions, both in sub- and superstructure, running smoothly. The actions of the administrative and ruling elite, especially those of the priest class, suggest that they knew that they would not have been able to run the state and govern the incipient class society without creating such ideological patterns. And they devised means that coerced the population into internalising these patterns.[20]

Neolithic society was based on the kinship organisation of significantly less complex agrarian communities. In these communities coordinating social activities was fairly straightforward and there was no need for complex rules and institutions to control thought and governance. Thus, the social necessity for elaborate mythological resources was not as developed as in Sumer. This era of human development found its mental expression in totems referring to the cult of female and male ancestors, and basic forms of symbolism pertaining to astral bodies. The necessity to adopt more complex forms of promoting group identity must have made itself felt to Uruk society as it turned into a stratified urban aggregate, with the institution of priesthood the most characteristic social phenomenon.

The ideological projections of Sumer appear rather fascinating to modern readers. Some studies have shown the seminal influence they had on later theology and literature. It should be appreciated that these projections have determined to a great extent the ideological structures that percolated through the history of civilisation. The Sumerian mindset can be found underlying all dogmas pervading present Middle Eastern societies. Sumerology and Assyriology are, therefore, branches of study that are of increasing value to us. The structure of early Mesopotamian thought is stunningly rich.

What follows are some of the basic elements of normative Sumerian thought as represented in extant documents.

STRUCTURE AND FUNCTION OF THOUGHT

Sumerian thought is of a primitive dialectical structure. Sky (*an* or Anu) and Earth (*ki*) are conceived as antagonists that represent the male and female principles respectively. According to one myth, *Enki* is the product of the union of Anu, the sky god, and Ki, the Earth.[21] In Enki, the masculine element prevails. He embodies the concept of the progenitor, and the cultural concept of fatherhood. In early myth, he copulates with, and engenders, successive generations of female deities. Finally – in the Babylonian tradition of the second millennium – he fathers Marduk, who slays Tiamat.[22]

From 2000 BCE onwards, the goddess cult and the mythological discourse pertaining to it were increasingly discredited and marginalised. This development must be seen in correlation with women's loss of social status. Even before the second millennium, the principle of masculinity, and with it male dominance, became prevalent in social structure and state policies. From the supreme state institution of royal authority to the smallest ward units and household establishments, the tenets of a masculine and uniform religion held sway, and mythological ideas hardened into fixed religious beliefs. Society underwent a major ideological and moral transformation. The kings would now either claim they were gods,[23] or assert they were divinely selected. The relationship between master and slave turned into one between god and creature. The transmutation of mythic thought into canonised creeds, and thus into religion proper and definite law, was a socio-historical development which had overwhelming ramifications. The ziggurats and scribal schools – among them the *Edubba* or "tablet houses", cultural academies that flourished in the Old Babylonian period – acted as centres for promoting the existing socio-political order and furthering the authority of the current king. The chief mission of the priests, scribes and thinkers was to establish what we now regard as mythology. This they did through the composition and promulgation of explicitly theological texts and epic prose and poetry. For millennia, the holy city of Nippur and, later on, Babylon were the cultural, religious and literary centres of these efforts.[24]

Celestial Order

The Sumerians' system of thought was based on the order they observed in the skies. Just as stars, moon and sun followed eternal, unchanging movements, the earthly laws had to express, and secure, an everlasting order. The state and the the ruler had to represent this order on behalf of the gods. Political authority was irrefutably sanctioned. All forces and features of nature were thought of as manifestations of specific deities, and so were all social forces. No feature, object or creature that could not have been associated with a god was thinkable. This theistic world-view was to undergo a remarkable evolution and form the point of departure for classical Greek philosophy, and by extension for modern European scientific thought. However much these modes of thinking contradict each other, they evolved in clear interconnectedness. Their interrelatedness must be accounted for when writing the histories of religion, of philosophy and of scientific thought. The Sumerian mode of thinking clearly amounted to a remarkable advancement in terms of early cultural achievements. Their "laws of the gods" still reverberate in the modern idea of scientifically established laws of nature.

Seminal Motifs

Familiar mythological topics, such as primeval man, heaven and nether world, the expulsion from paradise and the deluge occupy important places in

Sumerian thought. Problems and contradictions encountered in nature or society formed the subject matter of poetic compositions. These efforts at conceptualisation amount to a fully-fledged theoretical system that could be applied to any new event or discovered relation. The systematic approach culminated in an intellectual flowering, in which an amazing variety of phenomena were explored and categorised. The Sumerian conviction that everything in the universe constantly interacted has occupied, under different guises, a seat of honour in intellectual history throughout the ages, and informs the first principle of dialectics.[25] The earliest known utopias and legends go back to cuneiform tablets. The utopia of a paradisiacal garden, the life of a primal couple of human beings and their expulsion from this garden, as well as the conflict of the brothers Cain and Abel, were presaged in Sumerian texts. So was the narrative of the Deluge. This originally independent story was later incorporated into the Gilgamesh Epic, a story of a semi-divine hero's quest for immortality. Many of the motifs in these texts resound with a yearning for the old days of the neolithic society or refer to the peoples' struggles with the hardships caused by social contradictions.[26] Obviously, all these were expressed in ways that reflect how far removed the human mind of 5,000 years ago still was from a scientific understanding of reality. We should not forget that even in classical Greco-Roman civilisation, actual scientific thought was rather limited, and philosophical argumentation was never fully dissociated from mythology and theology.

EMPIRE AND COLONIALISM

The first emperor who conquered all of the Sumerian city states and united them under the centralist Akkad state was Sargon.[27] Prior to this, Sumerian city states had maintained outposts and waged military campaigns with the aim of securing trade interests or political influence.[28] Nevertheless, it was Sargon who first established an imperial capital as the heart of an expansive system in which vast lands within and beyond Mesopotamia were, by means of what appears to have been excessive violence, subdued into the status of colonies under Akkadian sovereignty. Subsequent imperial and colonial endeavours amounted to little more than enhanced applications of the Sargonic model. The slaughtering of people through a well-planned use of force, the appropriation of all their belongings and resources, the deportation of captives as slaves, and the creation of tiers of colonial dependence, became principal features of historical development. According to the way he presented himself and his rule to the world, Sargon had founded the universal empire of his times, extending his power to "the four corners of the world".[29] Thus, over and above being a class-based state society, Sumer had now turned into a multi-ethnic imperialist civilisation.

Legal norms were inscribed on obelisks that were erected in public places, and some effort was spent on making subjects understand and obey the fundamental rules of the social order imposed by the regime. The Laws of Ur-Nammu[30] and the Code of Hammurabi[31] are of timeless fame – or notoriety.

Apart from these inventions, some of the *maqams* (modal scales), melodic patterns and instruments in Middle Eastern music seem to go back to ancient Mesopotamian culture. Given that their demonstrable influence on south-west Asian culture – and on all civilisations informed by it – is unique, a great deal of speculation as to the ethnic origins of the Sumerians has taken place, often with a view to "finding" their contemporary ethnic successors.[32] I do not wish to debate the importance of furthering such research, but it seems to be fairly established now that the proto-Sumerians of the Ubaid culture consisted of communities that settled in the south Mesopotamian delta around 6000 BCE, most probably coming in *both* from the Arabian deserts to the south-west and from the fringes of the Zagros and Taurus mountains to the east and the north respectively. The fecund terrain must have been a decisive factor in the long-term transformation that brought about an "original" Sumerian culture and idiom, in which traces of Hurrian and Semitic Amorite word roots are found, although the language itself is not related to either of them. However, there is no positive evidence to exclude the possibility of the Ubaid people being of a different "ethnic origin". More important than the question of a pure origin seems to me the consideration that here, as in many instances in human history, different cultural units may have merged into a synthesis based on common cultural achievements. In fact, the Sumerians probably signify the historic "origin" of that very process. Their lands were situated in the most fertile valleys between the Arabian deserts and the Zagros–Taurus chain of mountains, and in the flux of development of their civilisation, they attracted a number of incursions and attacks. As was the case with the Roman Empire, the riches so ostentatiously displayed by Sumerian civilisation aroused the envy of neighbouring peoples, as well as incurring the wrath of those who had been on the receiving end of Sumer's expansive aggrandisement in the first place. A chain reaction was triggered that resulted in a dynamic and accelerated historical development. All regional peoples, including the Semitic tribes from the south and the west, and the Indo-European ones from the north and the east, were assimilated into the stratified mode of organisation of civilisation under the supremacy of the Mesopotamian empires, and by virtue of this assimilation they learned how to set upon the centre in unceasing waves.

3

The Lasting Effects of Sumerian Civilisation

Sumerian culture underwent remarkable transformations and in part endured within other civilisations, several of which were in part its offspring. The first verifiable example of such transformation is that of Sargon's dynasty in Akkad, which lasted from about 2350 to 2250 BCE. Although the official and cultic language and the hegemonic culture of Akkad were Sumerian, a progressive influx of Semitic elements can be discerned. Perhaps in reaction, the Hurrian tribes known to us as the Guti struck an alliance with the rulers of other Sumerian city states against the central authority of Akkad and established a new balance of power which contributed to a further transformation of Sumerian culture.

From around 2000 BCE, Sumer suffered the repeated incursions of Amorite tribes from the areas to the south and east of the south Mesopotamian heartlands, and following the fall of the Ur III Dynasty a period of principalities and city states ensued, dominated by Amorite ruling families. With the advent of the Amorite dynasty of King Hammurabi of Babylon, the original Sumerians lost all their former power and Sumerian was replaced as an official language by the Akkadian language of Babylon. This language, which is at the root of the Assyrian and Chaldean languages spoken in Mesopotamia up to the present day, became the new lingua franca of the Middle East. Babylonian culture became the new socio-cultural idiom.

Following this, the Hurrian-speaking Kassites, the Mitanni and the Hittites from the north claimed an increasing share in political power both inside and outside Babylon proper. Nevertheless, the brain and tongue of political power throughout the region remained Babylonian. The whole of Sumerian culture was selectively appropriated by the Babylonians, whose distinctive theology and literature epitomised a whole era of world history. Astonishing achievements were made in the fields of mathematics and astronomy. The Assyrian Amorite dynasty of Nineveh, north of Babylon, took this process a step further. Under the ideological and cultural leadership of Babylon and then the politico-military leadership of Assyria, the whole of the ancient Middle East was shattered, devastated and renewed.

The Babylonian and Assyrian periods thus amounted to a conversion of Sumerian civilisation into Akkadian, and ensured its direct expansion over most of the Middle East and its indirect transmission to regions far beyond. This process was, however, primarily affected by means of imperialist force. The ideological and cultural contributions at this stage were limited. Sumerian was taught as a liturgical language and, by virtue of translations and bilingual texts, was disseminated widely. Gradually it became absorbed into local idioms as it became assimilated with the various vernaculars. Towards the end of the first millennium BCE, Sumerian had all but vanished as a language.

The era of direct impact of Sumerian on world civilisation thus ran from about 4000 to 2000 BCE, followed by one of indirect impact that lasted perhaps equally long. No other civilisation has both sustained and exhausted humanity for so long. No other ideology could have prepared humankind for the system of slavery, installed its basis and superstructural institutions, secured its permanence, and, over and above all this, sanctioned slavery by means of dogma that was virtually unchangeable. A balance-sheet of its contributions to the process of civilisation is therefore pivotal to an understanding of this process as a whole. The following aspects, which I shall outline roughly, need to be taken into account.

THE ORIGIN OF SUMERIAN SLAVE-OWNING SOCIETY

Sumerian stratified civilisation was arguably based on the neolithic society in the Fertile Crescent, which had emerged over several millennia preceding the formation of what we would regard as urban settlements. Partly through trade, partly through force, but mainly through the development of its own highly productive economic system, Sumerian civilisation managed to adapt, absorb and lay claim to all the technological and scientific advances of the Stone Age. The differentiation of labour in its socially stratified towns led to an institutionalisation of handicrafts and various professional skills which made it possible for the Sumerians to reap the benefit of these earlier inventions. The neolithic communities of Sumer's hinterland must have been as overwhelmed in the face of the ascent of Sumerian slaveholding civilisation as are the oppressed peoples of today vis-à-vis contemporary United States imperialism, in the sense that the oppressed peoples experience the actions of the United States as imperialist. Their development must, to some extent, have been arrested. Especially in Assyrian times, the imperialistic policy of uprooting and deporting entire populations reached such proportions that its repercussions can be felt even today. Particularly cruel methods of torture and execution, enforced displacement, and slaughter and rape during the waging of gruesome military campaigns assumed nearly genocidal proportions. Their premeditated application indelibly marked the memory of humankind. The use of systematic violence to establish or uphold a class society became a pattern that has been refined and repeated over and over again. If the deliberate and systematic annihilation of human beings is still practised now, on a scale proportionate to technological progress, does this not suggest that these practices of the first civilisations are so deeply ingrained in human cultural memory that we may speak of them as genetically encoded? I believe that, like genes in biological organisms, social memory has ways of codifying and preserving collective experience in such a way that certain forms of behaviour or reactions are passed down to later societies.[1] Whilst the ruling and exploiting classes live in abundance, the ruled and exploited social groups grow ever weaker and experience ongoing immiseration. Once the dialectics of tyranny and exploitation are established, dynamics are brought into play to which we have not yet managed to call a halt. We may be able to split atoms, but we still cannot stop this fatal course of social development. But is not the accumulation of abundance as useless as its opposite, the lack of material, intellectual or social means and faculties? Humankind could live in a more balanced and happy way if neither of these existed.

It is precisely this inequality that gives rise to human suffering. Even in its basic form it draws on a form of consciousness that differentiates humans from animals. It also gives birth to the notion of dignity, and thus constitutes an impetus that would manifest itself in an alternative line of historical development – the tendency to resistance and liberation. For the Middle East, the institution of prophecy became the vessel of expression of this tendency. The early, but strong example of the hope of emancipation, based on prophecy, tells us how civilisation begins where communities are ruthlessly deprived of the comparatively peaceful and egalitarian structures of neolithic social organisation and the residues of these structures are then pushed out of the historical process, rendered non-historical. Human memory preserves a phantasmagorical vision of a paradise just as its real substrate loses its place in the historical process. By appropriating the values of neolithic society and inventing the apparatus of the state, civilisation swallows up any ill-equipped individual or community like a full-grown leviathan.

THE SUMERIAN STATE

The birth of the state at Sumer, in so far as it encapsulated the identity of class society, was truly an extraordinary event. It seems as though there was no fantasy that this tool could not realise; and to the present day, the dominant notion of the state is to the effect that any male who can claim affiliation to a state, and indeed any nation with a state, are endowed by their creator with unlimited rights over others. The example of Sumer can help us understand where this power of the state comes from. It provides invaluable material for an analysis of civilisation as a whole, because it is pristine. First and foremost, the institution assumes incomparable power over individuals, over the ethnic group, and over those factions that remain outside the body politic. The masterful creating of the state by the Sumerian priests established a social mentality whereby institutionalised political power was a worldly manifestation of the celestial order. The main purpose of any mythology or knowledge of the gods is to secure the hegemony of the dogma of a sanctioned and perennial class society as a part of the natural order. The divine authorities are simply the newly burgeoning monarchic dynasties. But to state this outright would neither serve the credibility of this authority, nor would it help entrench and preserve it. Thus, the state must first be established and grounded in the field of ideology. The state is born where ideological vindication is fused with the technical know-how of Neolithic society at the threshold of surplus product. It is through securing the former that the latter can be appropriated by a certain stratum of society. The fusion of the two indeed leads to unprecedented productivity.

Most scholars agree that the archaic Sumerian temple formed the template for the apparatus of the later, fully-fledged dynastic state. Despite the modernists' cherished opinion that the state is a rational expression of human reason, we might do better to take it as a theological, dogmatic expression of the human mind. I suggest that civilisation, and the state as its most essential feature, are tantamount to a theological manifestation of the dogmatic mode of comprehension predominant at the primitive stage of the formation of classes, where rational thinking has not yet evolved. In that respect, the state might be the most outdated tool we use today, especially in forms that lack legitimation through processes of grass roots decision making. I argue in Parts 3 and 4 that one important achievement of European societies is to have imbued the body politic of their countries with democracy. This, of course, has only become possible thanks to the extraordinary resistance and struggles for freedom of oppressed peoples, classes, nations and individuals.

Just as there is a direct correlation between the state and God in general, there is one between extremely centralised sovereignty and monotheistic thought and belief specifically. As the image of God that one projects becomes mightier and more inscrutable, this God assumes more attributes (and I shall argue that these are the traits of civilisation), and political authority becomes more powerful, awe-inspiring, incomprehensible and unapproachable, as do the masks behind which it hides its features. The king personifies all these characteristics. He is trained to represent them, for he is supposed to represent God. Prior to class society, the totem was the condensed identity or a kind of family name of the community it represented. But since social relations were not exploitative, the totems were neither truly terrifying nor actually divine. As self-aggrandising and exploitative behaviour on the part of the tribal chiefs grew, the totem slowly climbed up to the heights of divinity. As it changed its abode from the earth to the heavens, it lost its palpability, its proximity, and its quality of being something cared for. It gained properties associated with being remote, untouchable and fear-inducing. Thus the differentiation of social strata in society carried in itself a momentum irreconcilably antagonistic to the essence of social living.

Nevertheless, it is too limited to regard the state solely as a means for indirect theft and hoax. For one thing, its initial development could not be accounted for in this manner. The complexity of class society, with its tendency to continuously refine the division of labour and the collective security issues of its members, generates a demand for mandatory coordination that both prompts the ruling class to espouse the rigid institutionalisation of political authority and allows it to render itself indispensable. This ambiguity of the state needs to be taken into account, for it has given rise to two dogmatic patterns of interpretation, the first being the official view sanctioning nearly everything pertaining to institutionalised authority, the second being the non-conformist wholesale denunciation and demonisation of anything associated with state power. Obviously, those social classes that are linked to the state apparatus tend to favour the former pattern, their opponents the latter. Because of this polarisation, the state itself is an expression of an analytically irreducible social identity characterised by the antagonism between those who live in abundance and those who live in poverty, each section having interests conflicting with those of the other. The remarkable zeal with which state power has been both theoretically discussed and practically organised from ancient times to the present day may indicate how theologically charged this institution is. Modern civilisation may take pride in having, at least for the time being, banished God from the subject–object relation that it has established between science and nature. But when it comes to society, nothing of that kind has been achieved. Because wherever there's a state, there's a god.

THE TEACHING OF THE GODS

Any study of Sumerian civilisation entails an analysis of mythology and the teaching of the gods. This branch of knowledge would later be called *theology* in Greek and *ilahiyyah* in Arabic. I believe that a proper understanding of it is at least as important as a Marxian analysis of the state and money. Marxian theory has contributed much to the project of scientifically understanding state and society. And yet it seems to me that its propensity to regard the ideological power at the root of the state as a simple reflection of material factors constitutes its weakest point and, as it were, its most dangerous aspect. To me it seems that one of the central reasons for its failure to achieve what it envisioned lies in its tendency to limit the discussion of religion to a blunt "opium-for-the-people" type of sloganeering. Marxian theory in most of its interpretations treats religion as something ordinary and straightforward. I am convinced that just as thorough an analysis of the teaching of the gods (*ilahiyyah*) is needed as of money and state power. Sumer offers a striking illustration. Theology is the science of the class struggles of the Sumerians. No analysis of Sumerian ideology, and consequently of the whole of antiquity based on it, can be done without a scrutiny of the social projections of the concepts and patterns of argument involved in the teaching of the gods. Further, the same is indispensable for studying the monotheistic religions and the structural characteristics of the mentality and literature of the classical age, of the medieval Middle East and Europe, and indeed of present societies. The mental set-up of all societies bears the imprint of theology. Without uncovering this imprint and erasing it one cannot create a positive society on a scientific basis. Among the major shortcomings of "real socialism" was that it did not so much as acknowledge the existence of the historical and ideological dimension of social life and therefore encouraged extremely one-sided perceptions as to what constitutes the state. Social realities cannot be explained within the limits of a critique of money and capital. Indeed, such attempts have in many instances led straight to the predicaments of a slightly different version of that very idealism that it so vigorously opposes; just as real socialism ended up surrendering itself into the loving arms of capital. It now seems inescapable to me that reductionist applications of Marxian thought are detrimental to the interests of those who champion them.

The power of ideology, specifically of its theological form, is by no means less than that of money, or indeed of institutionalised force. The three are in fact closely intertwined and have fully penetrated each other, generating a historically unique synergy that makes me think of the relationship between the Father, the Son and the Holy Spirit. Beyond the level of random comparison, there are real parallels involved in the genesis of these two trinities. In each, one element incessantly urges for material emanation while another progressively spiritualises. But with the Sumerians, this trinity comes as a single substance. From one of them there emanates worldly power, whilst from another comes the empyrean. But there are indications that the elite of the ostensibly primitive Sumerians did not actually believe this. They may well have been aware that they themselves created the whole threesome and they certainly had a very precise idea of how to make use of it. Strangely enough, a typical scientist of today might be much more bigoted than they were, and we might be just as far from understanding Sumerian theology as Sumerians would have been from understanding modern science. Certainly there is "truth" in both of these dissimilar discourses, and to proceed we need to study them both in our search for this "truth" and to try to establish a historical correlation between them. Just as a child cannot be understood without reference to its mother, so science cannot be construed without reference to theology.

Having said this, I am not calling for a relapse into theology. But I do think that the academic disciplines of our age have shown a remarkable laziness in linking their specific endeavours to general issues arising from a critical understanding of civilisation, and thus of the impact of theology and state power on their field of operation. The result has been a situation similar to that of the sorcerer who fell victim to his own sorcery. In particular, those contemporary ideologues of society who claim a research-based underpinning for their ideas would do well to account for the effects of the intricate cross-connections of the trinity of theology, the state and money on human life. I suggest that such an account is a prerequisite for salvation from the grip of sorcery and indeed for formulating visionary projects for social change. Issues pertaining to such a task will be discussed in the following parts of this volume.

SUMERIAN CLASS SOCIETY

An account of the Sumerian class society, and of the history of civilisation at the beginning of which it is now situated by most scholars, would therefore have to shed light on its influence on the relation between science and philosophy on the one hand and mythology and theology on the other. The commonplace that science and philosophy are by-products of civilisation is by no means undisputed. What is maintained by most authors is that the quality and extent of the inventions made by the inhabitants of Halafian and Ubaid settlements of the sixth to the fourth millennium BCE is only paralleled by the spurt in cultural and technological change since the sixteenth century CE. The depiction of class society as a hotbed of intellectual innovation and technical development is open to discussion. I think that the example of Sumer actually shows us that the most substantial accumulation of knowledge happens in preclass societies and that the hegemony of the state has an impeding effect on this process. The knowledge and technique generated by Sumerian society beyond what was already available to its historical antecedents of the upper chalcolithic era were rather limited. The developments that did occur were mainly linked to the monopolisation of agriculture and social know-how, as well as to the establishment of an ideological hegemony on top of all that. This involved idealising knowledge as a set of concessions made by the gods to their faithful human servants rather than regarding it as a product of human labour and practical strife. This form of ideological distortion is one of the most severe in history. Thanks to their ideological faculty of deception, the Sumerian priests deserve to enter the historical record as the foremost architects of centralised political power and thus as the main agents of the growing weight of class as a characteristic of civilisation. Had it not been for the ideological hegemony established through Sumerian mythology and religion, a much earlier and quicker development of science, technology and philosophy under conditions of a free system of production might have been possible for humankind.

The historical archetype of Sumer is a case in point for any discussion of the correlation between knowledge and power. A higher level of freedom in social relations is conducive to intellectual creativity, while increasing pressure and ideological deception lead to a serious decline, in terms of the availability of verifiable information and the quality of overall interpretations of the world.

One portion of the population in class society is exempted from production, while another much larger portion is enslaved and dehumanised for the sake of exploiting their labour. This forms the basis for intellectual stagnation. Its maintenance requires legitimisation through ideological dogma. The principal role of the priestly class throughout history has been to uphold these dogmas. Priests elaborated and conserved the fictitious concepts of paradise and hell and of a punishing god, and presented those to the suffering people while securing hitherto unknown wealth for themselves and the political leaders. The initial centres of production of mythology were the temples. Eventually, their function would be taken over by the academies that were founded when a specific layer of intellectuals emerged. The academic order of the philosophers became a pre-eminent feature of Greco-Roman civilisation. But it actually goes back to the prototype academy of letters established in the Babylonian cultural centre of Nippur under the name of Edduba, an institution often described as the "first university" in history.

This is not to say that religion only arises with, and can be equated to, the emerging ruling class and its state apparatus. As is clear from cuneiform texts, the perception of the world in early Mesopotamia included a variety of primitive religious ideas involving tribal totemism and the spirits of both female and male ancestors. Animist beliefs were common, and so were various kinds of sorcery or witchcraft. With the progressive development of class divisions, however, the ensuing conflicts of interest brought about a division in religious and mythological systems of belief. The ideologues of the exploitative order sought to establish the hegemony of their own religious ideas, and they eventually discredited the old notions of spirituality – especially those identified as sorcery – as transgression, while introducing certain practices that were explicitly sanctioned. What might today be seen as a matter of individual worship was then an issue of power relations within a changing social order. In its further development, this social division also underlies the antagonism between Satan and God.[2] The antagonism is put most blatantly in Sumerian mythology. Comparative studies of Biblical narratives that have their origin in Sumerian myths provide us with valuable material for our view: the expulsion of Adam and Eve from Paradise is a terse and poetic parable illustrating the beginnings of class society, and the quarrel between Cain and Abel tells us of the contradictions between agriculturalists and pastoral nomads.[3]

There are other narratives that tell us of the degradation of woman. In poems, epics and myths, goddesses are dethroned, humiliated and killed, and gradually declassified; eventually they disappear from the Sumerian pantheon. One step beyond this, in monotheism woman is a deceitful creature, socially enslaved by the will of God. It befits her to remain secluded and to keep her mouth shut. Traces in cultural memory of the age of female goddesses are glossed over with accounts of the past of woman as the one who seduced Adam into committing the original sin. The allegorical woman is always guilty and responsible for something. One of the strategies applied in consolidating the stupendous superiority of the masculine gender was and is the legitimisation of social power relations by means of mythology and its derivate religions. Male dominance is sanctioned in every field of social practice, and the patriarch exalted as the next-to-sacred representative of religion itself. When reading ancient mythology and religion, one should therefore bear in mind the history of the sinister thriving of gender enslavement. The Babylonian creation myth *Enuma Elish* is of a double significance in this context. Whereas in early Sumerian mythology the cunning sage Enki, in his struggle for male dominance, used the stratagems of someone who is compelled to compromise with the powerful female deities, the later Babylonian myth glorifies the young, valiant city god Marduk, who mercilessly slaughters the demonised mother-goddess Tiamat. In the first reading, the epic tells of how the absolutist character of kingship has been consolidated (as is historically documented in the Code of Hammurabi). In the second reading, it is the self-representation of a dynastic culture that has left behind certain paradigms and a creed associated with early Sumerian mythology, establishing incontestable religious laws in its own right that constitute a major episode in the history of class and gender oppression. These codes should be read within the context of a sweeping institutionalisation of patriarchal and monarchic authority. The absolute power of the ruler is equated with that of a god. The sequestering of woman into the slavery of *the private and the public home*[4] has now been institutionalised and legally codified in such a way that the power relations involved in patriarchy can permanently penetrate the very fabric of society. As the polytheist religions with their female and male deities waned, the monotheist religions, as symbolised in Middle Eastern culture by the patriarchy of Father Abraham al-Khalil,[5] were already waxing.

All in all I would not want my brief account to be understood as though I view the part played by the Sumerians in history as a purely negative one. Sumerian texts do reflect something that appears to me as a pre-scientific, symbolic expression of the regular character of the occurrence of natural events and their equation with inter-human laws. I find it inadequate to reduce the Sumerian concept of the divine to totemic idolatry, but insist that it contains a notion that might be interpreted as a proto-form of the gradually evolving idea of a universal order of things. This idea would for a long time be symbolised in the concept of a supreme celestial god, and is today conveyed by the special and general theory of relativity. And yet, for the purpose of our analysis it makes sense to focus on the aspect of how this concept of the divine regulated class relations. The knowledge-based conceptualisation of the world of natural occurrences and of society as an integral part of it undergoes constant development. Ancient Mesopotamian civilisation, as mediated to us by the bulk of extant documents, funnelled this development along the lines of an official policy as expressed in a mythology designed to serve the interests of the ruling class, and later on in even more conservative, rigid religious doctrines. But at the same time there were factions accused of sorcery, witchcraft or demon worship by the authorities and ostracised for pursuing interests detrimental to those of the state. Their social role in the production of knowledge that would lead up to philosophical reasoning should not be underestimated. In brief, it is of crucial importance to an analysis of civilisation to account for both of these social factions' contributions to the development of mythology, religion, philosophy and science. The progressive and the backward elements involved in both of these forms of knowledge as well as their conflicting character should be kept in mind when doing so.

4

Some Methodological Issues Concerning Historical Development and Expansion

It seems appropriate to make some critical observations concerning methodological approaches to history at this stage. The discussion of method I am aiming at, however, does not refer to a proposed dual antagonism of materialism and idealism in the history of historiography. Projections based on the notion of such binary opposition of methods are far from coming to terms with the manifold factors involved in historical development. The idea of class being the prime mover in history has proved inapt for providing satisfactory explanations for real processes, as of heroic individuals. What should rather be discussed is the historicity of social development. How tenable would an analysis of society, or of civilisation in general, be if we were to discard the time factor? However, most of the approaches favoured in the social sciences are ahistorical. The parameters of processes analysed are mostly regarded as given; and economic, legal, political and military issues are often construed on the basis of a static model. This is being done with the air of supremely sober scientific spirit. A similarly abstract conceptualisation of frozen relations is often encountered, in which social developments are compartmentalised into historical periods. Historians, too, tend to treat a constellation from a certain epoch without explicitly reflecting on the often determining relations it forms with preceding or succeeding eras. Each epoch denies the one preceding it,[1] or at least presents us with a distorted outlook reflecting the subjective preferences of those who arrange the material.

Ultimately, history is essentially degraded to a reservoir of interpretations constricted by the regime of a paramount present. Overemphasis or neglect of certain moments tends to blur our vision of what different epochs take from, and give to, each other. This makes it difficult to arrive at a reasonably realistic picture of the interdependences of historical eras. The claim that a scientific outlook on history is still very much a work in progress, therefore, does have its merits. I found it highly enlightening to review my own approach in the light of this critical viewpoint. The textbook schematic outlook that we acquired in the formative period of our movement[2] turned out to bear quite precarious consequences in that it made us lose touch with reality. To present ready-made recipes as analyses of history and society is a habit that has always backfired on those who fall into it. This holds true even for the most distinguished socialist academics, who believe that their argumentation represents the cutting edge of their science. It was an extremely important learning process to see how socialist approaches that had set out with the claim of being at the pinnacle of scientific method produced results that were hardly any better than those of dogmatic idealist approaches. They, too, were pervaded with the egocentrism that is part of the lore of the Sumerians. Any set of ideas that is subject to ratification by a given political body – no matter how scientifically founded it may appear – is bound to become a tool for the justification of the existing order. Perhaps the quantity of scientific data employed renders it even more perilous than the preoccupations of the Sumerian priests ever were: the manipulation, exaggeration and belittlement done in the name of science in the age of rationality must have caused infinitely more harm to society than the mythical and religious palaver of old. If mythology and religion are an *opiate* for the people, manipulative science is a blade piercing at the heart of society. It is easier to overcome the intoxicating effect of the drug than to heal the gaping wounds inflicted by the knife.

The orders of exploitation and oppression that have reached gigantic proportions precisely by relying on modern science and technology did not thrive by virtue of the elaborate methods of torture that they resort to, but due to the way in which science is being pursued and employed. Representatives of the scientific and academic establishment are directly responsible for that, and to a greater degree than the Sumerian priests could reasonably be held "responsible" for the early Mesopotamian state-centred civilisation. With all the critical problems confronting humanity in the present and the immediate past – two world wars and a number of regional wars, poverty, environmental destruction, gender inequality, the threat posed by nuclear arms, uncontrolled population growth, and the derailment of technology – the part played by the scientific establishment is more notorious than that played by the political and military establishment. It is the priests of science who have endorsed this flow of events. The conservative and egotistical role of universities in our times renders them morally guilty of the evils riddling our age, no less than the ancient temple or the medieval religious establishment could be blamed for the evils of those ages. To raise accusations of cruelty, backwardness, superstition and darkness against earlier ages and wash oneself in the purifying waters of modern science does not cleanse anyone of the problems we have to tackle. The annihilation, torture, starvation and diseases that human beings had to suffer during the twentieth century were quantitatively more than those of all previous centuries taken together. This should be reason enough to apply radical self-criticism to the basic paradigms of our age, the techniques and appliances they rest upon, the achievements they claim, and the way in which science is being pursued and, what is most important, applied. A good way of starting this would be to rectify our outlook on historical and social development, and scrupulously adhere to the ethical consequences we can draw from this. An uncontrolled, perverted sect will scarcely be able to wreak more havoc than Chernobyl or Hiroshima did, and a sorcerer or preacher cannot really do more harm than a scientist. Behind any destructive and painful event, there is the plan and programme drafted at the desk of some scientist who has long since detached himself from moral values and does not question whom or what he serves. Behind this attitude, in turn, there lies an idea of history and society that may be characterised by its lack of proportion, its injustice and its manifest wrongs. The state of the world we live in is in itself the most eloquent criticism of science.

The importance I attach to founding the reconstruction of a development of civilisation on Sumer, and of founding our conception of Sumer on the neolithic society from which it emerged, may be understood better in the light of this critique. When we say that the history of civilisation begins at Sumer, we imply that it begins within the setting of the agrarian, village-based social environment that human beings created from the rich natural resources afforded by the mountain ranges from which the Tigris and the Euphrates spring, and by the valleys through which they take their course. Sumer, and all the civilisations that were informed by it, were nurtured for at least 10,000 years by this region, albeit at the price of the region itself falling barren. This, then, is the mother who gave birth to civilisation. It is here that, as far as it can be reconstructed by written history, the dialectic principle of historical development started to work. I am not dwelling on this point to satisfy patriotic sentiments. Rather, I attach importance to it because it allows us to properly establish the temporo-spatial aspect of the dialectics of history with a view towards developing a response to the commonly accepted criticism that I outlined above. At the danger of being repetitive, I point to this fact because it is necessary to set a correct starting point for an analysis of civilisation. It is impossible to correctly define a historical and social entity[3] without correctly determining its *beginnings*; and a historical and social entity that is not correctly conceived will never cease being a cause of hazard and crisis.

Once having set a starting point that is perceived as the source of historical development at large, the obvious question whether there are other, similar sources, and if so, what the correlation between them might be, comes to the fore. The most fatal error we could make in this respect is to present social formations in an inexorable scheme of monolinear successive development, as though their occurrence were a matter of predetermined fate. Unfortunately,

Marxian dialectical materialism has not done much to differentiate itself from Hegelian dialectical idealism in this very respect. Undoubtedly, both of these methodological projections have contributed much to the interpretation of history and still continue to do so. But this is exactly why the outlook they adopt must be thoroughly questioned, and they must be held accountable for the unsolved task of establishing the concrete realities of our history and our society. In both of these methods, the concrete has, to a large extent, been relegated to a place of secondary importance, or rather ascribed a concrete value only in relation to its usefulness in exemplifying and verifying the method. On the other hand, the trend in twentieth-century sciences and humanities to turn the most intricate details of the concrete into specialised branches or fields of research and lose sight of the main gist of things, and to disregard a number of highly relevant issues as "non-subjects of scientific research", has got academics into the unfavourable position of becoming scientific bigots. One reason for that might be that universities and academics never really parted from the role model of the temple and the priest. It should be kept in mind that even where individual academics question and oppose the peculiar egocentrism of our times, the institutional order remains one that is backward and, as it were, more harmful to social morale than comparable ancient and medieval institutions were. *Scientific socialism*, on the other hand, made the claim of defending labour and representing equality, and therefore being the true holder of a just and scientific approach to history. However, it is still far from deserving this title. The immeasurable ethical crisis and social injustice that actually existing socialism plunged into bears evidence to that effect. Its collapse seems to me to be the revenge taken by history, i.e. by concrete societies, on the socialist movement for its failure to approach these societies in a correct and fair way. History and society are living organisms, and whosoever misinterprets or neglects them will sooner or later receive an appropriate answer in the form of a well-deserved slap in the face. The dire consequences of resting social projects and political programmes on abstract schemes or faulty views of history have become manifest in actually existing socialism and actually existing fascism, as well as in various other social movements and state-building processes. Any edifice whose foundations are not laid out soundly will eventually collapse, unless the necessary corrections are made in time and at the right place. Our age has witnessed the inevitability of this rule more than any other.

There are multiple other sources by which historical development is informed, each having its own weight. But the central issue I am trying to focus on is that of the mainstream of the flow of historical events that has brought us to where we are now. There are, doubtless, other streams, brooks and backwaters. However, we are looking at the energy that is generated when running waters are held back by a dam, since history actually bears down on us as a mighty torrent, rather than in the form of a network of meandering histories or small self-contained pools of past experience. This main torrent of historical flux has been nourished by a plenitude of tributaries. It may, from time to time, rotate in whirlpools or stagnate on some plain, but, overall, it is continually growing and accelerating. One of the main functions of writing history, then, is to establish how, when and where a given social unit has contributed to this flow. This approach also allows us to establish whether a social formation is "non-historical" or outside history.[4] Against this backdrop, the question of whether historical development follows a linear path or moves in helicoid cycles is not centrally relevant.

This approach has the advantage of connecting to humanist rather than to nationalist notions of societal life. It can show how even a community whose self-perception, or self-portrayal by its ideologues, is permeated with images of a pure and separate national history is in reality constantly nurtured by the flux of history at large, which knows no ethnic or religious preferences. By way of example, it is often said that Jews throughout history have perceived themselves as members of an elect people or at least a truly special entity, often with overtones of superiority over others. However, Jewish culture carries a variety of influences partaking of the grand world civilisations, from Mesopotamia and Egypt via Phoenicia and Persia, Greece, Rome and the Islamic world, to modern Europe and the United States. As a matter of fact, Jews have always understood how to assimilate these influences to the benefit of their culture. By the same token, Jews have often been among the most conscious and active participants in, and contributors to, these civilisations. In that respect, Jewish history indeed has the privilege of providing a case in point for the highly intertwined development of the specific and the general in history. Another dimension of the approach I have tried to adopt is that it urges the historian to pay as much attention to each phenomenon as it deserves. Just as history may be conceived as a whole, each particle in it has its place and its value. Even the smallest community or the most ordinary individual are of a historical value that should not be negated. Just as history is reflected in a given society, and the life of this society is reflected in history, a society is reflected in a given individual, and an individual is reflected in the life of a society. This formula, which is the quintessence of historical materialism as the application of the dialectical method to history,[5] has become a basic scientific conviction of mine. Along these lines, I will discuss methodological issues as they arise in connection with the subjects we are going to deal with throughout the book.

5

The Expansion and Maturation of Slavery

The extraordinary fecundity of Sumerian economic production was apparently pointed to by Sumerians as proof of their superiority and, as in successive civilisations, regarded as a criterion for the display of power. It has been calculated from tablet texts that a seed-to-yield ratio of up to 50 to one on barley and wheat was achieved on irrigated lands.[1] With all the craftspeople and traders that could be supported on such surpluses and the rapid urbanisation processes that occurred around the major centres of production, profound socio-political transitions took place. The accumulation of material valuables posed problems in terms of security: they needed to be defended against raids. Bronze technology, which had principally served in the production of agricultural tools, became a means of producing weapons of war that promised to their holders a sweeping superiority in battle. Since surrounding non-urban communities that did not possess them would have been hopelessly inferior, the wielding of such bronze weapons also contributed to the political strengthening of the urban aggregates, in the same way as the possession of nuclear weapons today allows for certain political prerogatives. The exercise of this strength was, of course, embedded in the complex political organisation of society under a state that was powered by the efficient administrational and ideational *body hieratic*. Here was a system that proved not only capable of reproducing and protecting itself, but at the same time possessed an exceptional expansive power.

SOME TRAITS OF MESOPOTAMIAN EXPANSION

When this power was converted into the first planned and deliberate imperial expansion during the Akkadian dynasty of Sargon, an era began that I would label *the imperialist stage of slave-holding civilisation*. Excursions and campaigns that used to be the trajectory of individual heroic exploits – as related in the Sumerian version of the Gilgamesh Epic – gradually turned into a systematic expansion and, increasingly, long-term colonialism. In these endeavours, political domination went hand in glove with a thriving trade on land, sea and river. Here we can see the beginnings of the tidal rising and falling of political entities as caused by the expansion of the empire and the defiance of the communities that had to confront it. From the second half of the third millennium BCE, we have an imperial Sumerian colonialism, the exact nature of which is still the subject of extensive research and debate. It seems that wide lands to the east, the west and the north were militarily subdued and, through politico-military outposts, integrated into the imperial economy as tributaries. We may surmise the following as to the logic involved in this process:

1. *The expansion is based on the production surplus*: both raw materials and a market for produced goods are required in increasing proportions. The sales and acquisitions are clearly codified and seem to increase in number and quantity. A class of traders as the motor force of expansion may be postulated based on available evidence.
2. *A professional military contingent is established* with the development and quantitative growth of arms production. The well-trained and well-equipped military becomes an institution in its own right and grows proportionate to the expansion of the system. This enables the political elite to annihilate large numbers of human beings for the sake of pillaging and enslavement.

   This form of behaviour is completely unknown amongst other species and, in its planned and organised form, seems to arise with the consolidation of class society. There is no evidence of such behaviour in societies where social stratification is less developed or absent. Where cannibalism or ritual slaughter do occur, they are highly limited and embedded in a ritualistic context. Such instances of slaughter apparently occurred in prehistoric Mesopotamian society in connection with the enacting of the birth and death of the seasons and, apparently, in the form of infanticide. But premeditated killing for the sake of procuring booty only developed as a measure of the exploitative ruling class who then systematised it. This was done to give this unnatural behaviour the appearance of a legitimate, "normal" historical act. It was sanctioned through belief and ritual as an act of divine retribution and celebrated in epics and legends as a manifestation of the heroic virtues of the ruler. For a specific social class, these exploits became a principal aim and their pursuit was upgraded to the rank of a noble profession. This is how the age of *homo homini lupus*[2] began. (It was also the beginning of malediction. Perhaps one of the most important epics written in the Sumerian language, *The Curse of Agade* [Akkad], relates how the Akkadian king Naram-Sin wreaks havoc on the holy city of Nippur, and how, in reprisal, Akkad is cursed by the gods and left to disintegration and oblivion.)[3]

3. *The infighting of the small city states culminate in their forceful unification, and their growing needs give rise to the imperialist character of the system.* Former, less stratified communities may have expanded, but their expansion was not based on the subjugation and plunder of other entities. There is a qualitative difference between expansion on the basis of natural necessities and the establishment of colonial tiers on a political and economic level. It seems that the Sumerian ruling class adopted the policy of aggressive external orientation as a means for grappling with internal strife and, at the same time, an opportunity to enlarge their fortunes.
4. These three factors conflate into the reality of *a socially stratified civilisation maintaining itself by way of growth through expansion*, which becomes a quintessential trait of civilisation. There are different forms of expansion varying according to their objective: instantaneous looting, the establishment of permanent control over strategic resources such as ores and timber, or the establishment of trade colonies from which new cities might emerge. Apart from trade-based expansion serving the end of procuring raw materials and merchandising manufactured goods, there are many examples of ideological expansion, which gives priority to the erection of temples similar to those of the centre. Transient or permanent settlement, according to the nature of the location, accounts for another widespread form of expansion. Many of the more permanent settlements established on previously inhabited terrain were gradually transformed into sites of new civilisations as a result of mutual assimilation. These dynamics account for a considerable number of historical formations.

TERMS OF COMPARISON: EGYPT AND THE INDUS CIVILISATION

The situation is somewhat different in the second large civilisation of the ancient Middle East, the Egyptian empire. From the neolithic communities of the Fayum and Badarian culture that maintained a food-producing economy from at least the second half of the fifth millennium BCE, a complex urban civilisation with a coercive ruling class arose in the Nile valley by the end of the fourth millennium. Although it bears clear similarities with Mesopotamia in terms of socio-political organisation, state institutionalisation seems to have been much more centralised from the beginning. Initial polities were not based on one among numerous independent city states, but apparently on a few larger kingdoms and, ever since the first two dynasties preceding the Old Kingdom,[4] on administrative provinces spanning large areas. Within the framework set by a potent hierarchic predominance, absolute monarchy was exercised by reference to a mythology in which the ruler was deified. The Egyptian pantheon was arranged around a holy family consisting of father, mother and son.[5] The New Kingdom saw the introduction of a proto-form of monotheism, albeit only temporarily.[6] As in Sumer, the political system was idealised as an earthly reflection of the perennial celestial order. Its rigid structures were thus underpinned by a strong ideological hegemony over most subjects. However, imperial efforts at colonisation of surrounding areas remained somewhat more limited than in Mesopotamia, although they certainly included Nubia, Libya, the Sinai and, later on, Ethiopia. Egyptian civilisation did maintain trade links with the eastern Mediterranean coastal region and with Crete, and was integrated in a network of indirect relations with Mesopotamia. Trade via the Nile, the Red Sea and the Mediterranean helped spread the influence of Egypt, which was a major source of inspiration for early Greek civilisation. Similarly, north-east Africa's history bears the marks of ancient Egyptian expansion. The degree of entrenchment of slavery in Egyptian society and the use of slave labour in monumental architecture as its most striking extant document are particularly noteworthy. Not only did it encourage the ruling class of the Roman Empire to embark on projects of a similar scale, but it provided a model for the functionality of religious and political authority in the large-scale coercion of human labour that informed Middle Eastern despotism. The part played by ancient Egyptian civilisation in the maturation and perpetuation of slavery as an historical system is tantamount to that played by Sumerian civilisation in its initial formation and expansion.

The ancient Indus civilisation, associated chiefly with the rich finds from the sites of Harappa (Punjab) and Mohenjo-Daro (Sind), emerged from local settlements of the Early Harappan period dating back to the fourth millennium BCE, which in turn might have been influenced by the Neolithic culture of the sixth-millennium Baluchistan. The Mature Harappan civilisation that unfolded by 2600 BCE was the most extensive of the ancient riverine civilisations. Its influence spread from the Pamir Mountains of Central Asia. Yet, its central cities were not marked by monumental graves or palaces, and its temples apparently were not a focus of social bonding. Despite the Harappan culture's enormous territorial extension, military subjugation and colonial tiers seem not to have been on a scale comparable with Mesopotamia or Egypt. Communities of the Indus civilisation were engaged in trade with Mesopotamia via coastal shipping along the Gulf, and thus connected to the world system that had emerged. Research has not yet provided a clear explanation for the crisis that led to urban decline around 1750 BCE, but internal factors seem more likely to have been the cause than a purported invasion by "barbarians". Against the backdrop of this discontinuity, it may be asserted that the impact of ancient Indus civilisation on Middle Eastern history was limited. The specific Vedic Indian civilisation of antiquity is rather associated with the advent of Aryan agro-pastoralists by 1200 BCE.[7]

To the immediate east of Mesopotamia, in the province of Khuzestan of modern Iran, was the region of Elam or the Susiana, named after the Elamite capital Susa. Cultural development during the neolithic era was at least on a par with that of the Mesopotamian Ubaid culture. At 3100 BCE, a proto-Elamite culture emerged that was without doubt informed by Sumerian advances. However, it showed distinctly different traits, such as a specific form of cuneiform writing. Although Elam was incorporated into the Akkadian Empire under Naram-Sin, the very fact that even the earliest available written evidence indicates a conflict with the city of Ur (2700 BCE), as well as the spectacular defeat of the Ur III dynasty by the Elamites, suggests a high degree of independent socio-political development. However, there is no evidence of this in extant documents. The considerable political power of the Middle Elamite Empire (c. 1285–1103 BCE) is well documented.[8] Would Elam have become an early Middle Eastern civilisation in its own right if it hadn't been for Sumer? Or would urbanisation in the Susiana never have happened at all without the Mesopotamian influence? The often neglected example of Elam is of particular interest when examining the dialectics of an intrinsic development towards cultural complexity that occurs under the shadow of a neighbouring civilisation of superior power; in other words, the dialectics of expansion and resistance.

INTERDEPENDENT DEVELOPMENTS IN A COLONISED WORLD

The old spontaneous quietude of both the agrarian sedentary way of life and the nomadic existence of the herders was shaken in its foundations when the wealth and the power of urban Sumer increased. For the many communities that did not participate in the transition to urban civilisation, life may have been idyllic, but it certainly always involved a tough struggle for survival. Next to them, a paradisiacal garden arose, and they were confronted with the alternative of entering it either as subservient slaves or as occupying conquerors. Further to the west, Egypt posed a similar choice to yet other communities. For the urban polities, too, self-assertion against the raids of covetous rivals or non-urban tribal peoples became a critical matter, the handling of which could determine survival or demise.

These confrontations were decisive moments in a dialectical process characteristic of early history. Although the process that led to the initial formation of Sumerian civilisation must have been connected to the encounter of several tribal communities in that same area, the adaptation of new ways of life by some of them created a difference between stratified urban entities and tribal formations. This gave rise to clashes that in turn precipitated further developments.

When urbanisation reached its natural limits by the middle of the third millennium BCE, the wars for possession and predominance among the rival cities escalated. The dynasty of Sargon took this opportunity to assume power, introduce a new level of central intervention and install "sons of Akkad' as governors in the conquered cities. This new elite quelled internal antagonisms and mobilised the aggrandising drive of the upper classes towards external targets. Although inscriptions from this era are doubtless somewhat boastful, they indicate that by the second half of the third millennium there was a significant number of Mesopotamian trade colonies – from Syria to Central Anatolia and the inner parts of Iran, to the islands and southern coast lines of the Persian Gulf region. The development of culturally complex connections with the Phoenicians of the eastern Mediterranean, the Hittites of Anatolia, the Mitanni of Upper Mesopotamia and the Elamites of Iran occurred in the context of long-distance trade and colonial expansion. In some instances former colonies or tributary provinces of the superpowers attained political power and independent statehood after long periods of resistance. Little is known about the resistance and rebellion of communities, cities or tribal groups. However, the documents composed by the scribes of the imperial centres in order to glorify their rulers' war drive suggest that these clashes involved much bloodshed and travail. The strengthening of local structures outside the imperial cores added an important dimension to the historical process. The communities that formed them assimilated certain traits of the pre-existent class societies and adopted many of their institutions. The full development of class differences in their social structures produced distinct identities; growing rivalry with the centres developed into long-term friction and warfare, from which new local states emerged.

This aspect of the evolution of ancient civilisation accounts for many of the events unfolding throughout the second millennium BCE and, indeed, the first half of the first millennium BCE. It is a key development in Middle Eastern history. The newly stratified state societies were responsible for as many important developments as were the so-called "early high cultures" of Sumer and Egypt, and they certainly added local colours to the rich texture of Middle Eastern cultural life. But they also became vehicles for the ever deeper entanglement of humankind in the system of slavery. The repetition of patterns of coercion by newly emerging polities seemed all but inevitable. It is therefore useful to have a closer look at this new momentum in slave-owning civilisation.

6

Tribal Confederations, Local and Territorial States

Having proved their capacity to uphold their institutions over a long period of time, the Sumerian and Egyptian slave-owning societies spread their features over wider areas. Their expansion anticipated a tendency displayed by many other civilisations of high complexity, namely to branch out. The agriculturalist and pastoralist clan communities affected by this expansion were increasingly contained in tiers that restricted their traditional freedoms. The responsive patterns they developed were twofold.

Firstly, an impoverished section that could no longer be accommodated within the old communal structures migrated and settled in the immediate vicinity of the large imperial cities. There they were available to the urban upper strata as cheap labour. (In Egypt, these foreign paupers were called "*apiru*", a term from which the Semitic word "*ibri*", i.e. Hebrew, is thought to be derived. And in Mesopotamia the Kassite groups seem to be descendents of such poor, semi-urban labourers.) This early migration, boosted by deportation, is highly evocative of the situation of the myriad impoverished half-free labourers of rural origin that are flowing into the big cities of our time.

Secondly, the privileged section of the clan communities acted as intermediaries for the major powers. They would negotiate the relations between the imperial authorities and the populace within their own sphere of power, or, provided they were embedded in a native urban system, even function as intermediaries between the two superpowers. At times, this section remained in the position of comprador merchants, dependent on the centres of slave-owning imperialism. In other instances, the polities they controlled imitated the central model and transformed into small city states. Some prominent examples of the latter process are the towns of Byblos[1] and Ugarit[2] on the eastern Mediterranean coast line, Carchemish,[3] Samsat,[4] Ebla,[5] Harran[6] and Mari[7] in northern Syria or north-west Mesopotamia, Hattushas[8] and Kanesh[9] in central Anatolia, and, in a slightly different vein, Elam in the eastern Zagros foothills.

In contrast to the earlier neolithic settlements, some of which reached sizeable proportions, this new type of settlement was neither rooted in the ritual importance attached to its site nor in the cultivation of lands in its vicinity. They were in all stated cases situated at strategic passes or crossings along established trade routes, and principally functioned as sites for trade and, to a lesser extent, manufacture. They rapidly grew into fully-fledged towns or capital cities, coveted by the regional powers. Timber, metals, textiles and luxury goods were items in a complex and sophisticated foreign trade network that foreshadowed similar phases of mercantile prosperity in other places and at other times. Silver and gold were used for money, and trade letters assumed an important function in the exchange process.

The simplification of script devised in the Phoenician cities constitutes but one example of how trade not only generated an increase in the material prosperity of a certain class, but also fostered and helped spread cultural achievements throughout the ancient world system. Mainly by virtue of trade, a middle class differentiated itself from the coercive elite and the enslaved masses. This middle class, consisting of merchants and artisans, formed the backbone of class society in this new type of settlement. It gained a certain degree of independence from the bureaucracy in temple and palace, as well as from the large numbers of slaves and labourers who progressively lost their clan allegiances.

The tribal confederation is another important aspect of the history of local states. In most cases, this stage of social organisation preceded the formation of urban conglomerations. However, it should also be regarded as a long-term mode of social organisation in its own right. It might have arisen in response to the need for arbitration in conflicts among various tribes with common cultural ties. Furthermore, it served the aim of putting up an efficient defence against attacking urban forces, allowing the confederate tribes to secure a united stance and thus a stronger position vis-à-vis their neighbours.

Within the pattern of development discussed above, the tribal confederation functions as a transitory stage, where features such as a centralised military contingent stationed in urban centres, elaborate temples and palaces and a bureaucratic apparatus are still absent and the urban middle class has not yet formed. Tribal confederations are liable to break apart under internal or external pressures. They are the mode of organisation corresponding to the heroic age invoked in the epic traditions of most ancient peoples. Such mode of organisation may be postulated for the Hurrians of the late third and the Hittites of the early second millennium BCE and with more certainty for the Amorites and Canaanites of approximately the same era.

The tradition of clanship and tribalism is still a strong socio-political factor in today's Middle East. It derives its strength in part from the fact that some groups have been living under these forms of organisation for several thousand years. The history of the Middle East certainly deserves to be read as a history of tribal groups or "ethnic structures". The ethnic group comes before the dynasty, the religion and the class structure, and should be taken into account as an analytical category. The widespread preference for focusing on the category of dynasty in antiquity, religious affiliation in the Middle Ages, and nationhood in modernity serves an understanding of history that uncritically reflects the official self-representation of the ideological regimes of the respective ages. Social history is always more complex and varied than these categories suggest. It will take an attempt at rewriting the history of history for us to come to terms with the distortions inherent in our traditional treatment of written evidence.

No written evidence is available for the ethnic history of human groups. Yet, it represents much more real, and considerably more long-term structures than the history of any given religion, dynasty or "people" as it appears in the historical record. The most significant developments in structure of the Middle Eastern tribal and clan orders occurred during the neolithic age, when different forms of agriculturalist, pastoralist and transhumance food-producing economies evolved from the palaeolithic hunter–gatherer groups.

By the same token, the history of women, who played a major role in these developments, is equally inaccessible through written records, hidden, as it is, in the history of cereal cultivation, horticulture, small-scale cattle domestication, the hearth-centred village dwellings, textile fabrication and domestic tools. Little can be surmised as to how the expense of human labour in social production served as a structuring factor in group relations, how children were raised and domestic orders established. Perhaps even less will ever be known as to how primitive signs evolved into rich speech, how concepts emerged – perhaps from the meditation on certain aspects of material production – and how the mentality of the human groups of these ages was formed.

And yet, the ethnic history of the Middle East began with, and developed from, these primary processes. In historiography, women are mostly allocated a position that falls critically short of reflecting their actual role in social organisms. Because male dominance developed into a major aspect of socio-political authority during the civilisation process, and because women were increasingly excluded from the institutions of base and superstructure in ancient societies, there actually did arise a factual basis for the male tradition of writing "history without women": the historically evolved inequality between the sexes both effected and obscured the egregious distortions that form our common-sense notion of history.

Both in terms of ethnic groups and in terms of gender the nature of the written evidence that forms the focus of historical research is tainted by the hierarchical character of the social conditions under which it was produced. A valid study of Middle Eastern history will have to centre on rectifying these distortions. Some of the main questions that have occupied me in this respect relate to tribal confederations: Should tribal confederations be understood as a response to the development of stratified urban civilisation? To what extent were they transformed by urban civilisation?

Although, admittedly, the answers to these questions lie in the dark, it is nonetheless intriguing to hypothesise: different language groups and forms of material culture can be postulated even for the mesolithic and early neolithic times. At a stage when the neolithic communities of the Fertile Crescent established more or less permanent social institutions and clearly distinguishable material cultures, clans would have merged into phratries, as can be seen in the Halafian example. Those sharing certain cultural traits eventually would have formed ethnic groups. Let us now suppose communities belonging to such an ethnic group, or tribe, are attacked by other tribes, or indeed by contingents associated with expanding Sumerian civilisation. Affiliation to this ethnic group would now be a matter of life or death, since it would determine the availability of solidarity with other clans or village communities belonging to the same group. Intertribal conflicts about pastures and cultivatable lands made warfare a constant issue of tribal life. Tribes constantly had to defend themselves against the forces of civilisation and made counter-attacks on the rich cities. The strength of one's tribe would have been a decisive matter, but within the tribe, one's clan or family needed to be strong.

I would suggest that this material situation has had lasting repercussions on the mentality and social behaviour of the community members. The oral tradition of epic narratives that prevail in many societies, not only in the Middle East, has an identity-building function: the heroic deeds associated with the incessant tribal conflicts or the warding off of external attackers become the motifs of a poetic form of oral history that has permeated cultural memory over the ages. I believe that this ethnic history has been a major strand in the history of all kinship-based social groups, throughout the ages, and to some extent informs their self-perception to this day. The long perspective of this history – we are talking about a phenomenon that can be traced back over several thousand years – amid a terrain regularly shaken by the military campaigns of successive state forces, must be one of the reasons why kinship-based social groups in the Middle East are still so potent and unabatedly defiant of social change.

The Middle East was the leading geo-cultural region in the process that led to the establishment of slave-owning society as a world system. This process was not limited to the formation of the Mesopotamian and the Egyptian civilisations; the maturation and extension that occurred throughout a wider region, including Anatolia, Iran and the eastern Mediterranean, from the early second millennium to the second half of the first millennium BCE, was part of it.

Let us have a look at some prominent civilisations that flourished during this period.

THE HITTITES

The Old Hittite kingdom arose around 1700 BCE as a civilisation of central Anatolia. The earliest extant traces of this civilisation, the Nesitic inscriptions of Kanesh, are associated with the Assyrian trading colonies of the nineteenth century BCE onwards. The Indo-European Hittites initially copied Sumerian and Akkadian script, and much of their political and religious culture is reminiscent of the Sumerian model. The Hittite kingdom was not only an important trading centre, but controlled and exploited significant metal resources. It became a real competitor to the Babylonian, Assyrian and Egyptian empires. The Hittite king Mursilis conquered Babylon in 1595 BCE, and Hattusilis III concluded the peace treaty of Kadesh with Ramses II of Egypt in 1258 BCE. The kingdom may well have been founded as a tribal confederation, but gradually assumed the distinct character of a slaveholding civilisation.

Varied ethnic groups must have lived in its realm, among them the speakers of Hattic, Luwian, Palaic and Hurrian. The Hurrians first concentrated in the region around modern Mardin in Kurdistan proper, the Luwians in south and west Anatolia, the Pala in the Black Sea region, and the Hatti, whose name is preserved in that of the Hittite capital Hattushas, in the centre of Anatolia.[10] The Hittite religion was a hybrid of Sumerian mythology and Hurrian beliefs, which contain Indo-European strands also found in those of the Vedic Aryans. Hittite religion changed through the centuries, perhaps indicating changes in the social structure of the culture. The mountain goddess Kubaba (the Cybele of the Phrygians) was an important, but by no means dominant, figure in Hurrian and neo-Hittite tradition. She no longer occupied the prominent place in the pantheon that had once belonged to Sumerian goddesses. And yet, under the name of Cybele, she eventually became the "Great Mother of the Gods" of the Greco-Roman tradition, in whose veneration striking features of earlier Mesopotamian cults reoccurred.

Owing to its intense contacts with the Achaean and Mycenaean[11] settlements of the mid-second millennium, Hittite civilisation left an impression on the Greek culture of Ionia, the region of Asia Minor bordering on the New empire. Troy especially, the powerful city state that dominated the Gulf of Canakkale, functioned as a bridge between the nascent Greek world in the West and the great empires of the East. It was the centre from where the Middle Eastern civilisations spread into the Balkans and the Greek mainland, just as Kanesh had been the centre for the spreading of Mesopotamian culture into Anatolia. It is no wonder that the sack of this old city was a favourite motif in Greco-Roman tradition, which occurred both in Homer's *Iliad* and in Virgil's *Aeneid*. The account of the Trojan War was the narrative of a Greek victory over a powerful Eastern kingdom, and thus marked the beginning of a new era in history.[12]

THE HURRIANS, KASSITES, GUTIANS, MITANNI, URARTIANS AND MEDES

Due to their strategic importance, their metal resources and their produce, Upper Mesopotamia and the lands to the north of it were targeted by the Anatolian Hittite empire, as well as the Babylonian and Assyrian empires of Mesopotamia. This peculiar geopolitical situation is indicative of why no permanent centralised structures and institutions evolved in this region in ancient times. Even then it formed a buffer zone. From the long history of agrarianism in Upper Mesopotamia, it can be inferred that the mainly sedentary communities of this region had assumed fairly stable ethnic structures by the second millennium. Here, strong tribal cohesion might have been as detrimental to the formation of urban centres as the repeated incursions and occupations by the surrounding centralised civilisations were. It is interesting that the Hurrians showed a very strong presence throughout the second millennium as a confederation among interrelated tribes, but failed to undergo developments similar to those that account for a centralised Hittite civilisation. The Hurrians were engaged in constant relations with the Hittites and the other ethnic groups that formed the social basis of the northern civilisation. They formed a local dynasty in the region south of the Taurus, and were one of the links in the chain of long-distance trade and cultural transmission that linked the Aegean to East Asia.

The symbiotic, though tiered relationship between the Sumerian heartland and the areas east of the Tigris and in the mountain region of Zagros, inhabited by the Hurrians, goes back at least to the late third millennium. At that time, Hurrian personal and place names started to occur in Sumerian records. This reflects a cultural interchange that was well under way in the Halafian and Ubaidian chalcolithic, and some scholars hold that the Uruk system already maintained a tributary economy, in which this northern habitat would have been involved, by the mid-fourth millennium. Nevertheless, textual evidence of this relationship can be found in some myths concerning Inanna, and in the Sumerian Gilgamesh tablets, in which the hero undertakes an excursion into the Zagros mountains. In one way, it may be said that Sumer *was* the central civilisation of the Hurrians. This is not only a question of being the hinterland of an alien civilisation. If we look at our own[13] situation today, it is clear that there is simply no functional need for establishing a separate hierarchic centre where one, or indeed more than one, already exists just next door. Administrative relations may just as well be structured under a province, autonomous region or federal unit of the neighbouring centralised powers. And is today's situation not neatly anticipated in the years in which written history began?

The Guti were another ethnic group from the central Zagros range. Coming into Lower Mesopotamia from the East, they aligned themselves with one faction of the rivalling Sumerian city states, played their part in overthrowing the

Akkadian dynasty's central power, and took over some city states, until they were ousted by the Third Dynasty of Ur. Again, this type of alliance is well-known in present times.

The Kassites, too, entered Lower Mesopotamia from the northern and eastern mountainous areas. They had settled on the perimeter of the urban clusters, and a sizeable section of them had lived as poor, semi-urban or rural labourers for centuries before a Kassite dynasty in 1595 BCE took de facto power from the victorious Hittites in Babylon. Apparently, Kassites had been engaged in the Mesopotamian bureaucracy at various levels – including the upper echelons – in much the same way that the Barmakids during the Abbasid Empire or Nizam al-Mulk at the time of the Seljuks would exercise considerable power under dynasties of other ethnic origin.

Mitanni was a territorial state established around 1500 BCE by Hurrians in central Mesopotamia, in what is today Urfa, Diyarbakır, Mardin and Şırnak. Its capital, Wassukanni, was situated somewhere by the Habur River.[14] The Mitanni state was both militarily and politically stronger than earlier Hurrian federations. Horsemanship and a special military class, headed by charioteers, made them a formidable opponent to the Hittites and the Assyrians. But by the mid-first millennium, Hurrians had become dominant among the Hittites themselves, in south-west Anatolian Kizzuwatna[15] and in several city states in the region of Syria and Palestine. This position continued when Mitanni was incorporated into the New Hittite empire and finally annexed by the Assyrians under Shalmaneser I around 1250 BCE.

By the early first millennium, another territorial state, Urartu, was established by ethnic groups speaking a language akin to Hurrian. Mentioned as a country in Assyrian records from the time of Shalmaneser, Urartu grew into a powerful state, with Lake Van[16] at its centre. It included large parts of Armenia and the region up to Lake Urmia in Iran. Urartu controlled the trade routes from northern Mesopotamia and Iran to the Mediterranean and Anatolia. Long aqueducts were built for irrigation, probably with corvée labour. Huge storage areas for wine and grain were contained in the fortified administrative centres, built on natural heights. During the Assyrian campaigns of the thirteenth to ninth centuries BCE, the inhabitants of Urartu (amongst them the forebears of the modern day Armenians) suffered heavily from these invasions, while a small group at the top of their society collaborated with the Assyrians and was rewarded for this with the accomplishments of Assyrian civilisation. The ruling class initially used the Assyrian language and script and had their scribes trained in Sumerian cultic texts. Eventually, the Urartian language was employed, and a particular politico-religious culture established; but it is likely that, as in other earlier states, the tribes spoke other vernaculars that were never recorded in script. (This, too, is a characteristic that has survived to the present day: while the ruling elite and comprador administrators become the carriers of other, dominant idioms and cultures, the lower layers of the tribes preserve their vernaculars and often very distinct cultures.) It can be tentatively stated that by the sixth century BCE, the majority of the inhabitants of the country spoke Armenian, an Indo-European language.

Shortly after the demise of Urartu, and further to the east, another tribal confederation with its roots in the Zagros Mountains rose to political power – the Medes. They formed an alliance with Babylon to set an end to Assyrian domination. Their historical role will be discussed at length in Chapter 9.

EARLY EASTERN MEDITERRANEAN CIVILISATIONS

The rich arable lands at the western end of the Fertile Crescent were home to an abundance of early mesolithic and neolithic settlements, many of which continued to be inhabited until the late fourth and early third millennia – the advent of an expanding web of trade connections with the urban cultures of Egypt and Mesopotamia. Both of these civilisations were in need of the timber resources found in the Lebanese forests. The eastern Mediterranean, generally called the land of Canaan, was linked to trade networks involving Anatolia, Mesopotamia, Egypt and Crete.

The Phoenician cities emerged as aggregates of a civilisation centred around a fully-fledged class of traders. Most cities in Canaan evolved as hybrids of local chalcolithic cultures and colonisation efforts similar to those seen in the Anatolian Kanesh. From the outset, they were inhabited by ethnically mixed populations. City states such as Byblos, Tyre and Ugarit became sites of a vibrant cosmopolitan culture, to some extent anticipating the ethnic, cultural and religious multiplicity found in contemporary Lebanese society. Nevertheless, the Phoenician cities were synergetic cauldrons of a very distinct culture, whose reputation was based not only on seafaring trade, but also on refined artisanship and carpentry. From the twelfth to the eighth century BCE, the Phoenicians established an astonishing number of colonies throughout the entire Mediterranean region, from Libya to Spain, from Sicily to Cyprus.

The North Semitic alphabet gave rise to both the linear Phoenician and the Aramaic alphabets (which in turn were adopted and modified in the Greek and Latin alphabets) and the Hebrew, ancient Persian (Pahlavi), Armenian, Georgian and Indian scripts. The North Semitic alphabet can thus be said to be the ancestor of most alphabets used in the world today.

The extant ancient eastern Mediterranean mythologies and religions contain many elements of Sumerian myth, along with a number of specific, "original" elements. The different forms of Baal ("lord" or "owner") are reminiscent of various Sumerian, Hurrian and Egyptian deities. The cult of Astarte bears many resemblances to the veneration of Ishtar. Over and above these, there is a supreme being and father of gods who goes by the name of El.

While successive layers of Greek, Roman, Byzantine and Arab Islamic civilisation were added onto the Phoenician synthesis with its Egypto-Mesopotamian substrate, the culture of what is now Lebanon steadily evolved from the creative tension between the assimilation of different foreign influences and the emergence of specifically local traits. This hybrid eastern Mediterranean civilisation had, among others, an important impact on early Cretan culture and on the Punic civilisation of North Africa. It was one of the major geo-cultural points of transmission of ancient Middle Eastern culture to the emerging Greek world, which was not only provided with an alphabet, but also with forms and patterns of state formation and the mythology that goes with it.

A few miles inland from the Mediterranean coastline, cities like Jerusalem (Urusalim), Damascus (Dimashqa or Dammeshek) and Aleppo (Halab), with their comparatively large agricultural hinterlands, formed a second belt of cities which played a role in linking the Mediterranean trade to remoter regions in Arabia and Anatolia (especially after the demise of Ebla and Mari). Many historic journeys, most of them unrecorded, must have led through these cities. West Semitic idioms were predominant in these multicultural retail centres for material goods and cultural inventions. Due to their geopolitical position and partially owing to sophisticated diplomacy, these city states were able to retain a certain degree of independence from Babylonian–Assyrian, Hittite and Egyptian rule. This situation made them an attractive destination for tribes who sought to escape mounting pressures or miserable living conditions through migration.

Among these tribes were those that would later be remembered as Hebrews, and whose migration is associated with the narratives woven around the figure of Abraham. The Biblical references to Ur and Harran[17] – both places associated with Mesopotamian colonial culture – and some additional evidence suggest that the roots of these tribes should be sought in a region where Hurrian and Amorite elements coexisted and sometimes merged. The Ugaritic texts shed light on the greater cultural heritage of ancient Canaan, where small-scale movements of semi-nomadic tribes were a frequent occurrence.[18] It is not far-fetched to suggest that these communities, involved in herding livestock as well as in trade, would mostly have been at odds with the central authorities of the major empires and territorial states. Against this background, the old folk tale according to which Abraham had to leave Harran following a confrontation with the despotic king Nimrod (perhaps derived from the Assyrian Ninurta) is highly evocative.[19] We may thus lend an ear to oral tradition when it tells us that this Abraham was a tribal leader acquainted with the urban culture of wider Mesopotamia and its polytheistic religion, but who preferred to venerate the totem of his own tribe. Here we have a constellation of beliefs, the dialectical resolution of which would lead to a fusion of elements of tribal totemic beliefs with elements of the hegemonic religious culture of urban Mesopotamia and Canaan into the conception of a sole, sovereign, god particular to the tribal community.

The process of a tribal community exalting its totem to the rank of a god and then transforming this deity into the only God has for its social basis the liberty of the tribe vis-à-vis the institutionalised system of state power. This seems to me to account for the key moment in the transformation of the religious belief associated with the Abrahamic tradition. It was at the same time a revolutionary deed, a breakaway from the Sumerian system, fuelled by its antagonising oppressiveness. Many Amorite tribes were antagonised by the system, but the primitive tribal totemism of olden times would no longer correspond to the religious needs of their age. It was a model that had to be superseded. This historical dilemma is at the root of what later became the Abrahamic religion(s). Its supersession may appear to us a tiny step taken at some remote, hardly tangible time in history; but historically it played the role of a major ideological revolution.

It is not for nothing that Abraham is revered as the founding father of monotheistic religion in three different holy scriptures (the Torah, the Bible and the Qur'an). The narratives about him touch upon a strategic breakthrough that was crucial to the later religions' formative processes. At a more mature stage in history, polytheistic religions were perceived as backward fabrications. A God who defied idolatry and was himself invisible struck a different chord with the rapidly developing mental structures and logical faculty of humankind, as much as he served the purpose of political unity. This ideological revolution is a timely and progressive response to the contradictions posed by the historical process.

The story about Abraham *not* sacrificing his son Ishmael[20] also reflects a measure of revolutionary import. There is some evidence to the effect that child sacrifice was a widespread phenomenon in Phoenician religious cults. Priests apparently advised heads of families to ritually kill their sons in order to ward off plagues. Resistance against this cruel and binding custom would have taken a form different from that of a single, individual act. It expressed the awakening of human conscience in the face of extreme practices of primitive religious fanaticism.

All in all, the gradual transformation of the Canaanite sky god El into a sole God that favours one's own tribal community over all others was a development that would prove highly consequential to the system of slave-owning civilisation. We shall turn to this development and its ramifications in the next chapter, where we shall discuss it in the wider context of ancient religious reforms, prophecy and classical philosophy. My thesis will be that all of these movements of revolt and reform contributed to building up pressures that led firstly to ideological change and eventually to restructuring in the realm of political institutions.

CRETAN CIVILISATION

From around 2000 BCE, the island of Crete became the site of palace-centred economies that initially were replicas of the Middle Eastern ones. Throughout centuries of intense contact with Egypt, western Asia and Canaan, the inhabitants of this island at the westernmost extremity of the civilised world developed their own forms of culture – the Minoan – that in turn became an important source from which mainland Greece could draw throughout the Bronze Age. Apart from the glorious palaces and sophisticated material culture,[21] Minoan civilisation has left us an early form of a linear syllabic alphabet (from around 1800 BCE), perhaps inspired by Egyptian hieroglyphic writing. By around 1500 BCE, Crete was invaded by the Mycenaeans, groups of Minoanised Greeks from the mainland. The invasion took place while the Mycenaeans were in the process of establishing a hierarchical political and social system that recapitulated the process of state formation in the Middle East and Crete. The Mycenaeans put on the ready-made cloak of Minoan administration.

Thus the core unit of European civilisation emerged from a westward expansion of Middle Eastern civilisation, transmitted from four directions by Phoenicia, Egypt, Anatolia (Troy, the Hittites, the Phrygians and the Lydians) and Minoan Crete. We shall discuss the development of Greek civilisation, and the question of how Europe was born in a later chapter.

MESOPOTAMIAN AND EGYPTIAN CIVILISATION IN THE SECOND AND FIRST MILLENNIA

From as early as the beginning of the second millennium BCE, the glorious era of the birth and institutionalisation of ancient slaveholding civilisation faded, and with it faded the influence of the seminal cultures of the Middle East. After the downfall of the restorative regime of the Third Dynasty of Ur, the Sumerians exited the stage of world history, though not without leaving us moving compositions lamenting the loss of former glory. Motifs from these compositions reverberate in later holy scriptures, in classical tragedies and poetry. The Babylonian and Assyrian empires continued the heritage of Sumerian civilisation without adding much to it. Babylonian scribes spent painstaking efforts at writing down, preserving and systematising the Sumerian lore. From the rise of the Amorite Dynasty of Hammurabi in the nineteenth century to the surrender of the city of Babylon to the Persians in 539 BCE, Babylon was perhaps the world's foremost centre of political power and of learning. The mythical tower of Babylon is a representation of ancient cosmopolitanism, which obviously left deep and lasting impressions on the cultural memory of the peoples of the Middle East.

Assyrian sway was another aspect of the aggressive, militaristic expansion of the original Sumerian civilisation. Between the fourteenth and the seventh centuries BCE, Assyrian military prowess uprooted virtually every ethnic community in the Middle East. Many of the Assyrian campaigns were directed against ethnic uprisings or political rebellions of minor vassal states in regions as disparate as Sinai, the eastern Mediterranean, Anatolia, Upper Mesopotamia and Iran. Mass deportations were a notorious means of Assyrian warfare. In the aftermath of these campaigns, social unrest tended to take on the shape of religious or sectarian movements rather than ethnic uprisings. Assyrian imperialism certainly contributed to the acceptance of and the behaviour pertaining to slavery and to the spread of a strictly tiered, institutionalised trade system.

Assyria's power was challenged, more often than not, by the Hittites and their Anatolian allies, by a number of the eastern Mediterranean city states, by the Urartians, by the Mitanni, and by the Elamites and Medes. The legend of the blacksmith Kawa[22] has its historical roots in the long and bitter resistance of the Indo-European tribes against Assyrian military cruelty and political despotism. The politico-military history of Assyria finally ended when an alliance of Median and Babylonian forces sacked the capital Nineveh in 612 BCE. The Assyrian priests and scribes who left us the famous library of Nineveh, however, continued their activities. Assyrians adopted the Aramaic idiom and became prominent among the first Christians of the East, thus sustaining and spreading a social movement that was fighting against the system of slave-owning civilisation.

Egypt, too, lost its former radiance by the second millennium. After the invasion by the Asian Hyksos, who established a dynasty in the seventeenth century, the old elite set up the New Kingdom. However, the Egyptian empire lost many of its territorial prerogatives, and increasingly more of its original culture, throughout the centuries, until Egypt eventually fell under the domination of the Assyrians, the Greeks and the Romans.

7

Resistance to Slave-owning Civilisation and Its Reform

Our discussion of the process of transition to civilisation has been focused on two aspects: firstly the accumulation of means of production and secondly the question of mental preparation for this change.

The accumulation of means of production entailed the opening up of fertile lands to irrigation, the development of the crafts ushered in by the enormous increase in per capita productivity, the use of bronze technology, the rapid population boom and the appearance of urban settlements. This not only brought about changes in the physical structure of society, but also caused a revolution in its very fabric. The small units of the kinship-based mode of organisation could not persist in the new urban environment for long. Kinship organisation had developed in response to the needs of an economy based on agriculture and pastoralism. Consequently, this system had to be superseded when social labour was divided into specialised crafts and agricultural primary production. Such, in brief, was the material reality of the urban revolution.

The second aspect we have examined is the question of mental preparation for this change in the mode of material production. The rural ways of reproduction, which allowed for certain liberties, could not have been continued under urban conditions. As the temples functioned also as centres of production, one of their tasks was to establish and maintain a kind of administrative power over those who expended physical labour. In a way, the temple-centred economy had to create its own workforce, which involved controlling people's time and training them for the jobs they were allocated.

This position of the temple in the early complex society generated the need for a *revolution in mentality*. The individual torn away from the old tribal ways of living would presumably feel deprived in a stratified urban environment and would probably need to be motivated to continue his or her mere physical existence. Physical force alone cannot even confine an animal to its barn for long. To persuade anyone to trade the freedom of tribal life for an urban existence dedicated to production, will take inducement that goes beyond the use of sheer force. There was a need for ideological change, for a revolution in mentality. It was the dictate of the concrete working and living conditions that forced the priests to invent and run centres where the administration of production and the new ideology could be combined, the system diagnostic of the formation of Sumerian and Egyptian civilisations. This not only accounts for the existence of the priest in early society, but also gives us an idea of the immense efforts involved in creating the new ideology and teaching it. It explains the prominent role of the priest class in predynastic times, i.e. before the institutionalisation of the *body politic* and the establishment of kingship. This system of belief created by the priest class had to utterly convince people of the inexorability of the new system of production for it to run smoothly. Organised force was a secondary factor in its formation. It was the grandiosity of Sumerian mythology and religion that persuaded human beings into enslavement. The ideological system created by the priests marked a turning point in human history. It formed the foundations of the successive overlapping and interacting systems of civilisation that underlie the contemporary world order.

Studies in the history of mentalities in general, and analyses of mythological and religious structures in particular, are still far from having developed into a proper science. Religion is nowadays mostly discussed under the aspect of advocating or rejecting certain beliefs, and has thus become infertile terrain. The arid sociology that is taught in its place is all too often limited to a sophisticated pondering on basic facts and assumptions. But to confine the humanities' role to that of making analytical statements on material circumstances is hardly less irresponsible than immersion in metaphysics to the point of drowning in it: both approaches yield equally distorted images of reality. Philosophical and scientific education in our time suffers greatly from this disease. I emphasise this point to underscore my observation that an understanding of the functioning of the Sumerian temples is central to understanding the present. Not only mosque and church, but also the university have to retrace their origins to the Mesopotamian ziggurats. No matter how obsolete the ziggurats may seem to us, we should not forget that they were the seedbeds of literally thousands of the most cherished institutions of civilisation. They were the laboratories for the encoding of human mindsets, the first asylums where the *submissive creature* was created. The ziggurats were not only the first homes to gods and goddesses, but also the first patriarchal households and the first brothels. They formed the blueprints of all subsequent places of worship, schools, parliaments and public halls. I am neither qualified nor minded to come up with a definition of what Sumerology is or should be, or to give an in-depth appraisal of any of its subjects; my intention is merely to point to certain necessities I came across while trying to understand our own situation today. The rising interest in ancient Mesopotamia among the academic establishment in the United States might be an indication to the effect that the need for such knowledge is increasingly felt.

The creation of the human as a *creature*, as "subordinate" to the divine order, doubtless ranges among the greatest inventions of Sumerian mythology. These subjugated labourers or slaves[1] were the most fundamental *means of production*. The story of the creation of the "slave" as a living tool is equally worthy of examination as that of the wheel or the axe. Keeping in mind the fate of the countless millions born as peasant serfs or factory workers and what has been said and done in their name, the implications of this long-lasting, bitter and toilsome "order of creaturely subordination" may transpire for us in greater clarity. If we only consider the extreme extent of human labour spent on the construction of a single pyramid or a typical ancient city centre, we may get an idea of the sheer scale and the horror of what was effected with the inception of this order.

As far as I am concerned the principal task of historical and social studies should be to render this reality of human subordination intellectually intelligible and emotionally understandable. Subsequent stages of class society developed increasingly refined mechanisms for engendering and perpetuating the mentality of subordination. Present-day systems have devised rather subtle strategies for engineering their subjects. I cannot offer any detailed analysis of how mind, psyche and consciousness are historically structured and how they are affected by these strategies, since this would go far beyond the scope of my argument. But I do think that any discussion of historical processes will be incomplete if it fails to account for this dimension. I would refer to my earlier writings on relevant questions for an insight into how our movement discussed these issues in a more practice-oriented context.[2]

As is the case with all social formations in history, slaveholding class society underwent constant changes – induced by human practice – from its establishment and institutionalisation, via its adaptation to rather diverse sets of circumstances, to its eventual transformation enforced by both internal and external dynamics. Historical materialism teaches us that no given formation is permanent but, rather, permanently subject to change. Given that the issues I have raised are still entangled in gross misconceptions and the historical and social sciences often simply confront us with large amounts of unprocessed data, it is clear that we can hardly go beyond merely attempting to indicate certain distinct phenomena.

The Third Dynasty of Ur in Mesopotamia and the Egyptian Middle Kingdom were attempts at the restoration of the system of slavery-based civilisation amidst growing internal and external contradictions. Neither Sargon's ruthless exercise of force, nor his endeavours to impose the system on outlying areas, could stop his dynasty from becoming a victim of this same force after less than 100 years. The lifespan of the Middle Kingdom was equally short. It was impossible to continue the system as it was, and reform was not penetrating to its core. Accordingly, the attempts at reformation had few lasting, stabilising effects. The god–kings found it increasingly difficult credibly to promulgate their own divinity in the face of growing internal and external opposition and frequent power struggles. Within the Akkadian system, some local rulers or provincial governors attained considerable powers, which induced them to aspire to independence as kings in their own right. At the fringes of the system, they would find in the neighbouring tribes a growing number of potential allies. Experience made it clear to many that the order of the god–kings was in fact a man-made one. Provinces and cities gaining in significance demanded their share in power and sought to further their own influence. We find ample reference to conflicts between priests and kings: many a change of dynasty was concocted in the temples.

The monumental self-representation manifested in the architecture of palaces and graves, the ostentatious trappings of despotic hubris, and the obligatory displays of obeisance (that may even have involved the live interment of a king's attendants on his death) provoked defiance and prepared the ground for a revolution in belief and world-view. In a system relying on the unlimited availability of slave labour, advancements in technology that could potentially create surplus products were left idle or cast aside. The superimposition of relations of property and hegemony on all means of production generated by neolithic society had already led to a period of stagnation. Craftspeople in particular were constricted in their freedom and capacity to work for themselves due to their attachment to either a temple or a royal household. Whilst the number of those exempted from production grew rapidly, the actual producers were deprived of the fruits of their own labour. The class basis for an impending revolution in mentality and for physical uprisings thus expanded. The heavy mill in which people were ground moved on with sheer brutality; but with each of its turns, it progressed increasingly languidly. This, too, raised some doubts as to the tenets sanctifying it. The notion that the gods should not, nay could not, be so unscrupulous found increasing support, and many hearts and minds were filled with sentiments not of gratitude or obeisance, but of desperate invocation and revolt. The muffled murmurs that told of human suffering burst into cries announcing the end of endurance. There was more than just a single Job accusing the gods.[3] The Sumerian compositions relating to what we identify as the metaphor of Job are evidently the products of a time of crisis, suffering and hopelessness. Those years when the gods, that is the ruling elite, turned a deaf ear on the people's implorations and lamentations may just as well have fallen within the hurly-burly of the first half of the second millennium CE, the "Dark Age" in which it culminated. The defiant tone of the compositions makes clear that the ecumenical prophet of pain and patience, Job, initially was the prophet of a historic change in mental disposition. He stands for an epoch.

Outside the imperial cities, new windows of opportunity for rebellion and counter-attack had opened up. A number of ethnic groups penetrated the centres of power, some coming as slaves, some as labourers or bureaucrats, but some as raiders or invaders. The Amorites, Gutians, Kassites and Hyksos are merely those examples of a wider process that have left extant traces in the historical record. Most likely, there was a wider front of tribal confederations that put up resistance against slave-holding imperialism and eventually founded minor states that led to a completely different situation in Middle Eastern political relations. For their own protection, the weakened old powers had to step up aggression. During the millennium of military aggression spanning from Hammurabi's rule (in the eighteenth century BCE) to the fall of the Neo-Assyrian empire after the death of Ashurbanipal (towards the end of the seventh century BCE), there was scarcely an ethnic structure in the Middle East that would have been exempted from the uprooting terror of the imperial armies.

The historical answer to this world situation was the invention of unparalleled systems of religious belief. The vanguard of these systems, and of the movements of popular ancient "soul rebels", was the prophets and the architects of the monotheistic religions. Throughout the last centuries of the first millennium, the idea of a Messiah (God's Anointed) coming as redeemer and saviour spread among the people and kindled their expectations. But this historical epoch was not only one of new faiths; people were by now more than familiar enough with the god–kings to know that they were just humans made of flesh and blood like everyone else. Many were not satisfied with mythology and theology, and an intellectual current emerged that parted with this mentality – that of philosophical thought.

THE GENESIS OF MONOTHEISTIC RELIGIONS IN THE CONTEXT OF ANCIENT CIVILISATION

The birth of monotheistic religions has the significance of a revolution in the mental and ethical character of humankind. This significance is obscured where the discussion of religion is reduced to the question of whether or not there is a God. To put the question thus means to disregard the much more relevant issue of the historical function of religion in human society. Most adherents and many scholars of the monotheistic religions would rather focus on defending their respective tenets than try to expound the impressive social history connected with the genesis of these religions, or – what is even more important – discuss the impact they had on mental development, the formation of logical structures and the rise of philosophy and the sciences. The fact that each of the monotheistic religions emerged at a period of profound crisis in social development is indicative of their revolutionary character.

It will be useful to focus on the question of what exactly they were meant to overcome, and what kind of intellectual and institutional change their rise promoted. What follows is a discussion of the function of each of the monotheistic religions in terms of the transformation of class structures and political organisation. Much of this discussion will be included in the separate chapters devoted to Christianity and Islam respectively, but at this stage I shall attempt an exposition of the role of religion in slave-holding class society and the development of ancient civilisation, followed by some reflections on prophecy and the early history of Judaism.

The Mesopotamian Roots of Biblical and Qur'anic Motifs

The story of "the primordial man", called Adam ("*man*") in Judeo-Christian and Islamic tradition, occurs in a strikingly straightforward version in Sumerian mythology.[4] Here, too, human beings are formed from clay taken from the *abzu* (a kind of primordial mud or underground waters) at the behest of some gods who become weary of doing menial labour. It is interesting to note that in this most complete, and perhaps oldest, Sumerian creation myth, the myth of "Enki and Ninmah", humanity is not conceived as forming the climax of creation or the centre of the universe. According to this narrative, first the universe was created and divided, and for years the gods lived normal "human" lives, working according to the lot assigned to them in order to provide for themselves, and multiplying through coupling. They had to prepare their own food, carry baskets and dig canals. It was then that they complained about their lot and convinced the personified "prime matter", the goddess Nammu, to wake up her son Enki and ask him to create servants for the deities. Enki conceived of a plan, and realised it with the help of a team of goddesses. Once the demiurges had shaped the clay, they loftily decreed their creatures' eternal "fate": humankind was assigned hard work, and the gods and goddesses celebrated the completion of their task with a banquet. It does not take much interpretative skill to realise that the narrative suggests that these servants were created from the faeces of the gods, who themselves are made of the moon, the sun, the wind, etc. Needless to say, the gods have the discretion to admit certain favourite servants to their company; an early example of upward mobility!

Some scholars even argue that the template for the account of the creation of Eve (Semitic: Hawwa) from Adam's rib can be found in the Sumerian Dilmun myth, where Nin Hursag creates the goddess Nin Ti in order to heal a self-incurred illness in Enki's rib. The name Nin Ti can be read both as "Lady of the Rib" and "Lady of Life", and it has been suggested that these two meanings were conflated in the narrative of Hawwa, the "mother of all life". The Biblical Eve obviously is in a much more subordinate position than was Nin Hursag, the divine Lady of the (Zagros) Highlands, who possessed the superior powers of accepting or rejecting Enki's love, rebuking or healing him. The persona of Nin Hursag is associated with the old neolithic culture of the Zagros Mountains and foothills, in which women occupied a prominent place. Owing to a tradition of astral cult that goes back to pre-Sumerian times, the names of deities are preceded by a sign ("*") depicting a star. The word "star" itself is derived from an old Indo-European word that survives in the Kurdish *sterk*, and is assumed to be at the root of the name of Ishtar. The extant Sumerian accounts attest both to the power of the goddesses of the Neolithic agricultural revolution and to the transformations that this culture underwent in an increasingly complex, stratified society.

Much has been made of the Mesopotamian origins of the idea of Eden or paradise. A paradisiacal, sorrow-free time and place are conjured up in the motif of the primeval holy island of Dilmun, from where the gods came, the glorious E-unir shrine of Enki at Eridu and the even more palpable monumental palaces and parks, such as the royal gardens of Babylon. They evidently all added to the gradual construction of the idea of a paradise that is as sensually concrete as it is always out of reach. It has often been suggested that the islands of the Persian Gulf, perhaps Bahrain, and the lavish vegetation found along the shores of the rivers Tigris and Euphrates with their rich archaic shrines and communal buildings, provided the material sources of inspiration for these narratives.

The complex idea of paradise undoubtedly deserves a more thorough analysis than I can offer here. The essential dialectics underlying its construction seem to be that for those who are subjugated, it meant the yearning for a place and time when coercion, organised violence and hierarchies did not exist, when all people were considered of equal worth, and all lived in unity with nature. This early utopian vision was nourished by the mental projection of a lost neolithic social order. For the newly burgeoning ruling class, paradise meant a world where they were freed from the obligation to work, and where the services of a large number of creatures were freely available to them. Paradise, then, seems to be a concept that emerged as a product of the imaginative intermingling of what those who were pushed down dreamt of, and what those who rose above them luxuriously enjoyed, at the time of the unfolding of class society.

Those who designed its ideology and ran its institutions depicted this class society as an impeccable divine order where the *raison d'être* of the human creatures was to serve their masters. The formation of the Sumerian priest class, the political elite and the military and bureaucratic set-up was accompanied by the spreading of the mythical narratives that served the strategy of establishing hegemony over the hearts and minds of the populace. This strategy clearly outweighed that of the use of force in the initial establishment of a stratified society in lower Mesopotamia; cohesion and allegiance were secured by these discourses of power in myth, cult, architecture and arts. This strategy was certainly no less successful than the battles for supremacy and ideological hegemony waged by the American and European universities and think-tanks of our times. And historically speaking, it managed to secure much more permanent results than the latter!

Any ruling class or elite that wants to rise to power will firstly have to win over the hearts and minds of the masses. A number of historical examples indicate that where they fail to do so, and rely only on sheer force and blatant lies, their attempts will ultimately fail. The principal issue in a power struggle is this war over beliefs and emotions. In the Sumerian case, we are not talking about the promulgation of existing ideological beliefs or ready-made scientific knowledge. The issue at stake here is no less than the *creation* of a grand mythology as a material requirement needed for the construction of the whole set of sub- and superstructures of class society. The historic achievements of the Sumerian priests thus had a seminal influence on the entire history of civilisation that was to follow from it. They did not only serve the coercive ruling class that emerged in the Sumerian cities, but acted in the interest of all successive class societies – that is, of all those forces that came to represent what we call civilisation. The mechanisms and stratagems involved in the endeavours of the Sumerian priest class will not be discussed here at length. However, it should be noted that understanding their role can help us arrive at a narrative of Middle Eastern history that is critical of the various dogmas underlying our traditional interpretation.

The story of the expulsion from paradise does not occur in Sumerian mythology in a form comparable to the narratives we encounter in the Hebrew Bible and the Qur'anic literature. Nevertheless, analyses of the latter can only gain from references to the historical background of early Middle Eastern stratified societies. Underlying them was the experience of the process of class differentiation, repeated in every newly urbanised society: the ascending upper class would set itself off from the lower layers of the dissolving kinship organisation, to which it originally owed allegiance by blood. The layers that were pushed into the position of servile subordinate creatures experienced a veritable "fall" away from the realm of the upper class. The ban on eating certain fruits and the heavy penalty for transgression can be seen as a moralising account of the simple fact that the subjugated masses were not allowed to sit at the banquet tables of their rulers. There is no place for servants in paradise; this striking feature occurred already in the earliest Sumerian paradise myth. In the monotheistic versions, the expelled servants were attacked ideologically as well and made to feel guilty about their own exclusion.

The story of the Flood that appears in the Hebrew Bible and the Qur'an[5] has its commonly acknowledged predecessors in the Sumerian myth of Ziusudra, retold in the Akkadian Gilgamesh Epic (where the flood-hero is called Utnapishtim), and in the Old Babylonian story of Atra-hasis. There is some archaeological evidence for the devastating flooding of archaic cities situated in the south Mesopotamian delta area near the Persian Gulf. The myths present the event as a curse humankind incurred from the gods for unduly clamorous behaviour disturbing the peace of the gods, and for out-of-bounds reproduction leading to overpopulation in the towns. Natural disaster is represented in the guise of divine punishment. There is a popular tradition in Kurdistan according to which the vessel on which Noah embarked landed at Mount Cûdi,[6] one of the highest peaks overlooking Lower Mesopotamia from the north.

The etymology of the ancient Kurdish name of the mountain ("he saw land/a place")[7] is intriguing both for the suggestion that it may be related to a very old Mesopotamian flood myth, and for being one of the examples of the preservation of word roots that appear in many Indo-European languages but may have been used in the Fertile Crescent in prehistoric times.[8] More than anything else, this assumption underpins the centrality of neolithic social formations of the Fertile Crescent to the wider development of human cultures. There are numerous other elements in Biblical and Qur'anic narratives that have their roots in Mesopotamian civilisation, such as the symbol of Job, or Ayyub, mentioned above, or the Song of Solomon with its striking citations of Sumerian love poetry associated with Inanna and Dumurzi.[9]

Now that we have discussed the shared Middle Eastern background of the lore of different religions, let us look at the popular oral traditions according to which Urfa and its environment are the "home of the prophets". From the start of the second millennium, this region was a site of intense and strategically important Sumerian colonisation. At the same time, it falls within a wider region where two of the main tribal cultures of that era collided, interacted, exchanged material and cultural values, and to some extent coalesced: both the Semitic Amorite and the Hurrian ethnic groups that we find throughout almost the entire Middle East inhabited this area. Both of them were to some extent integrated in the Sumerian-centred system of long distance trade, and both of them were to some degree dispossessed and antagonised by it. The coming together of different cultural traditions is always a potential basis for opposition to the system, since it provides an opportunity for different world-views and cultural traditions to meet. The popular narrative of the uprising of Abraham against Nimrod, irrespective of its historical accuracy, can thus be taken as a prototype for the conflicts between semi-nomadic tribal communities and the hegemonic state system. Urfa's traditional fame as a hotbed of prophets can be an indication of the deep-rooted tradition of native resistance in the region.[10]

The same can be said about Jerusalem and its surroundings: if Urfa was one of the main sites of resistance against the Mesopotamian imperial system, then Jerusalem played a comparable, though somewhat better documented role vis-à-vis the Egyptian empire. Jerusalem, too, is renowned as a hotbed of prophecy. The two locations' respective positions as centres of opposition account for their traditional reputation as holy cities of monotheistic beliefs. They had held this position from the time of the legendary emigration of proto-Judaic tribes from Harran towards Palestine to the time of Jesus' uprising in Jerusalem: a very old, popular Eastern tradition has it that King Abgar of Osroëne invited Jesus to Urfa when his life was in danger.[11] Interaction and migration between these two regions continued throughout the last two millennia. As sites of the fermentation of monotheistic religious systems, they provided a cultural ambience in which hopes for liberation could flourish to the degree that the cities were ascribed a holy character. Even the present-day convictions as to the holiness of these places can be traced back to their position in the struggle against rigid systems of slavery. Cultural memory has preserved their historical importance in a religiously encoded way.

The Character of Prophecy[12]

Once we have lifted the heavy veil of religious zealotry that covers the historical phenomenon of prophecy and placed it in the context of ancient slave-holding civilisation, we can extrapolate the following traits of the social movements that form the undercurrent of what is known as prophecy:[13]

1. Prophecy evolved from within the two most deeply rooted, archaic slave-holding systems of the ancient Middle East. It was shaped by the ideological institutions that emerged with the social differentiation of antagonistic classes. However, it surfaced during crises and upheavals in the form of an ethical and eschatological rebellion of human conscience against the pressures the system exerted and legitimised through intellectual and psychological enculturation.
2. Rather than striving for a fully independent ideological enculturation, prophecy aimed at reshaping those aspects of hegemonic mythology and religion that blatantly contradicted social reality. It did not have the power to overcome the official doctrines and institutions prevalent at the time. Although prophecy did have revolutionary aspects, its overall character was reformist: prophecy supported developments that led to a renovation of the system and rendered it more tolerable.
3. The social basis of prophecy was mainly the impoverished layers of newly differentiated class societies and the non-privileged sections of ethnic structures at the point of their disintegration. In some instances, prophecy could assume the position of politico-ideological leadership in ethnic communities that were altogether at odds with the system. In the main, however, it would have been particularly attractive to individuals who were marginalised by the predominant social institutions and had no powerful peer group within the system.
4. Prophecy did not emerge primarily as a material, political force, but developed as an ideological vanguard with spiritual and moral aspects of social life as its emphasis.

The following points will suffice for sketching the nature of institutionalised prophetic religion. They will be exemplified in our discussion of the three great prophets[14] with a view to appreciating their historical importance. The developments initiated by early prophetic movements in the Middle East can be discussed under the following aspects:

1. Prophecy in the Abrahamic religions laid the foundations for a conception of religion based on the Oneness of God (Arabic: *tawhid*), i.e. monotheism

in the strict sense of the word. The God that appears in the narratives focusing on Abraham is totally distinct from the pantheons of the Sumerians and Egyptians. In a way, theological independence is achieved through this concept as a signifier of the freedom of humankind in general, and the ethnic or tribal community in particular. Notwithstanding all the references it makes to the mythological and religious lore of the two archaic slave-holding systems, the new divine identity does amount to a significant advance towards liberation.

2. This divine identity was completely other than human, immortal and hostile to idolatry. It was based on a high-level abstraction of the concept of the divine that superseded both the totemic concept of religion found in traditional tribal societies, and the "two-class" concept of religion prevalent in slave-holding societies as a reflection of kingship. It can be regarded as the core of a religious development that potentially appeals to the whole of humankind and relates to a more complex stage in the history of human intellect.
3. It represented a higher form of logical reasoning than the somewhat infantile polytheistic and totemic conceptualisations did. This would eventually make monotheistic beliefs particularly accessible to different groups and currents that formed due to awakening intellectual and ethical concerns.
4. The early Middle Eastern prophet movements were especially influential among kinship-based communities that struggled to preserve customs and forms of behaviour associated with tribal freedom and that were not integrated into the system. They also drew support from artisans and the small number of marginalised ecstatics, ascetics and hermits found in the ancient societies.[15] Prophecy accounts for some of the most important aspects of social movements in the crisis-ridden, post-Sumerian world.
5. The history of many of the smaller Middle Eastern city states that emerged outside the centralised territorial states of Egypt and Mesopotamia was intricately connected with these social movements led by guilds of prophets. The Hebrew kingdoms constitute the most striking and best-studied example.
6. Due to the influence of the hegemonic system of slavery and the patriarchal structure of the tribal communities, the position of women had greatly deteriorated and the veneration of goddesses completely vanished from the prophetic–monotheistic cults. From the time of the Babylonian empire, an unconcealed and coarse political patriarchate was firmly established. It corresponded with the primitive social patriarchy in semi-nomadic tribal societies, where male lineage was one of the principles underlying kinship organisation. All the prominent prophets starting from the Patriarch Abraham were males, and there was no place for women in this system. In the Genesis stories, woman is ascribed an affinity with Satan. The genesis of this Biblical tradition can only be explained by reference to

the Assyro-Babylonian influence (as metaphorically reflected in the story of Abraham) and the Egyptian influence (as reflected in the story of Moses) on the formative process of the Hebrew class society. The denigration and oppression of women was (and continues to be) a long-term process that visibly accelerated from the second millennium onwards. Growing gender inequality went hand in glove with the process of the overall development of class differences.

7. The idea of the one and only god occurred as a prominent ideological motif underpinning the consolidation of royal authority in later centuries. The divine rule of a single god is equated with the earthly rule of a single king. However, this function, which the doctrine acquired in the course of history, should not distract from the initial liberating tendency and the contribution to abstract reasoning inherent in the initial idea. Obviously, the ruling class would try to assimilate the positive god of the new religion and modify its teachings so as to serve its interests. But this does not contradict the observation that the historical function of the institution of prophecy was primarily that of significantly softening the systems of slavery that had evolved in ancient history. With their postulate that there is one single great god to whom even kings are accountable, the new religious currents dealt one of the fatal blows to the age of the god–kings, who were believed to have as much command over the souls of their subjects as they ostensibly had over nature.[16]

The new religious currents were the second major civilisation movement in the Middle East, and the progress with which they can be associated is clearly discernible despite the subsequent degeneration of both religious thinking and state rule exercised in the name of the laws of the only god. Especially the fact that the body politic was now bound in its actions by religious rules contributed to the moderation of the use of power; but the radical changes in thought and learning probably deserve at least as much mention. This new religious learning, from which developed the systematic theology of the Christian and Islamic traditions, certainly belongs to a different stage in the history of mentalities from the inveterate priestly and scribal school traditions of Mesopotamia and Egypt and of those states that copied and adapted them to their local cultures. The institution of prophecy had a central impact not only on the initial formation, but also on the reshaping and interpretation of the religious lore of Hebrew Yahwism. The struggles waged in the name of both Judaism and early Christianity must be recognised for what they were: major factors in the processes that led to the supersession of three of the largest and longest-lasting empires in world history – the Assyro-Babylonian, Egyptian and Roman empires.

The Formation of Judaism

The most consequential episode in the monotheistic revolution was the adoption of El by an increasing number of tribes from the Arabian Peninsula, who abandoned their totemic traditions in favour of the belief in "Allah".[17] But it took a long and by no means trouble-free historical process to get there. Centuries after the events reported in the narrative of Abraham, Moses also adopted this El as the only deity, and he became principally, if not exclusively, the god of the Hebrew tribes. The text of the Pentateuch emphasises that they formed a "chosen people" or "treasured possession" of the god,[18] whose name was changed into Yahweh from the time of Moses. He is described as a highly "jealous" god, and imagery of a patriarchal marital relationship between the god (male) and his chosen people (female) is evoked.[19] The divine verdict of being "chosen out of all the peoples on earth" played a central part in the formation of a tradition that has proved strong enough to sustain the distinctiveness of Jewish society to the present day. This special relationship with the divine entails, among others, the idea that the Hebrew tribes were strong enough to "wrestle with God" (which is the literal meaning of "*Israel*") – that is, participate in an intimate, face-to-face relation in which the ethnic community and its deity were nearly equally powerful.[20] The obvious differences between what is termed the religion of the patriarchs and the Mosaic faith are related to the social changes that occurred among the tribal groups throughout the centuries. One element of the relations between the different ethnic communities of Canaan would have been rivalry and some degree of internecine conflict, but any greater community with a nascent urban centre would have been liable to absorb members of different ethnic groups. It is interesting to note that according to the narrative, migration by no means came to an end when the tribes reached Canaan, but "famine" caused them (or, rather, some of them) to move on to Egypt.[21] Now, this migration of deprived communities into the orbit of the imperial centres is well attested and has been discussed in Chapter 6. It was here that the migrants from Harran turned into "*apiru*", the ostensibly dirty labourers, on the fringe of society, who came "from the desert", from non-urban backgrounds. Just as was the case with the Mesopotamian Kassites, some of the "*apiru*" would have attained positions within the imperial bureaucracy, like Joseph[22] and Moses. It is striking that this individual upward mobility is not only depicted as a gift of God, but that the narrative of Moses actually draws heavily on motifs that occur in the legends woven around the "biography" of the Akkadian king Sargon.[23] It seems that stories of this type were resorted to when members of tribes of little fame ascended to positions of high power, whether they were founders of imperial dynasties or monotheistic lawgivers.

Egyptian papyri tell us that "*apiru*" were employed in dragging stones for large-scale building programmes during the reign of Rameses II (ca. 1304–1237 BCE).[24] A group of them might well have been led out of Egypt by an ethnic kinsman employed at the court, perhaps someone who had fallen out of favour with the king for taking the wrong side in political power games or having supported a failed revolt. There is no data in known extra-biblical texts to illustrate further the tentative historical events underlying the Exodus narrative. The word "*mose*" simply means "is born" in Egyptian. The epithet "Pharaoh" is a metaphor in the oral tradition of the Canaanites, who had to endure Egyptian expansion, just as "Nimrod" is a metaphor for the northern Mesopotamian folk tales.[25] We do not know anything about the scale of this exodus of enslaved labourers, but the descendants of Abraham would have made up only a tiny fraction of them. Tradition has it that by the time of the exodus, or rather through the very event of it, the clans and tribes had been transformed into a fully-fledged "people". What can safely be asserted is that this *hijra*[26] or grand departure, whatever the actual scale and time of it, left deep and permanent marks in the cultural memory of the Hebrews, and indeed the whole of the Judeo-Christian world. It can be said to have been the first "long march to freedom" in history. Those who arrived in Canaan are likely to have created links with Hebrew groups already settled there. The undoubtedly long and painful migration through desert lands and especially the ideological and political norms and institutions promulgated by reference to it can justifiably be regarded as constitutive elements of a tribal confederation that quickly evolved into a state society in its own right. It is widely thought that Moses was influenced by the Egyptian cult of Aton, which involved the veneration of the sun as the sole deity. This cult had been forcefully imposed on the country during the reign of Akhenaton, also known as Amenhotep IV (1353–1336 BCE) but was subsequently abolished.[27] The biblical text itself contains allusions to the influence the Midianite cult of the Arabian Peninsula and the Sinai exerted on Moses through his father-in-law, the priest Jethro.[28] The interplay of strategies designed to resolve the problems of leadership and organisation in the runaway Hebrew groups and the syncretistic religious influences of the wider Levant amalgamated in the rise of the charismatic, inspired champion of monotheism who could enhance his authority through the performance of miracles. The resorting to miracles and the style of politico-ideological leadership that goes with it came at a historical juncture when the methods of traditional political authority and the world-view underlying them had lost their face value. It contained the encoded message that it was necessary to adopt a new world-view and new, perhaps drastic, measures of social governance. The fact that the historical requirements of the new era were rather demanding and could not easily be internalised by the community unless it underwent profound changes in mentality was expressed in the discourse of miracles, inspired leadership and divine revelations. It is a well-known fact that similar discourses of inspired leadership were produced at comparable junctures in the histories of different societies and ages, and we shall look at some of them further on in this book. Narratives of prophecy are arguably one way of giving meaning to highly complex, startling historical processes.

The socio-political problems expressed in the Mosaic tale of departure were of a tough nature and must have involved many uncertainties. It would have been impossible to solve these problems on the basis of the old, parochial patterns of kinship-based leadership when there was a multitude of tribal groups and scattered individuals, most of whom the text tells us were highly unsatisfied with their conditions and rather hostile towards the self-declared leadership.[29] And indeed, establishing a tribal confederation with a new ideology from groups of runaway *apiru* and mainly rural settlers and semi-nomads would have involved inter-clan rivalry, the hardships of prolonged migration, conflicts with settled communities over the use of their pastures and arable lands, and bloody battles with other ethnic groups. There is ample archaeological and textual evidence to the effect that ancient Canaanite cults and popular forms of worship inspired by Egyptian and Assyro-Babylonian religion were thriving among the Hebrew communities. Moses' putative response to the worshipping of the golden calf was draconian: he commanded the members of the priestly Levite clans to slay 3,000 people in retribution. The mode of organisation assumed by the society producing such narratives was something other than that of the typical tribal confederation. It underwent revolutionary changes in terms of ideology, ethics and governance. Change was precipitated by the increasingly tough conditions of national formation at the point of breaking away from the hegemonic systems.

Moses found answers to the questions puzzling him by withdrawing into seclusion on the peak of a mountain and meditating. This technique of deliberately abandoning fellow human beings and establishing an intense rapport with nature can be found in the preparative phase of any prophecy. It is reminiscent of the techniques of shamanism, a spiritual form of expression during an important stage in human socialisation. Shamanism functions in primitive societies as an institution that mixes techniques of sorcery and healing with rituals through which adolescents are initiated into, and encouraged to internalise, the beliefs and customs of the community. Shamans are the spiritual leaders and custodians of knowledge in societies without priests or sheikhs. Although some of the functions of the shaman and the prophet overlap, the two are distinct. The shaman and his Arabian counterpart, the sheikh, are responsible for upholding the dominant customs and mores and preserving the order of the clan or tribe. This entails not only the spiritual, but also the material aspects of community life. Prophecy, in contrast, amounts to a new departure. It formulates a utopian vision of the future. Its function is to reject and replace the past and invent an alternative future according to new concepts and plans. In that sense, prophets also differ from priests, who have the duty to represent an already established religious tradition.

The concept of God will be discussed later in this book. At this stage, it may be sufficient to remark that the identity of God does undergo significant changes in the historical process. The Mosaic Yahweh, for one thing, differed from the "God of Abraham" and his mythical forerunners in many respects. Moses was no more an exponent of Egyptian doctrines than he was a sheikh or priest of the Abrahamic faith. The historical conditions urged him to embark upon a prophetic calling. Having said this, the influence of Abrahamic tradition on the Hebrew tribes, limited though it may have been, was doubtless a decisive factor in determining the direction that this major advance in the history of the monotheistic religions was to take. The Mosaic faith was, in a way, a nationalisation of religion. Underlying this national Jewish understanding of religion was the desire to avoid being melted down in the cauldron of cultural hybridity, and to avoid perishing in the face of great dangers.

With the Ten Commandments that Moses received on the mountains, the new religious era assumed a distinct shape. A number of legal, financial and organisational measures are ascribed to Moses. According to the Scriptures, his brother Aaron had the task of representing the tribe before God; furthermore, the ideological authority was vested in him.[30] Joshua was assigned the post of military commander.[31] Moses installed a council for legal affairs governed by the new laws but retained an advisory body consisting of the elders of the tribes.[32] These reforms were aimed at creating cohesion and promoting group identity.

The holy and fertile lands that Yahweh promised were, of course, inhabited, and the established communities would have been far from warmly welcoming to the new arrivals.[33] The outcome of the encounters with them would be determined by force – pretty much as it is today. How entwined holiness and malediction are! The exodus narrative sets out the basic terminology and logic that later monotheistic religions were to follow. It is quite likely that things happened in a very different way from what is narrated, but the historical results of this putative exodus are striking nonetheless, and the textual account of it refers to the inception of many far-reaching developments.

The subsequent stages of the Hebrews' history are equally entangled with legend. It is held that the era of Saul (c. 1021–1000 BCE) marked the transition from the primacy of the clergy to an institutionalised monarchy. The age of David and Solomon seems to be something like the heroic age of Hebrew culture. Assyrian sovereignty and the destruction of Jerusalem by the Babylonians in 587/586 BCE put an end to the political existence of ancient Israel. The displacement of a large number of Jews to Babylon resulted in the assimilation of elements of Sumerian mythology and Babylonian learning and consequently the formation of a new layer of intellectuals, who counterpoised the impact of the prophets on education and governance in the post-exilic era.

When the Persian emperor Cyrus conquered Babylon in 538, the Jews attained their freedom. It is said that many returned to Jerusalem and engaged in rebuilding the city. Obviously, a part of the Jewish community voluntarily remained in Babylon or moved elsewhere, and some eventually made for Jerusalem after having spent several years in the Achaemenid Mesopotamia. Adding to all these cultural influences was that of Hellenism, which arrived with the campaigns of Alexander. It was through the synergetic influences of

Babylonian learning, Persian Zoroastrian teachings and Greek sources that the priests who redacted the Old Testament in its present shape were intellectually moulded.

By the time of Roman rule, Judaism had given rise to a number of sects: the conservative and collaborationist Sadducees (from Semitic *saduq*, "true"), the Pharisees (who cherished the Persian heritage), and the radical insurgents, dubbed the "fourth philosophy" by the chronicler Josephus. More than any of them, however, the apocalyptic movement of the Essenes, whose teachings reverberate in the words of John the Baptist, reflected the spirit of the new era. Conditions were ripe for humanity's acceptance of a universal religion to confront the universal slavery of the Roman Empire. The official Jewish religion with its nationalistic interpretation of the priestly diviners[34] failed to develop responses to the challenges posed by the overall political environment. Apocalyptic, Messianic world-views such as that voiced by John the Baptist found increasing support amongst the population and apparently caused anger amongst the authorities.[35] The renewed destruction of Jerusalem at the hands of the Roman army in 70 CE and the dispersal of the Jewish community ushered in a new period in history.

THE RESISTANCE OF ETHNIC GROUPS TO SLAVE-HOLDING CIVILISATION

Conscious ethnic groups account for a form of historical movement spanning the full duration of the system of slavery from its beginnings to its disintegration. Much of the energy of the greater territorial states of the ancient Middle East and Greco-Roman antiquity was absorbed by conflicts with adversaries of this type. Ethnic groups of the neolithic age were structured more or less spontaneously. They exist – to employ a Marxist simile – *in themselves*. There is scant cause to think that pre-state communities had an awareness of themselves as ethnic entities, since there was no enemy that would attack and try to subjugate them, and there were no social contradictions that would lead to the formation of such awareness. The target of a resistance that would demand and generate ethnic unity had to be both geographically and culturally external, and of a social structure that was other than that of like ethnic groups. These contradictions arose with the rise of stratified political societies in the immediate vicinity and from within kinship-based groups. While the upper strata of the ethnic communities would be assimilated into the emerging class society, the lower strata were left exposed to a multidirectional threat. At the initial, archaic stage, the units of class society were emerging like so many small islands from the vast ocean of the neolithic world. The threat that emanated from them was limited. But, as the landmasses of civilisation extended all over this old world, it was the agrarian and pastoralist communities' turn to find themselves in the position of isolated islets. In order not to be swallowed up, they had to isolate themselves and put up resistance. This historical development is at the root of the extraordinarily strong ethnic consciousness encountered in societies in the Middle East and comparable regions of the contemporary world. The imperialist stage of slave-holding civilisation was at the same time the stage of organisation of kinship communities as conscious ethnic groups.

I would like to come back to the thesis that tribal confederations emerged in response to the expansion of stratified urban civilization, as discussed in Chapter 6. According to this thesis, the colonisation moves of urban centres from the second half of the third millennium onwards caused ethnic communities to become aware of the significance of resources found in their native territories and to take up the cudgels for their trade interests. When the colonial administrations appropriated these resources by force, awareness changed to resistance, which in turn was met with bloody repression. Their own material interests compelled ethnic groups to reorganise both internally and against the external forces in order to secure defensive and offensive powers. Many communities appropriated the arms technology they found in the colonial outposts or with the intruding armies and developed a hierarchical group of warriors. Alliances with kindred groups facing the same contradictions were inevitable. They led to the formation of tribal confederations. In the long run, a tribal confederation had two choices. It could either be successful against its enemies and, by virtue of increasing centralisation, transform itself into a state with an urban centre in its own right, or disintegrate in the face of defeats, its members retreating into less accessible terrain such as mountain or desert regions. This terrain would offer a certain degree of protection against the drive on the part of the dominant class society to capture and enslave them. This latter fate would have been that of countless communities that have been subjugated and assimilated, most of them leaving not so much as a trace in the historical record. In the main, this is the way the wheel of history turned through the successive centuries leading up to our own.

Tribal consciousness was the proto-form of primitive national consciousness (not to be confused with that of the modern, capitalist age).[36] But even this primitive idea of nation emerged only at a later stage in history, and it did so by way of overriding tribal consciousness. In fact, the idea of nation did not emerge where there was a deep-rooted ethnical awareness; on the contrary, it arose where tribal structures proved insufficient or even detrimental to the process of developing responses to historical challenges. These responses were principally political and military in nature. As to the Middle East, it should be noted that the formation of different ethnic groups associated with either of the greater language groups of the region occurred – and interacted – at different points in history. Semitic-speaking groups were involved in the early history of Sumer and Egypt, and can be found among those who rebelled against these empires at a later stage in history. The Semitic Arabs appeared at the beginning of the feudal age as the main dynamic in the spread of Islam. Likewise, speakers of Indo-European languages appeared in the form of both tribal confederations and territorial states. The Hittites, Mitanni, Medes and Persians were but the more prominent among them.

The Assyrian and Babylonian empires had made it a stated, proudly documented policy to uproot and destroy local ethnic structures of any sort. Against this policy, both Semitic and Indo-European tribal groups resisted – each in a fashion prescribed by the historical conditions in which they were living.

In the final analysis, neither the ideological innovation of monotheism (which developed in reaction to slave-holding imperialism, though somewhat entwined with it) nor the political developments associated with the resistance put up by tribal alliances proved fatal to the classic centres of slave-owning civilisation. Neither of them succeeded in replacing it with an alternative form of civilisation. This only occurred with the transition to feudal civilisation. But both of these movements dealt shocks to the system and contributed significantly to its assuming new forms. They helped to moderate and reform the system. We must not underestimate the impact of these historical developments on the formation of norms of liberation – understood both spiritually and politically – at a time when human beings were regarded as mere things or shadows. They provided channels for the expressions of anguish, rebellion and apocalyptic hope on the part of a multitude of groups of disenfranchised and exploited people. They inspired the search for new ways of life.

In the course of the first millennium BCE mystical groups emerged in the Middle East as a new kind of social formation. They were no longer ethnocentric, but enabled people to accept each other as brothers and sisters on the basis of clandestine, mystical beliefs. They emerged as a *third form of social organisation* in the history of humankind, distinct from both the class society of the age of slavery and the kinship-based ethnic society. These social movements heralded a twofold development. They are of interest from the point of view that history at large eventually assumed the guise of a history of religions and sects. The history of the Middle East in particular can arguably be described as the history of religious and sectarian wars. In terms of its genealogy, the whole discourse of the history of religions, which was to become a master narrative of later ages, can be regarded as a product of developments connected with the rise of religious "brotherhoods". But the changes such groups underwent also led them to produce the prototypes of philosophical groups. The focus of intellectual interest shifted from the realm of religious belief to that of philosophical reasoning. If religion emerged from mythology, philosophical approaches first evolved from an atmosphere that owed as much to the development of the material base of civilisation as it did to the conscious activities of mystical or mystery groups.[37] The form of thinking called philosophy is a product of the interplay between, on the one hand, the need to reform the system of slavery and, on the other hand, the development of the human mind.

8

The Greco-Roman Contribution

When dealing with the subject of the beginnings of stratified civilisation, I tried to pay particular attention to the interconnections between seemingly unrelated subjects. In this I was guided by my hopes that the broken link between science and ethics could somehow be re-established. This priority entailed settling for short-cut arguments in many instances where in-depth discussion would have been desirable, and for repetitions where a more streamlined flow of argument could reasonably be expected.

While discussing slave-holding civilisation, my eyes were always set on the present. The rationale behind my delving into early history was that it would be methodologically insufficient to analyse capitalism as an isolated socio-economic form, especially where the objective of such analysis is to criticise it as a system. Capitalism, and even socialism, where it actually existed, preserved and encapsulated the products that constituted the base and superstructure of slave-owning society. The present world system runs on the basis of more generalised and sophisticated forms of these primary "features of civilisation". The sheer dimensions, the multiplicity and the degree of perfection of modern social institutions might be bewildering; but that should not make us overlook the fact that what really makes them work are the structures that arose with the seminal formation of civilisation.

For a variety of reasons, the social sciences are at odds with the common preoccupation of the natural sciences to arrive at general laws governing the phenomena they study. I believe that the reluctance to deal with wider contexts and overarching issues in historical and social studies has to do with the intellectual dictates of class hegemony, which demand the production of snappy ideological images, promoting the capitalist status quo. While science maintains an apodictic certainty concerning its knowledge about the world and its ability to explain the world, it seems to have become, however, a mere and enormous collection of data. Worse, science also seems to be unable to give any meaning to these data. The amazing manipulations permeating the mainstream approaches to the social sciences in Europe and the United States must be seen in the context of the influence of powerful social groups in the academic world which are working towards the requirements of increasingly crude global imperialist dominance.

My concern is that, if we want to counterpose a project called "scientific socialism", we will have to rediscuss its methodological basics. Some staunch leftists might not find this a particularly meaningful enterprise. But I dare say that unless it undergoes a thorough self-criticism and severe corrections, Marxism will inevitably end up being a mildly wayward plaything at the hands of capitalism. The idea of the "dictatorship of the proletariat", even where it can be implemented, will hardly open up any new horizons beyond its utilisation by capital as yet another model of domination after the fashion of crude Sargonic imperialism. Beneath the collapse of actually existing socialism, for which no theoretical model has yet sufficiently accounted, there runs a continuous line from the Sumerian hieratic state to the grand models of political organisation of the twentieth century. Discussing the lines of continuity in state-centred civilisations at large may offer an answer to the question:"Where and by whom were mistakes made and the cause betrayed?" It may also clarify the more haunting question: "How, when and by whom can a more viable form of socialism be realised?" My contribution to this discussion will be made in Part 3 of this book. It will constitute perhaps the most important aspect of my submissions, which were drafted as a defence against the hypocrisy of the twentieth century.

GREEK CIVILISATION

One of the key questions lying before anyone who seeks to understand human history in the long perspective is how to define and where to place the Greco-Roman form of slave-holding civilisation. Many of the errors and distortions found in historical and social studies are related to the fundamental failure to contextualise it historically. Most common is the exaggerated representation of Greco-Roman civilisation as the starting point of civilisation per se. This aspect is mainly encountered in Eurocentric discourse. Its direct opposite is the disparaging and often blatantly polemic, unscientific viewpoint advanced in "Eastocentric", notably Islamist, discourse. It should be noted that both of these outlooks are informed by a pattern of thought that can already be found in the cultural supremacism pervading much of Greek mythology and philosophy, *as well as* in the exclusive, nearly fanatical self-centredness of religious thought of Middle Eastern origin.

We have already mentioned that Greco-Roman civilisation was nourished by earlier forms of culture that developed in south-west Asia and north-east Africa. Neolithic economy in Greece started around 6500 BCE and repeated a process that had begun in the Middle East more than 2,000 years earlier. It is often argued that this new way of life was introduced by newcomers from

Anatolia. There are indeed many indications that the agricultural revolution throughout Europe benefited greatly from the inventions, tools and concepts that had reached it from the East. The archaeologist Gordon Childe was a pioneer in establishing this view among scholars of prehistory. It allows us to understand that the differentiation of cultures and the formation of ethnic groups in which a distinct material culture and perhaps a distinct language prevailed should not be linked with the notion of physical conquest of a stronger "people" subduing another, ostensibly "weaker" one. The differentiation of cultures should rather be explained in terms of the spread of the cultural know-how and the economic techniques of the agricultural revolution throughout a world shared by different communities who appropriated these tools in different ways.

This process, which had begun in the Fertile Crescent, was repeated in south-west Europe after it had taken place in North Africa, India, China and the Danube area. It was perhaps the most consequential instance of an event that repeatedly occurred throughout the ages of history: local cultures being nourished by the wave-like dissemination of cultural practices emanating from main sources. For the sake of an overall understanding of historical change, the dissemination of Indo-European languages ought to be construed in this way rather than through positing the wholesale migration of ready-made ethnic entities. The Hellenes of mainland Greece and the Latins of central Italy were products of thousands of years of cultural exchange, in the course of which certain communities acquired specific characteristics based on territorial and ethnic ties.

The fact that the non-Indo-European Western "Mediterranean" languages were replaced by Indo-European Greek and Latin is now commonly held as proof of a prehistoric influx of Eastern culture; but much more visible in the historical record is the influence of Eastern complex stratified *cultures* on Bronze Age Greece. I have already pointed out that this process of nourishing drew on four direct sources: second millennium Anatolia, Eastern Mediterranean, Egypt and Crete. The main point, however, is how these manifold influences amalgamated into a rich synthesis. It can be safely asserted that this happened on the basis of the neolithic foundations that early Greek society had already acquired. Doubtless the natural environment had an important impact on social development – to the same extent that it does on any early society. Reference to nature cannot therefore sufficiently explain the peculiar characteristics of ancient Greece. Its geographical position at the intersection of Asia, Africa and Europe may account for thc availability of the many cultural inputs drawn upon for the creation of a synergetic novelty. But the question of how this specific synthesis evolved can only be answered when discussed against the backdrop of the wider context of early human history.

The extraordinary richness of the synthesis can be addressed by specifying the quality and quantity of the incoming values. These values can then be considered as providing the raw materials out of which it was Greek civilisation's role to construct a higher stage of development in ancient history. Its original contribution, then, was its very capacity to turn this totality of cultures into something more than the sum of its component parts. But to depict this undoubtedly important contribution as the primary, original source from which all civilisation was born is an unacceptable distortion. Long before modern European civilisation created its own view of the classical heritage, the ancient Greek authors themselves pursued this manipulative self-representation with a chauvinism that could take on near-fanatical zeal. It became a tradition for the Greeks to construe anyone other than themselves as "barbarians", despite the fact that the "original" sources of civilisation had been established long before the Greeks made the transition from primitive clan society to civilised political power.

We have already discussed how mythology, writing and a variety of other intellectual abilities were introduced to Greece. The system collapse that led by 1200 BCE to the downfall of the Hittite Empire, the destruction of Troy and Ugarit, and the decline of Mycenaean civilisation created a vacuum into which new groups of settlers could easily move. Greek-speaking tribes began to settle in the eastern Aegean region. From the last century of the second millennium, the Aeolians and Ionians established numerous coastal and island towns and created a large permanent Greek presence in western Anatolia. This presence was to expand gradually. By the fourth century BCE the Hellenisation of wide parts of Anatolia progressed rapidly, and the Luwians, Phrygians and Lydians eventually became assimilated into Hellenic culture. Virtually the only "aboriginal" ethnic groups that preserved their culture were those that can be considered the ancestors of the Armenians and the Kurds in the region of Commagene. Reaching its early climax under the reign of Alexander, the long Hellenic presence in Anatolia came to a tragic end only when the Turks displaced the Anatolian Greeks at the beginning of the twentieth century CE.

Apart from Anatolia and Mediterranean islands such as Crete and Cyprus, Greek expansion also included Western areas like Macedonia and southern Italy. The seventh and sixth centuries BCE were the era of transition from ethnic federations to fully stratified slave-holding, centralised polities. By the early seventh century dozens of Greek communities had formed into city states. What is remarkable is that in these city states the priest class was secondary to the political class. Without passing through a period of a fully-fledged monarchy, the upper strata of the *polis* established a system that could be called a slave-holding republic. This assembly-based mode of political organisation was the most striking difference between the "exemplary" Greco-Roman polities and those of Mesopotamia, Egypt and other ancient Middle Eastern states. In these polities, the priest class and later the successive dynasties were indispensable features of political organisation.

Underlying this difference is the fact that, by the mid-first millennium, conditions for forming complex cultures were quite different from those of the third or second millennium BCE. On the ideological level, rationality was increasingly cherished; on the economic level, trade had outstripped agriculture in importance. The bulk of the population of archaic Greek city states consisted of a middle class that had connections with the seafaring trade and they shared in the considerable prosperity it brought. This middle class, diverse though it was in itself, showed an inclination for secular politics. Its interests would have been incompatible with a hieratic or dynastic government. This non-centrist, independent, philosophical way of thinking was strengthened by the affluence of the middle class while, at the same time, it strengthened the political position of this class.

The growing importance of trade also had bearings on the division of labour within the city states – not only those in the Greek sphere. Throughout the Mediterranean world and the adjacent areas regional specialisation in the production of certain tradeable goods developed, generating a new boom in craftsmanship. Networks of long-distance trade spanned the entire area from the Atlantic to the Pacific in the first millennium BCE – in a sense this was a global economy. Needless to say, ideas and beliefs were exchanged on the trade routes, too.

That such rich and complex economic, social and ideological developments led to the emergence of the *polis* and, at a later stage, of "democracy", should not come as a surprise. Although this "democracy" was a slave-holding polity, it was essentially different from the earlier, Eastern city state with its rigid monopoly of priestly and dynastic power. In fact, this difference was one of the factors that led to the creation of Western civilisation.

Before the development of the philosophical way of thinking, there were no institutionalised schools in Greece. The only "teachers" we know of were itinerant bards such as Homer and rhapsodists like Hesiod on the one hand, and, on the other hand, priests or laymen who acquired and introduced the knowledge of Babylon, Persia and Egypt to the Greek world. There are no indications of a native temple culture comparable to that of Mesopotamia. To a significant extent, ideology was imported from the East; even the Homeric tradition came from western Anatolia. This by no means depreciates the emergence of philosophical thought, but it does empasise the fact that philosophy is a common achievement of civilisation at large. Dialectically speaking, philosophy is the product of an environment where the old-fashioned explanations of Eastern mythology no longer satisfied the human intellect and even became the subject of ridicule. Eastern mythology became ideologically and politically obsolete in the emerging democracies of Greece.

The absence of the rigid religious apparatuses found in Mesopotamia and Egypt and a political regime centred on public debate created the conditions in which a new intellectual attitude could thrive. The complex structure of the

Greek city states demanded rational thought rather than fear of the gods. By the beginning of the classical era, slave-owning civilisation had been through nearly three millennia of development, maturation and decay. It had reached the limits of its growth as a system and approached its climax, which was at the same time its end. Greco-Roman civilisation was quintessentially the confession of this truth.

The merchant class of the western Mediterranean was inclined to venture and discover and, amid a world that was rapidly changing, had to rely on individual reason rather than divine laws. The new hegemonic class system created a hegemonic form of thought after its own fashion – one that did not do away with the underlying system of slavery. As we have seen, development in the material base of human civilisation never happened in isolation. Our discussion of the philosophical revolution illustrates that the development of ideologies and methods of communication and dissemination, in other words, of the central elements of the superstructure, must be regarded as a complex whole that similarly advanced in the form of chain reactions and dialectical constellations. Philosophy certainly was not the invention of a few geniuses starting their journey from scratch.

Nevertheless, the likes of Thales, Pythagoras, Parmenides, Heraclitus, Socrates, Plato and Aristotle occupy places in the history of human thought that are probably comparable to those of the prophets of faith. Their philosophy constituted indispensable sources for the historical activation of the individual human mind's power. It heralded the awakening of the individual in his or her struggle for freedom when religion confirmed the sanctity of the social status quo. Undoubtedly both of these modes of thought were indispensable for the development of civilisation. Going back to common roots in mythology, they have progressively differentiated and increasingly contradicted each other, their clashes giving birth to higher syntheses here and there. Development in human thought has been nourished by the very tension between these antagonisms, and by that between different strands of philosophical thinking with their conflicting methodological preferences. By the same token, philosophy has contributed to the development of science as much as it has been informed by it.

Since Socrates, moral philosophy has emphasised individual insight, individual perfection and individual responsibility to an extent that surpasses the ethical teachings of Zoroastrianism. Socrates espoused the view that the individual could determine his or her own destiny. He challenged the ideological world-view of archaic slavery, which had laid fetters on the intellectual faculty of the individual and hence on social development. The codes of moral conduct informed by mythology and religion interlocked with very old conventions and observances to establish absolute hegemony over individual behaviour. All of an individual's actions and thoughts were braided beforehand into an infinite chain of events that could never be altered.

This notion of fate was negating the freedom that people enjoyed in organic (non-state) societies, albeit on a collective basis. It implied a conception of morals that was implanted into ancient slave-holding society through the acts of the priests. It established the connective tissue of stratified social orders. Reformers such as Zoroaster, the Buddha and Socrates were among the first to disentangle human action from the heavy chain of fate and emphasise individual will. They ushered in a tradition that has grown, throughout the centuries, into the foremost conception of human agency and ethics.

When discussing the treatment of present-day problems in the following sections of this volume, we will discuss the tenacious moral ramifications of the age-old human subordination to political and divine power, and the importance of finding an antidote. But we will also discuss how its historical reverse, the ethical paradigm of individualistic freedom, now threatens to take the individual hostage. The individualist concept of ethics, which has reached its peak in Western modernity, deserves some closer scrutiny. I believe that it is absolutely critical to develop an alternative to this individualist understanding of ethics, which, bolstered by science and technology, is surely implicated in abhorrent catastrophes like the insane warfare of the twentieth century or the severe environmental destruction of the present. If it is not critically reflected upon, it may pull humanity into a chaos and savagery that easily outmatches the innocent primitive order of so-called "savage communities".

The role of Greek civilisation in this historical differentiation of ethical outlooks was to evolve the concept of individual morals. This was further elaborated by Roman authors and reached its climax in European modernity. On the other side of the divide was the Eastern behavioural culture and ethics. The gods of the Greeks became increasingly anthropomorphous (and were recognised for that by the Greeks) and the individual human being grew aware of his or her powers. On the other hand, the Eastern empires had unalterably entrenched a culture in which the ruler was given divine qualities and the order he represented was sanctified by reference to the cosmic laws. These opposing outlooks on individual will and agency had common roots in archaic Sumerian culture. The juncture where they separated was the reform movement associated with the teachings of Zoroaster.

The historical divide between East and West, and the numerous conflicts, contradictions and syntheses that these two major lines running through the history of civilisation were engaged in, must be discussed with reference to these two divergent ideas of ethics in the larger sense. Their appraisal is of a wider relevance to the questions we have to pose as to our own immediate future, especially since it has been established now that neither the liberal discourse of capitalism, nor the Marxist discourse of socialism can provide satisfying answers. The historical discussion will certainly not provide direct solutions to present issues, but I do hope that it will help us see things in a different light.

Where the divide between the two aforementioned mental attitudes widened through the rise of Greek civilisation, the Western way became discernible as heralding the advent of a new level of economic, social, cultural and political development, with the human being as its focus. It relied on the skills of the individual to penetrate nature and society for the purpose of furthering the individual's interest.

This culture found its highest ideological expression in Aristotle, and his pupil Alexander the Great was swift to utilise it in his Eastern campaigns. The expanding empire he commanded was to become the empirical proof of this new superiority. His success was that of a diligent, well-read student of the new thought. Traditional Eastern thought had become the obscure preference of a group of priests, who scarcely did more than copy old texts. Zoroaster's resolute yell had been insufficient to stop the decline of the ever-repetitive system of priests and kings that prevailed throughout Mesopotamia, Egypt, Persia and India.

The progress that had been achieved with the invention of monotheistic religion was too limited to shake the sound foundations of the inveterate hieratic order. The order of social identity woven around the temple had established an ideological and moral outlook according to which the formation and preservation of an ever unchanging type of state was regarded as an immutable necessity, and individual action left no traceable marks. Changes and renovations were assimilated into this pattern. The countermovement inspired by Zoroastrian thought did make it to the gates of Athens in the form of the Persian empire; but by then it had already been clad in the trappings of the very system it had set out to reform. Despite its clear military and material superiority, the Persian empire succumbed to a student in his mid-twenties. The mindset that relegated everything to the gods and equated its kings with them was unable to produce anything worthwhile against the onslaught of classical rationalism at its peak.

The vibrant reform experiment that was the birth of Islam at the beginning of the Middle Ages, for all its glory and longevity, eventually became bogged down on the same "Eastern path" and ultimately lost out to the "Western way".

In my discussion of Islam in Part 2, I shall further develop the argument that the ascent and disintegration of politico-cultural systems must be discussed with reference to the thought structures and patterns of moral behaviour at their root. It is only in connection with their overall direction that the material factors gain importance and that a material culture thrives or loses out. I believe that the example of classical Greece is a case in point.

THE ROMAN ERA OF SLAVE-HOLDING CIVILISATION

The transition from neolithic to Iron Age culture in the Italian peninsula happened in the wake of the first millennium BCE. Until very recently, scholars have debated the possible Anatolian origins of the Romans' political predecessors, the Etruscans.[1] The clearly discernible Middle Eastern influences in early Etruscan artefacts show that the values of those civilisations were well appreciated and eagerly imitated. The Etruscans and Latins entered the historical record amid an environment of ongoing Greek colonisation. To the south of the peninsula, the kingdom of Syracuse and the Phoenicio-African Carthage (Kart-hadasht) were engaged in rivalry and flourishing commerce. Rome itself was founded as a politically unified city, probably by the early sixth century, and during the initial regal period the ethnic structure of its inhabitants had already differentiated into patricians and plebeians. The fierce class struggle between them shaped the early republic and resulted in the laying down of written law and the creation of rather elaborate political institutions like the legislative popular assembly and the plebeian tribunate. It was with the expansion of Rome into an empire that the more powerful among the citizens reorganised under the banner of the principate.

In his epic account of the foundation myth of Rome, the poet Virgil depicted the emperor Augustus as the descendant of Aeneas, the Trojan hero who had fled the sacked city and migrated to Italy. The common myth that Virgil referred to ultimately ascribed the foundation of Rome to the lineage of Aeneas. By emphasising the Trojan, i.e. Anatolian origins of Rome, this discourse alluded to the cultural roots of the civilisation that was now to conquer the world. Although Roman civilisation was mainly nourished by the direct Greek influence and thus only indirectly by the Anatolian, Phoenician and Egyptian civilisations, it can justifiably be regarded as the third big link in the chain of cultural transmission from the Fertile Crescent to Europe. A direct comparison between Sumer and Rome will therefore be helpful. If the former was the primary, seminal, form of ancient slave-holding social organisation, the latter was its most perfected, and last, form. Whereas Sumerian base and superstructure in its entirety was clad in the trappings of temple culture and its mythological discourse, Roman society (undoubtedly undergirded by the Greek achievements) created somewhat more rational, and secular, republican structures.

After more than two millennia, the Mesopotamian god–kings had made way for the Roman deified emperors. Notwithstanding all the significant metamorphoses in social fabric and institutions, the overall nature of Roman imperial power was not altogether different from the Sargonic model. After all, Roman mythology too was merely yet another copy of the Sumerian original (a rather dull copy, eclectic and hardly convincing). The actual official religion of Rome was concentrated in politics, that sacrosanct institution elevated to the level that was reserved for religion in other polities. Roman ideology did not need a religious cover but preferred to promulgate its political values overtly. Here the ground was prepared for the transition from the *hieratic state* to the *secular state*.

A more detailed study could mention further similarities and differences to indicate the connections between early Mesopotamian and Roman civilisation. Rather than attributing obvious disparities to a supposedly dissimilar "essence", we should focus on analysing how the forms of social organisation varied according to the paramount conditions of time and space. The values of human civilisation that Inanna had claimed as her "*mé*" rolled down the slopes of the Taurus–Zagros foothills as a tiny snowball. By the time the snowball reached the plains of Mesopotamia and the Nile valley it had grown, and it rolled on to Anatolia and other regions of the Middle East, including, eventually, the Greek peninsula. Then it arrived in Italy and from there rolled northwards across the Alps. Civilisation is an ever-growing snowball that picks up and incorporates fresh values, generated by human labour, wherever it passes, and eventually turns into an unstoppable avalanche.

While the establishment of an upper-class democracy must certainly be credited to Athens, the development of republican institutions was a Roman achievement. The historical comparison shows that democracy and a republican regime cannot be simply equated. Not every democracy takes the form of a republic, and not every republic is a democracy! As a matter of fact, evidence suggesting a primitive assembly – that most important institution of class democracy – is available for early Mesopotamian society. Athenian democracy, too, can be read as a highly developed but rather short-lived form of tribal, ritual, democracy. The Roman system, however, established a long-lived institutional order which provided safeguards for the plebeian class, electoral procedures, differentiated permanent bodies and elaborate written legal codes.

The Roman republic was secular and multi-religious insofar as the rulers kept their distance from any form of religion and liberally accommodated, and utilised, any creed that did not threaten their interests. The examples of the officially condoned spread of Indo-Iranian Mithraism well into the north-west European parts of the Roman Empire and of the savage onslaught on early Christianity are well known. When the potentially consolidating function of the Christian faith for the disintegrating empire was recognised, the tables were turned and it was eventually adopted as the state religion.

The principles underlying the Roman system were not enshrined in any religious dogma, but in its secular legal codes. The Roman republic had evolved a legal system that reflected the complex structure of Roman society with its conflicting class interests. The concept of citizenship became a central element of this system. Allegiance to the polity was the condition of individual civil rights, although their actual availability was subject to class status. Class affiliation was officially encoded and each professional group ascribed a clearly outlined social status. Roman law negotiated power relations through mutually acceptable rules rather than by reference to customary mores or the divine will embodied in the person of the ruler. Although the legal order sprang by and large from the urban class conflicts between plebeians and patricians, it was grafted upon the conquered provinces.

Roman law thus became one of the major sources of medieval and modern law in many regions of the world. It fulfilled an important social function by establishing principles that were more permanent than the ever changing rules and requirements of daily politics. These principles were historically distilled from political conflicts and were meant to provide a consensual framework of mechanisms and remedies available to everyone. Needless to say, this framework hinged on the overall acceptance of Roman slave-holding domination, as was expressed in the "liberal" legal regime of the famous Pax Romana. Military authority had fully separated from the centres of civilian political authority.

Repeating a socio-political process that had earlier in history led to the separation of hieratic and dynastic power in Mesopotamia and Egypt, the autonomous institutionalisation of military power was the product of long and hard internal quarrels. The military profession became one of extremely high social esteem. Military leaders "naturally" aspired to political authority. The mentality bred by the social supremacy of the military elite vis-à-vis all other sections of the population can be discerned in countless post-Roman social formations, including the modern aspirations of generals to political power and the often concerted attempts to secure institutionalised predominance of the military over the political sphere. Bonapartism has its historical antecedents not only in Caesarism, but also in the Sargonic tradition. Although Napoleon Bonaparte was the last grand example of that historical tradition, its residues linger on as a potential tendency in present-day politics, especially in times of crisis or inner strife.

It was under this system that Roman expansion acquainted vast parts of Europe with the slave-holding mode of production. The estate economy of the *latifundia*, with its large-scale irrigation schemes, became the favoured occupation of the nobility. It outmatched urban handicrafts and trade in importance and became the main field of employment, with complex hierarchies of labour organisation. Nonetheless, the elaborate road system and the advancement of maritime traffic did facilitate international trade throughout the lands surrounding the "Roman lake" that the Mediterranean had become. All in all, the Roman era saw growth and modification of the existing economic structures of antiquity but little qualitatively new development.

In the Roman cities, the class called the proletariat formed as the historical ancestor of the modern urban working class. These cities, with their markets, shops, theatres, arenas, academies, assemblies, temples and palaces were somewhat different from the cities of the Egyptians and the Mesopotamians. In those earlier examples, huge settlements grouped around the temple and the royal household, with most economic activities integrated into one or the other of them.

Urban architecture in its fully-fledged form evolved with the polities of the Greco-Roman world, where a comparatively independent urban middle class determined the character of the settlement order. It was in that era, mainly at the early stage of Roman expansion, that cities became the paramount settlement type throughout the Middle East, and that wide parts of Europe first became acquainted with them. The hegemony of the city over human life has today acquired truly oppressive dimensions. Ironically enough, the term "civilisation" is itself derived from *civitas*, a Latin word used for city or urban polity, and its Arabic equivalent *madaniyyah* is likewise a derivate of *madinah*, the city. Nonetheless, urbanisation has generated fundamental problems that threaten human civilisation itself. Urban life is a mainstay of modern society; but is it also the stronghold of a striking conformity with the system that so harms society. The city is at once the symbol of civilisation and the agent that decomposes its very foundations. It is not only an enlarged settlement area, but a socio-historical issue that requires careful analysis. I have the impression that urban life has become a leading source of social ills. Not only environmental destruction, but also ways of life that completely contradict the flow of nature are among the problems that need to be discussed in connection with urbanisation. Progressive movements, too, have mainly regarded urban life as a criterion of progress. My concern with current development trends in human civilisation will be dealt with in Part 4 of this volume.

The glorious Roman era contributed remarkably little to the development of arts and sciences, apart from the obvious architectural achievements. The monumental and sophisticatedly engineered buildings of the Roman period bear witness to the ruthless, large-scale employment of servile labour. The amazingly vigorous presence of the remains of Roman urban architecture never fails to impress the spectator's senses as though she or he were confronted with a living, yet elusive, being. I can think of nothing that is as impressive as the masterworks of architecture from the age of slavery, and I am convinced that it is the unlimited, barbarous, employment of collective slave labour that accounts for the magic aura of these works. The labour, and the way in which it was used, evoke magnificence and horror at the same time. Latin poetry, prose and drama actually have a similar feel to them. It is well known that rhetoric acquired an outstanding importance in Roman public life and was fully institutionalised. The Latin power of expression, which I think has to some extent persevered in modern Italian,[2] was of course underpinned by the resoluteness of a political power that ruled half the world. The most powerful would naturally be the most eloquent; the slaves had little more at their disposal than that cursed, incomprehensible, Aesopian language.[3] Whenever I ponder upon the intricate connection between power, liberty and the faculty of eloquent speech,[4] I have to think of the learned rhetoric of the Roman ruling class, which is outstanding even in comparison to classical Arabic and Persian.

Its superior quality was soundly rooted in the merits of a "golden age" of Latin civilisation; a civilisation that was the synthesis of innumerable large and small achievements of known and unknown civilisations from Sumer to Egypt, from Persia to Greece. The heritage of nearly 3,000 years of stratified civilisation was absorbed into an ethnic formation that had hardly been able to provide for the living of its members under the neolithic mode of production. The specific historical constellation under which this happened turned the Romans into fortune's children. They quickly attained a high level of culture and built elaborate institutions. Similar "moments of chance" had been born to the early riverine civilisations (Sumer, Egypt, China, Harappan) that evolved from the prosperity brought on by the agrarian revolution.

I wish there were ways of accounting for the incredible toil and nameless bravery of the human beings who created the developments that accumulated into "moments of chance" for some. It is morally imperative to render visible this human labour and elucidate the mechanisms through which the sublime mythologies and earthly paradises were erected. If only the invisible subalterns of the human past could be reinstated in their rightful positions! If the cosmos of their hopes and their real, hellish, sufferings could be accounted for, justice could be done to history and, perhaps, "the truth" be told.

Ancient Greece was the first Western site of such a "moment of chance" for civilisation. Having devoured whatever reached it from the East, its nascent upper class assimilated pre-existent mythologies and institutions into a system that allowed for the development of a rationally motivated agency. Thus Greece became the cradle of Western civilisation and nursed a vigorous baby. By the time this baby, parented by a fusion of what we today perceive as East and West, reached the age of adolescence, it had acquired the name of Alexander and in its turn engaged itself in a further marriage with the East that came to be known under the name of Hellenism.

This union was symbolically expressed in the real marriage between Alexander and Roxana, whom he captured and married by force after having conquered her native Bactria in 327 BCE.[5] Beyond arranging for the highly symbolic residency of Roxana at Babylon and his further marriage with two Persian noblewomen in 324, the new emperor's policy included financial incentives for a reputed 10,000 Greek soldiers who married Asian women. The male children from these marriages were recruited as a new generation of loyal soldiers. These marriages formed the nucleus of a fusion of cultures. They were of the same kind as the unions (dictated by male interest) that the cunning god Enki entered into with the mountain goddess Nin Hursag and successive generations of her female offspring. We know that the actual child born from their coition was Sumerian civilisation. Generations later, Inanna would reclaim her holy *mé* from Enki in what can be interpreted as woman's attempt to re-appropriate the values of civilisation she had created throughout the neolithic age. By thus reading mythological narratives – and other sources of history – we can get an inkling of the human travails underlying the making of stratified civilisation. By doing so we can learn to discern and appreciate the fresh green buds of histories that have been blackened out for millennia, and we may discover that they grow from a live tree with healthy roots that might well yield further fruits after all.

Rome came across that tree when it was in its full blossom and went at it with such force that eventually its trunk collapsed. The Roman system mobilised all the potential energy of the regions it extended into. Its ruling class established power relations with the upper strata of the conquered areas in order to assimilate the existing local structures, slave-holding or otherwise, into its system. "Rome" is, at closer scrutiny, merely a conventional name for a much more complex and diverse systemic reality. It incorporated and preserved some aspects of the more backward local, stratified, structures and dissolved others. The outcome was in most cases the continuation of the old under new forms with new institutions fashioned after the spirit of Roman ruling-class culture. In that respect the Roman Empire can be compared to a gigantic grinding machine that ground down and assimilated into its own structural requirements all human communities it extended to, just as present-day globalisation under US hegemony does.

It can be argued that this strategy activated the slumbering potential of older stratified structures. It certainly galvanised the "uncivilised" communities of Europe that the Roman Empire first incorporated into a wider, tiered system of civilisation. Over the 1,000 years of its existence, Rome went as far as any socio-political system can go in terms of institutionalising its own principles and the value judgements informing its hierarchic organisation through vast parts of the world. Of all empires, it came closest to what can be called a world empire, thus realising the universality the Akkadians, Babylonians, Assyrians and others had claimed for their respective empires.

The Pax Romana was indeed a new world order. Although existing social entities were subdued to Roman sovereignty, they were granted considerable autonomy in internal matters. Local nobilities and other aspiring groups found that the Roman system offered them ideal opportunities, institutions and lifestyles to suit their aggrandising ambitions. Simply through pursuing their own interests, they contributed to the power and longevity of the Empire. The exertion of force on the part of the Empire was much less decisive than one would have thought. In fact, the system always offered the diverse populations points of identification and provided a univocal legal order that many would have found agreeable. In brief, many citizens of the Empire had their stakes in the system. Especially during the later Roman Empire, high officials and even emperors could come from Romanised families of any ethnic origin. One of the most crucial differences between the Roman and, say, the Assyrian or Persian empires, was that its power mechanisms were not based on dynastic rule but on individual merit. On the whole, when it came to upward mobility, religious and ethnic affiliation was a factor of little relevance in comparison to success in battle or rational political judgement. But the mechanisms thus outlined were as precarious as they were sophisticated, and once the system's creative quality was exhausted, they proved as prone to disintegration as they had been conducive to growth.

9

Medes, Persians and the Making of the East

The wider Zagros area had already come to our attention when we discussed the processes that led to the initial formation of civilisation in Mesopotamia. We now need to look at the area again to see how the centre of gravity of civilisation was for the first time transposed to places outside of Mesopotamia. Throughout the eras dominated by the Sumerians, Babylonians and Assyrians, the centre of civilisation was always situated in the lands between the Tigris and the Euphrates. If we add the stage of maturation of neolithic culture to that of the formation of complex stratified societies, we are looking at a period from around 6000 BCE to the fall of Assyria towards the end of the seventh century BCE.

Sedentary human history can be subdivided into three main periods; the agricultural village communes (roughly from 10000–3000 BCE), urban civilisation (3000 BCE–1950s CE), and the stage that we are struggling to pass through today, and yet have failed to name appropriately. Some call it the nuclear or electronic age, others simply the internet era. Some speak of the age of information and communication, others of postmodernism or trans-civilisation.

Whatever the details of this rough-cut compartmentalisation, Mesopotamia can be credited with having played a vanguard role over at least 10,000 formative years. Over this period of time, the river-like flow of history passed through five or six separate areas. Nonetheless, many scholars argue that the main body of the thoughts, beliefs and inventions that have given direction to history in general was created in the area of wider Mesopotamia over these first 10,000 years.

When a system is deeply rooted in its historico-geographical environment and has survived there for long, there is little chance for a new, antagonistic system to form on top of its roots. The new system would emerge, rather, from pristine soil. There are several historical examples to corroborate this observation, which would of course have to be tested against the evidence provided by more detailed research: the Greco-Roman civilisation evolved from an area that was hitherto nearly untouched; capitalist civilisation formed along the shores of the Atlantic Ocean and in the centres of Northern Europe. Even much of what makes up postmodernism comes not from Europe, but from the new world, the United States of America.

The oldest centres of world civilisation are Sumer and Egypt, in and around the Fertile Crescent. These areas are today amongst the most miserable on earth. They are unproductive and weak and people there are left with little less than the hopes of migrating to the West. This paradox ought to be one of the major issues of concern for anyone trying to understand what makes up civilisation.

The historical shift of the centres of civilisation to areas outside Mesopotamia thus raises an issue that can guide us to find urgent answers to present day questions. The way we approach the question of *centre and periphery* is of immediate relevance to the global action that anti-capitalist forces need to take today. Globalisation – and the opposition to it – should not be reduced to mere issues of economy. If the actual global system is not understood in the wider context of its historical and cultural flux, the anti-globalisation movement will find it difficult to develop realistic answers to the questions that scientific socialism, for all its accumulated knowledge of nearly two centuries, has left unsolved. Such wider historical perspective is needed if we are to surpass the superficiality most new social movements currently display towards key questions of human emancipation.

As discussed in previous chapters, the relations between Sumer and its periphery resulted in the foundation of semi-independent alternative centres of civilisation as well as in the influx of ethnic groups from the surrounding lands, which either attacked the wealthy cities for booty or served as a cheap labour force. We have seen that trade relations between the centre and the periphery were important from the outset, but these assumed a different character when systematic force and tiered political relations came into the equation.

From the time of the Akkadian empire onwards, the almost constant internecine warfare between the imperialist centre and the formations of its periphery, with weapons technology initially devised in the centre, left its imprint on the inner fabric of society both at the centre and on the periphery. Growing differences in wealth led to a worsening of social antagonisms and reinforced coercive political practices. Both often led to violent campaigns aimed at subduing external ethnic structures. The freedom struggle of the ethnic communities against colonisation became an inevitable feature of the process of civilisation: as a contradictory element particular to the growth of urban stratified society, resistance provided a major impetus to human history.

It is in that sense that the laws identified by dialectical and historical materialism became the laws of movement of society. Marxist theory has applied the laws it postulates mainly to analyses of the formation of capitalist civilisation.

I believe that this procedure is not only deficient, but harbours potentially serious methodological errors. Marxist writers have rarely analysed the reality of class society in the particular characteristics it assumed when and where it historically emerged. This shortcoming has made Marxist theory, ideology and practical politics prone to influences from the ideologies and practices of the ruling class, which it has left undeciphered. These influences had been formed much earlier in history than those of capitalism, and have been historically dominant throughout. Thus it will surely help if we analyse the structures underlying civilisation by way of focusing not on the latest form of society, but on the earliest one, and then cross-check the results obtained by comparing them to what we know of modern societies.

Evidently, the theoretical efforts of Marx and Engels could only draw from the comparatively limited reservoir of knowledge and philosophical instruments available in the early days of scientific socialism. It is therefore our responsibility to reassess and modify their work in the light of the material knowledge and theoretical sensitisation we have been exposed to since. Such a project would also have to be informed by the wealth of experience made in terms of the theory's social and political application. This is all the more urgent since the state of affairs of the socialist project, and the profound global crisis of capitalism, force all progressives to exercise constructive self-criticism. We should regard these terrible conditions as a chance for us to come forward with realistic solutions.

The time around 2000 BCE saw large-scale reactions on the part of the peoples of the periphery against the policies of the centres of Sumer and Egypt. Comparable phenomena have occurred in the second half of the twentieth century CE with its wars of national liberation on the periphery and mass migration movements to the capitalist centres. The constant interplay of action and reaction between centre and periphery in ancient history brought about the eventual, but thorough, reform of the polities of the centre under the sign of monotheistic religions. Another aspect that we are going to discuss is the creation of a historical divide between East and West, or what I would like to call the *divergence of civilisation*. We have already discussed how it became increasingly impossible for ethnic structures to survive the second millennium without adopting some of the features of centralised, stratified organisation. Thus, any major political victory on the part of a peripheral formation that has entered the historical record is bound to mean at least the partial loss of its former nature qua peripheral community. The same holds true for any initially emancipatory ideology once it has conquered the terrain of the centre.

With these caveats in mind, we can now turn to the immensely significant historical role of the Medes and Persians. But talking of caveats, it might be useful to underscore at this point that much of what has been said about the Indo-European or Aryan populations of Asia and Europe needs to be revised. The notion of a migration of blond and blue-eyed Aryans from northern

Europe or the fringes of the Russian steppes into northern Iran and hence to India, Media and Anatolia has been thoroughly discredited.[1] To begin with, most historians no longer believe in physical mass migration. Even though long-distance migration of smaller groups apparently did occur, it certainly was never on a scale that would have allowed an incoming group to replace an indigenous one. When we talk about the occurrence of Indo-European idioms in the first millennium BCE in regions as disparate as Italy and India, we must carefully consider how cultural dispersion usually happens through processes of mutual exchange and learning rather than conquest.

As a matter of fact, it is quite likely that Indo-European idioms were native to Upper Mesopotamia, and may even have dispersed from there to other regions, rather than having been brought in by immigrants from the steppes. Independently of the question of dispersion, we must scrupulously separate linguistic labels such as Aryan or Indo-European from racial constructs.

The wider Taurus and Zagros region at the periphery of the ancient Mesopotamian central states was populated by a variety of groups who, for all their diversity, probably had many characteristics in common owing to the shared geographic and cultural environment. Although their history is not well documented, these groups were, from the very outset, vital to the formation and development of the slave-holding central states of Mesopotamia. They supplied much of the raw materials and luxury goods upon which our image of Mesopotamian urban culture hinges, and performed a good part of the menial labour through which the accumulation of riches in the centre was made possible.

The sudden appearance of a hitherto unknown ethnic group (the Medes), conquering the heartlands of the major powers of the Middle East and establishing a vast empire (only to be swiftly taken over by another equally unheard of ethnic group (the Persians), can only be explained against the backdrop of the tradition of tribal resistance in Upper Mesopotamia and the Taurus–Zagros area. To be sure, the central polity of Elam to the south-east of the Zagros mountain range was established at about the same time as the Sumerian city states were. The Gutians, a group coming from the Zagros, held sway in the Akkadian heartlands towards the end of the third millennium. The Kassites from the same area formed the ruling dynasty of Babylon over centuries.[2] This suggests that the population of the area was not altogether unfamiliar with stratified urban civilisation. The state of Urartu, with its Hurrian and Mitanni heritage and evident Assyrian influences, might not exactly have been a precursor to Media, but its vicinity in space and time made it at least an elder cousin.

The different names given (mostly by the keepers of the literal traditions of the centre) to these groups whenever they meddled with state power may indicate that we are not talking about one single, identical ethnic group. But they should not confuse us as to the geopolitical and cultural links that existed (and still exist) among the inhabitants of the Taurus–Zagros area.

The tribal confederation established by the Medes should then be understood as part and parcel of this tradition of ethnic resistance against the expanding empires, rather than as the spontaneous creation of belligerent immigrants from the Caspian Sea. The shamanic or priestly group among the Medes, the Magi, may have fused elements of nature worship with Sumerian influences into a local religion that was clearly less hierarchical than the dominant Mesopotamian ones. By the time the Medes entered the realm of recorded history, they had embraced Zoroastrianism – a doctrine we have already discussed at length.

After Zoroastrianism became the official belief of the Median Empire, two historical tendencies in political ideology emerged: one equated monarchic political authority with divinity, thus continuing the foregoing system, and the other curtailed political (and divine) authority through norms of reason and republican institutions. While the former would be pre-eminent in the Eastern empires, the latter became an important momentum in the development of Greco-Roman civilisation in the West. However, both tendencies can be found in either strand of political tradition. Media constituted, as it were, the watershed between these two tendencies. Although we know very little about its organisation, it is safe to assert that one of its principal features was the lack of consolidated power structures. Media must have relied on vassal arrangements with local rulers rather than tight colonial mechanisms.

Historians believe that the Medes may not have commanded a fully-fledged state apparatus of the Mesopotamian kind, since their mode of organisation still owed much to that of tribal federalism. In this respect, it must have been a welcome alternative to the Assyrian style of occupation, extraction and deportation. By the time the Medes, in an alliance with the Scythians and the Babylonians, sacked Nineveh (612 BCE), the lot of most people throughout the Middle East would have been far worse than that of an average member of a pre-state agriculturalist or pastoralist community. Human freedom was far more curtailed than it had been in the neolithic era. The advent of a power that was barely centralised (the Median capital was newly established at Ecbatana) must have allowed the inhabitants of the region to take a deep breath and relax, if nothing else. This would have been because Media eschewed the Assyrian colonial system and relied on local indigenous administration. The Medes were apparently inspired by the resistance tradition symbolised by the Blacksmith Kawa, and guided by Zoroastrian teaching. This heralded the transition to a softer system of political rule, albeit one still based on corvée labour. In this sense, the Median–Persian advance did amount to a turning point in history, although it is true that the new rulers eventually assented to the logic of the dominant system. They perpetuated this dominant system, rather than toppling it and establishing a new one.

The continuity in the mode of production may be a key factor in this turn of events. To be sure, the Medes and many other tribes of the area had acquired iron-processing techniques and used the resources to craft weapons they could use against the central powers. I have called this the *democratisation* of technology in the Iron Age. The input of the victorious rebels was bound to bring a number of novelties and reforms to the otherwise decaying system. Zoroastrian tradition ideologically prepared the grounds for political developments that led to the divergence of civilisation, i.e. the separation of a Western and an Eastern strand.

Zoroastrianism's initial emphasis was on the individual's questioning the divine, and it offered new, revolutionary ethical principles based on free will rather than subordination. The Medes' rapid advance, and the Persians' takeover to consolidate and expand the empire thus built, had twofold consequences: on the one hand, the further eastward dispersion of the ancient slave-holding civilisation into central Asia and India; and on the other hand, the acceleration of the formation of Greek civilisation in the West. Media–Persia thus catalysed the development of a culture that was its enemy, but drew diligently on the tradition of questioning divinity and absolute kingship. The Median–Persian empire itself thus probably contributed to the extension of the lifespan of slave-holding imperial civilisation for another 1,000 years, rather than shortening it.

The transition of dynastic power from the Medes to the Persians can also be interpreted in the context of the former rebels turning rulers. The Persians were an ethnic group closely related to the Medes, and it is quite possible that these groups only developed noteworthy distinctive features by the mid-second millennium or later. They apparently shared in the same tribal confederation. It was at the point when the Median confederation, in which the Persians were included, transmuted into an integrated state that Persian tribes launched a counter-coup and seized power.

This process should not be viewed as the defeat of the Medes by the Persians, but rather as a change in dynasty amidst the manifold transformative processes involved in the shaping of a burgeoning imperial state. There is no evidence to support the assumption that one ethnic community was ousted by another. Although the Median upper class certainly came second to the Persian aristocracy in the Achaemenid administrative apparatus, by and large the Persian populace would not have been more privileged than the Median or indeed any other population group. Conflicts were much more likely to occur between different social groups, such as priests and chiefs, than between ethnic groups.

The Achaemenid Empire reached the Aegean Sea by 547, took Babylon in 539 and swiftly proceeded to conquer Egypt in 525. The Persians built an empire more extensive than any previous one had been, incorporating the Caspian region and large parts of Afghanistan, Central Asia and India. They were the first to establish an Armenian satrapy (province) in the Caucasus. Their skilful politics and the initially rather soft treatment afforded to the conquered peoples allowed the Persian rulers to establish a relatively stable empire that boasted an elaborate network of transport and communication. It is said that a message could be taken by horse riders via the Royal Road from Sardis in the Aegean to the Persian capital Persepolis in nine days thanks to a system of relays.

In contrast to its predecessors, the Persian empire acknowledged the variety of cultures, languages and ways of political organisation of its inhabitants. Although the mature empire did, for example, adopt the Babylonian system of levy, it did not forcefully assimilate and uproot the conquered peoples as the Assyrians had done. The impact of Persian material and intellectual culture on the development of the Middle East and the Mediterranean world is often underrated, although it is now widely acknowledged that post-exile Hebrew scripture owes much to Persian Mazdaism. It is well known that exiled Jewish authors viewed the Persians as their liberators from the Babylonian yoke. Overall, a great number of local ethnic cultures seem to have thrived during the times of Persian rule. The Persians established patterns of rule and administration that influenced the Middle East for many centuries to come.

But while the initially progressive character of Persian rule increased its strength, it also compounded the aggrandising and conservative aspects of the Achaemenid Empire, which eventually ossified into yet another slave-holding empire with its coercive administrative elite. While it is permissible to view the Persian era as a higher stage in the ancient history of the Middle East, brought about by the conflict between the antagonisms of the established slave-holding states of the centre and the oppressed ethnic groups of the periphery, the synthesis itself preserved much of the former structures.

Progressive in comparison to the Assyrian system, it was backward in comparison to the *poleis* of western Anatolia and mainland Greece. Rationality, social ethics and an emphasis on the will-power of the individual made up the ideological ammunition of the early classical Greek world. It is by using these that the Greeks managed to confront their militarily and politically superior arch-enemy. As the Persians got more and more embroiled in the trappings of absolute kingship, they became estranged from the initial idea of individual agency based on free will. In this lies the *ideological* reason for their final defeat. They had become despots resembling the Sumerian and Egyptian monarchs. Athens, in contrast, had established a system that in many repects depended on ethnic democracy. In one way, the battle was between the despotism of Persepolis and the democracy of Athens.[3] The Greek polities had invented many new institutions whereas the Achaemenids had taken over – or were taken over by – the huge, lumbering institutional apparatus they found in the territories they conquered.

I believe that even the cursory account I have tried to give suggests the intertwinement of antagonistic strands of development often regarded as disparate. Greek civilisation was deeply influenced by ancient Middle Eastern civilisation, but it also emerged as a reaction to developments inherent in the latter. The concrete shape Greek civilisation took owed much to the Persian reality at its front door.[4] There is a permanent dialectical relationship between victors and vanquished. Without this relationship, victory and defeat lose their meaning.

The most noteworthy aspect of Alexander of Macedon's forward thrust is neither the military nor the political skill he and his staff might have displayed. It lies in the cultural particulars and the philosophical mode of thought of the Greeks, which dictated patterns of behaviour and organisation that liberated much more energy than anything resting on the inveterate Mesopotamian state institutions and political practices ever could. The fact that these had undergone reforms at the hands of the Persians did not help them to stand a chance against the grand Hellenic campaign. What resulted was the first synthesis of East and West in history, with an ensuing continuum of more than 600 years of Greco-Roman predominance over the Middle East. It truly was a new stage in the cultural history of the region.

Alexandria, Pergamon and Ctesiphon are but a few of the urban centres this cultural synthesis generated. Another example is Zeugma, a site of considerable current interest.[5] Many people of the Middle East made their acquaintance with the city as the site of public spaces including *hamams* (baths), theatres, market places, schools, etc. during this epoch. The merchants and artisans of the Middle East gained social independence as a class considerably growing in numbers. Many scholars speak of a common market incorporating Rome, India and China. Slave trade became a pre-eminent facet of this vast market. The traditional dogmatic ideologies lost their grip and new ideas and sects blossomed like spring flowers. A new form of social organisation, based on creed or thought rather than ethnic affiliation or political loyalty, began to spread.

Acquiring the old always amounts to producing something new. For the new Middle East, the Persian influences might have been as momentous as the grafting of Hellenistic culture upon the local cultures of the region. The Parthian resurgence of Iranian culture during the time of the Roman occupation (third century CE) was not a counter-movement in the sense that there was a reverting to pre-Greco-Roman practices, but yet another aspect of this synthesis itself. The Middle East had profoundly changed. Under the successive Persian, Greek and Roman empires, the system of slave-holding economy had reached its peak. In the course of this sequence, various reformist tendencies had each made way for rigid, conservative structures. The Roman Empire of the third century CE was beyond repair. The popular belief in the Messiah Jesus had helped form the social tissue of a novel, antagonistic development. It was the oppositional ideology of its age. Before long, the religion of the prophet Muhammad would deal heavy political and military blows to the residues of that age, and struggle hard to consign all memory of the foregone epochs to oblivion.

10

The Demise of a Paradigm

All historiography divides the ever-changing flow of society into periods. The history of class society in particular is subject to such periodisation, through which individual periods can be interpreted as necessary parts or stages of an all-encompassing whole. Given the complexity of history, it is both desirable and necessary to divide ever-evolving long-term social processes into periods.

The trouble starts only when discussing the basic criteria employed to justify a certain periodisation or subdivision. According to the elements one places in the foreground of a particular historical narrative, different and even contradictory subdivisions can be made.[1] The one thing I find indispensable for a proper *critical analysis* of history is to apply the dialectical form of thesis, antithesis and synthesis, which has been successfully applied to a variety of natural processes and to social systems. This must be done with great care, however, considering the specific characteristics that differentiate social (and thus historical) processes from natural ones.

Anything said about the genesis of slave-holding civilisation is necessarily highly controversial. Views differ not only on the details of the formative processes, but also on the question of whether this was an inexorable stage in social development. To put the question differently: Was it necessary for some human beings to enslave others in order for complex social orders to be formed?

How can it be that the people of the neolithic age left their highly creative system, one that was potentially open to development, for the treadmills of slavery? After all, the neolithic way of life was largely free from coercion and more or less egalitarian. The agrarian mode of production was able to sustain even rather large communities on a permanent basis. For all the accumulated knowledge of social studies and anthropology, we have no answer to that question. The vulgar Marxist approach with its fixation on class divisions would be to postulate that the rulers subjugated the people by means of force and ruse. But then the question remains, how did the rulers arise in the first place?

Another approach, doubtless undergirded by the complacency of the actually privileged, would be to suppose that social differentiation and inequality amounts to a necessary precondition for the development of civilisation. But here we have to demand to know why a system that is supposed to lead into "civilisation" should generate conditions that speak so eloquently against it?

It would be unfair to claim that all theories ever propounded by the advocates of the positions thus caricatured are uselessly faulty. The second one, for example, still enjoys currency among anthropologists and archaeologists. But like the first one, it does have significant loopholes. These loopholes become all the more obvious when we consider how helpless the analytical acumen of social theory as provided by scientific method stands in front of the aggravated problems actual societies are facing today. Models defending the capitalist order, and thus focusing on individualist liberalism, seem to be neither better nor worse off than models advocating socialism and accordingly focusing on the well-being of society as a whole.

Granted, scientific theorising is always bound to deal with intractable contradictions and unsolvable problems. But the actually existing crisis of the world we live in confronts us with so many illnesses and dangers that in the absence of satisfactory historical explanations, the only theoretical position we can adopt is that human beings are simply monsters. This, however, would amount to a renouncing of the historical nature of human beings.

There have been various more or less successful attempts to devise models that can explain the origins of the dangerous tendency of humans to subjugate others. These attempts went back to the formative stage of early human societies, or even referred to relations between organisms in nature. But they will never be convincing enough to render *acceptable* to the human mind the grave contradictions of our social existence. It does not matter how convincingly one might argue for the supposedly necessary correlations between the growth of social inequalities and the development of civilisation – and rather convincing explanations have been given in naive mythological narratives, in imposing theological discourse, in philosophy and of course in scientific model building. Our intellect and conscience simply cannot regard the contradictory situations we are continually exposed to as "normal" material processes which humankind necessarily has somchow to go through.

Positions of this kind fly in the face of the existing level of awareness and claimable freedoms in society. There is thus an element in the de facto situation of humankind that will not readily allow a causal relationship between social inequality and the development of human civilisation. It is in fact possible for a historian to show that human beings have never at any stage in history totally surrendered to this line of reasoning, whether it was presented to them under the guise of sacred stipulations or of purest scientific sobriety. So it might be best to start the historical inquiry from the provable assumption that the ideological dogmatism propounded by world-views, faiths and theories to justify slavery has never gone unchallenged.[2]

There exists no commonly acceptable conception of human sociality in which the search for justice and compassion is integrated with a complete scrutiny of reality. While it is obviously essential to approach the analysis of the human past and present in a scientific manner, the acquisition of an ethical stance ought to be understood as being equally urgent. My way of looking at human history seeks to interlink theoretical effort with a moral stance, as I remain utterly convinced that it is of vital importance to link these two concerns; not merely as a matter of principle, but also because this has important methodological and practical implications.

To put the question in other words: Did the *slave-holding* form of civilisation amount to a historical necessity? Could the early complex societies have been organised differently? The overall relation between freedom and necessity appears to be one of the most fundamental antagonisms in human existence, since it both governs the relations among human beings and the relations human beings maintain with their natural environment. The antagonism is bound to continue for as long as there is life on earth. Just as permanent freedom is impossible given the natural conditions under which human beings exist, so it is unthinkable that people be condemned to permanent helplessness in the face of the dictates of fate. A state of permanent freedom can only exist in false utopias concocted by the idle minds of those social classes that have been exempted from the labour process. The notion of permanent bondage, in its turn, relates to the infernal languishing of slaves who have given up struggling and accepted their defeat. There is an obviously close connection between these two positions; but life itself is more intricate than this, and so is human history as a whole. Nevertheless, the vision of total freedom as much as the nightmare of complete subjection to outside forces can be seen as providing the catalyst for a variety of dogmatic outlooks.

Now early Middle Eastern civilisation was formed in close relation to the stratification of its people into social classes, and developed within the confines of this basic configuration. For Middle Eastern civilisation to develop further, these initial contradictions had to be intensified. The class structure of society was shaped and constantly reshaped by the struggles ensuing from social antagonisms. Where conflicts reached the level of open violence and wars, they often entailed a dramatic reshaping of society, whereas tranquillity or peace meant a more balanced – but still not stagnant – reshaping process. A critique of the ancient slave-holding system would have to take into account the human costs of the formative process of civilisation and ask not only what achievements we owe to this system, but also what we have *lost* through it. To answer these questions, such a critique would need to refer to the continuing aspects of human enslavement both in the relationships of production and within overall forms of social life, including behaviour, preferences, mindset, etc.

Nearly all scholars would agree that mature neolithic societies between 6000 and 4000 BCE utilised all the technical know-how and means of production necessary for a higher-yielding mode of production. Cultural preconditions for the transition to a complex society were there, and ecological conditions were also conducive. The crucial element seems to have been the social reorganisation into something that transcended clan structures, and allowed for the production of considerable surplus.

Apparently the "new" Sumerian and Egyptian societies achieved this particular transition through reorganisation around the central institution of the temple. This suggests the importance of belief in this process. The transition from shamanism to priesthood appears to have been pivotal. The priests supplanted the religious thought based on tribal ancestors represented through such things as totems with a more rational form of religion in what I call the initial ideological revolution. They introduced the collective use of labour force organised around the temple, which then developed into a world of small-scale, self-sustained economic units that tended to produce just enough to cover their direct needs.

Apart from the enhanced productivity it achieved, the new mode of organising labour also boosted the specialisation of crafts. The seeds of the new society thus formed in basis and superstructure alike; subsequent development consisted mainly of the maximal growth of the system, its branching out and the continual repetition of the patterns involved in this form of organisation. Sheer force was by no means the prime characteristic of this form of society – the intense appearance of violence in human history came only at a later stage.

Initially, people did not enter the new social relations *knowing* that this would be a form of society essentially based on the virtually irreversible enslavement of some by others. There is no reason to believe that even the priests acted with the full consciousness and cunning of an organised group of people luring others into submission. They might simply have opened up with their practice a path of development that appeared superior to the then predominant one – or was actually more viable – and galvanised others into adopting the novel cultic practices they promulgated.

Despite the sparse evidence concerning the transition to early hieratic society in Mesopotamia, everything seems to allow the hypothesis that the institutionalisation of hierarchies worked in this way rather than through organised force and deception. We are speaking of a superior social formation, which had to demonstrate its viability over and above previous formations. Otherwise it could not have been established, nor would it have been upheld and developed. Force cannot invent and realise something new; it can only help to preserve an order that has already lost its viability – or help its opponents to obliterate it and allow an alternative formation to spread.

I think the remarkable turning point must have been where the system grew and expanded, unfolding all the antagonistic characteristics that had been hidden from the start. In Sumer there occurred the differentiation of the upper strata of administrative and disciplining officials, which became the clergy proper – and which lost some of its power – and the political elite, followed by the fully-fledged military establishment. This process of transformation into a political kingship did not go without conflict, of which there is some evidence in the extant record. It mingled with the development of the patriarchal family, which led to the social downgrading of women and the corresponding vilification of female goddesses.

The case of Mesopotamia, as well as that of ancient Egypt, is one where ideological reconstitution is predominant over the use of force in the making of class society. We have found that class society initially played a progressive role,[3] manifested in its ideological superiority and the incommensurable surge in surplus product. Humankind can therefore not be "accused" of having accepted the yoke of slavery other than in a purely literary sense.

But the administrative class grew into a veritable ulcer and its coercive practices escalated and became callous. The growing of this ulcer was the unnecessary reality in the formation of classes. Living off the fruits of the system without exercising any indispensable function within it, the consolidated elite resorted to exploitation and coercion. While the initial administrative elite had a role to play in the division of labour, there gradually formed a kind of coercive political elite that would divert its full energy into the intermittent plundering and occupation of neighbouring areas, and the maximisation of the exploitation of the population it held sway over.

The system of servile labour became conservative and eventually altogether unnecessary. I am intrigued by the question of the extent to which "human nature" led to the *deification of human beings* in the person of the king.[4] What would the forms of "human nature" have been – for example, the basic psychological characteristics, or the particular mental disposition generated by an archaic society in the age of mythology? An in-depth reading of the religious reflections of political identity stands out as a fascinating task. Certainly the appearance of retributive functions of divine power (absent in the earlier conceptions of deities) relate to the ossification of the system of slavery at a stage when the ruling class institutionalised the systematic use of force when facing uneasiness amongst the subjugated.[5]

To decode the correlations between systems of belief and social orders remains one of the central tasks of social studies. Neglect in this respect categorically hints at the impact of ruling-class ideas on the researcher. As I have pointed out before, Sumerian society heuristically constitutes for me the archetype of all the codifications we encounter throughout the history of civilisation. In this sense, I maintain that the history of civilisation amounts to nothing else than the continuation of a Sumerian society grown in extension, branched out and diversified, but retaining the same basic configuration.

The rise of Babylon typifies a condition in which intensified brutalisation and conscious manipulation became standard practices of governance. The system's stability now hinged on the regular resort to them. This point in the Mesopotamian past is of significance since it accounts for the first instance where the issue of system collapse or reform was historically raised. As I have sought to establish in the previous chapters, all ensuing developments throughout the history of antiquity can be related to chronic, forcible attempts to prevent the system from collapsing on the one hand, and incessant prophetic initiatives designed to soften the system and render it more liveable on the other hand.

In theory, a social system would be expected to collapse only at the stage at which it has exhausted the full potential encapsulated in its ways of structuring the human relations of production, reproduction, etc. Any given system needs to prove viable under the concrete conditions arising at any time in any place it reaches out to. Where its viability is no longer given, an established, hegemonic system can temporarily be saved from decay to the extent that elements of the new are being forcibly suppressed and impeded in their formation. But where conditions are conducive to these elements forming an alternative system of superior viability, and especially where people acquire the awareness and will-power to assert their alternative, no established order of force and manipulation can prevent the new from arising.

The ancient elites ruling over servile labour managed to establish and uphold the most extensive and long-lived of all class-based social formations in human history so far. At the heart of their system was the regime of property that signified a radical departure from the previous form of collective ownership of the means of production.

While human beings became objects of property to other human beings, social identity was being constructed through mythological discourses proclaiming the subservience of human beings to the gods. The priests made people believe in these discourses and probably intimidated them, the political elite established mechanisms of disciplining and social organisation, and the bureaucratic elite applied the law that kept subjects in check.

But the system as a whole would have been perceived as a divine order. I have pointed out that I consider the holy, overpowering and fear-inducing force generated by the exaltation of religion into a hierarchical cult as being the crux of slave-holding class society. The submission of human beings into servile labour resulted in a system that tied all social relations to a network of unconditional and unquestionable codes. Not only slaves in the narrow sense, but all subjects, from rural workers to artisans and high-ranking officers, were unfree in the sense that they were entangled in this network. Strict codes of gender subordination relegated most women to positions at the very bottom of the social hierarchies, while the primary targets of enslavement by capture were women. Many scholars argue that women's enslavement reinforced, if it did not originally generate, wider patterns of social hierarchisation.

The ancient system based on the use of servile labour could only be superseded at the point where human beings as slaves, and the form of social relations human beings maintained with one another under this paradigm, became unproductive. As long as the relations of production centred on servile labour continued to remain more productive than the surrounding "non-civilised" communities' forms of behaviour, there was little chance for the system to collapse or for it to be superseded by external forces. Nor would it be overthrown in rebellion from below. On the economic level, the widespread use of iron technology in farming and the relative social independence of the artisans as a class in the Middle East of the first millennium did away with the predominance of the highly centralised royal and priestly households as units of production based on the large-scale employment of servile labour.[6] I think that the figure of the blacksmith Kawa also reflects the importance of independent iron-producing artisans for the peripheral communities. The other pivotal factor was the change in human mentality that we have discussed in detail in previous chapters. An increasing number of people would have seen that the laws governing them were not based on the absolute commandments of divinities, but simply on the edicts of rulers. In the midst of relations of production based on slavery, new human beings emerged. They emerged from a new productive and social basis, with thoughts and a faculty of will that made them act as something other than the meek subjects the system had relied upon. In other words, they became the force that was to dissipate this system, full of vigour and bursting with intelligence.

This immoral process can be witnessed at all levels, in all the institutions and at the basis and superstructure of the ancient societies. While accepting a multiplicity of interacting factors and setting aside any attempt at identifying a "prime mover", it is mostly accepted that developments in the material structure of social organisation do exert a fundamental impact on the outcome of transformative processes. The possession of all means of production, notably the slaves themselves, was concentrated in the hands of the few who ran the system, and inevitably was closely attached to the institutions of state power.[7]

It was precisely these relations that obstructed the adequate use of the potential inherent in the accumulated means of production. Such usage would have been detrimental to the interests of the owners.[8] Military campaigns gave rise to a surplus of slave population, while confiscations of land forced large numbers of the rural population into bonded labour or an existence among the urban proletariat.[9] The increase in enslaved and unemployed people over and above what the system could assimilate, along with the enhanced accessibility of means of production to small-scale producers outside the state monopoly, ushered in a mode of production based on serfdom in rural communities – the feudal mode of production.

The aggrandisement of the slave system had always been to the detriment of the agricultural communities. Now peasant labour found new opportunities for development, and pushed towards reorganisation along these lines. At this stage of transition, peasants would be either free or bound to their masters by virtue of relations that were based on the ownership of the land by the master, rather than the latter's command over the body of the former.[10] These peasants largely maintained their own households. Such conditions effectively provided an incentive to work more efficiently than a person compelled to work as a slave. The dissolution of the ancient system of slavery on the local level of rural communities occurred with the gradual ripening of the conditions for a more productive economic and social order. The decrepitude of the old order only led to its demise when a new material reality had asserted itself as a viable alternative.

What I have depicted as a general process of course took various forms in the different geographical areas of the Roman Empire. Vast parts of Europe had never been totally subjected to any slave system, and their almost pristine lands provided most favourable conditions for the new system, which led to what I would call the second agrarian revolution. Europe was one of the most energetic sites for the formative process of the feudal order. In the Middle East, lands already under cultivation over several thousands of years were reorganised and reinvigorated on the basis of serf relations. Here, the feudal revolution would inevitably have to be more profound before the long-standing and deep-rooted influences of the slave system could be wiped away. But conditions were conducive to that, and dynamised by the sacredness ascribed to the feudal relations and mode of production, the Middle East would eventually once again assume its leading role in the development of human civilisation.

The increasing availability of iron and other metal ores not only affected the peripheral communities but induced changes in the social fabric of the urban centres too. A wide array of merchants, artisans and other craftspeople had become emancipated from the major aggregates of slave-holding state economies and enjoyed the status of private entrepreneurs. The existence of these professional groups as independent social forces (with a sizeable proportion of freed men among them) now turned into a counterweight to the ancient slave system, which required central command over all forms of labour. If the property relations particular to slavery had initially catalysed the urban revolution, urban social relations in their new complexity now played the part of the undertaker of these outmoded dichotomisations.

While the de facto conditions for an urban order of the new type emerged from the fuzziness of social position, professional affiliation and legal status in the cities of late antiquity, the decline of the old order also entailed the dramatic shrinking of urban populations. Many of the vibrant cities of the classical Greco-Roman era turned into ramshackle settlements. The city as a site of social organisation was relegated to a position of minor importance under the feudal system, which infused the decentralised agricultural communities with new life. Never paralleling the imposing architecture, vitality and grandeur of the ancient cities, most medieval cities and towns were either downsized seats of government or enlarged villages.[11]

Both the number and the population density of medieval rural settlements, however, quickly outgrew those of late antiquity. In fact, humankind outgrew the fetters of the economic and social conditions of the slave system in terms of production, thought, and moral disposition. The quantitative and qualitative growth of human productive powers became antagonistic to the persisting forms of property, mentality and the ways of life of the slave system. On the one hand, the more viable mode of organisation, the superior understanding of the material world and human behaviour, and the more binding character of moral norms associated with the hieratic order seem to have been advantageous to the constitution of the archaic slave system. Force and ruse played a secondary part. On the other, it was precisely the system's failure to organise the means of production on a level with their potential capacity, its mental backwardness and moral eclipse that led to its demise. It was the inner degradation of the system on which the Roman Empire was founded that allowed the "barbarian" attacks during the third and fourth centuries to have such a huge effect. Raids by tribal warriors had been going on from the point of inception of the first slave-holding empire, but the fact that they shattered Rome at that particular moment is indicative of a structural crisis. The once-powerful military and political institutions failed to function, and the state terrorism resorted to by officials embroiled in corruption and intrigues may have delayed the collapse, or it may just as well have accelerated it.[12] What we do know is that nothing could reverse the process of economic and social transition.

Beyond the eastern frontier the situation was not very different. The Persian Sassanian empire – only established in 215 CE – had little to add to the history of humankind. Modelled on the old Achaemenid state, its classic dynastic organisation involved political self-importance and lacked any ideological or moral values. Its cumbersome structures would crumble under the Arab–Islamic attacks just as the Achaemenid empire had succumbed to Alexander's offensive. As with the Roman situation, an inwardly non-viable system was perpetuated by force. Despite the formidable military power at its disposal, the dominant ideology and ethics of empire failed to secure superiority over the new ideology and morality that came with early Islam, with its progressive elements, like Hellenic culture once before.

Beneath the clamour of battles lost and won, the stories of the rise and fall of political systems always hinge on the superior ideological and moral force of the new. Where an old system runs out of breath and becomes inoperable, it will sooner or later be overcome by a new force emerging from within or beyond its precincts, irrespective of the imbalance of power that may be perceived to exist between the two antagonistic forces. The histories of Mesopotamia, Egypt, the Greco-Roman world, China and India are full of telling examples.

The actual function of the violence that has been so abundantly resorted to in human history, ever since the politico-military institutions of the ancient slave system arose, is worthwhile reassessing. The system, which showed the unprecedented audacity to oppress fellow human beings in an organised and premeditated fashion involving the use of institutionalised violence, instated a tradition according to which history is written in blood. No animal species is known to exhibit a commensurable tendency to use force against fellow species members. It is therefore misleading to decry military and political force based on class, gender, ethnic and cultural differences as "inhuman", "savage" or "bestial", when these are clearly practices that evolved with the most cursed reality of class society, and are therefore highly "*inbestial*" and, sadly enough, human.

The primal character of institutionalised violence under the ancient slave system makes it all the more important to understand its causes and effects. Members of the administrative elite seeking sanctuary in the enchanting power of violence can be held liable for a host of consequential and highly dangerous developments; but the quintessential one seems to me to have been the madness of self-deification. Where political power is promulgated as being of divine nature, all doors to the pandemonium of reaction are flung wide open.

The slave-holding state is far too complex a phenomenon to be exhaustively penetrated by means of a vintage Marxian class analysis. Its constitution, covered with the ferment of ideology and permeated by violence, is the basic constitution of all states to the present day. I would not exempt real socialist states from this verdict. The espousal of secularism alone is not good enough to vanquish this reality: the *class character* of the state now entered the realm of the political as a sacrosanct claim. The secularism of modern states, informed by the French bourgeois revolution, is a superficial one anyway. The *essence* of the problem remains untouched, while the reformist postulates simply increase the threat that emanates from it.

But the mechanisms outlined here were as precarious as they were sophisticated, and once the system's creative quality was exhausted, they proved as prone to disintegration as they had been conducive to growth.

Part 2

The Age of Feudalism

Introduction to Part 2

Middle Eastern societies are still weighed down by feudalism. If they want to overcome the characteristics of this system, particularly the omnipresence of religion, the concepts *feudalism* and *feudal civilisation* have to be analysed. For, wherever the process of civilisation is hindered by painful and bloody conflicts, wherever despotic governments rule, wherever people suffer from a degenerated republicanism, there is a virulent influence at work that has its origins in an epoch we call the Middle Ages, an epoch characterised by feudalism. In the Middle Ages, feudalism was characterised by economic and social backwardness and crisis. Today it still is.

Historical development is not driven solely by the accumulation of capital and technological knowledge. This is made plain by the fact that a majority of the Arab peoples still maintains a degenerate medieval order, while they do not lack the accumulated capital and technological know-how of the European countries. The roots of this problem, therefore, must be sought elsewhere. The mere availability of money, knowledge, and technological capabilities by no means produces the same results here as in Western societies. Thus, the entire problem and the hopelessness of the situation must stem from ideological reasons. We can test this assumption by taking a close look at the feudal mentalities and ways of life in today's Middle Eastern societies. The crisis and the paralysis of these societies can hardly be resolved (in terms of progress, of reaching a higher level of dialectic synthesis) without analysing their ideological superstructure and then rebuilding it in order to make it compatible with the requirements of the present age.

The system of European capitalist civilisation owes its superiority to the disintegration of the feudal system. Contrary to popular opinion, the feudal system did not break up primarily under the influence of science and technology but rather because of the efficacy of an ideological revolution which simultaneously prepared the ground for scientific and technological development. At the heart of all progress was a revolution in which free intellect prevailed over clerical dogmatism.

The accumulation of knowledge and technology and the accumulation of material riches have certainly contributed to this process. However, they did not form its key element. On the contrary, many regions of the world have become wealthier than Europe. Their knowledge and technological capabilities have surpassed that of Europe. The same was true for the Islamic world in the eighth century. After the twelfth century, the leading position of the Islamic world continuously diminished. This fact, plus the successful European transformation, hint that there are ideological reasons behind the feudal character of today's Middle Eastern societies.

When analysing the concept of feudal civilisation, it is important to ask where and how feudalism came into being. Eurocentric historians, who still maintain a decisive influence on the writing of world history, believe that European history begins with the fall of the Roman Empire, i.e. it begins with itself. In this way, they intend to explain the present European superiority. The results of this reasoning are grave distortions and error. The feudal civilisation was born as a product of the cultural conditions of the Middle East, an environment where the maturation, development, and disintegration of the neolithic age and the age of slavery had taken place. It remains, even today, a very influential system of civilisation in the Middle East.

This observation is important for understanding how history works. It can be compared to a sequence of links in a chain, a logical sequence that we must not lose sight of. Civilisations do not rise and decline by chance. If there is a certain confusion in historiography concerning this point, it is rooted in the need of the politically powerful to create an egocentric view of history for their own purposes. Unfortunately, historical science has not yet obtained the level of objectivity typical of many other branches of the sciences. A closer look reveals close connections between a slave-holder system and feudalism as political systems. On the other hand, the antagonism between capitalism and feudalism is strong and their separation was correspondingly difficult and full of conflict. The nature of capitalism and the way it rules require that all feudal links are mercilessly destroyed. This is the origin of its revolutionary character.

The transition from slave-holder system to feudalism, on the other hand, is made (as per the Roman example) by way of a silent compromise with the feudal system. Instead of a harsh rejection or a confrontation between the old and the new, we find an internal transfer of power. The old system then decayed due to its own dynamics, while the new system slowly evolved. This was the case, for instance, in the transition from the slave-holder system in Rome to the feudal system in Byzantium. A similar development can be traced in India and China. It is the difference in the way the transition from one system to the next is made which is crucial here: there is only a slight difference of quality concerning the dependence of social relationships between the system of slave-holding and feudalism. Thus, a radical dissolution process is unnecessary. This non-radical nature of the dissolution process is responsible for the fact that the two systems are closely related and for the fact that their separation does not manifest itself in a fast sequence of radical events that we could call revolutionary. Instead, we find an evolutionary transformation process.

An essential task of historiography is realistically to define spatial and chronological parameters of evolutionary transformation regarding the different civilisations that we know. Until today historiography has not been able to develop a systematic framework for describing the flow of historical development in time and space. The observation that feudalism, too, has its roots in the Middle East will help to shed light on a number of important questions.

Secondly, this insight will contribute to a better understanding of monotheistic ideologies in their historical dimension. The discussion of religious ideologies is an important intellectual field that is still mostly neglected.

Thirdly, this approach will be of service to scientific method in determining Middle Eastern culture and its historical role. It might also prove to be a corrective in the writing of history.

Fourthly, it may lead to a diagnosis of the problems Middle Eastern societies are confronted with. And, one day, it might be able suggest solutions for other social communities in a similar state of backwardness, crisis, and hopelessness.

Today, because of its historical roots, the Israeli–Arab conflict causes more problems in the world than the confrontation between capitalism and socialism. This conflict illustrates impressively how our epoch inserts Gordian knots into the reality of the Middle East. In reality, this conflict – disguised as a conflict between religious beliefs – is a conflict between social orders which results in a confrontation between different systems of civilisation. Although this civilisation conflict looks like a tribal war, in fact it comprises the totality of historical continuity and the universal antagonism of our time. The diplomatic and military means used up by this conflict make it second in scope only to a world war.

This is why all serious powers of this world feel obliged to contribute by some means or other to this conflict or its solution. Therefore, the United Nations may as well go on making painstaking efforts at phrasing new resolutions, none of which will bear fruit until the lessons of the past are learnt. This is not an easy task when even our very recent history, such as World War II with all its horrors, is already blurring and becoming historical memory. However, the historically grown diseases of the Middle East, visible in the Israeli–Arab conflict, still determine today's explosive reality. The state of conflict between civilisations in the Middle East can assume an eschatological strength if we close our eyes to the dangers it contains.

Although Europe had only limited experience of the feudal system, and although it can ascribe the origins of its feudal system only to a small extent to an authentic, long-lasting period of slavery, it needed the epoch of an all-embracing renaissance to overcome that age. Nobody would claim that present-day Europe could have come about without the Renaissance of the fifteenth and sixteenth centuries. Is it not possible that the reason for the present state of hopelessness in the Middle East lies in the fact that there has never been such a renaissance in this part of the world? Despite its long-standing and deeply rooted system of slavery and feudalism, the Middle East has never experienced a renaissance.

The Islamic Awakening was the Middle East's last powerful contribution to civilisation. The creation of the Islamic order can be understood as a feudal Glorious Revolution. European feudalism is in no way superior to Eastern feudalism in its Islamic form. The crusades give evidence of the fact that the West could only establish superiority over the East by fighting a long chain of military campaigns. The variant of Eastern feudalism represented by the Ottoman Turks was still able to force European feudalism onto the defensive. Only with the arrival of capitalism was Europe able to free itself from this defensive position. Thus began the yet uninterrupted, and increasing, supremacy of Western civilisation over Eastern forms of civilisation. The East, in particular the Middle East, has been in a defensive position ever since. Its position is characterised by feelings of inferiority and a lack of concepts to explain this position. Any attempt at explanation using the methodologically narrow theories of imperialism and colonialism is insufficient in the extreme. Moreover, these theories are often nourished by a branch of Western historical understanding that we call "real socialism". Since theory cannot yet explain satisfactorily why real socialism has failed, it is even more important to question scientifically its narrow analytical framework.

Meanwhile, the East still suffers from its past. A renaissance of its own is beyond its imagination. But this is exactly what its progress depends upon, since neither unlimited amounts of oil nor technology transfer nor any Western-style enlightenment will be able to save it. The symptoms of this intellectual crisis are perfectly clear: dramatic population growth, unemployment, exploitation of its resources, betrayal of its history, failure even as epigones, ignorance of human rights and democracy, despotic isolationism, misleading religiousness, moral instability. With a view to a solution of its problems, the present political systems in the Middle East are even less capable of action than were primitive tribal communities.

All of this needs to be overcome, though, for the allegedly holy city of Jerusalem to stop being a city of death. Without a sense of the past, there will never be a rebirth, nor any progress towards higher levels of civilisation. The history of the Middle East first needs to catch up with the present modern age.

An understanding of the systems of civilisation formed in the Middle East will be at the heart of any mental revolution and deserves the utmost priority. The fragmentation of the intellect, which is so widespread in the social structure of the Middle East, can be stopped only by such an ideological revolution. The human crises and catastrophes we find in the Middle East can only be overcome by correctly analysing their feudal causes. We need to encourage change and the regeneration of intellectual life in order to bring about a mental revolution.

11

The Ideological Frame of Reference of the Feudal Age

Every human society or group can be described by a number of key characteristics that also reflect its self-conception. One of these is its ideological frame of reference – what we may call its ideological identity. When we need profound information on the state of a human group, on the way that it interacts with its environment, the group's ideological identity provides it. This is equally true for South American Indian tribes and for the inhabitants of a European metropolis.

Attempts to define societies by focusing on economic criteria seem unsatisfactory. The social sciences are still far from really understanding the function of ideological frames of reference. However, a close look at history shows us that, in the processes of the formation or disintegration of social groups, new frames of reference emerge or play a decisive part in such processes. Ideological identities form something like the brain of a society by providing a memory for the social past as well as by holding concepts and a vision of the social future. How these concepts are implemented will depend on economic factors. It will, however, be within a framework of variables that are independent of direct economic influence.

If we picture society as an organism, we will agree that it needs a central consciousness, an ideological centre where reflection takes place. This is the brain where the superstructure is created. In the institutionalisation of the substructure (under the decisive influence of economic factors) other extremities of the organism are more important. This is why we can call the ideological superstructure the basis of it all. Such an approach draws upon a naturalistic philosophical view of society, i.e. the basic concepts of nature also apply to human societies. When we described the slave-holder civilisation in the light of this philosophical approach as the first and probably most comprehensive form of a class society, Sumer served as our foremost example. It is the oldest historical example that we have and a large number of written sources allow us to take Sumer as a starting point for social analyses. It becomes clear at this point that an understanding of Sumerian society is indispensable. When the first civilisations arose, Sumer played an important part in the formation of some of the principal institutions of social super- and substructures. Sumer's authenticity, its fundamental ideological identity as a class society based on myths, is a blueprint for many civilisations. There may be other, seemingly contradictory examples, which nonetheless confirm the assumption that the Sumerian model has established strong and elementary rules.

Capitalist society can only be explained satisfactorily with the help of an analytical understanding of the accumulation of capital. In a similar way, a scientific explanation of the superstructures and ideological identities of all civilisations can only be accomplished with an analytical understanding of the Sumerian ideology. We have to know the archetype in order to understand its "hybrids", in order to recognise its variations, degenerations, or transformations. The reverse is much more difficult. Derivatives of the Sumerian concept, its hybrids or transformations, are the subject of virtually unlimited research in human philosophy and literature, while knowledge of the archetype is either lacking or regarded unnecessary. (This is also true for religious history. Although many religions have at least some roots in the Sumerian mythology, their origins are often adulterated or denied.)

It can be shown, though, that the Sumerians have in the same way absorbed elements of their ideology from the surrounding neolithic societies. (In fact, there is no system of ideology that has not taken from or given to other systems. We, as historians, must answer the question: Who has adopted what and for what purpose, and how have these adoptions been transformed? This remains a desideratum for the science of history.)

As we can see, it will be useful first to define the framework of ideological reference of feudal civilisations before we begin to discuss the formation processes of these civilisations. We shall benefit from this later when applying this method to such a complex topic as the Middle Ages.

When turning our focus to the Middle Ages we are immediately and strongly confronted with names such as Allah, Moses, Jesus and Muhammad. Their ideological identities need to be analysed. Who is this Allah, who is God? What is the relevance of such great prophets as Muhammad, Jesus or Moses? To which elements of social logic do they correspond? When we are trying to narrate history in the Middle East, these ideological frameworks are mostly ignored. The murderous fanaticism which bases itself all too often on these prophets and their religions demands that religion as such is seriously discussed. If we want to live a life of peace, such discussions of religion and theology are essential. *Secularism* will remain an empty word in the Middle East as long as we shy away from an analysis of religious ideologies. Secularism is deeply needed, however, as can repeatedly be seen from a number of terrible incidents. If we want to achieve a second renaissance, this time in the Middle East, we need to turn our attention to the first great reform movement.

Let me recall once more that the clan as the first known instance of a social formation had a view of the world that was dominated by animism and taboo beliefs. It was a view of the world that was based on the sacred but rather unintelligible power of the mana, a power that can only be sensed.

With the forming of a social group, an energy is generated that will make itself visible – at this stage of human history – in the form of animistic concepts and sacred taboos. (Although this phenomenon is extremely important, a fundamental condition to which all human life is bound, at this stage of human development it is but an intuitive realisation. It will take some thousand years before any scientific explanation for it can be offered.)

Mankind in its childhood feels that all objects are animated in the same way that people are, with the same emotions and wishes – all objects are personified. (In fact, the first social formation shows similar mental structures to those of a child – a fact which is confirmed by psychological research. Even ontogenetic models prove quite helpful for the social sciences in some respects.)

Hence, it becomes understandable why at this naive stage of clan ideology the belief that all things have a spirit gains momentum. All activities are given a sacred meaning, or, conversely, declared a taboo, which is ignored only at the cost of one's own well-being. In this way a social group or formation becomes a phenomenon that is understood as a sacred being with a spiritual identity of its own.

The totem becomes the symbol of the clan, it represents the clan. The totemic identity is filled with the sensation and the spirituality of the community it stands for. With the help of the totem, the power of the clan increases and the clan becomes aware of itself. Later, the concepts of the deities and the temple develop from this.

All that exists can only exist with an identifier, a designator, a name. Therefore, the clan, too, needs to identify itself with a name. This name is more complex than the mere form it is associated with, because the naming amounts to the recognition of everything the social formation in question stands for. The significance of the totem, therefore, is greater than the adoration of idols. With the totem, the clan-symbol has become language. It is the family name. Respect for the totem and a strong bond with the totem also mean respect and a strong bond among the clan members. The primitive religion becomes a fundamental ideological synonym of the community. In this way, the sacredness and immunity identified with the symbol heightens and strengthens the group and all its members. It is its ideology that provides the totemic identity with its meaning. Since it comprises the achievements, experiences and values of the clan, which lives under marginal conditions, the totem quite understandably attains the qualities of sacredness and taboo. The totemic existence contains the pain, the joy, the trouble and the labours of the past. It symbolises the group's entire past existence and its hopes for the future. According to this definition, the birth of religion takes place as the archetype of intellectual concepts, the mental and psychic formation of the clan, as the first ideological formation. Religion is the first attempt to reflect a social group's material existence on the intellectual level. It is this quality that has given religion its long-lasting and formative position in social history.

The concept of theistic religion, i.e. religion involving the idea of gods, succeeds the totemic concept. This step corresponds with the growth of social formations, which become more powerful and learn to develop their capabilities in order to continue their existence in greater safety. These developments find their symbolic expression in the identities of gods. The deity, as a general expression of all that the community in its continued existence experiences or gains from nature, becomes a being identified with all the powers of nature and society. It is an artificial concept. The deity becomes the collective term for the secrets and laws of nature, as the social group perceives them at this stage. When philosophy set out to explain nature, it went beyond this and largely parted with religious concepts. However, there is a relation between religion and philosophy, since theistic concepts are also attempts at interpreting nature and society. Philosophy externalises God, or more precisely, philosophy appreciates that theistic thought has become conservative and unproductive, and that society has left its childhood behind. Theistic thought is closely related to this childhood stage. While society develops and differentiates, the deity receives additional meanings apart from those related to the general existence of nature. Not only the power of the community in general, but also its particular strengths are regarded as divine. The deity grows, because the community is not satisfied with redefining it only as a general expression of nature or a set union of all its powers, but rather tries to furnish the rising and differentiating society with a new identity. This new identity is a reflection of all natural and social powers. In the religious fabric of the neolithic community, phenomena such as earth, plants, animals, waters, wind, weather and clouds gain particular importance, since they are always present and therefore biologically important for the reproduction and existence of the group. They are deified, because they govern life. These deities symbolically stand for concrete objects, which satisfy different needs. To a certain extent, this way of thinking is the first attempt at pursuing science or doing research. A science of the divine is created. At the totemic stage, the narrative remains limited, mythology has not yet been developed, and ideology does not go far beyond taking comfort in worshipping. The religious understanding of the neolithic age, where the deities are man's friends, mirrors the social qualities of this age. The fact that the deities are treated as man's loyal companions may hint at a relatively conflict-free society, with comparatively paradisiacal opportunities to draw from nature's resources whatever was needed. The deities are as immediately close to man as the community is close to the phenomena it has internalised with its deities. The gods are not yet regarded as completely different and separated from man. Even more important, all deities are female (maybe inspired by woman's capacity for childbearing) and woman is the mainspring of the agrarian revolution. Besides, in the early periods of Sumer, Egypt and ancient India, divinity is expressed by a feminine prefix – the masculine qualities of the deities arise only at a later stage. All known great goddesses, such as Ishtar, Inanna, Isis, Demeter and Kybele, come from this age. At the same time, this religion is an expression of the social unity of the family communities or tribes. There are deities for all the phenomena that are important in the life of the community and all the phenomena that have been recognised as useful or harmful powers of nature and have therefore been given names.

The conceptual order, the entire way of thinking, is expressed in terms of deities, which are ordered hierarchically according to their importance.

It is no surprise, therefore, that notions with an attributed magical content are deified. At this stage, every new found term marks a new opportunity and is consequently represented by a new deity. Woman's primary influence in the production processes as well as her child-bearing ability gave her an enormous social influence, which is reflected in this age of goddesses. Woman provides knowledge of helpful plants, fruit trees, domestic animals, field work, housebuilding, child raising, several tools, such as the pick and the quern, and probably the first two-wheeled ox-cart. The mother-goddesses symbolise woman's role in this age of innovations.

In previous chapters, arguments were put forward for the assumption that this agrarian revolution probably took place for the first time in the Tauros–Zagros region. It was argued that the Sumerians were the first people to make the transition to a class society after their adoption of these cultural techniques. The role of the priests in the ideology of Sumer and their ideological primacy at the time the class society was created was dealt with in detail. The priesthood is at the centre of this process and forms the ideological leadership, with the temple as their first headquarters and seat of government. The ideological formulas and religious rites forming there become the community's new social identity.

The class society is described and idealised in terms and concepts similar to the divine order. When they formulate the new class society, the priests are well aware of the fact that this society yields a much greater productivity. Accordingly, they actively take part in idealising the new order. The new divine identities need to be conceived in their concentrated sacredness and must be invested in their high offices. Soon the ziggurats come into being. Their uppermost floors are reserved for the deities, while the ground floors are for servants and slaves. The debate about the primacy of either economy or ideology must be challenged in view of the Sumerian example. There is much evidence for the assumption that the temples as command centres of the priesthood were, simultaneously, centres of material production and of ideological conception. The temples were the basis of civilisation, the basis of the city and the state.

There is no evidence anywhere for any kind of production that was not associated with a centre of the priesthood. We may safely conclude that religion as the ideological and identity-forming power of society had become an indispensable institution in the production process. This is clear at least for the formation phase of the class society. Later this religious configuration became redundant, or rather, it had to be expressed more adequately in a new form. In principle, the Sumerian deities, having their roots in the neolithic, are still the same anthropomorphic deities who share the world with man. They eat, drink and get married just like people. In the beginning there is a balance between male and female deities, but then competition and conflicts increase.

Adam and Eve's eviction from paradise and their condemnation to servitude originated at this time. It reflected society's division into classes. The Sumerian deities became creators, while their subjects were abased and became servants. The mythological conflict between Enki and Nin-Hursag/Inanna shows that woman's creativity is suppressed and forced to the background and that people are shaped into servants and slaves. In the entire later conflict between God and the believers, this Sumerian blueprint is still applicable. (This is an important statement. Where theology shies away from or denies the new inequality in the relationship between Man and God, this is evidence for a need to conceal the inner life of religion and its hidden interests.)

The divine identities created in Sumer led to a redefinition of the relation between the powers of nature and those of society. Now the social side came to the fore. Woman's dominance decreased and disappeared. The members of the community differentiated into priests and dignitaries, subjects, workmen and servants. This development was permanent. While the growing political powers in the community led to the rise of a number of deities, other identities disappeared or underwent substantial changes. At the time of Babylon, the absolute power of the ruler was reflected in the rise of the god Marduk. This last stage of Sumerian mythology had already reached the threshold of monotheism.

When the Semitic desert tribes became stronger and combined their homogenous and patriarchal life with the Sumerian civilisation, the war between the deities in Sumerian mythology intensified. The strong Sumerian influences now also covered woman's tracks in history. When the patriarchal tradition of the desert regions became a political power, it strove for despotism and absolute rule. As exemplified by Hammurabi, at the heart of rule as such lay these tribal traditions: the ruler was the law.

At the same time, however, increasing contradictions between and within the tribes resulted in opposition against the central political power, which identified itself with the deity – an opposition that took the form of the prophetic–Abrahamic tradition.

This prophetism produced a radical discontinuity in the Sumerian understanding of religion, because it devised a new image of man against the spirit of the time, when the gods still had the shape of people. Now man could never be God's equal any more. This image of man requires a closer look. The gods lost their human appearance. Furthermore, no man could be like God or be a god himself, not even the god–rulers of that age. The rulers lost their divinity and became representatives of the gods. In this way, the friendly deities of the neolithic, who had lived side by side with man, were turned into dominating and punishing gods by the slave-holder civilisation. This was an important conceptual transformation. The political power of the class society moved to the core of the concept of religion and correspondingly changed and reinterpreted mythology.

The differentiation of the tribes and their resistance resulted in a step forward ideologically by putting to the fore the identity of a god, who follows the interests of the oppressed and exploited, who appears as a saviour, and who, unlike the god-ruler, lavishes his people with blessings. This is the essence of the prophetic–Abrahamic tradition. People cannot be like God. They can only be his chosen messengers. The gods are not only damnatory and punishing gods; they can also bless and save people. They only punish severe crimes, but even then forgiveness is possible, humility provided. Hence, the monotheistic religious understanding is at its core an abstraction of natural and social powers onto a higher level, leaving behind the religious understanding of the slave-holder society, which had focused on the cult of the god–ruler. It was the ideological envelope of the class struggles and social conflicts of that time.

Although monotheism started from the slave-holder mythology and religion of the Sumerian type, little by little an antagonistic aspect emerged from it, containing radical opposition. Thus, the rise of non-anthropomorphic monotheism became the ideological foundation of the resistance against slavery.

The concept of a single god opened the way towards universalism and could, in principle, point beyond the narrow limits of the tribes at any time.

Since a similar situation showed similar results in other tribes, the ancient totems and idols of the clans and tribes had to be given up. They had become old-fashioned and did not contribute to the interests of the rising alliance of tribes. The god–rulers had caused enough suffering. Now a redeemer, a merciful god symbolising the unity of all people, entered the stage. His sphere grew wider and wider under the influence of growing contradictions and the wish for unification. Eventually, people attributed to him several new qualities and worshipped him as unique and without any counterpart in the human world. While the old system created particular deities for new qualities or phenomena, the new religion makes all these qualities the attributes of a single god. The 99 titles of Allah were qualities of civilisation just as binding as laws or moral codes.

The innovations Moses brought into monotheism consisted largely in estranging all Hebrew tribes from their former beliefs and in spreading the concept of religion as the exclusive concern of a single people. It was an advanced level of development when he structured Yahweh as a god who establishes a canon of rules, the Ten Commandments, and then demands that all Hebrew tribes should seriously commit themselves to these rules. This was also an expression of emancipation and rebellion against the Egyptian Pharaoh. Moses conceived an ideological framework that helped him unite the insubordinate but backward tribes in their struggle against the Babylonian and Egyptian supremacy. However, physical defence and friendly interaction were deeply intertwined, since there was both an exchange of goods and information and an attitude of resistance against the two great centres of slavery. The tribes converted the stores of knowledge they received from both centres into their new authentic ideology, which then became the basis for the historic reality of the Hebrew tribes and Israel. They experienced the dilemma that on the one hand they opposed the slave-holder system, while on the other hand they did not have the power to escape from its sphere of influence. Thus, permanent modernisation became a necessity for them. This becomes a continuous line of development. Although Jesus also belonged to this Judaic tradition, he rather took the opposite part. Like Abraham, who had been raised in the Babylonian–Assyrian tradition of Nimrod and later became its enemy and turned towards a new religion, Jesus demanded a breach with the official Judaism of the Pharisees and the scribes, who had become integrated into the Roman slave-holder society and had parted with the world of the poor. This position was a levelling of the Jewish tribal concept. It overcame the tribal view and addressed milieus, strata, even a class. In this way, however, Jesus also called into question the foundations of Roman power: Rome used the tribes as its material basis; it recognised their upper classes in order to establish and maintain a universal order. Against this background Jesus rose like the conscience of the world and challenged the Roman slave-holder system. In his person, Jesus united ideological and social rebellion against the slave-holder system. In Christianity, the triad of gods has not been reduced to a single god; it still shows influences from Sumer, ancient Egypt and even the neolithic. Only in this form can it overcome the tribal god Yahweh and the framework of the tribal religion. Jesus' religion is a religion of salvation. The oppression by the Roman slave-holder system had paved the way for it, and even before Jesus was born, people everywhere believed that the coming of the Messiah was about to happen at any time. Jerusalem was the melting pot of three Middle Eastern forms of religious thought. The Jewish tradition was deeply rooted; Alexander had brought the Hellenistic tradition; the Persian–Zoroastrian tradition also had its followers. The time of Jesus was a time of mystic brotherhoods; a conscious movement was seething, pressing for a new order of the oppressed against the universal order of Rome. By dividing the tribes and the small kingdoms and by tying them to the imperium, Rome left a great number of people without orientation. People needed a new reference point.

These were the conditions that formed Jesus, his character and his identity. His personal abilities did not contribute much. It was the long-awaited coming of the Messiah, so typical of this time, which was the main reason for Jesus' rise. Christianity became the name of this ideological movement and with it, perhaps for the first time in history, a universal party of humankind came into being. Initial religious struggles and social differences changed into political power. Three centuries later, the Christians had already conquered Rome. A bloodless revolution took place, or more precisely, a feudal civilisation was founded.

When in 380 Christianity rose to state religion, some important qualitative changes in the Roman civilisation took place. The cities, as the former sites of the slave trade, declined. Many people fled or moved to the countryside. Eventually, when order was re-established, serfdom emerged as some less rigid form of slavery and with it a new agricultural structure. This was not a return to the neolithic but a new type of civilisation, which re-associated people with a natural life. At the same time, the Roman emperors were no longer god–kings. This at least partly resulted from the enlightenment brought about by the monotheistic religion. Shrouded in religious and philosophical terms God had definitely been pushed off into heaven. Once more, the emperor's absolute power had also been challenged; the farther God was away from man, the greater was man's freedom.

While the predominant picture of God changed, Gnostics and mystics escaped into the old neolithic understanding of a god who is conciliatory towards man. The concept of unity between creator and creature, where the self has its identity in the transcendental God – as opposed to the concept of a punishing, dominating god far from man – pervaded early Christianity. Here, Jesus was the son of God because he was the Son of Man. Later, this line of thought was replaced by Aristotelian philosophy. It is important that Jesus was also regarded as the patron saint of the poor. These ideas paved the way for a civilisation that could at least promise some liberation.

There is no doubt that Christianity played a historical part in the development of feudalism and that it pervades humankind and its history in terms of faith and ethics. The early Christians had to make great sacrifices in order to overcome slavery. They had to resist and bear great sufferings. They started as a purely ideological spiritual movement and kept away from politics and violence for a long time. An important element in this was the collective life in the monasteries and churches, which was mostly based on asceticism, somewhat similar to the temple order of the Sumerian priesthood. These structures (monasteries, churches, etc.) were like schools where the new society tested its capabilities. Here, an alternative life, an alternative political power, was set up. Rather than being a place of contemplation, the churches and monasteries became schools and training places for the new social order. Of course, they did not remain untarnished by Roman rule. Rome enforced its universal claims upon the church, which soon lost its initial naivety. Exertion of influence and defence reactions account for each other mutually; their common product is a synthesis.

A development similar to the one caused by Jesus took place in the eastern centre of the slave-holder civilisation. At the heart of this was a man named Mani, from Ctesiphon in Mesopotamia. He was born in 216 CE, at about the time of the early Sassanids. We know that he made some progress at synthesising Zoroastrian, Hellenistic, and Christian culture. If his ideological movement had been able to overcome the reactionary class of priests, the Sassanian empire would certainly also have exerted some influence on Rome. Manichaeism or Maniism might have initiated a movement different from the dogmatism of monotheism. In certain respects, this movement might have been similar to the European Renaissance. If this had taken place, the Middle East would have experienced the "European" civilisation process much earlier. But the strong tradition of slavery on the part of the state and the official Zoroastrian priesthood, which were as reactionary as the Jewish Pharisees, did not permit such a development. They prevented the Manicheans from coming into power and cruelly suppressed them. Due to its ideological conservatism and its reactionary structure the Sassanian empire later lost ground, first to Byzantium and then to Islam, before it eventually decayed.

Elsewhere, rebellions were more successful. They took the shape of mass movements and in this way proved quite assertive. Slave-holder systems were gradually eroded, taken over and transformed. However, before Christianity was able to dispose of all layers of the slave-holder system, Islam came into being. Ideologically, Christianity may not have been sufficient. The dynamism of Islam generated a more radical ideological and practical solution. Islam began under conditions similar to those under which Christianity had begun. Its delayed development took place under the influence of the Assyrian Nestorian priesthood and the Jewish tribes in Arabia. Here, in the person of Muhammad, the nonconformist character of the Arab Bedouins manifested itself.

An analysis and thorough understanding of Islam is not only historically important, it is a precondition for understanding present Islamic societies. It is not understood yet that Islam has created certain personality structures. Its history is mostly described in political and military terms, while its ideological and social identity is often neglected. Even today, Islam remains an enigma. Its inner face concerning politics and religion is not even roughly understood. Its bright and its dark sides are deeply intertwined. Muhammad, the last prophet, and Islam, the last monotheistic religion, herald the end of the religious epoch. Contrary to any other assertions, Islam is concretised in the shape of a religion with a predominantly political and military character. Its religious aspects and its monotheistic content, on the other hand, are rather weakly developed. Islam as a higher-level ideological transformation of Sumerian mythology is furnished with very complex qualities. Despite great effort, Muhammad was able to overcome these mythological foundations and the two great religions stemming from it only to a very limited extent.

It seems to me that the monotheistic religion and its concept of God can be regarded as the ideological avant-garde of the Middle Ages. We should, therefore, take a closer look at this concept of God, at its social implications and at the time in which it originated. In my opinion, if we see the necessity of a Middle Eastern enlightenment and renaissance, we need to deconstruct the superstructure of the present Middle Eastern systems and assemble anew the building blocks we find.

12

Early Islam: a Revolutionising Force

Islam has been a subject of theoretical discussion and practical development ever since its inception. This is partly due to the fact that the reality which expresses itself through Islam, is not yet fully understood on an analytical level. To date, Islam has neither been forced into a rigid ideological framework, nor has it experienced institutional reforms. Thus, it has remained authentic, and continues to serve as a projection screen for diverse visions.

At the time of its origin, Islam did not have a large following. The prophet Muhammad had to go through long, tedious conflicts in order to establish this faith. His primary aim was to overcome the patriarchal ideology of the desert tribes. Whereas Moses had applied the new monotheistic belief for the unification of the Hebrew tribes, Muhammad strove to break up the Arabs' tribal structures, as tribalism had become a fundamental obstacle in the process of gaining and integrating power and building a coherent civilisation.

Muhammad was faced with 360 small, and three large idols represented in the Ka'aba. The continued existence of this colourful, heavenly panoptic made progress impossible. With the development of Mecca into an important trade centre, their disposal became a possibility. However, tension developed between the civilising influence of commerce and the primitive and reactionary zeal of the tribes. This tension was the real cause, the material and the social basis, for Muhammad's efforts. While one side pushed for progress and changes towards civilisation, the other was obstructive and persistently involved in tribal feuds.

Muhammad's thinking was deeply influenced by the three great centres of civilisation: the glorious Byzantium to the north, the powerful Sassanids to the east, and Ethiopia in east Africa. Muhammad made several caravan journeys between Mecca, Damascus and Jerusalem, during which he met Christian priests, especially Assyrian Nestorians. As Jewish tribes lived in his immediate vicinity, he would have known the Yahweh belief of the Jewish people quite well. The Hanifs, a Gnostic mystic sect descended from the Sabaeans, promoted monotheism in Mecca, and Muhammad is said to have been influenced by them in the same way that Jesus had been influenced by the Essenes. The Sassanid priesthood was influenced by Zoroastrianism to some extent. At the time of Mohammad's travels, all three of the monotheistic religions – Christianity, the Mosaic religion, and Zoroastrianism – were established religions, ideological frameworks, aspiring towards obtaining and preserving power. At the same time, the deities that Muhammad found in the Ka'aba represented the legitimate, dominant spiritual identities of the tribes.

Thus, surrounded on all sides by different ideological doctrines, Muhammad turned towards the mystical, Gnostic Hanifian movement.[1] He, too, was about to found a Gnostic sect.

Historically speaking, we have now arrived at the threshold of the transition from slavery to feudalism, which has some similarities with the later transition of European feudalism to capitalism.

Semitic tribes had often turned towards the centres of civilisation in Sumer and Egypt in order to pillage them. At other times, they had been carried off to these centres as slaves. The first known example is that of the Accadians in Sumer, but the Hebrews went to Egypt in similar circumstances. Once again, Semitic tribes that called themselves *Arab* (beautiful) started an offensive against these centres, believing that they were fulfilling a historical task: "*March, and you will win …*"

In this context, it becomes crucial to analyse the concept *Allah*, as used by the prophet Muhammad. Although a description of the essential material elements of this time is important, we first have to define the sociological context of this fundamentally ideological concept. However, the information available is limited. Today, *El* (spirit) is regarded as a Semitic term for the divine; a term that was probably developed only after the totemic interpretation of the world had proved anachronistic and inadequate. Under the influence of civilisation, this term was extended to refer to the concept of a dominant, divine being. Because the tribes of the Arabian peninsula call on him in many different names, we may say that we are dealing here with a concept that was formed at a time when the tribal community was starting to differentiate and the sheikhdom was established. This conceptual construction reflects a parallelism between the sheikh as the owner and ruler of the tribe, and El as the owner and ruler of nature. Both are cornerstones of the basic ideological identity of the Arabic tribes. The sheikh is the spiritual and political leader of the tribe and the growing strength of the tribe becomes visible in the sheikh's high office and authority. In a sense, he becomes a nobleman or primitive king. By his side, and complementing the sheikh's worldly power as it were, we find El or Allah, who rules all of nature. When the community began to differentiate, when the tribe learnt to secure its reproduction and continuance more efficiently within a natural world which they experienced as willing and even obedient, the age of totemism was over.

The totem was replaced by a dual world: nature was divided into earth and heaven. A new concept of god was formed: El is the ruler of heaven in the same way that the sheikh is the ruler of his tribe. This reflects a new understanding of "property" and "proprietor". The divine dignity is replenished with profane, material property. The term *malik* (king [of heaven]), derived from the root *mulk* (property, territory), connotes in all Semitic languages a distribution of property, which, in the case of the sheikhdom, takes on a meaning modelled on monarchy.

The Semitic Allah is a mirror image of the relationship between tribe and sheikh transferred onto earth and heaven. In Sumer, Egypt, Greece and India, where life is ruled by a multitude of influences, polytheism determined the development of society. Only after the political power had largely been centralised did the religious system shift towards monotheism. Similarly, the concept *El*, devised on the Arabian peninsula, became the influential ideological identity in the spiritual world of the Semitic tribes at about 2000 BCE. Its spreading and strengthening reflected the order of nature as the desert tribes experienced it. We may even say that *Allah*, as a basic ideological concept of the Middle East, derived largely from the region's geography.

At this early, childlike stage of human civilisation, new concepts assume a magical meaning, as though they were reality itself. Reality and concept are identified with each other. Later philosophers like Plato, on the other hand, regard ideas – concepts – as the key elements of existence. The material world is seen as their reflection and has no more value than the value of illusion and memory. This view springs from the increasingly rational and logical approach of philosophy to the analysis of nature and existing social conditions. A completely new and – for this age – wondrous phenomenon is the associative creativity increasingly used in the cognitive process. Here begins the classical age of cognition. With its monotheistic religious concepts, philosophical thought reaches a peak. Humanity enters a new stage. Analytical terms, helpful in describing and explaining the world, become the basis of religious thinking and philosophical schools. Priests and philosophers devise new concepts and ideas and turn them into tools for practical use. The most useful concepts, which contribute to the unity and strength of the community, assume the role of precious exchange values.

Humanity had begun its conscious existence by naming things and giving them meaning. Now, the process of civilisation was expanded with the ability to diagram actions with the help of basic terms and notions. The phenomena reflected in this way became key elements of social thought.[2]

Describing religious concepts in the context of their background, as was done above, makes it clear that these concepts are responsible for a society's strength in terms of explaining the world and filling it with meaning. It is extremely dangerous to reduce these questions to vulgar materialist assertions such as: *Religion is fraud; God does not exist.* Such statements are at least as deceitful and unscientific as those proclaiming God's existence and character in a poster-like fashion. It would serve us better to ask about the role of religion in a given social reality, and how we interact with it institutionally.

Later in history the question arises as to the powers through which the universe is controlled. Philosophy, in particular the philosophy of religion, tries to answer this question. For science, this is a matter of establishing the comprehensive laws determining the processes of production and their interaction with each other. The evolution of comprehension, it seems, is an infinite process.

In my opinion, it is narrow-minded, reactionary and even deceitful to describe the level of knowledge of a certain epoch as absolute and unchangeable, or as some kind of final truth for all humankind. This is what fuels religious dogmatism. Inquisition-like processes are a natural consequence of such constrictions. On the other hand, coarse denial of religious phenomena does not help societal development either. It merely provokes antagonism and will only strengthen religious dogmatism.

In so far as we are practising sociology within the framework described above, we shall have to answer questions concerning the creation, meaning and rules of religion. Thereafter, we shall need to discuss how religion functions, and what its functions are; whether it unites and consoles people, or whether it subjugates and enslaves them.

In this context, the conceptualisation of *Allah* should be seen as a fundamental socio-religious institution which is continuously developing and gaining power. Similar phenomena can be found in Sumer and Egypt, even in Zoroastrianism. The more centralised a society becomes in terms of power, the more monotheistic its religion becomes. Since religious notions and terms carry most of the thinking of this age, the evolution of concepts eventually results in the idea of the One God, and formulas such as "King on Earth", "God in Heaven" arise. When monotheism came into existence on the Arabian peninsula in the shape of *Allah*, this concept already contained a number of important social developments. Although the concept is largely derived from Sumerian and Egyptian tradition, an authentic part of it is in contrast to these cultures. Sumerian and Egyptian culture had always centred around combinations of man and god. Most of these Pharaohs and Nimrods presented themselves as god–kings. Endowed with such qualities, they also determined the qualities of the rising system of slavery. The Egyptian pyramids and the Sumerian royal graves are proof that the subjects of these rulers were merely there to serve their masters: when the masters died, the subjects were practically dead as well, and the servants were buried along with the ruler. It became a priority task for humanity to get rid of such barbarity. Thus, the ideological war against the god–kings, who presented themselves as most holy to their people, was one of the longest and most sacred wars in history. The destruction of the many gods and cults, and the subsequent decline of the god–kingdoms, was the reason why Abraham, the patriarch, could become such an important figure and the ancestor of three world religions. It also put an end to the practice of burying people alive. Even today, in the Urfa area, a man may violate marital faithfulness a hundred times and will only be regarded as a ladies' man; yet any girl who does as much as exchange a covetous glance with a man may immediately be killed by her family in accordance with the moral codex still valid there. Such rules may be seen as remnants of laws from the time of the god–kings.

Hence, Abraham is admired for good reasons. He was the result of laws brought forth by Egyptian and Sumerian, and maybe even much older customs, in which an individual had meaning only as part of the whole, without an identity of his own. Abraham, on the other hand, was associated with Allah. He became so important because he annulled these laws by saying that no man could become like God, like Allah. Since man could not be God, man could not be a part of some divine identity either.

As mentioned above, the Abrahamic tradition resulted from geographic conditions, the differentiating social structure of the tribes and the new concept of God. Its real legitimacy, however, lies in its opposition to the understanding of God and religion that had prevailed in Sumer and Egypt. Proclaiming that man cannot be like God, thus implying that neither Pharaoh nor Nimrod can be divine, is a declaration of war. The story of the destruction of the idols that has been passed down to us serves to illustrate how the age of god–rulers was brought to an end. In addition, the Abrahamic idea of God questions slavery, and thus is progressive and liberating. Moses makes it even more concrete. Later, when Allah's word is heard everywhere as the word of the God of all (Arab) tribes, the order of the god–kings is smashed and the conservative totemic phase of the tribes is overcome. This is what constitutes the intense revolutionary content of the monotheistic concept, and herein lies the reason why it is still important today. The power of Allah transcends everything and stands for a community gaining strength and freedom. The many wars that have been fought over the centuries in the name of Allah have a revolutionary content up to the point where they become reactionary. In the age of slave-holder societies and feudalism, the exclamation of the name of Allah, the One, has the same meaning as the propagation of slogans of liberalism, socialism or nationalism in the age of capitalism.

Any call of the muezzin tells of the chance of self-liberation. This is the sociological context of the phenomena we are discussing.

There are three levels in the rise and development, the evolution, of Allah. The first was influenced by Sumerian and Egyptian mythology and resulted in a still somewhat totemic deity. When trade and colonial relations between the two centres of civilisation became more intense, their identities changed and their ideologies needed to be transformed. El, the general god of the tribes, had gained importance and, together with Abraham, had started a historical offensive.

The second level was reached with Jesus. Moses had initiated processes that changed God into a God of the people, and led to a popular religion. The

Jewish belief had resulted in a Hebrew kingdom. However, it was only with Jesus that the Abrahamic tradition experienced an enormous boost. The Sumerian and Egyptian systems of slavery had had as their antagonists Abraham and Moses. The Greco-Roman slave-holder system experienced its antagonism with Jesus. Abraham and Moses had been leaders of their people when they had shaken the foundations of their own religion. Jesus, however, turned to all people oppressed by Rome. According to the scriptures, Jesus stood in the tradition of his father. This can be interpreted as the influence of Sumerian tradition. Marduk, the Babylonian god, is the son of the wise and cunning Enki. He is also the opposite pole to the Sumerian authority in Babylon. This opposition gave Marduk his ideological identity. Jesus, likewise, opposed the tradition of his time in a world of oppressed people. Therefore, we may regard him as a Jerusalem-born version of Marduk.

The third level was the level of monotheistic religions. The old gods had mostly been local or regional deities, or deities belonging to a certain tribe. The Lord (*rab*) Jesus, however, was introduced as the God of all people, of earth and heaven. This may have been influenced, at least in part, by the Roman Empire's claim of universality. In this way, material conditions were once again reflected in historical progress.

Jesus was the answer of the Jahweh-based tradition to the pressure that the *imperium* exercised on the human mind and soul. In this tradition, he represents a new level – where conscience and morals come to the fore, of standing up for and addressing the needs of the oppressed. This constitutes a break with the old, conservative religion, in which God was exclusively a god of the Jewish people. Jesus' overwhelming influence was closely related to the structures that he came from and to the structures that he aimed at. Rome was pressing hard on the conscience of the people. Jesus' radical approach towards the Jewish Pharisees and scribes provided the oppressed with an instruction for rebellion. In his person and in his teachings Jesus became the new ideological framework of the age. He triggered a new epoch.

In view of the social groups he addressed, Jesus' activities were not aimed primarily at political rule, but rather at a spiritual and moral reorientation. He did not take the precautions required for taking over political power. However, the prerequisites for a "kingdom of conscience" were there. Although there are hints that Jesus had initially had his eye on the kingdom of Jerusalem, his movement was eventually focused on a long-term project centred around a community based on social, ethical and religious coherence and solidarity. In the end, it was his resistance to the official Jewish priesthood and their inner degeneration and collaboration with Rome that led to rebellion. Originally, Jesus believed he could take care of Jerusalem with the support of the masses, before he was arrested due to betrayal by one of his twelve disciples, Judas Iscariot. The Roman governor might have released him nonetheless, but the priests saw their interests threatened and demanded his crucifixion. If he had not been sentenced to death, we probably would have seen only one of the many rebellions characteristic of that time. However, the anger that grew from a mixture of these events and the repression suffered by the people led to a rebellion of symbolic historicity. The proverbial spark, Jesus' crucifixion, ignited a historical development which spread like wildfire.

The pure and naive character of early Christianity was bound to be transformed into theological discourse under the influence of several Greek philosophical currents, neo-Platonism in particular. At the centre of the discussion was the triune god, the holy Trinity, which was subject to many interpretations. These interpretations, though, show mythological traces going back as far as Sumer. There is a basic Sumerian religious concept consisting in a triad of deities: a father–god, a mother–goddess, and a strong son. This concept is found both in the Enki myths and in the Babylonian Marduk myth. Behind this lies the triad of the first ancestor (the founder of the ancestral line), the son as a representative of tradition, and the grandson. Hegel has given a more modern explanation: he conceived trinity as thesis, antithesis, and synthesis, calling them the dialectic rule, which in his opinion is the fundamental law that brought forth the whole cosmos. And in fact, we can find the effects of this law in all the processes of nature. There are antecedents of this view, however. In Zoroastrianism, for instance, there is not a trinity but a duality, which can be understood as a first form of the dialectic law, since thesis and antithesis do not yet flow into a synthesis. In Greek philosophy, Heraclites carried this approach further and with Hegel it reached its present, modern formulation.

No less interesting is the role given to Jesus' mother, the Virgin Mary, later in Christianity. The Virgin Mary described here differs clearly from her precursors Inanna and Ishtar. This can be explained by assuming that a number of later developments had already been included in the legend, like the slaughter of the mother–goddess Tiamat by Marduk in the Babylonian creation myth. Mary's relative powerlessness can probably be ascribed to woman's degradation, her banishment from history and her restriction to the house – beginning with Moses. The severe rules of the male-centred tradition of the Semitic tribes were in clear contrast to the matriarchal cults of Inanna and Ishtar, who were essentially goddesses of the agricultural communities of the neolithic. In the Babylonian epoch, this antagonism was dissolved by disposing of the last remnants of female dominance inherited from the Sumerian culture. After that, the mother is only a former goddess and an obedient and chaste housewife. Her voice must no longer be heard, and her face must not be seen. By and by, she is banished behind the veil and handed over to the harem. This process had begun with Moses, and the extent of enslavement that women are exposed to in Arabia today is directly related to the development described here.

The Virgin Mary can be seen as having been derived from women from a previous era, women who had originally been goddesses. Incessant loss of status had turned woman into a mere breeding machine by the time Jesus was born. From 2000 BCE until 2000 CE woman's history, by contrast with man's seizure of power and his ruthless methods of exploitation, was told as a history of the lowest class. Woman had been subjected to multiple forms of enslavement. Even during the Babylonian epoch, though, the mother–goddess Tiamat had been in the front rank of those who put up resistance; and Moses had to overcome heavy resistance on the part of his female relative Miriam, who did not want to bow to his will.

Let us return to the Virgin Mary, Jesus' mother, the mother of God. The Lord's breath, it is said, inseminated her, and she bore a child. This is an allegory of man's absolute dominance over woman. Moreover, it makes clear that woman's role is limited to raising children. Another important fact is that this act was ascribed to the Holy Ghost. In this way the authorship of the creative act was taken away from Mary and from woman in general, who had represented it for so long. In Sumerian terms, the Holy Spirit would have corresponded to the mother–goddess. This is quite important, because the ideological framework created here was largely responsible for the fact that woman's influence continued to decrease during feudalism.

Since those days, all Marys have been without profile. They weep silently for their children, while they are completely obedient to their husbands, as though they have always been captives. This condition has nothing to do with "woman's nature"; it is solely the result of man's ambition for political power. Where the mother–goddesses had dominated during a previous epoch, male gods dominated in the age of classes and states. This reality, the reality of woman being denied her freedom, is often hidden behind so-called moral rules resulting in shame, veils and harems.

We must add that what we may call "Jesus' teachings" had only been turned into a philosophical discourse by the patristic philosophy of Church Fathers after the beginning of the fifth century. It was then that Christian ethics were transformed into a binding theology, from which we can derive the ideological framework of the feudal age. Christianity became the official doctrine of the state. It became a constitutive element of feudalism after it had been untied of its reservations about Rome's slave-holder society and its originally egalitarian impetus. The result was a compromise in respect of the reigning status quo. After that, the *imperium* was no longer a slave-holder empire, nor was Christianity the former naive, egalitarian, sacred religion of Jesus and his disciples.

With Christianity began the dominance of dogma over the thinking mind. Between the fifth and the fifteenth century 1,000 years went by during which philosophy was dominated by religious thought. This seems to be a step backwards in comparison to the classic time of antiquity, characterised by the high standards of Greco-Roman philosophy. One reason for this may be found in the dissolution of municipal communities and cities and a subsequent renaissance of rural economy. A city is a complex structure, an aggregate of growing communities demanding rational thought, a sophisticated form of government and the division of labour. Rural communities, on the other hand, are homogenous, restricted structures and are thus susceptible to dogmatic thought and rule by single persons. Their economy does not require division of labour. Since these communities do not change very much over time, they are a breeding ground for religious dogmatism.

The achievements of classical antiquity, however, are still valid today. They are closely related to the awakening of the human mind and will. The only permanent achievement of the dogmatic age, so to speak, was its success in keeping slavery alive in one form or another, and in making it a basic constant in human social relationships. Despite all the rurality of that time, there was no way back to the free neolithic state of life. This state had finally been overcome by the slave-holder systems. Although the new society was also mainly rural, it constituted a real progress compared to genuine slave-holder systems. Humankind had acquired structures of morals and thought which could not be put back in chains.

At the beginning of the Middle Ages man was no longer the human being that we had found in Sumer and Egypt. Although he was still dominated by religious belief, his piety by this time was only for Heaven. There was no submission to a god–ruler on earth. This would have been regarded as blasphemy. Religion had freed man from such tyranny. The backwardness we observe, however, was caused by the disintegration of urban spaces and the weakening of rational thought. Despite all this, there were still towns and cities much larger than in the neolithic era, and the works of classical philosophy were still copied and kept in libraries and monasteries. I believe that our modern times would not have been possible had we not passed through the school of the age of faith.

This, in principle, was the world and time when Islam came into being. It is true that Christianity had lost much of its original content already, but it had modernised the huge Roman Empire from within and had become Byzantium's state doctrine. Byzantium was now superior to the Sassanian empire. On the other hand, the new religion had begun a military campaign against all of Europe. Therefore, we cannot speak of convergence between East and West based on faith.

What was the role of Islam in this historical environment? Was it something genuinely new or was history just repeating itself? Was it filling a vacuum, or was it a power capable of transforming an old civilisation? These are not merely rhetorical questions, and they need to be answered when we define Islam.

One approach, I believe, towards explaining the fast rise of Islam lies in its – for the age of feudalism – radical and revolutionary tendencies. While Christianity had become the evolutionary, reformative line of feudalism, Islam had taken the radical, revolutionary turn. We have shown that, ideologically, they derived from the same sources. The New Testament and the Qur'an provide conclusive evidence for a common origin of the two religions: they are both unthinkable without the Old Testament and the Torah, which, in turn, are rooted in Sumerian and Egyptian mythology.

It would be a mistake, however, to see Islam only as a new interpretation of the Holy Scriptures (Old and New Testament). Rather, we should focus on the dynamics of the time when Islam came into being and on the influences exerted by Islam. Without doubt, the prophet Muhammad was a revolutionary personality, outstanding in his time. In contrast to the great preceding prophets recognised by Islam (Abraham, Moses and Jesus) Muhammad was a concrete, historical person who knew how to express his will in a logical, clear and structured way and who tried to put his thinking into practice. He succeeded in making his doctrine the prevailing ideological power of the Arabian peninsula in the course of his lifetime. In this respect, only a very small number of persons can be compared to him, maybe Alexander or Lenin. As soon as we approach Muhammad from a scientific point of view, rather than from a point of religious dogmatism, we find a man who was an astonishingly imaginative ideologue, politician and agitator. Muhammad does not need to appear as a person surrounded and protected by a shell of holiness. Contrary to popular opinion, the dogmatic development of Islam does not do him honour, but has distorted his image and rendered him as a person surrounded by religious dogma. This is a reduction of his historical personality unworthy of him.

If we want a real renaissance in the Middle East, it is utterly important to free the prophet Muhammad from the hands of past and present dogmatism and despotism. The history of his doctrine is the history of those who in his name refer to dogma, contrary to what he had taught himself.

Islam was compromised by its followers from the very beginning and Muhammad and his teachings were betrayed from the first day, his family (*ahli-bayt*) and his friends had to suffer, and his corpse could not be buried for three days.

The Karbala incident is not only a historical tragedy; it also bears witness to the treason at the heart of the founding of Islam.[3] It was, so to speak, an anticipation of the incredible cruelties and fanaticism yet to come. Therefore, I believe that the history and reality of Islam need to be evaluated anew. The Middle East suffers from a distorted historical discourse. Only through fundamental reforms can modern individuality become a possibility in this environment. A clear view of the person and the teachings of the prophet can only be possible after dogmatism and despotism have been cleared away and the modern-day reincarnations of the Pharaohs and Nimrods disposed of.

Therefore, and in order to contribute to a better understanding of Islam, we will have to discuss some of the foundations of Islam.

THE UNITY OF ALLAH (*TAWHID*)

This term gains its fundamental meaning from the assumption that Allah exists, that he is the only god and that Muhammad is his last prophet. This raises some questions: existence and unity remain undefined; why is Muhammad the *last* prophet?

Islamic theologians have, of course, always sought to answer these questions from within the confines of their religion. Attempts at scientific analyses offered explanations that were only partially useful, since they were undertaken either without information about Sumerian mythology, or from a biased Eurocentric point of view. A Middle Eastern enlightenment must address this task itself. However, this seems to be impossible without breaking taboos.

Let us go back once more to the Neolithic age and the beginning of Sumerian and Egyptian civilisation, i.e. the transition period.

The polytheistic communities had been centered around matriarchal customs and beliefs. When, at a later stage, they were transformed into structures with high economic productivity, class and gender divisions were introduced. Since these new structures proved reliable, they created an enormous trust in the workings and the mythological and religious teachings of the priesthood, whose temples were simultaneously the centres of production. The social changes were made acceptable by the high economic productivity. In a new process, astral religions arose, i.e. religions focusing on the starry sky and its phenomena. The stability and invariability of the order of the sky became intertwined with the faith. The rise of fanaticism and bigotry in the religions of the Middle East, I believe, is closely related to this immovability of the heavenly order. It produced terms like *unchangeable order, beginning of time*, and *eternity*.

There is one useful aspect, however, to the idea of an unchangeable order: it is open to the possibility of constant laws. The immovable order of the sky was projected onto earth, too. Although the polytheistic basis was retained, the number of deities was constantly reduced. The gods who now came to the fore represented elementary phenomena such as the earth, the sky, water, air, storm, etc. They were not yet anthropomorphic, but as a logical result of the rising class-conscious society and the division of labour, it is mythology that now had to explain how these new deities created man and why people must serve them and bow to their will. It was in particular Enki, the wise and cunning god, who proved to be extraordinarily imaginative in the creation of master–servant relationships. He also taught the other deities what he knew. Nin-Hursag, the goddess of the mountains, and Inanna, her later manifestation, were assigned only minor parts. A male-dominated council of gods was then created (which later became the Greek *pantheon*). At this moment, heavenly order and worldly rule were in complete agreement. And the story of Adam and Eve and their expulsion from Paradise announced man's future fate: never-ending servitude.

What then were the important contributions of the Sumerian priesthood to the evolution of the concept of God? They raised the gods to heaven, made them overseers over the basic forces of nature and masters of man, their subject. They also introduced the master–slave relationship into social life.

Their purpose in doing that was, quite obviously, the creation of ideological foundations for political power. The image of God in Sumerian theology developed hand in hand with a social need for the development of a political space.

God was the ideological counterpart of the material phenomenon of political power. He *created* man as his servant. In this way, the concept of God became identical with the concept of politics. I'd like to add that, in my opinion, political order couldn't exist without creating an ideological counterpart for itself. Politics came into being in the shadows of the gods. It cannot be separated from the intellectual framework of its time, nor from the mentality its dogma and ideology are rooted in.

Therefore, any attempt at secularisation would mean destruction of the classical political power – which makes it impossible. The *tawhid*-idea seems to be closely related to the homogeneous geography of the Arabian peninsula and the desire of the tribes for unity. Immediately after the totemic stage, the concept of god in the tribal order of Arabia became congruent with the Sumerian El, who was already a generalisation of the divine, resulting from the Sumerian invention of Heaven. Nonetheless, many tribes had their own ideas of El, which were both a constant source of conflict and a growing motivation to strive for unity. Hence, the desire for unity among the Arab tribes explains the importance of the *tawhid*-principle. It was exactly at the time when the tribes developed their desire for unity that this principle, the existence and unity of the one god, El, was postulated. The Book of Genesis already tells us about a strong desire for unity among the tribes related to Abraham's tribe.

As long as all tribes in the vicinity of Abraham's tribe worshipped a different El, unity could not be established. All the different shades of El, remnants of the vanquished polytheism, had to be united. At least for his own tribes Abraham was able to achieve this goal, and from that moment he presented himself to the surrounding tribes as El's ambassador. The new divine identity was *tawhid*, the one God. Man could only be his prophet.

Politically, the new religious development manifested itself in the rise of the sheikhdom as the upper level of tribal aristocracy. Unlike the Sumerian rulers, a sheikh could never become something like a god–king. The sheikh was usually a tribesman, socially still very close to the rest of his community. Thus, not even the prerequisites of his becoming a godlike person existed. Abraham himself was a sheikh who was turned into a symbol of rebellion against the godlike Nimrod. Man tried to formulate his own identity and the new divine identity in terms of the contrast between man and god. Hence, the *tawhid*-concept marks a real progress in the history of religious ideas: it became clear that it is man himself who was responsible for slavery and who, therefore, also had to take responsibility for the slaves as human beings. Thus, *tawhid* brought about a "milder" form of slavery. *Allah* became something like the family name of the tribes that united in his name. Allah became their source of power. Worshipping Allah is equal to begging for help from desperation and for strength, and it is the slogan for a life of unity. For centuries the cries of "*Ya Allah*" (Oh Allah!) were the essence of the formula: "Let us unite, let us become strong, let us be victorious!"

Worshipping Allah expresses the desire for unity and strength. Words like "his beloved believers will find their way into Paradise" are only the fantastic, the metaphorical side of this. There is a social and political reality underlying every ideological position, consisting of differing economic fundamentals and interests which will reveal themselves with closer analysis.

At the time of Jesus, this great ideological change was immensely advanced. In principle, all forms of religion in the Middle East were very close to each other, so that we may rightly speak of a common monotheistic tradition. Religious (Muslim) tradition tells us that there were 124,000 prophets in the millennium between Moses and Jesus. We have to understand this number as symbolic of the number of sensitive, intellectual people in the community who helped to keep alive traditions and customs, the hope for the promised land and the Paradise people dreamt of, and, eventually, for the day of redemption. Although there were a number of prophets who gained enormous importance at certain times, such as Moses, David, Solomon, Jeremiah, Ezra, John the Baptist and Jesus, we must also include in this chain the unknown majority of those who worked as teachers. The chain of prophets was a sacred tradition of the society just as with the ancestral cults preceding it. Ever since Abraham, there had always been a need for prophecy, as it triggered new beginnings, particularly in times of crisis. Those who passed down the Holy Scriptures, traditions and customs are called "rabbi" by the Jews, "patriarchs" by orthodox Christianity, and "sheikhs" (*shaykh-al-islam*) in Islam.

It would not be quite true to put the rapid spread and development of Islam down to the power of the sword. The sword could only be successful where the conditions were ready for violent change. Elsewhere, force or violence would not have led to new social developments but rather to destruction. Islam, however, where it was successful with its immense revolutionary offensive, brought economic, social, cultural, and political changes, in a new form and with new power.

Let us return to the time of Muhammad. The conditions under which the prophet was born and raised in the triangle between Mecca, Medina and Ta'if were those of an urban area with a flourishing trade. This area was rich compared to that of the Bedouin tribes of the desert. By the way, the Arabic word for "urban area" or "municipality" is *medaniyah*, which is also the word used for "civilisation". The city name Medina is derived from this term.

At Muhammad's time, the relatively well-developed economical and social conditions were accompanied by stagnating political structures. The prevailing official ideology was reactionary and aggressive. While slavery had almost been overcome on the level of social and economic institutions, the dominant political structures persisted in their conservatism. This was the main obstacle in the way of new methods of production and social power. Besides, a new passion for life and new dreams of the people demanded change.

Christianity, which had been the hope of the oppressed for salvation in its original, naive form, had long since ceased to be a religion of conscience and morals and had become the tool of the powerful in their political intrigues. It served largely as a means of expansion and repression. The traditional Messianic faith had turned into a search for signs and symbols which might announce where and when the new prophet, the Messiah, was expected to appear, as the Scriptures had announced.

Arabia was, geographically speaking, in a peripheral position as far as the three great empires of that time were concerned. This was a great advantage. None of the three empires was ever able to incorporate all of Arabia. The desert forms a natural wall of defence. The regular armies could not hold out against the Arab tribes with their horses and swords. Camels were a great advantage in the desert trade. This all contributed to the tribes' strategic advantage. Although there were a number of military campaigns against Mecca by each of the three empires, they had to pull back every time, suffering heavy losses. Conventional armies were obviously unsuitable for the desert conditions.

A verse in the Qur'an alludes to this, saying that swarms of tiny birds, by throwing stones, wore down the Ethiopian army and drove it apart.[4]

While the cities prospered due to the trade with the empires, the desert tribes developed guerrilla tactics, which made them even harder to fight.

Abraham had already brought this traditional civilisation to a high level of development, making it an authentic part of the overall civilisation of the Middle East. As long as they did not have swords and horses, the tribes were hardly able to influence their environment politically. Afterwards, at the start of the first millennium BCE, they became more influential and soon the first Hebrew kingdom was founded in the West. This led to constant attacks during the following centuries by Egypt and Babylon, and later by Assur, Persia, and Rome on this and other new centres of civilisation. The empires had to contain the tribes and their trade centres and prevent them from becoming too powerful. The tribes had already contributed in earlier times to the fall of Sumer and Egypt and, indirectly, through Jesus, they had brought about the end of Rome. At the time of Muhammad, however, their civilisational line culminated in a new order, the influences of which can still be felt today, namely, feudal civilisation.

THE PERSONALITY OF MUHAMMAD

From what we know, Muhammad's personality was quite contradictory, his development inconsistent.

During Muhammad's formative years, the cultures of the three empires, which were spreading everywhere, were far ahead of Arab tribal culture. The tribal totems gathered in the "pantheon" of the Ka'aba were lifeless, unable to inspire any initiative whatsoever. The reason for this was that the superstructure was characterised by institutions and mentalities relying on the conservatism of the tribal structures. Men were to be honoured for their tribal membership, women were despised, and female children were handed over to death.

Muhammad undertook several commercial journeys between Mecca and Damascus, journeys which were crucial for the maturing of his thoughts. We know that he often talked with Christian Nestorian priests. Khadijah's (Turkish Hatice) trust in Muhammad, her love and their marriage seem to have been decisive for his positive attitude towards women. Perhaps he would never have become a prophet without her influence. In this respect, Khadijah seems to have been much more influential than the Virgin Mary, and may be regarded as a temporary return of the culture of mother–goddesses. It is only because of the patriarchal social structure in Islam that her personality is not acknowledged in an appropriate way in Islam.

On the other hand, Khadijah was obviously the first person in the society of Mecca to support Muhammad. She was older than Muhammad, rich, and powerful enough to own a commercial caravan. From this we can conclude that Khadijah must have lived in permanent, serious conflict with the Meccan community, which despised women and abandoned its little girls alive in the desert. Since she would not have been able to cope with this mad society all on her own, her relationship with and marriage to Muhammad became quite important. It seems to have been the political and ideological nucleus of a developing organisation against the official Mecca. That the prophet did not marry a second woman during her life we must attribute to her material and spiritual power, rather than to his respect for her as a woman or for women in general. She was the first to recognise his calling as a prophet, followed by his cousin Ali and Ali's slave Zayd. This fact also underlines her contribution to the development of his thoughts.

The composition of this group also had some revolutionary aspects. Zayd was a slave who had been released,[5] and Khadijah was a successful woman in the midst of a traditionally male world. In fact, these four people personified an ideological programme.

Before receiving his calling, Muhammad had spent some time secluded on the mountain of Hira, where he underwent a phase of meditation and concentrated ideological insight. Nearly all prophets underwent such experiences. The book of Exodus, for example, gives a lengthy report about Moses and his meditation on the mountain of Sinai.

When Muhammad, already in his forties, accepted his calling, a new revolutionary movement came into being. It was a transition from ideology to political action and then to open war – war for rule of Mecca. Muhammad's verses of this time focus on the foundations of faith and morals. They sketch theoretical aspects of the revolution and define its principles. Meanwhile, danger was growing day by day, and with the upper class in Mecca seething with anger, Muhammad's life was no longer worth a cent.

In 622, at the age of 52, Muhammad left for Medina, which seemed to be the only option left to him after he had dismissed the thought of going to Ta'if, which was wealthier than Medina.

We have speculated above that Christianity might never have become more than a simple, mystic community without the crucifixion of Jesus. Something similar is true for Muhammad. Had he not been forced to leave Mecca, had he not been confronted with violent narrow-mindedness and bigotry, he might have preferred a life in just another Gnostic community. However, the law of action and reaction started a process which by and by turned into a historical development. Muhammad's time in Medina was a time of military and political organisation. His verses now primarily dealt with the question of how the new political system had to be organised. In Medina a new "social contract" was agreed upon and a new city state was founded.[6]

This new state, however, was founded at a time when trade and commerce were already highly developed, and it was surrounded by several great centres of civilisation. Therefore, expansion and growth would inevitably be to the disadvantage of the neighbouring states. It was a matter of life and death.

The desert tribes had always fancied the idea of conquering the surrounding centres of civilisation. Their relative poverty made Muhammad's ideological awakening quite attractive for them. From then on things moved very fast. When Muhammad approached the end of his life, the political system had already been established.

THE IDEOLOGICAL FRAME OF REFERENCE

All epochs and civilisations have their own ideological frame of reference, what I prefer to call their "ideological identity".

Again, it is the Sumerian mythological foundation on the basis of which the Arabs at the time of Muhammad formed their own ideology. After the Babylonians and the Hebrews, this is the third time Sumerian mythology was transformed and fitted into a different tradition. Let us take a look at the older forms in order to explain what I mean. Let me add that I do not intend to belittlc thc mcaning of the Qur'an, or discuss its dogmatisation as though it were just some minor religious phenomenon. On the contrary, I believe it is our high academic duty to treat the Qur'an with an appropriate sociological approach *and* to show what are the interests hidden behind the dogmatic mask of Islam. Any enlightenment of the Middle East depends on completing this duty successfully.

I regard it as inappropriate to begin a discourse on Islam by discussing questions of the faith, i.e. of God's existence and His oneness. That would be the sophistic method which Socrates had already warned about. *Understand yourself* was his approach, and, following him, the question must not be, if there is a carpenter, or if he is good or bad as a carpenter, but, rather, how the carpentry can be done in an exemplary way. That is, says Socrates, the method of philosophy, the way of the wise.

We have already stated above that God's existence and oneness is the central point of departure of Islam. What were the historical and social developments leading to this point? What is its practical meaning? These are elementary questions we need to answer.

Before we return once more to the origin of the term *Allah*, I want to make it clear that I do not find definitions like "cause of the universe", "creator" and the like, to be particularly helpful.

I am stressing this because today's reaction also instrumentalises religion against enlightenment according to practical political interests. In Turkey and many other Islamic countries the reactionary forces often rely on such methods, which mean nothing else but exploitation on a large scale, aimed at securing their own interests.

Therefore, it is quite probable that my present considerations might be abused for similar purposes in the foreseeable future. In view of this I wish to make it clear that the term *Allah* will – and in my opinion should – continue to exist also in the emerging information society. It is a term which developed and still develops along with society. Today it can only be the name for the one fundamental universal law. The better we know this law, the better we get to know Allah, who is the name of this law. Any additional definitions and discussions, which go beyond a practical interpretation, I believe, only serve the interests of reactionary forces and help defend exploitation and fear and injustice.

In the light of these considerations we analyse the term *Allah* with sociological methods. We examine its sociological contexts, its effects on society, and its consequences in history. We will try to uncover the social needs and necessities which contributed to this religious identity, how this religious identity developed, and how it was transformed.

Everything we know about the life of the prophet Muhammad shows that he was incessantly focused on the conceptualisation of *Allah*. His main problem was to explain God's existence and oneness, which was obviously no academic or artificial question considering the intense efforts he made. A key term had to be redefined. Allah was endowed with 99 predicates precisely describing his divine power and capabilities.

We have already seen that the tribes on the Arabian peninsula had begun to accept El, which in the Semitic etymology is equivalent to "spirit" or "high soul", as their religious identity or frame of reference already in the second millennium BCE. We have also seen that in the Mosaic tradition this term was transformed, making El a national god. Nation and God are particularly close to each other here. The meaning of *Israel* is evidence for that: Fighter for God. Under the kings David and Solomon, when the first centralisation of power took place, this name received official character. Now, Elohim became the expression for Israel's social existence.[7]

Considering the wars, inventions, innovations and ideas which are based on this God of Israel, it is easy to see what a great concept is involved here.

Christian tradition began, in terms of content, as a break, in the name of the poor, with the official Hebrew tradition. As social differentiation increased, this tradition was also increasingly interpreted from the point of view of the oppressed. In the Gospel a new hope, a new desire for redemption, along with a new ethics, gained a new ideological identity. Elohim becomes *rab* (the Lord) in Aramaic, the language Jesus used. Beginning with the Sumerians and their successors, the different terms for god almost always had the connotation "Lord", which also hints at the rise of a new master class.

It was Jesus who related the term *God* to a number of ethically connoted qualities, such as mercy, compassion, redemption, forgiveness, peace, justice, love, etc. The Lord, as the new ideological identity of the oppressed, was strengthened by these qualities and became the energy source of a new historical offensive. The Christians as God's children, including in particular his son Jesus, became the new blessed community. They would be protected from all evil by their Lord, he would help them realise their hopes, and all prayers were to him.

This is another example of how a society can bring forth abstract concepts which help it to develop and change. It is also an example of the fact that ideology cannot be separated from economic and social developments. They depend upon each other, but sometimes it is ideology which forms the avant-garde.

I am driving at the following: a life on the basis of concepts containing hopes, faith, and thoughts, a life following these concepts and trying to make them reality, will be successful and lead to great developments. A precondition is that these concepts should not be contradictory to their time, but rather should aim at progress. Otherwise the result will be a strengthening of reactionary forces, stagnation and decline.

Even more important here were the predicates Muhammad attributed to his God. He used them to prepare for the intellectual change resulting from the growth of feudal economic and social conditions. Muhammad became the manifestation of the new concepts and terms, of a new ideological identity, and he reflected the integrity of the moral behaviour of the new social structures that were being formed. The real revolution took place in him as a person when he made the new concepts part of his own mind and soul, part of his own will.

The revelation of the verses and the proclamation of the Sunna, which contains the moral life practice of the prophet, can be understood as the creation of a new man and a new community.

It is characteristic of all prophets that they refer to God as the basic reason and concept underlying their actions. This is just as true for the prophet Muhammad, who was also an important merchant. Trade as a fundamental form of human relationship was now loaded with divine meaning. It became a rule of religion that man had a right to exact and just remuneration for all his prayers, offerings, and piety, and everything else he gave to God. In the monotheistic religions, God took forms which had much in common with trading companies. The tendency of that time was towards urban communities and the formation of states. This is in particular true of the Hebrew communities. The stronger and more powerful they could imagine their god, the stronger they were themselves. This was a fantastic new formula: the more powerful your god, the more powerful are you. If you can destroy somebody's god, you can destroy that person. Confusing somebody's god will confuse that person.

Muhammad had added to Islam, with his concept of Allah, some attributes associated with the political and military qualities of his revolution. While the Jewish concept of God was mainly characterised by contents concerning the social education and control of the nation, and Christianity added primarily moral, ethical terms, Islam extended this concept by adding military and political terms. Islam was influenced considerably during the phase of its formation by a number of philosophical and theological terms and concepts, mainly of Greek origin and derived from Plato and Aristotle. These terms and concepts focused, essentially, on questions of eternity and existence.

We also need to ask why Muhammad called himself the *last prophet*. That was an important step in religious terms. Muhammad put an end to the age of the long chain of prophets. From now on, so Muhammad implied, societies would no longer need prophets to announce necessary change and implement it. Society had come of age. A human society, which was able and mature enough to install its government according to its own free will, did not need a prophet. In this sense, Islam concluded the age of religions, and was the last universal form of religion at the transition from religion to philosophy.

In a certain way these considerations have much in common with Marx's statement that socialism would end the age of state-based civilisations, when societies were free of unnecessary classes and strata, and had become socially rational and mature.

Muhammad advocated his convictions concerning the existence and oneness of Allah with an extraordinary enthusiasm. He listed his predicates, described his personal daily life and his working life, described eternity and creation and defined Allah in all possible ways. At this point one might ask, why Allah, the almighty, who knows everything, needed this last prophet to make himself heard? Therefore, I believe, it is not only Allah who is described by Muhammad, but also the new class society (new for the Arabs) and the features of a new epoch of civilisation for the Middle East. The difficulties of this undertaking were due to the difficult structure this new civilisation should take.

In particular, it was the new political and legal structures that posed an elementary problem. Therefore, Muhammad believed, it made sense to include a number of qualities in Allah's predicates to deal with laws, rules, command and power.

Ideology must be worked out and disseminated in association with material production. This must be a permanent process. There is, I believe, an inseparable relationship between ideological structure and production in all societies, historical or present. It determines the fundamental social reality.

As I have mentioned, Muhammad addressed the conceptualisation of Allah with tremendous enthusiasm. This is a hint of the importance he attached to the success of this task with respect to the success of his political intentions. Muhammad's thinking, and I want to emphasise this, was essentially sociological. He also knew that religion alone would not be enough for a new society, that, moreover, religion and philosophy were deeply interrelated, and that reason and religion were frequently in conflict with each other. Here lay the source of Muhammad's doubts. And he tried to overcome them by proving the existence of the one God. The one and only God then was to become the source of law and reason too.

We have to add here that Muhammad genuinely believed that his thought and his actions were rational and right. He had sincerely taken in all tenable values of religion. He had founded the system of Islam knowing that rational explanations and insights could no longer be evaded. However, the interdependence and interrelatedness of philosophy and religion made a synthesis very difficult. The ability to find a viable synthesis in difficult situations, though, has always been a fundamental quality of prophets and other visionaries. It took a near genius to foresee, as Muhammad did, that humankind in future times would overcome its present level of thought and develop what we call today philosophical–scientific methods. It was a painful disappointment that his system, even at an early stage, was compromised by religious reaction, which since then has lain like a film of oil over the mind and soul of the *ummah*, the religious community. There is a significant anecdote about Karl Marx in this context. Marx was very interested in the debates on Marxism in France and tried to follow them closely. On one occasion he is said to have exclaimed: "*Je ne suis pas Marxist!*" – "I am not a Marxist!" We may safely assume that Muhammad would have exclaimed with an even sharper voice: "I am not a Muslim!" if he could have seen the contradiction between the present modern times and his *ummah*.

What happens today in the name of Muhammad amounts to an insult of his person. In himself he concentrated contemporary religion, philosophy and science on the highest level in order to establish an optimum order of state, society and productivity. In his own lifetime he shook the world. How can the present Islamic societies be called Muhammadan? They generate personality structures and they are unable to recognise the state they are in. There can be no doubt that we need a movement in these societies for the destruction of all idols and false gods, like the movements that began with Moses, Jesus or Muhammad. Such a movement must comprise all levels of mind and soul and it must spread to all institutions of the sub- and superstructure.

THE MILITARY–POLITICAL REVOLUTION

From the beginning Islam expressed its ideological identity in military attacks on the surrounding states. These attacks resembled those earlier attacks by the barbarian Goths and Huns on Roman centres of civilisation. While the Byzantine, Sassanian and Ethiopian empires, with their unwieldy structures, controlled the economically most productive regions, the life of the Arab desert tribes, with their growing populations, became increasingly arduous. Thanks to commercial contacts and raids since earlier Sumerian and Egyptian times, the desert tribes were well informed about the treasures of civilisation and this nourished their fantasies of paradise. Life in the desert had become the symbol for the torments of hell, life in civilisation a source of inspiration for the benefits of paradise. The rise of Islam demonstrated to them credibly for the first time that their dreams about redemption from hell and admission into paradise might become true. Hand in hand with the creation of a new spirit, a new unprecedented faith emerged, and in its name boundless courage, the spirit of sacrifice, and thirst for action followed. These were very intense dreams and imaginations: people really began to believe that if they died as martyrs, they would immediately find their way into paradise. They believed they would receive heaven on earth for their wounds received in battle. This shows Muhammad's genius: after generating such intense faith, he only had to organise his battalions and plan for action.

Technically, as already mentioned, the ready availability of horses and iron swords as well as the open desert plains gave the Islamic conquerors nearly unlimited opportunities to attack. Since the laws of conquest (*jihad*, derived from Arab *fataha*, which originally means "to open", "to unlock") were sacred both here and in the beyond, and offered a tempting perspective to the poor, the Islamic armies spread like an avalanche. It was one of the best organised revolutionary movements in history, and was ideologically and militarily well prepared to conquer the entire world. It was not difficult for Islam to become a source of inspiration and redemption, not only for the desert tribes but for all peoples in the empires of its time. It only took some justice and respect for their cultures to procure its acceptance. The proverbial justice of the second caliph Omar (634–44) corresponded to historical necessities. At the same time, Islam's ideological superiority played an important part in the successful wars of conquest. People were ready and willing to abandon the reactionary ideological identities of their former rulers.

Islam is often depicted as a religion of the sword. As we have seen, however, the sword needed, and could not do without, the ideological superiority of the new faith. Christianity had formed a new social movement of faith and peace during its first centuries. Islam developed, as it were, from the top downwards as a political movement of armed warriors. Its ideological, military and political components were concentrated into a single aggregate. Conquest and rule appeared as a sequence of rapidly proceeding revolutionary events.

Islam's military campaigns had some of the features of guerrilla wars against conventional armies. In cases of failure, the Islamic warriors withdrew, then quickly re-formed and moved on to a new attack. In this way, they were able to attack a regular army from all sides and wear it down. They did not get involved in the kind of warfare that focuses on single decisive battles. Rather, they used a long-term strategy. They incessantly refined their tactics, which allowed them to neutralise even large armies with smaller forces of their own. From the beginning, regular armies were at a disadvantage, since their maintenance was costly and their progress awkward and slow.

The political order of Islam was set up immediately after the military victories. For the most part, the old system of satraps and provinces, passed down from the old Persian empire, was revived and filled with new ideological content. Islam did not exploit new areas for civilisation. Rather, it used the Arab desert tribes and other similar groups to revitalise the existing older civilisations and renew them with its own new ideological identity. At the heart of Islam's psychological superiority lay the mental and moral dissolution of the slave-holder structure and the establishment of a new identity in its place. This new identity promised people honour, respect and justice. There can be no doubt that Islam had taken on the most prominent military and political tasks of the feudal revolution.

Political theory takes an interesting place in Islamic thought. Whenever political structures were under consideration, the God concept of Islamic ideological identity interfered. The rulers, i.e. the sultans, were called *dhil al-Allah* (shadow of God). Allah was also given a number of names with political content, such as "the Ruler", "the Powerful", "the Punisher", "the Just". These names were later used as attributes of Islamic rulers.

The enormous number of political predicates, or names, formed the ideological basis for the dark absolutism that was to come, and this inevitably produced a much more rigid understanding of power than was the case with Christianity. Its only difference to slavery was that in a slave-holder system the ruler could eventually become a god, whereas in the Islamic system he could only become God's shadow. However, Islamic rulers took nearly all God's predicates, especially those related to politics, and thus, in a concealed way, came disturbingly close to divine authority.

Because of Islam's ideological structure, the separation of religion and philosophy has never been carried out completely, and herein lies the danger for Islamic political theory. The more the power of governments degenerated, the more openly they indulged in atrocities, surpassing even those of the slave-holder systems. In the age of slavery neither the deities, nor their god–kings, had been greatly developed. The Islamic Allah, however, is a highly developed god with multiple and very distinctive political attributes. When the rulers, acting in his shadow, began to participate in these predicates, a fiasco was unavoidable. This aspect of Islamic history negates many of its positive aspects. This danger was not too obvious in its initially progressive phase and in its jurisdiction by interpretation (*ijtihad*) and judicial precedents, as these had, until the tenth century, left the political structures still relatively open. However, when this way of interpretation and discussion was closed by the fatwas of Islamic sheikhs and by blind imitation of tradition (*taklid*), pushing the Islamic system as a whole onto reactionary and conservative ground, the political order, too, was reinforced and cemented. While, in the wake of the renaissance, European civilisation since the fifteenth century began to change its content and its appearance, taking a rapid upward trend on the basis of capitalism, the despotic political institutions of Islam were to enter the most reactionary phase of Middle Eastern history.

THE ECONOMIC AND SOCIAL CONTENT OF ISLAM

When the rise of Islam began, trade and commerce in the region were experiencing a golden age. Before that, the Hebrew tribes, which had witnessed the first religious changes towards monotheism, had still practised barter. While life in villages and cities tends to produce a static mythology and lazy gods, trade and commerce, as a result of the permanent change in their subjects, stimulate abstraction. The capacity for abstraction is an important stage in the development of logic and a primary element in the description of complex processes in language and thought. Commerce needs gods who do not act arbitrarily, who are bound by laws, whose actions are rational, intelligible and predictable. For an understanding of Muhammad's god concept his relation to trade is crucial. The prophet himself was the product of a life on the trade routes and of his relationship with a female trader.

Trade and commerce, like political institutions and the military, were part of the ideological identity of Islam. The rise of Islam was the imposing rationale and proper representation of trade. For the first time, a family of merchants had set out to establish their own state with the help of an independent ideological framework and, with magnificent effectiveness, had given the new body its own unique identity and had created a new type of civilisation. Since the attempt at establishing a Hebrew kingdom around Jerusalem, no new culture had exerted such worldwide influence, making the Arab tribes a new social power. They initiated an age dominated by merchants and the economy of trade. There are many verses in the Qur'an or in the Sunna of the Prophet praising and even honouring trade as a sacred value. The Middle East already knew the idea of usury and the money trade, and had instituted the practice of paying interest. Trade also brought about the development of the money system and with it that of arithmetic and mathematics. Barter and economic exchange are still reflected in abstract thought and the in symbolic or metaphorical meaning of many words.

At the social basis of civilisation far-reaching changes took place. The economy was rearranged around trade and money was put into circulation as a universal equivalent in barter trade. Islam appeared as the trading power of the civilised world. As a world power of its time, it played a similar role in the development of free trade to that played by the United States today when it removes obstacles to free trade in the process of globalisation. By establishing reliable states between the big centres of production, Islam became an indispensable power in the development of civilisations from the Atlantic to the Pacific, from the Indian Ocean to the Siberian steppes.

ISLAM'S INFLUENCE ON HUMANISM AND THE INDIVIDUAL

Christianity had already overcome the national and class-based aspects of its predecessors, a crucial step towards a religion for all and social strata. For the first time, the term humankind was used in such a way that belonging to different tribes, races or classes would no longer stand in the way of fraternity. Like Judaism, Islam, too, started as a real international movement. However, Christianity, having a disposition to progress, still has the leading role among world religions today. Judaism, on the other hand, belongs to those religions which have retained their tribal character quite fanatically to this day.

Islam takes a medium position. Whether Muhammad did or did not say that an Arab was superior to a non-Arab (*ajam*) only because of his piety, we can see that Islam, too, has not completely overcome its nation-based character.

The existence of an upper class amongst the Jews made a chauvinistic understanding of the term "nation" practically mandatory for them, if this upper class wished to maintain its privileged position. Otherwise they would not have been able to give reasons for their position in society nor for the claim of the Jews for leadership in the world as the chosen people. Even Yahweh showed chauvinistic qualities when he jealously stated that Israel was his chosen people, which he had married. The idea that the historic Jewry was an elite helped the Jews to accomplish great intellectual and social achievements. However, differences and jealousy produced by Jewish elitist thinking often enough stirred hatred and enmity. The present tragedy between Israel and Palestine has its roots not least in that kind of historical legacy.

Early Christianity took a different approach and thus contributed a great deal to fraternity and peace among people. It tried to treat all ethnic roots, nations and different schools of thought equally. In this way it was the first serious attempt at a still primitive kind of socialism and the formation of a humanist consciousness, in fact, the first great international socialist movement. More important still in this respect, it also did not discriminate against women. Later Christianity, in its now degenerated forms, lost this character. Thus Christianity also needs modernisation in line with what it originally intended.

Islam, however, with its class character and its ideological identity referring to merchants and trade as the elementary power of its social and political model, is neither as folkish as Judaism nor as internationalist as Christianity. It is this without doubt that contributed primarily to the unification of the desert tribes and hence to the development of an Arab nation.

There is no definite folkish idea inherent to Islam: Allah is the god of all humankind. In contrast with Yahweh, Allah treats all different nations and ethnic groups equally. However, Islam lacks any clear identifiable socialist aspects. From the beginning, as we can understand from the Qur'an and the Sunna, there was – it has to be conceded – a comparatively mild sexual and class discrimination at the basis of Islam. Nevertheless, it already knows the ideas of humanism and humanity and regards all other monotheistic religions as legitimate faiths. All people are invited to take part in its system provided they pay taxes. Whoever behaves with hostility towards Islam, though, is treated as a heathen (*kafir*). *Jihad*, war against the heathen, is waged to the bitter end and regarded as a kind of religious duty and a common task of the *ummah*. The term *ummah* itself refers to something like the international Islamic community. Today we would probably call the members of the *ummah* the liberal class. Hence we can summarise by saying that Islam was historically a religion of the middle classes, whereas Judaism was a religion of the upper class. Christianity, in this context, was a religion of the poor, the outcast, of those at the bottom of society.

By its unifying influence on the tribes, Islam played a positive role in the formation of the national communities of the Middle Ages (*milliyah*), quite comparable to the influence of capitalism on the formation of modern nations.

Those individuals who came to power in the Islamic countries of the Middle Ages contributed much to the development of the tribe they had come from. Most of the rulers of the Islamic world were ethnic Arabs, Persians or Turks. This may be one reason why today the leading Islamic nations are Arabic, Persian or Turkish. Obviously, without Islam their fate might have been completely different. If Islam could overcome religious and national chauvinism, and in so doing become somehow internationalist and receptive towards peace and fraternity, a constructive contribution could be made to the solution of many international problems. Islam as well as Christianity needs to turn to an internationalist understanding of humanity, enabling a broader understanding and ideal of justice, and a meaningful peace.

Islam calls the individual human being the most venerable of all creatures. This description gives evidence of a deep human understanding that was probably particularly employed against slavery. People had been enslaved and humiliated for thousands of years in the Middle East. Islam restored their dignity, an important and progressive achievement in its age. Individual freedom, at this point, seemed to be more valued than the general freedom of the society.

The people of this time understood these aspects of Islam. However, Islam could not completely eliminate slavery nor could it create an environment that was as favourable to individual freedom as capitalism was many centuries later. Nonetheless, Islam contributed to both considerably. More than Christianity, Islam overcame slavery by radical measures. Its rapid spread over most of the civilised world of its time actually involved a large number of tribes and other ethnic structures in its progressive approach and protected them from slavery before it could threaten them. In this way, Islam, more than any other civilised system, helped prepare the world for the international system of capitalism.

13

The Institutionalisation and Expansion of Feudal Civilisation

Once it was clear that the mentality and identity constructs as well as the political institutions of the slave-based systems had been surpassed by the advances of the two religions based on the Abrahamite tradition (Christianity and Islam), the process of feudal institutionalisation and expansion started. As the slave-based systems of the East and the West were dissolving under the grassroots evolutionary subversion of Christianity and the head-on revolutionary jolts dealt them by Islam, they made way for new forms of civilisation.

Ideological transformation processes generate personality structures that unfold with the new social formations. This, in a manner of speaking, is the programme and framework of the new order. Its mass propaganda and mass actions consist of efforts to obstruct the functioning of the old society. These periods can be generally characterised as revolutionary processes.

With Christianity, the ideological process and the years of the revolution lasted for a considerable time. The pronouncements of Jesus and his disciples formed the basic character, framework and programme of this revolution. The centuries leading up to its recognition as official religion were the years of action, based on mass propaganda. In the face of dreadful torture and persecution, the first Christians dissolved the old beliefs and social relations and substituted new ones in their place.

Islam found its leading personality in Muhammad. Following his first pronouncements, he started the small but formidable Mecca group and went on to embark on a highly activist, revolutionary process at a very early stage. This revolution by and large achieved victory within the 40 years or so of the acts of Muhammad and the Four Caliphs (*rashidun*).

Any significant revolution has comparable stages. Revolutions set out to accomplish the first stage of their envisaged goals within a rather short period (whereas the process of social change, where evolutionary developments take place, lasts longer).[1] After this, the gains of the revolution need to be institutionalised and the system created by the revolution needs to be expanded.

This is a time of consolidation and of spreading the principles of the revolution and the initial model relations it established. Ultimately, the system reaches its peak, enters a period of decline and disintegration, and finally makes way for newer formations.

THE PHASE OF THE INSTITUTIONALISATION OF CHRISTIANITY

The institutionalisation of Christianity was a protracted process that lasted for between five and eight centuries, following its recognition by the Roman Empire and the overt settling of its characteristics in the institutions of the latter. This institution-building process was quite a leap forward compared to the catacombs and semi-clandestine monasteries. Medieval cities were founded or re-established in often elaborate architecture around the churches, domes and cathedrals. It was mainly the church that prepared Europe for civilisation. Wherever it went, it would establish universities, the higher concentration of population it attracted would lead to urbanisation, and eventually either principalities or city councils would arise where there had been none before. These often formed the minimal skeleton of what we would today regard as state structures. Some of the new urban settlements would later make up the core of states.

In any event, the church created the groundwork for the medieval state (or consolidated it where there already was one) by educating the people in the spirit of obeisance to the will of God. New spiritual doctrine and moral values were to underpin the foundation of the *Holy Roman Empire of German Nations* of the Germans and the Franks when the original Roman Empire had collapsed due to the erosion of its religious and moral fundamentals. There would not have been a subsequent European civilisation if it hadn't been for the church reaching out to the barbarians of Europe and educating them. Ideology is the key factor in civilising barbarian tribes, and there was no ideology to hand apart from that of the church.

As the Christian Middle Eastern system of belief reached the remotest corners of Europe by the end of the first millennium CE, the door to civilisation was pushed open. One cannot ignore this historical mission of Christianity by way of reference to its period of reaction and decline. Europe is the magnum opus of Christianity. This doctrine that had become infused into the rough-hewn tribes of Europe had been distilled from thousands of years of cultural development in the Middle East. During this period values related to Middle Eastern civilisation were directly exported to Europe, just as values pertaining to European civilisation are today being exported to the rest of the world.

In the high Middle Ages, the church dominated all political life. In actual fact, the church was the state. It subsumed those ethnic communities it operated amongst. These communities resembled each other under administrative structures which promoted the formation of the major peoples of the Middle

Ages. The crystallisation of polities around the framework set up by the church contributed immensely to the genesis of certain political concepts that were to take on a central meaning in the initial stage of modernity, such as *homeland* and *national community*.

This favoured model of organisation proved conducive not just to the development of common idioms and cultures. It is perhaps even more important to note that the religious institutions were based on written culture, and thus were, for a long time, the major carriers of alphabetisation and the mediation of cultural pools. The theological and philosophical traditions that were conserved and passed on in this way, albeit with an accent on religious doctrine, were invaluable material for the blossoming of reason and learning. This in turn provided a sound basis for the sciences that eventually emerged, not least for Renaissance thought.

Although Christianity spread as far as the Ural Mountains in the north-east, it was less successful in its eastward expansion. The Persian Sassanian empire, and later on Islam, averted Christian institutionalisation in their realms. The Assyrian and Syriac monks did indeed play a part in the dissemination of Christian ideas in the East and at least paralleled the contribution of the Greeks in the initial promulgation of Christianity in the West. But, although the Nestorians fashioned an original brand of Christian theology based on the Greek classics, thus making the accumulated teachings of Eastern Christendom available to Islam in its formative years, theirs remained a minority religion. The Nestorian priests made invaluable contributions to the transmission of the cultural heritage of antiquity to the medieval Middle East. With their roots in ancient Assyrian culture and the primary teachings of Christianity, they were amongst the outstanding intellectuals of the Middle Ages.

I cannot help but ask myself what would have happened to Asia if a kind of enlightened Christianity had become dominant here. I think that Mesopotamia lost a lot in forfeiting the chances involved in the enlightening, renovating teachings of Mani of Ctesiphon and of the Nestorians. Perhaps the fate of the Middle East would have been different from what it was under the profligate regime that Islam became in the hands of the Umayyad and Abbasid rulers. Such questioning could, perhaps, become a part of a critical re-examination of history in its ostensibly inevitable succession of causalities.

INSTITUTIONALISATION AND EXPANSION FOLLOWING THE ISLAMIC REVOLUTION

This stage in the history of Islam occurs with the seizure of power by the Umayyad Dynasty. The ascent and the enthronement of the Umayyads was possible only on the basis of a counter-revolution. Whilst Muhammad had partially relied on the Hashemite branch of the Quraysh tribe, Uthman and Mu'awiya relied on the Umayyad branch of the same tribe, which traditionally had held administrative power in Mecca. What Muhammad did in the narrow sense was to wrest power from this tribal community and to form a new state through revolutionary action. Not only did he have a visionary perspective of progress, but he engaged in the building of new political and military institutions on the basis of a new ideological identity, manifested in the verses of the Qur'an and the Sunna.

The Umayyad branch converted to Islam only after the revolution was fully victorious. They were not really keen on this, and presumably proceeded with a view to securing their vested interests, all the while having a secret grudge against the Muslims. As soon as the prophet Muhammad passed away, they speeded up their preparations. The governorate of Damascus, run by Mu'awiya, operated as the central branch of the counter-revolution. Mu'awiya had learned all the plots and schemes of the Byzantine art of ruling and was an experienced politician who employed the Barmakids, a powerful family of bureaucrats from the Persian imperial tradition.

The House of the prophet (*ahli-bayt*) was represented by Ali, a sincere and devout man who wanted to preserve the essential values of the revolution. He was politically rather inexperienced and, like most honest people, somewhat naive. Principled though he was, he was inclined neither to serious institution building nor to the art of rulership. No matter how successful he may have been as a militant of early Islam, he was significantly inferior to Mu'awiya when it came to matters of exercising power and constructing a state. Ali must have believed that everyone would embrace the holy religion as wholeheartedly as he did, but he was wrong.

The counter-revolution staged in the name of the Umayyad dynasty may well be counted among the most consequential examples of its kind in history. The notables of this house were by no means genuine in their approach to Islam. However, for all their inner resentment, they knew how to jump onto a moving train and make the best of the landslide successes of the new movement. Having made some headway during the caliphate of Uthman, they irrevocably seized power after Ali was killed and his son Hussein gruesomely martyred at Karbala.

The painful consequences of this ruthlessly plotted counter-revolution from 640 to 680 have been borne by the entirety of the Islamic *ummah* for more than 1,300 years. What it amounted to was really a revival of tribalism and dynastism that capitalised on the invigorating force of the Islamic revolution. To a much greater extent than is commonly assumed, it was this move that nurtured reaction throughout the history of Islam and added to the strength of the oppressive and exploitative character of the old society. What it left behind is prescriptive, formal Islamism and this, in my humble opinion, is a betrayal of the essentials of Islam.

Movements like those of the Twelve Imams, the Shi'a and many of the Bateni sects were in search of these essentials and sought to preserve them.[2]

Without belittling their efforts, I shall refrain from claiming that they were successful. I would rather suggest we call the history of official Islam a *history of counter-revolution*, provided that in so doing we do not follow purely polemic intentions, but seek to establish criteria to make arguable distinctions between revolutionary Islam and reactionary Islam. Any monolinear history of Islam actually conceals the histories of betrayal and counter-revolution and critically blurs the vision of all those societies who think they are Islamic.

A reliable account of Islamic history is a prerequisite for having meaningful debates about Islam today. Neither of the last-mentioned distinctions can do without an in-depth analysis of the phenomenon of the Umayyad counter-revolution. I feel that the lack of such an analysis has been one of the main reasons why intellectuals of Muslim societies have been so fruitless over centuries. Karbala is not only a moment of disaster; it is a perpetual history of malediction – the repetition of catastrophe throughout the ages.

What happens today in countries like Iran or Algeria, and in fact many others, is inextricably linked to this cursed reality and shows us that what we have to deal with is not limited to a remote instance of seizure of power. What is more, it confronts us with the reality that we should dicuss how an incomplete and betrayed revolution might be reinterpreted in the light of today's knowledge and how its legacy might be fulfilled. Many revolutionary processes have undergone comparable stages. The effects of the revolutions and counter-revolutions that occurred in France and Russia, by way of example, can still be felt in everyday life far beyond these particular countries. Considering the proportions, the universality and the length of the effects of the Islamic revolution, the necessity for finding specific and up-to-date answers to the questions it raises becomes all the more evident. It entails the obligation to fathom analytically the painful, crisis-ridden and "underdeveloped" (in the sense of having been condemned to backwardness) reality of Muslim societies.

Having said all this, Islamic institutionalisation and expansion did accelerate visibly under the Umayyads. Their armies conquered territories from the Atlantic Ocean to India, from the Caucasus to the inner parts of Africa. Political institution building benefited from the traditions of Byzantium and the Sassanian empire, much of this mediated mainly through members of the old elite of the conquered territories. Many of these, like the illustrious Iranian family of Barmak, were instated as leading bureaucrats in the newly created state institutions in return for their establishing bonds between their own social formations and the central powers.

The Persian empire served as a model for the Arab Islamic empire in many respects. We see here a very early tendency to compromise with the political institutions of slavery, clearly reminiscent of the arrangements that every counter-revolution makes with the dominant institutions of the *ancien régime*. The less than 100 years of rule of the Umayyad dynasty proved sufficient to establish a powerful empire in the name of Islam. But the conquests, the occupations and the pillaging also antagonised many and there certainly was never a shortage of oppositional currents.

Not only the movement of the Twelve Imams, but also the Khariji, the Bateni and indeed many other Sufi orders started to form at around this time. The first successful resistance was started in the region of Khorasan, in what is now Iran, an area representing a long historical tradition of Parthian resistance against the Hellenes, leading up to the formation of the Arsakid dynasty that defeated Rome.

At a very early stage of Islamic history, the impoverished layers of many Arabian tribes revolted in the same way as the Khariji, and the partisans of Ali (Shi'ites and Alawis) became a rebel movement breaking out not only among the Arabs, but among all the forcefully Islamised peoples. Ever since the times of Sumer, the peoples of Iran knew how to fight back any attacks from the West. When the rotten Sassanian empire collapsed under a few jolts, this tradition was again revived. Abu Muslim of Khorasan led a resistance movement supported by Persians, Kurds, Azeris and some other communities – including Arabian ones – until it became large enough to topple the Umayyad rulers in 750 AD.

This moment was a chance for a renewal of Islam. The memories of the revolution were still fresh. But the dynasty that succeeded, the Abbasids, were not much different from their predecessors and instead of installing righteousness, they ignobly killed Abu Muslim, the leader of the rebellion that had brought them into power. The consequences of this murder were as adverse as that of the murder of the imam Ali: it greatly contributed to the premature development of a reactionary character of feudalism. Both Ali and Abu Muslim were militant representatives of a tendency in Islam that cherished justice and the concerns of the poor, that was principled and opposed to tribal fanaticism. But the fact that this tendency never set up any political institutions but had to operate within the narrow confines of mostly clandestine brotherhoods and *tariqas* brought along a variety of unhealthy effects.

There is ample evidence to the effect that revolutionary tendencies turning into sects can have as reactionary consequences the seizure of power by the counter-revolution. This inevitably opens the way to degeneration. It is at the point where they fail to successfully build a new order that revolutionary tendencies turn into sects, and it is for the reasons underlying their failure that they do so. The accumulated deficiencies of failed revolutions, shortcomings and errors make it impossible for a movement that has mutated into a sect to remain flexible. No matter how repetitively the gurus of such ossified movements declare their loyalty to the remembrance of the revolution, they will end up exploiting it in one way or another. Under any historical circumstance, this reactionary sectarianism of the revolutionary opposition is one of the main breeding-grounds for the counter-revolution. The marginalised position that socialist and nationalist democratic movements have been forced into vis-à-vis the foci of power under today's conditions is no different. One could give dozens of examples as to what happened to revolutionary currents in Turkey, for that matter.

The Abbasid period is practically the same as the period of maturity in Islamic history. This was the heyday of the endeavours to philosophically underpin the religious exegesis of Islam. Long before their reception in Europe, Aristotle, Plato and other Greek classics were translated into Arabic. Science and philosophy were alive and kicking. They were supported by a remarkable boom in trade. During this golden age of Islam that lasted from the ninth to the thirteenth century, the East was superior to the West in every respect. The central state model was active in every principality and was about to burst into a generation of new local states. The focal point of feudal civilisation that Islam constituted in this age spread into Spain and China, Siberia and Africa. A world system of trade was established that included security and economic infrastructure, roads and caravanserais.

Christian Europe had a hard time stopping Islam from expanding further to the West. But at the same time it drew upon Arabic–Islamic influences in the fields of philosophy, the sciences, and even statesmanship. To Europe, the East was the land of fantasy. Its dream worlds were ornamented with its particular civil values. A number of Arabic works were translated into Latin and other European languages and dialects. India had entered a new stage of civilisation under the influence of Islam. Parts of China and most of the Turkic tribes of Central Asia were likewise Islamised, and the Turkish and Mongol warrior clans that were to make both the Middle East and Europe tremble had their springboard prepared for them by Islam.

In terms both of its geographic expansion and of its institutional solidity and intellectual depth, the Middle East went through the final stage of its leadership position in civilisation, as inherited from the Sumerians. It seems that the energy involved in the creation of several successive layers of socio-cultural development, starting from the time around 10000 BCE, found its ultimate expression in the palaces of Baghdad, in the reveries and dances that movingly accelerated before they finally faded.

THE UNIVERSALITY OF FEUDAL CIVILISATION

The Islamic as well as the Christian formation of feudal civilisation represent its universality. Both are attempts at governing humanity (potentially all of humanity) through an ideology that regards the ruler not as a personified deity, but as the shadow of God, in other words as His spokesperson. It is this trait of feudalism that distinguishes it both from earlier, and more backward, forms of civilisation such as those associated with slavery, as well as from more developed forms. The unlimited enslavement of human beings under the system of god–kings, with all that that entailed – the ruthless consumption of human life as a labour force, most dreadful and disproportionate punishments, and the cruelty of warfare – must be kept in mind when discussing what feudal civilisation was, and what it may have meant to people whose collective memory was pervaded by their recollections of the old system. This, rather than comparing feudalism to capitalism or even socialism, gives us the key to understanding its historical importance.

I believe it is prerequisite for a tenable notion of history to consider the birth of ancient mythologies and that of the monotheistic religions in the systemic context of slavery. Unfortunately, I have not come across many satisfying accounts of the power of ideology in history. The uninteresting form of discourse that treats historical issues pertaining to the field of ideology as though it was talking about processes happening outside of the lives of human beings may actually contribute to the relative unpopularity of scientific explanations, especially when compared to the mass impact that religious patterns of interpreting history still have.

But if millions of people today are still faithful to the ideologies of certain prophets to such an extent that they are prepared to die for their sake, is not that precisely because they have to live under various forms of Nimrod and Pharaoh-like regimes? There is obviously a confusion on issues related to the interplay of political processes and religious convictions that I fear can only be resolved when the Middle East undergoes a cultural renaissance. I will argue in Parts 4 and 5 of this book that the European Renaissance could only be of superficial and limited importance to the Middle East because of the basis on which it rests. The cultural basis of the Middle East, in turn, does contain what might be construed as universality. Its renaissance will have to be more thorough, and more comprehensive than the European one was.

Monotheistic religious ideologies are political ideologies from head to toe. Actually, I suspect that they contain deeper political implications than even the most elaborate contemporary political thought. The discourse of religion, with all its concepts (including Allah, the Prophet and the angels) is that of the political literature of its time. These concepts are being used because in the time in question, politics was made on the basis of this terminology, and because the collective mindset of communities of those ages had been accustomed to this kind of discourse. But this discourse functions as a weapon in merciless political struggles. To lose sight of this fact, and of the relevance of this discourse to present-day politics, just because we miss in it the matter-of-fact language of today, would amount to self-delusion. One should rather translate the prophetic tradition into the political language of today. Any meaningful struggle for secularism will have to rely on such efforts for enlightenment.

To recount, the most realistic appraisal of the feudal revolution and the political institution building that followed would be the one that acknowledges the relative degree of emancipation it brought about as opposed to the system of slavery. The Middle Ages as the scene of a system established under the leadership of Christianity and Islam may appear "dark" to someone looking at them from the perspective of recent modernity, but they certainly amount to a true age of enlightenment in comparison to the millennia throughout which slavery held its worldwide sway.

Obviously, a number of scholars would be critical of the medieval order for its putting a purdah on the remnants of classical Greco-Roman culture, and justifiably so. But we also have to acknowledge that, however one might want to characterise what was erected upon the heritage of Jesus and Muhammad, it constituted material progress for all those communities that had been at the receiving end of the Roman Empire. Although the extant material culture of the Middle Ages, as manifested in urban architecture and artworks, might not be as glorious as that of the Classical Age, the deconstruction of slavery in the minds and souls of humankind as part of the consequential processes related to the history of mentality should be appreciated in its own right. It should also be appreciated for its capacity to form a dimension of socio-cultural developments that would actually lead to the vibrant urban culture and art production that is part of the modern world. The real magnitude of the Middle Ages becomes apparent once it is located in the field of dialectical relations that we perceive as historical development.

14

The Peak and Decline of Feudal Civilisation

Both Islam and Christianity reached their peak between the eleventh and thirteenth centuries. Both were relatively unthreatened, exerting power over major parts of the civilised world. The heavenly empire of the monotheistic religions had reached its goal and there seemed not much left to do but celebrate the great victories. Nor were there any new worlds left to conquer. The empires resembled each other so much that there also seemed not much sense in destroying each other by waging war. But there was a battle for intellectual superiority through philosophical discussion.

All civilising powers regard such phases as the accomplishment of their goals, the peak in their development, just like an organisation succeeding in completing its programmatic goals. Any step beyond that is already a step towards decline, as the ideological material at the basis of the system has been exhausted. History teaches us that social processes follow the rules of logic, even though they do not completely resemble the processes of nature. As though they wanted to confirm the level of development they had reached, both civilisations began to lead intense philosophical discussions. These debates were characterised by discourses on logic, Aristotelian thought, and Plato's abstract concept of the divine. Terms like *beauty, truth*, and *the good* appeared as sacred values.

In those times developing a doctrine about meaning, origin, etc. seemed extraordinarily attractive. The strength of the Muslim Allah was that he accumulated and condensed the religious concepts and ideas of the preceding epochs into one eternal single god. When the practical results caused by the influence of ideas began to show, philosophy was highly rated and exercised an enormous influence in preparing the intellectual atmosphere.

The need for mature political theory was satisfied by Aristotle. Soon Islam and Christianity valued him nearly as much as the Holy Scriptures. Ideas hitherto banned as dangerous were now welcomed as the last hope. This development was represented by Thomas Aquinas in Christianity and by Ibn Sina

(Latin: Avicenna) and Ibn Rushd (Latin: Averroes) in Islam. The latter, in particular, wrote in-depth commentaries on Aristotle.

The feudal society had become mature and more complex, creating a number of new institutions, concepts and ideas, and educating its members. The level of faith and ideas created initially became insufficient under new and changing conditions. People started to question causes and effects, reasons, purposes and means. Philosophical commentaries were viewed as remedies. The next stage was that philosophy had to make way for reactionary, conservative dogmatism. A new phase began, a phase of religious pressure and torture.

After institutionalisation and systematisation of the new social order, other problems arose as a result of both the inner structure of the order and external factors. The basic question was whether the system was able to overcome these problems and continue its existence. What were the problems? New ideas had produced new schools of thought, partly in opposition to the prevailing order, which was unable to respond satisfactorily to many questions. Subversion and decline emerged as new dangers. Controversial discussion became inevitable. Union and harmony gave way to ambivalence and ambiguity. This was not necessarily bad. Rather, we have to ask, using the terminology of dialectic materialism, whether the new thesis and antithesis were able to develop in a stable and effective way. When conditions are not ripe for them, new ideas and opposite concepts often share a common fate. An extreme state of decay may occur when the socio-economic system with its entire sub- and superstructure has lost the ability to last, while at the same time an opposite pole with new ideas cannot form due to the coincidental internal and external pressures. Such times are times of crisis and decline.[1]

Western civilisation is slowly entering a stage of superiority, largely because of a growing awareness of the dialectic relations mentioned above. These relations are already affecting all social processes. Problems are dealt with by scientific methods. They are described, named, and associated with possible solutions in order to get timely results and avoid heavy losses. In my opinion, these are dialectic approaches and processes. Whenever action is taken, it is already a dialectic synthesis, since the antithesis has been taken into consideration from the beginning. The aim is always useful improvement of the present conditions and order.

The intense philosophical discussions within Islam and Christianity in the course of the twelfth century were the result of serious problems they went through due to both internal and external causes. Internally, criticism and opposition grew as the old ideas and concepts had lost their credibility. Externally, the systems had developed by expansion and war. Now they came under fire themselves. Natural disasters and population growth led to decreasing wealth; economic problems and external attackers became increasingly successful. These circumstances, of course, triggered intellectual reflexes. Practical solutions were sought. Let us take a closer look at the political options available under such circumstances. A number of examples in history show us how such crises can be solved.

RENEWAL OF THE SYSTEM BY REFORMS

This also includes restoration, although it is only a rebuilding of the same structures on the same foundations using new stones and fresh mortar. A genuine reform, however, tries to adapt the system to new conditions, in order to achieve a far-reaching continuity.

THE CONSERVATIVE METHOD: CONTINUATION OF THE SYSTEM BY PRESSURE

This is a method we often find in history, specifically when a system is intellectually completely exhausted, emptied of its content, meaningless. Under such circumstances, external threats are often regarded as insolvable and unsuited to compromise; reform is rejected. Bold resistance leaves "Victory or death!" as the only alternatives.

Whenever a system loses its ability to change, it resorts to all kinds of brutal and despotic measures as its only options for as long as such measures will keep it alive. Such systems can only be disposed of by revolution. Whoever and whatever survives must surrender and there will be a radical break with the old identities. The new order provides a new identity for all its institutions and structures.

This is the tragic face of history: suffering and blood come to the fore wherever dogmatism prevails under backward social conditions that persist in a stubborn conservatism. Humankind needs to understand that the only continuity in nature is continuous change.

Islam and Christianity were the universal powers of the medieval civilisation. At this bottleneck of history, they audaciously resorted to philosophy. The philosophical debates in both systems referred to the faith being weakened and corrupted as a result of its shaken foundations.

At this stage many – even great – philosophers appeared who tried to prove the permanence of the existing order by proving the existence of God with the help of logical arguments. They held on to Aristotle and wrote commentaries on his theories because of his then still unsurpassed logic and authority. In this way the complexity of philosophy increased considerably. Amongst these philosophers, as we have seen, were Thomas Aquinas, Ibn Sina (who was also the most famous medical doctor of his age) and Ibn Rushd. They tried to save religion on its way between peak and descent with the help of philosophy.

Once Aristotle had intended to save the Greek *polis* with the help of his political thought. The medieval philosophers tried to save the endangered orders in their states. These orders had been instituted as earthly reflections of the divine, both in Islam and Christianity. When the theologians of this time tried to prove the existence of God logically, they aimed at securing the continuity of the existing (sacred) order. Hence, their activities were intended as a strengthening of the ideological identity, of the ideological frame of reference.

The question whether God exists or not seems rather abstract and not very practical from a modern point of view. These philosophers, however, were deeply convinced that they were discussing the highest truths. Sociologically, however, they were discussing whether the existing order was, and should be, the only possible one. It was their goal to provide the official order with a new ideological identity. Sociologically, this is what was behind the immense efforts meticulously to prove the existence of God. (We had already found traces of this principle in the Old Testament with Abraham and Moses. We then proceeded to Jesus and Muhammad and the establishing of the Christian and Islamic political orders. From there we proceed to the scholastic philosophy of the Middle Ages.)

Unfortunately, to date no Islamic theologian has been able to bring himself to express this simple principle. Even worse, no scientific approach in this direction has ever been the subject of a lecture at the theological or sociological faculties of Middle Eastern universities. The debate is still about the theological question "Does God exist?" and its primitive–materialist negation by the social sciences.

The theology of Thomas Aquinas was certainly a step in the direction of Protestantism and the Reformation in Christianity. Another, conservative branch of Christianity became increasingly reactionary and eventually tried to stop Christianity's decline through the Inquisition. Reforming priests and the new and still rare group of scientists and secular philosophers were treated even worse than Jesus had been. Giordano Bruno was burned alive. Galileo only escaped the same fate after renouncing his theses. The Czech monk Jan Huss was burned, like thousands of other members of mystic sects, people believing in magic or the co-founders of new church tendencies.

The courts of the Inquisition became machines of doom, allegedly in the name of God, to save and protect the rule of the church against dissenting, free-thinking people and the emerging national awareness of the peoples. The existing orders hid their interests behind the mask of religion and protected their interests in the name of the divine. Struggles of this kind dominated Europe until the beginning of modernity and ended only after many long, hopeless and incredibly bloody wars. Secularism was a result and a lesson of the religious wars, a product of devastating conditions, which were eventually only very narrowly overcome. Two different developments were eventually responsible for the step into modernity.

1. **The reformation of Christianity**

   This development was a result of both growing national awareness and democratisation within the church. From the start of the sixteenth century, a long phase of reformative changes began and these achieved rapid successes, which finally led to the modern, democratic rule of law. This process relied on a new and powerful social class, the bourgeoisie. We may safely call it one of the many historic examples of progressive, ideological change. The Reformation was a crucial step towards the end of the feudal medieval civilisation in Europe.

2. **The development of secular, scientific thought**
   We are talking here about a way of reasoning completely cut off from the church or theology in general. The individual who relies on science is able to determine his fate by himself without turning to any divine power whatsoever. This approach eventually grew into a new faith or a new kind of religion, characteristic of our epoch.

These developments paved the way for new national languages and cultures, and for literature and the arts and sciences, all of which make the individual seem so important. This process, which had originally started with a society fixated on the divine, has resulted in a godless multitude of people, where the individual is the individual's only god. A new and acute danger, it seems to me, has appeared here.

In Islam, the age of the Abbasids was the classical age of science and philosophy. Its interpretation of Islam is what we call the Sunni interpretation. The Islamic community is the state. Following its ideology, the Muslim idea of God, a huge sultanate is created and Islam becomes a monarchy. Skilfully masked and wrapped in religious terms and forms, material power is introduced into and established in the society.

The political system of feudalism would not work with the totemic masks of the Stone Age. Prophets and philosophers had taught that gods were not human and humans were not gods. Hence, the human consciousness, in the course of a historical process, had to decipher the divine images, demanding a new idea of God and new interpretations of nature.

When Muhammad devised his concept of *Allah*, he was also part of this historical process. Therefore, his definition of God was rooted in earlier divine concepts like the mythological concepts of Sumer and Egypt as well as the philosophical terminology of Greece and Rome. The feudal society experienced an advanced universality and deepening of cultural values, and its ideology had to correspond to this. This was particularly true of the concept of *God*, which had to be an elaborated and credible one. God had to be almighty and omnipresent and an inherent part of a person's identity. In this way, the feudal authority, i.e. the sultanate, was intellectually prepared. The actual finesse lay in the fact that the conditions of reality were reversed: God, who was actually a reflection of reality, was called almighty, whereas the feudal rule became the shadow of Allah. These explanations may illustrate how religious debates had been conducted for demagogic purposes in our region for centuries, while the identity of the societies was and still is kept unchanged with the help of the mechanisms described.

Let me add a personal remark. I do not want to belittle the term *Allah*. On the contrary, I want to illustrate its real meaning as a term with a social existence, which is therefore as real and influential as the economy. In my opinion, Muhammad contributed very much to the development of *Allah*. I do not agree with the flat denial of God on the part of some primitive materialists nor with the absolute truths of Idealism. These just distract from the true meaning of God as a concept within social existence, a meaning that, I believe, can only be unlocked by sociological analysis.

In general, ideological identity plays a fundamental role in the building of political power and its social fabric. Here lies an essential part of the answer to the question: Why don't Islamic societies develop into democracies and republics formed within the ideological frame discussed above? Before they can democratise, they will have to overcome this identity and undergo a coherent secularisation. A genuine secular society only becomes possible by understanding and overcoming the traditional ideological identity that has infiltrated all levels of society in the course of history. Thus, only because of such a process will a secular republic and a democratic society develop.

Nevertheless, the initial character of Muhammad's *Allah* concept was progressive and creative, a strengthening impetus calling for action. It was historically successful. Later, and already mature, the concept experienced severe difficulties in view of multicultural structures. Local ethnic groups and tribes kept their own religious ideas as passed on by their cultures, while outwardly pretending to be converted by Islam. Almost every group of the complex society had its own idea of Allah, depending on their interests and their level of development. Beside official Sunnism there were many more informal mystic Islamic groups.

Opposing factions, above all the Qaramita (Carmathians) and Fatimids, reached for power.[2] The Islamic philosophers at the peak of their influence were invited to come to the rescue of their society. Between the tenth and twelfth centuries, the complex social and political processes were integrated into the ideological superstructure.

Al-Kindi (801–66), al-Farabi (died 980), Ibn Sina (980–1037) and Ibn Rushd (1126–98) introduced a philosophy into Islam which, when the first symptoms of decay in society and state occurred, focused on ways out of the crisis. The more credibly God and religion could be presented – and in particular if logical proof could be provided – the greater their ideological superiority. These philosophers contributed to the continuity of the state in the same way that the priests in early history did.

Thus, Islam produced a theology which was in fact more advanced than Christian theology. The works of Ibn Sina were probably as extensive as Aristotle's. Methodical thought and the accumulation of knowledge were on a much higher level than in Europe. Today, scientific and philosophical works have usually to be translated from European into Eastern languages. At the time of Ibn Sina the Europeans had to translate the works of the East. In contrast with Christianity, methodical philosophical thought could not maintain its standard in the East. A conservative way of thinking in Islam began to take the existing scientific and philosophical achievements as an insult to religion and opposed them.

Al-Ghazali and al-Ashari were the last thinkers of that age of philosophy.[3] The twelfth century witnessed the beginning of a conservative phase, and a rigid dogmatism gained the upper hand in Islam. Reason was no longer trustworthy and the only way open to philosophy was faithfulness to the letter of the Qur'an and the Sunna. Although there was a similarly conservative wing in Christianity, which led eventually to the Inquisition, there were also reformative, independent, rationalist tendencies which opened a number of important ways of development. Islam entered a dark phase of its history when it failed to initiate a reformative process and philosophical thought independent of religion. In the context of overall historical development we may probably say that Middle Eastern culture from the beginning of the neolithic at about 10000 BCE until the thirteenth century CE was the leading example of human civilisation. Thereafter, it increasingly fell behind the developing capitalist civilisation in Europe. The reasons for this development have not yet been examined thoroughly. There are a number of works by Western historians such as Gordon Childe or S.N. Kramer that try to correct our view of the history of the Middle East. However, historiography in the region itself is still characterised by a narrow-minded defence of religion and a yearning after past superiority.

The regression and conservatism, which started in the name of Islam, began with an ideological development. This insight will help us to proceed in a methodically correct manner. Between the tenth and twelfth centuries the Middle East was superior to Europe regarding its material riches, social achievements and urban culture. These are not the fields where the decline began. (The Europeans probably regarded the Middle East with envy; its riches and splendour posed a higher quality of life that their own. Maybe this was one of the chief motivations for the crusades.) Hence, we must find the reasons for conservatism and regression in ideology.

As early as the thirteenth century Europe witnessed great advances in science. The fourteenth century brought the first reformation processes in religion, and the fifteenth century the Renaissance. The Islamic societies evolved just the other way round. Philosophical schools were accused of heresy. In law the traditional decision-making process by way of discussion of judicial precedents (*ijtihad*) was brought to an end. Deviants and heretics were tortured in many different ways. Al-Suhrawardi, for example, a man who stood for free thought and an unorthodox philosophy, was skinned alive (1191). Mistrust against science and reason became key elements of the faith. Philosophers like Farabi or Ibn Sina were condemned posthumously as heathens. An era of bigotry, solely relying on knowledge based on hearsay and rumour, had begun.

Memorising the Qur'an and the Sunna was thought to be science and any independent work of reason was regarded as diabolical. This bigotry was a disaster for the Middle East, and the main reason for the end of its glorious history and its slide into backwardness. Here, where civilisation had begun with the rise of religious culture, religion was perverted and betrayed, its meaning denied, and its achievements buried. And these graveyards of culture extended everywhere during that time of bigotry. Even today we do not know what lies hidden there.

Islam brings about only limited progress and little creative change to the history of the Middle East in general. From an ideological point of view, it can be interpreted as the third adaptation of Sumer. The oneness of Allah and the messenger function of his prophet are phenomena which had been realised conceptually and institutionally at a much earlier stage. In Islam these concepts came to control social tradition and the intellectual world.

Islam, however, employed revolutionary methods with great success and in this way catalysed and accelerated the development of a feudal civilisation resting on serfdom. Islam intensified this process and strengthened its institutions. This was a decisive factor in the expansion of feudalism and influenced and gave shape, even as an external power, to the development of feudal civilisations in Europe, India and China. In fact, Islam, being the religion of merchants, peasants and tradesmen, was an exporter of feudalism. The transcending of jihad, the sanctification of conquest, and the idea that those who die in the course of jihad immediately go into paradise as martyrs, as well as the fact that injured veterans receive a large share of the stolen goods, can only be understood in the context of exporting an ideology.

The period between the seventh and tenth centuries, when Islam came into being and matured, can be regarded as a time of expansion of the feudal revolution. This was followed by a period of bloody conflicts of interest, raids on neighbouring emirates and dynasties, and a complete lack of progress. Since the twelfth century, religion was used as a tool for various political interests and tendencies. Sunnism became the official and most conservative denomination, while Alevism developed as a religious movement closer to the oppressed people and with some rebellious characteristics. It also kept in touch with the cultural tradition of the people. Other denominations turned against tyranny and lies, and esotericism and Sufism regained strength. Mysticism as a reaction to institutionalised religion was characterised by introverted behaviour and a kind of idealism directed against the worldly power, while focusing all hopes on the world beyond.

These were mostly quietist movements arising as a result of defeat and powerlessness, and, let me add a personal impression, they resemble very much our present leftist groups. Alevist movements which came to power, such as the Iranian Shiites or the Fatimids in Egypt, succeeded in building their own political order. However, they are far from any Islamic reformism. Apart from persistently referring to the house of the prophet (*ahli-bayt*) as their origin they have no other ideological foundations and no developed philosophical or political programme. There are no ambitions either to create or advocate a new social basis. There is no capacity for progressive action. When they gain power the socio-economic patterns remain the same, the political programme remains practically the same, although its verbalisation gives it a place in what we would today call the left camp.

In this way, the centuries-long confessional wars could only produce deep-rooted divisions and political and economic exhaustion. This results not merely in backwardness, but also in blind quarrelling between numerous groups and factions. This mixture almost completely prevented economy and trade from developing.

During this time trade flourished in Europe and the system of mercantilism was created. A middle class came into being. In the Middle East such a middle class could not develop and, therefore, there was no counterweight to the central power. The system became, inevitably, more and more reactionary.

In principle, it was reliant on the fruits of wars and conquest for its existence. When the possibilities of conquest were exhausted, the political system turned into a degenerated, useless and superfluous institution. Conquest and expansion had taken up all its energy. Now it practically froze into a reactionary status quo, which manifested itself in the sultanates. There was no longer adherence to Islamic principles; the original ideology had been given up. The Islamic system had degenerated and was occupied with power struggles reminiscent of Byzantine intrigues. The epoch between the twelfth and the fifteenth centuries was characterised by decline and fall.

The following centuries, including our own, can only be described as an era of darkness for the Islamic societies. There is no sign of development anywhere. The decline is complete. In the words of the faithful, what the Holy Scriptures call eternal damnation seems to have seized all spiritual and material institutions. A dramatic contradiction becomes visible. For millennia, negation and antithesis have helped human societies overcome backward spiritual and institutional structures, requiring a new synthesis, creating something new. Here, in the Middle East, we find that the powers that had been negated and overcome in the past have returned and are preventing any development.

However, in my opinion it would be wrong to explain this phase of Middle Eastern history as solely caused by Islam. There must be reasons lying deeper than the surface of Islam: the more deeply a form of culture or civilisation is rooted in a certain place or region, the harder it is to create something new from it by simply antagonising it. New things need new soil.

Let me give an example. The Magdalenian culture represents a peak among the hunter–gatherer communities (until about 10,000 BCE). Traces of it can be found in particular in present-day Spain and France. Despite its cultural supremacy in the palaeolithic era this culture did not make the transition to the neolithic stage we find in the Middle East. One reason for this may be that this advanced palaeolithic civilisation did not contain the conditions and dynamics for its own negation. Its inner dynamics and its environment did not provide this community with properties enabling it to overcome its conditions and external influence was necessary. A civilisation that has deeply internalised its values and established and stabilised itself in its environment to such an extent that any other form of existence seems unthinkable can only be forced into change by external influence. Its dissolution and renovation need the impetus of external dynamics.

Conditions in the Middle East were different. Its geography and climate, its flora and fauna, the valleys of Tigris, Euphrates and Nile formed an environment of constant change, where alternatives to the neolithic communities could develop. The first state-like communities came into being based on slave-holder systems. For a long time different kinds of communities existed side by side. The systems did not follow or replace each other, but, rather, new developments can be found outside the old neolithic centres. Lower Mesopotamia was inhabited by backward clans of hunter–gatherers at the time when new groups from more advanced centres of neolithic culture first began to settle there. They realised that the soil was fertile and suitable for irrigation and thus a new civilisation came into being beside an older one. So we find two historical civilisations side by side in Mesopotamia, which is probably what makes this the most productive region in history.

Feudal civilisation also had its origin outside the area of the older contemporary civilisations in an urban centre in the midst of the desert, at a crossroads of caravan routes. It could not have come into existence in Mesopotamia or the Nile delta. Here the slave-holder system had incorporated itself into all aspects of life and the mentality of the people. These systems were not able to change from within in any fundamental way. Anything new, therefore, necessarily had to grow outside of them, although the two systems were in permanent contact and under mutual influence.

This finding is consistent with the dialectic rules. The negation of the negation is one of the laws of motion of history. Let me explain this in more detail. The new system comes into being as an alternative (negation) to the old system (which came into existence as a negation of a preceding order) in an area outside the old system. It then begins to neutralise the surrounding instances of the old system. It conquers them, materially and/or ideologically, and overcomes them.

After Islam had successfully played its part as the third great advance in the Middle East, it immediately began to lose touch with its history. This is sad but understandable. Muhammad's prediction that he would be the last prophet becomes quite meaningful in this context. After the rise of Islam there seems to be no more space left for utopias in the Middle East, no new contribution to civilisation possible from here. As a creative power, the Middle East, the mother of civilisations, withdraws behind the curtain of history. My hope is that it will rise again, and experience a renaissance in harmony with its past.

The mythological memory of the Middle East is fragmented, its religion long lost, and science never rose here. It only witnesses something like the proverbial dialogue at the foot of the tower of Babel, where everybody speaks a different language, and nobody understands anyone else.

The history of the Middle East in general and the history of Islam in particular can teach us a number of important lessons.

All these lessons run together in a single point, a desideratum for the Middle East: the region needs something similar to the European Renaissance, a rebirth of historical values and achievements now buried and forgotten. We must admit that the glorious ideological identities of the past and all the values they represent have long since decayed.

The first step of enlightenment will have to be a detailed scientific, sociological analysis of all the mythological and religious elements of our past by scholars of the region. Bold and versatile debates in the light of such analyses might then enlighten where opinions diverge. Apart from an appropriate understanding of history we will also need the courage to advance a new ideological identity based on a realistic view of the future. Revolutionary practice will lead to a (however belated) renaissance of the Middle East.

The Indian and Chinese examples of feudal civilisation are quite limited in their originality. Since the fourth millennium BCE both of them entered a process of adopting achievements and forms originating in the Middle Eastern neolithic. We may assume that the Harappa and Mohenja-Daro civilisations of about 2500 BCE had developed from originally Sumerian trade colonies. However, when after 1500 BCE the Aryans with their bronze weapons began to settle there, they contributed immensely to the rise of a continuous Indian civilisation. Similar developments are known to have happened at the banks of the Quang-Ho. Here, around 1500 BCE a political structure developed which was dominated by priests. This later resulted in a centralist regime with a god–king at the top. Several hundred years later these regimes entered a long phase of political and ideological confusion followed by a number of restorations, the last of which took place between 250 BCE and 250 CE. Then the slave-holder system slowly made way for a new civilising development: feudalism. Kung-Futse and Buddha played the role of reformation prophets and were the pioneers of a political system employing milder methods of exploitation.

Around 500 CE we find the characteristics of political change towards feudalism. The processes in the Middle East still exerted massive influence on East Asia at that time, and Islam's repressive impact in particular served as a catalysing element for the feudal development of India and China. Between 1000 CE and 1500 CE their feudal systems experienced a period of maturation followed by an increasing dependence on the rising European national states. Eventually their feudal systems declined.

Let me name the Aztec and Inca civilisations in South-America as final examples of the general model which went through a similar process beginning in about 500 BCE and ending in the sixteenth century, when they were terminated by the Spanish conquerors.

15

Some Concluding Remarks on the Preceding Chapters

The basic qualities and the historical position of feudal systems are still sociologically relevant. Slave work had lost its original productivity and had become an obstacle to new conditions of production. This was the fundamental antagonism leading to the end of the slaveholder system, as we can see from the Roman example. Slaves, not only as workers but as human commodities, had been the essential factor that had enabled the creation and rise of the slave-holder system. When the number of slaves exceeded what was needed for production purposes, and the club of slave-owners faced ruin, the system inevitably started to collapse; and at an increasing rate, because its cornerstone – slavery – had become the reason for its unproductivity and decay.

Additionally, there were continuous price rises in the cities and urban centres and permanent wars. The populations of the cities grew steadily and feeding them became a real problem. Now productivity stagnated, while the population grew. It became increasingly hard to maintain the cities, which had grown rapidly to their current size. Excessive urbanisation and high cost of living were central factors contributing to decay.

Similar considerations apply to the wars of that time: while they had initially been a source of productivity (when new regions were being opened up to civilisation) they later became necessary for border protection and the crushing of revolts, which made them a source of losses instead. The armies ceased to be stabilising factors and became the seat of unrest and internal power-plays.

Extensive landed property was another reason for unproductivity. Large *latifundia* had come into being covering every inch of cultivated soil. The peasants could no longer relate to the soil.

Hence, we can identify several different dissolution processes concerning basic elements of the system. These dissolution processes converged in a general crisis deactivating even those institutions and organisational structures still intact at that point. Additionally, internal revolts and hordes of barbarians flooding in from peripheral regions eventually put an end to the system.

The end seems to have been inevitable, neither increasing repression nor a far-reaching statism could prevent the transition to a new system.

This new system had to provide solutions for the open questions that had led to the decay of the old system. In particular, solutions had to be found for the great number of slaves dislocated from the production processes, unemployed soldiers, estates remaining uncultivated, the cities that had grown like abcesses, unproductive wars and a general atmosphere of insecurity and uncertainty. These were problems that could not be overcome by a restoration of the old system. The new system was characterised by an exodus from the cities, the disbandment of the large armies, avoidance of war, and the creation of limited but clearly defined areas where life was safe again. The overall picture resembles some kind of retreat, if not even a return to preclassical times. However, most cities continued to exist with smaller populations. The great *latifundia* were divided and granted in fief to the peasants, who in return had to pay certain taxes. In this way they were related to the production process again and able to support their families over the year. Slowly and within limits, new property was created. People turned away from the cities and rediscovered the soil as their main foundation for living and the wars of this epoch were no longer for slaves but for land. Man had (largely) ceased to be a commodity, and wealth and power were no longer measured by the number of slaves somebody owned, but by the number of acres his estate comprised.

This redistribution of land and estates led to the order of principalities and fiefdoms, which we call the feudal order. The basis of the principalities was the right to property and the peasants were tied to their feudal lord as serfs by means of the land that they worked. They were neither as free as in the neolithic nor as enslaved as in the classical age of slavery. The towns, which came into being around the seats of the liege lords, were rather small. Based on the new and more efficient order of production they grew only slowly to the size of cities. Both rural and urban areas were adapted to the new order. This was not a backward development but genuine progress. Civilisation had stepped back from a rapid and uncontrolled population growth under conditions where that growth could not be managed economically. Instead, the basis of production had been altered in such a way that civilisation could again begin a continuous line of development and progress.

This definition of feudalism is helpful in understanding why this age is not the source of new mythologies, religions or philosophies. Feudalism is a mixed system producing mixed ideologies resting on the known forms of both the neolithic and the class society. It refers to their ideological structures of identity and does not have the power to create anything really new. Feudalism differentiates and reforms the already available political, economic and ideological instruments and tools. Intellectually, Aristotelian philosophy remained the unsurpassable borderline of human thought for many centuries during the Middle Ages. The Arabs called him the "greatest master", *al-ustadh al-azim*.

Concerning faith, the intellectuals of the Middle Ages only reproduced religious dogma. Copying and memorising the Holy Scriptures (both in the East and in the West) was nearly equal to wisdom on the highest level. Dogmatism became a heavy burden for human thought. Creative thought was unwelcome. This is, in my opinion, what makes us call the Middle Ages "dark". Its intellectual efforts were centred around faith and metaphysics, which might never be questioned. The human mind seems to have been locked within their constraints.

However, man had risen from being the slave of a god–king to being the subject of a liege lord, who is only the earthly shadow of the Almighty. At the same time, the new system allows for the (albeit limited) free will of the individual. Man belongs to himself only in as much as he moves within the realms of divine mercy.

The inner face of the darkness attributed to the Middle Ages by modernity needs to be explored more precisely. (In my opinion this darkness has become even darker in modern times.)

I believe that it is the loss of ideological identity that lies at the heart of this medieval darkness.

The ideological equipment with which a political system comes into being, its soul so to speak, loses its meaning and becomes estranged from its original content as soon as this equipment has been materialised in visible economical, political and social structures. What follows, if there is no new movement of enlightenment, is ideological darkness. The ideological framework moves away from its original content. It bows to private interests, producing ideological deformations and aberrations, fake denominations, demagogic discourses – and schools, temples, and other ideological centres become the sources of spreading darkness.

In the Middle Ages, philosophy is made a tool of theology for proving the existence of God. In this way the pure, naive gospel gets lost, which originally had related to the individual's conscience, enabling awakening and an ethical attitude. So the political system is deprived of its legitimate foundation. It is reduced to struggles and wars about open material interests. Moreover, philosphy used as a kind of filling material for what theology has left unanswered only confuses people. As a reaction to this confusion, mysticism is advanced, followed by seclusive tendencies and ideological division. Real intellectual progress remains rare.

At this point we immediately recognise the function of the critical values of the Enlightenment in Europe.

A deepened study of nature and doubts about social conditions resulting from religious dogma were part of the foundation of the Renaissance. Light comes from two sides: the rise of the scientific method as a way of reasoning about nature frees the mind for new things, while the increasing individual search for freedom cuts off the ties of religious dogma and paves the way for an ethics free of religious constraints, and the free will of the individual.

Here, at last, we can't help asking if the civilisations originating in the Middle East were not and are not able to produce, by and out of themselves, something comparable – a question which can still be asked in today's political context. Do we not find considerable efforts and sacrifices towards such a development amongst the Arab scholars of the tenth to the twelfth centuries, in particular in the writings of al-Kindi, al-Farabi, Ibn Sina, al-Suhrawardi and Hallaj al-Mansur? All of them were passionate seekers after the truth, which they respected more than any political or economic interests. Love of the truth was their predominant motive. Great Sufis (Islamic mystics), such as Mawlana Jalal al-Din Rumi and Muhyi al-Din Ibn' Arabi (1165–1240), taught their followers to seek the truth with the help of their intuition.

Apart from a rich literature there was also scientific progress, particularly in mathematics, medicine, astronomy, botany and zoology.

Famous examples of the epic literature of the Middle Ages are the classics *Shahname* (Book of Kings), *Layla* and *Majnoun*. Ibn Khaldun's philosophy of history is even quite close to dialectic materialism.[1]

In practically every field, the East had overtaken the West. Nonetheless, nothing even remotely akin to the Renaissance in Europe ever took place in the Middle East. The invasions of the Mongols may have played a part in this, but I do not believe they were a decisive factor. Rather, we may contribute this to an ideological apathy, overwhelming dominance of dogmatism over the mind, and political intransigence and rigidity.

The Christian religion, however, which also originated in the Middle East, played quite a positive role in the intellectual and structural development of the European nations. These tribes, whose barbaric traditions were still alive, succeeded as the result of a rather superficial synthesis with the Christian religion. Christianity is the greatest gift the Middle East gave to Europe. It not only contributed to Europe's intellectual development but, more importantly, it formed a new and special ethics. Without the foundations created by Christianity, a civilised Europe would have been unthinkable. Europe profited from a combination of the qualities of Middle Eastern civilisation with the liberal tendencies of the barbarian (Germanic) communities.

Therefore, the fall of Rome was a positive development for Europe, as well as being the absence of such forms of rule as were characteristic of Byzantium or the Ottomans. Loose political confederations and principalities offered a better ground for development than the Middle East. The formation of a free mind and an individuality corresponding with it was favoured by the absence of ideologically and politically immovable structures. This is also the misfortune of the Middle East: its political culture made the formation of a bourgeoisie impossible and prevented loose federations and independent principalities. Deeply rooted dogmatism left no room for the individual, and wherever individuality was sought nonetheless, it was suppressed without mercy.

Civilisation was an old tree in the Middle East, which bore new fruit when its shoot was planted into the fresh European soil. Therefore, in my opinion, Europe is not the work of the Europeans. They took the seed of civilisation and planted it into their own environment and proved able to renew and refine the old plant. That is the great European accomplishment. This is an important distinction. The average Middle Eastern personality usually does not know what is its own achievement, nor does it know what it has given to Europe and what it may take from it. Herein lie the roots of the apparent hopelessness of the Middle East: its civilisation cannot bear itself anew.

But why does it seem impossible to dissolve the mental structures of Middle Eastern societies from outside, with the help of science and technology? If we take a look at China, Japan or India, we find that these countries at least were able to choose what they took from Europe: socialist China, liberal–conservative Japan and democratic India, with their rapidly developing material possibilities and capabilities, are more and more following the road of European civilisation.

The Middle East, however, stubbornly resists any change worth mentioning. It is, so to speak, history itself which resists here, history, society and culture as a whole. I shall discuss this phenomenon more thoroughly in the last part of this volume.

In this context, there are two terms which, ever since Muhammad, have had a key function: love of God, and love of truth. People believe that religion is a way to reveal truth, at least in part. Western (Greek) philosophy, however, maintains that truth can be found by means of reason, and in modern times has developed the scientific method and the experimental sciences.

The beginning of the Middle Ages in the East is marked by feelings of loss. The ancient world is gone, mythology has been forgotten, obvious social contradictions are not understood; nature is regarded as full of secrets and inscrutable; man is without orientation. There is a permanent search and longing for truth which eventually is projected onto Allah and his 99 qualities; He becomes the focus of all human dreams, of all love, and of all longing. His prophet Muhammad is seen as a mediator, who is expected to plead on behalf of His creatures. By focusing all their love onto God people hope for redemption from all human contradictions and for the fulfilment of all their desires. The ideological world of Islam provides the superstructure, the rest is accomplished by liturgical regulations, the laws of shariah and those who watch the keeping of these rules.

The prophet Muhammad himself, who was a progressive person in the context of his time, lived his relationships with women as a reflection of his love for God and thus raised woman and family for a short while to an unprecedented status and meaning.

Originally, the distance between love for God and love for a woman was not great. However, in the course of time sexual relationships lost their spiritual content and were subjected to quite unacceptable social measures and rules.

The deep longing and idealisation of love in the Middle Ages can be understood against the background of the lost past. All medieval pleading to God talks about this great loss, all love poems are full of metaphors of treason, powerlessness, painful losses. Middle Eastern culture is imbued with it.

It is described in the tragedy of Hallaj al-Mansur, and of many more, in the poetry of Mawlana Jalal al-Din Rumi as well as in the bitter love hymns of Yunus Emre. They all bemoan decline and values lost. The Middle East declines while Europe rises, and while it declines it suffers and moans, and produces martyrs and poetry. The entire high literature of the Middle Ages until Fuzuli is centred around this moaning and suffering, and life and love are hopeless in these writings. All loves end in fire and ashes. This reality also found its reflection in the popular tales of this time: Layla and Majnoun, Kerem and Asli, Ferhat and Shirin, Mem and Zin are names still known today even by uneducated people of the region.

In my opinion, the age-old Middle Eastern culture and civilisation passed slowly away between the tenth and the fifteenth centuries, and after that its remnants were buried in concrete. Whatever civilisational Middle Eastern values might have survived were eventually disposed of rapidly and violently by the Mongols. The Ottomans then only had to guard the cultural graveyard. The decline was complete after the conquest of Constantinople by Sultan Mehmet. Let me add some personal, and maybe quite emotional, remarks: from then on Arab Bedouins relieved themselves on the magnificent Egyptian works of civilisation and wild desert tribes performed their primitive rites and idiotic dances amid the ancient buildings.

In Turkey, the Ottoman palace order covered everything with deadly silence, including the death of newborn babies, which were slaughtered ritually for the sake of power. All of this happened in the name of Islam. The system of Islam had degenerated and in such degenerated systems everything is about death instead of life.

Such a morbid power was also in evidence when Jesus was murdered, and later when Nero burned Rome.

The Ottoman empire, painted in the colours of Islam, performed the final act of this theatre of death. Its palace music and court poetry seems only to be interested in moaning and the miserable delights of illegitimate concubinage.

Let me put it more clearly. While the palace indulged in bemoaning the great values of lost civilisation, the living, decadent and coarse, performed their primitive dances on the graves of the dead. The curse that seems to lie on the Middle East, therefore, is not simply caused by unemployment, heat, blind contradictions, and lack of education, but is also a consequence of the achievements of the past, which have been betrayed.

For this reason, analyses of the Middle Ages cannot monocausally focus on feudalism. They must also take account of increasing cultural loss and accelerating civilisational decline in the Middle East.

The seemingly everlasting regional war between Israel and Palestine illustrates perfectly the terrible mechanisms at work in the Middle East when it comes to delivering acts of revenge on both sides until nothing more remains but barrenness and destruction and, eventually, human life becomes impossible. In my opinion, it is civilisation itself that takes revenge here on those who betray it.

The history of the Middle East is like a chain of processes, each of which is the sum of all social and evolutionary powers at work. This chain ended somewhere during the Middle Ages. Genuinely new processes have not been added since. What can be done to continue this chain? My answer is that we should regard the rising European civilisation as helpful for our own culture instead of watching it with hostility as a competitor. There is no need for a war of civilisations. Civilisations can be friendly to each other as well. People in the Middle East should make their barren ground a holy land again and boldly and generously open their hearts to all that exists. Then, maybe, their own renaissance will become possible in accordance with the values of civilisation that were lost from this region countless ages ago.

Part 3

The Civilisation of the Age of Capitalism

Introduction to Part 3

The process of the formation of societies can be described as the accumulation of power within certain structures. This may sound highly abstract and needs some additional clarification.

Biologically, man is not a very strong or dangerous animal. How was it possible that such an animal could obtain such power over so many aspects of nature? The answer to this question can be found in the process of forming social groups and, eventually, complex societies. Consequently, it might be more important to ask, what is it that makes a social group more powerful than the individual and what, in turn, makes the individual stronger as part of a social group?

In nature, we find countless examples of mergings – ensembles of atoms or masses of organic and inorganic matter. Often the result of these mergings is the formation of new properties and qualities. This does not happen only in the inorganic world – there are even a number of well-developed social groups or formations in the animal kingdom, most notably among the ants and bees, the primates and the marine mammalians. However, none of these phenomena has developed anything comparable to a human society. Whether we talk about ants or apes, they do not have what of all animals man alone has: consciousness and creative power. Another important question in this context is to what extent does the individual deserve priority over the society, and vice versa? To what extent is the socialisation process an advantage to the individual and when will it become a disadvantage? Let me put it the other way round. How much individuality is useful and necessary for a society, and when does it become harmful? And why, in general, do most people not care about these questions?

Answering these questions will bring us closer towards defining capitalist society. In fact, capitalist society *has* to answer these questions.

Hence, we have to discuss the potential power that the individual can draw from the process of organising a society, from the permanent development of this society, and from its increasing dynamic creativity. We have to ask, what did people gain by forming a society and what did they lose?

The history of human social development shows that the individual always had to undergo a process of painful adaptation – painful because of the brute force applied. Even positive qualities, such as emotions like affection, were always intertwined with violence and threats in the adaptation process. The formation of societies was a continuous initiation ritual and a preparation for membership that rested on rewarding and intimidating the individual.

It was a merciless struggle, in which the losers might lose everything, including their lives. People were made to feel that their lives were at stake if they did not belong to the community in question. Therefore, they had to follow the rules and requirements of that community. Any person who did not comply with these conditions of dependence and who, therefore, had to remain outside the community, would not be able to lead a normal life but was going to die as a weakling or outcast.

In terms of survival, a human baby is for many years after birth at a great disadvantage compared to other animals. Yet, by belonging to even a small community, such as a tribe or a clan, the young child is raised under conditions that are far more positive. At this point, socialisation – social development – enters our consciousness like an extraordinary, magical power that can only have its origin in something divine. We can assume that the ideas of religion and divinity were the first and most significant reflections of this extraordinary and magnificent power potential in the social identity of man. In fact, the power resulting here formed a creative ability – creativity being regarded as one of the foremost qualities of the divine. This was not yet and not primarily a matter of religiousness, but since we do not have any evidence for creation out of nothing, tagging divinity to the creative power of societies seems an understandable concept. The better we understand its potential power, the more importance will we attach to the processes involved.

It is at this point that the vertebrate animal that man still is liberated itself from its existence as a passive creature in nature and passed through a development by which it gained a power that seems to enable man to actively control nature. The initial steps in this process of forming social communities produced a number of social extremes, involving numerous leaps in quality, passing from lower to higher forms, from one phase to the next. All difficulties and obstacles were answered by forming or re-forming corresponding social formations. Despite the limited anthropological and socio-historical evidence available, we may assume a permanent line of development. This tendency was not stopped by individual cases of stagnation or deviation from this line or even by the destruction of communities – such cases can be understood as remnants of the friction between the new and the old, no longer necessary in the evolutionary process of social development.

The principle underlying this development was the proper integration of the individual into the framework of the society. As this phenomenon became stronger, arbitrational power regarding social relationships and differences between individuals was vested in social conventions, customs and rituals. In this way, a society's social customs became its laws. When they eventually ended in rigid traditions, they often had a detrimental effect on the individual's initiative and motivation. At a certain point tradition became a force that made itself felt as counterproductive and paralysing. Nonetheless, in pre-capitalist societies social conventions, rules and customs were the only way to secure the survival of the individual. In class societies, official norms defined by the state supersede customs and social conventions. Compliance is enforced strictly by the state – if necessary by the use of violence. These conditions make the individual dependent on the state and its institutions and, eventually, lead him into captivity and slavery – materially as well as mentally.

Ideological and material realities had always been seen as a reflection of divine order. Pre-capitalist class societies and their inherent exploitation were characterised by constant structural dependencies. These were strengthened and consolidated by repression and torture and a belief in supernatural powers, myths and wonders. Over time, an increasing imbalance between society and the individual developed. Society and its rules – the limitations imposed on the individual's freedom – weighed heavily on the people, creating an increasing longing for liberation, which eventually led to resistance or rebellion. Man started to develop new ideas of God and new ways of living his social life in order to survive under the powers of the official order. Opposition formed.

The oppositive society was closer to the individual. The search for freedom was accompanied by new social movements and a search for new ideological frameworks and orders. A new ideology and its followers could take the place of the old, if they survived their opposition and were able to prove their productivity.

As we have seen, similar tendencies existed during the transition period from slave-holder society to feudal society. After a long phase of (enforced) social coherence and dominance of society over the individual, the individual's conscience and soul reawakened. People freed themselves from the age-old shackles of social customs and traditional laws. This tendency did not stop with the onset of feudalism, as can be seen in the writings of a later stage: the love for God expressed in mysticism and the medieval quests for love reflected the individual's flight from extreme social pressure and a search for freedom. Medieval literature describes romantic relationships as almost sacred and the quest for such relationships took fantastic forms and promised redemption for the individual.

If we regard the increasing importance of the individual as one of the main factors in the rise of capitalism, the deep, strong and widely branching roots of European liberalism become even clearer and more obvious. This also helps us understand why the doctrines about society put forward by scientific socialism could not prevail. As long as society continues to exist as a heavy immutable core, liberal individualism will always seem superior to socialism. Only if the core of the old society can be dissolved will we find the conditions for creating a real balance between individual and society.

Capitalism draws its creative power and energy mainly from the decay of social structures – societies – which, after thousands of years of constant growth, collided with the demands of the individual. In this respect, scientific socialism seems very narrow-minded to me. It even counteracts any striving for liberation by copying and tightening traditional social structures. Let us have a look at the geographic and chronological dimension in the genesis of capitalism. All matter is generally thought of as bound to a four-dimensional matrix of time and space. Social structures are also material phenomena, hence subject to the same physical conditions as any other matter. In particular, social formations are formed, develop, and decay when they are no longer well adapted and thus they will be replaced, or they are transformed into a new structure. A society in which these formations follow each other in a natural way can be said to have adapted its structures quite successfully to the changing demands and spirit of the times. This is why, in my opinion, a primitive tribal structure cannot jump directly into capitalism. If some clans or tribes are taken up in capitalist societies this does not mean that they have made such a jump by changing their old structures into new ones. On the contrary, their old structures have become meaningless and given way to seemingly more successful structures. A social formation will only then reach a stage of maturity – and simultaneously retain its own identity – when it corresponds well with the demands of its times.

Capitalism could only come into being as a result of and after the formation of all those social structures preceding it – i.e. it could only emerge when and where the necessary preceding links of the chain had already developed.

The same holds true for the spatial dimension of sociality. Any social formation is directly dependent on spatial conditions, primarily upon the general physical conditions crucial for human survival. The first social formations emerged in places suitable for hunting and gathering. Higher formations like those of the neolithic came into being where wild but tameable animals and plants suitable for cultivation could be found naturally. The great achievements of the neolithic produced the transition into the class society. Slave-holder society is a result of the dialectic process, in which the neolithic social structures were confronted with new conditions resulting from their growth and their achievements. The new social structures continued to exist and spread in time and space until they, too, were confronted with contradictions and physical limitations resulting from their own development.

Hence, *where* a social formation emerges is just as important as *when* it emerges. Social formations can only be understood in their temporal and physical context – i.e. they are part of their historical and geographical environment.

However, societies tend to portray themselves as original and different on account of their particular ideological identity. As a result, they are tempted to exaggerate their accomplishments and deny the successes of others. The ability to distort realities and write history correspondingly thus becomes a measure of historical success.

Social history resembles a living organism endowed with memory, imagination, will-power, drive and reason. Modern science has largely been developed in capitalist societies. European historiography never cared much for what the neolithic, with its centres in the Fertile Crescent, has given to all of humanity over thousands of years, nor does it care to discuss its fundamental contributions to all forms of social development. In my opinion, history cannot be written without taking into account the creative achievements of that age, which continued for millennia and played a fundamental part in the origin of the cultural matrix of mankind.

The Greco-Roman antiquity, which lies at the basis of European civilisation, is the zenith of a development that includes the Sumerian and Egyptian civilisations. It seems impossible to me that European antiquity could have developed without substantial transfer from the older civilisations. Their contributions to European civilisation are not limited to the spread of neolithic achievements into Europe since the fifth millennium BCE, but continued into the fifteenth century CE. Only then, with the Reconquista of Spain, did this transfer end – a transfer which included the social structures and cultural values which formed their sub- and superstructure. This short survey makes it clear that much of what Europe is, including its means of production, its mental patterns, its ethical values and its forms of faith and religion, originated in a different time and region.

To evaluate the accomplishments of capitalism, we thus need valid definitions of those civilisational values that resulted in the birth of capitalist society – both for the sake of history itself and for the knowledge of Europe's contribution to the stream of civilisation.

16

The Birth of Capitalism and Its New Ideological Identity

Social systems can be characterised by the material conditions of production within these systems and the distribution of property resulting from the production.

The predominant means of production usually gives the social system its name. In the first primitive local communities, tools of stone played the most decisive part. Hence, we call these communities *palaeolithic* and *neolithic* (from Greek *palaios* (ancient), *neos* (new) and *lithos* (stone)). During the time of the first class societies the enslaved human being had become an object of trade and had taken a crucial part in the production process. Hence the term *slave-holder societies*. During the Middle Ages, land became a means of production with increasing revenue. The *feudal form of society* is characterised by the spreading of the iron plough, thus making more and more land accessible to agricultural production. Slavery changed into serfdom. Now, people were no longer property that could be bought and sold, but belonged to the land that they lived and worked on and thus they belonged to the landowner. *Capitalist society* is characterised by industrial production. Here, man and land recede into the background. The factory is the main factor in production. An uninterrupted production process takes place, enabling an increase in productivity unknown to societies based on farming and trade.

Capitalism was the social system that emerged around these factories. The factory was the place of the highest concentration of capital, originating in the Mercantilist manufactories of the sixteenth to eighteenth centuries in Europe, where trade and money were concentrated. What we find here is a form of the accumulation of capital that we already know from Sumer. The transition from manufactories based on manual human labour to the industrial production in later factories became possible by the invention of the steam engine, i.e. by the introduction of a new technology. In other words, it was the transition from manufactories to industrial factories which caused an unprecedented increase in productivity. And this is where capitalism was born – and where our definition of capitalism begins.

As a real definition, the above description is inadequate and incomplete. It is, in my opinion, also too backward to be used to define any kind of society. Nonetheless, vulgar, materialistic approaches like these have been used and thus contributed in no small way to the early decline of so-called real socialism. The meaning of ideology and morals, historical understanding, even the concept of the state were simplified in a reductionist way. An approach with such deficits at its point of departure, namely in its definition, cannot be expected to lead to an alternative form of society.

This inadequate definition of capitalist society has resulted in a struggle against capitalism that has been incapacitated by mistakes and errors, a struggle which therefore remains unsuccessful. Capitalism is even gaining strength and inflicts painful defeats upon its opponents. The failure to comprehend social phenomena often yields myths and rough philosophical and quasi-religious views, rendering human life inevitably tragicomic. The great world wars caused by the capitalist system have at least some roots in such a lack of comprehension. Lack of knowledge produces ignorance, which in turn results in blind quarrels. Hence, overcoming ignorance lay at the origin of philosophy. Overcoming ignorance means overcoming pseudo-science and fears resulting from lack of knowledge. It even takes some of the pain from the prospect of death – as I can testify.

A careful consideration of its ideological identity and frame of reference may improve our concept of capitalist society. To create and uphold social systems requires a substantial amount of mind and will-power. Without an identity defined by an ideological frame of reference to order and channel the available will-power, the means of production are nothing but dead matter. Unfortunately, many social scientists do not seem to live up to their responsibilities. Participating in the social sciences is certainly different from participating in the natural sciences. However, as illustrated by the history of the atom bomb, even in the physical sciences an experiment that fails or an invention that goes astray can have catastrophic results. Studying and teaching the social sciences require at least as much responsibility towards and knowledge of the society as is required from a physician towards the human body. This knowledge, combined with a calm, critical analysis of social conditions and institutions, is a precondition for understanding and implementating the results gained. However, broad levels of society still lack these qualities for a progressive development and the tragic results can be seen day by day: irrational behaviour, torture, war …

Another important question about the formation of capitalist society is why the centre of its civilisation lies in Europe and by the shores of the Atlantic – and not in the Middle East. Islam had used up all political and ideological material, all the traditions of the Middle East and brought the region to a standstill. All religious myths and all forms of political authority that had been developed there ever since the Sumerians reached a dead end in Islam. In the high Middle Ages the Islamic Middle East was more highly developed than Christian Europe in terms of the material conditions of production and political systems and in terms of science and philosophy. It was not the Mongolian storm that shattered the Islamic empires but their decay from within – in much the same way as the collapse of the Roman Empire was not caused simply by a number of attacks by barbarian hordes. Islam's essence, its values, had been used up, leaving it an empty shell with increasingly fossilised political institutions. This internal decay determined the fate of civilisation in the Middle East.

At the end of the high Middle Ages, the development of Middle Eastern civilisation came to an end. Islam as an ideology was out of its depth with the advancement of civilisation because the simple exegesis of Islamic writers interpreting the Qur'an was out of its depth. This still holds true. Against this background of used up strength we also understand why Muhammad called himself the last prophet. Islam was the last act of a civilisation that lasted several thousand years, and which was fully aware that it was gathering all its strength for a final era. The Umayyad treason already indicated that the development would be rather short-lived – in spite of good conditions initially. At the end of the Middle Ages, the Middle Eastern decline was complete. Now the question is: How can a new civilisation in the Middle East be created? Mecca and its environment had been a piece of uncultivated soil in a remote corner of the Arabian desert. With the emergence and spread of Islam from this region, the desert culture gave its final civilisational push. Since the fifth century BCE, Greco-Roman civilisation, based on the achievements of the neolithic in the Middle East, became the basic blueprint for Europe. Christianity was the last educative measure Europe received from the Middle East. Islam, both by its transfer of ancient knowledge and by its conquests in the Iberian peninsula and the Balkans, served as midwife, assisting (rather violently) a new civilisation with its birth. This is the framework within which European civilisation developed. Let us now discuss some of the characteristics of its ideological identity.

A MIND BASED ON POSITIVE KNOWLEDGE

What we regard today as distinctive European thought is characterised mainly by the application of the scientific method and the knowledge gained this way. This method of reasoning is primarily what lies at the bottom of European civilisation and is, therefore, a basic condition for the rise of capitalism. The myth-bound mind-structure of the early days of mankind and the medieval world, marked by religion, were overcome step by step with progress towards capitalism. Gradually, a scientific way of thinking, which had been prepared for by the philosophy of Greco-Roman antiquity and the European Middle Ages, was to gain acceptance. It was based on the observation and explanation of nature and its phenomena. Its difference from traditional philosophy lay in the fact that philosophy hitherto had tried to explain all that exists in general terms and ideas, while the emerging new sciences aimed at explaining a more limited set of phenomena by referring strictly to observation and empirically gained data.

However, the two ways of thinking had something in common: their roots. In animistic societies all of nature is alive and animated. There is no difference between organic and inorganic matter, nature and society, man and animal. Any application of this world-view, any animist "technology" would result in what we call magic. The art of magic, therefore, produced the first leaders, the magicians – those who were more skilled and had more foresight than others. They were extraordinarily admired, even if their contributions could often only be small, since they helped their group to survive. As already mentioned in Part 1, the first social institution was the magicians. In the palaeolithic, this was replaced by shamanism.

The neolithic way of thinking was a more progressive social stage, partly animist and partly totemic–religiously structured. The tribe as a basic social unit became distinguishable as such and with it the meaning of affiliation to the tribe. The position of the mother, as a leader and creator, came to the fore. Woman in general gained recognition for her social role; she played a dominant part and enjoyed extraordinary power. Even today these mental structures are reflected as feminine elements in the grammar of many languages (and in feminist criticism!). The mindset of the neolithic, however, was characterised by a man–god structure, resting on a feminine basis and with the mother–goddess at the top. Under her, all important beings were ordered according to the importance attached to them by man.

With the rise of the class society in Sumer this way of thinking developed into a system based on myths and legends. Production of food and other vital resources as the most necessary and important abilities of society were reflected in a world of gods that corresponded to the master–slave relationship of the emerging social division into classes.

Philosophy was the next important step in the history of thinking. *Philosophy* originally means "love for wisdom" (from Greek: *philia* (love, friendship) and *sophia* (wisdom)). Even at this early stage, philosophy took a somewhat practical approach to the issues of nature and society.

Philosophy came into being when the mythic mindset lost its practical relevance, i.e. when mythology moved from everyday life into the realm of literary interpretation. The old mythological patterns of explanation became insufficient, new thinking was required. Gradually, religion and the gods lost their influence and no longer interacted with people or interfered directly with human affairs. This new way of thinking, this new world-view called philosophy, can be called the first non-religious, secular way of thinking. However, myth and religion had not completely been left behind.

It should be noted here that there is, of course, a difference between mythology and religion. Religion is structured theorems and dogma, obligatory rituals and a clearly defined faith. Within this religious structure, intellectual argument based on logic is possible.

Philosophy, then, is a methodical way of thinking, resulting in provable statements based on clearly defined principles and a chain of reasoning (i.e. the principles of logic). Philosophy brought forth a number of humanist and individualist approaches and developed into one of the most important prerequisites of the mindset of capitalist society. Philosophy provided the roots for what we call scientific thinking. It was not the only factor in the evolution of science, though.

Over time, the process of the production of goods resulted in an enormous amount of practical information concerning the production processes – it brought about an uninterrupted accumulation of knowledge based on empirical data. Seemingly different phenomena could be connected by cause and effect.

The establishment of new technologies initiated exploration and discovery in all areas of nature. Science gained importance: it became the synthesis of the struggle between myth religion and philosophy. The great battles in the intellectual world have come to an end with the victory of scientific thinking.

In thirteenth-century Europe, philosophy and the accumulation of practical knowledge seemed to have come to a dead end until Francis Bacon established experiments as sources of new and verifiable information and knowledge. In the fifteenth century, the Renaissance liberated man's mind and soul from religious dogma, opening his thoughts to human and secular issues. This path led directly into the avenues of science, not without demanding sacrifice and martyrs like Giordano Bruno. Their deaths rang in the age of the science, and humanity became acquainted with a new way of life. It appears to be too limited a view to identify capitalist civilisation with the age of science. As will be argued later, the victory of the scientific method can be said to have served as a catalyst for the present predominance of capitalist civilisation. The age of the scientific society – the rules of which are determined by the people themselves, guiding their own fates in this way – is a crucial step in the progressive evolution of human thinking.

While we call our present age the information or communication age, there are still laws and mechanisms at work in all political institutions that date back to the age of slavery. As will be shown later, mainly those social traditions that lie at the centre of what the state as an institution has been adhering to for 5,000 years, have been strengthened. The forming of such institutions is in principle contradictory to a scientific approach. But state repression has always prevented scientific insight from becoming the governing principle in organising social structures. Rationality nonetheless must demand it.

The age of information, as it is so often called today, has not yet produced its own unique social formation. Although science is in permanent progress, no principles amounting to an ethics of science have been formulated. It is, therefore, not impossible that science without control might result in even more dangerous regimes than those of the gods of mythology or the representatives of monotheistic religions on earth. We have already seen examples of extremely authoritarian or totalitarian regimes invoking science as the basis of their systems, while throwing all social and ethical principles overboard.

One of the most remarkable achievements of science has been to put the forces of nature into the service of society. No form of society could ever have existed without some form of knowledge or some knowledge-gathering process (which is for all practical purposes equivalent to *doing* science). The first use of a stone or club had already resulted in new knowledge. The mere calculation of a physical process in order to exploit it for production purposes meant doing science, even if the process in question had not yet been quantified in a mathematical formula. Ever since its birth, society has been accompanied by science and often in contradiction to it. The more these contradictions could be resolved, the more clearly science could become what it is today. It follows that with science, enlightenment becomes a permanent process, although its contribution varies over time.

The more science contributes to a society, the better developed are the information dissemination processes. It would be wrong to attribute this phenomenon to the development of capitalism as one of its unique qualities. Capitalism has only increased its contribution. But capitalist civilisation has not only been involved on an advanced level in the progress of science but also in imposing restrictions on it. The inner contradictions of capitalist society prevent science from using all its capabilities, which had played such a creative part in the birth of capitalism during the epochs of the Renaissance and the Enlightenment. The use of scientific methods means strength and, most importantly, enlightenment. Being enlightened means being able to approach matters effectively, successfully; it means qualitative and quantitative improvement of production. Increased productivity, in turn, means gaining strength and taking a leading position in all areas of economy and politics according to the old saying: knowledge is power. Hence, the emergence of the scientific method can be characterised as an aspect of the ideological identity of capitalist civilisation. Still, the relationship between science and society is marked also by strong contradictions. Society has not yet left its older frames of reference behind – it is not yet able to do without them; it is still dependent on religion and idealistic philosophy.

A crucial question is whether science, and science alone, can be a liberating power. Can science free man from man's human nature? Can science be "everything"? The thinking of the first men was determined by the divine – were they perhaps on the right path? Is science God? Would our transformation into a completely scientific nature be equivalent to our apotheosis, our becoming God? The statement *ana al-haqq* (I am God), attributed to an Arab mystic, might then be interpreted as if the nature of science might just as well be achieved by the power of intuition. Was it not Islam which expressed the equation *science = God* much earlier by calling God omniscient?

There is an imperative ethical principle which demands that the common interests, rights and safety of humanity are paramount. If we should prove unable to align the apotropaic power of science with this principle, we will probably have to suffer more dangerous authoritarian regimes than those of the biblical Nimrods and Pharaohs; regimes that will make us into robot-like creatures, suffering a servitude darker than that suffered by the slaves of those ancient times. The twentieth century teaches us much about the actuality of such dangers and the catastrophes that might result from them. Here we find the cruellest wars and at the same time science already spreading through many areas of society.

In view of the fact that both the slave-holder mythology and the feudal structures of the monotheistic religions have been overcome (while humanity is still not able to free itself of despotism), would not then a totalitarian world consisting of an enormous number of science-made, godlike beings mean an apocalypse?

INDIVIDUALISM

Capitalist society is based on the individual. Individualism, therefore, is an elementary psychological quality underlying this society. If the rational side of capitalist society is characterised by science, individualism determines its soul. Individualism, sometimes to the extent of near lunacy, is the outcry of the individual who has been freed of his chains by the birth of capitalism; an individual who no longer recognises anything as sacred except the interests of the ego. In capitalism, it is the ego which is the driving power of society: a force even stronger than science.

The capitalist individual is humanity's revenge on society as a social structure. The passions of the individual seem limitless. The more the ties with the past are cut, the freer the individual believes himself to be. Money takes the place of the divine. Money becomes the concrete expression of the soul of the capitalist system, assuming magical power – there is nothing that cannot be turned into money. While earlier societies sought to express their identities through totems, gods or god–kings, capitalist society expresses its identity through money. Money reflects the power of the society. It irresistibly attracts the individual's soul, having it accept even barbarous wars and genocide.

This transcending of the social structure by the individual has its explanation in thousands of years of socialisation. Previously, all social systems had formed their structures according to the interests of the dominating strata. Socialisation, or rather, the integration of the individual into a larger, quite rigid, given social context – openly, voluntarily or by force – was an inevitable and at times even sacred part of everybody's life. All of religion, ethics, production, politics were to serve this purpose. Every tradition, every person, invariably proclaimed this law. At the birth of capitalism these incredibly overloaded and rigid social structures were blown to pieces by the new power of the individual, setting free an enormous, hitherto unknown energy.

Society as people knew it was blown up, using individualism as an explosive, in the knowledge that this would offer fantastic opportunities – to some. When the first attempts were successful, the whole process was systematised. From then on it was no longer the temple where people turned their faces to God. Sin was abolished, or rather reduced to some kind of obstacle in the way of profit; the Ka'aba became the new factory, money the new god, and the individual's desires became sacred.

Of course, capitalism is not completely wrong in this respect. Over aeons the individual had been sacrificed for the sake of society. Indeed, many religions sacrificed their most precious creatures to their gods without batting an eyelid, in order to secure the community's welfare. Social history is in many respects the history of individual sacrifices for the good of society, which demanded service in the form of wars, rituals of worship, and the relinquishing of moral standards.

Much that was done in the name of the well-being of society seems irrational to us. The smallest violation of the least important of rules – even for innocent or justified reasons – might have been declared a deadly sin. In the name of society, the individual was deprived of his individuality.

Individualism became the defining characteristic of the capitalist ideological identity. Strengthening the individual – and thus effecting a just balance between individual and society – can release considerable power. This power can play a revolutionary and liberating role in times when conservative and reactionary societies, societies which suffocate the individual, are dissolving. This is the progressive and justified position of individualism in history. When the first societies emerged, they were surrounded by an unknown divine power. Now the power of the individual has been set free from the limitations of society. The individual himself seems to be heading for deification. At this historic turning point, the opportunity arises to establish the bitterly needed balance between individual and society. Capitalism does not seem to react to this need. However, the socialist reaction to capitalism gives some importance to this balance. Even this reaction seems to demand some energetic, individual awakening. The individual needs to revolutionise himself as a consequence of this historical necessity. With each chain of physical or mental slavery that the individual was able to cast off, a new window to the world was opened. What previously had been seen as sin or desire, in the Renaissance became a most desirable way of life. A wonderful secularisation began, life was brightened up by the arts. In fact, the magnificent works of art of antiquity partly inspired the Renaissance. Science encouraged people to live without the fear and threats originating from religious dogma. Freedom increased intellectual and emotional capabilities. The ideological framework of the Renaissance set new priorities. Important concepts emerged, for example, *country* in the sense of "home" or "homeland". Communities formerly held together by a shared faith disintegrated into separate nations. National states came into being. Secularisation meant enrichment of everybody's earthly existence. The break with the old and traditional for the sake of the new and creative was so radical that no institution of the old society was allowed to stand in the way of the emerging new society.

HUMANISM

Humanism is another part of the ideological framework of capitalist civilisation. The humanist principle attaches value to every human being and gives it priority above everything else. In the foregoing ages, man was inseparable from society and a relatively passive creature. This was a consequence of one class securing the rule and was supposed to preserve and strengthen society. However, it did not allow for the development of the concept of *man*.

Class society, eventually, saw man's only value in his contribution to the survival of his society. This became the chief objective of all social activity. Since it was man who needed to be integrated into social structures, it was man who could be sacrificed for the good of the social structure.

Man had no demands on the class society. Therefore, he was thought (by religious sanction) to be a meaningless creature, full of guilt, only worthy of servitude. This was the order of the slave-holder society, and this approach to human existence was refined again and again over the ages.

In spite of historical steps (from the rise of monotheistic religion to Jesus of Nazareth and to Islam) the degraded individual human being was still far from coming to the fore. (This was even worse for women. Whenever mankind was discussed, the considerations excluded women.) The ruling class, responsible for all the exploitation, decorated themselves with the attributes of the divine – apparently no longer part of the fallen human race. The development and construction of suitable ideological frameworks, therefore, became an important occupation, forming the basis of human existence in these past civilisations.

It is understandable that humanism was used to take revenge on the old society and its ruling class. Humanist thinking meant elevation and liberation, an opportunity to gain access to science and, hence, dignity. This is why humanism became one of the crucial aspects of the new ideological identity. It liberated people from oppression and from rule justified by religion; it bestowed value on every individual. The old society had always aimed at neutralising the individual and his desires by means of invented, non-human or superhuman beings. These tools were meant to place the spirit of servitude in the human mind. Humanism disposed of these beings. Man became the highest value. This was enough to cast a spell over the new society. Man was no longer a captive and subject to dogma and gods handed down through the centuries. He was given an identity of his own, by virtue of which he was able to form and create himself according to his own will. Man was allowed to recognise his emotions and senses and take responsibility for his own affairs. Creativity became a basic quality associated with man himself instead of being a quality of the divine. Man had entered a phase in which he was able to determine his own fate and be his own ruler. All preceding revolutions had led the individual from one form of servitude and dependency to the next. Now, however, man was to be liberated from all sorts of dependencies and given back to himself.

In view of this new human condition we have to repeat the question of balance. Will not man, who tore apart his social ties, become an animal – only even more dangerous? Will not the individual, now strengthened by money and science, see the world as his preserve, full of prey? Will this man not become even more harmful than the creature in social dependence? I am not asking these questions without reason. The age of individualism is marked by mass murders, massacres, genocide and other crimes against humanity – in the name of humanity. Mankind in its most bloodstained epoch has produced two world wars and many regional wars involving numerous nations, ethnic and religious communities and social classes. This epoch has also seen massive environmental problems, the decline of morals, idolisation of the stock exchange, and so on. The danger is real!

The one determining factor in the development process of European capitalist civilisation is the fact that class society had not yet been able to deepen its structures there. Older societies, which have experienced such structures for much longer, can only develop new forms with the help of external intervention and they find it rather difficult to adapt to new conditions. (Climate and geography may also influence the formation of new structures.)

Europe profited much from developments and achievements in other regions. From the agrarian revolution of the neolithic to the urban revolution and the slave-holder society to the accomplishments of feudalism – all this was passed on to Europe. The transfer process included ideological as well as scientific and technological development. Increasing trade opportunities familiarised the Europeans with products from all over the world. A suitable climate and fertile soil combined with the necessary knowledge produced a surplus, which could be used for trade and commerce, scientific and philosophical activities. Literacy increased and an educated class emerged.

Again, the crucial phenomenon underlying these developments was the fact that Europe had not really experienced class society. Apart from some bridgeheads in the form of colonies, the system of slavery had never really spread from the Greek and Italian peninsulas. Feudal civilisation only began to spread over Europe with the second millennium CE.

This freshness, combined with some surviving liberties from the clan societies, mingled with the accumulated accomplishments of civilisation. Thus, conditions were created for a great synthesis in the history of mankind. It did not take long for European civilisation to follow from this encounter.

The European example shows that all civilisations originate from mental revolutions. This cannot be accomplished by trade and commerce alone, although these are certainly necessary. As I see it, there is always a dialectical process going on. At first, there is some kind of new thinking, changes in the sphere of the mind and the soul, which lead to a feedback in the socio-economic area. This in turn leads to changes in the political structure and deepens the entire process in an attempt to render it irreversible.

17

The Development and Institutionalisation of Capitalist Civilisation

The heart of the capitalist system is the contracting of human labour, released from servitude and feudal chains, on the basis of payment for work. In the system of slavery, the slaves and all they had were the property of their owner until their death. They could be ordered to do any work; they could be sold, even killed. This gave them a status only slightly higher than that of cattle. The feudal system was based on the relation between lords and peasants, who worked their own land as well as that of the lords. The peasants, in return for their labour, received military protection. The lords also had extensive police, judicial and other rights over everybody on their land. The peasants were completely dependent upon their lord. They were only partly free. Although they could have families, they were, for all practical reasons, not able to leave the soil they worked on. In capitalism, however, man has left behind these personal dependencies on a single lord and his land. People are free to trade their own labour with any person they might choose, in exchange for a payment defined by the market. In comparison to the conditions of feudal bondage, this can certainly be regarded as an improvement and a step towards liberation.

A second decisive characteristic of the capitalist system is the industrial form of production with the factory at its centre. The transition from manufactory to industrial factory formed the crucial step in the development of capitalism. Manufactories generally used manual labour, concentrated in great workshops, making use of disciplinary rules.

Workshops, or proto-factories, albeit much smaller and without the imposition of rules, have been known since the late neolithic. The factory, however, is a form and place of production specific to capitalism. It is based on mass employment, the rational organisation of processes, and power-driven machines. The use of power-driven machines is the element that distinguishes capitalism and its factories from its predecessors. It largely contributed to the development of the capitalist form of production and thence was the cause of accelerated advance.

In trying to define different stages of human history, certain central technical achievements can be regarded as the chief criteria. The palaeolithic (the period which comprises about 98 per cent of human history) is viewed as the period when only rudimentary chipped stones were used as tools or weapons for hunting or fighting. Men lived as hunter–gatherers and stones were their most important technical means. The neolithic, as the second period in man's history, is defined by the use of sophisticated stone tools shaped by polishing or grinding. These tools enabled the revolutionary transition to agriculture and stockbreeding. At the beginning of the slave-holder period, the most important technologies in production, trade and war were those that used bronze. From the first millennium BCE to the rise of capitalism, the processing of iron was crucial to all technological development.

The development of technology, ever since the utilisation of the first tool, seems to have followed an exponential curve of development, reaching a peak with nuclear technology and space flight. The capitalist system corresponds with a qualitative technological revolution. In particular, mechanised production beginning with the use of steam engines and railways was responsible for the progress desired. Another factor just as important was the *scientific revolution*. It was understood that science and technology corresponded and were necessarily interconnected, leading to an explosion in the expansion of production facilities and structures. Many hitherto inaccessible natural resources could now be exploited. Apart from water and wind, electricity and nuclear energy were discovered and utilised. Gene technology today allows for the manipulation of living beings and seems to have the potential for creating unknown wonders.

However, technological progress cannot be allowed to go unbridled. Control of the development and use of technology is limited. It is derived from a probabilistic approach in which residual risks are inevitable. There is a near blind faith in the functioning of machines. A way of living that is extremely dependent on technology has produced a large number of dangerous physical and mental illnesses. Individualism and social coherence are endangered. It seems imperative that ethical boundaries should be drawn and that controls over both individualism and the harmful aspects of technology be implemented.

The capitalist way of production by means of mechanisation and power-driven machinery has led to a hitherto unheard-of level of development. In fact, with its ideological framework and its structures of production, capitalist civilisation represents a peak in human history. Production problems have been replaced by problems of consumption. Overproduction causes serious social problems. New ways in the processing of raw materials bring about a new system of foreign markets. Continuously decreasing production costs contribute to this. On the one hand, capitalism enables mankind to gain possession of seemingly unlimited resources. On the other hand, it renders this potential useless with regard to humane aspects, because the entire system depends on the exploitation of profit. The distribution of the means of production and the ownership of technology inhibit productive forces and result in the factual pressure to produce products of limited usefulness and importance for the sake of maximum profit – even beyond market saturation. Mankind once more is experiencing a situation where we cannot use our capabilities to serve our own needs and wishes – we are once again restricted by the will and capriciousness of those who own the profits drawn from these capabilities.

Despite these negative characteristics, we have to acknowledge the superiority of capitalist society. Its ideological and material framework has surpassed all past systems. The interrelatedness of production structures has resulted in far-going social and political changes and created corresponding institutions useful to them. Although social and political conditions seem to be generally the result of evolutionary processes, sometimes behaviour that is inflexible, rigid and conservative may require that the old status quo be overcome by some revolutionary action. This seems particularly true where the given conditions resist any form of evolutionary effort and reform. Under conditions like these, social depression may escalate. Such crises are phases of transition occurring when the old ideology and its institutions prove insufficient. We then find a situation where the old and the new fight each other on all levels in a conflict that we may characterise as a struggle between revolution and counter-revolution. Whenever the counter-revolution is successful, a hard regime is installed – where it is not successful, the new system is formed even faster. The content and shape of the newly formed institutions involve changes towards a better adaptation to the ideological and material aspects of the new order, also resulting in greater efficiency. Thus, the production facilities are enabled to restructure faster and more economically.

Hence, the forming of social and political institutions alone is useless. Only the creative influence of the ideological framework – both by the superstructure and by the pressure of the economical conditions of the substructure – can lead to a new framework describing the condition of the state and its institutions. In the end, the state is in itself just a neutral tool. It is subject to massive intellectual pressure from above by the ideological identity and from below by the economically dominant power. The alliance between the economic and social powers and those ideological identities that seem useful to their interests brings about the new system of government and supersedes the worn-out official structures of the old system. In this way the social and the class basis of the new system of government, as well as its ideological forms of expression, gain official status and can establish themselves as the legitimate governing power of the entire social order. By intense propaganda, then, support and approval from all parts of the population can be won. All class systems renew themselves in similar ways, differing only due to historical or geographical conditions.

The capitalist class society, it appears, largely rests on the accumulated structure of civilisational achievements. Where the monarchies in Europe were late, or too conservative, with political reforms during the seventeenth and eighteenth centuries, revolutionary, bloody and earth-shaking events took place (1640 in England, 1789 in France). We find similar events in the nineteenth and twentieth centuries in Europe and beyond. These revolutions under the leadership of the bourgeoisie substantially changed the nature and shape of civilisation. Consequently, this newly emerging class expressed its mission as the creation of political institutions specific to itself. In certain respects, the new social class was able to prove its maturity by becoming the state itself. The character of the class that could not be transformed into government machinery or state apparatus was controversial and indecisive, frozen in some kind of interrupted transition. It could either try to become the prevailing power and governing class, or it could be reduced to an indirectly controlled class, exploited for the interests of the class in control. The classes and strata dominating the productive structures could reposition themselves as the basic classes and strata of the state order, while their predecessors become increasingly marginalised. First among the concepts, in increasing order of their importance in the course of capitalist development, are *homeland, nation, citizenship, republic, secularism, democracy, rule of law* and *human rights*. All these concepts have undergone significant changes in content and meaning and by now have little or nothing to do with what they originally meant. The many different rulers all use them as empty shells to be filled with new meaning whenever it seems politically necessary, always aligning them with what *they* call the "new world order".

THE HOMELAND

We may define *home* as the name given to a geographic place, where similar social groups of a social system who have organic relationships with each other live together, earn their living, and share common experiences and memories of the past as well as hopes for the future. Since the first primitive communities consisted of nomads who did not cling to a certain place, notions like *home* did not exist. Later, when the agricultural revolution necessitated settling down, the place of settlement took on an essential meaning for the social life of the community. The seeds of economically useful plants and the breeding of animals increased the value of the soil and the place. The geographic area where memories were shared, and which yielded the material well-being of the group and their hopes for the future, became sacred. This sacredness was the basis of the notion of a home of the community, tribe or nation and became an inseparable part of the material and spiritual life of society.

This development continued in the class society with the creation of the holy temple, cities, property and commerce, and the state as a common administrative machine for them all. The idea of inner and outer borders emerged, for which the community had to take responsibility. The community regarded everything within these borders as completely their own, all that lay outside as somebody else's. The territory that was within the jurisdiction of the state was called "home", all that lay outside were foreign countries. The Sumerians raised the concept *home* to paradise level in the Dilmun myth.[1]

This is at least partly due to the fact that here, for the first time – simultaneously with urban life – a diverse and rich economy with surplus production came into being. In contrast, having no home (country), or the destruction or occupation of one's home, became the greatest possible disaster.

The second substantial change in the concept of *home* took place under the same conditions that produced the capitalist society. Sir Thomas Moore's *Utopia* (1616) and Tommaso Campanella's *The City of the Sun* (1602) stimulated the idea that the earthly society could be made an ideal place for people to live in.

The production structures and state facilities of capitalist society make the concept of *home* even more concrete. Since a national market together with a common language and history were closely connected with the idea of a common fatherland, borders increasingly became a serious problem. The capitalist focus on profit facilitates wars between such fatherlands.

Where more land meant more profit, the initially progressive love of one's country turned into a chauvinistic and aggressive sentiment. Thus, the inherent extremism in the capitalist concept of *homeland*, combined with extreme nationalism, generated the bloodiest wars in the history of mankind. Presently, the capitalist greed for profit seems to be resulting in a reverse trend, so-called globalisation.

By comparison, some societies with a common culture never had the chance to formulate their concept of *home*, as a result of medieval dogmatism, capitalist chauvinism or direct or indirect occupation. Their objective remains to lead a free life in a free country that is their home. Where they cannot accomplish such a life by peaceful methods, they resort to self-defence and eventually violence and war. To be left without home and subject to the arbitrary whims of others produces a loss of dignity, alienates the individual's thinking, destroys the human psyche and leads to social degeneration.

THE CONCEPT OF *NATION*

Both the concept *nation* and the social phenomenon of nationhood have undergone major changes under the influence of capitalism. National awareness and the emergence of national ties became fundamental characteristics of the new society. Nationhood in an ideological sense only became important with the arrival of capitalism.

A basic sense of belonging and fanaticism, which previously were expressed through religion, now attached themselves to the idea of the state. The development of the nation had played a progressive part in the overcoming of feudalism and in weakening the medieval Islamic idea of *ummah*[2] by replacing it with national markets.

These developments were influenced by capitalist structures of production. However, when nationalism degenerated into secession and practically into a new religion, it became reactionary. The chauvinist thinking in nationalist terms, with its claims of superiority over other peoples and nations, became the cause of new hostilities. We now find wars between ethnically defined nations. As class struggles became fiercer, the capitalist class increasingly used these ideologies for their own purposes, hiding their true interests behind the mask of the nation.

Those peoples that did not obtain their national identity can take a step towards freedom with the help of national awareness and national solidarity. Extreme nationalism fills the void in the individual's life left by the death of religion and assumes an utterly negative role. Particularly in the twentieth century this situation escalated and nationalism became the primary ideological fuel of bloody wars followed by separatism, racism and hatred – poisoning the international community and producing an anti-humanist attitude.

At the same time, the concept of *nation* went hand in hand with a tendency to establish nation states. A nation state in itself is an inconsistent phenomenon. Rather than by its ethnic composition a state's characteristics are determined by its dominant economic and social class. In the initial stages, when the interests of the entire national community could be united in a common struggle against the monarchy as a representative of the old regime, the term *nation state* might have been appropriate. However, as soon as interests began to diverge, the state ceased to be a nation state and became a means of repression in the interest of the dominant class. The concept of *nation*, it seems, is manipulated and subordinated in the same way as the concept of *god* – to the material interests of those in control.

THE REPUBLIC

The republic in modern times has been a tool of the bourgeoisie. It primarily has served to demolish the monarchy and the remaining feudal structures in Europe. The original republic, the *res publica* in the Roman sense, in its time meant nothing but a more or less unanalysed "public thing", a term used instead of *state*, or *nation*, etc. This understanding implied the participation of many in this *res publica*, and suggested a certain openness of its structures for a broad range of people. However, the republican idea could not spread and its real development in Europe only began with the French revolution.

The republican form of state and its history are quite instructive. The republic draws and involves all social strata and groups into a political discussion, enforces the founding of political parties and stimulates the learning of politics as an art. Republican tendencies are directed against monarchic, oligarchic, and dictatorial regimes and stand for revolutionary and democratic development. They usually represent a secular ideology, a non-religious, enlightened approach in contrast with all kinds of religious dogmatism. Contrasted with the Middle Ages, republicanism can refer to the Renaissance, the Reformation and the Enlightenment. These characteristics make the republic an important development. However, the egotistic interests of the capitalist class and their unwillingness to share power with the workers, hindered its development towards democracy and rendered it a conservative system, devoid of democratic content. Today, there is hardly any system which would not claim to be republican, but the concept *republic* has lost most of its original content. The republic is always in danger of being turned into something similar to the despotic state machinery of old. Dictators see no contradiction in presenting themselves as presidents of republics, although their whole populations obviously live in huge prisons.

The republic initially began its existence as a regime meant to overcome a crisis. But it needs to develop democratic structures in order to do this.

CITIZENSHIP

History shows that the individual's membership of social structures can take a variety of forms. There were the early clans and tribes, then city states, empires and religions. However, it was only with the rise of the civil order at the beginning of modernity that *nationality*, usually in the sense of "citizenship", became a commonly used term. People became members of a community, citizens of a country. Unlike membership in a tribe or a religious community, and in contrast to being the subject of a king or emperor, this citizenship formed the minimum basis for the legal equality of all citizens. Although this was not an immediate step towards greater freedom, citizenship represents a precondition for greater freedom, in particular for those people who educate themselves about individual liberties, enlightenment and political participation. Basic notions like democracy for all people and free individual citizenship seem to be concepts of increasing political importance today.

Throughout history, social powers have suppressed the individual for the benefit of their particular interests. In this way, the individual was supposed to adapt to the customs and laws of the societies in question. The whole spectrum of mythology, religion and all political institutions was utilised for the domination and control of the individual. Under the conditions of capitalist society, the influence of politics on the individual has become even more complex, going far beyond military service and taxes: a state ideology, certainly not second to religious dogma, is imposed on the people. An artificial citizen is to be created, with the help of technology, whose intellectual shape and mental composition are planned in advance, heralding a contemporary form of slavery. By means of the nearly unlimited capabilities of communication technology, an unprecedented degree of control over the individual and society is achieved. This is paradoxical and dangerous: the irrational excesses of individualism are to be balanced by an equally irrational degree of control.

During this balancing act severe problems occur, resulting in the most serious discussions that the capitalist system has ever seen. To what extent will their own language, culture, faith, their knowledge of history and their hopes of a free future enable citizens to cope with their fates? To what extent, and for how long, will the existing structures, with their concepts and norms, survive? Key terms, such as *civil society, human rights, the environment*, suggest a new definition of citizenship with the help of the major non-governmental organisations. In comparable historical epochs, Gnostic and mystic sects sought to help the individual who felt that the political and economic system was shutting off the air.

This has become a task for civil society. The highly developed and strictly executed idea of citizenship, as the modern state understands it, is not compatible with the idea of a free citizenship, a free identity, that has yet to be defined by civil society. A new ideological framework has to be created, and civil society will have to largely contribute to this, in order to steer civilisation in a new direction of development. Marxism, with its discussions restricted to the economy and the formation of a corresponding identity, has remained utterly unsuccessful. The new discussions addressed above may be more successful if they take into account and analyse the new dimensions and opportunities provided by the progress of information and communications technology.

SECULARISM AS A PRINCIPLE

Liberation from the tight grip of the church in particular, and religion in general, was a central principle of the ideology of the bourgeoisie. It can be understood as a reaction to the existing reality and mostly amounted to nothing more than flatly denying the existence of God. This approach was taken over practically unchanged by Marxism, which claimed to be representing the ideology of the working class. The weakest part of secularism in this form lies in the fact that it is not a result of a coherent analysis of religion. The rising natural sciences at the beginning of modernity fostered a separation from religious dogmatism. This was mercilessly punished by the Inquisition. Emotional, rebellious dissertations, referring to scientific insights, were published; dissertations similar to those of the philosophers of antiquity – such as Socrates – in their fundamental rebellion against dogmatism. There is a long line of martyrs killed for similar reasons.

The most difficult phase in helping a new society to be born is the struggle against dogmatism. Secularism is part of the political equipment in this struggle. The continuously developing state is the tool of power most often used by religious dogmatism. The Sumerians defined the chief principles of the state in its domination of the people, making them subjects of rule and slaves of the dominating class. This has not yet changed substantially. In Sumer, the state represented the political equivalence of a not even roughly understood heaven with its eternal stars and their unchangeable courses – stars, by the way, about which the Sumerian priests knew absolutely nothing. The state, however, served as a tool and justification for all kinds of injustice, force and deceit in the hands of the slave-holder class with their practically unlimited exploitation of human labour. The state was based on a superficial knowledge of nature and the seemingly boundless will-power of the gods, and presented itself as their worldly representative. It is based on the principle that everybody is accountable to the state, while the state itself can never be held accountable. It is based on the state's alleged sacredness, which may demand anything, including the lives of the citizens, without offering anything in return.

When the Sumerian priests created this dangerous social animal, they did not take any precautions. After all, things like the rights of an enslaved subject are hard to formulate. The Sumerians saw it this way: the state is everything, the individual nothing. The state becomes a dogma. Besides, the state can be ambivalent and cater to both the needs of the bourgeoisie and those of the proletariat, for its own benefit.

The Sumerian temples were also the first places where prostitution was conducted officially. The Sumerian-type state knew that both male and female prostitution were very helpful in exploiting society for its own purposes. Thus, people were taught to prostitute themselves. If the secular principle is to prevail completely, it has to be applied to Sumerian-type states and their historical derivatives in the Middle East too. The bourgeoisie, however, is neither able nor willing to accomplish this. Under capitalist conditions, real socialist measures too failed in overcoming the Sumerian-type state. On the contrary, they perfected it. A constructive debate on secularism is still a desideratum. It is not enough to turn against the state order, which employs religion in its own interests. It is the (Sumerian-type) concept of government itself, which rests on (religious) dogmatism that needs to be questioned. European civilisation has been content with only minimal criticism of the state, without radically trying to change its basic character. It has even strengthened it and made it more dangerous in some ways – a nuclear power is even worse than a state that hides behind religion and divine masks.

The state founded on dogmatism is a product of the Middle East. Therefore, many intense and violent discussions are waged over secularism in Middle

Eastern society. As long as the dogmatic state, the state dogma, is not approached radically, we cannot talk of a real struggle for secularism. If we say that a renaissance in the Middle East is necessary, then the state dogma must be critically analysed and overcome. This is a *conditio sine qua non*. Therefore, the struggle for freedom of speech must first be successful and people in this region must learn to value it. Even limited efforts towards democratisation – secularist or other – are valuable and deserve to be supported. The fate of a Middle Eastern renaissance, and with it the search for a new type of civilisation, is very much dependent upon the results of this struggle.

DEMOCRACY

The roots of the democratic system, which in principle is based on the selection of a government by all citizens, go back to pre-industrial tribal communities. The leaders of the tribes needed the approval of their community for their leadership. Democracy's present shape, however, didn't develop until the rise of capitalism. In present (class) societies, democracy is mostly a system handled by delegates or representatives (usually from the dominating class). All class societies have formed institutions which can either determine the composition of executive bodies according to their strength, or which function only as advisory bodies. In the past, we have often seen that, after a short period of democratic rule, monarchy regains power and democracy decays. After some early and unsuccessful attempts at democracy in Sumerian times it was the Attic *polis*, mainly in the fifth and fourth centuries BCE, that was responsible for its further development. Athenian democracy adopted its classical form of government that only involved male citizens of the dominating slave-owning class. It was strongly influenced by the philosophical thought of its time and based on thorough discussion of all issues relevant to the community. There is always only as much discussion and development of ideas as there is democracy.

The leadership bodies of a republic also are determined in elections. The citizens make their selection from a choice of candidates. Those who are elected in turn select a government. In this way, the democratic character of the entire system is rather limited. Hence, a republic need not be a democracy, and a democracy need not be a republic. Practically, democracy should mean that the interests of all citizens are taken into account; all citizens have the chance to influence the politics of their community; people elected into executive bodies are subject to public control; and the entire system has to stand regular elections. So far, democracy seems to be the best form of government. This, however, is the theory. Its application is more problematic.

The republican faction of the bourgeoisie is well aware of the fact that democracy would progressively restrict the power of their class. Therefore, if profit matters, the democratic institutions are ignored, while severe crises and decline seem to invite democratic solutions. The European bourgeoisie, at the height of its influence, had enough self-confidence to institute the hitherto most extensive and successful endeavour at democracy. They made it clear that democracy is a feasible form of government, able to set hidden potentials free. Democracy thus became a contemporary form of civilisation, and the goal and objective of many people. From that point of view, we may call our age the age of democratic civilisation.

However, more important than the form or structure of government is the way a community addresses and solves its problems. Today many regimes still use force or violence to solve all problems – that is, when they can no longer ignore or flatly deny them. The democratic approach, on the other hand, tries to build a social framework that also grants its weakest members the protection of the law, protection of their lives, freedom of thought, and a cultural existence. If science and technology can be put into the hands of a really democratic system, such a system will be able to establish the material conditions which allow for the solution of most problems. Contemporary civilisation has already created an ideal basis for democracy. In my opinion, the necessary changes and transformations are only possible within the framework of a thoroughly democratic regime, in a thoroughly democratic environment.

THE RULE OF LAW

Throughout history, all states have had systems of rules, sanctions or legal procedures which they call their codes of law. Law can have many different sources. It can be handed down by tradition or made by a legislative body. The state, on the other hand, is the structure which comprises and supersedes all other structures of the community. Therefore, it is the state which imposes and protects the law. In turn, the state can only act on the basis of this law, which cannot arbitrarily be changed. If such conditions obtain, we may speak of a state under the rule of law.

Another issue is the relationship between law and justice. This relationship is largely defined by the extent of participation of the citizens in the making of the laws. A government which does not accept the freedom of expression, and with it the free will and the interests of the population, cannot be said to be under the rule of justice. This holds true also when the law is not the same for all citizens.

The complex structure of capitalist society necessarily needs a highly developed system of laws, which has to be adapted continuously according to changes in society. Legal discussions are inevitable in capitalist systems and result in the establishment of constitutions and systems of law. The law moderates internal and external conflicts as much as possible and regulates the interests of differing groups, so that violence is avoided. It recognises the basic rights of all citizens and tries to build a peaceful society within a legal framework.

The legal dimension of European-led civilisation has developed enormously and influences the whole world. The brutal methods of old-style colonialism are passé, but the interests of the dominating class, nation or block of nations are, of course, always taken into consideration. Relying on its leading position in science and technology, its economic productivity and political power, European civilisation creates international law, establishing free trade and free markets worldwide. It imposes its own internal legal system on the world and declares it a universally valid paradigm.

Were democracy and law to be combined, the result would be the contemporary democratic state under the rule of law. The social system of modern-day civilisation, which is rooted in capitalism and at the same time is overcoming it in many respects, would then take its most advanced shape. By relying on the law, this system would be able to solve all kinds of social and political problems peacefully and with satisfactory and sustainable results.

HUMAN RIGHTS

Human rights, an institution of the modern era, are individual rights. They are an expression of basic values, transformed into written law. These values have become increasingly important with the advent of capitalism: freedom of thought, freedom of religion, the right to life. The term *human rights* refers to the protection of liberties which are indispensably and inalienably part of being human, regardless of differences of class, nation, religion, gender or ethnic group. These rights are the basis of the right to the free development of one's personality. From these basic rights secondary and tertiary rights can be derived, particularly concerning economic, social or cultural issues.

The most prominent of these basic human rights is the right to life, which forbids killing – even by the state – except in a state of war. In pre-capitalist times, the individual sought protection and safety within communities such as tribes, religious groups or, in the Islamic world, the so-called *waqfs*.[3] In principle, the individual was already endangered by the lack of social and physical security, education, health and work. He led an insecure existence.

The dissolution of traditional ties at the time of "wild" capitalism caused new difficulties for the individual. The old ways of solving problems had become inefficient. In theory, the resulting void was filled by human rights. However, these were no protection as long as they had not become codified as law in the relevant countries.

An important complex within the field of human rights is formed by the rights of women and children, and by environmental rights. Women may be viewed as the oldest of low classes and have been exposed to exploitation and oppression throughout history, an issue that has been addressed only in recent times. A worldwide discussion and efforts to rectify this are still ongoing. However, 5,000 years of class history make it all too clear that, whenever people were affected by some kind of inequality, discrimination or oppression, women were affected most. And yet, there is only a limited discussion – especially in the Middle East – about granting women all individual rights unconditionally. This is an issue important enough to be discussed everywhere in the world, and it has even become a special part of the social sciences. If ever a new kind of civilisation should emerge, woman and her freedom will play a decisive part in it.

The protection of the rights of the child should not be left to mother, father, or the authorities alone. Leading a child to full development requires humanity as well as knowledge. The ruthless order of the patriarchy has never been blessed with the necessary sensitivity. Therefore, apart from slaves, women and workers, children have became the favourite targets of oppression. In the early phases of class society, children were often sacrificed to the gods. Modern sacrifices in the age of capitalism take place on the altar of money. The rights of children, therefore, have to be clearly defined in an international declaration. Education, health, but also play, affection, and a life in peace are indispensable for the well-being of children.

The complex of environmental rights describes legal measures in the context of dangerous developments (for example, technology-caused pollution, contamination or intoxication of soil, ground water, atmosphere, climate, etc.) as a result of industrial or other capitalist activities; activities which might result in long-term damage or in making major parts of the world uninhabitable. A manifesto of environmental rights and an international environmental organisation should be recognised as an inseparable part of the general struggle for human rights and democracy and should be integrated into this struggle.

The concept of human rights exceeds the framework of law. It needs to be addressed as an ethical and political fundamental of philosophy. It needs to be politicised and institutionally controlled. Without an ongoing discussion about the contradiction between the individual and society, the growing crisis of civilisation cannot be solved. In order to achieve a balance between these two poles and between the poles of liberty and equality, humanity needs to take new measures.

There are scholars who call our present age "postmodern"; some already see the end of history. I, for my part, cannot agree with either. They originate from, and are limited to, the point of view of the modern *citoyen* or *bourgeois*. From this angle, the aporia, the exhausted potential of capitalist civilisation, seems to be the end of mankind. However, there are other possible interpretations. Some historians believe, for instance, that liberalism and, as a consequence, fascism as its complement, are part of an eternal order of things.

We have entered an epoch in history where problems cannot be solved on the traditional basis of state logic. Scientific knowledge and technology have invalidated the logic of states and classes. Today's so-called age of information and communication brings about a new dimension of development. It would be insufficient, though, to reduce the present to these characteristics, perhaps accompanied by an increasing environmental awareness. We need a historical awakening which takes these phenomena into account, while at the same time sketching a strategy and guidelines for such a historical change. I intend to give this issue a closer look and offer some proposals at the end of my discussion of civilisation.

18

Capitalist Expansion and the Climax of Capitalist Civilisation

Since its very beginning, human history and human life seem to have been continuously accelerated by scientific progress and technology. The palaeolithic, with its naive knowledge of nature, was the longest phase in the history of mankind and lasted until the most recent ice age. The mesolithic as an interim epoch then lasted until about 10000 BCE. The next phase, the neolithic, already technologically better developed, came and went even faster, making way for the slave-holder period (from 3000 BCE to 500 CE) an epoch full of new developments in all fields of human social, political, and religious life. The feudal age that followed lasted a mere 1,000 years. Progress, as a function of time, appears to accelerate exponentially.

Every epoch of human history strives to spread universally. We find traces of palaeolithic communities in almost all inhabitable regions of the earth. The kind of small community prevalent during this epoch therefore not only had the longest history but was also the most widespread. The neolithic communities, too, spread into almost all inhabitable regions. The feudal age and its newiron-based technologies spread even faster – with the help of Islam and Christianity.

In trying to describe how these different epochs spread so successfully, we encounter two important phenomena: colonialism and imperialism. All societies that are progressive and developed (in relation to other societies) spread and expand. Purposefully or not, more highly developed knowledge and technology fascinate and propagate.

The roots of colonialism go back to the neolithic, as we saw in our discussion of this epoch. However, during the early pre-modern epochs, colonial expansion was physical only to a small extent. Only minor parts of the population moved. What spread, rather, was knowledge, new technology, new methods of production, and the accompanying mythological and religious structures. Any attempt to explain history with reference to large migrations of peoples is, I believe, off the mark. A more highly developed community does not in the first place expand physically, but by imparting knowledge, technical know-how, ideology, and the power of its institutions.

However, colonialism does entail physical expansion in as much as it becomes necessary for trade and commerce. The power centre exerts its control through superiority of technology and knowledge of production rather than by means of violence.

In contrast, imperialism is mainly an occupying, hegemonic regime based on violence. Historiography informs us about the first known imperialist policies under the reign of Sargon, founder of the Sumerian–Akkadian dynasty. But even before that, there had been occupations. Wherever riches were building up, they became the target of poorer neighbours or of even richer and more powerful centres. In the slave-holder epoch as well as during feudalism, imperialism was a mighty phenomenon accompanied by huge territorial expansion and plunder. However, even in this context, it would not be quite true to equate expansion with the use of violence. An epoch can only spread into areas with inferior social systems and places of production. If, over time, the knowledge base and the technological basis of the spreading system can be made compatible with the colonised society, the expanding civilisation will be assimilated locally, making the use of violence unnecessary. In this way, the characteristics of the new epoch are eventually adopted. The most dangerous kind of imperialism is expansion through violent campaigns which are not followed and ideologically filled by a progressive system, but rather consist of plunder and slaughter. History provides many an example of such behaviour, which always had devastating results. The Mongols are a good example. Instances of expansion with a progressive character can be found too; expansion based on values which seemed superior and therefore were voluntarily accepted and adopted.

The (also physical) spreading of social systems through localisation and their becoming independent can only be observed where there are large uninhabited areas or weakened communities. Wherever an expansionist party moved into an area with a population equally great in number and with strong historical–cultural foundations, we find that the expansionist party is assimilated by the local culture. A kind of synthesis of a higher order emerges in the long run, which mostly bears, however, the characteristics of the old local culture. On the other hand, if a civilisation centre is conquered by a less developed culture, the occupying power will be absorbed in a very short time.

The seventeenth and eighteenth centuries provide ample evidence of the superiority of capitalist society. A conquest of the world began from the European shores of the Atlantic. A tradition that had begun with Sargon, then Darius, Alexander, Caesar and the Islamic conquerors, was carried on by Portuguese, Spanish, English and Dutch explorers, colonisers, and *conquistadores*. These capitalist conquests claimed to take their social and political system, ideology and, above all, their knowledge and technology, into the world.

After discovering America and reaching Australia and Indonesia during the fifteenth and sixteenth centuries, the Europeans founded numerous trading posts backed by powerful stock companies. The bourgeoisie, which in their countries of origin had been able to establish sustainable and strong institutions by way of evolution or revolution, now had the capacity to trade more than just goods: ideas, lifestyles, political institutions, etc. Hence, these areas, which had always been outside the world system, were opened to the influence of the old civilised regions. Subsequently, Europe has stamped its own characteristics upon the rest of he world.

The European expansion of trade was, in the same way as in old Sumer, in principle as much a conquest through a series of military campaigns. This kind of trade expansion reached its peak during the course of the eighteenth century. The nineteenth century experienced the transition from trade to capital export. At its heart, capital export is an export of the political system. The European expansion came at a time when the whole world lay open to it. In all the affected countries, a new bourgeoisie came into being that tried to emulate the European original. The emulation of civilisational structures spread by expansion, which can be traced back to the neolithic, reaches its peak with world trade and capital export. In the last quarter of the twentieth century, the world as a whole has become an area of expansion, where all borders are abolished. The attraction of capital renders the use of violence unnecessary. Worldwide, everybody seems to seek recognition by capitalism, whatever the cost may be. The capitalist tour of conquest produces the result that (mostly purely quantitative) economic growth, based on high-risk capital that passes quickly from hand to hand, produces crisis after crisis. A look at the geographic dimension of this expansion shows a number of surprising developments. Two great world wars, numerous internal wars and the classical colonial wars have left Europe largely exhausted and worn down. This condition is also a consequence, presumably, of the enormous civilisational stretch. After World War II, the United States became the main protagonist of capitalist civilisation, naive and high-spirited, as had been Europe before. Nearly all of North America was unified as a single civilisation under the leadership of the United States. America has pushed ahead with the scientific–technological revolution, potentially also outstripping Europe. With the help of technologies like the Internet, nuclear energy, space travel, in which the United States has the edge over the rest of the world, capitalist ideology is carried into the most remote corners in a neo-colonialist way under the guise of free world trade. It is a global attack and it is quite successful. The old nation state, however, like the feudal remainders some hundred years ago, is getting in the way of borderless globalisation and has to be overcome. In this way, the United States concludes a historic mission: the development of the entire world by means of a matured capitalism.

When the so-called *real socialist* attempt failed at the end of the twentieth century, the above process inevitably speeded up. In principle, the United States is undergoing a revision and restoration of the processes concluded in Europe. In particular, there is a tendency to support other regimes, regardless of former ideological differences (socialist versus capitalist), mainly on the basis of their democratic development and human rights standards. Capitalism now abstains from its once predatory character. The use of the fatherland as a *reservoir for exploitation*[1] is to be abandoned as a nineteenth-century practice. The final wave of globalisation has seized all countries and cultures.

A number of signs indicate that the present situation is similar to that of other civilisations at their peaks. This is suggested not only by historical comparisons but also by the internal state of the system, which does not seem to have any more leeway for positive development, only for crises and a new start. In order to understand why the present system has reached this state of crises, let us have one more look at its expansion and maturation phase. Although expansion from a centre outwards can be regarded as hinting at the maturity of the system, history indicates that expansion often serves as a means of overcoming internal crises and contradictions inherent in the system. In order to maintain successful internal economic and social levels, the system expands by increasing its supply of the products and resources necessary for the preservation of its productivity. This is the logic of colonialism. Additionally, and even more importantly, social struggles about the emerging values can also be channelled outwards and thus softened.

Amongst all known civilisations, capitalist civilisation has been the one that has succeeded in perfecting this method. Capitalism is undefeated in exhausting the possibilities of internal and external exploitation – compliance is achieved with the help of advertising. Its global expansion is historically accomplished: with the exception of space (for the time being, at least) there are no empty, unknown, profitable regions left. Technology, once the springboard of capitalism's military superiority, might no longer be required to fulfill that role: NATO, founded as a pact against the Soviet Union, has lost its original meaning. The nuclear balance of fear has become obsolete. Military technology and organisation place a heavy burden on the capitalist societies. The new objectives are mirrored in the initiative for the so-called European Security and Defence Identity (ESDI), which is supposed to be used as some kind of expedition force in smaller, local conflicts or as an operational peacekeeping force. Antagonism against the system, which had led to enormous armies and costly arms technology, has mostly been overcome. The struggle between the capitalist and the socialist bloc belongs to the past. The classic national liberation wars, too, have in principle been successful and can be regarded as completed. The internal class struggles have been reduced to a level where they can be continued through peaceful and democratic means. There has never been another epoch of civilisation leaving behind so many dead and so much destruction as the twentieth century. Humanity has (I am saying this with respect for all of mankind) experienced its own apocalypse. Thanks to the power of an enormously expanded science and technology, the end of the world – those heavens and hells that have been conjured up as myths since the early days of civilisation – has now, in the twentieth century, at the hands of numerous ordinary people, become a worldwide reality. When comparing science and mythology, we inevitably have to ask ourselves which of the two might be the more dangerous.

Capitalism has arrived at its zenith in the twentieth century. Large-scale wars are no longer necessary, nor would they be helpful in solving problems – rather, they might be suicidal. Wars of distribution have become futile, inefficient and even harmful because of the sophisticated state of science and technology and the boundless freedom of capital. This development has nothing to do with any philanthropist attitude of capitalism. Here, as ever, profit is the measure. Wars that would have been profitable in the past now involve major risks. Hence, the law of profit now enforces peace. Profit and technological development have gained a state of equilibrium. Wars for profit have become unnecessary. This may change again as soon as the conditions change and peace becomes more expensive than war. Therefore, the zenith of capitalism is also a phase of transition.

All systems of civilisation, as we saw, go through three historical phases: the foundation phase, the institution-forming phase and the zenith – just as a human being passes through childhood, adulthood and old age. All well-known historical civilisations – Sumer, Egypt, Rome, Persia, China, Islam, etc. – went through these phases, all with similar characteristics. All important systems of civilisation are confronted with a conflict during the last phase – civilisations age and wear out. If the system is in danger of being overthrown, they try to compensate for the effects of ageing by restoration, reform or both.

Usually, restoration is the more reactionary way. The term *restoration* is generally used for the time after a revolutionary movement has been defeated by counter-revolutionary measures. Good examples are the third Sumerian dynasty of Ur, the New Empire in Egypt, and the last two centuries of the Roman Empire in the West. A system of extreme state authority with strictly applied rules is introduced, as is some sort of co-operative agricultural system. There is justification for calling regimes like these, established to stop decline, "fascist". The different characteristics these regimes show originate in differing circumstances and starting conditions.

A reform process, on the other hand, is an attempt to prevent a violent putsch by way of compromise with the opposition and by initiating gradual change. Of this, too, we can find many historical examples.

A third possibility is a successful revolution. The old regime is overthrown and replaced with a new one, which sets off quick and radical measures in order to install a revolutionary social programme.

In reality, we often find all of these processes side by side or even merging with each other. Subdividing the capitalist system into phases, its starting point and the development of its basic characteristics can be located between the twelfth and sixteenth centuries. From the seventeenth to the nineteenth centuries followed the phase of institution forming and expansion. In the twentieth century, after the great wars, the expansion covered the whole world and the system reached its peak. The system's basic characteristics and institutions were formed during the first two phases. At the zenith of each civilisation, the next system is already discernible. The main contradictions develop and new syntheses can be discerned. Eventually the contradictions will end in conflict, a conflict that may pave the way for something new.

Until the epoch of bourgeois revolutions, the French middle class and proletariat were united by common interests against the feudal order. After the victory of the revolution, when the middle class took over the leadership in reorganising and re-institutionalising French society, this alliance came to an end. The French bourgeois revolution and the great ventures undertaken by Napoleon in order to spread it are typical examples of the phase of institution forming and expansion in the life of a civilisation. Even the temporary restoration between 1815 and 1830 of some fragments of the *ancien régime*, being the final offensive of the feudal order, could not prevent the bourgeois age of class societies. All areas of society were re-organised according to the priorities and the legislative will of the new dominant class – from mind to psyche, from economy to politics and the military. The ensuing phase of struggles with the working classes – over ideology and social and political practice – became increasingly visible.

In this sense, the nineteenth century was a time of differentiation and clarification of class identities. Liberalism, the ideology of the bourgeoisie, and socialism, the ideological expression of equality by the working classes, developed in quick succession. These new ideologies constituted the ideological struggle between the bourgeoisie and the working class. The latter for the first time in history had a systematic ideological basis, arrived at by using scientific methods. Karl Marx and his main work, *Das Kapital*, became for the working class what the Gospels had been for Christianity. There were frequent strikes and permanent industrial action in the civilisation centres. The first and second Internationales were founded and the new secular movement of the oppressed created new hope.

The twentieth century witnessed a broad wave of national liberation movements in areas on the periphery where nationalist ideologies had arrived and firearms were freely available. In Russia, an alliance of nationalists and workers took the first successful steps towards modern democratic civilisation when they overthrew the absolutist Russian monarchy. Although the attempt was unsuccessful in the long run, many lessons which can be helpful in clearing up contradictions and errors can be learned from it. The capitalist civilisation shrank back in horror from these incidents and developments and took a first serious attempt towards restoration. German nationalism under the leadership of Hitler can be read as the general response of a capitalist order lapsing into deep fear in the face of socialism. We may understand German nationalism as a restoration under counter-revolutionary conditions. In the end, European capitalism had to relinquish its leading position to the United States. In the second half of the twentieth century, North America grew into the most progressive centre of capitalism. The establishment of nation states all over the world led to a new political world map. In spite of weak points in its foundation, real socialism had some successes. It induced or influenced democratic developments in the United States and post-fascist Europe. After the fascist restorations, a democratic reform process began.

The twentieth century, with its imperialism and national liberation movements, its socialism and democracy, revolution and counter-revolution, restoration and reforms, putsches and counter-putsches and all its bloody wars, may well be called the age of madness. The cruellest weapons yet were invented and used, and all the values of faith and ethics were overthrown. Not only human society but the natural environment too is under threat of destruction. The capitalist drive for profit has taken the place of the divine will of old. At the beginning of the slave-holder era, an unprecedented surplus production had brought about the god–kings; the unprecedented capital-created surplus value has produced even more dangerous and godless kings which now torment humanity. In the twentieth century, capitalism attacked and oppressed all conceptions of a free and equal world that the workers – oppressed, imperfect and limited though they were – had wanted to create. Somehow, this reminds me of the Spartacus slave rebellion in ancient Rome, which was bloodily crushed in 70 BCE. The end of that rebellion saw 5,000 people crucified and exhibited along the Via Appia. The system had been threatened at its heart – and retaliated violently and madly.

It is true that socialism, revolution, and the national liberation movements have retreated and left an epoch behind them. However, it is just as true that capitalism cannot continue its customary course. Neither revolutionary tendencies nor counter-revolution, neither imperialism nor liberation movements were really successful. Nor can we say that either restoration or reforms have prevailed. What we have, in fact, is a completely new situation.

It is also true that capitalism strives to develop everywhere, including the former socialist countries. Unarguably, a government-controlled capitalist system is developing even in China, despite all claims to the contrary. Just as obviously, capitalist orders are being institutionalised in all minor and major countries in Africa, Asia and South-America, adapting remarkably well to local conditions. However, we should not be too astonished to find that what is happening there is quite different from the processes of the capitalist epoch in civilisation history. A number of symptoms is characteristic of this process, primarily the scientific–technological revolution beginning in the second half of the twentieth century. It seems that science and technology always play a major part in civilisation-related transformation processes. The new level of science and technology has created a new situation for profitability, most clearly expressed by computer and communications technology. Capital can be invested or withdrawn anywhere without difficulty. Working hours have significantly decreased. The former colonies are on their way towards a limited capitalist development. Everything, however, is dependent on financial capital, which has established worldwide rule with the help of the stock market. There is almost no government that does not respond somehow to developments at the stock market. Wars, in former times a proper means of gaining profits, have become an obstacle. Profitability requires the trouble-free, smooth functioning of the system.

The situation at the end of the twentieth century, therefore, is the result of antagonist ideological frameworks, capitalism and socialism, producing a society with characteristic features of both, a process which has been decisively influenced by the rapid development of science and technology. It seems that, for the first time in history, the forces dominating class society are in agreement about determining their fates themselves – albeit not yet under equal conditions – freely and in peace and under a democratic form of government.

I believe, therefore, that a democratic civilisation is not an illusion but is already materialising.

19

The Overall Crisis of Civilisation and the Age of Democracy

Understanding the relationship between the level of technological development and class formation is of the utmost importance for the social liberation struggle. However wrong the notion of the "end of history" seems to be, it appears that the type of civilisation which is based on a division between classes is coming to an end.

The emergence of the social formation which we call "class society" was rendered possible in the neolithic by the technological potential of that age. The division of people into those who rule and those who are ruled resulted in the state as a political entity. This is the social phenomenon we call "the civilisation process" – a phenomenon which first occurred in Lower Mesopotamia. Technology, obviously, is part of civilisation and, as a necessary momentum in the creation of classes, it has a dual effect. In the first phase, when the technological basis is still weak, it enforces a growing differentiation between the classes. People are used like pieces of equipment and property. The slave-holder society is born. Man's servitude is a consequence of the low technological basis. Later, when technology develops to a higher level, the gap between the classes decreases. (This even held true towards the end of the slave-holder age, when iron based technology ensured the widespread use of tools.)

Technological development is the material prerequisite for the development of political freedom. When industrialised factories replaced manufactories, a radical change occurred in the relation between classes. Advanced knowledge of production processes rendered slave labour unnecessary and required the free movement of workers with particular skills. People were able to offer their skills for sale. This is one of the key principles of the capitalist system.

The capitalist epoch added ground-breaking innovations to the history of technology. Moreover, with the reconciliation of science and technology each was able to advance the other's progress. In particular the twentieth century experienced a massive scientific and technological revolution, as a result of which we saw the rise of electronic and nuclear engineering apart from the highly developed mechanical engineering. When society came into contact with these radically new technologies, all traditional moral concepts were overthrown. Far-reaching changes – especially in politics, state systems and the military – were effected.

The state as a manifestation of concentrated and institutionalised politics was an invention of the age of slavery. Inadequate knowledge about its origin was kept alive by Marxist sociology when it focused its analysis of the state solely on the capitalist form. The first form of the state and its general principles were shaped by Sumerian priests without any kind of scientific basis. It was a tool of exploitation, justified by mythology and religion. The concept of the state as something sacred has been passed down in various disguises, from the Sumerian priests to the present. It is a dangerous concept, meant to preserve exploitation and oppression.

One might contend here that all of class history had only maintained and strengthened the Sumerian approach, with each new class in power refining it a little. The dominating and exploiting class protects existing institutions for its own interests. The state, and with it politics and the military, are functions used in perfecting the technology-based system of exploitation and directing its social structure.

The capitalist state bears the mark of its Sumerian priestly origin and the exploiting class in power is aware that it cannot survive without it. The state as such is not questioned or analysed, but safeguarded. Time and again it is restored and given a new identity. In this tradition, the Soviet revolutionaries created the much praised workers' state, ignoring, however, how much their state system resembled in style the historical blueprint found in ancient Sumer and Egypt. It was mere self-deception when they tried to sell the sacredness of their state, its repressive methods and the hard labour it required as a "dictatorship of the proletariat". However, this was understood only much later, but then very clearly.

The term *dictatorship of the proletariat* pretends to have something to do with working-class people. However, any kind of dictatorship, in my opinion, amounts to exploitation. The collapse of Soviet socialism was caused by such errors concerning state and dictatorship. The oppressed working classes do not need the state as a tool, because the state implicitly perpetuates class society, which is the true reason for its existence.

When I call the state "unchanged", I refer to its basic principles and functions. One of the main reasons for the failure of many honest efforts towards a free and equal world without oppression and of the great struggle of many revolutionaries throughout history can be found in their faulty conceptions of the state – both in theory and in practice. The countless different systems established by them became their undoing because they were not able to see through the two-faced character of the state. I am not arguing that we should get rid of the state – as long as there are people divided into classes we need the state at least for technical reasons. A life without the state in the present historical situation could only end back in the Stone Age or naked anarchy.

While class society and the state – civilisation, in other words – have been formed as products both of technology and of its weaknesses, we have to ask the crucial question: Is there any possible process in the development of technology which could render obsolete the division into classes and, at the same time, the system of civilisation based on this division?

If technology was responsible for the development of class divisions, a sufficiently sophisticated level of technology might one day be the instrument for overcoming class society. History shows that each instance of technological progress corresponds to a decrease in class differences and an increase in freedom.[1] One of the most significant historical consequences of the scientific–technological revolution of the twentieth century might thus turn out to be the abolition of the class system. Hence, it would be a grave error to continue using in an unmodified way the theoretical assessments that were formulated to combat the conditions and contradictions of the eighteenth and nineteenth centuries.

What distinguishes capitalism from feudalism is expressed in an accelerating curve of scientific–technological development, which subsequently brought about a number of socio-political institutions, such as the nation state, the republic and secularism, and which eventually led to nationalism and class struggles. We can assume that the social, political, and military consequences of the second big scientific–technological revolution – that of the twentieth century – will be considerably greater and more permanent. Its first consequence was the disbanding of the power blocs of the cold war. The second important consequence was that the nation state as we knew it lost much of its earlier relevance, due to the accelerating globalisation process. Thirdly, the transition towards an information society is gathering enormous speed with the revolutionary phenomenon of the Internet.

No theoretical analysis can understand the present age without taking into account the economic, social, political and military consequences of the unprecedented progress in almost all fields of technology. No viable political programme can ignore this.

THE DISINTEGRATION OF CAPITALISM AS A SYSTEM OF CIVILISATION

World War II destroyed the opposing systems of capitalism and socialism in so far so they were based on science and philosophy – or, more precisely, on an essentially mechanistic interpretation of science and technology.[2] At that stage, technology primarily meant the application of the laws of mechanics in industrial production processes, creating an enormous demand for manual labour. Science's contribution to philosophy consisted mainly of support for positivism. As we have already seen, people valued the old political institutions and mythology-derived beliefs. While bourgeois liberalism ended in fascism and chauvinistic nationalism, socialism led to authoritarianism and later even totalitarian statism and social nationalism. The Third Internationale, undefeated in the war and quite successful in many regions after the war, fell apart owing to ideological differences and ignorance.

While both systems did temporarily overcome their crises, neither was victorious over the other; the two existed in a state of equilibrium. It was evident that capitalism could no longer gain strength by means of war and that the time of its unconstrained domination was over. Moreover, both blocs adhered to an inadequate understanding of the class struggle and the struggle between imperialist capitalism and oppressed nations. This resulted in shortcomings and mistakes. In the end, the world has experienced neither the "end of history" nor the age of the "dictatorship of the proletariat", but a deep crisis which signifies the final stage of the class-based civilisation system. Moreover, the results of the post-war scientific–technological revolution (which had brought mankind new basic material and intellectual equipment and could have made possible a life of plenty) have not been made available to all of humanity. If not prevented by the prevalent ideologies and politics, the existing national and class-based contradictions could have been resolved peacefully with the help of technologies already at hand. However, the institutional superstructure of the system and the present-day distribution of property prevent the next system from actualising.

Capital's favourite tool for realising money is the international financial market or the stock market. Here, money multiplies with no intermediate working process – as in a casino. An averaged property distribution in combination with the existing conditions of production allow casino capitalism to pervade society and even prevent the system from reorganising and restructuring. With the current level of technology, if the available capital were used to satisfy basic needs, for the environment, health, education and employment, the class differences could have been greatly reduced and most current conflicts and social contradictions could have been peacefully resolved or avoided.

OUTLINES OF AN ALTERNATIVE

It seems that bloody revolutions cannot offer a viable alternative. Moreover, the present level of technological development makes them unnecessary. Clearly, today we have a situation where even a shepherd on a remote mountain plateau can make use of modern technology in order to communicate with the rest of the world and access the world's greatest information sources. At such a time, where everyone effortlessly communicates with each other, bloody methods – apart from self-defence – have become senseless. Technology offers unlimited opportunities for an increase in economic productivity. It can also create the awareness and necessary organisation to overcome the political obstacles blocking these opportunities. Also in *this* respect technology renders class-based government obsolete.

In the nineteenth century and in the first half of the twentieth century such technological possibilities were not yet available. Therefore, wars, rebellions and clandestine operations were inevitable and acceptable. The radical and historically new revolutions of the second half of the twentieth century have changed this completely. Today, some scholars divide history into three fundamental epochs. The first is the agricultural revolution and the rise of the rural communities that we have conjured up so often in the preceding chapters (from 10000 until 3000 BCE). The second, the emergence of cities and urban communities (lasting till the middle of the twentieth century). And lastly there is the epoch we live in and that has only just begun. It is characterised and determined by the technological leap we are witnessing. This concept, of course, has its shortcomings. Nonetheless, it is able to draw a consistent and fundamental line on the basis of the relationship between technology and human society.

We may safely assume, therefore, that a class-based society is irrelevant for new social and political structures which are emerging as a result of the development of science and technology. Rather, their shape will be determined by vocational and professional skills and knowledge. Nor will political qualities in the old sense be of prime importance any longer. The focus, so it seems, will shift to management skills and economic engineering. In future, the problem no longer will be how to impose labour and government on people, but how to qualify them adequately and insert them productively into the economic processes.

We are moving towards an epoch of voluntary participation by all in government, where pressure and displeasure have been overcome, rendering work a joy and pleasure inseparable from everybody's life. The original socialist idea, at least as far as work is concerned, can be realised. Mankind, for the first time in history, has developed tools and acquired the knowledge necessary for this.

POLITICS AND THE STATE

It has become clear that the classic forms of politics and state can no longer control the present civilisation system.

Military technology is developing to a degree which will permit mankind to completely destroy itself. The traditional political concepts could not prevent worldwide wars, thus demonstrating their inability to successfully lead and exercise government. The existing political institutions, therefore, need to be replaced. Political ethics have become bankrupt and the old civilisation is unable to solve problems. The state of the institutions, which rest on the ruling conditions of production, reflects this. The post-war balance – the nuclear stalemate between the blocs – ended with the fall of the Soviet Union. It became clear that the post-World War II geopolitical models had failed. Presently, both Europe, with its experimental, small expeditionary forces, and the United States, with its attempts at establishing a rocket defence shield, are unable to present appropriate alternatives to the failed balance of power. They prefer to safeguard their short-term interests.

An interim historical period seems inevitable, not least because the remainders of the old civilisation system are still extremely influential. The old and the new temporarily exist side by side in such transition periods – a phenomenon well known in history as we have seen in our consideration of the ancient slave-holding empires and medieval feudalism.

THE TRANSITIONAL PHASE

While the crisis of the old civilisation system escalates and the emergence of a new civilisation has not yet taken concrete form, we live in an interim period. I would like to call it "the epoch of democratic civilisation". At the end of the twentieth century, democratic governments have developed worldwide as regimes of compromise. This is not voluntarily, but a consequence of the failed option of fascism on the part of capitalism and the failed totalitarianism of real socialism. (I use the term *fascism* here in a sense that is not limited to Hitler's National Socialism but to denote conditions, emerging from the bloody regimes of reactionary capitalism, where the capital of the financial and stock markets became the predominant form of capital, spreading not only through the centres but also to and beyond the periphery.) In the face of threatening decay, confronted with the possibility that socialism might establish itself as a civilisation system, and driven by the chauvinistic character of nationalism, these regimes became extremely hard and cruel. Their failure, however, was caused by the extent of freedom humanity had achieved and by the new option scientific and technological progress presented to capitalism: a lasting compromise. This compromise was called *democracy*, and is, indeed, not completely unrelated to democracy. Owing to the enormous successes of the technological revolution, democracy was seen as rooted in this revolution and advancing it. It thus gained the confidence of the bourgeoisie. At the end of the twentieth century, this limited and restricted type of democracy is widely regarded as an adequate way of life and government. It keeps spreading over the world, seemingly on its way to become a universally accepted system.

The totalitarian tendencies of real socialism are contradicting the principle of freedom that socialism was supposed to uphold. Even though the integration of the individual into society results from its goal of equality, real socialism is bound to fail as soon as it becomes clear that the individual cannot be as creative within this system as within liberalism. Perfect equality only exists among slaves and slaves lack freedom. All progress ever since the age of slavery has been aimed at gaining more freedom, whether brought about by left or by right wing ideologists. State-based systems always sacrifice individual freedom for the sake of equality. The state itself is the living denial of freedom under the conditions of a class society. State-based control under real socialism is considerably stronger than under capitalism and allows much less individual freedom.

In contrast to regimes granting individual freedom, those oppressing freedom can only be successful through the use of violence. Reasons for the Soviet Union's failure may be found in its ideological framework. Without a philosophical concept to provide the individual with at least as much freedom as capitalism *and* with a realistic approach to equality, any talk about a new civilisation was so much nonsense. Equipped with a vulgar, materialist philosophy as their guide to life, people suddenly found themselves in a new kind of slave-based social order. A highly complex phenomenon like human life cannot simply be reduced to a number of materialistic clichés, ignoring people's emotions. The Soviet reality may serve as an example here. The various types of twentieth-century nationalism do not differ much from tribalism and do not contribute to a new kind of civilisation. In a totalitarian state under the nuclear balance of power, people become either soldiers or workers – an unbearable and intolerable situation, exceeding even the conditions in class-based societies. The functions of normal government cannot be exercised in such a state. No revolutionary or counter-revolutionary system can survive such structures in the long run.

There are numerous definitions for what today we call democracy. We might discuss in detail its class character and its degree of peacefulness, or contemplate its theoretical and historical origins. We might also point out that it is not a civilisation system per se. For the first time in history, all individuals, nations, cultures, ideologies, and economic and political ideas have the chance to develop together *and* in competition with each other. Since the end of the twentieth century, democracy has started to overcome its narrow class character. All former types of democracy were marked by the rule of a tightly restricted class of (mostly rich) people. (In some respects, the ancient Athenian class divisions have existed for a long time!) However, the democratic system emerging towards the end of the twentieth century was able to overcome these limitations to a large extent. Class differences have been substantially reduced, and the size of the ruling class has increased. In many fields formerly censored and controlled, there is now freedom of expression and freedom of association and organisation. Antagonisms and their supporters can develop and change without the use of violence.

I do not mean to say that all the known antagonisms – be they class-based, nation-based, intellectual, religious, cultural or social – have vanished into thin air. Of course not. Nor has solidarity come to an end. But, it seems to me, we have entered an epoch where all these conflicts can be resolved in a peaceful way according to laws.

There is no doubt that democracy is a more humane system than any of the barbarous, class-based traditions that regarded bloodshed as a criterion for heroism and greatness. No victory won by massacres can ever be sacred. If there is anything worth calling sacred, it is the advancement of humanity and progress that does not cause suffering; it is the emerging type of democracy that is replacing the bloody regimes of class history with freedom of expression for all groups – political, social, religious, ethnic or based on sexual preferences. Let me stress once more that this is a historical novelty. The development of contemporary history is an internal evolutionary process. It is not marked by spectacular occurrences, but grants mankind room for the creative development of psyche and mind.

A crucial fact that I wish to emphasise in our analysis of civilisation is that neither the creation nor the abolition of classes can be accomplished by the use of violence or force. Rather, the decisive factors are technological capacity and scientific knowledge. Wherever a community can increase productivity by means of technology, classes will inevitably form, since everyone can gain profit from this development. Class division stems from the creation of material opportunities. Its development in the course of history corresponds to the development of material productivity.

From a practical point of view, the abolition of classes in the capitalist system by revolution (i.e. by violence) seems possible. However, the experience of real socialism makes it clear that class-based institutions cannot be abolished in this way – they will be reformed or reproduced at the first opportunity. In situations of real socialism, some classes were abolished by force, but the emergence of new hybrid classes could not be prevented. Again, this was caused by the (insufficient) level of technological development. A social phenomenon created by technology can only be overcome when rendered obsolete by technology. Revolutions and violence may obstruct social phenomena but they cannot abolish them.

In the same way, as an inevitable consequence of technological development, societies will disappear or change. The absurd state of world affairs reigning before the rise of contemporary democracy resulted from ignorance of this fact. While neither fascism nor totalitarian real socialism could succeed, the fulfilment of many of their unrealised goals is now a possibility – thanks to technological development. In the same way, we no longer need gigantic armies of industrial and agricultural workers; their classes *too* have become obsolete because of technological development. Obviously, technology and not violence is the solution.

Contemporary democracy thus seems to be an essential interim stage for the development of technology to a level where true democracy can be accomplished through it. The power of democracy lies in the fact that it always includes a non-violent solution. Scientific surveys suggest that there might be a correlation between stable democracy and economic development.

Let us have a look at some aspects of the emerging democratic age.

Crisis

Contemporary democracy is a function of the deep crisis in which the civilisation system depending on class society finds itself – a class society that has been growing continuously since the time of the first slave-holder societies. The entire social system of basic principles and institutions has become inadequate and inefficient in the face of the enormous scientific revolution. This has resulted in an all-comprising reorganisation from economy to ideology, casting doubt on all principles and leaving all institutions dysfunctional. What the new social system will entail is not yet clear. Its ideological identity and its basic institutions cannot yet be made out. The only thing we know is that neither fascist restoration nor Soviet-type revolutionary change can offer a solution. During the current epoch, democracy as we have come to know it will determine the way we live and the way we are governed.

Class Society Has Become An Obstacle

The scientific–technological revolution has eliminated the necessity for class-based societies and civilisation processes based on them. The present (and still developing) level of technology requires the abolition of classes, which have become an obstacle to the way of social progress just as much as they were once a necessity. Technology demands the negation of class society and the emergence of a society based on professional skills and knowledge. In other words, the technological revolution is the strongest cornerstone of contemporary democracy. A determinate, interdependent relationship has formed between them. Contemporary democracy has not been arbitrarily established as some kind of political preference; it is a direct consequence of the material pressure exerted by technological development and scientific progress. Democracy and technology have arrived at a level where they can nourish each other and further each other's development.

Violence Is a Result of Scientific Ignorance

As argued before, the abolition or transformation of class society cannot be achieved by violence – this can only result from scientific–technological development. Whereas a single class *may* be created or abolished by force, it will inevitably disappear or reappear in the face of other pressures.

Throughout human history, violence has been a product of ignorance and insufficiently developed social practice. In particular, those mechanisms of violence and force which are at the disposal of class-based civilisation (the state, above all) will only lose their importance when the underlying ignorance can be disposed of. Scientific–technological development has made this a possibility, thus rendering theories about change through counter-revolutionary, reactionary, revolutionary or conservative violence irrelevant.

The exaggerated and merciless use of violence throughout history has surpassed and narrowed down evolutionary processes. Contemporary democracy refers to change in accordance with the natural evolution of society. It is aware of the fact that the scientific–technological foundations for this change are becoming available. It would be completely wrong, however, to draw the conclusion that democracy is a compromise between revolutionary and counter-revolutionary violence. Neither a compromise with violence nor a violent compromise is in the nature of democracy. On the contrary, democracy aims at removing violence and force from society. This has nothing to do with submission to pressure or circumstances. It is a result of the belief that true emancipatory development can only flourish in an environment where violence is not valid. Contemporary democracy thus requires criticism of all forms of civilisation based on force and violence. Democracy is the rule of self-criticism. It does not take a tactical or strategic but a fundamental position towards violence. It is a basic principle of democracy to reject force and violence, utilising knowledge and technology to this end. This principle expresses a fundamental philosophical assumption. Democracy's approach towards violence emphasises its peaceful character.

Peace should not be understood as a submission to violence. It entails the renunciation of violence and the embracing of a society, civilisation, and world free of violence. Self-defence, on the other hand, is an important principle of contemporary democracy. Defending one's own existence is a legitimate basic, and often constitutional, right. It is not democratic behaviour to submit to undemocratic laws or regimes. This does not include the destruction of anti-democratic forces in a counter-attack, but envisages the overcoming of injustice by general awareness and social organisation, which may amount to permanent protests and demonstrations. Resistance falls under the premise of self-defence and is, therefore, at the heart of law. Legitimate self-defence, including armed self-defence, is compatible with the principles of contemporary democracy. Any act beyond the constraints of these principles is not legitimate self-defence.

A Well-organised Social Mosaic

Democracy comprises not only a class, a clique, an estate or a dominant nation, but all of society. Many historical democratic institutions were unable to cross the boundaries of a single class or ethnic group. We may call them classical class democracies. Contemporary democracy, however, regards all different individual and group identities as legitimate. It also defends their right to freedom and equality, protecting minorities and asking them to contribute freely to society. In principle, this constitutes a dynamic, violence-free system based on the free association of individuals and groups and their activities in resolving all social conflicts. The basis of this democracy – and only then can we call it democracy – is a well-organised social mosaic forming a *democratic society*, which allows for any idea, religion, or cultural expression.

Justice

A democratic society requires a democratic state and a government that receives its authority – the authority of its basic legislative and executive organs – by society-wide elections. The history of civilisation is the history of the opposition between society and state, where the latter is almost always opposed to anything that smells of democracy. The state functions best where it effectively directs, controls and exploits society. A considerable portion of civilisation has been wasted on such activities on the part of the state.

Contemporary democracy, however, rearranges the relationship between state and society. Since it rests on increasingly complex social relations, it is at pains always to be transparent and open, and wishes to be perceived as an object of trust rather than a source of fear and exploitation; it presents the state as a guarantor of social justice. This is no longer the state in the classical sense. Its new objective is to effectively handle and coordinate the complex social relations on the highest level. The state structures are meant to be reorganised into a decision-making authority and administration for those areas which are not to be denationalised and with which the particular interest groups cannot deal on their own.

The body most resistant to democratic change is the state itself – to a large extent caused by its deeply rooted institutions and traditions, as old as civilisation itself. This will change, however, when it becomes clear that the state does not remain unaffected by the impetus of the scientific–technological revolution.

The Third Sphere

Those political institutions that are not part of the state will also have to become democratic. They will have to perform a bridge function between state and society. The democratisation of politics will create the necessary dynamics – both in theory and in practice. Until today, politics (especially in the Middle East) was a rigid institution, mostly outside society proper, with invariable roles, organs and traditional rules. Changes seemed possible only by force and violence. Democratic politics, though, is a system that allows for the peaceful and rapid realisation of changes. It is based on regular elections and a system of multiple parties, representing all kind of ideas and programmes within the constraints of a democratic society. Thus political parties, lobby groups and a great number of different organisations of civil society are sometimes able to exercise considerable influence on the decision-making processes. The institutions of civil society comprise the whole variety of political parties and all other organisations of civil society which participate in the democratic life. Beside society and state, they constitute something that we may call the *third sphere*.

It is exactly this sphere – which comprises the tools of democratic politics – that opens the door to developments hitherto impossible. In previous epochs, such organisations were forbidden and relegated to the realm of underground activities.

Human Rights and Women's Liberation

These are issues of central importance to the development of contemporary democracy. It would be insufficient to understand the terms *human rights* and *women's liberation* only as catchphrases of capitalist society. On the contrary, they became more important as the shortcomings of capitalism became obvious. Human rights and women's rights are two essentials of a general democratisation of society. They, too, can only develop in so far as the framework of classical, traditional civilisation is demolished. They are the results of the social conditions brought about by capitalism. Thus, they are criteria of contemporary democracy and a measure of its level of development. The legal framework of the new civilisation is described particularly in its handling of human rights, the cardinal concept of the modern age and as such unknown throughout class history. Its social basis is to a large extent determined by women's liberty.

Dialectical Materialism

The philosophical foundation of contemporary democracy is a system based on principles which cannot be interpreted randomly according to any group or class's own interest. It is a philosophy deeply intertwined with the history of science. One of the strongest pillars of contemporary democracy is the view of dialectical materialism concerning the existence, unity and transformation of contradictions. Its fundamental contradiction lies between the old class-based civilisation and the realities emerging from the new civilisational development. In this context we may regard the old civilisation as the dialectical thesis contradicted by the new phenomena as its antithesis. At the end of this process, we shall see a synthesis. Since contemporary democracy is still at the beginning of its development, the characteristics of the old and feeble, crisis-ridden civilisation still considerably outnumber the new phenomena. Nonetheless, they represent the future, for they are young, strong and vital. Thanks to the level of technological development and existing democratic structures, these much opposed tendencies might yet result in some kind of synthesis on a new and advanced level, certainly not without difficulties, but without too much use of violence.

By making use of this principle of philosophy, contemporary democracy attaches special importance to the terms *phenomenon*, *relation* and *transformation*. The philosophy of dialectical materialism is put into practice in the open system of contemporary democracy. It is open to change and participation in all areas of politics, society and state. Closed systems, in their inability to provide solutions, constantly cause serious harm to society as a whole. However, such systems will in the end dissolve nonetheless and comply with the dialectical law of history.

To sum up, the concept *epoch of democratic civilisation* denotes a long-term historical period, during which, in the course of scientific–technological evolution, the overcoming of class-based civilisation has not yet been completed and the new has not yet become concrete.

This concept assumes that the old and the new are intertwined and that the transformation process will be peaceful. It also assumes that the current level of technology has created conditions which form a material basis suitable for any form of violence-free change. It claims that the traditional state and the closed society are defeated in the sense that a third sphere – i.e. civil society – has gained more and more influence on state and society. The rise of civil society between the spheres of state and society as a whole brings to the fore a pluralist way of government and life. All kinds of differences (ideological, economical, social, ethnic, gender, racial and cultural) are regarded as the mutual riches of society as a whole. Each group enjoys freedom of expression and can participate actively in all aspects of social life, with its own identity, awareness and way of organising itself. This approach finds expression in building and rebuilding all the necessary institutions on a pluralist basis. If I were asked to give the age that I am describing here a general name, I would call it "the age of the democratic pluralist world".

THE ULTIMATE FORM OF CIVILISATION BASED ON CLASS SOCIETY

There is one phenomenon characterising the phase of decay of this age: the increasing avoidance, disapproval – even condemnation – of violent approaches to political problems. Violence for the sake of exploitation only produced destruction. The forceful occupation of property brought about violence when it had to be protected on the part of the ruling classes. The earliest gods of mythology did not know violence. However, with the emergence of class society and the coming of feudalism in particular, the gods were endowed with qualities of punishment and condemnation. The part of violence in social change is generally less crucial than we tend to think. It is sometimes important when it comes to qualitative leaps in social processes, performing transformative tasks, for example, in overcoming conservative hindrances. These phases are short and limited, though, and subsequently, when successful, the acts of violence have to be overcome. Violence, over the course of history, has mostly been employed in the service of unjust deeds such as conquest, occupation and plunder, which produced immense devastation and destruction. The injustice of such acts of violence was often justified with a reference to God. Those who died became martyrs, those who lived were praised as veterans, and the whole barbaric act itself was soon sung about in a heroic epic.

In the history of civilisation, the understanding of violence is a result of mythological, religious, and philosophical ideas in the service of those who exercised control as rulers and exploiters. In this way historiography is changed into something akin to fiction or a revisionist historical novel.

Above all, this way of writing history needs to be altered. Only then will history become accessible to genuine analysis. The greatest injustice is usually based on such unjust historiography. Distorted historiography results in practical errors as a consequence of misinformed analysis.

In the midst of a merciless epoch, it is a prime objective of my writings to contribute at least in outline to a well-informed analysis, and thus eventually to possible solutions in the conflicts of history and civilisation.

The recent phase of capitalism has become the subject of many assessments and evaluations. Representatives of a conservative view of history already see the "end of history". Authors of the left see the age of socialism dawning on the horizon. I have already emphasised that in my opinion such evaluations – on the one hand a static idealism, on the other a vulgar materialism – fail to grasp and conceive the complexity of the current age. Postmodern approaches, however, seem no more than a pragmatic way out of a conceptual dilemma and, in their unsystematic ways, merely seem to serve coping with every-day life.

Throughout history, working people and nations on the periphery have greatly struggled without being able to stop others from subduing and exploiting them harshly. This has not simply been as a consequence of their defeat, but as the result of a deficient knowledge and level of technology, which excluded them from a better participation in the distribution of resources. This no longer holds true today. Exploitation and abuse of power can be contained, and contemporary democracy is making a bold attempt to accomplish this. Conditions are emerging under which the corresponding political institutions and ideological identity can be established.

Contemporary democracy, from another angle, also stands for rearranging and restructuring of the manifold mechanisms of rule and exploitation, and that of all the institutions of capitalist civilisation. Society as a whole should do this in such a way that participation and redistribution of resources become possible. Such a system means that neither capitalism is able to exert one-sided power and exploitation nor can the working people overthrow capitalism by force in order to establish their own revolutionary system. Both sides, rather, have to accept a limitation of their one-sided utopian rigidity and interests. A life in peace according to the rules of a democratic state under the rule of law is made the basis of agreement for all. The objective of the envisaged change is productivity on the basis of technology and surplus production in all areas, while complying with the mechanisms of democratic politics. For this purpose, all groups of society receive the right of participation in political power. Such a system tries to encounter difficulties and conflicts by way of dialogue and reconciliation instead of through confrontation and division.

Obviously, capitalism cannot survive such a process in its traditional form. The consciousness created by technological progress and by the level of freedom obtained through the struggle of the workers, will not allow this. We might say that capitalism is satisfied with democratic change. Instead of making profit through bloody adventures and destruction, profit is made through an evolutionary process which involves the sharing of power and resources when required. Hence, there will be no return to traditional capitalism, nor its destruction through revolution. However, it seems possible for capitalism to dissolve slowly but surely, while a new civilisation gradually forms through a typical transformation process, driven by the progress of science and technology.

Capitalist civilisation needs to redefine its ideological identity on the basis of the criteria of contemporary democracy. It has to accept a way of life and government that rests on reconciliation with all parts of society in all of its economic, social and political institutions. The age of unrestricted rule and exploitation will be over then, and a new type of civilisation may enter the pages of history.

RELIGION AND SCIENTIFIC SOCIALISM

Socialist ideology and the unsuccessful socialist system based on it developed in opposition to the capitalist system. Whether it was a result of its ideological identity, premature birth or a series of accidental mistakes, it failed to turn the demand for freedom and equality by the workers and the oppressed into a different civilisational development. In spite of all claims to the contrary, it did not go beyond some kind of state capitalism. There have been a number of similar ideological tendencies or social movements in history.

Abraham and Moses attempted something like a tribal socialism with religious overtones in the framework of tribal–patriarchal social relations. In this social order, called "primitive socialism", the state was unknown. In some areas this order lasted for several millennia.

Jesus and the first Christians are among the foremost examples of religious socialism in terms of continuity and dissemination. The teachers of that time embodied this ideology and its practice in an unprecedented way.

The creation of Islam poses another prominent example for a community-based way of life. Equality and respect among its members take the form of a sacred family. The *ummah* in its pure form comes very close to the socialism of the feudal epoch.

Both Christianity and Islam departed from the socialism of the religious community after they became part of the state and came increasingly under the influence of individuals or dynasties. It was the development of private property that ruined the initial socialist character of these communities and made religion a simple and empty ideological shell.

Subsequently, the desire of the people for equality and freedom remained alive only on an imaginary level. They indulged in spiritual and human love and illusions of paradise and treasured their yearning for brotherhood. All this was expressed in a strong ethical and literary tradition.

Similar tendencies can be found in a number of philosophical schools that adhered to socialist approaches. Philosophical parties, some lasting for centuries, came into existence and often defended these ideas against harsh attacks in exemplary ways. These struggles for the protection of ideological awareness and beliefs can be described as social movements with egalitarian, libertarian intentions.

Even at the time when capitalism came into being, writings like Thomas More's *Utopia* (1515) or Tommaso Campanella's *La Città del Sole* (*The City of the Sun*, 1602) evoked ideas of an ideal socialism. For the dreams of liberty, which brought about capitalism, numerous people and communities took up the fight against religious dogmatism. They had no doubt that they were not fighting for some individual passion but for freedom, equality and fraternity – which became the main slogan of the French Revolution.

Karl Marx and Friedrich Engels founded the ideological framework for scientific socialism on elements from German philosophy, French socialism, English political economy and the English labour movement.

We can already see from this short discourse that there is continuity in the struggle for freedom and equality from the early stages of primitive neolithic communities to scientific socialism. This perpetual struggle for a community life based on fraternity was fought with great passion, suffering and resistance.

The organised labour movement that followed the *Communist Manifesto* (Karl Marx and Friedrich Engels, 1848) formed the latest link in the historical chain of movements for freedom and equality. The authors of the *Manifesto* were aware of the utopian character of previous movements and, therefore, attached great importance to their scientific approach. However, their concept of scientific work was very much affected by their own epoch. Capitalism experienced the height of its maturity and was confronted with its first crises. Socialism, in spite of its scientific nature, did not find a practical starting point and the labour movement was only just getting off the ground. Nonetheless, since the middle of the nineteenth century, it did not shrink from courageously announcing and spreading its point of view both ideologically and in practice. Even though they had not yet asked the question whether their strategies were adequate, these brave people had no doubts that their struggle could mean a turning point for mankind and for the cause of freedom. Its scientific attitude and its struggle for the rights of the working people demand our respect. Herein lies the prophetic impetus of this movement.

Neither the failure of the Commune of Paris nor the collapse of the Second Internationale could prevent scientific socialism from achieving its goal. That was officially reached when the leadership of the Soviet Union declared that a third of the world's population (thus also a third of the world's proletariat) had made the transition to socialism. Capitalism, they declared, could be defeated in all areas. For the first time in history there was a republic based on the principle of freedom and equality for the oppressed, a republic that was able to survive for some time by itself. Less than 80 years later, this republic had decayed and had lost its historical importance. Scholars in the service of capitalist propaganda called these events the failure of socialism; Marxists denounced it as betrayal by certain groups or interests; and those strictly faithful to socialism made it out as the collapse of their most sacred dreams. For those who try to analyse the problems soberly and scientifically, it ought to be clear that subjective evaluations – such as disillusionment or betrayal – are not very helpful. Whatever happened had to happen. Desires and dreams have decayed because reality could not live up to these dreams. Science, however, has to question these dreams. Instead of being happy or sad, it has to find out how much reality lies at the heart of the dreams. This is the only way to be successful.

The Soviet experience has not yet been analysed substantially. Neither have we yet seen all the consequences of this decay. Nonetheless, a look at those phenomena that are already visible can highlight some of the failed measures and unsuccessfully applied philosophical theorems. We have only just begun to examine the question whether these phenomena can be described as socialism, nationalism, liberalism, totalitarianism, egalitarianism or state capitalism. Such questions are in no way a simplification of the history of the solemn struggle of numerous people who fought for their belief in the reality of scientific socialism and the right of millions of working-class people. Nor do they imply that these struggles were futile. They demand, however, a full analysis of the practice of real socialism under the microscope of science as the only way to defend these values.

As long as there is human life, the high ideals of freedom and equality will need an ever closer examination of how their truth can be successfully realised. Since real socialism is an important reality, we need to take a closer look at its place and meaning in history.

The Ideological Framework of Real Socialism

Scientific socialism has a number of serious deficiencies, because of the level of historical, social and technological knowledge that forms its basis. Its founders could not fall back on the knowledge necessary for a general analysis of civilisation – it was not yet available. There was no information about the Sumerians, and even knowledge of classical antiquity contained many errors. There were no serious archaeological or theoretical works about the communities of the neolithic. Lewis H. Morgan's *Ancient Society* (1877), which was so highly esteemed by the founders of scientific socialism, was rather insufficient from today's point of view.[3]

The capitalist society these writers described was still very young. They mainly analysed its production structures and only touched upon its ideological identity and on the capitalist state. Moreover, they approached these important issues only in a vulgar-materialist philosophical way because they regarded them as mere reflections of the economy. This philosophical account was the basis for the building and decline of real socialism.

Without an analysis of the history of civilisation as a whole, analysing the economical aspects of a limited phase of capitalist civilisation does not allow for statements about possible developments. Society cannot be explained in this way and, therefore, such analysis cannot become an agenda for a revolutionary transformation of society. Later developments revealed the role of theoretically based errors in the failure of socialism.

Programmes exclusively referring to the working class lead to isolation and are unable to fully understand the relation between society and class reality. Even the bourgeoisie is only a small branch of social reality. What we find in these programmes is the notion that the working class and the bourgeoisie, two abstract classes, are the only determining constituents of social reality. It was not external violence that caused the fall of what had been established on the basis of narrow class concepts. It was the faulty perception of reality that made both counter-revolutionary fascism and real socialism fail.

Long-lived social transformations have always been able to put their trust in the level of technology available and the ideological and political institutionalisation made possible by it. This is true for all social forces, whether those of the oppressive, exploiting class or of the oppressed and exploited. The technological level of the nineteenth century was totally insufficient for the programme of scientific socialism. From the rapid decay of structures erected by socialism, we can easily conclude that the material basis for a classless society was not accessible yet.

Revolutionary Violence and Socialism

We can also observe a certain one-dimensional attitude on the part of socialism towards violence in general and revolutionary violence in particular. Its extreme esteem for violence becomes obvious when it is attributed the role of a “midwife at the birth of a new society”. Violence brought about by socialist revolutions and through real socialism, however, goes far beyond the role of a midwife. Sometime, it appears, rather, to be a sequel to the traditional line of Sargon, Hammurabi, Alexander, Caesar and Napoleon. The attempt at protecting the system by means of walls and barbed wire speaks volumes. A political system which acts in the interests of the people does not need such protection from its own citizens. On the contrary, if it really trusts its own ideological identity, it will try to attract the world and not to prevent its people from travelling. Furthermore, it became clear that the measures taken to prevent falling behind in the cold war arms race only contributed to the decline of the system. In this way, the socialist attitude towards violence and all the measures resulting from it were revealed as mistakes by the fact that they contributed to the fall of the system. Nobody will dispute the assertion that the armament policy and arms race were the chief causes for the fall of real socialism.

Extreme use of violence, as we have already discussed in detail, usually bears the mark of the ruling class. Any kind of violence directed at occupying other social existences or seizing their material and intellectual values and transforming and adopting them forcibly is reactionary by nature and has to be rejected. Such acts of violence – be they in the name of Allah, the sacred *patria*, or national liberation – are uncivilised plundering and murder.

Real socialism and many national liberation movements following in its tracks have made excessive use of violence, placing themselves at the mercy of a violent protection system. This attitude is doubtless a reflection of their belonging to the oppressed and exploited class. Since the use of violence occurs here in the name of socialism and progress, it also brings about serious degeneration. The bygone real-socialist regimes are clear evidence that such an attitude towards violence cannot be the way of the working people and the oppressed.

The right to use violence when necessary for self-defence exists only in the case of an attack on the constituting elements – material or ideological – of social existence. It is, furthermore, a legitimate answer to repressive violence against emancipatory processes, particularly in moments of qualitative change. Any other use of violence is probably only a means of profit, or a consequence of degenerate behaviour, and leads to unnecessary losses.

Although an erroneous theory of violence was among the grave mistakes leading to the fall of real socialism, there were many other cases where people went to war for the protection of their physical existence.

One-party Policy

The political and state-run institutions of real socialism never achieved independence. The forming and organising of soviets was much less a way of life than a propaganda means of the state, which became totalitarian and degenerated. The one-party structure superimposed a fascist-like black-and-white dualism upon the quite complex social structures. A number of side- and sub-organisations assumed the same functions: instead of serving the people and introducing their important demands into the politics of the state, they were turned into tools of the omnipresent siege of society by the state. While the state itself ought to have been a general means of coordination, it became a tool for the strict implementation of a totalitarian understanding of government. This government had been given more power and authority than had been the case even with theocratic concepts of the state. Inevitably, any vestige of the meaning of terms such as *democracy* and *republic* was lost.

Nonetheless, it was exactly in this field that real socialism ought to have proved itself superior to the capitalist system. Instead, we only find petrifaction and a development towards authoritarianism and totalitarianism in the socialist countries, whereas in the capitalist countries democratic criteria were developed. A party and a system of government that claimed to belong to the people should have contributed to a pluralist democratic system by doing much more in this respect than was done in the capitalist system. Just the opposite happened. The scientific work done under the banners of the *dictatorship of the proletariat* and the *people's republic* was anything but scientific and largely motivated by propaganda purposes. The state, with its excessive bureaucracy and ownership capital, became ubiquitous; it tried to make large profits to keep its machinery going. Quite apart from its failure to become superior to the capitalist system in respect of political and government institutions, real socialism remained clearly inferior in its overall efficiency and lost the trust of the people.

No Socialism Without Democracy

At a time when the capitalist system was trying to break with its former practice by means of democratic and non-government institutions, countries under real socialism implemented the opposite policy. They even disposed of the last remainders of traditional democracy and turned civil institutions into government agencies.

A socialist way of life and government can only be developed through a profound democratic awareness of society. It is not the state that needs to be strengthened, but society. This is what I call the democratic society, and its result will be democratic civilisation. State capitalism is the outcome of the very backward condition of a country, and the political system that falls back on it will tend to form a backward capitalistically structured state. However, such a political and economic framework will only permit the implementation of authoritarian or totalitarian concepts. It will not allow for the development of non-governmental organisations and institutions, and wherever such institutions already exist, they are turned into parts of the state-run propaganda machinery. Once more, it becomes clear that what we used to call real socialism is no socialism at all.

Socialism itself is a theory and a prognosis that can only be realised through overall democratisation. Societies without a developed democracy are not ready for socialism. Non-government institutions, if they are to be efficient democratic tools, must be cast loose from the state and, furthermore, have to exercise the function of specialised pressure groups permanently controlling the state institutions. This is the only way to monitor the increasingly complex relations between society and state. In the course of the decline of real socialism, the society which might have been expected to defend it did not hesitate to organise a broad social movement to get rid of it as fast as possible. This movement reflected the desire for a transition from a backward, undemocratic state capitalism to a moderate type open to democracy. This had nothing to do with the betrayal or deception of the people, but very much to do with a desire for more democracy, and it occurred in a system that was incapable of establishing a state under the rule of law.

In my opinion this is evidence for the thesis that socialism can only be built on the basis of a developed democracy. A *democracy of the people* cannot exist if is not superior to the current Western democracies. The claim to do better than Western democracies, however, will not live up to reality as long as such a *democracy of the people* has failed to implement pluralist structures, participation of all in the general will, ability to control the state institutions, tolerance externally and internally, and a policy on the basis of peace. In my opinion, one of the fundamental criteria characterising a socialist regime must be the level of democracy it enables. Any other criteria seem less important in comparison. Real socialism failed the test miserably. Worse, it denied democracy altogether and consequently was brought to an end in anger by the people themselves.

State Capitalism

Real socialism's economic system, being a part of the world economy as a whole, has never gone beyond state capitalism, which originally had only been thought to be an intermediate step. Although it made use of human labour in the fashion of some contemporary slave-holder state, it never attained the level of development of classical capitalism and, above all, it never satisfied the people. The productivity of the individual, estranged here from the products of his work, decreased continuously. Socialism, however, claims that work is a need and ought to be enjoyed. In fact, labour under real socialism mostly took the form of hard labour or even servitude. After its fall, people all over the world took on any lousy job for the lowest of wages and felt that to be a real blessing. There is absolutely no justification for bringing people to such a state. Such atrocities occurred, nevertheless, making it clear that the political system responsible for their situation had to be degenerate and anything but truly socialist.

Degenerate State Systems

National liberation movements, supported by the foreign policies of real socialist regimes, later brought about state systems mostly of poorer quality and even more degenerate than the preceding systems themselves. Even if they did bring liberation from classical colonialism, the ensuing regimes resembled the preceding colonial governments very closely.

Thcsc countrics, being in effect second hand copies of the classical blueprints of capitalism and real socialism, can only offer great sufferings to their people. These societies are doomed to experience the worst sides of history. The post-colonial regimes hopelessly, but mercilessly, try to copy their predecessors. In this way, through hitherto unknown iron-hard repression, they add to the feudal darkness that has just been overcome. People under such governance tend to get deeply estranged from themselves. They suffer from a lack of self-confidence, a poor awareness of history, ethical deprivation and blindness to their social situation. They are the most crisis-stricken societies of our age.

The Individual and Individualism

The rights of the individual, which should be regarded as a criterion of freedom in all stages of history, were treated as a problem in real socialism. The individual human being, emancipated intellectually and mentally from religious dogma, represents an important development only in part effected by capitalism. The value of any progressive attempt is proportional to the dignity of the individual it brings about, and the success should be measured against what they achieved. It can be judged from the individual's awareness and passion for life, by his creativity and productivity. A reliable measure for progress or decline is to determine where the individual stands at the beginning of such a process and where at the end. The same measure applies to the society and its way of government.

Capitalism conferred astonishing advances on the individual, the many positive and negative aspects of which deserve our full attention.

Real socialism, however, took individuality to pieces as a negative consequence of capitalism, and hence marched backward in this respect. As long as socialist individuality is not precisely defined and realised, the characteristics of the society and civilisation to be built will remain incomprehensible. The real value of a system of government can best be characterised by the qualities of the individual it brings forth. It is necessary that government centres around the human being as its most valuable subject. Man is the measure of all values and criteria. Particularly a system that claims to be the most progressive in its attitude towards freedom does not have any other certain measure.

It is not by accident that real socialism suffered heavy defeats in the field of individuality. It was the individual human being who was betrayed by socialism. In spite of all its visible deficiencies, capitalism was clearly preferred to socialism – exactly because of its sensitivity towards individual rights and its established standards of individual freedom.

Being an individual is a broad issue. After thousands of years it is still important to ask how much sociality is necessary and useful and when does it become useless and dangerous. Western civilisation has to thank its advancement of individuality for much of its progress. What may a human being win or lose by staying a member of his society, tribe, religious community, or some secular organisation? The answers given over time to these questions shed a realistic light on the process of individuation.

We have to clarify that individuality is different from individualism. Without individuation, I believe, a human being cannot become a socialist being. The process of individuation is as important as individualism is harmful.

Capitalism has turned individuality into individualism. A medieval, feudal mentality, perhaps mixed with capitalist thinking, prevents people from being democratic or socialist, so it seems.

Although the feudal age weakened the strict social order to some extent, dogma exerted a powerful rule, and man's fate was determined even before he was born. Mind and soul were paralysed by deep fatalism. There was no need to think or be creative when everything has already been determined in advance by divine will, and man needs not toil in vain. What is written will happen, and only what God has predestined can be accomplished. These are the roots of fatalism that, particularly at a time when Middle Eastern civilisation became increasingly conservative, exercised a deadly influence. It began when Platonic philosophy became theology. Christian and Islamic theology interpreted Plato's first ideas as religious dogmas.

Rising Western individualism mounted a merciless war against blind religious dogmatism, which churches and mosques piled up with the aim of subjugating the people. With the rise of the scientific method and the beginning of the Renaissance, this dogmatism was partly overcome. Furnished with the strength of this individuation process, capitalism started its remarkable development by using individualism as a weapon against the social structures. Individualism became so strong, it was unstoppable. Once the god–king had been a single man; now he appeared by the thousand. The situation rapidly changed from one extreme to another.

It was one of the greatest revolutions in history. The individual, liberated from dogma and the shadow of self-made gods, gained so much importance that now it is difficult to stop capitalists, who have gone mad in their passion for profit. The balance is lost and countermeasures are necessary to prevent social coherence – the result of thousands of years of human work – from being destroyed.

At this point, sociality became an indispensable social need. The forming of the socialist idea and scientific socialism are products of this historical need. If socialism can successfully overcome its narrow class-based approach, it will be able to carry out its mission in the name of all of society and express the will of the people to put an end to capitalist individualism. Real socialism exceeded the rightful reaction to individualism and profit orientation, resulting in a growing disrespect for individuality. It regarded individuation as a mere propaganda trick by Western civilisation, made individuality and human rights the target of ideological attacks, and took harsh measures against them.

There are certainly many more aspects open to criticism. The objective of this criticism was a clarification of the meaning of *socialist individual* and *socialist society*. I did not simply mean to discuss the negative aspects of socialism, but rather intended to free it from the ideal of utopia in order to make it practical again. Utopianism, and its strong historical foundation, vulgar materialism, I believe to be destroyed. They are obviously unfit as bases of scientific socialism. Scientific socialism has to overcome all the relics of utopian dogmatism and cleanse dialectic materialist philosophy from vulgar-materialist tendencies. Only then can it become an indispensable adviser to humankind on their way towards a new civilisation and will it be helpful in building a more coherent and usable ideological identity.

Such a new ideological identity will have to balance individuality and sociality as well as freedom and equality on the basis of what technology makes available and possible. The desired transformations will then be sustainable. Therefore, it has to establish itself strongly in the left tendencies of contemporary democratic civilisation.

Part 4

Ideological Identity and Time–Space Conditions of the New Development in Civilisation

Introduction to Part 4

There is no single coherent and comprehensive approach to defining the era in which we live. The very constitution of the era apparently does not allow that. What is rarely contended, though, is the notion that class society, and particularly capitalism, is in a state of crisis and disintegration. What people *do* disagree about, is how to define the newly emerging forms of civilisation – where they are detected. New forms do undoubtedly occur. Their nature, and thus the overall character of our era, is closely linked to the scientific–technological revolutions of the second half of the twentieth century and to their rapidly increasing applicability.

Most of the important changes in historical epochs are caused by intellectual and technical innovations, whether the wheel or the printing press, monotheism or the modern philosophy of nature. It is common knowledge that the technical invention that enabled the rise of capitalism was the steam engine (and subsequently, the internal combustion engine). Because the engine reduced the importance of manual labour, the existing class society was restructured and given new life. The influence of science and technology cannot be overestimated, nor the influence of the dialectic philosophy of nature that underpinned them. All this was radically new and reflected on all aspects of human life. Furthermore, it constituted conditions which made it possible to establish modern industrial modes of production. This, in turn, brought down the old social structures and brought new political institutions and substantial changes in the population's world-view. The technology that caused all this was largely based on theoretical mechanics, a branch of physics. Its applications were fundamental to the industrial revolution. In particular we should mention Albert Einstein's insights in the conversion of mass to energy, as it sparked off the most momentous scientific and technological revolution in history. Twentieth-century theoretical physics enabled us to bring electromagnetic and nuclear energy under control and to put them to use in technological appliances that radically changed the face of the world. Humankind is facing overwhelming developments – in terms of our practical life and in terms of the mental repercussions of the new technologies. These developments have turned the world into a global village, with a shepherd in the mountains of Kurdistan potentially enjoying the same access to information and communications technology as a businessman in New York. An all-out globalisation expands its reach 24 hours per day, seven days a week.

Technology has progressed far beyond the existing social, political and ideological structures. The medieval residues governing certain corners of this globe, and the regressing orders in the geopolitical centres of our age, fail to adapt to this tiger leap of technology. Due to this incompatibility, the contradictory situation arises, in which the unlimited opportunities offered by technology are not employed for the good of humanity. Even worse, their exploitation through the production, distribution and governance processes characteristic of vintage capitalism and traditional societies generates unprecedented dangers. Nuclear weapons, environmental disasters, climate change, Aids epidemics, overpopulation and egregious disparities in access to health and education facilities – these are just some of the key examples that illustrate my point. The global scope of these issues indicates that the character of the basic contradictions themselves has changed. Unless we understand this and take precautions, the abyss will grow even deeper. The only adequate precautions involve radical economic, social and political change. The contradiction in the age of classical capitalism manifested itself primarily in the structure of society. It led to developments regarding fair distribution of wealth. In our age, it has taken on the character of a contradiction between nature (the environment) and governments worldwide. Governments fail to make use of technological progress to establish social and environmental conditions fit to live in; in fact, they find it detrimental to their particular class, group or personal interests to do so. The social and political powers responsible for the nation states and the awkward, dysfunctional supranational order constitute a positive threat to the world we live in. There are still governments that regard nuclear deterrents and missile shields as the answer to all problems. Regional conflicts are fuelled in order to promote the sale of arms. Technology that causes environmental damage is conveniently overlooked. Budgets for global health and education problems – often generated by health and education policies – remain at negligible levels despite the fact that we have the technology to tackle these problems.

The blame for this irrational situation should be laid on the old form of production and the political powers behind it. The contradiction mentioned above thus boils down to the struggle between the masses and the forces that, through the lure of money, control politics for their own benefit. As a matter of fact, even command of the economic structure has become somewhat independent of the laws of motion and the control mechanisms of the old system of classical capitalism. Mutatis mutandis, it is subjected to the selfish interests of those who control the political superstructure and has thus become more dangerous than ever before.[1] Of course there is no shortage of contemporary oligarchies (masked as democracies) and of the kind of dictatorial regime that appears in any time of crisis and decay. Contemporary criteria of democracy do enforce themselves, but they exist next to, and entwined with, the very authoritarian oligarchic orders that constitute their antithesis. As far as economic structures are concerned, a handful of speculators on the stock market with no immediate connection to the production process have quite a number of manipulation tools at their disposal, enabling them to make almost any profitable coup that they desire. On the other hand, any interest group may bring their favourite oligarchy to power with the help of the powerful media. The deep antagonism between the representatives of those oligarchies and the rest of humanity causes a number of dangers and threats. The overwhelming power of technology allows for organised destruction and devastation on a scale reminiscent of Armageddon. Intellectually and psychologically, man is bombarded with concepts and forms alien to him by a system hostile to him. Technology, which for the first time in history could turn man's utopia into a reality, is abused by a minority uninterested in mankind's basic needs, turning man's reality into a living hell. Technology is becoming a monster, threatening to devour its creators.

A twofold contradiction results from this. Firstly, there is antagonism between the chauvinistic "owners" of the nation states (which have become modern tribes) and the cosmopolitan representatives of supranational capital. Secondly, both these groups are in opposition to the peoples and nations of the world. Hence, on the one hand the protective influence of the nation states screens their populations from the enrichment of modern democracy; on the other hand, they are in conflict with supranational capital over globalisation. In both cases, they play a reactionary role. They find themselves in a mediating position as *ultra-colonies* of the supranational orders. Whenever they are pressurised by their opponents, they will throw away the property of the people for small concessions. In this context, the institution building of the New Order has to take place. And this is to be accomplished within the triangle of imperialism, capitalism and the collaborative representatives of the nation states.

In the present age of information and communication, political borders become increasingly insignificant. Information sources can be accessed from everywhere at any time. As a consequence, peoples and nations get ever closer in an unprecedented way and the chances for international solidarity are better than ever. While this democratises society and strengthens the institutions of civil society, it also enables international solidarity on an advanced level. Hence, we have a situation which is considerably different from the contradictions of the twentieth (or even the nineteenth) century and the solutions to them. The controlling oligarchy is forced to adapt to contemporary democratic criteria. With the contradictions changing, the solutions too have to be changed. The criteria of contemporary democracy form the basis, the general framework, for any minimum consensus. Therefore, revolutionary or counter-revolutionary methods, which were the products of previous contradictions, have been overcome. The fascist or real-socialist regimes resulting from these methods have also for the most part disappeared.

Mankind's greatest challenge is the forming of ideological identities and the political institutions to support them in the context of the basic conditions and conflicts determined by the scientific and technological development of his time. This will be the starting point of our analysis and discussion on the following pages.

20

Ideological Identity in the Third Millennium

The new ideological framework will take shape in the process of overcoming both the philosophical foundations of capitalist civilisation and the methodological apparatus of real socialism. A permanent and urgent crisis has developed in the capitalist system through wars, revolutions and counter-revolutions. This crisis cannot be overcome by fascist restoration or real-socialist models. Hitherto, ideological identities did not include or take seriously technological development as a decisive factor, which is why they were unable to establish themselves in practice and reality. In my opinion, this is also why the ideological foundations of fascism and real socialism were insufficient. Hence, we need a new ideological framework.[1]

We are not confronted with the maturation or decay of economic, social or political conditions, nor with technological deficiencies. Everything we need for a new historical beginning is already there. We must, however, clearly define our ideological identities. Intellectual fragmentation is the result of defeat, of capitulation and submission. It is our foremost duty to bring about the birth of a new ideological identity in our minds and souls, an identity coherent and holistic, original and robust, an identity that will prevail. More precisely, we need to assess and analyse our present conditions in their historical and social entirety in order to develop a programme with tactical and strategic implications. Again, there is no successful practice without a valid theory underlying it.

All important historical epochs rested on strong ideological bases. In neolithic communities, the cult of the mother–goddess was ideologically fundamental. Later, Sumerian mythology formed the basis for all kinds of ideological identities, class society amongst others. Greek philosophy and the monotheistic religions left their weighty marks on classical antiquity and the Middle Ages. The Renaissance, Reformation and Enlightenment were essential stages in the formation of the ideological identity of capitalist civilisation. The socialist ideology was meant to become the ideology of a classless civilisation.

Each of these ideologies reflects the conflicts preceding the birth and development of a social system. The fate of such a system is settled primarily in the struggles over ideology. History does not know a single social system without such struggles. A society receives its ideological identity before its birth and the strength of its social system is directly connected to these ideological foundations.

Presently, theoretical analysis forms a substantial part of ideological identity, while in previous societies mythology, religion or philosophical views took the place of theory. The application of the scientific method in explaining nature and social conditions paved the way for the application of the scientific method in social theory. Such a theory entails an analysis of a given social order and makes predictions about the direction of its development. These predictions determine the reliability and success of its implementation in practice.

In Sumer and Egypt it was the priests in their temples who were responsible for ideology. Later, the first philosophers received their basic education in similar temples, before new institutions of learning (such as academies and gymnasiums) were created. Likewise, medieval churches and mosques fulfilled the role of institutions of learning. At the start of the modern age, this function was relegated to schools and universities, where traditional content was by and by mixed with scientific insight.

We need to learn how to decipher the flowing change of traditional ideological identities. The mere statement "religion is the opiate of the people" is totally insufficient in this respect. Any research into social history that doesn't include and evaluate the influence of mythology and religion on ideological identity over thousands of years is inevitably flawed. Notional conditions deserve the same analysis as material conditions – they mutually cause each other.[2] In order to cope with the problems of today's societies, we need to re-analyse how they emerged and developed historically. Part of this analysis should be the ideologies which accompanied these developments. This approach will also give a novel and unusually broad perspective on history and on our own time. At the same time it will contribute to the actualisation of new history. This method of analysis, followed by the application of its results, must necessarily be rooted in the beginnings of human civilisation, which, as far as we know, took its first steps in the Middle East.

Let us therefore summarise some of the important aspects of our analysis at this point in order to make them as clear as possible, even at the risk of some redundancy.

1. The identification of Greco-Roman antiquity with the historical source of European civilisation contains a number of deficiencies and mistakes. Greece and Rome and the civilisation they brought about can also be regarded as the last stages of slave-holder society, the origin of which was Middle Eastern civilisation. Thus, the true source was Sumerian and

Egyptian class society – Sumer, in a sense, being the blueprint for all that followed. However, the beginnings of history are not restricted to Sumer. Sumer only picked up the main tendency already present, namely a division of society into exploiters and exploited, oppressors and oppressed. This later developed into an East–West division with different forms of oppression and exploitation: while the East focused on rural forms, the West concentrated on the urban centres, which produced the more progressive methods and forced the agrarian areas to adapt themselves. This created an antagonism that can still be felt today. Whereas civilisations of Western origin are predominantly urban, with trade and commerce and manufactories and the polarity of a spiritual and a secular power centre, Eastern civilisations are concentrated in villages and small towns where peasants and nomads, tribes and principalities set the tone.

2. Without an analysis of the structure of Sumerian ideology, we can reliably describe neither monotheistic religions and ideologies, nor philosophical ideologies and the scientific way of thinking. Any study of the history of religion that does not take this into account will render a flawed and incoherent theory; so will claims that truth had only become accessible since the beginning of the age of science. Unfortunately, historiography has always been flawed in such ways. While there were attempts during the twentieth century to reveal these errors and distortions, it was the bloodiest epoch in history. If mankind ever wants to rid itself from such violence, it has to concede its guilt through self-criticism leading to a far-reaching ethical revolution. Any new civilisational development can only be accomplished following a theoretical and practical resolution to what already exists.
3. The history of class society is, in essence, reflected in the history of different ways of thought dialectically intertwined with each other. The way it is reflected is essentially the perspective of the ruling class. The oppressed and exploited, in contrast, create their own unofficial, heterodox view, which, of course, cannot be passed on openly but is nonetheless handed down through the generations.

The ideology of the first class of exploiters was enveloped in mythology referring to the general theme of light and darkness. Heaven, loftiness and sublimity were the attributes of the ruling class; lowliness, the nether world and hell the privileges of the exploited. The Sumerian priests contributed substantially to this. They rephrased mythology to suit their own purposes, influencing many following generations. When the formerly separate city states evolved into an empire the number of gods decreased to one. Natural attributes become social attributes. With the development of trade and commerce and urban communities monotheism emerged, being more compatible with a commerce-oriented society than polytheism. Such societies needed clear rules and laws. Hence, they developed their mythological foundation for religion. Myth is based on narrative and could not provide the rules and laws the community needed. The growing importance of constant exchange rates, even between distant places, rendered the merchants dependant on unambiguous rules based on unambiguous foundations. These rules, or laws, had to be obligatory.

4. The religion of the mother–goddess of the neolithic communities deeply influenced later so-called "secret", mystic ways of thinking. These religious forms on the one hand reflected the perceptions of the oppressed classes; on the other, they reflected the female gender and its qualities in life. It was both natural religion and manifestation of friendship and peace between man and god. Almost all sects and cults are closer to the oppressed parts of society and the female gender and follow a more egalitarian direction than mainstream religion. Although they later experienced intensive misuse, sects and brotherhoods in their original form can also be regarded as the opposition movements of antiquity and the Middle Ages. In spite of their widespread existence, their fates were usually determined by painful degeneration, persecution and elimination of their leaders, or by corruption. Nonetheless, from the neolithic to the present, brotherhoods and heretical confessions have reflected the faith, resistance and living conditions of the oppressed and exploited.
5. Philosophical thought, on the other hand, corresponded to a more developed urban community. It identified natural and social powers that influenced the practical lives of the people. Therefore, man became increasingly dissatisfied with the answers given by mythology and religion. More convincing explanations were called for. Learning about earth and heaven in ever-increasing detail, man discovered that the gods, who were supposed to be somewhere up there, could not be found. Understanding the laws of nature then took priority. A new way of questioning (which took a close look at the cause of the universe and creation, at the primordial matter and the appearance of the diversity visible today) brought about what we call philosophical thought. At the same time, the power of the god–king was questioned. When man learnt that the kings could not possibly be gods, and that their laws were only giving expression to their own interests, a philosophical discussion of social and political structures became inevitable. On the one hand, this progressive philosophical approach led to religious thinking which was more rational and hence paved the way for theology. On the other, it strengthened the natural sciences – which are based on empirical observation and try to give precise descriptions and formulate laws. Of course, philosophy was also used as a tool and weapon by the ruling class, resulting in the unification of philosophy and state religion with theological doctrine.[3] In the same way, there was a fusion of heretical beliefs and doctrines with philosophy. These expressed in a rational way the interests of the oppressed, who even learnt to use philosophical thought as some kind

of weapon, like the (Shi'ite) medieval communities adhering to the esoteric doctrine of *Batiniyah*[4].

6. Scientific thought gains the upper hand whenever concepts can be verified empirically and insight into nature and society becomes clear enough to render unnecessary any outside interference. This process is directly connected with the development of social structures. The more complex a community becomes (with increasing urban, mercantile or industrial characteristics), the greater its need for scientific thought.

   While the ruling exploitive class benefits from the growing productivity brought about by science, it shuns the enlightenment science brings. Enlightenment endangers its interests and thus the ruling class resorts to ideological means to suppress it. Hence, the emergence of scientific thought does not seem to bring about liberation automatically. Its effects on society depend on who (i.e. which class) controls it. If science is in the hands of private interest groups or reactionary circles, arbitrariness in decisions over society and the environment increases, resulting in the decay of both. Then again, science's productive, emancipationist and egalitarian potential can be realised all the better if it is in the hands of social forces that link it to progress and common wealth.

7. Western thought is a product of its historical predecessors, rooted in the mythological identity created in Sumer, ancient Anatolia and Greece. The influential cult of Zeus, between 1500 and 500 BCE, already carried many anthropomorphic characteristics. Fear and hope with respect to the gods had little more than moral meaning, hinting at rather weak class structures. Nature itself was quickly released from the sphere of the divine, and even social laws and conditions were eventually viewed as results of the human will. The Zeus cult represented the ruling classes. The common people, however, preserved their identity – their social difference – in the Dionysus cult. From the fifth century CE, mythology started to give way to philosophical thought. Individual enlightenment and will-power were strengthened. During this time, just the opposite was happening in the East: people increasingly became lowly subjects of the ruling class. The rise of the Hellenic civilisation made the differences visible for the first time. A real gap opened with the Medes. In north-west Iran and Upper Mesopotamia the different lines of development in East and West became easily discernible. The Zoroastrian tradition drew its strength from this difference.

   In the Roman Empire the divine will grew weaker and weaker and a more secular approach began to dominate. Stoicism with its cosmopolitan traits prepared the way for Christianity. The interpretation of holy Jewish texts in the light of Greek philosophy (Hellenistic Judaism) established the basic philosophical principles of Christianity and Islam. Between 500 and 1500 CE the church claimed to be the only representative of divine power on earth, thus forming the ideological foundations of Western feudalism. At a time when the superiority of Eastern thought came to an end, the church brought about a radical transformation of the moral and intellectual structures prevailing in the European societies of the time. All dissent was mercilessly persecuted. Clad in Roman armour, what had originally been a naive faith in Jesus was left far behind and merged with the interests of the ruling class. From the fifteenth century onward, science gained momentum, parted from theological thought and reduced it to a set of moral rules. In this era – the modern era – the Western mind became almost completely independent of religion and continued to develop, trusting in its own strength. As a consequence of this, the individual freed himself from social control. Excessive egoism, at the opposite extreme from dogmatism, became a disease. The modern Western individual feels as independent as a Sumerian god–king, positioning himself above society. This, in my opinion, is the basic danger and sickness of Western society, for which, hitherto, no remedy has been found.

In this epoch, the underprivileged of the West turned to scientific socialism. Socialism became the new ideological identity of the oppressed. It had its origins in class society, from which it was unable to free itself politically. Neither could it establish a true socialist character and true socialist administrative institutions. Its structures resembled those of the ruling class and, consequently, degenerated quickly. Hence, real socialism suffered the same fate as similar movements in antiquity and the Middle Ages, which were either suffocated or assimilated.

8. The Eastern line of thought took a different course. It tended towards an exaltation of the ruler, or some strong variant of monotheism. The evolution towards monotheism as it took place in Middle Eastern thought was a reflection of economic and political centralisation processes. Orders and dogmas following from the faith were absolute, and when they were turned into secular laws, they resulted in an intransigence that was to become characteristic of the growing backwardness of the entire East. It created a mentality even more backward than that of its starting point in Sumer. The Middle Eastern concept of God strengthened the division into rulers and subjects and contributed to the systematisation of feudal dependencies. This concept was the central idea behind medieval feudalism and ideological identity in the Middle East. It was a perfect expression of the mentality and the material interests of the merchants that formed the predominant class of the Arab communities. In a sense, Allah, who was loaded with the legacy of Greek philosophical thought as well as with Christian and Jewish theology, became the feudal manifesto of the Middle Eastern Middle Ages, its constitution and declaration.

The debate over the existence or non-existence of God is, in my opinion, a distortion of the real question: to what extent is God a reflection of social conditions? What does God stand for? Is God subject to evolution? What may become of God, eventually?

The answers that the West gave by returning God to earth amongst human beings resulted in the rise of science and democracy. In the Middle East, however, with its deeply rooted faith, God is placed like the sword of Damocles over the heads of the people. The ruling class adapted him to the circumstances of medieval feudalism as well as they were able to, giving expression to the ideological predominance of their class. The Sunni interpretation corresponded to official theology and was meant for the rising merchant class and landowners. All other denominations and sects (whose founders all in some way tied themselves to the family of the prophet in order to mask their sectarianism) were directed at the oppressed and exploited. These semi-secret heterodox tendencies posed a medieval form of class struggle and ethnic conflict which could not have taken place under any other label.

Intellectually, the Middle East declined after its blossoming between the eighth and the twelfth centuries. While the West laid the foundations for science and the Renaissance, the Middle East entered its intellectually most conservative and most reactionary phase. A way of life without principles or recognisable philosophical or moral guidelines, solely based on military strength, spread all over the region. Its influence can still be felt today in the alliance of Islam with feudal warlords.

9. We may safely conclude from the above review that what is needed is an ideological revolution in the Middle East. Opposition from neither the left nor the right was able to supersede the ideological identity of the Middle Ages. What it did manage to do was to suppress or hide it. Thus, something forged and artificial was produced. The struggle for an ideological identity of the Middle East must be continued. All the nationalist, communist and even neo-Islamic ideologies have failed, in that they never really defeated the medieval consciousness and, therefore, never really changed any fundamental phenomena. The Middle East needs to part from its reactionary ideological identity. Anything else is only whitewashing, which, as we know from the last two centuries, will only produce failure and backwardness.

The purpose of this analysis of civilisation was to contribute to defining the problems and the questions this concept poses. Whichever problem we address in the Middle East – the Iran–Iraq conflict, the Israeli–Arab confrontation, the internal Arab conflicts, the situation of the Kurds (which is probably more of a banishment from human dignity than a tragedy) or the Armenian tragedy – the problems of the region are deeply linked to each other.

The peoples and nations of the Middle East have to become part of the broad stream of the current democratic civilisation, which is much closer to freedom and equality than any preceding civilisation. They have to participate in a democratic movement that makes positive use of science and technology and frees itself from the residue of class society. What is needed is a real renaissance aimed at a democratic civilisation.

21

A New Programme for the Kurdish Movement

What are the programmatic consequences the Kurdish movement can draw from what we have discussed in the preceding chapters? What should the ideological identity that we are trying to form be like, and what kind of society do we want?

I will try to answer the above questions and describe some key characteristics of the political, economic, and social structures we envisage.

Our programme is meant to express our attachment to what I earlier called "contemporary democracy". It describes how our movement can internalise and foster it. The application of democratic criteria in the process of forming institutions in society, politics and state must become a priority.

The main points of our programme are women's freedom (which does not seem to be realisable under capitalism), environmental protection and measures for controlling the detrimental effects of technology.

The freedom and equality of women have to be essential values in the new civilisation. Woman, who has been practically eliminated from our society ever since the end of the neolithic, must take her place in society again as a respected, free and equal being. This objective must be pursued with all the theoretical, practical and organisational means available. Woman's reality is a problem more concrete and accessible to analysis than concepts like *proletariat* or *oppressed peoples*, which were so popular in the past. The extent to which social transformation takes place will be determined by the change women experience. Any part of society will enjoy freedom and equality to the same degree that women achieve freedom and equality. Women's participation in society will be decisive in establishing a permanent democracy. Hence, the new social movement will found its uniqueness largely on women's position in society.

For a truly new beginning, environmental issues should be included in the programme. Antagonism between man and environment can be as problematic as social issues. Conservation of the environment means protection and conservation of our natural living conditions, i.e. of soil, flora and fauna, water, air and climate. This is a fundamental challenge that needs to be adequately addressed.

In capitalist society, technology is often left unused and idle, or else turned into a scarcely controllable monster. We need an explicit policy on technology that corresponds to the basic needs of mankind while adhering to clear principles. A new beginning will be determined by both the state of technology and its adequate use. Nuclear technology, industrial processes contributing to the greenhouse effect, and genetically modified food are among those technologies which need to be strictly controlled or even prohibited. At the same time, it is necessary to achieve substantial progress in the fields of population control, health care and education. When working towards the democratisation of society, politics and state, technology and the economy have to be addressed as interlacing phenomena.

Children and elderly people also need special consideration. Their welfare cannot simply be left to their families.

Moral decline of a society is usually an expression of the crisis it is experiencing. When talking about morals, we are not referring to traditional manners and customs or religious codes of behaviour. We are talking about a particular social behaviour that our conscience is deeply convinced is right and good. In the same way as there is a reactionary or conservative ethics, there is a progressive and liberating ethics. We might call this the "conceptional institutionalisation of society".

A necessary characteristic of a new beginning is a new ethics. New ethical criteria have to be formulated, institutionalised and entrenched in law. The role of ethics and its institutions should be enshrined against all political measures and laws.

Ethics fulfils a bridge function in social systems: it allows art to complement the internal morally good with beauty. Therefore, the place of art in social life needs to be discussed in the same way as ethics. A society without art is a naked, primitive body, and hints at a disconnection between body and mind. Societies cannot exist without art. Art, however, should not be an occupation of the privileged, but rather should be understood as a response of the people to mythology, religion or philosophy. It describes the process of implementation and transformation that great thoughts and ethical concepts experience when they are rendered understandable and liveable for everybody.

22

Reflections on Strategic and Tactical Approaches

Undoubtedly, theory and programme should be followed by practical steps. While the theory only describes problem and solution, the programme formulates clear goals, distilled and critically extracted from the theory. The way towards these goals is determined by a long-term strategy defining a reliable way along which the necessary tactical steps can be implemented. Strategy can be understood as the art of determining which of many seemingly possible ways is the right one. Some are blind alleys, some will suddenly end in the middle of nowhere, others will offer nothing but suffering. An accurate strategy, therefore, demands a leadership that can identifying the misleading routes, changing course if necessary and bring society to the envisaged destination, where it will realise and legitimise its historical role. History is full of communities and organisations that failed because they lacked such strategy and leadership. In short, strategy is the art of effective leadership.

Strategy defines the social forces, the reserves and the temporary allies needed to achieve the goal successfully and without suffering heavy losses. This applies to a society marching towards its goal as much as it does to an athlete preparing for a sprint or a marathon. Any society or organisation that is unable to muster enough strength to achieve its goals is doomed to waste its vital energy and will stay behind and fall apart. In a way, defining a strategy for a community or organisation resembles the formation of brain functions. The level of simplicity of living with only lower neural functions can serve as a warning that a theoretical view and a social programme will only become really alive when they are endowed with strategic leadership. This is the case in any situation where the capability of decision making and acting is present. It includes the ability to recognise impracticable strategies, to critically analyse them and to define alternatives. The strategic framework also comprises competent military and political structures of leadership that are able to act independently and creatively. Otherwise they will lose orientation, stagnate and eventually degenerate. Thus, strategy is a crucial element of the ideological identity. Its final and completing element is called "tactics" and includes the tools and the energy necessary for achieving the goal.

A state makes every effort to implement the basic policies by organisation in the areas of legislature, executive authority and jurisdiction as well as by creating military and economic bodies. Societies have similar means at their disposal. Needs and goals determine the necessary means. Tactics determine which pioneering or side organisations are necessary and which methods they have to apply in order to pull a society out of a crisis.

Action has to correspond to the requirements of the goal and can comprise a broad spectrum of actions: from psychological to military, from peaceful to violent, from economic to political. A reliable, tactical leadership must be able to switch between different forms of organisation and action according to the requirements of the situation. If necessary, it must develop new forms with adequate speed. If an ideological identity fails to produce adequate organisational means and forms of action, it will be paralysed theoretically, programmatically and tactically. But if these can be applied in a timely manner, success is almost certain.

In conclusion, we need to mention the concept of ideological birth. The general crisis of class-based civilisation escalates and multiplies in the concrete reality of capitalism. In spite of many attempts, no viable ideology has yet developed. But the amount of knowledge available in the hands of individuals and communities increases the chances of such a development. We will have to view all ideological approaches – from the ancient mythologies to scientific socialism – as a dialectic whole. Everybody involved in these processes ought to feel respect at the accumulation of knowledge by mankind and be aware of the sacred value of every single word. As long as someone doesn't completely understand a particular idea it seems equally wrong for him either to denounce or to cherish this idea. This does not mean that one should remain silent in the face of wrong or inadequate ideas; convincing criticism, however, should be based on one's own appropriate behaviour.

Our zeitgeist is a mixture of, on the one hand, the general crisis of class-based civilisation and its symptoms of decline and, on the other hand, the characteristics of a transition phase in the course of which the identity of a new social civilisation is taking form. Although the differing qualities of the two worlds are in strong contrast, neither world can muster the strength to defeat the other. Besides, I believe such a black and white dualism contradicts the basic laws of nature. Nature – with social reality as one of its subdivisions – is undergoing permanent changes. It would be a dangerous distortion to describe different types of societies in terms of a simple black and white dualism. It is vital to have a wide perspective on social and civilisation-linked transformation processes – otherwise one would have the distinction of being either a fascist or a real socialist.

The terrible chain of suffering and bloodshed of the twentieth century has been broken by dialectic progress. Neither the black order of class society nor its alleged opposite (though in essence it is similarly single-coloured) of white communism have resulted in anything but failed utopias, which humanity is not willing to live in permanently.

Mankind needs to transfer the colourfulness we have come to know in nature to its societies. In this respect, Sumerian mythology was more flexible and humane than the monotheistic religions. Of course, the world is not black and white, and it never was – not even in systems based on mythologies or religious dogma.

Science has made us aware of nature's enormous diversity through its achievements in evolutionary theory, quantum physics and the theory of relativity. A look at social reality against this background makes it clear that opposites are connected to each other and dependent on each other over long periods of time. The victory of contemporary democracy to a large degree is based on its closeness to reality. It is based on a philosophy which orientates itself by the manifold formations of nature and on a practical approach that focuses on transformation through evolution. This type of democracy draws its power from its foundations in science and philosophy. Contemporary democratic civilisation sets out to become the possession of all mankind by imparting an understanding of the complexity of the laws of development. It has already begun to influence social change. This is not chance but an important consequence of the power of science. (Science is democratic!) However, in the same way that the dogmatic structures of the old society are able to retain their existence, some utopian models have partly assumed a physical existence and will be able to protect their structures.

It would therefore be completely wrong simply to regard contemporary democracy as the reconciliation of two extremes. Even the two extreme approaches have a right to exist as long as they comply with democratic criteria – contemporary democracy relies on the wealth of social forms. Contemporary democracy is thus not so much a compromise between two extremes as a reflection of the wealth of shapes a society has experienced in the past and will experience in the future. Contemporary democracy can be described as a system that allows free expression of all shapes and forms. It is characterised by a rich theory, practical approaches and the search for new forms. It is neither just a simple theory in the service of political power plays nor can it be reduced to a form of political rule. It is a long-lived and all-embracing type of civilisation containing elements both of class societies and of classless societies. It aims at unrestricted and free expression and listens to the voices of women and children. It is the theory and practice of free development, and thus refuses all forms of violence beyond legally determined self-defence. It tries to resolve the growing contradictions that exist both within society and between society and the environment through scientific–technological development, while always aiming at peaceful change.

One of the important elements of contemporary democracy is individuality – the right to live as a free individual, free from dogmatism and utopias, while knowing about their strengths. A second important element is the development or re-establishment of civil society, which can be referred to by the term *third domain* to illustrate that the present democratic civilisation rests on three pillars: democratic society, politics, and the state institutions. If it seems hard to democratise the old society, it will even be harder to democratise the state institutions, because of their classical structures. They are, however, forced to open themselves to democracy by the present democratic development. (In former times this goal would have been accomplished by rebellion!) In the meantime, the state institutions have largely gained the upper hand ideologically and practically over the democratic reflexes of society – it is not very hard to see through the classic forms of rebellion in order to know how to crush them successfully. Democratic politics is thus required to play its part in the mediation between state institutions and society.

The domains of society and state institutions are sufficiently well known from a historical point of view. While the power of rebellion was the voice of the people, the state – being the oldest authority – made its existence felt as something inevitable and fated. In particular the classical societies and nations outside the centres of capitalist civilisation took to an internal intransigence that was mirrored externally; this promoted and stimulated conservatism. (For a while, it seemed as if the emerging conservative balance could be destroyed by revolutions – a belief that was founded on a number of successful examples. However, capitalism and its imperialist companion learnt and took precautions.) This kind of state will not voluntarily democratise. It is necessary, therefore, to start a new movement. At the same time, the crisis of capitalism in its centres has taken such a dangerous and ecologically harmful character that we need a movement of the third domain here, too.

The third of the three domains is democratic politics. Any need brought about by the very complex conditions of civilisation must correspond to a civil counterpart. This should neither be a stern tool of revolution nor a state institution imposed on society to regulate communications between state and people. Rather, independent organisations, shaped according to the needs of the moment, are needed. These organisations should keep an equal distance from both sides (state and society) and maintain their own identity. I am not referring to fundamental social organisations with religious or ethnic purposes, but rather to organisations with only a limited number of members, each organisation focusing on specific problems. As soon as they have accomplished their objectives they should dissolve or transform themselves for other purposes. The model I have in mind avoids the blind alley of the old revolution versus counter-revolution pattern. The importance of these organisations will continue to grow from all areas of the economy to culture, sports, environmental protection, peace and human rights. Let me explain the theoretical and practical dimensions of the third domain somewhat more precisely.

This domain requires its own theory, programmatic foundations, strategy and tactics. In a way, it is a new practical approach. It enforces the transition from a classical understanding of political parties (as being formations nourished by and profiting from state and society) towards a functional understanding, orientating themselves towards the needs that arise. All organisations which – like classical political parties – lead the life of parasites, will have to restructure themselves according to the criteria posed by the theory of civil society. The success of contemporary democratic civilisation is largely dependent on a new definition of the roles and forms of action and organisation. Without progress in the third domain neither society nor state institutions will ever fully realise contemporary democracy. Only if this domain gains its freedom and becomes able to serve its purpose, only then will separatist tendencies and the element of violence cease to cause problems.

Democratic politics provides the opportunity for several peaceful solutions of a problem. The ability to plan and realise civil society projects is becoming increasingly important. Individuals or parties that adopt civil society projects will contribute immensely to the democratisation of state institutions and society. This involves relinquishing politics that rely on personal material profit in favour of creating values and implanting them into society and state institutions.

The creative potential of the third domain needs to be activated particularly in situations of crisis, when society has obviously entered a blind alley and cannot overcome its problems by traditional state-orientated approaches.

Hence, contemporary democratic civilisation is far from being another level of the (conservative) status quo and equally far from being the adventure playground of some utopian society engineers. Contemporary democracy, if I may use a metaphor, is not throwing the state institutions on the scrap heap of history but, rather, cuts them up and shreds them making good metal from old iron and scrap. This must be clearly communicated: we cannot replace the state, the civilisation machinery of old, by a new repression apparatus that continues to use the old state institutions or parts of them in some way or another. On the contrary, the state can only be a general means of communication relying on the contributions of all (the entire society and its institutions) while representing general criteria of freedom and justice and monitoring their compliancc. This state will not have batons, deadly weapons or dungeons for locking people away. In this way, according to Karl Marx's principle "from each according to his ability, to each according to his needs", society will by and by dispose of the last remnants of traditional state institutions. In the wake of the rise of science and technology mankind today is closer than ever to realising this idea.

23

Time as a Creative Element

Although every epoch has its own spirit, it is dependent on time and on the history preceding it. Time itself is an active and creative element influencing all dimensions of a historical process. The scientific basis of historical analysis is an accurate definition of the qualities of a given epoch and the dialectic influence one epoch may exercise upon another.

The decisive characteristic of the neolithic was the historical transition from nomadic hunter–gatherer communities to settled cattle-breeding and agrarian communities, as a consequence of technological development.

The slave-holder society was already a class society and relied on the enslavement of human beings, who became objects of commercial trade.

Feudalism was intellectually dominated by religion and this age is often called the age of theology. Slavery and enslavement took weaker forms and were tied to strict rules. Agriculture was still the most important element.

The age of capitalism is also the age of philosophy. The individual awakes. Hu-mankind becomes aware of itself and starts trying to solve its problems with the help of science and technology. However, this glorious age of individuality has deteriorated over time into an immoral individualism dominated by self-interest. This seems to be one of the most depressing and degenerate ideological epochs ever – even worse than epochs dominated by religious dogmatism, which at least had their own inherent logic and stringent moral codes. In the present general civilisational crisis, an all-dominant individualism is destroying any respect for historical values or utopian ideas. People no longer see beyond the immediate present, nor do they see anything beyond themselves. An irrational and anti-historical individualism has put the fulfilment of sexual instincts in the place of freedom.

In times of religious dogmatism the individual disappeared in the anonymity of the community, his fate predestined. The extreme anti-individuality (at least among the common people) was the most important reason for the rise of individuality in modern times. Now, with the crisis of capitalism, all values useful to the community are disappearing in a flood of extreme individualism. The defensive reaction against this development, organised in the name of socialism, took the form of a modern-day Sumerian priesthood. Obviously, the extremes nourished each other.

After World War II, it was inconceivable that mankind could survive without radical changes, not least because of the use of nuclear weapons. The intensifying scientific–technological revolution created a new spirit in the second half of the twentieth century. The continued and escalating crisis class-based civilisation experienced in the shape of capitalism could not be resolved by yet more wars nor by finding new variations of class societies.

A new age is clearly being-shaped by technology. The available technology has rendered possible a situation of total war that will leave neither victor nor victim, a situation where nothing new will be created but everything and everybody in existence will be destroyed. Ironically, technology has developed to a level that will permit mankind to solve all of its contradictions without the use of violence. The continuously increasing technological capabilities are creating a rich material basis for the new democratic age. They also permit the active realisation of all kinds of social transformations, e.g. the redistribution of income and other material goods, until all social class differences will disappear. The process of the transformation of matter into energy, i.e. the generation of energy, is becoming more and more effective. Permanently accessible energy sources offer revolutionary opportunities which are reflected in radical changes in the spirit of our age.

I believe it is justified to call this epoch, the foundations of which I have tried to describe here in detail, the age of democratic civilisation. It is, above all, an epoch in which the people can for the first time determine politics. Etymologically, democracy means "rule of the people". This will be achieved in several respects. Formerly, the people virtually did not exist as an agent of history. History was written in the name of kingdoms and dynasties and we learn nothing about those who really made history. Even the history of ideas is just a reflection of the reality of the ruling class – wherever their material power was lacking, they held sway through intellectual dominance and religious power. In capitalist society the idea of the nation state rapidly turned to chauvinism, which is only used as a disguise for class interests.

However, the time of unlimited rule – whether by individuals, dynasties or classes – is over: it has been upstaged by the people. Despite nationalist indoctrination and the many forms of fascism called forth by capitalism, today the people – the real actors in the drama of history – can no longer be barred from participation. Even the most selfish dictator can only obtain power with the support of the people. The post-World War II epoch, therefore, could mean a rebirth for all the people of all nations. The end of the twentieth century has seen the victory of democracy. The technical substructure and the political institutions have become crucial for the power of the people.

The price paid for entering this period was high. Throughout history the people have had to carry the burden of a civilisational process based on the formation of classes: they were subject to oppression, massacre, exploitation, plundering, deportation, expulsion, assimilation and similar methods, applied and completed by moral and ideological force. People were set at each other's throats. They fell victim to genocide in the many regional and local wars of the past century, particularly in the two world wars. The barbarism of the religious wars of the Middle Ages was surpassed by the wars in the name of nationalism in the capitalist age.

Certainly, the people did not simply endure all this over the ages. There were rebellions against, and strong criticism of slavery, religious power and semi-philosophical religious communities. All these were symptoms of resistance, albeit clad in tribal, religious or denominational movements. There is another history that has never been written or distorted: the history of the freedom of the people. The twentieth century is strongly marked by resistance movements on the part of the people. Despite all the errors of real socialism, those wars that were led in the name of socialism – as well as the wars of national liberation against colonial regimes – were in principle wars of resistance and liberation led by the people.

All these resistance movements helped the oppressed peoples and their cultures to survive. Even if they were not successful from a political point of view, they proved the strength, persistence and permanence of their cultures. Still, after World War II, the representation of the people in political institutions increased hugely. Hence, it was not capitalism that prevailed at the end of the twentieth century, but democracy. Contemporary democracy is an important first step towards a realisation of age-old hopes and dreams on the part of the people. In my opinion, contemporary democracy opens a way towards the end of exploitation. It should be regarded as a corrective for extreme class divisions. It can play a part in developing the wealth and the potential of the people and it can lead to a form of rule that is truly of the people – a form of rule that will include the traditions of peace and brotherhood. Religious, ethnic and national differences, which in the past led to secession and separation followed by violence, can be resolved peacefully through instruments available in contemporary democracy. The people would probably prefer some kind of world federation – sectionalism being the result of power plays among feudal rulers and chauvinistic bands with their own ethnic, nationalist or class interests. Contemporary democracy, on the other hand, supports the organisation and development of regional federations on a broad basis of common interest. In this way differences of language, culture, religion and nation lose their importance. Advanced democracies form unions, like the United States of America or the European Union.

Everywhere in the world we see an awakening of cultures and their adaptation to the present in order to participate in public life. For the first time, people are freeing themselves from the paralysing pressure of dogmatic ideologies and void utopias. They are bringing all they have to the great process that is taking place: the renaissance of the people. The fall of rigid class-based dictatorships is an immense gain for those peoples whose existence is determined by democracy.

Democratic society, its politics and its state institutions all resulted from the increasing influence of the people. If democracy has become an urgent point on the worldwide agenda, it is a reflection of the awakening and edification of the people and their obtaining increasingly more political power. Contemporary democracy is a mature form of life and government by the people, which can be permanent and successful because it has a real material foundation: it has developed as a reaction to the fascism and real socialism suffered by the people.

It should be clear from the above that the corrosion of capitalism and its antagonists is making way for the democratic civilisation of the people. It will be useful, therefore, to summarise the basic qualities of this civilisation-in-the-making and give some thought to how it may develop.

1. It rests on a foundation of science, technology and ideology. The material basis of society has radically changed in the wake of an accelerating technological development. It has become possible to eradicate poverty and thus all kinds of class differences and social injustice. Through complementing the technological foundations with appropriate economic and political institutions of government, we will be able to utilise them for the benefit of the entire society, creating freedom and equality. In this sense, technology is an emancipating factor. But in the hands of people with reactionary and egoistic tendencies, it can easily become destructive. Thanks to communications technology – another important phenomenon of the new democratic society – science, which was once an occupation for a chosen few, is entering the heart of society with impressive speed. Hence, the information society is accompanied by increasing democratisation and self-government. Wherever society, state or politics needs to access informational resources, they are forced into a framework of transparency and mutual democratic control. The concurrency of science and technology is very high; they nourish and accelerate each other's progress. This process brings about an explosion in production capabilities and opens vast resources to the whole of society. However, science – as indeed technology – has to be controlled by democratic means.

   In contrast to earlier epochs, the real importance of ideology today lies in communicating a perspective of hope. Ideology has to break dogmatic traditions while renouncing all kinds of utopian beliefs.

   The more science helps us to understand the world we live in, the more likely it is that this new understanding will result in increasing creativity.

A person, in my opinion, can be said to understand the spirit of the time when he has adapted his consciousness to society's knowledge of history and social phenomena and when he continuously tries to understand the dialectic processes of nature.

2. Democratic civilisation is a systematic democratisation of society: the people have to come to the fore with their own identity, authentic consciousness and will to freedom. Democratisation of society also means understanding the interests of an information society, expressing its demands and moulding them into political institutions. This is the first time in history that society has become aware of itself, understands itself and can freely determine its own fate. Hence, democratic civilisation corresponds with the democratisation of society.
3. Another key element is the democratisation of politics, which we fitted in above between state institutions and society as the third domain. As a mediating link between state institutions and society, democratic political tools safeguard the democratic and just character of the exchange between these two pillars, or domains. Without a variety of political parties and the many contemporary institutions of all social areas, democratisation of society and the state institutions is not possible. All the organisations of civil society – or the third domain as we named it – are indispensable for democratic civilisation.
4. The increasing readiness of modern-day states for democracy ought to be recognised as a revolutionary achievement. In our epoch earthly rule has been declared independent from divine power – state institutions exist in the service of the people and do not need any divine justification whatsoever. The fundamental point is that the state has changed into a democratic institution.

   The form democratic institutions take is of secondary importance; what seems to be of primary importance is to develop a wide range of optional and flexible structures – from confederate to more centralised forms – which countries and societies can choose from according to their needs. The complexity of today's problems and the diverse and varied institutions and political tools created to deal with these problems democratically provide the main impetus for the building of democracy. As soon as a state has to rely on such institutions, it inevitably loses its classical importance and meaning and takes up the role of chief co-ordinator between these institutions. Such a state can truly be called democratic. According to this understanding, democracy is the regime of diverse institutions; the state cannot but take a pluralistic approach. The growing influence of local institutions enforces the gravitating of politics from the centre to local subcentres. Centralism is becoming more and more of a burden. On all levels, from society to family, from state to economy, equal opportunities for all as well as freedom-oriented pluralistic structures seem to be within reach. This results in a continuing democratic evolution of the state and simultaneously produces a variety of state forms, from confederate to more centralised forms. It also counteracts the dangerous acts of forging disparate communities into a single state and the creation of numerous micro-states through secessionist tendencies. Phenomena such as the United States America, the European Union and the Commonwealth of Independent States represent historical developments and the urgent need for a new kind of society and democratic politics.

5. The age of democratic civilisation stands for the liberation of women as much as it stands for the liberation of the people. While endowed with divine characteristics in the neolithic, women have been subject to oppression throughout the history of class societies. History, hence, is male history. The dominant class character of the political rule grew hand in hand with the dominance of the male. The resulting essentially male character of society even today forbids research into gender questions; in particular in the Middle East, subjecting such research to taboos even stronger than religious taboos. Hidden behind the idea of honour, the rights and the lives of women have been violated and destroyed. Women were deprived of their personalities and identities and kept as prisoners and slaves of men. This had devastating effects, worse even than the formation of social classes. The degree to which the women of a society are enslaved is a measure and indicator of general degradation and enslavement of all the people in that society.

   Ending these conditions will inevitably have deep social consequences. The liberation of women will necessarily be followed by general liberation, enlightenment and justice. It will contribute to the insight that peace is more valuable than war. It signifies a victory for society and for the individual. If the twenty-first century can initiate women's awakening, liberation and gaining strength, this will be even more important than class or national liberation. The rise of a democratic civilisation must be accompanied by the rise of women into equality on all levels.

   A negative development caused by the dominance of male culture is an irresponsible approach towards children and elderly people. Children are exposed to vulgarities that make their lives a nightmare. The elderly are increasingly separated from their offspring. A general unscrupulousness and lack of sensitivity towards them increase the troubles of old age. In a democratic society these two aspects will have to be revised. Youth should be more than exposure to vulgarities. Children's right to their own lives should be respected. The elderly have wisdom and life experience to offer. A democratic society will have to include and respect both these groups.

6. Human rights and individuality will become increasingly valuable and inseparable parts of a new way of life. Despite the individualistic aberrations generated by capitalism, the scientific–technological progress of the

twentieth century practically forces both the individual and humanity on the road towards a more mature humanism and individuality. Besides bloodshed and inhumanity, the past century also offered a new humanism, resting on individuality. It has to be incorporated in the awareness of the possibilities of science and technology. For the first time in history, man's hope for true personhood can be realised on the strong material basis and the scientific foundations of our epoch. Mankind, until today so deeply divided in numerous ethnic, religious, or national groups, will be able to – and needs to – unite, using the common language created by science and democracy. The opportunity for true humanism is here. Internationalism has become a real and indispensable approach to life in contrast to former times. Human rights are no longer a showcase of the law. They are becoming a part of the consciousness of the individual who tries to institutionalise an optimum balance between the needs of the society and himself.

This is what the rule of law has brought into our lives: the balance between society and the individual. This is perhaps the most significant historical development in this epoch: that such a balance has become possible for the first time in history. In view of such an accomplishment it also seems justified to call the democratic civilisation a civilisation of true humanism, individuality and human rights.

24

Global Aspects and Perspectives

In contrast to former civilisations, the emerging democratic civilisation is not limited to particular regions or specific geographic conditions. Capitalism has ended the phase of regional civilisations and is attempting to replace it with global legal and economical norms and rules. This will provide conditions for trade and commerce that are similar worldwide. This process is generally known as globalisation. It is aimed at the removal of all restrictions to the forming of (capitalist) economic and political institutions. In this respect, capitalism has abandoned all nationalistic traits and pursues a cosmopolitanism or universalism. Nationalism and nation states seem, rather, to pose an obstacle for global capitalism. Everything is measured by its usefulness on a global scale, the global market. Values formerly derived from nationhood as a basic point of reference are now adapted to the process of globalisation. Wherever the old national values cannot adapt, they are described as "used up" or "antiquated".

In my opinion, these changes will not save capitalism as such – they may prolong its lifespan, however, and thus aid the transformation to contemporary democracy. We have to admit, though, that capitalism, in contrast to real socialism, has accomplished quite well the changes required by the scientific revolution.

The current model of institutionalised interstate relations, the United Nations, seems to need substantial reforms. Otherwise, this institution may not survive. Similar continental and regional organisations have similar needs. On a political level, the old interstate alliances or confederacies could neither withstand the demands of capitalist globalisation, nor live up to the criteria of the present democratic civilisation. These formations were established to bring a balance between the classic forms of capitalism and real socialism. As these two ideologies have been overcome, so must their legacy of political structures.

This obviously holds true for military alliances as well. The Warsaw pact is already history. NATO, having no real purpose any longer, is also losing its meaning. Other global institutions, such as the International Monetary Fund (IMF) and the World Bank, will have to undergo substantial reform. They were originally created in the context and within the logic of the cold war, in order to isolate the real-socialist countries economically and help tie developing countries to the economic centres of the West. These considerations are no longer valid. After World War II, with the experience of fascism behind it, the West focused politically on the well-known models of parliamentary democracy. It strove to adapt to the challenges of a new civil development, thus helping to create a democratic civilisation. The same capitalist centres that even in the recent past fled democracy and sought refuge in the realms of reaction and fascism are now adhering to democratic systems and criteria as though they had never known anything else. The idea of a democratic civilisation is certainly not a creation of capitalism. But capitalism, in contrast to real socialism, immediately grasped its value and managed to adapt to it fast.

All these processes occurred against the background of the scientific revolution, in the course of which a universal language with global consequences was created. From then on, the old power and distribution pattern became useless. Democratic civilisation should not be regarded as the authentic product of a certain region of the world. Rather, it is a creation just as universal as science and technology, to which it is very closely related.

In fact, the powerful capitalist centres were the first to muster the strength necessary to adopt the basic structures of democratic civilisation. This insight is also enlightening if we look at the relationship between democratic civilisation and economic, social, and political developments. The developed capitalist centres began to organise research into the theory and practice of democracy and started the adoption and application of the results. Hence, they also took a leading position in this field and cemented it.

Europe is playing an avant-garde role in this development. Despite their differences, the European countries are well aware of the fact that they need to truly adopt and develop the democratic system. After all the centuries of bloody religious and national conflicts in Europe, these countries now strongly support the aspects of peace and compromise inherent in the democratic system. It is an important quality of democracy's political culture that you can approach the most complex problems without having to resort to ideological, religious or racial motives. The European Union is a concrete and prominent example of this development. It represents not only a political union, but also a general civilisation principle. In spite of several problems concerning the enlargement and deepening of the Union, it seems highly probable that the unification of all the European nations under the federal roof of the European Union will be successful. A rollback presently seems inconceivable. However, Europe is getting old and will probably experience a similar fate to that of the ancient centres of civilisation in Sumer, Egypt, Greece and Rome. The periphery, at least partly, has already begun to outstrip Europe.

The United States was Europe's first-born child on another continent and there is certainly truth to the saying that the twentieth century was the American century. We should not underestimate its enormous contributions to science and technology as well as its part in the development of democracy. Although the United States is an extension and complement to Europe in these fields, it was able to move faster and more safely in the globalisation race. While the United States seemed to be at the zenith of its development at the end of the twentieth century, there were already visible signs of decay. Neo-colonialism has already been overcome in Vietnam. The globalisation policy currently practised experiences growing criticism and produces isolation. American dominance of the UN, NATO, and the IMF is very cumbersome and too costly to be worthwhile. It seems nearly inevitable that the US dominance will be overcome during the course of the twenty-first century.

Besides, there is presumably nothing new that the United States could add to the development of a democratic civilisation. It is no longer in the American interest to nourish authoritarian or fascist regimes nor is the United States strong enough for open intervention. This is why it has adopted the principle of globalisation in the name of democracy and relies on the scientific and technological potential as its fundamental strategy. Nonetheless, this strategy is increasingly being questioned and its influence is limited.

To a certain extent, the present situation and the relationship between the United States and Europe resembles the historical relationship between Greece and Rome. Naturally, their fates might be similar, too. Just as the influx of barbarians accelerated the fall of the Roman Empire, so the present flood of the underprivileged from all over the world towards the centre of power might contribute to the decline of the United States. Hence, the twenty-first century might confront us with a situation in which the United States experiences a similar process to that faced by the Soviet Union at the end of real socialism.

The development of Asia, the mother continent of civilisations, rests in different hands. Russia is the leading power in the north, China in the east and bordering the Pacific, and India in the south-east. Japan and Australia are only extensions of Western civilisation without a genuine position of their own in the development process.

Russia's position is ambivalent. It belongs entirely neither to Europe nor to Asia, but is far from representing a third model. It had to pay a high price for its leadership in the spreading of real socialism. Russia is jointly responsible for the destruction and bloodshed of the twentieth century. It is also responsible for the fact that senseless forms of dogmatism and utopianism became the goal of bloodshed and war in the name of socialism. When the experiment failed, the course was changed abruptly and in an irresponsible way from the bogey of communism to a Mafia-like capitalism. However, because of Russia's desire to exert decisive influence in central Asia and the Caucasus, it will continue to consolidate its position as a centre on the periphery without being able to make independent contributions to the democratic civilisation.

China might become the theatre of more interesting developments. Here, the ugly marriage between a capitalist economy with tremendous growth and a real socialist course in politics is proving quite successful. It remains an open question, however, whether this will result in an authentic independent civilisation one day, or whether the country will have to resort to its traditional historical role to seek greatness in the – albeit masterly – imitation of great civilisations. The Chinese development will influence Japan and Indo-China. Presently it seems that the Chinese copy of real socialism may be successful. China will probably continue to choose whatever may be useful from the political systems available. However, instead of a genuine new impetus or a novel synthesis of elements already available, the result will probably be progress by imitation, making China a rising world power of the twenty-first century.

India is in a similar situation. India has experienced many invasions and occupations and over time has established a tradition of assimilating the invading cultures. It follows a liberal democratic course and may in the future measure up to the United States in terms of science and technology. The country will probably preserve its manifold traditions while assimilating Western influence. New civilisational developments are not to be expected from there.

Besides India and China, there are a number of other marginal Asian cultures, such as the Turkish, Iranian, and Indonesian ones, which tend to follow the Middle Eastern pattern. An Asian union between Russia, China and India on the lines of the European Union or the United States is quite inconceivable in the near future.

Latin America is also a mixture of nations, cultures and political systems. Immigrants from Europe and the political power of the United States have left deep cultural and political marks, which makes it rather difficult for Latin America to be authentic. Great men such as Zapata, Bolivar, Che Guevara and Castro have also left their traces, but such men cannot simply be imitated. Nonetheless, it is Latin America that keeps alive the hope for change by its long and still continuing line of revolutionary endeavours. It would be quite a success if the people of Latin America were to make the transition to contemporary democracy in the twenty-first century.

Black Africa will doubtless continue to be a problem region in terms of development and progress. This is most drastically expressed by the extent of the Aids catastrophe in sub-Saharan Africa. Africa needs to get rid of the corrupt men, both African and foreign, who prevent change and hold back progress. Instead, it would do well to look to its strong female traditions in order to overcome the resistance put up by its still-powerful tribal structures. This will be a long struggle.

All over the world, the powers of dogmatism and utopianism have been severely weakened. The present societal models seem increasingly invalid and are accompanied by a pessimistic view of the future and an indefinite quest for new perspectives. The influence of a widespread pragmatism deprives people of their enthusiasm and renders them helpless. Pragmatism's ability to be successful depends directly upon the welfare of the consumer society, which, owing to its very nature, is incapable of creating a new philosophical tradition. It is only the pleasure of the moment that counts – a hedonistic attitude quite typical of times of crisis. Communism and real socialism, representatives of utopianism and dogmatism, have utterly failed. Confronted with this reality, man has set out anew on a quest for a future worth living. Today we experience an epoch filled with revolutions in science and technology and the beginning of a democratic civilisation based on this progress. However, we are still seeking, analysing, evaluating. Immature approaches (this much we have learned from real socialism) can be followed by disaster. The painful consequences of numerous revolutionary attempts at assumed higher goals can be ascribed to this simple fact.

The age of democratic civilisation, therefore, has to be determined by a complex, multidimensional synthesis of all of humanity's contradictions and conflicts and all its voices and longings. Admittedly, we are still far from that, far from a universal realisation of what humanity can accomplish. For me, it is helpful to look back on the cultural tradition of the region that made me and to ask my people if they have the strength and the potential to see beyond the horizon and to contribute to this synthesis.

Part 5

Can the Cultural Tradition of the Middle East Serve as a Source for a New Synthesis of Civilisations?

Introduction to Part 5

Presently, the Middle Eastern region has nothing to offer that might justify hopes for a positive future development – apart from the meagre fact that the region was once the historical source of civilisation. On the contrary, desertification, global warming and water deficiency might make this area even less hospitable than it already is. Recently discovered rich oilfields have not been able to play a positive part but only produced wars and conflicts. The considerable profits only serve to fill the purses of a handful of already rich people. The population goes away empty-handed. The land of the first civilisations between the Euphrates, the Tigris, and the Nile will remain a potential source of conflicts. Progress in irrigation techniques may help increase the efficiency of the region's agriculture. These are practically the only resources of the Middle East. Hence, it will not be the geography of the region that will advance a new synthesis of civilisation there, nor will it be science and technology: they are already global in their availability and application. What, then, can the region contribute to the democratic civilisation we have discussed above – a civilisation that will probably evolve a variety and richness of democratic forms, formations and processes? The democratic civilisation does not represent the synthesis itself but offers the framework from which the synthesis will emerge. Certainly, form and content go hand in hand, complement each other. A sustainable synthesis of humanity's many voices into a new civilisation, which comprises all of humanity, will have to be sought elsewhere. As we also saw, most of the world's currently important countries and nations can be said to be moving in roughly the same direction today. One region, the Middle East, takes quite a different position, however. What makes it that different? For one thing, there is the cultural tradition. The geographic influence only becomes visible when it is reflected by culture. After the first cultures had emerged, the external environment became secondary to the development processes and was replaced by internal dynamics. The history of civilisation is the history of cultural development and the accumulation of cultural knowledge. In this context, the definition of culture and its part in the development of civilisation is interesting. The nearly 10,000 years of the neolithic have seen the physical environment as a creative element. The civilisations that followed owe the Neolithic, with the first civilisations in Sumer and Egypt and their achievements, the basis for their development. This is what I have tried to describe in the preceding chapters: that there was a kind of initial spark of civilisation in the neolithic, which set off a chain reaction that continues until today. I also tried to describe how the Middle East slipped into a deep crisis between the tenth and fifteenth centuries, a crisis which has lasted into our time and has even deepened. We need to understand the identity of the Middle East, its *personality*, in order to relaunch it as a source of civilisation.

China, India, Russia, Latin America and also Europe and its successors are able to dress their identities in different ways, express them in different political systems. They do not really internalise them. For the personality of the Middle East, however, civilisation is not simply a dress, but life itself. Civilisation has become part of its genome, so to speak. Nowhere on earth can we find a similar situation. In the Middle East, history and culture, civilisation and life have produced societies and personalities more different and diverse than anywhere else. An agrarian culture of some 1,000 years has left its social traces. Mythological and religious thought have been alive all the time in the social subconscious. Dogmatism and fatalism have become inseparable parts of life. Independent and creative thought are fast asleep. Theological dogma are sacred taboos and must be believed unquestioningly. It is utter sin to live outside the realm of what the holy books say. Stories that once went from mouth to mouth as legends have become rules of faith, religion, God. The ideas and memories at the basis of civilisation have been forgotten. But they are still there. The cultural tradition of the Middle East is like a tree: its roots are deep and its seed has been carried into all corners of the world.

With its decline in the Middle Ages, the culture of the Middle East lost its originality. It became a graveyard and has been silent ever since. The Ottomans were merely the janitors of the graveyard. They lived from donations they could draw from funerals, from what they buried. The whole region is full of sorrow and sadness, which finds expression in its prayers and liturgy and does little more than convey the message of mortality to the people. Frightening people with death, preparing them for death by telling them about heaven and hell, has become the way of life, the core of civilisation in the region. Science and technology were dropped long ago. Society and politics have been repeating themselves in ever the same forms. The net of dogmatism and fatalism lying over the formerly creative and developed region causes depression and despair.

The people of the Middle East cry and weep a great deal. They had created so much and then they lost so much. During the past 1,000 years, sobbing was all that there was to hear in the dead silence that enveloped the region. A morbid sorrow resounds in prayers and songs, and in the sound of stringed instruments. Nothing of it is coincidence; it gives expression to what has happened to the region. This sorrow makes people drunk without drinking; they do not see what happens in the world around them, and death has become their daily companion. People shed blood for trivialities, as compensation for religious conflicts, for violations of what they believe to be their honour, for property conflict and family feuds. The tradition of the vendetta has a long history and is closely related to the custom of honour killings, in which male family members kill a female relative who is believed to have violated moral laws and thus to have brought into question the honour of the family.

The Middle East is a grave, and an inextricable knot of a grave, which remains the same while the rest of the world is constantly changing. It seems incapable of assimilating the elements and trends of contemporary development. The inextinguishable traces of past civilisations are in conflict with present civilisation, demanding a new synthesis. However, at present we find neither transformation nor erosion, both of which would need some creative potential. While all over the world ethnic, religious or national conflicts are within reach of a solution in one way or the other, here too the Middle East is different. If it appears to be possible to resolve a problem with the tools presented by contemporary democracy, then there lies hidden behind the surface of the problem the obstinate resistance of cultural difference.

This circumstance is not simply negative, but can also offer the chance for a way out of the accelerating crisis of capitalism. The true tragedy arises from the inability of the Middle East itself to analyse its own traditions in order to transform them into something more contemporary. The potential available must remain passive, because external influences are not internalised, resulting in conflicts and a deepening of the hopelessness.

This process has been continuing and intensifying for 500 years. Until about 1500, there was an uninterrupted cultural tradition of over 15,000 years, which was superior to other cultures most of the time. The material and intellectual superiority of all substructural and superstructural institutions was a source of great self-confidence and the feeling of representing the centre of the world. Everybody else was regarded as a foreign heathen. The last 500 years have not been enough to break this dogma. People in the Middle East notice the superiority of the West and its culture, they feel its material and intellectual power, but are unable to admit to themselves what they see and, hence, cannot learn from it. The newly formed classes, too, exercise their influence on this, although they are only perceived as artificial things. They are not able to tackle their historical foundations themselves, nor to analyse them in order to generate material for a new synthesis and a new approach, nor even to reject them altogether. They are only extensions of external political systems. These circles are even prevented from becoming influential in localisation or regionalisation efforts.

In the Middle East, capitalist modernisation has not yet been able to establish a dialogue with local cultures. It still appears as something foreign and alien. Society, on the other hand, still follows in part rules established in the neolithic, the slave-holder age, or feudalism. It has been dressed up in capitalist and real-socialist clothes, and this has produced chaos. There is no clear tendency nor are there any efficient institutions. Everything is left undecided and the only choice seems to be to escape or give up. The decay and the crisis of the Middle East must be taken seriously. The West underestimates how deeply the Middle East and its personality are rooted in the beginnings of civilisation. It has lived through all of it. This mistake throws away the possibility of a real dialogue with the past and prevents an appropriate dialectic relationship with the present. Presently there is no antithesis to Western civilisation. It could form in the Middle East.

The question how such an antithetical development could be accomplished remained unanswered during the twentieth century. Both nationalism and real socialism failed. The same was true for Islamism and its dated and empty doctrines. They can be compared to a private library which is driven around the Middle East on a donkey cart. They cannot produce a successful antithesis to the West. In the face of given social and state traditions, the institutions of democratic civilisation cannot easily be realised. There is a minimum set of conditions: at least some kind of enlightenment, a reformation of religions, some kind of renaissance of long-forgotten achievements – certain fundamental processes akin to what the West had to go through, in order to prepare a platform for democratic civilisation. At present, the Middle East's western-style institutions are alien bodies, imported from outside the region. Israel's existence, its reality, has been created from outside and, therefore, has not yet been accepted. The same applies to both liberal and communist parties. They are deeply alien to the strong traditions still prevalent. A revival of Islam, too, will not produce anything creative. It will only remind us of its history – which is, admittedly, better than forgetting it completely.

The many different interventions taking place in the Middle East appear to me like the treatment of a comatose patient with aspirin. Using artificial terms, an artificial entity has been simulated, which was then diagnosed and treated in the sincere belief that this would help the patient. Everything in the Middle East that comes in the name and shape of modernity has the character only of a model. The region has not yet understood itself. Its society is as little shapeable as concrete. Its political and state institutions resemble a metastasising cancer. However, the Middle East becomes understandable as soon as we examine its relationship with European civilisation and consider the dialectic entirety of the two civilisations: just as it is necessary for Europe to discover the foundations of its civilisation in the Middle East, so the Middle East needs to determine the rottenness of its own civilisation by understanding European civilisation and defining an antithesis in the course of this process of comprehension. I must stress, however, that such a comprehension must not amount to simple imitation or assimilation. What has happened during the past two centuries has been merely an imitation, albeit necessary, but devoid of any comprehension. In our present time it is useless to repeat this process. Self-respect and dignity cannot be obtained by naive and mindless imitation.

The process of assimilating European achievements unfortunately still persists, in rather an unhealthy way. It does not appear to be possible for the Middle East to adopt such things successfully. Rather, its seems, the forming of an antithesis will be necessary to help this process, too. Besides, any historical movement seeking to be of importance in the Middle East will have to leave adaptation and assimilation behind and instead formulate an antithesis. If it fails at this point, it will itself be left behind. The relationship with Europe during the past two centuries and the unsuccessful modernisation efforts confirm this conclusion. However, those current forms of resistance against European civilisation on the basis of tribalism, religion or nationalism are neither antithetic nor do they represent any synthesis. Any fairly successful imitation, some more advanced form of adaptation to local conditions, though, may already convey the impression of an antithesis. Some people grow a beard or wear a keffiyeh to demonstrate their attachment to roots in the past. This is foolish. Assimilation which amounts to a successful adaptation to local conditions does not possess any strength of its own and is unable to produce an antithesis. It can only claim to have communicated European values more profoundly by including given local facts.

Most of the existing monarchies and republics of the region are utterly backward with a view to adapting to European democratic criteria. They cannot be called monarchies or republics in the European sense of the word. Democratic and secular republicanism, in fact, only exist on a rhetoric or demagogic level. The prevailing superstructure of Middle Eastern societies is marked by personal self-interest in the disguise of tribal welfare, family welfare, or some primitive and chauvinistic nationalism, which is then presented to the masses by means of corruption. Their backwardness is even greater than was that of the tribal nobility 4,000 years ago. Additionally, there is an underlying primitive capitalism. Of course, the rulers have learnt from the past. Their beards are becoming to them as well as the robes, reminiscent of former times, which are required by Islam and its code of conduct. In the end, what they do is to use the despotic means handed down from the age of slavery to paint their medieval sultanates in the colours of Western modernity. This is even called reform by some, revolution by others. In reality, no such thing has ever taken place; the status quo, has merely been strengthened. European influence could never communicate reforms or revolution to the Middle Eastern culture. The pieces, the patchwork of European culture imposed and enforced on the region, represent not reform, but colonisation. This situation has not yet been overcome and is even presented as a rewarding goal to those countries hitherto most intensely influenced by European civilisation.

The waste of material resources makes it clear that these countries have not even been able to establish a genuine capitalist economy; their political institutions primarily operate as instruments of the well-known despotism of the sultanate, set up in the style of modern European-type bodies. Altogether, the European efforts of the last 200 years seem to have failed almost completely, in spite of vast civilisational and material resources, obviously wasted in the face of enormous ignorance and corruption. We will have to build a new relationship, a new approach towards European civilisation, based on a relation of thesis and antithesis, which will allow for the development of Middle Eastern civilisation.

This line-up has something to do with the nature of civilisations. Whosoever proves capable of establishing a dialectic relation with European civilisation in terms of forming a new synthesis deserves to claim the value of this synthesis not only for the whole region but for the world. The history of the Middle East, as we saw in previous chapters, is full of such syntheses: Gilgamesh, Zoroaster, Socrates, Jesus, Muhammad. In Europe there were the pioneers of the Renaissance.

The crucial point is whether the potential of these historical achievements can be revived into a new future. Is it possible to add another link to the chain of tradition, a link that does not stand for the mere assimilation of European civilisation but an adaptation and synthesis of both civilisations? The Middle East will have to live up to this challenge or it will be doomed to starve and suffer. It is not like Russia, China or India, nor can it become a "new America". Then, what could such a new relation to European civilisation look like? If life in this region fraught with history is supposed to go on in a meaningful and dignified way, it becomes necessary to respond to the question of *how to live*. We must neither be enveloped in European civilisation nor must we reject it categorically. We have to contribute to the development of humanity as a whole. We need a counter-offensive, in order to establish a life worth living on this planet. An expansion of the currently prevalent ideology in terms of a world constitution and a uniform global economy might always degenerate into a new worldwide black-and-white pattern, even if all of this could be accomplished by democratic means.

The world religions outside the Middle East have already to a large extent accepted adaptation. They follow the necessities of capitalism. More important is an awakening of the buried humanistic and civilisational values of the Middle East under new conditions. This region can neither simply adapt itself, nor can it easily be assimilated. If it succeeds in formulating an antithesis to European civilisation, it might become a hope for all of humankind.

25

Renewal of the Ideological Identity Will Be the Primary Historical Challenge

A change of consciousness in the Middle East needs to be initiated by a historical process similar to the Renaissance, the Reformation or the Enlightenment in Europe. The Middle East, however, has not yet even made acquaintance with these terms, and doesn't dare to. We have to clear up some misunderstandings in this context. The transfer of science and technology, the building of industrial structures, and the existence of a number of democratic institutions do not indicate that any of the above has taken place. These are eclectic developments, they remain superficial, poor experiments in the course of colonialism and assimilation. After two centuries of Westernisation we cannot but observe that there has not been any kind of authentic development beyond that. Any Islamist tendencies in response to Westernisation should be understood as nationalism painted green. There is no other way towards an authentic development but such an, admittedly belated, revolution. First of all, religion – a valuable, albeit hardly understood, part of Middle Eastern culture – must be tackled; but not with the simple means of laicism or by attacking the faithful. The aim is not the denial of God and the cursing of mosques, but the scientific analysis of these things in their historical development. The revolution will necessarily be an intellectual one; it will have to make an accurate analysis of the mythical origins of theology and regard theology as material for historiography.

After the twelfth century, orthodox Islam became inflexible.[1] Freedom of thought and individuality were destroyed. A person who is not allowed to think freely cannot really be creative. In a society unable to produce its own creative values, only oppressors and profiteers will benefit. Therefore, it is necessary to dispose of the dogmatic aspects of religion completely. Without such a reformation there will not be free individuals. Faith should not be dogma imposed on the individual.

Instead of the present form of liturgical prayers, profound and comprehensive analyses should be done of what the holy books have to say concerning all aspects of society. The verses of the Sunna should be interpreted on the basis of this analysis. Mosques and other holy places should be made local centres of science and art where, for instance, instructive and entertaining plays are performed. We should not forget that prayers (*namaz*) are only a later form of religious plays. Praying itself is theatre in a general sense. These remarks should not be distorted in the way of bigotry. I repeat: the origin of fasting and praying, sacrifices and holy days needs to be examined. All ceremonies should be given modern forms corresponding to the needs of our age but reviving the original meanings that underlie the fixed forms. Mosques and other holy places should become academies and places of learning and art. If scientists, artists and the wise of the surrounding area teach there, the people will not be left uneducated any longer. All other ritual forms should also be reconsidered. Instead of the cruel sacrificial slaughter of animals, donors might, more usefully, funnel capital into funds for the poor or for the benefit of other charities. Fasting should be performed only for the sake of self-discipline. In this way, all ceremonies and religious rituals should be ordered anew. Some people will ask where that leaves Allah. My answer is that, in the same way that we have evolved over the course of time, so our concept of Allah has evolved, that is, in accordance with the given conditions of the age we live in. Our present Allah is the essence of science; is everything that advances on its own on the basis of a universal dialectic; is everything that changes; is the endless process of change itself. Who could have a grander idea of God?

Baseless utopianism needs to be reformed in a similar way. Black-and-white fantasies about heaven and hell, purgatory, apocalypse, the coming of the Messiah, the chosen people, etc. should be given up. They only lead to oppression and exploitation. Just like the power of dogma, the power of utopia usually serves only the strongest. Moreover, religious paradises render the mind lazy.

A society that allows the unpunished murder of a 15-year-old girl because she is openly in love with somebody is terribly sick. All life is stifled in a society like this. No creative change can take place. Inspiration, poetry and love are made impossible. The revolution of the renaissance I am pleading for means curing this sickness. And we can learn many lessons from what Europe has already achieved.

There has been some accumulation of science and enlightenment which has to be put to practice now. We must get rid of the stale, egotistic fixation with tribe, clan, family, the life of a married woman, male existence, nation and piety. We must turn towards a universal understanding of mankind and we must live it. We must, therefore, do the things necessary for genuine love and a genuine understanding of the values of civilisation, our earth and the irreplaceability of man.

We must awaken our past with its Laylas, Majnouns, Kerems and others.[2] We must awaken the mythical founders of our civilisation, heroes and gods like Gilgamesh and Enkidu. We must recover the intellectual greatness of our famous scientists and philosophers, like Ibn Sina (Avicenna) and Ibn Rushd (Averroes). They had started something which we can continue; they can be examples we must try to live up to.

We are a part of history just as these names are part of our history. Beyond history we are nothing. Our present Middle Eastern literature is largely separated from the social and historical realities of the region. On the whole, it is an expression of individuals and groups assimilated by colonialism. Here, too, a renaissance of literature is crucial for the development of free personalities.

The role of religion should be limited to the sphere of ethics. Science should be left to consideration by philosophy. The problem of restructuring does not exist for philosophy and science: if we unify them in a common consciousness of history and make them the decisive momentum for free and creative minds, they will develop their enlightening strength. As soon as the scientific and philosophical achievements of Europe can be united with the historical reality of the Middle East, history and the human mind will be opened to an advanced enlightenment. This is what I understand by the term *developing an antithesis*.

The most important element in the creation of a free society is the development of individuality on the basis of argument. Individuality does not simply mean expressing oneself but, rather, realising society in oneself and oneself in society. A self-contented person, who is only concerned with his own advantage, cannot be called an individual person but, at best, a narcissist. With the development of individuality, the arts are provided with a new, creative dimension, driving civilisation and development onward.

To reflect our own origin more realistically; to answer to ourselves the question of how a person ought to live and how a person becomes a person; to muster the strength necessary for our lives – these are the essential criteria for an inspired thesis or antithesis. European civilisation cannot accomplish on its own a synthesis that brings about a new civilisation. The antithesis must come from the Middle East, just as the antithesis of the ancient East was the Greco-Roman civilisation. Their result, their synthesis, was the European civilisation of the modern age.

26

The Democratic Civilisation Project

Democratic civilisation is another important thesis of European civilisation which has to be experienced in the context of enlightenment and a new beginning. Intellectual renewal, which is an important part of it, actually keeps a safe distance from society and state and involves only a small number of determined and talented individuals. The democratic civilisation thesis, on the contrary, essentially refers to state and society, i.e. it obliges people to come to terms with them.

Unsuccessful real socialism both complicated the situation and required new options to be found. Europe forms the right wing of democratic civilisation and is at the same time holding it back. Further progress seems impossible, owing to the strength of capitalism. The right, according to capitalist logic, remains the most rational position. The experimental wing was left impotent by real socialism. It is not likely that the so-called "underdeveloped countries" will be able to fill this void – at best some are included as extensions on the periphery of the system.

In performing the democratic process, both on the social and the political level, the Middle East can become an antithesis. The democratisation of society, either by reform or by revolution, is the crucial issue.

As with all revolutionary mass movements, women and young people form the avant-garde of this process and represent its strongest democratic elements.

Women must take a special position in the democratic awakening of the Middle East. Despite their eminent and creative part in the neolithic community, women have been degraded and deprived of their rights ever since class societies were established. Their untapped strength might become the most vivid and active part of the struggle. Without it, democratic society will hardly prevail.

Women of the oppressed nations can position themselves as real initiators and mothers of the democratic offensive on the left of the rising democratic civilisation, thus establishing the necessary antithesis. They are the strongest pillar of a free and equal society. If in the Middle East the democratisation of society becomes an antithesis, it will primarily be due to women, and secondarily thanks to young people. The avant-garde role of women in the democratisation of Middle Eastern societies already bears the marks of an antithesis for the worldwide process.

Similarly, young people understand the contemporary world of the Middle East as something that renders them helpless and offers them no perspective. (Sacrificing one's life in the name of some nationalist or religious leader as a supposed martyr, thereby killing or injuring a great number of people, is definitely no perspective.) Today's communications and information technology allow young people to grow up and develop a consciousness very early. Because of this, democracy might grow roots in the Middle East in a very short time.

Geographic and cultural similarities throughout the region, and shared economic needs and water resources, might form the basis for a democratic federation of the entire region.

The only obstacle before us is the despotic state, the octopus at the centre of all political institutions. However, the more capitalist civilisation advances in its globalisation, the less chance there is of continuing the old ways. Globalisation from outside and the rising opposition of the people, stimulated by technology, seem to be dissolving despotism as a political means. This process has already started, and the antithetic existence is strengthened by an understanding of these conditions.

These are the crucial developments that lead me to believe that an intellectual revolution, hand in hand with democratic reformation, will open up the opportunity for the Middle East to become an antithesis.

27

The Theory and Practice of Middle Eastern Civilisation

The extreme alienation between the traditional structured state and society, brought about by permanent oppression, stifled almost all social initiatives and dynamics. The superficial modernity of capitalism worsened this situation. Nationalism and capitalism's reactionary totalitarian attitudes merged with the despotic structures existing in the state, while they were giving themselves airs of modernity. Any progressive elements within capitalism, for instance the already mentioned changes of the Renaissance and the Enlightenment, failed to reach society. Wherever the awakening of modernity failed, the traditional state became even more conservative and reactionary. Consequently, the hopelessness of the existing social structures of the Middle East was deepened.

Such states and societies do not have the strength to democratise themselves. Only the development of civil society as the third domain offers the opportunity to end the stasis. Civil society needs to accomplish democratisation in a sensible and independent way. Any form of violence will only serve as a pretext for repression, rendering society still more static. The extreme right and left have created a dreadful tradition of violence in the Middle East. Nonetheless, this does not make resistance useless, but stresses the importance of the form it assumes. The conservatism of state and society can only be overcome with the help of the third domain. For that, we need a comprehensive theory of civil society for the Middle East, including a programme and a strategy. The alternative society that we want to create must not be an extension of the state nor of traditional society. An independent philosophy of life, mutual coordination, a detailed programme, efficient organisations to address the needs for, and purposeful forms of action, might be able to soften intransigent positions and play an important part in the definition of a way for the future.

Institutions that until now have been marginalised should move to the centre. There are growing historical, technological, social and political reasons for the importance of the organisations of civil society. For the Middle East, it is important to implement the model within this framework and to establish up-to-date organisations of civil society as fundamental pillars of a democratic civilisation.

Organising people in matters of the economy can empower them to contribute to change. Even developed societies have seen the rise of formerly marginalised groups as a result of organising processes. These include consumer cooperatives, solidarity and aid organisations, charitable foundations, trade and commerce associations, all established on a legal basis. The classic structures of society and state can become almost secondary compared with these new structures.

If a community in the Middle Eastern region organises such social activities as education and health by itself, it gains influence. It becomes influential and attractive in the entire field of culture. The same applies in the field of sports, with opportunities and specific offers for women and young people. In particular, the cities have an increasing need for opportunities for mass and individual sports activities. Sport in which civil society actively participates is almost predestined to become one of its most important parts.

In view of increasing lawlessness and a general weakening of respect for the law, civil self-organisation in the field of law is indispensable and vital. Law offices as part of civil society are important institutions in the process of establishing a universal order of law. They communicate a consciousness of law, which is helpful in putting people on the road to democracy, and they contribute to the struggle against lawlessness.

Other necessary conditions for the establishment of a functioning third domain include the overcoming of the traditional relationship between political parties and the state, a relationship which is mostly focused on the mutual benefits it provides. Peace and a non-violent society also need their organisations and committees; these things can only be put across to people by activities and participation. Especially in the Middle East, where violence is part of everyday life, organisations and forms of action in the service of peace deserve a prominent place in the civil organising process.

Versatile organisations of women and young people contribute significantly to the development of the third domain. Umbrella organisations, like democratic federations comprising all the organisations and institutions of civil society on the national and international level, make the system complete.

Self-defence also needs to be discussed in the framework of civil society. It must be understood clearly and correctly in order to be applied ethically. It is by no means absurd to assume that civil society can be exposed to attacks from both the state and traditional society. They perceive democracy as a danger to their sources of profit and benefits. Since a number of institutions of the old society and of the state will no longer have a function and the positions of those who manage them will begin to sway, they may resort to illegal measures and even violence at any time. These are possible scenarios in which self-defence may become necessary and the law must provide for it. However, this term must be defined precisely. All individuals and groups have the right to defend constitutionally legal norms on the basis of universally recognised rights. They may exercise resistance by way of demonstrations, petitions, the use of the legal process, or other individual or collective methods, until their rights are granted. If neither the legal nor the political option is available, then people may resort to resistance in order to defend their rights against injustice done to themselves, their language or their culture. This is not rebellion, but legitimate protest based on inalienable rights. All individuals, communities and nations endowed with such rights in fact violate the law if they remain silent in the face of injustice. Defending existing claims, revolting if necessary, is part of the indefeasible right of resistance and is essential for the development of legal norms and justice. No person and no community has the right to remain silent in the face of lawlessness or even worse, to bow to it. This is where the real breach of law and with it the poisoning of society and state begins. Self-defence is a legal element of the development and application of law, and a cornerstone of democratic civilisation. Human rights, basic freedoms and the rights of the citizen have indispensably become part of universal law as laid down in international conventions and covenants. They have had to be fought for and now need to be fostered.

Another issue is the issue of leadership in civil society. This is a far-reaching responsibility, which needs centres of education, in particular for political cadres, functionaries and party officials. The model of society thus envisaged needs the help and contribution of people educated in matters ranging from ideology to technology. Such cadres cannot be produced by our present society or the education system of the state.

The theory and practice of civil society is enormously important in the Middle East. Traditional violent methods have done extreme harm to the Arabs, the peoples of Israel, Iran and Iraq, and the Kurds. They all have to admit that their violent endeavours over the centuries – and the theories which they still adhere to – have remained unsuccessful. Nationalism, for example, will never solve the Jerusalem problem. The solution of the Kurdish question will take another century if we continue as hitherto. Confessional wars and tribalism will never end. Violent societies waging permanent rebellion against well-armed states prevent any kind of progress.

If the Middle Eastern civilisation of nations historically close to each other can produce a civil society conforming to contemporary democratic criteria, then there might be hope for the region and for mankind. It is therefore important to take a look at the role of the nations in the Middle East. They are the main actors and the carriers of its culture and among the oldest nations of the world. What can they contribute to civilisation? How will they evolve in the future?

PALESTINE

The Arab–Israeli reality is the main problem of the region. There seems to be no solution to it. Its roots date back nearly 4,000 years. We know that the Semitic dialects formed between 9000 and 6000 BCE and spread all over the Arab peninsula, north Africa, the eastern Mediterranean, and the area between the Euphrates and the Taurus mountains. Semitic tribes provided a major part of the workforce needed in Sumer and Egypt. The Semitic tribes adhered to various kinds of polytheism until the time of Abraham and the rise of monotheism. Here lie the roots of the problem. As a consequence of the following struggles between the different religious factions, Judaism emerged, as the monotheistic religion of the Hebrew tribes. From now on, Arab and Hebrew tribes went different ways in respect of religion. While the Arabs continued their existence as desert tribes, the Jews created rich urban communities. The religious differences also became visible in social and class differences. Despite several setbacks, the Hebrew tribes flourished until about 70 CE, when the Romans destroyed Jerusalem and drove the Jewish population out of the region.

From now on, the Jews had to live in largely isolated societies, predominantly occupied with trade and commerce, and often persecuted. Eventually it was the holocaust which made a Jewish state inevitable and indispensable. However, the creation of the state of Israel led to another conflict within the fragile network of international relations. This conflict seems to be insoluble and has made the Near East a permanent "crisis region". Because of their historically enforced way of existence, the Jews, in order to survive, took part in the rise and spread of capitalism throughout Europe and the United States. In spite of sometimes terrible conditions, they gained increasing influence globally, holding important positions in commerce, finance, science, the arts, and politics all over the world. Therefore, Israel is backed by a majority of capitalist countries.

The conflict with the Arabs is a conflict about land. While the abolishment of Israel is unthinkable, the country will have to transform its nationalist basis in order to contribute to a solution, in the same way that Arab nationalism has to be transformed. Otherwise, the conflict will probably escalate until even the use of nuclear weapons is within reach. Of course, Israel would be strategically superior in such a conflict, but this cannot produce a viable and lasting solution. The whole conflict is typified in the merciless struggle over Jerusalem. The holy city lives under the curse of nationalism. Its name, however, means "sanctuary" (*al quds*) in Arabic and "place of peace" (*yerushaleim*) in Hebrew.

The Jews have had many experiences with and among different people as a consequence of their historical expulsion. These experiences amount to a considerable knowledge and capability in science, economy and the arts. Many intellectually outstanding people came from Jewish communities. Jewish culture has produced a formidable material and spiritual strength, which exercises a lasting influence on most of the fundamental ideologies and institutions.

The Arabs, on the other hand, have not had such experiences. They have been able, however, to spread over the entire peninsula and north Africa and have even become quite wealthy recently thanks to the oil under their soil. Hence, the Semitic strands have the means for fighting each other on a worldwide scale and have fallen victim to the religions and nationalism that they have created. If they ever want to achieve anything like a peaceful coexistence, they will have to leave their nationalism behind, and in its stead come to an agreement on the basis of the criteria of democratic civilisation. In my opinion, they should create a flexible federation overcoming the religious and nationalist division. In the long run, they need to cooperate, creating the conditions for cultural freedom and a free-market order, under the umbrella of an Israeli–Arab federation. Besides, such a federation also seems inevitable for the Arab world, which is divided into 23 (mostly small) states. The present Arab union doesn't work. An Israeli–Palestinian union, however, would force all Arabs to come together under one roof. Apart from some reactionary circles, the whole Middle East would benefit greatly from such a federation.

Another indispensable part of democratisation in the Middle and Near East is real secularisation. After thousands of years of destruction and repression in the name of religion, an all-embracing religious reform is needed. This will contribute enormously to the success of any democratisation efforts. At the same time, all nationalist ideologies, which presently determine the conflict in Palestine, must make way for scientifically based philosophies establishing freedom and unity and justice. Only such approaches will lead to mutual tolerance and peace. In this way, an Israeli–Arab compromise and a democratic whole can take the place of the present conflict. Such a development could also have a positive influence on the political situation worldwide.

In the Middle East itself, the civilisational antithesis of European civilisation would be strengthened and would probably radiate far beyond the region, triggering similar approaches elsewhere. The historical consequences of an Israeli–Arab compromise would catalytically push solutions for the other problems of the region. The present situation cannot last long. It is completely senseless and will probably not be tolerated for much longer on the local, regional, and international level. In the twenty-first century, I sincerely believe, we will see peace coming into the region as a consequence of democratisation followed by an economic and cultural impetus. This will have global implications, of course, and will advance the evolution of a new synthesis of democratic civilisation.

IRAN

The Iranian part of the Middle East still persists in its historically grown authenticity. Today, it seems to aim at developing further the experiment of democratising Islamic culture. The reformative character of the Iranian region dates back into early history, the Zoroastrian traditions, and the rise of the Persian empire. Iran played an important role both in the spreading of civilisation in Asia and in the reformation of the feudal aspects of Islamic civilisation. Shi'ite Islam came into being in Iran and was the first reformative approach. Subsequently, Iran experienced many revolts, rebellions and reformation attempts and was far less intransigent a political and religious construct than, for example, the Ottoman empire.

The last great revolution of the twentieth century also took place in Iran. Interestingly, it does not seem as though this Middle Eastern revolution will fade away easily. Rather, it seems that Islamic conservatism is dissolving while the political results of the Islamic revolution are being retained. Islamic reformative tendencies are gradually uniting with external influences. Therefore, the Islamic revolution will either destroy itself or fight with the conservatism of the Middle East in the name of an Iranian Islam. Presently we are witnessing a transition period. If the reformation of Islam is successful it will bring about a wave of democratisation in the Islamic world.

The Arab-dominated Islamic feudalism finds itself in a dilemma. It does not seem probable that a feudal anti-democratic Islam will survive in the long run. The transition period won't be a long one. The reformists are backed by the people, and the conservative tendencies are gradually losing influence and power.

It is obvious, therefore, that developments in Iran will deeply influence the progress expected for the Middle East in the twenty-first century. Iran, after Israel and the Arab countries, is the third important pillar of an emerging antithesis to the European model of civilisation.

ANATOLIA

The region called Anatolia, at the northern extreme of the Middle East, has always been part of it and has always contributed a great deal to its development. At the stage of contemporary civilisation, it lays claim to participate in the same way, now as a part of Turkey. Historically, Anatolia is a crossroads and transformation line in many different systems. The values and results of the long history of civilisation in the Middle East had to cross it on their way into the Caucasus, the Balkans and Europe, and in modern times from Europe into the Middle East.

At the end of the first millennium CE, Anatolia was inhabited by the Armenians in the north-west and the Kurds in the south-east. At the beginning of the second millennium, Anatolia witnessed the immigration of Turkish and Seljuk tribes. This settlement process lasted into the fourteenth century. Then, with the rise of the Ottoman civilisation, the Turks experienced a deep division into different classes. While the Turkmen in the mountainous areas continued their original culture, the Turks in the urban areas, formerly part of Byzantium, experienced a strong assimilation. Both Seljuks and Turks belonged to the Sunni denomination of Islam. They installed a conservative feudal regime. The Ottoman empire tried hard to keep the balance between feudalism and capitalism and was able to expand and exist comfortably until it came up against capitalist expansion, which led to its decline and fall. By the beginning of the twentieth century, the disintegration process was complete.

The conservative Islamic ideology of the Ottoman era was replaced by a Western-oriented nationalist ideology. Under the leadership of Mustafa Kemal (Ataturk) the new regime attacked Western colonialism and collaborating circles centred on the Sultanate as well as Armenian and Greek compradors.[1] An external alliance with the Bolsheviks and an internal alliance with the Kurds enabled it to win a national liberation war and establish the Republic of Turkey in Anatolia. So, the Kurds were actively involved in the foundation of the republic.

However, soon after that the new republic began its repressive policy towards the Kurds, who in turn responded with numerous rebellions. At this point already, the Turkish Republic had deprived itself of a historical chance to democratise itself. Confronted with the Kurdish question, the Turkish Republic suddenly came to a dead end.

Both geographically and in respect of its level of development, Turkey is the part of the Middle East closest to Europe. There are intense debates and discussions over the issue of democratisation in Turkey. Nonetheless, because of an obvious inability to democratise its structure, the EU-membership talks have not exactly been successful. The main reason is the existence of the Kurds. This fundamental problem with which Turkey is confronted has already taken grotesque proportions. Presently, the alternatives for Turkey seem to be a solution of the problem under the roof of a democratic republic or the refusal of membership by the EU, with Turkey retreating into its shell. A democratic approach will be the only way to solve the problem. All external and internal indicators support this view,

Still, among all countries in the Middle East, Turkey offers the best social conditions for a successful democratisation. Some steps have already been taken, and, if the rest follow, EU membership becomes possible. So, under the influence of European democratic civilisation, Turkey could strengthen the chances for democracy in the Middle East. It could also exert a dominant influence over the Turkish nations in central Asia. As a consequence of such a development, Turkey could become the fourth important cornerstone of democracy in the Middle East, together with the countries we discussed above. At the end of such a democratisation process, the Middle East might not only have solved its serious crisis in Palestine, but might even be able to form a democratic federation that comprises the whole region. Such a step would stress its antithetic development towards European-type civilisation, and would hopefully contribute to a successful synthesis of the two models, pointing beyond our contemporary understanding of democracy and civilisation.

THE KURDS AND KURDISTAN

The current stare of affairs is accompanied by an increasingly better understanding of the history of the region. As a result of this, the Kurds and Kurdistan have been able to claim an identity of their own in the Middle Eastern history of civilisation. It is necessary to describe the present situation of these people in the light of their history.

Written sources referring to their name go back to the Sumerians. They called the area which today is the geographical Kurdistan "mountainous country" and its inhabitants "mountain people". These terms are still used today. In the Sumerian language *kur* means "mountain" and the suffix *-ti* signifies relatedness. Hence, *kurti* means something like "the people from the mountains", or "the mountain race". However, the Sumerians also used other names, like *urarti*, "people from the highlands", or *guti*, which means "those who have oxen", because they used oxen to till the soil. Even today the Kurdish word for ox is *gudi*. Another name is *arya*, "those who work the soil with ploughs". Later the Assyrians coined the term *mata*, from which the Medes derived their name and which probably means "land of ore". The Pelasgians[2] called the country *Gondwana*, the Greeks called it *Kurdiana* or *Kommagene*. All these names refer to the inhabitants of the same region. After the first contact with Arab tribes, the name *Akraad* was coined, which is plural of *krd* (exactly as in modern Arabic). Later, the Seljuk Grand Sultan Sancar introduced the name *Kurdistan* (*i-stan* is the Persian suffix for "place" or "land"; cf. *Afghanistan, Pakistan*, etc.). Throughout the Ottoman epoch there is ample evidence for the use of the terms *Kurt* and *Kurdistan*. Mustafa Kemal, the founder of the Turkish Republic, mentioned the Kurds and Kurdistan by their name dozens of times, calling them a constitutional factor of the republic. Because of the great number of rebellions in Kurdistan, the name also found its way into the international literature of the nineteenth and twentieth centuries.

The Kurds and their homeland witnessed all kinds of military aggression, occupation and conquest during the slave-holder period – by the Sumerians, the Babylonians, the Arabs, the Mongols, and eventually the Turks. Nonetheless their tribal order remained undisturbed. Sometimes they were united; most of the time, however, they fought among themselves. This tradition continues today.

During the period of feudalism, Kurdish principalities flourished. Many of them were able to establish small states and local governments, tolerated by the Ottomans over a period of 400 years as allies of a sort. Some Kurdish individuals and also some families were quite successful under the rule of Islam as well during the pre-Islamic Iranian civilisations. Their upper class often experienced intense cultural assimilation by other nations. The undisturbed continued existence of their tribal order, however, ensured that their original culture was preserved.

Later, when the Turks invaded Anatolia, when under Sultan Selim Yavuz the Ottoman empire opened itself to the East, and during the Arabian campaigns of the empire, the Kurds played the part of auxiliaries. In return, they were allowed to preserve their free tribal order or their local governments. After World War II, the division of the Ottoman empire was rather disadvantageous for the Kurds. Although they actively participated in the liberation war and the foundation of the republic under the leadership of Mustafa Kemal, the new republic completely destroyed the order of the tribes and the Kurdish principalities. So the Kurds took to new rebellions and revolts, with devastating consequences for themselves. At the same time, repression of Kurds increased in Iraq and Iran as a result of growing nationalism and centralisation efforts. The crushing of the revolts was followed by a general phase of assimilation.

Today, the Kurds are the most visible of many oppressed small peoples in the Middle East. Their fragmentation, their tribal communities and their feudal social order are both the reason for and the result of their backwardness. They have never been able to free themselves from the stranglehold of external and internal factors. Unlike what happened among neighbouring peoples, neither religious nor nationalist ideologies could ever play a positive part here. While Islam and nationalism helped the Arabs, Persians and Turks to strengthen their nations and their states, the Kurds were always made to suffer from oppression and assimilation by them. They were unable to use the feudal Islamic religion or the capitalist national ideology as their national guidelines. All efforts in this direction failed, and people had to bear their poverty and backwardness. In short, democracy is their only hope. At the present time, now that nationalism and religion as ideologies have generally been overcome, and tribalism and feudalism are disappearing fast, their chances are quite good. Furthermore, democracy is in demand worldwide and democratic criteria are being spread even into remote spots of the world. At present, the world is forcing Iraq to become democratic, Iran is probably aiming at a democratic Islamism, and Turkey is beginning to change. The Kurds are surrounded by a ring of changing countries, offering them an opportunity to solve their problems according to democratic criteria. They are no longer an element of rebellion and separation for their neighbours but want to contribute democratically to the unity of these states. It seems clear to me that the time has now come to attempt a solution of the Kurdish question by peaceful and democratic means. This is the first time in history that the Kurds have had the chance to do this together with their neighbours.

It also seems an advantage today that the Kurds live divided across several nations, that they have never been poisoned by nationalism. By democratising themselves, the Kurdish people force the countries and nations among which they live to do the same. In former times the Kurdish movement had always seemed to be at the mercy of external powers. Now it has become a guarantee for peace, liberty and fraternity. No longer will the fate of the Kurds be ignorance, war, rebellion and destruction, but a democratic and developed civil society and unity in freedom.

Now the historic mission of the Kurds is to become democrats in a democratic Islamic Republic of Iran or, better, in a democratic federation of Iran. They will contribute to the continued existence of Iraq as part of a democratic federation of Iraq. In Turkey, they will play a major part in creating a real and coherently democratic and secular republic. They will also be of considerable influence in the democratisation of Syria. All in all, they will be a fundamental power of peace and democracy in the Middle East and a warrant for the continued peaceful existence of the Middle Eastern nations.

Apart from the Kurds, there are also the some other small nations with a similar historical fate: Armenians, Assyrians, Aramaeans, and people of Caucasian origin. They will also participate and contribute to the democratisation process for their own benefit, in order to safeguard their cultural existence and their liberties. These nations may be small in number, but their different cultures add to the colours and the richness of democracy.

Nonetheless, the Middle East, in comparison with many other regions of the world, is an area of backwardness. It is still in the hands of small groups of people who have no appreciation of history, but who have merely organised their private interests in the disguise of political institutions. Their political stance staggers between assimilation and a hypocritical rhetoric of independence. As long as the Middle East as a whole fails to undergo its own renaissance and enlightenment, it will remain extremely difficult to change its fate. However, at a time when all over the world regional and international federations are being created or are under consideration, the Middle East cannot simply be exempted from such developments and considerations. Throughout the history of the Middle East, many nations and peoples have lived there in close neighbourhood, almost as if in a natural federation. The present muddle is intolerable, and the internal condition of the Middle Eastern countries as well as the state of the region as a whole loudly demand a unified, democratic Middle East. The Kurds could be the tool for achieving this goal.

Editorial Team

Sonja Dekker studied history and English literature at the University of Stellenbosch (Western Cape, South Africa).

Arjen Harm studied political philosophy and English literature at the University of Stellenbosch.

Hendrika Harm holds an MA in linguistics of the University of Stellenbosch and is working as a freelance language practitioner.

Leendert Dekker studied in Amsterdam and is a retired professor of Dutch and Afrikaans literature and a lexicographer.

Klaus Happel studied biology and philosophy at the Universities of Düsseldorf and Cologne. He is working as a freelance translator and political consultant.

John Tobisch-Haupt has travelled extensively in the Middle East for many years. He is now a freelance translator and consultant.

I also wish to thank the many other people all over the world who have contributed to this work in many, many ways.

Notes

PART 1

1 The Birth of Civilisation on the Banks of the Tigris and the Euphrates

1. A term coined by the eminent Marxian archaeologist Gordon Childe in the 1930s. Although the term is sometimes contested, it remains in use. The processes it designates are now thought to have been slow and irregular, rather than instantaneous, with sedentism, the domestication of animals, and the cultivation of plants not necessarily always occurring at the same time and in the same place. It is established, though, that a burgeoning number of communities over vast areas adopted patterns involving a combination of the three within a relatively short span of time. Cf. Robert J. Wenke, *Patterns in Prehistory*, Oxford 1999, pp.294ff. and Roger Matthews, *The Archaeology of Mesopotamia*, London 2003, p.69.
2. These three sites were chosen by Ocalan because of their location in northern Kurdistan (the predominantly Kurdish areas of south-eastern Turkey). They are indeed among the oldest excavated so far.
3. Viz. the Halafian, Samarian and Ubaid cultures of the ceramic, neolithic and chalcolithic eras respectively.
4. *History Begins at Sumer* is the title of a book by the late Samuel Noah Kramer, first published in 1956.
5. The term itself is often shunned by recent anthropologists, who prefer to talk of *cultural complexity* in order to bypass the ideological connotations of "civilisation" vis-à-vis "lower" forms of social organisation.
6. This Greek word, coined by the fifth-century Syrian mystical theologian Dionysius Aeropagita (known as the Pseudo-Denys), is derived from a juxtaposition of *hieros* "sacred" and *arkhein* "to rule".
7. From it evolved the Semitic alphabetic script, in turn the ancestor of most known scripts from Greece to Georgia, from Arabia to India.
8. According to Gwendolyn Leick, *mè* is a Sumerian term that refers to all those institutions, forms of social behaviour, emotions and signs of office, which in their totality were seen as indispensable for the smooth operation of the world. The list of the *mè* includes kingship, priestly offices, crafts and music, as well as intercourse, prostitution, old age, justice, peace, silence, slander, perjury, the scribal arts and intelligence, among many others. Source: Gwendolyn Leick, *Mesopotamia: The Invention of the City,* London 2002, pp. 22–3.
9. These were the foothills of the Zagros mountain range in what is today Kurdistan.

2 The Historical Role of Sumerian Civilisation

1. Arabic and Persian historians of the ninth and tenth century such as al-Tabari, al-Mas'udi and al-Biruni did mention pre-Islamic Mesopotamian civilisations in their works, as does Ibn-Khaldun (1333–1406) in his *Introduction to History*; the Ottoman period is marked by complete silence on the subject of ancient Mesopotamia. Mesopotamia became a subject of

research in the West in the nineteenth century, but Sumerian cuneiform writing was only deciphered in the 1870s. Cf. Roger Matthews, *The Archaeology of Mesopotamia*, London 2003, p. 4.

2. Anthony Giddens reminds us that "if we were to think of the entire span of human existence thus far as a day, agriculture would have come into existence at 11.56pm and civilisations at 11.57" (*Sociology*, 4th edn., 2001, p. 40) – although 11.59 would be more accurate.
3. Ocalan critically revisits his idea of the historical relationship between nature and human communities in his second volume of prison writings, where he completely rejects the notion of a "savage" nature that needs to be subdued.
4. Hegel's *Philosophy of History* as well as his *Lectures on the Philosophy of World History* have been followed by many others, among them: Oswald Spengler, *The Decline of the West*; Arnold Toynbee, *Civilization on Trial*; Arnold Toynbee and D.C. Somervell, *A Study Of History*; Karl Jaspers, *The Future of Mankind*; Fernand Braudel, *A History of Civilisations*; Karl Popper, *The Poverty of Historicism*; and Francis Fukuyama, *The End of History and the Last Man*.
5. A paradigmatic problem at the heart of many newer studies suggesting that there either was no slavery in early Mesopotamia or that it wasn't socially relevant, is that they use the concept of slavery developed by classical scholars and seek for corresponding phenomena in Mesopotamia – a method which yields largely negative findings.
6. Although Ocalan gives no definition of slavery or servile labour at this point, it can be surmised from other parts of his text that he refers to any kind of commandeered, coerced or dependent labour in the context of institutional estates, such as the temples or the large households of powerful individuals. His focus is on the ideological and physical subjection of people by others rather than on the legal slave status as defined by Babylonian or Roman law.
7. "In centres like Uruk a highly significant segment of the population must have been given or won its freedom from more than a token or symbolic involvement in the primary process of food production" (R. McC. Adams, *Heartland of Cities*, Chicago 1981, p. 80).
8. According to Ocalan ideologues and leaders of all consecutive class societies drew upon this mythological system and adapted it to the specific conditions of their own environment. In other words, mythologies and theologies created at subsequent stages were modified copies of the Sumerian one.
9. Ocalan is referring here to narratives in Sumerian cuneiform script on clay tablets, which were created around the middle of the third millennium BCE and later. These include *Enki, Enlil, Inana, Inana and Dumuzi, Nanna-Suen, Ninurta, Gilgamesh, Lugalbanda and Enmerkar, Enki and Ninmanh*, and *Enki and the World Order*, all of which deal with Sumerian deities and heroes. The whole topic of Sumerian mythology is covered in depth in Jeremy Black, *Gods, Demons and Symbols of Ancient Mesopotamia: An Illustrated Dictionary*, Austin 1992; Samuel Noah Kramer, *Sumerian Mythology: A Study of Spiritual and Literary Achievement in the Third Millennium BC*, Philadelphia 1998; and Thorkild Jacobsen, *The Harps That Once ... Sumerian Poetry in Translation*, New Haven 1987.
10. Recent archaeological work has contested this view, maintained by most scholars since the excavation of the so-called "death pits" or "Royal Graves" at Ur by Woolley in 1928. It is evident that the burials in question are an expression of allegiance beyond life, but further details remain a matter of conjecture (Gwendolyn Leick, *The Babylonians: an Introduction*, New York 2003, pp. 113–16).
11. This observation is confirmed by Matthews, *Archaeology of Mesopotamia*, p. 89.
12. In the epic *Enuma Elish*, the Babylonian creation myth that substantially differs from earlier Sumerian myths.
13. i.e. *henotheism*, the worship of one main god while accepting the existence of others. Many theologians believe that the early proto-Judaic cult associated with Abraham, or even Judaism in general, were henotheistic.
14. Judaism, Christianity and Islam. Ocalan treats these religions, and his interpretation of the Abrahamite tradition, at length in the following chapters.

15. Another term introduced by Gordon Childe. Although recent authors would prefer the words "transition" or "conversion" rather than revolution, the notion that a qualitative change in social organisation is associated with the rise of early cities remains central to studies in ancient societies. What is contested, however, is Childe's belief that a set number of traits would evolve in a "coevolutionary fashion" in any social system at a certain level (Bruce Trigger, *Understanding Early Civilisations*, Cambridge 2003, p. 43). Many anthropologists use the concept of social or cultural complexity to describe what they think are fluid processes happening in various spheres of human activity and experience.
16. The city of Uruk-Warka may have numbered as many as 50,000 inhabitants by 3000 BCE. By the mid-third millennium, the overwhelming majority of the south Mesopotamian population must have lived in cities, including most farmers. Robert J. Wenke, *Patterns in Prehistory*, Oxford 1999, p. 404; Susan Pollock, *Ancient Mesopotamia*, Cambridge 1999, p. 72.
17. Pollock, *Ancient Mesopotamia*, p. 94.
18. The notable example of the Bau temple at Girsu is given by J. Nicholas Postgate, *Early Mesopotamia*, London 1992, p. 186.
19. Cf. Postgate, *Early Mesopotamia*, pp. 80–1. "Representative" here only means that not every inhabitant of the city was on those assemblies, not that the notable males sitting would have been accountable or even elected.
20. Susan Pollock, Irene Winter and Zainab Bahrani have each written subtle analyses showing how monuments and artworks should be regarded in this context as much as epic texts and mythology proper. See Pollock, *Ancient Mesopotamia*, pp. 173–95 or Z. Bahrani, *Women of Babylon*, New York 1999.
21. In another tradition, Enki's mother is the mother–goddess Nammu, who was also believed to have given birth to the primal human being.
22. i.e. the goddess associated with the primeval matter or *apsu* once signified by Nammu.
23. The first to do so was Naram-Sin of Akkad (2260–2223 BCE).
24. Nippur and the area around it, which includes Babylon, was settled around 5000 BCE and played a central role well into the first millennium BCE.
25. Allusion is made to Stalin's version of dialectical materialism. One undoubtedly important dimension of Ocalan's historical narrative is his own grappling with the dogmatism of Stalinist Marxism, which has informed his thought over years. As he emphasises in the second volume of this work, his own thinking was a melange of traditional Middle Eastern dogmatism and misunderstood Marxist modernism. The trope of Sumerian mythology thus becomes a figure for the Kurdish movement's outlook on the world, which he feels needs thorough revision.
26. "From some of the earliest written documents, those from Mesopotamia in the third millennium BCE, we hear the age-old complaints about poverty, taxes, oppressive rulers, governmental harassment, and other ills of cultural complexity. Little wonder that from these early records we also see the beginnings of Utopian movements, made up of those who yearn for a return to a hypothetical simpler place and time, when political, religious and economic hierarchies did not exist, when all people were considered of equal worth, where all had an equal share, and where no one had power over anyone else" Wenke, *Patterns in Prehistory*, pp. 337–8.
27. 2340–2284 BCE.
28. Colonies and trade outposts were already known to the tributary Uruk economy of the fourth millennium.
29. Cf. Gwendolyn Leick, *Mesopotamia: The Invention of the City*, London 2002, p. 93.
30. Ur-Nammu (2112–2095 BCE) was the first king of the Third Dynasty of Ur. The fragmentary body of law associated with his name deals mainly with civil and criminal matters.
31. Hammurabi ruled the Babylonian empire from 1792 to 1749 BCE and implemented significant administrative reforms. His *Code* is the vintage example of patriarchal civil law.
32. Many nationalistic Turkish scholars have taken pains to prove that the Sumerians were of Turkish origin, following a pronouncement of Mustafa Kemal Ataturk to that effect; but

Arabic, Persian and Kurdish nationalists have ventured into similar appropriations of Mesopotamian history.

3 The Lasting Effects of Sumerian Civilisation

1. The theme of cultural memory, a recurrent idea in Ocalan's book, is extensively discussed in Derrida, Jan Assmann and Maurice Halbwachs.
2. Ocalan's actual words mean "between Satan and Allah".
3. Such studies were made by Samuel N. Kramer, Muazzez I. Cig and Genevieve Lloyd, the latter arguing from a feminist perspective. Genesis 4: 2–5 mentions that Abel was a shepherd and Cain a cultivator of crops who envied his brother for his more God-beloved animal sacrifice.
4. A pun on the Turkish word "*genel ev*" (public home), the most common expression for the venue of prostitution. The allusion already occurred in earlier writings of Ocalan on the family and indicates that family home and brothel complement each other. To Ocalan, marriage entails the compulsion on the part of the woman (excluded, as she is, from social relations of production) to morally, socially and intellectually sell herself off to a man over and above the mere obligation to do housework and have sexual intercourse. Given that most women in Kurdish society are actually sold off into matrimony by their fathers (bride price), the conditions of a married life are fairly similar to those of prostitution. Many scholars hold that in ancient Mesopotamia prostitution emerges from the degradation of priestesses of goddesses who cherished forms of relations other than that of the monogamous, patriarchal family. They are pushed into the position of sex slaves available to any man bringing offerings to the priests. This process seems to be interconnected with the spread of patriarchal households.
5. Al-Khalil or the "friend of God" is the title of Abraham in Islam, where he is regarded as a prophet.

4 Some Methodological Issues Concerning Historical Development and Expansion

1. cf. Jules Michelet's statement "chaque époque rêve la prochaine" (each epoch dreams the one that follows), quoted in Walter Benjamin's essay on "Paris, the Capital of the 19th Century".
2. Readers who desire a deeper knowledge and understanding of the Kurdish issue are referred to the second volume of Ocalan's prison writings, in which the author's personal history and the history of the PKK (Kurdistan Workers' Party) are extensively discussed, and to another book by the present translator, *The Kurdish Rising* (forthcoming).
3. viz. the Kurds.
4. Which is what some Turkish authors inspired by Marxian ideas would say about the Kurds.
5. This reading of historical materialism is strongly reminiscent of Walter Benjamin's *Concept of History* (1939), especially Thesis 17.

5 The Expansion and Maturation of Slavery

1. This was done by T. Jacobson (1982), quoted in Guillermo Algaze's article "Initial Social Complexity in Southwestern Asia", *Current Anthropology*, vol. 42 no. 2 (2001).
2. Lat.: "man is a wolf to man"; the epitome of how T. Hobbes imagined the natural state of human beings.
3. This epic was presumably written during the time of the Ur III dynasty. There is no historical evidence that Naram-Sin actually sacked the temple of the god Enlil at Nippur, as the epic suggests. The gist of the story seems to be that royal hubris played a part in the self-fulfilling prophecy of the ruin of the Akkadian empire.
4. The first and second dynasties (3110–2665 BCE) achieved unification of the two kingdoms of Upper and Lower Egypt. The so-called Old Kingdom (2664–2155 BCE) started with the third dynasty. It was the first heyday of Egyptian monumental architecture, arts and sciences.
5. Osiris, Isis and Horus respectively.

6. Pharaoh Amenhotep IV (1353–1336 BCE) aka Akhenaton, husband to queen Nefertiti, banned inveterate religion and replaced it with the cult of the Sun as the sole deity, to be venerated by the name of Aton. The class of priests ensured that the successor to the throne, Tutankhamen, reinstated the traditional religion. Subsequently, Akhenaton was vilified and his name excluded from the list of kings.
7. This paragraph was rewritten based on information provided by Romila Thapar, *A History of India*, London 2002.
8. The considerable political power of the Middle Elamite Empire (c. 1285–1103 BCE) is well documented. The characteristics of this era will be discussed in the next chapter.

6 Tribal Confederations, Local and Territorial States

1. Mediterranean harbour town in North Lebanon, called Kubna in ancient Egyptian and Gubla in Akkadian, from which its modern Arabic name Jubayl is derived. After centuries of close relations especially with Egypt, it became the foremost city of Phoenicia by the eleventh century BCE.
2. Ancient coastal town at the site of Ra's Shamrah near Latakia in Northern Syria; evidence suggests links with Mesopotamia since the Ubaid period. Babylonian, Egyptian and Cretan wares from the first half of the second millennium were found in this cosmopolite town, where scribes used four languages – Ugaritic, Sumerian, Akkadian and Hurrian – and no less than seven different types of script, including Egyptian hieroglyphic and various forms of Mesopotamian cuneiform. A special alphabetic cuneiform script was invented here. Some of the texts found at Ugarit are regarded by scholars as sources of Biblical narratives. The apex of Ugarit's political and cultural prosperity was the period from about 1450–1200 BCE.
3. Ancient town situated at the Turkish–Syrian border southeast of Antep. Fortified trade centre involved in shipping timber from Anatolia down the Euphrates, city state from the early second millennium to the Hittite conquest in the fourteenth century BCE.
4. Site in Adiyaman province (south-east Turkey) that was a fortified city guarding an important crossing point of the river Euphrates on the east–west trade route since the time of the Hittites.
5. Modern Tell Mardikh near Aleppo in the predominantly Kurdish north of Syria. Ebla was a formidable regional power controlling 17 city states in the Levant and modern Turkish Kurdistan from about 2600 BCE to its first destruction, probably by Naram-Sin. The city proper was a centre for manufacturing, distribution and trade in various products and maintained relations with Egypt, Sumer and Elam. Under Amorite rule, Ebla retained some importance until about 1600 BCE.
6. Ancient city in the Urfa province of Turkish Kurdistan, inhabited to the present day. Centre of the veneration of the moon god Sin, Harran was a town of considerable economic and political importance to the Assyrian Empire.
7. Modern Tell al-Hariri in Syria. Mari was a city state of considerable prosperity, whose ruling class enjoyed close ties to the Assyrians. The rule of its king Zimri-Lim was ended when Hammurabi destroyed the city. The magnificent palace of Zimri-Lim contained one of the most important archives of Assyrian tablets found to the present day.
8. Modern Bogaskoy in Yozgat province of central Anatolia. Hattushas was made the capital of the Hittite Empire, but the town goes back to the Hattians, an earlier Anatolian people that must have established an urban culture at least by the beginning of the second millennium BCE.
9. Hittite city in central Anatolian Kayseri (Caesarea) province. The best known, and perhaps most important, of the Assyrian "karums", i.e. trade outposts where communities of merchants from Assur lived in a certain area of the main city and organised exchange relations between the native townspeople and their own imperial capital. Conditions and controls were imposed on the long-distance trade both by the Anatolian rulers and by the Assyrian governments.
10. The Hattic language, a non-Indo-European idiom, seems to have been extinct by the time of the New Hittite empire, which is sometimes referred to as the State of Hatti (1400–1180 BCE).

11. It is believed that the Hittite term Ahhiyawa is the cuneiform version of Mycenaean Akhaiwoi, i.e. Achaean, an inclusive term for proto-Greeks.
12. Archaeologists believe that the historical Troy was burned down around 1250 BCE, i.e. around the time of the decline of the Hittite Empire.
13. viz. the Kurds'.
14. It bears a Sumerian name (Khubur).
15. Near modern Iskenderun (Alexandrette) on the Mediterranean Turkish–Syrian border, a city state that became a Hittite vassal in the fourteenth century, only to exert major cultural and economic influence on the empire as a whole.
16. In modern day north Kurdistan, in the east of Turkey.
17. e.g. Genesis 11:31, 12: 4–5
18. The texts found at the mound of Ra's Shamrah (see note 2) reflect, among others, ancient Canaanite legends which contain many elements that occur in Biblical narratives composed at a much later date, but also make ample reference to the flourishing of debt-slavery in the mid-second millennium. "The only way out for the labourers was to fully abandon their communities, and this they seem to have done in great numbers. Throughout the Syro-Palestinian area there was an increased presence of men and women who had cut ties with their political and social communities and joined groups of outcasts beyond the reach of the states. They became semi-nomadic and lived in inaccessible areas in the steppe and the mountains" (Marc Van de Mieroop, *A History of the Ancient Near East ca. 3000–323 BC*, Oxford 2003, p.160).
19. This narrative strand occurs in the Jewish *Book of Jubilees* (second century BCE) and in the works of the Iranian historian al-Tabari (839–923 CE), who drew on pre-Islamic Middle Eastern sources, but also on the Qur'an 21:51–72, 29:15–27 and 37:89–94. It seems to be rooted in older oral traditions. Abraham destroys a number of earthen idols in Harran and is brought before Nimrod who sentences him to death. He is saved through divine intervention and sets off for Canaan.
20. Ishmael in Islamic tradition; Genesis 22:1–19 mentions Isaac as the potential victim. The Qur'an itself does not specify the name of the son (37:95–110).
21. Minoan artifacts were traded throughout the Mediterranean.
22. A popular Kurdish folk tale that provides the etiological explanation for the lighting of fires on the eve of the Kurdo-Persian New Year Festival Newroz (21 March). The tyrant Dehaq had two snakes growing from his shoulders. To appease them, he had to feed them the brains of two young lower-class men every day, until he was finally slain by Kawa, a blacksmith, who took the decapitated tyrant's head to a mountain top and lit a huge fire to indicate to the people that the time of tyranny was over and they could return to the villages which they had abandoned in fear.

7 Resistance to Slave-owning Civilisation and Its Reform

1. Here, as in other instances, Ocalan uses the term "slave" in a broader sense than it usually assumes in studies of, say, Greco-Roman antiquity. Owing to the peculiarities of the Turkish political literature, the term designates dependency and subordination in social relations based on hierarchy and coercion, rather than exclusively referring to the status of people who could be bought and sold.
2. Several volumes of selections from educational dialogues Ocalan held with activists of the PKK movement are available in Turkish; some of them focus on questions concerning the formation of consciousness and personality structures under the conditions of Kurdish socialisation, others on the contextualisation of gender relations in a wider analysis of political oppression or on what might be called a "psychology of the oppressed".
3. According to scholars such as the late S.N. Kramer and Muazzez İlmiye Çiğ;, the material informing the Book of Job of the Hebrew Bible goes back to motifs found on Sumerian tablets. The Biblical text itself contains a number of Akkadian word roots. Other scholars

argue that much of the material in the Book of Job goes back to Iranian Zoroastrian texts. In the Qur'an, Job appears as the patient and faithful one who ultimately trusts in the greatness of God despite his suffering (21:83–86 and 38:40–44). While this strand certainly does appear in the Hebrew Book of Job, the Marxist philosopher Ernst Bloch has offered an interpretation according to which the Biblical text is a narrative of defiance of an absolutist, almighty and wanton god and thus raises questions of theodicy and implies the rejection of the priestly conception of God (See *Atheismus im Christentum,* Frankfurt am Main 1967, (pp. 148–66). In the Sumerian proto-"Job" texts, the aspect of defiance and accusation of the gods is clearly discernible. Theodicy is likewise a preoccupation of Zoroastrian writings. A site near Viranşehir in Urfa province is hallowed by Kurds and Arabs as the tomb of the prophet Job, alias Ayyub.

4. See Eva Wasilewska, *Creation Stories of the Middle East,* London 2000, for a thorough comparative study of the Mesopotamian, Canaanite, Biblical and Qur'anic creation and paradise stories.
5. See, among others, 11:25–50.
6. The mountain is located between Mardin and Cizre (al-Jazirhe) at the border between modern Turkey and Iraq, which cuts through the Kurdish region of Botan.
7. "*cu*" – or "*cih*" in modern Kurdish – is thought to be cognate with the Greek "*geo*".
8. Many scholars have discarded the idea that the speakers of Indo-European migrated into Anatolia, Northern Mesopotamia and Iran from elsewhere. From the time when the textual sources inform us of the languages used in Anatolia, Indo-European idioms were among those used. Anything going beyond this observation remains speculative; cf. Marc Van de Mieroop, *A History of the Ancient Near East ca. 3000–323* BC, Oxford 2003, p. 113.
9. This thesis was already put forward by the late S.N. Kramer in 1956. See Yitschak Sefati, *Love Songs in Sumerian Literature*, Jerusalem 1998, for a recent in-depth discussion.
10. The social function of prophecy as a historical phenomenon will be discussed below, and in Part 2 in the context of the formation of Islam.
11. The kingdom of Osroene in Kurdistan was founded in the second century BCE. Its capital was Edessa, the modern Urfa. A letter of Jesus to King Abgar, which is mentioned in the Church History of the Palestinian bishop and historian Eusebius (fourth century CE), has been dismissed by Church authorities as a forgery since the fifth century. The legend of Abgar's invitation, however, was widely circulated in all languages spoken in the early medieval Middle East and enjoys continuing popularity. Edessa had been a focus of Christian culture since well before 200 CE, and a body of early Syriac patrist literature is known under the name "School of Edessa".
12. It should be kept in mind that although Ocalan employs the wider concept of prophecy as religio-political reform commonly accepted in scholarship, his *point of departure* is the Islamic concept of prophecy or prophethood as a quality associated with certain figures including Abraham, Moses, Job, Jesus and many of the figures who occur as prophets in the Hebrew Bible, since this is how his readership would at first understand the word.
13. The word "*nabi*" that is employed in both Hebrew and Arabic for "prophet" goes back to the Akkadian root "*nabu*", "to proclaim". Prophecy is believed to have been a more or less common phenomenon throughout the ancient Middle East.
14. In fact, Ocalan discusses four major "prophets": Abraham, Moses, Jesus and Muhammad, the latter two in Part 2 of this volume.
15. These also existed in all ancient Middle Eastern societies. The ecstatic or "frenzied one" was known to the Akkadians as *mahhu*, and to the Sumerians as *lú-gub-ba*, a group apparently associated with the cult of Inanna/Ishtar.
16. According to ancient Egyptian belief, the king had the duty – and by inference the capacity – to keep the universe going. His ritual actions were crucial to the perpetuation of the cosmic and earthly order, a breach resulting in total chaos (see Jan Assmann, *Ägypten in der*

Wissenskultur des Abendlandes, in J. Fried and J. Süßmann (eds) *Revolutionen des Wissens von der Steinzeit bis zur Moderne*, Munich 2001, p 56–8). This key position in the master plan entailed his absolute authority to dispose over the life and afterlife of his subjects. The deified Mesopotamian rulers were invested with comparable powers.

17. The word "Allah" itself is derived from the old Semitic word for "god", "*il*", which is also the root form of "El". In recent years scholars have asserted that the name of the Sumerian god *Enlil* is also derived from this old root (see Gwendolyn Leick, *A Dictionary of Near Eastern Mythology*, New York 2001, pp. 151f.).
18. See, for example, Deuteronomy 7:6–8 and 14:2.
19. The jealousy metaphor pervades especially Exodus (e.g. 20:5 and 34:11–17) and Deuteronomy (e.g. 5:9, 6:15 and 32:16–21), and prophetic texts of the ninth to seventh centuries such as Isaiah 62:4, Jeremiah 3:14 or Hosea 2:1–20 evoke the image of marriage.
20. See Genesis 32:22–32 for the story of how Jacob wrestled with the deity.
21. Genesis 12:10–20 and 20:1–18.
22. Genesis 39:1–6.
23. Babylonian tablets say about King Sargon: "She conceived me, my en-priestess mother, in concealment she gave me birth, / Set me in a wicker basket, with bitumen she made my opening watertight. / She cast me down into the river from which I could not ascend./ … / Aqqi the water drawer did raise me as his adopted son. / … / While I was still a gardener, Ishtar did grow fond of me" (quoted after Leick 2001, p 94), whereas Exodus 2:1–10 relates that "a Levite woman" (i.e. of priestly origin) "conceived and bore a son" and "hid him for three months" until "she got a papyrus basket for him, and plastered it with bitumen and pitch; she put the child in it and placed it among the reeds on the bank of the river". Moses is adopted by Pharaoh's daughter, and it is Yahweh who grows fond of him.
24. See Jonathan N. Tubb, *Canaanites*, London 1998, p. 81.
25. It still was in the oral traditions of the Afro-American slaves, and for Bob Marley in his powerful call for an "Exodus" from the Western system of oppression. Bob Marley is also one of the best known examples for contemporary, allegorical use of the metaphor of "Babylon" in a tradition very different from that of Western Orientalism.
26. The Arabic term for migration chosen in the Turkish original connotes the emigration of Muhammad from Mecca (spelt "hijra" or "hegira").
27. See e.g. Jan Assmann, *Moses the Egyptian*: *The Memory of Egypt in Western Monotheism*, Cambridge, Mass. 1997.
28. Exodus 3:1, and especially 18:10–24.
29. Exodus 16:2–3 and 17:2–4, but also 2:11–14.
30. Exodus 16:9–10 and 28:1–3.
31. Exodus 17:8–10.
32. Exodus 18:25–26 and 19:7 respectively.
33. See Exodus 34:11–16.
34. Rather than alluding to the groups that are the focus of the Gospels' polemics, Ocalan employs the (pre-Islamic) Arabic term for "diviner", "*kahin*", which is cognate with the Hebraic "*cohen*", the hereditary priests who administered the temple.
35. The Essene community of Qumran, which produced the Dead Sea Scrolls, for example, lived outside the boundaries of officially governed urban society. The legendary execution of John the Baptist may have been symptomatic of the authorities' policies towards such ideologies.
36. The Turkish language has different words for an ancient "nation" or "people", a medieval one ("*millet*") and a nation in the modern sense, where the English demands the indiscriminate use of the one Latinate word. Ocalan does make the distinction in parentheses in addition to the use of the distinct terms.
37. Both words are derived from the same root, Gr. *myein*, "to close [lips and eyes]", although they have acquired a somewhat different meaning by convention. The Turkish word Ocalan uses comes from the root "to hide, to veil".

8 The Greco-Roman Contribution

1. This claim was first made by the historian Herodotus in the fifth century BCE.
2. Ocalan had various meetings with high-ranking Italian officials during his stay in Rome, which was the longest interlude between his expulsion from Syria in October 1998 and his abduction from Kenya in February 1999. His own account of these events comes in the second volume of his prison writings.
3. An allusion to Lenin's famous complaint about Tsarist censorship in his 1920 preface to *Imperialism: The Highest Stage of Capitalism.*
4. Eloquent speech was an issue that Ocalan paid special attention to in his educational activities. He was enthusiastic about empowering the traditionally speechless groups in society: women, illiterate people from a peasant background, children, etc.
5. Modern north-east Afghanistan, Uzbekistan and Tajikistan.

9 Medes, Persians and the Making of the East

1. Views influenced by this thesis have for a long time been quite popular with bourgeois Kurdish historians, and even occurred in the first party programme of the Kurdistan Workers' Party (PKK), drafted in 1978.
2. The Kassites might account for the historical correlate of the "eight successive Median kings" who ostensibly ruled over Babylon in the third millennium according to Berosus, a Babylonian historian of the third century BCE, writing in Greek.
3. The classical Greek authors made a big point of depicting the conflict as one "between eastern slavery and western freedom" (Van de Mieroop, p 270) – a highly ideologically charged assertion that found resonance in the Orientalist discourses of modernity, where it served to legitimise colonialism.
4. Its significant Other, as recent authors such as Francois Hartog might have said.
5. Zeugma is one of the archaeological sites in south-east Turkey meted out the fate of flooding in the course of dam projects. It is situated in Belkis near Antep, i.e. the surroundings of ancient Aspendos.

10 The Demise of a Paradigm

1. This manuscript – which is based on the classical Marxian periodisation according to the slave-holding, feudal and capitalist modes of production – was finalised in 2001. In the second volume of his prison writings, drafted in 2004, Ocalan uses an entirely different periodisation when discussing social history from a different viewpoint.
2. This is what Ocalan has done in the previous chapters.
3. It is this thesis that Ocalan thoroughly revises in the second volume of his prison writings.
4. In the second volume of his prison writings, Ocalan ponders this question in depth.
5. Bernbeck remarks that Sumerians had to go to the netherworld irrespective of their conduct in life.
6. Throughout the Roman era, a considerable number of private elite households or estates fashioned along these lines reached vast proportions.
7. In a similar vein, Pierre Dockès argues that the centralised state as the masters' corporative tool of oppression was the pivot of the slave system, and the decay of the state – precipitated by the logic of the development of the relation of production itself – put an end to the slave system and gave rise to serfdom. Cf. his *Medieval Slavery and Liberation*, Chicago 1982.
8. It has to be kept in mind that in ancient Near Eastern societies wealth was the result of political power, and not vice versa. The production of wealth was therefore less relevant to the ruling-class individual than his social position and office.
9. Ocalan does not specify to which historical period this statement refers, but the use of the term *proletariat* allows us to infer that he alludes to the late Roman Empire.

10. The so-called *coloni* or tenant farmers, who accounted for more than 80 per cent of all peasant labour in Asia Minor according to A. Demandt.
11. The most important exception to this would be Baghdad, with an estimated half a million inhabitants at its heyday in the early ninth century CE. It surpassed Constantinople and was emulated in size and glory only by fourteenth-century Cairo.
12. "An army of officials – the late Roman system looks at first sight like corruption run riot. Everything was for sale, including government." Averil Cameron, *The Later Roman Empire*, London 1993, p. 106.

PART 2

12 Early Islam: a Revolutionising Force

1. The term Gnosticism is used here as a collective term for all the small but free sects striving for *gnosis*, or knowledge of God, which had distanced themselves from the slave-holder ideology and religious tradition since the fifth century, and had spread across the entire Middle East since then.
2. On a more general level, social development and the unfolding of language and terminology are closely intertwined. The reality of language and intellectual understanding expresses itself in the process of self-naming, self-recognition and conscious reproduction of a community. A community cannot reproduce rationally without intellectual consciousness; it can only reproduce on an instinctive, somewhat physiological level. Formation and development of a society become possible through language and reason. A society which loses its language or its reason stops being a society, becomes something completely different at best. Beyond mere perpetuation of its material–physical existence, the foundations of a society lie in its intellectual development, which uses the power of language and reason in order to link social memory, tradition, religion, philosophy and science. Religion and its concepts are the basic building blocks for the intellectual development and memory of a society. Without them the social process will not start. Formation and expansion of all economic and political ideas and institutions are made possible by language and conceptualisation. Societal thinking receives its first institutionalisation as collective memory when it is coded and standardised in the form of tradition, custom and moral behaviour. Concepts dealing with future social developments become a driving force in the shape of utopias and visions. A society's religion serves as its fundamental utopia and its memory of the past, while at the same time defining its traditions and morals, and structuring its hopes and desires for the future. It is this vital dialectic relation between religion and society that gives society its sociological meaning.
3. The fourth Caliph, Ali Ibn Abi Talip, who ruled from 656 to 661 CE and who belonged to the tribe of Muhammad had been assassinated and his enemy Muawiya ibn Abi Sufyan had proclaimed himself Caliph, founding the dynasty of the Umayyad by turning the office of the successor of the prophet into a hereditary monarchy. In 680, al-Hussayin Ibn Ali, the murdered Ali's son, led a revolt against the Umayyad, which was crushed bloodily at Karbala in today's Iraq. The martyrdom of Hussayin and other members of Muhammad's family has become the founding myth of the Shi'ites, the supporters of Ali, in their political opposition to the institutionalised Islam (of the Sunni line) under the absolutist Umayyad caliphate.
4. *Sura* 105, Al Fil (the elephant). This *sura* describes how the Coptic king Abraha of Ethiopia and his army, equipped with elephants, advanced on Mecca in the year the prophet was born (570).
5. He was later adopted by Muhammad, compare. sura 33:37 ff. (The Confederate Tribes). Ali, who is mentioned here, was a son of Abu Talib, who later became the fourth caliph Ali ibn Ali Talib, and who married Muhammad's daughter Fatima. He was eventually assassinated.
6. "Social contract" in the sense of Rousseau's *contrat social*.
7. Singular *Eloah* (Hebrew: God), the God of Israel in the Old Testament. The term *Elohim* is usually employed in the Old Testament for the one and only God of Israel, whose personal name was revealed to Moses as YHWH, or Yahweh. Though *Elohim* is plural in form, it is

understood in the singular sense. *Elohim* is monotheistic in connotation, though its grammatical structure seems polytheistic.

13 The Institutionalisation and Expansion of Feudal Civilisation

1. The distinction between revolutionary and evolutionary changes is made mainly according to the mode of operation employed to bring about the change.
2. The Twelver-Shi'ism recognises a certain line of descendants of Hussein, son to the Prophet's daughter Fatima and his cousin, the caliph Ali, as infallible spiritual leaders (*imam*), the twelfth in their line being expected to return to earth as the *mahdi* (the God-guided one) on the Day of Judgment. The Ismailis are another denomination of Shi'ism which accepts a different line of descent, today manifested in the position of the Aga Khan. The Alawi or Alevites also refer to Ali and Hussein but their beliefs differ from the Shi'a faith in many central points.

14 The Peak and Decline of Feudal Civilisation

1. These remarks are aimed at the present state of politics in Turkey, which the author regards as intransigent and, therefore, as being in a permanent state of crisis.
2. The Qaramita, an offshoot of the Ishmaelite Shi'ites, established some kind of republic in eastern Arabia in the ninth century. The Fatimids in 969 established a Shi'ite dynasty in Egypt, which had many followers in Yemen, Syria, Iran and western India.
3. Al-Ashari (died 935) stands for a traditional literal interpretation of the Qur'an in contrast to the Islamic philosophers influenced by Greek rationalism, such as Ibn Sina. However, he tried to give rational reasons for his method of interpretation. Al-Ghazali (1058–1111) represents the same tradition. He is the author of several political models of Islamic theocracy.

15 Some Concluding Remarks on the Preceding Chapters

1. Ibn Khaldun (1332–1406) in his main historical and sociological work *Book of Examples* (*Muqqadima*) sketched a cyclic idea of Arabian history kept in motion by economic contradictions.

PART 3

17 The Development and Institutionalisation of Capitalist Civilisation

1. According to Mesopotamian mythology, Enki, who lived on the island of Dilmun (modern Bahrein), is said to have given the world its order and helped with the creation of the human race. He gave the places where man lived, *inter alia* Sumer and Dilmun, their characteristics and blessed them.
2. *Ummah* is the community of all faithful Muslims who believe that Muhammad is their prophet and who follow his law.
3. *Waqfs* are institutions of the sharia, the Islamic law. They were widespread in the Ottoman empire. They were meant to make untaxed income from quite large estates in the possession of Islamic clergy available for charitable purposes, for instance the maintenance of mosques, schools and homes.

18 Capitalist Expansion and the Climax of Capitalist Civilisation

1. A literal translation of the Turkish word *sömürge*, which is often used in the sense of *colony*.

19 The Overall Crisis of Civilisation and the Age of Democracy

1. The growing differentiation of occupations and professions should not be seen as a progressive form of class division or an advancement of the state machinery. On the contrary, classical class division and the existence of the state are becoming increasingly obsolete.
2. World War II was anything but an ordinary war. It was caused by a radical attempt to restore capitalist civilisation against the background of a deep-going depression and crisis. It created an extreme statism – as all class-based systems do in an attempt to counteract decay.
3. The American Lewis H. Morgan published *Ancient society, or Researches in the Lines of Human Progress from Savagery through Barbarism to Civilization* in 1877. This was the first major scientific account of the origin and evolution of civilisation, and together with Johann Jakob Bachofen's *Das Mutterrecht* (*Mother Right*, 1871) it was among the first attempts at writing a history of family. Both publications contributed to Engels' treatment of the basic issues of civilisation *Der Ursprung der Familie, des Privateigenthums und des Staats* (*The Origin of the Family, Private Property and the State*, 1884).

PART 4

Introduction to Part 4

1. It is no longer production which determines the political superstructure, as Marx saw it, but just the other way round. In the hands of a capitalist oligarchy, the political superstructure direct the economy according to their own profits.

20 Ideological Identity in the Third Millennium

1. Ocalan here chiefly, albeit indirectly, refers to the debate within the Kurdish liberation movement, set against a Middle Eastern background.
2. Marxism gave preference to economic analysis, which is partly the reason why it eventually led to real socialism and decay.
3. A good example here is Aurelius Augustinus, also called Saint Augustine of Hippo, a native of Numidia and one of the Latin Fathers of the Church (354–430). Originally of Manichaean faith and an adept Neoplatonist, he converted to Christianity at the age of 32, six years after Christianity had become the state religion of the Roman Empire. Later he became bishop of Hippo Regius.
4. A Muslim sect, that interpreted religious texts exclusively on the basis of their hidden, or inner, meanings (Arabic: *batin*) rather than their literal meanings (*zahir*). For them, Muhammad was only the transmitter of the word of God, whereas it was the imam (leader) who was empowered to interpret its true, hidden meaning.

PART 5

25 Renewal of the Ideological Identity Will Be the Primary Historical Challenge

1. Different denominations and religious diversity developed within Islam from the start – the Shi'ites of Iran, the Alevites of the Kurds, the Bektashi and Mevlana orders of the Turks and many other heterodox confessions and sects.
2. These are figures from medieval love epics. All of them faced death for having violated social taboos.

27 The Theory and Practice of Middle Eastern Civilisation

1. Originally a term denoting agents for Western companies exploiting China. Here it is related to the Western exploitation of Ottoman Turkey, of course.
2. The "aboriginal" Aegean population, who inhabited Greece before the Greek tribes immigrated in the twelfth century BCE.

Bibliography

PART 1

Braidwood, Robert J., *Prehistoric Men*, New York 1975
Campbell, Joseph, *The Masks of God*, vols 1–4, London 1991
Childe, Vere Gordon, *Man Makes Himself*, Glasgow 1936
—— *Studies in the History of Civilization*, London 1947
—— *Social Evolution* (Josiah Mason lectures in anthropology), New York 1963
Dolukhanov, Pavel, *Environment and Ethnicity in the Middle East*, Aldershot 1994
Frazer, James George, *The Golden Bough*, Macmillan 1945
Gaster, Theodor H., *Thespis: Ritual, Myth, and Drama in the Ancient Near East*, New York 1961
Gibbon, Edward, *The Decline and Fall of the Roman Empire*, New York 1946
Guthrie, W. K. C., *A History of Greek Philosophy*, Cambridge 1991
Kramer, Samuel Noah, *Sumerian Mythology: Study of Spiritual and Literary Achievement in the Third Millennium BC*, New York 1961
—— *The Sumerians: Their History, Culture and Character*, Chicago 1971
—— *History Begins at Sumer: Thirty-Nine "Firsts" in Recorded History*, Philadelphia 1981
—— *Inanna: Queen of Heaven and Earth*, London 1984
—— and Maier, John, *Myths of Enki, the Crafty God*, Oxford 1989
Lewin, Roger, *The Origin of Modern Humans*, New York 1998
Maisels, Charles Keith, *The Emergence of Civilization: From Hunting and Gathering to Agriculture, Cities, and the State in the Near East*, New York 1993
Morgan, Lewis Henry, *Ancient Society*, Tucson 1985
Stone, Merlin, *When God Was a Woman*, San Diego 1978

PART 2

Bruno, Giordano, *Cause, Principle, and Unity: Five Dialogues*, Westport 1976
Corbin, Henry, *History of Islamic Philosophy*, London, 2001
Lewis, Bernard, *The Jews of Islam*, Princeton 1987
—— *Cultures in Conflict: Christians, Muslims, and Jews in the Age of Discovery*, Oxford 1996
—— *The Multiple Identities of the Middle East*, New York 2001
—— *The Arabs in History*, Oxford 2002
Nizam al-Mulk, *The Book of Government: Or, Rules for Kings: The Siyar al-muluk or Siyasat-nama of Nizam al-Mulk*, London 1978
Rodinson, Maxime, *Muhammad*, Norwalk, Conn. 1989
Schuré, Edouard, *Great Initiates: A Study of the Secret History of Religions*, Blaine, Minn.1961
Warner, Arthur George and Warner, Edmond, *The Shahnama of Firdausi*, London 2001

PART 3

Bakunin, Mikhail Aleksandrovich, *God and the State*, Whitefish, Mont. 2004.
Barber, Benjamin, *Strong Democracy: Participatory Politics for a New Age*, Berkeley 1984

Basalla, George, *The Evolution of Technology*, Cambridge 1989
Benhabib, Seyla (ed.), *Democracy and Difference: Contesting the Boundaries of the Political*, Princeton 1996
Bowles, Samuel and Gintis, Herbert M., *Democracy and Capitalism: Property, Community and the Contradictions of Modern Social Thought*, New York 1987
Campanella, Tommaso, *The City of the Sun*, Berkeley 1981
Chomsky, Noam, *World Orders: Old and New*, New York 1994
Feyerabend, Paul, *Against Method, Outline of an Anarchistic Theory of Knowledge*, St Louis 1975
Fukuyama, Francis, *Trust: The Social Virtues and the Creation of Prosperity*, New York 1996
Fuller, Graham E. and Lesser, Ian O., *A Sense of Siege: The Geopolitics of Islam and the West*, New York 1994
Guéhenno, Jean Marie, *The End of the Nation-State*, Minneapolis 1995
Kennedy, Paul, *The Rise and Fall of the Great Powers*, New York 1987
Lenihan, John, *Science in Action*, New York 1990
Lukács, Georg, *History and Class Consciousness*, Cambridge, Mass. 1972
Machiavelli, Niccolo, *The Prince*, London 2003
Mill, John Stuart, *On Liberty*, Oxford 1998
Pettit, Philip Noel, *Republicanism: A Theory of Freedom and Government*, Oxford 2000
Pierson, Christopher, *Beyond the Welfare State? The New Political Economy of Welfare*, Philadelphia 1998
Popper, Karl, *The Open Society and Its Enemies*, Princeton 1971
—— *The Poverty of Historicism*, London 1988
Shapin, Steven, *Scientific Revolution*, Chicago 1998

PARTS 4 AND 5

Bookchin, Murray, *Toward an Ecological Society*, Montreal 1988
—— *Urbanization Without Cities: Rise and Fall of Citizenship*, Montreal 1992
—— *The Ecology of Freedom: The Emergence and Dissolution of Hierarchy*, Warner 2003
Laclau, Ernesto and Butler, Judith, *Contingency, Hegemony, Universality: Contemporary Dialogues on the Left*, London 2000

Index

Compiled by Sue Carlton